**AN INTRODUCTION TO
DATA STRUCTURES
WITH APPLICATIONS**

## McGRAW-HILL COMPUTER SCIENCE SERIES

**McGRAW-HILL
BOOK COMPANY**
New York
St. Louis
San Francisco
Auckland
Bogotá
Hamburg
Johannesburg
London
Madrid
Mexico
Montreal
New Delhi
Panama
Paris
São Paulo
Singapore
Sydney
Tokyo
Toronto

**JEAN-PAUL TREMBLAY**
**PAUL G. SORENSON**
*Department of Computational Science*
*University of Saskatchewan, Saskatoon*

# An Introduction to Data Structures with Applications

## Second Edition

Dédié - Dedicated


A mes parents
Philippe et Anna
TREMBLAY

To my wife Linda
and our children; Kimberly,
Jill and Stephen
SORENSON

**Library of Congress Cataloging in Publication Data**

Tremblay, Jean-Paul, date
   An introduction to data structures with applications.

   Includes bibliographies and index.
   1. Data structures (Computer science) 2. Electronic
digital computers—Programming. I. Sorenson, P. G.
II. Title.
QA76.9.D35T73 1984      001.64'42      83-9895
ISBN 0-07-065157-4

**AN INTRODUCTION TO
DATA STRUCTURES
WITH APPLICATIONS**

567890HALHAL 898765

ISBN 0-07-065157-4

The editors were Eric M. Munson and Jon Palace; the production supervisor was Dennis
J. Conroy. New drawings were done by Alex Kozlow. Halliday Lithograph Corporation was
printer and binder.

# CONTENTS

# PREFACE

## PREFACE TO THE SECOND EDITION

At the time of the first writing of this book, a data structures course was central to most computer science curricula. Today most curricula contain more than one course in data structures that are of fundamental importance. Often these courses are taught at the first or second year of computer science programs.

This second edition contains several general improvements, including the following in particular:

*1*   An increased formalization of the algorithmic language to include procedures, functions, case statements, and exits from loops
*2*   Structured algorithms throughout the book
*3*   The use of Pascal in Chapters 2 to 6
*4*   Many new exercises
*5*   An increase in the analysis of algorithms

The emphasis on PL/I as the main programming language has decreased significantly in all chapters except for the last chapter, dealing with files.

Chapter 1 has been trimmed in size. The material on number conversion has been deleted and the tables on hardware specifics have been updated.

Chapter 2 has been reorganized. In particular, the text editing example has been changed to emphasize text formatting, and the application dealing with bit strings has been removed.

Chapter 3 contains a new section that describes structures and array of structures. The simulation application has been changed.

Chapter 4 contains little in the way of changes.

Chapter 5 contains many changes. In particular, Secs. 5-1, 5-2, and 5-4 have been changed substantially. The contents of Secs. 5-3 and 5-6 contain minor changes. The application of trees to decision tables has been dropped. New applications and materials include block-structured symbol tables, an augmented treatment of List structures, and an expansion of graph topics to include breadth first search, depth first search, and spanning trees.

Chapter 6 contains new material on weight-balanced binary trees, 2-3 trees, and tries. The hashing section has been rewritten.

Finally, Chapter 7 has been expanded to include sections on external sorting and searching.

This second edition assumes basic familiarity with assembly languages, Pascal, and combinatorial mathematics (including recurrence relations). The material dealing with these topics, however, can be ignored without loss of continuity.

We acknowledge the important assistance of Grant Cheston, who class-tested Chapters 5 and 6 and contributed to the analysis of the algorithms throughout the book.

We also acknowledge the invaluable assistance of Shane McDonald in the preparation of the manuscript for typesetting. He also assisted in the preparation of Chapter 6. Brad Willems assisted us with the preparation of Chapters 3 and 5, Karen Manson with Chapters 2 and 7, and Jim Tubman with Chapter 1. Howard Hamilton provided us with continual assistance in the preparation of Sec. 7-11. Beth Protsko helped prepare the index. We owe a very special thanks to Sue Wotton and Gail Walker for typing support.

JEAN-PAUL TREMBLAY

PAUL G. SORENSON

## PREFACE TO THE FIRST EDITION

Computer science is primarily concerned with the study of data (information) structures and their transformation by mechanical means. The importance of data structures is recognized in the ACM's "Curriculum 68" report[1]  and the ACM's curriculum-committee reports on computer education for management and information systems systems[2,3,4]  in courses entitled "Data Structures" and "Information Structures," respectively.

The first coherent and comprehensive treatment of data structures is due to Donald E. Knuth.[5]  His great contribution to the area of data structures has influenced the organization and notation in Chaps. 3, 4, 5 and 6 of this book.

Most computer-science curricula have at least one course in data structures. However, in many instances such a course is given in the junior or senior year of study. This condition makes it difficult for the student to apply data-structure con-

---

[1]  *CACM*, 11, No. 9, pp. 172-173, 1968.
[2]  *CACM*, 14, No. 9, pp. 573-588, 1971.
[3]  *CACM*, 15, No. 5, pp. 363-398, 1972.
[4]  *CACM*, 16, No. 12, pp. 727-749, 1973.
[5]  "The Art of Computer Programming: Fundamental Algorithms," Addison-Wesley, Reading, Mass., 1968.

cepts to material taught in advance courses involving the manipulation of information (e.g., information systems analysis and design, information storage and retrieval, operating systems, compiler construction, computer graphics, and artificial intelligence and heuristic programming). This book is an outgrowth of notes used in a two-semester course given in the second semesters of the first and second years at the University of Saskatchewan. The reason for its appearance so early in the program is that the course is intended to introduce the student to concepts and terminology used in later courses. A desirable set of goals for a course in data structures is:

*1*    To introduce the student to those aspects of data structures which are required in subsequent computer science courses

*2*    To motivate the student by illustrating the key concepts with various examples in computer science

*3*    To increase the student's intuitive understanding of basic concepts

New concepts should be introduced in a modular manner, i.e., in terms of previously understood concepts and in a way which permits the student to view computer science as a unified discipline. This cohesiveness can be achieved by trying to touch as many advanced courses as possible that require a knowledge of the basic structures introduced. Well-chosen applications can facilitate the realization of this goal and also greatly motivate the student. The course should attempt to introduce the student to terminology used in later courses. This approach will tend to generate a sense of familiarity at the beginning of such courses. We wish to emphasize that concepts and terminology should be introduced well before they are used. Otherwise, a student must invariably struggle with both the basic tools and the subject matter to which the tools are applied.

Although the applications which are discussed are meant to touch on as many areas of computer science as possible, an equally important goal is to emphasize the problem-solving process. Most students are employed by firms that require problem solvers. Many students find it difficult to formulate a problem by examining a particular situation within an organization. Frequently, such students upon finishing their studies are unable to structure a problem; indeed, they expect it to be already formulated.

Chapter 1 contains a discussion of the nature of information. Primitive data structures such as real, integer, character, pointer, etc. are introduced along with a number of storage representations which have been used on different computers. The concepts of number conversion and codes are briefly discussed.

The second chapter deals with the topic of string manipulation. A discussion of two formal systems for string manipulation is given—namely, the Markov formalism and the formal grammar. Using this approach a number of desirable primitive operations for string manipulation and pattern matching can be determined. Their derivations are also motivated by considering certain string-processing applications such as text-editing system and the KWIC (Key Word In Context) indexing system.

Chapter 3 is concerned with linear data structures such as arrays, stacks, queues, double-ended queues, etc., and the associated operations that can be performed on these structures. A number of possible storage structures, based on sequential allocation, are discussed. The topic of recursion (and its implementation) is dealt with in some detail, since many programming languages permit its use. The concept of recursion is important in its own right because students will encounter throughout their career problems where recursion is unavoidable, because of the recursive nature of the process or because of the recursive structure of the data. The

ALLOCATE and FREE features of PL/I are mentioned. A number of applications in linear data structures such as the compilation of expressions in Polish notation and the simulation of a simple "timesharing" system are given.

Chapter 4 deals with the storage representation of linear data structures based on linked storage allocation. The POINTER and BASED attributes of PL/I are described. Doubly linked and circular structures are also discussed. Applications such as symbol-table construction and multiple-precision arithmetic are presented.

Chapter 5 gives a comprehensive description of nonlinear structures and their sequential and linked representations in storage. The most important nonlinear structures are trees, and their representations and manipulations are discussed at some length. Furthermore, a number of applications such as dictionary construction and decision tables are included. Multilinked structures are also described. Graph structures and certain relevant applications such as PERT and CPM networks and computer graphics are presented. Finally, the topic of dynamic storage management is introduced.

Chapter 6 describes internal searching and sorting techniques. Searching methods based on binary trees and hashing techniques are introduced. Sorting methods such as the Quicksort, Heapsort, and Mergesort are described in some details. A comparison of these methods is made, and it is shown that the performance of certain methods can be significantly improved by choosing an appropriate data structure (and an associated storage structure).

Finally, Chap. 7 contains a rather comprehensive description of external files. External storage devices are described, since their characteristics are important in file design and manipulation. A number of file organizations such as sequential, index sequential, and random are introduced. Certain multiple-key file organizations such as multilists and inverted lists are also discussed. A number of applications are introduced for most of the types of files mentioned. Among the applications considered are a small billing system, an on-line banking system, and a student-records retrieval system. Data-base management systems are briefly introduced.

The emphasis of the course is on problem solving, algorithms, and, to a lesser extent, programming. We have strived to make sure that new concepts are well illustrated by examples and worked-out problems. The approach used in teaching the courses is modular—more complex structures are viewed in terms of simple structures. The ordering is primitive data structures, linear data structures, trees, multilinked structures, graphs (lists), and files.

The selection of the programming language(s) used to solve the problems in the exercises is an integral part of the problem-solving process. Ideally, the student should select the language which facilitates a "painless" formulation of the solution for a problem. While numerous special-purpose languages exist for particular application areas, it is unrealistic to expect the student to be fluent in all such languages. Special features from a wide variety of languages are discussed in the text; however, all the exercises are completed in a language with which the students are familiar and which contains the following features:

1　Character strings of dynamically varying length
2　Structure variables, i.e., variables which can contain elements with a mixture of data types
3　Facilities which allow the programmer to create and destroy instances of variables (including structure variables) dynamically
4　Recursion
5　Control structures which promote the proper structuring of programs

Suitable programming languages are ALGOL W, PL/I, and SNOBOL (although the control structures in SNOBOL are deficient in terms of feature 5). FORTRAN is the antithesis of the language to be used (it fails to have any of the five features). We have chosen PL/I as the main language because it provides the file-accessing facilities required.

Although a number of texts are available on data structures, few texts give a comprehensive treatment of files in terms of simpler structures that have been introduced in the same text. In addition, no text that we have encountered has been written adopting the philosophy and organization we are suggesting.

This book is suitable for course I1, Data Structures, of "Curriculum 68," [6] and for courses UC1 and UC3 in the "Curriculum Recommendations for Undergraduate Programs in Information Systems" report.[7] We do not follow the outlines of these courses exactly but the book is close enough to preserve their spirits. A basic familiarity with PL/I is assumed.

We owe a great deal to John A. Copeck, who made many valuable criticisms and suggestions throughout the entire preparation and proofreading of the book. In particular, John A. Copeck assisted in the preparation of Secs. 5-2.2, 5-5.1, and 5-6. We also owe a lot to Richard F. Deutscher, who formulated and tested many programs and assisted in the formulation of Secs. 4-3.3, 5-3.1, 5-5.4,7-1, and 7-3. We appreciate the efforts of Linda Nylander, who did many of the figures and assisted in the preparation of Secs. 3-7.1, 3-9, 5-2.4, 5-4.2, and 5-5.2.

We also acknowledge Walter Ridgeway for assisting us in the preparation of Secs. 2-5.4, 7-5, 7-7, and 7-9. Richard Cooper assisted us in the index-generation application and Lorna Stewart prepared all of the figures in Chap. 7. Allan Listoe proofread most of the manuscript and tested a number of programs. Finally, Robert Kavanagh assisted us in Sec. 5-5.2 and Richard Bunt proofread Secs. 3-9, 7-1, and 7-2. We owe a very special thanks to Dianne Good and Doreen Baker who did such an excellent job of typing the manuscript and to Gail Walker for providing typing support. This work would not have been possible without the support given by the University of Saskatchewan.

---

[6] Ibid 1

[7] Ibid 4

# 0

# INTRODUCTION

We begin this chapter with a discussion outlining the importance of structuring not only the data pertaining to the solution of a problem but also the programs that operate on the data. The task of formulating a solution to a problem is made simpler if the problem can be analyzed in terms of subproblems. This structuring process in problem solving is usually reflected in the program for the problem — the problem tends to be modular. This approach to problem solving and organization has had a profound impact on the design of many programming languages, in particular, the design of "goto-less" languages. Processes, or modules concerned with operations performed on data structures, are frequently represented by subroutines or functions. For the program implementation of any significant problem the organization of a program into suitable modules or subroutines is indispensable. The simple way to write programs is to organize them in such a modular fashion. The algorithms and programs presented in this text are written with this philosophy in mind.

In the second section of this chapter, a description of the algorithmic notation adopted throughout the text is introduced and illustrated with examples.

The third section introduces the notions of algorithm analysis. In particular, the time analysis of algorithms is emphasized.

## 0-1  STRUCTURE AND PROBLEM SOLVING

Problems solved on digital computers have become progressively larger and more complex. The computer programs providing the solutions to such problems have grown larger and more difficult to understand. The programmer(s) responsible for implementing the solutions to these large problems are given volumes of information consisting of problem specifications and flowcharts.

The task of writing a computer program is made simpler if the problem can be analyzed in terms of subproblems. The structuring process in problem solving is usually reflected in the program for the problem with the result being a modular program consisting of a number of small parts.

The concept of modularity in programs is not new. There have been for some years now a number of operating systems which have been constructed in a modular fashion. The computer manufacturer supplies the user with an operating system which consists of many program modules. The selected modules can be tuned to a particular operating environment by assigning system parameters representative of that environment. Also, since the operating system program is in a continual state of change, changes can be made more easily if the entire program is divided into a number of program modules whose interrelationships are simple and clearly defined.

A complex program usually cannot be written as a set of program modules unless its solution is structured or organized in that way. The programming of large problems usually involves many programmers, and the decisions made by one programmer, such as the choosing of labels and variable names, should not affect other programmers. This can only be accomplished if the description and specifications of each program module and its interfaces are made as clear and simple as possible. Indeed, for certain problems, the tasks of organizing and defining the problems are much more time consuming and costly than the task of programming them.

The modularity of most systems can be represented by a hierarchical structure (graph) such as that given in Fig. 0-1.1.

The structure has a *single* main module, with which we associate a level number of 1, that gives a brief general description of the system. The main module refers to a number of subordinate modules, with which we associate a level of 2, that give a more detailed description of the system than was done in the main module. The modules at level 2 refer to a further subdivision of modules at level 3, and so on. It is quite possible that modules at higher levels refer to modules at lower levels (this would be indicated by upward pointing arrows in the diagram), although this was not the case in Fig.0-1.1 and is not the case in general. The concept of hierarchically structuring a problem in this fashion is a fundamental one in problem solving. It is this form of organization or structuring which permits us to understand a system at different levels and allows us to make changes at one level without having to completely understand more detailed descriptions at higher levels. Also important in this hierarchical structuring process is the desirability of being able to understand a module at a certain level independently of all remaining modules at that same level.

Ideally, a program will be structured similar to that described in the previous diagram. This ideal modular structure does not necessarily imply that there is a direct correspondence between the flow of control in the program and the interconnections between subproblem modules. It is true that in most instances a module corresponds to a subroutine or procedure, but it is entirely possible that a problem module does not have any executable statements associated with it.

The best example of such a module is one which describes the organization of information required for communication between other modules. In such a module

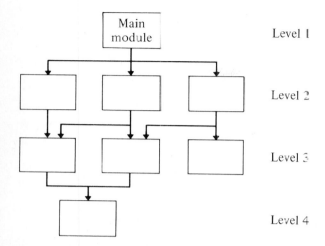

**FIGURE 0-1.1**   Hierarchical structure of a system.

we are concerned with structuring the information to facilitate easily understood and efficient methods of information access. Of course, such methods involve the use of appropriate data structures with efficient storage representations. Hence, the hierarchical structuring of program modules and submodules should not only reduce the complexity of the flow of control in program statements but also promote the proper structuring of information.

Thus far we have discussed the desirability of organizing the solution to a problem into a number of modules which can be understood independently. The modules in such a structural system correspond to concepts in the programmer's mind when he or she attempts to understand the problem. Indeed, the greater independency between the modules in general implies greater clarity and distinctness in these concepts.

In organizing a solution to a problem which is to be solved with the aid of a computer, we are confronted with at least four interrelated subproblems. The subproblems are:

1   To understand thoroughly the relationships between the data elements that are relevant to the solution of the problem
2   To decide on the operations that must be performed on the logically related data elements
3   To devise methods of representing the data elements in the memory of the computer such that (a) the logical relationships which do exist between data items can best be retained, and/or (b) the operations on the data elements can be accomplished easily and efficiently
4   To decide on what problem-solving (programming) language can best aid in the solution of the problem by allowing the user to express in a "natural" manner the operations he or she wishes to perform on the data

Let us examine, more closely, each of these subproblem areas.

To understand the logical relationships between the data items in the problem implies that we must understand the data itself. (Of course, to have a good understanding of the data, we must first of all take great care in the preparation and recording of the data!) Data in a particular problem consist of a set of elementary items or atoms. An atom usually consists of single elements such as integers, bits, characters, or a set of such items. A person solving a particular problem is concerned with establishing paths of accessibility between atoms of data. The choice of atoms of data is a necessary and key step in defining and then solving a problem. The possible ways in which the data items or atoms are logically related define different *data structures*. By choosing a particular structure for the data items, certain items become immediate neighbors, while other sets of items are related in a weaker sense. The interpretation of two items being immediate neighbors is that of adjacency relative to the ordering relation that may be imposed by the structure.

It is important to point out that the class of concepts dealing with data structures has become increasingly important in recent years. Initially, computers were used to solve primarily numerical scientific problems, but this has changed drastically with the emergence of many nonnumerical problems. Associated with the solution of numerical problems were rather primitive data structures such as variables, vectors, and arrays. These structures were, for most cases, adequate for the solution of numerical problems. However, in the solution of nonnumerical problems, these primitive data structures were clearly not sufficiently powerful to specify the more complex structural relationships in the data.

We turn to the second subproblem, that is, to decide on the operations which must be performed on the data structures that are to be used. A number of operations can be performed on data structures—operations to create and to destroy a data structure, operations to insert elements into and delete elements from a data structure, and operations to access elements within a data structure. Of course, these operations vary functionally for different data structures (for example, in Chap. 3 we will discover that the insert operation for a queue differs from the corresponding operation for a stack). The operations associated with a given data structure may be implemented as a set of fairly sophisticated algorithmic processes in a particular language, or these operations may be realized through basic instructions in the programming language that is used. Which situation occurs depends on the data structures being used and the programming languages that are available. For either case, the way in which data are manipulated is dependent on how the data structure is to be represented in memory—the third subproblem.

The representation of a particular data structure in the memory of a computer is called a *storage structure*. The distinction between a data structure and its corresponding storage structure is often confused. It frequently leads to a loss of efficiency and prevents problem solvers from making optimal use of their tools and resources. There are many possible memory configurations or storage structures corresponding to a particular data structure. For example, there are a number of possible storage structures for a data structure such as an array. It is also possible for two data structures to be represented by the same storage structure. In many instances, almost exclusive attention is directed toward the storage structures for certain given data and little attention is given to the data structure per se. In essence there is significant confusion between the properties that belong to the interpretation and meaning of the data on the one hand and the storage structures that can be selected to represent them in a programming system on the other hand.

In discussing storage structures, we will be concerned with representing data structures in both the main and the auxiliary memory of the computer. A storage structure representation in auxiliary memory is often called a *file structure*.

The fourth subproblem which we posed earlier related to the selection of a programming language to be used in the solution of the problem. If the representation of a data structure does not exist in the programming language being used, then the program for a particular algorithm may be quite complex. For example, in a payroll (data processing) application, a tree-like representation of information for an employee may be required. This structure does not exist in certain programming languages, such as FORTRAN. This does not mean that we cannot program a payroll application in FORTRAN. It could be done by writing programs to construct and manipulate trees; but this would be complex. It would be more suitable to use a data-processing language such as COBOL in this case. Ideally, the programming language chosen for the implementation of an algorithm should possess the particular representations chosen for the data structures in the problem being solved. In practice, the choice of a language may be dictated by what is available at a particular computing center, what language is preferred by some key personnel, etc.

It is clear from the above discussion that data structures, their associated storage structures, and the operations on data structures are all integrally related to problem solving using a computer. These three aspects will be examined in great detail in this text.

A fourth aspect, that of selecting an appropriate language in which to express a programmed solution to a problem, will not be rigorously pursued. However, whenever possible, we will be introducing programming language concepts from a variety of languages, especially as these concepts relate to the expressibility of a data structure and its associated operations.

A number of applications will be discussed in a comprehensive manner throughout the book. The problem-solving aspects of many applications will be examined in three stages, as follows:

*1* The selection of an appropriate mathematical model (including data structures)

*2* The formulation of algorithms based on the choice made in stage *1*

*3* The design of storage structures for the data structures obtained in stage *1*

The next section gives a description of the algorithmic notation which will be used to express the algorithms discussed throughout the book.

## 0-2 ALGORITHMIC NOTATION

In this section we present a full description of the algorithmic notation used in this book. Although parts of the notation will be introduced at various points throughout the book, the complete notation is given here as a reference. The algorithmic notation is best described with the aid of examples. Consider the following algorithm which determines the largest algebraic element of a vector:

**Algorithm GREATEST.** This algorithm finds the largest algebraic element of vector A which contains N elements and places the result in MAX. I is used to subscript A.

1. [Is the vector empty?]
    If $N < 1$
    then   Write('EMPTY VECTOR')
            Exit
2. [Initialize]
    MAX ← A[1]   (We assume initially that A[1] is the greatest element)
    I ← 2

3.   [Examine all elements of vector]
    Repeat thru step 5 while I ≤ N
4.   [Change MAX if it is smaller than the next element]
    If MAX < A[I]
    then   MAX ← A[I]
5.   [Prepare to examine next element in vector]
    I ← I + 1
6.   [Finished]
    Exit                                                                  □

The execution of an algorithm begins at step 1 and continues from there in sequential order unless the result of a condition tested or an unconditional transfer ('Go to', 'Exitloop', or 'Exit') specifies otherwise. In the sample algorithm, step 1 is executed first. If vector A is empty, the algorithm terminates; otherwise, step 2 is performed. In this step MAX is initialized to the value of A[1] and the subscript variable, I, is assigned the value 2. Step 3 leads to the termination of this algorithm if we have already tested the last element of A; otherwise, step 4 is performed. In this step, the value of MAX is compared with the value of the next element of the vector. If MAX is less than the next element, then MAX is assigned this new value. If the test fails, no reassignment takes place. The completion of step 4 is followed by step 5, where the next subscript value is incremented; control then returns to the testing step, step 3.

### 0-2.1  Format Conventions

The following subsections summarize the basic format conventions used in the formulation of algorithms.

#### 0-2.1.1  Name of Algorithm

Every algorithm is given an identifying name (**GREATEST** in the sample algorithm) written in capital letters.

#### 0-2.1.2  Introductory Comment

The algorithm name is followed by a brief description of the tasks the algorithm performs and any assumptions that have been made. The description gives the names and types of the variables used in the algorithm.

#### 0-2.1.3  Steps

The actual algorithm is made up of a sequence of numbered steps, each beginning with a phrase enclosed in square brackets which gives an abbreviated description of that step. Following this phrase is an ordered sequence of statements which describe actions to be executed or tasks to be performed. The statements in each step are executed in a left-to-right order.

#### 0-2.1.4  Comments

An algorithm step may terminate with a comment enclosed in round parentheses intended to help the reader better understand that step. Comments specify no action and are included only for clarity.

### 0-2.2 Statements and Control Structures

The following subsections summarize the types of statements and control structures available in the algorithmic notation.

#### 0-2.2.1 Assignment Statement

The assignment statement is indicated by placing an arrow ($\leftarrow$) between the right-hand side of the statement and the variable receiving the value. In step 2 of he sample algorithm, MAX $\leftarrow$ A[1] is taken to mean that the value of the vector element A[1] is to replace the contents of the variable MAX. Note that in this notation, the symbol "=" is used as a relational operator and never as an assignment operator. In step 5, I is incremented by I $\leftarrow$ I + 1. An exchange of the values of two variables (accomplished by the sequence of statements TEMP $\leftarrow$ A, A $\leftarrow$ B, B $\leftarrow$ TEMP) is written as A $\longleftrightarrow$ B. Finally, many variables can be set to the same value by using a multiple assignment; for example, I $\leftarrow$ 0, J $\leftarrow$ 0, K $\leftarrow$ 0 could be written as I $\leftarrow$ J $\leftarrow$ K $\leftarrow$ 0.

#### 0-2.2.2 If-statement

The if-statement has one of the following two forms:

*1*    If *condition*
    then    _____
             _____
                .
                .
                .
             _____

*2*    If *condition*
    then    _____
             _____
                .
                .
                .
             _____
    else    _____
             _____
                .
                .
                .
             _____

Following the "then" is an ordered sequence of statements which are all to be executed if the condition is *true*. These statements are referred to as the then-clause. After execution of the then-clause, control passes to the first statement after the if-statement. The range of the then-clause is indicated by indentation. If the tested condition is *false*, then either the next statement (type *1*) or the ordered sequence of statements following the "else" (type *2*) is executed. In the latter case, control goes to the next statement when the else-clause has been completed. Of course, any unconditional transfer ('Go to', 'Exitloop', or 'exit') in either the then- or else-clause must immediately be followed. If-statements can be nested within other if-statements, but for the sake of clarity, excessive nesting of if-statements should be avoided.

### 0-2.2.3 Case Statement

The case statement is used when a choice from among several mutually exclusive alternatives must be made on the basis of the value of an expression. The following segment of an algorithm contains an example of the case statement.

```
        .
        .
          .
4. [Process string beginning with either digit or letter]
        Select case (SUB(STRING, 1, 1))
                Case 'A' thru 'Z':
                Call WORD_OUT(STRING)
                Case '1' thru '9':
                Call DIGIT_OUT(STRING)
                DIGIT_CTR ← DIGIT_CTR + 1
                Case '□' or ',' or ';' or '.' or '?':
                (no action taken)
                Default:
                Write('ERROR -- INVALID STRING')
                Return
5. [Continue processing]
        .
        .
          .
```

In general, the case statement has the form:

```
Select case (expression)
        Case value 1:
        Case value 2:
            .
            .
              .
        Case value N:
        Default:
```

First, the expression is evaluated [in the example, Select case (SUB(STRING, 1, 1)) takes the first character of a string], and its value is compared to that of all the cases. A branch is then made to the appropriate case. If the value of the expression does not match that of any case, then a branch is made to the default case if there is one or to the next step if there is not.

### 0-2.2.4  Repeat Statement

For easy control of iteration (looping), a repeat statement has been provided. This statement has one of the following forms:

*1*    Repeat for INDEX = *sequence*
*2*    Repeat while *logical expression*
*3*    Repeat for INDEX = *sequence* while *logical expression*

Type *1* is used when a step is to be repeated for a counted number of times. INDEX is simply some variable used as a loop counter, and *sequence* is some representation of the sequence of values that INDEX will successively take. The starting value, the final value, and the increment size must be indicated in some way by the representation chosen: Repeat for I = 1, 2, . , 25, Repeat for TOP = N + K, N + K − 1, ..., 0, and Repeat for K = 9, 11, .., 2 * MAX + 1 are various examples of valid repeat statements. Once all statements in the range of the repeat statement have been executed, the index assumes the next value in the sequence, and the statements in the range are executed in order once again. We assume testing of an index for completion takes place prior to the execution of any statement; thus, a repeat statement may result in the loop being executed zero times. As an example, Repeat for I = −1, −2, .... 10 and Repeat for K = 5, 6, ..., −17 would no cause any statements to be executed; instead, the repeat statements would be treated as having completed their execution. Type *2* is used to repeat a step until a given logical expression is *false*. The evaluation and testing of the logical expression is performed at the beginning of the loop, and semantically the statement is similar to the while-clause of PL/I. As a special case of type *2*, we may write "Repeat while *true*." Since *true* is a valid logical expression, this is, in effect, an infinite loop. This possibility is rarely used but may be considered when we wish to exit a program. or just a loop, from within a loop. Consider the following segment:

.
.
.

5. [Loop to read data while there remains input]
        **Repeat while** *true*
           Read(ARRAY[I])
           If there is no more data
           then    **Exitloop**
           else    I ← I + 1

.
.
.

Type *3* is merely a combination of types *1* and *2* and is used to repeat a step for a sequence whose values are taken successively by INDEX until a logical expression is *false*. For each of the above types, the loop may extend over more than one step, in which case the repeat statement has the form "Repeat thru step N ... ."

As soon as a repeat statement has finished its execution, control is transferred to the first statement outside the range of the repeat statement. If, however, an 'Exitloop' statement is encountered during the execution of a repeat statement, control is transferred to the first step following the loop and the repeat statement is considered to have finished its execution. Here is another example of a repeat statement:

.

.

.

6. [Initialize counter]
   COUNT ← 0
7. [Processing loop]
   Repeat thru step 9 for I = 1, 2, ..., N
8. [Get number]
   Read(A[I])
9. [Count if negative]
   If A[I] < 0
   then COUNT ← COUNT + 1
10. [Output result]
    Write(COUNT)

.

.

.

If N has the value 5 and the first numbers in the data stream are 7, 4, –3, –2, 6, –17, 8, ..., then steps 8 and 9 would be executed five times and the number 2 would be printed in step 10 because there are two negative numbers among the first five. Control is *not* passed to step 10 after step 9 has been executed; instead, it is returned to the repeat statement where I is incremented, and steps 8 and 9 are allowed to execute once again if I is not greater than N.

### 0-2.2.5 Go To and Exitloop Statements

These two statements are rather extraordinary and are seldom used. The go to statement causes unconditional transfer of control to the step referenced. Thus, "Go to step N" will cause transfer of control to step N regardless of whether the statements of a loop or of a then- or else-clause have been completed. The exitloop statement is similar to the go to statement, but the range to which it can transfer control is limited. As the name implies, exitloop causes an immediate, unconditional exit from a loop. Note that an exitloop statement applies to only one level; thus, if one loop is nested within another, an exitloop from the inner loop will transfer control back to the outer loop. In general, go to and exitloop statements should be avoided since they lead to unstructured algorithms and, ultimately, to bad programming practice. Throughout the book we stress the importance of structured algorithms and use go tos and exitloops only when the alternatives are awkward.

### 0-2.2.6 Exit Statement

The exit statement is used to terminate an algorithm. It is usually the last step:

.

.

.

7. [Finished]
   Exit

However, there are often situations in which one may wish termination in midstream:

.
.
.

4. [ Check to see if processing can continue]

      If *condition*
      then   Exit

.
.
.

In any case, "Exit" causes immediate termination of an algorithm.

### 0-2.2.7 Variable Names

A variable is an entitiy that possesses a value, and its name is chosen to reflect the meaning of the value it holds (in the sample algorithm, MAX holds the largest algebraic element of a vector). For our purposes, a variable name always begins with a letter followed by characters which may be chosen from a set of possible characters including letters, numeric digits, and some special characters. Blanks are not permitted within a name, and all letters are capitalized. The following are examples of valid variable names:

      BLACK_BOX
      X_SQUARED
      ZEKE

The most useful of the special characters is "_" (called the *break character*), which may be used as a separator in names made up of several words; POT_OF_TEA is easier to read than POTOFTEA. The following are examples of invalid variable names:

| | |
|---|---|
| 4PLAY | Does not begin with a letter |
| A-Z | '-' is not one of the special characters allowed; otherwise, one could not differentiate this from the symbol for subtraction |
| TWO WORDS | Blanks are not allowed |

### 0-2.3 Data Structures

The following subsections summarize some of the nonprimitive data structures available in the algorithmic language. Structures and arrays of structures are introduced in Chaps. 3 and 4.

### 0-2.3.1 Arrays

Array elements are denoted by ARRAY[DIM1, DIM2, ..., DIMN], where ARRAY is the name of the array and DIM1 through DIMN are its subscripts. Array subscripts are always enclosed in square brackets.

#### 0-2.3.2 Dynamic Storage

The algorithmic notation facilitates the allocation of dynamic storage. Since this topic is dealt with in detail in Chaps. 4 and 5, we will only go into the notational aspects here.

One may define a block of storage to be made up of certain fields; for example, a block may have pointer (PTR, LINK, etc.) fields, information (INFO, DATA, etc.) fields, etc. The block is given an identifying name such as NODE. Schematically, a block of storage may look like one of the following:

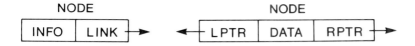

Definition of storage is informal, simply being described in the preamble to an algorithm.

The allocation symbol for dynamic storage is the heavy arrow ( ⟸ ), indicating that a pointer variable is to be given the address of an available block of storage (for example, X ⟸ NODE). Referencing a field of a given block is done by naming the field and following this by the pointer variable name enclosed in round parentheses; INFO(X) ← 'JUB JUB BIRD' sets the information field of node X to the given string. Finally, the freeing of a block of storage which is no longer needed is done by the restore statement; Restore(X) restores the block pointed to by X to the available storage area.

#### 0-2.4 Arithmetic Operations and Expressions

The algorithmic notation includes the standard binary and unary operators, and, of course, these are given the standard mathematical order of precedence. Table 0-2.1 should make this clear.

Arithmetic expressions may contain variables which have been assigned numeric values and are evaluated the same way as in mathematics. Thus, we may write GRADE ← 0.20 * LAB_WORK + 0.30 * MIDTERM + 0.50 * FINAL. In the notation we assume two types of numeric values, real and integer. As this implies, a real variable can hold any value, whereas an integer variable can only hold integer values with any fraction being truncated. As an example, if R is of type real and I of type integer, R ← 3 / 4 will assign a value of .75 to R while I ← 3 / 4 will assign a value of 0 to I.

#### 0-2.5 Strings and String Operations

Since many applications throughout the book are concerned with nonnumeric processing (i.e., symbol manipulation rather than "number crunching"), the algorithmic notation facilitates the processing of nonnumeric information. A character string is just that, a string of capitalized characters enclosed in single quotation marks ('THIS IS A VALID STRING'). For clarity, a blank is often denoted by a box; '☐☐' is a string containing two blanks. The null, or empty, string is denoted by two adjacent quotation marks, ''. Note that this is not the same as '☐' which is a string containing a single blank.

**Table 0-2.1**    Arithmetic Operators and Precedence

| | Operation | Symbol | Order of Evaluation |
|---|---|---|---|
| 1. | Parentheses | () | Inner to outer |
| 2. | Exponentiation | ↑ | Right to left |
| | Unary plus, minus | +, − | |
| 3. | Multiplication | * | Left to right |
| | Division | / | |
| 4. | Addition | + | Left to right |
| | Subtraction | − | |

The simplest string operation is that of concatenation denoted by '○'; for example, 'FRUMIOUS' ○ '□' ○ 'BANDERSNATCH' is equivalent to 'FRUMIOUS□BANDERSNATCH'. Just as variables may hold numeric constants or values of arithmetic expressions, so they may represent character strings, thus, we may write G ← 'GRYPHON'. More complex string manipulations are discussed in detail in Chap. 2. These include functions such as LENGTH, INDEX, and SUB, which are patterned after PL/I's LENGTH, INDEX, and SUBSTR functions, respectively.

### 0-2.6  Relations and Relational Operators

In this book the relational operators (<, >, ≤, ≥, =, ≠) are written the same way as, and have the same meaning as, their mathematical counterparts. Relations between variables and expressions will be considered valid if the variables have been assigned some value. A relation evaluates to a logical expression, that is, it has one of two possible values, *true* or *false*. Numerical relations are clear. Relations between strings are possible and depend on a colating sequence such as '□&#...ABC...Z01...9'. According to this sequence, special characters are lexically less than letters which, in turn, are lexically less than digits. Of course, relations between data types are not possible. In the following examples, Z has the value 10 and MT has the value 'MOCK TURTLE':

*1*    Z ≤ 9/3 + 2
*2*    Z ≠ Z + 5
*3*    MT < 'MOCK TURTLE SOUP'

Relations *1*, *2*, and *3* have the values *false*, *true*, and *true*, respectively.

### 0-2.7  Logical Operations and Expressions

The algorithmic notation also includes the standard logical operators. These are

| Operator | Notation |
|---|---|
| negation | not |
| logical and | and |
| logical or | or |

which are given in decreasing order of their precedence. These may be used to connect relations to form compound relations whose only values are *true* and *false*. In order that logical expressions be clear, we assume that operator precedence is as follows:

| Precedence | Operator |
|---|---|
| 1 | Parentheses |
| 2 | Arithmetic |
| 3 | Relational |
| 4 | Logical |

Consider the following, assuming that ONE is a variable whose value is 1:

*1*   (ONE < 2) and (ONE < 0)
*2*   (ONE < 2) or  (ONE < 0)
*3*   not(ONE < 2)

Expressions *1*, *2*, and *3* have the values *false*, *true*, and *false*, respectivly.

Just as we have numeric and character variables, so we have logical variables (for example, FLAG ← *true*). Logical expressions are most often used as conditions in repeat and if statements. In a repeat statement one might have:

3. [Loop on pass]
      Repeat thru step 6 while NUM ≠ MAX and not ERROR_FLAG

In an if statement one might have:

If X ≤ 100
then X ← X ↑ 2

**0-2.8  Input and Output**

In the algorithmic notation, input is obtained and placed in a variable by the statement "Read(*variable name*)." Output has the form "Write(*literal* or *variable name*)" with literals enclosed in quotation marks. For example, we may output the value of X by writing **Write(X)** if X is any variable, or we may output messages by writing Write( 'STACK UNDERFLOW'). Input and output are not limited to single variables; Read(X, Y, Z) is certainly valid and causes three consecutive pieces of data to be read into X, Y, and Z, respectively. In fact, we may extend input and output to arrays; for example:

    .
    .
    .

10. [Output data]
      Repeat for I = 1, 2, ..., N
      Write(A[I])

    .
    .
    .

Lastly, end of file may be used as the terminating condition of a repeat statement (e.g., Repeat while there is input data).

### 0-2.9  Subalgorithms

A subalgorithm is an independent component of an algorithm and for this reason is defined separately from the main algorithm. The purpose of a subalgorithm is to perform some computation, when required, under control of the main algorithm. This computation may be performed on zero or more parameters passed by the calling routine. The format used is the same as for algorithms except that a return statement replaces an exit statement and a list of parameters follows the subalgorithm's name. Note that subalgorithms may invoke each other and that a subalgorithm may also invoke itself recursively. Consider the following recursive function:

**Function** FACTORIAL(N). This function computes N! recursively. N is assumed to be a nonnegative integer.

1.   [Apply recursive defintion]
        If N = 0
        then    Return(1)
        else    Return(N * FACTORIAL(N–1))                                    ☐

In the algorithmic notation, as in Pascal, there are two types of subalgorithms: functions and procedures.

### 0-2.9.1  Functions

A function is used when one wants a single value returned to the calling routine. Transfer of control and returning of the value are accomplished by 'Return(*value*)'. A function begins as follows: Function NAME(PARM1, PARM2, ..., PARMN). The following example function should make clear the format of functions:

**Function** AVERAGE(VAL1, VAL2, VAL3). The purpose of this function is to compute the average of three values. We assume all variables to be real. AV is a local variable of type real used to return the computed value

1.   [Compute average]
        AV ← (VAL1 + VAL2 + VAL3) / 3.0
2.   [Return result]
        Return(AV)                                                            ☐

A function is invoked as an implicit part of an expression; for example, E ← AVERAGE(X, Y, Z) results in the returned value being put into E.

### 0-2.9.2  Procedures

A procedure is similar to a function but there is no value returned explicitly. A procedure is also invoked differently. Where there are parameters, a procedure returns its results through the parameters. Here is an example of a typical procedure:

**Procedure** DIVIDE(DIVIDEND, DIVISOR, QUOTIENT, REMAINDER). This procedure divides the **DIVIDEND** by the **DIVISOR** giving the **QUOTIENT** and REMAINDER. Assume all numbers to be integer.

1. [Perform integer division]
     QUOTIENT ← DIVIDEND / DIVISOR
2. [Determine remainder]
     REMAINDER ← DIVIDEND – QUOTIENT * DIVISOR
3. [Return to point of call]
     Return                                                                        ☐

Note that no value is returned explicitly but that the quotient and remainder are returned through two of the parameters. A procedure is invoked by means of a call statement: for example, Call DIVIDE(DDEND, DIV, Q, R).


### 0-2.9.3 Parameters

In all subalgorithms there is a one-to-one positional correspondence between the arguments of the invocation and the subalgorithm parameters. With the AVERAGE function we just looked at there is a one-to-one correspondence between the parameters VAL1, VAL2, and VAL3 and the arguments X, Y, and Z of the invocation E ← AVERAGE(X, Y, Z). All parameters are assumed to be called by reference (or address) unless otherwise specified; therefore, if parameters are to be call by value, this should be stated in the preamble, as should all other assumptions. Lastly, as mentioned before, there may not be any parameters. In this case, all variables are assumed to be global. Of course, there may be global variables as well as parameters.


## 0-3 INTRODUCTION TO ALGORITHM ANALYSIS FOR TIME AND SPACE REQUIREMENTS

As soon as one can write an algorithm, it is necessary to learn how to analyze an algorithm. The first type of analysis that one encounters is of the correctness of an algorithm. This analysis can be done by tracing the algorithm, reading the algorithm for logical correctness, implementing the algorithm, and testing it on some data, or using mathematical techniques to prove it correct. Another type of analysis is of the simplicity of the algorithm. Perhaps the algorithm can be expressed in a simpler way so that it is easier to implement and perform other analyses on the algorithm. However, the simplest and most straightforward way of solving a problem is sometimes not the best one. Usually this occurs when the simplest approach involves the use of too much computer time or space. Thus it is important to be able to analyze the time and space requirements of an algorithm to see if it is within acceptable limits. For example, if an algorithm to control the trajectory of a rocket required several seconds for each trajectory adjustment, it would be unacceptable. Time and space analyses are also important for comparison of algorithms to determine the best one. This section will provide an introduction to the basic concepts in analyzing the time and space requirements of an algorithm. The analysis will initially emphasize timing analysis and then, to a lesser extent, space analysis.


### 0-3.1 Rate of Growth

Unfortunately it is generally not possible to perform a simple analysis of an algorithm to determine the exact amount of time required to execute it. The first complication is that the exact amount of time will depend on the implementation of the algorithm and on the actual machine. We would like our analysis to be useful in as general a context as possible and not dependent on the language or machine that might be used to implement it. As a result we cannot expect our analysis to yield an exact value for the time required. Even if we did specify the language and machine to be used, the task of calculating the exact time would be very laborious. To do this task, we would need to know the exact instructions executed by the hardware and the time required for each instruction. Fortunately we are normally satisfied if our analysis is capable of giving the order of magnitude for the time required.

Yet another complication arises in doing a timing analysis in that the time requirements will normally depend on the amount of input. For example, an algorithm that sums the values in an vector can be expected to require more time for a vector of size 100,000 values than for one of size 100. As a result the estimate for the time required by an algorithm is usually expressed as a function of the size of the input. Thus if the input has size n, as in the above example, where there are n values in the vector, then the time is expressed as $T(n)$ and space as $S(n)$, where T and S are functions of the amount of data.

Before beginning our analysis of algorithms, it is beneficial to recall the rates of growth for some functions that are often used to express T and S. Figure 0-3.1 plots several functions. As is readily apparent, some functions grow much faster than others. The functions that involve n as an exponent, $2^n$, $n^n$, and $n! \sim (n/2.56)^n$ (using Stirling's approximation for n!), are called exponential functions. Any algorithm whose execution time grows proportionally to an exponential function is too slow for anything but small input sizes. Functions whose growth is less than or equal to $n^c$ for some constant c, for example, $n^3$, $n^2$, $n \log_2 n$, n and $\log_2 r$, are said to be polynomial. Algorithms with polynomial time can solve reasonable-sized problems if the constant in the exponent is small. For problems involving large amounts of data, it is necessary to find an algorithm whose execution time grows linearly, proportional to n, or sublinearly, for instance, proportional to $\log_2 n$.

### 0-3.2  Basic Time Analysis of an Algorithm

Let us begin our analysis of the time required for the execution of an algorithm with an example. First consider the following algorithm to sum the values in vector V that contains N values:

**Algorithm** SUM_VALUES. Given a vector V containing N elements, this algorithm computes the arithmetic sum (SUM) of these elements. I is an integer variable.

1.  [Sum the values in Vector V]
    SUM ← 0
    Repeat for I = 1, 2, ..., N
        SUM ← SUM + V[I]
2.  [Finished]
    Exit                                                                    ☐

As remarked in the previous section, rather than calculating the exact time, we want an estimate of it. Usually this is most easily done by isolating a particular operation, sometimes called an *active operation*, that is central to the algorithm and that is executed essentially as often as any other. In the above example, a good operation to isolate is the addition that occurs when another vector value is added to the partial sum. The other operations in the algorithm, the assignments, the mani-

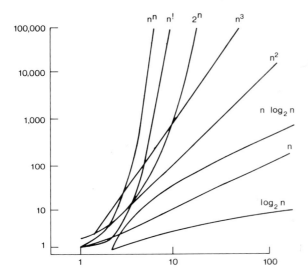

**FIGURE 0-3.1**

pulations of the index I, and the accessing of a value in the vector, occur no more often than the addition of vector values. These other operations are collectively called *bookkeeping operations* and are not generally counted. It is very important that none of the bookkeeping operations are executed significantly more often than the active operation. (Later we will see that it isn't a problem if one is executed slightly more often.) After the active operation is isolated, the number of times that it is executed is counted. If we follow this approach in the example, the number of additions of values in the above algorithm is N. As long as the active operation occurs at least as often as the others, then the execution time will increase in proportion to the number of times the active operation is executed. Thus the above algorithm has execution time proportional to N. Or expressed another way, the time required is linearly proportional to the size of the input.

As a second example, consider the matrix multiplication of two N×N matrices, A and B, to form an N×N matrix C. The matrix multiplication can be accomplished by the following algorithm:

**Algorithm** MATRIX_MULTIPLICATION. Given two-dimensional square matrices A and B, each containing N rows and columns, this algorithm computes the matrix product and places the result in matrix C. I, J, and K are integer variables.

1.   [Multiply matrices A and B, and store the result in matrix C]
      Repeat for I = 1, 2, ..., N
         Repeat for J = 1, 2, ..., N
            SUM ← 0
            Repeat for K = 1, 2, ..., N
               SUM ← SUM + A[I, K] * B[K, J]
            C[I, J] ← SUM
2.   [Finished]
      Exit

The actual size of the input for this algorithm is $2N^2$, but it is convenient to use N as our measure of the size of the input in order to simplify the calculations. For the active operation, we can select either the multiplication of A[I, K] and B[K, J], or the addition of the above product to SUM. This follows since both are central operations and essentially occur as often as any other. It is easy to see that either of these operations is executed $N^3$ times, so that the time for the algorithm is proportional to $N^3$.

Note that there are actually more assignments than multiplications or additions. There are N assignments to I, $N^2$ assignments to J and C, $N^3$ assignments to K, and $N^2 + N^3$ assignments to SUM. This yields a total of $N + 3N^2 + 2N^3$ assignments. Certainly assignment could have been selected as our active operation, although it is questionable whether it is as central to the problem as either multiplication or addition. If it were used as the active operation, we would conclude that the time was proportional to $N + 3N^2 + 2N^3$. Fortunately we are normally only interested in the order of magnitude of the time required. The order only considers the term (an additive part of the equation for the function) that grows the fastest, $2N^3$, and ignores the constant, 2, associated with it. Thus we obtain that the order of magnitude for the time required is $N^3$, independent of which operation is chosen as active, but that just happens in this problem. In other cases, maybe assignments would have to be active.

### 0-3.3 Order Notation

A notation has been developed to facilitate the handling of order of magnitude functions. A function f(n) is defined to be O(g(n)), that is. f(n) = O(g(n)), and is said to be of order g(n), if there exists positive constants $n_0$ and c such that

$$|f(n)| \leq c * |g(n)| \qquad \text{for all } n > n_0$$

Thus it is easy to verify the following:

$100n^3$ is $O(n^3)$
$6n^2 + 2n + 4$ is $O(n^2)$
$1 + 2 + 3 + \cdots + n = n * (n + 1)/2 = n^2 - O(r) = O(n^2)$
1024 is $O(1)$
$n + \log n$ is $O(n)$
$3n$ is $O(n^2)$ [and also of $O(n)$].

Using the definition of a limit from calculus, the above definition can be shown to be equivalent to

$$\lim_{n \to \infty} \frac{|f(n)|}{|g(n)|} = c$$

for some constant c. In this form, L'Hopital's rule is often useful for computing the limit. It states that if

$$\lim_{n \to \infty} f(n) = \infty \quad \text{and} \quad \lim_{n \to \infty} g(n) = \infty$$

then

$$\lim_{n \to \infty} \frac{f(n)}{g(n)} = \lim_{n \to \infty} \frac{f'(n)}{g'(n)}$$

where f' and g' are derivatives of f and g. Thus, as an example,

$$\lim_{n \to \infty} \frac{\ln(n)}{n} = \lim_{n \to \infty} \frac{1/n}{1} = \lim_{n \to \infty} \frac{1}{n} = 0 \qquad \text{so} \qquad \ln(n) = O(n),$$

where ln(n) is the natural logarithm of n. Using this notation we have

$$T_S(n) = O(n) \quad \text{and} \quad T_{MM}(n) = O(n^3)$$

where $T_S$ is the time for the vector sum algorithm and $T_{MM}$ is the time for the matrix multiplication algorithm.

### 0-3.4 More Timing Analysis

In this section two more algorithms will be analyzed to develop further techniques. First consider the following algorithm to search vector V of size N for the location containing value X:

**Algorithm** SEARCH. Given a vector V containing N elements, this algorithm searches V for the value of a given X. FOUND is a Boolean variable. I and LOCA-TION are integer variables.

1.  [Search for the location of value X in vector V]
    FOUND ← *false*
    I ← 1
    Repeat while I ≤ N and not FOUND
        If V[I] = X
        then   FOUND ← *true*
               LOCATION ← I
               Exit
        else   I ← I + 1
    Write ('VALUE OF', X, 'NOT FOUND')
2.  [Finished]
    Exit                                                                □

A reasonable active operation is the comparison between values of V and X. However, a problem arises in counting the number of active operations executed: the answer depends on the index of the location containing X. The best case is when X is equal to V[1] since only one comparison is used. The worst case is when X is equal to V[N] and N comparisons are used. Thus we obtain

$$T_{LS}^B(N) = O(1), \quad \text{and} \quad T_{LS}^W(N) = O(N),$$

where $T_{LS}^B$ is the best-case time for the linear search and $T_{LS}^W$ is the worst-case time for the linear search.

The important question is, "What time can be expected on the average?" To answer this question, we need to know the probability distribution for the value X in the vector, i.e., the probability of X occurring in each location. If we assume the vector is not sorted, it is reasonable to assume that X is equally likely to be in each of the locations. But X might not be in the list at all. Let q be the probability that X is in the list. Then using the above assumption, we have

probability X is in location I is q/N
probability X is not in the vector is 1 − q

The average time is given by

$$T_{LS}^A(N) = \sum_{s \text{ in } S} (\text{probability of situation } s) * (\text{time for situation } s)$$

where S is the set of all possible situations. Thus for the above algorithm we have

$$T_{LS}^A(N) = \text{(probability of X in location 1)} * 1$$
$$+ \text{(probability of X in location 2)} * 2 \quad \ldots$$
$$+ \text{(probability of X in location N)} * N$$
$$+ \text{(probability of X not in V)} * N$$

$$= \sum_{s=1}^{N} \frac{q}{N} * s + (1 - q) * N$$

$$= \frac{q}{N} \sum_{s=1}^{N} s + (1 - q) * N$$

$$= q * \frac{(N + 1)}{2} + (1 - q) * N$$

Thus if $q = 1$, then

$$T_{LS}^A(N) = \frac{(N+1)}{2}$$

and if $q = \frac{1}{2}$, then

$$T_{LS}^A(N) = \frac{(N+1)}{4} + \frac{N}{2} \sim \frac{3N}{4}$$

In either case, $T_{LS}^A(N) = O(N)$.

Unfortunately, as the above example indicates, the average-case timing analysis is generally more difficult than the best case or the worst case. The difficulties begin with the need to obtain a reasonable probability distribution of the possible situations. For many problems, this is difficult to do. As a result, only the worst-case timing analysis is done for many algorithms.

It is interesting to consider an alternate version of the linear search.

**Algorithm** ALTERNATE_SEARCH. This is a reformulation of Algorithm SEARCH given earlier. The vector V has been padded with an extra element.

1.  [Linear search when the value is initially placed at the end of the vector]
    V[N + 1] ← X
    I ← 1
    Repeat while V[I] ≠ X
        I ← I + 1
    If I = N + 1
    then   Write ('VALUE OF', X, 'NOT FOUND')
    else   LOCATION ← I
2.  [Finished]
    Exit                                                                    □

The number of comparisons between V and X is the same as for the previous algorithm, except that one more comparison is required for the present algorithm when X isn't in the vector. Thus using a count of executions of the active operation, we would conclude that the first algorithm is marginally better. But for algorithms with the same order, the constants associated with the largest term of the timing function should be estimated. In this example, it is easy to see that there are significantly more bookkeeping operations for the first algorithm than for the second. This results in a larger constant associated with the term for N in the equation for the time of the first algorithm. Thus the second algorithm will be more efficient. To determine how much larger the constant would be would necessitate a much more detailed analysis. For such comparisons, it is sometimes better to implement and time both versions. Nevertheless, it is frequently useful to try to give an order of magnitude estimate for the size of the constant associated with the largest term.

### 0-3.5 Space Analysis of an Algorithm

The analysis of the space requirements for an algorithm is generally easier than the timing analysis, but where necessary, the same techniques are used. Usually the space analysis is only done for the space to store the data values and hence does not include the space to store the algorithm itself. Also, as for timing analysis, the space function is usually expressed in order notation.

**BIBLIOGRAPHY**

BAASE, S.: "Computer Algorithms: Introduction in Design and Analysis," Addison-Wesley, 1978.
HOROWITZ, E., S. SAHNI: "Fundamentals of Computer Algorithms," Computer Science Press, 1978.

# 1

# INFORMATION AND ITS
# STORAGE REPRESENTATION

*To begin a study of data (or information) structures, we find it is necessary to establish clearly what is meant by information, how information is transmitted, and how (in its most basic form) information is stored in a computer. It is not our intention to delve deeply into questions concerning the nature of information and information transmittal, for to do so would involve an intensive study in information and communication theory. However, we do wish to discuss information and its transmission and storage from a clear and simplistic viewpoint so that the student of information structures can appreciate what information is and how it is physically handled.*

*In the latter part of this chapter, we relate the earlier discussion on information concepts to a description of the primitive data structures commonly used to solve problems with a computer. The primitive data structures we introduce are the integers, reals, logical data, character data, and pointer data. In the discussion of each primitive data structure, we will emphasize its storage representation.*

## 1-1 THE NATURE OF INFORMATION

It can be said that the study of any aspect in computer science involves the storage, retrieval, and manipulation of information. For example, information is stored when a student record is updated with term marks. Information is retrieved when a compiler requests, for translation, the next source-language instruction from a program-source file. And information is manipulated when two numbers are added together in the arithmetic unit of a computer. Hence, students' marks, program instructions, and numbers are all information. In this context, we can define information as recorded or communicated material that has some meaning associated with symbolic representation.

Can we measure information? For example, how much information is there in a student's mark? Does program A contain more information than program B? Because the answer to such questions are very basic to computer science, as well as to other areas of research (e.g., psychology, business management, and communication engineering), a separate field of study called *information theory* has evolved. In this section we introduce basic notions from information theory to provide some understanding of the nature of information.

In an attempt to discover a "yardstick" for measuring information, Hartley [1928], Kolmogoroff [1942], Wiener [1948], and Shannon [1949] have presented formal definitions for information content. In an information theoretic sense, information is viewed as the resolution of uncertainty. Suppose we are given a set of $n$ configurations (or data items) of any system in which each configuration has an independent probability of occurrence $p_i$. Then the *uncertainty* of the set is defined as

$$H = -\sum_{i=1}^{n} p_i \log_2(p_i)$$

(1-1.1)

To illustrate how Eq. (1-1.1) is applied, assume we have eight poker chips numbered on one side, 1 through 8. Suppose the chips are placed on a table, numbered-side down, and we select one chip from the set of eight. We might ask "What is the number on the selected chip?" Or, phrasing the question in terms of measurement of uncertainty, how much uncertainty is there associated with the identity of the chip before we turned the chip over? We know that with probability 1/8 the chip is marked with a given number for all numbers between 1 and 8. Therefore, if we apply Eq. (1-1.1), the average uncertainty associated with the nature of the selected chip is

$$H = -\sum_{i=1}^{8} \frac{1}{8} \log_2(\frac{1}{8}) = -\log_2(\frac{1}{8}) = \log_2(8) = 3 \text{ bits}$$

Notice that we have assigned a unit of measure, namely *bits*, to the measure of uncertainty of a set. A bit is a measure of uncertainty (or information) which represents the presence of a two-state condition, as exemplified by an on-off condition or a true-false condition. Observe that we have said a bit is a measure both of uncertainty and of information. This association is intentional, since the amount of information gained can be equated with the amount of uncertainty that is removed upon discovering the nature of information source, such as the number on the chip. If one asks the question "Is Bill's dog brown?," then the uncertainty involving the color of Bill's dog can be removed by answering correctly yes or no. Because an answer, whether it be yes or no, arises from a two-state condition, the amount of uncertainty removed or information gained by receiving a yes or no is one bit.

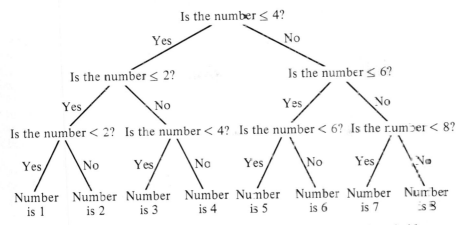

**FIGURE 1-1.1** Question tree for discovering the nature of a numbered chip.

For the case of the selected numbered chip, we calculated that three bits of information were necessary to remove the uncertainty of the number on the chip. From our definition of bit, this would imply that if we were allowed to ask three "yes-no questions," the nature of the chip would be uncovered. In fact this is true! The "question tree" in Fig. 1-1.1 illustrates how the number of the chip can be discovered assuming correct yes-no answers are received for the questions.

The three bits of information associated with the discovery of the chip's number can be represented by a message of length three, composed of 0's and 1's (where a 1 represents a "yes" answer and a 0 represents a "no" answer) In Table 1-1.1, message scheme A represents all possible paths in the question tree where the ith bit, $i = 1, 2,$ or 3, in a message represents the ith question asked. Message scheme B illustrates that scheme $A$ is by no means unique, i.e., many three-bit schemes could be devised to represent the identity of each of the eight chips.

**Table 1-1.1** Message schemes representing the eight numbered chips.

| Chip Number | Message Scheme A | Message Scheme B |
|:---:|:---:|:---:|
| 1 | 111 | 001 |
| 2 | 110 | 010 |
| 3 | 101 | 011 |
| 4 | 100 | 100 |
| 5 | 011 | 101 |
| 6 | 010 | 110 |
| 7 | 001 | 111 |
| 8 | 000 | 000 |

Note that if we had considered nine chips with numbers 1 to 9, a bit message of at least length four would be required. In fact, it has been shown (Reza [1961]) that for any coding scheme representing a set of $n$ elements which are equally probable of being selected, at least one of the codes must have its length greater than or equal to the information measure of the set, that is,

$$H = -\sum_{i=1}^{n} p_i \log_2 p_i$$

Messages consisting of 0's and 1's are very important in the study of information structures. As we will observe in the next section when discussing the transfer of information, messages in a computer are of this form (i.e., strings of 0's and 1's). Our measure of average information content $H$, which yields a bound on message length, can be helpful in determining a good storage structure for a given data structure. In Chap. 7, for example, we will use this information measure to compute the efficiency of certain storage structures used for record organizations in files.

It would be misleading to imply that all information is measurable. For example, we can ask whether the information content on this page is the same for an undergraduate student as it is for a child of six. Obviously, it is not. A main ingredient necessary for information to be transferred is understanding. In communication theory, messages that are received but not completely understood are said to contain "noise." It is the problem of deciding what is noise and what is meaningful information that has prevented the application of information theory to everyday situations—situations such as measuring the information content of a lecture or measuring the information flow through a company.

**Exercises for Sec. 1-1**

1.  Consider the probabilities associated with the event of rolling a pair of dice. The probability that a certain number shows is given in Table 1-1.2. Compute the average uncertainty $H$ that is associated with the event of rolling a pair of dice.

2.  Create a fixed-length binary code capable of representing each of the possible rolled amounts in Prob. 1. (By "fixed length" we mean that all codes are of the same length.) Compare the length of this code to the value computed in Prob. 1. Should it be higher or lower?

**Table 1-1.2**

| Rolled Amount | Probability | Rolled Amount | Probability |
|:---:|:---:|:---:|:---:|
| 2 | 1/36 | 8 | 5/36 |
| 3 | 1/18 | 9 | 1/ 9 |
| 4 | 1/12 | 10 | 1/12 |
| 5 | 1/ 9 | 11 | 1/18 |
| 6 | 5/36 | 12 | 1/36 |
| 7 | 1/ 6 | | |

3. Design a variable-length binary code representing the rolled amount in Prob.
   1. The code should be designed so that if a number of events are recorded
   using this code, the average length of a code for these events is less than that
   derived in Prob. 2.

## 1-2 THE TRANSMISSION OF INFORMATION

Shannon [1949] depicts the process of transmitting information as a five-element system: a *source,* or originator of a message; a *transmitter,* or encoder of the message to
be sent; a *channel,* the medium through which the message is conveyed; a *receiver,* or
decoder of the message received; and a *destination,* or recipient of the information.
These are illustrated in Fig. 1-2.1. An example of a communication system is a
human (or human brain) as a source, the mouth, tongue, and other speech organs as
a transmitter, air as the channel, the auditory system of another human as receiver,
and the brain of the receiving person as the destination. In a simple computer system, a video display terminal can be considered a source, the keyboard a
transmitter, a transmission line from the keyboard to the computer maintaining a
channel, a channel selector (or multiplexor) a receiver, and main memory of the
computer the destination.

   While the above discussion illustrates the physical components of an information transmission process, there are three aspects that must be considered to ensure
the transfer of information between the source and destination. These are the syntactic, semantic, and pragmatic aspects (Morris [1946]). The *syntactic* aspect concerns the physical *form* of the information transmitted. For example, the syntactic
aspect of the information received while reading this sentence is the form or shape
of the ink blots of which it is constituted. The ink blots are recognized as letters
from the English alphabet which are combined to form words, which in turn are
combined to form a sentence. Through a sentence, a concept or concepts are
expressed and meaning is associated with the syntactic form of the information. The
*semantic* aspect refers to this *meaning,* which is attached to the syntactic representation. The *pragmatic* aspect of information transmission involves the *action* taken as a
result of the interpretation (i.e., attached meaning) of the information. The actions
taken as a result of interpretation of the information often depend heavily on previous conditioning. For example, if we disagree with what is written in a particular
book (based on previous experience), we may choose to close the book—possibly
permanently.

   Successful communication must take all three aspects into consideration. If we
were to change the syntactic structure of the English language—as would be the case

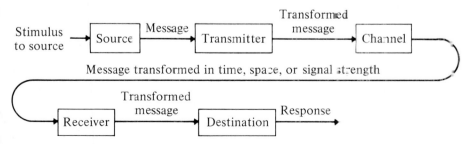

**FIGURE 1-2.1**   A diagram of a general communication system.

if "blanks" were inserted within words—proper communication would be inhibited. Similarly, communication is inhibited if it is impossible to associate any semantics with the words. For example, what is the meaning of "data evade lowly"? It is a syntactically correct English sentence but has no meaning. Of course, the pragmatic aspect (i.e., the action taken) depends on the semantic aspect just as the semantic aspect depends on the syntactic aspect. In the case of the sentence "Data evade lowly," the semantics are questionable. Hence, no action can be expected to follow—except possibly to reread the words.

A further example illustrating the relationship between the three aspects of information transfer can be drawn from the area of computer programming. For the successful execution of a Pascal program, the source statements must be syntactically correct. If a comma or semicolon is missing or appears in a wrong place, the statement is syntactically incorrect, and possibly an invalid interpretation may be given to the statement. (Again, the semantics depend on the syntactic form of the information). Even if a source statement is syntactically correct, the semantics interpretation that the programmer and the compiler attach to the statements may differ. For example, we may write the statement

    x := a + b * c;

wishing x to be assigned the expression *(a + b) * c*, whereas the compiler may interpret the assigned expression as *a + (b * c)*. Of course, the pragmatic result or action of the compiler is to generate the machine code associated with *x := a + (b * c);*. In summary, for information to be transferred successfully, it is necessary to have rules which are mutually accepted by the sender and the receiver regarding the syntactic and semantic aspects of the information, plus a set of appropriate actions taken in response to the meaning derived by the receiver.

In introducing the three aspects necessary for information transmission, we assumed that the transmission process should fall into the general class of communication systems as proposed by Shannon [1949] (see Fig. 1-2.1). It is interesting to note, however, that there are, in general, two methods of physically transmitting information: *continuous* and *discrete*.

Information transmitted in a continuous form appears as signals selected from a spectrum of amplitudal values, as illustrated in Fig. 1-2.2. The classical example

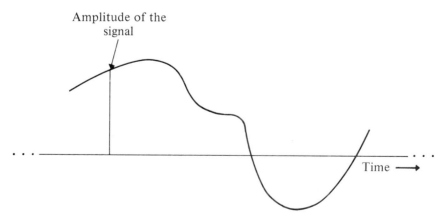

**FIGURE 1-2.2**    Continuous information transmission.

of continuous-information transmission takes place in verbal communication which relies on the frequency and amplitude of sound waves

Information transmitted in a discrete form appears as signals which may only assume a finite number of states within a continuum of amplitudal values. For example, the presence or absence of a pulse can represent a discrete form of information, such as a true-false or an on-off condition. This is illustrated in Fig. 1-2.3. Notice a cutoff point exists for determining if the pulse is on or off. Written text provides us with a classical example of a method of communication which relies on discrete-information transmission. That is, whether we write "DATA" or "data," we receive the same information. Even though each person has his or her own writing style, we always attempt, when interpreting a piece of written English text, to resolve each symbol to one of twenty-six different letters from the English alphabet. Of course, the twenty-six letters represent the finite number of states that characterize discrete information transmission.

Analog computers are designed to store, retrieve, and manipulate information that is continuous in nature. These types of computers are particularly well suited to the solution of linear, integral, and differential equations as might be required, for example, in controlling a fractionation process where the composition and amount of gas in a fractionation tower is regulated. Based on information representing the correct composition of raw materials entering the tower, plus current temperature and pressure readings, a new temperature setting is calculated via a control law. This control law has been programmed (i.e., hardwired) into the integrating and differentiating circuitry of the analog computer. All readings, settings, and calculations are in the form of continuous signals.

An analog computer does not have the speed, computational ability, and above all, accuracy to handle the processing needs of many of the common computer applications such as payroll accounting. In fact, even in process-control applications like the fractionation tower example, the analog computer is not completely satisfactory and has been replaced by the computationally superior digital computer or by a combination of digital and analog computers known as *hybrid computers* (see Smith [1970]).

In a digital computer, all information is transferred in a discrete form which involves signals representing one of two states. The binary signals are created by the presence or absence of an electric current or the presence of a positive or a negative current. Certain research efforts have been made toward the development of nonbinary computers (especially ternary computers); however, such computers are still in the testing stage, as to date they are much less reliable than binary computers.

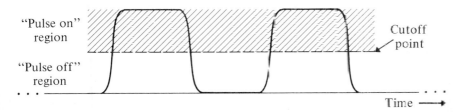

**FIGURE 1-2.3**  On-off (two-state) discrete information transmission.

Throughout the remainder of this text we are interested in the storage, retrieval, and processing of discrete information (more precisely, information represented in a binary encoded form) by digital computers. There are two types of discrete information present in digital computers, namely, machine instructions (or operations) and the data which are to be manipulated by these operations. In our study of data structures, we are primarily concerned with the organization of the data to solve a problem for a particular application. However, associated with a data structure is a particular set of operations needed to access properly information in that structure. Therefore, in discussing how information should be structured, we will also be concerned with the operations for accessing the information. The operations we consider will be presented in a high-level language such as Pascal; however, such high-level operations are translatable to a functionally equivalent set of machine-level operations.

## 1-3 THE STORAGE OF INFORMATION

In a digital computer there are two types of memory units, namely, operational units and storage units. The name that is commonly associated with an operational unit is a *register*. A register is used for the temporary storage and the manipulation of information.

Some of the most important registers are contained in the central processing unit (CPU) of the computer. The CPU contains registers (sometimes called accumulators) which hold the arguments (i.e., operands) of arithmetic computations. Some very complex integrated circuitry allows the information which is stored in the accumulators to be added, subtracted, multiplied, and divided. In addition, certain bits of the accumulator can be tested to determine if the normal sequence of control in a program should be altered (e.g., the testing of a particular bit in an accumulator designated as the sign bit of a number to see if a branch should be taken based on a negative value). Besides storing operands and the results from arithmetic operations, registers are also used to temporarily store program instructions and control information concerning which instruction is to be executed next. Because of their highly specialized nature, registers have a great deal of combinational logic (i.e., circuitry) associated with them. This makes them expensive relative to storage-type memory units in a computer. Consequently, registers are only used to store information temporarily.

The storage-type memory unit is designed to store information which is more permanent in nature. For example, a particular storage unit or set of storage units is associated with a particular variable in a program. However, before arithmetic computations involving a variable are performed, the value of the variable, as stored in the memory unit, must be transferred to a register unit. The transfer must take place because memory units do not have the necessary logic associated with them (or between them) to execute arithmetic operations. If the result of a computation is to be assigned to a variable, the resultant value must be transferred from an arithmetic register back to the memory unit associated with the variable.

When a program is executed, its instructions and data generally reside in storage units. The entire set of storage units in the main frame or main part of a computer is often called *main memory*. Later, in Chap. 7, we discover that in some instances programs can also reside in storage units which do not belong to main memory. Examples of such storage-unit devices (often called *secondary storage devices*) are magnetic disks and drums.

The most commonly used type of main memory storage is semiconductor memory. A semiconductor memory unit (see Fig. 1-3.1) is made up of special sequential and combinatorial circuitry, and it resides in a small block of material (commonly called a *chip*) along with many other such memory units. A semiconductor unit holds one bit of information. Information is input to a storage unit by the presence of a low or high voltage. If a low voltage represents a zero value, the high voltage represents a one value, or vice versa. The state of the information associated with a memory unit is stored in a piece of sequential circuitry called a *flip-flop*. A flip-flop is a simple two-state device and, hence, is ideal for storing binary information. A one value is stored in the flip-flop by simultaneously applying high pulses to the input line and the write line. This activates the line that sets the flip-flop (placing it in a one state). On the other hand, if a low input pulse is combined with a write pulse, the inverter causes a pulse to appear in the reset line of the flip-flop. This produces a zero state.

A read line is combined with the output line from the flip-flop. When the read line is pulsed, the state of the flip-flop can be determined and, hence, the binary value of the memory unit can be read.

A second type of main storage that was developed in the 1950s and was predominant until the late 1970s is *magnetic core memory*. A magnetic core is a doughnut-shaped toroid of magnetic material that holds one bit of information. The nature of the bit (that is, whether it currently represents a zero or one) is determined by the direction of the magnetic flux within the core. Semiconductor memory has become more popular than core primarily because of the tremendous decrease in price of integrated circuitry in recent years. Other considerations favoring semiconductor memory are its physical compactness its smaller energy demands (i.e., less electrical power is needed to read and write information and to keep the memory units cool), and its quicker response time to read and write commands. No doubt other more compact and functionally superior memory units will be used in the future. Techniques involving super conduction (i.e., Josephson technology) and biotechnology are among the more promising in the coming decade.

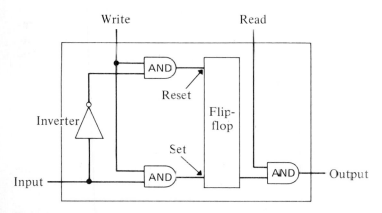

**FIGURE 1-3.1** A semiconductor storage unit.

## 1-4  PRIMITIVE DATA STRUCTURES

In this section we are concerned with the structuring of data at their most primitive level within a computer, that is, the data structures that typically are directly operated upon by machine-level instructions. We will present storage representations for these data structures for a variety of machines. The primitive data structures examined in this section form a basis for the discussion and composition of more sophisticated data structures introduced in the remaining chapters of this book.

Prior to a discussion of data structures, primitive or otherwise, we must be familiar with a number of common operations used to manipulate data structures and their elements.

### 1-4.1  Operations on Data Structures

An operation frequently used in conjunction with data structures is one which creates a data structure. This operation will be called a **CREATION** operation. For example, variables in Pascal, PL/I, FORTRAN, ALGOL, plus many other languages can be created by using a declaration statement. In Pascal, the declaration statement

**var** n : integer;

causes space to be created for *n* upon entering, at execution time, the block (i.e., **begin** block or **procedure** block) in which the declaration for *n* occurs. In contrast, a FORTRAN declaration such as

**INTEGER Z**

results in the creation of memory space for **Z** during the compilation of the declaration statement. Storage space for a variable can also be created at execution time when its name is first encountered in the source program. Programming languages such as SNOBOL, LISP, and APL use this form of data structure creation. As we progress through the text, we will discover still other ways of creating data structures. For now, the key point is that, irrespective of what programming language is used, the data structures present in a program are not manufactured "out of thin air," but are specified, either explicitly or implicitly, with creation statements.

Another operation, providing the complementary effect of a **CREATION** operation, is one which destroys the data structure. The operation is called a **DESTROY** operation. Certain languages, such as FORTRAN, do not allow a programmer to destroy data structures once they have been created, since all creations are performed at compile time and not at execution time. In Pascal, ALGOL, and PL/I, data structures within a block are destroyed when the block is exited during execution. While a **DESTROY** operation is not a necessary operation, it aids in the efficient use of memory.

Probably the most frequently used operation associated with data structures is one that the programmer uses to access data within a data structure. This type of operation is known as a **SELECTION**. The form of the **SELECTION** depends to a significant degree on the type of data structure being accessed. As more complex structures are introduced, we will see that the method of access is one of the most important properties of a structure—especially as this property affects the decision as to whether we should use a particular data structure.

Another operation used in conjunction with data structures is one which changes data in the structure. This operation will be called an **UPDATE**. An assignment operation is a good example of an update operation. Other more complicated forms of update operations exist (e.g., parameter passing operations). We will see that the cost of performing an **UPDATE** operation is an important property which must be considered in data-structure selection.

The four operations just discussed provide us with all the operations that are normally applied to the primitive data structures that will be discussed in this chapter. In procedure-oriented languages such as Pascal and FORTRAN, a primitive data structure is equated with a simple variable such as a real variable, integer variable, logical variable, etc. A simple variable is assigned a single value such as a real value. The single value associated with a simple variable is referenced through a simple identifier name such as **X**.

### 1-4.2 Number Systems

We begin a discussion of primitive data structures by examining integer and real numbers. To provide a proper perspective for a study of data structures that are numeric in nature, we find it is worthwhile to briefly examine the types of number systems that have arisen.

Numbers are used symbolically to represent quantities of objects. A very simple method of representing a quantity is through the use of tally symbols. In a tally system, a one-to-one correspondence is established between tally marks and the objects being counted. For example, six objects can be represented as ****** or 111111. It should be immediately obvious that this type of system is very inconvenient when attempting to represent large quantities.

Number systems, such as the Roman number system, provide a partial solution to the problem of representing a large number of objects. In the Roman system, additional symbols are available for expressing groups of tally symbols. For example, if I = 1, then V = IIIII, X = VV, L = XXXXX, etc. A given quantity is represented by combining symbols according to a set of rules which depend to some degree on the position of the symbols in a number. The disadvantage of a system which relies primarily on grouping one set of symbols to form a new symbol is that in order to represent extremely large quantities (e.g., the number of sand pebbles on a beach), a multitude (e.g., potentially infinite number) of unique symbols is required.

Positional number systems were created to avoid the problem of having to create and remember a large number of symbols. In a positional number system a finite number, say $R$, of unique symbols is used. $R$ is often referred to as the *radix* of the positional number system. A quantity is represented in a positional number system by the symbols themselves and the positions of the symbols. We can exemplify this point by examining the positional number system with which we are most familiar: the *radix ten* or *decimal* number system. To illustrate why the decimal system is a positional system, consider the number 1303. We interpret 1303 to mean

$$1 \times 10^3 + 3 \times 10^2 + 0 \times 10^1 + 3 \times 10^0$$

Note that while two 3's appear in the number, the left-most 3 represents the quantity three hundred, while the other 3 represents the quantity three. Clearly, the quantity represented by the symbol is position dependent.

Fractional values can also be represented in a positional system. For example, one-quarter is written as .25, which is interpreted as $2 \times 10^{-1} + 5 \times 10^{-2}$.

The rules for discovering the value of a decimal number are based on the position of symbols in the number. These same rules can be applied to other positional number systems such as the *binary number system*. A binary number 11001.101 represents a quantity equivalent to that represented by the decimal number 25.625. We can arrive at this equivalence by expanding the binary number according to its positional representation, that is,

$$1 \times 2^4 + 1 \times 2^3 + 0 \times 2^2 + 0 \times 2^1$$
$$+ 1 \times 2^0 + 1 \times 2^{-1} + 0 \times 2^{-2} + 1 \times 2^{-3}$$
$$= 16 + 8 + 1 + .5 + .125 = 25.625.$$

The number systems with which we will be most concerned will have radices of 2, 8, 10, and 16 and are commonly referred to as the binary, octal, decimal, and hexadecimal number systems respectively. Our interest in these number systems arises from the fact that many computers perform their operations in base 2, 8, and 16. We are especially interested in understanding how to convert between the decimal number system and any one of the three other number systems generally available in computers. Table 1-4.1 familiarizes us with the binary, octal, and hexadecimal representations of the integers from 0 to 17.

In the discussion to follow, we will distinguish between numbers in different systems by adding a subscript to the number (unless it is obvious by context in which base the number is represented, such as in Table 1-4.1.). When a subscript is not present, the number is assumed to be a decimal number. As an example, we say that $(11011)_2$, $(33)_8$ and $(1B)_{16}$ are all numerically equivalent to the number 27. One further point of notation—since our list of symbols from the decimal system is

**Table 1-4.1**  Binary, octal, and hexadecimal
numbers between 0 and 17.

| Number | Binary | Octal | Hexadecimal |
|--------|--------|-------|-------------|
| 0 | 0 | 0 | 0 |
| 1 | 1 | 1 | 1 |
| 2 | 10 | 2 | 2 |
| 3 | 11 | 3 | 3 |
| 4 | 100 | 4 | 4 |
| 5 | 101 | 5 | 5 |
| 6 | 110 | 6 | 6 |
| 7 | 111 | 7 | 7 |
| 8 | 1000 | 10 | 8 |
| 9 | 1001 | 11 | 9 |
| 10 | 1010 | 12 | A |
| 11 | 1011 | 13 | B |
| 12 | 1100 | 14 | C |
| 13 | 1101 | 15 | D |
| 14 | 1110 | 16 | E |
| 15 | 1111 | 17 | F |
| 16 | 10000 | 20 | 10 |
| 17 | 10001 | 21 | 11 |

exhausted, we use the letters A, B, C, D, E, and F to denote 10, 11, 12, 13, 14, and 15, respectively, in the hexadecimal system.

### Exercises for Sec. 1-4.2

1. Write the first 17 integers in base 3.
2. Write the first 17 integers in base 9. Is there any relationship between the numbers written in base 3 and those written in base 9?

### 1-4.3 Integers

We are all familiar with the concept of an integer and many of the operations commonly applied to integers (i.e., addition, multiplication, etc.). The set of integers can be defined rigorously (e.g., the set of nonnegative integers can be defined by applying the Peano axioms); however, whether the reader has seen a formal definition is not of major importance to the current discussion. It suffices to say that the set of integers $I$ is the set

$$\{\ldots -(n + 1), -n, \ldots, -2, -1, 0, 1, 2 \ldots, n, n + 1, \ldots\}$$

The importance of integer data in terms of computation is obvious. A quantity representing objects which are discrete in nature (i.e., the number of objects are countable) can be represented by an integer. The number of dollars in a bank account, the number of passengers on a flight, and the number of pieces on a chess board are all information items expressible as integers.

The uses of integers are many, varied, and obvious therefore, further motivation for their importance as data type is unnecessary. However, the method of representing integers as signed numbers is less obvious—especially if we are concerned with performing computations efficiently and inexpensively. In this section, we concentrate on several representations of integers as signed numbers and discover that the representation we are most familiar with is not necessarily the best representation for performing computations on a computer.

The conventional method for writing negative numbers is to place a sign symbol in front of a number. This method, often called the *sign and magnitude method*, has been used for representation of signed numbers in several computers. Generally, the sign is represented as the first or left-most bit of the binary number representation, and the magnitude portion of the number appears in the remainder of the representation. For example, +7 and - 6 are represented in binary as

| Number | Sign Bit | Magnitude |
|--------|----------|-----------|
| +7     | 0        | 00....0111 |
| −6     | 1        | 00....0110 |

Note that in this example 0 and 1 are used to represent the positive and negative signs, respectively. This sign representation is customary.

While the sign and magnitude representation has the advantage of being familiar and readable to the programmer, it is not the most economical representation. If we want to add or subtract two numbers, a special effort must be made to interpret the sign of each number in order to decide what operation should be performed. For example, the addition of +7 and - 6 really involves the subtraction operation, and the subtraction of - 6 from +7 really involves the addition operation. Special circuitry is required to examine the sign bit, and in addition, both subtractor and adder units are required when using sign and magnitude representation.

The most economical and popular representation of integers is the *radix complement representation*, in general, and *2's complement representation* as applied specifically to binary computers. In radix complement representation, all arithmetic operations are performed modulo $M$, for $M = R^N$, where $R$ is the radix in which the integer is expressed and $N$ is the maximum number of digits required to represent an integer modulo $M$. We can illustrate what is meant by modulo arithmetic, in general, with the following discussion. Assume that an operation * is performed on numbers $x$ and $y$, yielding result $z$ (that is, $z = x * y$). If the same operation is performed modulo $M$ (we designate this new operation by $*_M$), then the result of $x *_M y$ is $z_M = z \bmod M$. That is, $z_M$ is the remainder or *residue* when dividing $z$ by $M$.

In modulo $M$ arithmetic, the following relationship holds for addition on an integer $x$:

$$x = x + M \tag{1-4.1}$$

Employing some very simple algebra, we can find an expression for "the negation of $x$," namely,

$$-x = M - x \tag{1-4.2}$$

This equation holds providing both sides are computed modulo $M$ (i.e., both sides have the same result).

Equation (1-4.2) gives an indication as to how both positive and negative integers can be represented in radix complement form. As an example, assume that we are working with 2's complement numbers using modulo $M = 16$ arithmetic (implying the number of binary digits $N$ required to express an integer is 4—that is, $2^4 = 16$). Table 1-4.2 illustrates how the sixteen numbers representable in a 2's complement modulo 16 system are related to the integers from $-8$ to $+7$.

Note that the representation of the negative integers in complement form has been derived from applying Eq. (1-4.2). An alternative method of deriving the complemented form for negative integers is by performing the complementation using binary

**Table 1-4.2**  The 2's complement representation for integers expressed in modulo 16.

| Integer | 2's Complement Representation | Integer | 2's Complement Representation |
|---------|------------------------------|---------|------------------------------|
| 0 | 0000 | $-1$ $(16 - 1 = 15)$ | 1111 |
| 1 | 0001 | $-2$ $(16 - 2 = 14)$ | 1110 |
| 2 | 0010 | $-3$ $(16 - 3 = 13)$ | 1101 |
| 3 | 0011 | $-4$ $(16 - 4 = 12)$ | 1100 |
| 4 | 0100 | $-5$ $(16 - 5 = 11)$ | 1011 |
| 5 | 0101 | $-6$ $(16 - 6 = 10)$ | 1010 |
| 6 | 0110 | $-7$ $(16 - 7 = \phantom{0}9)$ | 1001 |
| 7 | 0111 | $-8$ $(16 - 8 = \phantom{0}8)$ | 1000 |

arithmetic. For example, the complemented form of $-2$ is

$$16 - 2 = (10000)_2 - (10)_2 = (1110)_2$$

Let us consider another example.

*Example 1-1.* What is the 2's complement representation for $-38$ expressed in a modulo 32 system?

First, we must express $-38$ as a modulo 32 number. We know that $-38$ mod $(32) = -6$. To find an equivalent 2's complement representation, we apply Eq. (1-4.2). That is

$$32 - 6 = 26 = (11010)_2$$

or $(100000)_2 - (110)_2 = (11010)_2$ ////

One of the major advantages of radix complement notation is that we can perform addition and subtraction operations using only addition and complementation. Note that a complementation operation for binary numbers is a very simple operation. It involves

*1* Copying the 0's to the right of the right-most 1
*2* Copying the right-most 1
*3* Writing the complement of all bits to the left of the right-most 1

Hence, the 2's complement of 6 expressed as a five-digit number is 2'sCOMP(6) = 2'sCOMP$((00110)_2)$ = $(11010)_2$. Thus, 2'sCOMP can be viewed as a function which accepts an integer expressed in some radix $R$ and converts it to its 2's complement form. The result $(11010)_2$ matches the result in Example 1-1.

The following example illustrates that only a binary addition and 2's complementation are required for the addition and subtraction of integers.

*Example 1-2.* Evaluate $3 + 4$, $3 - 4$, $-3 + 4$, $7 + 7$, and $-7 - 7$ using 2's complement representation and modulo 16 arithmetic.

(a) $3 + 4 = (0011)_2 + (0100)_2 = (0111)_2 = 7$

(b) $3 - 4 = (0011)_2 + 2'sCOMP((0100)_2) = (0011)_2 + (1100)_2$
    $= (1111)_2 = -1$

Recall that $(1111)_2$ is equal to $-1$ in 2's complement form.

(c) $-3 + 4 = 2'sCOMP((0011)_2) + (0100)_2 = (1101)_2 + (0100)_2$

    $= (0001)_2 = 1$

(d) $7 + 7 = (0111)_2 + (0111)_2 = (1110)_2 = -2$

(e) $-7 - 7 = 2'sCOMP((0111)_2) + 2'sCOMP((0111)_2)$

    $= (1001)_2 + (1001)_2 = (0010)_2 = 2$ ////

In Example 1-2, parts *(d)* and *(e)* yield invalid results. Remember that the range of integers we can represent in 2's complement form assuming a modulo 16 system is $-8$ to $+7$. Therefore, the evaluation of the expressions $7 + 7$ and $-7 - 7$ result in *overflows*. We will return to consider the problem of overflow after introducing another representation scheme used for integers in computers.

The *diminished radix-complement* form of a digit $d$ of radix $R$ number system is defined as $R - 1 - d$. Therefore, the binary digits 0 and 1 expressed in diminished radix-complement form are 1 and 0, respectively. An integer $I$ expressed in such a form is found by the following equation

$$\text{DRCOMP } (I) = R^n - 1 - I$$

Note that $R^n$ is expressed in the radix $R$ number system as a 1 followed by $n$ zeros.

The essential difference between the radix complement form and the diminished radix-complement form is that the modulo for complementation (that is, $R^n$) is diminished by 1 in the latter case. The diminished radix-complement form for integers expressed in binary is commonly called *1's complement*. The 1's complement of the integer 6 in a modulo 16 system is $16 - 1 - 6 = 9$ or $(10000)_2 - 1 - (0110)_2 = (1111)_2 - (0110)_2 = (1001)_2$. It is important to note that the 1'sCOMP($x$), where $x$ is a binary number, is found very simply by exchanging all the 0's in $x$ with 1's and all the 1's with 0's. Table 1-4.3 further illustrates this point.

One disadvantage of the diminished radix-complement system is the presence of both $+0$ and $-0$. The fact that both are numerically equivalent yet syntactically different can create many computational problems. However, with diminished radix-complement notation, we can perform addition and subtraction operations using addition and complementation (as was necessary using radix complement), plus the ability to "add the carry-out." We illustrate in Example 1-3 how addition and subtraction are performed on numbers represented in 1's complement notation.

*Example 1-3.* Evaluate $3 + 4$, $-3 + 4$, $7 + 7$, and $-7 - 7$ using 1's complement representation and modulo 16 arithmetic.

(*a*)  $3 + 4 = (0011)_2 + (0100)_2 = (0111)_2 = 7$

(*b*)  $3 - 4 = (0011)_2 + 1\text{'sCOMP}((0100)_2) = (0011)_2 + (1011)_2$

**Table 1-4.3**  The 1's complement representation for integers expressed in modulo 16.

| Integer | 1's Complement Representation | Integer | 1's Complement Representation |
|---------|------------------------------|---------|------------------------------|
| 0 | 0000 | $-1$(1'sCOMP$(0001)_2$) | 1110 |
| 1 | 0001 | $-2$(1'sCOMP$(0010)_2$) | 1101 |
| 2 | 0010 | $-3$(1'sCOMP$(0011)_2$) | 1100 |
| 3 | 0011 | $-4$(1'sCOMP$(0100)_2$) | 1011 |
| 4 | 0100 | $-5$(1'sCOMP$(0101)_2$) | 1010 |
| 5 | 0101 | $-6$(1'sCOMP$(0110)_2$) | 1001 |
| 6 | 0110 | $-7$(1'sCOMP$(0111)_2$) | 1000 |
| 7 | 0111 | $-0$(1'sCOMP$(0000)_2$) | 1111 |

$$= (1110)_2 = -1$$

Recall that $(1110)_2$ in 1's complement form is $-1$.

(c)  $-3 + 4 = (1'sCOMP((0011)_2) + (0100)_2) = (1100)_2 + (0100)_2 = 0$

Note that a carry-out of 1 takes place here.

(d)  $7 + 7 = (0111)_2 + (0111)_2 = (1110)_2 = -1$

(e)  $-7 - 7 = 1'sCOMP((0111)_2) + 1'sCOMP((0111)_2)$

$$= (1000)_2 + (1000)_2 = (0000)_2 = 0 \qquad \qquad ////$$

From Example 1-3, we see that part (c) does not yield the correct answer (that is, $-3 + 4$ should be 1, not 0). Note that if we add the carry-out to the final results of (a), (b), and (c), we obtain the correct answers of 7, $-1$, and 1, respectively. In 1's complement additions and subtractions, this end-around carry addition must be performed.

In parts (d) and (e) of Example 1-3 we again have overflow, as we did in parts (d) and (e) of Example 1-2. It is important, when performing computations, for a computer to detect overflow, and to post an overflow error message. To derive conditions for detecting overflow, we must realize

1  The addition of a positive number and a negative number can never cause an overflow.
2  The addition of two positive numbers or two negative numbers does not cause an overflow if the resulting sum has the same sign as the two operands.

These rules hold for 1's and 2's complement additions with the exception of a 2's complement addition of two $n$-bit negative numbers, $a$ and $b$, such that $|a| + |b| = 2^{n-1}$. To detect an overflow in this case, we must check for the magnitude bits being all zeros and for the carry-out bit value of 1. More detailed discussions concerning 1's complement end-around carry and overflow detection are found in Tremblay and Manohar [1975], Stone [1972], and Dietmeyer [1971]. Of course, these rules are violated when $7 + 7$ and $-7 - 7$ are evaluated using modulo 16 arithmetic.

It is also important to point out that a 2's complement representation is generally compatible with an unsigned integer representation. For example from Table 1-4.2, $-4$ can be interpreted as 12 in an unsigned representation and therefore 5 + 7 [which is equivalent to $(0101)_2 + (0111)_2$ ] is equal to $(1100)_2$ . The fact is most computers using 2's complement representation also accommodate an unsigned integer representation as shown in Table 1-4.4.

Overflow can take place when other arithmetic operations, such as multiplication and division, are applied as well. The classical example of an overflow situation arises when a number is divided by zero.

In this section we have intentionally concentrated on introducing two alternative systems of integer representation to the sign and magnitude representation with which we are familiar. We will now discuss the storage representation of integer data. It will be shown that because the radix complement and diminished radix-complement are efficient and inexpensive methods of representation, one of these two methods is generally adopted by computer manufacturers.

**Table 1-4.4** Storage structure for integer data from a sample of computers.

| Computer | Binary Representation | Decimal Representation |
|---|---|---|
| IBM 360-370, 4300, and 3030 Series | 2's complement 16- and 32-bit numbers or unsigned integer | Packed decimal nos. 7 decimal digits per 32-bit word |
| CDC CYBER 170 Series 800 | 1's complement 60-bit numbers | Does not exist |
| Burroughs B5000 and B6000 Series | Sign and magnitude 40-bit numbers (sign and magnitude) | Character mode (6 bits/character) 8 decimal digits per 48-bit word |
| PDP-10 or PDP-20 | 2's complement 36-bit numbers or unsigned integer | Does not exist |
| PDP-11 | 2's complement 16-bit numbers or unsigned integer | Does not exist |
| VAX 11/730, 11/750 and 11/780 | 2's complement 8-, 16-, 32-, 64-, and 128-bit numbers or unsigned integer | 0 to 31 packed decimal digits |
| Motorola MC68000 | 2's complement 16- and 32-bit numbers or unsigned integer | 8 packed binary-coded decimal digits per 32 bit word |
| Intel 8080 | Unsigned integer | 2 binary-coded decimal digits per 8 bit word |

Typically, one computer word is devoted to the storage representation of an integer. In assembly languages and in some programming languages (such as Pascal), the programmer is able to specify the amount of storage, less than the word size, in which an integer can be stored. The smallest directly addressable unit of memory, often called a *byte*, is the least amount of storage that can be used for integer representation.

Using a storage structure which is less than a word in length has some drawbacks, however. When computations are performed on an integer stored in less than a word of memory, the integer representation is brought into the arithmetic unit, expanded to a full-word representation, and computations are performed on this new representation. To store an integer in less than a word, the reverse procedure must be taken, i.e., the appropriate subfield of the full word is isolated in a register, and this subfield (which is at least as large as a byte) is assigned to a desired set of memory locations.

Generally, a 2's complement form of representation is preferred to a 1's complement form because the +0 and −0 controversy is avoided. Table 1-4.4 illustrates this fact for a representative sample of machines from the computer industry. A 32-bit 2's complement representation for the integer 12 is illustrated in Fig. 1-4.1. Examples of integers stored in 16-bit representation are shown in Table 1-4.5.

It is important to know the range of integer values that can be expressed using an $n$-bit storage representation. The summation formula for $2^0 + 2^1 + 2^3 + \cdots + 2^{n-1}$ is

$$\sum_{i=0}^{n-1} 2^i = 2^n - 1$$

(1-4.3)

In an $n$-bit 2's complement storage representation, the first bit expresses the sign of the integer. Therefore, we can represent positive integers in the range 0 to $1 \times 2^0 + 1 \times 2^1 + \cdots + 1 \times 2^{n-2}$ or (by Eq. 1-4.3) 0 to $2^{n-1} - 1$. In 2's complement notation, all other bit configurations are devoted to negative numbers in the range of $-2^{n-1}$ to −1. To summarize, in general, we find that an integer $N$ can be accommodated using an $n$-bit 2's complement storage representation if

$$-2^{n-1} \le N \le 2^{n-1} - 1$$

Because both +0 and −0 can be represented, the range of integers representable in 1's complement is one less than the range representable in 2's complement. Hence, if an $n$-bit 1's complement storage representation is used, then $N$ can be in the range

$$-2^{n-1} + 1 \le N \le 2^{n-1} - 1$$

We can illustrate the limitations placed on the representation of integers by examining storage representations of length 16 and 32 bits. A 16-bit word machine using 2's complement notation can represent an integer $N$ where $-2^{15} \le N \le 2^{15} - 1$ or $-32,768 \le N \le 32,767$. A 32-bit word machine using 2's complement

**Table 1-4.5**  Example of integers stored in 16-bit 1's and 2's complement representation.

| Decimal Integer | One's Complement Storage Representation | Two's Complement Storage Representation |
|---|---|---|
| 9613 | 0010010110001101 | 0010010110001101 |
| −9613 | 1101101001110010 | 1101101001110011 |
| 317 | 0000000100111101 | 0000000100111101 |
| −317 | 1111111011000010 | 1111111011000011 |
| 32767 | 0111111111111111 | 0111111111111111 |
| −32767 | 1000000000000000 | 1000000000000001 |
| −32768 | not representable | 1000000000000000 |

Sign

| 0 | 00000000000000000000000000001101 |

**FIGURE 1-4.1** 32-bit 2's complement storage representation of the integer 13.

notation can represent a much larger range, namely, $-2^{31} \leq N \leq 2^{31} - 1$ or $-2,147,483,648 \leq N \leq 2,147,483,647$.

In some of the large or more recently designed computers, a decimal form of storage representation is available for integers in addition to a binary form. Associated with the decimal representation are some basic decimal instructions which include at least add, subtract, and compare instructions. The main purpose for decimal instructions and decimal representations is to improve performance when there are few computational steps between source input and output. Conversions between source and a decimal form can be achieved without a conversion to an intermediate form, as is necessary in conversions between a source and binary form. In fact in some systems (e.g., IBM mainframes), the intermediate form necessary for source to binary conversions is the decimal representation.

All this discussion pertaining to the representation and manipulation of integer data in decimal form appears to be contrary to our earlier premise that information in a computer is stored in binary digits (i.e., bits). Not so! To represent integers in a decimal format, we encode the decimal digits using a 4-bit binary-coded decimal (often called "pure BCD") scheme. In pure BCD, each decimal digit is represented by its 4-bit binary equivalent. For example, the integer 9613 would be encoded as

$$\begin{array}{cccc} 1001 & 0110 & 0001 & 0011 \\ 9 & 6 & 1 & 3 \end{array}$$

Note that in pure BCD, the 4-bit codes 1010, 1011, 1100, 1101, 1110, and 1111 do not have decimal digit equivalents. Two of these extra codes often are used to represent the sign of the number.

A form of pure BCD representation (called *packed decimal*) is available on the IBM mainframe series. The general form of a packed-decimal number is given in Fig. 1-4.2. Some examples of integers represented in packed-decimal form are given in Table 1-4.6. Note that 1100 and 1101 are codes representing the plus and minus signs, respectively. Other forms of decimal representation are available; in particular, a 6-bit encoding scheme has been adopted by Burroughs (see Table 1-4.4).

**Table 1-4.6** Examples of packed-decimal representations.

| Integer | Packed-Decimal Form |
|---------|---------------------|
| 0149 | 00000001010010011100 |
| −0149 | 00000001010010011101 |
| 935 | 1001001101011100 |
| −6 | 01101101 |

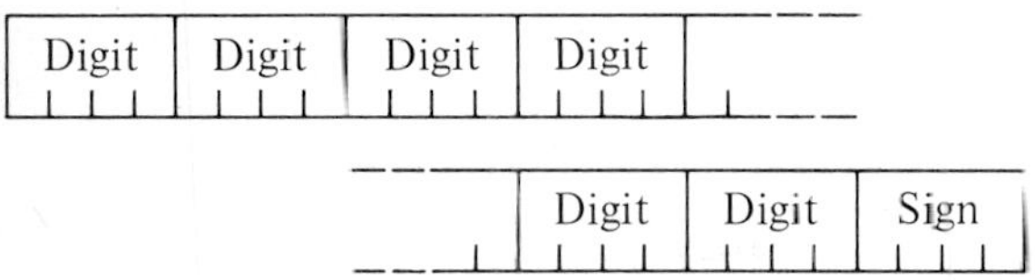

**FIGURE 1-4.2**

**Exercises for Sec. 1-4.3**

1. Express the following integers in 2's complement, assuming a 6-bit representation: (a) –33, (b) –52, (c) $(-33)_8$, (d) $(-E)_{16}$, (e) –241.
2. Evaluate the following expressions using 2's complement and modulo 16 arithmetic: (a) 6 – 1, (b) 7 – (–2), (c) –3 – 3.
3. Evaluate the following expressions using 1's complement and modulo 32 arithmetic: (a) 8 + 8, (b) 6 – 1, (c) 7 – 11.

**1-4.4 Real Numbers**

While not explicitly stating it, in Sec. 1-4.2 we introduced the *fixed-point representation* for a real number $A_R$ in radix system $R$ as

$$A_R = \pm (a_{N-1} a_{N-2} \cdots a_1 a_0 . a_{-1} \cdots a_{-(M-1)} a_{-M})_R$$

which has a literal expansion of

$$A = \pm \sum_{i=-M}^{N-1} a_i R^i$$

Fixed-point notation is sufficient to represent most of the real numbers normally arising when computations are performed on a computer. However, there exist computer applications which involve very large or very small real numbers. One such application area is astronomy. Large distance and mass measurements are used in computations concerned with the gravitational force between celestial bodies. Distances such as 16,800,000,000,000 kilometers are not abnormal. At an atomic level, on the other hand, calculations for energy emissions in a bubble chamber demand extremely small distance measurements. A typical distance might be .0000000000832 meters.

The cost of a computer is directly affected by the precision of the numbers that can be handled in computations. A major cost factor is in the central processing unit alone. The greater the precision allowed, the larger and more complex is the arithmetic unit. Arithmetic computations, involving both the real numbers just cited, would require a precision of 27 decimal digits. To obtain an equivalent precision in binary representation, a computer would require approximately ninety binary digits (or bits). Since most computers today provide from 16 to 64 bits of precision, a computer with a word size of ninety would not be economical as a general-purpose machine.

An alternative method of representation which overcomes this difficulty is the *floating-point* or *scientific* notation. In this shorthand notation, the two measurements given earlier would be expressed as $.168 \times 10^{14}$ kilometers and $.832 \times 10^{-10}$ meters.

The general form of a real number in radix $R$ expressed in floating-point notation is

$$f_{-1}f_{-2} \cdots f_{-M} \times R^E$$

where $f_{-1}f_{-2} \cdots f_{-M}$ is called the *fractional part* or *mantissa* and $E$, which is always an integer, is the *exponent*.

It is obvious that considerable effort is saved by expressing numbers in floating-point notation. Because computer designers are very conscious about the amount of "space" (i.e., the number of bits) required to represent a number, floating-point notation has been adopted as a means of representing real numbers.

It should be noted that the fractional part of a floating-point number is meant to contain only the most significant digits of a real number. For example, $.168 \times 10^{14}$ kilometers is expressed with a mantissa of three digits. That is, $.168 \times 10^{14}$ is an approximation of an accurate measurement such as 16,817,210,391,704 kilometers. The difference between the approximate measurement and the accurate measurement is called *round-off error*.

The previous discussion points out that floating-point notation allows for the efficient representation of extremely large and extremely small numbers which are assumed to contain few significant digits. Computers can only store a finite number of significant digits, and therefore, not all real numbers can be represented. In general, the number of significant digits retained in most computer applications is such that round-off error is negligible. However, if the computer we are using cannot represent all the significant digits of a real number with which we are working, then we are left with three alternatives.

The first alternative is to do our computation on a larger machine. Later in this subsection we discover that computers exist which provide almost twenty decimal digits of accuracy. However, as indicated earlier, such precision comes at a price, and the computing charge rates may be prohibitively high.

A second alternative is to use a multiple-precision program package. (In Sec. 4-3.3 we will be discussing in detail an example of multiple-precision arithmetic.) In a multiple-precision package, a real number is divided into several segments, each segment usually corresponding to a computer word. Operations such as additions are performed on individual segments, and the programs in the package are responsible for handling "carries" and "borrows" which take place between segment operations. Since each segment operation must be interpreted by the program package, the use of multiple-precision arithmetic can be very expensive as well.

The third alternative, and the one that is most often accepted, is to round the real number to as many significant digits as can be represented in the machine. Rounding is a very simple operation which can be described best by an example.

*Example 1-4.* What is the real number 21.833652 rounded to five decimal digits of accuracy?

21.833652 + .0005 = 21.834152

The rounded answer is 21.834.

The procedure we have adopted is simply to add 5 to the sixth decimal digit and then to isolate the five most significant digits for our answer. Of course, in general, to round a decimal number at the $n$th digit, we add 5 to the $(n + 1)$ digit and retain the left-most $n$ digits.    ////

We have already discussed two methods of representing real numbers (a floating-point representation, such as in .2364 × $10^2$, and fixed-point representation, such as 23.64). Floating-point representation is the most common storage structure used for real data and we will discuss it first. Fixed-point notation will be described later, at which time some of its advantages and pitfalls will be highlighted.

The floating-point format that is generally adopted for the representation of reals consists of one or two fixed-length fields (where a field is a computer word in length). The radix and the number of digit positions representable with a floating-point format vary from one computer to another. Nevertheless, a general format does exist and can be illustrated, as in Fig. 1-4.3.

Usually, the *sign* is the first bit in a floating-point representation, and by convention 0 denotes a positive number and 1 denotes a negative number. The *characteristic* or *biased exponent* is an expression of the exponent in a form of notation called *excess notation*. To illustrate what is meant by excess notation, let us assume that the characteristic part of the floating-point representation is seven bits in length (as it is in the IBM 3030 and 4300 series). In a 7-bit field, we are capable of representing integers in the range of -64 to +63 in 2's complement, for example. However, 2's complement notation is not a particularly good representation for exponents. When adding or subtracting floating-point numbers, left or right shifting is required in the fractional part of the floating-point number to ensure that the two operands are aligned. Shifting can be achieved by using a single counter which, when given a positive number, counts down to zero until the desired shifts have occurred. Because of hardware considerations such as these, it is desirable to use an exponent notation in which each exponent is expressed as a nonnegative integer. In a 7-digit field, we can express nonnegative integers in the range of 0 to 127. To achieve such a range, and yet be able to express positive and negative exponents, we find it is necessary to bias the true exponent by 64. Therefore, to derive the characteristic for a floating-point number from its exponent, we add the bias or excess factor, namely, 64 in this case. Hence, a floating-point number with an exponent of -48 would have a characteristic of -48 + 64 = 16 in what is commonly called *excess-64 notation*.

The third and final component in a floating-point storage representation is the *fractional part* or *mantissa*. A condition called *normalization* is often imposed on the storage structure of the fractional part to increase the number of trailing digits after the significant digits and to permit division without overflow. This condition dictates that the fractional part, $F$, must lie in the interval $R^{-1} \leq F < 1$, except in the instance of a fractional part which is identically zero. If we choose the radix $R$ of the fractional part to be 2, then a nonzero fractional part of any floating-point structure must begin with a $(1)_2$ (that is, $2^{-1} \leq F < 1$). However, of late, octal- and hexadecimal-based floating-point storage representations have become popular. They have definite advantages over binary-based floating-point representations. For example, in a hexadecimal-based storage structure, a nonzero fractional part $F$ need only lie in the interval $16^{-1} \leq F < 1$ or $(.0001)_2 \leq F < 1$ for the number to be in normalized form. Eight times as many binary fractions need normalization after computations as do hexadecimal fractions. The second advantage is that for a given number of bit

| Sign | Characteristic | Fraction | | |
|------|----------------|----------|---|---|

**FIGURE 1-4.3**

positions in the characteristic, a hexadecimal-based system permits the representation of numbers of much larger magnitude. That is, for a 7-bit characteristic, we can represent numbers as small as $16^{-64}$ and as large as $16^{+63}$ in a hexadecimal system, whereas the comparable magnitudes would be $2^{-64}$ and $2^{+63}$ in a binary system.

One advantage of a binary-based floating-point representation is that normalization always generates a fraction in which the first bit position is a $(1)_2$. Therefore, in some machines (in particular the PDP-11), this initial $(1)_2$ is assumed to be present at all times; however, it is never recorded in the fractional part. This extra bit is often referred to as the *hidden bit*.

In some computers the radix point is placed at the *right end* of the mantissa. In such cases, the mantissa is not necessarily treated as a fraction and normalization is not used (for example, in the Burroughs' machines). An advantage of this representation is that reals and integers are represented using the same storage structure. An integer is identified simply by having a zero exponent. In the CDC 170 series machines, a special instruction is provided for performing normalization (i.e., normalization is not automatically performed). For computations involving integers, normalization is not performed; and for computations involving reals, normalization should be requested explicitly to increase the number of significant digits attainable in the final answer. IBM machines supply two sets of floating-point instructions, one for normalized computations and one for computations which are not normalized.

Figure 1-4.4 illustrates how some real numbers would be stored in a machine using 32-bit floating point representation, which is composed of a 1-bit sign field, 7-bit characteristic (expressed in excess-64 notation), and a 24-bit fractional part (normalized hexadecimal number).

In most computers (see Table 1-4.7), the entire floating-point representation is contained in a computer word. However, for some scientific applications, the fractional part in a single-word representation is not large enough to yield the precision that is demanded. Consequently, many machines have a double-precision floating-point representation. For example, the double-precision floating-point storage structure for the IBM 3030 series is given in Fig. 1-4.5.

Before we complete our discussion of floating-point storage representation, it should be noted that in some smaller computers (i.e., minicomputers such as the PDP-11 and Nova series computers), floating-point operations may not be an integral part of the computer's instruction repertoire. In such instances, "add-on" hardware boxes may be purchased and attached to the CPU such as the coprocessor that is available on the Intel 8086 16-bit microprocessor. It is the case that most

| Decimal Number | Hexadecimal Number | 32-bit Floating-Point Number |
|---|---|---|
| $.0 \times 10^0$ | $(0)_{16} \times 16^0$ | 0 1000000 00000000000000000000000 |
| $-.17307 \times 10^5$ | $-.(439B)_{16} \times 16^4$ | 1 1000100 01000011100110110000000 |
| $.28692 \times 10^5$ | $.(1CB126E9)_{16} \times 16^2$ | 0 1000010 00011100101100010010110 |
| $-.75 \times 10^0$ | $-.(C)_{16} \times 16^0$ | 1 1000000 11000000000000000000000 |
| $.8317 \times 10^{-3}$ | $.(36819C4)_{16} \times 16^{-2}$ | 0 0111110 00110110100000011001110 |

**FIGURE 1-4.4**   Illustration of floating-point storage format.

**Table 1-4.7** Storage structures for real data from a sample of computers.

| Computer | Exponent | Base of Exponent | Mantissa (excluding sign) Single | Double | Radix Point | Normaliza-tion |
|---|---|---|---|---|---|---|
| IBM 360-370, 4300 and 3030 Series | 7 bits (excess-64) | 16 | 24 bits | 56 bits | left of mantissa | Yes/No |
| CDC CYBER 170 Series 800 | 11 bits, one as sign (excess-1024) | 8 | 48 bits | 96 bits | left of mantissa | by instruc-tion |
| Burroughs B5500 & B6500 | sign + 6 bits | 8 | 39 bits | 78 bits (B6500 only) | right of mantissa | No |
| PDP-10 | 8 bits* | 2 | 27 bits | — | left of mantissa | Yes |
| PDP-11 (45 model) | 8 bits (excess-128) | 2 | 23 bits + hidden | 55 bits + hidden | left of mantissa | Yes |
| VAX 11/730, 11/750 and 11/780 | (a) 8 bits, excess 128; (b) 11 bits, excess 1024; (c) 15 bits, excess 16384 | 2 | 23 bits + hidden | (a) 39 bits + hidden; (b) 52 bits + hidden; (c) 112 bits + hidden | left of mantissa | Yes |
| Motorola MC68000 | not inherently available on the microprocessor but the IEEE standard has been adopted | | | | | |
| Intel 8080 | not inherently available on the microprocessor but the IEEE standard has been adopted | | | | | |

\* Excess-128 notation for positive exponent, 1's complement notation for negative exponent.

| Sign | Characteristic | | Fractional Part | |
|---|---|---|---|---|
| 1 | 2 | 8  9 | 32  33 | 64 |

**FIGURE 1-4.5**

16-bit or larger microprocessors are being developed with floating-point coprocessors that are compatible with the IEEE floating-point standard as outlined in Coonen[1980]. Alternatively, software packages (i.e., programs) may exist which simulate the action of hardware floating-point instructions. Because the operations are simulated, floating-point computations are extremely slow and should be avoided, if possible.

In addition to a floating-point storage representation of real numbers, a fixed-point storage representation is possible. In general, the machine instructions performed on real numbers stored in a fixed format are identical to those involving integer numbers. There is a reason for this; namely, that the storage structure for fixed-point represented real numbers is the same as for integers. In fact, in the programming language PL/I, an integer must be declared as a fixed-point number in which the radix point is declared to be on the right-hand end of the fixed-point format.

It is very easy to cope with real numbers expressed in fixed-point format when computations are completed by hand (for example, 3.782 + 93.2 = 96.982), but this is not the situation in a computer. As already suggested, fixed-point hardware arithmetic operations do not exist, per se, in computers; rather, they are simulated using integer operations. As a hypothetical example, in a "decimal computer," 3.782 and 93.2 would be represented as 00 . . . 03782 and 00 . . . 00932, respectively. Of course, accompanying these storage representations is information kept as to the position of the radix point for each number (i.e., positions 3 and 1 in this example). If a computation such as an addition is performed involving these numbers, then the stored number 00 . . . 00932 must be shifted to the left two positions to make a correct summation possible. After the integer addition is complete, we would have a result of 00 . . . 96982 with an implied radix position of 3. While the previous discussion involves decimal integer operations, it is easy to visualize how comparable operations would be performed on fixed-point binary numbers.

When declaring a variable to be of type *integer* in Pascal, the precision of the number and the position of the radix point cannot be specified in the declaration. The programmer must take the responsibility for the assumed radix point and must specify the position of the radix point for output in the output format statements. In the language PL/I, the precision of the number and its radix point position can be specified in the declaration; the compiler takes the responsibility for correct arithmetic operations with the assumed radix point. Fixed-point operations such as addition, subtraction, and multiplication present few difficulties in PL/I, but **FIXED** division can result in nonintuitive quotients.

In the last two sections we have introduced, as primitive numeric data structures, the integers and reals. We have concentrated on presenting the storage structures commonly used to represent these data structures; we will continue this approach when examining the nonnumeric data structures in the following sections of this chapter.

**Exercises for Sec. 1-4.4**

1. Express the following integers in 16-bit (i) 1's complement representation and (ii) 2's complement representation: (a) 27, (b) –256, (c) –7, (d) 7, (e) 44.
2. Express the numbers given in Prob. 1 in a packed-decimal storage representation.
3. Express .250 as a floating-point number stored in (i) the IBM 3030 series of machines, and (ii) the CDC 170 Series 800 machines.
4. Express .625 as a floating-point number in the VAX 11/750.

### 1-4.5 Character Information

The first computers were actually sophisticated calculators in the sense that they were only capable of handling numeric data. Even the first computer programs were written in a strictly numeric form, i.e., machine code. It was soon realized that machine-code programming was cumbersome and the programs were difficult to read and correct. To overcome this problem, symbolic codes were developed to represent information items that were "character" rather than numeric in nature (by a character we mean the literal expression of some element selected from an alphabet). The use of character data led to the formation of mnemonics for operations and addresses, which in turn led to the development of assembly languages and, later, to the development of procedure-oriented programming languages.

A wide variety of character sets (or alphabets) are handled by the most popular computers. Two of the largest and most widely used character sets are those represented by EBCDIC (*Extended Binary Coded Decimal Interchange Code*) and ASCII (*American Standard Code for Information Interchange*). EBCDIC is a character coding system used primarily on the IBM 3030 series of computers. ASCII was developed as a standard coding scheme for the computer industry and is used on many non-IBM machines. The character sets provided by these two coding schemes are as follows:

*ASCII character set*

    *1*    English alphabet in both small and capital letters {a, b, c, ..., z, A, B, C, ..., Z}

    *2*    Decimal number characters {0, 1, 2, 3, 4, 5, 6, 7, 8, 9}

    *3*    Operation and special characters {+, -, *, /, >, =, <, |, space (SP), !, ", #, $, %, &, ', (, ), ,, ., :, ;, ?, @, ↑, ↓, →, ', {, }, [, , ], ~ }

    *4*    Control characters such as DEL (delete or rub out), STX (start of text), ETX (end of text), ACK (acknowledge), HT (horizontal tab), VT (vertical tab), LF (line feed), CR (carriage return), NAK (negative acknowledge), SYN (synchronous idle for synchronous transmission), ETB (end of transmission block), FS (file separator), GS (group separator), and RS (record separator)

*EBCDIC character set*

    *1* through *3* above, plus control characters which, although having different mnemonics and names than those given in *4*, perform the control functions.

Let us examine these character sets in terms of the function they commonly perform. English characters, decimal number characters, and special characters can be combined to form English text. Computer applications involving natural-language text are both wide-ranging and numerous. Of course, numbers are most often used in computations. Characters which are operational in nature (for example, +, -, *, /, =) are commonly used in programs to represent operations in the programming language such as addition, subtraction, multiplication, and division. The control characters are the set of characters with which programmers are least familiar. They are signal characters which aid in the transmission or storage of information. For example, the typical format for transmitting a block of data in which several records are included is illustrated in Fig. 1-4.6.

When one is storing information, control characters such as FS, GS, and RS are required to separate files, groups, and records of information. In Chap. 7, more will be said concerning the importance of control characters in the organization of files. The function of control characters is that of structuring information and not of

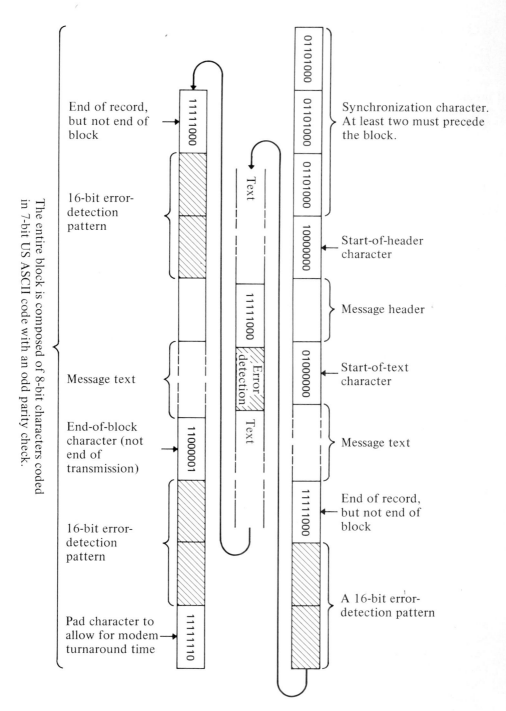

**FIGURE 1-4.6**

providing information relating to the solution of the problem. Therefore, control characters play an integral part in the storage representation of data structures but not in data structures per se.

Character sets have been created for special-purpose computer applications. Many computer graphic systems use operational-type characters for the manipulation of points and lines on a cathode ray tube. For example, special characters have been used to designate the rotation, translation, enlargement, or contraction of pictures on the screen. Another example of a special character set is the character set used in the APL (*A Programming Language*) programming system. APL a programming language designed originally by K. Iverson, is very effective for manipulating arrays. The APL character set includes the capital letters from the English alphabet, the decimal numerals, the special characters which are included in the EBCDIC and ASCII character sets, some Greek letters ($\alpha$, $\Delta$, $\varepsilon$, $\iota$, $\rho$, $\omega$) and a number of mathematically oriented characters ($\subset$, $\supset$, $\cap$, $\cup$, $\lceil$, $L$, $\bot$, $\top$, $\downarrow$, $\rightarrow$, $\div$, $\times$, $;$, $\leqslant$, $\geqslant$, $\neq$, $\bigcirc$, $\square$, $o$). Many other "nonstandard" alphabets exist for special-purpose applications, but it is beyond the scope of this text to document the number of such cases. In the earlier discussion in this section, it was pointed out that the introduction of character data was a necessary step toward the development of high-level languages. However, it is interesting to note that many of the first languages, such as FORTRAN and ALGOL 60, accommodate character data only to the limited extent of allowing the programmer to annotate the output with literal text. In languages which were developed later, such as SNOBOL, PL/I, and ALGOL 68, *character strings* along with instructions to manipulate string data were provided. A character string is simply a number of literal characters that are combined under concatenation to form a data structure which is more complex than a simple-character element (e.g., the four characters 'D', 'A', 'T', and 'A' when concatenated form the character string 'DATA'). It is worthwhile to note that in its "pure" form, Pascal does not provide character strings and strings operations. Sometimes these features are added to a particular Pascal compiler, while at other times it is the responsibility of the programmer to include these features if they are needed.

While it is worthwhile to investigate characters as primitive data structures, they are in many ways too primitive to be useful in expressing much of the nonnumeric information which can be processed by a computer. It was not purely coincidental that the designers of languages such as PL/I chose the character string as the basic data type as opposed to the character  The reasoning behind this design decision will be further illustrated in Chap. 2.

A character is represented in memory as a sequence of bits where a distinctive bit sequence is assigned to each character in the character set. Fixed-length bit sequences can be handled much more efficiently than variable-length bit sequences. Therefore, it is a generally adopted policy by computer manufacturers that character sets are encoded in fixed-length bit sequences.

In the discussion in Sec. 1-1, it was demonstrated that a bit sequence of length $n$ could be used to represent $x$ unique objects, where $\log_2 x = n$. If the objects we are considering are characters, then $x = 2^n$ characters can be represented using bit sequences of length $n$. Therefore, with $n = 6$ and $8$, we can encode up to 64 and 256 characters, respectively.

Previously, we presented a number of character sets which have been designed for use on computers. Most of these character sets include the decimal numerals, the letters from a natural-language alphabet, punctuation characters, and arithmetic operators. Unfortunately, the bit codes for representing identical or nearly identical character sets have not been standardized in spite of a considerable effort toward standardization in the computer industry. Some of the more commonly used codes for the FORTRAN character set are listed in Table 1-4.8. (We have chosen this particular character set since the FORTRAN language, and hence its character set, has been standardized and is available on a wide variety of computers.)

**TABLE 1-4.8**   Character codes in common use for the FORTRAN character set, given in octal.

| Character | ASCII | 360 EBCDIC | UNIVAC CPU Code | 6600 Display Code | External BCD | Hollerith Punch Positions |
|-----------|-------|------------|-----------------|-------------------|--------------|---------------------------|
| A | 101 | 301 | 06 | 01 | 61 | 12-1 |
| B | 102 | 302 | 07 | 02 | 62 | 12-2 |
| C | 103 | 303 | 10 | 03 | 63 | 12-3 |
| D | 104 | 304 | 11 | 04 | 64 | 12-4 |
| E | 105 | 305 | 12 | 05 | 65 | 12-5 |
| F | 106 | 306 | 13 | 06 | 66 | 12-6 |
| G | 107 | 307 | 14 | 07 | 67 | 12-7 |
| H | 110 | 310 | 15 | 10 | 70 | 12-8 |
| I | 111 | 311 | 16 | 11 | 71 | 12-9 |
| J | 112 | 321 | 17 | 12 | 41 | 11-1 |
| K | 113 | 322 | 20 | 13 | 42 | 11-2 |
| L | 114 | 323 | 21 | 14 | 43 | 11-3 |
| M | 115 | 324 | 22 | 15 | 44 | 11-4 |
| N | 116 | 325 | 23 | 16 | 45 | 11-5 |
| O | 117 | 326 | 24 | 17 | 46 | 11-6 |
| P | 120 | 327 | 25 | 20 | 47 | 11-7 |
| Q | 121 | 330 | 26 | 21 | 50 | 11-8 |
| R | 122 | 331 | 27 | 22 | 51 | 11-9 |
| S | 123 | 342 | 30 | 23 | 22 | 0-2 |
| T | 124 | 343 | 31 | 24 | 23 | 0-3 |
| U | 125 | 344 | 32 | 25 | 24 | 0-4 |
| V | 126 | 345 | 33 | 26 | 25 | 0-5 |
| W | 127 | 346 | 34 | 27 | 26 | 0-6 |
| X | 130 | 347 | 35 | 30 | 27 | 0-7 |
| Y | 131 | 350 | 36 | 31 | 30 | 0-8 |
| Z | 132 | 351 | 37 | 32 | 31 | 0-9 |
| 0 | 060 | 360 | 60 | 33 | 12 | 0 |
| 1 | 061 | 361 | 61 | 34 | 01 | 1 |
| 2 | 062 | 362 | 62 | 35 | 02 | 2 |
| 3 | 063 | 363 | 63 | 36 | 03 | 3 |
| 4 | 064 | 364 | 64 | 37 | 04 | 4 |
| 5 | 065 | 365 | 65 | 40 | 05 | 5 |
| 6 | 066 | 366 | 66 | 41 | 06 | 6 |
| 7 | 067 | 367 | 67 | 42 | 07 | 7 |

**Table 1-4.8**    Character codes in common use for the FORTRAN character set, given in octal. (Continued)

| Character | ASCII | 360 EBCDIC | UNIVAC CPU Code | 6600 Display Code | External BCD | Hollerith Punch Positions |
|---|---|---|---|---|---|---|
| 8 | 070 | 370 | 70 | 43 | 10 | 8 |
| 9 | 071 | 371 | 71 | 44 | 11 | 9 |
| + | 053 | 116 | 42 | 45 | 60 | 12 |
| – | 055 | 140 | 41 | 46 | 40 | 11 |
| * | 052 | 134 | 50 | 47 | 54 | 11-3-4 |
| / | 057 | 141 | 74 | 50 | 21 | 0-1 |
| blank | 040 | 100 | 05 | 55 | 20 | space |
| ( | 050 | 115 | 51 | 51 | 34 | 12-5-8 |
| ) | 051 | 135 | 40 | 52 | 74 | 11-5-8 |
| $ | 044 | 133 | 47 | 53 | 53 | 11-8-3 |
| = | 075 | 176 | 44 | 54 | 13 | 6-8 |
| , | 054 | 153 | 56 | 56 | 33 | 0-8-3 |
| . | 056 | 113 | 75 | 57 | 73 | 12-8-3 |

The codes adopted by the sample set of computers are listed as follows:

EBCDIC — IBM 3030 and 4300 series

ASCII — Burroughs 5000-6000 series, PDP-10, PDP-11, VAX-11 series

6000 Display Code — CDC 6000

The External BCD code is a 6-bit code which is used for storing information on magnetic tape. The Hollerith code is a standard code for representing information on punched cards. Both of these codes can be handled on a wide variety of machines.

The most widely accepted code for internal use (i.e., for character-string information in the main memory of the computer) is the ASCII, in spite of IBM's tremendous influence in the computer industry. Most computer manufacturers which have recently entered the industry have adopted ASCII. Established companies, such as IBM, hesitate to change their character codes because their new products will not be compatible with previously developed products.

Earlier in this section, we stated that a bit sequence of length 8 could represent up to 256 characters. While the EBCDIC code is 8 bits in length, the standard character set that is supported by IBM equipment contains only 105 characters (including control characters). Therefore, in most circumstances, the EBCDIC code is only $105/256 \times 100\% = 41\%$ efficient. However, if additional characters are needed for special-purpose applications (e.g., computer graphics applications), they can be readily assigned to the open codes existing in the coding scheme.

The ASCII scheme's use of 7 bits implies that a total of 128 characters are representable. Since each of these codes is assigned to a unique character, ASCII is a very efficient coding scheme. If, however, new characters are required for special-purpose applications, open codes are nonexistent. Undoubtedly, the designers of ASCII felt that the character set was universal enough for any application. Unfortunately, they did not allow for the advent of programming systems such as APL.

One method of extending a character set which is already 100 percent utilized is to use one or two of the existing characters as *escape* (or shift) *characters*. An excellent example of character-set extension can be seen in the 5-bit (32 character) telegraphy code shown in Table 1-4.9. In this case, two characters (a letter shift and a figure shift) extend the range of the character set. Whenever a figure-shift character appears, the characters following are upper-case characters, until a letter-shift character appears in a sequence of characters. Similarly, the characters following a letter shift are letters until a figure shift occurs.

For example, the text

OIL PRODUCTION (MAY 4) 94,247 BPD.

would be encoded as

lsOIL PRODUCTION fs(lsMAY fs4) 94,247 lsBPDfs.

where **ls** means letter shift and **fs** means figure shift.

A simple variation on this same scheme is to use an escape character to represent a change in mode. The appearance of an escape character indicates that all subsequent characters, up to the next appearance of the escape character, are taken from the extended character set. Using this scheme, the previous text would be represented as

OIL PRODUCTION es(esMAY es4) 94,247 esBPDes.

**Table 1-4.9**   Baudot 5-bit telegraphy code.

| Code | Lower Case | Upper Case | Code | Lower Case | Upper Case |
|------|-----------|-----------|------|-----------|-----------|
| 11000 | A | × | 11100 | Q | 1 |
| 10011 | B | ? | 01010 | R | 4 |
| 01110 | C | : | 10100 | S | , |
| 10010 | D | $ | 00001 | T | 5 |
| 10000 | E | 3 | 11100 | U | 7 |
| 10110 | F | ! | 01111 | V | ; |
| 01011 | G | & | 11001 | W | 2 |
| 00101 | H | # | 10111 | X | / |
| 01100 | I | 8 | 10101 | Y | 6 |
| 11010 | J | Bell | 10001 | Z | |
| 11110 | K | ( | 00000 | Blanks | |
| 01001 | L | ) | 11111 | Letter shift | |
| 00111 | M | . | 11011 | Figure shift | |
| 00110 | N | , | 00100 | Space | |
| 00011 | O | 9 | 00010 | Carriage return | |
| 01101 | P | 0 | 01000 | Line feed | |

where es means escape character.

Coding schemes involving escape characters are commonly used in the transmission or temporary storage of information. For applications requiring the manipulation of character text, characters are usually transformed into a "complete" code (i.e., a code not involving escape characters, such as ASCII) which can be handled more easily by the processing unit in a computer.

A final topic related to the storage representation of character data is that of conversion between numbers and characters. It is commonplace to find text which contains characters representing numerical information (e.g., the date, an address, or a quantity on order). Even applications which are generally considered to be non-numeric in nature, such as business data-processing applications, require the manipulation of numeric information using arithmetic operators. To perform such operations, we find it is necessary to convert the numeric characters into a fixed-point or floating-point internal representation. In some machines (e.g., IBM 3030 series), hardware instructions are provided to do the conversion. In most instances, however, conversions between character and numeric representation must be implemented by programs.

Through our examination of the character-coding schemes that have been developed, it is obvious that the majority of character codes are designed with conversion in mind. Adjacent numerals (for example, 6 and 7) are assigned adjacent codes [for example, $(066)_8$ , $(067)_8$ in ASCII, and $(F6)_{16}$ , $(F7)_{16}$ in EBCDIC]. This adjacency property facilitates conversion in the following manner. By subtracting the character code for zero from the given character code, we arrive at the numeric value of the character. For example, the ASCII representations of the characters '0' and '9' are $(060)_8$ and $(071)_8$ , respectively. The result of subtracting the encoded value of '0' [that is, $(060)_8$ ] from the encoded value of '9' [that is, $(071)_8$ ] is $(11)_8$ , which of course is the correct fixed-point representation for 9 in octal.

The following algorithm handles character to fixed-point numeric conversion for any coding scheme that has the adjacency property. More precisely stated, the algorithm is generalized so as to handle the conversion of multidigit character strings, such as '4937', to a fixed-point representation.

**Function** CONVERT_CHARACTER_TO_NUMERIC(NUMBCHAR). Given a multidigit character string designated as NUMBCHAR, this function finds its equivalent integer representation and stores this value in NUMBER. NUMBCHAR[I] denotes the Ith character starting from the left in the multi-digit string NUMBCHAR. The function DECODE returns the code representation for its character argument [e.g. if the character '0' is encoded in ASCII, then DECODE('0') returns $(060)_8$ or an equivalent numeric representation. The integer variable ZEROREP is used to hold the code representation of the character '0'. This is subtracted from the code representation of each character to yield the fixed point octal representation of the integer corresponding to the character [for example, $(067)_8 - (060)_8 = 7]$.

1.  [Initialize the integer value and the constant ZEROREP]
    NUMBER ← 0
    ZEROREP ← DECODE('0')
2.  [Convert all characters in the string NUMBCHAR]
    Repeat for I = 1, 2, 3, ..., LENGTH(NUMBCHAR)
        NUMBER ← 10 * NUMBER + DECODE(NUMBCHAR[I])
            − ZEROREP

3.  [Finished]
        Return(NUMBER)                                                        ☐

The problem of converting a positive number to a sequence of numeric characters involves a process which is basically the converse of the previous conversion algorithm. The following algorithm is a solution to this conversion problem in general.

**Function** CONVERT_NUMERIC_TO_CHARACTER(NUMBER). Given an integer NUMBER, this function finds its equivalent character-string representation and stores this string in NUMBCHAR. The function ENCODE returns the character equivalent of the encoded representation of its argument [e.g., ENCODE$((071)_8)$ is '9' in ASCII]. MOD is a function which returns the remainder in the division of its first argument by its second argument [e.g., MOD(23, 10) is 3].

1.  [Initialize]
        NUMBCHAR ← ''
2.  [Build a character string of digits from right to left]
        Repeat through step 4 while NUMBER $\neq$ 0
3.  [Concatenate new numeric equivalent to the part of the number already formed]
        NUMBCHAR ← ENCODE(DECODE('0') + MOD(NUMBER, 10))
                ○ NUMBCHAR
4.  [Remove the least significant digit]
        NUMBER ← NUMBER / 10
5.  [Finished]
        Return(NUMBCHAR)                                                      ☐

In this section we have concentrated upon the storage representation of character data. We have by no means completed our discussion of character information. In Chap. 2 we will consider the character as part of a more complex data structure—namely, the character string.

**Exercises for Sec. 1-4.5**

1.  Given a single-character argument, write a Pascal function CONVBIT that returns a sequence of bit values which is representative of the internal storage representation for that character. For example, CONVBIT('1') returns '11110001' and CONVBIT('*') returns '01011100'.
2.  Write a Pascal procedure for converting an integer into a decimal-digit character (that is, 4 to '4').

**1-4.6  Logical Information**

A logical data item is a primitive data structure that can assume the values of either "true" or "false." (In a programming situation, true and false are expressed in many different ways, depending on the programming language used—for example, FORTRAN—.TRUE. and .FALSE., ALGOL—true and false, Pascal—true and false, PL/I—'1'B and '0'B, LISP—T and NIL, etc.) Logical quantities represent constant truth values (for example, "2 divides exactly into 4" is always true and "2 divides exactly into 5" is always false), or values which change depending on time or circumstances (e.g., "Peters is twenty years old"). Only two logical constants exist:

*true* and *false*. Logical situations which are subject to change can be represented by logical variables. However, to properly motivate the need for logical variables, first we should discuss the logical operations that can be applied to logical data.

Just as operations exist for arithmetic data (i.e., operations such as addition, subtraction, multiplication, etc.), operations exist for logical data. The three most common logical operations are "anding," "oring," and "complementing" which are popularly represented by the operators $\wedge$, $\vee$, and $\sim$, respectively. If X and Y depict logical variables, then $\wedge$, V, and $\sim$ are defined as follows.

$\wedge$   The result of X $\wedge$ Y is true if and only if X and Y both have the value true; otherwise, the result is false.

V   The result of X V Y is false only if X and Y have the value false; otherwise, the result is true.

$\sim$   The result of $\sim$X (note that $\sim$ is a unary operator with one operand) is true if X has the value false, and the result of $\sim$X is false if X has the value true.

Table 1-4.10 defines the results of the three logical operations.

Expressions involving logical operands commonly arise when using the *relational operators*: $<$, $\leq$, $=$, $\neq$, $\geq$, $>$. We are familiar with the application of relational operators to arithmetic operands. The results of relational operators are the logical values "true" and "false," as exemplified in expressions like $(1 + 5) = 6$ (which is true) and $5 < 4$ (which is false). Relational operators can also be used in conjunction with character and pointer data (in a restricted sense), and we will encounter examples of these relational operators later on in the book.

As computer programmers, we will continually face problems that involve logical decisions. When formulating an algorithm, our ideas are organized in terms of logical steps that lead to the solution of the problem to be solved. These logical steps are reflected in the control structure of the programs for the algorithms which are formulated. For example, in programming an accounts-payable application part of the problem statement might be: "If the current balance is negative, then calculate and add the interest charge." The condition "current balance is negative' is a logical one, and as part of the program, it could be written as 'CURRENT_BAL < 0''.

The value of such a condition may be variable because it is dependent upon the values of the operands, which may change during program execution. Sometimes it is convenient to represent logical conditions which vary during program exe-

**Table 1-4.10**   Tabular definition of the logical operators $\wedge$, V, and $\sim$.

| X | Y | X $\wedge$ Y | X V Y | $\sim$X |
|---|---|---|---|---|
| T | T | T | T | F |
| T | F | F | T | F |
| F | T | F | T | T |
| F | F | F | F | T |

cution, such as "CURRENT_BAL < 0", by logical variables. Logical variables are used most often to represent the values of complex logical expressions [for example, (A < B ∧ C < D) V (B < A ∧ D < C)], which might needlessly require reevaluation several times during the execution of a program. Also, logical variables are popularly used to represent terminating conditions on loop constructs in which the terminating condition depends on a logical expression (e.g., the while <logical condition> do group in Pascal).

The storage representation of logical values is dependent upon the language translator (i.e., compiler or interpreter) that is processing the program and the machine for which the translator is designed. The most obvious storage structure that can be applied to logical data is the single bit. In this scheme it is conventional to represent the value *true* by an "on" bit (i.e., a bit with the value of 1) and the value for *false* by an "off" bit (i.e., a bit with a value of 0). The IBM PL/I Optimizing compiler attempts to use a bit storage structure for logical values whenever possible.

Most machines do not have instructions which allow direct access of a given bit in memory. Therefore, the isolation of the value of a particular logical data item may involve the execution of several machine instructions. Consequently, other storage representations have been adopted. One of the most inefficient ways (in a storage sense) of representing logical data is to assign an entire word of memory to a logical item. In the WATFIV compiler, for example, the values .TRUE. and .FALSE. are represented by eight 1 bits and eight 0 bits in the left-most byte of a 32-bit word, respectively. In Pascal, it is also necessary to use four bytes to represent a logical variable—the notion of a logical bit string does not exist. While such full-word representations are extremely wasteful of memory space, they facilitate fast access of logical information. Of course, fast access is achieved because most machine instructions operate on words of data, as opposed to specific bits of information.

Other compilers, such as the PL/C compiler for the IBM 3030 series computers, utilize the smallest addressable unit of memory (i.e., the 8-bit byte) to represent logical values. This storage representation has the advantage of quick access and relatively small storage requirements.

This section completes a brief description of logical data and their representation. In subsequent chapters, we will return to a discussion of logical data when describing more complex data structures, in particular, logical arrays.

### 1-4.7 Pointer Information

A *pointer* (or *link*) is a reference to a data structure. We can illustrate how a pointer might be used by considering a problem which often arises when compiling a program. Suppose a program contains four occurrences of the real constant, 3.1459. During the compilation process, four copies of 3.1459 could be created. However, it is more efficient to use one copy of 3.1459 and three pointers referencing the single copy, since less space is needed to represent a pointer than a real number in floating-point representation (see Fig 1-4.7).

Probably the most important property of a pointer is that, as a single fixed-size data item, it provides a homogeneous method of referencing any data structure, regardless of the structure's type or complexity. In the previous example, the three pointers could point to an integer constant, a character constant, or a logical constant, and the method of referencing would have been the same, i.e., an address pointing at the required data item.

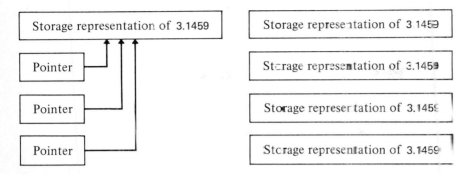

**FIGURE 1-4.7** Multiple references to a real number through a pointer versus multiple copies of a real number.

A final important characteristic of pointers is that, in some instances, they permit faster insertion and deletion of elements to and from a data structure. In later chapters, in particular Chaps. 4, 5, and 7, we will see that this restructuring property is an extremely important one.

It is crucial to realize that, with the introduction of the pointer, we are now provided with two methods of accessing a data structure. The method we are most familiar with is commonly called the *computed address method*. In this method, a data structure is accessed directly through an address (either an absolute or a relative address). This address is computed by the language translator (i.e., compiler, interpreter, or assembler) which is processing the source program. In the second method, the *pointer* or *link addressing method*, the address of a data object is not computed, but is assigned to a pointer. To access a data-structure element, we first load a pointer value. The pointer value (i.e., address) provides a reference to the data structure of interest. Access to a particular data element within the data structure may require some additional computation, depending upon the complexity of the data structure. We will be more concerned with this aspect as we introduce more complex data structures. The pointer addressing method is, in general, more time-consuming than the computed address method, since access to an item is always done via a pointer. However, there are situations in which the flexibility provided by indirectly referencing a data object using a pointer is well worth any time inefficiencies that are generated.

The difference between the two addressing modes is clearly identified by examining a subject that is too often misunderstood by programmers—parameter passing in subroutines (i.e., procedures) and functions. Consider the program segment given in Fig. 1-4.8.

In this program, **EXAMPLE** is the name of a module (i.e., procedure), X is a *formal parameter*, and Y is the *actual parameter* in the call statement. One method of parameter passing which is available in programming languages such as SNOBOL, LISP, and ALGOL W is *call-by-value*. In call-by-value, the value of an actual parameter is assigned (at execution time) to a predetermined location that has been allocated to the corresponding formal parameter (see Fig. 1-4.9).

Whenever access to a formal parameter is required, it is done directly via the predetermined *computed address*. Any assignment to the formal parameter affects only the value of the formal parameter and *not* the value of the actual parameter.

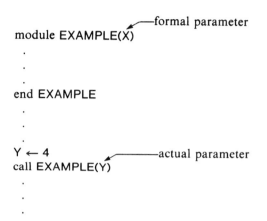

FIGURE 1-4.8

Therefore, in the example program, when execution returns from the module to the statement following the call statement, Y retains the same value it had prior to the call.

Two other parameter-passing schemes (*call-by-name* in ALGOL 60 and ALGOL W, and *call-by-reference* in FORTRAN and PL/I) make use of the pointer method for accessing parameter values. Instead of the value of the actual parameter, a pointer to the location of the actual parameter is passed and is assigned to the formal parameter. This association is shown in Fig. 1-4.10. Therefore, when the value of X is desired in the module EXAMPLE, the value of Y is retrieved via the pointer assigned to X.

Problems can arise when using parameter-passing methods which involve pointers. If the actual parameter is an expression, such as Y + 4, instead of a simple variable, then it does not make sense to assign a value to the corresponding formal parameter, since the effect would be to assign a value to the expression Y + 4.

Such meaningless assignments have created problems when using call-by-reference in FORTRAN. For example, if we call the module EXAMPLE with the expression 2 as the actual parameter, then the address of the constant 2 is assigned to the formal parameter X (see Fig. 1-4.11). If X is assigned the value 4, then the effect is to assign 4 to the memory location at which the constant 2 resides, that is, 2 now becomes 4. When a return is made to the statement following the call to EXAMPLE, the statement Y ← 2 + 2 is executed. However, the constant 2 now has the value 4, and Y will take on the value 4 + 4 or 8. Amazing but true! This situation was eliminated in PL/I by creating a dummy location for the value of the evaluated expression which appears as an actual parameter. Hence, if a formal parameter is assigned a value of 4, the value of the dummy location is changed, not the constant 2.

Location for value of Y 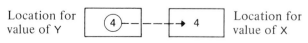 Location for value of X

FIGURE 1-4.9

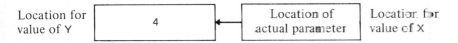

| Location for value of Y | 4 | | Location of actual parameter | Location for value of X |

**FIGURE 1-4.10**

In call-by-name parameter passing, assignments to formal parameters with expressions as actual parameters are disallowed. A special routine, called a *thunk*, is set up to perform the evaluation of the actual parameter. The address of the thunk is assigned to the location of the formal parameter. Therefore, whenever the value of the formal parameter is required, the thunk is located via the pointer assigned to the formal parameter location and then is evaluated. Hence, while both call-by-reference and call-by-name use a pointer addressing scheme, a basic difference does exist. In call-by-reference, an actual parameter is evaluated only once—before the procedure is called. In call-by-name, an actual parameter is evaluated each time the formal parameter is referenced.

Some of the first programming languages developed, such as COBOL, FORTRAN, and ALGOL 60, did not have a pointer data type. However, the effect of a pointer can be simulated in these languages using an index into an array. (We will discuss this idea in Chap. 4.) Languages which were developed later, such as Pascal, PL/I, SNOBOL, ALGOL W and ALGOL 68, have a pointer type which can be controlled explicitly by the programmer. The advantages of a pointer type will become clearer when we consider the algorithms for accessing linked data structures in later chapters.

In the previous discussion on pointer data, it was indicated that a pointer is an address which references a data structure. In terms of storage representation, addresses are generally assigned a word or half-word of storage in most computers. Of course, the larger the number of addresses (i.e., the address space) in the computer, the larger the amount of storage needed to represent an address.

The address of a pointer may reference a data structure in one of two modes—*absolute* or *relative*. Absolute mode implies that the value of the pointer is an absolute memory location, such as 7632, at which the data structure being pointed at may reside. A relative pointer carries as a value an offset into a region of

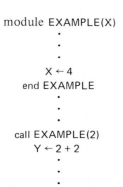

```
module EXAMPLE(X)
        .
        .
        .
     X ← 4
   end EXAMPLE
        .
        .
        .
  call EXAMPLE(2)
     Y ← 2 + 2
        .
        .
        .
```

**FIGURE 1-4.11** Algorithm segment illustrating pitfalls of call-by-reference form of parameters passing that exists in FORTRAN.

memory relative to some base location for that region. (This base location is often stored in a special register called a *base register*.) Hence, if the value of a pointer is 5 and the base location of the data area for a program is 7627, then the effective absolute address of the pointer is 7627 + 5 = 7632.

In early computers only an absolute mode of addressing was available. Today, however, all but very unsophisticated mini and microcomputers have relative-mode addressing capabilities. Most computer systems allow more than one program to reside in memory at one time. Therefore, if a program is executed twice, there exists a good possibility that it is not allotted the same memory locations. If a relative mode of addressing is used, then programs can be relocated in memory by simply changing the base location rather than all the pointer values, as would be necessary in an absolute mode. Hence, relative-mode addressing is more popular than absolute-mode addressing.

At the machine instruction level, the accessing of a data structure via a pointer is generally accomplished in one of two ways. The first method involves the loading of the pointer's value (i.e., the address of the first element in the data structure) into an accumulator or index register. A machine-level instruction whose operand refers to this index register is then used to provide access to the desired data structure. This use of an index register is illustrated in machine-level instructions as follows:

(LD means "load" and LDI means "load with index")
LD X, R1     — load the pointer X into register R1
LDI R1, R2   — load the contents of the memory location specified by
               the pointer (i.e., address) contained in R1 into register
               R2

The second method involves the use of *indirect addressing*. In this method, the operand of a machine instruction is used to derive directly the address of the information we wish to access. For example, consider a machine-level instruction such as

LD @X, R2

If the contents of memory location X are an address, say Y, then the contents of memory location Y are loaded into register R2 upon execution of the above instruction. Therefore, the net effect is to load directly into R2 the contents of the memory location Y. The one instruction involving an indirect address is equivalent to the two instructions given previously involving an index register.

Indirect addressing provides a quicker single access to a data structure than a method using index registers. However, if accesses are required for a large number of data elements, the index-register method is superior to indirect addressing. The reason for this superiority is that the index register need only be loaded once, and once loaded, the contents of an index register can be changed more quickly to account for the different offsets for a number of data elements than an indirect address. (An indirect address resides in main memory, not in a register.) Table 1-4.11 exhibits some of the addressing capabilities available in a sample set of computers.

Throughout Chaps. 4, 5, and 7, the pointer plays an integral role in the expression of linked and multilinked structures which are presented. In these chapters the flexibility provided by pointers for accessing, deleting, and inserting data-structure elements will become very evident.

**Table 1-4.11**  Addressing capabilities for the set of sample computers.

| | Indirect Addressing (Yes or No) | Number of Index and Base Registers | . Addressable Space |
|---|---|---|---|
| IBM 360-370, 4300, and 3030 Series | No | 16 index and base registers | Memory access via index and base registers. Largest offset relative to a base register is 4095 bytes. |
| CDC CYBER 170 Series 800 | Yes | 8 address registers; 8 increment registers; 8 general-purpose registers | Access via address and increment registers. Addressable space of 2,097,152 words. |
| Burroughs 5500 | No | 8 base registers | Can access 32,768 words directly; can use base register with maximum offset of 4095 words. |
| PDP-10 | Yes | 15 index registers, memory locations 1-15 can be used as index registers also | Access via base registers has maximum offset of 8192 or 16384 words depending on implementation. |
| PDP-11 | Yes | 8 index registers, one is used as the program counter | Access via index register and indirect addressing. Range of valid offsets for indexed operation is -32768 to +32767 bytes. |
| VAX 11/730, 11/750 and 11/780 | Yes | 16 index registers, 4 reserved: one as program counter, one as stack pointer, one as argument pointer, and one as frame pointer | Access via index register and indirect addressing. Range of valid offsets for indexed operation is 2,147,483,647 bytes. |
| Motorola MC68000 | Yes | 16 general purpose registers, 8 of which are base registers, and all of which can be used as index registers. | 14 addressing modes including memory access via index and base registers; addressing range of 16,777,216 bytes. |
| Intel 8080 | Yes | Three 16 bit base registers; no index registers | 64 K bytes. |

## BIBLIOGRAPHY

COONEN, J. T.: "An Implementation Guide to a Proposed Standard for Floating-Point Arithmetic," *Computer*, Jan., 1980, pp. 68-79.

DIETMEYER, D. L.: Logic Design of Digital Systems, Allyn and Bacon, Inc., Boston, 1971.

FOSTER, C. C.: Computer Architecture, Van Nostrand Reinhold Co., New York, 1970.

HARTLEY, R. V. L.: Transmission of Information, *Bell Systems Tech. J.*, **7**, 1928, p. 535.

IVERSON, K. E.: A Programming Language, John Wiley & Sons, Inc., New York, 1962.

KOLMOGOROFF, A.: Interpolation and Extrapolation von Stationarem Sufalligen Folgen, *Bull. Acad. Sci. U.S.S.R. ser. math.*, **5**, 1942, pp. 3-14.

MANO, M. M.: Computer Logic Design, Prentice-Hall, Englewood Cliffs, N.J., 1972.

MORRIS, C. W.: Signs, Language, and Behavior, Prentice-Hall, Inc., New York, 1946.

REZA, F. M.: An Introduction to Information Theory, McGraw-Hill Book Company, Toronto, 1961.

SHANNON, C. E., and W. WEAVER: The Mathematical Theory of Communication, University of Illinois Press, Urbana, 1949.

SMITH, C. L.: Digital Control of Industrial Processes, *Computing Surveys*, Vol. 2, No. 3, Sept., 1970, pp. 211-242.

STONE, H. S.: Introduction to Computer Organization and Data Structures, McGraw-Hill Book Company, New York, 1972.

TREMBLAY, J. P., and R. P. MANOHAR: Discrete Mathematical Structures with Applications to Computer Science, McGraw-Hill Book Company, New York, 1975.

WIENER, N.: Cybernetics, The Technology Press of M.I.T. and John Wiley & Sons, Inc., New York, 1948, 2nd ed., M.I.T. Press, Cambridge, Mass., 1961.

# 2

# THE REPRESENTATION AND
# MANIPULATION OF STRINGS

*In the previous chapter we introduced the character as a primitive data structure. It was pointed out that the character string, and not the basic character element is the more useful data structure of the two for programs involving nonnumeric applications. In this chapter, we see how the character string can be built from character elements. We begin by introducing the Markov algorithm, a classical system for manipulating strings. Using this presentation as a basis, we discuss string manipulation and pattern matching, especially as they relate to the programming languages Pascal and SNO-BOL. Next, a variety of storage representations for strings is examined. Finally, string applications which involve text formatting, lexical analysis, and KWIC indexing are discussed.*

## 2-1 DEFINITIONS AND CONCEPTS

In this chapter, we are concerned with the type of operations (or manipulations) that can be performed on strings. There are many interesting properties exhibited by string operations, just as there are interesting properties for arithmetic operations over the natural numbers. To refamiliarize ourselves with some of the properties associated with operations, let us consider the operation of addition on the natural numbers. This operation can be represented in general by a functional system in two variables:

$$f(x,y) = x + y$$

where $x$ and $y$ are natural numbers. This system is well known to us and exhibits certain interesting properties. Firstly, the sum of any two numbers is a natural number. This property is called *closure*. Closure is a necessary property for a system (i.e., a set and an operation on that set) to be classified as an algebra or algebraic system. Secondly, $(x + y) + z = x + (y + z) = x + y + z$ when $x$, $y$, and $z$ are natural numbers; accordingly the operation of addition is said to be *associative*. Thirdly, there exists a number $i$ such that for every natural number $x$, $x + i = x$. This number is zero and is called the unit element or *identity* of the additive system. There are many other important properties, such as distributivity and commutativity, which exist when arithmetic operations such as addition and multiplication are applied to the set of natural numbers.

We begin a discussion of strings by formally defining a string. To do so, we must introduce the notion of an alphabet and the operation of concatenation. Simply stated, an *alphabet* V is a finite nonempty set of symbols. The set $V = \{a, b, c, ..., z\}$ is a familiar example of an alphabet and $\{\alpha, \beta, \gamma, \varepsilon\}$ is a four character alphabet (which is a subalphabet of the Greek alphabet).

The *concatenation* of two alphabetic characters, say 'a' and 'b', is said to form a sequence of characters, namely, 'ab'. (Note that henceforth when we refer to a character from an alphabet or a sequence of such characters, they are enclosed in single quote marks.) The operation of concatenation also applies to sequences of characters. For example, 'ab' concatenated with 'ab' is 'abab'. We denote the concatenation operator by the special symbol $\bigcirc$. This allows us to write expressions such as 'ab' $\bigcirc$ 'a' which is identical in value to 'aba'.

A *string* over an alphabet V is (1) a letter from the alphabet V, or (2) a sequence of letters derived from the concatenation of characters from the alphabet V. Examples of strings over an alphabet $V = \{ 1, 2, 3 \}$ are '1', '31', '3321', and '222'.

Let $V \bigcirc V = V^2$ designate all strings of length two on V, $V \bigcirc V \bigcirc V = V^2 \bigcirc V = V^3$ designate all strings of length three on V, and, in general, $V \bigcirc V \bigcirc ... \bigcirc V = V^n$ designate all strings of length n on V. Then the closure of V, denoted as $V^+$, is defined as

$$V^+ = V \cup V^2 \cup V^3 \cup ....$$

For completeness, a special string $\Lambda$ called the empty or NULL string is often combined with $V^+$ to form the closure set $V^*$ of V. That is, $V^* = \Lambda \cup V \cup V^2 \cup V^3 \cup ... = \Lambda \cup V^+$. The string $\Lambda$ has the *identity* property (that is, $x \bigcirc \Lambda = \Lambda \bigcirc x = x$ for any string x which is an element of $V^*$), and it is called the identity element in the algebra formed by the set $V^*$ and the operation of concatenation. Associativity is another property of this algebra [that is, $(x \bigcirc y) \bigcirc z = x \bigcirc (y \bigcirc z) = x \bigcirc y \bigcirc z$ for x, y, z $\varepsilon$ $V^*$].

As an example, consider the set of strings V* that can be generated from an alphabet $V = \{a, b\}$. Some subsets of V* are

$V^2 = \{$ 'aa', 'ab', 'ba', 'bb' $\}$
$V^3 = \{$ 'aaa', 'aab', 'aba', 'abb', 'baa', 'bab', 'bab', 'bbb' $\}$
$V^4 = \{$ 'aaaa', 'aaab', 'aaba', 'aabb', 'abaa', 'abab', 'abba', 'abbb', 'baaa', 'baab', 'baba', 'babb', 'bbaa', 'bbab', 'bbba', 'bbbb' $\}$

.
.
.

We will, on many occasions, refer to the closure set V* of an alphabet.

As a final example of a string, let us examine the FORTRAN programming language. The FORTRAN alphabet consists of 26 letters, 10 digits, and a set of special characters, such as '(', ')', ',', '=', '+', etc. It is only these characters that are used in writing a FORTRAN program. Hence, a program can be viewed as the concatenation of characters over an alphabet to yield an arbitrarily long string. In Sec. 2-5.2, we see that the problem of ensuring that only the proper set of characters appears in a program is handled by the scanning phase of a compiler.

## 2-2 STRING MANIPULATION AND PATTERN MATCHING

We begin this section by discussing the Markov formalism in Sec. 2-2.1. It will provide us with a good introduction to the concepts relating to string manipulation and pattern matching. The Markov system, however, is not a practical system from a programming and data manipulation point of view. Nevertheless, later in this section, we propose an enhanced set of primitives and a set of composite string-handling functions which are modeled, in part, on the string-handling capabilities exhibited in the Markov formal system. Next, string-handling facilities in the general-purpose language Pascal and the string manipulation language SNOBOL are described and related to the string-handling functions proposed earlier. The section concludes with a discussion of recursive pattern matching.

### 2-2.1 Markov Algorithms

The Markov algorithm, named for the Russian mathematician A. A. Markov, is a formal system for string manipulation that was originally developed to support a theory of computation. While the Markov algorithm appears formal and mathematical in nature, the first string-processing language, COMIT, was based to a significant extent on the Markov formalism. There is a striking similarity between the Markov model and the SNOBOL programming language, which is a widely used successor of COMIT. Later, in Sec. 2-2.5, we introduce some of the string manipulation functions in SNOBOL, and it becomes clear that both the data and control structures of Markov algorithms are modeled very closely in SNOBOL.

The general strategy in a Markov algorithm is to take as input a string x and, through a number of steps (or productions) in the algorithm, transform x to an output string y. This transformation process is commonly performed in computer application areas such as text editing or program compilation. In particular, the compilation process can be thought of as the transformation of strings from a source language (such as Pascal) into strings of object code (such as an assembly language program or machine code).

The single input string x is the only data structure operated on by the algorithm; however, this string is flexible in its capacity to grow or shrink in length as transformations are applied to it. Both x and the transformed output string y contain characters from an alphabet V. Hence, x and y belong to V*.

A *simple* (Markov) *production* is a statement of the form u → w where u and w represent strings in V*, where V does not contain the symbols "→" and ".". In the production, u is called the *antecedent* and w is called the *consequent*. A production with antecedent u and consequent w is *applicable* to a string z ε V* if there is at least one occurrence of u in z; otherwise, the production is *not applicable*. If the production is applicable, then the first (i.e., left-most) occurrence of u in z is replaced by w. For example, if a production 'ba' → 'c' is applied to the input string 'ababab', then the resulting string is 'acbab'. However, the production 'baa' → 'c' is not applicable to 'ababab'.

A Markov algorithm consists of an ordered set of productions $P_1$, $P_2$, $P_n$. The flow of control through a Markov algorithm depends on whether productions are applicable. Execution starts with the first production. If a production is applicable, execution resumes with the first production. On the other hand, if a production is not applicable (i.e., a substring to be replaced is not found), execution continues to the next production.

A Markov algorithm terminates in one of two ways:

*1*    The last production is not applicable.
*2*    A *terminal production* is applicable.

A terminal production is a statement of the form x → y., where x and y represent strings in V* and the symbol "." immediately follows the consequent.

*Example 2-1* Consider the Markov algorithm having the productions

$P_1$:      'ab' → 'b'
$P_2$:      'ac' → 'c'
$P_3$:      'aa' → 'a'

on the alphabet V = {a, b, c}. This algorithm deletes all occurrences of 'a' in a string with the exception of an 'a' if it appears as the last character in the subject string. Let us trace through the execution of this algorithm given an input string 'bacaabaa'. The symbol "⟹" is used to indicate the result of a transformation, and the substring being replaced (or matched) is underlined.

'baca<u>ab</u>aa'      ⟹ 'bacabaa'(by $P_1$)
'bac<u>ab</u>aa'       ⟹ 'bacbaa'(by $P_1$)
'ba<u>ac</u>baa'       ⟹ 'bcbaa'(by $P_2$)
'bcb<u>aa</u>'         ⟹ 'bcba'(by $P_3$)

Since all productions, including the last production ($P_3$), are not applicable to the string 'bcba', the algorithm terminates.                              ////

We are now able to define, more formally, the execution of a Markov algorithm in terms of our algorithmic notation.

**Algorithm** MARKOV. We are given a Markov algorithm with a finite sequence $P_1$, $P_2$, $P_n$ of productions which are to be applied to an input string $z_0$ ε V*. Variables i and j are indices and $z_i$ denotes the result after the application of the ith transformation to the input string $z_0$.

1.    [Initialize i, the intermediate string index]
         i ← 0

2.    [Initialize j, the production index]
   $j \leftarrow 1$
3.    [Establish conditions for execution]
   Repeat step 4 while $j \leq n$
4.    [Check for production applicability and terminal production]
   If $P_j$ is applicable
   then apply production $P_j$
       set $i \leftarrow i + 1$ to obtain a new string z
       If $P_j$ is a terminal production
       then write $z_i$
          Exit
       else $j \leftarrow 1$
     else $j \leftarrow j + 1$
5.    [The algorithm is blocked]
   Write $(z_i)$
   Exit                    □

In Example 2-1, the productions $P_1$: 'ab' → 'b', $P_2$: 'ɛc' → 'c', and $P_3$: 'aa' → 'a' can be expressed in a compressed form 'a'x → x (x ɛ V) by using a variable x in the algorithm. The variable x in this production assumes a role similar to that of a variable in a program (that is, x can take on any value from a defined range of values, which in this case is the set {a, b, c}. A formal description of the Markov algorithm for deleting all occurrences of 'a', except for one on the end of the string, is simply

  MA: DELETE_A (x ɛ V)
  $P_1$:  'a'x → x

Note that we have included an algorithm header MA (Markov Algorithm) and a declaration for the variable x along with its range set V.

*Example 2-2* Let V be a certain alphabet and let y represent a character from this alphabet. We would like to write Markov algorithms to transform any string z ɛ V* (1) into the string yz, and (2) into the string zy as follows:

  MA: YZ (y ɛ V)
  $P_1$:
  $\Lambda$ → y.

Given as input a string z, y is inserted on the front of the string and the algorithm YZ is completed.

  The second problem is not as trivial. Since the first occurrence of $\Lambda$ in z is to the left of the first symbol in z, a production of the form $\Lambda$ → y. will not work. An algorithm consisting of the production z → zy. is not appropriate because z is an arbitrary string in V* and variables in a Markov algorithm can only assume single-letter values and cannot take on string values. For the algorithm to work for all possible strings z, it would require an infinite number of productions.

  A production is always applied to the first occurrence of x (where x → y is a production) in string z. A problem arises when we desire to apply a production to the second, third, fourth, or last occurrence of x. To overcome this problem, we create a set of *auxiliary symbols* which are used as *markers*. Markers allow us to mark a particular point within a string, thus making possible the application of a production at that point.

Returning to the second part of this example, let V be the alphabet and $\alpha$ be a marker, $\alpha \notin V$. The result of applying the following Markov algorithm to a string z is the string zy.

MA:  ZY $(x, y \; \varepsilon \; V)$
$P_1$:  $\alpha x \rightarrow x\alpha$
$P_2$:  $\alpha \rightarrow y.$
$P_3$:  $\Lambda \rightarrow \alpha$

Since the input string z does not initially contain the auxiliary symbol $\alpha$, production $P_3$ is applied to z, yielding $\alpha z$. Production $P_1$ is used repeatedly to move $\alpha$ to the right of the symbols in z. If z contains $m$ characters, then the result of applying $P_1$ $m$ times is $z\alpha$. $P_1$ no longer applies at this stage, but $P_2$, which is terminal, does apply. Hence, the result of the Markov algorithm is zy.     ////

Let us consider a final example which also involves the use of marker symbols.

*Example 2-3* Given a string $z \; \varepsilon \; V^*$ such that $z = z_1 z_2 z_3 \ldots z_{n-1} z_n$, we want to generate an output string $z'$ which is the reverse of z (that is, $z' = z_n z_{n-1} \ldots z_3 z_2 z_1$). We employ $\alpha$ and $\beta$ as auxiliary symbols.

MA:  REVERSE $(x, y \; \varepsilon \; V)$
$P_1$:  $\alpha\alpha \rightarrow \beta$
$P_2$:  $\beta\alpha \rightarrow \beta$
$P_3$:  $\beta x \rightarrow x\beta$
$P_4$:  $\beta \rightarrow \Lambda.$
$P_5$:  $\alpha xy \rightarrow y\alpha x$
$P_6$:  $\Lambda \rightarrow \alpha$

Initially, $\alpha$ is placed in front of z by the application of $P_6$. Then $P_5$ moves the $\alpha$ until the last character of the string z is encountered or until another $\alpha$ is reached. This process (i.e., the application of $P_6$ and $P_5$) is continued until the first symbol remains as $\alpha$. The symbol $\beta$ is used to delete all occurrences of $\alpha$. This is accomplished by the application of $P_1$, $P_2$, and $P_3$. After all $\alpha$'s are removed, the $\beta$ is removed via $P_4$ and the algorithm terminates.

Given $z = 'abc'$, the sequence of transformations applied to z by the algorithm REVERSE is as follows:

| | |
|---|---|
| $'abc' \Rightarrow \alpha'abc'$ | (by $P_6$) |
| $\Rightarrow 'b'\alpha'ac'$ | (by $P_5$) |
| $\Rightarrow 'bc'\alpha'a'$ | (by $P_5$) |
| $\Rightarrow \alpha'bc'\alpha'a'$ | (by $P_6$) |
| $\Rightarrow 'c'\alpha'b'\alpha'a'$ | (by $P_5$) |
| $\Rightarrow \alpha'c'\alpha'b'\alpha'a'$ | (by $P_6$) |
| $\Rightarrow \alpha\alpha'c'\alpha'b'\alpha'a'$ | (by $P_6$) |
| $\Rightarrow \beta'c'\alpha'b'\alpha'a'$ | (by $P_1$) |
| $\Rightarrow 'c'\beta\alpha'b'\alpha'a'$ | (by $P_3$) |
| $\Rightarrow 'c'\beta'b'\alpha'a'$ | (by $P_2$) |
| $\Rightarrow 'cb'\beta\alpha'a'$ | (by $P_3$) |
| $\Rightarrow 'cb'\beta'a'$ | (by $P_2$) |
| $\Rightarrow 'cba'\beta$ | (by $P_3$) |
| $\Rightarrow 'cba'$ | (by $P_4$) |

////

From the examples in the previous discussion, it should be obvious that the order in which we arrange the productions totally determines the flow of execution in a Markov algorithm. For example, if we had decided to place production $P_6$ (that is, $\Lambda \rightarrow \alpha$) as $P_1$ in Example 2-3, then the REVERSE algorithm would generate an infinite number of $\alpha$'s in front of the input string and the algorithm would never terminate. Although the control structure for Markov algorithms is simple, it allows virtually no flexibility in the organization of productions.

As an alternative to the Markov model just proposed, we introduce a model which allows the labeling of productions to affect a more flexible transfer of control between productions. Labeling changes the original Markov model in two ways:

*1* If a production is applicable and a label is appended to it, then the transfer of control is to the production bearing that label name.

*2* If a production is not applicable or if no label is appended to the production, execution continues to the next production if there is a next production or halts if there is no next production.

*Example 2-4* Let us rewrite the REVERSE Markov algorithm as presented in Example 2-3 in the form of a labeled Markov algorithm (henceforth referred to as an LMA).

> LMA:  REVERSE (x, y $\varepsilon$ V)
> $P_1$:    $\alpha xy \rightarrow y\alpha x$    $(P_1)$
> $P_2$:    $\alpha x\beta \rightarrow \beta x$    $(P_4)$
> $P_3$:    $\alpha x \rightarrow \beta x$    $(P_6)$
> $P_4$:    $\alpha\beta \rightarrow \Lambda$.
> $P_5$:    $\alpha\alpha \rightarrow \Lambda$.
> $P_6$:    $\Lambda \rightarrow \alpha$    $(P_1)$

An execution trace for this LMA given an input string 'abc' is shown in Table 2-2.1.

For an input of z = 'abc', 27 tests for production applicability are required in the LMA formulation, while 57 such tests are needed for the MA in Example 2-3. (By the number of tests for production applicability, we mean the number of attempted production applications during the execution of the algorithms.) Not only does the addition of labels provide increased flexibility in algorithm design, but it also allows for more efficient algorithm execution. Much more efficient algorithms exist for reversing a string, and one such algorithm is now given.

> LMA:  REVERSE1 (x, y, $\varepsilon$ V)
> $P_1$: $\alpha\alpha \rightarrow \Lambda$    $(P_4)$
> $P_2$: $\alpha xy \rightarrow y\alpha x$    $(P_2)$
> $P_3$: $\Lambda \rightarrow \alpha$    $(P_1)$
> $P_4$: $\alpha \rightarrow \Lambda$    $(P_4)$

This algorithm has two fewer productions, one fewer marker symbols, and reverses the input string 'abc' using only 18 tests for production applicability. ////

*Example 2-5* Let us consider one more example of a labeled Markov algorithm. Consider the problem of deleting the first character 'a' from a string along with all other characters to the left of 'a'. If there are characters to the left of 'a', a 'c' is to be concatenated to the front of the resulting string; otherwise, a 'd' is concatenated to the front of the string.

**Table 2-2.1**

| Intermediate String | Production Applicable | Number of Attempted Applications |
|---|---|---|
| 'abc' $\Rightarrow \alpha'$abc' | (by $P_6$) | 6 |
| $\Rightarrow$ 'b'$\alpha'$ac' | (by $P_1$) | 1 |
| $\Rightarrow$ 'bc'$\alpha'$a' | (by $P_1$) | 1 |
| $\Rightarrow$ 'bc'$\beta'$a' | (by $P_3$) | 3 |
| $\Rightarrow \alpha'$bc'$\beta'$a' | (by $P_6$) | 1 |
| $\Rightarrow$ 'c'$\alpha'$b'$\beta'$a' | (by $P_1$) | 1 |
| $\Rightarrow$ 'c'$\beta'$ba' | (by $P_2$) | 2 |
| $\Rightarrow \alpha'$c'$\beta'$ba' | (by $P_6$) | 3 |
| $\Rightarrow \beta'$cba' | (by $P_2$) | 2 |
| $\Rightarrow \alpha\beta'$cba' | (by $P_6$) | 3 |
| $\Rightarrow$ 'cba' | (by $P_4$) | 4 |

Total = 27

(Note that production $P_5$ is only applicable if z is initially $\Lambda$).

To construct such an algorithm, we need an auxiliary symbol $\alpha$ to mark the location of the first 'a' in the input string. Once the marker is placed, it is a simple matter to remove all previous characters and place the appropriate character 'c' or 'd' in front of the resulting substring. Two algorithms to do this are given in Table 2-2.2.

Notice that in the algorithm to the right in Table 2-2.2, we have dropped the convention of labeling every production and have chosen to label only where necessary. Also, we have used more meaningful label names. Hereafter, we adopt this more readable form of expressing LMAs.    ////

One might question if the introduction of labels to Markov algorithms alters the computational power of the Markov model. Galler and Perlis [1970], from whom we have borrowed our labeling technique, have constructively demonstrated that the two models (i.e., the MA model and the LMA model) are equivalent in computational power (i.e., any function computable using an MA is computable

**Table 2-2.2**  Algorithms for Example 2-5.

| LMA: | LEFTSUBSTR1(x $\varepsilon$ V) | | LMA: | LEFTSUBSTR2(x $\varepsilon$ V) | |
|---|---|---|---|---|---|
| $P_1$: | x'a' $\rightarrow \alpha$ | | | x'a' $\rightarrow \alpha$ | |
| $P_2$: | x$\alpha \rightarrow \alpha$ | ($P_2$) | DELETE: | x$\alpha \rightarrow \alpha$ | (DELETE) |
| $P_3$: | $\alpha \rightarrow$ 'c'. | | | $\alpha \rightarrow$ 'c'. | |
| $P_4$: | 'a' $\rightarrow$ 'd' | | | 'a' $\rightarrow$ 'd' | |

using an LMA, and vice versa). By "constructively demonstrated," we mean that they have produced a Markov algorithm which takes as its input string a labeled Markov algorithm and translates this LMA into an equivalent MA. It is obvious that every MA can be converted to an LMA by simply appending the label $(P_1)$ to each production that is not terminal. Hence, labels are a convenience which help us to write more efficient algorithms, but they provide no additional computing power.

In addition to providing string-processing functions, Markov algorithms can be used with some difficulty to compute arithmetic functions. For example, if we represent a number N by a string of tally symbols (for example, 111 . . . 1), then the LMA for addition can be accomplished by:

LMA: ADD
$'+' \rightarrow \Lambda$

assuming an input string of the form '11 . . . 1+11 . . . 1'. However, the LMA for multiplication (given an input string of the form '11 . . . 1*1 . . . 11') is more difficult.

|  | LMA: | MULT |  |
|---|---|---|---|
|  | ADD$\gamma$: | $'1*' \rightarrow '*'\gamma$ | (CREATE$\beta$) |
|  | REMOVE1: | $'*1' \rightarrow '*'$ | (REMOVE1) |
|  | REPLACE$\beta$: | $\beta \rightarrow '1'$ | (REPLACE$\beta$) |
|  |  | $'*' \rightarrow \Lambda.$ |  |
|  | CREATE$\beta$: | $\gamma'1' \rightarrow '1'\beta\gamma$ | (CREATE$\beta$) |
|  | MOVE$\beta$: | $\beta'1' \rightarrow '1'\beta$ | (MOVE$\beta$) |
|  |  | $\gamma \rightarrow \Lambda$ | (ADD$\gamma$) |

In the algorithm, $\gamma$ marks the number of additions of the multiplicand (i.e., the right-hand set of tally marks—for example, '11' in '111*11') and $\beta$ represents a digit in the product (i.e., the resulting string). An intermittent trace of the multiplication of '111*11' is as follows:

$$'111*11' \Rightarrow '11*'\gamma'11' \Rightarrow '11*1'\beta\gamma'1' \Rightarrow '11*1'\beta'1'\beta\gamma \Rightarrow '11*11'\beta\beta\gamma$$
$$\Rightarrow '11*11'\beta\beta \Rightarrow '1*'\gamma'11'\beta\beta \Rightarrow \ldots \Rightarrow '*11'\beta\beta\gamma\beta\beta\beta\beta$$
$$\Rightarrow '*_11'\beta\beta\beta\beta\beta\beta \Rightarrow '*1'\beta\beta\beta\beta\beta\beta \Rightarrow '*'\beta\beta\beta\beta\beta\beta \Rightarrow \ldots$$
$$\Rightarrow '*11111'\beta \Rightarrow '*111111' \Rightarrow '111111'$$

It is easy to appreciate that the calculation of an arithmetic expression such as 25 * 26 / (31 + 10) would be tedious but not impossible using Markov algorithms.

Other features can be added to the Markov algorithm computation model to make it more convenient to use, e.g., subalgorithms, formal parameters and the creation of special addressable-storage cells that can be used to store temporary results. While it appears to be very restrictive, the Markov model is powerful enough to enable the computation of any computable function (i.e., any function we would care to compute). However, the Markov model is awkward, especially for arithmetic computations. Nevertheless, the Markov algorithm helps illustrate string manipulation at a primitive and understandable level; as we will see in Sec. 2-2.5, it is the basis for the very powerful string manipulation language SNOBOL.

### Exercises for Sec. 2-2.1

1. Design a Markov algorithm which examines an arbitrary string x on a given alphabet (say V = {a, b, c}) to determine if it is equal to some specified string w (say w = 'abb'). If x equals w, the string x is replaced by a specified string

y (say y = 'b' ); otherwise, x is replaced by the specified string z (say z = 'c'). Use a marker symbol.

2. Design a Markov algorithm which transforms a string $x_1 x_2 \ldots x_n$ where each $x_i \; \varepsilon \; \{a, b\}$ to the string $x_1 x_2 \ldots x_n x_n x_{n-1} \ldots x_1$.

3. In many instances, it is required to know the number of symbols in a particular string. This can be accomplished using the tally notation by replacing every symbol in the string by the tally symbol "1". For example, the algorithm consisting of the production scheme

$$x \rightarrow 1 \quad (x \; \varepsilon \; V)$$

transforms an arbitrary string to a sequence of tally symbols. Since $1 \notin V$, the algorithm terminates when every symbol has been transformed to the tally symbol. Given two strings $x_1 x_2 \ldots x_n$ and $y_1 y_2 \;\; \ldots \; y_m$, where each $x_i$ and $y_i$ are tally symbols, design a Markov algorithm which transforms the string $x_1 x_2 \; \ldots \; x_n - y_1 y_2 \ldots y_m$ to a string $z_1 z_2 \ldots z_{n-m}$, which represents the difference of the tally symbols. For example '111-11' is transformed to '1'. Assume $n \geqslant m$.

4. Design a Markov algorithm (labeled or unlabeled) which recognizes a palindrome. A palindrome is a string of the form $x_1 x_2 \; \ldots \; x_n x_n x_{n-1} \ldots x_1$ in which each $x_i \; \varepsilon \; V$ for some specified alphabet V. If the input string is a palindrome, the output should be the string 'a' where $a \; \varepsilon \; V$. If it is not, the output should be 'b' where $b \; \varepsilon \; V$.

5. Write a Markov algorithm which takes an input string z of the form $x_1 x_2 \; \ldots x_n$ '#' $y_1 y_2 \; \cdots \; y_m$ in which $x_i$, '#', $y_j \; \varepsilon \; V$ for $1 \leqslant i \leqslant n$, $1 \leqslant j \leqslant m$. The algorithm should output '#' if x is a substring of y or y is a substring of x; otherwise, the string '##' should be output.

6. Formulate an LMA which performs the integer division of two numbers x and y. The input is in a tally form with the two operands separated by the symbol '/'. Therefore, $5 \div 2$ is represented as '11111/11'. The answer must appear in strict tally notation (that is, '11' for the example given).

7. Write a Markov algorithm which receives as input a string and determines whether it is valid. If it is valid the result string should be 1; if not, the result should be 0. A valid string consists of a string of characters enclosed in single quotes. Within the string only double quotes may be used. The alphabet V is assumed to be $\{A, B, \ldots, Z, 0, 1, \ldots, 9, ', \#, !, *, -, +, /\}$. An example of a string is

      'RALPH''S  IGUANA  DOESN''T  LIKE  NEWTS'

8. Design a Markov algorithm that replaces in the subject string all occurrences of more than one blank by a single blank.

9. Consider an expression consisting of the symbols ), (, >, and < where < > and ( ) are used as matching brackets. A proper expression is defined as an expression that is correctly balanced and nested. For example

| | |
|---|---|
| < ( ) > | is proper |
| ( < > < ( ) > ) | is proper |
| ( > < ) | is not correctly balanced |
| ( < ( > ) ( | is not correctly nested. |

Give a Markov algorithm that determines whether a string is a proper expression. This Markov algorithm should indicate that the string is proper (or not) by converting it to a null string if it is proper and a nonnull string if i is not.

10. Design a Markov algorithm that counts the number of words in the subject string. You may assume that the words are separated by one or more blanks with no blanks at the end of the string. Let V be the vocabulary, where $1 \varepsilon V$, and $V - \{ \square \}$ is the set of non-blank characters. Express the answer in tally notation, i.e., a sequence of 1's.

11. Let $V = \{a, b, c, (, )\}$ be an alphabet. Write a labeled Markov algorithm LEFT_PAR that isolates the first (i.e., leftmost) parenthesized string in $x$, and then terminates with this leftmost string. If there is not a parenthesized string, the algorithm should terminate with the empty string as output. For example, 'a(bc)b' should terminate with '(bc)', and '() ac (c)a' should terminate with '()'; whereas 'ac' and 'a((b' both should terminate with the empty string.

12. The Markov formalism discussed in the text does not represent a programming language as such. What additional facilities should be added to the formalism to make it a programming language?

## 2-2.2 Primitive Functions

A close analysis of the essential string-handling facilities required of any tex creation and editing system (formal or otherwise) should lead to the following list of primitive functions:

*1* Create a string of text.
*2* Concatenate two strings to form another string.
*3* Search and replace (if desired) a given substring within a string.
*4* Test for the identity of a string.
*5* Compute the length of a string.

In this subsection we discuss the importance of each of these functions in a string-handling system and incorporate into our algorithmic notation operations which affect these functions.

The creation of a string implies not only the ability to construct a representation for a string but also the ability to retain the value of a string in a variable (or memory-cell location). This feature is inherent in the Markov algorithm model, where one string is created (the subject string) and transformed to eventually become the output string.

In the algorithmic notation, a string is expressed as any sequence of charac ers enclosed in single quote marks. We can provide a transparent representation for strings: e.g., a single quote contained within a string is represented by two single quotes. Therefore, the string "It is John's program." is represented as 'IT IS JOHN''S PROGRAM.'. Variables can be used to retain string values. Therefore, to assign the string 'CAT' to the variable PET, we write

PET ← 'CAT'.

The empty (or null) string is denoted by either two single quotes ('') or the symbol Λ.

*Concatenation* is the most important operation on a string. At the beginning of this chapter, we defined a string to be the concatenation of individual characters. In a Markov algorithm productions contain right- and left-hand sides made up of strings and/or character elements concatenated together. Concatenation is so important and natural to string manipulation that in many systems (e.g., the SNOBOL programming language), an explicit operator is omitted and concatenation is implied through the juxtapositioning of string arguments. However, in an effort to represent operators in a consistent manner, we use $\bigcirc$ to denote concatenation in our algorithmic notation. Therefore, to concatenate the string 'STRUCTURES' to 'DATA$\square$' and assign the result to the variable SUBJECT, we write

> SUBJECT ← 'DATA$\square$' $\bigcirc$ 'STRUCTURES'

Observe that we denote a blank character as '$\square$' whenever it is important to show distinct blanks in a string. Also note that string variables as well as string constants can appear as operands (e.g., PET ← PET $\bigcirc$ 'DOG' ).

When one is searching for a substring within a given string, there must be some method of returning the position of the substring within the string, if the substring is found. This position is often called the *cursor position,* and it is given by an integer value indicating the character position of the left-most character of the substring being sought. The name of the function used in the algorithmic notation to perform this operation is INDEX. INDEX (SUBJECT, PATTERN) returns (as a value) the cursor position of the left-most occurrence of the string, PATTERN, in the string SUBJECT. If PATTERN does not occur in SUBJECT, the value 0 is returned. As examples, if SUBJECT = 'BACABABA', then INDEX(SUBJECT, 'ABA') is 4, INDEX(SUBJECT, 'A') is 2, and INDEX(SUBJECT, 'ABC' ) is 0.

The variable name PATTERN is used as the second argument in the description of INDEX for a definite reason. The string associated with PATTERN is searched for in the subject string on a character-by-character basis from the first character of the subject string to the last. This process of applying a pattern string to a subject string is commonly called *pattern matching.* The INDEX function is our first example of a pattern-matching operation. A wide variety of pattern-matching operations exist, and many of these are illustrated in this chapter. However, INDEX provides the most primitive form of pattern matching, and it is a basis upon which more sophisticated pattern-matching operations can be built. Observe that the application of a Markov production relies on a form of pattern matching (e.g., given a subject string 'ABCDE', the application of the Markov production 'CD' → 'E' requires that pattern 'CD' be found in the subject string before the replacement string 'E' can be assigned).

The ability to extract a substring from a subject string is another important function. In the Markov model, substring designation was provided through the use of marker symbols and character variables. For example, the productions

> {$\alpha xy \rightarrow y\beta x$
> $\beta \rightarrow \Lambda.$
> $\Lambda \rightarrow \alpha$ }

reverse the first two characters of the subject string. In the algorithmic notation, rather than using special marker symbols, we use the cursor position plus a substring length to isolate a substring. The name given to this function is SUB.

SUB(SUBJECT, i, j) or SUB(SUBJECT, i) returns as a value the substring of SUBJECT that is specified by the parameters i and j, or i and an assumed value of j. The parameter i indicates the starting cursor position of the substring, while j specifies the length of the required substring. If j is not provided, j is assumed to be equal to $k - i + 1$, where k is equal to the length of the argument SUBJECT. To complete a definition of SUB, some additional cases must be handled.

*1*    If $j \leq 0$ (regardless of i), then the null string is returned.
*2*    If $i \leq 0$ (regardless of j), then the null string is returned.

3    If i > k (regardless of j), then the null string is returned.
4    If i + j > k + 1, then j is assumed to be k − i + 1.

Consider the following examples for the function SUB. SUB('ABCDE' 2) and SUB('ABCDE', 2, 7); both return 'BCDE', SUB('ABCD', 3, 2) returns 'CD', and SUB('ABCDE', 0 3) and SUB('ABCDE', 6) both return ' '.

The function SUB can also be used on the left-hand side of an assignment (i.e., in a replacement mode of operation). For example. if SUBJECT = 'ABCDE', then SUB(SUBJECT, 2, 2) ← 'A' would change the value of SUBJECT to 'AADE'. If SUB (SUBJECT, i, j) appears on the left-hand side of an assignment and i ≤ 0 or j ≤ 0, then the assignment is not executed. If i > k or i + j > k + 1, then characters are assigned to positions beyond the right-hand end of the subject string. Intermediate character positions which are unassigned are set to blank characters.

The next two primitive functions are not basic operations to the Markov algorithm system. Nevertheless, they are important in practical applications involving string editing and formatting, and they can be realized as Markov algorithms.

Testing the identity of a string implies the existence of some form of predicate which returns a *true* or *false* value when a comparison is made between a subject string and a known string. In the algorithmic notation we are supplied with two relations, = and ≠ . To illustrate how each is defined, consider the following examples:

'XMAS' = 'XMAS' is *true*, and 'XMAS' ≠ 'CHRISTMAS' is *true*

while

'XMAS' = 'CHRISTMAS' is *false* and 'XMAS' ≠ 'XMAS' is *false*.

It is easy to expand this comparison feature to include all of the commonly used relational symbols (that is, <, ≤, >, ≥, ≮ and ≯). We do so by defining a character *collating sequence* upon which a lexical (i.e., word) ordering can be made The collating sequence which is applicable to most character sets is: blank ¢ . < ( + | & ! $ * ) ; − / , % _ > ? : # @ ' =    A through Z, 0 through 9. This sequence is based on the internal representation of the characters. as discussed in Sec. 1-4.5. The lexical ordering on strings is similar to the one found in a dictionary or a telephone directory. Hence, 'XMAS' > 'CHRISTMAS', 'XMAS' ≤ 'XMAS1984', and 'XMAS' ≮ 'XMA' are all *true*, while 'XMAS' > 'XMAS', 'Y' ≯ 'XMAS', and 'X' ≥ 'XMAS' are all *false*. From these examples, it is clear that comparisons are made on a character-by-character basis starting from the left-most character of each string in the comparison. The presence of any character (even a blank) is always considered to be greater than the omission of a character (that is, 'X␣' > 'X' is *true*).

The length of a string is important in the formatting of character strings for output. This is why formal systems do not bother to include this operation as a basic feature. In the algorithmic notation, the computation of the length of a string is achieved by the function LENGTH. If SUBJECT is a character variable, then LENGTH(SUBJECT) returns as a value the number of symbols in the string represented by SUBJECT. The value 0 is returned if SUBJECT is the empty string. As examples, LENGTH('TOP') is 3, LENGTH(SUBJECT), where SUBJECT is 'ABAB', is 4, and LENGTH(SUB(SUBJECT, 1, 0)) is 0.

### 2-2.3 Composite Functions

In the previous section, we identified interesting and useful primitive string-handling functions—primitive in the sense that most string-handling functions can be composed in a modular manner from these functions. We now turn our attention to a discussion of four functions: LEN, MATCH, SPAN, and FIND, which are examples of functions that are nonprimitive, yet basic, to string-handling problems. These functions are presented in algorithmic notation and are described in terms of the primitive functions just discussed. We make extensive use of forms of these functions in the application section at the end of this chapter.

Since all the functions are of a pattern-matching nature, we are able to characterize them by using the same set of arguments throughout. Each of the pattern-matching algorithms have the following arguments:

*1*   SUBJECT — the string in which a pattern match is made.
*2*   PATTERN — the string for which a pattern match is sought within the subject string. (In Algorithm LEN, PATTERN is replaced by NUM, which is the number of characters to be matched.)
*3*   CURSOR — the character position in SUBJECT at which the pattern matching is to begin. Therefore, from CURSOR to the last character of the SUBJECT is that portion of the subject string which is considered in the pattern-matching operation.
*4*   MATCH_STR — the variable that is set to the value of the substring that is successfully matched. If the pattern match is unsuccessful, MATCH_STR is left unchanged.
*5*   REPLACE_STR — the string that replaces the characters which are matched providing REPLACE_FLAG is *true*.
*6*   REPLACE_FLAG — a flag indicating whether a replacement should be made for that portion of the subject string that is matched. If REPLACE_FLAG is *true*, a replacement is made; if *false*, no replacement is made.

The four pattern-matching functions are truth-valued functions (i.e., predicates) in the algorithmic descriptions that follow. In all cases, a value of *true* is returned if a pattern match is achieved; otherwise, a value of *false* is returned.

**Function LEN(SUBJECT, NUM, CURSOR, MATCH_STR, REPLACE_STR,**
         **REPLACE_FLAG).**
The Function LEN returns true if there are NUM characters in SUBJECT following and including the CURSOR character. If there are NUM characters, MATCH_STR is assigned the matched character string which is NUM in length. If REPLACE_FLAG is *true*, then the NUM characters are replaced by REPLACE_STR.

1.   [Check for NUM characters]
        If CURSOR + NUM > LENGTH(SUBJECT) + 1
        then   Return(false)
2.   [Set match and replace if specified]
        MATCH_STR ← SUB(SUBJECT, CURSOR, NUM)
        If REPLACE_FLAG
        then   SUB(SUBJECT, CURSOR, NUM) ← REPLACE_STR
               CURSOR ← CURSOR + LENGTH(REPLACE_STR)
        Return(true)
3.   [No replacement]
        CURSOR ← CURSOR + NUM
        Return(true)                                                  □

To illustrate how the LEN algorithm works, let us examine its evaluation assuming parameters of SUBJECT = 'TO□BE□OR□NOT□TO□BE', NUM = 3, CURSOR = 10, MATCH_STR = unknown value, REPLACE_STR = 'NEVER', and REPLACE_FLAG = true. Since CURSOR + NUM (equaling 13) is less than or equal to the length of the subject string plus 1 (equaling 19), the test for a possible pattern match is *true* in step 1 of the algorithm. In step 2, MATCH_STR is set to the substring 'NOT'. Since the REPLACE_FLAG is set, that part of the subject string that is matched (i.e., 'NOT') is replaced by the value of REPLACE_STR (i.e., 'NEVER') to yield a new subject string of 'TO□BE□OR□NEVER□TO□BE'. Finally, CURSOR is updated to a value of 15, which is the cursor position of the character following the last character in the replacement string.

A number of additional examples demonstrating the effect of the LEN function follow. In all examples, the initial value of SUBJECT is
'TO□BE□OR□NOT□TO□BE'.

LEN(SUBJECT, 1, 19, MATCH_STR, REPLACE_STR, false) returns a value of *false* since the SUBJECT string is only 18 characters in length, and hence cannot contain a substring beginning at position 19.

LEN(SUBJECT, 2, 7, MATCH_STR, REPLACE_STR, false) returns a value of *true* and MATCH_STR is set to 'OR'. CURSOR is set to 9, and SUBJECT is left unchanged.

LEN(SUBJECT, 6, 1, MATCH_STR, '', true) returns a value of *true* and MATCH_STR is set to 'TO□BE□', CURSOR is set to 1, and SUBJECT becomes 'OR□NOT□TO□BE'.

We now consider the second of our composite pattern-matching functions. MATCH is a function which tests for a pattern match of a given pattern string with a substring of SUBJECT, beginning at the character position indicated by CURSOR.

**Function MATCH(SUBJECT, PATTERN, CURSOR, MATCH_STR, REPLACE_STR, REPLACE_FLAG).**
The Function MATCH returns a value of true if the pattern string (PATTERN) is found in the string SUBJECT starting at the CURSOR position. If the match is successful, MATCH_STR is set to PATTERN, and if REPLACE_FLAG is set, then that portion of the subject string that is matched is replaced by REPLACE_STR.

1. [Check if PATTERN fits within string bounds]
     If CURSOR + LENGTH(PATTERN) > LENGTH(SUBJECT) + 1
     then   Return(false)
2. [Check for pattern match]
     If SUB(SUBJECT,CURSOR,LENGTH(PATTERN)) ≠ PATTERN
     then   Return(false)
3. [Perform replacement]
     MATCH_STR ← PATTERN
     If REPLACE_FLAG
     then   SUB(SUBJECT,CURSOR,LENGTH(PATTERN)) ← REPLACE_STR
            CURSOR ← CURSOR + LENGTH(REPLACE_STR)
            Return(true)

4.   [No replacement]
         CURSOR ← CURSOR + LENGTH(PATTERN)
         Return(true)                                                          □

As an example of how the MATCH function works, consider the initial parameters of SUBJECT =

   'SHAKESPEAREAN□SONNETS□ARE□IN□IAMBIC□PENTAMETER',

PATTERN = 'SHAKESPEARE', CURSOR = 1, REPLACE_STR = 'ELIZABETH', REPLACE_FLAG = true. In step 1, CURSOR + LENGTH(PATTERN) (equaling 12) is less than LENGTH(SUBJECT) + 1 (equaling 47), and therefore, a check is made in step 2 to see if the pattern match is possible. The substring, beginning with cursor position 1 and of length equal to the length of the pattern string, matches the string represented by PATTERN. In step 3, MATCH_STR is set to PATTERN, and because the REPLACE_FLAG is set, the SUBJECT is assigned

   '' ○ 'ELIZABETH' ○ 'AN□SONNETS□ARE□IN□IAMBIC□PENTAMETER',

or

   'ELIZABETHAN□SONNETS□ARE□IN□IAMBIC□PENTAMETER',

CURSOR is set to 10, and a value of true is returned.

Some further examples illustrating how MATCH performs are as follows. In all cases, SUBJECT is

   'SHAKESPEAREAN□SONNETS□ARE□IN□IAMBIC□PENTAMETER'.

MATCH(SUBJECT, 'ELIZABETH', 2, MATCH_STR, REPLACE_STR, false) does not result in a match, thus leaving SUBJECT, CURSOR, and MATCH_STR unchanged.

MATCH(SUBJECT, '', 47, MATCH_ST,
'□AND□CONSIST□OF□THREE□QUATRAINS', true) results in a match with the empty string at the end of subject. Hence, SUBJECT becomes 'SHAKESPEAREAN□SONNETS□ARE□IN□IAMBIC□PENTAMETER□AND□ CONSIST□OF□THREE□QUATRAINS', CURSOR is set to 77 (i.e., one more than the length of the new subject string), and MATCH_STR is assigned the empty string.

The next pattern-matching function we examine allows us to match all characters in the subject string, beginning with the character at the cursor position and ending at the first character that is not in the pattern string. A form of this function is particularly useful in text-formatting, as will be demonstrated in Sec. 2-5.1.

**Function SPAN(SUBJECT, PATTERN, CURSOR, MATCH_STR, REPLACE_STR, REPLACE_FLAG).**
The Function SPAN returns true if the CURSOR character matches any of the characters in PATTERN. If there is such a match, MATCH_STR is set to the string of characters, including and following the CURSOR character, all of which match a character in PATTERN. The pattern match ends when a character not in PATTERN is encountered, or when the last character in the subject string is reached. The sequence matched is replaced by REPLACE_STR if REPLACE_FLAG is set to true.

1. [Check if the pattern fits in the bounds of the subject string]
   If CURSOR > LENGTH(SUBJECT)
   then  Return(false)
2. [Initialize the subject string index I to CURSOR]
   I ← CURSOR
3. [Check to find if character I is in PATTERN]
   Repeat while I ≤ LENGTH(SUBJECT) and
     INDEX(PATTERN, SUB(SUBJECT, I, 1)) ≠ 0
       I ← I + 1
4. [Character not found in PATTERN]
   If I = CURSOR
   then  Return(false)
5. [Set match and replace]
   MATCH_STR ← SUB(SUBJECT, CURSOR, I − CURSOR)
   If REPLACE_FLAG
   then  SUB(SUBJECT, CURSOR, I − CURSOR) ← REPLACE_STR
     CURSOR ← CURSOR + LENGTH(REPLACE_STR)
     Return(true)
6. [No replacement]
   CURSOR ← I
   Return(true)                                                            □

Consider the string 'HE□WALKED....□ANDWALKED....□AND□WALKED'. Assume we want to edit this string by replacing the first substring of '.'s by a comma. We set PATTERN = '.', CURSOR = 10, REPLACE_STR = ',' and REPLACE_FLAG = true and invoke the function SPAN. Clearly, CURSOR is less than the length of the subject string. The index I is set to the cursor position 10 in step 2. The "while" condition specified in step 3 is true for I = 10, 11, 12, and 13. These positional values correspond to the substring '....' the first such substring in SUBJECT. The while condition is false for I = 14, since SUB(SUBJECT, 14, 1) is equal to '□' and this has a zero INDEX in PATTERN. Because I is not equal to CURSOR in step 4, MATCH_STR is set to '....' in step 5. REPLACE_FLAG is set, and SUBJECT is assigned 'HE□WALKED□AND□WALKED....□AND□WALKED'. Finally, CURSOR is set to the value of 11 and the value of true is returned.

Some further examples exhibiting the capabilities and limitations of the SPAN function are as follows. In all cases, SUBJECT is 'HE□WALKED....□AND□WALKED....□AND□WALKED'.

SPAN(SUBJECT, '', 1, MATCH_STR, REPLACE_STR, false)
does not result in a pattern match since there is not a blank character at the cursor position of 1.

SPAN(SUBJECT, 'ADEKLW.', 4, MATCH_STR, REPLACE_STR, false)
results in a pattern match with the substring 'WALKED....', and this substring is assigned to MATCH_STR. Since REPLACE_FLAG is not set, no replacement is made and CURSOR becomes the value 14.

SPAN(SUBJECT, 'ADEHKLNW□.', 1, MATCH_STR, '', true)
results in a pattern match of the complete subject string, which is assigned to MATCH_STR. Since REPLACE_FLAG is set, the entire subject string is

replaced by the value REPLACE_STR, which is the empty string, and CUR-SOR has the value of 1.

The final pattern-matching function we discuss is called FIND. FIND matches the first instance of a substring equal to the given pattern lying anywhere between (and including) the initial cursor position and the end of the subject string.

**Function** FIND(SUBJECT, PATTERN, CURSOR, MATCH_STR, REPLACE_STR, REPLACE_FLAG).

Function FIND returns true if the string PATTERN is found anywhere in the subject string from the CURSOR character to the end of the subject string. If a match occurs, MATCH_STR is set to the string, beginning with the CURSOR character and including all characters to the left of the first character of the pattern matched. If PATTERN is found starting with the CURSOR character, MATCH_STR is set to the empty string. If REPLACE_FLAG is set, then all characters starting from the CUR-SOR character up to the right-most character of the matched substring are replaced by REPLACE_STR.

1. [Check if the pattern fits in the bounds of the subject string]
   If CURSOR > LENGTH(SUBJECT)
   then   Return(false)
2. [Search for pattern match]
   I ← INDEX(SUB(SUBJECT, CURSOR), PATTERN)
   If I = 0
   then   Return(false)
3. [Set MATCH_STR and replace]
   MATCH_STR ← SUB(SUBJECT, CURSOR, I – 1)
   If REPLACE_FLAG
   then   SUB(SUBJECT, CURSOR, LENGTH(PATTERN) + I – 1)
           ← REPLACE_STR
   CURSOR ← CURSOR + LENGTH (REPLACE_STR)
   Return(true)
4. [No replacement]
   CURSOR ← CURSOR + I + LENGTH(PATTERN) – 1
   Return(true)                                                   □

As an example illustrating the FIND function, consider SUBJECT = 'I□MET□HER□THE□SUMMER□BEFORE□I□WAS□TO□ENTER□COLLEGE', PATTERN = 'I', CURSOR = 2, REPLACE_STR = '', and REPLACE_FLAG = true. If FIND is called with these parameters, then execution proceeds in the following manner. CURSOR is less than the length of the subject string, so a search for a pattern match is undertaken in step 2 using the INDEX function. A pattern match is found, and the occurrence of the left-most character in the match is at position 29. Since a match is achieved (that is, I = 28), step 3 is executed setting MATCH_STR to '□MET□HER□THE□SUMMER□BEFORE□'. Because the REPLACE_FLAG is set, the substring corresponding to MATCH_STR ○ PATTERN (i.e., '□MET□HER□THE□SUMMER□BEFORE□I') is replaced by the REPLACE_STR '' to yield a new subject string of 'I□WAS□TO□ENTER□COLLEGE'. CURSOR is set to CURSOR plus the length of the replacement string (i.e., CURSOR = 2) and a value of true is returned.

Additional examples using the FIND function and involving the subject string
'I⯀MET⯀HER⯀THE⯀SUMMER⯀BEFORE⯀I⯀WAS⯀TO⯀ENTER⯀COLLEGE'
follow:

FIND (SUBJECT, 'ENTERED', 1, MATCH_STR, REPLACE_STR, false)
does not result in a pattern match because the pattern 'ENTERED' is not in the
subject string.   Hence SUBJECT, MATCH_STR and CURSOR remain
unchanged.

FIND(SUBJECT, 'I', 1, MATCH_STR, 'HE', true)
results in a pattern match and replacement.  SUBJECT becomes
'HE⯀MET⯀THE⯀SUMMER⯀BEFORE⯀I⯀WAS⯀TO⯀ENTER⯀COLLEGE',
MATCH_STR is assigned the empty string and CURSOR is set to 3.

It is important to realize that the composite functions described in this section
have been presented in their most general form, i.e., as functions with six parameters.  It is *not necessary to include all the parameters* when applying the functions in
special case applications.  For example, if we want to use the SPAN function when
it is never necessary to replace the matched string, then the last two parameters
REPLACE_STR and REPLACE_FLAG are not required.  Their removal will also
simplify the implementation of composite functions.  In addition, the composite
functions can be written as procedures—as opposed to functions—for situations in
which it is not necessary to know if the pattern match succeeds or fails.  These
notions will be illustrated in Sec. 2-5.

This concludes the subsection on examples of composite string manipulation
functions.  In the next two subsections, we examine the string-manipulation facilities
available in two programming languages, Pascal and SNOBOL, and we relate these
facilities to the primitive and composite functions described thus far in this section.

## 2-2.4  STRING MANIPULATION IN PASCAL

To provide effective string-manipulation facilities, a programming language should
at least contain the primitive facilities and functions described in Sec. 2-2.2.  Unfortunately, these facilities are not provided in standard Pascal (Jenson and Wirth [75])
and therefore need to be added to the language by writing special functions.

In Pascal a string is commonly simulated using a single-dimensioned array (or
vector) of characters (Boswell, et al. [82]).  In order to pass arrays as the parameters
of functions and procedures, they must be defined as a **type**.  This can be done with
a **type** declaration at the beginning of the main program such as

**type** string = **array**[1..256] **of** char;

Thus *string* is used as the type identifier for an array of 256 characters.  One consequence of this declaration is that all variables declared to be of type *string* must be
of a specific fixed length (in this case length 256).

The vector representation of strings also implies that the character elements in
the array must be handled on an individual basis.  For example, the reading of a
string requires a loop to read the input data character by character into the array.  In
addition, the use of a delimiter to mark the end of the string aids in printing out the
string and in performing the string manipulation operations to follow.  Typically, the
delimiter is placed in the array when the string is read in as input data.

Use of the delimiter to mark the end of the string in an array also allows for
strings to be of varying length.  This must, of course, be within the bounds of the

array size. Using a single-character delimiter such as '|' with an array of type string as defined previously would mean that strings could be of any length up to 255 characters.

An array of characters can be assigned to another array, but the type descriptors must match exactly. This method of assignment is illustrated later in this subsection in the function match.

The primitive string operations must be developed as procedures and functions. Therefore the type *string*, as defined earlier, will be used for arguments during parameter passing. Another important aspect about parameters is that any parameter which is preceded by **var** is passed by address (i.e., by reference, see Sec. 1-4.7 ) and its changed value is thus returned to the calling program. Any parameter not preceded by **var** is only passed by value.

The operation to perform concatenation of two strings has as parameters the two strings to be joined together and the resultant string. In the algorithmic notation, the concatenation of two strings can be assigned to another string variable. Only scalars can be returned by Pascal functions, however, which means that the arrays of type *string* must be returned through the parameter list of a called procedure. A procedure to perform the concatenation operation is presented in Fig. 2-2.1.

An important aspect of Pascal which should be noted is that a string of characters such as 'abc' is not an acceptable argument. All the parameters are arrays defined to be of type *string*.

To illustrate the *concat* procedure, consider the following strings which are used as example strings throughout this subsection:

s contains   'This is a string.' ;

t contains  ' This is another one!';

and st contains '' (the empty string). The quotes are used to show the bounds of strings. It is assumed that each array has a '|' at the end of it.

The procedure *concat* is invoked by:

concat(s, t, st);

resulting in s and t remaining the same and st containing the following:

'This is a string. This is another one!'.

As a final note on concatenation, it should be observed that the checks for missing delimiters may not be required if the routine used for reading in the strings from the data always inserts the delimiter '|'. Unfortunately, it is difficult to guarantee that the end marker will not be destroyed by some other string manipulation function.

A very necessary part of many string-manipulation functions and procedures is a knowledge of the length of a string. Figure 2-2.2 exhibits the function *length*, with a single parameter of type *string*, that returns an integer giving the length of that string.

This function simply looks at each character in the string until it finds the delimiter. The length of the string is one less than the position of the delimiter. For example, using s as defined previously, *length* could be invoked as follows:

len := length(s);

The result is that *len* (an integer variable) is assigned the value 17.

The extraction of a substring from a string is performed by the procedure *sub* given in Fig. 2-2.3. Once again, it is necessary to use a procedure rather than the functional form used in the algorithmic notation. The parameters include the original string, the starting position of the substring, the number of characters in the sub-

```pascal
procedure concat(var s1,s2,result: string);
{ This is a procedure which performs the concatenation of 2 strings.}

var i, j: integer;        { indexes }

begin
    {Set first string except delimiter to result string.}
    i := 1;
    while (s1[i] <> '|') and (i < 256) do
    begin
        result[i] := s1[i];
        i := i + 1
    end;
    { Check if no delimiter in string.}
    if (i = 256) and (s1[256] <> '|')
    then begin
            writeln;
            writeln(' Error - missing delimiter on first argument.');
            writeln('Delimiter added; length of first string is 255.');
            s1[256] := '|';
            i := 256
        end;
    { Add second string unless result becomes too large. }
    j := 1;
    while (s2[j] <> '|') and (i < 256) do
    begin
        result[i] := s2[j];
        i := i + 1;
        j := j + 1
    end;
    { Add delimiter to end and check for overflow.}
    if i >= 256
    then begin
            result[256] := '|';
            writeln;
            writeln('Error - concatenation results in too long ',
                'character string. String truncated to length 255.')
        end
    else result[i] := '|'

end;
```

**FIGURE 2-2.1** Pascal procedure for concatenation.

**function** length (**var** str: string): integer;

{This is a function which computes the length of a given string.}

**var** i: integer;

```
begin
    { Compute length of string.}
    i := 1;
    while (str[i] <> '|') and (i < 256) do
        i := i + 1;
    { Check for no delimiter.}
    if (i = 256) and (str[256] <> '|')
    then begin
            writeln;
            writeln('Error - delimiter missing.');
            writeln('Delimiter added; length of string is 255.');
            str[256] := '|';
            length := 255
        end
    else { Return the length of string.}
        length := i - 1

end;
```

**FIGURE 2-2.2** Pascal function for the length of a string.

string, and a result string to return the substring. It is a fairly simple procedure that places the appropriate characters of the original string into the result and marks the end with a delimiter.

An example illustrating how the procedure *sub* is applied follows:

sub(s, 11, 6, rslt);

The string *rslt* would then contain 'string'.

It is also often necessary to replace a certain substring within a string. In the algorithmic notation, it is possible to simulate a substring assignment by using the normal function SUB and concatenation, but this is very awkward in Pascal. Instead, a procedure *psdsub* (meaning pseudo substring) can be designed to perform this task as shown in Fig 2-2.4. In *psdsub*, the subject string is altered based on the value of the substring being assigned. The parameters of *psdsub* are the same as for *sub* with the exception of the last one. A result string is not needed since the original string is altered. The fourth parameter in *psdsub* is a string containing the characters to be used as replacements in the string.

If the first position for the replacement string is beyond the end of the original string, intermediate blanks are added between the end of the original string and the start of the replacement string. When characters are to be inserted within the string, the remainder of the string is saved and then concatenated at the end after the inserted characters.

```
procedure sub(var s: string; pos, num: integer. var result: string);

{ This procedure takes a substring of the string s, starting at
  position pos for num characters and returns it in the
  parameter result. }

var lnth: integer;      { length of string }
    j, k, m: integer;       { indexes }

begin
      { Check if the value of pos or num is out of bounds.}
      lnth := length(s);
      if (pos <= 0) or (num <= 0) or (pos > lnth)
      then result[1] := '|'
      else begin
                { If num goes beyond end of substring, reset.}
                if pos + num > lnth + 1
                then m := lnth - pos + 1
                else m := num;
                { Obtain the substring.}
                j := pos;
                for k := 1 to m do
                begin
                    result [k] := s[j];
                    j := j + 1
                end;
                { Add the delimiter and return the string.}
                result[m + 1] := '|'
        end

end;
```

FIGURE 2-2.3  Pascal procedure for finding a substring.

```
procedure psdsub (var s: string; pos,num: integer; rplace: string).

{ Given string s, and a position for num characters, this procedure
  changes those characters of s to the characters contained in the
  string rplace. }

var save: string;
    j, k,
    lnth, svlnth,
    last: integer;
```

FIGURE 2-2.4  Pascal procedure for psdsub.

```
begin
     { Process if pos and num > 0.}
     if (pos > 0) and (num > 0)
     then begin
                    {Replace intermediate blanks and reset.}
                    lnth := length(s);
                    last := lnth;
                    if pos > lnth
                    then begin
                                    for k := lnth + 1 to pos do
                                    begin
                                        s[k] := ' ';
                                        lnth := pos + length(replace) - 1
                                    end
                          end;
                    { Save end of string after characters to be
                      substituted, including the delimiter. }
                    svlnth := 0;
                    for k := pos + num to last do
                    begin
                        svlnth := svlnth + 1;
                        save[svlnth] := s[k]
                    end;
                    save[svlnth + 1] := '|';
                    svlnth := svlnth + 1;
                    { Replace the characters in string by those
                      in replace if replace is not the null string.}
                    j := 1;
                    last := pos + length(replace) - 1;
                    for k := pos to last do
                    begin
                        s[k] := replace[j];
                        j := j + 1
                    end;
                    { Replace the end of string, svlnth is length of
                      saved characters.}
                    for k := 1 to svlnth do
                    begin
                        last := last + 1;
                        s[last] := save[k]
                    end;
                    { Set characters following the end of string
                      to blanks.}
                    for k := last + 1 to 256 do
                        s[k] := ' '
           end

end;
```

**FIGURE 2-2.4**    (continued)

Given the string *t* described earlier and a string *repl* containing 'string', the statement

psdsub(t, 17, 3, repl);

results in a new value *t* of ' This is another string!'.

Another necessary function for string manipulation is *index*. The purpose of *index* is to find the starting cursor position of the first (left-most) occurrence of a pattern string in a given string. A Pascal function for *index* is given in Fig. 2-2.5.

The function *index* contains only two parameters, the subject string and the pattern string. Given the string *s* as defined before and the string *pttn* containing a blank, the function *index* would be invoked in the following manner:

in := index(s, pttn);

which would set the value of *in* to 5.

In order to make use of the functions or procedures discussed thus far in the subsection, we find that they must be placed directly in the program before being referenced. This is not necessary if external declarations are allowed, but some versions of Pascal do not allow such declarations.

Once the primitive string operations have been developed, it is possible to create more advanced functions such as the composite functions described previously in Sec. 2-2.3. Three of those functions, *len*, *match*, and *span*, are given in Fig. 2-2.6 to 2-2.8.

```
function index (var s, pattern: string): integer;

{ This function returns the starting position of the leftmost
  occurrence of the pattern string in the string s.}

var lnth,
    ldif,
    i, j, k,
    flag: integer;

begin
    { Search for the pattern string.}
    lnth := length(pattern);
    ldif := length(s) - lnth + 1;
    index := 0;
    { Not found if either is null string.}
    if (lnth > 0) and (ldif > 0)
    then begin
            {Search for first character of pattern string.}
            i := 1;
            while i <= ldif do
            begin
                { Use flag to check if pattern is found
                  in the position starting at i for
                  number of characters in pattern.}
```

**FIGURE 2-2.5**    Pascal function for *index*.

```
        j := i;
        k := 1;
        flag := 0;
        while (k <= lnth) and (flag = 0) do
        begin
            if s[j] <> pattern[k]
            then flag := 1;
            k := k + 1;
            j := j + 1
        end;
        { Check if pattern has been found.}
        if flag = 0
        then begin
                    index := i;
                    i := ldif + 1
                end
            else i := i + 1
        end
    end

end;
```

**FIGURE 2-2.5**   (continued)

```
function len (var subject: string; var num, cursor: integer; var
        matchstr: string; replaceflag: boolean; replacestr:
        string): boolean;

begin
    { Check for num characters.}
    if cursor + num > length(subject) + 1
    then len := false
    else begin
                { Set match and replace, if specified.}
                len := true;
                sub(subject, cursor, num, matchstr);
                if replaceflag
                then begin
                            psdsub(subject, cursor, num, replacestr);
                            cursor := cursor + length(replacestr)
                        end
                else cursor := cursor + num
            end

end;
```

**FIGURE 2-2.6**   Pascal function for *len*.

```
function match (var subject, pattern: string; var cursor:
            integer; var matchstr: string; replaceflag:
            boolean; var replacestr: string): boolean;
```

{ This function returns a value of true if the pattern string
  (pattern) is found starting at the character position specified
  by cursor in the subject string; otherwise, it returns a value
  of false. If the pattern match succeeds, matchstr is set to
  the value of pattern and if replaceflag is true, the substring
  matched in subject is replaced by the value in replacestr. }

```
var temp: string;          { temporary string variable }

begin
      { Does the pattern fit within the search bounds of the
        subject string? }
    if cursor + length(pattern) > length(subject) + 1
    then match := false
    { Perform pattern match.}
    else begin
                sub(subject, cursor, length(pattern), temp);
                if (temp <> pattern)
                then match := false
                { Set matchstr and perform indicated replacement.}
                else begin
                            matchstr := pattern;
                            if replaceflag
                            then begin
                                        if cursor <> length(subject) + 1
                                        then psdsub(subject, cursor,
                                            length(pattern), replacestr)
                                        else begin
                                                {replacement of empty string}
                                                sub(subject, 1, cursor, temp);
                                                concat(temp, replacestr, subject);
                                            end;
                                        cursor := cursor + length(replacestr)
                                    end
                            else cursor := cursor + length(pattern);
                            { Successfully return.}
                            match := true
                        end
            end
      end

end;
```

**FIGURE 2-2.7**   Pascal function for *match*.

**function** span (**var** subject, pattern: string; **var** cursor:
    integer; **var** matchstr: string; replaceflag:
    boolean; **var** replacestr: string): boolean;

{ This function returns true if the character denoted by cursor matches any
  of the characters in pattern.  If the pattern match succeeds, matchstr becomes
  a sequence of characters containing the character at the position specified by
  cursor and all other characters which are contained in pattern.  The pattern
  match process terminates on encountering a character not in pattern or the end
  of the subject string.  If a replacement operation is specified, the sequence
  of characters is replaced by the value of replacestr. }

**var** i: integer;
    temp: string;

**begin**
    { Does the pattern fit within the bounds of the subject string? }
    **if** cursor > length(subject)
    **then** span := false
    **else begin**
            { Initialize the pattern match. }
            i := cursor;
            { Is character i in the pattern string?}
            sub(subject,i,1,temp);
            **while** (i <= length(subject)) **and**
                    (index(pattern,temp)<> 0) **do**
            **begin**
                i := i + 1;
                sub(subject,i,1,temp)
            **end**;
            { Unsuccessful pattern match? }
            **if** i = cursor
            **then** span := false
             **else begin**
                    { Set up matchstr and perform indicated replacement.}
                    sub(subject,cursor,i − cursor,matchstr);
                    **if** replaceflag
                    **then begin**
                            psdsub(subject, cursor, i − cursor,
                            replacestr);
                            cursor := cursor + length(replacestr)
                        **end**
                    **else** cursor := i;
                    { Successfully return.}
                    span := true
                **end**
    **end**

**end**;

**FIGURE 2-2.8**    Pascal function for *span*.

**Exercise for Sec. 2-2.4**

1.   Write and test a Pascal program for the composite function FIND as defined in Sec. 2-2.3.

### 2-2.5   String Manipulation in SNOBOL

Our discussion of Markov algorithms in Sec. 2-2.1 provides an excellent background for an introduction to the SNOBOL language. SNOBOL was first developed in 1962 at Bell Laboratories specifically to help solve problems involving string manipulation. We examine the fourth major version of SNOBOL, SNOBOL 4. From this examination it will become clear that SNOBOL has string-handling capabilities which are far more powerful than the primitive string-manipulation functions outlined in Sec. 2-2.2

A statement in SNOBOL is similar in form and definition to a Markov production. Its general form is

label subject pattern = replacement branch-label

The *label* is identical in purpose to that in a labeled Markov production. It differs in form since it must begin in the first character position of a SNOBOL statement, and it does not have a colon following it. A SNOBOL statement with a blank in the first character position is an unlabeled statement.

The *subject* is a variable or constant which represents the subject string for the pattern-matching operations performed in that statement. This feature allows a program to have as many subject strings as statements. Hence, the flexibility which is achieved by introducing the addressable storage-cell concept to the Markov model is realized.

The *pattern* plays the role of the "antecedent" in the Markov production. That is, the pattern is a string which is sought in the subject string. A pattern is "matched" if the pattern string is present anywhere in the subject string. An exception arises in a mode of operation, called *anchored mode*, in which the match must start from the first character of the subject string.

The *replacement* represents the string which replaces the matched portion of the subject string, providing a pattern match is successful. Therefore, its role is identical to that of the "consequent" in a Markov production.

The *branch label* differs from the branch label in a Markov production in the sense that a branch can be specified for a pattern-match failure as well as a success. The form of the branch is a colon followed by an F(label), an S(label), a (label), or both F(label) and S(label). F(label) means branch to "label" if the pattern match is a failure, S(label) means branch to "label" if the pattern match is successful, and (label) is interpreted as an unconditional branch (i.e., branch to "label" regardless of whether the pattern match is successful or not). The sequence of control is the same as in the labeled Markov production in the sense that, if a branch does not apply, the next statement in the program is executed.

The following set of SNOBOL statements outputs a string represented by SUBJECT which has had all the 'A's removed.

```
             SUBJECT = INPUT
AGAIN        SUBJECT 'A' = ''      :S(AGAIN)
             OUTPUT = SUBJECT
END
```

Program input is achieved through the pseudo variable INPUT, and output is attained by assigning the string intended for output to the pseudo variable OUTPUT. In the second statement of the program, the single character string 'A' is matched with the contents of SUBJECT. The left-most 'A' is matched first and replaced by the empty string. A successful match results in an immediate return to the second statement, and a pattern match is again attempted. This process continues until no more 'A's are present in the string represented by SUBJECT. At this point, the pattern match fails and control transfers to the third statement, where the current value for SUBJECT is output. The program halts upon executing the END statement.

This program illustrates an important point, namely, that the pattern portion of a statement need not always be present in a SNOBOL statement (as is demonstrated in the first and third statements). Note also that a pattern match always begins from the first character in SUBJECT. That is, if SUBJECT is initially 'CABBAC', then after the first pattern match and replacement, it has the value 'CBBAC'. The second time the statement labeled AGAIN is executed, the pattern-matching cursor is reset to point at the first character 'C', and pattern-matching attempts begin here, not at where the last pattern match succeeded (i.e., at the first 'B'). Hence, some rescanning must be done before achieving the second pattern match. While this may appear to be inefficient, rescanning of the subject string is necessary in some applications.

SNOBOL is substantially different from Pascal in many ways. One fundamental difference is that variables do not have to be declared in a program. While there are integer, real, and character-string data types in SNOBOL, the exact type of variable at a given point in a program is dictated by the context in which that variable appears. For example, the variable X takes on three different types (namely, integer, real, and character string) in the context of an integer addition, a real multiplication, and a string concatenation, as exhibited in the following three statements:

```
X = X + 2
X = X * 2.0
X = X 'STRING'
```

Notice that because concatenation is performed so frequently, there is no explicit operator for it. Strings to be concatenated are simply written down, one after the other, with one or more blanks separating each string.

Two very important concepts in SNOBOL are *pattern variables* and *pattern structures*. A pattern variable is assigned a pattern structure. The simplest form of pattern structure is a string. For example, in the statements

```
PAT = 'ERE'
SUBJECT = 'THERE HOME IS OUR HOME'
SUBJECT PAT = 'EIR'
OUTPUT = SUBJECT
```

PAT is a pattern variable which has the pattern structure 'ERE'.

Pattern structures can be made more complex with the introduction of the two pattern operations *alternation* and *concatenation*. The alternation operation (denoted by |) is useful in the formulation of a pattern which allows for the application of a number of patterns to the same subject string in a given pattern-matching situation. For example, if we want to replace all digits in a string by the character '#', then the following program can be used. (The variable TEXT holds the string value.)

```
            DIGIT = '0' | '1' | '2' | '3' | '4' | '5' | '6' | '7' | '8' | '9'
            TEXT = INPUT
LOOP        TEXT DIGIT = '#'     :S(LOOP)
            OUTPUT = TEXT
END
```

We interpret the pattern structure for DIGIT to mean that a match is made if either a '0', or a '1' or a '2', ..., or a '9' is found in the subject string to which it is applied. The match is made to the left-most digit, and this digit is replaced by '#'. Hence, if we trace the value of TEXT through the execution of the program, assuming an initial value of 'May 14, 1942' for TEXT, we have 'May 14, 1942' ... 'May #4, 1942' ... ' May ##, 1942' ... ... 'May ##, ####'.

To illustrate how concatenation can be used, let us assume we wish to construct a program which counts the number of words that end in a vowel in a given string represented by the variable TEXT.

```
            ENDING = 'A ' | 'E ' | 'I ' | 'O ' | 'U '
            TEXT = INPUT
LOOP        TEXT ENDING = '#'          :F(PRINT)
            COUNT = COUNT + 1          :(LOOP)
PRINT       OUTPUT = 'NUMBER OF WORDS ENDING IN A VOWEL'
+               ' IS: ' COUNT
END
```

In the "LOOP" statement, a scan is made of TEXT in an effort to detect a two-character sequence containing a vowel followed by a blank. If such a sequence is found, it is replaced by the string '#', and COUNT (which is automatically initialized to the empty string which, in turn, is implicitly converted to the integer zero in the context of the fourth statement) is incremented by 1. A return is made to the "LOOP" statement to attempt another pattern match. This looping process continues until no further pattern matches are successful, and a transfer is made to the statement which outputs the result. Note that in SNOBOL, if a statement must be continued on another line, the continuation line must begin with a plus (+) in column one.

The pattern ENDING can be simplified by using concatenation. We can write ENDING as

        ENDING = ('A' | 'E' | 'I' | 'O' | 'U' ) ' '

in which case, each of the alternatives are concatenated with the blank character. Note that we cannot use

        ENDING = 'A' | 'E' | 'I' | 'O' | 'U' ' '

since concatenation has precedence over alternation, and this statement would be interpreted as

        ENDING = 'A' | 'E' | 'I' | 'O' | 'U '

Two operations which are extremely helpful and sometimes necessary when using pattern structures involving alternation are the *conditional value assignment* and *immediate value assignment*. In the previous example, we have no way of determining which of the alternative patterns is matched, given that a match takes place. If we desire this information, the conditional-value-assignment operator (denoted by .) can provide it. If ENDING is expressed as

        ENDING = (('A' | 'E' | 'I' | 'O' | 'U') ' ' ) . RESULT

then the pattern string that is matched from the set of alternatives is assigned to the variable RESULT. A list of all pattern matches can be constructed by placing the statement

LIST = LIST RESULT

between the "LOOP" statement and the statement for updating the COUNT.

If it is desirable to obtain temporary results during a pattern-matching process, then the immediate assignment operator (denoted by $) is used to obtain this information. For example, if a printout of all vowels is desired in the program for detecting words that end in vowels, then the pattern ENDING should be formulated as

ENDING = ('A' | 'E' | 'I' | 'O' | 'U') $ OUTPUT ' '

In this instance, any partial pattern match involving a vowel is assigned to the pseudo variable OUTPUT, and hence is printed. Therefore, if TEXT = 'THE DOG RAN HOME' and ENDING is defined as just indicated, then

E
O
A
O
E
NUMBER OF WORDS ENDING IN A VOWEL IS: 2

would be output from the execution of the last programming example.

A comparison between the MATCH function, which was described algorithmically in Sec. 2-2.3, and the pattern-matching facilities in SNOBOL described thus far reveals that both have the capabilities of matching a pattern string with a substring of the subject string, of replacing the matched pattern with a replacement string (i.e., using the REPLACE_STR in MATCH and the assignment operator "=" in SNOBOL), and of assigning the matched string to a string variable (i.e., using MATCH_STR in MATCH and the conditional value assignment operator "." in SNOBOL). The major difference between these two facilities is that the MATCH function must match the pattern string to the substring of the subject string starting at a specified CURSOR position; whereas, in the basic SNOBOL pattern-matching statement, a match is attempted in a left-to-right scan, for all substrings of the subject string.

We are now prepared to describe and to give examples of some of the more powerful pattern-matching functions available in SNOBOL.

LEN(integer) returns a pattern defined to match any string of a length indicated by the integer-valued argument. Therefore,

SUBJECT LEN(5) · X =

matches the first five characters of SUBJECT and assigns these characters, via the conditional-value-assignment operator, to the variable X (providing SUBJECT is of length greater than 4). If a pattern match is achieved, the matched part of the subject string is replaced by the empty string. An empty string assignment can be denoted by an empty right-handed side, as well as by assigning ''.

The statement

LOOP TEXT (' ' LEN(3) ' ') · WORD = ' '      :S(LOOP)

results in the match and removal of all three-letter words in TEXT which are not followed by a punctuation mark.

The LEN function described in algorithmic notation in Sec. 2-2.3 and the LEN function in SNOBOL are almost identical in function differing only in the manner in which the pattern-matching cursor is controlled. In the algorithmic case, the CURSOR value is an explicit parameter, while in the SNOBOL LEN the cursor always refers to the next character position in the pattern matching scan. Note also that the algorithmic LEN returns *true* or *false*, while the SNOBOL LEN returns a pattern.

SPAN(string) returns a pattern defined to match the longest substring of the subject string, beginning at the current cursor position and containing only characters of the string argument. Therefore,

```
NUMB_STR = SPAN('0123456789')
TEXT NUMB_STR . NUMBER
```

creates the pattern which matches the first string of numbers in the string represented by TEXT. Hence, if TEXT = 'A0932-716', then the substring '0932' is matched and assigned to the variable NUMBER. However, if TEXT = 'ABC-DC', then the pattern match fails. Note that we can always express this and any other pattern-matching function in-line in the SNOBOL statement [e.g., TEXT SPAN('0123456789') · NUMBER]; however, the reading of a program is often simplified by separating the formation of the pattern structure from the pattern-matching statement.

The SPAN function in SNOBOL and the SPAN function algorithmically described in Sec. 2-2.3 are identical in purpose; however. they differ in effect. The SNOBOL SPAN function begins spanning at the position of the first character which matches a character in the argument string. The SPAN function which was described algorithmically begins pattern matching from the specified cursor position. Also, the algorithmic SPAN returns *true* or *false*, while the SNOBOL SPAN returns a pattern.

BREAK(string) returns a pattern defined to match the longest substring containing only characters not in the argument string. Hence, it is the converse function of SPAN. The program

```
AGAIN    TEXT BREAK(' ,.!?:;') · WORD =              :F(END)
         OUTPUT = WORD
         TEXT SPAN(' ,.!?:;') =                      :(AGAIN)
END
```

can be used to output all the words in TEXT, excluding surrounding blank characters. Note that the pattern-matching process continues until the entire TEXT is set to the empty string assuming TEXT ends in a punctuation mark. Once this happens, the pattern returned by the BREAK function fails to match TEXT and the program ends.

Observe that the BREAK function is quite similar to the FIND function as described in Sec. 2-2.3. The primary difference is that in the FIND function, the pattern-matching process is concluded when the entire PATTERN string argument is matched, and not just a character from that pattern argument. All characters up to and *including* the pattern portion of the matched string can be replaced by REPLACE_STR in the case of the FIND function.

TAB(integer) returns a pattern defined to match all characters from the current cursor position up to the tab position indicated by the integer argument. TAB can be used to move the cursor to specific positions when handling highly formatted subject strings. For example,

TEXT TAB(10) 'SEX:' LEN(1) · SEXTYPE

produces a successful match if the substring 'SEX:' immediately follows the first ten characters in TEXT. If 'SEX:' is matched, then the character following is matched by the LEN function and assigned to the variable SEXTYPE.

A function RTAB also exists, and it matches all characters from the current cursor position up to, but *excluding,* the tab as specified by an integer argument indicating the number of positions from the end of the string. Combining TAB and RTAB, we can write

TEXT TAB(10) RTAB(10)  · MIDDLE

to assign to **MIDDLE** the substring of TEXT which excludes the first ten characters and last ten characters of TEXT. Of course, if TEXT is fewer than twenty characters in length, the pattern match fails.

POS(integer) returns a pattern which matches the empty string, if the cursor is located at the position of the subject string indicated by the integer argument. Therefore,

TEXT 'SEX:' POS(14) LEN(1) · SEXTYPE

produces a successful match if the substring 'SEX:' appears immediately prior to and including the fourteenth character in TEXT. This example and the first example statement for TAB are functionally equivalent. Note, however, that POS is used to test the current position of the cursor, whereas TAB moves the cursor. The statement

TEXT BREAK(' ') POS(5)

results in a successful pattern match only if the first four characters are non-blank and the fifth is a blank.

A function RPOS is also available which matches the empty string at an integral number of positions from the end of the string, as specified by the integer argument.

Before concluding our discussion of string-handling facilities in SNOBOL, we should introduce a number of functions which are not pattern matching in nature, but are, nevertheless, important in string handling.

SIZE(string) returns the length of its string argument. Therefore, if TEXT has the value 'DATA', then SIZE(TEXT) returns the value 4. SIZE is identical to the LENGTH primitive function.

DUPL(string, integer) returns a string containing a specified number of duplications of its argument string. Thus, DUPL('ABC', 3) is 'ABCABCABC'.

A predicate function in SNOBOL returns an empty string if the condition tested is *true*; otherwise, the statement containing the condition fails. Besides the arithmetic predicates such as LT, LE, GT, GE, EQ, and NE, there exist the string predicates LLT, LLE, LGT, LGE, LEQ, and LNE. The prefix L means "lexically," and as an example, the predicate function LGT returns the empty string (i.e., *true*) if its first argument is greater than its second argument according to the lexical ordering determined by the collating sequence of the computer's character set. Therefore, LGT('B','A') is *true*, while LGT('A', 'B') is *false*.

Predicates can appear on the right-hand side of assignment statements, thus making the assignment conditional on the value of the predicate. For example,

```
BEGIN   LINE = INPUT                       :F(OUT)
        J = LT(J, 5) J + 1                 :S(BEGIN)
        OUTPUT = 'MORE THAN 5 LINES'       :(END)
OUT     OUTPUT = 'LESS THAN 6 LINES'
END
```

continues reading in records until six records (i.e., LINES) have been read or there are no more records to be read in. The latter case is detected by a failure in the input statement.

As a final example, let us consider the problem of converting an input item of the form

CHARLES W  SMITH      9872

to an output item of the form

SMITH, C. W.       S98.72

An input item consists of a name (composed of a first name, an initial, and a surname) followed by an expenditure in cents. No format can be assumed about the input item, except that one input item appears per input record. The end of the input items is designated by a record with an '*' in column 1.

An output item consists of a name (composed of a surname, a comma, and two initials) followed by an appropriately formatted expenditure. An output item begins in column 5, and the formatted expenditure starts in column 50.

The following SNOBOL program accomplishes the desired changes in formatting:

```
*COMMENTS IN SNOBOL ARE DESIGNATED BY USING AN * IN THE
* FIRST COLUMN.
*CONSTRUCTION OF PATTERNS USED IN THE PROGRAM
    BLANKS = SPAN(' ') | ''
    FIRST_INITIAL_PATTERN = BLANKS LEN(1) · FIRST NIT BREAK(' ') BLANKS
    SECOND_INITIAL_PATTERN = LEN(1) · SECONDINIT BREAK (' ') BLANKS
    SURNAME_PATTERN = BREAK(' ') · SURNAME
    AMOUNT_PATTERN = BLANKS BREAK(' ') · AMOUNT
*MAIN BODY OF PROGRAM
START LINE = INPUT
    LINE POS(1) '*'    : S(END)
    LINE FIRST_INITIAL_PATTERN =
    LINE SECOND_INITIAL_PATTERN =
    LINE SURNAME_PATTERN =
    LINE AMOUNT_PATTERN
```

```
*SEPARATE AMOUNT INTO DOLLARS AND CENTS
    AMOUNT RTAB(2) · DOLLARS LEN(2) · CENTS
*CONSTRUCT OUTPUT FORM
    NEWNAME = DUPL ( ' ',4)  SURNAME ', ' FIRSTIN '. ' SECONDINIT '.'
    EXPENDITURE = '$' DOLLARS '.' CENTS
    OUTPUT = NEWNAME DUPL(' ', 49 – LENGTH(NEWNAME)) EXPENDITURE
+                                   :(START)
END
```

SNOBOL is a very powerful and interesting programming language. The discussion in this subsection provides only a brief introduction to the language with a concentration on some of the more important string-handling capabilities.  To acquire a complete knowledge of the language, the interested reader is directed to "A SNOBOL4 Primer" by Griswold and Griswold [1973].  It is not surprising that the primitive and composite string-handling facilities presented in Sec. 2-2.3 are all available in the SNOBOL language; indeed, SNOBOL provides many additional facilities.  One other such facility we will examine in Sec. 2-4 is that of a recursively defined pattern structure.

**Exercises for Sec. 2-2**

1.  In the discussion of primitive string-manipulation functions, we introduced the operation of concatenation and the functions INDEX, SUB, and LENGTH. Can any one of these functions or operations be implemented in terms of the remaining functions? If possible, give the implementation.

2.  Design an algorithm for duplicating a given character string N times.  For example, given the argument string 'WAKA' and N = 2, Algorithm DUPL should generate the string 'WAKAWAKA'.

3.  Design an algorithm which trims off all the trailing blanks of a character string.  For example, given the argument 'HE□ENDED□IT□ALL!□□□□', Algorithm TRIM returns the string 'HE□ENDED□IT□ALL!'

4.  Construct an algorithm which effects the "break" pattern-matching operation. Given a subject string, a pattern string, an initial cursor position, an initially empty matched string, a replacement string, and a replacement condition (*true* or *false*), the algorithm scans the subject string on a character-by-character basis, starting at the given cursor position and proceeding to the first instance of a character which is also a character in the pattern string.  If such a character is found: *(a)* the algorithm exits with a value of *true*; *(b)* the matched string argument is assigned the substring of the subject from the initial cursor position up to, but excluding, the character found; *(c)* the replacement string replaces the matched string in the subject if the replacement condition is *true* ; and *(d)* after a replacement is completed, the cursor value is updated to point at the break character found. If a pattern character is not found, the algorithm returns *false,* and no changes are made.  Therefore, given a subject string (SUBJECT) of ' "THIS". □HE□SAID. □ "CANNOT□BE□SO".', a pattern string (PATTERN) of '.,;:?!', a cursor position (CURSOR) of 1, and a replacement string (REPLACE_STR) of the empty string '', BREAK(SUBJECT, PATTERN, CURSOR, MATCH_STR, REPLACE_STR, true) sets the subject string to

    '.□HE□SAID,□"CANNOT□BE□SO".'

the MATCH_STR to ' "THIS" ', and the CURSOR to 1.

5. Write a Pascal program called DELETE to delete all occurrences of each character contained in one given string from another given string. The two strings are as follows:

    (a) STR, the string from which deletions are to be made
    (b) LIST, the string providing the characters whose occurrences in STR should be deleted.

For example, if STR = 'THE□EZNZZXDX' and LIST = 'XZ', then the required answer is STR = 'THE□END'.

6. Write (a) a Pascal program or (b) a SNOBOL program to determine whether or not a sentence conforms to a particular pattern. For example consider the following.

    THE _____ BELONGS TO THE _____.

Sentences which would match this pattern are:

    THE BOOK BELONGS TO THE LIBRARY.
    THE CAT BELONGS TO THE FORD FAMILY.

7. An interesting problem in linguistics is the analysis of textual material. Let us assume that we are interested in developing an algorithm which is designed to analyze a manuscript to obtain:

    (a) the number of sentences in the manuscript
    (b) the average number of words in a sentence
    (c) the average number of symbols in a word

We will assume that:

    (a) Each sentence within the text is delimited by a period followed by two blanks and embedded periods are not permitted.
    (b) Each word within a sentence is delimited by one blank space.
    (c) Commas, semicolons, periods, and hyphens are not to be counted as characters.
    (d) The last sentence in the manuscript is indicated by a slash in the first position following a period-blank-blank sequence.
    (e) Words are not divided from one line to the next and the last word on each line is followed by at least one blank.
    (f) The first word on each line is preceded by blanks only if it is the first word in a paragraph.

Write a Pascal or SNOBOL program to perform the above.

## 2-3 GRAMMARS

In this section we describe a second formal system for string manipulation, the grammar. In this model we are less interested in performing manipulations on strings and are more interested in generating or recognizing a specific subset of strings generated from an alphabet. Grammars can be applied in practical situations, especially lexical and syntactic analysis, as will be illustrated in Sec. 2-5.2.

    In Sec. 2-1 we introduced the notion of the closure set of strings $V^*$ in which a string z is an element of $V^*$ if every character in z belongs to the alphabet V. For example, '10011' is an element of $V^*$ given that $V = \{0, 1\}$. In many instances we are interested only in a specific subset of the strings in $V^*$. For example, we may be concerned with only those strings of $V^*$ (given that $V = \{0, 1\}$) which contain one or more character sequences of a form '0' followed by one or more '1's. A string of one or more '1's is commonly denoted as '$1^+$'. Hence, the subset of interest contains strings of the form '$01^+01^+... 01^+$' or ('$01^+$')$^+$. Let us denote this special subset by L. Then '011010111' $\varepsilon$ L, and '01001' $\notin$ L, because it contains adjacent '0's.

Typically, the set of strings L can be used in an application involving the transfer of binary-encoded information from a source to a destination. The number of '1's in a particular subsequence (a subsequence is delimited by zeros) indicates the value of a transmitted number. For example, '011010111' is interpreted as 2 1 3. From our discussion in Chapter 1, we realize that this is not a very efficient coding scheme. However, the example given here is sufficient to illustrate that in some applications we are not interested in all strings generated from a given alphabet, but only a subset of such strings. Such a subset is often called a *language*. More formally, we define a language L to be a set of strings over some finite alphabet V, such that $L \subseteq V^*$.

Both a natural language, such as English, and a programming language, such as Pascal, adhere to our definition of a language. In both instances, the language is defined as a specific subset of the strings $V^*$ from alphabets such as $V = \{A, B, C, ..., Z, 1, 2, ..., 9, 0, \$, \textcent , !,$ and other special symbols$\}$. The strings which form the language are called *sentences*.

The question that immediately comes to the fore is: "How can we represent a language?" We can present a form of verbal description of the strings that are of interest to us—but this is neither an accurate nor a concise representation. A language-description mechanism must be able to represent an infinite set of strings, for some languages have an infinite number of sentences [e.g., the set of strings ('$01^+$')$^+$]. Such a mechanism must be able to exhibit the structural relationships (or syntax) that exist between the substring elements which, when properly combined, form sentences of the language. For example, the string

'I DATA STRUCTURES'

is incorrect syntactically because of the absence of a verb, while the sentence

'I LOVE DATA STRUCTURES'

possesses an obvious meaning. Note that in natural languages and programming languages, we must be concerned with two levels of structural interrelationships— namely, the word level (i.e., the substrings which form words from the vocabulary of that language) and the sentence level (i.e., the substring sequences which combine to form sentences of the language). This distinction will be brought up again in this section and in Sec. 2-5.2 during a discussion of *lexical analysis*.

A method of specification which takes into account these syntactic properties of a language is a *grammar*. A grammar consists of a finite set of replacement rules or *productions*. A grammar production and a Markov algorithm production (as discussed in Sec. 2-2.1) are quite similar in function—namely, that of a replacement specifier. However, they differ in purpose, since a grammar production is used to generate strings (i.e., sentences) from languages whereas a Markov production is used in the manipulation of a given subject string.

Before giving a more formal definition of a grammar, we examine a metalanguage for expressing a grammar. A *metalanguage* is a language used to describe another language; for example, English can be considered as a metalanguage when it is used to teach French. In the area of computer science, at least four such metalanguages have been developed for representing the syntax of programming languages—namely, BNF, syntax charts, ALGOL 68 notation and the Vienna language definition notation. BNF (meaning either Backus Naur Form or Backus Normal Form) was first made popular when it was used to describe the syntax of ALGOL 60 (Naur [60]). It is still commonly used, and we adopt it as the metalanguage used throughout this book.

We begin a description of BNF by citing an example of a BNF rule (or production) for describing a digit as follows:

<digit> ::= 0 | 1 | 2 | 3 | 4 | 5 | 6 | 7 | 8 | 9

Since confusion between the symbols of the metalanguage and symbols of the language itself must be avoided, four special metalinguistic symbols (<, >, ::=, | ) are used which are not part of the language's alphabet. A grammar is written as a set of productions, each of which has a left part, followed by the metasymbol ::=, followed by a list of right parts. The left part is a *nonterminal symbol* (e.g., <digit>) which is a variable representing a syntactic class within the grammar. Nonterminals are always parenthesized with the metasymbols < and >. The right parts, which are separated by the metasymbol |, are strings containing terminal and/or nonterminal symbols. A *terminal symbol* is a character from an alphabet or a string of characters from an alphabet. For example, the numerals 0, 1, 2, ... 9 are terminal symbols in the production for <digit>. We interpret the example production to mean that "a digit is composed of a 0, or 1, or 2, or ..., or 9."

We more formally define a grammar by a 4-tuple $G = (V_N, V_T, S, P)$ where $V_N$ and $V_T$ are disjointed sets of nonterminal and terminal symbols, respectively. S is the distinguished symbol of $V_N$, and it is commonly called the *goal* or *starting symbol*. P is a finite set of productions. The set $V = V_T \cup V_N$ is called the *vocabulary* of the grammar.

**Example 2-6** Let $G_1 = (V_N, V_T, S, P)$ be a grammar representing the syntax for a small subset of the English language. Then

$V_N$ = { <sentence>, <subject>, <predicate>, <article>, <noun>, <verb>, <object>},
$V_T$ = {a, the, Linus, Charlie, Snoopy, blanket, dog, song, holds, pets, sings},
S = <sentence>,
P = {1 <sentence> ::= <subject> <predicate>
    2 <subject> ::= <article> <noun> | <noun>
    3 <predicate> ::= <verb> <object>
    4 <article> ::= a | the
    5 <noun> ::= Linus | Charlie | Snoopy | blanket | dog | song
    6 <verb> ::= holds | pets | sings
    7 <object> ::= <article> <noun>   <noun>}

The sets of productions have been numbered from one to seven for future references.

                                                                           ////

The language, say $L_1$, generated from the grammar $G_1$, as described in Example 2-6, consists of a number of sentences (in fact, 972 sentences in all). An enumeration of some of these sentences is as follows:

'Charlie pets the dog'
'Linus holds the blanket'
'Snoopy sings a song'
'The blanket holds a dog'

There are two important things to note concerning the generation of strings (i.e., sentences) from a grammar. First, we have neglected (for legibility reasons) to put into the terminal symbols of the grammar the blank characters which normally appear between the words in the sentences. Throughout the book, we assume, unless it is obvious from context of the text, that a blank delimits all terminal symbols.

Second, it should be noted that not all strings composed of terminal symbols form sentences (e.g., 'Linus the a holds' is not syntactically correct). Hence, it is necessary to devise a method of analyzing the various parts of a string to determine whether the string is a sentence in the language. Such a process exists and is called *parsing*. For a given sentence, we can construct a parse, and for a string which is not a sentence, we cannot construct a parse. The diagram of a parse displays the syntax of a sentence in a manner similar to a tree and is, therefore, called a *syntax tree*. A parse of the sentence 'Linus holds the blanket' is shown in Fig. 2-3.1

How do we construct a parse? Or, equivalently, how do we derive a syntax tree? In general, there are two methods of parsing—top-down and bottom-up. Let us examine both of these methods in some detail.

In *top-down parsing*, an attempt to construct a syntax tree is initiated by starting at the root of the tree (i.e., the distinguished symbol) and proceeding downward toward the leaves (i.e., the symbols forming the string). The effect of such a process is to generate sentences systematically from the language until a match can be found with the string in question. Of course, if no match can be found, the string is not a sentence of the language. This generation of sentences can be mapped with the aid of a special relation $\Rightarrow$ in which x $\Rightarrow$ y is interpreted as "string x produces y (or y reduces to x)" during a step of a parse. We illustrate the steps in the generation of the sentence 'Linus holds the blanket' given the grammatical rules for $G_1$:

| | | | |
|---|---|---|---|
| <sentence> | $\Rightarrow$ | <subject> <predicate> | ... by production 1 |
| | $\Rightarrow$ | <noun> <predicate> | ... by production 2 |
| | $\Rightarrow$ | Linus <predicate> | ... by production 5 |
| | $\Rightarrow$ | Linus <verb> <object> | ... by production 3 |
| | $\Rightarrow$ | Linus holds <object> | ... by production 6 |
| | $\Rightarrow$ | Linus holds <article> <noun> | ... by production 7 |
| | $\Rightarrow$ | Linus holds the <noun> | ... by production 4 |
| | $\Rightarrow$ | Linus holds the blanket | ... by production 5 |

A circled number on the syntax tree in Fig. 2-3.1 represents the production number that is used in that part of the construction of the syntax tree. It is easy to see how the construction of the tree parallels the sentence generation process just given.

In practice, the construction of a syntax tree using a top-down parsing strategy may involve a number of wrong production steps before the correct tree results. For example, the rule <subject> ::= <noun> is used in the second step of the sentence generation. We could have chosen, with the same conviction, to use the production step <subject> ::= <article> <noun>. Of course, to do so leads to the generation of a sentence which is not the input string. This fact can be discovered in the next production step of <article> ::= a or <article> ::= the, since neither 'a' or 'the' are equivalent to 'Linus'. Such errors in production selection can be recovered from

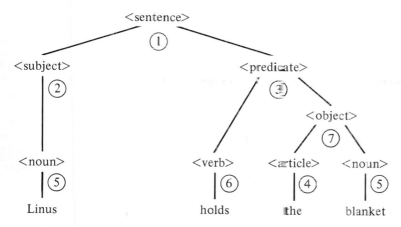

**FIGURE 2-3.1**    A parse of the sentence 'Linus holds the blanket'.

relatively easily by simply retracing our steps up the syntax tree and trying an alternative production step. Such an alternative step s the application of <subject> ::= <noun>. We continue in this manner during the entire parse until the correct sentence is generated. More will be said about top-down parsing and backtracking strategies in Sec. 5-2.3.

In the second method of parsing, *bottom-up parsing*, the completion of the syntax tree is attempted by starting at the leaves and moving upward toward the root. Relating this strategy to the grammar $G_1$ given in Example 2-6, the following series of derivations results in a bottom-up parse of 'Linus holds the blanket' (remember that x $\Rightarrow$ y also means "y reduces to x" and this is the interpretation used in bottom-up parsing):

| | | |
|---|---|---|
| <noun> holds the blanket | $\Rightarrow$ Linus holds the blanket | ... by prod.5 |
| <subject> holds the blanket | $\Rightarrow$ | ... by prod.2 |
| <subject> <verb> the blanket | $\Rightarrow$ | ... by prod.6 |
| <subject> <verb> <article> blanket | $\Rightarrow$ | ... by prod.4 |
| <subject> <verb> <article> <noun> | $\Rightarrow$ | ... by prod.5 |
| <subject> <verb> <object> | $\Rightarrow$ | ... by prod.7 |
| <subject> <predicate> | $\Rightarrow$ | ... by prod.3 |
| <sentence> | $\Rightarrow$ | ... by prod.1 |

Observe that the same syntax tree is constructed (see Fig. 2-3.1), and the same productions are invoked as for the top-down method; however, the production steps take place in a completely different order. In particular, because we parsed the sentence in a left-to-right manner using both methods the productions are not applied in the reverse order. If our parsing strategy for the top-down method had worked from right-to-left, then the productions would have been applied in the reverse order in which they were applied using the left-to-right bottom-up strategy. Similarly, a bottom-up right-to-left parse applies productions in the reverse order to that of a top-down left-to-right strategy. Because a bottom-up left-to-right parse is so commonly used in compilers for parsing statements from a programming language, it is often called a *canonical parse.*

The basic parsing strategy in a canonical parse begins with the isolation of a special substring in the given input string or the resulting string that has been transformed by a number of production applications to the input string. Such a transformed string is often called a *sentential form,* and the special string which is isolated is commonly called a *handle.* In the bottom-up parse of the sentence 'Linus holds the blanket', the initial string 'Linus holds the blanket', the final derivation '<sentence>', and all intermediate derivations are examples of sentential forms. The handle should be the left-most simple phrase (a *simple phrase* is a substring of the sentential form that matches the right-hand side of a production) corresponding to a production that can be applied given the context of the handle in the sentential form. For example, 'Linus' is the handle in the sentential form 'Linus holds the blanket', and '<verb> <object>' is the handle in the sentential form '<subject> <verb> <object>'. In an example given later in this section, we illustrate how an examination of the context of a phrase affects the decision as to whether that phrase is the handle.

Once the handle has been isolated, its corresponding left-hand side (in our example, <noun>) is substituted at the position of the right-hand side to create a new sentential form (i.e., the sentential form '<noun> holds the blanket', in the case of our example). This process is continued until the goal symbol ('<sentence>', in the example) is reached, if possible. If the goal symbol is the only remaining symbol in the transformed string, then the original input string is a sentence from the language described by the grammar; otherwise, it is not.

An important concept in a discussion of grammars and, indeed, in a discussion of many other topics is that of *recursion.* Recursion can be loosely defined as a process by which we define something in terms of itself. An example of a grammar which recursively defines a simple language is as follows:

$G_2 = (V_N, V_T, S, P)$ where
$V_N = \{<digit>, <no>, <number>\}$
$V_T = \{0, 1, 2, 3, 4, 5, 6, 7, 8, 9\}$
$S = \{<number>\}$
$P = \{1 \ <number> ::= <no>$
$\qquad 2 \ <no> ::= <digit> \ | \ <no> <digit>$
$\qquad 3 \ <digit> ::= 0 \ | \ 1 \ | \ 2 \ | \ 3 \ | \ 4 \ | \ 5 \ | \ 6 \ | \ 7 \ | \ 8 \ | \ 9\}$

In the productions labeled 2, the syntactic phrase <no> can be defined as <no> <digit>. This is a recursive definition. To see how it is applied, let us assume we are to generate the string '694' of the language for $G_2$. We begin with the distinguished symbol <number> and proceed as follows:

| <number> | ⇒ | <no> |
|---|---|---|
| | ⇒ | <no> <digit> |
| | ⇒ | <no> <digit> <digit> |
| | ⇒ | <digit> <digit> <digit> |
| | ⇒ | 6 <digit> <digit> |
| | ⇒ | 69 <digit> |
| | ⇒ | 694 |

The production step of <no> ::= <no> <digit> is a very powerful one, since we are effectively creating a two-digit entity from a one-digit entity. This process of expansion allows us to express any integer we desire, regardless of its value. Of course, for a given integer, this recursive step, and hence the expansion, must cease. This occurs with the application of a nonrecursive production such as <no> ::=

<digit>. This nonrecursive production step is called the *basis step* in the recursive process.

Recursively defined productions are used in instances in which certain substrings may appear repeatedly in a sentence of a language. For example in the language which we introduced at the beginning of this subsection (i.e., the language with sentences of the form '01$^+$ ... 01$^{+\prime}$), two substrings repeatedly appear; namely, '01$^{+\prime}$ and within this substring, the substring . These substrings form the basis for a recursive definition of the language, as is illustrated in the productions with the syntactic phrases <ones> and <zero ones> in the grammar $G_3$:

$G_3 = (V_T, V_N, S, P)$ where
$V_N = \{<L>, <zero\ ones>, <ones>\}$,
$V_T = \{0, 1\}, S = <L>$
$P = \{1\ <L> ::= <zero\ ones>$
    $2\ <zero\ ones> ::= <ones>\ |\ <zero\ ones>\ <ones>$
    $3\ <ones> ::= 0\ |\ <ones>\ 1\}$

The power of recursive productions in a grammar cannot be underplayed, and the following two statements, which can be proved as theorems, illustrate this point:

*1*   Any grammar containing a recursively defined production describes an infinite language (i.e., a language with an infinite number of sentences).
*2*   Any grammar containing no recursively defined productions describes a finite language (i.e., a language with a finite number of sentences).

Hence in this section the language described by grammars $G_2$ and $G_3$ are infinite, while the language described by $G_1$ is finite.

As another example illustrating the use of recursively defined productions, consider the problem of formulating a grammar for describing an identifier name. An identifier name in many programming languages consists of a single alphabetic character or an alphabetic character followed by a finite number of alphabetic, numeric, and special characters. An example grammar can be given as

$G_4 = (V_N, V_T, S, P)$ where
$V_N = \{<identifier>, <ident>, <letter>, <others>\}$
$V_T = \{A, B, ..., Z, 0, 1, ..., 9, \_, \#, \$\}$
$S = <identifier>$
$P = \{1\ <identifier> ::= <ident>$
    $2\ <ident> ::= <letter>\ |\ <ident>\ <letter>\ |\ <ident>\ <others>$
    $3\ <letter> ::= A\ |\ B\ |\ C\ |\ ...\ |\ Z\ |\ \#\ |\ \$$
    $4\ <others> ::= 0\ |\ 1\ |\ 2\ |\ 3\ |\ 4\ |\ 5\ |\ 6\ |\ 7\ |\ 8\ |\ 9\ |\ \_\}$

A syntax tree for the parse of 'LAB_1' is given in Fig. 2-3.2.

In most programming languages, there is a practical limit to the length of an identifier name (e.g., the length of a PL/I identifier name can be at most 31) The grammar $G_4$ allows for any length of identifier. By a slight modification in the BNF metalanguage, we can accommodate a production which is to be applied iteratively 30 times (at most). The set of productions labeled 2 can be rewritten as

$2\ <ident> ::= <letter>\ |\ <letter>\ [\ <letter>\ |\ <others>]^{30}$.

In general, a production of the form $x ::= y[z]^n$ is interpreted as

$$x ::= yz\ |\ yzz\ |\ yzzz\ |\ ...\ |\ \underbrace{yzz\ ...\ z}_{n\ times}$$

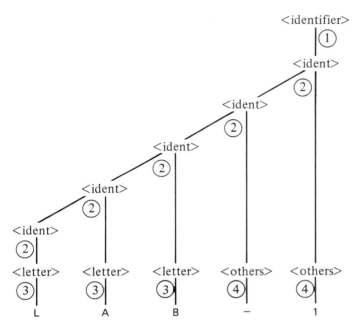

**FIGURE 2-3.2**   The parse of the string 'LAB_1' using the productions of $G_4$.

*Example 2-7*   As a final example in this subsection, let us construct a grammar for simple arithmetic expressions in a programming language like Pascal. A simple arithmetic expression can be a simple identifier, a numeric constant (for simplicity, we only allow unsigned integer constants), or an expression involving constants and identifiers as operands of addition (+), subtraction (–), multiplication (*), and division (/) operations. Remember that in Pascal, multiplication and division have precedence over addition and subtraction (that is, X * 2 – 3/Y + 1 is interpreted as (X * 2) – (3/Y) + 1). We will illustrate how we can account for this precedence in a grammar description.

$G_5$   = ($V_N$, $V_T$, S, P) where
$V_N$  = {<expr>, <term>, <form>, <primary>}
$V_T$  = {+, –, *, /, i, n}
S = <expr>
P = {1 <expr> ::= <term>
    2 <term> ::= <form> | <term> + <form> | <term> – <form>
    3 <form> ::= <primary> | <form> * <primary>
                | <form> / <primary>
    4 <primary> ::= i | n}

Note that i (equivalent to <identifier>) and n (equivalent to <number>) are considered as terminal symbols in this grammar. Both of these terminals have been defined previously as goal symbols in the grammars $G_2$ and $G_4$. Therefore, these two grammars can be thought of as subgrammars in $G_5$, and hence the entire grammar can be defined to the detail of an individual character if so desired.                                                                          ////

The breakdown of $G_5$ into the subgrammars corresponding to <number> and <identifier> is a conceptual breakdown with which most compiler writers must deal. One module of the compiler, called a *scanner*, handles string recognition at the word (or lexical) level; that is, the character strings forming sentences of the language are analyzed and grouped into word-like constructs such as <number>s and <identifier>s.

A second compiler module, the *parser*, takes as input representations or tokens of the word-like constructs which have been resolved by the scanner. The parser is only responsible for identifying syntactically correct sentences which are perceived as being composed of words from the language. Therefore, the exact value of a word-like construct (i.e., whether a <number> is 26 or 3782) is of no consequence to the parser, since these values are identified by the scanner. It is quite clear that the grammars needed to describe word-like constructs for the scanner are appreciably simpler than grammars for the parser (as illustrated in $G_5$). If the syntax analysis phase of a compiler is broken into two modules, the scanner and the parser, a great amount of effort can be expended in the production of a very efficient scanner. This efficiency is important because the scanner is called much more often than the parser.

From the previous discussion it should be clear that the grammars $G_2$ and $G_4$ are grammars describing syntactic units which are processed by the scanner, while $G_5$ is a grammar suited to a parser.

Let us perform a canonical (left-to-right bottom-up) parse of the expression 2 + X * Y. Within the framework of $G_5$, this expression appears as the string

'<number> + <identifier> * <identifier>'

Therefore, we can write in shorthand notation (that is, n = <number>, i = <identifier>, <p> = <primary>, <f> = <form>, <t> = <term>, and <e> = <expr>) the following trace of the parse:

| | | | |
|---|---|---|---|
| <p> + i * i | $\Rightarrow$ | n + i * i | ... by production 4 |
| <f> + i * i | $\Rightarrow$ | | ... by production 3 |
| <t> + i * i | $\Rightarrow$ | | ... by production 2 |
| <t> + <p> * i | $\Rightarrow$ | | ... by production 4 |
| <t> + <f> * i | $\Rightarrow$ | | ... by production 3 |
| <t> * i | $\Rightarrow$ | | ... by production 2 |

Note that the last sentential form begins with the string '<t> *'. By examining the productions of $G_5$, we see that a <term> must have either the terminal symbols + or – or no symbol at all following it. Therefore, the string cannot be resolved to the goal symbol given the current state of the parse.

Consider that point in the parse in which we have the sentential form '<t> + <f> * i'. By using lookahead, we observe that the symbol '*' follows <f> in the string. If we make all the reductions of the substring '<f> * i' before combining the result of these reductions with the substring '<t> – ', we can achieve a parse.

Let us pick up the parse at the sentential form '<t> + <f> * i' and continue in the manner just proposed.

| | | |
|---|---|---|
| <t> + <f> * <p> | ⇒ | <t> + <f> * i    ... by production 4 |
| <t> + <f> | ⇒ | ... by production 3 |
| <t> | ⇒ | ... by production 2 |
| <e> | ⇒ | ... by production 1 |

We have our parse!

The necessity for lookahead within the parsing strategy occurs because certain dependencies exist in the grammar's structure. For example, in $G_5$ the syntactic form <term> is dependent upon <form> (i.e., <term> ::= <form> | <term> + <form> | <term> – <form>). Hence, all possible reductions that can be made to <form> should be made prior to reductions for <term>. This is the rule we adopted in the parse for '2 + X * Y'. This example clearly indicates the importance of lookahead in the decision as to whether a particular phrase of the sentential form is the handle.

The syntax tree shown in Fig. 2-3.3 illustrates that the multiplication operator and its operands are grouped prior to the grouping of the addition operator and its operands. Therefore, the expression is considered evaluated as '2 + (X * Y)' and, within the grammar, the precedence of * and / over + and – has been attained.

As a general rule, the more "complex" a grammar is, the more lookahead is required in the parsing strategy (in fact, some authors have used the amount of look-ahead which is required in a parse as a measure of the complexity of a grammar). The grammar $G_5$ requires a one-symbol lookahead. There are grammars which require k symbols of lookahead for a finite k, and still others which require a potentially infinite amount of lookahead.

Before concluding this subsection, we wish to discuss briefly two additional points—the notations of syntax and semantics and their relationship to grammars,

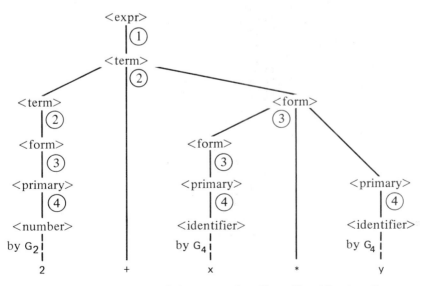

**FIGURE 2-3.3 The parse of the expression '2 + X * Y' using the productions of $G_5$.**

and the relationship between Markov algorithms and grammars. A grammar is only capable of specifying the structure (i.e., syntax) of a sentence. For some languages it is not always convenient or possible to express exactly that set of strings which forms sentences in a language. A good example of this situation is the subset of the English language defined by $G_1$. Sentences generated by $G_1$ include

'Snoopy sings the blanket' and
'The song pets Charlie'

Both of these sentences are syntactically correct, but they have little or no meaning, and from a semantic point of view they are not sentences. It is very often the case that strings which are sentences in a formal grammatical sense are not sentences of a language, and additional checking for semantic correctness must accompany a parse of the sentence. Semantic checking is very often done by compilers when translating a program.

The grammars we have described in this subsection are called *context-free grammars*. A context-free grammar is a grammar in which there is only one nonterminal allowed on the left-hand side of a production. An example of a grammar which is not context free is $G_6$ as follows:

$G_6 = (\{<S>, <B>, <C>\}, \{a, b, c\}, <S>, P)$ where
$P = \{$ 
$\qquad\qquad <S> ::= a<S> <B> <C>$
$\qquad\qquad <S> ::= a <B> <C>$
$\qquad <C><B> ::= <B> <C>$
$\qquad\quad a <B> ::= ab$
$\qquad\quad b <B> ::= bb$
$\qquad\quad b <C> ::= bc$
$\qquad\quad c <C> ::= cc\}$

$G_6$ describes the language containing strings of the form $a^n b^n c^n$ for $n \geq 1$ (e.g., for n = 3, $a^3 b^3 c^3$ = aaabbbccc). The generation of the string $a^2 b^2 c^2$ is $<S>$ $\Rightarrow a <S> <B> <C> \Rightarrow$ aa $<B> <C> <B> <C> \Rightarrow$ aa $<B> <B> <C> <C>$ $\Rightarrow$ aab $<B> <C> <C> \Rightarrow$ aabb $<C> <C> \Rightarrow$ aabbc $<C> \Rightarrow$ aabbcc.

It can be shown that any *phrase-structure grammar* is expressible as a Markov algorithm. A phrase-structure grammar is the most general class of grammars in the sense that no restrictions, such as allowing only one symbol on the left-hand side, are placed on the productions. Using Markov algorithms, we can easily write both a generator and a recognizer for strings of the form $a^n b^n c^n$.

```
LMA:      GENERATE
START:    Λ → 'abc'
MOVE:     'ba' → 'ab'     (MOVE)
          'ca' → 'ac'     (MOVE)
          'cb' → 'bc'     (MOVE)
          output string   (START)
```

The command *output string* is introduced to allow for the presentation of each string. Note that the algorithm GENERATE produces the set of strings $\{a^n b^n c^n$ for every $n \geq 1$.

```
LMA:        RECOGNIZE
            'a' → α'a'
            'b' → β'b'
            'c' → γ'c'
```

| START: | $\alpha'a' \rightarrow \alpha$ | (DELETEB) |
|---|---|---|
|  | $\alpha\beta\gamma \rightarrow {}'s'.$ |  |
|  | $\Lambda \rightarrow \Lambda.$ |  |
| DELETEB: | $\beta'b' \rightarrow \beta$ | (DELETEC) |
|  | $\Lambda \rightarrow \Lambda.$ |  |
| DELETEC: | $\gamma'c' \rightarrow \gamma$ | (START) |
|  | $\Lambda \rightarrow \Lambda.$ |  |

Upon the termination of RECOGNIZE, a string value of 's' indicates that the string is a sentence. Any other value indicates that it is not a sentence.

Markov algorithms and phrase-structure grammars are equivalent with respect to computational power. However, both these formal models are designed for different purposes. The Markov model exhibits properties which are basic to string handling and rudimentary pattern matching, as discussed in Sec. 2-3.2. The grammar is a model for string recognition and generation, and we investigate these two functions more fully in Sec. 2-5.2. By this point in the chapter, the importance of pattern matching as a string-manipulation facility should be very clear. We would now like to extend the previous discussion on grammars and their relationship to pattern matching by introducing the *recursive pattern structure* construct that is available in the SNOBOL language.

The fact is we have already encountered several examples of recursively defined patterns through the introduction of a recursively defined production in a grammar. Recall that the recursive definition of an unsigned integer is given as

<unsigned integer> ::= <digit> | <unsigned integer> <digit>
<digit>                ::= 0 | 1 | 2 | 3 | 4 | 5 | 6 | 7 | 8 | 9

Hence, an unsigned integer is defined to be a single digit, or an integer consisting of a single digit followed by a digit, or an integer composed of two digits followed by a digit, etc. While the productions for an unsigned integer provide a concise definition, they are capable of representing any member of the infinite set of unsigned integers. Of course, the process of string recognition is a form of pattern matching.

Recursive pattern structures can be defined in SNOBOL with the aid of the *unevaluated-expression operator* *. This operator delays evaluation of its operand until a pattern value is required during pattern matching.

We begin a description of * by illustrating how it is used in defining a nonrecursive pattern structure. In a pattern definition such as

PAT = TAB(N) LEN(1) . X

the pattern constructed for PAT is determined, in part, by the value of N at the time the assignment statement is executed. In SNOBOL, it is convenient and conventional to define all pattern structures at the beginning of the program, and thus avoid the continual re-evaluation which takes place if the patterns are used "in-line." To maintain this convenience and convention, and yet allow a pattern to change based on a parameter such as N, we use the * operator. For example, if PAT is defined as

PAT = TAB(*N) LEN(1) . X,

then the * operator prevents the evaluation of the assignment statement until PAT is used as a pattern in another SNOBOL statement, such as

LAB SUBJECT PAT =

However, each time the statement labeled LAB is executed, the pattern assignment is re-evaluated, thus allowing a different value of N and, hence, the construction of a different pattern each time PAT is used.

This ability to defer the evaluation of a pattern is necessary in the construction of a recursive pattern structure. For example, the SNOBOL statements

DIGIT = '0' | '1' | '2' | '3' | '4' | '5' | '6' | '7' | '8' | '9'

UINTEGER = DIGIT | *UINTEGER DIGIT

define a pattern for an unsigned integer. Therefore, in the statements

SUBJECT = 'A13982'
SUBJECT UINTEGER =

the pattern UINTEGER is evaluated initially as the pattern alternative DIGIT, which matches the character '1'. The second numeric character '3' is matched along with '1' by the second alternative for UINTEGER—namely, UINTEGER DIGIT. This is possible because UINTEGER evaluates to DIGIT, and hence the second alternative is the pattern DIGIT DIGIT. In a similar fashion, the string '139' is matched by the alternative *UINTEGER DIGIT, where *UINTEGER now evaluates to DIGIT DIGIT. It is easy to see how this pattern evaluation process is extended recursively to pattern match the entire digit string '13982' and, indeed, any digit string forming an unsigned integer.

Consider, as another example, the recursive pattern structure that might be used to define an identifier.

LETTER = 'A' | 'B' | 'C' | 'D' | 'E' | 'F' | 'G' | 'H' | 'I' | 'J' | 'K' | 'L' | 'M' | 'N' |
     'O' | 'P' | 'Q' | 'R' | 'S' | 'T' | 'U' | 'V' | 'W' | 'X' | 'Y' | 'Z'
DIGIT = '0' | '1' | '2' | '3' | '4' | '5' | '6' | '7' | '8' | '9'
IDENTIFIER = LETTER | *IDENTIFIER LETTER | *IDENTIFIER DIGIT

These statements describe a pattern structure consisting of a set of strings, in which each string consists of a single letter or a letter followed by an arbitrary number of alphanumeric characters.

There is no operator or function in the list of primitive and composite character-manipulation functions, given in Secs. 2-2.2 and 2-2.3, which performs a role similar to that of the unevaluated expression operator (*) in SNOBOL. Nevertheless, pattern-matching functions can be called recursively to simulate the effect of a recursive pattern structure. For example, an unsigned integer can be scanned for recursively by using two functions. The first function, UINTEGER, isolates the initial digit in the subject string. UINTEGER calls the function, DIGIT_SCAN, which matches the string of digits forming the left-most unsigned integer in the subject string. The matching is achieved by recursive calls to DIGIT_SCAN.

**Function** UINTEGER(SUBJECT). A given string, SUBJECT, is scanned until the first (i.e., left-most) digit is found. The function DIGIT_SCAN is invoked to isolate the left-most unsigned integer. The six pattern-matching parameters assume the roles defined in Sec. 2-2.3.

1.   [Initialize CURSOR]
      CURSOR ← 1

2.   [Scan for first numeric character]
        Repeat while
                LEN(SUBJECT, 1, CURSOR, MATCH_STR, REPLACE_STR, false)
                and MATCH_STR < '0'
        (In the string-comparison operation involving <, it is assumed that the
        numeric characters 0 through 9 are higher than all other characters in the
        collating sequence. CURSOR is automatically incremented in the **LEN**
        function when the pattern match is successful.)
3.   [Do we have a numeric character?]
        If MATCH_STR < '0'
        then   Return('')   (No digit exists in SUBJECT)
        else   Return(DIGIT_SCAN(SUBJECT, CURSOR))
                (Otherwise, return digit string as unsigned integer.)            ☐

The DIGIT_SCAN function recursively concatenates numerical characters from
SUBJECT to form the string of digits making up the unsigned integer.


**Function** DIGIT_SCAN(SUBJECT, CURSOR). Given a string SUBJECT and a
cursor value CURSOR, isolate the longest string of numerical characters starting
from the cursor character of SUBJECT.

1.   [Test for end of digit string]
        If LEN(SUBJECT,1,CURSOR,MATCH_STR,REPLACE_STR,false)
                and MATCH_STR ⩾ '0'
        then Return(MATCH_STR ○ DIGIT_SCAN(SUBJECT,CURSOR))
        else Return('')                                                          ☐

In the Function DIGIT_SCAN, digits are isolated and concatenated with the
results of previous invocations of DIGIT_SCAN. For example, if SUBJECT = 'MAY
1980' and CURSOR initially has the value 5, then a trace of the DIGIT_SCAN
function is illustrated in Table 2-3.1.


**Table  2-3.1**

| *Step* | CURSOR | MATCH_STR | DIGIT_SCAN |
|---|---|---|---|
| 1 | 5 | '1' | ? |
| 1 | 6 | '9' | ? |
| 1 | 7 | '8' | ? |
| 1 | 8 | '0' | ? |
| 1 | 8 | '' | '' |
| return to 1 and exit | 8 | '0' | '0' |
| return to 1 and exit | 8 | '8' | '80' |
| return to 1 and exit | 7 | '9' | '980' |
| return to 1 and exit | 6 | '1' | '1980' |
| return to UINTEGER | | | |

Note that four recursive calls of Function DIGIT_SCAN are made during the process of scanning the SUBJECT string. For each such call, a return is made to the point of invocation in step 1 and the value returned is concatenated with the value that MATCH_STR has at that particular invocation of DIGIT_SCAN. It is important that intermediate values be retained for MATCH_STR during the recursive calls of DIGIT_SCAN. A more in-depth discussion of recursive functions is undertaken in Sec. 3-5.1, where it will be explained how these intermediate values are stored from one invocation of a recursive function to the next.

Observe that Function DIGIT_SCAN can be implemented without the use of recursion. An iterative approach, such as the approach used for removing leading nonnumerical characters in Function UINTEGER, can be adopted. However, the given version of DIGIT_SCAN illustrates how recursive pattern matching can be achieved using composite string-handling functions. For many problems, it is easier to formulate a recursive algorithm than an iterative algorithm. We will encounter examples of such problems in Chap. 5 when discussing the traversal of trees.

**Exercises for Sec. 2-3**

1. Consider the following grammar with the set of symbols {a, b}:

    <S> ::= a | b | <S>a | b<S>

   Describe the set of strings generated by this grammar.
2. Write grammars for the following languages:
    (a) The set of *nonnegative odd integers*
    (b) The set of *nonnegative even integers* with *no* leading zeros permitted.
3. Write grammars for the following languages:
    (a) $\{ a^i ba^i \mid i \geqslant 0 \}$
    (b) $\{ wbw^R \mid w \; \varepsilon \; \{0, 1\} \; * \}$ where $w^R$ is the reverse of w, i.e., if w = 001, $w^R = 100$.
    (c) {<name>   <name> is a FORTRAN name}. (Note that FORTRAN names must have no more than six characters.)
4. Write a grammar (using BNF) which describes a PL/I <procedure head> statement. An example of a procedure head is

    Example: PROCEDURE (X, Y, Z) RECURSIVE
             RETURNS (CHARACTER (*) VARYING);

   Assume that only one of FIXED, FLOAT, BIT(*) VARYING or CHARACTER(*) VARYING can appear as a RETURNS argument. You may assume <identifier> to be a terminal in the grammar.
5. The following grammar generates simple arithmetic expressions involving addition (+), subtraction (−), multiplication (*), and division (/). The symbol i represents a variable name:

    <factor>     ::= (<expression>) | i
    <term>       ::= <factor> | <term> * <factor> | <term> / <factor>
    <expression> ::= <term> | <expression> − <term>
                   | <expression> > − <term>

   Give the derivations for the following expressions:

       i + i, i − i/i, i * (i + i), i * i + i.

6. Suppose we want to implement a DDC compiler for the DDC (decimal digit calculator) language which performs arithmetic operations on integer arguments. The BNF grammar description below was written to describe the DDC language syntactically. Unfortunately, the grammar is ambiguous. (A grammar for a language is ambiguous if a sentence from the language can be parsed in more than one way.)

$$
\begin{aligned}
<\text{DDC expr}> &::= <\text{DDC term}> \\
&\mid <\text{DDC expr}> <\text{opl}> <\text{DDC expr}> \\
<\text{DDC term}> &::= <\text{decimal arg}> \\
&\mid <\text{DDC term}> <\text{op2}> <\text{decimal arg}> \\
<\text{decimal arg}> &::= <\text{digit}> \\
&\mid <\text{decimal arg}> <\text{digit}> \\
<\text{digit}> &::= 0 \mid 1 \mid 2 \mid 3 \mid 4 \mid 5 \mid 6 \mid 7 \mid 8 \mid 9 \\
<\text{opl}> &::= + \mid - \\
<\text{op2}> &::= * \mid /
\end{aligned}
$$

   (a) Demonstrate that the grammar is, indeed, ambiguous.
   (b) Correct the grammar so that it is unambiguous.
   (c) According to your grammar, what is the value of 7 + 6 * 3 / 2?
   (d) If we change the BNF description of <opl> and <op2> to read

$$
\begin{aligned}
<\text{opl}> &::= * \mid / \\
<\text{op2}> &::= + \mid -
\end{aligned}
$$

   what is the value of the expression 7 + 6 * 3 / 2 in the language described by your corrected grammar?

7. Write grammars for the following:
   (a) $\{a^n b a^m\}$ for n, m $\geq$ 1
   (b) $\{a^n b^n a^n\}$ for n > 1 (*Hint*: You may have to use more than one symbol on the left-hand side of a production)

8. Given expressions of the form

$$
\begin{aligned}
<\text{expression}> &::= <\text{expression}> + <\text{term}> \\
&\mid <\text{term}> \\
<\text{term}> &::= <\text{form}> * <\text{term}> \\
&\mid <\text{form}> \\
<\text{form}> &::= I
\end{aligned}
$$

formulate a recursively defined SNOBOL pattern to recognize the strings 'I + I', 'I * I + I' and 'I'. A string, such as 'I + I I', should not be matched by the pattern.

## 2-4 STORAGE REPRESENTATION OF STRINGS

A string is a sequence of characters, and as such, it is most conveniently represented using a sequence of storage locations in memory. In Sec.1-4.5 it was pointed out that characters are binary encoded in fields which are typically 6, 7, or 8 bits in length. Therefore, in almost all machines, an integral number of characters, say n, are stored in a computer word, where n = $\lfloor w/f \rfloor$ and w is the word size in bits and f is the field length in bits of the binary encoded character. For the IBM 3030 series computer w = 32 bits, f = 8 bits (for the EBCDIC code), and hence n = 4 characters per word.

In this section, we discuss the storage representation of three types of character strings, namely, fixed-length strings (available in PL/I), "varying"-length strings (available in (PL/I), and variable-length strings (available in SNOBOL). The idea of using a sequence of memory words or locations to represent a string is applied to the storage representation of all three types of character strings.

The amount of storage required by a *fixed-length string* is known when the string is created. For example, the PL/I statement,

DECLARE S CHARACTER (6) INITIAL('*A1');

declares a field of six binary-encoded characters (which for an IBM 3030/370 implementation implies a field of six bytes). An initialization of S to '*A1' implies that S is assigned '*A1☐☐☐'. This assignment is represented in Fig. 2-4.1, where X'5C', X'C1', X'F1', and X'40' are read as "hexadecimal 5C, C1, F1, and 40" [i.e., $(5C)_{16}$, $(C1)_{16}$, $(F1)_{16}$, and $(40)_{16}$. and are the EBCDIC representations of '*', 'A', '1', and blank, respectively. Observe that there are two bytes in $word_{i+1}$ which are not assigned to S. Extra bytes, such as these, may be assigned to another character string if the string storage area is managed efficiently by the compiler or interpreter.

The maximum length of a PL/I *"varying"-length string* is also known at creation time. Enough storage is allocated to accommodate up to this maximum number of characters along with storage for an information field which contains the current length of the string. The execution of the PL/I declaration

DECLARE C CHARACTER(6) VARYING INITIAL ('*A1');

results in an allocation of storage as illustrated in Fig. 2-4.2.

The EBCDIC representation which is adopted in Fig. 2-4.2 allows a string to assume a current length of up to 65535 (that is, $2^{16} - 1$), subject to the restriction that the current length is less than the maximum allowable length. In some implementations, it is necessary to add a second length field which contains the maximum length. This second field is used in checking for a string overflow condition (e.g., the assignment of a string which is larger than the predefined maximum length).

The most dynamic and powerful type of string is the *variable-length string*. In this case, neither the precise length nor maximum length is known at creation time. The storage structure for this type of string can be handled in many ways, but two popular methods of representation employ *boundary markers* and *string descriptors*. A boundary marker is a character which need not be printable, and which does not appear in the text of a string. For example, the printable character '↑' is used in the ASCII storage representation for the string '*A1', as shown in Fig. 2-4.3. A 7-bit ASCII character representation on a 16-bit word machine, such as the PDP-11, is assumed in Fig. 2-4.3. Note that the first bit of each half-word (i.e., byte) can be

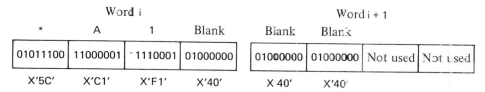

|       | Word i |         |       |  | Word i + 1 |          |          |
|-------|--------|---------|-------|--|------------|----------|----------|
| *     | A      | 1       | Blank |  | Blank      | Blank    |          |
| 01011100 | 11000001 | 1110001 | 01000000 |  | 01000000 | 01000000 | Not used | Not used |
| X'5C' | X'C1'  | X'F1'   | X'40' |  | X'40'      | X'40'    |          |          |

**FIGURE  2-4.1**  Fixed-length  EBCDIC  character  string  representations  for '*A1☐☐☐'.

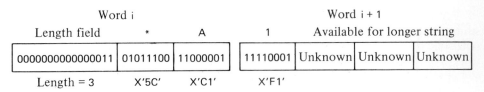

| Word i | | | Word i + 1 | | | |
|---|---|---|---|---|---|---|
| Length field | * | A | 1 | Available for longer string | | |
| 0000000000000011 | 01011100 | 11000001 | 11110001 | Unknown | Unknown | Unknown |
| Length = 3 | X'5C' | X'C1' | X'F1' | | | |

**FIGURE 2-4.2** Varying-length EBCDIC character-string representation for '*A1'.

either a "zero" or "one" depending on the type of parity error checking that is adopted in the computer. If all binary encodings of characters must have *even parity*, as is the case in Fig. 2-4.3, then the number of "ones" in an encoded character must be an even number. If *odd parity* is adopted, then the number of "ones" must be an odd number. Of course, if the parity of an encoded character disagrees with the adopted convention, an error has occurred in the transmission or storage of that character.

A string descriptor is a two-field element which contains a length field and a pointer field. The length field contains the current length of the variable-length string. The pointer field contains the address of the first character of the string in a large data area called *string space*. String space holds the encoded character information for all strings in the program. For example, in Fig. 2-4.4, the string '*A1' is represented using a descriptor. Note that to reference a string, we first must reference the descriptor which, in turn, provides the string address via the pointer field.

To aid in the understanding of the string storage structures presented in this section, it is worthwhile to examine how some of the primitive string-manipulation operations and functions (i.e., assignment, concatenation, LENGTH, SUB, INDEX) are realized using the different storage representations. A string assignment results in the copying of the string or a reference to the string formed by the right-hand side (or subject) of the assignment to the storage location(s) referenced by the left-hand side (or object) of the assignment. Problems do not arise when assigning values to fixed-length and "varying"-length string variables because enough storage is allocated for these variables when they are created. If the string value to be assigned is longer than the length allotted to the fixed or "varying"-length string variables, then the extra characters are removed from the right-hand end of the string so as to assign a string equal to the maximum length for the variable. When a string value is assigned to a fixed-length string variable, the value must be padded to the right with blanks before the assignment if its length is less than the predetermined fixed length allotted the string variable. The string value is padded until it is equal in length to the fixed length of the variable.

Assignments to variable-length string variables present some storage allocation problems. The space currently allocated to the string variable may be insufficient to

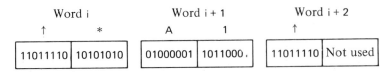

| Word i | | Word i + 1 | | Word i + 2 | |
|---|---|---|---|---|---|
| ↑ | * | A | 1 | ↑ | |
| 11011110 | 10101010 | 01000001 | 1011000, | 11011110 | Not used |

**FIGURE 2-4.3** Variable-length ASCII 7-bit character-string representation for '*A1' using boundary markers.

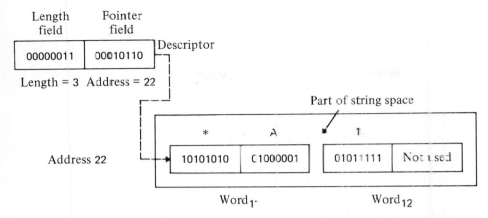

**FIGURE 2-4.4**    Variable-length ASCII 7-bit character-string representation for '\*A1' using descriptors.

store the string value being assigned. To illustrate this fact, suppose the assignments S1 = 'CAT' and S2 = 'ANIMAL' are executed. The resulting effects on the string space, when using the boundary-marker method, are depicted in Fig. 2-4.5a. Figure 2-4.5b illustrates the effects on the string space when using the descriptor method. For brevity and clarity, we have used characters and not a binary-encoded representation of the characters in Fig.2-4.5 and the remaining figures in this section.

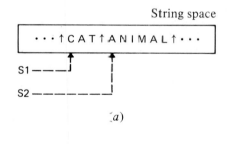

(a)

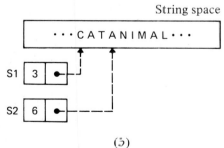

(b)

**FIGURE 2-4.5**   Assignments of the variable-length strings 'CAT' and 'ANIMAL' to S1 and S2, respectively.

String space

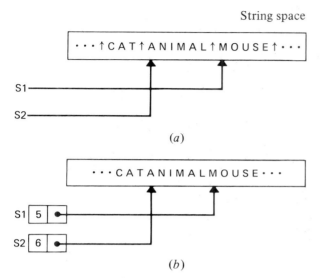

(a)

(b)

**FIGURE 2-4.6** Effect of the variable-length string assignment S1 = 'MOUSE'.

The assignment S1 = 'MOUSE' necessitates the creation of new space in the string area for the variable S1, as is illustrated in Figs. 2-4.6a and 2-4.6b.

Observe in Fig. 2-4.7 that an assignment of the value of one variable to another, such as S1 = S2, does not require the allocation of additional space in the string area. Instead, the assignment can be accomplished by assigning the reference to (in the boundary-marker method) or the description of (in the descriptor method) the subject string S2 to the object string S1.

If this policy is adopted for variable-to-variable assignments, new string storage must be allocated in instances involving string-expression and string-constant assignments. Otherwise, if S2, as depicted in Fig. 2-4.7, is assigned 'DOG' as shown in Fig. 2-4.8, then a side effect from this assignment would occur. Assigning 'DOG' to S2 changes the value of S1 to 'DOG' when using boundary markers, and to 'DOG-MAL' when using descriptors, which are, of course, both erroneous. Therefore, a correct assignment policy is to allocate additional string space for the new value of S2, as shown in Fig. 2-4.9.

The operation of concatenation results in the formation of a new string from two argument strings. Because the argument strings are not necessarily adjacent in memory and may not be stored in the order specified by the concatenation, storage is required to copy the argument strings into adjacent storage locations in order to perform the concatenation. In the case of a fixed-length or "varying"-length string storage structure, this storage may already exist if the concatenated string is being assigned to a variable. For variable-length string concatenations, additional storage must always be allocated—thereby adhering to the policy related to variable-length string assignments involving string expressions. Assume that S1 and S2 are as indicated in Fig. 2-4.9. Fig. 2-4.10 illustrates the effect of executing the statement S1 = S1 ○ 'HORSE'.

String space

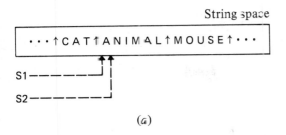

(a)

String space

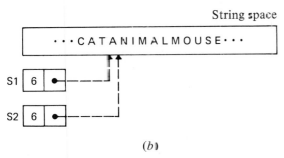

(b)

**FIGURE 2-4.7**   Effect of the variable-length string assignment S1 = S2.

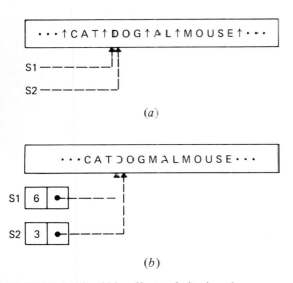

(a)

(b)

**FIGURE 2-4.8**   Side effects of altering the contents of the storage assigned to S2.

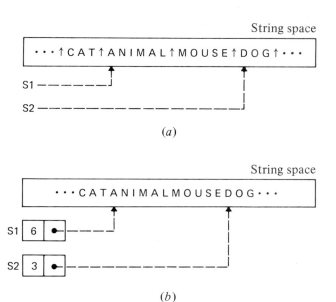

**FIGURE 2-4.9** Effects of allocating additional string space for the variable-length string assignment S2 = 'DOG'.

The **LENGTH** function is easily computed for fixed-length strings, since the length must be known in order to allocate storage for such strings. The lengths of a "varying"-length string and a variable-length string using the descriptor method are explicitly available through a field in the storage structure for each string type. The entire string must be scanned in order to calculate the length of a variable-length string bracketed with boundary markers.

The **SUB** function, when used to return a substring of a subject string, is implemented in a similar fashion for all string storage structures (i.e., once the sequence of storage locations for a string is discovered, it is a simple matter to isolate the appropriate subsequence indicated by the arguments of the SUB function). A check must be made to determine if the index and length, i.e., the second and third arguments of the SUB functon, are plausible for the given subject string. A similar check must be made on the arguments of SUB when it is used in a replacement mode such as in SUB(X, 1, 1) = '?'. If the index or length arguments specify a substring beyond the limited length of the fixed-length or "varying"-length string variable, an error occurs. For variable-length string variables, such a check is not necessary on the subject string, since such "SUB" assignments are valid.

As in the case with the SUB function, the **INDEX** function is implemented in a similar fashion for all string storage structures once the sequence of storage locations for a string is known. It is a simple yet time-consuming process to examine the subject string on a character-by-character left-to-right basis in an effort to match the pattern argument of the INDEX function.

Before we conclude this section, it is important to point out that while variable-length strings are extremely flexible, they present some problems from a storage management point of view. For example, in Fig. 2-4.6, the assignment of 'MOUSE' to S1 leaves the string 'CAT' inaccessible, and "garbage" is created in the

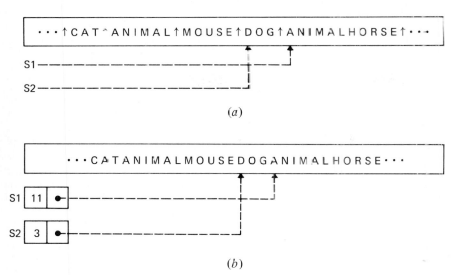

**FIGURE 2-4.10** Effects of executing the variable-length string assignment S1 = S1 ○ 'HORSE'.

string area. More and more garbage results after a number of string assignments. Some method of collecting this garbage must be used in order to utilize the string area efficiently. In Sec. 5-6, we will examine some garbage-collection techniques that can be applied to string areas for variable-length strings. In the next section, we look at some of the applications to which character manipulation can be applied.

**Exercises for Sec. 2-4**

1. Give storage representations for the string S which has the value 'STRING' assuming S is a
   (a) Fixed-length string
   (b) "Varying"-length string with maximum length of 8
   (c) Variable-length string
   Use an EBCDIC internal character representation for (a) and (b) and an ASCII internal character representation for (c). Recall that the EBCDIC and ASCII character codes are given in Chap 1.

2. In this subsection, the following rule was established for variable-length character strings.
   "... a correct assignment policy is to allocate additional string space for each new value assigned to a character string variable, unless the assignment is variable-to-variable (such as S1 ← S2). In this case S1 can simply be assigned the reference or descriptor of S2"
   (a) Illustrate the effects of variable-to-variable assignments like
       S1 ← 'DATA', S2 ← S1.
       using the descriptor method of storing variable-length strings.
   (b) Consider the algorithm statement
       S1 ← SUB(S1, 1, 2).

Can or cannot substring assignments, such as the one above, be handled without requesting new string space when using:

(i)  the boundary marker method
(ii) the descriptor method

3.  When using variable-length strings, a tremendous amount of "garbage" space accumulates as string variables are assigned new values. One suggestion for collecting this garbage and reusing it appropriately when using the descriptor method is to keep a vector of "old" descriptors which point to sections of available free space. If a request for new string space occurs, then a search is made first of the availability list of descriptors and, if possible, some of the garbage space is reclaimed for use. Elaborate on the feasibility of such a system—specifically, how do you decide what is garbage and how would you set up and  manage such a "garbage collection agency?"

## 2-5  STRING MANIPULATION APPLICATIONS

This section contains three applications illustrating how the concepts and, specifically, the string-handling functions discussed in this chapter can be applied.  In the first application, we introduce a text formatter TEXT_FORM and describe the text-handling operations that TEXT_FORM provides. It is an excellent, classical application because it involves a wide variety of character string-manipulation problems. The second application deals with the development of a lexical analyzer that is representative of scanners which perform low-level character by character analysis of source program input in a programming language compiler or interpreter. The final application discusses the problem of KWIC (*Key-Word-In-*Context) index generation which is an interesting and practical application in information retrieval.

### 2-5.1  Text Handling

One of the most common application areas in which string manipulation is used is text handling. Newspaper editing and typesetting, book and report generation, and computer program and data preparation are all applications involving on-line text-handling facilities. Rather than storing text on paper and then manually revising it, the text in each of these applications can be stored in a character form on an external storage medium (such as a disk unit) on a computer. Text-handling programs are then used to add to, delete from, or change the text, and to output the text in a desired format.

Text handling encompasses the two basic areas of *text editing* and *text formatting*. Text editing involves the ability to alter the given text by such operations as adding text, deleting portions of text, and changing or replacing text.  The text formatting area deals with the production of output in a desired layout.

In this section we concentrate our discussion on the text formatting area.  A simple formatter, TEXT_FORM, with a relatively small set of formatting commands, is presented.  The commands begin in character position one of a line of input.  In order to clearly identify a command as opposed to textual material, all commands begin with a dot(.). It is assumed that a line of text never begins with a '.'. The commands appear on a separate line of input from text and some have arguments accompanying them on that line while others do not.  The form of the commands is very similar to those encountered in *nroff* or *troff* on the UNIX operating system.

The commands are summarized in the following table:

| Command | Description |
|---|---|
| .RJ [n] | right justify text<br>n (optional) gives new right margin |
| .NJ [n] | text not right justified<br>n (optional) gives new right margin |
| .NP | begin a new paragraph |
| .CN | center text on next input line |
| .SL [n] | skip a line<br>n (optional) gives number of lines to be skipped |
| .IL | indent a level (5 positions) |
| .RL | return from a level of indent |
| .TB x/y/z/... | tabbing – includes tab setting list |
| .TE | end of tabbing |
| .ED | end of text |

The following example provides a clear indication of how the TEXT_FORM commands are used. The example is a memo describing recent changes in stock quotations.

```
.NJ 62
MEMO: To all COFUND's investors
.SL
FROM: Michael Broker
.SL
DATE: September 16, 1983
.SL
.CN
* * * * * * * * *
.SL 2
.CN
IMPORTANT RECENT STOCK QUOTATIONS
.SL
.RJ 62
The following table contains the most active
quotations from our twenty most sensitive firms. Notice
that in general the market is good, which is a relief
considering the next Board Meeting is on Monday.
.SL
.TB 5/21/37/
FIRM/QUOTATION/CHANGE/
```

```
----/---------/------/
.TE
.SL
.TB 5/24/38/
Amtred/58.5/+3.5/
CALTOIL/148.0/+4.5/
Moneytalk/36.0/-2.5/
UBM/342.5/+3.0/
.TE
.SL
.NP
May I also remind you of the Tenth Annual Share-holders Meeting
on January 10th.
.NJ 62
.IL
Signed:
.RL
.SL 2
REPORT RJ-103
```

The formatted output of this report after being submitted to the TEXT_FORM processor would be printed as shown in Fig. 2-5.1.

The processing of the TEXT_FORM commands can be achieved through the use of functions and procedures where each performs a certain task required in the

```
MEMO: To all COFUND's Investors

FROM: Michael Broker

DATE: September 16, 1983

              * * * * * * * * * *


          IMPORTANT RECENT STOCK QUOTATIONS

The following table contains the most active  quotations  from
our twenty most sensitive firms. Notice that  in  general   the
market is good, which is a relief considering the   next   Board
Meeting is on Monday.

        FIRM            QUOTATION        CHANGE
        ----            ---------        ------

        Amtred          58.5             +3.5
        CALTOIL         148.0            +4.5
        Moneytalk       36.0             -2.5
        UBM             342.5            +3.0

     May I also remind you of the Tenth   Annual   Share-holders
Meeting on January 10th.

     Signed:


REPORT RJ-103
```

**FIGURE 2-5.1** Sample TEXT_FORM output.

processing. Specifically, functions and procedures can be designed for tasks such as printing out a justified line of text, printing out a nonjustified line of text, centering text in a line, setting tabs, and printing out lines constructed with tabs. The following discussion illustrates how these functions can be designed to handle formatting commands corresponding to the tasks just listed.

The *right justification* of text requires manipulation of the contents of a line such that the printed output ends exactly at the right margin. In some cases a dictionary or syllabus is used to assist in the automatic hyphenation of words that can be broken at the right margin, but this is more complicated than we wish to present here. In typesetting, altering the spacing between letters is used as an aid in justification, but this is not possible on a line printer or teletype. Justifying a line on these latter types of fixed-space devices relies on changing the spacing between words.

An algorithm is presented which uses the adjustment of between-word separations to construct and output a line of right-justified text from a line of unformatted-input text.

**Function** JUSTIFY(PRINTLINE, RMARGIN). Given a character string PRINTLINE containing text of length greater than the right end position RMARGIN, the text is right justified and any excess text is returned. BLANKS holds the number of blanks to be introduced into the line. BFIELD is a character string of blank characters equal in length to the size of the field of blanks separating words and is initially of length 1. The indices used are J and K.

1.  [Is text immediately right justifiable?]
       If SUB(PRINTLINE, RMARGIN, 1) ≠ '☐' and SUB(PRINTLINE,
          RMARGIN + 1, 1) = '☐'
       then   Write (SUB(PRINTLINE, 1, RMARGIN))
              OUTLINE ← SUB(PRINTLINE, RMARGIN + 1)
              Return (OUTLINE)
2.  [Determine the position of first blank character to the left of position RMAR-
    GIN.]
       J ← RMARGIN − 1
       If SUB(PRINTLINE,RMARGIN,1) ≠ '☐'
       then   Repeat while SUB(PRINTLINE,J,1) ≠ '☐'
                 J ← J − 1
3.  [Look for next nonblank.]
       J ← J − 1
       Repeat while SUB(PRINTLINE, J, 1) = '☐'
          J ← J − 1
4.  [Set up loop for adding blanks.]
       BLANKS ← RMARGIN − J
       BFIELD ← '☐'
       Repeat step 5 for K = 1, 2, 3,..., BLANKS
5.  [Successively add blanks to the blank field separating the words.]
       Repeat while not MATCH(PRINTLINE, BFIELD, J, '', BFIELD ○ '☐', true)
          J ← J − 1
          If J = 0
          then   J ← RMARGIN − BLANKS + K − 1
                 BFIELD ← BFIELD ○ '☐'
       J ← J − LENGTH(BFIELD) − 2

6.  [Output justified text.]
    Write (SUB(PRINTLINE, 1, RMARGIN))
    OUTLINE ← SUB(PRINTLINE, RMARGIN + 1)
7.  [Finished.]
    Return (OUTLINE)                                  □

The first step of the function handles text which does not require the insertion of blanks to achieve right justification. As a simple example, assume PRINTLINE has the value

'THE BOOK IS AUTHORED BY W. M. FINDLING.  HE DISCUSSES
DATA MANAGEMENT...'

and RMARGIN is 20. Then SUB(PRINTLINE,20,1) is 'D' and SUB(PRINTLINE,21,1) is '□'.  Therefore, by step 1, the string

'THE BOOK IS AUTHORED'

can be printed and the remainder of the string is returned from Function JUSTIFY in the variable OUTLINE.

Let us assume that outside the JUSTIFY function the leading blank is removed from the returned string and this new string is assigned to PRINTLINE and considered for justification. In this case, SUB(PRINTLINE, 20, 1) is '□', making immediate justification impossible. In step 2, J is set to 19, and the nineteenth position of PRINTLINE contains the '□' before the 'H' in 'HE'. Therefore, the repeat loop in step 2 is avoided, and we proceed to find the right-most nonblank character. Such a character (namely, a period) is found at position 18, as denoted by the value of J. In step 4, BLANKS is set to 20 - 18 or 2, and BFIELD is initialized to '□'. Step 5 is repeated for K with values 1 and 2. In step 5, the basic pattern-matching function MATCH (as described previously) is invoked. Subfields of PRINTLINE are examined while scanning right to left in an effort to match the current value of BFIELD. For our example, a match succeeds when J is 9, at which point a blank is inserted just prior to the 'F' in 'FINDLING'. Therefore, PRINTLINE now has the value

'BY W. M. □FINDLING.  HE DISCUSSES DATA MANAGEMENT...'

The value of J is tested to see if it is zero, which it is not. Then J is set to 11 − 1 − 2 = 8, and step 5 is repeated for a final time with K = 2. Again a search is initiated for the next right-most blank from the current position represented by J. A blank is found at character position 6, and another blank is inserted just prior to the initial 'M', making PRINTLINE equal to

'BY W. □M. □FINDLING.  HE DISCUSSES DATA MANAGEMENT...'

In step 6, the twenty-character line

'BY W. □M. □FINDLING.'

is printed and the string '  HE DISCUSSES DATA MANAGEMENT...' is returned.

As before, we assume the preceding blanks of the returned string are removed, and this new string is assigned to PRINTLINE for further right justification. In this case, PRINTLINE is

'HE DISCUSSES DATA MANAGEMENT...'

Upon examining the twentieth character in both steps 1 and 2, we discover that it is the first 'A' in 'MANAGEMENT'. To right justify this text, we look for the first nonblank character to the left of the first field of blanks immediately preceding 'MANAGEMENT'. The second 'A' in 'DATA' is the character we are searching for, and it is found at character position 17 in PRINTLINE. Steps 2 and 3 of the function accomplish this search. Therefore, it is the string

'HE DISCUSSES DATA'

which must be expanded to 20 characters.

In step 4, J has the value 17, implying that the number of blanks which must be inserted is 3 (i.e., BLANKS = 3). Step 5 is repeated three times. The first two times blanks are inserted between 'DISCUSSES' and 'DATA', and 'HE' and 'DISCUSSES'. The third time through step 5, J is eventually decremented to zero, at which point it is reset to 19 and BFIELD is set to '☐☐'. A right-to-left rescan of the text is made while looking for the first occurrence of a field with two blank characters. Such a field is found between the words 'DISCUSSES' and 'DATA'. The two blanks are replaced by a field of three blanks, and the function terminates by printing

'HE ☐DISCUSSES ☐☐DATA'

and returning a value of 'MANAGEMENT...' in the variable OUTLINE.

There are cases where text is to be printed without justification on the right side. This can be performed by a function NO_JUSTIFY that is similar to JUSTIFY and requires the same parameters. Once again excess text is returned in this new function.

**Function** NO_JUSTIFY(PRINTLINE, RMARGIN). Given the character string PRINTLINE, a line of text is printed subject to the restriction of a right margin as specified by RMARGIN. Any excess text is returned, and the text is not justified on the right side.

1. [Is the line within limit of right margin?]
      If LENGTH(PRINTLINE) ≤ RMARGIN
      then   Write (PRINTLINE)
             OUTLINE ← ''
             Return (OUTLINE)
2. [Is there already a break at RMARGIN?]
      If SUB(PRINTLINE, RMARGIN, 1) ≠ '☐' and SUB(PRINTLINE,
         RMARGIN + 1, 1) = '☐'
      then   Write (SUB(PRINTLINE, 1, RMARGIN)
             OUTLINE ← SUB(PRINTLINE, RMARGIN + 1))
             Return (OUTLINE)
3. [Check to see if RMARGIN is a nonblank character.]
      J ← RMARGIN − 1
      If SUB(PRINTLINE, RMARGIN, 1) ≠ '☐'
      then   Repeat while SUB(PRINTLINE, J, 1) ≠ '☐'
                 J ← J − 1
4. [Output the line.]
      Write (SUB(PRINTLINE, 1, J))
      OUTLINE ← SUB(PRINTLINE, J + 1)
      Return (OUTLINE)                                                    ☐

In step 1 of Function NO_JUSTIFY the situation in which PRINTLINE is shorter than the maximum length of a line is dealt with easily. The PRINTLINE is written out and the value returned in the variable OUTLINE is an empty string.

The second step handles the case in which a word ends exactly on the right margin position. PRINTLINE is simply printed out up to the end of the line, and the rest of PRINTLINE is returned in OUTLINE as described in the final step of the procedure.

If step 3 is reached we must end the line with the last nonblank character to the left of the RMARGIN position. In this step, a backward search is undertaken from the position denoted by RMARGIN until a blank character is reached. This gives the position where PRINTLINE will be split such that the first portion is printed and the remainder is returned in OUTLINE in step 4.

Another commonly performed function available in text formatting is the capability of *centering* a piece of text in a line. It is assumed that the piece of text to be centered is shorter than the maximum allowable line length that is currently in effect. The parameters to the procedure are an input line and the right margin position.

**Procedure**  CENTER(INPUT_LINE, RMARGIN).  Given the character string INPUT_LINE containing text and RMARGIN an integer giving the position of the right margin character, the text is centered and printed out. LEADBL is an integer indicating the number of leading blanks required before the text on the line.

1.  [Find the number of leading blanks necessary.]
      LEADBL ← TRUNC((RMARGIN − LENGTH(INPUT_LINE))/2)
2.  [Print out.]
      INPUT_LINE ← DUPL('□', LEADBL) ○ INPUT_LINE
      Write (INPUT_LINE)
3.  [Finished.]
      Return                                                              □

The CENTER procedure begins by computing the number of blanks that must precede the title text. The line is then reconstructed with that many blanks followed by the text. A function DUPL, identical in nature to SNOBOL's DUPL, is used to add the blanks. This line is then printed out and control returns to the calling algorithm.

A final function that we will consider for the text formatter involves the *setting of tabs* and retaining them for their use in tabulation. This cability is described in the procedure SET_TABS. The parameters include TABLIST, a string containing the tab settings, TAB, a vector containing tab settings, and NO_TABS, an identifier indicating the number of tab settings applicable. TABSET is the flag showing when tabs are in effect. In TABLIST the tab settings are separated by '/'.

**Procedure**  SET_TABS(TABLIST, TAB, NO_TABS, TABSET).  Given TABLIST, a string containing the new tab settings, the individual settings are placed in the vector TAB. NO_TABS indicates the number of tab settings in the vector. The function CONV_CH_TO_NUM is used to convert the values to numeric before storing them in the vector.

1.  [Initialize.]
      CUR ← 1

2.  [Get the tab settings and place in the vector.]
    Repeat while FIND(TABLIST, '/', CUR, MATCH_STR, '', false)
        If SUB(TABLIST,CUR+1,1) = '/'
        then   Write ('MISSING A TAE SETTING.')
               TABSET ← false
               NO_TABS ← 0
               Return
        else   NO_TABS ← NO_TABS + 1
               TAB[NO_TABS] ← CONV_CH_TO_NUM(MATCH_STR)
3.  [Finished.]
    Return                                                                   □

   It is also necessary to print properly a line in which the tab settings are
applied. Items that are to be separated by tabs are also separated in the input line
by the character '/'. The line to be output is constructed by placing the individual
items at the positions denoted by the successive tab settings stored in the vector
TAB. The procedure to follow does this task

**Procedure** TABPRINT(PRINTLINE, TAB, NO_TABS). Given the character string
PRINTLINE and the tab settings stored in vector TAB, the text in PRINTLINE is
printed out according to the tab settings. The separator symbol in the list is '/'.
LINEOUT is a string variable that contains the line to be printed in tab form.
NO_TABS is the current number of tab settings applicable and I is a loop counter.

1.  [Initialize.]
    I ← 1
    LINEOUT ← ''
    CURSOR ← 1
2.  [Loop searching for separator symbol, '/'.]
    Repeat step 3 while
        FIND(PRINTLINE, '/', CURSOR, MATCH_STR, '', false)
3.  [Check for / in text represented as //]
    If SUB(PRINTLINE, CURSOR + 1, 1)='/'
    then   TEMP_STR ← TEMP_STR ○ MATCH_STR ○ '/'
           CURSOR ← CURSOR + 2
    else   (construction of a line)
           TEMP_STR ← TEMP_STR ○ MATCH_STR
           SUB(LINEOUT, TAB[I], LENGTH(TEMP_STR)) ← TEMP_STR
           TEMP_STR ← ''
           I ← I + 1
           If I > NO_TABS
           then   PRINTLINE ← SUB(PRINTLINE,CURSOR)
                  Write (LINEOUT)
                  I ← 1
                  LINEOUT ← ''
4.  [Output the tab set line.]
    Write (LINEOUT)
    Return                                                                   □

   We are now in a position to describe an algorithm to perform the text formatting operations.

**Algorithm** TEXT_FORM. This algorithm reads in text which contains formatting commands and processes these commands to produce the formatted output. CURSOR is a position in the string, and RMARGIN indicates the position of the right margin. IND gives the level of indentation currently in use on the page. LINES is the number of lines to be skipped if a skip command is being executed. JUST and TABSET are flags indicating the status for justification and tabbing. INPUT_LINE and PRINTLINE are strings of the text that are used during the execution of the algorithm. Several small functions and procedures that have been defined previously are called in this algorithm.

1.  [Initialize.]
        CURSOR ← 1
        RMARGIN ← 80
        IND ← 0
        NO_TABS ← 0
        JUST ← false
        TABSET ← false
        PRINTLINE ← ''
2.  [Read first line of input.]
        Read (INPUT_LINE)
3.  [Set up loop to process.]
        Repeat thru step 5 while true
4.  [Is it a command?]
        If SUB(INPUT_LINE,1,1) = '.' and SUB(INPUT_LINE,2,2) ≠ 'TE'
        then   (A formatting command that is not an end of tab command.)
               If TABSET
               then   (tab is in effect)
                      Write ('INVALID COMMAND WHEN TABSET IS ON')
                      Exit
               else   (process the command)
                      PRINTLINE ← NO_JUSTIFY(PRINTLINE, RMARGIN)
                      CMD ← SUB(INPUT_LINE, 1, 3)
                      Select case (CMD)
                      Case '.RJ':
                              JUST ← true
                              If LENGTH(INPUT_LINE) > 4
                              then   CURSOR ← 5
                                     FIND(INPUT_LINE,'□',CURSOR,ITEM,'',false)
                                     RMARGIN ← CONV_CH_TO_NUM(ITEM)
                      Case '.NJ':
                              JUST ← false
                              If LENGTH(INPUT_LINE) > 4
                              then   CURSOR ← 5
                                     FIND(INPUT_LINE, '□', CURSOR, ITEM, '',
                                       false)
                                     RMARGIN ← CONV_CH_TO_NUM(ITEM)
                      Case '.NP':
                              PRINTLINE ← DUPL('□', 4)
                      Case '.CN':
                              Read (INPUT_LINE)
                              Call CENTER(INPUT_LINE, RMARGIN)

Case '.SL':

    If LENGTH(INPUT_LINE) > 4

    then  CURSOR ← 5

        FIND(INPUT_LINE, '□', CURSOR, ITEM, '',

          false)

        LINES ← CONV_CH_TO_NUM(ITEM)

    else  LINES ← 1

    Repeat I = 1, 2, ..., LINES

        Write (blank line)

Case '.IL':

    IND ← IND + 1

Case '.RL':

    If IND > 0

    then  IND ← IND - 1

Case '.TB':

    If LENGTH(INPUT_LINE) ≤ 4

    then  Write ('ERROR - NO TAB SETTINGS.')

    else  CURSOR ← 4

        SPAN(INPUT_LINE, '□', CURSOR, BLANKS, '',

          false)

        SPAN(INPUT_LINE, '0123456789/', CURSOR,

          TABLIST, '', false)

        TABSET ← true

        Call SET_TABS(TABLIST, TAB, NO_TABS,

          TABSET)

Case '.ED':

    Exit

Default:

    Write ('INVALID COMMAND :', CMD)

    Write ('STOP FORMATTING.')

    Exit

else  If SUB(INPUT_LINE, 1, 3) = '.TE'

then  Repeat while PRINTLINE ≠ ''

    Call TABPRINT(PRINTLINE, TAB, NO_TABS)

    TABSET ← false

    NO_TABS ← 0

else  If TABSET

then  PRINTLINE ← PRINTLINE ○ INPUT_LINE

else  If PRINTLINE = ''

    then  PRINTLINE ← DUPL('□',5 * IND) ○ INPUT_LINE

    else  PRINTLINE ← PRINTLINE ○ '□' ○ INPUT_LINE

    Repeat while LENGTH(PRINTLINE) ≥ RMARGIN

        If JUST

        then  PRINTLINE ← JUSTIFY(PRINTLINE,

            RMARGIN)

        else  PRINTLINE ← NO_JUSTIFY(PRINTLINE

            RMARGIN)

        (Remove all leading blanks.)

        SPAN(PRINTLINE, '□', 1, '', '', true)

        (Add proper indentation.)

        PRINTLINE ← DUPL('□', 5 * IND) ○ PRINTLINE

5.  [Get next input line.]
  Read (INPUT_LINE)
  CURSOR ← 1
6.  [Finished.]
  Exit               □

Because this algorithm is of considerable length, some explanation is necessary to aid in its comprehension. Steps 1 to 3 are basically initialization steps. Steps 4 and 5 are the main body of the algorithm and are repeated until an end of text command or termination on an illegal command is encountered.

When the first character of an input line is a '.' a case statement is executed with the basis of selection being the format command. For each command there is a set of statements to be executed. In all cases except the command '.TE', the line of text saved in PRINTLINE is written out before the new command is put in place. In the cases '.RJ','.NJ', and '.SL', provision is made to read the optional argument from the input line. In case '.TB' the list of tab settings must also be read from the input line.

In the cases for changing the indentation, the variable IND giving the current level of indentation is updated. This variable is used as lines are prepared for output. Another input line is read only for the case of centering. In this instance, the next line holds the text to be centered.

If the line does not begin with a command, it is processed as a line of text. When tabs are in effect (i.e., TABSET is true), the input line is simply concatenated to PRINTLINE, which is eventually printed when the case '.TE' is encountered.

In the situation of no tabs, a longer process is required. If PRINTLINE is empty, it is assigned the current contents of INPUT_LINE prefixed by the proper number of blanks for indentation. The function DUPL, which is borrowed from SNOBOL, is used to place the correct number of blanks at the beginning of PRINTLINE. If PRINTLINE is not empty, a blank and then INPUT_LINE are concatenated onto the end of it. When the new PRINTLINE has been constructed, a repeat loop is entered to print lines until the length of PRINTLINE falls within RMARGIN. As each line is printed, PRINTLINE is adjusted with the current indentation once more placed at the beginning of the line.

Step 5 merely gets a new input line and prepares for the next processing loop.

This section has dealt with text formatting as it relates to basic string manipulation concepts. There are many more complex problems involved as the sophistication of a formatter increases. The whole area of text editing also requires extensive use of string manipulation. The exercises provided at the end of this section suggest some further extensions to the material in this section. Exercises to do a few more complicated operations with an editor are left to Chap. 4 where linked lists are introduced as a storage representation which can be used in the storage of text.

**Exercises for Sec. 2-5.1**

1.  The procedure CENTER centers a piece of text in a full-length line of text. Define a revised procedure which enables the text to be centered in an already-indented line.
2.  The problem of text editing also requires string manipulation. Assuming that LINE is a vector containing the lines of a file of text, write an algorithm which adds lines of text after the last line of text in the file. In conjunction with this

algorithm, write additional algorithms to perform the deletion of a line of text from the file, and for finding and changing the first occurrence of a word or phrase in the file.

### 2-5.2 Lexical Analysis

In our discussion of grammars in Sec. 2-3, we pointed out that often the description of a language must be viewed at two levels—the "word" level and the "sentence" level. For example, in the English language only certain combinations of characters from the English alphabet can be combined under concatenation to form a word. If a string of symbols contains a form which is not an English word, then this string cannot be a sentence from the English language. On the other hand, even if a string of symbols from the English alphabet is made up of English words, the entire string does not necessarily form a sentence from the English language (as illustrated by the string 'The sang the girl.'). Therefore, the decision as to whether a string forms a sentence from a "natural-like" language involves some analysis at the word (or lexical) level to decide if the string is composed of a set of legitimate symbols and words, followed by some analysis at the sentence (or syntactic) level to determine if the words in the string combine to form sentences from the language.

In this subsection we are concerned with the lexical analysis of source strings (or statements) from a subset of a hypothetical high-level programming language. Nevertheless, many of the techniques presented are applicable to the lexical analysis of natural language machine translation.

In Sec. 5-2.3, a discussion of the second part of the analysis phase, namely the syntactic analysis, will be undertaken. At that time we concentrate on the syntactic analysis of a programming language as performed in a compiler or interpreter.

In a compiler or an interpreter, the module which separates the source input into basic "word-like" constructs, such as identifier names, numeric constants string constants, keywords or reserved words, operators, etc., is commonly called the *scanner*. In the discussion to follow, we consider the design of a scanner for a simple language which is only composed of arithmetic expressions. The words or lexical components for such a language are identifiers, numeric constants, and the addition, subtraction, multiplication, division, and exponentiation operators, as well as parentheses and the assignment operator. The syntax for each of these primitive lexical classes is given by the grammatical descriptions:

| | | |
|---|---|---|
| &lt;identifier&gt; | ::= | &lt;name&gt; |
| &lt;name&gt; | ::= | &lt;letter&gt; |
| | | \| &lt;name&gt; &lt;letter&gt; |
| | | \| &lt;name&gt; &lt;digit&gt; |
| &lt;letter&gt; | ::= | A \| B \| C \| D \| E \| F \| G \| H \| I \| J \| K \| L \| M \| N |
| | | \| O \| P \| Q \| R \| S \| T \| J \| V \| W \| X \| Y \| Z |
| &lt;numeric&gt; | ::= | &lt;digit&gt; |
| | | \| &lt;numeric&gt; &lt;digit&gt; |
| &lt;digit&gt; | ::= | 0 \| 1 \| 2 \| 3 \| 4 \| 5 \| 6 \| 7 \| 8 \| 9 |
| &lt;add/sub op&gt; | ::= | + \| − |
| &lt;mult/div op&gt; | ::= | * \| / |
| &lt;exponent op&gt; | ::= | ↑ |
| &lt;(&gt; | ::= | ( |
| &lt;)&gt; | ::= | ) |
| &lt;=&gt; | ::= | = |

The terminals of the grammar (that is, A, B, ..., Z, 0, 1, ..., 9, +, −, *, /, ↑, (, ), =) plus the blank character form the alphabet for our sample language. The non-terminal symbols which appear in the left part of each rule (i.e., <identifier>, <numeric>, <add/sub op>, <mult/div op>, <exponent op>, <(>, <)>, <=>, etc.) represent the lexical classes which the scanner must identify. Once the lexical class of a source form is identified, the class name (or some token representative of the class name) plus the source form is passed on to the parser, which is responsible for the syntactic analysis phase. The class names appear as terminals to the grammar which describes the sentences of the language. It is this grammar which forms the basis of the syntactic analysis phase. For our example language, the grammar for the parser might be:

<assign stat>   ::=  <identifier> <=> <expression>
<expression>    ::=  <term> | <expression> <add/sub op> <term>
<term>          ::=  <form> | <term> <mult/div op> <form>
<form>          ::=  <primary> | <form> <exponent op> <primary>
<primary>       ::=  <identifier> | <numeric> | <(> <expression> <)>

In most instances it is inefficient to pass a lexical class name, such as '<identifier>', to the parser. Instead, a unique representation number is associated with each class and it is this number along with the source form (e.g., the identifier name) which is handed to the parser. For our example language, we adopt the following representation number assignments: <identifier> is 1, <numeric> is 2, <add/sub op> is 3, <mult/div op> is 4, <(> is 5, <)> is 6, <=> is 7, and <exponent op> is 8.

A class of symbols called delimiters must be handled by a scanner, and yet their presence is not passed on to the parser. In our example assignment-statement language, the blank character is such a delimiter (that is, X=A*Z is syntactically equivalent to X = A * Z).

We are now prepared to present an algorithm for scanning a source statement from the assignment statement language given earlier. A modified version of the SPAN composite function with only four parameters is used. Since string replacement is not required, the last two parameters of the original function are not required.

**Algorithm**  SCAN(SOURCE). This algorithm breaks a given source statement SOURCE into tokens, and then prints the tokens and their corresponding representation numbers. CHAR represents the current character being examined in source, TOKEN contains the present token being isolated, and REP_NO contains the representation number of that token. LETTERS and DIGITS are character variables which contain the strings 'ABCDEFGHIJKLMNOPQRSTUVWXYZ' and '0123456789', respectively. The integer variable CURSOR denotes the position of the character being examined in SOURCE. DUMMY is a logical variable which is used to hold the logical value returned by the function SPAN. ALPHA_NUM is a string variable which contains all letters and digits.

1.  [Initialize]
        CURSOR ← 1
        ALPHA_NUM ← LETTERS ○ DIGITS
2.  [Print source statement]
        Write(SOURCE)

3.    [Scan source statement]
      Repeat step 4 while CURSOR ≤ LENGTH(SOURCE)
4.    [Obtain next token]
      If not SPAN(SOURCE, '', CURSOR, TOKEN)
      then    (check for nonblank symbol)
          CHAR ← SUB(SOURCE, CURSOR, 1)
          (isolate next character)
          If NDEX(LETTERS, CHAR) ≠ 0    (check for identifier)
          then    DUMMY ← SPAN(SOURCE, ALPHA_NUM, CURSOR,
                TOKEN)
                Write(1, TOKEN)    (output identifier)
          else    (check for integer)
                If INDEX(DIGITS, CHAR) ≠ 0
                then    DUMMY ← SPAN(SOURCE, DIGITS, CURSOR,
                      TOKEN)
                      Write(2, TOKEN)
                else    (check for +, *, (, ), =, or ↑)
                      REP_NO ← INDEX('+*() = ↑', CHAR)
                      If REP_NO ≠ 0
                      then    Write(REP_NO + 2, CHAR)
                      else    (check for – or /)
                          REP_NO ← INDEX('–/', CHAR)
                          If REP_NO ≠ 0
                          then    Write(REP_NO + 2, CHAR)
                          else    Write('ILLEGAL CHARACTER', CHAR)
          CURSOR ← CURSOR + 1
5.    [Finished]
      Exit                                    ☐

If Algorithm SCAN is called with a source statement '  Z1 = 2+Y', then Z1
= 2+Y is printed in step 2 after the variables CURSOR and ALPHA_NUM are initialized in step 1. In the loop defined in step 3 the initial two blanks are removed
by the SPAN function. On the next try SPAN returns *false* (there is no blank at cursor position 3) and CHAR becomes 'Z'. 'Z' is then identified as a letter and a span is
made which incorporates both 'Z' and '1' in the parameter called TOKEN. A
representation number of 1 and the token string 'Z1' is then printed and control is
transferred back to step 3.

A complete trace of the algorithm for the source statement 'Z1 = 2+Y' yields
the following output:

```
Z1 = 2+Y
 1    Z1
 7    =
 2    2
 3    +
 1    Y
```

Output from the lexical analysis of the source statements 'TAX = RATE *
(INCOME – DEDUCTIONS)' and '1 = XY Z + ↑2' is

```
TAX = RATE * (INCOME – DEDUCTIONS)
 1    TAX
 7    =
```

```
1   RATE
4   *
5   (
1   INCOME
3   −
1   DEDUCTIONS
6   )
1  = XY Z + ↑ 2
2   1
7   =
1   XY
1   Z
3   +
8   ↑
2   2
```

The last example illustrates that the scanner is responsible only for recognizing properly formed lexical units, and not for identifying sentences from the source language. The problem of parsing sentences from a programming language will be discussed in more detail in Sec. 5-2.3.

In some compilers (especially one-pass "student" language compilers), the representation number and source form are passed directly to the parser. The parser uses the class representation number in the parsing routines. The production number corresponding to the reduction made by the parser is passed to a code-generation phase. In this phase, the source form along with the production number are used in the generation of object code which involves specific variable names, constant values, arithmetic operators, etc.

In a multipass compiler, the representation number and source form are often passed to a table-generating routine. This routine generates, in the first pass of the source statements of the program, a number of tables such as an identifier name table, a source statement-number table, a programmer-defined function table, a "macro" or preprocessor table, etc.

Step 4 in Algorithm SCAN is a language-dependent step. It is possible to encode the information relevant to the logical decisions involved in this step into a tabular form. If a new scanner is desired, then the contents of these tables are changed to suit the new language and the general scanning algorithm remains unchanged. These "table-driven" scanners are particularly useful when more than one scanner is needed for a compiler. Such a situation arises when a compiler must handle input from two or more different input devices which have different character sets (e.g., teletype and a card reader).

As a final note on lexical analysis, it should be remarked that we have neglected to discuss two very important functions of a scanner—namely, the removal of comments and the creation of line numbers. Two of the exercises to follow involve these functions.

**Exercises for Sec. 2-5.2**

1. Write a Pascal program which scans source statements from the assignment language discussed in this subsection. The program should handle Pascal-type comments. Of course, comments should be printed by the scanner along with the assignment statements, but no indication of the presence of comments

should be passed to the parser. Therefore,

$$X := \{*SQUARE \text{ of } X\} \ X \uparrow 2;$$

should only generate the following token strings:

$$'1 \ X', \ '6 \ :=', \ '1 \ X', \ '8 \uparrow', \ '2 \ 2'.$$

2. Add the capability of automatically numbering source statements to the scanner in Prob. 1. Therefore, if the first two assignment statements of a program are 'X := Y' and 'Y := Z*4', then they should be output as

    ```
    1  X := Y;
    2  Y := Z*4;
    ```

3. As a term project, write a scanner for a subset of the Pascal language which includes string and numeric assignments, procedures, for loops, begin groups, while do's, if-then-else statements, and formatted I/O statements.

4. As an extension to Prob. 3, add automatic paragraphing to the scanner. With automatic paragraphing, the bodies of procedures and grouping constructs are automatically indented by a certain number of character positions, say four. if, then, and else clauses are automatically aligned vertically. Therefore, if a source statement such as

    ```
    'if x := y
    then begin x := z; y := 0
    end else x := 0;'
    ```

it should be printed as

    ```
    if x = y
    then begin
            x := z;
            y := 0
          end
    else  x := 0;
    ```

by the scanner.

### 2-5.3 KWIC Indexing

An important area in computer science is information retrieval. In information-retrieval applications, a data base, which may contain a wide variety of data struc-tures, is maintained on an on-line basis using large random-access (e.g., disk) files. These files are searched for requested information based on index items generated from a user query. One of the problems associated with information-retrieval sys-tems (and especially automated library systems) is that of creating a good *indexing scheme*.

One method of indexing that is widely used in library systems is the permuted or KWIC (key-word-in-context) indexing scheme. A KWIC index provides the con-text surrounding each occurrence of each word. In practice KWIC indexing is most often applied to phrases, especially titles, selected from the documents of interest. While KWIC indexing allows us to determine the role of a word quickly, it is an indexing method which requires a large amount of storage due to the amount of contextual information that must be stored.

To illustrate this point, let us consider an example involving the title of a certain book "Introduction to Data Structures with Applications." In a KWIC indexing scheme, each item of the phrase (in this case the title) is scanned for keywords and reproduced once in a permuted fashion for each keyword. In our example, the list of permuted indices are:

<u>Introduction</u> to Data Structures with Applications// An
<u>Data</u> Structures with Applications// An Introduction to
<u>Structures</u> with Applications// An Introduction to Data
<u>Applications</u>// An Introduction to Data Structures

We refer to the underscored first word in each index as the *index word*. The set of index words generated from a title form the set of key words for that title (i.e., Introduction, Data, Structures, Applications are the key words in the example). Key words are considered to be those words which impart some meaning as to the nature of the document. Ordinary words such as 'a', 'for', 'to', 'the', 'an', 'and', 'with', 'its', etc. tell little about the subject of a document. In the implementation of a KWIC index generator, keywords are those words which are not the prepositions, conjunctions, pronouns, and, in many instances, the adverbs, adjectives, and verbs which form the ordinary word list.

In the following description of the KWIC generator, it is assumed that the information necessary to generate the indices is stored in four one-dimensional arrays. The first array, ORD_WORDS, holds an ordered list of ordinary words for the index generating system—one word per array location. In the examples used in the discussion to follow, assume that ORD_WORDS contains 'a', 'an', 'and', 'for', 'its', 'the', 'to', and 'with'. The second array, TITLE, contains complete book titles as input to the generator. A third array, KEYWORD, contains an ordered list of the keywords that are present in the titles currently stored in the system. Associated with these keywords, and stored in a fourth array called T_INDEX, is a list of array indices which refer to titles stored in the TITLE array. If a given keyword is stored at position i in the KEYWORD array, then T_INDEX[i] contains a character string which holds the TITLE array indices for all titles possessing that keyword. The array indices in the character string are separated by blank characters.

To illustrate the relationships between the arrays TITLE, T_INDEX, and KEYWORDS, assume TITLE[1], TITLE[2], ..., TITLE[5] are assigned the five titles:

'AN INTRODUCTION TO DATA STRUCTURES WITH APPLICATIONS//'
'AN INTRODUCTION TO PROGRAMMING//'
'PL/I PROGRAMMING WITH APPLICATIONS//'
'A SNOBOL4 PRIMER//'
'A PRIMER FOR LISP PROGRAMMING//'

Then KEYWORD[i] and T_INDEX[i] hold the information as shown in Table 2-5.1 for i ranging from one to the total number of keywords. Therefore, the titles which contain the keyword PROGRAMMING, for example, are TITLE[2], TITLE[3], and TITLE[5].

We now present the Procedure KWIC_GEN which is capable of generating a KWIC index listing for all titles currently entered in the system.

**Procedure** KWIC_GEN(TITLE, ORD_WORD, KEYWORD, T_INDEX). Given the four string vector parameters, this procedure generates a KWIC index ordered lexically by keywords. All TITLE indices for a particular keyword are combined as a single string. Each of these strings is stored as an element of T_INDEX. KEY-

**FIGURE 2-5.1**

| i | KEYWORD | TITLE#S |
|---|---------|---------|
| 1 | 'APPLICATIONS' | '1 3' |
| 2 | 'DATA' | '1' |
| 3 | 'INTRODUCTION' | '1 2' |
| 4 | 'LISP' | '5' |
| 5 | 'PL/I' | '3' |
| 6 | 'PRIMER' | '4 5' |
| 7 | 'PROGRAMMING' | '2 3 5' |
| 8 | 'SNOBOL4' | '4' |
| 9 | 'STRUCTURES' | '1' |

STRING is used to contain the string of indices for the current keyword. INDEX_NO is an integer variable which contains a particular TITLE vector index. KWIC_LINE is a temporary string variable which contains a line of output and I is a counter variable.

1. [Establish loop in which keywords are used as index words]
   Repeat thru step 5 for I = 1, 2, ..., LAST_KEY
2. [Obtain index list for current keyword]
   KEYSTRING ← T_INDEX[I] ○ '□'
3. [Process all title indices in KEYSTRING]
   Repeat thru step 5 while LENGTH(KEYSTRING) > 1
4. [Obtain and delete next title index]
   INDEX_NO ← SUB(KEYSTRING, 1, INDEX(KEYSTRING, '□') − 1)
   KEYSTRING ← SUB(KEYSTRING, INDEX(KEYSTRING, '□') + 1)
5. [Obtain and output KWIC line]
   KWIC_LINE ← TITLE[INDEX_NO]
   CURSOR ← 1
   If FIND(KWIC_LINE, KEYWORD[I], CURSOR, MATCH_STR)
   then    KWIC_LINE ← KEYWORD[I] ○ SUB(KWIC_LINE, CURSOR) ○ '□'
                ○ MATCH_STR
           Write(KWIC_LINE)
   else    Write('ERROR − KEYWORD NOT FOUND IN TITLE')
6. [Finished]
   Return                                                      □

Let us proceed through a partial trace of Procedure KWIC_GEN using the five titles given previously as data. Step 1 sets up a repeat loop for I running from 1 to 9. The first time step 2 is executed, KEYSTRING has the value '1 3 '. In step 3, a check is made to see if all TITLE indices corresponding to a given keyword have been used. INDEX_NO is set to 1 and KEYSTRING is reduced to '3 ' in step 4. In step 5, KWIC_LINE is temporarily set to

'AN INTRODUCTION TO DATA STRUCTURES WITH APPLICATIONS/,'

and then reset, using the FIND function described in Sec. 2-2.3, to

'APPLICATIONS// AN INTRODUCTION TO DATA STRUCTURES WITH '

The while condition in the repeat loop in step 3 is reexamined and the loop is repeated with KEYSTRING equal to '3 '. The output after the loop is completed a second time is

'APPLICATIONS// PL/I PROGRAMMING WITH '

If a complete trace was provided, then the next three and last two items to be printed by the KWIC_GEN routine for the given data would be:

'DATA STRUCTURES WITH APPLICATIONS// AN INTRODUCTION TO '
'INTRODUCTION TO DATA STRUCTURES WITH APPLICATIONS// AN '
'INTRODUCTION TO PROGRAMMING//AN '

.
.
.

'SNOBOL4 PRIMER// A '
'STRUCTURES WITH APPLICATIONS// AN INTRODUCTION TO DATA '

Procedure KWIC_GEN produces a proper KWIC index listing given that the appropriate information is stored in the three arrays TITLE, KEYWORD, and T_INDEX. Algorithm KWIC_CREATE, which we now describe, analyzes the input phrases and creates the three arrays needed in Procedure KWIC_GEN. KEYFIND is used as an index into the array KEYWORD.

**Algorithm** KWIC_CREATE. Given an input sequence of phrases (that is, titles) in the form of character strings and the ordered list of ordinary words, ORD_WORDS, as described earlier, this algorithm constructs the vectors TITLE, KEYWORD, and T_INDEX. PHRASE is a string variable which contains the current title being input. ORD_SEARCH is a function which searches the vector ORD_WORDS to determine whether or not a word in a particular title is an ordinary word. If the word in question is ordinary, its vector index is returned; otherwise, a value of zero is returned. Similarly, KEY_SEARCH is a function which searches the vector KEYWORD to determine whether or not a keyword has previously been encountered in the titles. If it has, the vector index of the keyword is returned; otherwise, the new keyword is inserted appropriately in KEYWORD and the index associated with the position occupied by this keyword is returned. The integer variable LAST_TITLE denotes the index of the last title to be added to the vector TITLE. WORD is an intermediate string variable which contains the current word being processed in a title. KEYIND is an integer variable which is used as an index for vector KEYWORD. BLANKS is a temporary string, and SPAN is used as a procedure because its functional form is not required in this algorithm.

1. [Initialize]
   LAST_TITLE ← 0
2. [Process all titles]
   Repeat thru step 8 while there is still an input title
3. [Read a document title]
   Read(PHRASE)
4. [Remove any leading blanks and append end markers '//' to title]
   SPAN(PHRASE, '□', 1, BLANKS, '', true)
   PHRASE ← PHRASE ○ '//'

5.  [Store current document title]
    LAST_TITLE ← LAST_TITLE + 1
    TITLE[LAST_TITLE] ← PHRASE
6.  [Process all words in current title]
    Repeat thru step 8 while SUB(PHRASE, 1, 2) ≠ '//'
7.  [Scan and remove next word from current title]
    WORD ← SUB(PHRASE, 1, INDEX(PHRASE, '□') – 1)
    PHRASE ← SUB(PHRASE, INDEX(PHRASE, '□') + 1)
    (Remove leading blanks.)
    SPAN(PHRASE, '□', 1, BLANKS, '', true)
8.  [Is WORD a keyword?]
    If ORD_SEARCH(WORD) = 0
    then   KEYIND ← KEY_SEARCH(WORD)
           T_INDEX[KEYIND] ← T_INDEX[KEYIND] ○ '□' ○ LAST_TITLE
9.  [Finished]
    Exit                                                                □

A trace of steps 3 through 8 is as follows. If an input phrase is the title 'A SNOBOL4 PRIMER', then in step 3 of Algorithm KWIC_CREATE, this itle is assigned to the variable PHRASE. If the input phrase has leading blanks, they are removed by the SPAN function, as defined in Sec. 2-2.3, and the markers '//' are concatenated to the end of the value for PHRASE in step 4. PHRASE is stored in the TITLE array at the next open location in step 5. Steps 7 and 8 are repeated until all word forms in the input phrase are examined as to their identity (i.e., whether they are keywords or not). If the word is not a keyword, as in the case of 'A', then a return is made to the repeat statement in step 6. If the word is a keyword, as in the case of 'SNOBOL4', ORD_SEARCH returns a nonzero value and the keyword is placed at its appropriate position in the KEYWORD array by the Algorithm KEY_SEARCH. (Note that both ORD_SEARCH and KEY_SEARCH are left as exercises to be completed at the end of this subsection.) Finally, in step 8, the T_INDEX array is updated by concatenating the TITLE array index onto the end of the other TITLE indices for the given keyword.

The algorithms KWIC_GEN and KWIC_CREATE allow us to store titles, or any type of descriptive phrase, and to produce a KWIC index listing. The KWIC index generator is a simple yet practical application of character-string manipulation. In an exercise to follow, there is an interesting extension to the basic index generator in this subsection.

**Exercises for Sec. 2-5.3**

1.  Given as input a word form assigned to the variable WORD, derive Function ORD_SEARCH which searches the ORD_WORDS array looking for the word form. If the word form is present, its index location in ORD_WORDS is returned; otherwise, a value of zero is returned. (There are a number of search procedures which can be used for ORD_SEARCH and these are discussed in Chap. 6. A simple linear search is a sufficient answer to this question.)

2.  As more and more documents are added to a KWIC-index generating system, it becomes less attractive to receive a KWIC index printout for the complete list of documents. Instead, it is more desirable to receive a KWIC-index listing for those documents which contain in their title (or some other representable

phrase) certain select index words. For example, we might pose a command of the form

LIST KWIC FOR <index word expression>

where <index word expression> is defined to be:

<index word expression> ::= index
| (<index word expression> <oper> index)

<oper>                     ::= OR | AND

The terminal "index" can be any index word we choose to search on. Therefore, example commands are

LIST KWIC FOR PRIMER
LIST KWIC FOR (APPLICATIONS AND PROGRAMMING)
LIST KWIC FOR ((DATA AND STRUCTURES) OR PASCAL)

Write an algorithm or Pascal program which interprets the "LIST KWIC" commands and outputs only the KWIC index terms as specified in the index-term expression for the command.

3. Given as an input parameter a keyword assigned to the variable WORD, construct Function KEY_SEARCH which searches the KEYWORD array looking for the keyword. If the keyword is present, its index location in KEYWORD is returned; otherwise, the keyword is inserted in the KEYWORD array at the appropriate location as determined by the lexical ordering of keywords. Note that space must also be left at the corresponding location in the T_INDEX array to hold the string of TITLE array indexes for keyword. Again, a simple linear search and linear insertion procedure is adequate for this question. Better procedures will be presented in Chap. 6.

## BIBLIOGRAPHY

BOSWELL, F. D., M. J. CARMODY, and T. R. GROVE: "A String Extension for Pascal," A.C.M. Sigsmall Newsletter, vol. 8, no. 4, Nov. 1982, pp. 22-23.

GALLER, B. A., and A. J. PERLIS: "A View of Programming Languages," Addison-Wesley, Reading, Mass., 1970.

GRIES, D.: "Compiler Construction for Digital Computers," John Wiley & Sons, Toronto, 1971.

GRISWOLD, R. E. and M. T. GRISWOLD: "A SNOBOL Primer," Prentice-Hall, Englewood Cliffs, N.J., 1973.

HARRISON, M. C.: "Data Structures and Programming," Scott, Foresman, and Co., Glenview, Ill., 1972.

"IBM System/360 Operating System PL/I(F) Languages Reference Manual," file no. S360-29, order no. GC28-6594.

JENSEN, K. and N. WIRTH: "Pascal User Manual and Report," second edition, Springer-Verlag, New York, 1975.

MARKOV, A. A.: "The Theory of Algorithms" (tr. form Russian), U.S. Dept. of Commerce, Office of Technical Services, no. OTS 60-51085.

NAUR, P. (ed.), "Revised Report on the Algorithm Language ALGOL 60," *Communications of the* ACM, vol. 6, no. 1, Jan. 1963, pp. 1-17.

# 3

# LINEAR DATA STRUCTURES AND
# THEIR SEQUENTIAL STORAGE REPRESENTATION

*The previous chapters have dealt with primitive data structures such as integers, reals, and strings. In this chapter we are concerned with nonprimitive data structures which are linear. A number of possible storage representations for these linear structures will be given. All such representations are based on sequential allocation.*

*The first part of the chapter discusses the concepts and terminology associated with nonprimitive data structures. These structures are classified into arrays, lists, and files. A number of associated operations on certain linear structures are described. The storage representations of arrays in row-major and column-major order are given in Sec. 3-2. Structures and arrays of structures are discussed in Sec. 3-3.*

*An important linear structure, the stack, is discussed in Sec. 3-4. The programming aspects of stacks in PL/I using controlled storage and the associated ALLOCATE and FREE statements are introduced.*

*Section 3-5 describes certain classical applications of stacks such as recursion, the compilation of arithmetic expressions, and stack machines. Recursion is available in many programming languages such as ALGOL 60 and Pascal. The compilation of infix expressions into Polish notation and their subsequent conversion into some object language are important applications in the area of compiler writing. A number of computers such as the PDP-11 and the Burroughs 5000 have stack memories, and some of their properties are described in this section.*

*Another important data structure known as a queue is introduced in Sec. 3-6. Certain variations of a basic queue are also mentioned. A simple application of queues is given in Sec. 3-7. It is concerned with the simulation of a grocery store application and is followed by a discussion of priority queues.*

### 3-1 CONCEPTS AND TERMINOLOGY FOR NONPRIMITIVE DATA STRUCTURES

A brief discussion of the importance of structure in problem solving was given in Sec. 0-1. The often confused distinction between a data structure and a storage structure was also mentioned. Chap. 1 was concerned with the description of primitive data structures such as integers, real numbers, characters, and pointers, and their corresponding storage representations. In Chap. 2, we saw how characters can be combined under concatenation to form a string — a data structure basic to most programming applications. We now proceed to extend our discussion to more complex data structures.

Nonprimitive data structures can be classified as arrays, lists, and files. An *array* is an ordered set which consists of a fixed number of objects. No deletion or insertion operations are performed on arrays. At best, elements can be changed to a value which represents an element to be ignored. The setting of an element in an array to zero to delete it is an example. A *list,* on the other hand, is an ordered set consisting of a variable number of elements to which insertions and deletions can be made.

A list which displays the relationship of adjacency between elements is said to be *linear.* Any other list is said to be *nonlinear.* In the remainder of this chapter we are concerned with linear lists.

Operations performed on lists include those which are performed on arrays. However, there is one important difference in that the size of a list may be changed by updating. Indeed, updating may insert or delete elements, as well as change existing elements. The insertion and deletion of elements in a list is specified by position. For example, we may want to delete the $i$th element of a list or insert a new element before or after the $i$th existing element. Frequently, it may be required to insert or delete an element whose position in a list is based on the values of the other elements in the list (as in sorting). It may be required to insert or delete a given element to or from a list, respectively. Such an element may precede or follow an element having a specified value or satisfying a particular relationship.

There are other important operations besides insertion and deletion that are commonly performed on lists. Each element in a list is composed of one or more *fields.* A field can be considered to be the smallest piece of information that can be referenced in a programming language. A number of operations include the following:

1   Combine two or more lists to form another list.
2   Split a list into a number of other lists.
3   Copy a list.
4   Determine the number of elements in a list.
5   Sort the elements of a list into ascending or descending order, depending on certain values of one or more fields within an element.
6   Search a list for an element which contains a field having a certain value.

These operations will be discussed for various structures throughout the text.

A *file* is typically a large list that is stored in the external memory of a computer (e.g., on magnetic disk). In addition, a file may be used as a repository for list items (commonly called *records*) that are accessed infrequently and/or must be stored between various invocations of a program. In external memory, as opposed to main memory, the time to access different list items may not be equal. As a result, new types of information organizations and access techniques are necessary for files. These new types of organizations, called *file structures,* are the subject of Chap. 7.

In discussing sequential storage structures in this chapter, we will be primarily concerned with the main memory of the conventional digital computer. Main memory is organized into an ordered sequence of words. As was pointed out in Chap. 1, each word contains from 8 to 64 bits and its contents can be referenced by using an address. For efficiency reasons, it is desirable to arrange data in a manner in which a particular element of the data can be referenced by computing its address rather than searching for it.

In Chap. 1 we discussed two possible ways that could be used to obtain an address of an element. The first method of obtaining an address was by using the description of the data being sought. This type of address is known as a computed address. Such a method of obtaining an address is used very extensively in many programming languages to compute the address of an element of an array and in the acquisition of the next instruction to be executed in the object program. The second method of obtaining an address was to store it somewhere in the memory of the computer. This type of address is referred to as a link or pointer address. In FORTRAN the addresses of the actual arguments of a subroutine are stored in the computer memory. The return address which is used by a subroutine to return to the calling program is also stored, and not computed. Certain structures require a combination of computed and link addresses.

In this chapter storage structures based on the computed-address principle will be discussed. The next chapter deals with storage structures based on the link-address technique. In discussing files in Chap. 7, we will be concerned primarily with storage structures on disk and magnetic-tape storage devices.

There are many data structures which can be represented so as to permit the referencing of any element by knowing its position in the structure. The selection operation associated with such a structure is said to possess an *addressing function*. An *addressing function* for a data structure consisting of $n$ elements is a function which maps the $i$th element of the data structure onto an integer between one and $n$. In the case of a vector, the addressing function $f$ maps the $i$th element onto the integer $i$, that is,

$$f(i) = i$$

which is a *linear addressing function*. We are particularly interested in data structures having linear addressing functions that are computationally simple. Addressing functions are discussed further in the next section of this chapter. A very important class of data structures which has a linear addressing function is discussed in Chap. 5. Another associated class of functions, known as *hashing functions*, is briefly introduced in Sec. 4-3.2 and discussed in detail in Chap. 6.

## 3-2 STORAGE STRUCTURES FOR ARRAYS

The simplest data structure that makes use of computed addresses to locate its elements is the one-dimensional array we have called a vector. Normally, a number of (contiguous) memory locations is sequentially allocated to the vector. Assuming that each element requires one word of memory, an n element vector will occupy n consecutive words in memory. A vector size is fixed and, therefore, requires a fixed number of memory locations. In general, a vector A with a subscript lower bound of "one" can be represented pictorially as in Fig. 3-2.1, where $L_0$ is the address of the first word allocated to the first element of A, and c represents the number of words allocated to each element. The address of $A_i$ is given by the following equation:

$$loc(A_i) = L_0 + c * (i - 1)$$

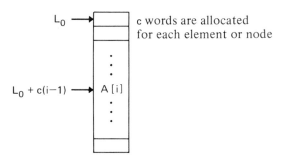

**FIGURE 3-2.1**   Storage representation of a vector.

Let us consider the more general case of representing a vector A whose lower bound for its subscript is given by some variable b.  The location of $A_i$ is then given by

$$loc(A_i) = L_0 + c * (i - b)$$

In FORTRAN, memory allocation is performed at *compile time* where the size of the vector obtained in the DIMENSION statement is saved along with the starting address $L_0$.  The size of a vector cannot be defined in FORTRAN during execution, as can be done in ALGOL and PL/I.  A programming language which can read a value for n at run time and declare a vector of n elements during the execution of the program is said to be able to allocate memory *dynamically*.

A multidimensional array can be represented by an equivalent one-dimensional array.  For example, in FORTRAN a two-dimensional array consisting of two rows and four columns is stored sequentially by columns as

A[1,1] A[2,1] A[1,2] A[2,2] A[1,3] A[2,3] A[1,4] A[2,4]
↑
$L_0$

The address of element A[i,j] can be obtained by evaluating the expression

$$L_0 + (j - 1) * 2 + i - 1$$

For element A[2,3], the address is given as $L_0 + 5$.  In general, for a two-dimensional array consisting of n rows and m columns (which is stored by column), the address of element A[i,j] is given by the linear expression

$$L_0 + (j - 1) * n + (i - 1)$$

In many programming languages, a two-dimensional array will be stored row by row (sometimes referred to as *row-major order*) instead of column by column (*column-major order*).  An array with subscripts having a lower bound of "one" consisting of n rows and m columns will be stored sequentially as

A[1,1] A[1,2] ... A[1,m] A[2,1] A[2,2] ... A[2,m]
... A[n,1] A[n,2] ... A[n,m]

The address of matrix element A[i,j] is given by the expression

$$L_0 + (i - 1) * m + (j - 1)$$

The representation of a two-dimensional array can be generalized to arbitrary lower and upper bounds on its subscripts. Assume that $b_1 \leq i \leq u_1$ and $b_2 \leq j \leq u_2$. The location of element $A_{ij}$ is given by

$$loc(A_{ij}) = L_0 + (i - b_1) * (u_2 - b_2 + 1) + (j - b_2)$$

where each row of A contains $u_2 - b_2 + 1$ elements. For example, the location of $A_{03}$, when $b_1 = -2$, $b_2 = 2$, and $u_2 = 3$, is given as

$$loc(A_{03}) = L_0 + (0 - (-2)) * (3 - 2 + 1) + (3 - 2)$$

$$= L_0 + 5$$

A similar type of formula can be obtained for the representation of a two-dimensional array in column-major order.

Consider the storing of a three-dimensional array B whose typical element is denoted by B[i, j, k] and whose subscript limits are given by $1 \leq i \leq 2$, $1 \leq j \leq 3$, and $1 \leq k \leq 4$. The row-major-order storage representation of this matrix will be

B[1,1,1] B[1,1,2] B[1,1,3] B[1,1,4] B[1,2,1] B[1,2,2] B[1,2,3] B[1,2,4]
B[1,3,1] B[1,3,2] B[1,3,3] B[1,3,4] B[2,1,1] B[2,1,2] B[2,1,3] B[2,1,4]
B[2,2,1] B[2,2,2] B[2,2,3] B[2,2,4] B[2,3,1] B[2,3,2] B[2,3,3] B[2,3,4]

This array is pictorially represented in Fig.3-2.2 as a cube consisting of two planes with each plane having 12 points. If the base address $L_0$ is ignored, the addressing function for the element B[i, j, k] of the array is given as

$$f(i, j, k) = (i - 1) * 12 + (j - 1) * 4 + k - 1$$

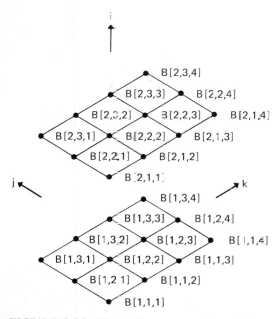

**FIGURE 3-2.2** Pictorial representation of the three-dimensional array B[i, j, k] for $1 \leq i \leq 2$, $1 \leq j \leq 3$, and $1 \leq k \leq 4$.

which is linear in i, j, and k. The lower limits on subscripts i, j, and k above could have been all made zero, and for the same upper limits, the new addressing function would now be

$$f(i, j, k) = 20 * i + 5 * j + k$$

Consider the generalization of the above to an n-dimensional array whose typical element is denoted by $A[s_1, s_2, ..., s_n]$ and subscript limits given by $1 \leq s_i \leq u_i$ for $1 \leq i \leq n$. The storage representation of this array in row-major order will be of the form

$$A[1,1,...,1,1] \; A[1,1,...,1,2] \; ... \; A[1,1,...,1,u_n]$$
$$A[1,1,...,2,1] \; A[1,1,...,2,2] \; ... \; A[1,1,...,2,u_n]$$
$$.......................................................$$
$$A[u_1,u_2,...,u_{n-1},1] \; A[u_1,u_2,...,u_{n-1},2] \; ... \; A[u_1,u_2,...,u_{n-1},u_n]$$

The addressing function for the element $A[s_1,s_2,...,s_n]$ is given as

$$f(s_1,s_2,...,s_n) = u_2 u_3 \cdots u_n(s_1-1) + u_3 u_4 \cdots u_n(s_2-1) + \cdots + u_n(s_{n-1}-1) + (s_n-1)$$

The function can be rewritten in the more convenient form

$$f(s_1,s_2,...,s_n) = \sum_{1 \leq i \leq n} p_i(s_i - 1)$$

where $p_i = \prod_{i < r \leq n} u_r$ and is a constant, and $\sum$ and $\prod$ are symbols which represent mathematical summation and product, respectively. Again, the addressing function is linear. In general form, the row-major addressing function is given by

$$f(s_1,s_2,...,s_n) = \sum_{1 \leq i \leq n} p_i(s_i - b_i)$$

where

$$p_i = \prod_{i < j \leq n} (u_j - b_j + 1) \qquad \text{for } b_i \leq s_i \leq u_i$$

Of course, the same approach could have been used to obtain the addressing function of the n-dimensional array if it had been stored in column-major order instead. Some compilers allocate storage in a sequentially decreasing fashion from the "high" end of memory. Here, we have assumed that memory is allocated in an increasing address sequence. Both methods are equivalent, with the exception that the value of the addressing function f is subtracted from the base location $L_0$.

Although many applications exist where arrays can be used to represent the structural relationships present in the data, there are an increasing number of applications where arrays are just not suitable. We shall briefly discuss such an unsuitable application. Consider the familiar symbol-manipulation problem of performing various operations on polynomials such as addition, subtraction, multiplication, division, differentiation, etc. Let us direct our attention, in particular, to the manipulation of polynomials in two variables. It may be required, for example, to write a program which subtracts polynomial $x^2 + 3xy + y^2 + y - x$ from polynomial $2x^2 + 5xy + y^2$ to give a result of $x^2 + 2xy - y + x$.

We are interested in finding a suitable representation for polynomials so that the operations mentioned above can be performed in a reasonably efficient manner. If we are to manipulate polynomials, it is clear that individual terms must be selected. In particular, we must distinguish between variables, coefficients, and exponents within each term.

It is possible to represent a polynomial as a character string and solve he problem by searching for individual terms and then searching for the various parts of a term. This approach tends to be complex, especially if one tries to program this approach in FORTRAN or Pascal.

A two-dimensional array can be used to represent a polynomial in two variables. In a programming language that permits subscripts to have zero values, the coefficient of the term $x^i y^j$ would be stored in the element identified by row i and column j of the array. If we restrict the size of an array to a maximum of 5 rows and 5 columns, then the powers of x and y in any term of the polynomial must not exceed a value of 4. The array representing polynomial $2x^2 + 5xy + y^2$ is given as

```
0 0 1 0 0
0 5 0 0 0
2 0 0 0 0
0 0 0 0 0
0 0 0 0 0
```

and the array for $x^2 + 3xy + y^2 + y - x$ is

```
 0 1 1 0 0
-1 3 0 0 0
 1 0 0 0 0
 0 0 0 0 0
 0 0 0 0 0
```

Once we have an algorithm for converting the input data to an array representing a polynomial and another for converting an array to an appropriate output form, then addition and subtraction of polynomials reduce to the adding and subtracting of corresponding elements in the two arrays, respectively.

A number of disadvantages are evident in using this representation. In the first case, the array tends to be sparsely filled with nonzero elements. Secondly, the exponents within each polynomial term are restricted in size. In the next chapter, a more efficient representation of such polynomials will be given. This can be accomplished by using a type of storage allocation other than sequential allocation.

In a number of applications involving matrices, there are instances where (because of certain properties) only a part of each matrix need be stored. An example of such an application will now be discussed. Suppose that the solution to the specialized system of equations which follows is sought:

$$A_{11}X_1 \qquad\qquad\qquad = b_1$$
$$A_{21}X_1 + A_{22}X_2 \qquad\qquad = b_2$$
$$A_{31}X_1 + A_{32}X_2 + A_{33}X_3 \qquad = b_3$$

$$\cdots\cdots\cdots\cdots\cdots\cdots\cdots\cdots\cdots\cdots\cdots\cdots$$

$$A_{n1}X_1 + A_{n2}X_2 + \cdots + A_{nn}X_n = b_n$$

This problem can be solved by the usual methods of setting up a two-dimensional array of $n^2$ coefficient elements in storage. In so doing, however, nearly half of the matrix coefficients are not used. We could solve a larger system of equations if we could represent this "triangular" array by an equivalent one-dimensional array. In the given system, there are $[n(n + 1)]/2$ coefficient elements. Therefore, a vector representation must contain at least an equivalent number of elements.

The elements of the triangular array can be stored as a vector in the order

$$A_{11}\ A_{21}\ A_{22}\ A_{31}\ A_{32}\ A_{33}\ \cdots\ A_{nn}$$

i.e., row by row. It is easily verified (assuming $A_{11}$ is at location 1) that the addressing function for element $A_{ij}$ is given by

$$\frac{(i-1)*i}{2} + j$$

For example, the addressing function yields $[(3-1)(3)]/2 + 1 = 4$ for the element $A_{31}$. The addressing function is not linear but quadratic. It is still a simple addressing function. Symmetric arrays which have every $A_{ij} = A_{ji}$ can also be represented in the same manner.

Using this representation for a triangular matrix, we can formulate an algorithm which solves the system of equations.

**Algorithm** TRIANGULAR. Given a system of N equations whose coefficient matrix A is triangular and is stored in a vector R and the right-hand side vector B, this algorithm obtains the solution vector X. SUM is a temporary variable. I and M are integer variables.

1. [Compute and print X[1]]
       X[1] ← B[1] / R[1]
       Write(X[1])
2. [Repeat for all values of the row index]
       Repeat thru step 5 for I = 2, 3, ..., N
3. [Initialize SUM]
       SUM ← 0
4. [Repeat for all values of the column index]
       Repeat for M = 1, 2, ..., I − 1
           SUM ← SUM + R[I * (I − 1) / 2 + M] * X[M]
5. [Calculate and output X[I]]
       X[I] ← (B[I] − SUM) / R[I * (I + 1) / 2]
       Write(X[I])
6. [Finished]
       Exit                                                                   □

The algorithm is easy to follow. $X_1$ is first computed from the first equation and then substituted in the second to obtain $X_2$, and so on.

Another common application is one in which most (greater than 95 percent) of the elements of a large matrix are zeros. In such a case, only the nonzero elements need be stored along with their row and column subscripts. A representation of a matrix based on this idea will be given in Sec. 5-3.1.

**Exercises for Sec. 3-2**

1. A dynamically declared array A is defined with row subscripts varying from 0 to N − 1 and column subscripts varying from 1 to 6. Give the storage mapping function to map A into memory assuming column-major storage.
2. Assume that 4 bytes of storage are required to hold each element of the following Pascal array:

       **var** values : **array** [1..8,1..3] **of** integer;

   Assuming further that storage for the array begins at byte 2000 in memory, give the actual address of element *values [4,2]*.

3. Consider the Pascal program given in Fig. 3-2.3. In the program, he 2d column of *a* is associated with the vector *b*. In procedure *p*, *b[i]* must address the appropriate location of an array *a*. Assuming that each integer value occupies 4 bytes, give the expression for the location of *b[i]* in terms of *i* and the base address of *a*.

4. Consider a three dimensional array X whose subscript limits are

$$1 \leq i \leq 3, \quad 1 \leq j \leq 3, \quad -1 \leq k \leq 0$$

Give the addressing function for the element X[i, j, k] where the storage representation is in row-major order.

## 3-3 STRUCTURES AND ARRAYS OF STRUCTURES

A detailed discussion of certain primitive data structures such as the integer, real number, and character was given in Chap. 1. A number of possible representations of these primitive structures in the main memory of a typical digital computer (i.e., possible storage structures) was also described. We will now turn to the representation in storage of more complex data structures. Actually, a complex (nonprimitive)

---

```
type vector = array [1..4] of integer;

var a : array [1..3] of vector;
    { a is actually a 4x3 array of integers }
    .
    .
    .

procedure p (var b : vector);

    var i : integer;

    begin
       .
       .
       .

          b[i] := i;
       .
       .
       .

    end; { p }

begin {main}
   .
   .
   .

   p( a[2] ); {call to procedure p}
   .
   .
   .

end.
```

**FIGURE 3-2.3**

---

data structure can be considered to consist of a structured set of primitive data structures. For example, a vector may consist of an ordered set of integers.

Recall that we have called integers, real numbers, and character elements primitive because the instruction repertoire of a computer has instructions which will manipulate these primitive structures. We can perform the common arithmetic operations on numbers. A word which contains a number of characters can be modified by using a number of machine-language instructions.

Let us concern ourselves with a nonprimitive yet very simple data structure — a complex number. A complex number is not considered a primitive since very few computers, if any, have machine-language instructions which add, subtract, multiply, and divide complex numbers. Many higher-level languages, however, such as PL/I and FORTRAN, permit the handling of complex numbers. Before we comment on the programming aspects of complex arithmetic, the definitions of the four complex operations are given.

Let $U = x + yi$ and $V = m + ni$ be two complex numbers where $i = \sqrt{-1}$ and x, y, m, and n denote real numbers. Then the complex arithmetic operations which can be performed on these numbers are defined as follows:

$$U \oplus V = (x + m) + (y + n)i$$

$$U \ominus V = (x - m) + (y - n)i$$

$$U \circledast V = (x * m - y * n) + (x * n + y * m)i$$

$$U \oslash V = (x * m + y * n) / (m * m + n * n) +$$

$$(y * m - x * n) / (m * m + n * n)i$$

where the operators $\oplus$, $\ominus$, $\circledast$. and $\oslash$ denote complex addition, subtraction, multiplication, and division, respectively. From this it is clear that complex numbers can be used in complex arithmetic operations using the ordinary arithmetic operators. Note, however, that the multiplication of two complex numbers, for example, consists of a sequence of many (six) machine-language instructions, while in the case of real numbers, it consists of only one such instruction. The same applies for the remaining arithmetic operators. Also, a complex number is considered to consist of an ordered pair of real numbers. Each number in this ordered pair is treated differently.

The trend in certain modern programming languages is to make available to the programmer a number of primitive operators and data structures. The programmer then uses these primitives to define additional more powerful operators and data structures. Among the languages which possess this facility are ALGOL 68 and ADA.

At this point our algorithmic notation will be expanded to accommodate structures (or records) and arrays of structures. As an example, the structure for a complex number can be specified in the following manner:

```
1 Z
  2 R real
  2 I real
```

The structure which consists of two real variables R and I is a hierarchical collection of three names. The hierarchical information is given by the level numbers (1 and 2 in the example). The name of the entire hierarchy (specified by a level number 1) is Z. The names at the bottom of the hierarchy (specified by a level number 2) are R and I that are considered to be indivisible data or fields that are real numbers.

The current structure can be interpreted as a complex number with R and I representing the real and imaginary parts of a complex number, respectively.

Suppose that we specify an additional structure X that is similar to Z in composition as follows:

```
1 X
    2 R real
    2 I real
```

Now assume that we want to refer to the variable R in structure X. How can this be accomplished? If we simply refer to R, there is an ambiguity since R is a variable name in the two structures X and Z. In order to make the desired reference unambiguous or unique, the qualified name X.R specifies that a part of structure X is being selected. The period separates the qualifier (X) from the variable being qualified (R). This name-qualification approach avoids the necessity of having to create different variable names for essentially the same class of items, each item of which may be associated with a different but similar hierarchical structure.

The two structures just described each have two component variables which are of the same type, i.e., real. In general, however, structures can be described whose components are of mixed type. As an example, the following statement creates a simplified structure for an employee:

```
1 EMPLOYEE
    2 NAME
        3 FIRST string
        3 M_I string
        3 LAST string
    2 ADDRESS
        3 STREET string
        3 CITY string
        3 PROVINCE string
    2 DEDUCTIONS
        3 NO_OF_DED integer
        3 DEDUCTION_NAME(5) string
        3 AMOUNT(5) real
```

The name of the structure is EMPLOYEE. Such a structure is called a major structure. It can be used to refer to the whole structure. EMPLOYEE.NAME refers to the part of the structure dealing with the employee's name and is called a minor structure. The names EMPLOYEE.NAME.FIRST, EMPLOYEE.NAME.M_I, and EMPLOYEE.NAME.LAST refer to first name, middle initial, and last name of an employee, respectively, and are called fields. As mentioned earlier fields cannot be further subdivided. Similarly, EMPLOYEE.ADDRESS is a minor structure which refers to the employee's address. Finally, EMPLOYEE.DEDUCTIONS refers to a minor structure consisting of three fields (NO_OF_DED, DEDUCTION_NAME, and AMOUNT) which describes an employee's deductions. Note that two parts of the DEDUCTIONS structure are arrays. The first array (DEDUCTION_NAME) is a character array, while the second (AMOUNT) is a numeric array. The qualified name of the deduction array is

EMPLOYEE.DEDUCTIONS.DEDUCTION_NAME

To refer to the Ith deduction of this array, we use

EMPLOYEE.DEDUCTIONS.DEDUCTION_NAME[I]

Observe that only fields and arrays have data types. In other words, major and minor structures cannot have data types. Also note that hierarchy of the items shown in the previous example can be viewed as having different levels. At the highest level (i.e., level 1) is the major structure name. At an intermediate level are substructures or minor structures. Each substructure name at a deeper level is given a greater number to specify the level depth. Fields within a minor structure must be given a higher level number than that of the structure. Finally, the indentation of level numbers in the declaration of a structure is used only to improve the readability of the structure. Moreover, the level numbers do not have to be successive. Each item, however, must be assigned a higher number than that of the level it is subdividing.

The notion of an array has been illustrated widely throughout the book. Their storage representations were discussed in the previous section. A sometimes undesirable property of an array is that all of its elements must be of the same data type. As mentioned earlier, the parts of a structure can be nonhomogeneous, i.e., they can be of different data types. We now extend the notion of a structure to include arrays of structures.

An *array of structures* is simply an array whose elements are structures. These elements have identical names, levels, and subparts. For example, if a structure MONTH_SALES was used to represent the sales performance of a salesperson for each month of the year, it might be declared as follows:

```
1 MONTH_SALES(12)
    2 SALESPERSON
        3 NAME string
        3 REGION string
    2 SALES_DETAIL
        3 QUOTA real
        3 SALES real
        3 COMMISSION real
```

Thus, we can refer to the sales data for the month of May by specifying MONTH_SALES[5]. Parts of the May sales are referred to by SALESPERSON[5] and SALES_DETAIL[5]. SALES_DETAIL.SALES[2] (or equivalently, SALES_DETAIL[2].SALES), which refers to the sales for the month of February, is called a *subscripted qualified name*. This extension to the algorithmic terminology will be used where required in subsequent algorithms throughout the remainder of the book.

Pascal does not permit the programmer to define additional operations in terms of primitive operators, but it does permit the definition of data structures in terms of primitive data structures. Pascal contains certain basic data structures such as characters, integers, real numbers, arrays, and nonhomogeneous data aggregates called *structures*. Certain aspects of programmer-defined data structures will be discussed throughout the book. Let us now simulate complex arithmetic by using Pascal structures. Such structures can be extended to an array of structures.

The declaration statement

```
type complex =
        record
            r,
            i : real
        end;
var z : complex;
```

creates a new data type *complex*, consisting of two fields *r* and *i*, each of which can store real values. The variable *z* is defined to be a structure of type *complex* and is made up of two fields. Thus, *z* can be interpreted as a complex number as mentioned earlier.

Suppose that we declare two additional complex number structures called *x* and *y* using the statement

    x,y : complex

The name-qualification approach used in the algorithmic notation also holds for Pascal. Note, however, that even if no ambiguity may occur, the qualifier must still be given in Pascal. For example, for the complex number $-1.5 + 2.3$, where $i = \sqrt{-1}$, the sequence of assignment statements

    z.r := -1.5;
    z.i := 2.3;

assigns the complex number $-1.5 + 2.3i$ to the structure *z*.

The writing of fully qualified names in Pascal can soon become tedious. Pascal, however, provides a statement for use with records that alleviates this problem. Such a statement is the "with statement." Within the "scope" of a with statement field names may be denoted by the field identifiers alone. For example, the previous structure *z* can be assigned a complex number as follows:

    with z do
        begin
            r := -1.5;
            i := 2 3
        end;

Note the fields *r* and *i* are within the scope of the structure variable *z*.

It is an interesting exercise to formulate a procedure for simulating the addition of two complex numbers. Let us assume that this procedure is to have three structure variables. as previously described, called *a*, *b*, and *c*. The procedure of Fig. 3-3.1 simulates the desired addition. The mainline statement

    cadd (x,y,z)

invokes the procedure, and the desired result is placed in the real and imaginary parts of the structure *z*. Similar procedures can be written to simulate other complex arithmetic operations.

---

```
procedure cadd (var a,b,c : complex);
{ This procedure adds the complex numbers a and b, which are stored
  in structures, and returns the result through the parameter c }

begin
    c.r := a.r + b.r;
    c.i := a.i + b.i
end;
```

**FIGURE 3-3.1**    Pascal procedure to simulate complex number addition.

---

The structures described in this example each have two variables which are of the same type. As an example of a nonhomogeneous structure, the statement in Fig. 3-3.2 creates a simplified structure for an employee. The names of the structures or record data types are *addresstype, deductype,* and *employeetype.* Within *employeetype,* the fields *address* and *deductions* are defined to be of types *addresstype* and *deductype,* respectively, which are both structures. The *name* field is also defined to be a structure, but the declaration for this structure is given immediately following the identifier *name.* This example illustrates two different methods of nesting structures or records within other records.

Pascal also allows arrays of structures. An array of structures is simply an array whose elements are structures. These elements have identical names, levels, and subparts. For example, if a structure *monthsales* were used to represent the sales performance of a salesperson for each month of the year, it might be declared as in Fig. 3-3.3. Subscripted qualified names in Pascal are of the same form as that described for the algorithmic notation outlined above.

As an application of an array of structures, let us consider a simplified system for gathering and reporting student grades. Let us assume that the data are comprised of two parts. The first part contains the number of all students enrolled in courses followed by the details (such as student name, student number, and

```pascal
type string = array [1..10] of char;

    addresstype =
        record
            street,
            city : array [1..20] of char;
            province : array [1..15] of char
        end;

    deductype =
        record
            number : integer;
            name : array [1..10] of string;
            amount : array [1..5] of integer
        end;

    employeetype =
        record
            name :
                record
                    first : array [1..10] of char;
                    mi : char;
                    last : array [1..19] of char
                end;
            address : addresstype;
            deductions : deductype
        end;
var employee : employeetype;
```

**FIGURE 3-3.2**   A nonhomogeneous structure.

```
var monthsales : array [1..12] of
      record
            salesperson :
                  record
                        name : array [1..30] of char;
                        region : array [1..5] of char
                  end;
            salesdetail :
                  record
                        quota,
                        sales,
                        commission : real
                  end
      end
```

**FIGURE 3-3.3**   An array of structures.

address) for each student in student number order. The second part of the data specifies the number of courses whose examination results are being reported, followed by the examination results for each course. The results of each course contain the course name and the course enrollment. A list of student descriptions (with grades) follows its course description. For example, an outline of the data which describe a total of 100 students enrolled in three courses follows (comments are enclosed in parentheses):

```
100 (number of students)
'Shane McDonald' 1 '2503 Blain Ave' 'Saskatoon' 'Sask' 'S7J 2B7'
      .
      .           (student details in student number order)
      .

'Janelle Harms' 100 '123 Elm St' 'Yorkton' 'Sask' 'S9K 5E6'
3 (number of courses)
'CMPT 180A' 60      (first course)
1 'Shane McDonald' 91

      .

      .

72 'Brad Willems' 43
'CMPT 181B' 40      (second course)
3 'Jim Tubman' 76

      .

      .

      .
90 'Marvin Paetsch' 55
'CMPT 212A' 25      (third course)
17 'Tim Brecht' 65

      .

      .

      .
75 'Doug Murray' 86
```

---

```
type string = array [1..10] of char;
    studentdata =
        record
            name : array [1..20] of char;
            number : integer;
            address :
                record
                    street : array [1..20] of char;
                    city : array [1..15] of char;
                    province : array [1..15] of char;
                    postalcode : array [1..7] of char
                end;
            transcript :
                record
                    numcourses : integer;
                    coursename : array [1..5] of string;
                    grade : array [1..5] of integer
                end
        end;
var student : array [1..100] of studentdata;
```

**FIGURE 3-3.4**   Array of structures for grade example.

---

The statements given in Fig. 3-3.4 define an array of structures for representing the personal and course data for 100 students.  Observe that the number of elements in the array of structures is specified by the number of students taking courses. Also, the transcript associated with each student consists of the number of courses he or she has taken (*numcourses*) and the course descriptions.  Each course description contains a course name and a grade for that course.  We assume that each student cannot take more than five courses.  The vectors *coursename* and *grade* represent the course names and the associated grades, respectively.

A general algorithm for constructing the array of structures from the input data given in the form described earlier follows:

1. Input number of students
2. Repeat for each student
       input student's name, number and address
       initialize transcript portion of the student's record
3. Input number of courses
4. Repeat through step 6 for each course
5. Input course title and class size
6. Repeat for each student in this class
       input student in this class
       update transcript portion of student's record
7. Output student file

For convenience, we assume that the student numbers are sequentially ordered from 1 to *numstudents*.  In this way a particular student number can be used directly to access that student's record in the array of structures.

The Pascal program given in Fig. 3-3.5 performs the required task.  Two subprograms are used in the program, the function *min* and the procedure *readstr*. The function *min* accepts as parameters two integer values and returns the smaller of the two. The procedure *readstr* reads in a string from the file data and stores it in *instr*. The following variables are needed due to the use of the *readstr* procedure:

| | |
|---|---|
| *instr* | the string read in from the data file by *readstr* |
| *len* | the length of the string read in from the data file by *readstr* |
| *k* | index to a particular character in *instr* |

In languages such as PL/I, it is possible to read directly in a string from a data file. However, Pascal does not support this. It is possible, however, to read in characters one at a time; *readstr* uses this capability. It begins by scanning to the first quotation mark (′), then reads in and stores everything up to the next quotation mark. This allows strings and numbers to be mixed in the file.

After returning from the procedure, the integer variable *len* contains the length of the string read in. This may then be used to assign the string to the variable desired. For example, with *name* defined as **array** [1..20] **of** char, and *k* integer.

```
readstr;
len := min(len,20);   { can't exceed size of name }
for k := 1 to len do
     name[k] := instr[k];
for k := len+1 to 20 do
     name[k] := ' ';
```

reads in a string, assigns it to *name*, and pads *name* with blanks.

**Exercises for Sec. 3-3**

1.  One-dimensional arrays and structures can each be thought of as a group of items. What are the principal differences between them? (Be sure to include address calculations for access of an item.)

2.  Consider the following Pascal declaration, where *n* and *m* are integer constants.

    ```
    type emptype =
            record
                    name : array [1..n] of char;
                    adr  : array [1..m] of char
            end;

            var emp : array [1..100] of emptype;
    ```

    Suppose the address of the beginning (first byte) of this array of structures is denoted as *BASE*. Note that each *name* requires *n* bytes of storage and each *adr* requires *m* bytes of storage.

    a) Draw a diagram of the way *emp* is stored in memory.
    b) Express the location of the first byte of the array *emp[i].adr* in terms of *BASE*, *i*, *n*, and *m*.

3.  A western farm currently produces several feed grains. In particular, wheat, barley, oats, rapeseed, and flax are produced. The production level (in bushels) and the price per bushel (in dollars and cents) received during the year are recorded. Use a structure to describe the data.

4.  A university book store maintains a list of up to twenty requests for any book which is currently out of stock. The information kept for such a book consists

```
program grade ( data , output );
{ This program inputs a series of students
  and the course lists for the students, storing the
  student statistics in an array of structures. }

const arraysize = 10;     { total number of students possible }
      namelen = 20;       { maximum length of student name }
      streetlen = 20;     { maximum length of street address }
      citylen = 15;       { maximum length of city name }
      provlen = 15;       { maximum length of province name }
      codelen = 7;        { maximum length of postal code }
      courselen = 10;     { maximum length of course name }
      cardlen = 80;       { maximum length of string read in
                            - it is the length of one line }

type string = array [1..courselen] of char;
     studentdata =
        record  { structure for students }
            name : array [1..namelen] of char;
            number : integer;
            address :
                record
                    street : array [1..streetlen] of char;
                    city : array [1..citylen] of char;
                    province : array [1..provlen] of char;
                    postalcode : array [1..codelen] of char
                end;
            transcript :
                record
                    numcourses : integer;
                    coursename : array [1..5] of string;
                    grade : array [1..5] of integer
                end
        end;

var data : text;       { the input file }
    numstudents,       { number of students }
    classsize,         { size of class }
    studentnum,        { student number }
    mark,              { student grade }
    courses,           { number of courses }
    temp,              { number of courses student is taking }
    len,               { length of string read from data file }
    i,j,k : integer;   { counted loop variables }
    coursetitle : array [1..courselen] of char;
                       { title of course }
    studentname : array [1..namelen] of char;
                       { student name }
    student : array [1..arraysize] of studentdata;
                       { array structure for the students }
```

**FIGURE 3-3.5**    Program *grade*.

```
instr : array [1..cardlen] of char;
                    { the string read in from data file }
```

**function** min(par1, par2: integer): integer;
{ This procedure returns the lower value of the two parameters. }

```
begin
    if par1 < par2
    then min := par1
    else min := par2
end;  { min }
```

**procedure** readstr;
{ This procedure reads a string in from the file data. The string
  is enclosed in single quotation marks, and may not extend over
  more than one data line. Upon return from readstr, the string
  read in is contained in the variable instr, and the length of
  this string is in len. }

**var** ch : char;  { the current input character }

```
begin
    len := 0;

    { scan to first quotation mark }
    repeat
        read(data, ch)
    until ch = #'#;

    { read in the string, up to the last quotation mark }
    repeat
        read(data, ch);
        if ch <> #'#
        then begin
                len := len + 1;
                instr[len] := ch
            end
    until ch = #'#
end;  { readstr }
```

**FIGURE 3-3.5**  (Continued)

---

of the book title (80 characters), book price (in dollars and cents), and the
requests for the book. Each request consists of a person's name (40 characters)
and address (100 characters). Use a structure to describe a book with its associated information.

5.  Use a Pascal structure to represent each of the following documents.
    a)  Airline ticket                  d)  Driver's license
    b)  Blue Cross or Medicare card     e)  Student identification card
    c)  Gasoline credit card

Make realistic assumptions about the contents of each document.

```
begin  { main program }

    { input enrolled students }
    reset(data);
    read(data, numstudents);
    for i := 1 to numstudents do
        begin
            readstr;
            len := min(len, namelen);
            { This statement ensures that the name read does not
              exceed the max. length of the input variable. }

            for k := 1 to len do
                student[i].name[k] := instr[k];
            for k := len + 1 to namelen do
                student[i].name[k] := ' ';

            read(data, student[i].number);

            readstr;
            len := min(len, streetlen);
            for k := 1 to len do
                student[i].address.street[k] := instr[k];
            for k := len + 1 to streetlen do
                student[i].address.street[k] := ' ';

            readstr;
            len := min(len, citylen);
            for k := 1 to len do
                student[i].address.city[k] := instr[k];
            for k := len + 1 to citylen do
                student[i].address.city[k] := ' ';

            readstr;
            len := min(len, provlen);
            for k := 1 to len do
                student[i].address.province[k] := instr[k];
            for k := len + 1 to provlen do
                student[i].address.province[k] := ' ';

            readstr;
            len := min(len, codelen);
            for k := 1 to len do
                student[i].address.postalcode[k] := instr[k];
            for k := len + 1 to codelen do
                student[i].address.postalcode[k] := ' ';

            student[i].transcript.numcourses := 0;
```

**FIGURE 3-3.5**   (Continued)

```
            for j := 1 to 5 do
                begin
                    for k := 1 to courselen do
                        student[i].transcript.coursename[j][k] := ' ';
                    student[i].transcript.grade[j] := 0
                end
        end;  { counted loop of i }

    { process courses offered }
    read(data, courses);
    for i := 1 to courses do
        begin

            readstr;
            len := min(len, courselen);
            for k := 1 to len do
                coursetitle[k] := instr[k];
            for k := len + 1 to courselen do
                coursetitle[k] := ' ';

            read(data, classsize);

            for j := 1 to classsize do
                begin

                    read(data, studentnum);

                    readstr;
                    len := min(len, namelen);
                    for k := 1 to len do
                        studentname[k] := instr[k];
                    for k := len + 1 to namelen do
                        studentname[k] := ' ';

                    read(data, mark);

                    student[studentnum].transcript.numcourses
                        := student[studentnum].transcript.numcourses
                            + 1;
                    temp :=
                        student[studentnum].transcript.numcourses;

                    for k := 1 to courselen do
                        student[studentnum].transcript.coursename[temp][k]
                            := coursetitle[k];

                    student[studentnum].transcript.grade[temp]
                        := mark

                end
        end;
```

**FIGURE 3-3.5**   (Continued)

```
      { output array of structures }
      for i := 1 to numstudents do
         begin
             writeln('Name: ', student[i].name, ' Student number: ',
                 student[i].number: 5);
             writeln('Address: ', student[i].address.street);
             writeln(' ': 9, student[i].address.city, ', ',
                 student[i].address.province, ' ');
             writeln(' ': 9, student[i].address.postalcode);
             writeln;
             writeln(' ': 9, 'Course Name', ' ': 4, 'Grade');
             for j := 1 to student[i].transcript.numcourses do
                 writeln(' ': 10, student[i].transcript.coursename[j],
                     ' ': 5, student[i].transcript.grade[j]: 3);
             writeln
         end

end.   { of program }
```

```
Name: Shane McDonald      Student number:    1
Address: 2503 Blain Ave
         Saskatoon      , Sask
         S7J 2B7

         Course Name   Grade
            CMPT 180A      91
            CMPT 212A      79
            CMPT 228B      87
            CMPT 313B      69

Name: Eric Neufeld        Student number:    2
Address: 123 Elm St
         Yorkton       , Sask
         S9K 5E6

         Course Name   Grade
            CMPT 180A      85
            CMPT 181B      79
            CMPT 212A      93
            CMPT 220B      77
            CMPT 313B      98

Name: Tim Ayers           Student number:    3
Address: 19 Sloughwater Cres
         Regina        , Sask
         S2N 5C9
```

**FIGURE 3-3.5**   (Continued)

Course Name    Grade
   CMPT 181B    54
   CMPT 220B    66
   CMPT 377A    68

Name: John Johnstone    Student Number:    4
Address: 2 Madison Cres
   Prince Albert  , Sask
   S3K 4P7

Course Name    Grade
   CMPT 181B    49

Name: Jennifer Murphy    Student number:    5
Address: 1137 117th St
   Toronto        , Ontario
   P3J 7F6

Course Name    Grade
   CMPT 180A    73
   CMPT 181B    77
   CMPT 220B    83

**FIGURE 3-3.5**  (Continued)

---

6.  A liquor store has the following kinds of alcoholic beverages on hand:

      50 brands of wine of which:
          10 brands are champagne
          5 brands are sherry
          20 brands are red
          10 brands are white
          5 brands are sparkling
      15 brands of whiskey of which:
          6 brands are rye
          6 brands are scotch
          3 brands are bourbon
      10 brands of rum
      5 brands of cognac
      7 brands of gin
      5 brands of vodka

Design a structure to store this information.

## 3-4 STACKS

One of the most important linear data structures of variable size is the stack. The first subsection introduces the concepts associated with this structure. Next, the associated insertion and deletion algorithms for a stack are given. The vector representation of a stack is described. The programming aspects of stacks in PL/I using CONTROLLED storage and the ALLOCATE and FREE statements are introduced.

### 3-4.1 Definitions and Concepts

In the most general form of a linear list, we are allowed to delete an element from and insert an element to any position in the list. An important subclass of lists permits the insertion or deletion of an element to occur only at one end. A linear list belonging to this subclass is called a *stack*. The insertion operation is referred to as "push," and the deletion operation as "pop." The most and least accessible elements in a stack are known as the *top* and *bottom* of the stack, respectively. Since insertion and deletion operations are performed at one end of a stack, the elements can only be removed in the opposite order from that in which they were added to the stack. This phenomenon will be observed in conjunction with recursive functions in Sec. 3-5.1, and such a linear list is frequently referred to as a *LIFO* (last-in, first-out) list.

A common example of a stack phenomenon, which permits the selection of only its end element, is a pile of trays in a cafeteria. These are supported by some kind of spring action in such a manner that a person desiring a tray finds that only one is available to him or her at the surface of the tray counter. The removal of the top tray causes the load on the spring to be lighter and the next tray to appear at the surface of the counter. A tray which is placed on the pile causes the entire pile to be pushed down and that tray to appear above the tray counter. Such an arrangement of trays is shown in Fig. 3-4.1.

Another familiar example of a stack is a railway system for shunting cars, as shown in Fig. 3-4.2. In this system, the last railway car to be placed on the stack is the first to leave. Using repeatedly the insertion and deletion operations permits the cars to be arranged on the output railway line in various orders.

The update operation associated with a stack may be restricted to the examination of the top element of a stack with a view to altering (not inserting or deleting) it. This operation is sometimes extended to other elements of the structure (in addition to the top element of a stack).

### 3-4.2 Operations on Stacks

Initially, the operations on a stack are simulated by using a vector consisting of some large number of elements which should be sufficient in number to handle all possible insertions likely to be made to the stack. A representation of such an allocation scheme is given in Fig. 3-4.3.

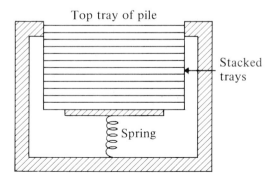

**FIGURE 3-4.1**  A cafeteria-tray holder.

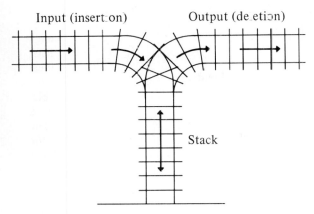

**FIGURE 3-4.2** A railway shunting system representation of a stack.

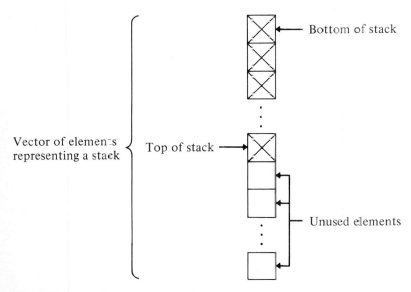

**FIGURE 3-4.3** Representation of a stack by a vector.

A pointer TOP keeps track of the top element in the stack. Initially, when the stack is empty, TOP has a value of zero and when the stack contains a single element, TOP has a value of "one," and so on. Each time a new element is inserted in the stack, the pointer is incremented by "one" before the element is placed on the stack. The pointer is decremented by "one" each time a deletion is made from the stack.

An alternative, and for our purposes, a more suitable representation of a stack is given in Fig. 3-4.4. The rightmost occupied element of the stack represents its top element. The leftmost element of the stack represents its bottom element.

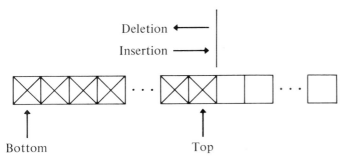

**FIGURE 3-4.4**  Alternative representation of a stack.

The algorithm for inserting an element in a stack follows.

**Procedure** PUSH(S, TOP, X). This procedure inserts an element X to the top of a stack which is represented by a vector S containing N elements with a pointer TOP denoting the top element in the stack.

1.  [Check for stack overflow]
        If TOP ⩾ N
        then   Write('STACK OVERFLOW')
                Return
2.  [Increment TOP]
        TOP ← TOP + 1
3.  [Insert element]
        S[TOP] ← X
4.  [Finished]
        Return                                                    □

The first step of this algorithm checks for an overflow condition. If such a condition exists, then the insertion cannot be performed and an appropriate error message results.
    The algorithm for deleting an element from a stack is given as follows.

**Function** POP(S, TOP). This function removes the top element from a stack which is represented by a vector S and returns this element. TOP is a pointer to the top element of the stack.

1.  [Check for underflow on stack]
        If TOP = 0
        then   Write('STACK UNDERFLOW ON POP')
                take action in response to underflow
                Exit
2.  [Decrement pointer]
        TOP ← TOP − 1
3.  [Return former top element of stack]
        Return(S[TOP + 1])                                        □

An underflow condition is checked for in the first step of the algorithm. If there is an underflow, then some appropriate action should take place. In many applications involving stacks, an underflow may occur repeatedly and is checked for as elements are inserted on and deleted from the stack.

Another algorithm commonly used is one to obtain the value of the $i$th element from the top of a stack without deleting it.

**Function** PEEP(S, TOP, I).   Given a vector S (consisting of N elements) representing a sequentially allocated stack, and a pointer TOP denoting the top element of the stack, this function returns the value of the Ith element from the top of the stack. The element is not deleted by this function.

1.  [Check for stack underflow]
       If TOP − I + 1 ≤ 0
       then   Write('STACK UNDERFLOW ON PEEP')
              take action in response to underflow
              Exit
2.  [Return Ith element from top of stack]
       Return(S[TOP − I + 1])                                                    □

Note that the first step of the algorithm checks for a possible underflow due to some improper value of I.

A fourth algorithm which changes the contents of the $i$th element from the top of a stack is also useful.

**Procedure** CHANGE(S, TOP, X, I).   As before, a vector S (consisting of N elements) represents a sequentially allocated stack and a pointer TOP denotes the top element of the stack. This procedure changes the value of the Ith element from the top of the stack to the value contained in X.

1.  [Check for stack underflow]
       If TOP − I + 1 ≤ 0
       then   Write('STACK UNDERFLOW ON CHANGE')
              Return
2.  [Change Ith element from top of stack]
       S[TOP − I + 1] ← X
3.  [Finished]
       Return                                                                   □

Let us now consider a simple example which involves the use of a stack. The set

$$L = \{ wcw^R \mid w \; \varepsilon \; \{a, b\}^* \}$$

(where $w^R$ is the reverse of w) defines a language which contains an infinite set of strings. For example, if w = ab, then $w^R$ = ba. A grammar which generates the above language is

$$G = (V_N, V_T, <S>, P)$$

where

$$V_N = \{<S>\}$$
$$V_T = \{a, b, c\}$$
$$P = \{ <S> ::= a<S>a, <S> ::= b<S>b, <S> ::= c \}$$

Some of the strings generated by the grammar are c, aca, bcb, abcba, bacab, abbcbba, abacaba, aabcbaa, etc. It is required to formulate an algorithm which, given an input string on the alphabet {a, b, c}, will determine whether this string is in the language L. This algorithm requires a stack in order to accomplish the task. We assume that the input string is padded on the right end with a blank (denoted by □). For example, the string aabcbaa is given as aabcbaa□.

**Algorithm** RECOGNIZE. Given an input string named STRING on the alphabet {a, b, c} which contains a blank in its rightmost character position, and a function NEXTCHAR which returns the next symbol in STRING, this algorithm determines whether the contents of STRING belong to the above language. The vector S represents the stack, and TOP is a pointer to the top element of the stack.

1.  [Initialize stack by placing a letter 'c' on the top]
    TOP ← 1
    S[TOP] ← 'c'
2.  [Get and stack symbols until 'c' or blank is encountered]
    NEXT ← NEXTCHAR(STRING)
    Repeat while NEXT ≠ 'c'
        If NEXT = ' '
        then    Write('INVALID STRING')
                Exit
        else    Call PUSH(S, TOP, NEXT)
                NEXT ← NEXTCHAR(STRING)
3.  [Scan characters following 'c'; compare them to characters on stack]
    Repeat while S[TOP] ≠ 'c':
        NEXT ← NEXTCHAR(STRING)
        X ← POP(S, TOP)
        If NEXT ≠ X
        then    Write('INVALID STRING')
                Exit
4.  [Next symbol must be a blank]
    If NEXT = ' '
    then    Write('VALID STRING')
    else    Write('INVALID STRING')
5.  [Finished]
    Exit                                                                    □

The algorithm operates in the following way. Initially, the symbol 'c' is placed on the stack. Until a 'c' is encountered in the input string, all symbols are placed on the stack. When 'c' is encountered in the input, a transfer to step 3 occurs. At this point, the remaining input symbols are compared with the stack by removing an 'a' from the top of the stack each time the input symbol is 'a', and a 'b' each time the input symbol is a 'b'. Should the top element of the stack not match the input symbol, the algorithm terminates and no further processing of the input string is performed. If all symbols match the inputs, the symbol 'c' at the bottom of the stack will become the top element of the stack. All symbols can be removed from the stack only for the case where the string read in after the symbol 'c' is the reverse of the input string processed before the 'c'.

The tracing of the contents of the stack for a number of input strings is given in Table 3-4.1.

In the section thus far we have illustrated the operations on a stack by using a vector representation. Now we are going to examine an alternative method of stack representation.

In some programming languages, such as PL/I and ALGOL W, we are allowed explicit control (i.e., control through instructions) of when and how much storage is to be allocated for certain variables in the program. Storage which can be controlled in this manner is called CONTROLLED storage in PL/I. Whenever additional storage is required for a new copy of some CONTROLLED variable or set of

**Table 3-4.1.** Trace of contents of stack for Algorithm RECOGNIZE.

| Input String | Character Scanned | Contents of Stack (top element of stack is the rightmost character) |
|---|---|---|
| abcba☐ | none | c |
| | a | ca |
| | b | cab |
| | c | cab |
| | b | ca |
| | a | c |
| | ☐ | c |
| | valid string | |
| aabcaab☐ | none | c |
| | a | ca |
| | a | caa |
| | b | caab |
| | c | caab |
| | a | caa |
| invalid string since a ≠ b | | |
| aabcbaaa☐ | none | c |
| | a | ca |
| | a | caa |
| | b | caab |
| | c | caab |
| | b | caa |
| | a | ca |
| | a | c |
| | a | c |
| invalid string since c is top element of stack and NEXT ≠ ' '. | | |

variables, this storage can be obtained by using an ALLOCATE statement. When the storage for the latest copy of a variable is no longer needed, it can be released by the execution of a FREE statement. Let us consider an example which illustrates how these programming constructs work.

Suppose we declare in a PL/I program a variable named IDENTIFICATION which consists of two subidentities, a student's name and a student's ID number. If it is desired that the storage allocation for IDENTIFICATION be under direct programmer control, the following declaration should be used:

```
DECLARE 1  IDENTIFICATION CONTROLLED,
           2  NAME CHARACTER(30),
           2  IDNO FIXED DECIMAL(6);
```

To obtain storage for a new copy of IDENTIFICATION, we use the instruction

```
ALLOCATE IDENTIFICATION;
```

Note that the **ALLOCATE** statement only provides storage and that the subentities NAME and IDNO do not have values assigned to them. Assignment of values can be achieved through the execution of assignment statements such as

```
NAME = 'JERRY KOOSMAN';   IDNO = 673129;
```

Consider what happens if, following the above assignment statements, another allocate statement plus two more assignment statements are executed: for example, statements such as

```
ALLOCATE IDENTIFICATION;
NAME = 'SHANE MCDONALD';   IDNO = 802688;
```

After the execution of these statements, any reference to NAME or IDNO would bring forward values assigned to the latest storage to be allocated (i.e., the value 'SHANE MCDONALD' and 802688). Note that the storage for the identification of 'JERRY KOOSMAN' is not lost; however, it is at this point inaccessible. To access this identification record requires that the latest storage for IDENTIFICATION be released. We achieve this through execution of the statement

```
FREE IDENTIFICATION;
```

Now a reference to NAME would have the value 'JERRY KOOSMAN'. If a second FREE IDENTIFICATION statement is executed, then storage would not exist for IDENTIFICATION and any reference to NAME or IDNO would result in an error.

It should be evident that the allocating and freeing of CONTROLLED storage is performed in a "last-in, first-out" manner. Elements are inserted and deleted from a stack in this same manner, and, consequently, it is easy to effect the operations of a stack using the ALLOCATE and FREE instructions. To PUSH an element onto a stack S (which should be declared to be of storage-type CONTROLLED) involves the following sequence of PL/I statements:

```
/* PUSH(S,X) - PUSH ELEMENT X ONTO STACK S */
ALLOCATE S;
S = X;
```

To POP an element involves the instruction

```
/* POP(S) - REMOVE TOP ELEMENT OF S */
FREE S;
```

Note that there are some major differences between representing a stack with CONTROLLED storage as opposed to a vector representation. The notion of a stack as a possible multiple-element data structure is less apparent when using controlled allocation. The declaration of a "stack-like" structure involves the declaration of a prototype element which is used in allocating and freeing CONTROLLED storage for each instance of the declared variable. Not only can elements be inserted or deleted just from the top of the stack, but only the top element can be referenced in a CONTROLLED storage representation (i.e., the Algorithms PEEK and CHANGE are not applicable in the CONTROLLED storage case).

The location of the top element in a stack represented in CONTROLLED storage is handled implicitly by the PL/I compiler. Hence, as we saw earlier, the operations of PUSH and POP do not require knowledge of the index TOP when the implementation involves CONTROLLED storage. While in the remainder of this chapter we use the Algorithms PUSH and POP as described for the vector representation, it should be remembered that a CONTROLLED storage representation provides the same insertion and deletion capabilities without the necessity of updating the index TOP. In Sec. 3-5.1, we give an example illustrating how a stack can be represented using programmer-defined data structures.

Pascal does not allow a "pure" stack as does PL/I. However, a stack based on linked-allocation techniques can be constructed. These programming details are left to the next chapter, which deals with linked allocation.

Quite often a program contains more than one stack. In such a situation, it can happen that one stack has encountered an overflow condition, while others are far from being full. Instead of imposing a maximum size on each stack, it would be preferable to allocate a common pool or maximum block of memory which all stacks can use.

The particular case of two stacks leads to a simple memory layout which permits them to exist together, as shown in Fig. 3-4.5. The first stack grows to the right, while the second stack grows to the left. With this arrangement it is possible for one stack to occupy more than half of the memory allocated to both stacks. An overflow will occur only if the total size of the two stacks exceeds the allocated memory space.

It is not possible to have more than two stacks sharing a common block of memory that still preserve the overflow property of the above configuration and the property of each stack having a fixed bottom element. If the overflow property is to be maintained, then the fixed-bottom property must be sacrificed. The amount of bookkeeping involved in keeping track of the bottom and top elements of a number of sequentially allocated stacks sharing a common block of memory is very significant. At certain times, entire stacks must be moved in order to preserve the sequential allocation property. The details of this approach are left to the exercises. A more convenient storage-allocation scheme for such a situation will be discussed in the next chapter.

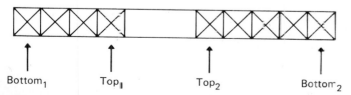

Bottom$_1$        Top$_1$          Top$_2$           Bottom$_2$

**FIGURE 3-4.5**   A sequential allocation scheme for two stacks.

**Exercises for Sec. 3-4**

1.  Suppose you need to use two stacks in a program. A simple memory layout for a single vector S containing the two stacks was given in Fig. 3-4.5.

    Give a procedure to PUSH a value stored in variable TEMP onto the second stack. What would be the difference between this procedure and one to PUSH a value TEMP onto the first stack?

2.  Suppose we wish to have n > 2 sequentially allocated stacks occupying a single vector, S[1..m]. This vector is divided into n segments, and each stack i is allocated a segment. Also, we have two vectors, T[1..n] and B[1..n], where T[i] and B[i] are used to indicate the top and bottom of stack i, respectively. So, if T[i] = B[i], stack i is empty. Thus, the vector S may look like the representation given in Fig. 3-4.6. To avoid special cases when pushing and popping stack n, let B[n+1] = m.

    To allocate the n segments, we set the elements of B and T initially by the assignments

    B[i] ← T[i] ← (TRUNC(m / n))(i – 1),  1 ≤ i ≤ n

    Stack i can grow from B[i] + 1 to B[i+1] before overflowing onto the next stack.

    Write two functions PUSHI and POPI to handle the pushing and popping of a given stack I, assuming the stacks have already been allocated.

**3-5 APPLICATIONS OF STACKS**

This section contains three applications in which stacks are used. The first application deals with *recursion*. Recursion is an important facility in many programming languages such as ALGOL 60 and Pascal. There are many problems whose algorithmic description is best described in a recursive manner. Such instances are given throughout the text and occur frequently in Chap. 5. The second application of a stack is classical; it deals with the compilation of infix expressions into object code. The section ends with a brief discussion of stack machines. Certain computers perform stack operations at the hardware or machine level, and these operations enable insertions to and deletions from a stack to be made very rapidly.

**3-5.1 Recursion**

Often in mathematics, a property or a set $P$ can be specified by an inductive definition. An inductive definition of a set can be realized by using a given finite set of elements $A$ and the following three clauses:

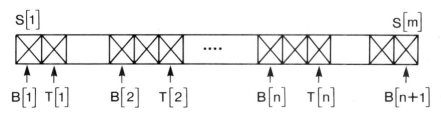

**FIGURE 3-4.6**   A vector representation of n stacks.

*1* Basis clause — the elements of $A$ are in $P$.
*2* Inductive clause — the elements of $B$, all of which are constructed from elements in $A$, are in $P$.
*3* Extremal clause — the elements constructed as in cases *1* and *2* are the only elements in $P$.

The inductive definition of the natural numbers which uses the operation of successor $S(x) = x + 1$ to produce new integers can be written as

*1* 0 is an integer (basis clause).
*2* If x is an integer, so is the successor of x (inductive clause).
*3* The natural numbers are the only elements constructed from cases *1* and *2*.

The natural numbers have been defined *recursively* through the process of *induction*. Recursion is the name given to the technique of defining a set or a process in terms of itself.

The factorial function, whose domain is the natural numbers, can be recursively defined as

$$FACTORIAL(N) = \begin{cases} 1, \text{ if } N = 0 \\ N * FACTORIAL(N-1) \text{ , otherwise} \end{cases}$$

Here FACTORIAL(N) is defined in terms of FACTORIAL(N − 1), which in turn is defined in terms of FACTORIAL(N − 2), etc., until finally FACTORIAL(0) is reached, whose value is given as "one." A recursive definition of a set or process must contain an explicit definition for particular value(s) of the argument(s); otherwise, the definition would never converge. The basic idea is to define a function for all its argument values in a constructive manner by using induction. The value of a function for a particular argument value can be computed in a finite number of steps using the recursive definition, where at each step of recursion we get nearer to the solution.

An important facility available to the programmer is the *procedure* (function or subroutine). Procedures in programming languages are a convenience to the programmer since they enable him or her to express just once an algorithm which is required in many places in a program. Corresponding to a recursive step in the definition of a function, we have n certain programming languages, such as Pascal, ALGOL, PL/I, and SNOBOL4 (but not FORTRAN), the opportunity to use a procedure which may contain a procedure call to any procedure (including itself). A procedure that contains a procedure call to itself, or a procedure call to a second procedure which eventually causes the first procedure to be called, is known as a *recursive* procedure.

There are two important conditions that must be satisfied by any recursive procedure. First, each time a procedure calls itself (either directly or indirectly), it must be "nearer," in some sense, to a solution. In the case of the factorial function, each time that the function calls itself, its argument is decremented by "one," so the argument of the function is getting smaller. Second, there must be a decision criterion for stopping the process or computation. In the case of the factorial function, the value of *n* must be zero.

There are essentially two types of recursion. The first type concerns *recursively defined functions* (or *primitive recursive functions*); an example of this kind is the *factorial* function. The second type of recursion is the *recursive use of a procedure* (*nonprimitive recursive*). A typical example of this kind of recursion is Ackermann's function, which is defined as

$$A(M,N) = \begin{cases} N + 1, \text{ if } M = 0 \\ A(M - 1, 1), \text{ if } N = 0 \\ A(M - 1, A(M, N - 1)), \text{ otherwise} \end{cases}$$

The recursion in Ackermann's function arises because the function A appears as an argument for a call of A; and this is typical of this type of recursion.

Many people believe that recursion is an unnecessary luxury in a programming language. This is based on the fact that any primitive recursive function, and therefore any function we would normally like to compute, can be solved iteratively.

An *iterative process* can be illustrated with the aid of the flowchart given in Fig. 3-5.1. There are four parts in the process: initialization, decision, computation, and update. The functions of the four parts are as follows:

1   *Initialization.* The parameters of the function and a decision parameter in this part are set to their initial values. The decision parameter is used to determine when to exit from the loop.
2   *Decision.* The decision parameter is used to determine whether to remain in the loop.
3   *Computation.* The required computation is performed in this part.
4   *Update.* The decision parameter is updated and a transfer to the next iteration results.

It is possible to transform mechanically any primitive recursive function into an equivalent iterative process. However, this is not the case for nonprimitive recursive functions. Although there does exist an iterative solution for Ackermann's function, in general there are many problems of that form for which iterative solutions either do not exist or are not easily found. Certain inherently recursive processes can be solved in programming languages that do not permit recursion only by essentially setting up a recursive framework. We will have occasion to return to this topic later. Recursion is becoming increasingly important in symbol manipulation and nonnumeric applications.

Throughout the text we will encounter problems where recursion is unavoidable because of the recursive nature of the process or because of the recursive struc-

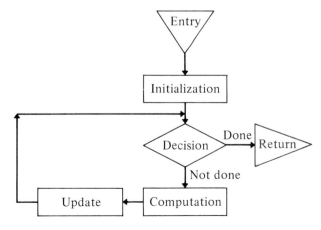

**FIGURE 3-5.1** Flowchart for an iterative process.

ture of the data which have to be processed. Even for cases where there is no inherent recursive structure, the recursive solution may be much simpler (though sometimes more time consuming) than its iterative counterpart.

There are special problems associated with a recursive procedure that do not exist for a nonrecursive procedure. A recursive procedure can be called from within or outside itself, and to ensure its proper functioning, it has to save in some order the return address so that a return to the proper location will result when the return to a calling statement is made. The procedure must also save the formal parameters, local variables, etc., upon entry and restore these parameters and variables at completion.

The general algorithm model for any recursive procedure contains the following steps:

*1*   [Prologue] Save the parameters, local variables, and return address.

*2*   [Body] If the base criterion has been reached, then perform the final computation and go to step 3; otherwise, perform the partial computation and go to step 1 (initiate a recursive call).

*3*   [Epilogue] Restore the most recently saved parameters. local variables, and return address. Go to this return address.

A flowchart model for this algorithm is given in Fig. 3-5.2. The model consists of a prologue, a body, and an epilogue. The purpose of the prologue is to save the formal parameters, local variables, and return address, and that of the epilogue is to restore them. Note that the parameters, local variables, and return address that are restored are those which were most recently saved, i.e., the last saved are the first to be restored (last-in, first-out). The body of the procedure contains a procedure call to itself; in fact, there may be more than one call to itself in certain procedures.

It is rather difficult to understand a recursive procedure from its flowchart, and the best we can hope for is an intuitive understanding of the procedure. The key box contained in the body of the procedure is the one which invokes a call to itself. The dotted-line exit from this box indicates that a call to itself is being initiated within the same procedure. Each time a procedure call to itself is executed, the prologue of the procedure saves all necessary information required for its proper functioning.

The procedure body contains two computation boxes — namely, the partial and final computation boxes. Frequently, the partial-computation box is combined with the procedure call box. (This is the case for computation of the factorial function.) The final-computation box gives the explicit definition of the process for some value or values of the argument(s). The test box determines whether the argument value(s) is that for which explicit definition of the process is given.

Associated with each call to (or entry into) a recursive procedure is a *level number*. The entry into the procedure due to the initial call from the main program is given the level number "one," as the main program is assumed to have level number "zero." Each subsequent entry into the procedure has an associated level number "one" higher than the level number of the procedure from which the call was made. Another characteristic of recursive procedures is the *depth* of recursion, which is the number of times the procedure is called recursively in the process of evaluating a given argument or arguments. Usually, this quantity is not obvious, except in the case of extremely simple recursive functions, such as FACTORIAL(N), for which the depth is N.

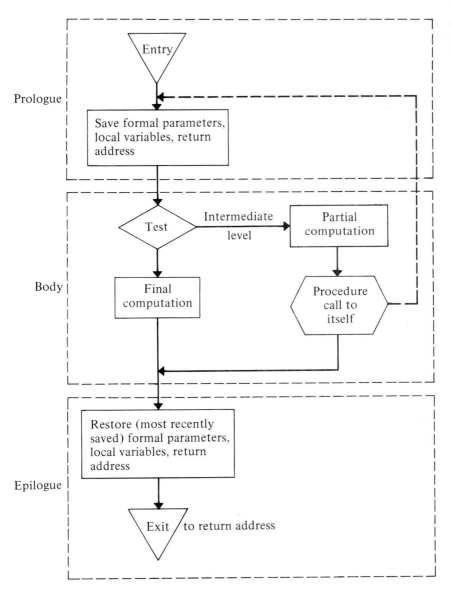

**FIGURE 3-5.2** Flowchart for mode of a recursive process.

The last-in and first-out characteristic of a recursive procedure suggests that a stack is the most obvious data structure to use to implement steps 1 and 3 of this procedure. At each procedure call (or level of recursion), the stack is pushed to save the necessary values; upon exit from that level, the stack is "popped" to restore the saved values of the preceding (or calling) level.

The recursive mechanism is best described by an example. Consider an algorithm to calculate FACTORIAL(N) recursively which explicitly shows the recursive framework. (The recursive definition of FACTORIAL is given at the beginning of Sec. 3-5.1.)

**Algorithm** FACTORIAL. Given an integer N, this algorithm computes N!. The stack A is used to store an activation record associated with each recursive call. Each activation record contains the current value of N and the current return address RET_ADDR. TEMP_REC is also a record which contains two variables (PARM and ADDRESS). This temporary record is required to simulate the proper transfer of control from one activation record of Algorithm FACTORIAL to another. Whenever a TEMP_REC is placed on the stack A, copies of PARM and ADDRESS are pushed onto A and assigned to N and RET_ADDR, respectively. TOP points to the top element of A and its value is initially zero. Initially, the return address is set to the main calling address (i.e., ADDRESS ← main address). PARM is set to the initial value of N.

1.  [Save N and return address]
        Call PUSH(A, TOP, TEMP_REC)
2.  [Is the base criterion found?]
        If N = 0
        then   FACTORIAL ← 1
               Go to step 4
        else   PARM ← N – 1
               ADDRESS ← step 3
               Go to step 1
3.  [Calculate N!]
        FACTORIAL ← N * FACTORIAL        (the factorial of N)
4.  [Restore previous N and return address]
        TEMP_REC ← POP(A, TOP)
            (i.e., PARM ← N, ADDRESS ← RET_ADDR, pop stack)
        Go to ADDRESS                                                    ☐

Steps 1 and 4 are the prologue and epilogue of this algorithm, respectively. Steps 2 and 3 make up the body; the test and final computation are in step 2. Step 3 contains the partial computation and the recursive call. A trace of Algorithm FACTORIAL with N = 2 is given in Fig. 3-5.3. A recursive Pascal formulation of the factorial function together with a main procedure to test the function for a series of input values are given in Fig. 3-5.4.

Let us now consider a more complex recursion example. A well-known algorithm for finding the greatest common divisor of two integers is Euclid's algorithm. The greatest common divisor function is defined by the following:

$$GCD(m, n) = \begin{cases} GCD(n, m), & \text{if } n > m \\ m, & \text{if } n = 0 \\ GCD(n, MOD(m, n)), & \text{otherwise} \end{cases}$$

Here $MOD(m, n)$ is $m$ modulo $n$ — the remainder on dividing $m$ by $n$. The first part of the definition interchanges the order of the arguments if $n > m$. If the second argument is zero, then the greatest common divisor is equal to the first argument. This defines the base values of the function. Finally, the GCD is defined in terms of itself. Note that the process must terminate since $MOD(m, n)$ will decrease to a value of zero in a finite number of steps. As an example, the GCD(20, 6) is obtained from the following computation:

$$20 = 6 * 3 - 2$$

| Level Number | Description | Stack 'A' Contents |
|---|---|---|

Enter level 1 (main call)

Step 1: PUSH(A,0,(2,main address))

Step 2: N ≠ 0
PARM ← 1, ADDR ← Step 3

| 2 | | |
|---|---|---|
| Main address | | |

↑
TOP

Enter level 2 (first recursive call)

Step 1: PUSH(A,1,(1,Step 3))

Step 2: N ≠ 0
PARM ← 0, ADDR ← Step 3

| 2 | 1 | |
|---|---|---|
| Main address | Step 3 | |

↑
TOP

Enter level 3 (second recursive call)

Step 1: PUSH(A,2,(0,Step 3))

Step 2: N = 0
FACTORIAL ← 1

| 2 | 1 | 0 |
|---|---|---|
| Main address | Step 3 | Step 3 |

↑
TOP

Step 4: POP(A,3), go to Step 3

| 2 | 1 | |
|---|---|---|
| Main address | Step 3 | |

↑
TOP

Return to level 2

Step 3: FACTORIAL ← 1 * 1

Step 4: POP(A,2), go to Step 3

| 2 | | |
|---|---|---|
| Main address | | |

↑
TOP

Return to level 1

Step 3: FACTORIAL ← 2 * 1

Step 4: POP(A,1), go to main address

| | | |
|---|---|---|
| | | |

↑
TOP

**FIGURE 3-5.3** Trace of Algorithm FACTORIAL.

```
{ program to test the recursive factorial function }
program runfact(output);

const startval = 3;
      stepval  = 2;
      endval   = 7;

var loopval: integer;

function factorial(n: integer): integer;

begin
  if n = 0
  then factorial := 1
  else factorial := n * factorial(n - 1)
end;  { factorial }

begin
    loopval := startval;
    while loopval <= endval do
        begin
            writeln('factorial(',loopval: 1,') is ', factorial(loopval));
            loopval := loopval + stepval
        end
end.

factorial(3) is        6
factorial(5) is      120
factorial(7) is     5040
```

**FIGURE 3-5.4**    Recursive formulation of the factorial function.

By the Euclidean algorithm, the GCD(20, 6) is the same as the GCD(6, 2). Therefore,

$$6 = 2 * 3 + 0$$

and the GCD(6, 2) is the same as the GCD(2, 0), which is 2. If we were required to find the GCD(6, 20), this could be solved by finding a solution to the GCD(20, 6) instead.

The Pascal program for the GCD function is given in Fig. 3-5.5. Pascal also has a MOD function which is a convenience in programming the GCD function.

Another complex recursive problem is that of the Tower of Hanoi, which has a historical basis in the ritual of the ancient Tower of Brahma. The problem is as follows:

Given $N$ discs of decreasing size stacked on one needle and two empty needles, it is required to stack all the discs onto a second needle in decreasing order of size. The third needle may be used as temporary storage. The movement of the discs is restricted by the following rules:

1    Only one disc may be moved at a time.
2    A disc may be moved from any needle to any other.
3    At no time may a larger disc rest upon a smaller disc.

A pictorial representation of the problem is given in Fig. 3-5.6.

The solution to this problem is most clearly seen with the aid of induction. To move one disc, merely move it from needle $A$ to needle $C$. To move two discs, move the first disc to needle B, move the second from needle $A$ to needle $C$, then move the disc from needle $B$ to needle $C$. In general, the solution of the problem of moving $N$ discs from needle $A$ to needle $C$ has three steps:

*1*    Move $N - 1$ discs from $A$ to $B$.
*2*    Move disc $N$ from $A$ to $C$.
*3*    Move $N - 1$ discs from $B$ to $C$.

A close examination of the first and third steps will reveal that these are recursive in nature; i.e., the first step is the implementation of the solution using needles $A$

---

```
{ program to test the euclidean algorithm }
program rungcd(input, output);

var i, j: integer;

function gcd(m, n: integer): integer;

begin
    if n > m
    then { reverse the call }
        gcd := gcd(n, m)
    else if n = 0
        then { m is the greatest common divisor }
            gcd := m
        else gcd := gcd(n, m mod n)
end; { gcd }

begin
    read(i);
    while not eof do
        begin
            read(j);
            if not eof
            then begin
                writeln('the greatest common divisor of ', i: 3,
                        ' and ', j: 3, ' is ', gcd(i, j));
                read(i)
            end
        end
end. { rungcd }
```

the greatest common divisor of  84 and 246 is        6
the greatest common divisor of   6 and  20 is        2
the greatest common divisor of 121 and  33 is       11

**FIGURE 3-5.5**   Recursive formulation of the GCD function.

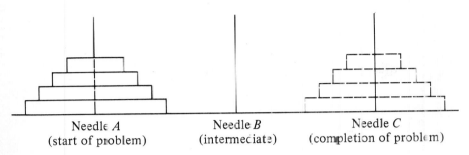

Needle *A*
(start of problem)

Needle *B*
(intermediate)

Needle *C*
(completion of problem)

**FIGURE 3-5.6**   Tower of Hanoi.

and *B* in place of needles *A* and *C* and *N* − 1 discs in place of *N*, while the third step is the implementation of the solution using needles *B* and *C* in place of needles *A* and *C* and *N* − 1 discs in place of *N*. Therefore, a recursive procedure can be formulated to solve the Tower of Hanoi problem. A Pascal recursive procedure which implements this solution, along with a mainline program to test it with three discs are given in Fig. 3-5.7.

To show more clearly the recursive path of the solution to the Tower of Hanoi problem, we describe an algorithm which simulates the recursive-procedure solution. This solution explicitly constructs the recursive framework using a stack mechanism. A general algorithm for solving the Tower of Hanoi problem is now given.

1.   Push parameters and return address on stack
2.   If the stopping value has been reached
     then pop the stack to return to previous level
     else move all except the final disc from starting to intermediate needle
3.   Move final disc from start to destination needle
4.   Move remaining discs from intermediate to destination needle
5.   Return to previous level by popping stack

The detailed algorithm can now be formulated.

**Algorithm** HANOI.   Given N_VALUE, the number of discs to be moved; SN_VALUE, the starting needle; IN_VALUE, the intermediate needle; and DN_VALUE, the destination needle, Algorithm HANOI performs the steps necessary to move N_VALUE discs from needle SN_VALUE to needle DN_VALUE, according to the rules of the Tower of Hanoi problem.

The stack ST is used to implement the recursive framework; each element of ST has five fields — N, SN, IN, DN, and RET_ADDR, which are used to store the values of N_VALUE, SN_VALUE, IN_VALUE, DN_VALUE, and the return address, respectively. TEMP_REC is a five-element temporary variable consisting of N_VALUE, SN_VALUE, IN_VALUE, DN_VALUE, and ADDRESS, which is needed to simulate the proper transfer of control from one activation of HANOI to the next. TOP points to the top element of ST. The Algorithms PUSH and POP, previously described, are used to manipulate the stack ST. ADDRESS is initially set to the main calling address; TOP is initially set to zero.

1.   [Save parameters and return address]
        Call PUSH(ST, TOP, TEMP_REC)
        (The effect of the PUSH operation is as follows:

    TOP ← TOP + 1, N[TOP] ← N_VALUE, SN[TOP] ← SN_VALUE,
    IN[TOP] ← IN_VALUE, DN[TOP] ← DN_VALUE,
    RET_ADDR[TOP] ← ADDRESS)

2. [Test for stopping value of N; if not reached, move N − 1 discs from starting needle to intermediate needle]

    If N[TOP] = 0
    then   Go to RET_ADDR[TOP]
    else   N_VALUE ← N[TOP] − 1
           SN_VALUE ← SN[TOP]
           IN_VALUE ← DN[TOP]
           DN_VALUE ← IN[TOP]
           ADDRESS ← step 3
           Go to step 1

3. [Move Nth disc from start to destination needle; move N − 1 discs from intermediate needle to destination needle]

    TEMP_REC ← POP(ST, TOP)
    Write('DISC ', N, 'FROM NEEDLE ', SN, 'TO NEEDLE ', DN)
    N_VALUE ← N[TOP] − 1
    SN_VALUE ← IN[TOP]
    IN_VALUE ← SN[TOP]
    DN_VALUE ← DN[TOP]
    ADDRESS ← step 4
    Go to step 1

4. [Return to previous level]

    TEMP_REC ← POP(ST, TOP)
    Go to RET_ADDR[TOP]                     □

    The algorithm compares N[TOP] to zero. If N[TOP] is not zero, a recursive call to move N[TOP] − 1 discs from SN[TOP] to IN[TOP] is simulated. That being completed, the N[TOP] disc is moved from needle SN[TOP] to DN[TOP]. Finally, a recursive call to move N[TOP] − 1 discs from IN[TOP] to DN[TOP] is simulated. If we assume that Algorithm HANOI is called with N = 2, SN = 'A', IN = 'B', DN = 'C', and ADDRESS = MAIN, Fig. 3-5.8 is a trace of the execution of Algorithm HANOI(2, 'A', 'B', 'C'). Figure 3-5.9 is a PL/I program which implements Algorithm HANOI. This program uses the implicit stacking mechanism provided by the PL/I ALLOCATE-FREE feature rather than a stack simulation like the one used in the algorithm. The statements ALLOCATE ACTIVATION_RECORD and FREE ACTIVATION_RECORD are used to effect the PUSH and POP operations of the algorithm.

    The correspondence between the programs in Figs. 3-5.7 and 3-5.9 should be clear from the comments and statement labels. The variables N_VALUE, SN_VALUE, IN_VALUE, and DN_VALUE in Fig. 3-5.9 take the place of the passed parameters in the *hanoi* statements in Fig. 3-5.7. The application of a stack in this section has been concerned with the storage of values for parameters and local variables in the evaluation of recursive functions. Stacks, however, can be used to control the allocation of storage in many block-structured languages (see Sec. 5-6).

**Exercises for Sec. 3-5.1**

1. a) The median of a set of an odd number of scores is defined as that score which has the property that the number of scores greater than it is equal to the number of scores smaller than it. Suppose there is a set of NUM

```
{ program to solve the tower of hanoi problem }

program testhano (input,output);

const snvalue = 'a';    { starting needle }
      invalue = 'b';    { intermediate needle }
      dnvalue = 'c';    { destination needle }

var nvalue : integer;   { number of disks to be moved }

procedure hanoi(n :integer; sndl, indl, dndl : char);

begin
   if n <> 0
   then begin

           { move n-1 disks from starting needle to intermediate needle }
           hano (n-1, sndl, dndl, indl);

           { move disk n from start to destination }
           writeln('move disk ', n: 1, ' from ', sndl, ' to ', dndl);

           { move n-1 disks from intermediate needle to destination needle}
           hanoi(n-1,indl, sndl, dndl)
       end;
end; { hanoi }

begin
   repeat
      begin
         readln(nvalue);
         writeln('tower of hanoi problem with ',nvalue: 1 ' disks');
         hanci(nvalue, snvalue, invalue, dnvalue);
         writeln
      end
   until eof
end.  { testhanoi }
```

```
tower of hanoi problem with 3 disks
move disk 1 from a to c
move disk 2 from a to b
move disk 1 from c to b
move disk 3 from a to c
move disk 1 from b to a
move disk 2 from b to c
move disk 1 from a to c
```

**FIGURE 3-5.7**   Recursive formulation of Tower of Hanoi problem.

| *Step Executed* | *Description* | *Stack Contents* |
|---|---|---|

| Step Executed | Description | | Stack Contents | | |
|---|---|---|---|---|---|
| 1 <br> 2 | PUSH(ST,0,(2,A,B,C,Main)) <br> N ≠ 0, perform equivalent of call <br> HANOI(1,A,C,B) with ADDRESS = Step 3 | N <br> SN <br> IN <br> DN <br> RET_ <br> ADDR | 2 <br> A <br> B <br> C <br> Main <br> ↑ <br> TOP | | |
| 1 <br> 2 | PUSH(ST,1,(1,A,C,B,3)) <br> N ≠ 0, perform equivalent of call <br> HANOI(0,A,B,C,) with ADDRESS = Step 3 | | 2 <br> A <br> B <br> C <br> Main | 1 <br> A <br> C <br> B <br> 3 <br> ↑ <br> TOP | |
| 1 <br> 2 | PUSH(ST,2,(0,A,B,C,3)) <br> N = 0, go to step 3 | | 2 <br> A <br> B <br> C <br> Main | 1 <br> A <br> C <br> B <br> 3 | 0 <br> A <br> B <br> C <br> 3 <br> ↑ <br> TOP |
| 3 | POP(ST,3), move disk 1 from A to B, <br> perform equivalent of call <br> HANOI(0,C,A,B) with ADDRESS = Step 4 | | 2 <br> A <br> B <br> C <br> Main | 1 <br> A <br> C <br> B <br> 3 <br> ↑ <br> TOP | |
| 1 <br> 2 | PUSH(ST,2,(0,C,A,B,4)) <br> N = 0, go to step 4 | | 2 <br> A <br> B <br> C <br> Main | 1 <br> A <br> C <br> B <br> 3 | 0 <br> C <br> A <br> B <br> 4 <br> ↑ <br> TOP |

**FIGURE 3-5.8** Trace of Algorithm HANOI.

| Step Executed | Description | Stack Contents |
|---|---|---|

| Step Executed | Description |
|---|---|
| 4 | POP(ST,3), go to Step 3 |

| | |
|---|---|
| 2 | 1 |
| A | A |
| B | C |
| C | E |
| Main | 3 |

↑ TOP

| 3 | POP(ST,2), move disk 2 from A to C, perform equivalent of call HANOI(1,B,A,C) with ADDRESS = Step 4 |
|---|---|

| |
|---|
| 2 |
| A |
| B |
| C |
| Main |

↑ TOP

| 1<br>2 | PUSH(ST,1,(1,B,A,C,4))<br>N ≠ 0, perform equivalent of call HANOI(1,B,C,A) with ADDRESS = Step 3 |
|---|---|

| | |
|---|---|
| 2 | 1 |
| A | E |
| B | A |
| C | C |
| Main | 4 |

↑ TOP

| 1<br>2 | PUSH(ST,2,(0,B,C,A,3))<br>N = 0, go to Step 3 |
|---|---|

| | | |
|---|---|---|
| 2 | 1 | 0 |
| A | E | B |
| B | A | C |
| C | C | A |
| Main | 4 | 3 |

↑ TOP

| 3 | POP(ST,3), move disc 1 from B to C, perform equivalent of call HANOI(0,A,B,C) with ADDRESS = Step 4 |
|---|---|

| | |
|---|---|
| 2 | 1 |
| A | B |
| B | A |
| C | C |
| Main | 4 |

↑ TOP

**FIGURE 3-5.8**   (Continued)

| Step Executed | Description | Stack Contents |
|---|---|---|

| 1 | PUSH(ST,2,(0,A,B,C,4)) |
| 2 | N = 0, go to Step 4 |

| 2 | 1 | 0 |
|---|---|---|
| A | B | A |
| B | A | B |
| C | C | C |
| Main | 4 | 4 |

↑
TOP

| 4 | POP(ST,3), go to Step 4 |

| 2 | 1 | |
|---|---|---|
| A | B | |
| B | A | |
| C | C | |
| Main | 4 | |

↑
TOP

| 4 | POP(ST,2), go to main call |

| 2 | | |
|---|---|---|
| A | | |
| B | | |
| C | | |
| Main | | |

↑
TOP

**FIGURE 3-5.8** (Continued)

scores in the array SCORE. Then a recursive solution to computing the median score would be to eliminate successively the highest score and the lowest score until only one score remained. That score would then be the median score. Assume NUM is odd.

Formulate a recursive function called MEDIAN which takes the parameters LOWBOUND and HIGHBOUND which indicate that the search for the median is to take place in the part of the array SCORE from position LOWBOUND to position HIGHBOUND. If there is only one value in SCORE(LOWBOUND:HIGHBOUND), the function MEDIAN prints out that value; otherwise it finds the smallest score, exchanges it with SCORE(LOWBOUND), finds the largest score, exchanges it with SCORE(HIGHBOUND), "shrinks" the table to exclude those two values and repeats the procedure. Assume the existence of two functions MAX and MIN, which each take LOWBOUND and HIGHBOUND, and return the largest and smallest score, respectively, in the array SCORE(LOWBOUND:HIGHBOUND).

```
HAN1:  PROCEDURE OPTIONS(MAIN);
/*  EXAMPLE 3-7.1  */
/*  RECURSIVE PROCEDURE SIMULATION SOLUTION OF  */
/*  TOWER OF HANOI PROBLEM  */

     DECLARE M FIXED BINARY(31),
           1 ACTIVATION_RECORD CONTROLLED,
              2 RET_ADDR LABEL,
              2 N FIXED BINARY(31),
              2 SN CHARACTER (1),
              2 IN CHARACTER (1),
              2 DN CHARACTER (1),

           N_VALUE FIXED BINARY(31),
           (SN_VALUE,IN_VALUE,DN_VALUE) CHARACTER (1),
           ADDRESS LABEL;

     /* READ IN NUMBER OF DISCS ON NEEDLE  */
     GET LIST(M);

     /* INITIATE CALL TO HANOI - INITIALIZE CALL PARAMETERS */
     /*     MOVE 'N_VALUE' DISCS FROM NEEDLE 'SN_VALUE' */
     /*     TO NEEDLE 'DN_VALUE' USING NEEDLE 'IN_VALUE' */
     /*     AS AN INTERMEDIATE */

     PUT EDIT ('TOWER OF HANOI PROBLEM WITH ',M' DISCS')
          (SKIP,A,F(2),A);
     N_VALUE = M;
     SN_VALUE = 'A';
     IN_VALUE =  B';
     DN_VALUE = 'C';
     ADDRESS = MAIN_ADDR;
     GO TO HANOI_CALL;

MAIN_ADDR: STOP;

HANOI_CALL:
     ALLOCATE ACTIVATION_RECORD;
     N = N_VALUE;
     SN = SN_VALUE;
     IN = IN_VALUE;
     DN = DN_VALUE;
     RET_ADDR = ADDRESS;
     IF N = 0
     THEN GO TO RET_ADDR;
     ELSE DO;

        /*  MOVE N-1 DISCS FROM START NEEDLE  */
        /*  TO INTERMEDIATE NEEDLE  */
```

**FIGURE 3-5.9** PL/I implementation of Algorithm HANOI.

```
          N_VALUE = N - 1;
          SN_VALUE = SN;
          IN_VALUE = DN;
          DN_VALUE = IN;
          ADDRESS = H_ADDR1;
          GO TO HANOL_CALL;
      END;


H_ADDR1:
      FREE ACTIVATION_RECORD;

      /*  MOVE DISC N FROM START TO DESTINATION NEEDLE  */
      /*      MOVE N-1 DISCS FROM INTERMEDIATE  */
      /*      TO DESTINATION NEEDLE  */
      PUT EDIT('MOVE DISK ',N,' FROM ',SN,' TO ',DN)
          (SKIP,A,F(2),A,A(1),A,A(1));
      N_VALUE = N - 1;
      SN_VALUE = IN;
      IN_VALUE = SN;
      DN_VALUE = DN;
      ADDRESS = H_ADDR2;
      GO TO HANOL_CALL;


H_ADDR2:
      FREE ACTIVATION_RECORD;
      GO TO RET_ADDR;


END HAN1;
```

**FIGURE 3-5.9**  (Continued)

---

b)  Describe concisely (using point form) the steps involved in tracing a recursive function, and illustrate by tracing Function MEDIAN for the set of scores 26, 67, 31, 88, 12.

c)  It can be shown that the average deviation from the median is given by

$$\frac{(Sum\ of\ the\ top\text{-}half\ scores) - (Sum\ of\ the\ bottom\text{-}half\ scores)}{Number\ of\ scores}$$

Indicate clearly and concisely how you could easily modify Function MEDIAN to compute the average deviation from the median by adding two parameters to the function definition and modifying the body of the function.

2.  The following is a solution strategy for a recursive function to find the kth smallest of a set S of integers.  If |S| (the number of elements in S) is odd, and if k is set to $\frac{|S|+1}{2}$, this function will find the median of the set S.  Let |S| be given by N.

```
          function FIND(k, S, N)
          Let m be the first element in S
          Divide S into three sequences:
```

$S_1$ composed of elements $< n$
$S_2$ composed of elements $= m$
$S_3$ composed of elements $> m$.

If $k \leq |S_1|$
then return FIND($k$, $S_1$, $|S_1|$)
else if $k \leq |S_1| + |S_2|$
    then return m
    else return FIND($k - |S_1| - |S_2|$, $S_3$, $|S_3|$)

Write a function FIND, and trace its execution on the values

$$k = 4 \quad S = \{4,7,3,6,6,2,5\}.$$

3.   Sometimes a problem can be solved most efficiently by utilizing a divide-and-conquer approach. For example, for the problem of simultaneously finding the largest and smallest elements in a set S of values, the following extremely efficient algorithm follows this approach:

Given a set or array S containing n constants in no particular order (say integer constants, although character constants would serve equally well), find the range of values by splitting S into two disjoint sets $S_1$ and $S_2$ of approximately equal size letting the maximum value of S be the maximum of MAX($S_1$) and MAX($S_2$) and the minimum value of S be the minimum of MIN($S_1$) and MIN($S_2$). Thus, we have reduced the problem to two problems of half the size. For each of $S_1$ and $S_2$, we use the same strategy to find their maxima and minima, and so on. Eventually, we get to the subproblem of finding the maximum and minimum of many sets of size 2 or size 1. For each such set, this only requires at most one comparison operation.

Altogether, this algorithm uses about $\frac{3}{2}n - 2$ comparison operations. It can be shown that no comparison-oriented algorithm can be more efficient than this divide-and-conquer algorithm.

a)   Write a recursive procedure MAXMIN which takes an array S and the size N of the array and returns a pair of values LARGE and SMALL, the largest and smallest entries in S, respectively.

b)   Give an algorithm for a reasonably efficient stack implementation of the procedure in (a). Give a trace of this stack implementation along the lines of the traces given in the text for the following set S of integer scores:

21, 86, 72, 13, 99, 51

4.   Consider the problem of calculating a "binomial coefficient" BC. The binomial coefficient refers to the Kth coefficient of the polynomial resulting from the expansion of a binomial term of the form A + B raised to the Nth power.

$$(A + B)^N = \frac{A^N}{0!} + \frac{(N * A^{N-1} * B)}{1!}$$

$$+ \frac{(N * (N - 1) * A^{N-2} * B^2)}{2!}$$

$$+ \frac{(N * (N - 1) * (N - 2) * A^{N-3} * B^3)}{3!} + \ldots$$

An explicit formula for the coefficient of the Kth term of that Nth degree polynomial is

$$BC(N, K) = \frac{N * (N - 1) * (N - 2) * \ldots * (N - K + 1)}{K!}$$

or

$$BC(N, K) = \frac{N!}{K!(N - K)!}$$

Note that we can expand this formula to

$$BC(N,K) = \frac{(N - 1) * (N - 2) * \ldots * (N - K)}{K!}$$

$$+ \frac{(N - 1) * (N - 2) * \ldots * (N - K + 1)}{(K - 1)!}$$

Equivalently, $BC(N, K) = BC(N - 1, K) + BC(N - 1, K - 1)$

Note that when $N = K$, $BC(K, K) = 1$, and that $BC(N, 0) = 1$ for any value of N.

a)   Write a recursive procedure based on the above identities for calculating the Kth binomial coefficient of the polynomial of degree N given by $(A + B)^N$.

b)   Illustrate how the contents of the run-time stack change as your program for calculating BC(N, K) computes BC(3, 2).

5.   What is the purpose of a stack in implementing a recursive procedure?

6.   Write a *recursive* procedure TRIM which removes all blanks from the front and rear of a string of text. Therefore, TRIM('☐☐CMPT☐181☐☐') returns 'CMPT☐181'.

7.   a)   Write a recursive function to convert decimal integers to their radix r representation by successive divisions. The name of the function is to be CONVERT, with two formal parameters NUMBER and RADIX. NUMBER denotes the integer to be converted and RADIX the base to which the integer is to be converted. The radix r representation is returned in string form.

   For example, computing the radix 6 representation of 184 entails that it be repeatedly divided by 6 and the resulting remainders are concatenated.

$$504 = 5 * 6^2 + 0 * 6^1 + 4 * 6^0 = 184_{10}$$

   Thus, CONVERT(184, 6) returns the value '504'. Use the MOD function.

b)   Draw a stack description (similar to that done for the factorial function in the text) of the recursive process for the case NUMBER = 153 and RADIX = 6.

8.   Sometimes recursive programming techniques can reduce the apparent complexity of a problem. This is particularly true for the problems which are most naturally described recursively or inductively.

One problem where a recursive description is fairly natural is that of converting an integer to a string of characters. Iterative methods have two "unnatural" attributes of which you should all be aware, i.e., they

a)  proceed from the rightmost digit to the leftmost, where most humans would prefer to process numbers from left to right

and they

b)  first determine the number of digits in the number, then remove digits from left to right by dividing by a successively smaller power of 10. The manual process need not explicitly determine the number's size.

A more "natural" recursive technique for converting positive integers to character strings is the following:

i)    Repeat this procedure with the rightmost digit of the number parameter removed until the parameter is less than 10. Then, once this leading (leftmost) digit has been isolated,

ii)   compute its value to modulo 10,

iii)  look up the appropriate character and save it in the next position to the right in any output string, and

iv)   return to the calling procedure.

a)  Write a recursive procedure to convert an integer to a character string.

b)  Trace the execution of your procedure on 1054 using the format in the text.

9.  Converting a decimal fraction into some other base requires the fraction to be repeatedly multiplied by the base. The digits that appear to the left of the decimal point become the digits of the answer in the order left to right. For example, 0.1 is converted to base 3 as follows:

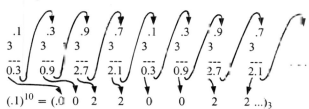

$$(.1)^{10} = (.0\ 0\ 2\quad 2\quad 0\quad 0\quad 2\quad 2\ ...)_3$$

Write a recursive function to convert decimal fractions to a specific base. The name of the function is to be CONVERT and it is to have 3 parameters, FRACTION, BASE, and N. FRACTION is a real variable containing the fraction to be converted. BASE is an integer variable containing the base to which the fraction is to be converted. Finally, N is the number of significant digits required. The result returned from the function will be a character string containing the first N significant figures of the conversion. For example,

CONVERT ( 0.1, 3, 7)

should return

'0022002'

10.  The usual method used in evaluating a polynomial of the form

$$P_n(x) = a_0 x^n + a_1 x^{n-1} + a_2 x^{n-2} + \cdots + a_{n-1} x + a_n$$

is by using the technique known as nesting or Horner's rule. This is an iterative method that can be described as follows:

$$b_0 = a_0$$

$$b_{i+1} = x * b_i + a_{i+1}; i = 0, 1, ..., n - 1$$

from which one can obtain $b_n = p_n(x)$. An alternate solution to the problem is to write

$$p_n(x) = x * p_{n-1}(x) + a_n$$

where

$$p_{n-1}(x) = a_0 x^{n-1} + a_1 x^{n-2} + \cdots + a_{n-2} x + a_{n-1}$$

which is a recursive formulation of the problem. Write a recursive-function program to evaluate such a polynomial. Use as data

$n = 3$, $a_0 = 1$, $a_1 = 3$, $a_2 = 3$, $a_3 = 1$, and $x = 2$.

11.  Consider the set of all valid, completely parenthesized, infix arithmetic expressions consisting of single-letter variable names, nonnegative integers, and the four operators $+$, $-$, $*$, and $/$. The following recursive definition gives all such valid expressions:

   *1*   Any single-letter variable ($\dot{A}$ – $\bar{Z}$) or a nonnegative integer is a valid infix expression.
   *2*   If $\alpha$ and $\beta$ are valid infix expressions, then $(\alpha + \beta)$, $(\alpha - \beta)$, $(\alpha * \beta)$, and $(\alpha / \beta)$ are valid infix expressions.
   *3*   The only valid infix expressions are those defined by steps *1* and *2*.

Write a recursive-function program that will have as input some string of symbols and which is to output "VALID EXPRESSION" if the input string is a valid infix expression and "INVALID EXPRESSION" otherwise. Write a main program to read the input data and invoke this function.

12.  Write a recursive-function program to compute the square root of a number. Read in triples of numbers N, A, and E, where N is the number for which the square root is to be found, A is an approximation of the square root, and E is the allowable error in the result. Use as your function

$$\text{ROOT(N, A, E)} = \begin{cases} \text{A, if } |A^2 + N| < E \\ \text{ROOT(N, } \dfrac{A^2 + N}{2A}, \text{ E), otherwise} \end{cases}$$

Use the following triples as test data:

|     |      |      |
| --- | ---- | ---- |
| 2   | 1.0  | .001 |
| 3   | 1.5  | .001 |
| 8   | 2.5  | .001 |
| 225 | 14.2 | .001 |

13.  Another common application for recursion is the problem of generating all possible permutations of a set of symbols. For the set consisting of symbols A, B, and C, there exists six permutations — namely, ABC, ACB, BAC, BCA, CBA, and CAB. The set of permutations of N symbols is generated by taking each symbol in turn and prefixing it to all the permutations which result from the remaining

N – 1 symbols. It is therefore, possible to specify the permutations of a set of symbols in terms of permutations of a small set of symbols. Write a recursive-function program for generating all possible permutations of a set of symbols.

14. In many applications it is required to know the number of different partitions of a given integer N, that is, how many different ways can N be expressed as a sum of integer summands. If we denote by $Q_{MN}$ the number of ways in which an integer M can be expressed as a sum, each summand of which is no larger than N, then the number of partitions of N is given by $Q_{NN}$. The function $Q_{MN}$ is defined recursively as

$$Q_{MN} = \begin{cases} 1, \text{ if } M = 1 \text{ and for all } N \\ 1, \text{ if } N = 1 \text{ and for all } M \\ Q_{MM,} \text{ if } M < N \\ 1 + Q_{M,M-1}, \text{ if } M = N \\ Q_{M,N-1} + Q_{M-N,N}, \text{ if } M > N \end{cases}$$

Write a recursive-function program and use values of N = 3, 4, 5, and 6 as data.

### 3-5.2  Polish Expressions and Their Compilation

In this section we are primarily concerned with the mechanical evaluation or compilation of infix expressions. We shall find it to be more efficient to evaluate an infix arithmetical expression by first converting it to a suffix expression and then evaluating the latter. This approach will eliminate the repeated scanning of an infix expression in order to obtain its value. We shall use examples of expressions found in scientific programming languages in this section, although the theory developed applies to any type of expression.

It was seen in Sec. 2-3 that a language consisting of the set of all valid infix expressions can be precisely described by a grammar. The same can be done for the corresponding set of all valid Polish expressions (suffix or prefix). When we convert a sentence in a language, say $L_1$, to a sentence in another language $L_2$ by some mapping, it is required that $L_2$ have many of the properties possessed by $L_1$. Properties such as "well-formed expression," associativity, and commutativity of operators in the conversion of expressions from one type to another must be preserved by the mapping.

Initially, a theorem which permits us to determine whether a Polish expression is well-formed (and consequently its corresponding infix counterpart) will be given. The translation of infix expressions to Polish notation is examined in detail and represents one of the classical applications of a stack. Finally, the generation of assembly-language instructions for Polish expressions is discussed at some length. The properties of the operators can be used in achieving some degree of code optimization (normally, a program consisting of fewer instructions than an unoptimized one).

### 3-5.2.1  Polish notation

In this subsection we introduce the notation for Polish expressions. This notation offers certain computational advantages over the traditional infix notation. Initially, an inductive definition of the set of valid suffix Polish expressions is given. A simple theorem which can be used to determine the validity of Polish expressions is then discussed. Also, the evaluation of Polish expressions is briefly introduced.

Consider the set of all valid, completely parenthesized arithmetic expressions consisting of single-letter variable names, nonnegative integers, and the four operators +, −, *, and /. The following recursive definition gives all such valid expressions:

1    Any single letter variable (a - z) or a nonnegative integer is a valid infix expression.
2    If $\alpha$ and $\beta$ are valid infix expressions, then $(\alpha + \beta)$, $(\alpha - \beta)$, $(\alpha * \beta)$, and $(\alpha / \beta)$ are valid infix expressions.
3    The only valid infix expressions are those defined by steps 1 and 2.

This is an inductive definition where expressions such as (a + b), ((a + b) − 5), and (10 + ((b * c) / d)) are considered valid (according to the definition), while expressions like a + 5, (a + b * c), etc., are considered to be invalid.

In writing a valid expression, complete parenthesization must be used. Such a requirement is somewhat severe, and in order that the number of parentheses does not become excessively large, certain conventions have been developed. An obvious convention is one in which the outermost parentheses of an expression are dropped so that (p + q) * r can be taken to be a valid formula instead of ((p + q) * r), as required by the original definition.

One method of reducing the number of parentheses further is to prescribe an order of precedence for the connectives. Once this is done, further reductions can be made by requiring that for any two binary operators appearing in a formula having the same precedence, the left one is evaluated first. The same requirement can be stated by saying that the binary operators are left-associative. Such a convention is commonly used in arithmetic; for example, 4 + 6 * 3 − 7    stands for (4 + (6 * 3)) − 7. If an evaluation of such an expression is to be done mechanically, it is important that the number of parentheses be reduced so that an excessive number of scannings of the expression is avoided.

Let us consider, initially, the mechanical evaluation of unparenthesized arithmetic expressions consisting of single-letter variables, nonnegative integers, and the four operators +, −, *, and /. The precedence of the operators * and / is considered to be equal and of higher value than that of + and −. An example of such an unparenthesized arithmetic expression is

a + b * c + d * e
          ⏝        ⏝
          1        2
⏝⏝⏝
    3
⏝⏝⏝⏝⏝
        4

According to our convention, the above expression stands for (a + (b * c )) + (d * e). For the evaluation of this expression, we must scan from left to right repeatedly. The numbers below the subexpressions indicate the steps of such an evaluation. This process of evaluation is inefficient because of the repeated scanning that must be done.

If there are parentheses in an expression, then the order of precedence is altered by the parentheses. For example, in (a + b) * c we first evaluate a + b and then (a + b) * c. In fact it is possible to write expressions which make the order of evaluation of subexpressions independent of the precedence of the operators. This is accomplished by parenthesizing subexpressions in such a way that, corresponding to each operator, there is a pair of parentheses. This pair encloses the operator and its operands. We now define the parenthetical level of an operator as the total number of pairs of parentheses that surround it. A pair of parentheses has the same parenthetical level as that of the operator to which it corresponds, i.e., of the operator which is immediately enclosed by this pair. Such an expression is called a *fully parenthesized expression*. For example, in the fully parenthesized expression

$$(a + ((b * c) * (d + e)))$$

$$1 \qquad 3 \quad 2 \quad 3$$

the integers below the operators specify the parenthetical level of each operator. When such an expression is evaluated, the subexpression containing the operator with the higher parenthetical level is evaluated first. In the case of more than one operator having the highest parenthetical level (as in the above example), we evaluate them one after the other from left to right. Once the subexpressions containing operators at the highest parenthetical level have been evaluated, the subexpressions containing the operators at the next highest level are evaluated in the same way. Thus in the above example, the subexpressions are evaluated in the following order:

$$(b * c), (d + e), ((b * c) * (d + e)), (a + ((b * c) * (d + e)))$$

As we mentioned earlier, for a fully parenthesized expression no convention regarding the order of precedence of an operator is needed.

In the case when the order of precedence of the operators is prescribed and the expressions are partly parenthesized, or in the other case when the expressions are fully parenthesized, a repeated scanning from left to right is still needed in order to evaluate an expression. The reason is that the operators appear along with the operands inside the expression. The notation used so far is to write the operator between the operands, for example, a * b. Such a notation is called an *infix notation*. Repeated scanning is avoided if the infix expression is first converted to an equivalent parenthesis-free *suffix* or *prefix* expression in which the subexpressions have the form

|  | operand | operand | operator |
|----|---------|---------|----------|
| or | operator | operand | operand |

in place of an infix form where we have

| operand | operator | operand |
|---------|----------|---------|

This type of notation is known as Łukasiewicz notation (due to the Polish logician Jan Łukasiewicz), or "reverse Polish" and "Polish" notation, respectively. For example, the expressions given in each row of Table 3-5.1 are equivalent.

Note that in both the suffix and prefix equivalents of an infix expression, the variables are in the same relative position. The expressions in suffix or prefix form are parenthesis free, and the operators are rearranged according to the rules of precedence for the operators.

A fully parenthesized infix expression can be directly translated to suffix notation by beginning with the conversion of the inner parenthesized subexpression and

**Table 3-5.1**

| Infix | Suffix (Reverse Polish) | Prefix (Polish) |
|---|---|---|
| a | a | a |
| a + b | ab+ | +ab |
| a + b + c | ab+c+ | ++abc |
| a + (b + c) | abc++ | +a+bc |
| a + b * c | abc*+ | +a*bc |
| a * (b + c) | abc+* | *a+bc |
| a * b * c | ab*c* | **abc |

then proceeding towards the outside of the expression. In the case of the fully parenthesized expression

$$(a + ((b * c) * d))$$

$$1 \quad\quad 3 \quad 2$$

the innermost parenthesized subexpression of level 3 is

$$(b * c)$$

and is converted to bc*. This suffix subexpression becomes the first operand of the operator * at level 2. Therefore, the subexpression bc**d of level 2 is converted to the suffix equivalent of bc*d*, and finally at level 1, the term a + bc*d* is converted to the final suffix form of abc*d*+.

Programmers, of course, do not program expressions in fully parenthesized form. Certain FORTRAN (and other) compilers initially convert partially parenthesized expressions to a fully parenthesized form before conversion to a suffix form is performed. (Suffix form seems to be most convenient for compilers.)

Let us consider the problem of mechanically converting a parenthesis-free expression (containing +, −, * and /) into suffix form. As was mentioned previously, only the operators are rearranged in order to obtain the suffix Polish equivalent. If we scan the infix string left to right, the leftmost operator having the highest precedence will be the first operator to be encountered in the suffix string. The next-highest-precedence operator will be the second operator to be encountered in the expression. Note that for infix expressions, if we do not specify that a leftmost operator has precedence over other operators of equal precedence, then the suffix equivalent is not unique. For example, the expression a + b + c would be converted to ab+c+ or abc++ if no mention was made that the leftmost operator + in the infix string has precedence over the remaining operator. From this it is clear that when we scan a suffix expression from left to right, we encounter the operators in the same order in which we would have evaluated them by following the precedence convention for operators in the infix expression. For example, the suffix equivalent of a + b * c, abc*+, where the operator * is encountered before + in a left-to-right scan, indicates that the multiplication is to be evaluated before addition.

In practice it is often necessary to evaluate expressions, i.e., to determine their value for a given set of values assigned to the variables appearing in the expressions. This can be done more easily by using a suffix representation of the expression, because scanning of the expression is required in only one direction, viz. from left to right, and only once, whereas for the infix expression the scanning has to be done several times and in both directions. For example, to evaluate the suffix expression abc* +, we scan this string from left to right until we encounter *. The two operands, viz. b and c, which appear immediately to the left of this operator are its operands, and the expression bc* is replaced by its value. Let us assume that this value is denoted by $T_1$. This reduces the original suffix string to $aT_1+$. If we continue to scan beyond $T_1$, the next operator encountered is + whose operands are a and $T_1$ and the evaluation results in a value which we will denote by $T_2$.

This method of evaluating suffix expressions can be summarized by the following four rules, which are repeatedly applied until all operators have been processed:

*1*    Find the leftmost operator in the expression.
*2*    Select the two operands immediately to the left of the operator found.
*3*    Perform the indicated operation.
*4*    Replace the operator and operands with the result.

As a further example, the suffix expression abc/d*+ corresponding to the infix expression a + (b / c) * d is evaluated below for values of a = 5, b = 4, c = 2, and d = 2:

| Suffix Form | Current Operator | Current Operands |
| --- | --- | --- |
| abc/d*+ | / | b, c |
| $aT_1d*+$ | * | $T_1$, d |
| $aT_2+$ | + | a, $T_2$ |
| $T_3$ | | |

Note that in this example $T_1 = 2$, $T_2 = 4$, and $T_3 = 9$.

As previously mentioned, there are a number of compilers that convert infix arithmetic expressions into Polish notation. In such compilers invalid Polish expressions, and consequently their invalid infix-expression counterparts, must be detected in the compiling phase of translation. The remaining pages of this section will be concerned with the description of a method that can be used to detect such invalid expressions. We will restrict ourselves to suffix Polish expressions, although an analogous method can also be developed for prefix Polish expressions. Let us first describe by induction the set of valid suffix Polish expressions.

Suppose S is a set of symbols $s_1, s_2, ..., s_q$ (typically variable names and literals), and the set $o_1, o_2, ..., o_m$ consists of operators for constructing expressions using elements of S. The *degree* of an operator is the number of operands which that operator has; e.g., the degree of the multiplication operator is two. A suffix expression is defined by the following:

*1*    A single symbol $s_i$ is an expression.
*2*    If $x_1, x_2, ..., x_n$ are expressions and $o_i$ is of degree n, then $x_1x_2 \cdots x_no_i$ is an expression.
*3*    The only valid expressions are those obtained by steps *1* and *2*.

To determine whether an expression is valid, we next associate a *rank* with each expression, which is determined as follows:

*4*    The rank of a symbol $s_j$ is "one."

*5*    The rank of an operator $o_j$ is $1 - n$, where n is the degree of $o_j$.

*6*    The rank of an arbitrary sequence of symbols and operators is the sum of the ranks of the individual symbols and operators.

For example, let the sets of symbols and connectives consist of single-letter variables (a - z) and the four arithmetic operators, respectively. The rank function, which is denoted by r, is given as

$$r(s_j) = 1, \text{ for } 1 \leqslant j \leqslant 26$$
$$r(+) = r(-) = -1, r(*) = r(/) = -1$$

The rank of the formula ab+cd-* is obtained from the computation

$$r(a) + r(b) + r(+) + r(c) + r(d) + r(-) + r(*) = 1$$

A theorem to follow is very important since it can be used to determine whether a given expression is valid. Before the theorem is stated, some mention of the terminology required is in order. If $z = x \bigcirc y$ is a string, then x is a *head* of z. Finally, x is a proper head if y is not empty (y is not '').

### 3-5.2.2 Conversion of infix expressions to Polish notation

We shall first develop an algorithm for translating unparenthesized infix expressions to suffix Polish. This algorithm will be subsequently modified to handle parenthesized expressions. Note that one can also have completely parenthesized infix expressions which do not require any rules of precedence except the usual rule for parentheses. Such expressions are inconvenient to use because of the large number of parentheses which are required.

The evaluation of an infix expression as well as a suffix Polish expression was discussed in the previous section. Recall that in an unparenthesized infix expression the evaluation is performed in such a manner that the operator with the highest precedence is evaluated before the others. If more than one operator has the same precedence in the expression, then the leftmost operator (for left-associative operators) or rightmost operator (for right-associative operators such as exponentiation and negation) with that precedence is evaluated first. Of course, in such an evaluation process, we need to scan the expression repeatedly, thereby making the process inefficient. The same idea can be applied to partially parenthesized infix expressions. The subexpression that is evaluated first is located by scanning up to the first right parenthesis and moving left until a left parenthesis is detected. The subexpression can then be evaluated using the rule of precedence.

Theorem.   A Polish suffix (prefix) formula is well-formed if and only if the rank of the formula is "one" and the rank of any proper head of a Polish formula is greater than (less than) or equal to "one."      ////

This theorem is very important in the compilation of infix expressions since it permits us to detect an invalid Polish expression (and, consequently, a corresponding invalid infix expression). Table 3-5.2 contains a number of valid and invalid expressions.

We shall next consider the mechanical conversion of infix expressions to Polish notation. Let us now define in BNF the infix expression containing single-letter variables, natural number constants, and the four binary arithmetic operators +, −, *, and /:

```
<identifier> :: = a | b | c ... | z
<digit> :: = 0 | 1 | 2 ... | 9
<digit string> :: = <digit string> <digit> | <digit>
<primary> :: = <identifier> | <digit string> | (<infix expression>)
<term> :: = <primary> | <term> * <primary> | <term> / <primary>
<infix expression> ::= <term> | <infix expression> + <term> |
                       <infix expression> − <term>
```

The above grammar inherently specifies that the operators * and / have equal precedence that is greater than the precedence of + and −.

On the other hand, in a parenthesis-free suffix expression, the subexpressions have the form

<operand 1> <operand 2> <operator>

and a suffix Polish expression can be specified by the following rules:

```
<reverse Polish> ::= <reverse Polish> <reverse Polish> <operator> |
                     <identifier> | <digit string>
<operator> ::= + | − | * | /
```

For example, the following expressions are equivalent:

| Infix | Reverse Polish |
|---|---|
| b | b |
| a + b | ab+ |
| a + b + c | ab+c+ |
| a + b * c | abc*+ |
| a * (b + c) | abc+* |
| a / b * c | ab/c* |

**Table 3-5.2**

| Infix | Suffix Polish | Rank | Valid or Invalid |
|---|---|---|---|
| a + * b | ab*+ | 0 | invalid |
| a − b * c | abc*− | 1 | valid |
| ab + c | abc+ | 2 | invalid |
| (a + b) * (c − d) | ab+cd−* | 1 | valid |
| a + b / d − | abd/+− | 0 | invalid |

It is an easy matter to devise an algorithm which will convert an infix expression without parentheses into Polish. This conversion is based on the precedence of the operators and requires the use of a stack. The Polish expression will be stored in some output string which will be used later in the generation of object code. Recall that all variables and constants are not reordered in any way when the infix expression is converted to Polish. The operators, however, are reordered in the output string, depending on their relative precedence, and it is for this reason that a stack is required.

Let us initially assign precedence values to the four arithmetic operators displayed in Table 3-5.3. The precedence associated with multiplication and division is greater than the precedence of addition and subtraction. Also included in the table is a precedence value for variables (which are restricted to a single letter for simplicity) and the rank function. The reason for this will be explained shortly.

Assume that the stack contents have been initialized to some symbol (# in Table 3-5.3) which has a precedence value less than all other precedence values given in Table 3-5.3. A general algorithm for the conversion process might take the following form:

1. Initialize stack contents to the special symbol #
2. Scan the leftmost symbol in the given infix expression and denote it as the current input symbol
3. Repeat thru step 6 while the current input symbol is not #
4. Remove and output all stack symbols whose precedence values are greater than or equal to the precedence of the current input symbol
5. Push the current input symbol onto the stack
6. Scan the leftmost symbol in the infix expression and let it be the current input symbol

The detailed algorithm can now be given.

**Algorithm** UNPARENTHESIZED_SUFFIX. Given an input string INFIX representing an infix expression whose single character symbols have precedence values and ranks as given in Table 3-5.3, a vector S representing a stack, and a string function NEXTCHAR which, when invoked, returns the next character of the input string, this algorithm converts the string INFIX to its reverse Polish string equivalent, POLISH. RANK contains the value of each head of the reverse Polish string, NEXT contains

**Table 3-5.3**

| Symbol | Precedence $f$ | Rank $r$ |
|---|---|---|
| +, − | 1 | −1 |
| *, / | 2 | −1 |
| a, b, c, ... | 3 | 1 |
| # | 0 | − |

the symbol being examined, and TEMP is a temporary variable which contains the unstacked element. We assume that the given input string is padded on the right with the special symbol '#'.

1. [Initialize the stack]
   TOP ← 1
   S[TOP] ← '#'
2. [Initialize output string and rank count]
   POLISH ← ''
   RANK ← 0
3. [Get first input symbol]
   NEXT ← NEXTCHAR(INFIX)
4. [Translate the infix expression]
   Repeat thru step 6 while NEXT ≠ '#'
5. [Remove symbols with greater or equal precedence from stack]
   Repeat while f(NEXT) ≤ f(S[TOP])
       TEMP ← POP(S, TOP)   (this copies the stack contents into TEMP)
       POLISH ← POLISH ○ TEMP
       RANK ← RANK + r(TEMP)
       If RANK < 1
       then   Write('INVALID')
              Exit
6. [Push current symbol onto stack and obtain next input symbol]
   Call PUSH(S, TOP, NEXT)
   NEXT ← NEXTCHAR(INFIX)
7. [Remove remaining elements from stack]
   Repeat while S[TOP] ≠ '#'
       TEMP ← POP(S, TOP)
       POLISH ← POLISH ○ TEMP
       RANK ← RANK + r(TEMP)
       If RANK < 1
       then   Write('INVALID')
              Exit
8. [Is the expression valid?]
   If RANK = 1
   then   Write('VALID')
   else   Write('INVALID')
   Exit                                                                    □

The algorithm operates in a straightforward manner. Initially, a special symbol '#' is placed on the stack. The purpose of this symbol is to ensure that upon the detection of '#' at the end of the string INFIX, the remaining elements of the stack (except '#') are put in POLISH. The main portion of the algorithm is concerned with the precedence value comparison of the incoming symbol NEXT and the top element of the stack. If the precedence value of NEXT is greater than that of the top element of the stack, then the symbol NEXT is inserted on the stack and the next input symbol is scanned. If, on the other hand, the precedence value of NEXT is less than or equal to that of the top element of the stack, then the latter element is removed from the stack and placed in string POLISH, after which the precedence values for NEXT and the new top element of the stack are compared, etc. The rank of the Polish string is updated each time a symbol is written in POLISH.

Note that since a variable has the highest precedence, it will be placed on the top of the stack. On scanning the very next input symbol, we see that the variable will be deleted from the stack and copied into POLISH (since in a valid infix expression, no two consecutive variables are permitted). Actually, it is a very easy matter to alter the algorithm so that the precedence value of NEXT is tested for a value of 3. If this test succeeds, then NEXT is a variable and it can be written out directly into POLISH without being placed on the stack. We do not do this, however, for reasons of generality which become important as the infix expression is permitted to be more complex than those which we are presently considering.

An incoming symbol with a precedence value greater than that of the top element of the stack will result in the operator (or variable) being inserted in the stack. This is understandable since the operation corresponding to this incoming operator should be performed before any other operations corresponding to the other operators on the stack. This will be reflected by the last operator to be placed on the stack being the first to be deleted from the stack and placed in string POLISH. Notice that when the precedence of an incoming operator is equal to the precedence of the operator on the top of the stack, then the latter is placed in the string POLISH. This preserves the property that in an expression containing operators with the same precedence, the leftmost operator is executed first. Therefore, the above algorithm will convert a + b + c to ab+c+ and not to abc++. The Polish string ab+c+ corresponds to the infix (a + b) + c and, abc++ corresponds to a + (b + c). A trace of the stack contents and the Polish string POLISH for the infix expression a + b * c – d/e * h is given in Table 3-5.4.

Let us now consider the problem of converting an infix expression containing parenthesized subexpressions. When a programmer writes an expression containing parentheses, he does not normally write it in a completely parenthesized form. When a left parenthesis is encountered in the infix expression, it should be placed on the stack regardless of its present contents. However, when it is in the stack, it should only be removed and discarded when a right parenthesis is encountered in the infix expression, at which time the right parenthesis is also ignored. A left parenthesis can be forced on the stack by assigning to it a precedence value greater than that of any other operator. Once on the stack, the left parenthesis should have another precedence value (called its *stack precedence*) which is smaller than that of any other operator. We can get rid of the left parenthesis on the stack by checking for an incoming right parenthesis in the infix expression. The right parenthesis is never inserted on the stack. Actually, we can modify the previous algorithm in such a manner that the left and right parentheses can perform the same function as the special symbol '#' used earlier. The original table of precedence values (Table 3-5.3) can be revised to have both an input- and stack-precedence value for each operator and operand. This is done in addition to getting rid of the symbol '#', in order to make the algorithm more general in the sense that the algorithm does not grow significantly in complexity when we add other operators such as relations, logical, unary, and ternary operators. Table 3-5.5 is a revised table which includes parentheses. Each symbol has both input-symbol and stack-symbol precedence, except for a right parenthesis which does not possess a stack precedence since it is never placed on the stack. Table 3-5.5 also contains the exponentiation operator denoted here by the symbol ↑. All arithmetic operators except exponentiation have an input precedence which is lower in value than their stack precedence. This preserves the left to right processing of operators of equal precedence in an expression. The exponentiation operator in mathematics is right-associative. The expression a ↑ b ↑ c is equivalent to the parenthesized expression a ↑ (b ↑ c) and not to the expression (a ↑ b) ↑ c.

**Table 3-5.4**   Translation of infix string a + b * c – d / e * h
to Polish.

| Character Scanned | Contents of Stack (rightmost symbol is top of stack) | Reverse-Polish Expression | Rank |
|---|---|---|---|
|   | # |   |   |
| a | #a |   |   |
| + | # + | a | 1 |
| b | # +b | a | 1 |
| * | # + * | ab | 2 |
| c | # + *c | ab | 2 |
| – | # – | abc * + | 1 |
| d | # –d | abc * + | 1 |
| / | # –/ | abc * +d | 2 |
| e | # –/e | abc * +d | 2 |
| * | # – * | abc * +dϱ/ | 2 |
| h | # – *h | abc * +dϱ/ | 2 |
| # | # | abc * +de/h * – | 1 |

The conversion of an infix expression into reverse Polish operates in much the same way as the previous algorithm. A left parenthesis is initially placed on the stack, and the infix expression is padded on the right with a right parenthesis. The new algorithm is formulated as follows:

**Algorithm** REVPOL. Given an input string INFIX containing an infix expression which has been padded on the right with ')' and whose symbols have precedence values given by Table 3-5.5, a vector S, used as a stack, and a function NEXTCHAR, which, when invoked, returns the next character of its argument, this algorithm converts INFIX into reverse Polish and places the result in the string POLISH. The integer variable TOP denotes the top of the stack. Algorithms PUSH and POP are used for stack manipulation. The integer variable RANK accumulates the rank of the expression. Finally, the string variable TEMP is used for temporary storage purposes.

1. [Initialize stack]
      TOP ← 1
      S[TOP] ← '('
2. [Initialize output string and rank count]
      POLISH ← ''
      RANK ← 0
3. [Get first input symbol]
      NEXT ← NEXTCHAR(INFIX)
4. [Translate the infix expression]
      Repeat thru step 7 while NEXT ≠ ''
5. [Remove symbols with greater precedence from stack]

```
            If TOP < 1
            then   Write('INVALID')
                   Exit
            Repeat while f(NEXT) < g(S[TOP])
                TEMP ← POP(S, TOP)
                POLISH ← POLISH ○ TEMP
                RANK ← RANK + r(TEMP)
                If RANK < 1
                then   Write('INVALID')
                       Exit
  6.    [Are there matching parentheses?]
            If f(NEXT) ≠ g(S[TOP])
            then   Call PUSH(S, TOP, NEXT)
            else   POP(S, TOP)
  7.    [Get next input symbol]
            NEXT ← NEXTCHAR(INFIX)
  8.    [Is the expression valid?]
            If TOP ≠ 0 or RANK ≠ 1
            then   Write('INVALID')
            else   Write('VALID')
            Exit                                              □
```

A trace of the stack contents and the Polish string POLISH for the infix expression

$$(a + b \uparrow c \uparrow d) * (e + f / d))$$

is given in Table 3-5.6. The reader is encouraged to trace the algorithm for the not well-formed expression (a * + b) + c)).

It is possible to extend precedence functions to handle relational operators, conditional statements, unconditional transfers (go to), subscripted variables, and

**Table 3-5.5**

| | | Precedence | |
|---|---|---|---|
| Symbol | Input Precedence Function f | Stack Precedence Function g | Rank Function r |
| +, − | 1 | 2 | −1 |
| *, / | 3 | 4 | −1 |
| ↑ | 6 | 5 | −1 |
| variables | 7 | 8 | 1 |
| ( | 9 | 0 | − |
| ) | 0 | − | − |

**Table 3-5.6** Translation of infix string (a + b ↑ c ↑ d) * (e + f / d)) to Polish.

| Character Scanned | Contents of Stack (rightmost symbol is top of stack) | Reverse-Polish Expression | Rank |
|---|---|---|---|
|   | ( |   |   |
| ( | (( |   |   |
| a | ((a |   |   |
| + | ((+ | a | 1 |
| b | ((+b | a | 1 |
| ↑ | ((+↑ | ab | 2 |
| c | ((+↑c | ab | 2 |
| ↑ | ((+↑↑ | abc | 3 |
| d | ((+↑↑d | abc | 3 |
| ) | ( | abcd↑^+ | 1 |
| * | (* | abcd↑↑+ | 1 |
| ( | (*( | abcd↑↑+ | 1 |
| e | (*(e | abcd↑↑+ | 1 |
| + | (*(+ | abcd↑↑+e | 2 |
| f | (*(+f | abcd↑↑+e | 2 |
| / | (*(+/ | abcd↑↑+ef | 3 |
| d | (*(+/d | abcd↑↑+ef | 3 |
| ) | (* | abcd↑↑+efd/+ | 2 |
| ) |   | abcd↑↑+efd/+* | 1 |

many other features found in present programming languages. Some exercises at the end of this section will deal with these extensions.

We have been concerned until now with the conversion of an infix expression to reverse Polish. The motivation behind this conversion is that reverse Polish can be converted into object code by linearly scanning the Polish string once. The next section deals with the problem of generating code from the Polish string.

The problem of converting infix expressions to prefix Polish will not be discussed in this section. A simple algorithm based on the scanning of an infix expression from right to left can be easily formulated. In many cases the entire infix string is not available, but it is obtained one symbol at a time in a left-to-right manner (because this is the way we write programs). Therefore, a practical algorithm for converting infix to prefix must be based on a left-to-right scan of the infix string. To facilitate such an algorithm, however, the use of two stacks instead of the usual one is permitted. This is left as an exercise.

### 3-5.2.3 Conversion of Polish expressions to code

It will be assumed throughout this discussion that the object code desired is assembly-language instructions. Without getting deeply involved in a description of a hypothetical machine, assume that the object computer which will execute the object code produced by the compiling process is a single-address single-accumulator machine having main memory that is sequentially organized into words. The instructions in a program are executed in a sequential manner unless a transfer instruction is encountered. The following are some of the assembler instructions which are available in the assembly language:

LOD a   — Loads the value of variable a in the accumulator and leaves the contents of a unchanged.

STO a   — Stores the value of the accumulator in a word of memory denoted by a. The accumulator contents remain unchanged.

ADD a   — Adds the value of variable a to the value of the accumulator and leaves the result in the accumulator. The contents of a remain unchanged.

SUB a   — The value of variable a is subtracted from the value of the accumulator, and the result is stored in the accumulator. The contents of a remain unchanged.

MUL a   — The value of variable a is multiplied by the value of the accumulator, and the result is stored in the accumulator. The contents of a remain unaltered.

DIV a   — The value of the accumulator is divided by the value of variable a, and the result is placed in the accumulator. The contents of a remain unaltered.

JMP b   — This is an unconditional branching instruction. The next instruction to be executed is located at a location (word) denoted by label b.

BRN b   — This is a conditional branching instruction. The location of the next instruction to be performed is given by the label b if the accumulator content is negative; otherwise, the instruction following the BRN instruction is next.

The above instructions are sufficient for our purpose. A simple example of evaluating a Polish string was given in the previous section. Consider, initially, a "brute-force" algorithm for converting a Polish expression consisting of the four basic arithmetic operators and single-letter variables to assembly language. Assume that the following code will be generated for the basic arithmetic operators:

```
x + y (xy+)    LOD x
               ADD y
               STO Tᵢ
x - y (xy-)    LOD x
               SUB y
               STO Tᵢ
x * y (xy*)    LOD x
               MUL y
               STO Tᵢ
x / y (xy/)    LOD x
               DIV y
               STO Tᵢ
```

Each operator generates three assembly-language instructions. The third instruction in the group has the form of STO $T_i$ where $T_i$ represents an address of a location (word) in memory that is to contain the value of an intermediate result. These addresses are created by the Polish-to-assembly-language algorithm which is to follow. A general algorithm for generating assembly language statements from a Polish string is the following.

1. Repeat thru step 3 for all characters in the Polish string
2. Obtain the current input symbol
3. If the current input symbol is a variable
   then push this variable on the stack
   else remove the two topmost operands from the stack
       generate the sequence of assembly language instructions which
         corresponds to the current arithmetic operator
       stack the intermediate result

The detailed algorithm can now be formulated.

**Algorithm** ASSEMBLY_CODE. Given a string POLISH representing a reverse Polish expression (which contains the four basic arithmetic operators and single-letter variables) equivalent to some well-formed infix expression, this algorithm translates the string POLISH to assembly language instructions as previously specified. The algorithm uses a stack S as usual. The integer variable I is associated with the generation of an intermediate result. The string variable OPCODE contains the operation code which corresponds to the current operation being processed.

1. [Initialize]
       TOP ← I ← 0
2. [Process all symbols]
       Repeat thru step 4 for J = 1, 2, ..., LENGTH(POLISH)
3. [Obtain current input symbol]
       NEXT ← SUB(POLISH, J, 1)
4. [Determine the type of NEXT]
       If 'A' ≤ NEXT and NEXT ≤ 'Z'
       then   Call PUSH(S, TOP, NEXT)     (push variable on stack)
       else   Select case (NEXT)     (process current operator)
                   Case '+':
                   OPCODE ← 'ADD□'
                   Case '−':
                   OPCODE ← 'SUB□'
                   Case '*':
                   OPCODE ← 'MUL□'
                   Case '/':
                   OPCODE ← 'DIV□'
               RIGHT ← POP(S, TOP)     (unstack two operands)
               LEFT ← POP(S, TOP)
               Write('LOD□' ○ LEFT)     (output load instruction)
               Write(OPCODE ○ RIGHT)     (output arithmetic instruction)
               I ← I + 1     (obtain temporary storage index)
               TEMP ← 'T' ○ I
               Write('STO□' ○ TEMP)     (output temporary store instruction)
               Call PUSH(S, TOP, TEMP)     (stack intermediate result)
5. [Finished]
       Exit

□

**Table 3-5.7** Sample code generated by Algorithm ASSEMBLY_CODE for the Polish string abc*+de/h*−.

| Character Scanned | Contents of Stack (rightmost symbol is top of stack) | Left Operand | Right Operand | Code Generated |
|---|---|---|---|---|
| a | a | | | |
| b | ab | | | |
| c | abc | | | |
| * | $aT_1$ | b | c | LOD b<br>MUL c<br>STO $T_1$ |
| + | $T_2$ | a | $T_1$ | LOD a<br>ADD $T_1$<br>STO $T_2$ |
| d | $T_2d$ | | | |
| e | $T_2de$ | | | |
| / | $T_2T_3$ | d | e | LOD d<br>DIV e<br>STO $T_3$ |
| h | $T_2T_3h$ | | | |
| * | $T_2T_4$ | $T_3$ | h | LOD $T_3$<br>MUL h<br>STO $T_4$ |
| − | $T_5$ | $T_2$ | $T_4$ | LOD $T_2$<br>SUB $T_4$<br>STO $T_5$ |

One very important point should be noted. In general, variables and constants (and indeed operators) can be more than one character in length. Instead of storing the variable names, values of constants, etc., in the string POLISH, integer pointers (giving the index of a variable or constant or operator) to a vector containing these names and constants are used. In this way, each item in POLISH is of the same length. The label $T_i$, in practice, would be a pointer to a vector containing all created variable names in storing temporary results.

The algorithm performs one linear scan of the string POLISH looking for an operator. Once one is found, it unstacks two symbols, outputs the indicated operation, and stores the intermediate result on the stack. The process is repeated until no operators are left in POLISH. The trace of the translation for the reverse Polish string 'abc*+de/h*−' is given in Table 3-5.7. The assembly language generated by the process is given in the rightmost column of the table. There are a number of obvious inefficiencies in the code generated. First, there exist redundant pairs of instructions such as

   STO $T_3$
   LOD $T_3$

in the sequence of output instructions. A second point is that no advantage is taken of the commutative property of the addition and multiplication operators. The result of this is contained in the code generated for the subexpression a + b * c, namely, the sequence

```
LOD b
MUL c
STO T₁
LOD a
ADD T₁
STO T₂
```

which could obviously be replaced by the equivalent sequence

```
LOD b
MUL c
ADD a
STO T₁
```

since the right operand is already in the accumulator and the values of a + b * c and b * c + a are equal. This last sequence takes advantage of the commutative property of addition. Finally, there is no effort made to economize the number of temporary locations required to store intermediate results. Indeed, if m such results are evaluated, the same number of temporary variables are created. The sequence of instructions

```
LOD b
MUL c
STO T₁
LOD a
ADD T₁
STO T₂
```

can obviously be replaced by the equivalent sequence where all instructions are the same except the last which becomes STO T .

The number of temporary variables required can easily be reduced by performing the following simple test. Before generating instructions for the arithmetic operators, a test is performed on the contents of the left (LEFT) and right (RIGHT) operands associated with the operator in question. For each operand (LEFT,RIGHT) corresponding to a created ($T_i$) variable, the temporary variable counter I is decremented by "one."

The redundant pairs of store and load instructions and the unnecessary temporary storing and subsequent reloading of a right operand for commutative operators can be eliminated by the following technique. Instead of always storing a partial result in temporary storage, as is done in step 4 of Algorithm ASSEMBLY_CODE, one can delay the generation of such an instruction until it is deemed absolutely necessary. The previous algorithm can be altered so as to place an intermediate result marker, '@', on the stack instead of always generating a store instruction. If this marker is never pushed down in the stack deeper than the next-to-the-top position, then an intermediate result need not be saved by the generation of a store instruction. An algorithm based on these comments is left as an exercise.

**Exercises for Sec. 3-5.2**

1. Write a recursive routine which will recognize if a particular expression is well-formed reverse Polish. Assume that the expression consists of single-letter variable names and the four basic arithmetic operators.

2. Thus far, we have only been concerned with the binary subtraction operator. In mathematics there are three usages of the minus sign, namely, to indicate the binary subtraction operator, the unary minus operator (such as −x), and the sign of a constant (such as x + (−5). Obtain a precedence table capable of handling assignment statements containing the unary minus (denoted by −) and the assignment operator (denoted by ←). (Hint: It is an easy matter to distinguish the different occurrences of minus. A minus symbol will denote a binary operator if it does not occur either at the beginning of an expression or immediately after a left parenthesis. A minus symbol at the beginning of an expression or immediately after a left parenthesis will be a unary operator unless it is followed by a digit or decimal point.)

3. Consider expressions which can contain relational and logical operators. Formulate the precedence functions required to convert such expressions to reverse Polish.

4. As we mentioned earlier, for certain applications the scanning of the infix expression is restricted to a left-to-right one-character-at-a-time scan. In an infix to prefix conversion, two stacks instead of one (as for infix to suffix conversion) are required, namely, an operator stack and an operand stack (to store temporarily the intermediate operands). Recall from Sec. 3-5.2.1 that all variables and constants retain their relative order when an infix expression is converted to prefix form. The operators, however, are reordered according to their relative precedence, and the operator stack is used in this reordering. The operand stack is used for temporary storage of intermediate operands so that, when finally the operator which connects them is found to be applicable, it can be placed in front of the concatenated operands. Formulate an algorithm to perform the translation assuming infix expressions consisting of single-letter variables and the four arithmetic operators.

5. Program Algorithm ASSEMBLY_CODE in the text and use suitable data to verify it.

6. Based on the discussion following Algorithm ASSEMBLY_CODE in the text, formulate an algorithm which will generate more efficient code based on the commutativity of the operators * and +.

7. Program the algorithm obtained in Prob. 6 and use suitable data to verify it.

8. Modify the algorithm obtained in Prob. 6 so as to incorporate the assignment operator.

9. Modify the algorithm obtained in Prob. 8 to generate code for the six relational operators.

10. Modify and program the algorithm obtained in Prob. 6 so that it will also handle the unary minus operator.

11. Describe how conditional and unconditional statements might be implemented in the reverse-Polish framework.

12. Write an algorithm to convert prefix Polish assignments into assembler code. The BNF grammar for a Polish assignment is

        &lt;assign&gt; ::= = &lt;id&gt; &lt;term&gt;
        &lt;term&gt; ::= &lt;id&gt; | &lt;op&gt; &lt;term&gt; &lt;term&gt;
        &lt;op&gt; ::= + | − | * | /
        &lt;id&gt; ::= &lt;letter&gt; | &lt;id&gt; &lt;letter&gt; | &lt;id&gt; &lt;digit&gt;

The conversion for a &lt;term&gt; should be done by a *recursive* procedure which prints out the assembler code for an input Polish assignment. You may assume that each assignment is contained on its own separate line. The assignment is in the Polish (prefix) notation described by the above grammar with an arbitrary number of blanks between the tokens and operators.

### 3-5.3 Stack Machines

In the previous section we discussed code generation for reverse-Polish expressions using fast register-type machines. One of the main problems with using machines which have a very limited number of registers is how to handle the storage of intermediate results. In particular, we must be very cognizant of the generation of wasted store/load instruction sequences. In this subsection, we illustrate how the presence of the simple stack operations of POP and PUSH can enhance the process of generating code from a reverse-Polish string.

Many of the machines which are appearing on the market include in their architecture hardware stacks or stack mechanisms. Two such machines are the PDP-11 and the Burroughs 5000. Both machines are particularly well suited for the stacking of local variables and parameters that arise in procedure calls of block-nested languages, as discussed in Sec. 3-5.1 on recursion. The B5000 and its successors have zero address instructions which make it very attractive when generating code from a suffix-Polish expression. Rather than describing a particular machine, we present a simple hypothetical stack-machine which is sufficient to illustrate the important concepts related to the code generation for reverse-Polish strings of arithmetic expressions. The instructions available for this machine are given in mnemonic form as follows:

1. PUSH <name> — Load from memory onto stack  This instruction loads an operand from the memory location named <name> and places the contents of <name> on the stack.
2. POP <name> — Store top of stack in memory. The contents of the top of the stack are removed and stored in the memory location referenced by <name>.
3. ADD, SUB, MUL, DIV — Arithmetic operation.

The indicated operation is applied to the top two values on the stack and the result is left at the second-from-the-top stack location. The top element of the stack is then popped off. Therefore,

ADD means S[TOP − 1] ← S[TOP − 1] + S[TOP], and TOP ← TOP − 1.
SUB means S[TOP − 1] ← S[TOP − 1] − S[TOP], and TOP ← TOP − 1.
MUL means S[TOP − 1] ← S[TOP − 1] * S[TOP], and TOP ← TOP − 1.
DIV means S[TOP − 1] ← S[TOP − 1] / S[TOP], and TOP ← TOP − 1.

As an example, consider the stack-machine instructions generated for the source statement:

A = B * C + A

This can be transformed to the reverse-Polish expression:

'ABC*A+='

For 'ABC*A−=', the set of stack-machine instructions (left side) and the set of register-machine instructions as produced using Algorithm ASSEMBLY_CODE of Sec. 3-5.2 (right side) are as follows:

```
PUSH B      LOD B
PUSH C      MUL C
MUL         STO T₁
PUSH A      LOD T₁
ADD         ADD A
POP A       STO T₂
            STO A
```

Figure 3-5.10 illustrates the effects of the execution of the given sequence of stack machine instructions.

The set of register-machine instructions can be reduced to

```
LOD B
MUL C
ADD A
STO A
```

if we eliminate the store/load sequence for $T_1$ and the needless store in $T_2$. However, the algorithm to generate such a sequence of code for a register machine is quite complex when compared to the algorithm for generating stack-machine code. Let us examine the stack-machine code generation algorithm.

**Algorithm** STACK_CODE.  Given a string POLISH consisting of symbols representing a reverse-Polish expression which is composed of the four basic arithmetic operators and single-letter variables, this algorithm translates the string POLISH into assembly language stack-machine instructions. I is a temporary index variable.

1. [Initialize]
       POP_SYMB ← SUB(POLISH, 1, 1)
2. [Scan through string]
       Repeat thru step 4 for I = 2, 3, ..., LENGTH(POLISH)
3. [Get the next symbol]
       NEXT ← SUB(POLISH, I, 1)

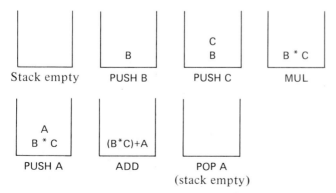

**FIGURE 3-5.10**   Effects of executing the stack-machine code generated from 'ABC*A+='.

4.  [Process current symbol]
          Select case (NEXT)
                    Case 'a' thru 'z':
                    Write('PUSH□' ○ NEXT)
                    Case '+':
                    Write('ADD')
                    Case '−':
                    Write('SUB')
                    Case '*':
                    Write('MUL')
                    Case '/':
                    Write('DIV')
                    Case '=':
                    Write('POP□' ○ POP_SYMB)
                    Default:
                    Write('ILLEGAL CHARACTER')
                    Exit
5.  [Finished]
          Exit                                                             □

    In step 1 of Algorithm STACK_CODE, the first symbol is saved under the assumption that it contains the variable name to which the arithmetic expression is assigned. If this name is not saved, but instead its value is pushed onto the stack (as in the case for all other variable names), then the generated PUSH instruction is a wasted instruction. Step 3 establishes the next character to be examined from the string POLISH. In step 4, the appropriate instruction which corresponds to NEXT is emitted. If NEXT is a variable name, then the name is emitted as the operand of a PUSH instruction. Finally, if NEXT is an assignment operator, the first symbol of the POLISH expression is emitted as the operand of a POP instruction.

    The important point to observe is that, as simple as Algorithm STACK_CODE is, no wasted instructions are generated (such as store/load sequences for temporaries). By tracing through Algorithm STACK_CODE, we see clearly that the stack operations PUSH and POP fit perfectly into the process of generating object code from a reverse-Polish form.

## 3-6  QUEUES

Another important subclass of lists permits deletions to be performed at one end of a list and insertions at the other. The information in such a list is processed in the same order as it was received, that is, on a first-in, first-out (FIFO) or a first-come, first-served (FCFS) basis. This type of list is frequently referred to as a *queue*. Figure 3-6.1 is a representation of a queue illustrating how an insertion is made to the right of the rightmost element in the queue. and how a deletion consists of deleting the leftmost element in the queue. In the case of a queue, the updating operation may be restricted to the examination of the last or end element. If no such restriction is made, any element in the list can be selected. The familiar and traditional example of a queue is a checkout line at a supermarket cash register. The first person in line is (usually) the first to be checked out.

    Another perhaps more relevant example of a queue can be found in a time-sharing computer system where many users share the system simultaneously. Since such a system typically has a single central processing unit (called the *processor*) and one main memory, these resources must be shared by allowing one user's program

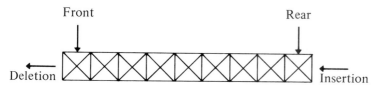

**FIGURE 3-6.1**    Representation of a queue.

to execute for a short time, followed by the execution of another user's program, etc., until there is a return to the execution of the initial user's program. The user programs that are waiting to be processed form a waiting queue. This queue may not operate on a strictly first-in, first-out basis, but on some complex priority scheme based on such factors as what compiler is being used, the execution time required, the number of print lines desired, etc. The resulting queue is sometimes called a *priority queue* and is the topic of discussion in Sec. 3-8.

A final example of a queue is the line of cars waiting to proceed in some fixed direction at an intersection of streets. The deletion of a car corresponds to the first car in the line passing through the intersection, while an insertion to the queue consists of a car joining the end of the line of existing cars waiting to proceed through the intersection. This particular example is discussed in an exercise at the end of Sec. 3-7.

We now wish to formulate algorithms for the insertion of an element to and the deletion of an element from a queue. The vector is assumed to consist of a large number of elements, enough to be sufficient to handle the variable-length property of a queue. In Sec. 4-3.1 another representation of a queue will be given which will be truly variable in size. The vector representation of a queue requires pointers f and r which denote the positions of its front and rear elements, respectively. An illustration of such an allocation scheme is given in Fig. 3-6.2. An algorithm for inserting an element in a queue is given as follows:

**Procedure** QINSERT(Q, F, R, N, Y). Given F and R, pointers to the front and rear elements of a queue, a queue Q consisting of N elements, and an element Y, this procedure inserts Y at the rear of the queue. Prior to the first invocation of the procedure, F and R have been set to zero.

1.  [Overflow?]
    If R ≥ N
    then    Write('OVERFLOW')
            Return

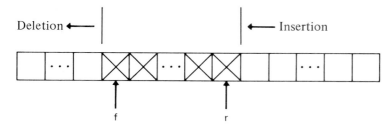

**FIGURE 3-6.2**    Representation of a queue by a vector.

2. [Increment rear pointer]
   $R \leftarrow R + 1$
3. [Insert element]
   $Q[R] \leftarrow Y$
4. [Is front pointer properly set?]
   If $F = 0$
   then $F \leftarrow 1$
   Return ☐

The following algorithm deletes an element from a queue:

**Function** QDELETE(Q, F, R). Given F and R, the pointers to the front and rear elements of a queue, respectively, and the queue Q to which they correspond, this function deletes and returns the last element of the queue. Y is a temporary variable.

1. [Underflow?]
   If $F = 0$
   then Write('UNDERFLOW')
        Return(0)    (0 denotes an empty queue)
2. [Delete element]
   $Y \leftarrow Q[F]$
3. [Queue empty?]
   If $F = R$
   then $F \leftarrow R \leftarrow 0$
   else $F \leftarrow F + 1$    (increment front pointer)
4. [Return element]
   Return(Y) ☐

This pair of algorithms can be very wasteful of storage if the front pointer F never manages to catch up to the rear pointer. Actually, an arbitrarily large amount of memory would be required to accommodate the elements. This method of performing operations on a queue should only be used when the queue is emptied at certain intervals.

Consider an example where the size of the queue is four elements. Initially, the queue is empty. It is required to insert symbols 'A', 'B', and 'C', delete 'A' and 'B', and insert 'D' and 'E'. A trace of the contents of the queue is given in Fig. 3-6.3. Note that an overflow occurs on trying to insert symbol 'E', even though the first two locations are not being used.

A more suitable method of representing a queue, which prevents an excessive use of memory, is to arrange the elements Q[1], Q[2]..., Q[n] in a circular fashion with Q[1] following Q[n]. Pictorially, this can be represented as in Fig. 3-6.4. The insertion and deletion algorithms for a circular queue can now be formulated.

**Procedure** CQINSERT(F, R, Q, N, Y). Given pointers to the front and rear of a circular queue, F and R, a vector Q consisting of N elements, and an element Y, this procedure inserts Y at the rear of the queue. Initially, F and R are set to zero.

1. [Reset rear pointer?]
   If $R = N$
   then $R \leftarrow 1$
   else $R \leftarrow R + 1$

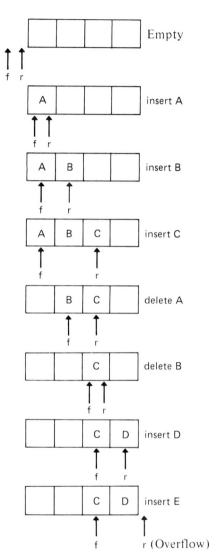

**FIGURE 3-6.3**    Trace of operations on
a simple queue.

2.   [Overflow?]
      If F = R
      then    Write('OVERFLOW')
           Return
3.   [Insert element]
      Q[R] ← Y
4.   [Is front pointer properly set?]
      If F = 0
      then    F ← 1
      Return

**Function** CQDELETE(F, R, Q, N).  Given F and R, pointers to the front and rear of a circular queue, respectively,  and a vector Q consisting of N elements,  this function deletes and returns the last element of the queue.  Y is a temporary variable.

1.  [Underflow?]
        If F = C
        then   Write('UNDERFLOW')
                Return(0)
2.  [Delete element]
            Y ← Q[F]
3.  [Queue empty?]
        If F = R
        then   F ← R ← 0
                Return(Y)
4.  [Increment front pointer]
        If F = N
        then   F ← 1
        else   F ← F + 1
        Return(Y)                                                            □

Consider an example of a circular queue that contains a maximum of four elements. It is required to perform a number of insertion and deletion operations on an initially empty queue.  A trace of the queue contents, which is not shown as circular for convenience, is given in Fig. 3-6.5.

A single queue has been described as behaving in a first-in, first-out manner in the sense that each deletion removes the oldest remaining item in the structure.  A

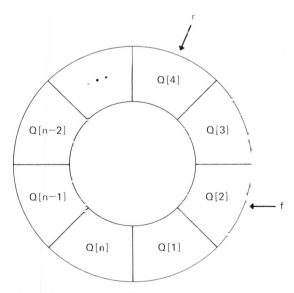

**FIGURE 3-6.4**   A vector representation of a circular queue.

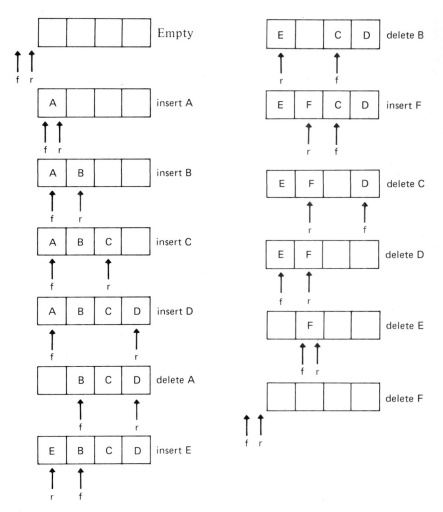

**FIGURE 3-6.5**    Trace of operations on a circular queue.

*deque* (double-ended queue) is a linear list in which insertions and deletions are made to or from either end of the structure. Such a structure can be represented by Fig. 3-6.6. It is clear that a deque is more general than a stack or a queue. There are two variations of a deque, namely, the input-restricted deque and the output-restricted deque. The input-restricted deque allows insertions at only one end, while an output-restricted deque permits deletions from only one end.

**Exercises for Sec. 3-6**

1.  Formulate an algorithm for performing an insertion into an input-restricted deque.
2.  Formulate an algorithm for performing a deletion from an input-restricted deque.
3.  Repeat Probs. 1 and 2 for an output-restricted deque.

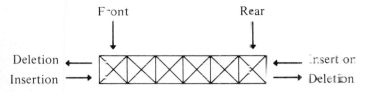

**FIGURE 3-6.6** A deque.

4. Given the circular queue of Fig. 3-6.4 with F = 6 and R = 2, give the values of R and F after *each* operation in the sequence: insert, delete, delete, insert, delete.

5. Give a procedure that uses a stack in order to reverse the elements of a circular queue which is stored in an array. For example, if the initial queue is that given in Fig. 3-6.7a, then the resulting queue is that given in Fig. 3-6.7b. You may assume that

    CALL PUSH(X);

automatically pushes the value of X onto a stack and

    X ← POP;

pops a value from the stack and assigns it to X. On the other hand, you may *not* assume procedures to handle the insertions and deletions from the queue. You must take whatever action is necessary to carry out these tasks yourself. Use appropriate parameters for the procedure so that it is independent of the calling algorithm.

## 3-7 SIMULATION

This section presents a brief, basic introduction to some of the more common terms and concepts used in simulation, a major application area for queues. A general algorithm for processing event-driven simulations is also discussed. A programmed grocery checkout simulation is included as a specific example. The section concludes with a brief discussion on the results of the simulation.

One of the classical areas to which queues can be applied is that of simulation. *Simulation* is the process of forming an abstract model from a real situation in order to understand the impact of modifications and the effect of introducing various strategies on the situation. The main objective of the simulation program is to aid the user, most often an operations research specialist or systems analyst, in projecting what will happen to a given physical situation under certain simplifying assumptions. It allows the user to experiment with real and proposed situations otherwise impossible or impractical. Simulation is a very powerful tool if applied correctly.

The major advantage of simulation is that it permits experimentation without modifying the real situation. Areas such as military operations are safer to simulate than to field-test. Large numbers of alternative modifications to a situation may be included in a simulation, and their results can be studied systematically in a comparative fashion.

Along with the advantages there are dangers. Large detailed simulations are expensive to run on a computer. There is a trade-off between having a program simple, to reduce computer costs, and yet detailed enough to be reasonably accurate.

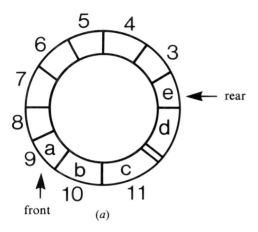

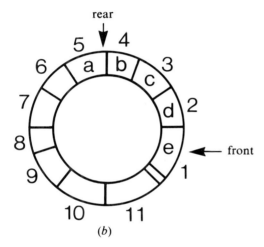

**FIGURE 3-6.7**

Assumptions made in order to simulate some process tend to be a key to the accuracy of the results. The more simplifying the assumptions, the less reliable the results, whereas the more detail included, generally the better the results. No matter how detailed the program, the prediction obtained will be inaccurate if the initial assumptions are incorrect or the situation being studied changes over time. In either of these cases, the simulation program becomes invalid as a prediction tool.

Any process or situation we wish to simulate is considered a system. A *system* is a group of objects interacting in order to produce some result. For example, a factory is a group of people and machines working together to produce some product. A system can be either discrete or continuous, depending upon how the status of the objects in the system changes. A *continuous system* has parameters which can take any real value in some given interval (such as temperature or pressure measurements). Simulations of continuous systems operate on these continuous parameters. *Discrete systems* have parameters which can only take values from a fixed number of choices (such as produce in a grocery store). A discrete system simulation processes discrete parameters. The solar system is a continuous system, since the planets move in smooth continuous motion, whereas a blender is an example of a discrete system, being either off or operating at one of a fixed number of speeds

A system can also be either deterministic or stochastic depending on the relationship between its input and output. A *deterministic system* is one where the final outcome can be predicted if the initial state and input to the system are known. In a true *stochastic system* there is no known explanation for its randomness. A system which requires too much effort to simulate deterministically may be easier to represent stochastically. Many systems contain both stochastic and deterministic parameters, but the random effects of the stochastic parameters cause the whole system to become stochastic. For example, when a feather is dropped off a building, it rarely lands in the same spot, since it is affected by many unpredictable factors. A keyboard is a deterministic system, since pressing the same key will always result in the same letter being displayed.

In order to simulate a system, a model of the system must be produced. A *model* is a body of information used to present the system in a different form. There is no unique model, since the form the model takes depends on the information selected from the system. A major element in solving a problem is the formation of a model, since the model is simpler than the system it represents. It must be kept in mind that the model is finite and therefore cannot produce reliable information on every aspect of the original system.

In order to determine the structure of a model for some situation, the entities, attributes, and activities of the system should be determined. *Entities* represent the components and workload of the system and are the objects (i.e., persons, places or things) of interest in the simulation. *Attributes*, of which there may be many, denote characteristics of these entities. The state of the system at any given time is specified by the attributes of the system's entities and the relations among the entities at that time. An *activity* is a process which causes a change of system state, in other words, the entities engage in activities. An *event* is the occurrence of an activity at a particular instant of time. The program must schedule the events in the simulation so the activities will occur in the correct time sequence. If we consider a bank system as an example, some of the entities would be the customers. The attributes for the customers could be the balance in their account and their credit rating, whereas the activities might include deposits and withdrawals. An event would occur when a customer enters or leaves a queue for a teller.

In simulating systems such as those just described, time is a quantity which is common to all. While there are many different methods by which the time clock can be handled in a simulation, only two will be discussed. In a *time-driven* simulation, a main clock is used to keep track of simulation time. The clock is allowed to increase one unit at a time. After each increase the program must examine each event to determine if it is to occur at this time. If the event is to be processed, the activity associated with the event is performed. This approach is often used in continuous simulations and where many events may occur at once.

A more efficient but less obvious method is an *event-driven* simulation. The program in this case must examine all events in the model to determine which is to happen next. In order to accomplish this, each event must have its own clock to keep track of the next time it will occur. After the main clock is updated, the activity associated with the event is performed and the event clock is set to the next occurrence of the event. This method is mainly used in discrete simulations.

In the remainder of this section event-driven discrete deterministic simulations will be further examined. In the study of simulations of this type, a general algorithm for a common model can be developed.

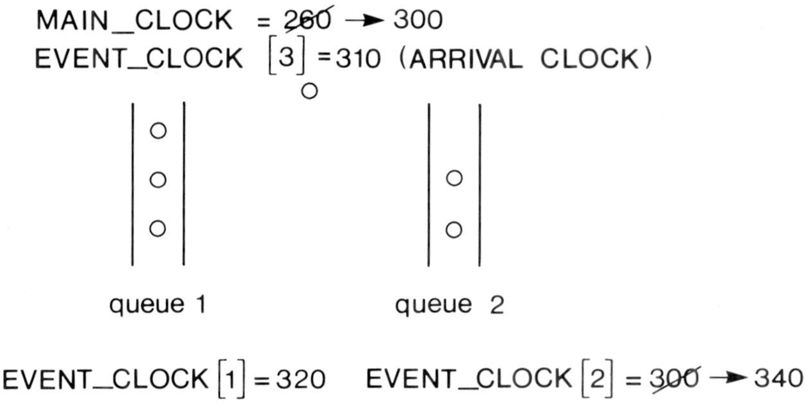

MAIN_CLOCK = ~~260~~ → 300
EVENT_CLOCK $\begin{bmatrix} 3 \end{bmatrix}$ = 310 (ARRIVAL CLOCK)

queue 1                    queue 2

EVENT_CLOCK $\begin{bmatrix} 1 \end{bmatrix}$ = 320    EVENT_CLOCK $\begin{bmatrix} 2 \end{bmatrix}$ = ~~300~~ → 340

**FIGURE 3-7.1**  Sample model.

Let us begin by considering a situation where entities (students) arrive and choose one of two queues (e.g., lines for course registration). The events in this model are an arrival (which includes joining one of the two queues) or a departure from one of the two queues. In order to represent this model there must be an event clock for each of the three events (one arrival and two departures).

Examine the state of the model as shown in Fig. 3-7.1. The next event to occur is determined by selecting the minimal EVENT_CLOCK, in this case EVENT_CLOCK[2] containing the value 300. In the diagram, the MAIN_CLOCK would be set from its previous value of 260 to 300, indicating the present time in the simulation. Next, the entity would be removed from the queue and statistics relevant to this activity would be updated. Finally EVENT_CLOCK[2] would be set to the time of the next departure from this queue, say at time 340. This process continues until MAIN_CLOCK exceeds some value. A general algorithm for controlling this process is now presented.

**Algorithm** SIMULATE. This algorithm provides a basic framework for an event-driven simulation with one arrival queue and N – 1 departure queues. N is the number of EVENT_CLOCKs used to store the time of the next occurence of the specific event. The Nth clock is the arrival event clock which is set to zero to ensure this will be the first event to occur. MAIN_CLOCK is used to record the current time in the simulation. ARRIVAL and DEPART are unspecified procedures that insert and remove objects from a queue, respectively. MIN is a procedure that selects the next event which is to occur. The simulation halts after handling the first event after the main clock has run past the total SIMULATION_TIME.

1.  [Initialize all simulation clocks]
        Repeat for I = 1, 2, ..., N–1
            EVENT_CLOCK[I] ← 99999   (a large number)
        EVENT_CLOCK[N] ← 0    (clock N is arrival clock)
        MAIN_CLOCK ← 0
2.  [Main loop]
        Repeat while MAIN_CLOCK < SIMULATION_TIME
            J ← MIN(EVENT_CLOCK)

```
        MAIN_CLOCK ← EVENT_CLOCK[J]
        If J = N
        then   Call ARRIVAL
        else   Call DEPART(J)
3.   [Print statistics, finished]
        Output relevant statistics for simulation
        Exit                                                          □
```

The previous algorithm is a general method for conducting event-driven simulations. For a detailed example, consider the following problem. Saskatchewan Groceteria (SASKGROC) is considering the addition of a new service counter in one of its stores. Currently, the store has three checkouts, but customer volume has increased to the point where a new counter is warranted. So that management can determine if the new counter should be a regular counter or an express counter (i.e., eight or fewer items), a simulation of customer flow through the checkout area will be undertaken.

The first simulation will be of a checkout area consisting of one express counter and three regular counters, as shown in Fig. 3-7.2. All customers with eight or fewer items are assumed to proceed to an express counter. Customers with more than eight items go to the standard counter with the shortest waiting line. In the second simulation, the express counter will be replaced by a standard counter, and

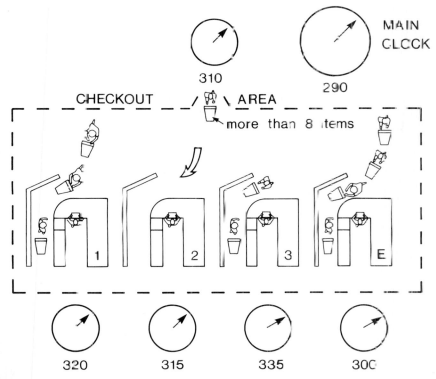

**FIGURE 3-7.2**   SASKGROC model.

the statistics from the two simulations will be compared to determine the most efficient system.

Customers enter the checkout area based on next arrival time, a figure determined by selecting a random number in the range [0, 300] seconds. The number of items bought by each customer will be approximated by selecting a random number in the range [1, 50]. The time taken for a customer to proceed through a counter once the cashier begins processing the groceries will be calculated by using an average rate of 30 seconds per item (pricing plus wrapping time). If more than 15 customers are in a line, the next customer gets discouraged and leaves. In order for us to determine which of the two systems is superior, the following statistics will be kept for each of the counters: average waiting time in lineups, number of customers per hour, and the number of items processed per hour.

In order for us to produce the required simulation, a model of the checkout area must be formed. The entities in this model are the customers whose movements through the system will be modeled. The attributes of the customers include number of items purchased, time at which the customer entered queue, and the time of departure from the queue. There are two activities in the model, entering and exiting the queues, which correspond to the events of the system. With this rough overview of the model the finer programming details can now be discussed.

The program to run the simulation consists of a main program and three procedures. The main program's structure is identical to the general algorithm introduced previously. Procedure *arrival* is a modified version of the QINSERT algorithm given earlier in this chapter with additional logic to determine the queue in which the customer is to be placed. In this procedure, the number of items purchased and arrival time are calculated for each customer. A special built-in function, *random*, returns a random number which is used for these calculations. Procedure *depart* follows the framework of the QDELETE algorithm with additional logic to calculate statistics for customers leaving a queue. The final procedure, *print*, displays the collected statistics.

The data structures for the program are as follows. Identifier *ctr* is a two-dimensional array of structures used to represent the queues. Variable *stat* is a vector of structures containing front and rear indexes into the queues, event clock values, and the accumulated statistics. The bounds of these data structures are declared as constants at the beginning of the program, allowing easy modification of the model. Identifier *arrivalclock* is initially set to zero, while all other event clocks are set to *maxint*, a large number. This ensures an arrival will be the first event to occur. Variable *flag* indicates the existence of the express counter and thus controls which of the two separate runs are to be executed. The Pascal program to run the simulation can now be presented in Fig. 3-7.3.

The results of the simulation with the assumptions and restrictions stated above are given in Fig. 3-7.4. Notice that inclusion of an express counter results in a significant drop in the length of wait for customers with eight or fewer items. The most revealing statistic is the total number of items processed per hour. Without the express counter 496 items are punched through per hour, but its inclusion causes this figure to rise to 614 items. This indicates that adding an express counter would be beneficial to both customers and management. On the basis of this simulation, a recommendation that the new counter should be an express counter would be made to the owners of SASKGROC.

The SASKGROC program was designed under a simplifying set of assumptions. If more accurate results are desired, some of these assumptions would have to be removed. For example, customers do not arrive randomly, but instead tend to arrive according to a pattern. At lunch hour the number of customers with eight or fewer items may rise sharply. Also, customers do not always pick the shortest queue, and checkout clerks do not work at a uniform speed. The simulation program must have enough detail to give accurate results and yet remain economical.

Although the point is not stressed throughout our discussion of the simulation example, it is obvious from an examination of the program in Fig. 3-7.3 that queues are the predominant data structures in a simulation. Specifically, a queue is required for each activity in a simulation. For major simulations such as those created for urban planning studies thousands of activities may be required.

There exist programming languages such as SIMULA, SIMSCRIPT and GPSS for the specific purpose of easily representing simulations. When one is programming in these languages, it is only necessary to specify what activities can take place in a modeled system and the queues associated with these activities will be automati-

---

```
program saskgroc(input,output);

{ This program runs the grocery simulation
  as described in the preceding text }

const numctrs = 4;           {number of regular checkout counters}
      express = 4;           {index number of express counter}
      simulationtime = 7200; {length of simulation}
      qsize = 15;            {size of all checkout queues}

type counter =
        record
            enter,           {time customer entered queue}
            itemno,          {number of items purchased}
            leave: integer   {time customer leaves queue}
        end;

     statistics =
        record
            ctrclock,              {clocks for checkout counters}
            numcust,               {number of customers in each queue}
            custhr,                {number of customers processed}
            wait,                  {time spent in queue waiting}
            totitems,f,r: integer  {total items processed}
        end;

var mainclock,                  {main simulation clock}
    nextevent,                  {index to next event}
    flag,                       {indicates if express counter present}
    i,min,                      {temporary variables}
    arrivalclock: integer;      {time of next arrival}
    x: real;                    {random number}
    ctr: array[1..numctrs, 1..qsize] of counter;
    stat: array[1..numctrs] of statistics;
```

FIGURE 3-7.3    Pascal program for SASKGROC simulation.

```
procedure arrival;
{ Procedure arrival is a modified version of qinsert, with additional
  pieces of code to determine the shortest queue and code
  to update the various clocks}

var items,        { number of items to be purchased }
    num,          { temporary value }
    min: integer;  { number of queue customer to enter }

begin
    min := maxint;
    items := round(random(x) * 50);

    { determine which queue customer to be added to }
    if (items <= 8) and (flag = 0)
    then num := express
    else begin
            for i := 1 to numctrs do
                begin
                    if stat[i].numcust < min
                    then begin
                            min := stat[i].numcust;
                            num := i
                        end
                end
        end;

    { add customer to queue }
    if stat[num].r = qsize
    then stat[num].r := 1
    else stat[num].r := stat[num].r + 1;

    ctr[num, stat[num].r].enter := arrivalclock;
    ctr[num, stat[num].r].itemno := items;
    ctr[num, stat[num].r].leave := arrivalclock + items * 30;

    mainclock := arrivalclock;

    if stat[num].f = 0
    then begin
            stat[num].f := 1;
            stat[num].ctrclock := ctr[num, stat[num].r].leave
        end;

    { update number in queue and calculate next arrival }
    stat[num].numcust := stat[num].numcust + 1;
    arrivalclock := arrivalclock + round(random(x) * 300)
end; { arrival }
```

**FIGURE 3-7.3**   (Continued)

**procedure** depart(num: integer);
{ procedure depart is a modified version of qdelete, with additional
  code to update statistics about customers leaving the
  store. Num contains the index to the queue where the next
  departure is to occur }

**begin**
    stat[num].custhr := stat[num].custhr + 1;
    stat[num].wait := stat[num].wait + ctr[num, stat[num].f].leave
                   - ctr[num, stat[num].f].enter;
    stat[num].totitems := stat[num].totitems
                      + ctr[num, stat[num].f].itemno;

    mainclock := stat[num].ctrclock;

    **if** stat[num].f = stat[num].r
    **then begin**
        stat[num].f := 0;
        stat[num].r := 0;
        stat[num].ctrclock := maxint
      **end**
    **else begin**
        stat[num].f := stat[num].f + 1;
        stat[num].ctrclock := ctr[num, stat[num].f].leave
      **end**;

    stat[num].numcust := stat[num].numcust - 1
**end**; { depart }

**FIGURE 3-7.3**  (Continued)

---

cally maintained by the run-time system that supports the simulation language.
Clearly, simulations are much more easily constructed using these special purpose
languages.

**Exercises for Sec. 3-7**

1.  This exercise discusses an application from this area which describes the simulation of a time-sharing computer system. Most students have been exposed to
some variation of such a system in their undergraduate courses. Since the
early 1960s, increasingly more computing is being done through on-line terminals which are connected to time-shared computer systems. A typical configuration for such a computer system is shown in Fig. 3-7.5.

    The important thing to note from the diagram is that a number of com-
puter users are sharing the computer simultaneously. Since we have but one
CPU (processor) and one main memory, we have to share these resources
among our $n$ users. We can share the processor by allowing one user's program to execute for a short time, then allowing another user's program to execute, and another, etc., until there is a return to the execution of the initial
user's program. This cycle is continued repeatedly on all active user programs.
This method of sharing the CPU among many users is often referred to as

```pascal
procedure print;
{ procedure print outputs the accumulated statistics from
  the simulation runs }
var totalcust,totalwait,totalitem: integer;

begin
    writeln;
    if flag = 0
    then begin
            writeln('SIMULATION WITH ONE EXPRESS QUEUE': 54);
            writeln;
            writeln('1': 30, '2': 11, '3': 11, 'express': 13, 'total': 9)
        end
    else begin
            writeln;
            writeln;
            writeln('SIMULATION WITH NON EXPRESS QUEUE': 54);
            writeln;
            writeln('1': 30, '2': 11, '3': 11, '4': 11, 'total': 11)
        end;

    writeln;
    write('No. customers/hr   ');
    totalcust := 0;
    for i := 1 to numctrs do
        begin
            write(round(stat[i].custhr / simulationtime * 3600): 11);
            totalcust := totalcust + stat[i].custhr
        end;
    write(round(totalcust / simulationtime * 3600): 11);

    writeln;
    write('Avge. waiting time ');
    totalwait := 0;
    for i := 1 to numctrs do
        begin
            write(round(stat[i].wait / stat[i].custhr / 60): 11);
            totalwait := totalwait + stat[i].wait
        end;
    write(round(totalwait / totalcust / 60): 11);

    writeln;
    write('Items processed/hr ');
    totalitem := 0;
    for i := 1 to numctrs do
        begin
            write(round(stat[i].totitems / simulationtime * 3600): 11);
            totalitem := totalitem + stat[i].totitems
        end;
    write(round(totalitem / simulationtime * 3600): 11)
end; { print }
```

**FIGURE 3-7.3**   (Continued)

{ The main program repeats the simulation twice, once for three
checkouts, one express, and the next with four regular
checkout stands }
**begin**

    **for** flag := 0 **to** 1 **do**
        **begin**

                { initialize vectors to zero }
                **for** i := 1 **to** numctrs **do**
                    **begin**
                        stat[i].ctrclock := maxint;
                        stat[i].f := 0;
                        stat[i].r := 0;
                        stat[i].numcust := 0;
                        stat[i].custhr := 0;
                        stat[i].wait := 0;
                        stat[i].totitems := 0
                  **end**;

                mainclock := 0;
                arrivalclock := 0;

                { determine which event is to occur next in time }
                **while** mainclock < simulationtime **do**
                    **begin**
                        min := maxint;
                        **for** i := 1 **to** numctrs **do**
                            **begin**
                                **if** stat[i].ctrclock < min
                                **then begin**
                                    min := stat[i].ctrclock;
                                  nextevent := i
                              **end**
                        **end**;

                      **if** arrivalclock < min
                      **then** arrival
                      **else** depart(nextevent)
                **end**;
            print
        **end**

**end**. { saskgroc }

**FIGURE 3-7.3**    (Continued)

## SIMULATION WITH ONE EXPRESS QUEUE

|                    | 1   | 2   | 3   | express | total |
|--------------------|-----|-----|-----|---------|-------|
| No. customers/hr   | 6   | 6   | 4   | 8       | 24    |
| Avge. waiting time | 17  | 15  | 16  | 8       | 14    |
| Items processed/hr | 186 | 170 | 131 | 127     | 614   |

## SIMULATION WITH NON EXPRESS QUEUE

|                    | 1   | 2   | 3   | 4   | total |
|--------------------|-----|-----|-----|-----|-------|
| No. customers/hr   | 6   | 6   | 4   | 4   | 20    |
| Avge. waiting time | 12  | 12  | 15  | 13  | 13    |
| Items processed/hr | 135 | 140 | 120 | 101 | 496   |

**FIGURE 3-7.4**  Output from SASKGROC program.

*time-sharing*. Of course, we can also share memory among the user programs simply by dividing memory into regions and allowing each user program to execute in its own region when it receives CPU control. (There are more sophisticated ways of sharing both the CPU and main memory, but we need not discuss them here.) In a system such as this, each user is unaware of the presence of other users. In fact, each terminal appears like a separate computer to the user.

Let us look at a simple example of how a time-sharing system might work. Suppose three users, Tremblay, Sorenson, and Bunt, sit down at their terminals and begin an on-line session with the computer. The following statistics are gathered concerning their session:

| Relative Session Starting Time | Program ID | Requested CPU Time Periods |
|:------------------------------:|:----------:|:--------------------------:|
| 0                              | TREMBLAY   | 4, 8, 3                    |
| 1                              | SORENSON   | 2, 1, 2, 2                 |
| 2                              | BUNT       | 4, 6, 1                    |

We interpret these figures in the following manner. After logging on the system at time 0 (the first number given in the statistics is the relative time, in seconds, at which each user begins his session), Tremblay initially is allotted 4 seconds of CPU time before he receives a typed response at his terminal. After examining the response, he then thinks momentarily and types in a new input to his program in memory. A further 8 seconds of CPU time is required before another response can be printed at Tremblay's terminal. Again there is a period of head scratching and of typing in a new input to his program. (We will refer to this total period of thinking then typing as the *user delay period*.)

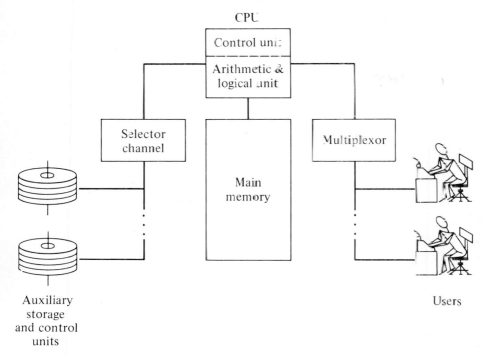

**FIGURE 3-7.5**  A typical time-shared computer system.

Finally, Tremblay's program uses 3 additional seconds of CPU time and then Tremblay logs off, terminating his session.

What we ignored in the above discussion is the fact that Sorenson and Bunt logged on at times 1 and 2, respectively, and their programs also require immediate CPU attention. Because we have only one CPU, Sorenson's program and Bunt's program will be made to wait until Tremblay's program has finished its first requested CPU time period of 4 seconds. We can indicate the fact that the Sorenson and Bunt programs are waiting for the processor by placing the program ID's (say, SORENSON and BUNT) in a queue behind Tremblay's program ID (i.e., TREMBLAY). Hence the queue at time 2 would appear as in Fig. 3-7.6.

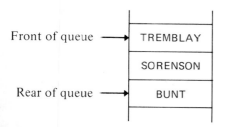

**FIGURE 3-7.6**  Processor queue at time 2.

When Tremblay's program has completed its first requested CPU time period, a reasonable scheduling strategy would be to allocate the CPU to Sorenson's program while Tremblay is scratching his head during a user delay period. Of course, when Sorenson's program has finished its CPU time period, Bunt's program should be allowed to execute a CPU time period. This type of scheduling strategy is often called a "first-come, first-serve" (FCFS) scheduling strategy. The rules for the FCFS strategy in this application are as follows:

*1*   When a program requests CPU time, it is placed at the back of the processor queue.

*2*   The program at the head of the processor queue is the program that is currently being executed. It remains at the head of the queue for its entire CPU time period.

*3*   When an executing program completes its current requested CPU time period, it is removed from the processor queue and is not placed back into the queue until a further request is made (i.e., rule *1*).

Following the above rules, the three user programs would behave in the manner graphically described in Fig. 3-7.7. Note that we have allowed a 5-second user delay period throughout.

The problem facing us is to simulate the activity of such a time-sharing system, given data relevant to user starting time and CPU time-period requests. The simulation must place users in the processor queue according to rule *1* and remove them as in rule *3*.

The purpose of such a simulation is to gain information about the efficiency of the time-sharing system. To this end, data are collected for the calculation of the following statistics:

*1*   CPU utilization $= \dfrac{\text{total CPU time}}{\text{total session time}} * 100$

(for each user)

*2*   Total user waiting time = total time − total CPU time
                                                                      − total user delay

(for each user)

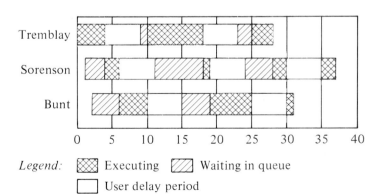

Tremblay

Sorenson

Bunt

0   5   10   15   20   25   30   35   40

*Legend:*   ▨ Executing   ▨ Waiting in queue
            ☐ User delay period

**FIGURE 3-7.7**

*3*   Total user delay = 5 * (number of CPU requests − 1)
     (for each user)

In order to simulate a system, we must thoroughly investigate the actions which take place within the system. These actions must be imitated in some manner such that certain characteristics of the simulated model are the same as in the real system. For example, users should begin execution in the model at the same time as they would in the real time-sharing system.

The primary actions which occur in this system, and the manner in which the simulation imitates the actions, are as follows:

*1*   *User requests service.*  In the real system this request would be a teletype signal which would alert the processor. In the model we use a variable set to the time at which the user will require service. When the simulation time reaches or passes this time, the user is added to the processor queue.

*2*   *User program in execution.*  To imitate this action, we update the simulation time by the length of the time requested by the user.

*3*   *User completes current executing period requested.*  At this point the user is removed from the queue for the delay or "thinking and typing" period. We will assume a delay period of five time units for all users. At this point the variable used to signal service requests, described in action *1*, is updated to indicate that the user is in the delay period.

If, at any point of time in the simulation, all users are in the delay phase and no users are in the processor queue, the simulation time is updated to the earliest service request time.

Formulate an algorithm for the simulation of this system.

2.   A tool frequently used by transportation and city planners is the computer simulation of traffic systems. The systems modeled range from the traffic network of a nation, a city, or area of a city right down to the traffic flow in one bridge or intersection. The models are used to pinpoint present or future bottlenecks and to suggest and test proposed changes or new systems.

A light-controlled intersection is one example of a traffic system for which the simulation model is relatively simple. Such a model would be used to evaluate intersection performance. The primary quantity measured would be the length of time motorists were stopped at the intersection. The performance of the intersection would be indicated by the average and maximum waiting times experienced by the motorists.

The specific model we will consider consists of an intersection of 2 two-lane streets each lane being controlled by a three-color traffic light. The street and lane codes used throughout this section are shown in Fig. 3-7.8.

To simplify the model, we make some assumptions about traffic flow and driver behavior. First, we assume that all traffic entering the intersection proceeds straight ahead; no right or left turns are allowed. Second, we assume that the car and driver response times are the same for all vehicles, i.e., given that the path is clear, it takes the same length of time for each car to respond and enter the intersection. The possibilities of stalling cars and accidents are ignored. We assume that all drivers are extremely law-abiding and thus, stop for both red and amber lights.

At this point we acknowledge the reader's comment that no such intersection exists. That is true; however, for the sake of clarity of description. such a

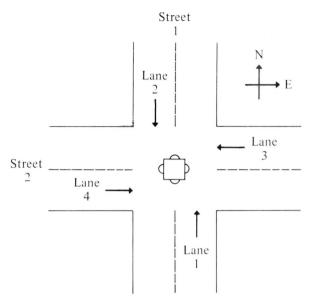

**FIGURE 3-7.8**   A traffic-light intersection.

simplistic intersection will be our subject. The traffic lights are assumed to have the following characteristics:

1   The traffic lights for the two lanes on each street have identical signal timing and are viewed as a set.

2   The light cycle times for both sets of lights are equal.

3   There are no right- or left-turn arrows and no four-way walk signal.

4   There is a short length of time, known as the *delay time*, between one set of lights turning red and the other set turning green.

5   The red-light period on each set of lights is longer than the combined periods of the green light, amber light, and delay of the other set of lights.

We now consider the problem in greater detail and amplify some ideas that were introduced earlier. Recall that one step in the creation of a simulation model is to subdivide the system under consideration into its component parts or entities. In the intersection system we are studying, the primary entities are the traffic lights and the cars. Each entity has attributes associated with it. For example, the light color is a property of the traffic lights; the important attributes of the cars could be the lane in which the car is traveling and the time at which it arrives at the intersection. Other attributes that could be considered for a car would be the speed at which it is traveling, its color, etc., but these are not relevant to the model we have described.

In an accurate computer simulation, the modeled entities should resemble their real counterparts as closely as possible, within the limits of computational efficiency. The methods by which this goal is achieved in the system under consideration are discussed next.

In this model, the intersection lights must change in the same time sequence as the real light signals. Given the initial configuration and the light-timing patterns (i.e., the length of time for each color of light), the configuration of the lights at any time can be determined. For example, if a street light initially turned red at time zero, and the red light period was 60 seconds, then at time 61 we know the light would be green.

The pattern of the cars in the model must closely resemble that of cars at an actual intersection with respect to frequency of arrival and direction of approach. If we have statistical data about an intersection, such as the number of cars entering from each direction and the average time between arrivals, a procedure can be used to introduce into the simulation cars with attributes statistically similar to those of the real traffic. This procedure is termed *Monte Carlo sampling*, and it determines outcomes at random at decision points in the simulation process.

The first decision regarding a car is the direction in which it is traveling toward the intersection. There are four possible results to this decision, say $E_1$, $E_2$, $E_3$, and $E_4$, representing north, south, west, and east, respectively. If we know the probabilities $p_1$, $p_2$, $p_3$, and $p_4$ $(p_1 + p_2 + p_3 + p_4 = 1)$ associated with each result, then a random number can be used to determine which result is chosen by the following procedure. A random number $R$ is obtained using a random-number generator that yields numbers uniformly distributed between 0 and 1. Then the result of the decision is

$$
\begin{aligned}
&E_1 \quad \text{if} \quad R < p_1 \\
&E_2 \quad \text{if} \quad p_1 \leqslant R < p_1 + p_2 \\
&E_3 \quad \text{if} \quad p_1 + p_2 \leqslant R < p_1 + p_2 + p_3 \\
&E_4 \quad \text{if} \quad p_1 + p_2 + p_3 \leqslant R
\end{aligned}
$$

If we assume that certain characteristics hold true for the traffic flowing through the intersection, then we can also assume that the time between consecutive arrivals (the interarrival time) is exponentially distributed. This means that the function

$$F(x) = 1 - e^{-\alpha x}$$

is the probability that the interarrival time is less than or equal to $x$, and $\alpha$ is equal to $1/ATI$ where $ATI$ is the average time interval between arrivals. We can generate a random value for $x$, the interarrival time, from this function by generating a random number $R$ to represent a probability and by using the formula

$$x = -ATI \log R$$

A more detailed discussion of exponential distributions and associated characteristics can be found in Naylor, Balinty, Chu, and Burdick [1968].

Having discussed the manner in which the light signals and car arrivals will be handled, we now turn out attention to that segment of the model which applies to the relationship between the lights and the cars. It is this segment which is most directly related to the data structures discussed in Sec 3-6.

This controlling segment of the model will either move cars through a green light (i.e., remove them from the model) or simulate the car stopping at an amber or red light. It is not difficult to realize that a queue is the obvious representation for the cars stopped at the red light. Our model will use four queues to represent the traffic buildup in the four directions. A car is added to the queue when it is stopped; it is deleted from the queue when it passes through the intersection. A queue overflow signals a traffic jam.

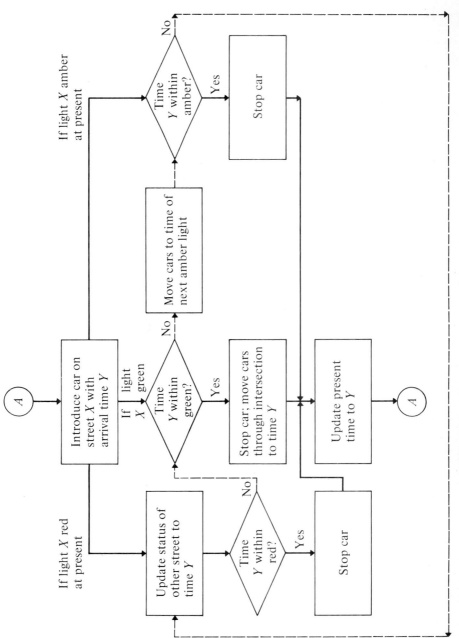

**FIGURE 3-7.9** Event flowchart for traffic-light intersection.

The general simulation model has the following steps:

*1*  Introduce a car into the model.
*2*  Update the lights and traffic flow to the arrival time of the car.
*3*  Dispose of the car as indicated by the light signal at the car's arrival time, i.e., move the car through the intersection or add the car to a waiting queue.
*4*  Go to step *1*.

This general solution is graphically represented by the flowchart in Fig. 3-7.9. Three branches emanate from the first event box (labeled *A*). The branch chosen depends on the color of the lights (at the present simulation time) on the street on which the car approaching the intersection is traveling. Note also the flow of control from the red-to-green-to-amber segments indicated by the broken line. This looping halts only when the light sequences that would occur between the present time and time *Y* have been simulated. The problem is to devise algorithms which implement the simulation of the intersection described, and to program and test these algorithms. The output of the model should include the maximum and average waiting time in each direction and the maximum and average queue length in each direction.

3.  Alter the algorithms and program in Prob. 2 to simulate an intersection in which vehicles make both right and left turns, as well as proceeding straight through. Use the following rule to decide right-of-way: A vehicle turning left may leave the waiting queue only if there are no vehicles in the approaching queue, or if the front vehicle of the approaching queue is also turning left. Note that an additional value, the direction of turn, must be saved for each car in the waiting queues. The same type of sampling method as that used to determine the vehicle's lane of travel can be used to determine the direction in which the vehicle will proceed.

## 3-8 PRIORITY QUEUES

A queue in which we are able to insert items or remove items from any position based on some property (such as priority of the task to be processed) is often referred to as a *priority queue*. Figure 3-8.1a represents a priority queue of jobs waiting to use a computer. Priorities of 1, 2, and 3 have been attached to jobs of type real-time, on-line, and batch, respectively. Therefore, if a job is initiated with priority i, it is inserted immediately at the end of the list of other jobs with priority i, for i = 1, 2, or 3. In this example, jobs are always removed from the front of the queue. (In general, this is not a necessary restriction on a priority queue.)

A priority queue can be conceptualized as a series of queues representing situations in which it is known a priori what priorities are associated with queue items. Figure 3-8.1b shows how the single-priority queue can be visualized as three separate queues, each exhibiting a strictly FIFO behavior. Elements in the second queue are removed only when the first queue is empty, and elements from the third queue are removed only when the first and second queues are empty. This separation of a single-priority queue into a series of queues also suggests an efficient storage representation of a priority queue. When elements are inserted, they are always added at the end of one of the queues as determined by the priority. Alternatively, if a single sequential storage structure is used for the priority queue, then insertion may mean that the new element must be placed in the middle of the struc-

Task identification

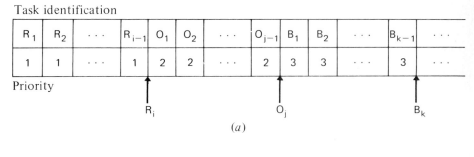

| $R_1$ | $R_2$ | $\cdots$ | $R_{i-1}$ | $O_1$ | $O_2$ | $\cdots$ | $O_{j-1}$ | $B_1$ | $B_2$ | $\cdots$ | $B_{k-1}$ | $\cdots$ |
|---|---|---|---|---|---|---|---|---|---|---|---|---|
| 1 | 1 | $\cdots$ | 1 | 2 | 2 | $\cdots$ | 2 | 3 | 3 | $\cdots$ | 3 | $\cdots$ |

Priority

(a)

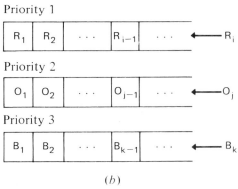

Priority 1

Priority 2

Priority 3

(b)

**FIGURE 3-8.1** A priority queue (a) viewed as a single queue with insertions allowed at any position, and (b) viewed as a set of queues.

ture. This can require the movement of several items. It is better to split the priority queue into several queues, each having its own storage structure.

In Chap. 7 we encounter another example involving queues of buffers as used by the data management facilities in most operating systems. In the next chapter, we examine an efficient form of storage representation for list structures such as the priority queue.

**Exercises for Sec. 3-8**

1. Assume we have a priority queue split into several queues as discussed in the text. To access these queues we might have vectors of pointers to the front and rear of each queue and one to indicate the length of each. Diagrammatically, this might look like Fig. 3-8.2. Thus, to access the front of the queue representing, say, priority 2, one merely starts at PRIORITY_F[2]. Note that this representation allows each queue to be of a different length: quite a conceivable situation since there are usually only a few jobs of priority 1 and so on. Given this representation, devise algorithms to insert into and delete from a priority queue.

2. Suppose we wish to have $N > 2$ sequentially allocated queues occupying a single vector, Q[1..M]. This vector is divided into N segments and each queue I is allocated a segment. Also, we have two vectors, F[1..N] and R[1..N], where F[I] and R[I] are used to indicate the front and rear of queue I, respectively. So, if F[I] = R[I], queue I is empty. Thus, the queue Q may look like that

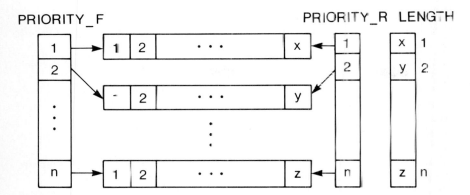

**FIGURE 3-8.2**

shown in Fig. 3-8.3. To allocate the N segments, we set the elements of R and F initially by

$$F[I] \leftarrow R[I] \leftarrow (TRUNC(M \ / \ N))(I - 1), \ 1 \leqslant I \leqslant N$$

Queue I can grow from F[I] + 1 to F[I+1] before overflowing onto the next queue.

Write two algorithms Q_INS_I and Q_DEL_I to handle insertion and deletion of the queues, assuming the queues have already been allocated.

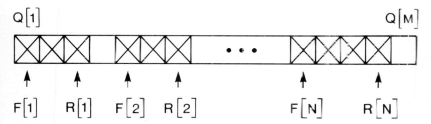

**FIGURE 3-8.3** A vector representation of n queues.

**BIBLIOGRAPHY**

COHEN, D. J. and P. J. BRILLINGER: Introduction to Nonnumeric Computation, Prentice-Hall, Englewood Cliffs, N.J., 1970.

FORSYTHE, A. I., T. A. KEENAN, E. I. ORGANICK, and W. STENBERG: Computer Science: A First Course, John Wiley & Sons, Inc., New York, 1969.

GRIES, D.: Compiler Construction for Digital Computers, John Wiley & Sons, Inc., New York, 1971.

HARRISON, M. C.: Data-Structures and Programming, Scott, Foresman and Company, Glenview, Ill., 1973.

D'IMPERIO, M. E.: Data Structures and Their Representation in Storage, *Annual Review in Automatic Programming, vol. 5, pp. 1-75*, Pergammon Press, Oxford, 1969.

KNUTH, D. E.: The Art of Computer Programming, vol. 1, Fundamental Algorithms, Addison-Wesley Publishing Company, Inc., Reading, Mass., 1968.

LEE, J. A. N.: The Anatomy of a Compiler, Reinhold, New York, 1967.

MARTIN, F. J.: Computer Modelling and Simulation, John Wiley & Sons, Inc., New York, 1968.

MCKEEMAN, W. M., J. J. HORNING, and D. B. WORTMAN: A Compiler Generator, Prentice-Hall, Englewood Cliffs, N.J., 1970.

NAYLOR, T. H., J. L. BALINTY, K. CHU, and D. E. BURDICK: Computer Simulation Techniques, John Wiley & Sons, Inc., New York, 1968.

TREMBLAY, J. P., and R. M. MANOHAR: Discrete Mathematical Structures with Applications to Computer Science, McGraw-Hill Book Company, New York, 1975.

TREMBLAY, J. P. and R. B. BUNT: An Introduction to Computer Science: An Algorithmic Approach, McGraw-Hill Book Company, New York, 1979.

# 4

# LINEAR DATA STRUCTURES AND
# THEIR LINKED STORAGE REPRESENTATION

*The previous chapter described the representation of linear data structures by using the sequential-allocation method of storage. Although this method of allocation is suitable for certain applications, there are many other applications where the sequential-allocation method is unacceptable. The latter class of applications usually has the following characteristics:*

1. *Unpredictable storage requirements. The exact amount of data storage required by a program in these areas often depends on the particular data being processed, and consequently, this requirement cannot be easily determined at the time the program is written.*
2. *Extensive manipulation of the stored data. Programs in these areas typically require that operations such as insertions and deletions be performed frequently on the data.*

*The linked-allocation method of storage can result in both the efficient use of computer storage and computer time. Therefore, in this chapter the concepts of linked allocation, as applied to linear data structures, are introduced.*

*The first section describes the basic notions of pointers and linked allocation by using a simple polynomial-manipulation application.*

*In the next section, a number of algorithms associated with linked linear structures are given. The programming aspects of certain commonly performed operations on these linked structures are initially discussed by using arrays. The reasons for this approach are twofold. First, certain programming languages such as ALGOL 60, FORTRAN, and BASIC do not allow linked structures per se, and arrays can be used to simulate them. Second, by using low-level structures such as arrays to simulate linked structures, insight into the manipulation of such structures can be gained. A number of operations are also programmed by using the Pascal new and dispose statements. These statements permit the programmers to control the allocation and definition of their own structures.*

*Finally, a number of applications involving linked linear structures such as symbol-table construction and multiple-precision arithmetic are described*

## 4-1 POINTERS AND LINKED ALLOCATION

The previous chapter discussed at some length how the address of an element in a data structure could be obtained by direct computation. The data structures discussed were linearly ordered, and this ordering relation was preserved in the corresponding storage structures by using sequential allocation. There was no need for an element to specify where the next element would be found.

Consider a list consisting of elements which vary individually in size. The task of directly computing the address of a particular element becomes much more difficult. An obvious method of obtaining the address of a node (element) is to store this address in the computer memory. In Chap. 1 we referred to this addressing mode as pointer or link addressing. If the list in question has $n$ nodes, we can store the address of each node in a vector consisting of $n$ elements. The first element of the vector contains the address of the first node of the list, the second element contains the address of the second node, and so on.

There are many applications which, by their very nature, have data which are continually being updated (insertions, deletions, etc.). Each time a change occurs, significant manipulation of the data is required. In some instances, the representation of the data by sequentially allocated lists results in an inefficient use of memory, wasted computational time, and indeed, for certain problems this method of allocation is totally unacceptable. The representation of polynomials by arrays discussed previously (see Sec. 3-2) had a number of obvious drawbacks. The arrays contained only a few nonzero elements, and this was far from being a compact representation of polynomials. Furthermore, the memory requirements associated with certain operations were not always predictable (as in the case of polynomial division), so one was faced with the situation of not knowing in advance how much memory to reserve for the polynomial generated by such an operation.

Recall from Sec. 1-4.7 that the interpretation of a pointer as an address is a natural one. Most computers use addresses to find the next instruction to be executed and its operand(s). In many hardware configurations, special registers are used to store such addresses. Pointers are always of the same length (usually no longer than a half-word), and this property enables the manipulation of pointers to be performed in a uniform manner using simple allocation techniques, regardless of the configurations of the structures to which they may point.

In the sequential-allocation method one is able to compute an address of an element provided that the storage structure is organized in some uniform manner. Pointers permit the referencing of structures in a uniform way, regardless of the organization of the structure being referenced. Pointers are capable of representing a much more complex relationship between elements of a structure than a linear order.

The use of pointers or links to refer to elements of a data structure (which is linearly ordered) implies that elements which are logically adjacent (because of the linear ordering) need not be physically adjacent in memory. This type of allocation is called *linked allocation*. We now turn to the problem of representing structures by this type of allocation.

A list has been defined to consist of an ordered set of elements which may vary in number. A simple way to represent a linear list is to expand each node to contain a link or pointer to the next node. This representation is called a *one-way chain* or *singly linked linear list,* and it can be displayed as in Fig. 4-1.1a. In that figure, the variable FIRST contains an address or pointer which gives the location of the first node of the list. Each node is divided into two parts. The first part

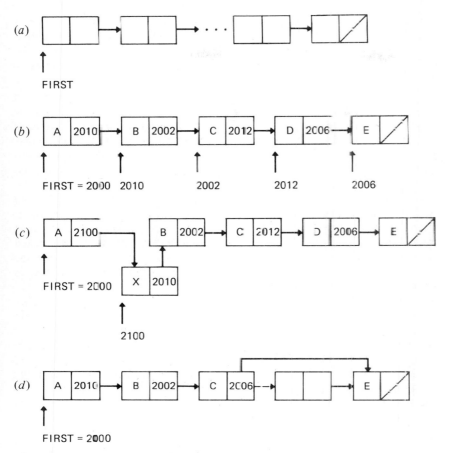

**FIGURE 4-1.1** Linked representation of a linear list.

represents the information of the element, and the second part contains the address of the next node. The last node of the list does not have a successor node, and consequently, no actual address is stored in the pointer field. In such a case, a null value is stored as the address. The arrow emanating from the link field of a particular node indicates its successor node in the structure. For example, the linked list in Fig. 4-1.1b represents a five-node list whose elements are located in memory locations 2000, 2010, 2002, 2012, and 2006, respectively. We again emphasize that the only purpose of the links is to specify which node is next in the linear ordering. The link address of NULL (indicated by the slash) in the last node signals the end of the list. NULL is not an address of any possible node, but is a special value which cannot be mistaken for an address. For this reason, NULL is used as a special list delimiter. It is possible for a list to have no nodes at all. Such a list is called an empty list, and this is denoted by assigning a value of NULL to FIRST in the current example.

Let us compare the operations commonly performed on sequentially allocated and linked lists. Consider the operations of *insertion* and *deletion* in the case of a sequentially allocated list. If we have an r-element list and it is required to insert a new element between the first and second elements, then the last n − 1 elements of the list must be moved so as to make room for the new element. For a list that contains many nodes, this is a rather inefficient way of performing an insertion — especially if many insertions are to be performed. The same principle applies in the case of a deletion, where all elements after the element being deleted must be moved up so as to take up the vacant space caused by the element being removed from the list.

In the case of linked allocation, an insertion is performed in a straightforward manner. If a new element is to be inserted following the first element, this can be accomplished by merely interchanging pointers. This is illustrated in Fig. 4-1.1c for a five-element list. The deletion of the fourth element from the original list can be performed by using the pointer change as shown in Fig. 4-1.1d. It is clear that the insertion and deletion operations are more efficient when performed on linked lists than on sequentially allocated lists.

There are a number of other comparisons we can make between the linked and sequentially allocated storage schemes for lists. If a particular node in a linked list is required, it is necessary to follow the links from the first node onward until the desired node is found. This is clearly inferior to the computed-address technique associated with sequential allocation. In some applications, however, it is required to examine every node in the list. In such a situation, it is only slightly more time consuming to go through a linked list than a sequential list.

It is easier to join or split two linked lists than it is in the case of sequential allocation. This can be accomplished merely by changing pointers and does not require movement of nodes.

The pointers or links consume additional memory, but if only a part of a memory word is being used, then a pointer can be stored in the remaining part. It is possible to group nodes so as to require only one link per several nodes. These two factors make the cost of storing pointers not too expensive in many cases.

The memory address in the link field has been used for illustration purposes in the present discussion. However, in practice, this address may be of no concern (and indeed unknown) to the programmer. Therefore, in much of the discussion to follow, a directed arc is used to denote a successor node.

We mentioned the use of pointers in this section only to specify the linear ordering (adjacency) among elements, but pointers can be used to specify more complex relations between nodes, such as that of a *tree* or a *directed graph*. This is difficult and indeed, for certain graphs, impossible to specify by using sequential allocation. These more complex structures can be specified by placing in the nodes a number of pointers. It is possible for a particular node to belong to several structures using this technique. A greatly expanded discussion of this will be given in Chap. 5.

From this discussion and some of the applications which follow, it will become clear that for certain operations, linked allocation is more efficient than sequential allocation; and yet for other operations, the opposite is true. In many applications, both types of allocations are used.

A *pool* or *list* of *free* nodes, which we refer to as the *availability list*, is maintained in conjunction with linked allocation. Whenever a node is to be inserted in a list, a free node is taken from the availability list and linked to the former list as required. On the other hand, the deletion of a node from a list causes its return to the availability list, where it can be used for insertion purposes at a later time. The advantage of this scheme of memory management is obvious. At any particular time, the only space which is used is what is really required.

The management of available storage in the case of a singly linked list is simple. For structures whose nodes can contain several pointers, this simplicity vanishes. A particular node can belong to many lists, and the deletion of this node from one list does not mean that it can be returned to the available storage list. The algorithm for managing memory, which is often called the *garbage collector*, tends to be nontrivial. This topic will be discussed in detail in Sec. 5-6. We are now prepared to examine some of the operations performed on linear linked lists.

Consider the familiar symbol-manipulation problem of performing various operations on polynomials such as addition, subtraction, multiplication, division, differentiation, etc. Let us direct our attention, in particular, to the manipulation of polynomials in three variables. It may be required, for example, to formulate an algorithm which subtracts polynomial $x^2 + 3xy - x + y^2 + 2z^3$ from polynomial $2x^2 + 5xy + y^2 + yz$ to give a result of $x^2 + 2xy + x + yz - 2z^3$. We are interested in finding a suitable representation for polynomials such that the operations mentioned above can be performed in a reasonably efficient manner. If we are to manipulate polynomials, it is clear that individual terms must be selected. In particular, we must distinguish between variables, coefficients, and exponents within each term.

It is possible to represent a polynomial by a three-dimensional array through an extension of the discussion of Sec. 3-2. From the discussion at the beginning of this section, it follows that this method of representation is unsatisfactory, and hence linked allocation should be used in this case. Before describing how it can be used, we consider the different classes of operations we can perform on linked linear lists.

Data in any type of application are required to be manipulated according to certain operations. If this processing is to be performed by the use of a computer, the first task to be accomplished is the adequate representation of the data in the computer memory. The difficulty and complexity of this task depend to a large extent on the particular programming language that is used to program the algorithms associated with an application. Certain languages have been specifically designed for manipulating linked lists. One such prominent language is LISP 1.5 In other cases, common procedures or functions to be performed on linked lists have been written as subprograms in a simple "host" language. An example of such a case is the list-processing language SLIP, which consists of a number of subprograms which are written in the FORTRAN language. We make use of the Pascal language to represent certain common operations performed on lists.

There are a number of classes of operations which are associated with linked lists. The first class contains those operations which are independent of the data contained in the nodes of a list. These operations include the creation, insertion, deletion, and selection of nodes. Programming languages which possess list-processing capabilities usually have these operations built-in.

Another class of operations associated with list structures is the one containing the operation which converts the raw data from a human readable form to a corresponding machine form. The inverse operation of converting an internal structure to a suitable human readable form is also required. These operations are clearly data dependent, and attention must be given to the operation that is associated with the structures. List-processing languages have some standard basic routines for such operations, but any additional routines must be programmed.

Finally, there are operations that must be programmed to manipulate the data according to what is required in a particular application at hand. In the case of polynomial manipulation, for example, such operations would include the addition, subtraction, multiplication, division, differentiation, and integration of polynomials. Once programmers have access to all the routines for the three classes mentioned above, their task of programming an algorithm is much simpler.

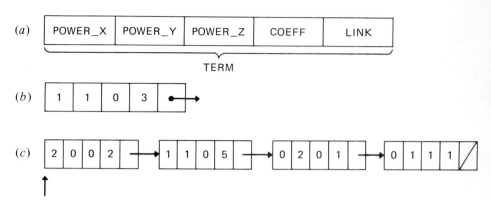

**FIGURE 4-1.2** Linked-list representation of a polynomial in three variables.

Let us consider the problem of describing singly linked linear list representations and operations in an algorithmic notation. A node consists of a number of fields, each of which can represent an integer, a real number, etc., except for one field (usually the last for purposes of illustration), called a *pointer*, which contains the location of the next node in the list.

Consider the example of representing a term of a polynomial in the variables x, y, and z. A typical node is represented as in Fig. 4-1.2a, which consists of five sequentially allocated fields that we collectively refer to as TERM. The first three fields represent the power of the variables x, y, and z, respectively. The fourth and fifth fields represent the coefficient of the term in the polynomial and the address of the next term in the polynomial, respectively. For example, the term 3xy would be represented as in Fig.4-1.2b.

The selection of a particular field within a node for the polynomial example is an easy matter. Our algorithmic notation allows the referencing of any field of a node given the pointer P to that node. COEFF(P) denotes the coefficient field of a node pointed to by P. Similarly, the exponents of x, y, and z are given by POWER_X(P), POWER_Y(P), and POWER_Z(P), respectively, and the pointer to the next node is given by LINK(P).

Consider as an example the representation of the polynomial

$$2x^2 + 5xy + y^2 + yz$$

as a linked list. Assume that the nodes in the list are to be stored such that a term pointed to by P precedes another term indicated by Q if POWER_X(P) is greater than POWER_X(Q); or, if the powers of x are equal, then POWER_Y(P) must be greater than POWER_Y(Q); or, if the powers of y are equal, then POWER_Z(P) must be greater than POWER_Z(Q). For our example, the list is represented by Fig. 4-1.2c.

Let us now consider the more difficult problem of inserting a node into a linked list. There are a number of steps necessary to accomplish this. First, the values for the various fields of the new node must be obtained either from an input operation or as the result of a computation. Second, we must somehow obtain a node from available storage. Finally, the values of the fields obtained in the first step are copied in the appropriate field positions of the new node, which is then placed in the linked list. The linking of the new node to its successor in the existing list is accomplished by setting the pointer field of the former to a value giving the location of the latter.

In the algorithms to be discussed in this section, assume that we have an available area of storage and that we can request a node from this area. In the polynomial example, the special assignment statement

P $\Leftarrow$ TERM

creates a new node consisting of the five fields previously described, with the location of the first of these being copied in the pointer variable P. At creation, the fields POWER_X(P), POWER_Y(P), POWER_Z(P), COEFF(P), and LINK(P) have undefined values. When a node is no longer required, we can return it to available storage. This we specify by stating, "Restore node P to the availability area." After we take this action, the node is assumed to be inaccessible and P is undefined. We will discuss in more detail the request of nodes from and the return of nodes to the availability area of storage in the next subsection.

We can now formulate an algorithm which inserts a term of a polynomial into a linked list.

**Function** POLYFRONT(NX, NY, NZ, NCOEFF, POLY). Given the definition of the node structure TERM and an availability area from which we can obtain such nodes, it is required to insert a node in the linked list so that it immediately precedes the node whose address is designated by the pointer POLY. The fields of the new term are denoted by NX, NY, NZ, and NCOEFF, which correspond to the exponents for x, y, and z, and the coefficient value of the term, respectively. NEW is a pointer variable which contains the address of the new node.

1.  [Obtain a node from available storage]
    NEW $\Leftarrow$ TERM

2.  [Initialize numeric fields]
    POWER_X(NEW) $\leftarrow$ NX
    POWER_Y(NEW) $\leftarrow$ NY
    POWER_Z(NEW) $\leftarrow$ NZ
    COEFF(NEW) $\leftarrow$ NCOEFF

3.  [Set link to the list]
    LINK(NEW) $\leftarrow$ POLY

4.  [Return first node pointer]
    Return(NEW)                                                     $\square$

Function POLYFRONT performs all its insertions at one end of the linked list. In general, it is also possible to perform insertions at the other end or in the middle of the list. The zero polynomial (polynomial with no terms) is represented by the NULL pointer. Before any term of a polynomial has been added to a list, its first node pointer, which we call POLY, has a value of NULL. Note that it is quite possible to get cancellation of terms in adding and subtracting polynomials, and that this can result in a zero polynomial.

When POLYFRONT is invoked, the address of the created node is returned, and it is this value that replaces the function call [(i.e., POLY $\leftarrow$ FOLYFRONT(NX, NY, NZ, NCOEFF, POLY)].

Given that it is possible to invoke the Function POLYFRONT, the construction of a linked list for a polynomial is achieved by having a zero polynomial initially and by repeatedly invoking Function POLYFRONT until all terms of the polynomial are processed. For the polynomial $2x^2 + 5xy + y^2 + yz$, this must be done four times. Since we want the first element of the list to be $2x^2$, we start by inserting the term $yz$ followed by the insertion of $y^2$, etc. If the pointer to the first node of the list is POLY, then a trace of the invoking Function POLYFRONT is given by Fig. 4-1.3.

Let us now consider an algorithm which performs an insertion at the end of a linked list.

**Function** POLYEND(NX, NY, NZ, NCOEFF, POLY). Given the definition of the node structure TERM and an availability area from which we can obtain such nodes, it is required to insert a node at the end of the linked linear list whose address is designated by the pointer POLY. The fields of the new term are denoted by NX, NY, NZ, and NCOEFF which correspond to the exponents for x, y, and z, and the coefficient value of the term, respectively. NEW is a pointer variable which contains the address of the new node. SAVE is a temporary pointer variable.

1.  [Obtain a node from available storage]
        NEW ⟸ TERM
2.  [Initialize numeric fields]
        POWER_X(NEW) ← NX
        POWER_Y(NEW) ← NY
        POWER_Z(NEW) ← NZ
        COEFF(NEW) ← NCOEFF
        LINK(NEW) ← NULL
3.  [Is the list empty?]
        If POLY = NULL
        then    Return(NEW)

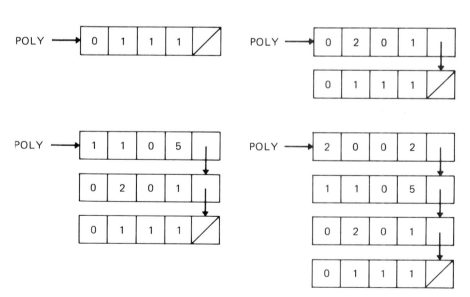

**FIGURE 4-1.3** Trace of the construction of polynomial $2x^2 + 5xy + y^2 + yz$ using Function POLYFRONT.

4.    [Initiate search for last node]
          SAVE ← POLY
5.    [Search for end of list]
          Repeat while LINK(SAVE) ≠ NULL
             SAVE ← LINK(SAVE)
6.    [Set LINK field of last node to NEW]
          LINK(SAVE) ← NEW
7.    [Return first node pointer]
          Return(POLY)                                                    □

The Function POLYEND must deal with two situations when inserting a new node at the end of a list whose pointer address is given by the variable POLY. In the first case, the value of POLY is NULL (there are no nodes in the list). A new node is created, and its address is assigned to the variable NEW. The information contents of the node are copied in the appropriate fields. The LINK field of the new node is set to NULL. In the second case, the value of POLY is not NULL, and in order to insert the new node at the end of the list, the end node of the original list must be found. This is accomplished by chaining through the list until a node with a LINK field of NULL is found. The chaining is performed with the help of the temporary variable SAVE, which is successively assigned the value of the LINK field of each node. Eventually, the value of the LINK field of the node pointed to by SAVE is NULL. The LINK field of this node is now assigned a value which points to the new node. Note that in the first case, the pointer variable POLY is assigned a value which points to the new node while, in the second case, the first node of the list after the insertion remains the same as that before the insertion.

By repeatedly invoking the Function POLYEND, we can easily achieve a linked-list representation of a given polynomial. This process is very similar to the one described previously using Function POLYFRONT. Note, however, that the terms of the polynomial need not be reversed in order to obtain the desired list. A trace of building a linked list for polynomial $2x^2 + 5xy + y^2 + yz$ is given in Fig. 4-1.4, where POLY is a pointer to the first node in the list.

Note that Function POLYEND becomes inefficient when the number of nodes in the list is large. In such a case, the entire list must be traversed in order to perform an insertion and as such is an algorithm of order n. This problem can be easily corrected by keeping the address of the last node that was inserted in the list. The next insertion can be performed without chaining through the entire list. The link field of the previously inserted node need only be changed to the address of the new node to be inserted. This obvious modification of Function POLYEND is implemented in the following algorithm.


**Function** POLYLAST(NX, NY, NZ, NCOEFF, POLY). Given the definition of the node structure TERM and an availability area from which we can obtain such nodes, it is required to insert a node at the end of the linked linear list whose address is designated by the pointer POLY. The global pointer variable LAST denotes the address of the last node in the list. The fields of the new term are denoted by NX, NY, NZ, and COEFF, which correspond to the exponents for x, y, and z, and the coefficient value of the term, respectively. NEW is a pointer variable which contains the address of the new node.

1.    [Obtain a node from available storage]
          NEW ⇐ TERM

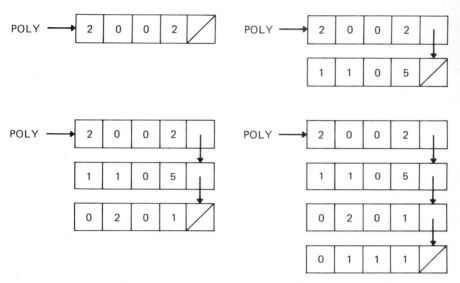

**FIGURE 4-1.4** Trace of the construction of polynomial $2x^2 + 5xy + y^2 + yz$ using the Function POLYEND.

2.   [Initialize numeric fields]
          POWER_X(NEW) ← NX
          POWER_Y(NEW) ← NY
          POWER_Z(NEW) ← NZ
          COEFF(NEW) ← NCOEFF
          LINK(NEW) ← NULL
3.   [Is the list empty?]
          If POLY = NULL
          then    LAST ← NEW
                  Return(NEW)
4.   [Insert node in nonempty list]
          LINK(LAST) ← NEW
          LAST ← NEW
          Return(POLY)                                                   □

In this section, we have introduced the basic concepts of linked allocation. As a motivating example, these concepts were applied to the representation of polynomials so as to facilitate their symbolic manipulation. A further discussion of this application is given in Sec. 4-3.1.

The next section is concerned with the description of certain storage structures for linear lists and their associated algorithms. Furthermore, the programming aspects of linked structures are discussed in some detail.

## 4-2  LINKED LINEAR LISTS

The basic notions of linked allocation as applied to the storage representation of linear lists were briefly discussed in the previous section. In this section linked allocation is dealt with in greater detail.

The first subsection is concerned with the formulation of algorithms such as insertion, deletion, traversal, and copying that are associated with linear lists. The programming aspects of these operations are also discussed in detail. In particular, the simulation of linked allocation by using arrays is introduced. This discussion is followed by describing the programmer-defined data-type facility which is available in Pascal for the linked representation of linear lists. The second subsection deals with the circularly linked representation of linear lists.

Since the traversal of a linked linear list is performed in one direction, the deletion operation in such a structure can be inefficient. Moreover, there are a number of applications which require the traversal of a linear list in both directions. For these reasons the "doubly" linked representation of a linear list along with its associated operations is introduced in the last subsection. The programming details of doubly linked linear lists are considered

### 4-2.1 Operations on Linear Lists Using Singly Linked Storage Structures

This subsection describes in detail the representation of linear lists using linked allocation. Algorithms such as the insertion of nodes into and the deletion of nodes from a linked linear list are given. The request for nodes from and the return of nodes to the available area of storage are described more fully than in Sec 4-1.

The programming aspects of linked allocation are discussed both from the simulation point of view, using arrays, and from the programmer-defined data-type facility available in Pascal. The first approach is the one which is usually taken in programming linked represented structures in languages that do not have pointer or link facilities, such as FORTRAN, ALGOL 60, and BASIC, while the second approach is used in languages that do have pointer facilities, such as Pascal, PL/I, SNOBOL, ALGOL 68, and ALGOL W.

Unless otherwise stated, we assume that a typical element or node consists of two fields, namely, an information field called INFO and a pointer field denoted by LINK. The name of a typical element is denoted by NODE. Pictorially, the node structure is given as follows:

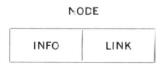

It is further assumed that an available area of storage for this node structure consists of a linked stack of available nodes, as shown in Fig. 4-2.1a, where the pointer variable AVAIL contains the address of the top node in the stack.

The task of obtaining a node from the availability stack can now be formulated. Assume that the address of the next available node is to be stored in the variable NEW. For practical reasons the availability stack contains only a finite number of nodes; therefore, it must be checked for an underflow condition. This condition is signaled by the value of AVAIL being NULL. If a node is available, then the new top-most element of the stack is denoted by LINK(AVAIL). The fields of the node corresponding to the pointer value of NEW can now be filled in and the field LINK(NEW) is set to a value which designates the successor node of this new node. The availability stack before and after a free node has been obtained is given in Fig. 4-2.1.

A similar procedure can be formulated for the return of a discarded node to the availability stack. If the address of this discarded node is given by the variable FREE, then the link field of this node is set to the present value of AVAIL and the value of FREE becomes the new value of AVAIL. This process is shown in Fig. 4-2.2.

We can now formulate an algorithm which inserts a node into a linked linear list in a stack-like manner.

**Function** INSERT(X, FIRST). Given X, a new element, and FIRST, a pointer to the first element of a linked linear list whose typical node contains INFO and LINK fields as previously described, this function inserts X. AVAIL is a pointer to the top element of the availability stack; NEW is a temporary pointer variable. It is required that X precede the node whose address is given by FIRST.

1. [Underflow?]
   If AVAIL = NULL
   then Write('AVAILABILITY STACK UNDERFLOW')
   Return(FIRST)
2. [Obtain address of next free node]
   NEW ← AVAIL
3. [Remove free node from availability stack]
   AVAIL ← LINK(AVAIL)
4. [Initialize fields of new node and its link to the list]
   INFO(NEW) ← X
   LINK(NEW) ← FIRST
5. [Return address of new node]
   Return(NEW)                                                      □

When invoked, INSERT returns a pointer value to the variable FIRST [i.e., FIRST ← INSERT(X, FIRST)]. Function INSERT is very similar to Function POLY-FRONT in Sec. 4-1, except for the additional detail of handling a request for a new node from the availability area of storage.

We now give a function which performs an insertion at the end of a linked linear list. Again, except for the detail of requesting a free node from the availability area, this function is almost identical to Function POLYEND of Sec. 4-1.

**Function** INSEND(X, FIRST). Given X, a new element, and FIRST, a pointer to the first element of a linked linear list whose typical node contains INFO and LINK fields as previously described, this function inserts X. AVAIL is a pointer to the top element of the availability stack; NEW and SAVE are temporary pointer variables. It is required that X be inserted at the end of the list.

1. [Underflow?]
   If AVAIL = NULL
   then Write('AVAILABILITY STACK UNDERFLOW')
   Return(FIRST)
2. [Obtain address of next free node]
   NEW ← AVAIL

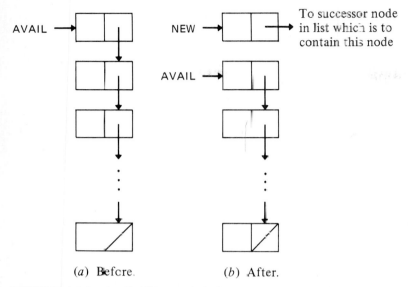

(a) Before.    (b) After.

**FIGURE 4-2.1** Availability stack before and after obtaining a node from it.

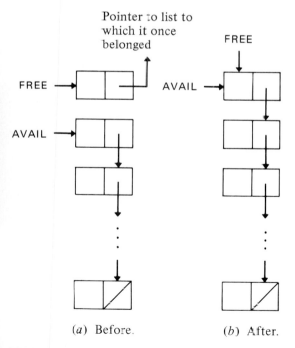

(a) Before.    (b) After.

**FIGURE 4-2.2** Availability stack before and after a free node has been returned.

3.  [Remove free node from availability stack]
    AVAIL ← LINK(AVAIL)
4.  [Initialize fields of new node]
    INFO(NEW) ← X
    LINK(NEW) ← NULL
5.  [Is the list empty?]
    If FIRST = NULL
    then    Return(NEW)
6.  [Initiate search for the last node]
    SAVE ← FIRST
7.  [Search for end of list]
    Repeat while LINK(SAVE) ≠ NULL
        SAVE ← LINK(SAVE)
8.  [Set LINK field of last node to NEW]
    LINK(SAVE) ← NEW
9.  [Return first node pointer]
    Return(FIRST)                                                            □

There are many applications where it is desirable to maintain an ordered linear
list. The ordering is in increasing or decreasing order on the INFO field. Such an
ordering often results in more efficient processing. For example, in the polynomial
example discussed in the previous section, the number of operations required to add
two polynomials each of degree n is reduced from order $n^2$ to order n if the terms of
each polynomial are kept in some decreasing order that depends on the powers of x, y,
and z.

A general algorithm for inserting a node into an ordered linear list is now
presented.

1.  Remove a node from the availability stack
2.  Set the fields of the new node
3.  If the linked list is empty
    then return the address of the new node
4.  If the node precedes all others in the list
    then insert the node at the front of the list and return its address
5.  Repeat step 6 while information content of the node in the list
    is less than the information content of the new node
6.  Obtain the next node in the linked list
7.  Insert the new node in the list and return address of its first node

The following detailed algorithm performs an insertion in a list according to the ordering that all terms are kept in increasing order of their INFO field.


**Function** INSORD(X, FIRST). Given a new term X, this function inserts it into a
linked linear list whose typical node contains INFO and LINK fields as previously
described. AVAIL is a pointer to the top element of the availability stack; NEW and
SAVE are temporary pointer variables. It is required that X be inserted so that it
preserves the ordering of the terms in increasing order of their INFO fields.

1.  [Underflow?]
    If AVAIL = NULL
    then    Write('AVAILABILITY STACK UNDERFLOW')
            Return(FIRST)

2.  [Obtain address of next free node]
        NEW ← AVAIL
3.  [Remove node from the availability stack]
        AVAIL ← LINK(AVAIL)
4.  [Copy information contents into new node]
        INFO(NEW) ← X
5.  [Is the list empty?]
        If FIRST = NULL
        then    LINK(NEW) ← NULL
                Return(NEW)
6.  [Does the new node precede all others in the list?]
        If INFO(NEW) ≤ INFO(FIRST)
        then    LINK(NEW) ← FIRST
                Return(NEW)
7.  [Initialize temporary pointer]
        SAVE ← FIRST
8.  [Search for predecessor of new node]
        Repeat while LINK(SAVE) ≠ NULL and INFO(LINK(SAVE)) ≤ INFO(NEW)
            SAVE ← LINK(SAVE)
9.  [Set link fields of new node and its predecessor]
        LINK(NEW) ← LINK(SAVE)
        LINK(SAVE) ← NEW
10. [Return first node pointer]
        Return(FIRST)                                              □

The algorithm considers the case of a null or empty list first of all, and its presence causes the LINK field of the new node to be set to NULL. In the second case, the new node is to precede the first node in the original list. This results in the new node becoming the first node in the updated list, and the LINK field of the new node is assigned a pointer value which corresponds to the location of the first node of the original list. In the third and final case, the pointer value of FIRST is not NULL and the INFO value of the node designated by FIRST is less than the INFO value of the new node to be inserted in the list. The value of the variable FIRST is assigned to temporary pointer variable SAVE. The temporary variable is assigned the LINK field values of successive nodes until the value of INFO(LINK(SAVE)) is greater than the value of the INFO field for the new node, or the LINK field of the node designated by the temporary variable value is NULL. In either case, the LINK field of the new node is assigned the address of the node indicated by the old LINK field of the temporary variable. The address of the new node is then assigned to the LINK field of the node indicated by the temporary variable. The average time for such an insertion is O(n / 2).

By repeatedly invoking Function INSORD, we can easily obtain an ordered linked linear list. For example, the sequence of statements

        FRONT ← NULL
        FRONT ← INSORD(29, FRONT)
        FRONT ← INSORD(10, FRONT)
        FRONT ← INSORD(25, FRONT)
        FRONT ← INSORD(40, FRONT)
        FRONT ← INSORD(37, FRONT)

creates a five-element list. A trace of this construction is given in Fig. 4-2.3.

Now that a number of insertion algorithms have been discussed, let us look at another equally important algorithm — that of deleting a node from a linked linear list. A general algorithm for deleting a node from a linked list is as follows.

1. If the linked list is empty
    then write underflow and return
2. Repeat step 3 while the end of the list has not been reached and the node has not been found
3. Obtain the next node in the list and record its predecessor node
4. If the end of the list has been reached
    then write node not found and return
5. Delete the node from the list
6. Return the node to the availability area

The detailed algorithm is now given.

**Procedure** DELETE(X, FIRST). Given X and FIRST, pointer variables whose values denote the address of a node in a linked list and the address of the first node in the linked list, respectively, this procedure deletes the node whose address is given by X. TEMP is used to find the desired node, and PRED keeps track of the predecessor of TEMP. Note that FIRST is changed only when X is the first element of the list.

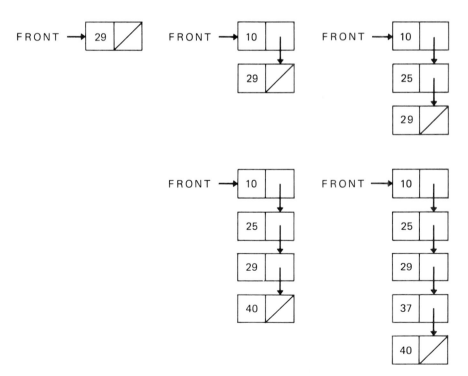

**FIGURE 4-2.3** Trace of the construction of an ordered linked linear list using Function INSORD.

1.  [Empty list?]
        If FIRST = NULL
        then    Write('UNDERFLOW')
                Return
2.  [Initialize search for X]
        TEMP ← FIRST
3.  [Find X]
        Repeat thru step 5 while TEMP ≠ X and LINK(TEMP) ≠ NULL
4.  [Update predecessor marker]
        PRED ← TEMP
5.  [Move to next node]
        TEMP ← LINK(TEMP)
6.  [End of the list?]
        If TEMP ≠ X
        then    Write('NODE NOT FOUND')
                Return
7.  [Delete X]
        If X = FIRST    (Is X the first node?)
        then    FIRST ← LINK(FIRST)
        else    LINK(PRED) ← LINK(X)
8.  [Return node to availability area]
        LINK(X) ← AVAIL
        AVAIL ← X
        Return                                              □

The first step in this procedure checks for an underflow. Next, a search is made for the desired node. Note that the repeat condition in step 3 fails either when X is found (i.e., TEMP = X) or when the end of the list is reached [i.e., LINK(TEMP) = NULL], thus, in step 6, TEMP ≠ X indicates the end of the list was reached without X being found. Step 7 performs the deletion. If X is the first node, the second node becomes the new first node of the list. Of course, this handles the situation in which there is only one node in the list in which case its deletion results in FIRST being set to NULL. When X is not the first node, its predecessor is set to LINK(X). Finally, X is returned to the availability area.

Procedure DELETE assumes that the address of the node to be deleted is known initially. Such, however, is not always the case. A node to be deleted is very often specified by giving its INFO value. A search is then made for the node with this value. The previous procedure can be easily modified to accommodate this change.

As a final example, we formulate a function which copies a linked linear list. A general algorithm to copy a linked list is now presented.

1.  If the list is empty then return null
2.  If the availability stack is empty
    then write availability stack underflow and return
    else copy the first node
3.  Repeat thru step 5 while the end of the old list has not been reached
4.  Obtain next node in the old list and record its predecessor node
5.  If the availability stack is empty
    then write availability stack underflow and return
    else copy the node and add it to the rear of the new list
6.  Set link of the last node in the new list to null and return

The following algorithm contains the details of the preceding general algorithm.

**Function** COPY(FIRST). Given FIRST, a pointer to the first node in a linked list, this function makes a copy of this list. A typical node in the given list consists of INFO and LINK fields; the new list is to contain nodes whose information and pointer fields are denoted by FIELD and PTR, respectively. The address of the first node in the newly created list is to be placed in BEGIN. NEW, SAVE, and PRED are pointer variables.

1. [Empty list?]
        If FIRST = NULL
        then    Return(NULL)
2. [Copy first node]
        If AVAIL = NULL
        then    Write('AVAILABILITY STACK UNDERFLOW')
                Return(0)
        else    NEW ← AVAIL
                AVAIL ← LINK(AVAIL)
                FIELD(NEW) ← INFO(FIRST)
                BEGIN ← NEW
3. [Initialize traversal]
        SAVE ← FIRST
4. [Move to next node if not at end of list]
        Repeat thru step 6 while LINK(SAVE) ≠ NULL
5. [Update predecessor and save pointers]
        PRED ← NEW
        SAVE ← LINK(SAVE)
6. [Copy node]
        If AVAIL = NULL
        then    Write('AVAILABILITY STACK UNDERFLOW')
                Return(0)
        else    NEW ← AVAIL
                AVAIL ← LINK(AVAIL)
                FIELD(NEW) ← INFO(SAVE)
                PTR(PRED) ← NEW
7. [Set link of last node and return]
        PTR(NEW) ← NULL
        Return(BEGIN)                                               □

The first step of the function checks for the empty case. In the second step, the first node of the original list is copied. The remaining steps of the function traverse the remaining nodes in the original list. Note that as each new node is created, its address must be placed in the PTR field of the predecessor of this node.

We now turn to the programming aspects of linked structures. These structures are first simulated by using only arrays. This discussion is followed by a description of the programmer-defined data-type facility that is available in Pascal for the linked representation of linear lists.

Let us consider the problem of implementing linked linear lists using arrays. As we mentioned previously, linked structures cannot be programmer-defined in a number of programming languages, such as FORTRAN, ALGOL 60, and BASIC, since there are no pointer-type variables in these languages. Although the Pascal language has pointer facilities, we nevertheless use it throughout the discussion on linked allocation with arrays. The concepts presented are directly applicable to languages without pointer data types.

In an array implementation, a node consists of a number of fields, each of which can represent an integer, a real number, a character string, etc., except for one field (usually the last field) which represents a pointer to the next node in the linear list. This pointer is an index (or subscript) of the array. This index points to the next node (i.e., array element) in the linear list. It is easy to see how an index together with a field name allows us to select a field from a particular node.

Consider the example of representing a term in a polynomial of the variables x, y, and z, which was discussed in Sec. 4-1. Assuming that any polynomial has at most 25 terms, we can declare five vectors: *powerx*, *powery*, *powerz*, *coeff*, and *link*, each representing a subscript giving the location of the next node in the list. Let us examine the representation of the polynomial $2x^2 - 5xy + y^2 + yz$ as a linked linear list.

Suppose that the representation of this ordered polynomial is represented in terms of the five vectors as follows:

| | | | | |
|---|---|---|---|---|
| *powerx[2]* = 2 | *powery[2]* = 0 | *powerz[2]* = 0 | *coeff[2]* = 2 | *link[2]* = 10 |
| *powerx[5]* = 0 | *powery[5]* = 1 | *powerz[5]* = 1 | *coeff[5]* = 1 | *link[5]* = 0 |
| *powerx[10]* = 1 | *powery[10]* = 1 | *powerz[10]* = 0 | *coeff[10]* = 5 | *link[10]* = 21 |
| *powerx[21]* = 0 | *powery[21]* = 2 | *powerz[21]* = 0 | *coeff[21]* = 1 | *link[21]* = 5 |

The first node of the list is specified by storing the index value of 2 in a variable called *first*. The value of *link[2]* gives the index value of the element of the second node in the polynomial. Knowing that *link[2]* has a value of 10 permits us to access the fields of the second node by writing *coeff[link[2]]*, etc. The index of the third node in the list is given by *link[10]*, which has a value of 21. Once the index value of the first node is known, it is an easy matter to follow the link pointers to obtain all the nodes in the list. The last node in the list has an index value of 5, and its link value is zero. Note that when using arrays, the NULL link is represented by the number zero.

Another point needs clarification here. By definition, the fields within a node are sequentially allocated. This is not the case in the above representation of linked lists. The field represented by *powerx[2]* is not adjacent in memory to the field denoted by *powery[2]*. The reason for this is the sequential allocation of vectors in the memory.

An alternative representation of linked lists is accomplished by using a double subscripted array. Let us declare a table called *node* consisting of 25 rows and 5 columns. Each occupied row of the matrix represents a node and, in particular, each element in a row designates a field of that node. The representation of our example polynomial is

| | | | | |
|---|---|---|---|---|
| *node[2,1]* = 2 | *node[2,2]* = 0 | *node[2,3]* = 0 | *node[2,4]* = 2 | *node[2,5]* = 10 |
| *node[5,1]* = 0 | *node[5,2]* = 1 | *node[5,3]* = 1 | *node[5,4]* = 1 | *node[5,5]* = 0 |
| *node[10,1]* = 1 | *node[10,2]* = 1 | *node[10,3]* = 0 | *node[10,4]* = 5 | *node[10,5]* = 21 |
| *node[21,1]* = 0 | *node[21,2]* = 2 | *node[21,3]* = 0 | *node[21,4]* = 1 | *node[21,5]* = 5 |

where *node[i,1]*, *node[i,2]*, *node[i,3]*, *node[i,4]*, and *node[i,5]* correspond to the fields *powerx*, *powery*, *powerz*, *coeff*, and *link* of some node, respectively. The above representation does make the five fields represented by a row of the matrix adjacent in memory because arrays are stored in row-major order in Pascal. The advantage of this approach is debatable, however, since the running time of the program is increased because of the use of double subscripting, and the programming effort is not diminished by this alternative representation.

An obvious representation which has the property that each node is sequentially allocated uses a vector consisting of 125 elements. A group of five consecutive elements of the vector represents a node whose subscript value is a multiple of five. If the vector is denoted by *poly*, and *i* represents the subscript value of the first field in a node, then the following correspondence holds with respect to the original formulation:

> $poly[i]$ $\longleftrightarrow$ *powerx*
> $poly[i+1]$ $\longleftrightarrow$ *powery*
> $poly[i+2]$ $\longleftrightarrow$ *powerz*
> $poly[i+3]$ $\longleftrightarrow$ *coeff*
> $poly[i+4]$ $\longleftrightarrow$ *link*

This method of representing a linked linear list for a polynomial is nearly as efficient as the case where five vectors were used.

Returning to the five vector representation *powerx*, *powery*, *powerz*, *coeff*, and *link*, we can select any field of a node given the index *p* to that node. The coefficient of the term pointed to by *p* is denoted by $coeff[p]$, the exponent of *x* is given by $powerx[p]$, and the pointer to the next node is given by $link[p]$. The selector for any field of a node is complete; that is, $powerx[p]$, $coeff[p]$, or $link[p]$, etc. can be used as either a left or right operand in an assignment statement.

Using arrays, let us now consider the programming of some of the algorithms discussed earlier in this chapter. Each of these algorithms obtained a node of available storage from the area of available storage. When using arrays to program linked linear lists, the programmer must control the list of available storage, which is usually maintained as a linked stack. When a free node is required, the top node of the availability list is deleted from the stack and is used as a new node. The availability list in the case of the polynomial example can be constructed by the Pascal procedure *alist* given in Fig. 4-2.4. This initialization program creates a linked linear list of 100 nodes. At the beginning, the values of the link fields are ordered in the sense that $link[i] > i$, where *i* is the subscript or address of the *i*th node. This, however, changes as nodes are removed from and returned to the availability list. The pointer *avail*, which is initially set to "one," gives the subscript corresponding to the top node in the stack. The vector *link* is assumed to be global to the procedure, as is the pointer *avail*.

The task of obtaining a node from the availability list can now be formulated. It is assumed that the address of the next available node is to be stored in the variable *new*. Recall that for practical reasons, the availability list contains only a finite number of nodes (100 in this case), so an underflow test must be made. The program to obtain a free node from the availability stack is given as follows:

```
{ program to obtain a free node from the availability stack }

{ check for underflow }
  if (avail = 0) then
     underflow;
```

{ obtain pointer value for a new node and store it in new }
new := avail;

{ obtain address of new top of stack node }
avail := link[avail];

The stack underflow error routine, *underflow*, has been omitted. The nature of this procedure will depend on what sort of corrective action (if any) is to be taken when the availability stack underflows. The fields of the node corresponding to the pointer value of *new* can now be filled in, and the field *link(new)* is set to a value which designates the successor node of this new node.

A similar program can be written which returns a node to the availability stack. If the pointer to this discarded node is given by the variable *free*, then the link field of this node is set to the present value of *avail*, and the value of *free* becomes the new value of *avail*. The program for this operation follows:

{ program to return a discarded node to availability stack }

{ change the link field of the discarded node to point to
  the previous top element in stack }
link[free] := avail;

{ the discarded node becomes the new top element of stack }
avail := free;

---

{ procedure to construct a linked stack of available
  nodes for a polynomial in three variables }
**procedure** alist;

**var** i: integer;

**begin**

    { set the link field of each node
      to point to its successor }
    **for** i := 1 **to** 99 **do**
        link[i] := i + 1;

    { set pointer field of last node to empty }
    link[100] := 0;

    { set top of stack pointer 'avail' to one }
    avail := 1

**end**;  { alist }

**FIGURE 4-2.4**  Procedure for constructing a linked stack of available nodes using vectors.

The previous programming techniques can be incorporated in a procedure for Function POLYFRONT of Sec. 4-1 as shown in the Pascal function given in Fig. 4-2.5. It is assumed that the five vectors *powerx*, *powery*, *powerz*, *coeff*, and *link* and the variable *avail* are global to the function.

Now that it is possible to invoke the function *polyfront*, all that is required to build a linked linear list for a polynomial is to start with a zero polynomial and repeatedly invoke the insertion function until all terms of the polynomial are processed. For the polynomial $2x^2 + 5xy + y^2 + yz$, we must invoke the insertion function four times. Since we want the first element of the list to be $2x^2$, we start by inserting the term yz followed by the insertion of $y^2$, etc.

If the pointer to the first node of the list is *poly*, an integer, then the following program steps will construct this polynomial:

---

```
{ function to insert a term of a three variable
  polynomial at the front of a linked linear list }


function polyfront(nx, ny, nz, ncoeff, first: integer): integer;


var p: integer;


begin
      { check for availability stack underflow }
      if avail = 0
      then begin

            writeln('availability stack underflow');
            polyfront := 0

        end
      else begin

            { obtain node from available storage }
            p := avail;
            avail := link[avail];

            { initialize numeric fields }
            powerx[p] := nx;
            powery[p] := ny;
            powerz[p] := nz;
            coeff[p] := ncoeff;
            link[p] := first;
            polyfront := p
        end
end;   { polyfront }
```

**FIGURE 4-2.5** Function *polyfront*.

---

```
{ initialize list pointer to null }
poly := 0;

{ insert the last term of polynomial }
poly := polyfront (0,1,1,1,poly);

{ insert the third term of polynomial }
poly := polyfront (0,2,0,1,poly);

{ insert second term of polynomial }
poly := polyfront (1,1,0,5,poly);

{ insert first term of polynomial }
poly := polyfront (2,0,0,2,poly);
```

A Pascal procedure based on Procecure DELETE is given in Fig.4-2.6. It is assumed that the two vectors *info* and *link* and the pointer variable *avail* are defined outside the procedure and are global to it.

The previous procedures are included in a main program whose label is *test* in the program segment of Fig. 4-2.7. As we mentioned earlier, the five vectors and the variable *avail* are global to the subprograms *alist*, *polyfront*, and *delete*.

The representation of linked linear lists by vectors has been discussed at some length to give some insight into their construction and manipulation. The programming of linked lists in Pascal using programmer-defined structures is the topic of the remainder of this subsection.

Thus far, we have been primarily concerned with data elements, such as simple variables, and array elements. The facility which allows the programmer to define his own classes of data objects was mentioned briefly in Chap. 3. This idea is pursued further in this section and in particular is applied to the representation of linked linear lists.

The problem of data representation in many applications is often complex. Arrays are not always well suited for easily expressing the relationships that exist among elements. A tree, for example, which is discussed in detail in the next chapter, is difficult to represent using arrays.

Consider an application concerning student registration at a university. Each student can be considered, in a structural sense, as an entity or record. Associated with each entity is a set of properties such as student number, student name, year of study, and many other items. For a particular student, each property has a certain value. A student can have a name of 'JOHN BROWN', a student number of '89107' and a year of study of '1982'. Conceptually, all the properties or fields in an entity belong together, thus reflecting their relationship to one another. One could use arrays to represent such a system, where an array element could represent the value of each property. A more desirable situation would be the representation of the entity by a single structure containing a number of fields, each field representing a property.

In Pascal, a programmer can create a template for a desired data entity by using a dynamically allocated structure. This facility permits the programmer to specify what fields are to be grouped together and in what order. This also gives a name to the grouping.

```
procedure delete (x: integer; var first: integer);

var pred, next: integer;
    deleted: boolean;

begin
    if first = 0
    then { check for empty list }
        writeln('attempting to delete from empty list')
    else begin
            deleted := false;
            if x = first
            then { delete first node }
                begin
                    first := link[first];
                    deleted := true
                end
            else begin

                    { search for predecessor of x }
                    next := first;
                    while (next <> x) and (next <> 0) do
                        begin
                            pred := next;
                            next := link[next]
                        end;

                    if next = 0
                    then { reached end of list }
                        writeln('node not found')
                    else { delete node }
                        begin
                            link[pred] := link[x];
                            deleted := true
                        end
                end;

            if deleted
            then { return node to availability area }
                    begin
                        link[x] := avail;
                        avail := x
                    end
        end

end; { delete }
```

**FIGURE 4-2.6** Procedure *delete*.

**program** test(input, output);

{ declare five vectors representing typical nodes }
**type** vector = **array** [1..100] **of** integer;

**var** powerx, powery, powerz, coeff, link: vector
avail: integer;

**procedure** alist;

**begin**
{ main body of procedure alist }
**end**; { alist }

**function** polyfront(nx, ny, nz, ncoeff, first: integer): integer;

**begin**
{ main body of function polyfront }
**end**; { polyfront }

**procedure** delete(x, first: integer);

**begin**
{ main body of procedure delete }
**end**; { delete }

**begin**

{ construct availability stack }
alist
**end**. { test }

**FIGURE 4-2.7** Main procedure containing procedures *alist, polyfront,* and *delete.*

For example, the statement

**type** pointer = ↑student;
student =
**record**
number : integer;
name : **array** [1..20] **of** char;
year : integer
**end**.

**var** p : pointer;

declares a structure with a name of *student* which consists of the fields *number*, *name*, and *year*. Such a declaration results in the definition of a data structure consisting of an ordered sequence of fields. In the above example, the data structure name is *student*. The declaration does not allocate storage for the fields named but merely indicates the makeup of the structure. As many copies of the data structure as required can be created elsewhere in the program by using **new** statements. If a specific copy of a data structure is desired, the programmer must use a pointer to this particular type of data structure in a **new** statement. For example, the execution of the statement

   **new**(p);

would create a storage area which allocates space for three fields, namely, *number*, *name*, and *year*. Since many copies of the dynamically allocated structure can be created in this way, a field name such as *number* is not enough for unambiguously specifying a certain field. We must be able to reference, by the use of an address or pointer, an instance of a field within a particular structure. This reference designator is a variable which has as its value the address of the created entity. The variable *p* is defined as a pointer to the *student* data structure, and the address of the node created is assigned to *p* by the **new** instruction.

   The referencing of a particular node of a dynamically allocated structure or of a field within this node is accomplished by using pointer qualification. For example, *p↑.student* denotes the node generated by the **new***(p)* statement. The fields can be referenced as *p↑.number*, *p↑.name*, or *p↑.year*.

   The sequence of assignment statements

   p↑.number := 89107;
   p↑.name := 'John Brown ';
   p↑.year := 1982;

initializes *number*, *name*, and *year* of the created node to values of 89107, 'John Brown', and 1982, respectively. This process can be represented by Fig. 4-2.8. The address of the created element is stored in the pointer variable *p* and is represented in the figure by the arrow from *p* to the element.

   Having created a node as in the previous **new** statement and placed its address in a reference variable, the programmer is now in a position to use or change the values of the fields of the node. This is illustrated in the simple Pascal program of Fig. 4-2.9 which creates a node, assigns values to the three fields *number*, *name*, and *year*, and outputs the results.

   Pascal not only allows the allocation of dynamic structures, but also permits the freeing of such structures to available storage. This is accomplished by the statement

   **dispose**(p);

when the node indicated by pointer *p* is to be restored to the availability area.

   It was mentioned that pointer variables usually specify an address. An exception is that they may be assigned the value returned by Pascal's built-in **nil** function.

P | 89107 | JOHN BROWN | 1982

**FIGURE 4-2.8**

This value cannot be related to any address and, therefore, cannot be interpreted as a pointer to a node. The function nil returns the same value on each invocation, and therefore, it can be used as an end-of-list delimiter. The comparisons "equal" and "not equal" can be made between nil and a pointer variable, as well as between two pointer variables. Furthermore, values for pointer variables cannot be read or output.

As another example consider the following problem. It is required that we write a program which reads in *n* sets of data consisting of employee number, employee name, hourly wage, and hours worked. A node is created for each set of data consisting of an input set and an additional field denoting gross pay. The addresses of the created nodes are to be stored in a reference array which is indexed by the employee number. Assume that the employee numbers are unique and that their values are between one and fifty. A program which performs the above task is given in Fig. 4-2.10.

The first part of the program defines a data structure class with the name *employee* whose typical node consists of four items having names of *name*, *rate*, *hours*, and *pay*. Note that the first item, *name*, is a vector.

---

{ program to create a node and output its contents }

```
program sample(output);

type pointer = ↑ student;
     student =
         record
             number: integer;
             name: packed array [1..20] of char;
             year: integer
         end;

var p: pointer;

begin
    new(p);
    with p↑ do
        begin
            number := 2100;
            name := 'Mike Pearson         ';
            year := 1923;
            writeln('number is ', number: 4);
            writeln('name is   ', name);
            writeln('year is   ', year: 4)
        end
end.

number is 2100
name is   Mike Pearson
year is    1923
```

**FIGURE 4-2.9**  Creation of a node using Pascal.

---

{ sample payroll program. for each employee there are two input
lines: the first has the employee's number, pay rate, and
hours - the second has the employee's name. }

**program** payroll(input, output);

**const** size = 20;

**type** vector = **packed array** [1..size] **of** char;
    pointer = ↑ employee;
    employee =
        **record**
            name: vector;
            rate, hours, pay: real
        **end**;

**var** member: **array** [1..50] **of** pointer;
    i, n, number: integer;
    p: pointer;

{ procedure to fill an array of characters, i.e., to read a string }
**procedure** readarray(**var** arr: vector);

**var** i: integer;
    b: char;

**begin**
    **if not** eof(input)
    **then begin**
            b := input↑;
            get(input);
            **while not** eof(input) **and** (b = ' ') **do**
                **begin**
                    b := input↑;
                    get(input)
                **end**;
            **if not** eof(input)
            **then begin**
                    i := 1;
                    **while not** eof **and** (i <= size)
                        **and not** eoln(input) **do**
                        **begin**
                            arr[i] := b;
                            b := input↑;
                            get(input);
                            i := i + 1
                        **end**;
                    **if** i <= size

FIGURE 4-2.10  Payroll program.

```
                then begin
                        arr[i] := b;
                        i := i + 1;
                        while i <= size do
                            begin
                                arr[i] := ' ';
                                i := i + 1
                            end
                    end
                end
        end
end; { readarray }

begin

    { read in number of employees }
    readln(n);
    for i := 1 to n do
        begin

            { create an employee record }
            new(p);
            with p↑ do
                begin
                    readln(number, rate, hours);
                    readarray(name);
                    readln;

                    { place address of created node in the element
                      of array member with a subscript given by
                      the employee number obtained from the input }
                    member[number] := p;
                    pay := hours * rate {compute gross pay}
                end
        end
end.
```

**FIGURE 4-2.10**  (Continued)

---

Next, a 50-element reference array named *member* is declared whose associated subscripts can be any employee number.

The new statement creates a node and stores its address in the pointer variable *p*. This address is then used to assign values to the four fields of the newly created node. The subscript of the array element is given by the employee number read from the employee input. For example, the input lines read in which contain the information

```
3
2 2.50 40
John Doe
```

11 3.00 45
Sam Smith
20 3.50 44
Tom Brown

result in the creation of three nodes whose addresses are stored in array elements *member[2]*, *member[11]*, and *member[20]*. Pictorially, this can be described by Fig. 4-2.11.

Let us now discuss the representation of linked linear lists. This can be accomplished by having a reference field in a certain node contain the address of another node. The programming of linked lists using arrays required the management of available space. When programmer-defined data types are used, all available space is allocated by the compiler. Similarly, the return of an unused node from a linked list to the availability list is handled by the compiler. We are therefore not concerned with available storage in the discussion to follow.

Returning to the polynomial example, the declarations

```
type pointer = ↑term;
     term =
        record
            powerx : integer;
            powery : integer;
            powerz : integer;
            coeff : real;
            link : pointer
        end;

    var p : pointer;
```

defines the structure of the polynomial term. The node *term* collectively represents the four fields *powerx*, *powery*, *powerz*, and *coeff*, which are capable of containing the required numeric data. The fifth field *link* is given the *pointer* attribute which specifies that the value of *link* will denote the address of a *term* data type. The variable *p* is also an address to a *term*, and its purpose is discussed shortly.

The execution of the statement

**new**(p);

creates a node and assigns the address of the new node to *p*. Note that many *term* nodes may be in use at one time, but each one must be generated by the execution of a **new** statement.

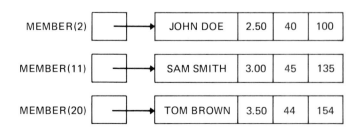

**FIGURE 4-2.11**

As before, the referencing of a node or a particular field is accomplished by using pointer qualification. For example, $p\uparrow.term$ would denote the node generated by the preceding **new**$(p)$ statement. Each field could also be referenced as $q\uparrow.powerx$, $q\uparrow.powery$, $q\uparrow.powerz$, $q\uparrow.coeff$, or $q\uparrow.link$ where $q$ is assumed to be a pointer variable associated with the structure *term*. As an example, we can add the coefficients of two polynomial terms, indicated by $p$ and $q$, using the statement

$x := q\uparrow.coeff + p\uparrow.coeff;$

These Pascal programming concepts should provide an adequate background for the list-processing programs in this and other sections. A Pascal implementation of Function POLYFRONT is given in Fig. 4-2.12. In function *polyfront* and also the subprogram of Fig. 4-2.14 (*delete*), the structure *term* is not declared. It is assumed that these procedures are nested within an invoking routine in which the necessary declarations are made.

If the pointer to the first node of the list is *poly*, then the program in Fig. 4-2.13 will construct the polynomial $2x^2 + 5xy + y^2 + yz$

A Pascal implementation of Procedure DELETE is given in Fig. 4-2.14.

### Exercises for Sec. 4-2.1

1. Given a linked list whose typical node consists of an INFO and LINK field, formulate an algorithm which will count the number of nodes in the list.
2. Formulate an algorithm that will change the INFO field of the kth node to the value given by Y.
3. Formulate an algorithm which will perform an insertion to the immediate left of the kth node in the list.
4. Formulate an algorithm which appends (concaterates) a linear list to another linear list.

---

```
{ function to insert a node at the front of a linked
  list and return a pointer to the new node. of
  course, pointer is a user-defined data type }
function polyfront(nx, ny, nz: integer;
            ncoeff: real; first: pointer): pointer;

var p: pointer;

begin new(p)
    with p↑ do
        begin powerx := nx;
            powery := ny;
            powerz := nz;
            coeff := ncoeff;
            link := first
        end;
    polyfront := p
end; { polyfront }
```

**FIGURE 4-2.12** Program for Function POLYFRONT using dynamically allocated storage.

---

```
{ construct a linked list representation of
  a polynomial using the insert procedure }
program polyst(input, output);

type pointer = ↑term;
     term =
         record
             powerx,
             powery,
             powerz: integer;
             coeff: real;
             link: pointer
         end;

var poly: pointer;

function polyfront(nx, ny, nz: integer; ncoeff: real;
                   first: pointer): pointer;

begin
     { body of function polyfront }
end; { polyfront }

begin

     { initialize }
     poly := nil;

     { insert last element of polynomial }
     poly := polyfront(0, 1, 1, 1, poly);

     { insert 3rd element of polynomial }
     poly := polyfront(0, 2, 0, 1, poly);

     { insert 2nd element of polynomial }
     poly := polyfront(1, 1, 0, 5, poly);

     { insert 1st element of polynomial }
     poly := polyfront(2, 0, 0, 2, poly);
end.
```

**FIGURE 4-2.13** Program for construction of polynomial $2x^2 + 5xy + y^2 + yz$.

5.  Given a simple linked list whose first node is denoted by the pointer variable FIRST, it is required to deconcatenate (or split) this list into two simply linked lists. The node denoted by the pointer variable SPLIT is to be the first element in the second linked list. Formulate a step-by-step algorithm to perform this task.

```
{ procedure to find and delete node x from
  the polynomial list pointed to by first }
procedure delete (x: pointer;  var first: pointer);


var pred,
    next: pointer;
    deleted: boolean;


begin


    { check for empty list }
    if first = nil
    then writeln('attempting to delete from empty list')
    else begin
            deleted := false;


            if x = first
            then { delete first node }
                begin
                    first := first↑.link;
                    deleted := true
                end
            else { search for predecessor of x }
                begin
                    next := first;
                    while (next <> x) and (next <> nil) do
                        begin
                            pred := next;
                            next := next↑.link
                        end;
                    if next = nil
                    then { reached end of list }
                        writeln('node not found')
                    else { delete node }
                        begin
                            pred↑.link := x↑.link;
                            deleted := true
                        end
                end;


            if deleted
            then { free node }
                dispose(x)
        end


end; { delete }
```

**FIGURE 4-2.14** Program for Procedure DELETE using dynamically allocated storage.

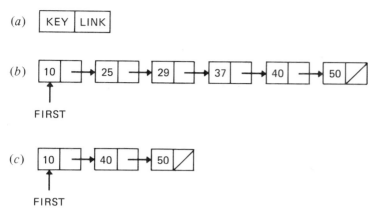

**FIGURE 4-2.15**

6. Suppose that you are given a linear linked list whose first node is denoted by the pointer variable FIRST and whose typical node is represented by Fig. 4-2.15a, where the variables KEY and LINK represent the information and link fields of the node, respectively. The list is ordered on the field KEY so that the first and last nodes contain the smallest and largest values of the field. It is desired to delete a number of consecutive nodes whose KEY values are greater than or equal to KMIN and less than KMAX. For example, an initial list with KMIN and KMAX having values of 25 and 40, respectively, could look like Fig. 4-2.15b. After deleting the designated nodes, the updates list would reduce to Fig. 4-2.15c. In this example, we dropped the nodes whose KEY field values are 25, 29, and 37. Formulate an algorithm and write a program which will accomplish the deletion operation for an arbitrary linked list.

7. An unknown number of input data lines are created, each of which contains a student record with the following information: student number, name, college, sex, and year of study. Each field is separated by at least one blank, in the order just given. The sex is entered as M (male) or F (female). A sentinel line, with student number of 999999 and "dummy" information in the other four fields, is used to signal the end of the data.

    The college and year of study of a student may change. A series of update lines follows the initial data. Update lines contain students who made changes. The update data are also followed by a trailer line having a student number of 999999 and random information in the other two fields. The update data are then followed by a series of lines on which a college name is entered.

    Design an algorithm to create a linked list of the student records which is ordered by student numbers (smallest to largest). The algorithm should then read the update data and modify this list accordingly. Once all update lines have been read in, the college names should be read and a well organized report of all students in each college should be output in alphabetical order. List the student number, name, sex, and year of study for each of these students.

    Note that neither the original file data nor the update data are ordered. It is possible that there may be an update line for a student who is not in the original file, in which case an appropriate error message is to be printed.

8. In the discussion on text handling in Sec. 2-5.1, we concentrated primarily on the text formatting functions and essentially ignored problems in text editing. One of the major problems in text editing is to store efficiently the lines of text such that this text can be modified later prior to the output of the text in a formatted form. In this question, we examine the insertion function in a *Screen-Oriented TEXT Editor* that we will call SOTEXTE In SOTEXTE lines of text are stored as 90 character strings in a character string array that is called FREE_TEXT. The first five character positions of an element of FREE_TEXT contains the line number for an 80 character line of text. The 80 character line of text is stored at positions 11 through 90 in the element of the FREE_TEXT array. Positions 6 through 10 of an array element are reserved for an array element index that acts as a link field in a manner to be illustrated shortly.

In SOTEXTE, lines of text are displayed on the screen along with their associated line number as follows:

```
00320I   These are lines of example text which help
00330    This is the line to follow the inserted text
         .
         .
         .
```

To insert a line of text after a given line (say line 00320), all that is required is to move the cursor to the sixth position of a given line and enter an "I" meaning insertion as shown in the previous text. A newly-numbered blank line will then be created just below the insertion line on the screen in the following manner.

```
00320I   These are lines of example text which help
00321    _
00330    This is the line to follow the inserted text
```

The text to be inserted can then be typed on this and subsequent lines as illustrated in the following text.

```
00320I   These are lines of example text which help
00321    illustrate how the insert command behaves
00322    when given a number of lines to be placed between
00323    two lines that are already in the SOTEXTE system._
00330    This is the line to follow the inserted text
```

Internally, within the SOTEXTE command handler, the effect of an insertion command is to establish a link in positions 6-10 of the element in the FREE_TEXT array corresponding to the insertion line (i.e., line 00320 in the example). The inserted text is placed in the open locations at the end of the FREE_TEXT array and line number increments of 1 are assigned. Therefore, if the next FREE_TEXT location which is open is 24, then the insertion command alters the stored text in line 320 to

0032000024These are lines of example text which help

and the text associated with line numbers 321, 322, and 323 are stored in locations 24, 25, and 26 respectively of the FREE_TEXT array.

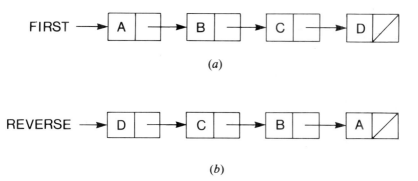

(a)

(b)

**FIGURE 4-2.16**

Devise the Algorithm INSERT_LINES that is capable of processing text insertions. Your algorithm can ignore the problem of cursor control on the screen (i.e., assume an input parameter is the line number of the line preceding the point of insertion). The algorithm should check to ensure that a line number associated with an inserted line of text does not equal a line number already in use.

9. Construct Algorithm RENUMBER which renumbers the entire stored text in the FREE_TEXT array such that the line number increments of ten are restored in a SOTEXTE text file as described in Prob. 8. For example, if a line number sequence is . . ., 320, 321, 322, 323, 330, . . . due to line insertions, then a new line number sequence of 330, 340, 350, 360, . . . should be created.

10. Formulate an algorithmic function which will reverse a singly linked list. For example, the reverse of the list of Fig. 4-2.16a is given in Fig. 4-2.16b. Assume a typical node consists of an INFO and LINK field. The parameter to the function should be a pointer to the original list, and the function should return a pointer to the reversed list.

11. Write a recursive procedure to insert a value into an ordered linked list. The parameters for the procedure are a pointer to the linked list and the value to be inserted into the list. Assume the nodes have INFO and LINK fields. For example, if we have the list of Fig. 4-2.17a and the call is

    Call INSERT (START,10);

then the result is the list given in Fig. 4-2.17b.
Note: As recursion is used, there should be no need for a loop within the procedure.

12. The search time for an item stored in a linear list necessarily varies with its position in the list. In many applications it is advantageous to place frequently referenced items near the start of the list. However, in many situations it cannot be determined in advance which items will be referenced most often. In cases like these a dynamic reorganization of the list, based on current reference activity, can reduce expected search time.

    Assume you have a singly linked linear list pointed at by the pointer variable START. Each node consists of a search key, KEY, an information field, INFO, and a pointer to the next node, NEXT. Formulate a logical func-

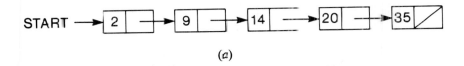

(a)

(b)

**FIGURE 4-2.17**

tion SEARCH(X DATA) that simultaneously searches and reorganizes the list in the following fashion. A node with search key X is sought. The nodes of the list are examined in turn. If the node is found, it is deleted from its current position and moved to the start of the list. Information contents of the node are then returned as parameter DATA. The value of the function SEARCH is *true* if the requested element is found and *false* if it is not.

13. The purpose of this exercise is to set up a data structure to maintain a company's list of customers with outstanding bills. For each customer with an outstanding bill, the customer name, address, and total outstanding amount is stored. Also a list of items for which the customer has an outstanding debt is stored.

Because the debtors list and items list are constantly changing, it is appropriate to store these as linked lists. For the purpose of searching and printing of reports, it is most appropriate to order the customer list by customer name. Similarly it has been decided that it is most appropriate to order the item lists in chronological order according to purchase time. As an item is added to the appropriate list at time of sale, this means that additions to the item lists occur at the end of the list. In order to facilitate this operation, a pointer should be maintained that points to the last node in each item list. Thus a diagram of the data structure is given in Fig. 4-2.18.

The operations that your algorithms should be able to perform on the data structures are the following:

(-)  Customer purchase

e.g., 'PURCHASE' 'WILSON' '3401 1st AVE N.'
        2
        'CHAIR' 190
        'TABLE' 250

e.g., 'PURCHASE' 'TARALA' '507 MAIN STREET'
        1
        'BED' 250

The first example indicates that WILSON purchased 2 more items so that they should be added to the end of the item list for WILSON. The second example

CUSTOMER LIST

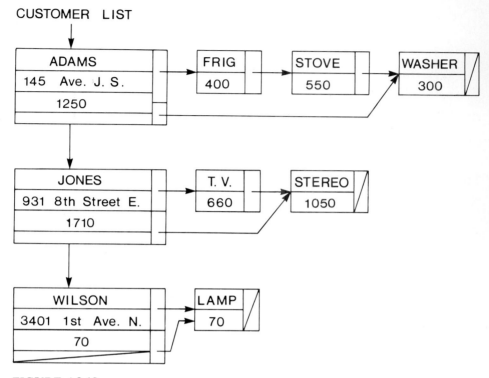

**FIGURE 4-2.18**

is for a new customer, thus the name TARALA will have to be added to the customer list, in alphabetical order, and the items purchased used to form an items list. Note that the number following the customer information specifies the number of items.

    (ii)   Customer payment

         e.g.,  'PAYMENT'  'JONES'  'STEREO'
                 'PAYMENT'  'JONES'  'T.V.'

These examples show that first JONES paid for his stereo and then for his television. Thus each of these items should be deleted from JONES's item list. You may assume that the customer pays for one item at a time and specifies the item by name. When a customer has paid all his debts, as for JONES above, then the customer should be deleted from the customer list.

    (iii)   Customer bill

    e.g., 'BILL'  'ADAMS'

Print out a list of the items and amounts for which ADAMS has an outstanding debt.

(iv)   Debtors list

e.g.,   'DEBTORS'

Print out the list of customers with outstanding debts.

Initially you should start with no customers in the list. Then read in the operations one by one and carry them out on the data structure.

### 4-2.2   Circularly Linked Linear Lists

The previous sections have been concerned exclusively with linked linear lists in which the last node of such lists contained the null pointer. We now wish to discuss a slight modification of this representation which results in a further improvement in processing. This is accomplished by replacing the null pointer in the last node of a list with the address of its first node. Such a list is called a *circularly linked linear list* or simply a *circular list*. Figure 4-2.19 illustrates the structure of a circular list.

Circular lists have certain advantages over singly linked lists. The first of these is concerned with the accessibility of a node. In a circular list every node is accessible from a given node. That is, from this given node, all nodes can be reached by merely chaining through the list.

A second advantage concerns the deletion operation. Recall from Procedure DELETE of Sec. 4-2.1 that in addition to the address X of the node to be deleted from a singly linked list, it is also necessary to give the address of the first node of the list. This necessity results from the fact that in order to delete X, the predecessor of this node has to be found. To find the predecessor requires that a search be carried out by chaining through the nodes from the first node of the list. It is obvious that such a requirement does not exist for a circular list, since the search for the predecessor of node X can be initiated from X itself.

Finally, certain operations on circular lists, such as concatenation and splitting (see Probs. 4 and 5 in Exercises for Sec. 4-2.1), become more efficient.

There is, however, a disadvantage in using circular lists; namely, without some care in processing, it is possible to get into an infinite loop! In processing a circular list, it is important that we are able to detect the end of the list. We can help guarantee the detection of the end by placing a special node which can be easily identified in the circular list. This special node is often called the *list head* of the circular list. This technique has an advantage of its own — the list can never be empty. Recalling from Secs. 4-1 and 4-2.1 that most algorithms require the testing of a list as to whether it is empty, we see that this advantage is certainly important. The representation of a circular list with a list head is given in Fig. 4-2.20, where the variable HEAD denotes the address of the list head. Note that the INFO field in the list head node is not used, which is illustrated by shading the field. An empty list is represented by having LINK(HEAD) = HEAD.

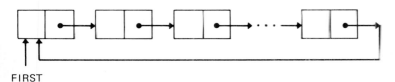

FIRST

**FIGURE 4-2.19**  A circularly linked linear list.

The algorithm for inserting a node at the head of a circular list with a list head consists of the following steps:

```
NEW ⇐ NODE
INFO(NEW) ← Y
LINK(NEW) ← LINK(HEAD)
LINK(HEAD) ← NEW
```

Circular lists will be used in a number of applications throughout the remainder of the text.

**Exercises for Sec. 4-2.2**

1. Formulate a deletion algorithm for a circular list with a head node.
2. Formulate an algorithm to concatenate two circular lists. (See Prob. 4 in Exercises for Sec. 4-2.1.)
3. Design an algorithm to split a circular list into two circular lists. (See Prob. 5 in Exercises for Sec. 4-2.1.)
4. Formulate insertion and deletion algorithms for a queue which is represented by a circular list.
5. Obtain an algorithm for the return of a circular list to the availability area of storage.
6. String manipulation can be easily accomplished by storing strings as linked lists. In a simple (and slightly space-inefficient) implementation, each node in a circular singly linked list represents a character in the string. For example, we could represent two strings S1 and S2 as shown in Fig. 4-2.21. S1PTR and S2PTR are the respective pointers to the last characters in the strings S1 and S2.

    Write a procedure to implement the instruction

    S1 ← SUB(S1, 1, K) ○ S2 ○ SUB(S1, K + 1)

    The input parameters to the procedure are S1PTR, S2PTR, and K.

**4-2.3  Doubly Linked Linear Lists**

Thus far, we have been restricted to traversing linked linear lists in only one direction. In certain applications, it is very desirable and sometimes indispensable that a list be traversed in either a forward or reverse manner. This property of a linked linear list implies that each node must contain two link fields instead of the usual one. The links are used to denote the predecessor and successor of a node. The link denoting the predecessor of a node is called the *left* link, and that denoting its successor its *right* link. A list containing this type of node is called a *doubly linked linear list* or a *two-way chain*. Pictorially, such a linear list can be represented by

HEAD

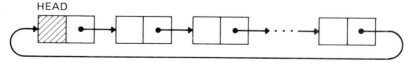

**FIGURE 4-2.20**  A circularly linked linear list with a head node.

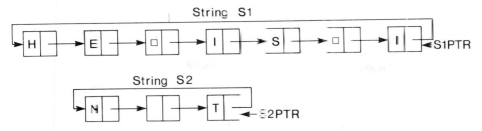

**FIGURE** 4-2.2

Fig. 4-2.22, where L and R are pointer variables denoting the left-most and right-most nodes in the list, respectively. The left link of the left-most node and the right link of the right-most node are both NULL, indicating the end of the list for each direction. The left and right links of a node are denoted by the variables LPTR and RPTR, respectively.

Consider the problem of inserting a node into a doubly linked linear list to the *left* of a specified node whose address is given by variable M. A number of cases are possible. First of all, the list could be empty. This is denoted by setting both L and R pointers to the address of the new node and by assigning a NULL value to the left and right links of the node being entered.

A second possibility is an insertion in the middle of the list. The list before and after an insertion can be represented by Fig. 4-2.23, where NEW is the address of the new node being inserted.

Finally, the insertion can be made to the left of the left-most node in the list, thereby requiring the pointer L to be changed. The list before and after such an insertion is shown in Fig. 4-2.24. The insertion algorithm can now be precisely formulated.

A general algorithm for inserting a node to the left of a given node in a doubly linked linear list is as follows.

1.   Obtain a new node and set its fields
2.   If the list is empty
      then insert the node in the list
        update left and right pointers to the list and return
3.   If the node is to be inserted at the front of the list
      then insert the node
        update the left pointer to the list and return
4.   Insert the node in the middle of the list and return

The details of this algorithm are now given.

**Procedure** DOUBINS(L, R, M, X). Given a doubly linked linear list whose left-most and right-most node addresses are given by the pointer variables L and R, respectively, it is required to insert a node whose address is given by the pointer variable NEW. The left and right links of a node are denoted by LPTR and RPTR, respectively. The information field of a node is denoted by the variable INFO. The name of an element of the list is NODE. The insertion is to be performed to the left of a specified node with its address given by the pointer variable M. The information to be entered in the node is contained in X.

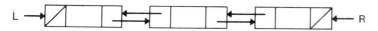

**FIGURE 4-2.22** A doubly linked linear list.

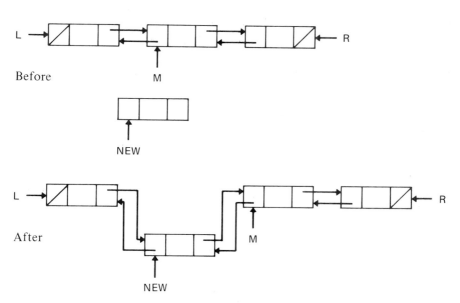

**FIGURE 4-2.23** Insertion in the middle of a doubly linked linear list.

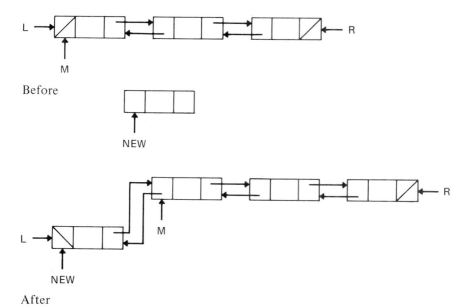

**FIGURE 4-2.24** A left-most insertion in a doubly linked linear list.

1.  [Obtain new node from availability stack]
        NEW ⇐ NODE
2.  [Copy information field]
        INFO(NEW) ← X
3.  [Insertion into an empty list?]
        If R = NULL
        then    LPTR(NEW) ← RPTR(NEW) ← NULL
                L ← R ← NEW
                Return
4.  [Left-most insertion?]
        If M = L
        then    LPTR(NEW) ← NULL
                RPTR(NEW) ← M
                LPTR(M) ← NEW
                L ← NEW
                Return
5.  [Insert in middle]
        LPTR(NEW) ← LPTR(M)
        RPTR(NEW) ← M
        LPTR(M) ← NEW
        RPTR(LPTR(NEW)) ← NEW
        Return                                              □

    We now examine the problem of deleting a node from a doubly linked list.
You may recall that the deletion of a node in a singly linked list entailed finding the
predecessor of the discarded node. The search was performed by chaining through
successive nodes. This search was necessary in order to change the link of the
predecessor node to a value that would point to the successor of the node being
deleted. Such a search could be very time consuming, depending on the number of
deletions and the number of nodes in the list. In a doubly linked list, no such
search is required. Given the address of the node which is to be deleted, the predecessor and successor nodes are immediately known. Doubly linked lists are much
more efficient with respect to deletions than singly linked lists.

    A number of possibilities arise. If the list contains a single node then a dele-
tion results in an empty list with the left-most and right-most pointers being set to
NULL. The node being deleted could be the left-most node of the list. In this case
the pointer variable L must be changed. An analogous situation can arise at the
right-most node of the list. Finally, the deletion can occur in the middle of the list.

    A general algorithm for deleting a node from a doubly linked linear list is as
follows.

    1.  If the list is empty then write underflow and return
    2.  If a single node exists in the list
            then set the left and right pointers of the list to null
            else if the leftmost node in the list is being deleted
                then delete the node and update the left pointer to the list
                else if the rightmost node in the list is being deleted
                    then delete the node and update the right pointer to the list
                    else delete the node from the middle of the list
    3.  Restore the deleted node to the availability area and return

The detailed deletion algorithm can now be formulated.

**Procedure** DOUBDEL(L, R, OLD). Given a doubly linked list with the addresses of the left-most and right-most nodes given by the pointer variables L and R, respectively, it is required to delete the node whose address is contained in the variable OLD. Nodes contain left and right links with names LPTR and RPTR, respectively.

1.  [Underflow?]
    If R = NULL
    then   Write('UNDERFLOW')
           Return
2.  [Delete node]
    If L = R      (Single node in list)
    then   L ← R ← NULL
    else   If OLD = L     (Left-most node being deleted)
           then   L ← RPTR(L)
                  LPTR(L) ← NULL
           else   If OLD = R     (Right-most node being deleted)
                  then   R ← LPTR(R)
                         RPTR(R) ← NULL
                  else   RPTR(LPTR(OLD)) ← RPTR(OLD)
                         LPTR(RPTR(OLD)) ← LPTR(OLD)
3.  [Return deleted node]
    Restore(OLD)
    Return                                                               □

The Pascal procedure given in Fig. 4-2.25 performs an insertion in a doubly linked linear list according to Procedure DOUBINS. The declarations

**type** pointer = ↑ structure;
    vector = **array** [1..20] **of** char;
    structure =
        **record**
            lptr: pointer;
            info: vector;
            rptr: pointer
        **end**;

are assumed global to the procedure. A similar procedure can be written for Procedure DOUBDEL and is left as an exercise.

Doubly linked linear lists can be easily used to represent a queue whose number of elements is very volatile. Such a representation is given in Fig. 4-2.26a, where R and F are pointer variables which denote the rear and front of the queue, respectively. The insertion of a node whose address is NEW at the rear of the queue is shown in Fig. 4-2.26b, where R' denotes the address of the rear of the queue after the update. The following sequence of steps accomplishes such an insertion:

    RPTR(R) ← NEW
    RPTR(NEW) ← NULL
    LPTR(NEW) ← R
    R ← NEW

Similarly, a deletion from a doubly linked queue can be represented by Fig. 4-2.26c, where F' denotes the address of the front node of the updated queue. The deletion from the front of the queue is achieved by the following algorithm steps:

```
F ← RPTR(F)
LPTR(F) ← NULL
```

Let us consider the possibility of simplifying the insertion and deletion algorithms associated with doubly linked linear lists. The case of an empty list can be
dispensed with by never permitting a list to be empty. This can be accomplished by
using a special node that always remains in the list. Hence, it is the only node in an
empty list. The special node is called the *head node* of the list and was described in
the previous subsection. By using the head node, we can realize a certain degree of

---

```
{ procedure for inserting a node into a doubly linked linear list.
  pointer and vector are user-defined data types with vector being
  a character string. }
procedure doubins (var left, right, m: pointer; info: vector):

var predm,  { predecessor of m }
    node: pointer;

begin
    new(node);
    node↑.info := info;
    if right = nil
    then { insert into empty list }
        begin
            left := node;
            right := node;
            node↑.lptr := nil;
            node↑.rptr := nil
        end
    else if m = left
        then { leftmost insertion }
            begin
                node↑.lptr := nil;
                left := node;
                node↑.rptr := m;
                m↑.lptr := node
            end
        else { insert in middle }
            begin
                node↑.lptr := m↑.lptr;
                node↑.rptr := m;
                predm := m↑.lptr;
                predm↑.rptr := node;
                m↑.lptr := node

            end
end; { doubins }
```

FIGURE 4-2.25  Pascal implementation of the Procedure DOUBINS.

(a) Doubly linked representation of a queue.

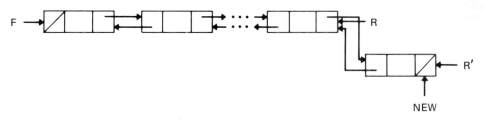

NEW

(b) Insertion in a doubly linked queue.

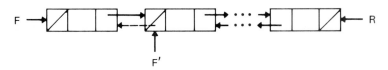

F'

(c) Deletion in a doubly linked queue.

**FIGURE 4-2.26**  Representation of and operations on a doubly linked queue.

symmetry in the structure by making the list circular, as shown in Fig. 4-2.27. Note that the right link of the right-most node contains the address of the head node and the left link of the head node points to the right-most node. The empty list is represented as in Fig. 4-2.28, where both left and right links of the head node point to itself. The algorithm for inserting a node to the left of a specified node M now reduces to the following sequence of steps:

    RPTR(NEW) ← M
    LPTR(NEW) ← LPTR(M)
    RPTR(LPTR(M)) ← NEW
    LPTR(M) ← NEW

The insertion of a node into an empty list can be represented before and after the insertion by Figs. 4-2.29a and b, respectively.

In a similar manner, the corresponding deletion algorithm for a node with an address given by the variable OLD consists of the following steps:

    RPTR(LPTR(OLD)) ← RPTR(OLD)
    LPTR(RPTR(OLD)) ← LPTR(OLD)

HEAD

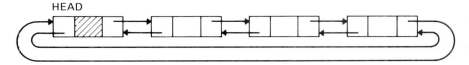

**FIGURE 4-2.27**  A doubly linked circular list with a head node.

**FIGURE 4-2.28** An empty
doubly linked circular list
with a head node.

The doubly linked method of allocating storage will be used extensively
throughout the remainder of the book. In particular, it will be used repeatedly in
Sec. 5-1.2 to represent trees, in Sec. 5-5.2 to represent graphs in computer graphics,
in Sec. 5-6 to represent the availability area in dynamic-storage management techniques, in Chap. 6 in certain algorithms for searching and sorting, and in Chap. 7 to
represent overflow areas for file structures.

**Exercises for Sec. 4-2.3**

1. Design insertion and deletion algorithms for a deque that is represented by a
   doubly linked linear list.
2. Repeat Prob. 1 for an input-restricted deque.
3. Repeat Prob. 1 for an output-restricted deque.
4. Derive a function that constructs a doubly linked list with a list head from a
   singly linked list that is accessed through a pointer FIRST. That is, given the
   list of Fig. 4-2.30a, the doubly linked list of Fig. 4-2 30b is generated. Note
   that the original singly linked list need not be destroyed.
5. To help manage the design and implementation of a number of software projects, a project management system has been developed by the Datapro Cor-

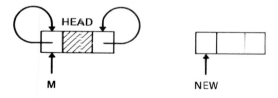

(*a*) Before.

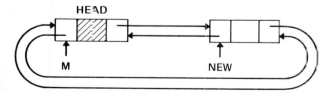

(*b*) After.

**FIGURE 4.2.29** Insertion into an empty doubly linked
circular list.

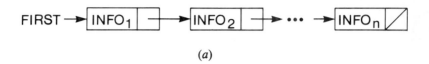

*(a)*

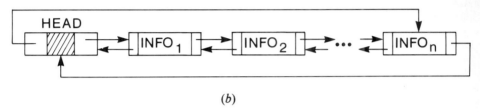

*(b)*

**FIGURE** 4-2.30

poration. The primary purpose of the system is to keep track of which analysts and programmers are working on which projects or are available for work but are currently not assigned to a project.

Consider the example data structure of Fig. 4-2.31*a*. In the figure, three projects (XR3, Raynac, Algoma) are active currently and the personnel for each are listed below the project name code. The list of personnel available for work is kept under the project node labeled Ready.

You are to assume a node structure that contains LPTR, NAME, and RPTR fields where the Ready node is pointed to by the variable FIRST.

a)  Write an algorithm that handles a project termination — in which case all the personnel associated with the project are returned to the ready list. The example data structure given earlier would be modified as in Fig. 4-2.31*b* if the Raynac project was terminated. Note that the input parameters to the algorithm are the name of the terminated project and the value of the variable FIRST.

b)  Write an algorithm to move an analyst or programmer in one project to another project. For example, if Cook is moved from the Algoma project to the Raynac project, given the original project assignment, then the new data structure representation would be as given in Fig. 4-2.31*c*. The input parameters to the algorithm are a pointer to the node of the employee that is to be moved, a pointer to the project node of the project the employee is currently working on, and a pointer to the project node of the project the employee will be moved to.

6.  Write a procedure which handles the updating of an ordered linear list of computer manufacturers and their current stock market quotations. For example, a current list of companies and their quotations might be

| | |
|---|---|
| WANG | 3.72 |
| DIGITAL | 9.83 |
| HONEYWELL | 15.21 |
| BURROUGHS | 16.13 |
| CONTROL DATA | 18.92 |
| IBM | 132.15 |

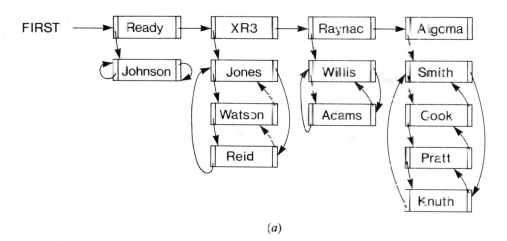

(a)

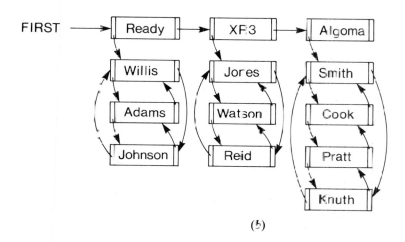

(b)

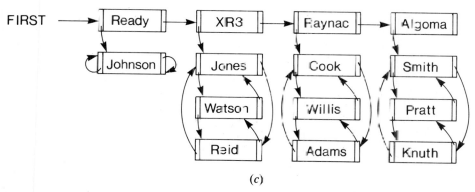

(c)

**FIGURE** 4-2.31

An input command of the form 'UPDATE' '<company name>' <latest quotation> should result in the updating of the list so as to preserve its order by quotation. Therefore, 'UPDATE' 'DIGITAL' 17.75 results in the new list

| | |
|---|---|
| WANG | 3.72 |
| HONEYWELL | 15.21 |
| BURROUGHS | 16.13 |
| DIGITAL | 17.75 |
| CONTROL DATA | 18.92 |
| IBM | 132.15 |

It should be assumed that the list is highly volatile in the sense that quotations are continually being changed and companies (plus quotations) are continually being added or removed from the list (*note*: you are not responsible for implementing DELETE and INSERT commands in this question). Assume that in the implementation of your update routine, a company's name is in the list. Note that a company can move *up* or *down* the list depending on the latest quotation; therefore, choose your data structure carefully.

Note that you need only write a procedure for the update command. You may assume that a company list already exists upon which you can perform an update. Note also that a number of comparisons are necessary for this procedure and that to be more efficient than a straightforward deletion and reinsertion of a node, a node is to be moved only a few positions.

### 4-3 APPLICATIONS OF LINKED LINEAR LISTS

This section will be concerned with a number of applications of linear linked lists. Many examples could be given, but only a few will be described in this section.

We have in our discussion of linked lists used as a typical node a term of a polynomial. A more thorough discussion of polynomials is the first application to be discussed. The need to automate polynomial manipulation has led to the design of special-purpose languages to satisfy the need. Common operations performed on polynomials are addition, subtraction, multiplication, division, integration, and differentiation. Of these operations, addition and subtraction are much easier to implement than the others. The implementation of polynomial addition is the only operation that will be discussed in this chapter. We will discuss algorithms to perform other operations in Sec. 5-2.1.

The second subsection describes the organizations and associated algorithms for maintaining a dictionary of names. This problem occurs in many application areas such as in compiler construction and information organization and retrieval.

Another application, which is closely related to polynomial evaluation, is performing arithmetic operations to some arbitrary precision. In certain problems (such as the matrix inversion of ill-conditioned matrices), we may be required to carry a large number of digits in the computation in order to obtain a modest number of significant digits. The number of significant digits required may be specified at program run time, and from this can be computed the number of digits which must be carried. This problem is the last to be discussed in this section.

#### 4-3.1 Polynomial Manipulation

We have in our discussion of linked lists often used, as a typical node, a term of a polynomial. A more thorough discussion of polynomials is now given. The implementation of polynomial addition is the only operation that is discussed in this subsection. Multiplication of polynomials can be obtained by performing repeated additions.

In order to achieve greater efficiency in processing, each polynomial can be stored in decreasing order by term according to the criterion briefly described in Sec. 4-1. Recall that a polynomial term $D_1 x^A y^B z^C$ will precede the term $D_2 x^A y^B z^C$ if $A_1 > A_2$; or, if the $A$'s are equal, then $B_1 > B_2$; or if the $B$'s are equal, then $C_1 > C_2$.

This ordering of polynomials makes the addition of polynomials easy. In fact, two polynomials can be added by scanning each of their terms only once. The previous comparison method can easily be used to add corresponding terms in two polynomials. If $A_1 = A_2$, $B_1 = B_2$, and $C_1 = C_2$, then the coefficient of the sum term can be obtained directly as $D_1 + D_2$.

The ordering just described will be used in Function POLY_ADD. This function has as input two ordered linked linear lists which represent two polynomials to be added. Each ordered list is constructed by the Function PINSERT, which is very similar to the Function INSORD given in Sec. 4-2.1. Since the two polynomials are ordered, the sum polynomial can be constructed by using a function that is essentially identical (except for the handling of the availability area) to Function POLYLAST of Sec. 4-1. Also needed is a function that is essentially identical (except for the information fields of a node) to Function COPY of Sec. 4-2.1. Function POLY_ADD does not alter its two input polynomials, and the address of the sum polynomial is returned to the main algorithm which invoked the function. We now formulate the function that adds two polynomials.

A general algorithm for summing two polynomials is now presented.

1. Repeat thru step 3 while there are terms in both polynomials yet to be processed
2. Obtain the values for each term
3. If the powers associated with the two terms are equal
   then if the terms do not cancel
           then insert the sum of the terms into the sum polynomial
           obtain the next terms in both polynomials to be added
       else if the power of the first polynomial > power of the second
           then insert the term from first polynomial into sum polynomial
               obtain the next term in the first polynomial
           else insert the term from second polynomial into sum polynomial
               obtain the next term in the second polynomial
4. Copy remaining terms from the nonempty polynomial into the sum polynomial
5. Return the address of the sum polynomial

The specifics of the algorithm follow.

**Function** POLY_ADD(P, Q). Given two polynomials whose first terms are referenced by pointer variables P and Q, respectively, an insertion function as described in Function POLYLAST of Sec. 4-1, and a copying function as described in Function COPY of Sec. 4-2.1, it is required to add these polynomials and store their sum in a third polynomial which is referenced by the pointer variable R. The original polynomials are to remain unchanged. PSAVE and QSAVE are pointer variables. A1, A2, B1, B2, C1, C2, D1, and D2 are temporary variables. LAST (used in POLYLAST) is assumed to be a global variable.

1. [Initialize]
   R ← NULL
   PSAVE ← P
   QSAVE ← Q
2. [End of any polynomial?]
   Repeat thru step 4 while P ≠ NULL and Q ≠ NULL
3. [Get values for each term]
   A1 ← POWER_X(P)
   A2 ← POWER_X(Q)
   B1 ← POWER_Y(P)
   B2 ← POWER_Y(Q)
   C1 ← POWER_Z(P)
   C2 ← POWER_Z(Q)
   D1 ← COEFF(P)
   D2 ← COEFF(Q)
4. [Compare terms]
   If (A1 = A2) and (B1 = B2) and (C1 = C2)
   then   If D1 + D2 ≠ 0
          then   R ← POLYLAST(A1, B1, C1, D1 + D2, R)
          P ← LINK(P)
          Q ← LINK(Q)
   else   If (A1>A2) or ((A1=A2) and (B1>B2)) or
          ((A1=A2) and (B1=B2) and (C1>C2))
          then   R ← POLYLAST(A1, B1, C1, D1, R)
                 P ← LINK(P)
          else   R ← POLYLAST(A2, B2, C2, D2, R)
                 Q ← LINK(Q)
5. [Not at end of one of the polynomials?]
   If P ≠ NULL
   then   LINK(LAST) ← COPY(P)
   else   If Q ≠ NULL
          then   LINK(LAST) ← COPY(Q)
6. [Restore initial pointer values for P and Q]
   P ← PSAVE
   Q ← QSAVE
7. [Return pointer to sum polynomial]
   Return(R)                                                                □

The first step of the function initializes the pointer variable associated with the sum polynomial to NULL and saves the pointer variable values of P and Q in PSAVE and QSAVE, respectively.

The second step determines whether there are terms in the polynomials which remain to be processed; if both polynomials have not been completely processed, then the third and fourth steps of the function are executed.

The third step gets the values for A1, A2, B1, B2, C1, C2, D1, and D2. Step four is concerned with comparing a term of each polynomial. If the powers associated with the two terms are equal [i.e., (A1=A2), (B1=B2), and (C1=C2)], then the sum term is inserted in polynomial R, provided the terms do not cancel. This insertion is performed by invoking Function POLYLAST. Note that in order to avoid chaining to the end of the linked list for each insertion, the pointer variable LAST has been used to denote the address of the last node inserted. This technique was described in Sec. 4-1. If the powers of the P term are greater than those of the Q term, then the P term is inserted at the end of the sum polynomial; otherwise, the Q term is inserted.

The fifth step checks to see if the end of one of the polynomials has not been reached. If this is the case, then the remaining terms are copied onto the end of the sum polynomial by invoking Function COPY. Finally, the original values of the pointer variables P and Q are restored and the address of the sum polynomial is returned.

We now give the function which is used to build an ordered linked representation of a polynomial.

**Function** PINSERT(NX, NY, NZ, NCOEFF, FIRST). Given an ordered linked list whose typical node contains the information fields POWER_X, POWER_Y, POWER_Z, and COEFF, and a pointer field LINK, as previously described in this chapter, and given a new term, this function inserts that term so as to preserve the order of the list. The fields of the new term are denoted by NX, NY, NZ, and NCOEFF, which correspond to the exponents for x, y, and z and the coefficient value of the term. The address of the first term in the list is given by FIRST. NEW and SAVE are pointer variables. A, B, and C are auxiliary variables.

1. [Create a node]
   NEW ⇐ TERM
2. [Copy information contents into new node]
   POWER_X(NEW) ← NX
   POWER_Y(NEW) ← NY
   POWER_Z(NEW) ← NZ
   COEFF(NEW) ← NCOEFF
3. [Is list empty?]
   If FIRST = NULL
   then    LINK(NEW) ← NULL
           Return(NEW)
4. [Initialize search for new node's position]
   A ← POWER_X(FIRST)
   B ← POWER_Y(FIRST)
   C ← POWER_Z(FIRST)
5. [Does new node precede first node of list?]
   If (NX>A) or ((NX=A) and (NY>B)) or
      ((NX=A) and (NY=B) and (NZ>C))
   then    LINK(NEW) ← FIRST
           Return(NEW)
6. [Initialize temporary pointer]
   SAVE ← FIRST
7. [Search for predecessor of node]
   Repeat while LINK(SAVE) ≠ NULL
       A ← POWER_X(LINK(SAVE))
       B ← POWER_Y(LINK(SAVE))
       C ← POWER_Z(LINK(SAVE))
       If (NX<A) or ((NX=A) and(NY<B)) or
          ((NX=A) and (NY=B) and (NZ<C))
       then    SAVE ← LINK(SAVE)
       else    Exitloop

8.  [Set link fields of new node and its predecessor]
        LINK(NEW) ← LINK(SAVE)
        LINK(SAVE) ← NEW
9.  [Reset first node pointer]
        Return(FIRST)                                                            □

This function is very similar to Function INSORD of Sec. 4-2.1, and no further explanation should be required.

The last algorithm to be discussed reads in the two polynomials and repeatedly invokes Function PINSERT in order to construct the linked representations of these polynomials. Each term is given by four successive pieces of input data. The first three correspond to the powers of x, y, and z, and the fourth to the coefficient of the term. The end of a polynomial in the data is signaled by a dummy coefficient value of 0.

**Algorithm**    POLYNOMIAL.    Given    Functions    POLY_ADD,    PINSERT,    and POLYLAST, as previously described, it is required to read two polynomials and obtain their sum.  POLY1, POLY2, and POLY3 are pointer variables associated with the three polynomials. The variables X, Y, Z, and C are used to denote the powers of x, y, z and the coefficient of the term.

1.  [Initialize]
        POLY1 ← POLY2 ← NULL
2.  [Create first polynomial list]
        Read(X, Y, Z, C)
        Repeat while C ≠ 0
            POLY1 ← PINSERT(X, Y, Z, C, POLY1)
            Read(X, Y, Z, C)
3.  [Create second polynomial]
        Read(X, Y, Z, C)
        Repeat while C ≠ 0
            POLY2 ← PINSERT(X, Y, Z, C, POLY2)
            Read(X, Y, Z, C)
4.  [Add polynomials]
        POLY3 ← POLY_ADD(POLY1, POLY2)
5.  [Check results]
        Print polynomials
        Exit                                                                     □

We note in terminating this section that a circular linked representation of a polynomial could have been used throughout the associated algorithms. In certain cases this representation would have resulted in somewhat simpler algorithms.

**Exercises for Sec. 4-3.1**

1.  Assuming that a polynomial in three variables is represented by a linked linear list as discussed in this section, formulate an algorithm which traverses the linked list and evaluates the polynomial for given values of x, y, and z.
2.  Formulate an algorithm to subtract two polynomials in three variables.
3.  Formulate an algorithm to create an ordered linear list with no duplicate

terms. The input is a polynomial in three variables that is unordered and may have repeated terms.

4.  Formulate an algorithm to produce a copy of a polynomial in three variables.
5.  Formulate an algorithm to multiply two polynomials in three variables. (*Hint:* This can be achieved by repeated additions.)
6.  Formulate an algorithm to divide polynomial P by polynomial Q. The quotient polynomial is to be placed in a linked list whose first term is given by the pointer variables QUOTIENT, while the remainder polynomial is to be stored in a linked list whose first node address is given by the pointer variable REMAINDER.
7.  Formulate an algorithm to integrate a polynomial in three variables with respect to one of these variables. Create a linked list for the result.
8.  Repeat Prob. 7 for the differentiation of the polynomial with respect to a given variable.
9.  Formulate an algorithm to print the polynomials of Step 5 in Algorithm POLYNOMIAL.

## 4-3.2 Linked Dictionary

An important part of any compiler is the construction and maintenance of a dictionary containing names and their associated values. Such a dictionary is also called a *symbol table*. In a typical compiler there may be several symbol tables corresponding to variable names, labels, literals, etc.

The constraints which must be considered in the design of symbol tables are processing time and memory space. Usually, there exists some inverse relationship between the speed of a symbol-table algorithm and the memory space it requires.

There are a number of phases associated with the construction of symbol tables. The principal phases that we discuss at this time are *building* and *referencing*. The building phase involves the insertion of symbols and their associated values (if known) into a table, while referencing is the fetching or accessing of values from a table. We will deal in much more detail with these topics in Sec. 5-2.2 and Chap. 6.

The ratio of the expected number of insertions to references is very important. In many symbol-table systems, insertion time and access time are closely related, but in the absence of such a relationship and in the case where the expected number of references or accesses is high with respect to insertions, it may be advantageous to allocate more time and space to the insertion function in order to improve the referencing function.

It is an easy matter to construct a very fast symbol-table system, provided that a large section of memory is available. In such a case, a unique memory address is assigned to each name, where the address is obtained from the arithmetic value of the characters making up the name. If names were restricted to the set of valid FORTRAN names consisting of, at most, six characters, then some two billion words of storage would have to be allocated to such a dictionary system — a totally unacceptable situation.

The most straightforward method of accessing a symbol table is by using the *linear search* technique. This method involves arranging the symbols sequentially in memory via a vector or by using a simple linear linked list. An insertion is easily handled by adding the new element to the end of the list. When it is desired to access a particular symbol, the table is searched sequentially from its beginning until it is found. It will take, on the average, $N/2$ comparisons to find a particular symbol in a table containing $N$ entries. The insertion mechanism is very fast, but the referencing is extremely slow. In the case where few references are made, this method would be efficient. If many references to symbols in the table are required, then some other method should be used. For example, for a table containing 1,000 entries, it would take, on the average, some 500 comparisons to locate a specified element.

Another relatively simple method of accessing a symbol table is the *binary search* method. The entries in the table are stored in alphabetical or numerically increasing order. A search for a particular item resembles the search for a name in a telephone directory. The middle entry of the table is located and its value is examined. If its value is too high, then the middle entry of the first half of the table is examined and the procedure is repeated on the first half until the required item is found. If the value is too low, then the middle entry of the second half of the table is tried and the procedure is repeated on the second half. An average of $\log_2 N$ comparisons is required in order to locate an entry. This is considerably better than the search time for the linear search method.

The binary search technique has certain undesirable properties. First, it appears that the number of memory words allocated to the table is a function of the number of items which is to be stored in the table, namely, the smallest power of two which is greater than or equal to the number of entries that are to be stored in the table. This can be quite wasteful of memory. The basic method, however, can be changed to get around this restriction. Second, an insertion of an entry requires that a search be done in order to locate the position or address in the table where the entry will be stored. The ratio of insertion time to access time is quite high for this method. This method would be suitable if few insertions are to be made. A rather detailed discussion of the binary search method and other search methods is given in Chap. 6.

Since a fast symbol-table method is not possible by associating a unique memory address that is computed from the arithmetic value of the characters making up the name, let us look at an obvious modification. Suppose that we have a function which maps a name into an integer. This type of function will be called a *hashing function*. Let us consider the set of FORTRAN names that can be used in a computer program and a hashing function H which maps each name into an integer between 0 and 9. Such a function can be obtained by dividing the internal representation of the name (binary coded decimal) by the number 10. The remainder of this division must be less than 10. This function obviously maps many names into the same number, and so the mapping is many-to-one. The hashing function partitions all names into a set of classes. Two names are in the same class if, and only if, they are mapped into the same number, i.e., they have the same remainder upon division by 10. A name cannot be in two distinct classes, since it can only be mapped into one number. The partition that is induced by such a hashing function is called an *equivalence relation*, and the classes formed in this way are called *equivalence classes*.

An efficient symbol-table method is to represent each equivalence class in memory as a simple linked linear list. The insertion algorithm consists of mapping the name into a number. This number determines which equivalence class or linked list the name should be in. If the name is not already in that linked list, it is appended to the end of the list. The search for a name can be performed in a similar manner. The name is mapped into a number which is used to locate the linked list in which this name must belong. A sequential search of this list yields the desired entry.

As an example, let us assume the following:

The names NODE, BRAND, OPERATIONS, and PARAMETERS are all mapped into the number 0

The name STORAGE is mapped into the number 1
The names AN and ADD are mapped into the number 2
The names FUNCTION and B are mapped into the number 8

Let us use a one-dimensional array called EQUIV consisting of 10 elements. Each element of EQUIV contains the address of the first node of the linked list representing a particular equivalence class. If there are no names in a certain equivalence class, then the corresponding element in the array EQUIV has a value of NULL. Figure 4-3.1a shows the structure for the equivalence class consisting of the names NODE, BRAND, OPERATIONS, and PARAMETERS which are mapped into zero. A similar representation is given in Fig. 4-3.1b for the remaining equivalence classes.

The importance of a suitable hashing function cannot be overemphasized. Ideally, it would be desirable to have a function which results in all equivalence classes having the *same* number of symbols. The worst possible case is one where all names would be mapped into the same number (one equivalence class), thereby causing the insertion and fetching algorithms to be no more efficient than those in a linear search method. It is a nontrivial matter to obtain the "proper" hashing function, since the size of the equivalence classes that it induces depends on the names being used (i.e., on the domain of the hashing function). A more complete discussion of the class of hashing functions will be given in Chap. 6.

Another important factor in attaining a reasonable efficiency is keeping the size of each equivalence class relatively small. For example, if it is known that, on the average, a dictionary will have 125 entries at any given time, then one would want approximately 100 classes. In such a case, the average number of comparisons for accessing an entry is slightly greater than "one," and a similar figure also holds for insertions. These average figures are based on the assumption that all names are mapped into the 100 classes in a uniform manner.

The hashing functions to be used should not be too complex since the time taken to evaluate the function for a particular argument must be added to the insertion and fetch times. It is usually possible to live within this constraint because of the great speed of a computer in doing arithmetic computations.

We now turn to the formulation of an insertion algorithm for the symbol-table procedure. A general algorithm for entering a name into a symbol table is as follows.

1. Compute the hash number
2. Allocate a new node and set its fields
3. If the equivalence class is empty
   then add the node to the equivalence class and return
4. Repeat step 5 while a duplicate name is not found and the end of the equivalence list is not reached
5. Obtain the next name in the equivalence class
6. If a duplicate name was not found
   then add the node to the equivalence class
7. Return

A procedure for this algorithm follows.

**Procedure** ENTER(NAME, EQUIV). Given a one-dimensional reference array, EQUIV, each element of which contains a pointer to an equivalence class and a hashing function HASH, which maps a name into an integer, it is required to

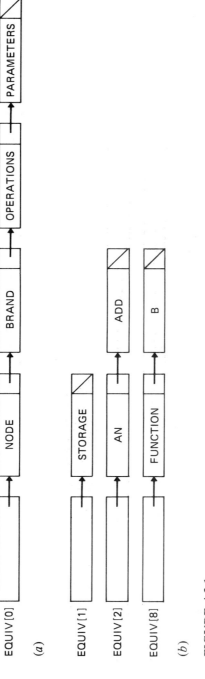

EQUIV[0]

NODE   BRAND   OPERATIONS   PARAMETERS

(*a*)

EQUIV[1]

STORAGE

EQUIV[2]

AN   ADD

EQUIV[8]

FUNCTION   B

(*b*)

**FIGURE 4-3.1**

append the entry denoted by NAME to the end of the appropriate equivalence class (if it is not already there). The typical node in a list consists of an information field (SYMBOL) and a pointer field (LINK). The node structure is referred to as RECORD. RANDOM is the hash number for a name. POINTER is a pointer variable.

1.  [Compute the hash number]
    RANDOM ← HASH(NAME)
2.  [Allocate a node and set its fields]
    NEW ⇐ RECORD
    SYMBOL(NEW) ← NAME
    LINK(NEW) ← NULL
3.  [Is the equivalence class empty?]
    If EQUIV[RANDOM] = NULL
    then   EQUIV[RANDOM] ← NEW
           Return
4.  [Initiate search for NAME]
    POINTER ← EQUIV[RANDOM]
5.  [Search]
    Repeat while SYMBOL(POINTER) ≠ NAME and LINK(POINTER) ≠ NULL
           POINTER ← LINK(POINTER)
6.  [NAME already there?]
    If SYMBOL(POINTER) ≠ NAME
    then   LINK(POINTER) ← NEW
    Return                                                         □

The Pascal program in Fig. 4-3.2 constructs a symbol table. It consists of a hashing function, a procedure based on the preceding algorithm, and a mainline program. The hashing function finds the remainder on dividing the bit representation of *name* by *n*. The *mod* function is used to find the remainder when *number* is divided by *n*.

The hashing function used in the procedure *hash* takes the first and last characters in the name to be hashed and converts them to an integer *value* by taking the ASCII value of the last character and adding it to the ASCII value of the first character * 256. (For a name containing a single character. the last character is a duplicate of the first.) This integer is then multiplied by the length of the name. Examples of this process are given in Table 4-3.1.

The main program is written such that up to *m* (a constant) equivalence classes can be handled in the symbol table. Each name to be inserted is on one input line. On an end-of-file, each simple linked linear list representing an equivalence class is scanned, and each name in it is printed.

Table 4-3.1

| Name | Part | Value | Hash Number |
|------|------|-------|-------------|
| B    | BB   | 16962 * 1 = 16962 | mod 11 + 1 = 1 |
| AN   | AN   | 16718 * 2 = 33436 | mod 11 + 1 = 3 |
| LINK | LK   | 19531 * 4 = 78124 | mod 11 + 1 = 3 |

```
program hashing(input, output);
{ this program builds a dictionary of names consisting of
  1 to n alphanumeric characters. each name is hashed into
  an integer which is between 1 and m inclusive and
  denotes to which of m possible equivalence classes name
  belongs. procedure enter puts name in the symbol field
  of a node which is placed at the end of the list pointed
  to by an element of the pointer array equiv. }

const m = 11;  { size of hash table }
      n = 12;  { maximum length of name }

type vector = packed array [1..n] of char;
     pointer = ↑ recordstructure;
     recordstructure =
         record
             symbol: vector;
             link: pointer
         end;

var equiv: array [1..m] of pointer;
        { pointer vector representing hash table }
    ptr: pointer;  { used to print lists }
    name: vector;
    i: integer;   { counted loop variable }

function hash(name: vector; namesize,
             tablesize: integer): integer;
{ this function maps name to a number
  between 1 and tablesize }

var length,      { length of symbol }
    value: integer;  { preconditioned value }

begin

    { compute the length of the symbol }
    length := namesize;
    while (name[length] = ' ') and (length > 0) do
        length := length - 1;

    { compute the preconditioned result }
    value := (ord(name[1]) * 256 +
             ord(name[length])) * length;

    { return the hashed value }
    hash := value mod tablesize + 1
end; { hash }
```

FIGURE 4-3.2  Program for symbol-table algorithm.

```
procedure enter(name: vector);
{ each element of the array equiv is a pointer to a list of
  names which have been mapped into the equivalence class
  referenced by the subscript of the element. this procedure
  puts name in a node at the end of the list which belongs
  to the equivalence class denoted by the integer random }


var random: integer;    { hashed value of key }
    temp, p: pointer;   { temporary pointer variables }
    stop: boolean;      { logical flag }


begin


  { compute the hash number }
  random := hash(name, n, m);
  writeln(name, ' hashed into ', random: 2);


  if equiv[random] = nil
  then { equivalence class empty }
      begin
          new(temp);
          temp↑.symbol := name;
          temp↑.link := nil;
          equiv[random] := temp
      end
  else { search for end of list }
      begin
          stop := false;
          p := equiv[random];
          while (p↑.link <> nil) and not stop do
              if name = p↑.symbol
              then { x is already present }
                  stop := true
              else p := p↑.link;
          if name = p↑.symbol
          then { check last in chain }
              stop := true;
          if not stop
          then { name is not in the list }
              begin
                  new(temp);
                  temp↑.symbol := name;
                  temp↑.link := nil;
                  p↑.link := temp
              end
      end
end; { enter }
```

**FIGURE 4-12**   (Continued)

```
begin { main program }

    { initialize hash table }
    for i := 1 to m do
        equiv[i] := nil;

    { input variables to enter into table }
    writeln('records hashed into table');
    writeln;
    readarray(name);
    while not eof do
        begin
            enter(name);
            readarray(name)
        end;

    { print out contents of each equivalence class }
    writeln;
    writeln('linked lists formed by procedure enter');
    writeln;
    for i := 1 to m do
        begin
            ptr := equiv[i];
            write('equivalence class number ', i: 2);
            while ptr <> nil do
                begin
                    write(' ': 2, ptr↑.symbol);
                    ptr := ptr↑.link
                end;
            writeln
        end
end.   { hashing }
```

**FIGURE 4-3.2**    (Continued)


**Exercises for Sec. 4-3.2**

1.  The midsquare hashing method follows:
    (a) Square part of the key, or the whole key if possible.
    (b) Either (i) extract n digits from the middle of the result to give
        $h(key) \in \{0, 1, ..., 10^n - 1\}$, or (ii) extract n bits from the middle of the
        result to give $h(key) \in \{0, 1, ..., 2^n - 1\}$.
    Write a program which uses this procedure to hash a set of variable names. The
    midsquare method frequently gives satisfactory results, but in many cases the
    keys are unevenly distributed over the required range.
2.  A hashing method often implemented, called *folding*, is performed by dividing
    the key into several parts and adding the parts to form a number in the required
    range. For example, if we have eight-digit keys and wish to obtain a three-digit
    address, we may do the following:

    $$h(97434658) = 974 + 346 + 58 = 378$$
    $$h(31269857) = 312 + 698 + 57 = 67$$

records hashed into table

| frog | hashed into | 9 |
| lion | hashed into | 10 |
| pelican | hashed into | 10 |
| whale | hashed into | 3 |
| lynx | hashed into | 6 |
| snake | hashed into | 9 |
| bluejay | hashed into | 2 |
| beetle | hashed into | 6 |
| salmon | hashed into | 3 |
| duck | hashed into | 1 |
| monkey | hashed into | 5 |
| wolf | hashed into | 11 |

linked lists formed by procedure enter

| equivalence class number | 1 | duck | |
| equivalence class number | 2 | bluejay | |
| equivalence class number | 3 | whale | salmon |
| equivalence class number | 4 | | |
| equivalence class number | 5 | monkey | |
| equivalence class number | 6 | lynx | beetle |
| equivalence class number | 7 | | |
| equivalence class number | 8 | | |
| equivalence class number | 9 | frog | snake |
| equivalence class number | 10 | lion | pelican |
| equivalence class number | 11 | wolf | |

**FIGURE 4-3.2**   (Continued)

---

(Note that the final carry is ignored.)  Implement this method in a computer program.

3.   Compare the results of applying the division, midsquare, and folding hashing functions to a fixed set of keys. Make sure the range is the same or almost the same in each case.  Which method distributes the keys most evenly over the elements of the range?

### 4-3.3 Multiple-Precision Arithmetic

There are a number of applications in which a particular accuracy in the results must be obtained. This accuracy, however, depends on the data that are manipulated. For example, a certain accuracy may be required in the solution of a set of simultaneous equations.  The program to solve this problem can be run on a computer using single- or double-precision numbers, but this technique may not be accurate enough.  In many cases, the desired accuracy can be obtained only through the use of routines which perform multiple-precision operations. The number of digits used in such routines can depend on the number of equations being solved and the ill-conditioned matrix of the floating-point coefficients. The same problem presents itself in obtaining the inverse of an ill-conditioned matrix

In this section we wish to formulate algorithms for performing multiple-precision arithmetic on the integers. Although this construction is done only for the operations of addition and subtraction, these techniques can easily be extended to the operations of multiplication and division.

Let us consider the problem of performing multiple-precision integer arithmetic. Most digital computers have a certain maximum number of bits or digits for the representation of an integer. The number of bits varies from a minimum of 8 to a maximum of 64, the upper bound representing an integer of approximately 20 decimal digits. In certain applications, the size of the integers used may be considerably greater than this upper bound. If we want to manipulate these integers, we must find a new way to express them.

Let $m - 1$ be the largest integer that can be stored in a particular computer. Then it is possible to express any integer, say A, using a polynomial expansion of the form

$$A = \sum_{i=0}^{k} a_i m^i \quad \text{where } 0 \leqslant |a_i| < m \text{ for every } i$$

For example, assume that the largest integer that can be stored in a particular computer is 999. An integer A having a value of 12,345,678 can be represented, in the above form, as follows:

$$\begin{aligned} A &= 678 * 1{,}000^0 + 345 * 1{,}000^1 + 12 * 1{,}000^2 \\ &= 678 + 345{,}000 + 12{,}000{,}000 \\ &= 12{,}345{,}678 \end{aligned}$$

In this example, $k = 2$, $a_0 = 678$, $a_1 = 345$, and $a_2 = 12$. If A is a negative integer, then each nonzero $a_i$ will be negative. For example, if A is $-2,000,342$, then it can be represented as

$$A = (-342 * 1{,}000^0) + (0 * 1{,}000^1) + (-2 * 1{,}000^2)$$

Arbitrarily large integers are of little use unless we are able to perform operations on them. In this section we consider the operation of addition, and we present an algorithm for the addition of signed multiple-precision integers. For the algorithm, we require that the above polynomials be represented as linear linked lists. Before describing the lists used, we consider the different cases that occur in adding two polynomials representing integers.

Given integers

$$A = \sum_{i=0}^{k} a_i m^i \quad \text{and} \quad B = \sum_{i=0}^{k} b_i m^i$$

it is required to obtain a polynomial representing the sum

$$S = \sum_{i=0}^{k+1} s_i m^i = A + B$$

Note that k is the exponent of the highest-degree term in either polynomial A or B that is nonzero; that is, $a_k \neq 0$ or $b_k \neq 0$. The maximum degree possible for polynomial S is $k + 1$. Some of the coefficients $s_i$ of S may be zero. As an extreme example, if A is equal to $-B$, then all coefficients of the polynomial are zero.

We now list the five distinct cases which may arise in adding these multiple-precision integers. In all examples given, m is chosen to be 1,000 for the purpose of illustration.

*Case 1:* $A = 0$ or $B = 0$. If one of $A$ or $B$ is zero, then $S$ is set equal to the number which is nonzero. If $A = B = 0$. then $S = 0$.

*Case 2:* $A > 0$ and $B > 0$. In this case, we have

$$s_i = (a_i + b_i + c_{i-1}) \bmod n \quad \text{for } 0 \leqslant i \leqslant k$$

and

$$s_{k+1} = c_k$$

Here, $c_i$ is a "carry value" propagated at the $i$th stage; $c_{-1}$ is equal to zero in this and all cases in which it is used. If $a_i + b_i + c_{i-1} \geqslant m$, then $c_i$ is assigned a value of 1; otherwise, $c_i$ is assigned a value of 0. We may formulate this statement as

$$c_i = \lfloor (a_i + b_i + c_{i-1}) / m \rfloor \quad \text{for } 0 \leqslant i \leqslant k$$

since

$$0 \leqslant a_i + b_i + c_{i-1} \leqslant (m - 1) + (m - 1) + 1 = 2m - 1 < 2m$$

where the notation $\lfloor P \rfloor$ = largest integer $\leqslant P$.

As a first example, let $A = 12,345$ and $B = 6,890$. To get $S = A + B$, we write

$$A = a_0 m^0 + a_1 m^1 = 345 * 1,000^0 + 12 * 1,000^1$$
$$B = b_0 m^0 + b_1 m^1 = 890 * 1,000^0 + 6 * 1,000^1$$

The calculations proceed as follows:

$$c_{-1} = 0$$
$$s_0 = (a_0 + b_0 + c_{-1}) \bmod m$$
$$= (345 + 890) \bmod 1,000 = 235$$
$$c_0 = \lfloor (a_0 + b_0 + c_{-1}) / m \rfloor = \lfloor 1,235 / 1,000 \rfloor = 1$$
$$s_1 = (a_1 + b_1 + c_0) \bmod m$$
$$= (12 + 6 + 1) \bmod 1,000 = 19$$
$$s_2 = c_1 = \lfloor (a_1 + b_1 + c_0) / m \rfloor = \lfloor 19 / 1,000 \rfloor = 0$$

Thus,

$$S = \sum_{i=0}^{1} s_i m^i = 235 * 1,000^0 + 19 * 1,000^1 = 19,235$$

As a second example, let $A = 650,125$ and $B = 425,975$. The calculations are

$$c_{-1} = 0$$
$$s_0 = (125 + 975 + 0) \bmod 1,000 = 100$$
$$c_0 = \lfloor 1,100 / 1,000 \rfloor = 1$$
$$s_1 = (650 + 425 + 1) \bmod 1,000 = 76$$
$$c_1 = \lfloor 1,076 / 1,000 \rfloor = 1$$
$$s_2 = c_1 = 1$$

and

$$S = 100 * 1,000^0 + 76 * 1,000^1 + 1 * 1,000^2 = 1,076,100$$

*Case 3:* $A < 0$ and $B < 0$. We calculate

$$s_i = -(|a_i + b_i + c_{i-1}| \bmod m) \quad \text{for } 0 \leqslant i \leqslant k \text{ and } s_{k+1} = c_k$$

In this case, $c_i$ must be a carry of $0$ or $-1$, so

$$c_{-1} = 0 \quad c_i = -\lfloor |a_i + b_i + c_{i-1}| \, / \, m\rfloor \quad \text{for } 0 \leqslant i \leqslant k$$

Consider the example which has $A = -96$ and $B = -99,934$. We find S as follows:

$$
\begin{aligned}
c_{-1} &= 0 \\
s_0 &= -(|-96 - 934 + 0| \bmod 1{,}000) = -30 \\
c_0 &= -\lfloor |-96 - 934 + 0| \, / \, 1{,}000 \rfloor = -1 \\
s_1 &= -(|0 - 99 - 1| \bmod 1{,}000) = -100 \\
s_2 &= c_1 = -\lfloor |0 - 99 - 1| \, / \, 1{,}000 \rfloor = 0
\end{aligned}
$$

We have

$$S = -100,030$$

*Case 4:*  $A < 0$, $B > 0$, $B \geqslant |A|$; or $B < 0$, $A > 0$, and $A \geqslant |B|$.  In this case, we add integers of opposite sign to obtain a nonnegative result.  The calculations are the same as in *case 2*, that is,

$$
\begin{aligned}
s_i &= (a_i + b_i + c_{i-1}) \bmod m \quad \text{for } 0 \leqslant i \leqslant k \\
s_{k+1} &= c_k \\
c_{-1} &= 0 \quad c_i = \lfloor (a_i + b_i + c_{i-1}) \, / \, m \rfloor \quad \text{for } 0 \leqslant i \leqslant k
\end{aligned}
$$

In this case, $c_i$ is not a "carry" but is a "borrow" since we are actually subtracting a positive number from a greater or equal positive number.  Since either $a_i$ or $b_i$ is negative, $c_i$ will have a value $0$ or $-1$.

As an example, consider $A = -10,700$ and $B = 12,300$.  Then

$$
\begin{aligned}
c_{-1} &= 0 \\
s_0 &= (-700 + 300 + 0) \bmod 1{,}000 \\
&= -400 \bmod 1{,}000 = 600 \\
c_0 &= \lfloor -400 \, / \, 1{,}000 \rfloor = -1 \\
s_1 &= (-10 + 12 - 1) \bmod 1{,}000 = 1 \\
s_2 &= c_1 = \lfloor 1 \, / \, 1{,}000 \rfloor = 0
\end{aligned}
$$

Thus $S = 1,600$.  The final borrow is always zero when the positive number is greater than or equal to the absolute value of the negative number.

*Case 5:*  $A < 0$, $B > 0$, and $B < |A|$; or $B < 0$, $A > 0$, and $A < |B|$.  We initially proceed as in *case 4*.  Again, the $c_i$'s are borrows.  For example, given $A = -789,300$ and $B = 400,700$, we calculate

$$
\begin{aligned}
c_{-1} &= 0 \\
s_0 &= (-300 + 700 + 0) \bmod 1{,}000 = 400 \\
c_0 &= \lfloor 400 \, / \, 1{,}000 \rfloor = 0 \\
s_1 &= (-789 + 400 + 0) \bmod 1{,}000 \\
&= -389 \bmod 1{,}000 = 611 \\
c_1 &= \lfloor -389 \, / \, 1{,}000 \rfloor = -1
\end{aligned}
$$

At this point we have a borrow, but there is nothing that it can be borrowed from.  This serves as an indication that our procedure is incomplete.

Our result is in the form of

$$-1,000,000 + 611,400$$

One way to obtain the answer is to use the same procedure again to add 0 and $-611,400$. This procedure will result in

$$-1,000,000 + 388,600$$

and neglect the "borrow" of $-1$ and negate the number $388,600$ to get the right value of $-388,600$. Thus, $S = -388,600$.

This concludes the discussion of the different cases that arise in adding two integers. All cases except the first use the formulas (or variations of them) given in *case 2*. Care must be taken to ensure that the correct signs are used, and the significance of a final borrow of $-1$ should be noted. Before devising a formal algorithm, we must consider a representation of multiple-precision integers suitable for computer implementation.

Given the integer A, we can form a singly linked list representing its polynomial expansion. Each node in the list consists of a coefficient $a_i$ and a pointer to the next node in the list. This value field and pointer field are denoted as COEF and LINK, respectively.

A list representing the number $A = 12,345,678$ is given in Fig. 4-3.3. The number $-1,280,000,129$ can be represented by the list of Fig. 4-3.4. Note that for this integer, all the nonzero coefficients are negative. Such will always be the case for negative integers. Zero will be represented by a null list.

Several subalgorithms are required in the Function ADDITION. We will refer to the first as INSERT. It is similar to the algorithm of the same name in Sec. 4-2.1, but it allocates the node structure just described. INSERT places the node at the front of a list and fills in the COEF field. As an example of its use

$$R \leftarrow INSERT(N, R)$$

will cause a node to be allocated, place the value of N in the COEF field, set the LINK field to R's pointer value, and assign the address of the new node to R.

A second subalgorithm we require is SIGN. Given that R points to a list representing an integer,

$$N \leftarrow SIGN(R)$$

will assign $-1$ to N if the integer is negative; otherwise (if the integer is nonnegative), 1 is assigned to N.

Given two lists pointed to by P and Q that represent the integers A and B, respectively, it is required to construct a list pointed to by SUM and representing A +

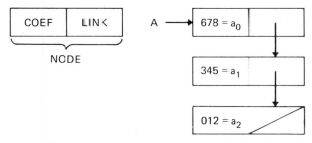

**FIGURE 4-3.3** List representation of a multiple-precision integer.

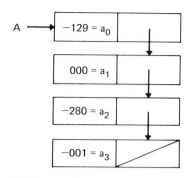

**FIGURE 4-3.4**

B. Function ADDITION will construct the reverse of list SUM and then employ Function REVERSE to reverse the order of the nodes. REVERSE also negates each coefficient value if· requested, as will be necessary for additions of the type given in *case 5*. (This will be made clear when Function ADDITION is presented.) A third function performed by it is to delete any nodes having a zero COEF value when they are representative of leftmost zeros in a number, such as 000,125,789. We will first formulate this function.

**Function** REVERSE(R, NEGATE). Given a pointer R to the first node in a list, it is required to reverse the order of the nodes in the list R. Each node has a COEF and a LINK field. The variable NEGATE has the value *true* when each field must be negated. Any nodes containing a zero coefficient field and situated at the beginning of the list will be deleted. OLD marks a node to be deleted. S and Q are auxiliary pointer variables.

1.  [Valid list?]
        If R = NULL
        then    Write('INVALID LIST')
                Return(NULL)
2.  [Delete leading zeros]
        Repeat while COEF(R) = 0
            OLD ← R
            R ← LINK(R)
            Restore(OLD)
            If R = NULL
            then    Return(NULL)
3.  [Initialize]
        S ← NULL
4.  [Continue to end of list]
        Repeat thru step 6 while R ≠ NULL
5.  [Negate coefficient?]
        If NEGATE
        then    COEF(R) ← –COEF(R)
6.  [Reverse next node]
        Q ← S

```
        S ← F
        R ← LINK(R)
        LINK(S) ← Q
```
7.    [Return pointer to front of linked list]
      Return(S)                                                                □

In step 1 a check is made for the validity of the list to be reversed. Step 2 deletes all the leading zeros of the polynomial expansion. Step 3 initializes S which is used to mark the node whose pointer is to be changed. Steps 4 through 6 perform the reversing of the list. Step 5 negates the coefficients of terms if the flag indicates this is to be done. In step 6, R is moved down the original list, S points to the node previously pointed to by R, and Q points to the predecessor of S. Setting LINK(S) ← Q has the effect of making S point to the node which will follow it in the reversed list. Function REVERSE is invoked as

      SUM ← REVERSE(SUM, *true*)

if the COEF fields must be negated. Otherwise

      SUM ← REVERSE(SUM, *false*)

is used. The variable NEGATE is assigned *true* or *false*.

Given the preceding functions, we can formulate a function for the addition of multiple-precision signed integers. A general algorithm which performs the desired addition is now presented.

1.  If either of the two lists to be added is null
    then return the address of the nonempty list
2.  Repeat thru step 5 until the end of one of the two lists is reached
3.  Perform the calculations for addition cases 2 thru 5
4.  Obtain the next terms in the lists
5.  Repeat thru step 9 for the first pass and second pass if necessary
6.  Repeat thru step 8 until the end of the shortest list is reached
7.  Perform the calculations for addition cases 2 thru 5
8.  Obtain the next term in the list
9.  If a case 5 addition exits
    then if this is the second pass through the loop
          then exit the loop
          else reverse the sum list
                initiate a second pass to add negative number to zero
    else exit the loop
10. Process the final carry if present
11. Reverse the resulting list and return

A detailed algorithm is now given.


**Function** ADDITION(P, Q). Given pointers P and Q to lists representing multiple-precision integers, it is required to construct a list pointed to by SUM which represents the sum of the integers. Variable MAX has a value such that $0 \le |COEF(R)| < MAX$ for all nodes R. Variable C represents a carry or borrow value, and SUMCF is used to contain the sum of corresponding COEF fields and C. NEG has value 1 when at least one integer is nonnegative, or −1 when both are negative. SECOND_PASS is a flag used in handling additions of the type in *case 5*.

1.  [Trivial case]
        If P = NULL
        then   Return(Q)
        If Q = NULL
        then   Return(P)
2.  [Initialize]
        If SIGN(P) = −1 and SIGN(Q) = −1
        then   NEG ← −1
        else   NEG ← 1
        SUM ← NULL
        C ← 0
        SECOND_PASS ← *false*
3.  [End of a list?]
        Repeat thru step 5 while P≠ NULL and Q ≠ NULL
4.  [Calculate value for, and insert, next node]
        SUMCF ← NEG  * (COEF(P) + COEF(Q) + C)
        C ← NEG * ⌊ SUMCF/MAX ⌋
        SUM ← INSERT(NEG * (SUMCF mod MAX), SUM)
5.  [Obtain addresses of next terms]
        P ← LINK(P)
        Q ← LINK(Q)
6.  [Scan remainder of list or perform second pass?]
        Repeat thru step 7 while *true*
            If P ≠ NULL
            then   Q ← P
            If Q ≠ NULL
            then   Repeat while Q ≠ NULL
                     SUMCF ← NEG * (COEF(Q) + C)
                     C ← NEG * ⌊ SUMCF/MAX ⌋
                     SUM ← INSERT(NEG * (SUMCF mod MAX), SUM)
                     Q ←LINK(Q)
7.  [Second pass required?]
        If C = −1 and NEG = 1
        then   If SECOND_PASS
            then   C← 0
                Exitloop
            else   SECOND_PASS ← *true*
                Q ← REVERSE(SUM, *true*)
                SUM ← NULL
                C ← 0
        else   Exitloop
8.  [Final carry?]
        If C ≠ 0
        then   SUM ← INSERT(C, SUM)
9.  [Reverse the resulting list]
        If SECOND_PASS
        then   Return(REVERSE(SUM, *true*))
        else   Return(REVERSE(SUM, *false*))      ☐

    On termination of this function, P and Q have the value NULL. It is assumed that their original values have been saved for future reference.

Step 1 handles the trivial case when one or both lists are null (one or both integers are zero). In certain cases, it may be desirable to copy the nonzero list and return its pointer instead of making the pointer SUM equivalent to P or Q. In the latter case, a change in the list SUM will result in a change of the list P or Q.

In step 2 the variables are initialized. If both integers to be added are negative, then NEG is set to −1; otherwise, it is set to 1. NEG is used to modify the calculations in steps 4 and 6, so that they include *case 3*, as well as the previously described cases.

In general, lists P and Q may not have the same length. Step 3 detects the end of either list and passes control to step 6 when this occurs. Step 4 performs the calculations for *cases 2 to 5* inclusive. Note how NEG is used, particularly when it has value −1. This step adds a node with the required value to the front of the list SUM. In step 5, the pointers P and Q are moved down the list, and control transfers to recheck their values in step 3.

In step 6, the remainder of the longer list is scanned. All calculations are the same as in step 4, except that COEF(P) has been eliminated. When list Q is finished, control transfers to step 7. This step detects an addition as described in *case 5*; the borrow is −1 when both lists have been scanned and NEG is 1. When these conditions are satisfied, the flag SECOND_PASS is set to *true*, the list SUM is reversed, and each COEF field is negated. Q points to the inverted list and SUM and C are reinitialized. Control transfers back to step 6 which essentially adds the negative integer, represented by list Q, to zero. The next time step 7 is executed, SECOND_PASS has the value *true*, and the borrow C is set from −1 to 0 and the loop is exited. Of course, if the conditions checked in step 7 are not met, no second pass is necessary and the loop is exited immediately.

In step 8, the final carry, if any, from the addition of integers possessing the same sign is put in the list SUM. Step 9 reverses this list, negating each COEF field if SECOND_PASS has the value *true* (otherwise, we would have the absolute value of the correct answer).

It is instructive to trace this function using several pairs of integers and a low value for MAX. The reader should carefully study the following examples:

Example 4-1  Let P and Q represent integers −99,012 and −915,995, respectively. A list representation of these numbers is given in Fig. 4-3.5. Figure 4-3.6 traces the execution of important steps in Function ADDITION. We have MAX equal to 1,000 and NEG equal to −1. The final list represents the integer −1,015,007. ////

Example 4-2  Let P and Q represent integers 75,198 and −1,079,239, respectively, with a list representation given in Fig. 4-3.7. Again, MAX is 1,000, but in this case NEG will be 1. A trace of the algorithm is given in Fig. 4-3.8. This final list represents the sum −1,004,041.    ////

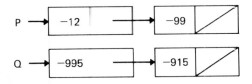

**FIGURE 4-3.5**

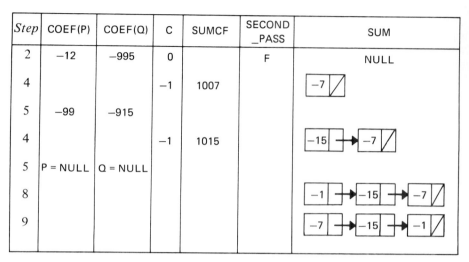

| Step | COEF(P) | COEF(Q) | C | SUMCF | SECOND _PASS | SUM |
|------|---------|---------|---|-------|--------------|-----|
| 2 | −12 | −995 | 0 | | F | NULL |
| 4 | | | −1 | 1007 | | $-7$ |
| 5 | −99 | −915 | | | | |
| 4 | | | −1 | 1015 | | $-15 \rightarrow -7$ |
| 5 | P = NULL | Q = NULL | | | | |
| 8 | | | | | | $-1 \rightarrow -15 \rightarrow -7$ |
| 9 | | | | | | $-7 \rightarrow -15 \rightarrow -1$ |

**FIGURE 4-3.6** Trace of Function ADDITION with operands −99,012 and −915,995.

### Exercises for Sec. 4-3.3

1. Give the list representations of 75,198 and −1,079,238 with MAX equal to 128.
2. Trace Function ADDITION as in Figs. 4-3.6 and 4-3.8 by using the lists constructed in Prob. 1. Convert the list SUM to its base 10 equivalent in order to check your result.
3. Devise an algorithm for multiplying two list-represented integers.
4. Devise an algorithm for dividing two list-represented integers.

## 4-4 ASSOCIATIVE LISTS

In this subsection the notion of an associative list (or structure) is introduced, and a comparison is made between such a data structure and the linear list which we have discussed in Chap. 3 and thus far in Chap. 4. Some examples are presented, and the storage representation of associated lists is examined.

An associative list can be thought of as a special form of linear list. It is special in the sense that a particular element of the list is generally not referred to as "the first element of the list" or "the last element of the list" (as in the case of a stack or queue) or "the *n*th element of the list" (as is commonly done for a general linear list). Instead, a particular element is referenced via an associated name.

As an example of an associative structure, consider the problem of analyzing text and counting the number of occurrences of each word in the text. If we use the

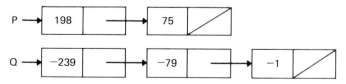

**FIGURE 4-3.7**

| Step | COEF(P) | COEF(Q) | C | SUMCF | SECOND_PASS | SUM |
|---|---|---|---|---|---|---|
| 2 | 198 | -239 | 0 | | F | NULL |
| 4 | | | -1 | -41 | | [959 /] |
| 5 | .75 | -79 | -1 | -5 | | [959]→[959 /] |
| 4 | | -1 | -1 | -2 | | [998]→[995]→[959 /] |
| 5 | P = NULL | Q = NULL | | | | |
| 6 | | | -1 | -959 | T | NULL |
| 7 | | -959 | 0 | | | [41 /] |
| 6 | | -995 | -1 | -996 | | [4]→[41 /] |
| 6 | | -998 | -1 | -999 | | [1]→[4]→[41 /] |
| 6 | | Q = NULL | -1 | | | [-41]→[-4]→[-1 /] |
| 7 | | | 0 | | | |
| 9 | | | | | | |

FIGURE 4-3.8  Trace of Function ADDITION with operands 75,198 and -1,079,239.

last sentence for our example text, the words and their associated counts can be tabulated as shown in Table 4-4.1.

An associative list can be viewed as a linear list in which each element or node of the list contains two or more information items. One of the items in a list node, usually the first item, is unique over all nodes of the associative list. We will refer to this special item as the *associative item*. The remaining item or items of a node will be called the *list item* or *list items*.

As an example, consider the list composed of the words of text and their associated word count as presented previously. In a parenthesis form of list notation, which will be used more extensively in Chap. 5, we can represent this list as ((as, 1)(an, 2)(example, 1) ... (word, 1)(in, 1)). The words, 'as', 'an', 'example', etc., are the set of associative items for this list.

Because of the manner in which elements of associative lists are generally accessed, we consider such a list as a special case of a linear list. In the example given previously, the word count is accessed via its associated word. It is this form of access that is primarily used in an associative list.

In the algorithmic notation, a particular element of an associative list, say the list WORDCNT, is accessed using the form WORDCNT<WORD>, where WORD is a variable containing an associative item (in this case a word). The braces <> are used to denote the associative item and differentiate clearly an associative-list form of element specification from an array element specification. Therefore, as an example taken from Table 4-4.1

$$X \leftarrow \text{WORDCNT} <\text{'AS'}>$$

assigns the list element 1 to X and

$$X \leftarrow \text{WORDCNT} <\text{'OF'}>$$

assigns the list element 4 to X.

As noted in Chap. 3, an important property of a list is its capacity to grow or to shrink by the removal or addition of elements to the list. In an associative list, this property is available as well. In our algorithmic notation, a new list element is created by an assignment statement. For example,

$$\text{WORD} <\text{'NEW'}> \leftarrow 3$$

**TABLE 4-4.1**

| Word | Count | Word | Count |
|---|---|---|---|
| as | 1 | analyzing | 1 |
| an | 2 | text | 2 |
| example | 1 | and | 1 |
| of | 4 | counting | 1 |
| associative | 1 | number | 1 |
| structure | 1 | occurrences | 1 |
| consider | 1 | each | 1 |
| the | 3 | word | 1 |
| problem | 1 | in | 1 |

establishes the new element with a value of 3 and associates the character string 'NEW' with it.

To alter an element also involves an assignment. Again, using the word count example

WORDCNT <'AN'> ← WORDCNT <'AN'> + 1

assigns a new value to the list item of an element of WORDCNT.

If we attempt to reference a list item or items by using a name which is not associated with any element in the list, then either a zero or the empty string is the value returned from the reference. This convention is consistent with the convention adopted in the programming language SNOBOL, which has an associative data structure. For example, if 'DATA' is a name which is not associated with an element of WORDCNT, then

X ← WORDCNT <'DATA'> + 1.

assigns the value 1 to X, while

X ← 'THE WORD COUNT OF NEW IS' ○ WORDCNT <'DATA'>.

assigns the string 'THE WORD COUNT OF NEW IS' to X.

The following procedure performs a word frequency analysis on a given piece of text. The words present in the text, plus the associated word counts, are printed at the end of the analysis.

**Procedure** WORD_ANALYSIS(TEXT). Given the input text TEXT, a word frequency analysis is made by placing in the associative structure, WORDCNT, the word counts of all words in the text. ALPHABET is the character string 'ABCDEFGHIJKLMNOPQRSTUVWXYZ'. CURSOR is an index to the current symbol being scanned. WORD contains the current word being processed.

1.  [Initialize]
    CURSOR ← 1
2.  [Continue to end of text]
    Repeat thru step 4 while CURSOR ≤ LENGTH(TEXT)
3.  [Find next alphabetic character]
    Repeat while INDEX(ALPHABET, SUB(TEXT, CURSOR, 1)) = 0
        CURSOR ← CURSOR + 1
4.  [Isolate word and increment its associated count]
    SPAN(TEXT, ALPHABET, CURSOR, WORD, '', *false*)
    WORDCNT<WORD> ← WORDCNT<WORD> + 1
5.  [Output results]
    Print words and associated word counts.
    Return                                                    □

After the cursor used for the scanning of TEXT is initialized to 1, the first alphabetic character (i.e., the first letter of a word) is located in step 3. In step 4, the alphabetic field which follows is pattern-matched using the SPAN function, as described in Sec. 2-2.3, and this character-string field is assigned to the variable WORD. The WORD element of the associative list WORDCNT is then updated by 1. Note that the first time a word appears, a value of zero is created for it in the associative list. The procedure terminates in step 5 when the value of CURSOR becomes greater than the length of the given text. Just prior to termination, the words and the associated word counts are printed. The manner in which both words and word counts are output depends on the programming system in use. Since SNOBOL has an associative type of data structure, let us examine how the output might be accomplished.

In SNOBOL the term that is used for describing an associative structure is a TABLE. To illustrate how TABLEs are created and used, let us consider the following SNOBOL program which handles the text-analysis problem as described previously in this subsection.

```
              LETTER = 'ABCDEFGHIJKLMNOPQRSTUVWXYZ'
              PAT = BREAK(LETTER) SPAN(LETTER)  WORD
              WORDCNT = TABLE(5, 4)
READIN        TEXT = TEXT INPUT                           :F(BEGINOUT)
NEXTWORD      TEXT PAT =                                  :F(READIN)
              WORDCNT <WORD> = WORDCNT <WORD> + 1   :(NEXTWORD)
BEGINOUT      OUTFORM = CONVERT(WORDCNT, 'ARRAY')
              I = 1
PRINT         OUTPUT = OUTFORM <I, 1> ' ' OUTFORM <I, 2>  :F(END)
              I = I + 1                                   :(PRINT)
END
```

In the SNOBOL program, WORDCNT is initialized as a TABLE by the assignment statement WORDCNT = TABLE(5, 4). (The significance of the parameters 5 and 4 will be described shortly.) The text is input to the variable TEXT. The pattern PAT is then applied to TEXT. PAT locates the first letter and then spans the substring of alphabetic characters which follows. This substring is assigned to the variable WORD. The TABLE element associated with the word is then updated.

The text analysis continues until all the text is processed. The CONVERT instruction in SNOBOL automatically converts a table to a two-dimensional array. (We shall see in the discussion dealing with the storage structure of associative lists that this type of conversion is relatively easy to accomplish.) The converted table is the output, and the SNOBOL program ends.

A discussion of the storage representation of associative lists is now presented. Two representations are considered; the first is a method for representing tables in SNOBOL (the method is similar to that given by Griswold[1972]), and the second involves the application of a hashing function in a manner similar to that described for the linked dictionary in Sec. 4-3.2. Both methods involve a linked form of storage representation.

In SNOBOL, tables can be implemented as blocks of storage cell pairs. Each storage cell pair holds a descriptor or value of the associative item and the table (or list) item of the list. As elements are inserted into the table, a block of storage cells may become full. When a block becomes full, a new block is allocated and is linked on to the end of the previous most recently allocated block. As an example, consider the representation of the first nine elements in the list of word frequencies as derived from the example given earlier in this subsection. Assume the initial block is of size (2 * M) + 1 or 11 for M equal to 5, and any extended block is of size (2 * N) + 1 or 9 for N equal to 4. In the SNOBOL program presented earlier, we declared the initial size of the table plus the size of extent using the statement

    WORDCNT = TABLE(5, 4).

Figure 4-4.1 shows the storage representation for parts of the word count list. In Fig. 4-4.1, the first cell in each block contains the block size less 1 and a pointer to the next block if a next block has been allocated. The first field of all other storage cells represents the type of the item associated with that cell (for example, "S" means string and "I" means integer). The second field contains a string descriptor or a numeric value, depending on the type of the item.

The locating of a list item involves a linear search of the associative items which are located in the first cells of the cell pairs. If the search name does not match an associative item in the first block, a search is made of subsequent blocks via the link field in the first cell of a block.

A second method of representing an associative list is to apply a hashing function to the associative items of the list elements. In Sec. 4-3.2, we illustrated how hashing functions can be used to build a linked dictionary. Let us use the hashing function discussed in that section and show how an associative list can be represented. The hashing function involves the product of the length of a name and a number derived from the internal representations of the first and last characters of a name. This product is divided by the table size, which was chosen to be 10. The remainder from this division is used as the hash value. The hashing process was illustrated in Table 4-3.1. Figure 4-4.2 depicts how our example associative list of word counts can be stored using the hashing function just described and assuming a primary table size of 10. Again, the storage of only the first nine elements of the list is shown.

After a word is scanned and isolated, it is hashed into the primary table as shown in Fig. 4-4.2. If the hash table entry corresponding to the hash value is empty, then the word is placed at that location and the list item entry is initialized to zero. If the hash value location is occupied, a check is made to determine if the associative item stored at this location is the same as the isolated word. If it is, the value of the list item associated with the word is returned. If the associative item is not the word, then a check of the pointer field is made to determine if it is null or a pointer to the overflow table. If the pointer field is null, then the word is placed in

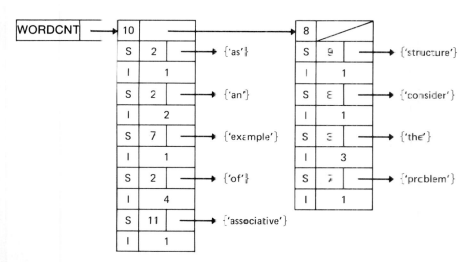

**FIGURE 4-4.1** Block representation of an associative list.

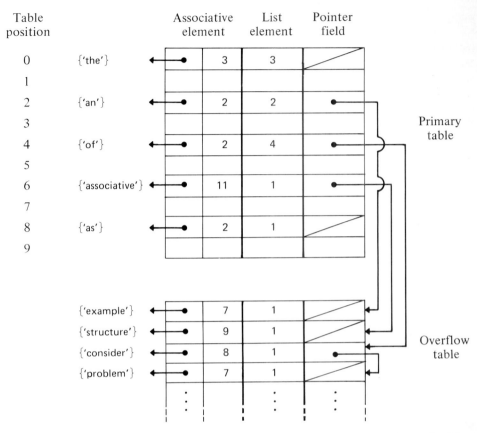

**FIGURE 4-4.2** Storage representation of an associative structure using a hashing function.

the associative item field of the first open location in the overflow table and the pointer field at the primary table location is updated. If the pointer field contains an address in the overflow table, then the associative item in the overflow table location is examined in a manner identical to that in which the primary table location was examined. The linked list of colliding associative items is followed until either the word is found as an associative item or the word is inserted at the end of the linked list of colliding elements. In the example illustrated in Fig. 4-4.2, 'the' has a hash value of 0; 'an' and 'example' have hash values of 2; 'of', 'consider', and 'problem' have a hash value of 4; 'associative' and 'structure' have hash values of 6; and 'as' has a hash value of 8.

In this subsection the associative list involving word counts of a piece of text has been used throughout as a motivating example. Associative structures are applicable to any problem which involves the association of a particular item (such as a word count) or items (such as in a student record) with a uniquely identifying associative item (such as a word or a student name). In Chap. 7 we discuss a particular file organization called *index sequential* which also utilizes the property of list associativity.

**Exercises for Sec. 4-4**

1. Design an algorithm (which should contain a number of subalgorithms) to handle the processing of class records using an associative list called STUDENT. The associative item is the student's name (initials plus surname). The ID number (ID), the college (COLLEGE), marks for up to ten assignments (MARK[I] for I = 1, 2, ..., 10), and the grade-to-date (GRADE) form the list items of a record. To refer to a particular list item, such as John Brown's mark on the sixth assignment, use the notation

   MARK[6] OF STUDENT <'J. BROWN'>

   The class records system should handle four input commands:
   (a) An insert command of the form

   INSERT <student's name> <ID number> <college>

   which inserts the ID number and college into the student's record.
   (b) A delete command of the form

   DELETE <student's name>

   which deletes a student record.
   (c) An update command of the form

   UPDATE <student's name> <assignment number> <mark>

   which updates the student's record with the given mark for the given assignment.
   (d) An output command of the form

   OUTPUT <student's name> or the form OUTPUT ALL

   which prints either a particular student's record or all students' records.
2. Program in Pascal the class record system as described in Prob. 1.

**BIBLIOGRAPHY**

BERZTISS, A. T.: Data Structures: Theory and Practice, Academic Press, Inc., New York, 1971.

D'IMPERIO, M. E.: Data Structures and Their Representation in Storage, *Annual Review in Automatic Programming*, vol 5, pp. 1-75, Pergamon Press, Oxford, 1969.

GRISWOLD, R. E.: The Macro Implementation of SNOBOL4: A Case Study of Machine-Independent Software Development, W H. Freeman and Company, San Fransisco, 1972.

HARRISON, M. C.: Data Structures and Programming, Scott Foresman and Company, Glenview, Ill., 1973.

KNUTH, D.E.: The Art of Computer Programming, vol. 1, Fundamental Algorithms, 2d ed., Addison-Wesley Publishing Co., Inc., Reading, Mass., 1973.

KNUTH, D.E.: The Art of Computer Programming, vol. 2, Seminumerical Algorithms, 2d ed., Addison-Wesley Publishing Co., Inc., Reading, Mass., 1973.

# 5

# NONLINEAR DATA STRUCTURES

Thus far we have been concerned with linear lists. The relationships that can be expressed by such data structures are essentially one dimensional. In this chapter we will introduce data structures which are nonlinear and are, therefore, capable of expressing more complex relationships than that of physical adjacency. The most important nonlinear data structure is probably a tree. Trees are used to represent the relationships among data elements in so many applications that a substantial portion of this chapter is concerned with their manipulations, representations, and associated applications.

The chapter begins with a detailed description of trees from basic concepts to their representations and manipulations. Section 5-2 contains a number of important applications to which trees have been frequently applied. Multilinked structures and their applications are dealt with in Sec 5-3. More general data structures (graphs) which can contain loops or closed paths are the topics of Sec. 5-4. This section is concerned with the manipulation and storage of graphs by bit matrices and list structures. Section 5-5 contains a number of applications to which graphs can be applied. These complex data structures require sophisticated storage-management techniques, and a number of such techniques are described in Sec. 5-6.

## 5-1 TREES

The section deals with a very important data structure, the *tree*. The first subsection introduces the basic notions of graph theory which are used throughout the chapter. The reader may want to only skim over the graph portion on first reading. When graphs are encountered in Sec. 5-4, the reader may want to reread the first part of this subsection. In particular, trees are discussed in detail. A number of associated operations on trees, such as their traversals and equivalence, are introduced in Sec. 5-1.2. In Sec. 5-1.3, the storage representations and manipulations of binary trees are discussed. Various storage representations for trees based on linked allocation are described. Iterative and recursive algorithms are given throughout the subsection. Section 5-1.4 describes and gives an algorithm for the conversion of general trees to binary trees. The last subsection introduces sequential and other representations of trees.

### 5-1.1 Definitions and Concepts

We first consider the definition of a general graph and its associated terminology. A tree can be viewed as a restricted graph. The restriction imposed on a graph to define a tree yields a general tree. For a number of reasons, however, it is convenient to define and manipulate binary trees instead of general trees. Each general tree can be represented by an equivalent binary tree.

   Consider the diagrams shown in Fig. 5-1.1. For our purpose here, these diagrams represent graphs. Notice that every diagram consists of a set of points which are shown by dots or circles and are sometimes labeled $v_1$, $v_2$, . . ., or 1, 2, . . .. Also in every diagram, certain pairs of such points are connected by lines or arcs. The other details, such as the geometry of the arcs, their lengths, the position of the points, etc., are of no importance at present. Notice that every arc starts at one point and ends at another point. A definition of the graph, which is essentially a mathematical system, will now be given. Such a mathematical system is an abstraction of the graphs given in Fig 5-1.1.

   A *graph* G consists of a nonempty set V called the set of *nodes* (*points*, *vertices*) of the graph, a set E which is the set of edges of the graph, and a mapping from the set of edges E to a set of pairs of elements of V.

   We shall assume throughout that both sets V and E of a graph are finite. It is also convenient to write a graph as $G = (V, E)$. Notice that the definition of a graph implies that to every edge of the graph G, we can associate a pair of nodes of the graph. If an edge $x \in E$ is thus associated with a pair of nodes (u, v) where u, $v \in V$, then we say that the edge x connects or joins the nodes u and v. Any two nodes which are connected by an edge in a graph are called *adjacent* nodes.

   In a graph $G = (V, E)$, an edge which is directed from one node to another is called a *directed edge*, while an edge which has no specific direction is called an *undirected edge*. A graph in which every edge is directed is called a *directed graph*, or a *digraph*. A graph in which every edge is undirected is called an *undirected graph*. If some of the edges are directed and some are undirected in a graph, then the graph is a *mixed graph*.

   In the diagrams, the directed edges are shown by means of arrows which also show the directions. The graphs given in Figs. 5-1.1b, e, and g are directed graphs. Those given in Figs. 5.1-1c and f are undirected, while the one given in in Fig 5-1.1d is mixed. The graph given in Fig. 5-1.1a could be considered either directed or undirected. In Fig. 5-1.1f, the nodes 1 and 2, 2 and 3, 3 and 1, 2 and 4, and 3 and 4 are adjacent.

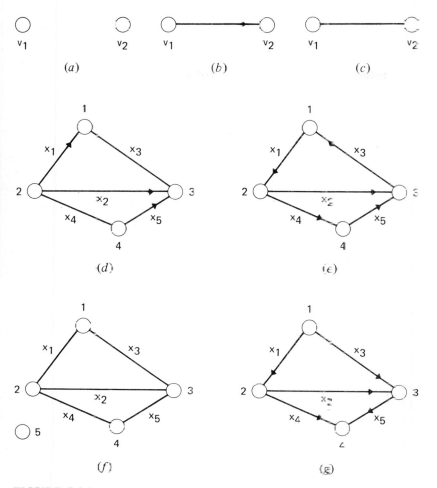

**FIGURE 5-1.1**

A city map showing only the one-way streets is an example of a directed graph in which the nodes are the intersections and the edges are the streets. A map showing only the two-way streets is an example of an undirected graph, while a map showing all the one-way and two-way streets is an example of a mixed graph.

Let $(V, E)$ be a graph and let $x \in E$ be a directed edge associated with the ordered pair of nodes $(u, v)$. Then the edge $x$ is said to be *initiating* or *originating* in the node $u$ and *terminating* or *ending* in the node $v$. The nodes $u$ and $v$ are also called the *initial* and *terminal* nodes of the edge $x$. An edge $x \in E$ which joins the nodes $u$ and $v$, whether it be directed or undirected, is said to be *incident to* the nodes $u$ and $v$.

An edge of a graph which joins a node to itself is called a *loop (sling)* (not to be confused with a loop in a program). The direction of a loop is of no significance; hence, it can be considered either a directed or an undirected edge.

The graphs given in Fig. 5-1.1 have no more than one edge between any pair of nodes. In the case of directed edges, the two possible edges between a pair of nodes which are opposite in direction are considered distinct. In some directed as well as undirected graphs, we may have certain pairs of nodes joined by more than

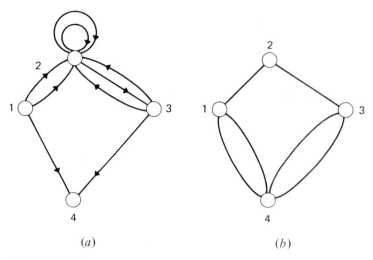

(a)                                          (b)

**FIGURE 5-1.2**

one edge, as shown in Figs. 5-1.2a and b. Such edges are called *parallel*. In Fig. 5-1.2a, there are two parallel edges joining the nodes 1 and 2, three parallel edges joining the nodes 2 and 3, while there are two parallel loops at 2.

Any graph which contains some parallel edges is called a *multigraph*. On the other hand, if there is no more than one edge between a pair of nodes (no more than one directed edge in the case of a directed graph), then such a graph is called a *simple graph*. The graphs given in Fig. 5-1.1 are all simple graphs.

The graphs in Figs 5-1.2a and b may be represented by the diagrams given in Figs. 5-1.3a and b in which the number on any edge shows the multiplicity of the edge.

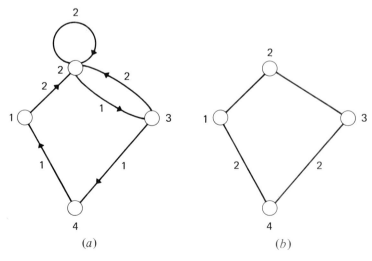

(a)                                          (b)

**FIGURE 5-1.3**

We may also consider the multiplicity as a weight assigned to an edge. This interpretation allows us to generalize the concept of weight to numbers which are not necessarily integers. A graph in which weights are assigned to every edge is called a *weighted graph*.

A graph representing a system of pipelines in which the weights assigned indicate the amount of some commodity transferred through the pipe is an example of a weighted graph. Similarly, a graph of city streets may be assigned weights according to the traffic density on each street.

In a graph, a node which is not adjacent to any other node is called an *isolated node*. A graph containing only isolated nodes is called a *null graph*. In other words, the set of edges in a null graph is empty. The graph in Fig. 5-1.1c is a null graph, while that in Fig. 5-1.1f has an isolated node. In practice, an isolated node in a graph has very little importance.

The definition of graph contains no reference to the length or the shape and positioning of the arc joining any pair of nodes, nor does it prescribe any ordering of positions of the nodes. Therefore, for a given graph, there is no unique diagram which represents the graph. We can obtain a variety of diagrams by locating the nodes in an arbitrary number of different positions and also by showing the edges by arcs or lines of different shapes. Because of this arbitrariness, it can happen that two diagrams which look entirely different from one another may represent the same graph, as in Figs. 5-1.4a and a'.

In a directed graph, for any node v the number of edges which have v as their initial node is called the *outdegree* of the node v. The number of edges which have v as their terminal node is called the *indegree* of v, and the sum of the outdegree and indegree of a node v is called its *total degree*. In the case of an undirected graph, the *total degree* or the *degree* of a node v is equal to the number of edges incident with v. The total degree of a loop is 2 and that of an isolated node is 0. We now introduce some additional terminology associated with a simple digraph.

Let G = (V, E) be a simple digraph. Consider a sequence of edges of G such that the terminal node of any edge in the sequence is the initial node of the next edge, if any, in the sequence. An example of such a sequence is

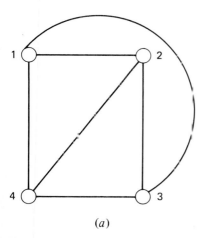

(a)

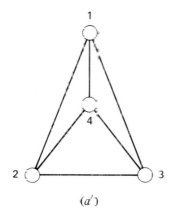

(a')

**FIGURE 5-1.4**

$$((v_{i_1}, v_{i_2}), (v_{i_2}, v_{i_3}), \ldots, (v_{i_{k-2}}, v_{i_{k-1}}), (v_{i_{k-1}}, v_{i_k}))$$

where it is assumed that all nodes and edges appearing in the sequence are in V and E, respectively. It is customary to write such a sequence as

$$(v_{i_1}, v_{i_2}, \ldots, v_{i_{k-1}}, v_{i_k})$$

Note that not all edges and nodes appearing in a sequence need be distinct. Also, for a given graph, any arbitrary set of nodes written in any order does not give a sequence as required. In fact, each node appearing in the sequence must be adjacent to the nodes appearing just before and after it in the sequence, except in the first and last nodes.

Any sequence of edges of a digraph such that the terminal node of any edge in the sequence is the initial node of the edge, if any, appearing next in the sequence defines a *path* of the graph. A path is said to *traverse* through the nodes appearing in the sequence, *originating* in the initial node of the first edge and *ending* in the terminal node of the last edge in the sequence. The number of edges appearing in the sequence of a path is called the *length* of the path.

Consider the simple digraph given in Fig. 5-1.5. Some of the paths originating in node 2 and ending in node 4 are

$$P_1 = ((2, 4))$$

$$P_2 = ((2, 3), (3, 4))$$

$$P_3 = ((2, 1), (1, 4))$$

$$P_4 = ((2, 3), (3, 1), (1, 4))$$

$$P_5 = ((2, 3), (3, 2), (2, 4))$$

$$P_6 = ((2, 2), (2, 4))$$

A path in a digraph in which the edges are distinct is called a *simple path (edge simple)*. A path in which all the nodes through which it traverses are distinct is called an *elementary path (node simple)*.

Naturally, every elementary path of a digraph is also simple. The paths $P_1$, $P_2$, $P_3$, and $P_4$ of the digraph in Fig. 5-1.5 are elementary, while paths $P_5$ and $P_6$ are simple but not elementary. We shall show here that if there exists a path from a node, say u, to another node v, then there must be an elementary path from u to v.

A path which originates and ends in the same node is called a *cycle (circuit)*. A cycle is called *elementary* if it does not traverse through any node more than once.

Note that in cycle, the initial node appears twice if it is an elementary cycle. The following are some of the cycles in the graph of Fig. 5-1.5:

$$C_1 = ((2, 2))$$

$$C_2 = ((1, 2), (2, 1))$$

$$C_3 = ((2, 3), (3, 1), (1, 2))$$

$$C_4 = ((2, 1), (1, 4), (4, 3), (3, 2))$$

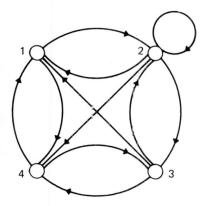

**FIGURE 5-1.5**

Observe that any path which is not elementary contains cycles traversing through those nodes which appear more than once in the path. By deleting such cycles, one can obtain elementary paths. For example, in the path $P_5$, if we delete the cycle $((2, 3), (3, 2))$, we obtain the path $P_1$, which also originates at 2 and ends in 4 and is an elementary path. Similarly, if in the path $P_6$, we delete the cycle $((2, 2))$, we get the elementary path $P_1$. Likewise, it is possible to obtain elementary cycles at any node from a cycle at that node. Because of this property, some authors use the term "path" to mean only the elementary paths, and they likewise apply the notion of the length of a path to only elementary paths.

A simple digraph which does not have any cycles is called *acyclic*. Naturally, such graphs cannot have any loops. We now consider a class of diagrams which are acyclic.

An important class of digraphs called directed trees and their associated terminology will be discussed in the remainder of this section. Trees are useful in describing any structure which involves hierarchy. Familiar examples of such structures are family trees, the decimal classification of books in a library, the hierarchy of positions in an organization, an algebraic expression involving operations for which certain rules of precedence are prescribed, the structure of this chapter to the subsection level as given in Fig. 5-1.6, etc. Applications of trees are given in Sec. 5-2.

A *directed tree* is an acyclic digraph which has one node called its *root*, with indegree 0, while all other nodes have indegree 1. Note that every directed tree must have at least one node. An isolated node is also a directed tree.

In a directed tree, any node which has outdegree 0 is called a *terminal node* or a *leaf*; all other nodes are called *branch nodes*. The *level* of any node is the length of its path from the root. The level of the root of a directed tree is 0, while the level of any node is equal to its distance from the root. Observe that all the paths in a directed tree are elementary and that the length of a path from any node to another node, if such a path exists, is the distance between the nodes, because a directed tree is acyclic.

Figure 5-1.7 shows three different diagrams of a directed tree. Several other diagrams of the same tree can be drawn by choosing relative positions of the nodes with respect to its root. The directed tree of our example has two nodes at level 1, five nodes at level 2, and three nodes at level 3. Figure 5-1.7a shows a natural representation, namely, the way the tree grows from its root up and ending in the leaves at different levels. Figure 5.1-7b shows the same tree drawn upside down. This is a convenient way of drawing a directed tree and is commonly used in the literature. Figure

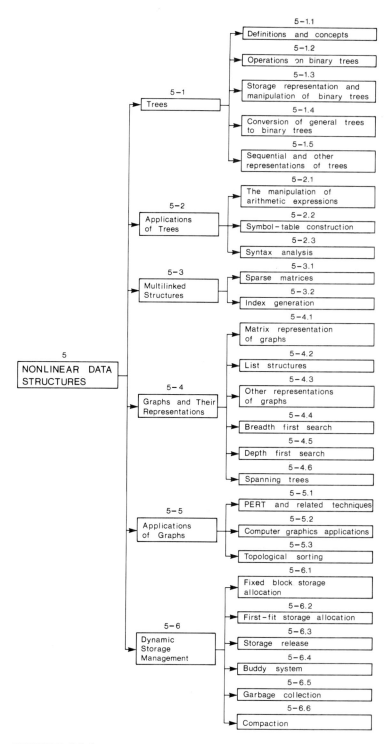

**FIGURE 5-1.6**

5.1-7c differs from Fig. 5-1-7b in the order in which the nodes appear at any level from left to right. According to our definition of a directed tree. such an order is of no significance. We shall, however, consider certain modifications so that an ordering of the nodes becomes relevant in a tree.

In many applications the relative order of the nodes at any particular level assumes some significance. In a computer representation such an order, even if arbitrary, is automatically implied. It is easy to impose an order on the nodes at a level by referring to a particular node as the first node, to another node as the second, and so on. In the diagrams the ordering may be done left to right. Instead of ordering the nodes, we may prescribe an order on the edges. If in a directed tree an ordering of the nodes at each level is prescribed, then such a tree is called an *ordered tree*. According to this definition, the diagrams given in Figs. 5-1.7b and c represent the same directed tree but different ordered trees. Note that the ordered trees as such are no longer directed graphs because the concept of order does not exist in a directed graph. We are mostly concerned with ordered trees in this section, and therefore, we use the term "tree" to mean ordered tree unless otherwise stated.

In both directed and ordered trees, it is important to decide whether the root is shown on top or at the bottom because the terminology used to describe the relative positions of the nodes as above or below may assume different meanings according to

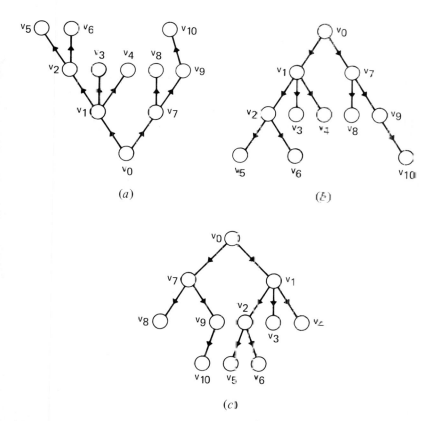

(a)

(b)

(c)

**FIGURE 5-1.7**

the choice made for locating the root. In our discussion we shall assume that the root is at the top and that all other nodes are below the root.

From the structure of the directed tree it is clear that every node of a tree is the root of some subtree contained in the original tree. In fact, if we delete the root and the edges connecting the root to the nodes at level 1, we get subtrees with roots which are the nodes at level 1. For the tree in Fig. 5-1.7, the node $v_7$ is the root of the subtree $\{v_7, v_8, v_9, v_{10}\}$, $v_1$ is the root of $\{v_1, v_2, v_3, v_4, v_5, v_6\}$, $v_2$ is the root of $\{v_2, v_5, v_6\}$, $v_5$ is the root of $\{v_5\}$, and $v_9$ is the root of $\{v_9, v_{10}\}$, etc. The number of subtrees of a node is called the *degree* of the node. Naturally, the degree of a terminal node is 0. The degree of $v_2$ is 2 because $v_5$ and $v_6$ are its subtrees, while the degree of $v_1$ is 3 because $\{v_2, v_5, v_6\}$, $\{v_3\}$, and $\{v_4\}$ are its subtrees.

If we delete the root and its edges connecting the nodes at level 1, we obtain a set of disjoint trees. A set of disjoint trees is a *forest*. We have also seen that any node of a directed tree is a root of some subtree. Therefore, subtrees immediately below a node form a forest.

At this stage we shall give another definition of directed trees that is recursive. According to this definition, a tree contains one or more nodes such that one of the nodes is called the root while all other nodes are partitioned into a finite number of trees called subtrees. This definition permits the formulation of algorithms associated with trees to be simpler. This will be shown in the following subsections.

Here, a tree with n nodes has been defined in terms of trees with fewer than n nodes. For the tree in Fig 5-1.7, the tree $\{v_0, ..., v_{10}\}$ is defined in terms of trees $\{v_1, ..., v_5, v_6\}$ and $\{v_7, ..., v_{10}\}$, while the tree $\{v_1, ..., v_5, v_6\}$ can be defined in terms of $\{v_2, v_5, v_6\}$, $\{v_3\}$, $\{v_4\}$, and so on. Finally, we get trees with one node each which are their terminal nodes.

There are several other ways in which a directed tree can be represented graphically. These methods of representation for the directed tree of Fig. 5-1.7 are given in Figs. 5-1.8a, b, c and d. The first method uses the familiar technique of Venn diagrams to show subtrees; the second uses the convention of nesting parentheses; and the third method is the one used in the table of contents for a book. The last method, which is based on a level-number format, is similar to those techniques used in PL/1 and COBOL. In this format, each node is assigned a number. The root of the tree has the smallest number. The number associated with a given node must be less than the numbers associated the root nodes of its subtrees. Note that all the root nodes of the subtrees of a given node must have the same number.

The method of representation given in Fig. 5-1.8b immediately shows how any completely parenthesized expression can be represented by a tree structure. Naturally, it is not necessary to have a completely parenthesized expression if we prescribe a set of precedence rules, as discussed in Sec. 3-5.2. As an example, consider the expression

$$v_1 * v_2 - (v_3 + v_4 \uparrow v_5)$$

The tree corresponding to this expression is shown in Fig. 5-1.9.

In the diagrams representing trees, we have chosen to show the roots on top and the edges pointing downwards. All the nodes at any particular level are shown on a horizontal line. In the case of an ordered tree, the nodes at any particular level are ordered from left to right. This ordering distinguishes an ordered tree from other directed trees. It is sometimes convenient to borrow terminology from a family tree. Accordingly, every node that is reachable from a node, say u, is called a *descendant* of u. Also, the nodes which are reachable from u through a single edge are called the *children* of u.

So far we have not placed any restriction on the outdegrees of any node in a

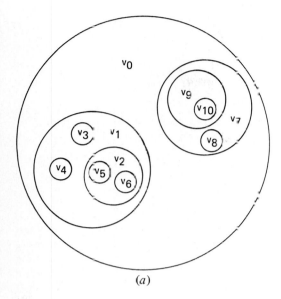

(a)

$$(v_0(v_1(v_2(v_5)(v_6))(v_3)(v_4))(v_7(v_8)(v_9(v_{10}))))$$

(b)

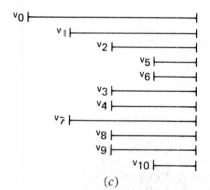

(c)

```
1  v0
  2  v1
    3  v2
      4  v5
      4  v6
    3  v3
    3  v4
  2  v7
    3  v8
    3  v9
      4  v10
```

(d)

**FIGURE 5-1.8**   Different representations of trees.

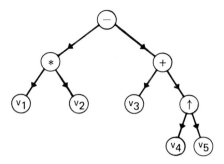

**FIGURE 5-1.9**

directed or an ordered tree. If in a directed tree the outdegree of every node is less than or equal to *m*, then the tree is called an *m-ary tree*. If the outdegree of every node is exactly equal to *m* or 0 and the number of nodes at level i is $m^{i-1}$ (assuming that the root node has a level number of 1), then the tree is called a *full* or *complete m-ary tree*. For *m* = 2, the trees are called *binary* and *complete binary trees*. We shall now consider *m*-ary trees in which the *m* (or fewer) children of any node are assumed to have *m* distinct positions. If such positions are taken into account, then the tree is called a *positional m-ary tree*.

Figure 5-1.10*a* shows a binary tree, Fig. 5-1.10*b* shows a complete binary tree, and Fig. 5-1.10*c* shows all four possible arrangements of children of a node in a binary tree. The binary trees shown in Figs. 5-1.10*a* and *d* are distinct positional trees, although they are not distinct ordered trees. In a positional binary tree, every node is uniquely represented by a string over the alphabet {0, 1}, the root being represented by an empty string. Any child of node u has a string which is prefixed by the string of u. The string of any terminal node is not prefixed to the string of any other node. The set of strings which correspond to terminal nodes forms a *prefix* code. Thus, the prefix code of the binary tree in Fig. 5-1.10*b* is {00, 01, 10, 11}. A similar representation of nodes of a positional *m*-ary tree by means of strings over an alphabet {0,1, ..., *m* – 1} is possible.

The string representation of the nodes of a positional binary tree immediately suggests a natural method of representing a binary tree in a computer. It is sufficient for our purpose at this stage simply to recognize that such a natural representation exists.

Binary trees are useful in several applications. We shall now show that every tree can be uniquely represented by a binary tree such that for the computer representation of a tree, it is possible to consider the representation of its corresponding binary tree. Furthermore, a forest can also be represented by a binary tree.

In Fig. 5-1.11 we show in two stages how one can obtain a binary tree which represents a given ordered tree. As a first step, we delete all the branches originating in every node except the left-most branch. Also, we draw edges from a node to the node on the immediate right, if any, which is situated at the same level. (This is done only for nodes which were formerly brothers — children of the same root node.) Once this is done, then for any particular node we choose its left and right children in the following manner. The left child is the node which is immediately below the given node, and the right child is the node to the immediate right of the given node on the same horizontal line. Such a binary tree will not have a right subtree.

The above method of representing any ordered tree by a unique binary tree can

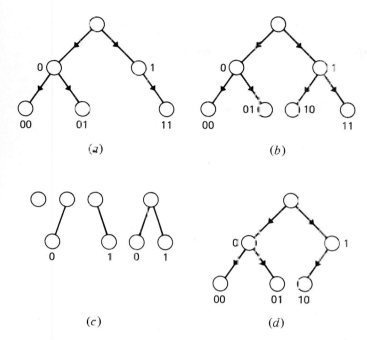

**FIGURE 5-1.10** Examples of binary trees and complete binary trees.

be extended to an ordered forest, as shown in Fig. 5-1.12. Both of these representations can be defined by algorithms. This correspondence is called the natural correspondence between ordered trees and positional binary trees. An algorithm which will convert a general tree into an equivalent binary tree will be given in Sec. 5-1.4.

**Exercises for Sec. 5-1.1**

1. Show that the sum of the indegrees of all the nodes of a simple digraph is equal to the sum of outdegrees of all its nodes and that this sum is equal to the number of edges of the graph.

2. Draw all possible digraphs having three nodes. Show that there is only one digraph with no edges, one with one edge, four with two edges, four with three edges, four with four edges, one with five edges, and one with six edges. Assume that there are no loops.

3. Give three different elementary paths from $v_1$ to $v_3$ for the digraph given in Fig. 5-1.13. What is the shortest distance between $v_1$ and $v_3$? Is there any cycle in the graph?

4. Find all the indegrees and outdegrees of the nodes of the graph given in Fig. 5-1.14. Give all the elementary cycles of this graph. Obtain an acyclic digraph by deleting one edge of the given digraph. List all the nodes which are reachable from another node of the digraph.

5. Show by means of an example that a simple digraph in which exactly one node has indegree 0 and every other node has indegree 1 is not necessarily a directed tree.

6. How many different directed trees are there with three nodes? How many different ordered trees are there with three nodes?

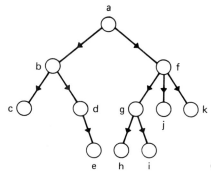

Given directed tree

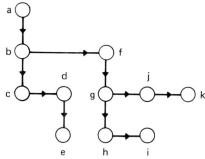

Stage 1

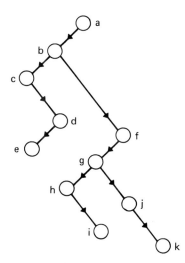

**FIGURE 5-1.11**   A binary representation of a tree.

7. Give a directed tree representation of the following formula: (a + b) * (c + d) ↑ e.

8. Show that in a complete binary tree, the total number of edges is given by $2(n_t - 1)$, where $n_t$ is the number of terminal nodes.

9. Obtain the binary tree corresponding to the directed tree and forest given in Figs. 5-1.15 and 5-1.16, respectively.

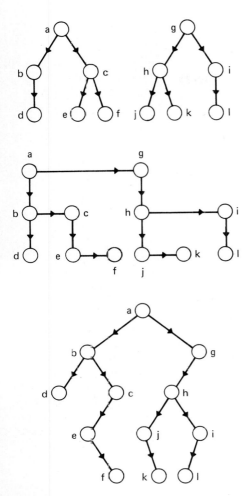

**FIGURE 5-1.12** Binary representation of a forest.

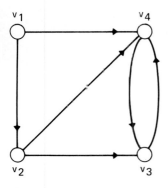

**FIGURE 5-1.13**

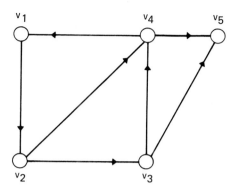

**FIGURE 5-1.14**

### 5-1.2 Operations on Binary Trees

The previous section introduced the notion of a binary tree structure. Little mention, however, was made of what types of operation are performed on such structures. In this section we introduce several of these operations, such as the traversal of trees, insertion, deletion, searching, and copying.

One of the most common operations performed on tree structures is that of traversal. This is a procedure by which each node in the tree is processed exactly once in a systematic manner. The meaning of "processed" depends on the nature of the application. For example, a tree could represent an arithmetic expression. In this context the processing of a node which represents an arithmetic operation would probably mean performing or executing that operation. There are three main ways of traversing a binary tree: in preorder, in inorder, and in postorder. We now examine each traversal order. The easiest way to define each order is by using recursion.

The *preorder traversal* of a binary tree is defined as follows:

1. Process the root node.
2. Traverse the left subtree in preorder.
3. Traverse the right subtree in preorder.

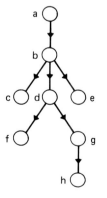

**FIGURE 5-1.15**

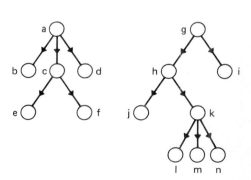

**FIGURE 5-1.16**

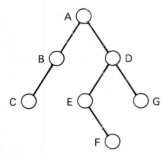

**FIGURE 5-1.17**

If a particular subtree is empty (i.e.. a node has no left or right descendant), the traversal is performed by doing nothing. In other words, a null subtree is considered to be fully traversed when it is encountered. The preorder traversal of the tree in Fig. 5-1.17 gives the following processing order:

    A B C D E F G

The *inorder traversal* of a binary tree is given by the following steps:

1. Traverse the left subtree in inorder.
2. Process the root node.
3. Traverse the right subtree in inorder.

The inorder traversal of the example tree given in Fig. 5-1.17 results in the following processing order:

    C B A E F D G

This traversal order gives the infix form of the expression.
Finally we define the *postorder traversal* of a binary tree as follows:

1. Traverse the left subtree in postorder.
2. Traverse the right subtree in postorder.
3. Process the root node.

The postorder traversal of the sample tree gives the following processing order:

    C B F E G D A

If the words "left" and "right" are interchanged in the preceding definitions, we obtain three new traversal orders, which are called the *converse preorder, converse inorder*, and *converse postorder*, respectively. The converse traversal orders for the example tree of Fig. 5-1.17 are

    A D G E F B C     (converse preorder)

    G D F E A B C     (converse inorder)

    G F E D C B A     (converse postorder)

We will not, however, pursue the applicability of these converse traversals in this book.

So far, we have conveniently assumed that a tree somehow already exists. Let us now examine the problem of constructing such a binary tree. The approach taken in constructing a tree is often application-dependent. For example, the binary tree representation of a mathematical expression, such as that given in Fig. 5-1.18a, depends on the right and left operands associated with each binary operator. In this particular example, an algorithm based on the Polish notation discussion of Sec. 3-5.2 could be formulated.

As another example, the creation of a binary tree could be based on the information associated with each node. This ordering could be numerical (either ascending or descending), or it could be a list of names to be kept in lexicographical order as shown in Fig. 5-1.18b. That is, the left subtree of the tree (or subtree) is to contain nodes whose associated names are lexically less than the name associated with the root node of the tree (or subtree). Similarly, the right subtree of the tree (or subtree) is to contain nodes whose associated names are lexically greater than the name associated with the root node of the tree (or subtree).

So far we have assumed that a binary tree exists. Such a tree, however, must be constructed. This construction can be realized by the repeated use of an insertion operation that adds a new node into an existing tree. For example, the insertion of

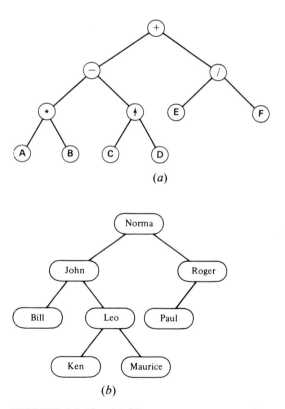

(a)

(b)

**FIGURE 5-1.18**   (a) Binary tree representation of an expression; (b) a lexically ordered binary tree; and (c) behavior of creating a lexically ordered tree.

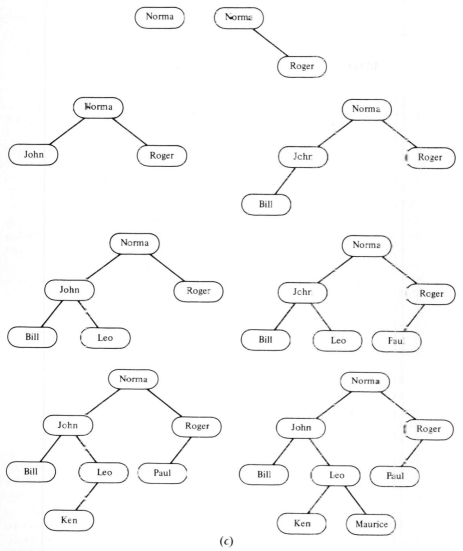

(c)

**FIGURE 5-1.13** (continued)

a node into a lexically ordered tree must maintain that ordering. Such an insertion can be performed at the leaf level. Two cases arise. First, as a special case, an insertion into an empty tree results in appending the new node as the root of the tree. The more general case involves inserting a new node into a nonempty tree. The new name is first compared with the name of the root node. If the new name lexically precedes the root name, then the new node is appended to the tree as a left leaf to the existing tree if the left subtree is empty; otherwise, the comparison process is repeated with the root node of the left subtree. If on the other hand, the new name lexically follows the root node name, then the new node is appended as a right leaf to the present tree if the right subtree is empty; otherwise the comparison process is repeated with the root node of the right subtree. This informal algorithm assumes that no attempt has been made to enter duplicate name entries. Assuming the insertion sequence of names

Norma, Roger, John, Bill, Leo, Paul, Ken, and Maurice

a trace of the construction of the tree given in Fig. 5-1.18*b* is exhibited in Fig. 5-1.18*c*. This topic is discussed in more detail in Sec. 5-2.2 where an algorithm for maintaining a tree-structured symbol-table is introduced.

Another common operation which is performed on a binary tree is the deletion of an arbitrary node. By an arbitrary node, we mean that any node in the tree can be deleted, even its root. The searching strategy to find the node to be deleted depends on the ordering of the binary tree, but once the appropriate node is found, a number of cases can arise. If the node to be deleted has no offspring, it can simply be deleted. If the node has either a right or left empty subtree, the nonempty subtree can be appended to its grandparent node. When the node to be deleted has both a right and left subtree, the deletion strategy may differ for unordered and ordered binary trees. For an unordered tree, one subtree can be attached to its grandparent node while the other can be attached to some node with an empty subtree. Another alternative is to use the ordered deletion strategy described below.

The situation becomes more difficult when a node with two subtrees is removed from an ordered tree, since the ordering of the binary tree must be kept intact. First we can obtain the inorder successor of the node to be deleted. Then the right subtree of this successor node is appended to its grandparent node, and the node to be deleted is replaced by its inorder successor. This is accomplished by appending the left and right subtrees (with the aforementioned successor node) of the node marked for deletion to the successor node. Also, the successor node is appended to the parent of the node just deleted.

Consider the lexically ordered binary tree given in Fig. 5-1.19, where John is marked for deletion. In this case the inorder successor of John is Ken. This latter node replaces the former in the revised tree. In the deletion process, the right subtree of Ken (that is, Kirk) becomes the left subtree of Ken's parent (Leo). Also, Ken becomes the new left offspring of John's parent (that is, Norma). An algorithm for deleting a node from a lexically ordered binary tree is given in the following section.

Probably the most frequently performed operation on a binary tree is that of searching. A search of a nonordered binary tree requires that the tree be traversed using one of the six traversals (inorder, postorder, preorder, and their converses) until the appropriate node is found. However, if the tree is lexically ordered, the number of comparisons needed to determine if an item exists in the tree and to pinpoint its location are reduced. The strategy behind such a search is to start at the root of the tree and branch either left or right repeatedly (depending if the item being searched for is lexically greater or smaller than the node being examined). The search continues until either the item is found or an empty subtree is encountered. If the search ends with an empty subtree, the item is not present in the tree. More details and algorithms for search trees are given in Sec. 6-2.3.

Another operation used with binary trees is the copy operation. This involves traversing a binary tree using one of the traversals while building a duplicate copy of the information found in each node. This operation produces two *equivalent* trees, i.e., both trees have the same structure or shape with corresponding nodes containing the same information.

This subsection has discussed certain operations which are common to binary

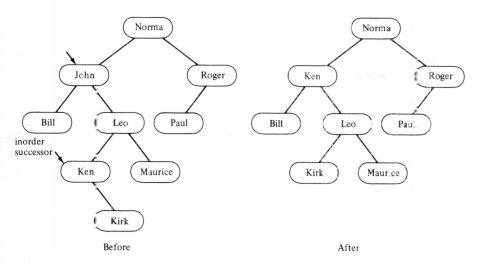

**FIGURE 5-1.19**   Deletion of a node from a lexically ordered binary tree.

trees. In the following subsection, the storage representation of binary trees will be introduced. Also, algorithms for the operations previously introduced will be discussed.

### 5-1.3  Storage Representation and Manipulation of Binary Trees

Throughout the previous chapters the computer representation of certain elementary data structures such as linear lists and arrays was discussed. In this subsection we extend these concepts to binary tree structures.

Linked and sequential allocation techniques will be used to represent these tree structures. The advantages and disadvantages of each allocation technique were discussed in Sec. 4-1. In this subsection we will give emphasis to linked storage structures. These linked structures are more popular than their corresponding sequential structures because, in performing insertions and deletions, the former structures are more easily altered than the latter. Furthermore, since the size of a tree structure is often unpredictable, linked allocation techniques are more appropriate.

The linked storage representation of binary trees is introduced first. Based on this representation, several algorithms, such as those for traversing and copying tree structures, are given. The concept of 'threaded" binary trees is then introduced. The storage representation of a tree based on the threading concept is efficient from both time and space considerations, and is the final topic discussed in this subsection.

### 5-1.3.1  Linked Storage Representation for Binary Trees

Since a binary tree consists of nodes which can have at most two offspring, an obvious linked representation of such a tree involves having storage nodes of the form shown in Fig. 5-1.20, where LPTR and RPTR denote the addresses or locations of the left and right subtrees, respectively, of a particular root node. Empty subtrees are represented by a pointer value of NULL. DATA specifies the information associated with a node.

Figure 5-1.21 contains an example of the linked storage representation for the binary tree given in Fig. 5-1.17. The pointer variable T denotes the address of the root node. The two forms are remarkably similar. This similarity illustrates that the linked storage representation of a binary tree very closely reflects the logical structuring of the data involved. This property is very useful and desirable in designing algorithms that process binary tree structures.

We can now fill in the details of the general algorithms given in the previous section for the preorder, inorder, and postorder traversals of a binary tree. These algorithms are written as procedures with one parameter. The only parameter required is a pointer variable which contains the address of the root of the tree. Although recursive algorithms would probably be the simplest to write for the traversals of binary trees, we will formulate algorithms which are both iterative and recursive.

Let us consider the traversal of binary trees by iteration. Since in traversing a tree it is required to descend and subsequently ascend parts of the tree, pointer information which will permit movement up the tree must be temporarily stored. Observe that the structural information that is already present in the tree permits the downward movement from the root of the tree. Because movement up the tree must be made in a reverse manner from that taken in descending a tree, a stack is required to save pointer variables as the tree is traversed. A general algorithm for a preorder traversal of a binary tree using iteration is now given.

1. If the tree is empty
   then write tree empty and return
   else place the pointer to the root of the tree on the stack
2. Repeat step 3 while the stack is not empty
3. Pop the top pointer off the stack
   Repeat while the pointer value is not null
      Write the data associated with the node
      If right subtree is not empty
      then stack the pointer to the right subtree
      Set pointer value to left subtree

We will now give a procedure for traversing a tree in preorder.

**Procedure** PREORDER(T). Given a binary tree whose root node address is given by a pointer variable T and whose structure is the same as previously described, this procedure traverses the tree in preorder, in an iterative manner. S and TOP denote an auxiliary stack and its associated top index, respectively. The pointer variable P denotes the current node in the tree.

| LPTR | DATA | RPTR |
|------|------|------|

**FIGURE 5-1.20**

1. [Initialize]
   > If T = NULL
   > then    Write('EMPTY TREE')
   >         Return
   > else    TOP ← 0
   >         Call PUSH(S, TOP, T)

2. [Process each stacked branch address]
   > Repeat step 3 while TOP > 0

3. [Get stored address and branch left]
   > P ← POP(S, TOP)
   > Repeat while P ≠ NULL
   >     Write(DATA(P))
   >     If RPTR(P) ≠ NULL
   >     then    Call PUSH(S, TOP, RPTR(P)) (store address of nonempty
   >                                             right subtree)
   >     P ← LPTR(P)    (branch left)

4. [Finished]
   > Return                                                              □

Step 1 checks for an empty tree and exits if T = NULL. Otherwise, it stacks the address of the root node. Step 2 controls the processing of the tree. The addresses of yet untraversed subtrees are kept on the stack. In the third step of the algorithm, we visit and process a node. The address of the right branch of such a node, if it exists, is stacked and a chain of left branches is followed until this chain ends. At this point, we reenter step 3 and delete from the stack the address of the root node of the most recently encountered right subtree and process it according to step 3. A trace of the algorithm for the binary tree given in Fig. 5-1.21 appears in Table 5-1.1, where the right-most element in the stack is considered to be its top element and the notation "NE," for example, denotes the address of node E. The visit of a node in this case merely involves the output of the label for that node.

An equivalent procedure for a recursive preorder traversal of a binary tree is easily formulated.

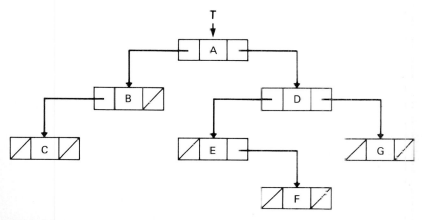

**FIGURE 5-1.21**    Linked representation of a binary tree.

**Table 5-1.1**  Trace of Procedure PREORDER for Fig. 5-1.21

| Stack Contents | P | Visit P | Output String |
|---|---|---|---|
| NA | | | |
| | NA | A | A |
| ND | NB | B | AB |
| ND | NC | C | ABC |
| ND | NULL | | |
| | ND | D | ABCD |
| NG | NE | E | ABCDE |
| NG  NF | NULL | | |
| NG | NF | F | ABCDEF |
| NG | NULL | | |
| | NG | G | ABCDEFG |
| | NULL | | |

**Procedure**  RPREORDER(T).  Given a binary tree whose root node address is given by a pointer variable T and whose node structure is the same as previously described, this algorithm traverses the tree in preorder in a recursive manner.

1.  [Process the root node]
      If T $\neq$ NULL
      then    Write(DATA(T))
      else    Write('EMPTY TREE')
             Return
2.  [Process the left subtree]
      If LPTR(T) $\neq$ NULL
      then    Call RPREORDER(LPTR(T))
3.  [Process the right subtree]
      If RPTR(T) $\neq$ NULL
      then    Call RPREORDER(RPTR(T))
4.  [Finished]
      Return    □

A Pascal procedure for Procedure RPREORDER is given in Fig. 5-1.22.  The node structure is assumed to be global to the procedure and is defined in the main program by the statement:

**type** pointer = ↑ node;
    node =
       **record**
          data: char;
          rptr, lptr: pointer
       **end**;

**procedure** rpreorder(t: pointer);

{ Recursive procedure for printing data content of each node in a }
{ binary tree which is traversed in preorder }

**begin**

    { check for empty tree }
    **if** t = nil
    **then writeln**('EMPTY TREE')
    **else begin**

        { Print the data content of the node }
        **writeln**(t↑.data);

        { Print the left branch of node t if one exists }
        **if** t↑.lptr <> nil
        **then** rpreorder(t↑.lptr);

        { Print the right branch of node t if one exists }
        **if** t↑.rptr <> nil
        **then** rpreorder(t↑.rptr)

    **end**
**end;** { rpreorder }

**FIGURE 5-1.22**  Recursive procedure for the preorder traversal of a binary tree.

---

The procedure in Fig. 5-1.22 has one parameter which receives the address of the root node of the tree. If this pointer variable *t* is nil, then the tree is empty. The remainder of the procedure follows the recursive Procedure RPREORDER given earlier.

A general algorithm for an iterative postorder traversal of a binary tree is now presented.

  1.  If the tree is empty
      then write empty tree and return
      else initialize the stack and initialize pointer value to root of tree
  2.  Start an infinite loop to repeat thru step 5
  3.  Repeat while pointer value is not null
        Stack current pointer value
        Set pointer value to left subtree
  4.  Repeat while top pointer on stack is negative
        Pop pointer off stack
        Write data associated with positive value of this pointer
        If stack is empty
        then return
  5.  Set pointer value to the right subtree of the value on top of the stack
      Stack the negative value of the pointer to the right subtree

The next algorithm iteratively traverses a binary tree in postorder.

**Procedure** POSTORDER(T). The same node structure described previously is assumed, and T is a variable which contains the address of the root of the tree. A stack S is also required again, but this time each node will be stacked twice, once when its left subtree is traversed and once when its right subtree is traversed. On completion of these two traversals, the particular node is processed. Consequently, we need two types of stack entries, the first indicating that a left subtree is being traversed, and the second that a right subtree is being traversed. For convenience we will use negative pointer values to indicate the second type of entry. This, of course, assumes that valid pointer data are always nonzero and positive.

1.  [Initialize]
        If T = NULL
        then    Write('EMPTY TREE')
                Return
        else    P ← T
                TOP ← 0
2.  [Traverse in postorder]
        Repeat thru step 5 while true
3.  [Descend left]
        Repeat while P ≠ NULL
            Call PUSH(S, TOP, P)
            P ← LPTR(P)
4.  [Process a node whose left and right subtrees have been traversed]
        Repeat while S[TOP] < 0
            P ← POP(S, TOP)
            Write(DATA(-P))
            If TOP = 0   (Have all nodes been processed?)
            then    Return
5.  [Branch right and then mark node from which we branched]
        P ← RPTR(S[TOP])
        S[TOP] ← -S[TOP]                                            □

The first step checks for an empty tree. In step 2 an infinite loop is initiated to ensure that the entire tree is processed. In the third step, a chain of left branches is followed and the address of each node encountered is stacked. Step 4 prints out the data associated with those nodes whose right and left subtrees have been traversed, indicated by a negative pointer value. In step 5, the right subtree of the node on top of the stack is placed in P to be traversed in the next iteration of the loop. The address of this node is negated, indicating that both left and right subtrees have been traversed and that its data may be printed.

The recursive algorithm for postorder traversal is now introduced.

**Procedure** RPOSTORDER(T). Given a binary tree whose root node address is given by a pointer variable T and whose node structure is the same as previously described, this procedure traverses the tree in postorder, in a recursive manner.

1.  [Check for empty tree]
        If T = NULL

```
            then   Write('EMPTY TREE')
                   Return
2.   [Process the left subtree]
            If LPTR(T) ≠ NULL
            then   Call RPOSTORDER(LPTR(T))
3.   [Process the right subtree]
            If RPTR(T) ≠ NULL
            then   Call RPOSTORDER(RPTR(T))
4.   [Process the root node]
            Write(DATA(T))
5.   [Finished]
            Return                                                  □
```

A Pascal procedure for Procedure RPOSTORDER is given in Fig 5-1.23. We now present a recursive algorithm for traversing a binary tree in inorder.

**Procedure RINORDER(T).** Given a binary tree whose root node address is given by a pointer variable T and whose node structure is the same as previously described, this algorithm traverses the tree in inorder, again in a recursive manner.

---

```
procedure rpostorder(t: pointer);

{ Recursive procedure for printing data content of each node in a }
{ binary tree which is traversed in postorder }

begin

    { check for empty tree }
    if t = nil
    then writeln('EMPTY TREE')
    else begin

        { Print the left branch of node t if one exists }
        if t↑.lptr <> nil
        then rpostorder(t↑.lptr);

        { Print the right branch of node t if one exists }
        if t↑.rptr <> nil
        then rpostorder(t↑.rptr);

        { Print the data content of the node }
        writeln(t↑.data)

    end
end;   { rpostorder }
```

**FIGURE 5-1.23** Recursive procedure for the postorder traversal of a binary tree.

---

1.  [Check for empty tree]
       If T = NULL
       then    Write('EMPTY TREE')
              Return
2.  [Process the left subtree]
       If LPTR(T) ≠ NULL
       then    Call RINORDER(LPTR(T))
3.  [Process the root node]
       Write(DATA(T))
4.  [Process the right subtree]
       If RPTR(T) ≠ NULL
       then    Call RINORDER(RPTR(T))
5.  [Finished]
       Return                                                        ☐

A similar iterative algorithm can be formulated for the inorder traversal of a tree, but this task is left as an exercise. If the terms LPTR and RPTR are interchanged in the previous algorithms, the algorithms for converse-preorder, converse-postorder, and converse-inorder traversals result.

Another familiar operation that is required in manipulating binary trees involves making a duplicate copy of a tree. Frequently, the original tree may be destroyed during processing. Therefore, a copy of the tree is produced before such processing begins. The following recursive subalgorithm generates a copy of a tree.

**Function** COPY(T). Given a binary tree whose root node address is given by the pointer value T and a node structure (NODE) as previously described, this subalgorithm generates a copy of the tree and returns the address of its root node. NEW is a temporary pointer variable.

1.  [Null pointer?]
       If T = NULL
       then    Return(NULL)
2.  [Create a new node]
       NEW ⇐ NODE
3.  [Copy information field]
       DATA(NEW) ← DATA(T)
4.  [Set the structural links]
       LPTR(NEW) ← COPY(LPTR(T))
       RPTR(NEW) ← COPY(RPTR(T))
5.  [Return address of new node]
       Return(NEW)                                                   ☐

Again, the subalgorithm is simple and requires no further comment. An iterative formulation of this operation is also possible. This version, however, is left as an exercise.

Recall from Sec. 4-2 the notion of a head node. A head node is a node with the same structure as the nodes making up the binary tree. The left pointer of the head node points to the root of the binary tree, while the right pointer points to the head node itself. Any other fields, such as DATA, are empty.

As was mentioned in the previous section, trees can be created through the repeated use of an insertion operation. A general algorithm for performing such an insertion into an existing lexically ordered binary tree is as follows:

1.  If the existing tree contains no nodes
    then append the new node as the root of the tree and Exit
2.  Compare the new name with the name of the root node
    If the new name is lexically less than the root node name
    then If the left subtree is not empty
          then repeat step 2 on the left subtree
          else append the new name as a left leaf to the present tree
             Exit
    else If the right subtree is not empty
          then repeat step 2 on the right subtree
          else append the new name as a right leaf to the present tree
             Exit

Note that the general algorithm assumes that no attempt is made to enter a duplicate entry. The detailed algorithm is left as an exercise.

Deletion is one of the most common binary tree operations  However, the deletion algorithm depends on the ordering of the tree. If the tree is not lexically ordered, then a traversal is done to find the location of the node and it is removed. If the tree is lexically ordered, recall from the previous section that essentially two different cases arise. The first case, which is the simplest, involves deleting a node which has at least one empty subtree. The second (and more difficult) case concerns deleting a node whose two subtrees are nonempty. As was mentioned in the previous section, we must find the inorder successor of the node to be deleted in order to perform the indicated deletion. A general algorithm for deleting an arbitrary node from a lexically ordered tree follows:

1.  Determine the parent node of the node marked for deletion, if it exists; note that it will not exist if we are deleting the root node
2.  If the node being deleted has either a left or right empty subtree
    **then append the nonempty subtree to its grandparent node**
        (that is, the node found in step 1) and Exit
3.  Obtain the inorder successor of the node to be deleted
    Append the right subtree of this successor node to its grandparent
    Replace the node to be deleted by its inorder successor
          This is accomplished by appending the left and right subtrees
          (with the aforementioned successor node) of the node marked for
          deletion to the successor node
          Also, the successor node is appended to the parent of the node
          just deleted (that is, the node obtained in step 1)

A procedure for the deletion of a node from a lexically ordered tree is now given.

**Procedure** TREE_DELETE(HEAD, X). Given a lexically ordered binary tree with the node structure previously described and the information value (X) of the node marked for deletion, this procedure deletes the node whose information field is equal to X. PARENT is a pointer variable which denotes the address of the parent of the node marked for deletion. CUR denotes the address of the node to be deleted. PRED and SUC are pointer variables used to find the inorder successor of CUR. Q contains the address of the node to which either the left or right link of the parent of X must be assigned in order to complete the deletion. Finally, D contains the direction from the parent node to the node marked for deletion. Also, the tree is assumed to have a list head whose address is given by HEAD. FOUND is a Boolean variable which indicates whether the node marked for deletion has been found.

1. [Initialize]
   If LPTR(HEAD) ≠ HEAD
   then   CUR ← LPTR(HEAD)
          PARENT ← HEAD
          D ← 'L'
   else   Write('NODE NOT FOUND')
          Return

2. [Search for the node marked for deletion]
   FOUND ← *false*
   Repeat while not FOUND and CUR ≠ NULL
        If DATA(CUR) = X
        then   FOUND ← *true*
        else   If X < DATA(CUR)
               then   (branch left)
                      PARENT ← CUR
                      CUR ← LPTR(CUR)
                      D ← 'L'
               else   (branch right)
                      PARENT ← CUR
                      CUR ← RPTR(CUR)
                      D ← 'R'
   If FOUND = *false*
   then   Write('NODE NOT FOUND')
          Return

3. [Perform the indicated deletion and restructure the tree]
   If LPTR(CUR) = NULL
   then   (empty left subtree)
          Q ← RPTR(CUR)
   else   If RPTR(CUR) = NULL
          then   (empty right subtree)
                 Q ← LPTR(CUR)
          else   (check right child for successor)
                 SUC ← RPTR(CUR)
                 If LPTR(SUC) = NULL
                 then   LPTR(SUC) ← LPTR(CUR)
                        Q ← SUC
                 else   (search for successor of CUR)
                        PRED ← RPTR(CUR)
                        SUC ← LPTR(PRED)
                        Repeat while LPTR(SUC) ≠ NULL
                             PRED ← SUC
                             SUC ← LPTR(PRED)
                        (connect successor)
                        LPTR(PRED) ← RPTR(SUC)
                        LPTR(SUC) ← LPTR(CUR)
                        RPTR(SUC) ← RPTR(CUR)
                        Q ← SUC
   (Connect parent of X to its replacement)
   If D = 'L'

```
then   LPTR(PARENT) ← Q
else   RPTR(PARENT) ← Q
Return                                                              □
```

The first step of the algorithm checks for an empty tree. If the tree is empty, then the required node cannot be found and the algorithm terminates; otherwise, a left branch is taken and the direction D is set to 'L' (indicating a left branch). Step 2, although lengthy, is not complex. This step searches for the node to be deleted. If it is not found, then the Repeat statement fails and control passes to the following statement, where we print the appropriate message. When the desired node is found, it must be deleted from the tree. This is done in step 3. As we mentioned earlier, two cases arise. The second case is exhibited in Fig. 5-1.19. The tracing of the algorithm is left as an exercise.

As we examine the previously chosen storage representation for a binary tree, it is evident that there are many NULL links. In fact, it can be shown that there are exactly n + 1 such links for a tree of n nodes. This wasted memory space can be used in the reformulation of the previous representation of a binary tree. This representation is the topic of the next subsection.

### 5-1.3.2 Threaded Storage Representation for Binary Trees

The wasted NULL links in the storage representation of binary trees introduced in the previous subsection can be replaced by *threads*. A binary tree is threaded according to a particular traversal order. For example, the threads for the inorder traversal of a tree are pointers to its higher nodes. For this traversal order, if the left link of a node P is normally NULL, then this link is replaced by the address of the predecessor of P. Similarly, a normally NULL right link is replaced by the address of the successor of the node in question. Because the left or right link of a node can denote either a structural link or a thread, we must somehow be able to distinguish them. Upon the assumption that valid pointer values are positive and nonzero, structural links can be represented as usual, by positive addresses. Threads, on the other hand, will be represented by negative addresses. Also, it is often desirable in processing a tree to have a list head as discussed in Sec. 4-2.3. This head node is simply another node which serves as the predecessor and successor of the first and last tree nodes with respect to inorder traversal. Such an approach, in essence, imposes a circular structure on the tree in addition to its tree structure. Prior to tree creation, the head node is defined as shown in Fig. 5-1.24, where the dashed arrow denotes a thread link. The tree is attached to the left branch of the head node making the pointer to the root node of the tree LPTR(HEAD). The threading of the binary tree for inorder traversal is given in Fig. 5-1.25.

Another way of distinguishing a thread link from a structural link is to have a separate boolean flag for each of the left and right pointers. The node structure

HEAD

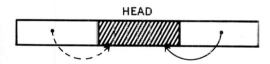

**FIGURE 5-1.24** Representation of an empty threaded binary tree.

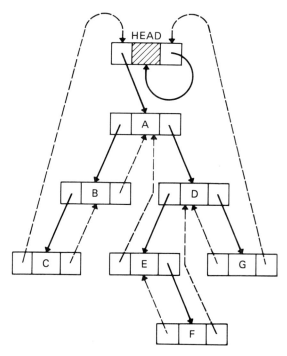

**FIGURE 5-1.25**   Inorder threading of a binary tree.

using this approach is shown in Fig. 5-1.26, where LTHREAD and RTHREAD are boolean indicators associated with the left and right links, respectively. The following coding scheme is used to distinguish between a structural link and a thread.

LTHREAD = true(1)    Denotes a left thread link
LTHREAD = false(0)   Denotes a left structural link
RTHREAD = true(1)    Denotes a right thread link
RTHREAD = false(0)   Denotes a right structural link

This method of distinguishing between a thread and a structural link is preferred over the previous method if the programming language used does not allow negative-valued pointers. Note, however, that the negative-valued pointer approach is more efficient from the point of view of storage than is the flag method. In the remainder of our discussion we will use a negative pointer to denote a thread.

Given a threaded tree for a particular order of traversal, it is a relatively simple task to develop algorithms to obtain the predecessor or successor nodes of some particular node P. These algorithms are given here for inorder traversal.

| LPTR | LTHREAD | DATA | RTHREAD | RPTR |
|------|---------|------|---------|------|

**FIGURE 5-1.26**   Alternate node structure for a threaded binary tree.

**Function** INS(X). Given X, the address of a node in a threaded binary tree, this function returns the address of its inorder successor. F is a temporary pointer variable.

1.  [Return the right pointer of the given node if a thread]
    P ← |RPTR(X)|
    If RPTR(X) < 0
    then    Return(P)
2.  [Branch left repeatedly until a left thread]
    Repeat while LPTR(P) > 0
        F ← LPTR(P)
3.  [Return address of successor]
    Return(P)                                                    □

Step 1 initializes P to the absolute value of the right link of X. If the original link value is negative (that is, denotes a thread), then the inorder successor of X has been found and the value of P is returned If this test fails, however, control passes to step 2. In this step we repeatedly branch left until a left thread is encountered. At this point we enter step 3 where the required address is returned.

**Function** INP(X). This function is similar to the previous one except that the address of the given node's inorder predecessor is returned.

1.  [Return the left pointer of the given node if a thread]
    P ← |LPTR(X)|
    If LPTR(X) < 0
    then    Return(P)
2.  [Branch right repeatedly until a right thread]
    Repeat while RPTR(P) > 0
        P ← RPTR(P)
3.  [Return address of predecessor]
    Return(P)                                                    □

This algorithm operates in a manner similar to that of the previous algorithm. The roles of LPTR and RPTR are simply interchanged.

The successor subalgorithm can be used repeatedly to traverse the threaded tree in inorder.

**Algorithm** TINORDER. Given the address of the list head (HEAD) of a binary tree which has been threaded for inorder traversal and subalgorithm INS previously discussed, this algorithm traverses the tree in inorder. P is a temporary pointer variable.

1.  [Initialize
    P ← HEAD
2.  [Traverse threaded tree in inorder]
    Repeat while true
        P ← INS(P)
        If P = HEAD
        then    Exit
        else    Write(DATA(P))                                  □

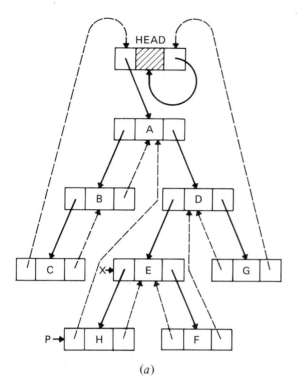

(a)

**FIGURE 5-1.27**    Insertion of a node to the left
of a given node.

The algorithm is simple. Observe that we have set up, in step 2, a Repeat
statement which seems to control an infinite loop. This, however, is not the case,
since when the successor node becomes the list head, the entire tree has been
traversed. At this point the algorithm terminates.

From this algorithm it can be seen that the threaded tree has certain advantages over its unthreaded counterpart. First, the inorder traversal of a threaded tree
is somewhat faster than that of its unthreaded version because a stack is not
required in the former. The second advantage is more subtle. With a threaded tree
representation, we can efficiently determine the predecessor and successor nodes for
inorder traversal order for any node P. In the case of an unthreaded tree representation, however, this task is more difficult. A stack is required to provide upward-
pointing information in the tree, which threading provides. Thus, with a threaded
tree representation, it may be possible to generate the successor or predecessor of
any arbitrarily selected node without having to incur the overhead of using a stack
mechanism.

Naturally, a price must be paid for these advantages. Threaded trees are
unable to share common subtrees, as can unthreaded trees. Second, if negative
addressing is not permitted in the programming language being used, two additional
fields are required to distinguish between thread and structural links. Finally, insertions into and deletions from a threaded tree are more time-consuming, since both
thread and structural links must be maintained.

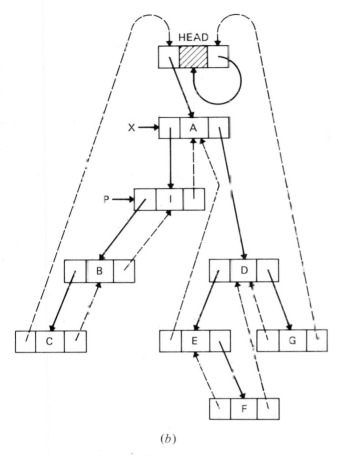

*(b)*

**FIGURE 5-1.27** (continued)

The following subalgorithm inserts a node into a threaded binary tree to the left of a designated node. There are two possible cases. The easiest case involves inserting the new node as a left subtree of the designated node, if that node has an empty left subtree. The remaining (and more difficult) case inserts the new node between the given node, say X, and LPTR(X). An insertion of node H to the left of node E (whose left subtree is null) is shown in Fig. 5-1.27a. Figure 5-1.27b gives an example of the remaining case in which node I is inserted to the left of node A.

**Procedure** LEFT(X, INFO). Given the address of a designated node (X) in an inorder threaded binary tree and the information associated with a new node (INFO), this procedure inserts a new node to the left of the designated node. P is a temporary pointer variable which denotes the address of the node to be inserted.

1. [Create new node]
   P ⟸ NODE
   DATA(P) ← INFO

2.  [Adjust pointer fields]
        LPTR(P) ← LPTR(X)
        LPTR(X) ← P
        RPTR(P) ← –X
3.  [Reset predecessor thread if required]
        If LPTR(P) > 0
        then    RPTR(INP(P)) ← –P
        Return                                                          ⫐

The first step creates a new node and initializes its information field. Step 2 handles the case where the new node becomes the left subtree of node X. The last step handles the second insertion case where the right link of the inorder predecessor of X (before insertion) is set to a thread which points to the new node.

The notion of threading a binary tree can also be extended to preorder and postorder traversals. In these cases, however, thread pointers need not always point to higher nodes in the tree. Also, the algorithms associated with these traversals may sometimes be more complex than those obtained earlier for inorder traversals.

Thus far we have been concerned with the storage representation of binary trees. Clearly, there are applications in which the tree structures are not binary. These more general tree structures can be converted easily to equivalent binary trees. This topic is described in detail in the next subsection.

**Exercises for Sec. 5-1.3**

1.  Prove that a binary tree with n nodes has exactly n + 1 null branches.
2.  Formulate an iterative algorithm for traversing a binary tree in inorder.
3.  Trace through Procedure POSTORDER, using the binary tree of Fig. 5-1.21, and construct a table similar to Table 5-1.1.

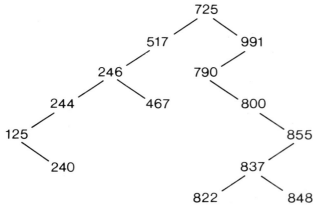

**FIGURE 5-1.28**

4.  Given the binary tree in Fig. 5-1.28, determine the order in which the nodes will be visited if the tree is traversed in inorder, in postorder, and in preorder. Repeat this exercise for the converse traversals.

5.  Obtain an algorithm to obtain the "swapped" version of a binary tree. Figure 5-1.29b gives the swapped version of Fig. 5-1.29a.

6.  Given a threaded binary tree for inorder traversal, construct an algorithm (similar to Procedure LEFT) for inserting a node to the immediate right of a designated node.

7.  Investigate the threading of a binary tree for preorder traversal. In particular, attempt to formulate algorithms for obtaining the preorder predecessor and successor of a designated node.

8.  Repeat Prob. 7 for postorder traversal.

9.  Create an iterative algorithm to copy a binary tree.

10. In the presentation of inorder threaded binary trees, algorithms were developed for producing the inorder predecessor and successor of an arbitrary node P. Develop similar algorithms for producing the preorder predecessor and successor and the postorder predecessor and successor of an arbitrary node P in an inorder threaded binary tree with a list head node as presented.

11. Formulate algorithms similar to Functions INP and INS for postorder threading of trees.

12. Devise an algorithm for determining whether two trees A and B are similar, based on the traversal methods discussed in this section.

13. Is every binary tree uniquely defined by its preorder and inorder traversals? How about by its preorder and postorder traversals? Would it be uniquely defined by its inorder and postorder traversals? If yes, formulate an algorithm or algorithms which constructs a doubly-linked representation of the tree. Assume the same notation as used in the text and that each node has an information field of a single letter.

14. Given a threaded binary tree (as in Fig. 5-1.25), formulate an algorithm which will compute the number of leaf nodes in that tree.

15. Formulate an algorithm for finding the kth element in the preorder traversal of an unthreaded binary tree.

16. Construct an algorithm and write a Pascal program which constructs and traverses a "lexically ordered" threaded binary tree for inorder traversal. Your approach should be modular. That is, you should use an appropriate insertion

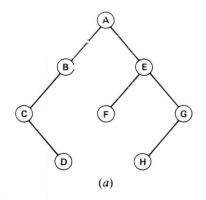

(a)

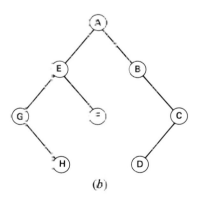

(b)

**FIGURE 5-1.29**

routine and a routine to find the inorder successor of a node in order to traverse the given tree.

17. The *diameter* of a tree is the length of a longest path in the tree from the root to any leaf. Write an algorithm which takes the value of a pointer to the root of the tree, then computes and prints the diameter of the tree and a path of that length (i.e., a sequence of nodes from the root node to some leaf which is of that length). Hint: try to modify Procedure POSTORDER for your purposes.

18. In what order is the tree in Fig. 5-1.30 threaded? Node P is to be inserted immediately to the right of node F. Give a diagram of the tree (threaded in the same order) which results when node P is inserted.

19. Obtain a recursive algorithm for deleting a node from a lexically ordered tree.

20. Formulate a detailed iterative algorithm for the insertion of a new entry into an existing lexically ordered binary tree. Assume that a duplicate entry insertion is possible.

21. Repeat Prob. 20 but obtain a recursive algorithm.

22. Obtain algorithms for the converse-preorder, converse-inorder, and converse-postorder traversals of a given binary tree.

### 5-1.4 Conversion of General Trees to Binary Trees

A general tree, or more generally, a forest of trees can be converted into an equivalent binary tree. This conversion process is called the natural correspondence between general and binary trees. Furthermore, this correspondence is a one-to-one relationship. In this subsection we formulate a detailed algorithm for converting general trees to binary trees. Before this algorithm is given, however, the specification of the input format to the algorithm must be given.

Perhaps one of the most popular and convenient ways to specify a general tree (or forest) is to use a notation similar to that used in several programming

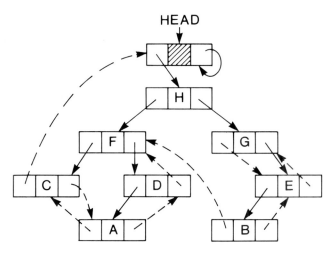

**FIGURE 5-1.30**

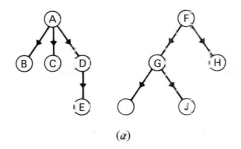

(a)

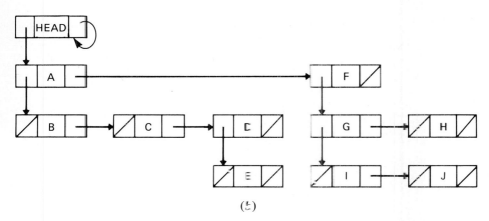

(b)

**FIGURE 5-1.31** (a) A forest of two trees; and (b) binary tree representation of a forest.

languages. As an example, the two trees of Fig. 5-1.31a can be specified in the following manner:

```
1    A
        2    B
        2    C
        2    D
                3    E
1    F
        2    G
                3    I
                3    J
        2    H
```

In this notation the numbers associated with the nodes indicate the subtree relationship. For example, those nodes with an associated number of 1 denote root nodes. Those with higher numbers indicate their lower position in the tree structure. The equivalent binary tree for this forest is given in Fig. 5-1.31b.

In the formulation of an algorithm for converting a forest to a binary tree, we must connect a parent to its left offspring and connect from left to right all the siblings at the same level within the same tree. This latter requirement implies that a stack must be maintained. We assume that the input to the algorithm consists of a sequence of nodes for each tree in preorder. The representation of each node takes the form of a pair of elements; the first and second elements represent the level number and name associated with that node, respectively. Each entry in the stack is made up of two items. The first item represents the level number associated with a node, and the second item denotes the address of that node.

A general algorithm for this conversion process is as follows:

1. Create a head node for the binary tree and push its address and level number on stack
2. Repeat thru step 6 while there still remains data
3. Input a current node description
4. Create a tree node and initialize its contents
5. If the level number of the current node is greater than that of the node on top of the stack
   then connect parent to its left offspring (current node)
   else Remove from the stack all nodes whose level numbers are greater than that of the current node
   Connect left child on the stack to current node
   Remove left child from stack
6. Push current node description onto the stack
7. Finished

The following algorithm implements the notion of natural correspondence.

**Algorithm** CONVERT. Given a forest of trees whose input format is in the form just described, it is required to convert this forest into an equivalent binary tree with a list head (HEAD). Each element of the stack consists of two fields. The vectors NUMBER and LOC denote the level number and address associated with a node. TOP denotes the top of the stack. The variables LEVEL and NAME represent the level number and name of an input node, respectively. PRED_LEVEL and PRED_LOC give the level number and address of a node which has previously been encountered. NEW is a temporary pointer variable.

1. [Initialize]
   HEAD ⇐ NODE
   LPTR(HEAD) ← NULL
   RPTR(HEAD) ← HEAD
   NUMBER[1] ← 0
   LOC[1] ← HEAD
   TOP ← 1
2. [Process the input]
   Repeat thru step 6 while there remains input
3. [Input a node]
   Read(LEVEL, NAME)
4. [Create a tree node]
   NEW ⇐ NODE
   LPTR(NEW) ← RPTR(NEW) ← NULL
   DATA(NEW) ← NAME
5. [Compare levels]
   PRED_LEVEL ← NUMBER[TOP]

PRED_LOC ← LOC[TOP]
If LEVEL > PRED_LEVEL
then    LPTR(PRED_LOC) ← NEW    (connect parent to its left-most offspring)
else    (remove nodes from stack)
        Repeat while PRED_LEVEL > LEVEL
            TOP ← TOP − 1
            PRED_LEVEL ← NUMBER[TOP]
            PRED_LOC ← LOC[TOP]
        If PRED_LEVEL < LEVEL
        then    Write('MIXED LEVEL NUMBERS')
                Exit
        RPTR(PRED_LOC) ← NEW    (connect siblings together)
        TOP ← TOP − 1
6.    [Push a new node onto the stack]
        TOP ← TOP + 1
        NUMBER[TOP] ← LEVEL
        LOC[TOP] ← NEW
7.    [Finished]
        Exit    ☐

The first step of this algorithm creates a list head for the required binary tree and places the level number and address of this node on the stack. Observe that a level number of zero is associated with the list head. This convenient choice will later cause the root of the tree to be appended to the list head. Step 2 controls the input of the given forest, and step 3 inputs a pair of values which represent a node in the tree. The fourth step creates a new node and initializes its links to NULL. The label of the new node is also copied. Step 5 first copies the level number and address of the top element in the stack into PRED_LEVEL and PRED_LOC, respectively. If the level number of the new node is greater than the level number of the top-most node on the stack, then the left link of the latter is set to the address of the former. This assignment connects a parent to its left-most offspring. A transfer to step 6 then results. If, however, the level number of the new node is less than or equal to that of the top of the stack, then successive elements are removed from the stack until the level number of the top-most element is less than or equal to the level number of the new node. If the comparison gives a less than result, then an error exists in the numbering of the tree structures; otherwise, in the case of equality, the right link of the stack top node is set to NEW and removed from the stack. Step 6 stacks the level number and address of the new node.

A trace of the algorithm using the forest of Fig. 5-1.31a is given in Table 5-1.2, where NA denotes the address of a node with name A, NB denotes the address of a node with name B, etc. A stack entry written as, for example, 1NA means that we have placed on the stack level number (1) and the address (NA) of some node with name A. The stack top is to the right. Note that if a forest happens to have several nodes with the same name, say B, then each of these nodes will have a different address, even though our notation will refer to each address as NB. The table shows only changes which have occurred since the previous steps.

The preorder and inorder traversals of a binary tree which corresponds to a forest have a natural correspondence with these traversals on the forest. In particular, the preorder traversal of the associated binary tree is equivalent to visiting the nodes of the forest in *tree preorder*, which is defined as follows:

**Table 5-1.2**

| Current Input | Stack | Level | X | PRED_LEVEL | LOC | LPTR (PRED_LOC) | RPTR (PRED_LOC) |
|---|---|---|---|---|---|---|---|
| | ONT | | | | | NULL | NULL |
| 1,A | ONT 1NA | 1 | NA | 0 | NT | NA | NULL |
| 2,B | ONT 1NA 2NB | 2 | NB | 1 | NA | NB | NULL |
| 2,C | ONT 1NA 2NC | 2 | NC | 2 | NB | NULL | NC |
| 2,D | ONT 1NA 2ND | 2 | ND | 2 | NC | NULL | ND |
| 3,E | ONT 1NA 2ND 3NE | 3 | NE | 2 | ND | NE | NULL |
| 1,F | | 1 | NF | 3 | NE | | |
| | | | | 2 | ND | | |
| | ONT 1NF | | | 1 | NA | | NF |
| 2,G | ONT 1NF 2NG | 2 | NG | 1 | NF | NG | NULL |
| 3,I | ONT 1NF 2NG 3NI | 3 | NI | 2 | NG | NI | NULL |
| 3,J | ONT 1NF 2NG 3NJ | 3 | NJ | 3 | NI | NULL | NJ |
| 2,H | | 2 | NH | 3 | NJ | | |
| | ONT 1NG 2NH | | | 2 | NG | | NG |

1. Process the root of the first tree.
2. Traverse the subtrees of the first tree in tree preorder.
3. Traverse the remaining trees of the forest in tree preorder.

The tree traversal of the forest of the two trees given in Fig. 5-1.31a gives the sequence

A B C D E F G I J H

This is exactly the same sequence obtained during the preorder traversal of the equivalent binary tree of Fig. 5-1.31b.

Similarly, the *tree inorder* traversal of the example forest is defined as follows:

1. Traverse the subtrees of the first tree in tree inorder.
2. Process the root of the first tree.
3. Traverse the remaining trees of the forest in tree inorder.

The tree inorder traversal of the example forest of Fig. 5-1.31a yields the sequence of labels

B C D E A I J G H F

Again, this is the same sequence as that obtained by traversing the binary tree of Fig. 5-1.31b. No such direct correspondence exists for postorder traversal.

Now that we have discussed how to handle general trees in terms of binary trees, the topic of the next subsection is the sequential storage representation of general trees and binary trees.

**Exercises for Sec. 5-1.4**

1. Using the forest of Fig. 5-1.12, trace (as in Table 5-1.2) the Algorithm CONVERT.

2. Formulate a recursive algorithm for converting a forest into an equivalent binary tree.

3. This problem concerns the operations of subtree insertion and deletion, as applied to general trees. Remember that a general tree can be converted to a binary tree using the natural correspondence algorithm discussed in this section. It is most natural to discuss insertion or deletion of a subtree in terms of its relation to the parent node. Thus we define our two operations as follows:

   DELETE(N, I)
   INSERT(N, I, T)

   DELETE deletes the Ith subtree of the node given by N. INSERT inserts the tree, with root T, as the new Ith subtree of the node given by N. For example, consider the general tree shown in Fig 5-1.32a. If we execute INSERT(P, 2, Q) where Q identifies the tree given in Fig. 5-1.32b, we obtain the tree shown in Fig. 5-1.32c. The complimentary operation for restoring our original tree is then DELETE(P, 2). You are required to formulate algorithms for INSERT and DELETE, assuming that you are given the binary tree equivalent to the general tree (this is obtained by the natural correspondence algorithm). State any assumptions that you make. Also examine what happens to the binary-tree equivalent of the general tree when these operations are performed.

4. A preorder traversal for an $m$-ary forest (and, subsequently, an $m$-ary tree) was defined at the end of the subsection. The result of a preorder traversal on the $m$-ary tree given in Fig. 5-1.33 is ABECFGHD. Given a natural correspondence binary representation of an $m$-ary tree, formulate an algorithm which lists the nodes of this tree in $m$-ary preorder. The nodes should be prefixed by an appropriate level number, as shown earlier in this section.

### 5-1.5 Sequential and Other Representations of Trees

In this subsection we describe several representations of trees that are based on sequential-allocation techniques. These representations are efficient and convenient, provided that the tree structure does not change very much (as to insertions, deletions, etc.) during its existence. The particular representation chosen also depends on other types of application-dependent operations that are to be performed on the tree structure. Some of the representation methods that we examine are for binary trees, others are for general trees.

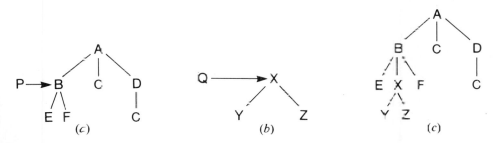

FIGURE 5-1.32

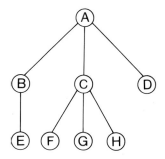

**FIGURE 5-1.33**

Perhaps one of the better known subclasses of binary trees is the set of complete binary trees. A *complete binary tree* is a binary tree in which there is one node at the root level, two nodes at level 2, four nodes at level 3, etc. An example of such a tree structure, together with its sequential representation, is shown in Fig. 5-1.34. In this representation the locations of the left and right children of node i are 2i and 2i + 1, respectively. For example, in Fig. 5-1.34 the index of the left child of the node in position 3 (that is, E) is 6. Similarly, the index of the right child is 7. Conversely, the position of the parent of node j is the index TRUNC(j/2). For example, the parent of nodes 4 and 5 is node 2.

In the previous example we conveniently chose a tree with $2^3 - 1$ nodes. In general, a tree with $2^n - 1$ nodes for a particular value of n is easily represented by a vector of $2^n - 1$ elements. Binary trees which have more or less than $2^n - 1$ nodes for some $n$, however, can also be represented using the previous approach. An example of a tree which contains nine nodes is given in Fig. 5-1.35. Note that a substantial amount of memory is wasted in this case. Therefore, for large trees of this type, this method of representation may not be efficient in terms of storage.

A common method for the sequential representation of binary trees uses the physical adjacency relationship of the computer's memory to replace one of the link fields in the linked representation method introduced earlier. For example, consider

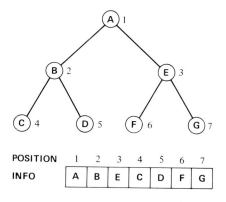

**FIGURE 5-1.34**   Sequential representation of a complete binary tree.

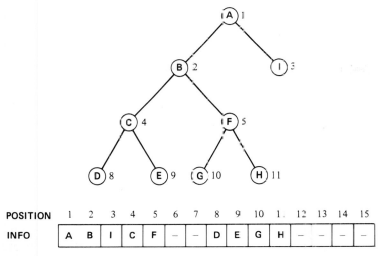

| POSITION | 1 | 2 | 3 | 4 | 5 | 6 | 7 | 8 | 9 | 10 | 11 | 12 | 13 | 14 | 15 |
|---|---|---|---|---|---|---|---|---|---|---|---|---|---|---|---|
| INFO | A | B | I | C | F | – | – | D | E | G | H | – | – | – | – |

**FIGURE 5-1.35**  Sequential representation of an incomplete binary tree.

an alternative representation of a tree structure, in which the left link (LPTR) from the usual doubly linked representation has been omitted. One possibility involves representing the tree sequentially, such that its nodes appear in preorder. Using this approach, we find that the tree of Fig. 5-1.36a is represented by Fig. 5-1.36b, where

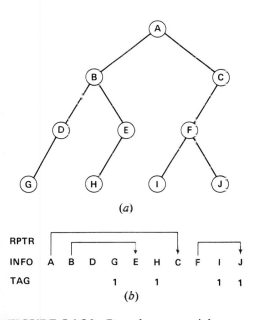

(a)

| RPTR | | | | | | | | | | |
|---|---|---|---|---|---|---|---|---|---|---|
| INFO | A | B | D | G | E | H | C | F | I | J |
| TAG | | | | 1 | | 1 | | 1 | 1 | |

(b)

**FIGURE 5-1.36**  Preorder sequential representation of a binary tree.

RPTR, INFO, and TAG are vectors. Observe that in this representation we do not require the LPTR pointer, since for a nonnull link, it would point to the node to its immediate right. The bit (logical) vector TAG denotes, with a logical value of 1, a leaf node.

Another popular method of representing a general tree sequentially is based on its postorder traversal. Such a representation takes the form of one vector, which represents the nodes of the tree in postorder, and a second vector, which denotes the number of children of the nodes. An example of the postorder representation is given in Fig. 5-1.37. Recall that this postorder representation of a tree is useful in evaluating functions that are defined on certain nodes of the tree. Section 3-5.2.3 contained an example of such a case where object code was generated from the reverse Polish representation of an expression.

As a final and straightforward sequential method of representing a tree, consider a vector which contains the father of each node in the tree. As an example, the tree of Fig. 5-1.38 is represented as follows:

$$
\begin{array}{ccccccccccc}
\text{i} & 1 & 2 & 3 & 4 & 5 & 6 & 7 & 8 & 9 & 10 \\
\text{FATHER[i]} & 0 & 1 & 1 & 1 & 2 & 2 & 4 & 4 & 4 & 6
\end{array}
$$

where the branches in the tree are given by

$$\{(\text{FATHER}[i], i)\} \quad \text{for } i = 2, 3, \dots, 10$$

Observe that the root node (1) of the tree has no father; consequently, we have used a value of zero for its father. This method of representation can be extended to represent a forest. An obvious disadvantage of this method is that it fails to reflect certain orderings of the nodes. For example, if we interchange nodes 5 and 6, the representation of this new tree is the same as that of the previous tree.

In the preceding pages we have been concerned with the representations and manipulations of trees. In the next section we will discuss certain applications in which trees are used.

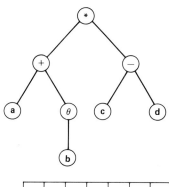

| POST   | a | b | $\theta$ | + | c | d | − | * |
|--------|---|---|---|---|---|---|---|---|
| DEGREE | 0 | 0 | 1 | 2 | 0 | 0 | 2 | 2 |

**FIGURE 5-1.37**  Postorder sequential representation of a tree.

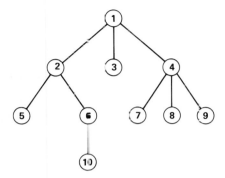

**FIGURE 5-1.38**

**Exercises for Sec. 5-1.5**

1.  Based on the sequential representation of a complete binary tree, formulate an algorithm for its inorder traversal.
2.  Based on the storage representation of a binary tree given in Fig. 5-1.36b, construct an algorithm for its postorder traversal.
3.  Formulate an algorithm based on the sequential representation of a tree using the FATHER vector which finds the path between node x and node y.

## 5-2  APPLICATIONS OF TREES

The present section contains three applications of trees. The first describes methods for the mechanical manipulation of arithmetic expressions. An interesting application of trees concerning the construction and maintenance of symbol tables is discussed in Sec. 5-2.2. The tree also plays an important role in the area of syntax analysis, where it is used to display the structure of a sentence in a language and is used in defining unambiguous languages. Such topics are dealt with in Sec. 5-2.3, along with a description of top-down parsing by using recursive descent.

### 5-2.1  The Manipulation of Arithmetic Expressions

In this subsection we will first discuss the relationship between binary trees and formulas in prefix or suffix notation. Next, we will describe the mechanical manipulation of expressions that are represented by binary trees. Recall that in Sec. 4-3.1, we discussed the formal manipulation of polynomials. In the remainder of this subsection we will extend this previous discussion of manipulating expressions and introduce algorithms for differentiation of expressions. The discussion here, however, is based on the tree representation of expressions. Therefore, certain operations and properties of such expressions will be described in terms of their tree representation. A discussion of variant records in Pascal is included.

In Sec. 3-5.2 we observed that formulas in reverse Polish notation are very useful in the compilation process. There is a close relationship between binary trees and formulas in prefix or suffix notation. Let us write an infix formula as a binary tree, where a node has an operator as a value and where the left and right subtrees are the left and right operands of that operator. The leaves of the tree are the vari-

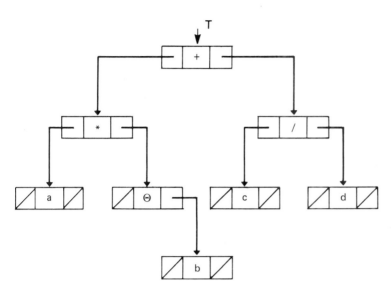

**FIGURE 5-2.1**   The formula a \* *θ*b + c / d as a binary tree.

ables and constants in the expression. Let Θ represent the unary minus. There are
rules given in the Exercises for Sec. 3-5.2 that can distinguish a unary minus from a
binary minus and the negative sign of a constant. The operand of Θ is considered
to be a right subtree. The binary tree in Fig. 5-2.1 represents the formula
a\*Θb+c/d. If we traverse this tree in preorder, we visit the nodes in the order
+\*aΘb/cd, and this is merely the prefix form of the infix formula. On the other
hand, if we traverse the tree in postorder, then we visit the nodes in the order
abΘ\*cd/+, which is the formula written in suffix notation. Observe that if we had
represented the formula as a general tree, as in Fig. 5-2.2*a*, and then applied the
natural correspondence algorithm of Sec. 5-1.4 to convert this tree into an equivalent
binary tree, we would have the structure shown in Fig. 5-2.2*b*. The prefix form of
the formula is obtained by traversing the binary tree in preorder, while the suffix
form is generated by an inorder traversal of the binary tree (not a postorder traversal).

   In the following portion of this subsection we shall discuss the mechanical
manipulation of expressions which are represented as binary trees. Since we have
already introduced this topic in Chap. 4, it should be obvious that the expressions
themselves are to be manipulated (symbolically) and not their values. We may want
to symbolically add, subtract, multiply, divide, differentiate, integrate, compare for
equivalence, etc., such expressions.

   There are a number of programming languages which permit the declaration
of expressions. For example, an expanded version of ALGOL 60, called FOR-
MULA ALGOL, is such a language where a new data type called FORM was
added to basic ALGOL. Expressions in this language are stored as trees, and a
number of related operations are available in the language. SNOBOL4 is another
language which permits "unevaluated expressions" to be used in a program. These
unevaluated expressions can represent a pattern or an expression, and these can be
evaluated later in the program. If the unevaluated expression represents a pattern,

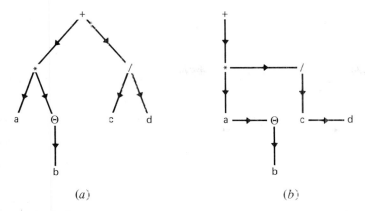

**FIGURE 5-2.2**  The general and binary tree representations of
a * θb + c / d.

then this pattern is only evaluated at pattern-matching time (see Sec. 2-3.4) or by
using the function EVAL. If the unevaluated expression does not represent a pattern, but some arithmetic or string expression, then the reference EVAL(EXPR),
where EXPR denotes the expression string, returns the value of EXPR. LISP is
another language which permits the evaluation of symbolic expressions.

Let us now describe a binary tree representation for symbolic expressions.
Such a representation is given for the expression a * ⊖ b + c ↑ 2 in Fig. 5-2.3,
where ⊖ and ↑ represent the unary minus and exponentiation operations, respectively. In this figure, E is a pointer variable which denotes the root of the tree, each
node of which consists of a left pointer (LPTR), a right pointer (RPTR), and an
information field (TYPE). The TYPE field indicates, in the case of a nonleaf node,
the arithmetic operation which is associated with that node. The values of TYPE
associated with the operators +, −, *, /, ↑, and ⊖ are 1, 2, 3, 4, 5, and 6, respectively.
For a leaf node, however, TYPE denotes a variable or a constant (by having a value of
0). In such a case, the right pointer of the leaf gives the address in the symbol table
which corresponds to that variable or constant. Note that the type of the operator
(and not the operator itself) is stored in the tree. This choice makes the processing of
such trees simple. The symbol table used contains the name of the variable (SYMBOL)
or constant and its value (VALUE).

Initially, let us consider the evaluation of an expression which is represented by a
binary tree. That is, we want to obtain the value of this expression. The simplest way
of accomplishing this is to formulate a recursive solution. Such a solution is given in
the following recursive function.

**Function**  EVAL(E).  Given a pointer E that denotes the address of the root node
expression as discussed previously, this function returns the value of this expression.
F is a local pointer variable.

1.  [Evaluate the symbolic expression]
        Select case (TYPE(E))
            Case 0:   (a variable or a constant)
                F ← RPTR(E)
                Return(VALUE(F))

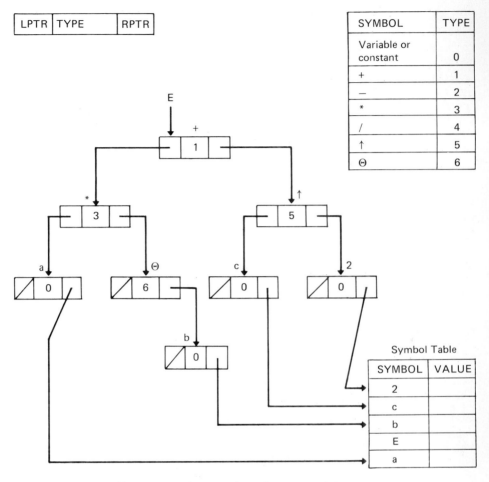

**FIGURE 5-2.3** A binary tree representation of an expression.

Case 1: (an addition operator)
   Return(EVAL(LPTR(E)) + EVAL(RPTR(E)))
Case 2: (a subtraction operator)
   Return(EVAL(LPTR(E)) − EVAL(RPTR(E)))
Case 3: (a multiplication operator)
   Return(EVAL(LPTR(E)) * EVAL(RPTR(E)))
Case 4: (a division operator)
   Return(EVAL(LPTR(E)) / EVAL(RTPR(E)))
Case 5: (an exponentiation operator)
   Return(EVAL(LPTR(E)) ↑ EVAL(RPTR(E)))
Case 6: (a unary minus operator)
   Return(−EVAL(RPTR(E)))
Default:
   Write('INVALID EXPRESSION')
   Return(0)

The function is simple. It contains one case statement. Its result is a transfer of control to the appropriately labeled statement. If the current node is a leaf, then the value of the variable or constant denoted by this node is returned. This is accomplished by using the right table pointer of that node to reference the associated entry in the symbol table. For a nonleaf node, however, the recursive evaluation of the subtree(s) of this node which represent the operand(s) of the current operator is initiated. This is achieved by invoking the Function EVAL with the left and right pointers of that operator node as arguments in the case of a binary node; otherwise, only the right pointer is used in the case of a unary minus operator. This process continues until a leaf node is encountered. For a given leaf node, a value from the associated entry in the symbol table is located.

Now that we are able to evaluate an expression which is represented by a binary tree, let us next consider the operation of symbolically adding two such expressions. For example, assume that it is required to add the expressions EXPR1 and EXPR2. Let E1 and E2 be the pointer variables which denote the roots of the binary trees for EXPR1 and EXPR2, respectively. The required addition is easily achieved by creating a root node for the sum expression and using the values of E1 and E2 as the left and right pointer values, respectively, for this new node. The type field of the new root node is also set to 1. The statements to accomplish this construction are

```
P ⇐ NODE
LPTR(P) ← E1
RPTR(P) ← E2
TYPE(P) ← 1
```

with P containing the address of the root node for the expression EXPR1 + EXPR2. The algorithm is trivial when it is compared with the algorithm developed in Sec. 4-3.1 for essentially the same application.

In practice, however, we would like the addition function to perform certain obvious simplifications. For example, if the expressions being added are constants, then we should create a new constant node representing this constant sum. Moreover, if one of the expressions being added is zero, then no new root node is required. Similar rules can be devised for the other arithmetic operators and are left as exercises.

As a second example, let us consider the problem of determining whether or not two expressions (which are represented by binary trees) are similar. Two binary trees associated with such expressions are said to be similar if they are *identical* for all node types except for those which represent the commutative operators + and *. In this latter case, we can accept the case where the left subtree of the first tree is identical to the right subtree of the second tree and the right subtree of the first tree is identical to the left subtree of the second tree. The following logical function accomplishes this similarity check.

**Function** SIMILAR(A, B). Given two expressions whose equivalent binary trees' root nodes can be denoted by A and B, respectively, this logical function determines whether the given expressions are, according to the previous discussion, similar.

1.  [Check the types of the root nodes]
    If TYPE(A) ≠ TYPE(B)
    then    Return(*false*)

2. [Check the trees for similarity]
    Select case (TYPE(A))
        Case 0:  (compare leaf nodes)
          If VALUE(RPTR(A)) $\neq$ VALUE(RPTR(B))
          then   Return(*false*)
          else    Return(*true*)
        Case 1, 3:  (check for commutativity of + and *)
          Return(SIMILAR(LPTR(A), RPTR(B)) and
                            SIMILAR(RPTR(A), LPTR(B))
          or SIMILAR(LPTR(A), LPTR(B)) and
                            SIMILAR(RPTR(A), RPTR(B)))
        Case 2, 4, 5:  (check for identical binary trees)
          Return(SIMILAR(LPTR(A), LPTR(B)) and
                            SIMILAR(RPTR(A), RPTR(B)))
        Case 6:  (check for identical unary subtrees)
          Return(SIMILAR(RPTR(A), RPTR(B)))        □

This function assumes the node structure and binary representation of Fig. 5-2.3. Note that the operators are divided into three categories — namely, the binary commutative operators, the binary noncommutative operators, and the unary operator.

As a final example, we will consider symbolic differentiation. Algebraic differentiation is one of the earliest symbolic manipulation applications to be computerized. Programs to obtain the derivative of an algebraic expression were written in the early 1950s. In this portion of the subsection we are concerned with the formulation of an algorithm for this application.

The problem can be described briefly as follows. Given the rules for differentiation with respect to x,

$$D(x) = 1$$
$$D(a) = 0; \text{ where a is a constant or variable other than x}$$
$$D(\ln u) = D(u)/u$$
$$D(-u) = -D(u)$$
$$D(u + v) = D(u) + D(v)$$
$$D(u - v) = D(u) - D(v)$$
$$D(u * v) = D(u) * v + D(v) * u$$
$$D(u/v) = D(u)/v - (u * D(v))/v^2$$

create an algorithm which will accept an algebraic expression composed of valid operators and operands and construct the derivative of this expression with respect to a given variable.

For the purposes of this example, we assume that the valid operators are LN (natural logarithm), $\Theta$ (unary minus), +, -, *, and /; the valid operands are variables of 1 to 5 characters in length, the first of which must be a letter; and constants are 1 to 5 digits in length, which may include a decimal point and a minus sign.

The primary aspect of the solution to this problem is choosing an appropriate data structure to represent the algebraic expressions. We shall use a binary tree structure to represent such expressions.

A typical node for such a structure is given in Fig. 5-2.4, in which LPTR and RPTR are pointers, SYM is the character representation of the element represented by the node, and TYPE is a code number which indicates the type of the element. The values of TYPE are given in Table 5-2.1. Note that the ↑ symbol, which denotes

| LPTR | SYM | TYPE | RFTR |
|------|-----|------|------|

**FIGURE 5-2.4**  Node structure for symbolic differentiation

exponentiation, is not allowed in the input expressions, but is used in the derivative and is therefore listed here.

Using this binary representation, if a node represents a binary operator, then the left subtree denotes the first operand and the right subtree denotes the second operand. For unary operators, however, the right subtree represents the single operand. A binary tree representation of the expression (a + x) * 3.1 + (ln $\Theta$y) is shown in Fig. 5-2.5.

We shall now develop a number of simple algorithms which will be used in the main differentiation routine. The first of these creates a node and sets its TYPE field to a value which depends on the kind (i.e., constant, variable, etc.) of symbol which is passed to the algorithm.

**Function  MAKE_NODE(VAL).**  Given VAL, a variable that contains the character representation of an algebraic element such as a constant or an operator, this function creates a node whose LPTR and RPTR pointers are set to NULL. The TYPE field of this node is determined from VAL. The address of the new node is returned. X is a pointer variable, OPS is a string which represents the alphabet of valid operators, and DIGITS is a string which contains the alphabet of symbols for constants.

1.  [Initialize]
       OPS ← '+-*/↑$\Theta$LN'
       DIGITS ← '-.0123456789'
2.  [Create a node]
       X ⇐ NODE
       LPTR(X) ← RPTR(X) ← NULL
       SYM(X) ← VAL
       TYPE(X) ← 0
3.  [Determine node type]
       If VAL ≠ ' '
       then    TYPE(X) ← INDEX(OPS, VAL)
               If TYPE(X) ≠ 0
               then    TYPE(X) ← TYPE(X) + 2
               else    If INDEX(DIGITS, SUB(VAL, 1, 1)) ≠ 0
                       then    TYPE(X) ← 1    (VAL is a constant)
                       else    TYPE(X) ← 2    (VAL is a variable)
4.  [Finished]
       Return(X)                                                     □

The function creates a leaf node and initializes its contents. In particular, the TYPE field is set to 0. If this value isn't changed later then it signals an error to the invoking algorithm. Step 3 determines the node type. If the character representation of the given element is illegal (i.e., it's not an operator, constant, or variable) then a value of zero is returned. Otherwise, the INDEX function is used to determine the type of the given element according to the values given in Table 5-2.1.

**Table 5-2.1**    Values for TYPE

| Type | Meaning |
|------|---------|
| 1 | constant |
| 2 | variable |
| 3 | + (add) |
| 4 | − (subtract) |
| 5 | * (multiply) |
| 6 | / (divide) |
| 7 | ↑ (exponentiation operator) |
| 8 | Θ (unary minus) |
| 9 | LN (natural logarithm) |

The following two algorithms are specialized tree creation algorithms which are designed to create trees with one or two subtrees:

**Function** CREATE1($N_1$, $N_2$). Given $N_1$ and $N_2$, the first a pointer to a single node and the second a pointer to a binary subtree, this function joins them such that $N_2$ becomes the right subtree of $N_1$ in the resultant tree. It is assumed that a unary operation will have this operand as its right subtree. A pointer to $N_1$ is returned.

1.  [Join nodes]
        $RPTR(N_1) \leftarrow N_2$
2.  [Finished]
        Return($N_1$)                                    □

**Function** CREATE2($N_1$, $N_2$, $N_3$). Given $N_1$, $N_2$, and $N_3$, the first a pointer to a single node and the other two pointers to binary subtrees, this function joins them such that

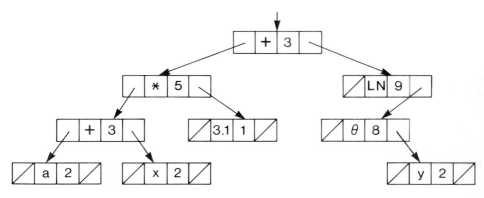

**FIGURE 5-2.5**

$N_2$ and $N_3$ become the left and right subtrees of $N_1$, respectively. The address of $N_1$ is returned.

1.  [Attach subtrees]
    $LPTR(N_1) \leftarrow N_2$
    $RPTR(N_1) \leftarrow N_3$
2.  [Finished]
    $Return(N_1)$                                                                ☐

From the differentiation rules given earlier, it is easily seen that the derivative of the operand(s) must first be found before a rule corresponding to a particular operator can be applied. This process is readily described in a recursive manner within the tree traversing framework. The general differentiation strategy is as follows:

1.  Check for a null expression
2.  If current node is a constant
    then create a type 0 node and return
3.  If current node is a variable
    then create a type 0 or type 1 node and return
4.  Obtain differentiated operand(s) for the current operator
5.  Apply the appropriate rule depending on the current operator type
    a)  Addition—create a binary tree with an addition node and return
    b)  Subtraction—create a binary tree with a subtraction node and return
    c)  Multiplication—create a binary tree with an addition node as its root (see Fig. 5-2.6a) and return
    d)  Division—create a binary tree for the division operator (see Fig. 5-2.6b)
    e)  Unary minus—create a binary tree with a unary subtraction node as its root and return
    f)  Natural logarithm—create a binary tree with a division operator node as its root and return

A detailed algorithm corresponding to this general algorithm can now be given.

**Function** DIFFER(ROOT, VAR). Given ROOT, the address of the root node of a binary tree structure (like the one given in Fig. 5-2.5) representing an algebraic expression, and VAR, the variable with respect to which the expression is to be differentiated, this function creates a binary tree structure representing the derivative. The value returned is the address of the derivative binary tree structure. OPERAND1 and OPERAND2 are pointers to the derivatives of the first and second operands, if the operands exist. OP2 is a pointer to a copy of the second operand. If an operation has only one operand, it is assumed that this operand is the right subtree. COPY is assumed to be a function which duplicates a given binary tree. Functions MAKE_NODE, CREATE1, and CREATE2 which have been previously described, are used in this function. TEMP1, TEMP2, TEMP3, and TEMP4 are pointer variables.

1. [Check for null expression]
       If ROOT = NULL
       then    Return(NULL)
2. [Is current node a constant?]
       If TYPE(ROOT) = 1
       then    Return(MAKE_NODE('0'))
3. [Is current node a variable?]
       If TYPE(ROOT) = 2
       then    If SYM(ROOT) = VAR
               then    Return(MAKE_NODE('1'))
               else    Return(MAKE_NODE('0'))
4. [Obtain operand(s) of operator]
       OPERAND2 ← DIFFER(RPTR(ROOT), VAR)
       If LPTR(ROOT) ≠ NULL
       then    OPERAND1 ← DIFFER(LPTR(ROOT), VAR)
5. [Process an operator node]
       Select Case(TYPE(ROOT))
               Case 3:   (Addition)
                   Return(CREATE2(MAKE_NODE('+'), OPERAND1, OPERAND2))
               Case 4:   (Subtraction)
                   Return(CREATE2(MAKE_NODE('-'), OPERAND1, OPERAND2))
               Case 5:   (Multiplication)
                   TEMP1 ← CREATE2(MAKE_NODE('*'), OPERAND1,
                                                   COPY(RPTR(ROOT)))
                   TEMP2 ← CREATE2(MAKE_NODE('*'), OPERAND2,
                                                   COPY(LPTR(ROOT)))
                   Return(CREATE2(MAKE_NODE('+'), TEMP1, TEMP2))
               Case 6:   (Division)
                   OP2 ← COPY(RPTR(ROOT))
                   TEMP1 ← CREATE2(MAKE_NODE('/'), OPERAND1, OP2)
                   TEMP2 ← CREATE2(MAKE_NODE('*'), COPY(LPTR(ROOT)),
                                                   OPERAND2)
                   TEMP3 ← CREATE2(MAKE_NODE('↑'), OP2, MAKE_NODE('2'))
                   TEMP4 ← CREATE2(MAKE_NODE('/'), TEMP2, TEMP3)
                   Return(CREATE2(MAKE_NODE('-'), TEMP1, TEMP4))
               Case 8:   (Unary minus)
                   Return(CREATE1(MAKE_NODE('Θ'), OPERAND2))
               Case 9:   (Natural logarithm)
                   Return(CREATE2(MAKE_NODE('/'), OPERAND2,
                                                   COPY(RPTR(ROOT))))
               Default:
               Write('ERROR')
               Return(NULL)                                              □

The algorithm is straightforward and follows the rules of differentiation which
were introduced earlier.  Steps 2 and 3 correspond to the constant and variable
cases, respectively.  Step 4 obtains the operand(s) associated with a particular operator.  In the case of a unary minus, only one operator is required, which must be
present as a right subtree.  The differentiation for the operators is performed in step
5.  This step contains a case statement which causes the appropriate operation to be
processed.

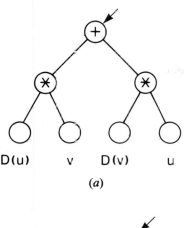

(a)

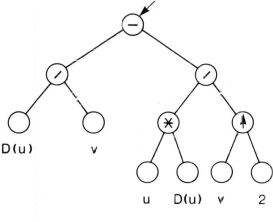

(b)

**FIGURE 5-2.6** Differentiation trees for
(a) multiplication; and (b) division.

The node structure used in the current application was of one form (see Fig. 5-2.3). However, there are two kinds of nodes; namely, branch nodes and leaf nodes which represent operators and variables or constants, respectively. In the remainder of this subsection, we discuss the representation of and manipulation of expressions in Pascal. Pascal allows the definition of record types that have alternative structures (or record variants) within the same record declarations.

Records with alternative structures are called *variant records* in Pascal. A variant record contains two parts: a fixed part (which is optional) and a variant part. The fixed part (if present) is a common front part to all the alternative record structures.

As an example, consider a simplified student registration system which requires two alternative record structures. Both record variants are to contain a common or fixed part such as name, student number, and year of study. Two variant parts are possible. For a resident of a province, the high school attended and the city of permanent residence are recorded. For out-of-province students, his/her home province is noted. A Pascal declaration for such a variant record structure is as follows.

```
type string = packed array [1..25] of char;
     student = (resident, nonresident);
     studenttree =
          record
               name : packed array [1..25] of char;
               studentnumber : integer;
               yearofstudy : integer;
               case studenttype : student of
                    resident : (highschool : string;
                                        city : string);
                    nonresident : (province : string)
          end;
```

The variable *studenttype*, which has two possible values (resident or nonresident), is called a *tag field*. To each of these values there corresponds a variant part of the record structure.

In general, a variant record declaration has the following form.

```
record-name =
     record
          field₁ : type₁;
          field₂ : type₂;                          ⎫
               .                                    ⎬  fixed part
               .                                    ⎭
               .
          fieldₘ : typeₘ;
          case tag-field : tag-type of
               label₁ : (field–list₁);             ⎫
               label₂ : (field–list₂);             ⎪
                    .                               ⎬  variant part
                    .                               ⎪
                    .                               ⎭
               labelₙ : (field–listₙ)
     end;
```

The field list for the part which is common to all record alternatives occurs first. The variant part of the declaration follows. This part begins with the word case and is followed by a tag field. The tag field can have the values $label_1$, $label_2$, . . ., $label_n$. To each value label there corresponds a field list enclosed in parentheses. Every element in such a list contains a name and associated type. Elements are separated by semicolons.

Returning to the symbolic manipulation discussion, a variant record can be used to distinguish between branch nodes and leaf nodes. The node structures for these two types of nodes are exhibited in Figs. 5-2.7a and b. Note that both structures have a common field called *nodetype*. A branch node contains three additional fields. A leaf node, on the other hand, has one additional field. Using two variant record structures the expression tree of Fig. 5-2.3 can be redrawn as that shown in Fig. 5-2.7c. The declaration for such a tree structure follows:

```
type varrec =
     record
          symbol : packed array [1..12] of char;
          value : integer
     end;
```

```
operation = (plus, minus, mult, divide, expon, unary);
nodekind = (op, vc);
exprtree = ↑treenode;
treenode =
    record
        case nodetype : nodekind of
            op : (lptr : ↑treenode;
                  optype : operation;
                  rptr : ↑treenode);
            vc : (tableptr : ↑varrec)
        end;

var expr : exprtree;
        .
        .
        .
```

Note that the symbol table entries each contain two elements — *symbol* and *value*. The enumerated type *operation* contains appropriate names for the arithmetic operators. Observe that the variant record structure *treenode* has no fixed part. The tag

(*a*)

(*b*)

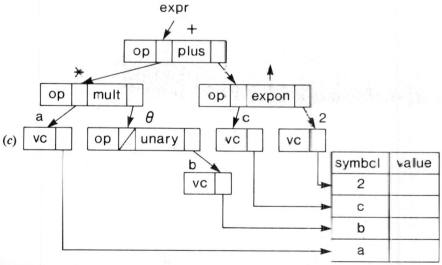

**FIGURE 5-2.7**    A binary tree representation of an expression using variant records.

field that is common to both alternative record structures is *nodetype*. This field has either a value of *op* or *vc* denoting a branch node or leaf node, respectively.

A Pascal recursive function which evaluates a tree structure of the form given in Fig. 5-2.7*c* appears in Fig. 5-2.8.

### Exercises for Sec. 5-2.1

1. Formulate simplification rules, similar to those developed for addition in the text, for the other arithmetic operations.
2. Modify Function DIFFER to incorporate the exponentiation rule which is given as follows:

$$D(u \uparrow v) = D(u) * (v * (u \uparrow (v - 1))) + (\ln(u) * D(v)) * (u \uparrow v)$$

3. Modify the algorithm obtained in Prob. 2 so as to include the trigonometric functions, sin(u), cos(u), tan(u), etc.
4. Optimize the algorithm obtained in Prob. 3 such that expressions such as (x + 0), (0 − x), (1 × x), (x / 1), (x ↑ 1), (x ↑ 0), etc., are simplified.
5. Obtain an algorithm, based on the binary tree representation of an expression, which will symbolically integrate a given expression containing variables, constants, and the ordinary arithmetic operators.
6. Formulate an algorithm, which when given the address of a tree expression, prints the equivalent infix notation of that expression such that it contains a minimum number of parentheses.

### 5-2.2  Symbol-Table Construction

As an application of binary trees, we will formulate algorithms that will maintain a stack-implemented tree-structured symbol table. Recall that a brief introduction to symbol tables was given in Sec. 4-3.2. One of the criteria that a symbol-table rou-

---

```
function eval(e : exptree) : real;

begin
    if e↑.nodetype = vc
    then eval := e↑.tableptr↑.value
    else case e↑.optype of
            plus: eval := eval(e↑.lptr) + eval(e↑.rptr);
            minus: eval := eval(e↑.lptr) – eval(e↑.rptr);
            mult: eval := eval(e↑.lptr) * eval(e↑.rptr);
            divide: eval := eval(e↑.lptr) / eval(e↑.rptr);
            expon: eval := power(eval(e↑.lptr), eval(e↑.rptr));
            unary: eval := –eval(e↑.rptr)
        end
end;
```

**FIGURE 5-2.8**   Pascal function for evaluating a symbolic expression.

---

| LPTR | SYMBOLS | INFO | RPTR |
|------|---------|------|------|

**FIGURE 5-2.9**

tine must meet is that the table searching must be performed efficiently. This requirement originates in the compilation phase where many references to the entries of a symbol table are made. The two required operations that must be performed on a symbol table are insertion and look-up, each of which involves searching. A binary tree structure is chosen for two reasons. The first reason is because if the symbol entries as encountered are uniformly distributed according to lexicographic order, then table searching becomes approximately equivalent to a binary search, as long as the tree is maintained in lexicographic order. Second a binary tree is easily maintained in lexicographic order in the sense that only a few pointers need be changed.

For simplicity we assume the use of a relatively sophisticated system which allows variable-length character strings. Very little effort is required on the part of the programmar to handle such strings. We further assume that the symbol-table routine is used to create trees for variables which are local to a block of program code. This implies that an attempt to insert a duplicate entry is an error. In a global context, duplicate entries are permitted as long as they are at different block levels. In a sense, the symbol table is a set of trees—one for each block level.

A binary tree is constructed with typical nodes of the form given in Fig. 5-2.9, where LPTR and RPTR are pointer fields. SYMBOLS is the field for the character string which is the identifier or variable name (note that string descriptors might well be used here to allow fixed-length nodes, but it is assumed that this use is transparent to the user), and INFO is some set of fields containing additional information about the identifier, such as its type.

Finally, it is assumed that prior to any use of the symbol-table routine at a particular block level, the appropriate tree head node is created with the SYMBOLS field set to a value that is greater lexicographically than any field identifier. HEAD is a vector of pointers to the head nodes of each block level, thus, HEAD[N] points to the HEAD node of the Nth block level. Hence, when a block is entered, a call is made to a main routine which administers to the creation of new tree heads. Similarly, when a block is exited, a routine which deletes tree heads is invoked.

Because both the insertion and look-up operations involve many of the same actions (e.g., searching), we will actually produce only one routine, TABLE, and distinguish between insertion and look-up by the value of a logical parameter, INSERT. On invoking subalgorithm TABLE, if INSERT is true, then the requested operation is insertion; NAME and DATA contain the identifier name and additional information, such as symbol type, respectively. If the insertion is successful, a value of *false* is returned to indicate an error (because the identifier is already present in the table at that level). On the other hand, if the algorithm is invoked with INSERT set to *false*, then the requested operation is look-up. In this case, NAME contains the identifier name to be searched for and DATA is irrelevant. On a successful search, DATA is set to the INFO fields of the matching SYMBOLS entry, and a return with a value of *true* is made to the invoking algorithm. An unsuccessful search during a look-up operation causes a value of *false* to be returned. In this latter case, it is the responsibility of the invoking main routine to try the look-up procedure at lower block levels (trees headed by HEAD[N - 1], HEAD[N - 2], etc.).

A general algorithm to perform an insertion or a search in a specified level of a stack-implemented tree-structured symbol table is as follows.

1. Determine the root node for the current symbol table level
2. Repeat step 3 until the end of the current symbol table level is reached
3. If name precedes the root node entry of the current subtree
   then branch left
           If the left branch of the current root node is empty
           then if name is to be inserted
                   then create a new leaf node
                           insert leaf as a left subtree and return
                   else write search is unsuccessful and return
   else If name follows the root node entry of the current subtree
           then branch right
                   If the right branch of the current root node is empty
                   then if name is to be inserted
                           then create a new leaf node
                                   insert leaf as a right subtree and return
                           else write search is unsuccessful and return
           else if name is to be inserted
                   then write name already present and return
                   else return

A detailed algorithm to perform this function is now given.

**Function** TABLE(HEAD, N, INSERT, NAME).   Given the parameters as described previously, this function performs the required operation, insertion or look-up, on the tree-structured symbol table local to block level N. PARENT denotes the address of the parent node of the new item which is to be inserted. T and P are temporary pointer variables. The function returns *true* when a successful search or insertion has taken place, or *false* for an unsuccessful search or when a duplicate entry is found during an insertion.

1. [Initialize search variable]
       T ← HEAD[N]
2. [Perform indicated operation]
       Repeat step 3 while T ≠ NULL
3. [Compare given item with the root entry of the subtree]
       If NAME < SYMBOLS(T)
       then   (branch left)
               PARENT ← T
               T ← LPTR(T)
               If T = NULL
               then   If INSERT
                       then   (create a new leaf and insert as a left subtree)
                               P ← NODE
                               SYMBOLS(P) ← NAME
                               LPTR(P) ← RPTR(P) ← NULL
                               LPTR(PARENT) ← P
                               Return(*true*)
                       else   (search unsuccessful)
                               Return(*false*)

```
else    If NAME > SYMBOLS(T)
        then    (branch right)
                PARENT ← T
                T ← RPTR(T)
                If T = NULL
                then    If INSERT
                        then    (create a new leaf and insert as a right subtree)
                                P ⇐ NODE
                                SYMBOLS(P) ← NAME
                                LPTR(P) ← RPTR(P) ← NULL
                                RPTR(PARENT) ← P
                                Return(true)
                        else    (search unsuccessful)
                                Return(false)
        else    (a match has occurred)
                If INSERT
                then    Return(false)
                else    Return(true)
```

This function is simple to understand. In step 3 we compare NAME against a symbol-table entry. If they match, we have found the required entry or we have attempted to enter a duplicate name. In either case, we then exit. If no match is found, then, depending on whether NAME is less than or greater than the symbol table entry being examined, we prepare to take the left or right node descendent and repeat for further comparison. However, since a tree ordered in this manner is such that every node in a left or right subtree precedes or follows lexicographically the root node, respectively, we know that whenever an attempt is made to go down an empty subtree, then no match is found. Thus, we have determined where the entry should be. In such a case, an error is reported if the request was a look-up; otherwise, a new node is created, pertinent information copied into it, and it is inserted either to the left or to the right of the current node being examined in the existing tree structure.

As previously mentioned, symbol-table construction for a block structured language consists of forming a new tree for each new block encountered during compilation. Such a construction uses the *static* scope rule based on the block structure. Consider the program segment from a nested language such as that given in Fig. 5-2.10. A separate lexically ordered binary tree would have to be formed for the declarations in the blocks labeled *1*, *2*, *3*, and *4*, and once the compilation of the block is completed its symbol table must be removed. In order to manage a large number of symbol tables, a stack-implemented tree-structured symbol table is now introduced.

The stack-implemented tree-structured organizations for the program segment at points labeled ⓐ and ⓑ in Fig. 5-2.10 are given in Fig. 5-2.11a and b, respectively. In this organization the BLOCK_INDEX stack points to the root nodes of each of the trees making up the symbol table. The node structure is the same as given in Fig. 5-2.9, where the left pointer (LPTR) and right pointer (RPTR) fields indicate the structural links in each of the tree structures.

Consider the process of constructing the symbol tables for the program segment in Fig. 5-2.10. The start of a new block (BBLOCK), causes the main controlling program to invoke the set operation. The *set* operation is invoked when the beginning of a block is recognized during compilation. Since the symbol table is

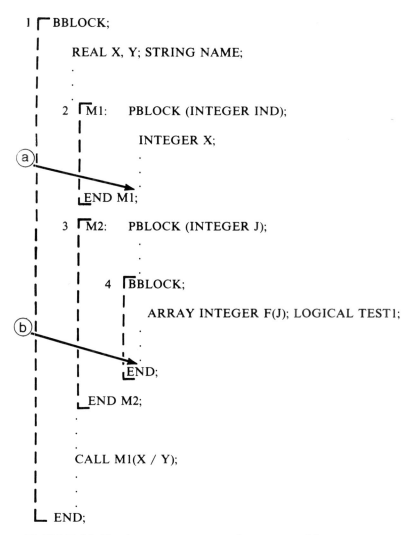

**FIGURE 5-2.10**   A program segment from a nested language.

being maintained as a stack, the current value of TOP is placed in the BLOCK_INDEX to indicate the root of the symbol table for this block. In the example, initially the BLOCK_INDEX is set to 1, this being the first symbol table entered on the stack. Now all variable declarations in this block (X, Y, NAME) are added to the stack using Function **TABLE** to form a lexically ordered tree structure. When the compilation process reaches the next block (M1), its definition is added to the current block's (BBLOCK) list of variable definitions. The set operation is then invoked to create a new symbol table for the block M1. The set operation places the current value of TOP (5) in the BLOCK_INDEX, indicating the root of the new symbol table. Now the variable declarations for the block M1 are added to the stack using Function **TABLE**. At this point the current contents of the stack are as shown in Fig. 5-2.11a.

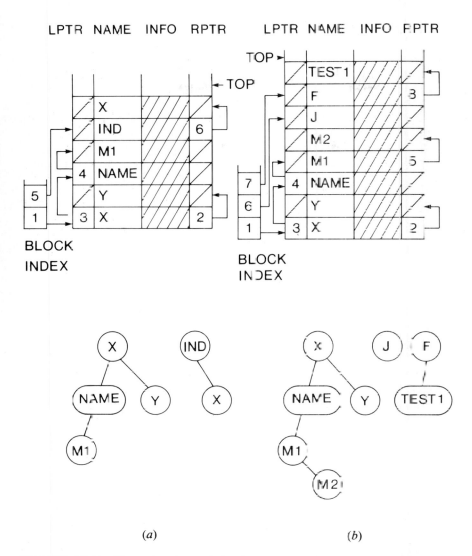

FIGURE 5-2.11   Example of a stack-implemented tree-structured symbol table.

When the end of a block is encountered (i.e., END M1;), a *reset* operation logically deletes the associated tree structure by setting TOP to the value of the top-most element in the BLOCK_INDEX, 5, and then removing this element from the BLOCK_INDEX. If the entire symbol table is to be kept for the duration of the compilation process, then the records from the compiled block should be moved to an inactive area. An alternative to moving the records is simply not to readjust the index TOP during the reset operation, and thereby continue to add records to previously unused symbol locations. This latter approach, however, can cause problems.

Continuing on from point (a) in Fig. 5-2.10, an end statement for block M1 is reached. A reset operation as described above removes this symbol table. The compilation process now reaches the third block (M2), and a new symbol table is begun. Inside this block another block (4) is reached. Once all the variables local to this block are added to the current symbol table, the stack is as shown in Fig. 5-2.11*b*. Following this, all the end statements for the current blocks are encountered, emptying the stack.

A look-up operation for this structure must follow a particular search strategy in order to guarantee that the latest occurrence in time (as in the *dynamic most recent association* scope rule is some languages) of a variable name is located. The search must begin at the tree structure for the last block to be entered (i.e., begin with the tree to which the top-most block index element points), and proceed to the tree for the first block to be entered (i.e., end with the tree to which the bottom-most block index element points). This ensures that the most recent declaration for a variable is found first.

In order to simplify the SET, RESET, and SYMBOL_TABLE algorithms, we will assume the form of the input is as follows:

```
1□A□B□C
   2□X□Y□Z
      3□E□A□N
   2□P□Q□R□D
```

where the numbers indicate the block number and the letters represent the variable names at this level.

Two stacks are needed to maintain a stack-implemented tree-structured symbol table. BLOCK_INDEX is a stack of pointers which point to the root nodes of the separate symbol table trees. LEVEL_INDEX is a parallel stack used to keep track of the level numbers of those symbol trees already created.

A general algorithm for controlling the creation of stack-implemented tree-structured symbol tables is as follows.

1.  Initialize the stacks
2.  Repeat thru step 7 while there remains data
3.  Skip over initial blanks and remove level number from input line
4.  Repeat step 5 while level number remains ≤ stacked level number
5.  Pop symbol table off stack
6.  Push new symbol table on stack
7.  Insert all variables for this block in current symbol table

The set procedure is now introduced.

**Procedure** SET(DEPTH, STRING, BLOCK_INDEX, LEVEL_INDEX, TOP).  This procedure creates a root node for a new lexically ordered binary tree and stores its address in the stack, BLOCK_INDEX. STRING is the input name stripped of preceding and following blanks, and DEPTH is the level number of the new symbol table. NODE is the structure introduced earlier. The stack manipulating routine PUSH is used. TOP is the stack index.

1.  [Create root node for tree]
        NEW ⇐ NODE
        NAME(NEW) ← STRING
        Call PUSH(BLOCK_INDEX, TOP, NEW)
        Call PUSH(LEVEL_INDEX, TOP, DEPTH)

2.   [Set links]
         LPTR(NEW) ← RPTR(NEW) ← NULL

3.   [Finish]
         Return                                                                     ☐

The reset operation is invoked when an input level number is less than the previous level number. This procedure is now introduced.

**Procedure** RESET(BLOCK_INDEX, LEVEL_INDEX TOP). This procedure is invoked when a program block has been completely processed and is no longer needed. BLOCK_INDEX contains the pointers to the roots of the symbol table trees and LEVEL_INDEX holds the level numbers of those trees. The stack routine POP is used, with TOP representing the stack index. X and Y are temporary variables.

1.   [Remove current symbol table tree]
         X ← POP(BLOCK_INDEX, TOP)
         Y ← POP(LEVEL_INDEX, TOP)
2.   [Finished]
         Return                                                                     ☐

The only remaining algorithm necessary to the stack-implemented symbol table is the main routine which controls those algorithms already discussed.

**Algorithm** SYMBOL_TABLE. This algorithm controls the creation of a stack-implemented tree-structured symbol table using the SET, RESET, and TABLE routines. IN is a logical value returned from function TABLE. TOP is the stack index.

1.   [Initialize stacks]
         TOP ← 0
         Call PUSH(BLOCK_INDEX, TOP, NULL)
         Call PUSH(LEVEL_INDEX, TOP, 0)
2.   [Process each input line]
         Repeat thru step 6 while there still remains data
3.   [Input current symbol table]
         Read(INPUT)
4.   [Skip over initial blanks]
         LEVEL ← SUB(INPUT, 1, 1)
         Repeat while LEVEL = '☐'
             INPUT ← SUB(INPUT, 2)
             LEVEL ← SUB(INPUT, 1, 1)
5.   [Create or destroy symbol tables]
         Repeat while LEVEL ≤ LEVEL_INDEX[TOP]   (remove symbol tables)
             Call RESET(BLOCK_INDEX, LEVEL_INDEX, TOP)
         CHAR ← SUB(INPUT, 3, 1)   (remove first variable name)
         INPUT ← SUB(INPUT, 5)
         Call SET(LEVEL, CHAR, BLOCK_INDEX, LEVEL_INDEX, TOP)
6.   [Insert remaining variables for this block]
         CHAR ← SUB(INPUT, 1, 1)
         INPUT ← SUB(INPUT, 3)

```
            Repeat while CHAR ≠ '□'
                IN ← TABLE(BLOCK_INDEX, LEVEL, true, CHAR, '□')
                If not IN   (duplicate entry)
                then   Write('VARIABLE IS ALREADY AT THIS LEVEL')
                CHAR ← SUB(INPUT, 1, 1)
                INPUT ← SUB(INPUT, 3)
    7.   [Finish]
            Exit                                                    □
```

The algorithm is fairly simple to understand. In step 1, the stacks are initialized. The next step is the main input loop which continues while there remains data. Step 3 inputs a list of names for the current symbol table. Step 4 removes all leading blanks from the input line. In step 5, the current level number is compared to the top level number on the stack (the previous level). If the current block level is less than or equal to the previous block level, then symbol tables must be removed using RESET until the appropriate level is reached. If the new block level is greater than the level number on the top of the stack, no symbol tables are removed. In all cases, a new symbol table is formed by a call to SET. In step 6 the remaining symbols in the input line are then added to the symbol table.

### Exercises for Sec. 5-2.2

1.   Trace Function TABLE using as data the following set of names: DO, ELSE, GET, PUT, THEN, DECLARE, FIXED, FLOAT, BINARY, CHARACTER, BASED, and POINTER.
2.   Write a Pascal function for Function TABLE and use the data of Prob. 1 to verify your program.
3.   Develop an algorithm LOOKUP which examines a stack-implemented tree-structured symbol table to determine if a variable is present in the entire structure.

### 5-2.3  Syntax Analysis

In Sec. 2-3 the notions of a grammar as a mathematical system for defining languages and as a device for giving some useful structure to sentences of a language were discussed. Also, the problem of obtaining a parse for a particular sentence of a language was introduced. Recall that a parse consisted of finding a sequence of productions that would generate a given sentence from the starting symbol of the grammar. The concept of a syntax tree and its relationship to the parse of a sentence of a language were mentioned briefly. The syntax tree (or derivation) corresponding to a sentence of a language could be found in a top-down or bottom-up manner.

This section deals with the use of grammars in syntax analysis or parsing. We will therefore be concerned with the syntax-recognition phase of the compiler. The data structure which is central to syntax analysis is the syntax tree. From such a tree and its semantics can be derived object code for a sentence. Furthermore, a syntax tree is a convenient representation which can be used in the derivation of many important relations for certain classes of grammars.

Initially, the important concept of syntactic ambiguity and its relationship to the parsing problem are mentioned. Next, the top-down method of parsing introduced earlier is discussed in more detail. The approach that is used is informal and

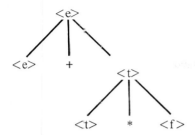

**FIGURE 5-2.12**   Syntax tree for
<expr> + <term> * <factor>
in $G_1$.

very general, but also very slow because of all the backtracking or backup that must be performed. Certain improvements are suggested which can eliminate, for certain grammars, the amount of backtracking that is required. Finally, this modified top-down method of parsing is given in an algorithmic description.

As we previously discussed in Sec. 2-3, syntax trees are an important aid to understanding the syntax of a sentence  A syntax tree for a sentence of some language has a distinguished node called its *root* which is labeled by the starting symbol of the grammar. The leaf nodes of the syntax tree represent the terminal symbols in the sentence being diagrammed. All nonleaf nodes correspond to nonterminal symbols. Each nonterminal node has a number of branches emanating downward, each of which represents a symbol in the right side of the production being applied at that point in the syntax tree.

More generally, any sentential form can have a syntax tree. The leaf nodes in such a tree can designate terminal and nonterminal symbols. Let A be the root of a subtree for a sentential form $\sigma = \phi_1 \beta \phi_2$, where $\beta$ forms the string of leaf nodes emanating from that subtree. Then, $\beta$ is the phrase for A of the sentential form $\sigma$. $\beta$ is a simple phrase if the subtree whose root is A consists of the application of the single production $A \rightarrow \beta$.

Consider the example grammar

$G_1 = (\{<expr>, <factor>, <term>\}, \{i, +, *, (, )\}, <expr>, \Phi)$

where $\Phi$ consists of the productions

    <factor> ::= i | (<expr>)
    <term> ::= <factor> | <term> * <factor>
    <expr> ::= <term> | <expr> + <term>

and i stands for an identifier or variable name. The syntax tree for the sequential form <expr> + <expr> * <factor> is given in Fig. 5-2.12, where <expr> + <term> * <factor> and <term> * <factor> are its phrases, while <term> * <factor> is a simple phrase.

An important question which arises in formal languages is whether a sentential form has a unique syntax tree. Consider the simple grammar $G_2$ which has the following productions:

    S ::= S * S
    S ::= a

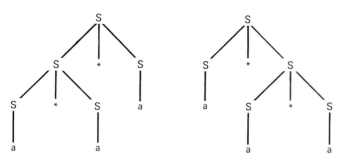

**FIGURE 5-2.13**   Two distinct syntax trees for the sentence
a * a * a in $G_2$.

where a is a terminal symbol. Let us find a derivation for the sentence a * a * a.
One such derivation is

$$S \Rightarrow S * S \Rightarrow S * S * S \Rightarrow a * S * S \Rightarrow a * a * S \Rightarrow a * a * a$$

where the left-most S in the second step has been rewritten as S * S. Another possibility, of course, is that the right-most S in the same step is rewritten as S * S.
Both possibilities are diagrammed in Fig. 5-2.13. It is clear that the two syntax trees
are different. That is, we have two different parses for the same sentence. The
existence of more than one parse for some sentence in a language can cause a compiler to generate a different set of instructions (object code) for different parses.
Usually, this phenomenon is intolerable. If a compiler is to perform valid translations of sentences in a language, then that language must be unambiguously defined.
This concept leads to the following definition.

A sentence generated by a grammar is *ambiguous* if there exists more than one
syntax tree for it. A grammar is ambiguous if it generates at least one ambiguous
sentence; otherwise, it is *unambiguous*.

It should be noted that we called the *grammar* ambiguous, and not the
language which it generates. There are many grammars which can generate the
same language; some are ambiguous and some are not. However, there are certain
languages for which no unambiguous grammars can be found. Such languages are
said to be *inherently ambiguous*. For example, the language { $x^i y^j z^k$ | i = j  or j =
k} is an inherently ambiguous context-free language.

The question which naturally arises at this point is: does there exist an algorithm which can accept any context-free grammar and determine, in some finite
time, whether it is ambiguous? The answer is no! A simple set of sufficient conditions can be developed such that when they are applied to a grammar and found to
hold, then the grammar is guaranteed to be unambiguous. We wish to point out
that these conditions are sufficient but not necessary. In other words, even if a
grammar does not satisfy the conditions, it may still be unambiguous.

Let us examine another example of an ambiguous grammar. In particular,
consider the grammar $G_3$ for arithmetic expressions consisting of the operators +
and * with single-letter variables:

<expr> ::= i | <expr> + <expr> | <expr> * <expr> | (<expr>)

Assume that the sentence i + i * i is to be diagrammed. Two possible derivations are as follows:

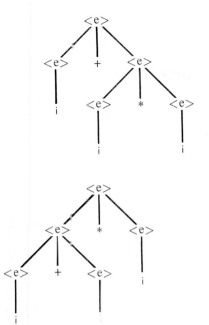

**FIGURE 5-2.14**  Two syntax trees
for i + i * i in $G_3$.

$$
\begin{aligned}
\text{<expr>} &\Rightarrow \text{<expr> + <expr>} \\
&\Rightarrow \text{<expr> + <expr> * <expr>} \\
&\Rightarrow \text{i + <expr> * <expr>} \\
&\Rightarrow \text{i + i * <expr>} \\
&\Rightarrow \text{i + i * i} \\
\text{<expr>} &\Rightarrow \text{<expr> * <expr>} \\
&\Rightarrow \text{<expr> + <expr> * <expr>} \\
&\Rightarrow \text{i + <expr> * <expr>} \\
&\Rightarrow \text{i + i * <expr>} \\
&\Rightarrow \text{i + i * i}
\end{aligned}
$$

Their corresponding syntax trees are given in Fig. 5-2.14. Since there exists two distinct syntax trees for the sentence i + i * i, the grammar is ambiguous. Intuitively, this grammar is ambiguous because it is not known whether to evaluate * before + or conversely. The grammar can be rewritten in such a manner that the multiplication will have precedence over addition. This revision is accomplished in the following grammar $G_4$:

<expr> ::= <term> | <expr> + <term>
<term> ::= <factor> | <term> * <factor>
<factor> ::= i | (<expr>)

Recall from Sec. 2-3 the two methods discussed for constructing a parse tree for a sentence generated by a grammar—namely, bottom-up parsing and top-down parsing. The remaining pages of this section are concerned with giving a more detailed discussion of the top-down method of parsing. The term top-down parsing is derived from the idea that an attempt is made to construct a parse tree for some given input string by starting from the root of the tree and working down to the symbols in the sentence. This task is accomplished by initially numbering in some fashion the different right-hand sides (or alternatives) associated with each metavariable in the grammar. For example, if $S ::= \alpha_1 \mid \alpha_2 \mid \cdots \mid \alpha_n$ are the productions that have the common left-hand side S in the grammar, then we assign some ordering to the alternatives of S (the $\alpha$'s).

As an example, consider the grammar

```
<e> ::= <t> + <e> | <t>
<t> ::= <f> * <t> | <f>
<f> ::= (<e>) | i
```

and let us order them as shown. That is, <t> + <e> is the first alternative for <e>, and <t> is the second; <f> * <t> is the first alternative for <t>, and <f> the second, etc. In the informal discussion of the top-down parsing method which follows, an input pointer that initially points to the left-most symbol of the input string is used.

Recall that a top-down parser tries to construct a syntax tree for the input string in the following manner. Initially, the tree consists of a node labeled S which is called the initial active node of the tree. The following steps are then performed recursively:

1   If the active node denotes a variable A, then we choose its first alternative, say $X_1 X_2 \cdots X_r$ for A and extend the tree by creating r direct descendants for A labeled $X_1 X_2 \cdots X_r$. The symbol $X_1$ is then considered to be the new active node.

2   If the active node denotes a terminal symbol, say a, then it is compared with the current input symbol. If they match, then the node to the immediate right of a is considered to be the new active node and the input pointer is moved one symbol to the right. Otherwise, a return is made to the node where the previous rule was applied, the input pointer is changed when required, and the next alternative is tried. If no such alternative exists, a return to the previous node is made, etc. When such a mismatch occurs, the parser has to backup.

During the parsing process, the leaves of the part of the syntax tree that has been generated so far always match that part of the input string which has been processed.

The informal top-down parsing method given above is very general but can be very time-consuming. A more efficient (though less general) method that does not allow backup can be devised. This method of parsing is known as *recursive descent*. It should be noted, however, that this highly recursive technique does not work on all context-free grammars. That is, certain grammars require backup in order for successful parsing to occur.

In the recursive-descent method of parsing, a sequence of production applications is realized in a sequence of function calls. In particular, functions are written for each nonterminal. Each function returns a value of *true* or *false* depending on whether it recognizes a substring which is an expansion of that nonterminal. The programming mechanism for the handling of recursive function calls provides the stacking capability required, thus freeing the user from having to establish and manipulate a stack explicitly, assuming that the language used supports recursion.

The remainder of this subsection presents an algorithm for the recursive-descent parsing method for the following context-free grammar:

<factor> ::= (<expr>) | i
<term> ::= <factor> * <term> | <factor>
<expr> ::= <term> + <expr> | <term>

Note that the alternatives of <term> and <expr> have been ordered in such a way as to check for the longest alternative first. This approach is important when one alternative is a substring of another alternative and such is the case for the alternatives of both <term> and <expr>.

A recursive-descent parser for this example grammar contains one recursive function for each nonterminal in the grammar (i.e., <factor>, <term>, and <expr>) which parses phrases for that nonterminal. Each function specifies where to begin a search for a phrase of its associated nonterminal. The function looks for a phrase by comparing the input string beginning at a specified point with the alternatives of its associated nonterminal and invoking other functions to recognize the subgoals when required.

The following algorithm and its associated functions parse without any backup the strings of the language described by the example grammar. This is accomplished easily by using one context symbol following the part of the phrase which has already been parsed. The context symbol in question can be either a + or a *. Note that there are four functions, namely, GET_CHAR, EXPR, FACTOR, and TERM. Also note that each function has no parameters or local variables.

**Algorithm** RECDSNT.    This algorithm calls four programmer-defined functions, namely, GET_CHAR, EXPR, FACTOR, and TERM. The first one, GET_CHAR, always returns the next character in the input string, INPUT, and assigns it to the global variable NEXT. CHAR is local to GET_CHAR and contains the value to be returned. The latter three functions are all recursive and return either Boolean *true* or *false*. The variable CURSOR is also global to all routines and denotes the present character position in the input string. The variable I is a local index variable. SUB and LENGTH are built-in string manipulation functions which return a specified substring of a string and the number of characters in a string, respectively.

1.  [Initialize]
        Read(INPUT)
2.  [Loop through all input strings]
        Repeat while there still remains an input string
            Repeat for I = 1, 2, ..., LENGTH(INPUT)
                STRING[I] ← SUB(INPUT, I, 1)
            CURSOR ← 1
            NEXT ← GET_CHAR
            If EXPR
            then    If NEXT = '#'
                    then    Write(INPUT, ' VALID')
                    else    Write(INPUT, ' INVALID')
            else    Write(INPUT, ' INVALID')
            Read(INPUT)
3.  [Finished]
        Exit

**Function** EXPR.

1.  [<expr> ::= <term> + <expr> | <term>]
        If not TERM
        then   Return(false)
        If NEXT = '+'
        then   NEXT ← GET_CHAR
               If  NEXT = '#'
               then   Return(false)
               If not EXPR
               then   Return(false)
               else   Return(true)
        else   Return(true)                                    □


**Function** TERM.

1.  [<term> ::= <factor> * <term> | <factor>]
        If not FACTOR
        then   Return(false)
        If NEXT = '*'
        then   NEXT ← GET_CHAR
               If NEXT = '#'
               then   Return(false)
               If not TERM
               then   Return(false)
               else   Return(true)
        else   Return(true)                                    □


**Function** FACTOR.

1.  [<factor> ::= (<expr >) | i]
        If NEXT = '#'
        then   Return(false)
        If NEXT = '('
        then   NEXT ← GET_CHAR
               If NEXT = '#'
               then   Return(false)
               If not EXPR
               then   Return(false)
               If NEXT ≠ ')'
               then   Return(false)
               else   NEXT ← GET_CHAR
                      Return(true)
        If NEXT ≠ 'i'
        then   Return(false)
        else   NEXT ← GET_CHAR
               Return(true)                                    □

The final function GET_CHAR returns the next character in the input string assigning it to the global variable NEXT.

**Function GET_CHAR**

1. [Returns the next character from the input string]
    CHAR ← STRING[CURSOR]
    CURSOR ← CURSOR + 1
    Return(CHAR)                                                        □

The following points are made concerning the algorithm:

*1*  The variable NEXT is global and contains the next symbol of the input
    string which is being processed. When a function to find a new goal is
    called, the first symbol to be examined is already in NEXT. Similarly,
    before returning from a function after a successful match, the symbol fol-
    lowing the substring found by the function is put into NEXT. Note the
    input string to be parsed is padded on the right with the symbol '#'.
*2*  The function GET_CHAR obtains the next input symbol.
*3*  To begin parsing, the main algorithm invokes the function GET_CHAR
    which in turn places the left-most symbol in the input string in NEXT.

A trace of the parse for the input (i + i) * i# is given in Fig. 5-2.15.

Note that the example grammar used in this subsection has contained right-
recursive rules instead of the more popular and natural left-recursive rules used in
grammars earlier in the text for the same language. A grammar which contains
left-recursive rules causes infinite loops to occur when a top-down method of parsing technique, like the ones introduced in this subsection, is used. For example, a
left-recursive production such as <expr> ::= <expr> + <term> will cause the
parser to try for an <expr> which in turn will cause the parser to try for another
<expr>, etc , resulting in an infinite loop. Such pitfalls can be avoided, but we will
not go into the remedies in this subsection.

**Exercises for Sec. 5-2.3**

1.  Show that the grammar consisting of the rules

    <e> ::= (<e>) | <e> + <e> | <e> - <e> | <e> * <e> | <e> / <e> | i

    is ambiguous by constructing all possible trees for the sentences i + i + i and i
    + i * i

2.  Trace Algorithm RECDSNT (similar to Fig. 5-2.15) in order to parse the string
    (a) i + i * i, (b) i + (i + i), and (c) i * (i + i).

3.  Formulate a grammar for generating the set of parenthesized arithmetic expres-
    sions consisting of the binary operators +, −, *, /, and ↑ (exponentiation), the
    unary minus operator Θ, and the single letter variable i. Write a top-down parser
    based on recursive descent.

4.  Expand the recursive-descent parser given in this subsection to include the divi-
    sion and subtraction operators (i.e , / and −).

5.  The following grammar describes a string manipulation language:

    <string assign> ::= I ← <substr expr>
    <substr expr> ::= <concat expr> ! <position> : <position>
    <concat expr> ::= S | I | S || <concat expr> | I || <concat expr>
    <position> ::= <length expr> | <substr expr> ? <substr expr>
    <length expr> ::= T | @ <substr expr>

| CURSOR | Activity |
|---|---|
| 1 | Perform Main |
| 1 | Call EXPR |
| 1 | Call TERM |
| 1 | Call FACTOR |
| 1 | check for #. No. |
| 1 | check for (. Yes. CURSOR ← 2. |
| 2 | check for #. No. |
| 2 | Call EXPR |
| 2 | Call TERM |
| 2 | Call FACTOR |
| 2 | check for #. No. |
| 2 | check for (. No. |
| 2 | check for i. Yes. CURSOR← 3. |
| 3 | Return true from FACTOR. |
| 3 | check for *. No. |
| 3 | Return true from TERM. |
| 3 | check for +. Yes. CURSOR ← 4 |
| 4 | check for #. No. |
| 4 | Call EXPR |
| 4 | Call TERM |
| 4 | Call FACTOR |
| 4 | check for #. No. |
| 4 | check for (. No. |
| 4 | check for i. Yes. CURSOR ← 5. |
| 5 | Return true from FACTOR. |
| 5 | check for *. No. |
| 5 | Return true from TERM. |
| 5 | Return true from EXPR. |
| 5 | Return true from EXPR. |
| 5 | check for ). Yes. CURSOR ← 6. |
| 6 | Return true from FACTOR. |
| 6 | check for *. Yes. CURSOR ← 7. |
| 7 | check for #. No. |
| 7 | Call TERM |
| 7 | Call FACTOR |
| 7 | check for #. No. |
| 7 | check for (. No. |
| 7 | check for i. Yes. CURSOR ← 8. |
| 8 | Return true from FACTOR. |
| 8 | check for *. No. |
| 8 | Return true from TERM. |
| 8 | Return true from TERM. |
| 8 | check for +. No. |
| 8 | Return true from EXPR. |
| 8 | check for #. Yes. CURSOR ← 9. |
| 9 | Return  VALID  from MAIN. |

**Figure 5-2.15**   Trace of Algorithm RECDSNT for the string (i + i) * i#.

Note that ←, !, ||, ?, @, I (meaning "identifier"), S (meaning "string"), and T (meaning "integer") are all terminals in this grammar. Formulate a recursive-descent parser for this language.

## 5-3 MULTILINKED STRUCTURES

The data structures we have discussed to this point in the text have contained one or two pointer fields. Except for the tree structures, the structures which contained two pointer fields specified the relation of physical adjacency.

In this section we generalize the structures in the sense that more than two pointer fields can be used in the node structure. The first application is concerned with the representation and manipulation of sparse matrices. Section 5-3.2 discusses the problem of generating an index of terms for a book.

### 5-3.1 Sparse Matrices

A useful application of linear lists is the representation of matrices that contain a preponderance of zero elements. These matrices are called *sparse matrices*. They are commonly used in scientific applications and contain hundreds or even thousands of rows and columns. The representation of such large matrices is wasteful of storage, and operations with these matrices are inefficient if the sequential allocation methods of Chap. 3 are used for their storage. In this section we describe a representation of sparse matrices using linked allocation and formulate an input algorithm and a multiplication algorithm for matrices in this form. First, however, a different type of sequential allocation scheme for representing matrices is discussed.

Consider the matrix

$$A = \begin{bmatrix} 0 & 0 & 6 & 0 & 9 & 0 & 0 \\ 2 & 0 & 0 & 7 & 8 & 0 & 4 \\ 10 & 0 & 0 & 0 & 0 & 0 & 0 \\ 0 & 0 & 12 & 0 & 0 & 0 & 0 \\ 0 & 0 & 0 & 0 & 0 & 0 & 0 \\ 0 & 0 & 0 & 3 & 0 & 0 & 5 \end{bmatrix}$$

Of the 42 elements in this $6 \times 7$ matrix, only 10 are nonzero. These are

$A[1, 3] = 6, A[1, 5] = 9, A[2, 1] = 2, A[2, 4] = 7, A[2, 5] = 8,$
$A[2, 7] = 4, A[3, 1] = 10, A[4, 3] = 12, A[6, 4] = 3,$ and $A[6, 7] = 5.$

One of the basic methods for storing such a sparse matrix is to store nonzero elements in a one-dimensional array and to identify each array element with row and column indices, as shown in Fig. 5-3.1a.

The ith element of vector A is the matrix element with row and column indices ROW[i] and COLUMN[i]. Note that the matrix elements are stored in row-major order with zero elements removed. A more efficient representation in terms of storage requirements and access time to the rows of the matrix is shown in Fig. 5-3.1b. The ROW vector is changed so that its ith element is the index to the first of the column indices for the elements in row i of the matrix.

We assume that the ROW and COLUMN vectors consist of half words. The representations of matrix A in Fig. 5-3.1 have cut storage requirements by more than one half. For large matrices the conservation of storage is very significant. The

| | ROW | COLUMN | A |
|---|---|---|---|
| 1 | 1 | 3 | 6 |
| 2 | 1 | 5 | 9 |
| 3 | 2 | 1 | 2 |
| 4 | 2 | 4 | 7 |
| 5 | 2 | 5 | 8 |
| 6 | 2 | 7 | 4 |
| 7 | 3 | 1 | 10 |
| 8 | 4 | 3 | 12 |
| 9 | 6 | 4 | 3 |
| 10 | 6 | 7 | 5 |

(*a*)

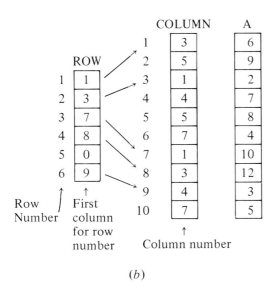

(*b*)

**FIGURE 5-3.1**    Sequential representation of sparse matrices.

sequential-allocation scheme for sparse matrices is also of value in that matrix operations can be executed faster than possible with a conventional two-dimensional array representation, particularly when matrices are large.

A general algorithm for adding two matrices is as follows.

1.  Repeat thru step 8 until all rows have been processed
2.  Obtain current row indices for matrix A and B
3.  Obtain starting position in vectors of next row in matrix A and B
4.  Repeat thru step 6 until either the end of matrix A's or B's row is reached
5.  If elements exist in the same column in matrix A and B

then sum elements and move on to the next column in matrix A and B
else if matrix A column number is less than matrix B's column number
  then move on to the next column in matrix A
  else move on to the next column in matrix B

6. Add new element to matrix C
7. If the end of matrix A's row has not been reached
  then add remaining elements in row to matrix C
8. If the end of matrix B's row has not been reached
  then add remaining elements in row to matrix C

The following detailed algorithm adds two matrices that are represented as in Fig. 5-3.1*b*.

**Algorithm** MATRIX_ADDITION. Given sparse matrices A and B represented by vectors A and B with row and column indices AROW and ACOL BROW and BCOL, respectively, it is required to form the matrix sum C = A + B. C must be represented in the same manner as A and B, so CROW and CCOL are formed. A and B have the same dimensions, M × N, and contain R and S nonzero elements, respectively. The number of nonzero elements in C on completion of the algorithm is T. Auxiliary variable I is used to index the rows of the matrices and J and K index the matrix elements in vectors A and B, respectively. Variables SUM and COLUMN are used to contain each new element for matrix C and its column position.

1. [Initialize]
  I ← 1
  T ← 0
2. [Scan each row]
  Repeat thru step 9 while I ≤ M
3. [Obtain row indices and starting positions of next rows]
  J ← AROW[I]
  K ← BROW[I]
  CROW[I] ← T + 1
  AMAX ← BMAX ← 0
  If I < M
  then Repeat for P = I + 1 I + 2, ..., M while AMAX = 0
     If AROW[P] ≠ 0
     then AMAX ← AROW[P]
    Repeat for P = I+1, +2, ..., M while BMAX = 0
     If BROW[P] ≠ 0
     then BMAX ← BROW[P]
  If AMAX = 0
  then AMAX ← R + 1
  If BMAX = 0
  then BMAX ← S + 1
4. [Scan columns of this row]
  Repeat thru step 7 while J ≠ 0 and K ≠ 0
5. [Elements in same column?]
  If ACOL[J] = BCOL[K]
  then SUM ← A[J] + B[K]

```
                COLUMN ← ACOL[J]
                J ← J + 1
                K ← K + 1
        else    If ACOL[J] < BCOL[K]
                then    SUM ← A[J]
                        COLUMN ← ACOL[J]
                        J ← J + 1
                else    SUM ← B[K]
                        COLUMN ← BCOL[K]
                        K ← K + 1
6.  [Add new elements to sum of matrices]
        If SUM ≠ 0
        then    T ← T + 1
                C[T] ← SUM
                CCOL[T] ← COLUMN
7.  [End of either row?]
        If J = AMAX
        then    J ← 0
        If K = BMAX
        then    K ← 0
8.  [Add remaining elements of a row]
        If J = 0 and K ≠ 0
        then    Repeat while K < BMAX
                        T ← T + 1
                        C[T] ← B[K]
                        CCOL[T] ← BCOL[K]
                        K ← K + 1
        else    If K = 0 and J ≠ 0
                then    Repeat while J < AMAX
                                T ← T + 1
                                C[T] ← A[J]
                                CCOL[T] ← ACOL[J]
                                J ← J + 1
9.  [Adjust index to matrix C and increment row index]
        If T < CROW[I]
        then    CROW[I] ← 0
        I ← I + 1
10. [Finished]
        Exit                                                    □
```

For each pair of corresponding rows in matrices A and B, steps 3 to 9 are executed to add matrix elements from those rows. When J or K is zero, the nonzero elements in the row of matrix A or B, respectively, have all been accounted for. When both J and K are zero, the algorithm can proceed to add the next rows of the matrices. If J or K are not initially zero, they are set to zero when they reach the values AMAX or BMAX, respectively. AMAX and BMAX are the positions in the ACOL and A and BCOL and B vectors where the next row starts. However, if there is no next row, AMAX and BMAX have values $R + 1$ and $S + 1$, respectively (see steps 3 and 7).

Steps 5 to 7 inclusive perform the required additions of matrix elements. A number of different cases arise, depending on whether the row of one matrix has

MATRIX ELEMENT

**FIGURE 5-3.2**    Node structure for linked-allocation representation of a sparse matrix.

been completely scanned, the column indices are equal, or one column index is less than the other. Step 6 checks for an element having a value of zero before adding it to matrix C. If no elements are added to row I of matrix C, then CROW[I] is set to zero in step 9

Sequential-allocation schemes for representing sparse matrices generally allow faster execution of matrix operations and are more storage efficient than linked-allocation schemes. Representing sparse matrices sequentially, however, has the shortcomings we have discussed earlier. The insertion and deletion of matrix elements necessitates the displacement of many other elements. In situations where insertions and deletions are common, a linked-allocation scheme such as described in the following discussion should be adopted.

A basic node structure called MATRIX_ELEMENT as depicted in Fig. 5-3.2 is required to represent sparse matrices. The V, R, and C fields of one of these nodes contain the value, row, and column indices, respectively, of one matrix element. The fields LEFT and UP are pointers to the next element in a circular list containing matrix elements for a row or column, respectively. LEFT points to the node with the next smallest column subscript, and UP points to the node with the next smallest row subscript. A multilinked structure that uses nodes of this type to represent the matrix A described previously in this section is given in Fig. 5-3.3.

A circular list represents each row and column. A column's list can share nodes with one or more of the rows' lists. Each row and column list has a head node such that more efficient insertion and deletion algorithms can be implemented. The head node of each row list contains 0 in the C field; similarly, the head node of each column list has 0 in the R field. The row head nodes are pointed to by respective elements in the array of pointers AROW. Elements of ACOL point to the column head nodes. A row or column without nonzero elements is represented by a head node whose LEFT or UP field points to itself

The pointers in this multilinked structure arouse suspicion because they point up and to the left. In scanning a circular list we therefore encounter matrix elements in order of decreasing row or column subscripts. This approach is used to simplify the insertion of new nodes to the structure. We assume that new nodes being added to a matrix are usually ordered by ascending-row subscript and ascending-column subscript. If this is the case, a new node is inserted following the head node all the time and no searching of the list is necessary. This is illustrated by the matrix multiplication algorithm at the end of this section.

A general algorithm to construct a multilinked representation of a sparse matrix is now presented.

1. Allocate and initialize head nodes for matrix
2. Repeat thru step 6 until there is no more input
3. Read new column, row, and value information
4. Allocate and initialize a new node
5. Find position for new node in row list and insert node in list
6. Find position for new node in column list and insert node in list

We now present a detailed algorithm for constructing a multilinked structure representing a matrix, as exhibited in Fig. 5-3.3. It is assumed that input records for the algorithm consist of row, column, and nonzero matrix-element values in arbitrary order. No duplicate elements are input to the algorithm.

**Algorithm** CONSTRUCT_MATRIX. It is required to form a multilinked representation of a matrix using the MATRIX_ELEMENT node structure previously described. The matrix dimensions M and N, representing the number of rows and number of columns, respectively, are known before execution of the algorithm. Arrays AROW and ACOL contain pointers to the head nodes of the circular lists. X and Y are used as auxiliary pointers. A row index, column index, and value of a matrix element are read into variables ROW, COLUMN, and VALUE, respectively.

1. [Initialize matrix structures]
       Repeat for I = 1, 2, ..., M
           AROW[I] ⇐ MATRIX_ELEMENT
           C(AROW[I]) ← 0
           LEFT(AROW[I]) ← AROW[I]
       Repeat for I = 1, 2, ..., N
           ACOL[I] ⇐ MATRIX_ELEMENT
           R(ACOL[I]) ← 0
           UP(ACOL[I]) ← ACOL[I]
2. [Loop until there is no more input]
       Repeat thru step 6 until input records are exhausted
3. [Obtain the next matrix element]
       Read(ROW, COLUMN, VALUE)
4. [Allocate and initialize a node]
       P ⇐ MATRIX_ELEMENT
       R(P) ← ROW
       C(P) ← COLUMN
       V(P) ← VALUE
5. [Find new node's position in row list]
       Q ← AROW[R(P)]
       Repeat while C(P) < C(LEFT(Q))
           Q ← LEFT(Q)
       LEFT(P) ← LEFT(Q)
       LEFT(Q) ← P
6. [Find new node's position in column list]
       Q ← ACOL[C(P)]
       Repeat while R(P) < R(UP(Q))
           Q ← UP(Q)
       UP(P) ← UP(Q)
       UP(Q) ← P
7. [Finished]
       Exit                                                             □

In step 1 of Algorithm CONSTRUCT_MATRIX, the required head nodes are allocated and initialized. For each ROW, COLUMN, and VALUE triplet subsequently read, a node is allocated and initialized. Steps 5 and 6 insert the new node in the appropriate row and column lists, respectively.

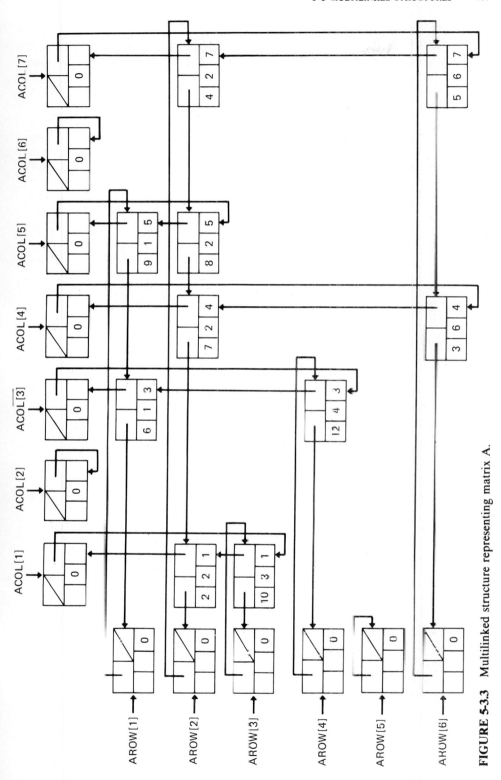

**FIGURE 5-3.3**  Multilinked structure representing matrix A.

We now formulate an algorithm for multiplying two matrices, as represented in Fig. 5-3.3. When two matrices A and B are multiplied to form matrix C, that is, C = A × B, it is necessary that the number of columns in A equal the number of rows in B. If A has m rows and n columns, and B has n rows and t columns, then the product matrix C will have m rows and t columns. The elements of the matrix C are

$$C[i, j] = \sum_{k=1}^{n} (A[i, k] * B[k, j]) \qquad 1 \le i \le m, 1 \le j \le t$$

A general algorithm to perform matrix multiplication with multilinked structures is as follows.

1. Allocate and initialize head nodes for matrix C
2. Repeat thru step 6 for each row of matrix A
3. Repeat thru step 6 for each column of matrix B
4. Repeat step 5 until either the end of a row list or a column list is reached
5. If the current column number of matrix A is greater than the current row number of matrix B
   then obtain next left column in matrix A
   else if current row number of matrix B is greater than the current column number of matrix A
      then obtain the next higher row in matrix B
      else update the product
         obtain the next left column in matrix A and the next higher row in matrix B
6. If the product is not equal to zero
   then allocate and initialize a new node
      insert the node in matrix C

A detailed algorithm for this function is now presented.

**Algorithm** MATRIX_MULTIPLICATION. Given the pointer arrays AROW, ACOL, BROW and BCOL pointing to multilinked representations of sparse matrices A and B with dimensions M × N and N × T, respectively, it is required to form the representation of the product matrix C = A × B. Pointer arrays CROW and CCOL are used to point to rows and columns of the matrix C, which has dimensions M × T. Variables I and J are used to count the rows of matrix A and the columns of matrix B, respectively. A and B are used as pointers for scanning the rows of matrix A and columns of matrix B. P is an auxiliary pointer.

1. [Set up head nodes for row lists]
   Repeat for I = 1, 2, ..., M
      CROW[I] ⇐ MATRIX_ELEMENT
      C(CROW[I]) ← 0
      LEFT(CROW[I]) ← CROW[I]
2. [Set up head nodes for column lists]
   Repeat for J = 1, 2, ..., T
      CCOL[J] ⇐ MATRIX_ELEMENT
      R(CCOL[J]) ← 0
      UP(CCOL[J]) ← CCOL[J]

3.  [Use M rows of matrix A]
       Repeat thru step 7 for I = 1, 2, ..., M
4.  [Use T columns of matrix B]
       Repeat thru step 7 for J = 1, 2, ..., T
5.  [Initialize for scanning row I of matrix A and column J of matrix B]
       A ← LEFT(AROW[I])
       B ← UP(BCOL[J])
       PRODUCT ← 0
6.  [Move pointers as necessary and multiply matching elements]
       Repeat while R(B) ≠ 0 and C(A) ≠ 0
          If C(A) > R(B)
          then   A ← LEFT(A)
          else   If R(B) > C(A)
                 then   B ← UP(B)
                 else   PRODUCT ← PRODUCT + V(A) * V(B)
                        A ← LEFT(A)
                        B ← UP(B)
7.  [If product is nonzero add it to matrix C]
       If PRODUCT ≠ 0
       then   P ⇐ MATRIX_ELEMENT
              R(P) ← I
              C(P) ← J
              V(P) ← PRODUCT
              LEFT(P) ← LEFT(CROW[I])
              UP(P) ← UP(CCOL[J])
              LEFT(CROW[I]) ← P
              UP(CCOL[J]) ← P
8.  [Finished]
       Exit                                                   □

Steps 1 and 2 initialize the head nodes for the product matrix C. Steps 3 and 4 provide the repetitions necessary to multiply each row of matrix A by each column of matrix B in steps 5 to 7, inclusively. Step 5 initializes pointers A and B to scan the circular lists of row I of matrix A and column J of matrix B, respectively. The variable PRODUCT is initialized in this step, and it will be used to total the products of corresponding row and column elements.

In step 6, note that row I and column J are being scanned in order of decreasing column and row subscripts, respectively. If the column subscript and row subscript of the nodes pointed to by A and B, respectively, are not equal, then one pointer is moved to the next node in the circular list. If those row and column subscripts are equal, however, then the variable PRODUCT is updated and both pointers A and B are changed to point to the next elements in each list. When the head node in either list is reached, the required product of row I and column J has been computed.

Step 7 allocates and initializes a new node if PRODUCT is nonzero. Because rows and columns are being scanned according to increasing subscript values, and because pointers in the nodes point left and up in the list structure, the new node can be inserted as successor to the head nodes of row I and column J.

A Pascal implementation of Algorithm MATRIX_MULTIPLICATION as a procedure is given in Fig. 5-3.4. An intermediate assignment to an element pointer must first be made.

{ This procedure multiplies two sparse matrices represented by multilinked }
{ structures. Matrices A and B with dimensions m × n and n × t }
{ respectively are multiplied to form matrix C with dimensions m × t. }
{ Matrix has been declared to be type array of pointers to a structure as }
{ described previously in this section. }

**procedure** matrixmult(**var** arow, acol, brow, bcol, crow, ccol: matrix;
                             m, n, t: integer);

**var** i, j, product: integer;
    a, b, p: pointer;

**begin**
    { Allocate row head nodes}
    **for** i := 1 **to** m **do**
        **begin**
            new(p);
            p↑.c := 0;
            p↑.left := p;
            crow[i] := p
        **end**;

    { Allocate column head nodes }
    **for** j := 1 **to** t **do**
        **begin**
            new(p);
            p↑.r := 0;
            p↑.up := p;
            ccol[j] := p
        **end**;

    **for** i := 1 **to** m **do**
        { scan rows of matrix A }
        **begin**
            **for** j := 1 **to** t **do**
                { scan column of matrix B }
                **begin**
                    { Initialize for scanning row i of matrix A
                      and column j of matrix B }
                    a := arow[i]↑.left;
                    b := bcol[j]↑.up;
                    product := 0;

                    { move pointers as necessary and
                      multiply matching elements }
                    **while** (b↑.r <> 0) **and** (a↑.c <> 0) **do**
                        **begin**
                            **if** a↑.c > b↑.r
                            **then** a := a↑.left

**FIGURE 5-3.4**    Pascal procedure for Algorithm MATRIX_MULTIPLICATION.

```
                    else if b↑.r > ε↑.c
                        then b := b↑.up
                        else begin
                                product := product + a↑.v * b↑.v;
                                a := a↑.left;
                                b := b↑.up
                            end
                end;

            if product <> 0
            then { then add it to matrix C }
                begin
                    new(p);
                    p↑.r := i;
                    p↑.c := j;
                    p↑.v := product;
                    p↑.left := crow[i]↑.left;
                    p↑.up := ccol[j]↑.up;
                    crow[i]↑.left := p;
                    ccol[j]↑.up := p;
                end
        end
    end
end; { matrixmult }
```

**FIGURE 5-3.4** (continued)

---

**Exercises for Sec. 5-3.1**

1. Write and test a computer program for Algorithm MATRIX_ADDITION. Trace this algorithm for matrix A given at the beginning of this section and the matrix

$$B = \begin{bmatrix} 0 & 0 & 0 & 4 & 0 & 0 & 1 & 0 \\ 9 & 0 & 0 & 0 & 0 & 0 & 0 & 3 \\ 0 & 0 & 0 & 0 & 0 & 0 & 0 & 0 \\ 0 & 6 & 7 & 8 & 0 & 0 & 0 & 0 \\ 20 & 0 & 0 & 0 & 0 & 0 & 2 & 0 \\ 0 & 0 & 0 & 0 & 1 & 0 & 0 & 0 \\ 5 & 7 & 0 & 0 & 0 & 13 & 0 & 0 \end{bmatrix}$$

   with the last row and last column deleted.
2. Program Algorithm CONSTRUCT_MATRIX in Pascal.
3. Trace Algorithm MATRIX_MULTIPLICATION using matrix A and matrix B given in Prob. 1.
4. Create an algorithm to multiply two matrices using the vector representation of a matrix.
5. Develop an algorithm for adding two matrices using the multilinked representation for the matrices.
6. Obtain an algorithm that will form the transpose of a sparse matrix, assuming a multilinked representation.

**5-3.2  Index Generation**

When writing a book we are confronted with the task of compiling an index. In the index, the major terms used throughout the book must be presented in lexical order. Several subterms may be associated with a major term and are written in lexical order immediately following that major term. Also, each subterm could have its own subterms, which we will refer to as sub2terms. Each major term, subterm, and sub2term is followed by a set of numbers that identifies the pages where the corresponding term is discussed. In this section, algorithms are presented that process a number of arbitrarily ordered major terms, subterms, and sub2terms, and their associated page numbers in a book, and subsequently print the required index.

The data to be processed must be presented to the algorithm in a standard format. It is convenient to adopt a BNF notation, discussed in Sec. 2-3, for the description of this format. A <term> is a string of any characters, excluding #, %, and @. In most cases <term> consists of alphabetic characters. Using <term> we can describe the input format as follows:

<page number> ::= 1 | 2 | 3 | ... | n − 2 | n − 1 | n
(We assume the book has n pages)
<major term> ::= <term>
<major term string> ::= <major term> |
                           <major term string> @ <page number>
<subterm string> ::= #<term> | <subterm string> @ <page number>
<sub2term string> ::= %<term> | <sub2term string> @ <page number>
<major, subterm and sub2term string> ::= <major term> <subterm string>
                                                   <sub2term string>

One <major term string>, <subterm string>, <sub2term string>, or <major, subterm, and sub2term string> is input to the index-generation algorithm at a time. A <subterm string> always corresponds to the <major term> most recently encountered in the input. A <sub2term string> always corresponds to the <major term> and <subterm string> encountered last.

As an example, some input strings may be

OBJECT CODE@483@478@484
#OPTIMIZATION@531
OBJECT CODE#GENERATION@549@539
OBJECT CODE#GENERATION%PDP/11@496

Subterms OPTIMIZATION and GENERATION correspond to the major term OBJECT CODE. Sub2term PDP/11 corresponds to the subterm GENERATION and the major term OBJECT CODE.

In order to print the required index, the index must first be represented in computer memory. A multilinked structure with three types of nodes is used for this purpose. Such a structure is illustrated in Fig. 5-3.5.

To each major term there corresponds a node with four fields that we describe as MAJORNODE. The major term name is stored in the field TERM. The field MJLINK is a pointer to the node containing the next major term in a sequence of increasing major terms (according to the computer's collating sequence). MJPAGE is a pointer to a linked linear list of page numbers where the major term is discussed. SUBLIST is a pointer to a linked linear list consisting of nodes, each of which is denoted as SUBNODE.

In each SUBNODE, the field SUBTM contains a term which is subsidiary to the major term in the MAJORNODE predecessor. SUBLINK points to the next

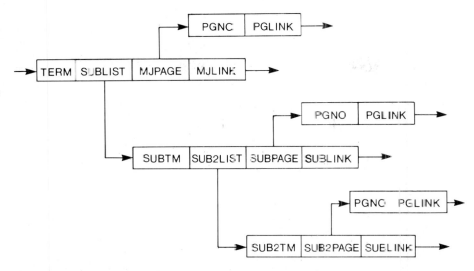

**FIGURE 5-3.5** Multilinked structure for representation of an index.

SUBNODE. This linked linear list containing subterms is ordered according to the increasing lexical value of subterms. SUBPAGE is a pointer to a linked linear list of page numbers where the subterm is discussed. SUB2LIST is a pointer to a linked linear list consisting of nodes, each of which is denoted as SUB2NODE.

In each SUB2NODE, the field SUB2TM contains a term which is subsidiary to the subterm in the SUBNODE predecessor. SUB2LINK points to the next SUB2NODE. This linked linear list containing sub2terms is also ordered according to the increasing value of its sub2terms. SUB2PAGE is a pointer to a linked list of page numbers where the sub2term is discussed.

The lists of page numbers consist of nodes, each of which is a PAGENODE. The field PGNO contains a page number for the predecessor major term or subterm. PGLINK is a pointer to the next PAGENODE. The nodes are ordered according to increasing page numbers.

Using these node structures, we can represent the major term OBJECT CODE and its subterms and sub2terms as in Fig. 5-3.6.

Algorithms are required for allocating and initializing the node structures MAJORNODE SUBNODE, SUB2NODE, and PAGENODE.

**Function** ALLOCATE_MJ(MAJORTERM). Given a major term, MAJORTERM, it is required to allocate a MAJORNODE structure and initialize the TERM field to MAJORTERM and all pointer fields to NULL. P is a local pointer variable.

1. [Allocate a node]
   P ⇐ MAJORNODE
2. [Initialize a new node]
   TERM(P) ← MAJORTERM
   SUBLIST(P) ← MJPAGE(P) ← MJLINK(P) ← NULL
3. [Return pointer to new node]
   Return(P)                                                    □

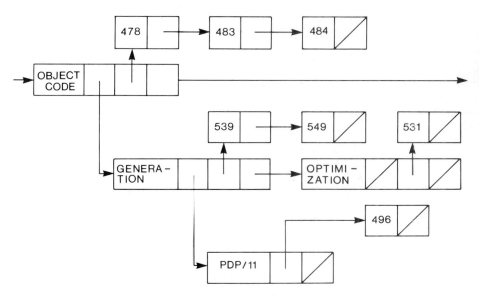

**FIGURE 5-3.6**    Representation of OBJECT CODE and its subterms.

**Function** ALLOCATE_SUB(SUBTERM). Given a subterm, SUBTERM, it is required to allocate a SUBNODE structure and initialize the SUBTM field to SUB-TERM and the pointer fields to NULL. P is a local pointer variable.

1. [Allocate a node]
   P ⇐ SUBNODE
2. [Initialize new node]
   SUBTM(P) ← SUBTERM
   SUB2LIST(P) ← SUBPAGE(P) ← SUBLINK(P) ← NULL
3. [Return pointer to new node]
   Return(P)                                                     □

**Function** ALLOCATE_SUB2(SUB2TERM). Given a sub2term, SUB2TERM, it is required to allocate a SUB2NODE structure and initialize the SUB2TM field to SUB2TERM and the pointer fields to NULL. P is a local pointer variable.

1. [Allocate a node]
   P ⇐ SUB2NODE
2. [Initialize new node]
   SUB2TM(P) ← SUB2TERM
   SUB2PAGE(P) ← SUB2LINK(P) ← NULL
3. [Return pointer to new node]
   Return(P)                                                     □

**Function** ALLOCATE_PG(PAGE). Given PAGE, a page number, it is required to allocate a PAGENODE structure and to initialize its fields. P is a local pointer variable.

1.  [Allocate a node]
        P ⇐ PAGENODE
2.  [Initialize new node]
        PGNO(P) ← PAGE
        PGLINK(P) ← NULL
3.  [Return pointer to new node]
        Return(P)                                                    ☐

These four algorithms are invoked using the assignments

        PTR ← ALLOCATE_MJ(MAJORTERM)
        PTR ← ALLOCATE_SUB(SUBTERM)
        PTR ← ALLOCATE_SUB2(SUB2TERM)
        PTR ← ALLOCATE_PG(PAGE)

In all cases, the address of the node allocated and initialized is assigned to PTR.

When sub2terms, subterms, and major terms are input to the algorithms for
index generation, it is possible that duplicate terms will be encountered. In these
situations, an existing list of page numbers must be updated. The following algorithm does this, and it also has the capability to construct a new list of page
numbers.


**Procedure** PAGING(PAGEPTR, PAGES).  Given PAGEPTR, a pointer to a linear
list of page numbers that is possibly empty, it is required to add to this list any page
numbers from the string PAGES that are not in the list. It is assumed that PAGES
has the form

        PAGES ::= <page number> | PAGES @ <page number> | ''

P is an auxiliary variable used to index the '@' delimiters. PAGE contains a page
number which is a candidate for insertion into the linked list.

1.  [All page numbers processed?]
        Repeat thru step 3 while PAGES ≠ ''
2.  [Obtain a page number]
        P ← NDEX(PAGES, '@' )
        If P = 0
        then   PAGE ← PAGES
               PAGES ← ''
        else   PAGE ← SUB(PAGES, 1, P − 1)
               PAGES ← SUB(PAGES, P + 1)
3.  [Process this page]
        If PAGEPTR = NULL   (Empty linear list?)
        then   PAGEPTR ← ALLOCATE_PG(PAGE)
        else   If PAGE < PGNO(PAGEPTR)   (Should PAGE be first in list?)
               then   SAVE ← ALLOCATE_PG(PAGE)
                      PGLINK(SAVE) ← PAGEPTR
                      PAGEPTR ← SAVE
               else   SAVE ← PAGEPTR (Get first node)
                      (Not duplicate page number?)
                      Repeat while PAGE ≠ PGNO(SAVE)

(End of list?)
If PGLINK(SAVE) = NULL
then    PGLINK(SAVE) ← ALLOCATE_PG(PAGE)
        Exitloop
else    LAST ← SAVE
        (Get next node)
        SAVE ← PGLINK(SAVE)
        (Should a new node precede SAVE node?)
        If PAGE < PGNO(SAVE)
        then    PGLINK(LAST) ← ALLOCATE_PG(PAGE)
                PGLINK(PGLINK(LAST)) ← SAVE
                Exitloop

4.   [Finished]
     Return                                                             □

In Algorithm PAGING, '' denotes the null string. In step 2, the first page number in the string PAGES is obtained and deleted from PAGES. Step 3 scans the list referenced by PAGEPTR and inserts a node containing PAGE in its proper position according to an ascending sequence of page numbers. If PAGE has previously been added to the list, however, it is ignored and the next page number is processed. This algorithm can be invoked using PAGING(PAGEPTR, PAGES). Changes made to PAGEPTR, PAGES, and also the node structures designated PAGENODE are effective in the algorithm that invokes Algorithm PAGING, because PAGEPTR and PAGES are considered to be passed by name and the PAGENODE structures are global.

We require an algorithm that adds sub2terms to the sub2term list of a subterm. In this algorithm it is also necessary to invoke Algorithm PAGING to construct or update a list of page numbers for a sub2term. A general algorithm to insert a sub2term is now presented.

1.   If the sub2term list is empty
     then insert the sub2term in the list
     else if the sub2term < first sub2term in the sub2term list
          then insert the sub2term at the front of the sub2term list
          else repeat while no duplicate sub2terms are encountered
               if the end of the sub2term list is encountered
               then insert the sub2term at the end of the sub2term list
                    exit the loop
               else if the sub2term < current sub2term being examined
                    then insert the sub2term before the current sub2term
                         exit the loop
2.   Update the page number list

The detailed algorithm is now given.

**Procedure** SUB2_INSERT(SUB2PTR, SUB2TERM, PAGES). Given SUB2PTR, a pointer to a possibly empty linear list of subterm nodes, this algorithm adds SUB2TERM to that list if it was not added previously. Page numbers in the string PAGES are added to the list of page numbers for the subterm using Procedure PAGING.

1.  [Add SUB2TERM to the list]
        If SUB2PTR = NULL  (Is sub2term list empty?)
        then   SUB2PTR ← ALLOCATE_SUB2(SUB2TERM)
               SAVE ← SUB2PTR
        else   (Should sub2term be first in list?)
               If SUB2TERM < SUB2TM(SUB2PTR)
               then   SAVE ← ALLOCATE_SUB2(SUB2TERM)
                      SUB2LINK(SAVE) ← SUB2PTR
                      SUB2PTR ← SAVE
               else   SAVE ← SUB2PTR
                      (Get first node)
                      Repeat while SUB2TERM ≠ SUB2TM(SAVE)
                          If SUB2LINK(SAVE) = NULL   (End of list?)
                          then   SUB2_INK(SAVE)
                                     ← ALLOCATE_SUB2(SUB2TERM)
                                 SAVE ← SUB2LINK(SAVE)
                                 Exitloop
                          else   (Get next node)
                                 LAST ← SAVE
                                 SAVE ← SUB2LINK(SAVE)
                                 (Should a new node precede SAVE node?)
                                 If SUB2TERM < SUB2TM(SAVE)
                                 then   SUB2LINK(LAST)
                                            ← ALLOCATE_SUB2(SUB2TERM)
                                        LAST ← SUB2LINK(LAST)
                                        SUB2LINK(LAST) ← SAVE
                                        SAVE ← LAST
                                        Exitloop
2.  [Update page number list]
        Call PAGING(SUB2PAGE(SAVE), PAGES)
3.  [Finished]
        Return                                                        □

We also require an algorithm that adds subterms to the subterm list of a major
term. In the algorithm it is also necessary to invoke Algorithm PAGING to construct
or update a list of page numbers for a subterm.


**Procedure** SUB_INSERT(SUBPTR, SUBTERM, SUB2TERM, PAGES).  Given
SUBPTR, a pointer to a possibly empty linear list of subterm nodes, this algorithm
adds SUBTERM to the list if it was not added previously.  Page numbers in the
string PAGES are added to the list of page numbers for the subterm using Procedure PAGING.

1.  [Add SUBTERM to the list]
        If SUBPTR = NULL  (Is subterm list empty?)
        then   SUBPTR ← ALLOCATE_SUB(SUBTERM)
               SAVE ← SUBPTR
        else   (Should subterm be first in list?)
               If SUBTERM < SUBTM(SUBPTR)
               then   SAVE ← ALLOCATE_SUB(SUBTERM)
                      SUBLINK(SAVE) ← SUBPTR

             SUBPTR ← SAVE
     else    SAVE ← SUBPTR
             (Get first node)
             Repeat while SUBTERM ≠ SUBTM(SAVE)
                If SUBLINK(SAVE) = NULL    (End of list?)
                then    SUBLINK(SAVE) ← ALLOCATE_SUB(SUBTERM)
                      SAVE ← SUBLINK(SAVE)
                      Exitloop
                else    (Get next node)
                      LAST ← SAVE
                      SAVE ← SUBLINK(SAVE)
                      (Should a new node precede SAVE node?)
                      If SUBTERM < SUBTM(SAVE)
                      then    SUBLINK(LAST)
                             ← ALLOCATE_SUB(SUBTERM)
                         LAST ← SUBLINK(LAST)
                         SUBLINK(LAST) ← SAVE
                         SAVE ← LAST
                         Exitloop
2.    [Update sub2term and page number lists]
       If SUB2TERM ≠ ''
     then    Call SUB2_INSERT(SUB2LIST(SAVE), SUB2TERM, PAGES)
     else    Call PAGING(SUBPAGE(SAVE), PAGES)
3.    [Finished]
       Return                                            □

     This algorithm is invoked using SUB_INSERT(SUBPTR, SUBTERM, SUB2TERM, PAGES). Any changes made to SUBPTR, PAGES, and the node structures are valid in the invoking algorithm, because of call-by-reference argument passing and the globality of the structures.

     The final algorithm necessary for the formation of the index structure can now be presented. It inputs data in the format previously described and determines the major term, subterm, sub2term, and page number components. The list of major terms is constructed by the following algorithm, and Algorithms SUB_INSERT and PAGING are invoked to construct subterm and page number lists.

**Algorithm** CONSTRUCT_INDEX. This algorithm reads one <major term string>, <subterm string>, <sub2term string>, or <major, subterm, and sub2term string> at a time into STRING. STRING is scanned to obtain the components MAJORTERM, SUBTERM, SUB2TERM, and PAGES. The multilinked structure representing the index is constructed. FIRSTMJ is a pointer to the first MAJORNODE in the linear list of major terms; it is initially NULL, but eventually points to an existing index structure. A, B, and C are temporary variables holding positions of special characters in the input line.

1.    [Loop until all input has been exhausted]
       Repeat thru step 8 until input records are exhausted
2.    [Input next input term string]
       Read (STRING)
3.    [Locate special symbols]
       A ← INDEX(STRING, '#')

```
          B ← INDEX(STRING, '%')
          C ← INDEX(STRING, '@')
4.  [Obtain page numbers]
        If C ≠ 0
        then  PAGES ← SUB(STRING, C + 1)
              STRING ← SUB(STRING, 1, C - 1)
        else  PAGES ← ''
5.  [Obtain the sub2term]
        If B ≠ 0
        then  SUB2TERM ← SUB(STRING, B + 1)
              STRING ← SUB(STRING, 1, B - 1)
        else  SUB2TERM ← ''
6.  [Obtain the subterm]
        If A ≠ 0
        then  SUBTERM ← SUB(STRING, A + 1)
              STRING ← SUB(STRING, 1, A - 1)
        else  SUBTERM ← ''
7.  [Obtain the major term]
        If STRING ≠ ''
        then  MAJORTERM ← STRING
              If FIRSTMJ = NULL   (Empty list?)
              then  FIRSTMJ ← ALLOCATE_MJ(MAJORTERM)
                    SAVE ← FIRSTMJ
              else  (Should MAJORTERM be first in list?)
                    If MAJORTERM < TERM(FIRSTMJ)
                    then  SAVE ← ALLOCATE_MJ(MAJORTERM)
                          MJLINK(SAVE) ← FIRSTMJ
                          FIRSTMJ ← SAVE
                    else  SAVE ← FIRSTMJ   (Get first node)
                          (While not a duplicate major term)
                          Repeat while MAJORTERM ≠ TERM(SAVE)
                              If MJLINK(SAVE) = NULL   (End of list?)
                              then  MJLINK(SAVE)
                                        ← ALLOCATE_MJ(MAJORTERM)
                                    SAVE ← MJLINK(SAVE)
                                    Exitloop
                              else  (Get next node)
                                    LAST ← SAVE
                                    SAVE ← MJLINK(SAVE)
                                    (Should a new node precede SAVE node?)
                                    If MAJORTERM < TERM(SAVE)
                                    then  MJLINK(LAST)
                                              ← ALLOCATE_MJ(MAJORTERM)
                                          LAST ← MJLINK(LAST)
                                          MJLINK(LAST) ← SAVE
                                          SAVE ← LAST
                                          Exitloop
8.  [Update subterm and page number lists]
        If SUBTERM ≠ ''
        then  Call SUB_INSERT(SUBLIST(SAVE), SUBTERM, SUB2TERM, PAGES)
        else  Call PAGING(MJPAGE(SAVE), PAGES)
```

9.  [Finished]
        Exit                                                            □

    Steps 1 to 6 of this algorithm breaks the input string into its various components. SAVE is a pointer to a MAJORNODE whose subterm and page number lists are to be updated. SAVE is a local variable, so if no major term is included in the string, SAVE will already have been set on an earlier iteration and will be pointing to the MAJORNODE for the major term recently input. It is assumed that the first input string must have a major term component. Algorithms PAGING, SUB_INSERT, SUB2_INSERT, and CONSTRUCT_INDEX could be made more efficient with certain modifications. Also, different multilinked structures would enable more efficient index construction. Some modifications of these algorithms are suggested in the exercises of this section.

    We now give the algorithms for scanning the multilinked representation of the index and printing the index terms. An example of the output produced by these algorithms for the terms in Figure 5-3.6 is as follows:

> OBJECTCODE, 478, 483, 484
>    GENERATION, 539, 549
>       PDP/11, 496
>    OPTIMIZATION, 531

The first algorithm is a subalgorithm for formatting page numbers.


**Function**  PAGE_STRING(PAGEPTR).  Given PAGEPTR, a pointer to a linked linear list of PAGENODE structures, it is required to form a string PAGES consisting of the page numbers in the list. The numbers are to appear in increasing order from left to right and each number is preceded by ',□'.

1.  [Initialize string and auxiliary pointers]
        PAGES ← ''
        SAVE ← PAGEPTR
2.  [Scan the linear list]
        Repeat step 3 while SAVE ≠ NULL
3.  [Add page number to string]
        PAGES ← PAGES ○ ',□' ○ PGNO(SAVE)
        SAVE ← PGLINK(SAVE)
4.  [Transfer string]
        Return(PAGES)                                                   □

    This function is invoked using PAGE_STRING(PAGEPTR), and a string of page numbers is returned. The following algorithm employs PAGE_STRING for printing the entire index.


**Procedure**  PRINT_INDEX(FIRSTMJ).  Given FIRSTMJ, a pointer to the multilinked structure representing an index, it is required to print the index. SAVE stores the pointer to the current major term being printed. SUBSAVE stores a pointer to the current subterm being printed, and SUB2SAVE stores the pointer to the current sub2term being printed.

1.  [Initialize]
        SAVE ← FIRSTMJ

2. [Scan the major terms]
   Repeat thru step 5 while SAVE ≠ NULL
3. [Write major term]
   Write(TERM(SAVE) ○ PAGE_STRING(MJPAGE(SAVE)))
4. [Write subterms sub2terms]
   SUBSAVE ← SUBLIST(SAVE)
   Repeat while SUBSAVE ≠ NULL
      Write('☐☐☐☐☐' ○ SUBTM(SUBSAVE)
            ○ PAGE_STRING(SUBPAGE(SUBSAVE)))
      SUB2SAVE ← SUB2LIST(SUBSAVE)
      Repeat while SUB2SAVE ≠ NULL
         Write('☐☐☐☐☐☐☐☐☐' ○ SUB2TM(SUB2SAVE)
               ○ PAGE_STRING(SUB2PAGE(SUB2SAVE)))
         SUB2SAVE ← SUB2LINK(SUB2SAVE)
      SUBSAVE ← SUBLINK(SUBSAVE)                               ☐
5. [Update pointer to MAJORNODE structure]
   SAVE ← MJLINK(SAVE)
6. [Finished]
   Return                                                      ☐

The execution of this procedure is simple.  SAVE is used to scan each MAJOR-
NODE, SUBSAVE is used to scan each SUBNODE of a subterm list, and
SUB2SAVE is used to scan each SUB2NODE of a sub2term list.

**Exercises for Sec. 5-3.2**

1. Index terms are often referred to for a range of page numbers, for examples,
   37–41, 29–70, 23–24, etc.  Change Procedure PAGING so that it also accepts
   page numbers of the form

   <page number list> ::= <page number> – <page number>

   For a particular page number list, a page number is a duplicate if it lies in the
   specified range of numbers, for example, 40 is a duplicate page number if
   37–41 is already in the index structure.  Also, modify Function PAGE_STRING
   such that two or more consecutive page numbers in a list are printed as a range
   of numbers.
2. Algorithm CONSTRUCT_INDEX is more efficient if major terms are organized as
   a binary tree.  Modify the algorithm to accomplish this.  Also, change Procedure
   PRINT_INDEX so that it can scan the binary tree of major terms.
3. Suggest and implement error-checking devices for the algorithms in this section.
   In particular, how can input data be validated?

## 5-4 GRAPHS AND THEIR REPRESENTATIONS

A discussion of graph terminology was given in Sec. 5-1.1 where terms such as
graph, node, edge, path, cycle, etc., were introduced.  This section is concerned with
a further discussion of graphs and their representations.

A diagrammatic representation of a graph may have a limited usefulness.
However, such a representation is not feasible when the number of nodes and edges
in a graph is large.  The first subsection presents an alternative method of representing graphs by using matrices.  This method of representation has several advantages.

It is easy to store and manipulate matrices and hence the graphs represented by them in the computer. Certain well-known operations of matrix algebra can be used to obtain paths, cycles, and other characteristics of a graph.

The second subsection deals with the representation of a graph by a list structure. Several programming languages have been developed to allow easy processing of structures similar to those that will be described. The need for list processing arose from the unpredictable nature of the storage requirements of computer programs and data. It is shown that a list structure can be used to represent a directed graph.

The third subsection discusses other representations for graphs. Adjacency lists and edge lists are introduced as alternative representations for graphs. Various computer representations of these storage methods will also be discussed. A sample storage representation for a grammar is given as an example.

The final four subsections give several operations which can be applied to a graph. The first of these, breadth first search (BFS), can be used to find the shortest distance between some node in a graph and all remaining nodes. Depth first search (DFS), to be dealt with in Sec. 5-4.5, is used to determine the cutvertices of a graph. The third subsection introduces the notion of a spanning tree for a graph, which is a tree that contains the minimum number of edges necessary to connect all the nodes of the graph. The final subsection gives an example of a time consuming problem.

A number of applications of graphs and their specific representations are discussed in Sec. 5-5.

### 5-4.1 Matrix Representation of Graphs

Given a simple digraph $G = (V, E)$, it is necessary to assume some kind of ordering of the nodes of a graph in the sense that a particular node is called a first node, another a second node, and so on. A matrix representation of G depends upon the ordering of the nodes.

Let $G = (V, E)$ be a simple digraph in which $V = \{ v_1, v_2, ..., v_n \}$ and the nodes are assumed to be ordered from $v_1$ to $v_n$. An $n \times n$ matrix A whose elements $a_{ij}$ are given by

$$a_{ij} = \begin{cases} 1 \text{ if } (v_i, v_j) \in E \\ 0 \text{ otherwise} \end{cases}$$

is called the *adjacency matrix* of the graph G.

Any element of the adjacency matrix is either 0 or 1. Any matrix whose elements are either 0 or 1 is called a *bit matrix* or a *Boolean matrix*. Note that the ith row in the adjacency matrix is determined by the edges which originate in the node $v_i$. The number of elements in the ith row whose value is 1 is equal to the outdegree of the node $v_i$. Similarly, the number of elements whose value is 1 in a column, say the jth column, is equal to the indegree of the node $v_j$. An adjacency matrix completely defines a simple digraph.

For a given digraph $G = (V, E)$, an adjacency matrix depends upon the ordering of the elements of V. For different orderings of the elements of V we get different adjacency matrices of the same graph G. However, any one of the adjacency matrices of G can be obtained from another adjacency matrix of the same graph by interchanging some of the rows and corresponding columns of the matrix. We shall neglect the arbitrariness introduced in an adjacency matrix because of the ordering of the elements of V. Therefore, any adjacency matrix of the graph will satisfy a

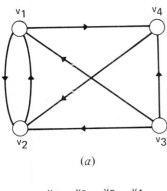

$$\begin{array}{c c} & \begin{array}{cccc} v_1 & v_2 & v_3 & v_4 \end{array} \\ \begin{array}{c} v_1 \\ v_2 \\ v_3 \\ v_4 \end{array} & \left[ \begin{array}{cccc} 0 & 1 & 0 & 1 \\ 1 & 0 & 0 & 0 \\ 1 & 1 & 0 & 1 \\ 0 & 1 & 0 & 0 \end{array} \right] \end{array}$$

(b)

**FIGURE 5-4.1**    A digraph and its adjacency matrix.

given purpose. In fact, if two digraphs are such that the adjacency matrix of one can be obtained from the adjacency matrix of the other by interchanging some of the rows and the corresponding columns, then the digraphs are equivalent.

As an example representation, consider the digraph given in Fig. 5-4.1a in which the order of the nodes is given as $v_1$, $v_2$, $v_3$, and $v_4$. The adjacency matrix for this digraph is given in Fig. 5-4.1b.

We can extend the idea of matrix representation to multigraphs and weighted graphs. For simple undirected graphs, such an extension simply gives a symmetric adjacency matrix. In the case of a multigraph or a weighted graph, we write $a_{ij} = w_{ij}$, where $w_{ij}$ denotes either the multiplicity or the weight of the edge $(v_i, v_j)$. If $(v_i, v_j) \notin E$, then we write $w_{ij} = 0$.

For a null graph which consists of only n nodes but no edges, the adjacency matrix has all its elements zero; i.e., the adjacency matrix is the null matrix. If there are loops at each node but no other edges in the graph, then the adjacency matrix is the identity or the unit matrix.

Let us now consider the powers of an adjacency matrix. Naturally, an entry of 1 in the ith row and jth column of A shows the existence of an edge $(v_i, v_j)$, that is, a path of length 1 from $v_i$ to $v_j$. Let us denote the elements of $A^2$ by $a_{ij}^{(2)}$. Then

$$a_{ij}^{(2)} = \sum_{k=1}^{n} a_{ik} a_{kj}$$

For any fixed k, $a_{ik} a_{kj} = 1$ if and only if both $a_{ik}$ and $a_{kj}$ equal 1; that is, $(v_i, v_k)$ and $(v_k, v_j)$ are the edges of the graph. For each such k we get a contribution of 1 in the sum. Now $(v_i, v_k)$ and $(v_k, v_j)$ imply that there is a path from $v_i$ to $v_j$ of length 2. Therefore, $a_{ij}^{(2)}$ is equal to the number of different paths of exactly length 2 from $v_i$ to $v_j$. Similarly, the diagonal element $a_{ij}^{(2)}$ shows the number of cycles of length 2 at the node for $v_i$ for $i = 1, 2, ..., n$.

By a similar argument, one can show that the element in the ith row and jth column of $A^3$ gives the number of paths of exactly length 3 from $v_i$ to $v_j$. In general, the following statement can be shown:

Let A be the adjacency matrix of a digraph G. The element in the ith row and jth column of $A^n$ $(n > 1)$ is equal to the number of paths of length $n$ from the ith node to the jth node.

The matrices $A^2$, $A^3$, and $A^4$ for the graph given in Fig. 5-4.1 are given as follows:

$$A^2 = \begin{bmatrix} 1 & 1 & 0 & 0 \\ 0 & 1 & 0 & 1 \\ 1 & 2 & 0 & 1 \\ 1 & 0 & 0 & 0 \end{bmatrix} \qquad A^3 = \begin{bmatrix} 1 & 1 & 0 & 1 \\ 1 & 1 & 0 & 0 \\ 2 & 2 & 0 & 1 \\ 0 & 1 & 0 & 1 \end{bmatrix} \qquad A^4 = \begin{bmatrix} 1 & 2 & 0 & 1 \\ 1 & 1 & 0 & 1 \\ 2 & 3 & 0 & 2 \\ 1 & 1 & 0 & 0 \end{bmatrix}$$

For the graph given in Fig. 5-4.1, we see that there are two paths of length 2 from $v_3$ to $v_2$ hence the entry 2 in the third row and second column of $A^2$. Similarly, there are three paths of length 4 from $v_3$ to $v_2$, hence the corresponding entry in $A^4$.

Given a simple digraph $G = (V, E)$, let $v_i$ and $v_j$ be any two nodes of G. From the adjacency matrix of A we can immediately determine whether there exists an edge from $v_i$ to $v_j$ in G. Also from the matrix $A^r$, where $r$ is some positive integer, we can establish the number of paths of length $r$ from $v_i$ to $v_j$. If we add the matrices A, $A^2$, $A^3$, ..., $A^r$ to get $B_r$,

$$B_r = A + A^2 + \cdots + A^r$$

then from the matrix $B_r$ we can determine the number of paths of length less than or equal to $r$ from $v_i$ to $v_j$. If we wish to determine whether $v_j$ is reachable from $v_i$, it would be necessary to investigate whether there exists a path of any length from $v_i$ to $v_j$. In order to decide this, with the help of the adjacency matrix, we would have to consider all possible $A^r$ for $r = 1, 2, ....$ This method is neither practical nor necessary, as we shall now show.

It is easily shown that in a simple digraph with n nodes, the length of an elementary path or cycle does not exceed n. Also, for a path between any two nodes, one can obtain an elementary path by deleting certain parts of the path that are cycles. Similarly (for cycles), we can always obtain an elementary cycle from a given cycle. If we are interested in determining whether there exists a path from $v_i$ to $v_j$, all we need to examine are the elementary paths of length less than or equal to $n - 1$. In the case where $v_i = v_j$ and the path is a cycle, we need to examine all possible elementary cycles of length less than or equal to n. Such cycles or paths are easily determined from the matrix $B_n$ where

$$B_n = A + A^2 + A^3 + \cdots + A^n$$

The element in the ith row and jth column of $B_n$ shows the number of paths of length $n$ or less which exist from $v_i$ to $v_j$. If this element is nonzero, then it is clear than $v_j$ is reachable from $v_i$. Of course, in order to determine reachability, we need to know the existence of a path, and not the number of paths between any two nodes. In any case, then matrix $B_n$ furnishes the required information about the reachability of any node of the graph from any other node.

**Table 5-4.1**

| $\Lambda$ | 0 | 1 | V | 0 | 1 |
|---|---|---|---|---|---|
| 0 | 0 | 0 | 0 | 0 | 1 |
| 1 | 0 | 1 | 1 | 1 | 1 |

Let $G = (V, E)$ be a simple digraph which contains n nodes that are assumed to be ordered. An $n \times n$ matrix P whose elements are given by

$$p_{ij} = \begin{cases} . & \text{if there exists a path from } v_i \text{ to } v_j \\ 0 & \text{otherwise} \end{cases}$$

is called the *path matrix* (*reachability matrix*) of the graph G.

Note that the path matrix only shows the presence or absence of at least one path between a pair of points and also the presence or absence of a cycle at any node. It does not, however, show all the paths that may exist. In this sense a path matrix does not give as complete information about a graph as does the adjacency matrix. The path matrix is important in its own right.

The path matrix can be calculated from the matrix $B_n$ by choosing $p_{ij} = 1$ if the element in the ith row and jth column of $B_n$ is nonzero, and $p_{ij} = 0$ otherwise. We shall apply this method of calculating the path matrix to our sample problem whose graph is given in Fig. 5-4.1. The adjacency matrix A and the powers $A^2$, $A^3$, $A^4$ have already been calculated. We thus have $B_4$ and the path matrix P given by

$$B_4 = \begin{bmatrix} 3 & 5 & 0 & 3 \\ 3 & 3 & 0 & 2 \\ 6 & 8 & 0 & 5 \\ 2 & 3 & 0 & 1 \end{bmatrix} \qquad P = \begin{bmatrix} 1 & . & 0 & 1 \\ 1 & . & 0 & 1 \\ 1 & . & 0 & 1 \\ 1 & . & 0 & 1 \end{bmatrix}$$

It may be remarked here that if we are interested in knowing the reachability of one node from another, it is sufficient to calculate $B_{n-1}$, because a path of length n cannot be elementary. The only difference between P calculated from $B_{n-1}$ and P calculated from $B_n$ is in the diagonal elements. For the purpose of reachability, every node is assumed to be reachable from itself. Some authors calculate the path matrix from $B_{n-1}$, while others do it from $B_n$.

The method of calculating the path matrix P of a graph by calculating first A, $A^2$, ..., $A^n$ and then $B^n$ is cumbersome. We shall now describe another method which is based upon a similar idea but which is more efficient in practice. Observe that we are not interested in the number of paths of any particular length from a node, say $v_i$ to a node $v_j$. This information is obtained during the course of our calculation of the powers of A, and later it is suppressed because these numbers are not needed. This unwanted information is not generated so as to reduce the amount of calculation involved. This is achieved by using Boolean matrix operations in our calculations, which will now be defined. The operators $\Lambda$ and V on E are given in Table 5-4.1. For any two $n \times n$ Boolean matrices A and B, the Boolean sum and

Boolean product of A and B are written as A V B and A ∧ B, which are also Boolean matrices, say C and D. The elements of C and D are given by

$$c_{ij} = a_{ij} \text{ V } b_{ij} \quad \text{and} \quad d_{ij} = \overset{n}{\underset{k=1}{\text{V}}} (a_{ik} \wedge b_{kj}) \quad \text{for all } i,j = 1, 2, ..., n$$

Note that the element $d_{ij}$ is easily obtained by scanning the ith row of A from left to right and simultaneously the jth column of B from top to bottom. If, for any k, the kth element in the row for A and kth element in the column for B are both 1, then $d_{ij} = 1$; otherwise, $d_{ij} = 0$.

The adjacency matrix is a Boolean matrix, and so also is the path matrix. Let us write A ∧ A = $A^{(2)}$, A ∧ $A^{(r-1)}$ = $A^{(r)}$ for any r = 2, 3, .... The only difference between $A^2$ and $A^{(2)}$ is that $A^{(2)}$ is a Boolean matrix and the entry in the ith row and jth column of $A^{(2)}$ is 1 if there is at least one path of length 2 from $v_i$ to $v_j$, while in $A^2$ the entry in the ith row and jth column shows the number of paths of length 2 from $v_i$ to $v_j$. Similar remarks apply to $A^3$ and $A^{(3)}$ or in general $A^r$ and $A^{(r)}$ for any positive integer r. From this description, it is clear that the path matrix P is given by

$$P = A \text{ V } A^{(2)} \text{ V } A^{(3)} \text{ V } \cdots A^{(n)} = \overset{n}{\underset{k=1}{\text{V}}} A^{(k)}$$

If we take the sum $k = 1$ to $k = n - 1$, we get a matrix which may differ (if at all) from P in the diagonal terms only.

For our sample example of the graph given in Fig. 5-4.1, we find

$$A^{(2)} = \begin{bmatrix} 1 & 1 & 0 & 0 \\ 0 & 1 & 0 & 1 \\ 1 & 1 & 0 & 1 \\ 1 & 0 & 0 & 0 \end{bmatrix} \qquad A^{(3)} = \begin{bmatrix} 1 & 1 & 0 & 1 \\ 1 & 1 & 0 & 0 \\ 1 & 1 & 0 & 1 \\ 0 & 1 & 0 & 1 \end{bmatrix} \qquad A^{(4)} = \begin{bmatrix} 1 & 1 & 0 & 1 \\ 1 & 1 & 0 & 1 \\ 1 & 1 & 0 & 1 \\ 1 & 1 & 0 & 0 \end{bmatrix}$$

$$A \text{ V } A^{(2)} \text{ V } A^{(3)} = \begin{bmatrix} 1 & 1 & 0 & 1 \\ 1 & 1 & 0 & 1 \\ 1 & 1 & 0 & 1 \\ 1 & 1 & 0 & 1 \end{bmatrix} = A \text{ V } A^{(2)} \text{ V } A^{(3)} \text{ V } A^{(4)} = P$$

This method of obtaining the path matrix of a simple digraph can easily be computed by using the following algorithm due to Warshall.

**Algorithm WARSHALL.** Given the adjacency matrix A, this algorithm produces the path matrix P.

1. [Initialize]
    P ← A
2. [Perform a pass]
    Repeat thru step 4 for k = 1, 2, ..., n
3. [Process rows]
    Repeat step 4 for i = 1, 2, ..., n
4. [Process columns]
    Repeat for j = 1, 2, ..., n
    $P_{ij} \leftarrow P_{ij} \text{ V } (P_{ik} \wedge P_{kj})$
5. [Finished]
    Exit

□

{ Given the adjacency matrix A, produce the path matrix P. }
{ Matrix is an array of type boolean }

**procedure** warshall(**var** a, p: matrix; n: integer);

    **var**
        k, i, j: integer;

    **begin**
        p := a;
        **for** k := 1 **to** n **do**
            **for** i := 1 **to** n **do**
                **for** j := 1 **to** n **do**
                    p[i, j] := p[i, j] **or** p[i, k] **and** p[k, j]
    **end**; { warshall }

**FIGURE 5-4.2**    Pascal procedure for Algorithm WARSHALL.

To show that this algorithm produces the required matrix, we note that step 1 produces a matrix in which $p_{ij} = 1$ if there is a path of length 1 from $v_i$ to $v_j$. Assume that for a fixed k, the intermediate matrix P produced by steps 3 and 4 of the algorithm is such that the element in the ith row and jth column in this matrix is 1 if and only if there is a path from $v$ to $v_j$ through the nodes $v_1, v_2, \ldots, v_k$, or an edge from $v_i$ to $v_j$. Now with an updated value of k, we find that $p_j = 1$ either if $p_{ij} = 1$ in an earlier step or if there is a path from $v_i$ to $v_j$ which traverses through $v_{k+1}$. This means then $p_j = 1$ if and only if there is a path from $v_i$ to $v_j$ through the nodes $v_1, v_2, \ldots, v_{k+1}$ or an edge from $v_i$ to $v_j$.

A Pascal program for this algorithm is given in Fig. 5-4.2. Notice that Boolean values are used and the input adjacency matrix describes the graph given in Fig. 5-4.1. A timing requirement of the algorithm is $O(n^3)$. The space requirement is $O(n^2)$.

Algorithm WARSHALL can be modified further to obtain a matrix which gives the lengths of shortest paths between the nodes. For this purpose, let A be the adjacency matrix of the graph. Replace all those elements of A which are zero by $\infty$, which shows that there is no edge between the nodes in question. The following algorithm produces the required matrix which shows the lengths of minimum paths.

**Algorithm MINIMAL.** Given the adjacency matrix, B, in which the zero elements are replaced by infinity or by some very large number, the matrix C produced by the following algorithm shows the minimum lengths of paths between the nodes. MIN is a function that selects the algebraic minimum of its two arguments.

1. [Initialize]
    C ← B
2. [Perform a pass]
    Repeat thru step 4 for k = 1, 2, ..., n
3. [Process rows]
    Repeat step 4 for i = 1, 2, ..., n
4. [Process columns]
    Repeat for j = 1, 2, ..., n
        $c_{ij} \leftarrow MIN(c_{ij}, c_{ik} + c_{kj})$

5. [Finished]
   Exit ☐

Here, + in step 4 means the ordinary adding of integers. In practice we are often interested not only in the length of the minimum path between any two nodes but also in the actual path. It is a simple matter to modify the previous algorithm to obtain such a path, and therefore it is left as an exercise.

We shall end this subsection by showing how the path matrix of a digraph can be used in determining whether certain procedures in a program are recursive.

In some programming languages, a programmer must explicitly state that a procedure is recursive. For example, in PL/1 the RECURSIVE option must be specified. In other languages which do not require any such specification, it is possible to use concepts from graph theory to determine which procedures are recursive. A recursive procedure is not necessarily one which invokes itself directly. If procedure $p_1$ invokes $p_2$, procedure $p_2$ invokes $p_3$, ..., procedure $p_{n-1}$ invokes $p_n$, and procedure $p_n$ invokes $p_1$, then procedure $p_1$ is recursive.

Let $P = \{ p_1, p_2, ..., p_n \}$ be the set of procedures in a program. In a directed graph consisting of nodes representing elements of P, there is an edge from $p_i$ to $p_j$ if procedure $p_i$ invokes $p_j$. Figure 5-4.3 shows a directed graph and its adjacency matrix representing the calls made by the set of procedures $P = \{ p_1, p_2, ..., p_5 \}$.

A procedure $p_i$ is recursive if their exists a cycle involving $p_i$ in the graph. Such cycles can be detected from the diagonal elements of the path matrix Q of the graph. Thus $p_i$ is recursive if and only if $q_{ii} = 1$. The matrix Q can be obtained by using Warshall's Algorithm. The matrix Q is given by

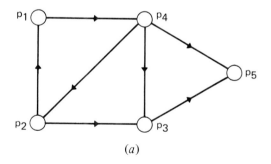

(a)

|      | $p_1$ | $p_2$ | $p_3$ | $p_4$ | $p_5$ |
|------|-------|-------|-------|-------|-------|
| $p_1$ | 0 | 0 | 0 | 1 | 0 |
| $p_2$ | 1 | 0 | 1 | 0 | 0 |
| $p_3$ | 0 | 0 | 0 | 0 | 1 |
| $p_4$ | 0 | 1 | 1 | 0 | 1 |
| $p_5$ | 0 | 0 | 0 | 0 | 0 |

(b)

**FIGURE 5-4.3** Procedure calls among $p_1$, $p_2$, $p_3$, $p_4$, and $p_5$.

$$Q = \begin{bmatrix} 1 & 1 & 1 & 1 & 1 \\ 1 & 1 & 1 & 1 & 1 \\ 0 & 0 & 0 & 0 & 1 \\ 1 & 1 & 1 & 1 & 1 \\ 0 & 0 & 0 & 0 & 0 \end{bmatrix}$$

which shows that the procedures $p_1$, $p_2$, and $p_4$ are recursive.

### Exercises for Sec. 5-4.1

1. Obtain the adjacency matrix A of the digraph given in Fig. 5-4.4. Find the elementary paths of length 1 and 2 from $v_1$ to $v_4$. Verify the results by calculating $A^2$, $A^3$, and $A^4$.

2. For any $n \times n$ Boolean matrix A, show that

$$(I + A)^{(2)} = (I + A) \wedge (I + A) = I + A + A^{(2)}$$

where I is the $n \times n$ identity matrix and $A^{(2)} = A \wedge A$. Show also that for any positive integer $r$

$$(I + A)^{(r)} = I + A + A^{(2)} + \cdots + A^{(r)}$$

3. Using the result obtained in Prob. 2, show that the path matrix of a simple digraph is given by $P = (I + A)^{(n)}$, where A is the adjacency matrix of the digraph that has $n$ nodes.

4. For a simple digraph $G = (V, E)$ whose adjacency matrix is denoted by A, its *distance matrix* is given by

$$d_{ij} = \infty \quad \text{if } (v_i, v_j) \notin E$$

$$d_{ii} = 0 \quad \text{for all } i = 1, 2, \ldots, n$$

$$d_{ij} = k \quad \text{where k is the smallest integer for which } a_{ij}^{(k)} \neq 0$$

Determine the distance matrix of the digraph given in Fig. 5-4.4. What does $d_{ij} = 1$ mean?

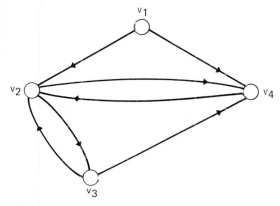

**FIGURE 5-4.4**

5.  Modify Algorithm **MINIMAL** so that all minimum paths are computed.
6.  Assume that a digraph has all its edges labeled. Write a program which will display all minimum paths between all pairs of nodes.

### 5-4.2  List Structures

In this subsection we are concerned with the representation of a structure called a *list structure*. The manipulation of such a structure is known as *list processing*. It will be shown that a list structure can be used to represent a directed graph.

The development of list-processing structures, techniques, and programming languages was primarily a response to the requirements of a particular computer application field, namely, symbolic manipulation. Various problem areas such as artificial intelligence, algebraic manipulation, text processing, and graphics are included in this field. Recall that these all have in common the following characteristics:

*1*  Unpredictable storage requirements. The exact amount of data storage required by a program in these areas often depends on the particular data being processed, and consequently, this requirement cannot be easily determined at the time the program is written.

*2*  Extensive manipulation of the stored data is required. Programs in these areas typically require that operations such as insertions and deletions be performed frequently on the data structures used.

Taking into consideration the high costs of computer storage and computing time, a data structure was required which would utilize the available storage space to provide maximum problem-solving capacity and would support efficient (meaning time-wise efficient) manipulation algorithms. The list structure to be discussed satisfies both these criteria.

In the context of list processing, we define a *list* to be any finite sequence of zero or more *atoms* or *lists*, where an atom is taken to be any object (e.g., a string of symbols) that is distinguishable from a list by treating the atom as structurally indivisible. If we enclose lists within parentheses and separate elements of lists by commas, then the following can be considered to be lists:

(a, (b, c, d), e, (f, g))
()
((a))

The first list contains four elements, namely, the atom a, the list (b, c, d) which contains the atoms b, c and d, the atom e, and the list (f, g) whose elements are the atoms f and g. The second list has no elements, but the null list is still a valid list according to our definition. The third list has one element, the list (a), which in turn contains the atom a. A graphic representation of these examples is given in Fig. 5-4.5.

Another notation which is often used to illustrate lists is similar to that used in the linked representation of trees. Each element of a list is indicated by a box; the arrows or pointers indicate whether the boxes are members of the same list or members of sublists. Each box is separated into two parts. The second part of an element contains a pointer to the next element in the same list or a slash (denoting a null pointer) to mark the end of a list. This "horizontal" pointer represents the relation of physical adjacency in a list. The first part of an element contains either the name of an atomic element or a pointer to the list representation for a list element.

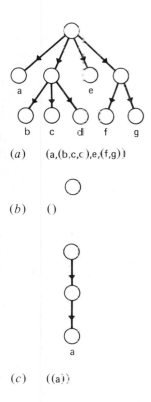

(a)    (a,(b,c,c ),e,(f,g) )

(b)    ()

(c)    ((a))

**FIGURE 5-4.5**    Graphic representation of list structures.


For a nonatomic element the pointer specifies the "vertical" or hierarchical relationship in a list.

The box and arrow representations of the previous lists are shown in Fig. 5-4.6. The symbol ⇒ indicates the root or first element of the list.

The following three properties are associated with list structures:

*1 Order* A transitive relation defined on the elements of the list and specified by the sequence in which the elements appear within the list. In the list (x, y, z), x precedes y and y precedes z implies that x precedes z. This list is not equal to the list (y, z, x).

In the box and arrow notation, order is defined by the horizontal arrows. Each horizontal arrow is interpreted to mean that the element from which the arrow originates precedes the element to which it points.

*2 Depth* The depth of a list is the maximum level attributed to any element within the list or within any sublist in the list. The level of an element is indicated by the nesting of lists within lists, i.e., by the number of pairs of parentheses surrounding the element. In the list of Fig. 5-4.5a, the elements a and e are at a level of 1, while the remaining elements b, c, d, f, and g have a level of 2. The depth of the entire list is 2.

In the box and arrow notation, the concepts of depth and level are easiest to understand if a number $d$ is associated with each atomic and list element in the list. The value of $d$ for an element x, denoted by $d(x)$, is the number of vertical arrows that must be followed in order to reach the element from the first element of the list. In Fig. 5-4.6a, $d(a) = 0$, $d(b) = 1$, etc. In general the level of any element x is given by $d(x) + 1$, and the depth of the list is the maximum value of this level over all the atoms in the list.

*3 Length* The number of elements at level 1 in a list. For example, the length of list (a, (b, c), d) is 3.

As an example, let us consider a common occurrence of a list structure that is seldom recognized as such. An English sentence construction consists of a subject, verb, and object. Any such sentence can be interpreted as a three-element list whose elements can be atoms (single words) or lists (word phrases). The following sentences and their corresponding list representations are examples:

Man bites dog. = (Man, bites, dog)

The man bites the dog. = ((The, man), bites, (the, dog))

The big man is biting the small dog. =

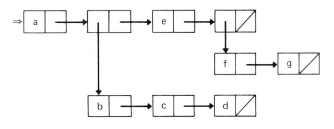

$(a)$    $(a,(b,c,d),e,(f,g))$

$\Rightarrow$    (null pointer)

$(b)$    $()$

$(c)$    $((a))$

**FIGURE 5-4.6**  Storage representation of list structures.

((The, big, man),(is, biting),(the, small, dog))

The subject and object of the last example can be further separated into nouns and qualifiers as in

(((The, big), (man)), (is, biting), ((the, small), (dog)))

The box and arrow representation of this sentence is given in Fig. 5-4.7
The properties of this list are as follows:

the length is 3
the depth is 3
the level of 'man' is 3, the level of 'is' is 2, etc.

There is a distinct relationship between a list structure and a digraph. In particular, a list is a directed graph with one *source* node (a node whose indegree is 0) corresponding to the entire list and with every node immediately connected to the source node corresponding to an element of the list — either by being a node with outdegree 0 (for atoms) or by being a node that has branches (for elements which are lists) emanating from it. Every node except the source node has an indegree of 1. The edges leaving a node are considered to be ordered lists. This means that we distinguish the first edge, second edge, etc., which corresponds to the ordering of list elements by the first element, second element, etc. Furthermore, there are no cycles in the graph. The graphs of example lists are given in Fig 5-4.5.

The preceding list definition could apply equally well to trees. However, lists are in fact extensions of trees in that a list can contain itself as an element and a tree cannot. Hence, there are some lists that cannot be represented as trees, but every tree can be represented as a list. Lists can have essentially recursive nesting structure that no tree can have, and thus there are some lists that have a finite representation in our parentheses-comma notation, but which correspond to infinite graphs. For example, the graph of the list structure M = (a, b, M) is shown in Fig. 5-4.8.

Next, we discuss the storage representation of list structures. When we consider the criteria which such structures are designed to satisfy, a linked storage representation is certainly the most effective. It provides dynamic allocation of nodes as needed, ease in manipulation, and the ability to share sublists. A list is generally represented by some variation of the binary tree representation of natural

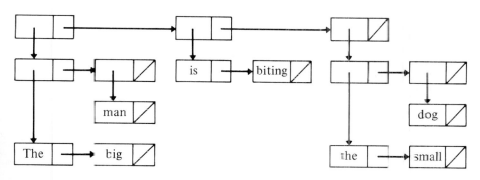

**FIGURE 5-4.7**

trees, i.e., by using two link fields — one to indicate membership within a list and one to indicate nesting.

A typical list node is shown in Fig. 5-4.9. DPTR is the link pointing to the first element of the sublist; RPTR points to the next element in the same list; and INFO contains information about the list (e.g., an alphabetic name). An atomic node is indicated by an empty DPTR, in which case INFO contains the atomic information.

This node format is sufficient for lists whose atomic information requires small storage space. In such a case, little storage space is wasted in the list nodes which do not require a large INFO field.

A more typical situation is one in which the atomic information requires a relatively large amount of storage space. A more practical node format in this case is given in Fig. 5-4.10, where RPTR performs the same task as in the previous format. The ATOM field is a flag which allows atomic and list nodes to be distinguished. If ATOM equals 1, the node is an atomic node, and DPTR is used to point into some auxiliary information storage structure (e.g., a vector of structures). However, if ATOM equals 0, the node is assumed to be a list node and DPTR points to the first element of some sublist.

This format allows all nodes within the list structure to be of one size, and yet avoids wasting information space unnecessarily in the list nodes. It is for this reason, and for reasons of diagrammatic and algorithmic simplicity, that this second format is used in the remainder of this subsection. The figures will show atomic nodes in the same manner as Fig. 5-4.11 where the "x" in the DPTR field denotes a pointer to the information related to atom x. As an example, the list (a, (b, c), d) is represented by Fig. 5-4.12.

Recall from Fig. 5-4.8 that the graphic representation of a recursive list contains an infinite repetition of the graph nodes. This practice is impractical for computer implementation. A more sensible method is to implement the list M = (a, b, M) as shown in Fig. 5-4.13. This representation of a recursive loop is obviously efficient; however, great care must be exercised in order to avoid infinite loops in programs which manipulate such structures.

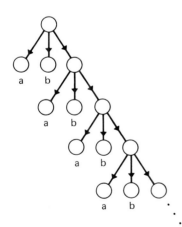

**FIGURE 5-4.8**

| DPTR | INFO | RPTR |
|------|------|------|

**FIGURE 5-4.9**   Node representation of a list element.

| ATOM | DPTR | RPTR |
|------|------|------|

**FIGURE 5-4.10**   Alternate node representation of a list element.

The space-conserving attribute of lists is not restricted to only recursive structures. A more common situation involves duplicate lists, which occur frequently in practical applications. For example, the list (y, (z, w), (2, (z, w), a)). is represented by Fig. 5-4.14.

Let us consider what changes are required to delete the element z from the sublist (z, w) of Fig. 5-4.14 in order to create the list (y, (w), (2, (w), a)). It is necessary to locate and change both pointers to the element z. This is not a desirable feature since the backtracking necessary to locate the pointers is extremely time-consuming. Because the operation of removing the first element of a list is quite common, it is desirable to derive a storage structure on which such manipulations can be accomplished more efficiently.

In this revised representation, a *list header node* is associated with each list. Using the same node format as before, a list header node has RPTR pointing to the first element of the list and DPTR set to NULL. A value of a 0 is associated with the ATOM field to indicate the node is a list node. An empty list is indicated by DPTR = RPTR = NULL. In this representation each pointer to a list emanates from its list head rather than from its first element. Using this representation the deletion of the first element of the list requires only changing the RPTR field of its header node. Using this header node representation, we find that Fig. 5-4.14 would appear as in Fig. 5-4.15.

**FIGURE 5-4.11**   Atomic node representation

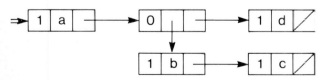

**FIGURE 5-4.12**   Storage representation of (a, (b, c), d).

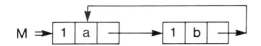

**FIGURE 5-4.13**    Storage representation of a recursive list.

Although this representation requires slightly more storage, this drawback is more than compensated for by the manipulative efficiencies it allows.

The remainder of this section is concerned with list operations. The process of creating, inserting, and deleting elements of a list are similar to the equivalent tree operations and will be discussed in the following pages. The copying, traversal and output operations are also similar to the corresponding tree operations. Exercises dealing with these list operations are given at the end of the section.

Creation of a list structure from a parenthesized representation is logically the first algorithm to be presented. If we assume that the input string contains no blanks, one letter names for nodes, and disallow circular or shared list representations, the algorithm is straightforward. The process can be performed either iteratively or recursively. A general algorithm for the iterative method is now presented.

1.  If the first symbol in the input string is a '('
    then create a list header node
    else write invalid list and exit
2.  Repeat thru step 5 until all symbols in the input string have been processed
3.  If the current symbol is a '('
    then create a sublist connecting node and attach the node to the current
        sublist
        push the address of the sublist node onto the stack
        create a list header node for the new list and attach it to the sublist
        node
4.  If the current symbol is a ')'
    then end current sublist by popping a higher list address off the stack
5.  If the current symbol is any of A thru Z
    then create a list node and attach it to the current sublist

In the first algorithm, the iterative method will be presented using the stack algorithms of Sec. 3-4.

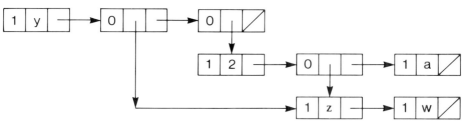

**FIGURE 5-4.14**

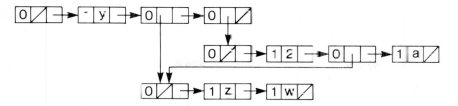

**FIGURE 5-4.15**  Storage representation of a list using a list head.

**Function**  CREATE(INPUT).  Given INPUT, a valid string describing a list, this function creates the corresponding list structure with list heads.  The stack S, used to create the list structure, is represented by a vector of pointers and is manipulated by the stack algorithms PUSH and POP.  CURSOR is used to keep track of current position in the input string.  P and Q are temporary pointer variables  The name of the node structure is NODE.  The function returns a pointer to the head node.

1.  [Check for valid list and set up list head node]
      If SUB(INPUT, 1, 1) = '('
      then    P ⇐ NODE
              RPTR(P) ← DPTR(P) ← NULL
              ATOM(P) ← 0
              Call PUSH(S, TOP, P)
      else    Write('INVALID LIST')
              Return(NULL)
2.  [Repeat until entire input string has been processed]
          CURSOR ← 1
          Repeat step 3 while CURSOR < LENGTH(INPUT)
3.  [Update cursor and handle each symbol]
          CURSOR ← CURSOR + 1
          Select case (SUB(INPUT, CURSOR, 1))
                  Case '(':   (a new sublist)
                          Q ⇐ NODE
                          RPTR(Q) ← NULL
                          ATOM(Q) ← 0
                          RPTR(P) ← Q
                          Call PUSH(S, TOP, Q)
                          P ⇐ NODE
                          RPTR(P) ← DPTR(P) ← NULL
                          ATOM(P) ← 0
                          DPTR(Q) ← P
                  Case ')':   (end current sublist)
                          P ← POP(S, TOP)
                  Case ',':
                          (no action)
                  Case 'A' thru 'Z':   (enter on current sublist)
                          Q ⇐ NODE
                          RPTR(Q) ← NULL
                          ATOM(Q) ← 1
                          DPTR(Q) ← SUB(INPUT, CURSOR, 1)

> (actually a pointer to this information)
> RPTR(P) ← Q
> P ← Q
> Default:
> Write('INVALID CHARACTER')
> Return(NULL)

4.    [Return]
      Return(P)                                                    □

The algorithm creates the list structure, including list heads, using the node structure as previously described. In the case statement of step 3, notice that the name of the node is assigned to DPTR. In an implementation this would be replaced by a pointer to the information stored in some other structure. The function returns NULL on invalid input data and a pointer to the head of the list otherwise. A trace of the function on the list ((a, b), c) is given in Fig. 5-4.16. Commas that do not separate names of nodes have been left out of the trace in order to shorten it.

The recursive algorithm for creating a list structure is similar to its iterative counterpart, assuming the same input restrictions. The stack procedure PUSH is replaced by a recursive call, and POP is substituted by a return statement. The creation of the head node is assumed to be done in the calling program. A pointer to this node is passed down to the procedure. CURSOR, a global variable, is initialized to a value of 1 outside the procedure. The algorithm terminates when control is returned to the calling program.

**Procedure**  RCREATE(INPUT, P). Given INPUT, a valid string describing a list, this procedure recursively creates the corresponding list structure with list heads. P is a pointer set to the list header node created outside the procedure. CURSOR is used to keep track of current position in the input string and is initially set to 1 outside of the procedure. Q is a temporary pointer variable.

1.    [Repeat until control returns to calling program]
      Repeat thru step 5 while true
2.    [Update cursor]
      CURSOR ← CURSOR + 1
3.    [Process each symbol]
      Select case (SUB(INPUT, CURSOR, 1))
            Case '(':   (start a new sublist)
                  Q ⇐ NODE
                  RPTR(Q) ← NULL
                  ATOM(Q) ← 0
                  RPTR(P) ← Q
                  P ← Q
                  Q ⇐ NODE
                  RPTR(Q) ← DPTR(Q) ← NULL
                  ATOM(Q) ← 0
                  DPTR(P) ← Q
                  Call RCREATE(INPUT, Q)
            Case ')':   (End current sublist, return one level)
                  Return

```
Case ',':
        (no action)
Case 'A' thru 'Z':   (Add to current sublist)
        Q ⇐ NODE
        RPTR(Q) ← NULL
        ATOM(Q) ← 1
        DPTR(Q) ← SUB(INPUT, CURSOR, 1)
        (actually a pointer to this information)
        RPTR(P) ← Q
        P ← Q
Default:
        Write('INVALID CHARACTER')
```
4.   [Return to calling program]
     Return                                                   □

The next algorithms to be examined deal with list-splitting operations, which are generally unique to list processing. A list is considered to consist of two logical entities, a *head* and a *tail*. Consider the list ((a, b), c, (d, e)) shown in Fig. 5-4.17 in which the head is the list (a, b) and the tail is (c, (d, e)). The graphic representation of the head and tail is given in Fig. 5-4.18. Note the effect of the splitting operation on the level of the elements in the resultant lists. The elements of the head of the list have their level reduced by 1, while the level of the elements of the tail are unaltered.

Given a list structure which uses header nodes, the following functions return pointers to the head and tail, respectively.

**Function** HEAD(ROOT). Given ROOT, a pointer to the list header node of a list structure, this function returns a pointer to the head of the list. If the head is an atom, the pointer is to the description of the atom. P is a pointer variable.

1.   [Check validity of list structure]
         If ROOT = NULL or DPTR(ROOT) ≠ NULL
         then   Write('INVALID LIST')
                Return(NULL)
2.   [Is the list null?]
         P ← RPTR(ROOT)
         If P = NULL
         then   Write('NULL LIST')
                Return(NULL)
3.   [Return pointer to HEAD]
         Return(DPTR(P))                                      □

**Function** TAIL(ROOT). Given ROOT, a pointer to the list header node of a list structure, this function creates a list header node and returns its address. The RPTR field of this header node points to the tail of the list. P and Q are temporary pointer variables. The name of the node structure is NODE.

1.   [Check validity of list structure]
         If ROOT = NULL or DPTR(ROOT) ≠ NULL
         then   Write('INVALID LIST')
                Return(NULL)
```
```

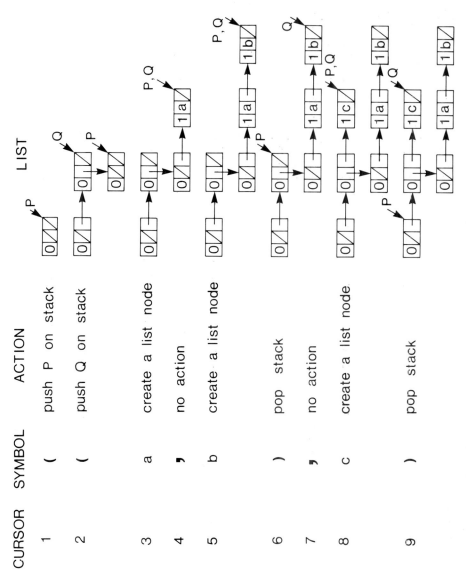

**FIGURE 5-4.16**  Trace of Function CREATE for the list ((a, b), c).

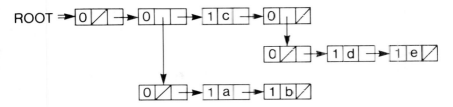

**FIGURE 5-4.17**

2.  [Is the list null?]
    P ← RPTR(ROOT)
    If P = NULL
    then   Write('NULL LIST')
         Return(NULL)
3.  [Create a list head and return]
    Q ⇐ NODE
    ATOM(Q) ← 0
    DPTR(Q) ← NULL
    RPTR(Q) ← RPTR(P)
    Return(Q)        □

    The operation which provides the opposite effect of the HEAD and TAIL operations is the construct operation, also unique to list processing. Given two operands, the first either an atom or a list, the second a list, this operation creates a list structure using the first argument as the head of the created list and the second argument as the tail. For example, if A is the list (q) and B is the list (d, e), then the construct of A and B is the list ((q), d, e). As another example, if A is the atom s and B is the list (t, u), then the construct of A and B is the list (s, t, u).

    Note that the level of each element in the first argument is increased by 1 as a result of the construct operation, while the level of all elements in the second argument are left unchanged. The construct operation is invalid if the second argument is not a list, although it may be the null list. For example, if A is the atom x and B is the list (), then the construct of A and B is (x).

    In the following algorithm, we assume that if A is an atom it is represented by a node with DPTR pointing to the information and RPTR equal to NULL. The list header node for list B becomes the list header node for the new list structure.

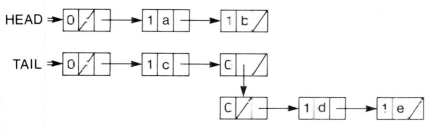

**FIGURE 5-4.18**  The head and tail representations of the list ((a, b), c, (d, e)).

**Procedure** CONSTRUCT(A, B). Given A, the pointer to the list header node of a list structure or to an atom, and B, a pointer to the list header node of a list structure, this procedure joins the two lists. The list header node for list B becomes the list header node for the new list structure. The list L created is such that HEAD(L) = A and TAIL(L) = B. P and Q are temporary pointer variables.

1.  [Check validity of list structures]
     If A = NULL or B = NULL
        then   Write('INVALID LIST')
               Return
2.  [Is B a list?]
     If DPTR(B) $\neq$ NULL
        then   Write('INVALID LIST B')
               Return
3.  [Add A to list B]
     If ATOM(A) = 1
        then   P ← RPTR(B)   (if A is an atom, join node to list B)
               RPTR(B) ← A
               RPTR(A) ← P
        else   Q $\Leftarrow$ NODE   (if A is a list, create joining node and add to list B)
               P ← RPTR(B)
               RPTR(B) ← Q
               RPTR(Q) ← P
               DPTR(Q) ← A
     Return                                                              □

Another familiar operation performed on list structures is the concatenation operation which we denote by APPEND. For example, if A is the list (a, (b, c)) and B is the list (d, f), then their concatenation is the list (a, (b, c), d, f). Note that the level of each element in both lists remain the same, and that A and B cannot be atoms. This operation is shown graphically in Fig. 5-4.19.

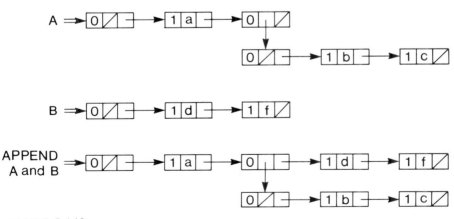

**FIGURE 5-4.19**

**Procedure** APPEND(A, B). Given A and B, the pointers to the list header nodes of two list structures, this procedure joins the lists so that elements at level 1 are the level 1 elements of both lists A and B. The elements of list A precede those of list B. The list header node for list A becomes the list header node for the new structure. Since A is altered in the algorithm, it is assumed to be passed by reference.

1. [Check validity of list structures]
    If A = NULL or DPTR(A) ≠ NULL
    then    Write('INVALID LIST A')
            Return
    If B = NULL or DPTR(B) ≠ NULL
    then    Write('INVALID LIST B')
            Return
2. [Find last node in top level of list A]
    Repeat while RPTR(A) ≠ NULL
        A ← RPTR(A)
3. [Join lists and free list header node for B]
    RPTR(A) ← RPTR(B)
    Restore(B)
    Return                                                    ☐

A less common list operation is counting the number of atoms in a list. For example, the list (a, b, (c, d)) has four atoms, while the list (()) has no atoms. The procedure to count atoms could be either iterative or recursive. The recursive approach is as follows. The procedure is invoked recursively until the basis condition of a NULL RPTR is encountered. The procedure then returns to the previous list and continues on until control is returned to the calling program after traversal of the top level list. We will present the recursive approach and leave the iterative as an exercise.

**Procedure** COUNTER(A, COUNT). Given A, a pointer to the list header node, this recursive procedure calculates the number of atoms in a list, returning the result in COUNT. COUNT is set to zero outside of the procedure.

1. [Repeat until the entire list has been examined]
    Repeat step 2 while A ≠ NULL
2. [Process the current node and move along list]
    If ATOM(A) = 1
    then    COUNT ← COUNT + 1
    else    If DPTR(A) ≠ NULL
            then    Call COUNTER(DPTR(A), COUNT)
    A ← RPTR(A)
3. [Return to last list examined]
    Return                                                    ☐

The next algorithm deletes an atomic node containing certain information, assuming no shared or recursive sublists. We also assume that there is only one copy of the information node (i.e., more than one pointer may access the same position in the auxiliary storage structure). For example, if a is the node to be removed from the list (b, a, (a)), the result would be (b, ()). Notice that the removal of the only node in a list does not cause the list to disappear. The procedure may be implemented either iteratively or recursively, however, we will present only the recursive formulation.

**Procedure** DELETE(REMOVE, Q, P). Given REMOVE, a pointer to the name of the atomic node to be deleted, this recursive procedure removes all instances of this node. The procedure is initially called with Q set to the list header node and P set to the RPTR of this value.

1. [Repeat until the entire list has been examined]
   Repeat step 2 while P ≠ NULL
2. [Search for nodes to be removed]
   If ATOM(P) = 1 and DPTR(P) = REMOVE
   then  (node has been found)
         RPTR(Q) ← RPTR(P)
         Restore(P)
         P ← RPTR(Q)
   else  If ATOM(P) = 0 and DPTR(P) ≠ NULL
         then  (move deeper in list recursively)
               Call DELETE(REMOVE,DPTR(P),RPTR(DPTR(P)) )
         Q ← P   (move across list)
         P ← RPTR(P)
3. [Return to last list examined]
   Return                                                                  □

The destruction of a list is more complex than the destruction of a tree. A list cannot automatically be returned to the pool of available storage, since other lists may be referencing the list to be destroyed. This topic is discussed in detail in Sec. 5-6.

As we mentioned previously, several programming languages have been developed to allow easy processing of list structures. LISP 1.5 is one of the most powerful of these. In LISP 1.5 there are five basic or "pure" LISP functions, namely, CAR, CDR, CONS, EQ, and ATOM. The functions CAR, CDR, and CONS are equivalent to the list operations HEAD, TAIL, and CONSTRUCT, as discussed previously in this subsection. EQ and ATOM are logical functions (i.e, predicates). EQ tests for equality of two atoms, and ATOM determines whether a list element is an atom. Any function provided in LISP 1.5 can be expressed in terms of the five "pure" LISP functions. For a thorough discussion of LISP 1.5, the reader is invited to read McCarthy et al., [1969].

**Exercises for Sec. 5-4.2**

1. Give the storage representation for the following lists:

   (a, (b, (c, d)), e, f)
   ((x), y, A, z)    where A = (a, b, (c, d))

2. Represent the graph of Fig 5-4.20 by a list structure. Draw its storage representation.
3. Give an algorithm for the function EQ which tests to see if two atomic arguments are equal.
4. Using the Algorithm EQ, plus HEAD, TAIL, and CONSTRUCT, derive algorithms for the UNION and INTERSECTION of two lists. For example,

UNION((a, b, (c, d)), (a, (b))) is (a, b, (c, d), (b)), and INTERSECTION((a, b, (c, d)), (a, (b))) is (a).

5. Construct an Algorithm REVERSE for reversing a given list. For example, REVERSE((a, b, (c, d))) is ((d, c), b, a). Use the "pure" LISP functions in your algorithm.

6. Create an Algorithm LEVEL, which determines the depth of a specific node. For example, b in the list (a, (b, c)) is at level 2.

7. Construct an Algorithm COPY which takes an existing list structure and builds a duplicate copy without destroying the original list.

8. Develop an algorithm which does the reverse of CREATE, i.e., takes a list structure and prints out the parenthesized expression.

9. The *depth* of a list is the maximum level of all the sublists. Create an Algorithm DEPTH which calculates this number.

10. Two list structures are said to be *equal* if they have the same structure and the same data in corresponding fields. Given pointers to the heads of two lists, create an Algorithm EQUAL which determines if these two lists are identical.

### 5-4.3 Other Representations of Graphs

We will now discuss other storage methods for graphs. The best storage representation for some general graph depends on the nature of the data and on the operations which are to be performed on these data. Furthermore, the choice of a suitable representation is affected by other factors, such as number of nodes, the average number of edges leaving a node, whether a graph is directed, the frequency of insertions, and/or deletions to be performed, etc.

The use of an adjacency matrix to represent a graph as described in Sec. 5-4.1 has several drawbacks. This representation makes it difficult to store additional information about the graph. If information about a node is to be included, it would have to be represented by an additional storage structure. Weighted graphs could have their edge values stored in place of a bit value, but such a configuration would preclude the use of the Warshall algorithm described in Sec. 5-4.1. The most severe problem with using a matrix to represent a graph is its static implementation. In order to use this representation, we find that the number of nodes must be known

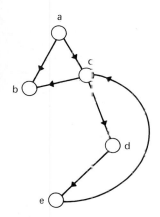

**FIGURE 5-4.20**

beforehand to set up the storage array. Also, an insertion or deletion of a node requires changing the dimensions of the array, both difficult and inefficient with large graphs. This approach is not very suitable for a graph that has a large number of nodes or has many nodes which are connected to only a few edges.

A graph can be represented in many different ways, the most appropriate depending on the application. In the following section we will use an adjacency list. An *adjacency list* is a listing for each node of all edges connecting it to adjacent nodes. For a graph G = (V, E), a list is formed for each element x of V, containing all nodes y such that (x, y) is an element of E.

If there are a number of edges between a pair of nodes and a considerable number of nodes that are connected to only a few other nodes, then the storage representation for the adjacency list of the graph in Fig. 5-4.21a, where the adjacency list is given in Fig. 5-4.21b, could be as shown in Fig. 5-4.21c. Undirected graphs can also be stored using this data structure; however, each edge will be represented twice, once in each direction. Observe that the graph is weighted, that the storage representation consists of a node table directory, and that associated with each entry in this directory we have an edge list. A typical node directory entry consists of a node number, the data associated with it, and a pointer field which gives the address of the list of edges for this node. Each list of edges, stored as a linked list, has an entry which contains the weight of the edge (optional) and the node number at which the particular edge terminates. For a completely dynamic representation, the node table directory could be replaced by a linked list, where the terminating node number in the edge list is changed to a pointer to the appropriate node in the linked list table directory. This representation would simplify the insertion and deletion of nodes (see Prob. 5).

Perhaps one of the conceptually simplest representations of a graph is by an *edge list*. Each pair of nodes (u, v) connected by an edge are included in the listing. If the graph being stored is a digraph, then u is the initiating node and v is the terminating node. If the graph is undirected, no ordering is imposed on the pairs. The edge list for the sample graph is given in Fig. 5-4.21d. A simple data structure to represent this listing would be a linked list. Fields could be added to this structure to store information about the edges, but adding information about the nodes would require an additional structure.

To demonstrate the effect of the choice of a graph representation on the efficiency of an algorithm, consider the following problem. Suppose we wish to determine whether a graph contains at least one edge. If the graph is stored as an adjacency matrix, the matrix must be searched until a '1' bit is found. In the worst case there are $n^2$ elements to be examined, where n is the number of nodes. If an adjacency list representation is used, each node in the node table directory must be searched to determine if a linked list is present, requiring n comparisons. However, if an edge list is used, all that is necessary is to check for an entry on the list, one comparison.

As another example, let us examine the storage representation of a grammar. Such a representation becomes important in applications where grammars must be examined and manipulated as in top-down parsing (see Sec. 5-2.3). In this application an efficient storage representation for the grammar is required, since various alternative rules must be tested for their applicability during each stage of the construction of the parse.

An example of an efficient representation uses a multilinked structure to represent the grammar. In this representation the node structure used is as shown in Fig. 5-4.22.

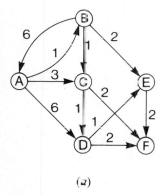

(a)

| a | b | c | d |
|---|---|---|---|
| b | a | c | e |
| c | d | f |   |
| d | e | f |   |
| e | f |   |   |
| f |   |   |   |

(b)

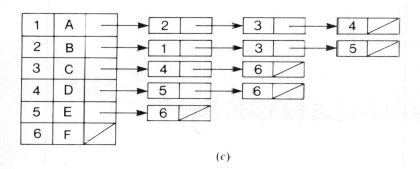

(c)

(a, b), (a, c). (a, d), (b, a),
(b, c), (b, e)  (c, d), (c, f),
(d, e), (d, f). (e. f)

(d)

FIGURE 5-4.21    (a) Sample graph; (b) adjacency list for graph; (c) storage representation for adjacency list; and (d) edge list for graph.

| NAME | | |
|---|---|---|
| TYPE | ALTER | NEXT |

**FIGURE 5-4.22**

Each node represents some symbol X in the right-hand side of some rule and consists of four fields NAME, TYPE, ALTER, and NEXT where

*1*    NAME is the name of symbol X.
*2*    TYPE is a pointer variable which is NULL if X is a terminal symbol; otherwise, since in this case X is nonterminal, it points to the node which corresponds to the first symbol in the first right-hand side for X.
*3*    ALTER is a pointer variable which points to the first symbol of the next alternate right-hand side following the one in which the node is situated. This only applies for the first symbol in a right-hand side. Otherwise, the value is NULL.
*4*    NEXT is a pointer variable that denotes the next symbol in the right-hand side or NULL.

Furthermore, each metavariable is represented by a pointer variable that points to the first symbol in its first right-hand side. Figure 5-4.23 represents the graph of the following grammar:

$$
\begin{aligned}
&\text{<e>} &&::= \text{<e> <aop> <t> | <t>} \\
&\text{<t>} &&::= \text{<t> <mop> <f> | <f>} \\
&\text{<f>} &&::= \text{<f> ↑ <p> | <p>} \\
&\text{<p>} &&::= \text{(<e>) | i} \\
&\text{<aop>} &&::= \text{+ | –} \\
&\text{<mop>} &&::= \text{* | /}
\end{aligned}
$$

**Exercises for Sec. 5-4.3**

1.   Represent the graph of Fig. 5-1.5 by a list structure. Draw its storage representation.
2.   Draw a storage representation for the following grammar:

$$
\begin{aligned}
&\text{E ::= a | b | (E + E)} \\
&\text{B ::= R | (B)} \\
&\text{R ::= E = E}
\end{aligned}
$$

3.   Represent the graph of Fig. 5-1.5 by an adjacency list. Diagram its storage representation and design an algorithm to construct the structure.
4.   Formulate an algorithm to:
     (a) Produce a completely dynamic representation of an adjacency list as described previously in this section.
     (b) Create an algorithm to insert a node in this structure.
     (c) Create an algorithm to delete a node from this structure.
5.   Produce an algorithm to transform an adjacency matrix to an adjacency list.

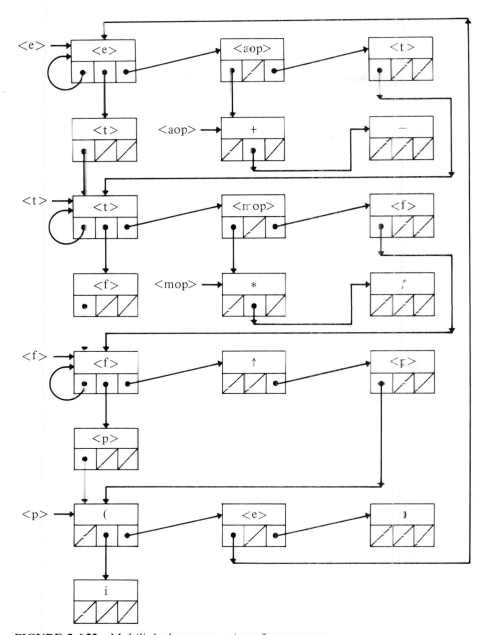

**FIGURE 5-4.23**   Multilinked representation of a grammar.

### 5-4.4 Breadth First Search

In general, breadth first search (BFS) can be used to find the shortest distance between some starting node and the remaining nodes of the graph. This shortest distance is the minimum number of edges traversed in order to travel from the start

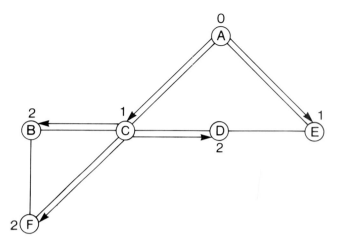

**FIGURE 5-4.24**   Breadth First Search traversal.

node to the specific node being examined. Starting at a node v, this distance is cal-culated by examining all incident edges to node v, and then moving on to an adja-cent node w and repeating the process. The traversal continues until all nodes in the graph have been examined.

Using the BFS strategy described above on the graph in Fig. 5-4.24, the indi-cated traversal results, assuming node A is the start position and each edge is assigned a value of one. The shortest distance from the start is given by the number associated with each node. All nodes adjacent to the current node are numbered before the search is continued. This ensures every node will be examined at least once.

The efficiency of a BFS algorithm is dependent on the  method used to represent the graph. The adjacency list representation discussed in Sec. 5.4-3 is suit-able for this algorithm, since finding the incident edges to the current node involves simply traversing a linked list, whereas an adjacency matrix would require searching the entire matrix many times.

We will use the data structure introduced in the previous section for the algo-rithm. The node table directory will be represented by a vector of records with node structure as in Fig. 5-4.25a. REACH specifies whether a node has been reached in the traversal and its initial value is *false*. NODENO identifies the node number, DATA contains the information pertaining to this node, and DIST is the variable which will contain the distance from the start node. Finally, LISTPTR is a pointer to a list of adjacent edges for the node. The edges are represented by a structure of the form given in Fig. 5-4.25b. DESTIN contains the number of the terminal node for this edge, and EDGEPTR points to the next edge in the list. The storage representation for the graph in Fig. 5-4.24 is presented in Fig. 5-4.26, after the BFS traversal (before BFS traversal all REACH values would be *false*).

The following algorithm to calculate BFS distances uses two helping pro-cedures, QINSERT and QDELETE as introduced in Sec. 3-6. QINSERT enters a value onto the rear of a queue, in this case a node whose incident edges have not yet been examined. The procedure has two parameters, the queue name and the

| REACH | NODENO | DATA | DIST | LISTPTR |
|-------|--------|------|------|---------|

(a)

| DESTIN | EDGEPTR |
|--------|---------|

(b)

**FIGURE 5-4.25** (a) Node table directory structure; and (b) edge structure.

value to be inserted. QDELETE removes a value from the front of a queue specified, placing it in INDEX. In the algorithm, this value is the next node which will be processed. An algorithm to calculate shortest distance from a start node using a breadth first search strategy can now be presented.

**Procedure** BFS(INDEX). Given the structure as described above and the queue handling procedures, QINSERT and QDELETE, this algorithm generates the shortest path for each node using a breadth first search. INDEX denotes the current node being processed and LINK points to the edge being examined. It is assumed that the REACH field has been set to *false* when the structure was created. QUEUE denotes the name of the queue.

1. [Initialize the first node's DIST number and place node in queue]
   REACH[INDEX] ← *true*
   DIST[INDEX] ← 0
   Call QINSERT(QUEUE, INDEX)
2. [Repeat until all nodes have been examined]
   Repeat thru step 5 while queue is not empty
3. [Remove current node to be examined from queue]
   Call QDELETE(QUEUE, INDEX)
4. [Find all unlabeled nodes adjacent to current node]
   LINK ← LISTPTR[INDEX]
   Repeat step 5 while LINK ≠ NULL
5. [If this is an unvisited node, label it and add it to the queue]
   If not REACH[DESTIN(LINK)]
   then   DIST[DESTIN(LINK)] ← DIST[INDEX] + 1
          REACH[DESTIN(LINK)] ← *true*
          Call QINSERT(QUEUE, DESTIN(LINK))
   LINK ← EDGEPTR(LINK)   (Move down edge list)
6. [Finished]
   Return                                                          □

Using the graph representation in Fig. 5-4.26, the algorithm initially places node A into the queue. Step 3 removes the front element from the queue (initially, node A). Nodes C and E are placed in the queue during the list traversing loop of

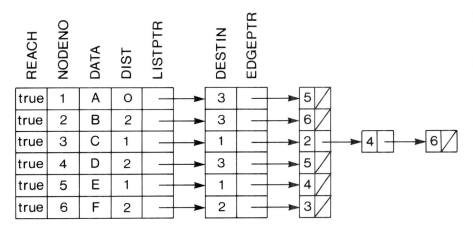

**FIGURE 5-4.26** Storage representation of sample graph.

step 4. The algorithm then removes C from the queue and begins processing its incident edges. Since the first node in the list (A) has already been labeled, it is ignored. This ensures that the algorithm will not examine any node after it has been labeled. The algorithm terminates when the queue is emptied.

The algorithm calculates the distance of every node from a starting node. If all that is required is the distance for one specific node, an extra condition can be inserted in the loop at step 5, comparing the current node being labeled to the specific node required. If the values are equal the algorithm can be stopped, saving a traversal of the remaining portion of the graph.

Let us now examine the timing analysis of Procedure BFS. Step 1 is performed once. The "then part" of the if statement in step 5 is performed $n - 1$ times. This follows from the fact that "then part" is executed only when the REACH value of a node is *false*. Note that the REACH value is set to *true* in the "then part". Hence, the queue contains one node from step 1 and $n - 1$ nodes from step 5 for a total of n nodes. Consequently, step 2 is repeated n times. The adjacency lists contain 2 * e edges where e denotes the total number of edges in the graph. It then follows that step 4 and the assignment statement in step 5 are each performed 2 * e times since all edges in the adjacency lists are examined. Consequently the time analysis for the procedure is $O(n + e)$.

**Exercises for Sec. 5-4.4**

1. Produce the input structure and BFS shortest path numbering for the graph in Fig. 5-4.27 starting at node 1.
2. For the dynamic adjacency list representation of a graph described in Sec. 5-4.3, develop an algorithm to perform a shortest path BFS on the new structure.
3. A graph is connected if for every two nodes x and y, there is either a path from y to x or from x to y. Modify Algorithm BFS to determine if a graph is connected.

**5-4.5 Depth First Search**

A depth first search (DFS) of an arbitrary graph can be used to perform a traversal of a general graph. As each new node is encountered, it is marked (in our case with

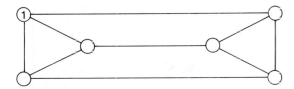

**FIGURE 5-4.27**

*true* indicating the order in which the nodes were encountered) to show that the node has been visited. The DFS strategy is as follows. A node s is picked as a start node and marked. An unmarked adjacent node to s is now selected and marked, becoming the new start node, possibly leaving the original start node with unexplored edges for the present. The search continues in the graph until the current path ends at a node with outdegree zero or at a node with all adjacent nodes already marked. Then the search returns to the last node which still has unmarked adjacent nodes and continues marking until all nodes are marked.

If we use the graph in Fig. 5-4.28 as an example, the DFS strategy results in the traversal indicated by the arrows, assuming each edge has been assigned a value of one. Starting at node A, the search numbers all nodes down until node F, where all adjacent nodes have already been marked. The algorithm returns to node C, which still has an unlabeled adjacent node D. After node D and E are labeled, all nodes are numbered and the search is complete.

Since adjacent nodes are needed during the traversal, the most efficient representation again is an adjacency list. The same data structure as presented in algorithm BFS will be used, changing the DIST variable in the node table directory to DFN (for depth first search number). The procedure to calculate the depth first numbering scheme can be iterative using a stack, or recursive, as we will present.

**Procedure** DFS(INDEX, COUNT). Given the structure as described before, this recursive procedure calculates the depth first search numbers for a graph. INDEX is the current index into the node table directory table and is assumed to be initialized to one outside the procedure. COUNT is used to keep track of the current DFN number and is initially set to zero outside the procedure. Finally, it is assumed the DFN field was initialized to zero when the adjacency list structure was created.

1.  [Update the depth first search number, set and mark current node]
    COUNT ← COUNT + 1
    DFN[INDEX] ← COUNT
    REACH[INDEX] ← *true*
2.  [Set up loop to examine each neighbor of current node]
    LINK ← LISTPTR[INDEX]
    Repeat step 3 while LINK ≠ NULL
3.  [If node has not been marked, label it and make recursive call]
    If not REACH[DESTIN(LINK)]
    then   Call DFS(DESTIN(LINK), COUNT)
    LINK ← EDGEPTR(LINK)   (Examine next adjacent node)
4.  [Return to point of call]
    Return                                                             □

The algorithm checks if the REACH field has been set to *true* before traversing the remaining part of the graph. This will both prevent renumbering of any node

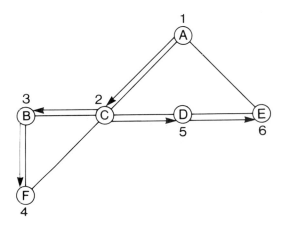

**FIGURE 5-4.28**    Depth First Search traversal.

and save from traversing any part of the graph twice. Once a null pointer is encountered in an edge list, the algorithm returns (i.e., backs up one level), repeating this until all edge lists have been traversed. Control is then returned to the calling program.

The timing analysis for this procedure is similar to that obtained for Procedure **BFS**. The worst-case analysis results in at most n − 1 recursive calls since a recursive call is performed only once for each unreached node. Step 2 and the assignment statement in step 3 are performed a maximum of e times. Therefore, the worst-case time bound is O(n + e).

A graph is *connected* if for every pair of nodes x and y, there exists a path between x and y. By applying a depth first search (or breadth first search) and examining the REACH field, we can determine if the graph is connected. A REACH value of *false* indicates the search could not reach this node (or nodes). This proves there is no path to this node, therefore the graph cannot be connected.

A graph is called *biconnected* if there is no single node whose removal causes the graph to break into two or more pieces. A node whose removal causes the graph to become disconnected is called a *cutvertex* (node C in Fig. 5-4.29). To determine if a graph has any cutvertices and which nodes they represent, we must remove one node at a time from the graph, applying either a DFS or BFS algorithm, and

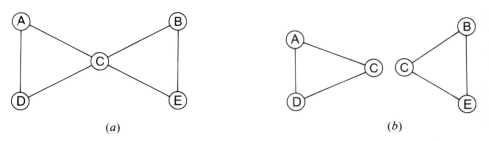

**FIGURE 5-4.29**    (*a*) Sample graph; and (*b*) graph with node C removed.

determine whether the graph is still connected. Obviously this is a very time-consuming method.

A more efficient approach is as follows. A DFS is performed on the graph. Then a DFS tree is created by redrawing the graph with only the edges used to traverse the graph during the search. These tree edges and are represented by solid lines in Fig. 5-4.30. Now those edges not traversed are inserted as back edges, indicated by dashed lines. The graph of Fig. 5-4.28 redrawn as a DFS tree is presented in Fig. 5-4.30a, the nodes now numbered with their DFN value.

For every node we calculate a lowpoint. A *lowpoint* is the DFN number of the lowest numbered node which can be reached by tracing through zero or more tree edges, followed by at most one back edge. For example, in Fig. 5-4.30a node 2 has a lowpoint of one. This is obtained by following tree edges from node 2 to node 5 to node 6, and one back edge up to node 1. This value results in a lowpoint of one. The lowpoints for the sample graph are given in Fig. 5-4.30b. The cutvertices can now be determined using these values.

The root node of the DFS tree is a cutvertex if it has two or more sons attached to it. Any other node v is a cutvertex if there is some son u of v such that the lowpoint of u is greater than or equal to the DFN of v. For example, node 2 has a son, node 3, with a lowpoint of two. Node 2 itself has a DFN number of two, and since the values are equal, node 2 is a cutvertex. Upon further examination of the graph in Fig. 5-4.30b, no other node is a cutvertex. However, the graph is not biconnected since there is at least one cutvertex.

This application of DFS is useful in many real-world situations. A vital communications network may be represented by a graph, allowing each node to represent a communication line and each edge indicating the presence of an interconnection between the lines. If a cutvertex is present, destruction of the line represented by the cutvertex would result in a breakdown of communications. If the graph is biconnected, the removal of one line (node) would not affect communications, since there will remain at least one other link.

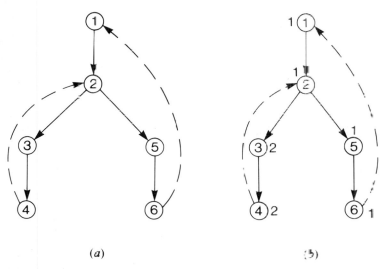

(a)                              (b)

**FIGURE 5-4.30**   (a) DFS tree; and (b) with lowpoints.

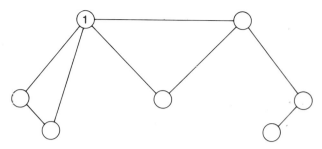

**FIGURE 5-4.31**

**Exercises for Sec. 5-4.5**

1.  Produce the input structure and DFN numbers for the graph in Fig. 5-4.31. Also determine the lowpoints and find the cutvertices starting at node 1.
2.  For the dynamic adjacency list representation of a graph described in Sec. 5-4.3, develop an iterative algorithm using a stack to perform a DFS on this new structure.
3.  Using the approach described in this subsection, formulate an algorithm which will generate the lowpoints and determine the cutvertices of an arbitrary graph.

### 5-4.6 Spanning Trees

A spanning tree of a graph is an undirected tree consisting of only those edges necessary to connect all the nodes in the original graph. A spanning tree has the properties that for any pair of nodes there exists only one path between them, and the insertion of any edge to a spanning tree forms a unique cycle. Those edges left out of the spanning tree that were present in the original graph connect paths together in the tree.

The particular spanning tree for a graph depends on the criteria used to generate it. If a depth first search is used, those edges traversed by the algorithm form the edges of the tree, referred to as a depth first spanning tree. If a breadth first search is used, the spanning tree is formed from those edges traversed during the search, producing a breadth first spanning tree. Examples of a breadth first spanning tree and a depth first spanning tree are given in Fig. 5-4.32 for the graph of Fig. 5-4.24.

When determining the cost of a spanning tree of a weighted graph, the cost is simply the sum of the weights of the tree's edges. A minimal cost spanning tree is formed when the edges are picked to minimize the total cost.

The remainder of this section is devoted to the development of an algorithm to determine a minimal cost spanning tree for a weighted graph. The most efficient graph representation for this algorithm is an edge list sorted by increasing order of weight. An adjacency matrix could be used, but this would require the entire matrix to be searched for each edge participating in the spanning tree in order to find the edge with minimal weight.

The input graph will be stored as a linked list with each edge in the list being represented by a node structure as shown in Fig. 5-4.33. The field START is the initial node number and TERMIN is the terminal node number for this edge. WEIGHT contains the cost associated with the edge, and FLAG determines if the edge is to be

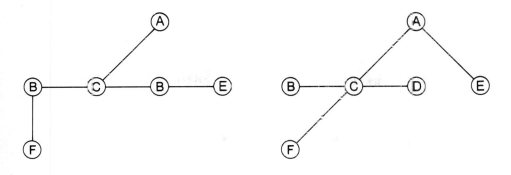

**FIGURE 5-4.32**   (*a*) DFS spanning tree; and (*b*) BFS spanning tree.

included in the minimal cost spanning tree. A vector CHECK is used to indicate if a specific node has already been joined to the spanning tree. A general algorithm to calculate the minimal spanning tree is now presented.

1.   Mark off the starting and terminating nodes for the first edge
2.   Repeat until all edges have been examined
   if the current edge has not already been included in the minimal spanning tree
   then if the starting and terminating nodes have been checked off
    then mark edge to indicate path exists between these nodes
    else if both the starting and terminating nodes have not been checked off
     then add this edge to the minimal spanning tree
      restart the examination from the beginning of the edge list
   Examine next edge

Integers have been used for names of nodes to simplify the detailed algorithm, which may now be presented.

**Algorithm** MIN_SPAN.   Given the structure described previously, sorted in increasing order of cost, this algorithm calculates the minimal spanning tree. CHECK is a vector of size equal to the number of nodes. HEAD, defined outside the algorithm, points to the beginning of the linked list of edges. We assume the FLAG field has been set to zero when the structure shown in Fig. 5-4.33 was created.

1.   [Check off nodes in the first edge]
  CHECK[START(HEAD)] ← 1
  CHECK[TERMIN(HEAD)] ← 1
  FLAG(HEAD) ← 1
2.   [Set loop and repeat until all edges have been examined]
  P ← HEAD
  Repeat while P ≠ NULL
   f FLAG(P) = 0   (those edges not already in tree)

```
then   If (CHECK[START(P)] = 1) and (CHECK[TERMIN(P)] = 1)
       then   FLAG(P) ← -1   (there is a path between these two nodes
                                   already)
       else   If (CHECK[START(P)] ≠ 0) and (CHECK[TERMIN(P)] ≠ 0)
              Then CHECK[START(P)] ← 1   (add the edge to the tree)
                   CHECK[TERMIN(P)] ← 1
                   FLAG(P) ← 1
                   P ← HEAD   (restart search)
            P ← LINK(P)   (examine next edge)
3.   [Finished]
     Exit
```

Several simple modifications can be added to this algorithm to change its function. If the edge list were to be sorted in decreasing order of weight, the maximum cost spanning tree can be calculated. The total cost of the tree can be found by summing the weights of the edges as they are inserted in the spanning tree. This algorithm can also be used to determine if the original graph was connected. An edge with a flag value of zero after the entire edge list has been traversed indicates the edge was never connected with the graph.

**Exercises for Sec. 5-4.6**

1. Modify both the breadth first search and depth first search algorithms to generate spanning trees.
2. Create a procedure which reads in an edge list in no particular order and creates a linked-list representation sorted by increasing order of weight.
3. Develop an algorithm that creates a minimal cost spanning tree, where the graph is represented by an adjacency matrix.

**5-4.7 An Example of a Time-Consuming Problem**

In this subsection we give an example of a problem which can be very time consuming to solve. Such a famous problem is the so-called travelling salesperson problem. In this problem, a salesperson must start at a specified city, visit each of $n-1$ other cities exactly once, and then return to the initial city. The cost of going from city i to city j is represented as C[city i, city j]. The objective is to find a route through the cities that minimizes the total cost. As an example consider a travelling salesperson living in Montreal who must visit several cities and then return home. The distance chart (in kilometers) in Table 5-4.2 is available to the traveller. Two round trips are illustrated in Fig. 5-4.34. In particular, these trips are as follows:

$$M \to O \to T \to L \to S \to W \to H \to K \to M$$

$$M \to O \to T \to S \to W \to L \to H \to K \to M$$

One approach to obtaining a path with the shortest distance is to generate all possible round trips and to record one of the shortest trips. There is a fairly straightfor-

| START | TERMIN | WEIGHT | FLAG | LINK |
|-------|--------|--------|------|------|

**FIGURE 5-4.33**   Edge list structure.

ward, but time consuming, recursive algorithm for the problem that uses this approach. We will now develop this algorithm and analyze its time requirements.

Given that the salesperson has already visited some cities by some partial route, the idea is to extend the route by going to a city not already visited. This is continued until all cities have been visited and the route is completed by returning to the initial city. The problem is to determine which city to visit next. To make sure that we find the best route, we shall try each of the possible cities next. Using these ideas, let SUBROUTE(I, CURRENT) be a procedure that, given N - I cities have already been visited by the initial part of the route leading to CURRENT, will determine the best route to visit the remaining I cities. It does this by visiting an unvisited city NEXT, and then calling SUBROUTE( I-1 , NEXT) to continue the route. This is done for each of the possible next cities, that is, each city not already visited. Thus the subroutine has the general form:

**Procedure** SUBROUTE(I, CURRENT). Complete a partial route by visiting the I cities not already visited. START is the specified start city. CURRENT is the last city on the current partial route. PARTIAL_COST is the cost of the current partial route. MIN_COST is the cost of the least cost route found so far. CUR_ROUTE is the current partial route where CUR_ROUTE(city i) gives the city that follows city i on the route. VISITED is a logical vector that indicates whether each city has been visited on the current partial route.

1. [Determine a route through the cities which minimizes total cost]
   If I = 0
   then   (All cities have been visited so compare the cost of the route
          obtained by returning to the start city with the previous minimum
          cost)
          TOTAL_COST ← PARTIAL_COST + C[CURRENT, START]
          If TOTAL_COST < MIN_COST
          then   MIN_COST ← TOTAL_COST
                 MIN_ROUTE ← CUR_ROUTE


**Table 5-4.2**   Distance Chart

|   |          | 1<br>H | 2<br>K | 3<br>L | 4<br>M | 5<br>O | 6<br>T | 7<br>S | 8<br>W |
|---|----------|--------|--------|--------|--------|--------|--------|--------|--------|
| 1 | Hamilton | 0      | 325    | 125    | 570    | 465    | 70     | 440    | 310    |
| 2 | Kingston | 325    | 0      | 440    | 290    | 170    | 255    | 605    | 625    |
| 3 | London   | 125    | 440    | 0      | 720    | 565    | 190    | 555    | 195    |
| 4 | Montreal | 570    | 290    | 720    | 0      | 205    | 540    | 670    | 905    |
| 5 | Ottawa   | 465    | 170    | 565    | 205    | 0      | 395    | 490    | 755    |
| 6 | Toronto  | 70     | 255    | 190    | 540    | 395    | 0      | 375    | 380    |
| 7 | Sudbury  | 440    | 605    | 555    | 670    | 490    | 375    | 0      | 745    |
| 8 | Windsor  | 310    | 625    | 195    | 905    | 755    | 380    | 745    | 0      |

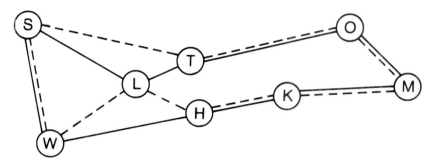

**FIGURE 5-4.34**

       **else**   (Determine the continuation of the route by selecting the next
               city and using recursion to continue from there)
               Repeat for each city, NEXT
                   If not VISITED[NEXT]
                   **then**   (Try the route obtained by extending the current partial
                             route to NEXT)
                             CUR_ROUTE[CURRENT] ← NEXT
                             VISITED[NEXT] ← *true*
                             Call SUBROUTE(I−1, NEXT)
                             (Delete the visitation just tried so that another can be tried)
                             VISITED[NEXT] ← *false*
2.   [Finished]
       Return                                                  □

Now the solution to the problem can be obtained by starting with all cities unvisited
except the start city, and using the procedure call

     Call SUBROUTE(N−1, START)

Further details of the algorithm can be filled in without much difficulty.

     To analyze the time needed by the algorithm, we need to isolate an active
operation. Picking an operation within the loop of SUBROUTE, the operation
"VISITED[NEXT] ← *true*" seems to be central to the algorithm. We begin by calculating the number of occurrences of "VISITED[NEXT] ← *true*" resulting from the call
SUBROUTE(I, CURRENT).   The   "then"   part   of   the   loop   within
SUBROUTE(I, CURRENT) is traversed I times since there are I unvisited cities to try
when the call is made. The number of executions of "VISITED[NEXT] ← *true*"
resulting   from   each   loop   traversal   is   1   +   the   number   of   executions   of
"VISITED[NEXT] ← *true*" resulting from the call SUBROUTE(I−1, NEXT). Let F(I) be
the number of executions of "VISITED[NEXT] ← *true*" resulting from the call
SUBROUTE(I, CURRENT). Thus we have

     F(I) = (number of traversals of the loop) * (number of executions per traversal)
           = I * (1 + F(I−1))
           = I + I * F(I−1)   for I > 0

Also

     F(0) = 1

since for I = 0 a return visit is done to the initial city. These equations form what is called a recurrence relation for function F, since they define the value of F on an argument in terms of the values of the function on smaller arguments. Note that

$$F(I) \geq I * F(I - 1) \quad \text{for } I > 0$$
$$F(I) = 1 \quad \text{for } I = 0$$

so we immediately have $F(I) \geq I!$. Thus the time for the travelling salesperson algorithm $T_{TS}(n)$ satisfies the relation

$$|T_{TS}(n)| \geq c * |F(n-1)| \geq c * (n-1)!$$

for $n > n_0$ and constant c. The notation used for this is $T_{TS}(n) = O((n - 1)!)$. To see what this means, suppose we have a computer that can execute $10^9$ instructions per second (this is somewhat faster than present day machines). Then the following gives a lower bound on the execution time of the algorithm on various problem sizes:

| problem size n | 9 | 12 | 15 | 18 | 21 |
|---|---|---|---|---|---|
| $\frac{(n-1)!}{1 \times 10^9}$ sec | $4 \times 10^{-5}$ sec | $4 \times 10^{-2}$ sec | 1.4 min | 4 days | 7.7 years |

Obviously this algorithm is useless for problems of size larger than 15. Also we are fortunate that we performed this analysis to estimate the execution time of the algorithm rather than implementing the algorithm and wasting much computer time trying to run the algorithm on some sample data.

It turns out that the travelling salesperson problem is a member of a very infamous class of problems known as the NP-Hard class. Problems in the NP-Hard class are known to have execution times in the worst case at least as long as problems in a class known as NP-Complete. This latter class contains several hundred interesting problems. Also this NP-Complete class has the special feature that if an algorithm with worst case execution time bounded by a polynomial exists for any problem in the class, then such an algorithm can be obtained for all the problems in the class. However it is widely believed that no algorithm which is polynomially bounded will ever be found for any of them, and hence that the best algorithm for each of them is exponential in execution time. By implication, it is widely believed that the best algorithm for the travelling salesperson problem requires exponential time. Nevertheless, there are much better algorithms for the travelling salesperson problem than the above one, although they are still exponential in the worst case.

For recursive algorithms, space required to store the stack must also be counted. Thus the space for a recursive routine is given by the space for its local variables plus the space for the local variables of all the recursive calls from it. A separate count must be made of the space for variables global to all the recursive routines. Applying this approach to the SUBROUTE algorithm used for the travelling salesperson problem is fairly easy. The global variables will consist of the matrix of costs C, the vectors VISITED, CUR_ROUTE, and MIN_ROUTE, and variables START, PARTIAL_COST, TOTAL_COST, and MIN_COST. This entails $O(n^2)$ storage for global variables. Only a constant amount of storage, O(1), is needed for variables local to the procedure. Thus including the storage for the recursive calls, the local storage for SUBROUTE is given by

$$S_{SR}(I) = O(1) + S_{SR}(I-1)$$

since all the recursive calls that occur in one routine can reuse the same stack storage. Also

$S_{SR}(0) = O(1)$.

Solving the recurrence relation we obtain $S_{SR}(l) = O(l)$. Thus we obtain

$$S_{TS}(n) = \text{global storage} + S_{SR}(n-1)$$
$$= O(n^2) + O(n-1)$$
$$= O(n^2).$$

From the previous discussion, it is clear that the effort in determining the shortest round trip by choosing the shortest distance trip from all possible trips is too costly. A more realistic approach is to use some intuitive and common sense approach in determining a reasonably short round trip. Such an approach is called a *heuristic* approach. Note that the shortest round trip is not usually obtained by using a heuristic approach.

One heuristic strategy is to proceed to the nearest city that has not yet been visited from a current position. When you arrive at this new position, you can again look for the nearest city that has not been visited. This process is repeated until a round trip distance is determined.

The round-trip distance obtained using this heuristic approach depends on which city that is used as the starting point. Starting at a different city will usually yield a different, and possibly shorter, round-trip distance.

One problem with the previous heuristic approach is that a city like Sudbury, which is further away from the more centrally located cities, is visited towards the end of a round trip. Such a shortcoming, however, can be avoided by including a remote city in a round trip immediately after its nearest neighbor has been visited. A modified heuristic which alleviates this shortcoming is as follows:

Given that you are at a particular city (e.g., A), proceed to its nearest neighbor providing that there is no other city (e.g., B) which has the first (A) as its nearest neighbor. Otherwise, we proceed to city B.

The implementation of heuristics is left as an exercise.

### Exercise for Sec. 5-4.7

1. Write a Pascal program which implements the heuristic strategy just suggested. Also implement its suggested modification. Use Table 5-4.2 as data.

## 5-5 APPLICATIONS OF GRAPHS

Section 5-4.3 discussed a number of possible storage structures for graphs. In this section we have selected three applications in which graph structures are extensively used. One of the first applications of graphs to be computerized was concerned with project scheduling, a technique which is often known as PERT or CPM. This topic is covered in the first subsection. Complex data structures are often used in computer graphics systems, and consequently, these are introduced in Sec. 5-5.2. The problem of topological sorting is described in the last subsection.

### 5-5.1 PERT and Related Techniques

A directed graph is a natural way of describing, representing, and analyzing complex projects which consist of many interrelated activities. This project might be, for example, the design and construction of a power dam or the design and erection of an apartment building. In this section we are interested in determining the critical path of a digraph. Such a critical path is a very important management tool that can be applied to many situations. There are a number of management techniques such as PERT (program evaluation and review technique) and CPM (critical path method) which employ a graph as the structure on which analysis is based. The problem of finding a minimal path between two nodes was discussed in Sec. 5-4.1. A critical path, however, involves finding the longest path between two nodes in a weighted digraph.

This section will introduce certain basic terminology associated with finding the critical path of a graph. An informal algorithm will be given for computing the critical path(s) of a weighted graph.

Formally, a PERT graph is a finite digraph, with no parallel edges or cycles, in which there is exactly one source (i.e., a node whose indegree is 0) and one sink (i.e., a node whose outdegree is 0). Furthermore, each edge in the graph is assigned a weight (time) value. The directed edges are meant to represent activities, with the directed edge joining nodes which represent the start time and the finish time of the activity. The weight value of each edge is taken to be the time it takes to complete the activity.

Although there will be a number of independent activities in the graph, there will usually be certain essential dependencies, with respect to time which have the form that activity $a_i$ must be completed before activity $a_j$ can begin. If all such time dependencies are available, then they can be conveniently displayed in a directed graph such as in Fig. 5-5.1. The project has eight activities, and the activities follow a particular order in the sense that certain activities must be completed before certain other activities can begin. Each node is called an *event* and represents a point in time. In particular, node $v_1$ denotes the start of the entire project (its source) and $v_6$ its completion (its sink). The numbers associated with the edges represent the number of days required to do that particular activity. From the graph we see that before activity $<v_3, v_4>$ can begin, activity $<v_1, v_3>$ must be completed. Similarly, before activity $<v_4, v_6>$ can begin, activities $<v_2, v_4>$ and $<v_3, v_4>$ must both be done, etc. Finally, in order to complete the project, activities $<v_5, v_6>$, $<v_3, v_6>$, and $<v_4 v_6>$ must all be completed.

We process the PERT graph by computing the earliest completion time for each activity under the restriction that, before an activity can begin, every activity upon which it depends must be completed. In terms of the graph, this corresponds to the assignment of time values to each node in such a manner that the value assigned to a node is the length of time to complete the activities along the longest path leading into that node. That is, we assign to a node the value which is the maximum, over all the incoming edges, of the weight of an edge plus the time associated with that edge's source node. By definition, the value of 0 is assigned to the source node.

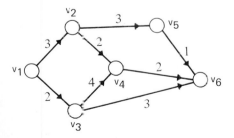

**FIGURE 5-5.1**  A PERT graph.

In summary, we can associate a time value with each event node in the following manner:

$$TE(v_1) = 0$$

$$TE(v_j) = \max \{t(P)\} \qquad j \neq 1$$

where $t(P)$ denotes the sum of time durations for a path $P$ and where the maximum is taken over all paths from $v_1$ to $v_j$. When we finally assign a value to the sink node, this value is the earliest completion time for the entire project.

Referring to Fig. 5-5.1, node $v_2$ has only one incoming edge, and consequently, a value of 3 ($= 0 + 3$) is assigned to that node. Node $v_4$ has two incoming edges, so we must take the temporally longer path length $(v_1, v_3, v_4)$ ($= 2 + 4$) rather than the path $(v_1, v_2, v_4)$ ($= 3 + 2$) and assign 6 to node $v_4$. Node $v_6$ has four incoming paths $(v_1, v_3, v_6)$, $(v_1, v_3, v_4, v_6)$, $(v_1, v_2, v_5, v_6)$, and $(v_1, v_2, v_4, v_6)$. The value for the first path is 5, while that of the second is 8, and that of the third and fourth is 7; therefore, a value of 8 is assigned to $v_6$. Since $v_6$ is the sink node, assigning $v_6$ a value of 8 indicates that the project will require at least eight days to complete. The network with the earliest completion time, TE, assigned to each node is given in Fig. 5-5.2.

Having progressed this far, we can next calculate the latest completion time associated with each node. This is the latest time an activity can be completed without causing a delay in the earliest completion date of the project (i.e., they are the latest completion times associated with the activities that do not cause the TE value of the sink node to be increased). These latest completion times, TL, are assigned to nodes in such a way that the assigned TL value is the largest value which will still allow every activity starting at that node to be completed without an overall time increase. In terms of the graph, we assign to a node the value which is the minimum, over all outgoing edges, of the edge's destination node TL value minus the edge weight. By definition, the TL value of the sink node equals its TE value.

In summary, we can associate a time value with each event node in the following manner:

$$TL(v_n) = TE(v_n)$$
$$TL(v_j) = TE(v_n) - \max \{t(P)\} \qquad j \neq n$$

where $t(P)$ denotes the sum of time durations for a path $P$ from $v_j$ to $v_n$ and where the maximum is taken over all such paths and subtracted from $TE(v_n)$.

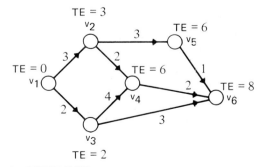

**FIGURE 5-5.2**

Returning to Fig. 5-5.2, since $v_5$ has only one outgoing edge, we assigned to $v_5$ a TL value of 7 (= 8 – 1). Likewise, node $v_4$ has only one outgoing edge, so a TL value of 6 (= 8 – 2) is assigned to $v_4$. Node $v_3$ has two outgoing edges, $<v_3, v_4>$ and $<v_3, v_6>$. The minimum of 2 is assigned to that node. Continuing this process yields a TL value of 0 for the source node. The PERT graph of our example with its TE and TL values is given in Fig. 5-5.3.

After having computed the TE and TL values for each node in a graph, we can determine its critical path(s). A *critical path* is a path from the source node to the sink node such that if any activity on the path is delayed by an amount t, then the entire project is delayed by t. Each node on the critical path has its TL value equal to its TE value. This means that, if the project is to be completed by its earliest completion time, the nodes on the critical path must be reached at their earliest completion times. For our example graph, the nodes on the critical path are: $v_1$, $v_3$, $v_4$, $v_6$ and the critical path is $(v_1, v_3, v_4, v_6)$. Nodes that are not on the critical path have slack time associated with them. *Slack time* of a node is merely the difference between its TL and TE values, and it indicates the amount of spare time which is available in doing a particular activity. In our example, node $v_2$ has a slack time of one day. This means that the activities that must be completed at node $v_2$ can be delayed one day if necessary without causing a delay in the project.

In order to reduce the earliest completion time for the project, we find only those activities on the critical path must be speeded up. Since in practice the number of activities which lie on the critical path in large graphs is a small percentage of the total number of activities, say 10 percent, only those 10 percent need be improved.

We shall now consider the representation of a PERT graph according to the method suggested in Sec. 5-4.3 using arrays. For the node access directory, there will be four one-dimensional arrays, DATA, TE, TL, and POINTER. For node i, DATA[i] contains label data and information about i, TE[i] and TL[i] are the earliest and latest completion times for node i, and POINTER[] is the index into the table of edges where the edges originating at node i are listed in successive array positions. For the table of edges, there will be two one-dimensional arrays, TIME and DEST, with TIME[j] being the weight of edge j in time units and DEST[j] being the destination node of edge j. The originating node for edge j is node i, where i is the largest number such that POINTER[i] ≤ j. Figure 5-5.4 illustrates the storage structures that we are now describing.

The following algorithm will create the desired storage structures by reading edge data from an input file. For convenience, this algorithm assumes that the

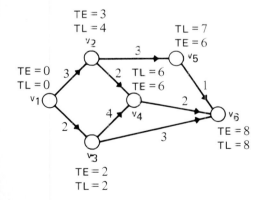

**FIGURE 5-5.3**

| NODE NO. | DATA | TE | TL | POINTER |
|---|---|---|---|---|
| 1 | $v_1$ | 0 | $\infty$ | 1 |
| 2 | $v_2$ | 0 | $\infty$ | 3 |
| 3 | $v_3$ | 0 | $\infty$ | 5 |
| 4 | $v_4$ | 0 | $\infty$ | 7 |
| 5 | $v_5$ | 0 | $\infty$ | 8 |
| 6 | $v_6$ | 0 | $\infty$ | 9 |

| EDGE NO. | TIME | DEST |
|---|---|---|
| 1 | 3 | 2 |
| 2 | 2 | 3 |
| 3 | 2 | 4 |
| 4 | 3 | 5 |
| 5 | 4 | 4 |
| 6 | 3 | 6 |
| 7 | 2 | 6 |
| 8 | 1 | 6 |

**FIGURE 5-5.4**   The data arrays after Algorithm CREATE has read the input file.

input data has been sorted into ascending order by originating node number, with node 1 being the source node (the start of the project) and with the highest numbered node being the sink node, corresponding to the completion of the project. The edge data items are the following: ORIGIN, the node number of the originating node: INFO, data or information about the originating node; WEIGHT, the edge weight in time units; and END, the node number of the destination node. Note that INFO need be given only once for a particular originating node; it can be a null string other times. In order to input information and label data for the project sink node, we will have to use an extra set of edge data items since the sink node has outdegree 0. The destination node number will be zero in this case, and this input record will be functioning like a "trailer record," thus providing a second means of terminating data input. A general algorithm to accomplish this procedure is as follows.

1. Read the first set of data items
2. Repeat thru step 5 until there is no more data
3. If the new node number is less than the previous node number
   then write data is out of sequence and exit
4. If the new node number is greater than the previous node number
   then create a new originating node
      insert it in the structure
      insert the edge in the structure according to the new node's location
   else insert the edge in the structure according to the previous nodes location
5. Read the next set of data items

A detailed algorithm to create the desired structure is now presented.

**Algorithm CREATE.** Given the global array structures DATA, TE, TL, POINTER, TIME, and DEST, this algorithm reads edge data from an input file and assigns values to the elements of these arrays so as to reflect the relationships existing in a PERT graph. The variables NO_NODES and NO_EDGES are also considered to be global, and they give the number of different nodes and edges, respectively, that have been encountered in the graph.

1.  [Initialize]
        TE ← POINTER ← 0
        DATA ← ' '
        NO_NODES ← NO_EDGES ← 0
        TL ← ∞   (or some very large number)
2.  [Read the first set of data items]
        Read(ORIGIN, INFO, WEIGHT, END)
3.  [Continue processing until there is no more data]
        Repeat thru step 5 until input file is exhausted
4.  [Assign to array elements]
        If ORIGIN < NO_NODES
        then   Write('DATA OUT OF SEQUENCE')
                Exit
        If INFO ≠ ' '
        then   DATA[ORIGIN] ← INFO
        If ORIGIN > NO_NODES
        then   (new originating node)
                NO_NODES ← NO_NODES + 1
                POINTER[NO_NODES] ← NO_EDGES + 1
                If END ≤ 0
                then   Exit
                else   NO_EDGES ← NO_EDGES + 1
                        TIME[NO_EDGES] ← WEIGHT
                        DEST[NO_EDGES] ← END
        else   (same originating node)
                If END ≤ 0
                then   Write('NONSINK NODE HAS AN EDGE WITH
                                INVALID DESTINATION')
                        Exit
                else   NO_EDGES ← NO_EDGES + 1
                        TIME[NO_EDGES] ← WEIGHT
                        DEST[NO_EDGES] ← END
5.  [Get next input data]
        Read(ORIGIN, INFO, WEIGHT, END)
6.  [Finished]
        Exit                                                    □

Step 1 initializes the arrays and counters appropriately. In step 4, label information is stored if necessary. Then, if a new originating node has been encountered, the node counter is updated and the entry in the POINTER array is set. These actions are omitted if the node is a previously encountered one. At this time, the edge counter is updated if it is a valid edge, and the appropriate data is stored in the arrays.

In order to determine the critical path, we must compute the TE and TL values for each node. A general algorithm to calculate these values is now given.

1.  Repeat thru step 3 for each node starting at the source node and ending at the sink node
2.  Repeat step 3 for all edges associated with the current node
3.  Set TE of the terminating node to the maximum of either its current TE value, or the TE of the start node plus the connecting edge's time

4.  Repeat thru step 6 for each node starting at the sink node and ending at the source node
5.  Repeat step 6 for all edges associated with the current node
6.  Set TL of the source node to the minimum of either its current TL value, or the TL of the terminating node minus the connecting edge's time
7.  Output the nodes on the critical path

The following algorithm computes the critical path and then prints out the nodes on the path.

**Algorithm** PROCESS. Given the global arrays as previously described, along with NO_NODES and NO_EDGES, the number of different nodes and edges in the PERT graph, this algorithm computes and stores the TE and TL values for each node and then prints those nodes which lie on the critical path. NODE# and EDGE# indicate which node and which edge are currently being examined.

1.  [Initialize to compute TE values]
    NODE# ← 1
    EDGE# ← POINTER[1]
2.  [Compute TE value for each node]
    Repeat while NODE# < NO_NODES
      Repeat while EDGE# < POINTER[NODE# + 1]
        TE[DEST[EDGE#]] ← MAX(TE[DEST[EDGE#]], TE[NODE#]
                    + TIME[EDGE#])
        EDGE# ← EDGE# + 1
      NODE# ← NODE# + 1
3.  [Initialize to compute TL values]
    TL[NODE#] ← TE[NODE#]
    NODE# ← NO_NODES - 1
    EDGE# ← NO_EDGES
4.  [Compute TL values for each node]
    Repeat while NODE# ≥ 1
      Repeat while EDGE# ≥ POINTER[NODE#]
        TL[NODE#] ← MIN(TL[NODE#], TL[DEST[EDGE#]]
               - TIME[EDGE#])
        EDGE# ← EDGE# - 1
      NODE# ← NODE# - 1
5.  [Output the nodes on the critical path]
    Repeat for NODE# = 1, 2, ..., NO_NODES
    If TE[NODE#] = TL[NODE#]
    then    Write(NODE#, DATA[NODE#])
6.  [Finished]
    Exit                    □

The operation of this algorithm is quite straightforward. In step 2 the elements $TE[v_j] = \max \{t(P)\}$ $j \neq 1$ are computed, thereby assigning to each node $v_j$ the time taken along the longest path P from node $v_1$ to node $v_j$. In step 3 the latest completion time for the project finish node is defined to be the earliest completion time for the project, and the counters are reset. In step 4 the values $TL[v_j] = TE[v_n] - \max \{t(P)\}$ $j \neq n$ are computed, thereby assigning to each node $v_j$ (other than the sink node $v_n$) the latest time value such that adding this time value to the time associated with the longest path from $v_j$ to $v_n$ does not exceed the project finish date. In step 5 the nodes on the critical path (those nodes whose TE and TL values are equal) are printed, along with the appropriate labeling information.

It is also possible to use linked lists as the method of representing a PERT graph. For example, each event node of the graph could be represented by a node structure as shown in Fig 5-5.5a, where OUT is a pointer to the first node in a list of the edges originating at this event node, IN is a pointer to the first node in a list of the edges whose destination is this event node, DATA is label information for this event node, TE and TL are the earliest and latest completion times for this event node, and LINK is a pointer to the next structural node in the list of event nodes. For the edges, a structure of the form shown in Fig. 5-5.5b could be used. OUTL is a pointer to the next edge in the list of edges originating at the event node to which SOURCE points, INL is a pointer to the next edge in the list of edges whose destination is the event node to which DEST points, and TIME is the weight in time units of this edge which joins the nodes to which SOURCE and DEST point.

Algorithms to create such a representation of a PERT graph and determine the nodes on the critical path are relatively easy to construct. The computational logic is the same as that used in the array representation algorithms, but naturally the logic dealing with the manipulation of the storage structures will differ.

**Exercises for Sec. 5-5.1**

1.  Trace Algorithms CREATE and PROCESS using as data the graph given in Fig. 5-5.4

2.  Given node structures for the event nodes and edges of a PERT graph as described at the end of Sec. 5-5.1, construct an algorithm that will create a linked-list representation of this graph. The algorithm should have the input edge data in the following form:

    ORIGIN, the label of the source node for some edge
    END, the label of the edge's destination node
    WEIGHT, the weight of the edge in time units

    The algorithm should create and insert nodes ORIGIN and END into the event node list, if they are not already there. It must then create an edge node and insert it into the proper incoming and outgoing edge lists and update all pointers correctly.

3.  Given a linked representation of a PERT graph as constructed by the algorithm in Prob. 2, write an algorithm that will traverse this representation, com-

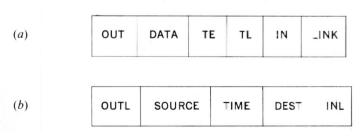

(a) | OUT | DATA | TE | TL | IN | LINK |

(b) | OUTL | SOURCE | TIME | DEST | INL |

**FIGURE 5-5.5**

puting the TE and TL values for the event node. The algorithm should 'then print out the nodes that are on the critical path.

4. Write Pascal procedures that implement Algorithms CREATE and PROCESS in Sec. 5-5.1 and the algorithms of Probs. 2 and 3. Evaluate the two representations, arrays and linked lists, in terms of storage use and processing speed for small and large PERT graphs.

### 5-5.2 Computer Graphics Applications

"*Computer graphics* is the general term applied herein to the use of a digital computer to form an internal model representation of an externally perceived graphical entity." (Abrams [1971].) Such modeling makes possible the modification, manipulation, or other such processing of the entity and the subsequent display of the entity in a visible format. Some typical applications of computer graphics include graph plotting, map drawing, and cartoon drawing, as well as building, road, aircraft, and automobile design.

There are two extreme modes in computer graphics—interactive and passive. As an introduction to many facets of the subject, we will discuss a system typical of each mode. The reader should be aware that this distinction is primarily for pedagogic purposes; a typical practical system would be a hybrid of the two extremes.

*Interactive computer graphics* is that mode of graphics in which the user and the computer interact or converse on-line. An on-line display device and manual input devices are used, providing very fast computer response to the user commands.

The most commonly used display is the cathode ray tube (CRT), a familiar device used in noncomputer equipment such as radar scopes and television screens. The method by which the CRT can display a computer-drawn picture is quite simple. Digital electrical signals generated by the computer are transformed, by a digital-to-analog converter, into a continuous signal. This signal controls the quantity and direction of electrons·emitted by one portion of the CRT; these electrons create the visible spots on the phosphorescent surface of the tube.

The major drawback with the CRT is that the points produced by the electron bombardment are extremely temporary, i.e., they quickly fade. In order to maintain a picture, a process by which the picture was created must be constantly repeated. This process is called "refreshing" the display and must be repeated about 30 times a second to avoid a flickering picture.

Other output devices in which the picture does not vanish have been developed. These include the direct-view storage tube and the plasma panel. At present these devices have technical problems which make them less popular than the conventional CRT for most applications.

In an *interactive system*, the user must communicate quickly and effectively with the computer. The input device used must provide for issuing commands, positioning symbols on the screen, and specifying items to be deleted or changed. Devices created for this purpose include the keyboard, the light pen, and the tablet.

A typical interactive system is illustrated in Fig. 5-5.6. A tablet and keyboard are used as input devices; a CRT is the output device. Note the *display processor*. This processor interacts with the CPU and accesses main memory to obtain the instructions describing the picture to be generated. The display processor can interpret these instructions and pass the appropriate signals to the CRT. The display processor is also responsible for refreshing the CRT, thus relieving the CPU of this

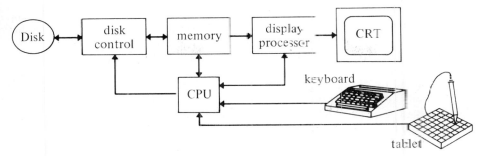

**FIGURE 5-5.6** A typical interactive graphics system.

time-consuming task. Sophisticated display processors may have the capability to generate simple geometric shapes.

The second graphics mode is noninteractive, or passive. In this mode a system usually operates in a batch environment; the input devices are typically card, disk, or tape files, and the output devices are usually "hard copy," that is, they provide a permanent picture. Examples of such output devices are line printers, plotters, and drafting machines. The most common passive output device is the moving pen plotter. This device moves a pen in the $xy$ plane, under computer control.

The hard-copy devices generate pictures very slowly and are thus seldom used in interactive systems. The only exception would be the case where a permanent record of the final product is desired.

A typical off-line system configuration is shown in Fig. 5-5.7. The processor generates the analog signals, which control the plotter, from the tape created by the main computer.

We will now discuss an aspect of computer graphics which is of greatest interest in this book—the data structures aspect. First consider some basic concepts.

All the computer graphics output devices provide a two-dimensional surface on which the pictures are to be created. This surface is treated as a cartesian coordinate system; the only points which can be specified are those addressed by an $x$ coordinate and $y$ coordinate of the system. All the devices can display any point so

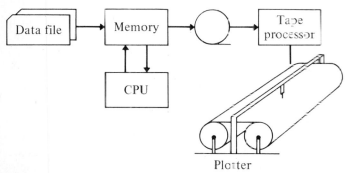

Plotter

**FIGURE 5-5.7** A typical off-line system configuration.

addressed.  Some of the more sophisticated devices have the capability to generate a continuous line between two addressable points; however, many create a line by displaying equally spaced points that lie along the line.

The earliest computer graphics systems were designed for graph plotting and data display.  Simple data structures such as the one- and two-dimensional array were sufficient for this complexity of graphical display.  The structure would be either a vector of the $(x, y)$ coordinates of all points to be displayed, a vector of $y$ coordinates corresponding to implicit $x$ coordinates, or a two-dimensional array A in which A[i, j] would be set to indicate that the point (i, j) was to be displayed.

This type of structure is adequate for applications in which the display are relatively static; however, much of the subsequent developments of computer graphics has been in applications requiring more versatile displays.  Some of the more promising areas are the design of buildings, aircraft, and automobiles, and this has led to the development of general graphics systems which can be used for any purpose.

Such applications require a versatile display that can be easily changed— deleting from, transforming, and adding to the display must be accommodated.  The simple data structures previously discussed are not adequate for these operations.  In order to provide the display capabilities desired, a more versatile data structure is necessary.  An adequate data structure should satisfy the following criteria:

1    The structure must provide a conceptual model of the subject; that is, the ordering and relationships between the subject parts must be preserved.
2    The structure must support the displaying, manipulation, transformation, and analysis of the subject.
3    The structure must be satisfactory in terms of memory requirements and processing speeds.

The reader's knowledge of data structures at this point should indicate that some type of linked structure could satisfy these requirements.

Consider two instances of the simplest type of list structure, i.e., two linear lists, one with the coordinates of points to be displayed, and the other with the coordinates of endpoints of lines to be displayed.

When a linked representation is used, the deletion or addition of a point or line is trivial, requiring only the changing of a few pointers rather than the shifting of many elements of an array.  The concatenation of two pictures is also simple; the line and point lists of each need only be linked.

This structure would satisfy the three requirements for a simple system like interactive graph plotting.  However, for more complex applications, a more complex data structure is necessary to satisfy the three criteria.

In order to satisfy the first criterion, the data structure must be capable of specifying the relationships between entities within the picture.  One important concept in graphics is the notion of a subpicture, that is, a segment of a picture.  Consider Fig. 5-5.8, which is an electrical circuit composed of the combination of two simpler circuits.  This hierarchical structure is illustrated by the tree diagram of Fig. 5-5.9.

Consider this structure with respect to the third criterion.  Obviously, this data structure results in the inefficient use of storage because of the repetition of certain nodes.  This inefficiency can be removed by using a directed graph.  Such a structure, equivalent to Fig. 5-5.9, is shown in Fig. 5-5.10.  This type of structure conserves memory space; by applying the subpicture concept, it also provides an implicit subroutine property.  Each copy of a picture or subpicture is created by passing

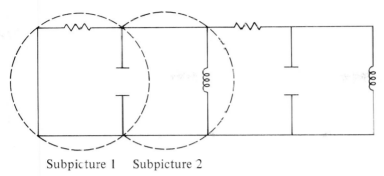

Subpicture 1     Subpicture 2

**FIGURE 5-5.8**

parameters to a subroutine which is responsible for generating all occurrences of an entity. For example, each node in Fig. 5-5.10 would contain scale and positional data characteristics of the subpicture.

A data structure similar to this is used by the Bell Telephone Laboratories GRAPHIC 2 system. Such a structure is sufficient for some limited on-line design but is not suitable for applications where frequent searching and updating are performed. As an example, consider the problem of finding all occurrences of a particular basic element, like the line element in Fig. 5-5.10. This would require that the entire graph be traversed, which would represent a significant amount of computing time.

The problem of providing for more efficient searching and updating can be solved by introducing a data structure that allows rapid access to graphical topology information. The hierarchical ring structure provides this facility to some extent. The hierarchical ring structure has levels, similar to the tree or directed graph discussed previously in this chapter, but the elements at any level are connected in a ring. Logically related elements are linked such that any data item can be accessed from any other item. Figure 5-5.11 shows a ring structure equivalent to the directed graph in Fig. 5-5.10.

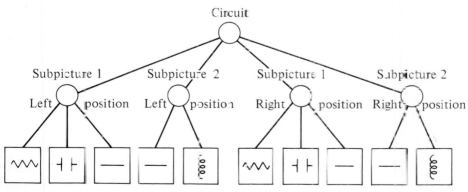

**FIGURE 5-5.9**

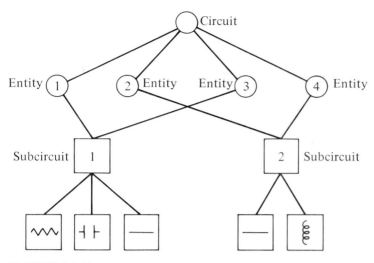

**FIGURE 5-5.10**

Note that the occurrences of similar basic elements, i.e., the lowest-level elements, are linked together. It is this feature that improves the access efficiency of the structure. Insertion is relatively simple in such a structure; however, deletions must be executed with care to ensure that all relevant pointers are changed correctly.

Systems that use structures similar to this are the General Motors Graphics System (Williams [1971]), the 3DPDP system (van Dam [1971]), and the SKETCHPAD system (Sutherland [1963]).

The major drawback of the hierarchical ring structures is the amount of memory space required for the multitude of pointers. For many applications this problem is compensated for by the improved flexibility and accessibility of the structure.

As a detailed example of a possible data structure for an interactive graphics system, we will consider a structure similar to, but less complex and less general than, the structure used by the SKETCHPAD system. The basic elements of this system are points and lines, and it is assumed that we have an output device capable of displaying these two elements. The data structure is a variation of the hierarchical ring structure and uses double linkage to enable easy manipulation of the lists. The data structure makes use of four types of nodes, which are illustrated in Fig. 5-5.12. For each picture or subpicture (entity), there is a MASTER node which has four fields. The PLINK, LLINK and ELINK fields are the pointers to the rings of points, lines, and entities, respectively, which make up the picture. The TMATRIX field is the master transformation matrix, the purpose of which is explained later.

The POINT, LINE, and ENTITY nodes are ring nodes, and therefore, each has a LLINK and a RLINK field to point to the previous and next elements of the node, respectively. The LINE node only has fields which are pointers to the nodes representing the endpoints of the line.

Each POINT node has X and Y fields which contain the x and y coordinates of the point. As well, there are three fields named LLINK1, LLINK2, and LLINK3 which are NULL or point to line nodes if the point is an endpoint. The LLINK4 field is used if the point is an endpoint to more than three lines; LLINK4 contains

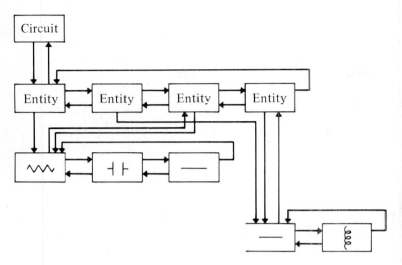

**FIGURE 5-5.11**

the address of a BUCKET node which consists of five fields, LLINK1, LLINK2, LLINK3, LLINK4, and BULINK, a pointer to the next bucket.

The MLINK field of the ENTITY node points to the MASTER node of the structure representing the subpicture. The only field not discussed is the TMATRIX field. TMATRIX contains data pertinent to the particular occurrence of the subpicture that the ENTITY node represents.

To understand properly the use of the TMATRIX field, we must digress somewhat and present a brief discussion of the subject of picture transformations. The three most common picture transformations are rotation about a point, and shifting or translation in the x and/or y direction.

The shifting or translation of a point (x, y) can be expressed algebraically as

$$\left.\begin{array}{l} x' = x + T_x \\ y' = y + T_y \end{array}\right\} \tag{1}$$

where $T_x$ and $T_y$ are the translation amounts in the x and y directions, respectively. The translation of the diagram in Fig. 5-5.13a by $T_x = 5$ and $T_y = 3$ is shown in Fig. 5-5.13b.

The rotation of a point (x, y) about the origin through a clockwise angle $\theta$ can be expressed as

$$\left.\begin{array}{l} x' = x \cos \theta + y \sin \theta \\ y' = -x \sin \theta + y \cos \theta \end{array}\right\} \tag{2}$$

The rotation of a point (x, y) about any other point (p, q) can be expressed as a combination of rotation and translation:

*1*   Shift the points such that (p, q) lies on the origin to give

$$x' = x - p$$
$$y' = y - q$$

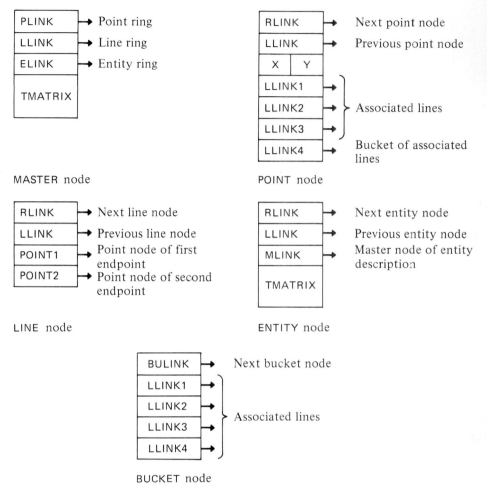

FIGURE 5-5.12

2    Rotate this point about the origin

$$x'' = x' \cos \theta + y' \sin \theta$$
$$y'' = -x' \sin \theta + y' \cos \theta$$

3    Shift the points such that (p, q) is returned to original position

$$x''' = x'' + p$$
$$y''' = y'' + q$$

Figure 5-5.13c shows the original diagram rotated about the point (4, 0) by 10 degrees.

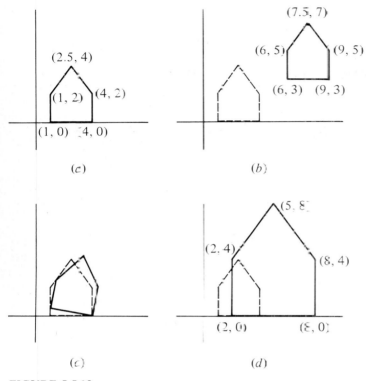

**FIGURE 5-5.13**

The scaling of a point is the changing of the $(x, y)$ coordinates by the factors $S_x$ and $S_y$.

$$\left.\begin{array}{l} x' = x \ S_x \\ y' = y \ S_y \end{array}\right\} \tag{3}$$

To double a picture choose $S_x = S_y = 2$. If $S_x \neq S_y$, the picture will appear distorted. Figure 5-5.13$d$ shows the original diagram scaled with $S_x = S_y = 2$.

These two-dimensional transformations can be represented in a matrix format. The transformation of the point $(x, y)$ to $(x', y')$ can be represented as

$$[x' \ y' \ 1] = [x \ y \ 1]\begin{bmatrix} a & d & 0 \\ b & e & 0 \\ c & f & 1 \end{bmatrix}$$

The $3 \times 3$ matrix completely specifies any transformation consisting of any sequence of translations, rotations, and scalings. The matrix format of the transformations given by Eqs. (1), (2), and (3) is as follows:

*Translation:* $[x' \ y' \ 1] = [x \ y \ 1]\begin{bmatrix} 1 & 0 & 0 \\ 0 & 1 & 0 \\ T_x & T_y & 1 \end{bmatrix}$

*Rotation*:
$$[x' \; y' \; 1] = [x \; y \; 1] \begin{bmatrix} \cos\theta & -\sin\theta & 0 \\ \sin\theta & \cos\theta & 0 \\ 0 & 0 & 1 \end{bmatrix}$$

*Scaling*:
$$[x' \; y' \; 1] = [x \; y \; 1] \begin{bmatrix} S_x & 0 & 0 \\ 0 & S_y & 0 \\ 0 & 0 & 1 \end{bmatrix}$$

Note that a $3 \times 3$ matrix is required in order to specify point translations.

A sequence of transformations can be specified by multiplying together the independent matrices specifying each. If matrix A represents the first transformation and matrix B the second, the matrix $A \cdot B$ will represent the first transformation followed by the second. The matrix $B \cdot A$ is not the same, as it represents the second transformation followed by the first. This multiplication can be repeated so that any sequence of transformations can be represented by one matrix.

As an example, consider the rotation of a point about any other point. The sequence of transformations necessary for this was discussed previously. This sequence can be represented as

$$[x''' \; y''' \; 1] = [x \; y \; 1] \begin{bmatrix} 1 & 0 & 0 \\ 0 & 1 & 0 \\ -T_x & -T_y & 1 \end{bmatrix} \begin{bmatrix} \cos\theta & -\sin\theta & 0 \\ \sin\theta & \cos\theta & 0 \\ 0 & 0 & 1 \end{bmatrix} \begin{bmatrix} 1 & 0 & 0 \\ 0 & 1 & 0 \\ T_x & T_y & 1 \end{bmatrix}$$

Now that we understand some of the operations necessary to effect picture transformation, we turn our attention to the data structure needed to accomplish these transformations.

The data structure corresponding to the picture in Fig. 5-5.14 is shown in Fig. 5-5.15. The node with the label PICTURE is the master node for the entire picture; note that the PLINK and LLINK fields are NULL, indicating that there are no independent lines or points in this picture. The two subpictures from which the picture is composed are SQ and TRI. Each subpicture is composed of three lines. Note that neither subpicture has an independent point. The transformation matrices in the second and fourth nodes of the PICTURE entity ring contain the information necessary to shift and expand the top figure to the location and size of the bottom figure.

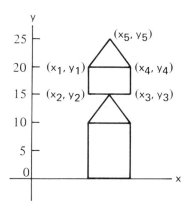

**FIGURE 5-5.14**

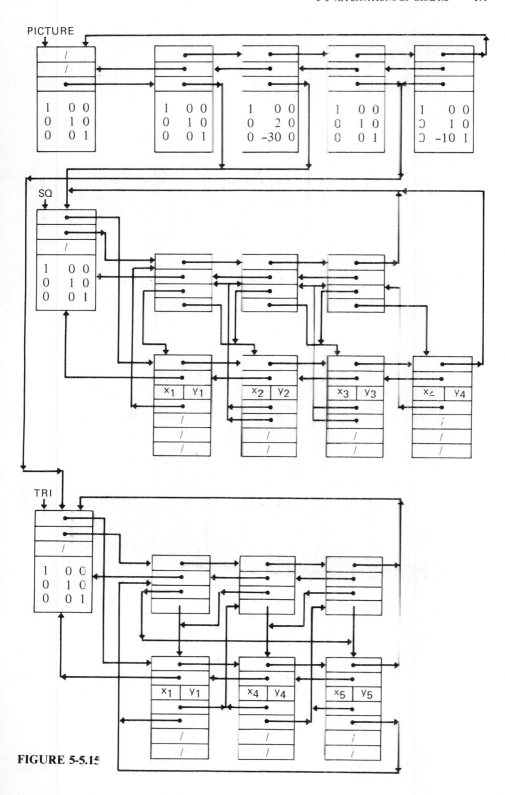

PICTURE

$$\begin{array}{ccc} 1 & 0 & 0 \\ 0 & 1 & 0 \\ 0 & 0 & 1 \end{array}$$

$$\begin{array}{ccc} 1 & 0 & 0 \\ 0 & 1 & 0 \\ 0 & 0 & 1 \end{array}$$

$$\begin{array}{ccc} 1 & 0 & 0 \\ 0 & 2 & 0 \\ 0 & -30 & 0 \end{array}$$

$$\begin{array}{ccc} 1 & 0 & 0 \\ 0 & 1 & 0 \\ 0 & 0 & 1 \end{array}$$

$$\begin{array}{ccc} 1 & 0 & 0 \\ 0 & 1 & 0 \\ 1 & -10 & 1 \end{array}$$

SQ

$$\begin{array}{ccc} 1 & 0 & 0 \\ 0 & 1 & 0 \\ 0 & 0 & 1 \end{array}$$

$x_1$ $y_1$

$x_2$ $y_2$

$x_3$ $y_3$

$x_4$ $y_4$

TRI

$$\begin{array}{ccc} 1 & 0 & 0 \\ 0 & 1 & 0 \\ 0 & 0 & 1 \end{array}$$

$x_1$ $y_1$

$x_4$ $y_4$

$x_5$ $y_5$

**FIGURE 5-5.15**

The basic manipulations to be performed on a graphic data structure are

*1*   Insertion of elements
*2*   Deletion of elements
*3*   Transformation of structure or substructure
*4*   Display of elements

Algorithms to perform these manipulations are presented, but first some preliminary discussion is necessary. We assume the existence of an AVAIL function which, given a parameter description of nodes such as POINT_NODE, LINE_NODE, etc., returns the pointer to a node taken from the availability list. This node is the correct size, as derived from the parameter to the AVAIL function. We also assume that the statement 'AVAIL ← X' returns the node to an appropriate location in the availability list.

We use three insertion algorithms: PINSERT, LINSERT, and ENTINSERT, which along with the algorithm MASTER can be used to create and make additions to picture displays. A general algorithm for inserting a point into the previously described structure is as follows.

1.   Find the start of the point list
2.   Repeat step 3 until a pointer to the master node is encountered
3.   If the point to be added already exists
     then return its address
4.   Create a new point node and insert the node at the front of the point list
5.   Return the address of the new point node

Inserting a new line into the previously described structure is somewhat more difficult than inserting a point. A general algorithm to perform this function is now given.

1.   Create and insert the new point nodes for the endpoints of the line
2.   If no line definition already exists for the line to be added
     then create a new line node and insert it at the front of the line list
          attach the line node to the point nodes created previously
3.   Repeat step 4 for both line endpoints
4.   If no pointer already exists from the point node to the new line node
     then if one of the first three links in the point node is null
          then insert a pointer to the line node in the first null field
          else repeat to check all buckets belonging to this point
                    if the bucket already contains a pointer to this line node
                    then exit loop
                    if one of the line links in the bucket node is null
                    then insert a pointer to the line node in the first null field
                         and exit loop
                    if the bucket link is null
                    then create a new bucket
                         insert a pointer to the line node in the first link field
                    else move on to the next bucket
5.   Return the address of the new line node

Detailed algorithms are now presented for the insertion operations.

**Function** PINSERT(HEAD, $X_1$, $Y_1$). Given HEAD, a pointer to the master node of the structure into which the point is to be inserted, and $X_1$ and $Y_1$, the coordinates of the point to be inserted, this function creates a node to represent the point if one such node does not already exist. A pointer to the point node is returned. P is a pointer.

1.  [Start of point ring]
     P ← PLINK(HEAD)
2.  [Check for node representing point]
     Repeat while P ≠ HEAD
         If X(P) = $X_1$ and Y(P) = $Y_1$
         then   Return(P)
         else   P ← RLINK(P)
3.  [Create node]
     P ← AVAIL(POINT_NODE)
     RLINK(P) ← PLINK(HEAD)
     LLINK(P) ← HEAD
     PLINK(HEAD) ← P
     X(P) ← $X_1$
     Y(P) ← $Y_1$
     LLINK1 ← LLINK2 ← LLINK3 ← LLINK4 ← NULL
     LLINK(RLINK(P)) ← P
4.  [Return pointer to the point node]
     Return(P)                                                          □

**Function** LINSERT(HEAD, $X_1$, $Y_1$, $X_2$, $Y_2$). Given HEAD, a pointer to a master node, and ($X_1$, $Y_1$), ($X_2$, $Y_2$), the endpoints of the line, this function inserts the line represented by the endpoints. New nodes are created if the points are not represented. The value returned is the pointer to the line node. P, Q, R, S, and T are pointer variables. REPLACE_FLAG is a Boolean variable.

1.  [Create new nodes for endpoints using Function PINSERT]
     P ← PINSERT(HEAD, $X_1$, $Y_1$ )
     Q ← PINSERT(HEAD, $X_2$, $Y_2$ )
2.  [Check if line already defined]
     R ← LLINK(HEAD)
3.  [Match line node with points]
     Repeat while R ≠ HEAD and not (POINT1(R) = P
                 and POINT2(R) = Q or POINT1(R) = Q
                 and POINT2(R) = P)
         R ← RLINK(R)
4.  [Create line node]
     If R = HEAD
     then   (no line)
             R ← AVAIL(LINE_NODE)
             RLINK(R) ← LLINK(HEAD)
             LLINK(HEAD) ← R
             LLINK(R) ← HEAD
             LLINK(RLINK(R)) ← R
             POINT1(R) ← P
             POINT2(R) ← Q

5.   [Initialize loop control variable]
     T ← P
6.   [Repeat for both endpoints]
     Repeat step 7 while T ≠ NULL
7.   [Make sure the point nodes point to the line node]
     T ← P
     P ← Q
     Q ← NULL
     If T = NULL
     then   Exitloop
     If LLINK1(T) ≠ R and LLINK2(T) ≠ R and LLINK3(T) ≠ R
     then   If LLINK1(T) = NULL
            then   LLINK1(T) ← R
            else   If LLINK2(T) = NULL
                  then   LLINK2(T) ← R
                  else   If LLINK3(T) = NULL
                       then   LLINK3(T) ← R
                       else   (Check the buckets belonging to a point)
                            S ← LLINK4(T)
                            (Loop control)
                            REPEAT_FLAG ← *false*
                            Repeat while S ≠ NULL
                                If LLINK1(S) = R or LLINK2(S) = R
                                    or LLINK3(S) = R or LLINK4(S) = R
                                then   REPEAT_FLAG ← *true*
                                           Exitloop
                                else   If LLINK1(S) = NULL
                                        then   LLINK1(S) ← R
                                              REPEAT_FLAG ← *true*
                                           Exitloop
                                  If LLINK2(S) = NULL
                                  then   LLINK2(S) ← R
                                              REPEAT_FLAG ← *true*
                                           Exitloop
                                If LLINK3(S) = NULL
                                  then   LLINK3(S) ← R
                                              REPEAT_FLAG ← *true*
                                           Exitloop
                                If LLINK4(S) = NULL
                                  then   LLINK4(S) ← R
                                              REPEAT_FLAG ← *true*
                                           Exitloop
                                T ← S
                                S ← BULINK(S)
                        If not REPEAT_FLAG
                        then   (Create a new bucket)
                                S ← AVAIL(BUCKET_NODE)
                                LLINK1(S) ← R
                                BULINK(S) ← NULL
                                LLINK2(S) ← LLINK3(S) ← NULL
                                LLINK4(S) ← NULL

If POINT1(R) = T or POINT2(R) = T
then    LLINK4(T) ← S
else    BULINK(T) ← S

8.  [Return value]
    Return(R)    □

**Function  ENTINSERT(HEAD, ENT, TRANS).**  Given HEAD, the pointer to the master node for the structure in which the entity is to be inserted; ENT, the pointer to the substructure representing the entity; and TRANS, the transformation matrix to be applied to the substructure, Function ENTINSERT creates an entity node and links it to the entity ring. The value returned is the pointer to the entity node.

1.  [Create node]
    P ← AVAIL(ENTITY_NODE)
    RLINK(P) ← ELINK(HEAD)
    LLINK(P) ← HEAD
    MLINK(P) ← ENT
    TMATRIX(P) ← TRANS
    ELINK(HEAD) ← P
    LLINK(RLINK(P)) ← P

2.  [Return pointer to entity node]
    Return(P)    □

**Function  MASTER.**  This function creates and returns a pointer to a master node which is initialized so that the TMATRIX is the identity matrix and the links point to the node itself.

1.  [Create node]
    P ← AVAIL(MASTER_NODE)
    PLINK(P) ← LLINK(P) ← ELINK(P) ← P

    $$TMATRIX(P) \leftarrow \begin{bmatrix} 1 & 0 & 0 \\ 0 & 1 & 0 \\ 0 & 0 & 1 \end{bmatrix}$$

2.  [Return the pointer to the master node]
    Return(P)    □

As an example of the use of these algorithms, the structure shown in Fig. 5-5.15 could be created by the following sequence of algorithm steps:

1.  [Create structure to represent triangle]
    TRI ← MASTER
    LINSERT(TRI, $X_1$, $Y_1$, $X_4$, $Y_4$)
    LINSERT(TRI, $X_4$, $Y_4$, $X_5$, $Y_5$)
    LINSERT(TRI, $X_1$, $Y_1$, $X_5$, $Y_5$)

2.  [Create structure to represent three-sided square]
    SQ ← MASTER
    LINSERT(SQ, $X_1$, $Y_1$, $X_2$, $Y_2$)
    LINSERT(SQ, $X_2$, $Y_2$, $X_3$, $Y_3$)
    LINSERT(SQ, $X_3$, $Y_3$, $X_4$, $Y_4$)

3.    [Create picture by combining the 4 occurrences of the entities]
        PICTURE ← MASTER

$$\text{ENTINSERT(PICTURE, SQ, } \begin{bmatrix} 1 & 0 & 0 \\ 0 & 1 & 0 \\ 0 & 0 & 1 \end{bmatrix})$$

$$\text{ENTINSERT(PICTURE, TRI, } \begin{bmatrix} 1 & 0 & 0 \\ 0 & 1 & 0 \\ 0 & 0 & 1 \end{bmatrix})$$

$$\text{ENTINSERT(PICTURE, SQ, } \begin{bmatrix} 1 & 0 & 0 \\ 0 & 2 & 0 \\ 0 & -30 & 1 \end{bmatrix})$$

$$\text{ENTINSERT(PICTURE, TRI, } \begin{bmatrix} 1 & 0 & 0 \\ 0 & 1 & 0 \\ 0 & -10 & 1 \end{bmatrix})$$

The deletion algorithms are based on the following assumptions:

*1*    The deletion of a point requires that all lines for which that point is an endpoint be deleted as well. (Note that the other endpoint is not deleted, though it must no longer refer to the deleted line node.)

*2*    The deletion of a line does not cause the deletion of the endpoint.

*3*    The deletion of an entity causes only one entity node to be deleted.

To accomplish these deletions we use four algorithms. LINEDELETE deletes a line node referenced by a pointer; LDELETE deletes a line referenced by its endpoints; PDELETE deletes a point referenced by coordinates; and ENTDELETE deletes an entity node referenced by a pointer to the entity substructure and the entity transformation matrix.

Note that the removal of a node from a ring requires special checks for the first and last nodes in order that the master ring node is correctly changed. These special checks could be eliminated by using a ring header node of the same type as the nodes in the ring. This would be a wise decision if adequate storage space were available.

A general algorithm for deleting a line referenced by a pointer is now given.

1.    Delete the line node from the line list
2.    Repeat thru step 6 for both line endpoints
3.    Find the point or bucket node in which a reference to the line is found
4.    Find the last node which contains any line references at all
5.    Replace line references to the deleted line with line references from the last node
6.    If a bucket becomes empty
        then return it to free storage
7.    Return line node to free storage

The line deletion algorithms are as follows.

**Procedure** L NEDELETE(HEAD, P). Given HEAD, the master node of the structure in question, and P, the pointer to the line to be deleted Procedure LINEDELETE deletes the node referenced and removes the reference to the line from the associated line field. Q, R, S, T, and V are auxiliary pointer variables.

1.  [Delete node]
        If RLINK(P) $\neq$ HEAD
        then    LLINK(RLINK(P)) $\leftarrow$ LLINK(P)
        If LLINK(P) = HEAD
        then    LLINK(HEAD) $\leftarrow$ RLINK(P)
        else    RLINK(LLINK(P)) $\leftarrow$ RLINK(P)
2.  [Remove line reference from endpoints]
        Repeat thru step 5 for Q = POINT1(P), POINT2(P)
3.  [Find S, the node or bucket containing the line reference]
        S $\leftarrow$ Q
        If not (LLINK1(S) = P or LLINK2(S) = P or LLINK3(S) = P)
        then    T $\leftarrow$ LLINK4(S)   (prepare to look in buckets)
                Repeat while T $\neq$ NULL
                    S $\leftarrow$ T
                    T $\leftarrow$ BULINK(T)
                    If LLINK1(S) = P or LLINK2(S) = P or LLINK3(S) = P
                      or LLINK4(S) = P
                    then   Exitloop
                (has P been found?)
                If LLINK1(S) $\neq$ P and LLINK2(S) $\neq$ P
                        and LLINK3(S) $\neq$ P and LLINK4(S) $\neq$ P
                then Write('ERROR - NO LINE REFERENCE FOUND')
                     Return
4.  [Replace line reference in node S with last line reference]
        If S = Q  (prepare to find last bucket, T)
        then    T $\leftarrow$ LLINK4(S)
        else    T $\leftarrow$ BULINK(S)
        If T = NULL
        then    T $\leftarrow$ S
        else    (look for last reference, R)
                Repeat while BULINK(T) $\neq$ NULL
                    T $\leftarrow$ BULINK(T)
                If T $\neq$ Q and LLINK4(T) $\neq$ NULL
                then    R $\leftarrow$ LLINK4(T)
                        LLINK4(T) $\leftarrow$ NULL
                else    If LLINK3(T) $\neq$ NULL
                        then   R $\leftarrow$ LLINK3(T)
                               LLINK3(T) $\leftarrow$ NULL
                        else   If LLINK2(T) $\neq$ NULL
                               then   R $\leftarrow$ LLINK2(T)
                                      LLINK2(T) $\leftarrow$ NULL
                               else   If LLINK1(T) $\neq$ NULL
                                      then   R $\leftarrow$ LLINK1(T)
                                             LLINK1(T) $\leftarrow$ NULL
                                      If S $\neq$ Q or T $\neq$ Q
                                      then   (delete empty bucket)

```
                                    If LLINK4(Q) = T
                                    then    LLINK4(Q) ← NULL
                                            AVAIL ← T
                                    else    V ← LLINK4(Q)
                                            Repeat while BULINK(V)
                                                               ≠ T
                                                V ← BULINK(V)
                                            BULINK(V) ← NULL
                                            AVAIL ← T
                            else    Write('ERROR - NO EMPTY BUCKET
                                       SHOULD HAVE BEEN FOUND')
                            Return
```

5.   [Make actual replacement if necessary]

```
        If R ≠ P   (note: if R = P, we have already deleted it)
        then    If LLINK1(S) = P
                then    LLINK1(S) ← R
                else    If LLINK2(S) = P
                        then    LLINK2(S) ← R
                        else    If LLINK3(S) = P
                                then    LLINK3(S) ← R
                                else    If S ≠ Q and LLINK4(S) = P
                                        then    LLINK4(S) ← R
                                        else    Write('ERROR - NO LINE
                                                    REFERENCE IN S')
                            Return
```

6.   [Return line node after deleting references to it]

```
        AVAIL ← P
```

7.   [Finished]

```
        Return                                                      □
```

In step 1 of the algorithm, the line node to be deleted is removed from the chain of line nodes belonging to HEAD. Then, in steps 3 through 5, all references to this line node are removed from the two endpoint point nodes. In step 3, the pointer S is set to point to the node (point node or bucket node) in which a reference to the line is found. In step 4, the pointer T is set to point to the last node (point node or bucket node) that contains any line references at all. Having determined T, the line reference fields in T are searched for the last non-NULL reference. This reference is saved in R, and the field is set to NULL. If this action happened to empty a bucket node, the bucket node is returned to available storage. If no reference was found in T, this is an error. In step 5, the line reference in node S is replaced by the last line reference, R, which was obtained from node T. Note that if the last reference in T was, in fact, the reference to the deleted line, then no replacement need take place. The reference has already been set to NULL. These steps are then repeated for the other endpoint. In step 6, the unchained line node is returned to available storage and in step 7, control returns to the calling procedure.

The method of line-reference deletion chosen, namely, overwriting by the last line reference in a point node's set of line references, has certain advantages. First, it avoids gaps in the list of line references still available for a point node, and secondly, it enables better storage management because empty bucket nodes can be returned when they are no longer needed.

**Procedure** LDELETE(HEAD, $X_1$, $Y_1$, $X_2$, $Y_2$). Given HEAD, the master node of the structure, and $X_1$, $Y_1$, $X_2$, $Y_2$, the coordinates of the endpoints of a line, Procedure LDELETE finds the node corresponding to the line and uses the LINEDELETE function to delete the node and references to it. P is a pointer variable.

1. [Find endpoints]
   $P \leftarrow$ LLINK(HEAD)
2. [Test endpoints vs. arguments]
   (test until found or have searched all endpoints)
   Repeat while P $\neq$ HEAD
       if X(POINT1(P)) = $X_1$ and Y(POINT1(P)) = $Y_1$ and
           X(POINT2(P)) = $X_2$ and Y(POINT2(P)) = $Y_2$
       or X(POINT1(P)) = $X_2$ and Y(POINT1(P)) = $Y_2$ and
           X(POINT2(P)) = $X_1$ and Y(POINT2(P)) = $Y_1$
       then Exitloop
       else P $\leftarrow$ RLINK(P)
   If P = HEAD
   then Write('ERROR - NO ENDPOINT MATCH')
       Return
3. [Delete node]
   Call LINEDELETE(HEAD, P)
   Return                                              □

Algorithms PDELETE and ENTDELETE are left as exercises.

The transformation of a picture or subpicture is relatively simple using this data structure. One need only multiply the TMATRIX of the appropriate master with the transformation matrix corresponding to the desired transformations and place this new value in the TMATRIX field. That is, you set TMATRIX $\leftarrow$ TMATRIX * [new transformation].

In order to display the picture stored by this data structure, one multiplies each point vector in the point ring with the TMATRIX field of the picture master node and makes the proper line or point display requests. The entity subpictures are displayed recursively; the transformation matrix applicable to a point is the product of the TMATRIX field of the subpicture master node with the TMATRIX field of the master node

**Procedure** DISPLAY(PICTURE, MAT). Given PICTURE, the master node of the picture to be displayed, and MAT, the transformation matrix applicable at the present level, Procedure DISPLAY recursively traverses the data structure in order to create the visual representation of the picture. The procedure assumes the existence of two routines: LINEWRITE($X_1$, $Y_1$, $X_2$, $Y_2$), which creates a line on the graphics device with endpoints $(X_1, Y_1)$ and $(X_2, Y_2)$; and POINTWRITE(U, V), which creates a point on the same device with coordinates (U, V). The main level reference to DISPLAY should have the identity matrix as the argument for the MAT parameter.

1. [Create corresponding transformation matrix]
   MAT $\leftarrow$ TMATRIX(PICTURE) * MAT
2. [Traverse line ring to display lines]
   P $\leftarrow$ LLINK(PICTURE)

> Repeat while P $\neq$ PICTURE
> $\quad$ $[X_1, Y_1, N] \leftarrow [X(POINT1(P)), Y(POINT1(P)), 1] * MAT$
> $\quad$ If N $\neq$ 1
> $\quad$ then $\quad$ Write('INVALID MATRIX')
> $\quad\quad\quad$ Return
> $\quad$ $[X_2, Y_2, N] \leftarrow [X(POINT2(P)), Y(POINT2(P)), 1] * MAT$
> $\quad$ If N $\neq$ 1
> $\quad$ then $\quad$ Write('INVALID MATRIX')
> $\quad\quad\quad$ Return
> $\quad$ Call LINEWRITE($X_1, Y_1, X_2, Y_2$)
> $\quad$ P $\leftarrow$ RLINK(P)

3. [Traverse point ring to display points that are not endpoints]
> $\quad$ P $\leftarrow$ PLINK(PICTURE)
> Repeat while P $\neq$ PICTURE
> $\quad$ If LLINK1(P) = NULL
> $\quad$ then $\quad$ $[U, V, N] \leftarrow [X(P), Y(P), 1] * MAT$
> $\quad\quad\quad$ If N $\neq$ 1
> $\quad\quad\quad$ then $\quad$ Write('INVALID MATRIX')
> $\quad\quad\quad\quad\quad$ Return
> $\quad\quad\quad$ Call POINTWRITE(U, V)
> $\quad$ P $\leftarrow$ RLINK(P)

4. [Traverse entity ring recursively displaying each]
> $\quad$ P $\leftarrow$ ELINK(PICTURE)
> Repeat while P $\neq$ PICTURE
> $\quad$ Call DISPLAY(MLINK(P), TMATRIX(P) * MAT)
> $\quad$ P $\leftarrow$ RLINK(P)

5. [Finished]
> $\quad$ Return $\hfill\square$

### Exercises for Sec. 5-5.2

1. Construct an algorithm which, given HEAD, the pointer to the master node, and $X_1$ and $Y_1$, the coordinates of a point, deletes the node representing the point and deletes all lines of which the point is an endpoint.

2. Given ENT, the master node of a substructure, and TRANS, a transformation matrix, construct an algorithm which finds the entity node which references ENT and has TMATRIX = TRANS and deletes this node.

3. Formulate Algorithms PDELETE and ENTDELETE alluded to at the end of Sec. 5-5.2.

### 5-5.3 Topological Sorting

The earliest use of topological sorting with computers was in conjunction with network analysis, for example, with techniques such as PERT. A PERT graph consists of directed edges corresponding to activities and nodes corresponding to events. A certain activity must be accomplished to move from one event to another. The PERT graph is used to analyze interrelated activities of complex projects. Activities may be taking place in parallel, and one event may be the starting or ending point for a number of activities. The purpose of a topological sort is to order the events in a linear manner, i.e., first, second, third, and so on, with the restriction that an event cannot precede other events that must first take place.

In general, a topological sort defines a linear ordering on those nodes of a directed graph that have the following property: If node P is a predecessor of node Q, then Q cannot be the predecessor of node P. This property must hold even if P = Q, that is, P cannot be its own immediate predecessor and successor. In other words, a topological sort cannot order the nodes in a cycle.

As an example of the results of a topological sort, consider Fig. 5-5.16. Part (a) shows a graph containing no cycles, and part (b) shows a linear ordering that could possibly result from a topological sort applied to this graph. The successors of each node P always appear to the right of P. (Note that other linear orderings could be defined.)

Another application of topological sorting is the ordering of terms that must be defined in a book. Suppose we have a number of terms $T_1, T_2, ..., T_n$ that are related by pairs $(T_i, T_j)$ such that $T_i$ is used in the definition of $T_j$. Then, we wish to order the terms so that each term $T_i$ appears before each term $T_j$ that uses $T_i$ directly or indirectly in its definition. It is possible to have circular definitions, for example, $(T_i, T_j)$, $(T_j, T_k)$, and $(T_k, T_i)$. In this case, a complete linear ordering of the terms cannot be made. Consider the examples in Fig. 5-5.17; the relationships between the definitions of record, file, field, key, and transaction (as found in two different books) are shown. An edge points from term $T_i$ to $T_j$ if $T_i$ is used in definition of $T_j$. In part (a) of Fig. 5-5.17, a linear ordering cannot be defined. For part (b), a topological sort could define the linear ordering

record – field – file – key – transaction

An alternative ordering is

record – file – field – key – transaction

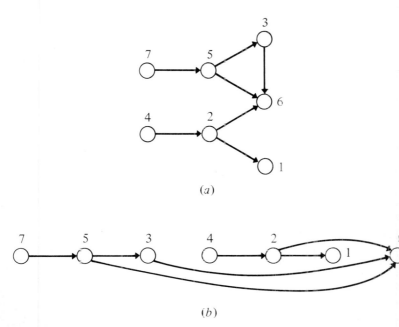

(a)

(b)

**FIGURE 5-5.16**   Example of a topological sort.

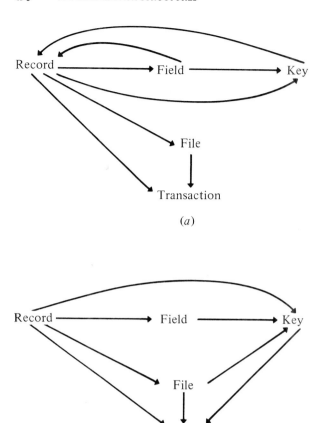

(a)

(b)

**FIGURE 5-5.17**   Relationships between definitions.

In part (a), even though we cannot successfully apply a topological sort, the attempt to do so can be useful in detecting the circular definitions.

In general with a topological sort we wish to specify a linear ordering for a set of nodes identified by descriptors, given a number of edges identified by ordered pairs of descriptors. The linear ordering must be such that all of a descriptor's successors appear after that descriptor. If it is not possible to specify a complete linear ordering, then the loops that exist among the nodes or descriptors must be accounted for. In this section, we give an algorithm that performs a topological sort on nodes with any type of descriptors (character string or numeric). We also give an algorithm that detects one loop following an unsuccessful sort. Although we can only deal with small examples here, the number of descriptors or nodes in a typical application of topological sorting may be in the order of thousands.

The graph to which the topological sort is being applied can be represented using the structure shown in Fig. 5-5.18. In this figure, the graph shown in Fig. 5-5.17b is represented.

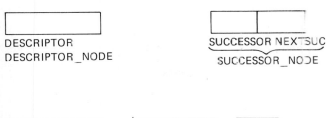

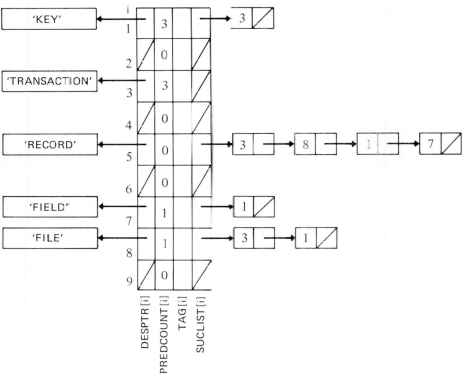

**FIGURE 5-5.18**   Data structure for representing a graph.

A value I between 1 and 9 is assigned to each descriptor in Fig. 5-5.17*b*. This assignment is done using a hashing function which will be described shortly. The value I is used to reference the array elements DESPTR[I], PREDCOUNT[I], TAG[I], and SUCLIST[I]. DESPTR[I] is a pointer to a DESCRIPTOR node containing the descriptor corresponding to I. PREDCOUNT[I] is the number of immediate predecessors that the descriptor has. SUCLIST[I] is a pointer to a singly linked list of SUCCESSOR_NODE structures that contain the numbers corresponding to the immediate successors of the descriptor represented by I. The use of TAG[I] will be described later. Note that the positions 2, 4, 6, and 9 in the arrays are not used. These empty locations are necessary so that an efficient searching algorithm based on a hashing function can be adopted in selecting an array position for each descriptor. The general algorithm for the searching function follows.

1.   Calculate the index of the descriptor using a hashing function
2.   Repeat thru step 6 until all locations in the structure have been examined

3. If the location being examined in the structure is empty
   then insert the descriptor and return the index value
4. If the descriptor in the location being examined is equal to the one to be entered
   then return its index value
5. If the end of the structure has been reached
   then restart the search at the first location in the structure
6. If no empty location is encountered
   then write overflow of descriptor arrays and return

The detailed algorithm to perform this search follows.

**Function** STORE(STRING). We are given a structure exemplified by Fig. 5-5.18 that contains M array elements and that currently has N descriptors. Given a descriptor STRING, it is required to find STRING in the structure and to return the array position corresponding to STRING. If STRING cannot be found, then it is allocated an unused array position, N is incremented, and the array position is returned. A hashing function HASH is used in the search process. The variables D and K are auxiliary indices.

1. [Initialize for search]
   $D \leftarrow K \leftarrow$ HASH(STRING)
   (HASH returns a value between 1 and M inclusive)
2. [Continue until STRING or an empty position is found]
   Repeat thru step 5 while K $\neq$ D or K = HASH(STRING)
   (K = D and K = HASH(STRING) on first iteration)
3. [Check descriptor pointer for indication of unused array location]
   If DESPTR[K] = NULL
   then   P $\Leftarrow$ DESCRIPTOR_NODE
          DESCRIPTOR(P) $\leftarrow$ STRING
          DESPTR[K] $\leftarrow$ P
          N $\leftarrow$ N + 1
          Return(K)
4. [Check descriptor to see if it matches STRING]
   If DESCRIPTOR(DESPTR[K]) = STRING
   then    Return(K)
5. [Update and test index]
   K $\leftarrow$ K + 1
   If K > M
   then    K $\leftarrow$ 1
   If K = D
   then    Write('OVERFLOW OF DESCRIPTOR ARRAYS')
           Return(0)                                              □

Hashing functions that could be used to map the descriptor STRING to a number between 1 and M are described in Sec. 4-3.2. The search mechanism used in this algorithm is termed linear probing. Consecutive array locations are scanned until STRING is found or an empty array location in encountered. If the array index K ever exceeds M, then it is reset to 1. In this manner, the entire array can be scanned if necessary. If all M array positions are scanned without finding STRING or an empty location, then an error message is printed and the algorithm halts. If the number of descriptors N is almost equal to M. linear probing is an inefficient search method. It is wise to choose an M at least 25 percent greater than the maximum value of N.

Function **STORE** is invoked by the assignment

I ← STORE(STRING)

It is assumed that the structure in Fig. 5-5.18 and parameters M and N can be accessed by all algorithms discussed in this section. A general algorithm for the construct operation is now given.

1. Initialize the arrays
2. Read first predecessor-successor pair of descriptors
3. Repeat thru step 7 while there remains data
4. Store the predecessor and successor in the structure
5. Update the predecessor count of the successor
6. Add the successor to the successor list of the predecessor
7. Read next pair of descriptors

The following algorithm constructs the structure described previously.

**Procedure** CONSTRUCT. Given a number of descriptor pairs (PRED, SUC) such that **PRED** is the immediate predecessor of SUC, it is required to construct the structure exemplified by Fig. 5-5.18. The number of unique descriptors N is counted. The user of this algorithm must ensure that M, the number of array locations, is greater than or equal to the maximum value of N.

1. [Initialize arrays]
    N ← 0
    Repeat for K = 1, 2, ..., M
        DESPTR[K] ← SUCLIST[K] ← NULL
        PREDCOUNT[K] ← 0
2. [Read first predecessor-successor pair of descriptors]
    Read(PRED, SUC)
3. [Continue until input data are exhausted]
    Repeat thru step 7 while there are input data
4. [Store or find descriptors and determine indices for them]
    I ← STORE(PRED)
    J ← STORE(SUC)
5. [Update predecessor count of successor]
    PREDCOUNT[J] ← PREDCOUNT[J] + 1
6. [Update successor list of predecessor]
    Q ⇐ SUCCESSOR_NODE
    SUCCESSOR(Q) ← J
    NEXTSUC(Q) ← SUCLIST[I]
    SUCLIST[I] ← Q
7. [Read the next predecessor-successor pair]
    Read(PRED, SUC)
8. [Finished]
    Return                                                                 □

In order to construct the structure shown in Fig. 5-5.18, the following descriptor pairs must be read by Procedure CONSTRUCT. These pairs must correspond to the edges of the graph in Fig. 5-5.17*b*.

| KEY | TRANSACTION |
| FIELD | KEY |
| RECORD | FIELD |
| RECORD | KEY |
| RECORD | FILE |
| FILE | KEY |
| RECORD | TRANSACTION |
| FILE | TRANSACTION |

An algorithm for performing a topological sort is quite simple now that the structure for representing a directed graph is available. The descriptors are to be printed in a linear order by the sort. If a descriptor's predecessor count is zero, then it can be printed. After this, the predecessor count of each of the descriptor's successors can be decremented by one. Each time a descriptor's predecessor count reaches zero, it is eligible to be printed. Since more than one descriptor may have a zero predecessor count simultaneously, a control mechanism is required to keep track of these descriptors. We use a linked queue, and the following algorithm is required to add an element to the end of a queue.

**Procedure** LQINSERT(K). Given a number K corresponding to a descriptor as defined by Procedure CONSTRUCT, it is required to add K at the rear of a linked queue that has front and rear pointers F and R, respectively. Each QUEUE_NODE has an information field V and a link field LINK.

1.  [Allocate queue node]
    $\quad$ P $\Leftarrow$ QUEUE_NODE
    $\quad$ V(P) $\leftarrow$ K
    $\quad$ LINK(P) $\leftarrow$ NULL
2.  [Add node to rear of queue]
    $\quad$ If R = NULL
    $\quad$ then $\quad$ F $\leftarrow$ R $\leftarrow$ P
    $\quad$ else $\quad$ LINK(R) $\leftarrow$ P
    $\quad\quad\quad\quad$ R $\leftarrow$ P
3.  [Finished]
    $\quad$ Return $\qquad\qquad\qquad\qquad\qquad\qquad\qquad\qquad\qquad\qquad$ □

A general algorithm for performing a topological sort is as follows.

1.  Insert all descriptors without predecessors at the rear of the queue
2.  Repeat thru step 5 while the queue is not empty
3.  Print the first descriptor in the queue and delete it from the structure
4.  Decrease the predecessor count of each node in the successor list of the deleted descriptor by one
5.  If any predecessor count reaches zero
    then add the descriptor to the rear of the queue

The following procedure performs the sort.

**Procedure** TOPOLOGICAL_SORT. Given the structure for representing a directed graph as previously described, it is required to print the descriptors of the nodes in a linear order such that each descriptor is printed before its successors. A queue and Procedure LQINSERT are used to accomplish this. The variable N is global.

1.  [Initialize queue pointers]
    F ← R ← NULL
2.  [Scan for descriptors without predecessors and add them to the queue]
    Repeat for K = 1, 2, ..., M
        f DESPTR[K] ≠ NULL and PREDCOUNT[K] = 0
        then   Call LQINSERT(K)
3.  [Process each descriptor in queue]
    Repeat thru step 5 while F ≠ NULL
4.  [Write and delete front descriptor in queue]
    K ← V(F)
    N ← N - 1
    F ← LINK(F)
    Write(DESCRIPTOR(DESPTR[K]))
    DESPTR[K] ← NULL
    If F = NULL
    then   R ← NULL
5.  [Scan successor list of descriptor printed]
    Q ← SUCLIST[K]
    SUCLIST[K] ← NULL
    Repeat while Q ≠ NULL
        PREDCOUNT[SUCCESSOR(Q)] ← PREDCOUNT[SUCCESSOR(Q)] – 1
        f PREDCOUNT[SUCCESSOR(Q)] = 0
        then   Call LQINSERT(SUCCESSOR(Q))
        Q ← NEXTSUC(Q)
6.  [Finished]
    Return                                                   □

In step 4, N is decremented by 1 every time that a descriptor is output. If N is not equal to zero on completion of the algorithm then N descriptors are not included in the linear ordering and at least one cycle or loop exists among these descriptors.

A general algorithm for determining cycles among descriptors is as follows.

1.  Initialize the arrays
2.  Repeat step 3 for all locations in the storage structure
3.  If a successor list for this location exists
    then set the predecessor count of the successor to the location of the predecessor in the structure
4.  Determine the subscript of the first descriptor which has not been printed
5.  Mark all descriptors composing cycle
6.  Reverse cycle so successors follow predecessors
7.  Print descriptors in cycle

A detailed algorithm for finding cycles is now presented.

**Procedure** DETECT_CYCLE. Given a structure similar to that described in Fig. 5-5.18, with one or more descriptors among which one or more cycles exist, it is required to detect and print the descriptors in one cycle.

1. [Initialize arrays]
    Repeat for I = 1, 2, ..., M
        PREDCOUNT[I] ← 0
        TAG[I] ← *false*
2. [Check each descriptor and process those that were not printed]
    Repeat step 3 for I = 1, 2, ..., M
3. [Place subscript of predecessor in PREDCOUNT element of successor]
    If DESPTR[I] ≠ NULL
    then   P ← SUCLIST[I]
           SUCLIST[I] ← NULL
           Repeat while P ≠ NULL
                If PREDCOUNT[SUCCESSOR(P)] = 0
                then   PREDCOUNT[SUCCESSOR(P)] ← I
                P ← NEXTSUC(P)
4. [Find the first I whose descriptor has not been printed]
    Repeat for I = 1, 2, ..., M
        If PREDCOUNT[I] ≠ 0
        then   Exitloop
5. [Mark the predecessors with true TAG fields]
    Repeat while not TAG[I]
        TAG[I] ← *true*
        I ← PREDCOUNT[I]
6. [Reverse the list defined by the marked array elements starting at PREDCOUNT[I]]
    J ← 0
    Repeat while PREDCOUNT[I] ≠ 0
        K ← J
        J ← I
        I ← PREDCOUNT[J]
        PREDCOUNT[J] ← K
    PREDCOUNT[I] ← J
7. [Write the descriptors in a cycle]
    Repeat while TAG[I]
        Write(DESCRIPTOR(DESPTR[I]))
        TAG[I] ← *false*
        I ← PREDCOUNT[I]
8. [Output the first and last descriptor in the cycle]
    Write(DESCRIPTOR(DESPTR[I]))
    Return          □

     This algorithm continues when Procedure TOPOLOGICAL_SORT terminates, provided that a cycle exists among the descriptors. If the pointer SUCLIST[I] is not null in step 3, then it points to a list of numbers of descriptors not printed. The array element PREDCOUNT of a successor descriptor is set to the predecessor number I in this step. This effectively constructs a linked list in which predecessors can be accessed via the PREDCOUNT values. In step 4 an array subscript is found that corresponds to a descriptor not yet printed. The list containing this subscript is scanned, and each node is marked using the TAG elements which were shown in Fig. 5-5.18. When a TAG element with a value of *true* is encountered in step 5, the subscript I corresponds to the first descriptor in a completely marked cycle. Step 6 reverses the list corresponding to this cycle so that step 7 can print the descriptors with predecessors before successors. The first descriptor in the cycle or loop is printed in step 8.

In Fig. 5-5.19a, the data structure established by Procedure CONSTRUCT as applied to the descriptor pairs

| | |
|---|---|
| FIELD | KEY |
| RECORD | FIELD |
| RECORD | KEY |
| RECORD | FILE |
| RECORD | TRANSACTION |
| FILE | TRANSACTION |
| KEY | RECORD |
| FIELD | RECORD |

is shown. These pairs correspond to the edges of the graph in Fig. 5-5.17a. This data structure is unchanged after Procedure TOPCLOGICAL_SORT is executed because none of the predecessor counts are zero for the elements corresponding to descriptors.

Figure 5-5.19b shows the state of the arrays in the data structure following execution of step 3 in Procedure DETECT_CYCLE. In the figure, we show the true and false values for the TAG fields as 1 and 0, respectively. The nonzero values in the PREDCOUNT array indicate the predecessors of the array locations' descriptors. Following step 5 of this algorithm, part (c) of the figure shows the state of the arrays. TAG[1] and TAG[5] have been set to 1 and indicate the elements in the cycle. After step 6 of Procedure DETECT_CYCLE is executed, the arrays remain the same. Since the cycle detected consists of only two descriptors, it was not possible to reverse their order, as one item is always both the predecessor and the successor of the other item in a two-element cycle. Steps 7 and 8 print

KEY
RECORD
KEY

and reset the TAG field to *false* as in Fig. 5-5.19b.

A final algorithm illustrates the implementation of the preceding algorithm for topological sorting with loop detection.

**Algorithm** TOPSORT. Given the arrays DESPTR, PREDCOUNT. TAG, and SUCLIST and node structures DESCRIPTOR_NODE, QUEUE_NODE, and SUCCESSOR_NODE as previously defined, this algorithm attempts a topological sort, and if it fails to define a complete linear ordering one cycle is then detected among the descriptors.

1. [Initialize data structures]
   Read(M)
   Allocate M elements for each array
   Call CONSTRUCT
2. [Attempt to sort the descriptors]
   Call TOPOLOGICAL_SORT
3. [Is detection of a cycle necessary?]
   If N > 0
   then   Call DETECT_CYCLE

4.  [Finished]
    Exit                                                                    □

   We must restate that the arrays and node structures and the variables **M** and **N** are global to all algorithms in this section.


**Exercises for Sec. 5-5.3**

1.  List all the valid linear orderings that could result if a topological sort is applied to the graph in Fig. 5-5.16a.
2.  Trace Procedure TOPOLOGICAL_SORT using the directed graph from Fig. 5-5.16a. Assume that the edges are read by the algorithm in the order (7, 5), (5, 3), (3, 6), (5, 6), (2, 1), (2, 6). (4, 2).
3.  Eliminate the edge from KEY to RECORD in Fig. 5-5.17 and now trace Procedures CONSTRUCT, TOPOLOGICAL_SORT, and DETECT_CYCLE as in Fig. 5-5.19.
4.  Could Procedure TOPOLOGICAL_SORT completely order a set of descriptors if two pairs of descriptors read by Procedure CONSTRUCT are duplicates? Explain. (Assume that the corresponding directed graph of descriptors has no cycles.)


**5-6  DYNAMIC STORAGE MANAGEMENT**

In many of the preceding sections we have made free use of structures that require a form of memory management in order to handle requests for storage and releases of storage. For example, for the lists in Chap. 4 and the trees in this chapter, we simply requested nodes whenever we needed them, and never bothered to indicate when or how these nodes were to be released when they were no longer needed. A similar approach was taken for strings in Chap. 2, except that there we never even asked for storage. We simply proceeded as if the creation of any new string was invariably accompanied by enough storage space to hold the string.

   Such conveniences definitely make it easier for an application programmer. In fact, it might be argued that these conveniences are almost a necessity now that certain applications have become so complex. As might be expected, a price must be paid. This price consists of the development cost of the requisite systems programs for such dynamic storage management and (in all likelihood) the slower execution of application programs. Consequently, in this section we wish to examine some of the techniques and algorithms that could be used to provide various levels of storage management and control. Most of the dynamic storage-management methods that are commonly used are variants of the techniques presented here.

   The first subsection discusses the simplest case of dynamic storage allocation, fixed block allocation. The following subsection deals with the first-fit allocation scheme for variable-sized blocks and introduces various enhancements to the basic scheme. Methods for returning storage once it is no longer needed are studied in Sec. 5-6.3. In Sec 5-6.4, we introduce the buddy system for both allocation and release of storage. The final two subsections cover the topics of garbage collection and compaction methods for releasing unwanted allocated storage.


**5-6.1  Fixed Block Storage Allocation**

In this subsection we look briefly at two of the simplest storage management systems where the amount of storage needed is known beforehand.

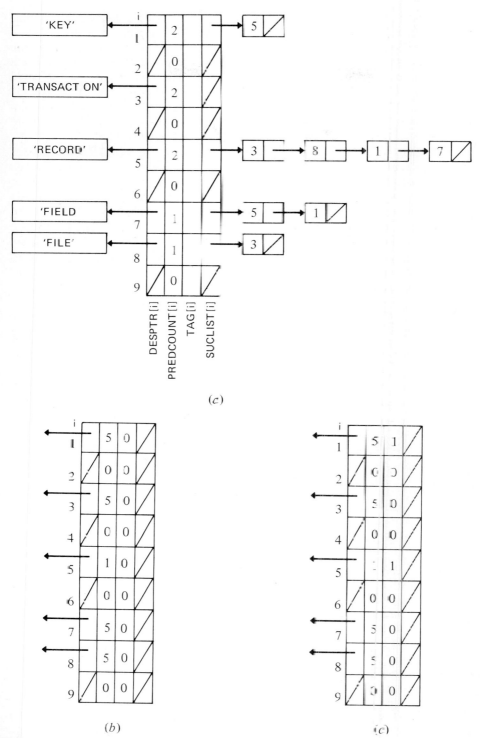

(c)

(b)                                    (c)

**FIGURE 5-5.19** Applications of the algorithms to Figure 5-5.17a

In FORTRAN storage allocation is remarkably simple because all storage requirements are known explicitly at compile time. For example, programmers cannot write a FORTRAN program in which the arrays' sizes are determined at run time. They must have already dimensioned them at compile time. Recursion is not permitted. There are no programmer-defined data structures whose creation could take place at data-determined times during execution, such as provided by SNOBOL's DATA statement together with an assignment or Pascal's structure declarations together with **new** statements. As well, there are no string operations provided, and hence string-handling capabilities are virtually nonexistent.

All these restrictions produce a situation in which the FORTRAN compiler, when translating a source program, is able to determine exactly how much storage will be required for the execution of that program. Storage management then ceases to be a problem because there is no dynamic storage management required by FORTRAN programs. The required amount of storage is allocated for each program and subprogram at loading time. Storage is freed only when the program has executed to completion and is being purged from the system.

In contrast to FORTRAN, in which there is no dynamic storage management, ALGOL 60 provides an example of a more sophisticated system that does provide storage management, though not really under the control of the programmer. A stack is used to hold the blocks of storage, each of which is an activation record of a program or block invocation. Because of the nested structure of program and block calls, their invocations follow a LIFO discipline, and hence a stack is ideally suited for the maintenance of the storage blocks in use at any particular time. Programs can be invoked recursively, but because a stack is being used, this presents no difficulties. This aspect was discussed is Sec. 3-5.1.

Storage for program code is allocated at loading time and remains until the entire job is purged. The stack is used for the data and the run-time control information associated with blocks and procedures as they are invoked during execution. Since ALGOL 60 requires that all data structures be declared upon block entry, all array declarations are processed immediately upon entering a subprogram or block for execution. Such an approach provides the information regarding array sizes, and this, together with the compile-time information about storage needs, serves to define exactly the storage requirements for a particular block. The appropriate amount of space is reserved on the run-time storage stack, and the block can be executed. When the block is finally exited, the stack is popped and the storage allocated for this block is freed.

Use of a stack to provide the dynamic storage management capability is reasonably efficient, in that little computation is involved in determining the amounts of storage to allocate or in updating stack pointers. Such a stack mechanism is quite commonly used in cases, such as ALGOL programs, where the language exhibits a nested block structure, where subprogram invocations follow a LIFO discipline, and where exact storage requirements can be determined at the time of execution upon block entry.

There are, however, many applications which involve list, graph, or tree processing. With such processing the programmer is often made responsible for creating and removing nodes as the data require. In addition, many applications require a string-handling capability of a more powerful nature then that provided by FORTRAN or ALGOL. In particular, variable-length strings may be needed. As pointed out in Sec 2-4, variable-length strings require some form of dynamic storage management. It is to this topic that we now turn.

In considering dynamic storage-management techniques, we find that there are many factors which influence the selection of methods. For example, the statistical distribution of the sizes of the storage areas requested, the distribution of the lengths of time that blocks of storage are required, and the frequency of requests and releases of storage are important factors. Furthermore, the features of the language which necessitate dynamic storage management, and the language implementor's philosophy regarding the degree to which a programmer is to be allowed to control storage, are important considerations.

The simplest case is that involving storage requests which are always for a fixed number of storage locations. Such a situation might arise in a language like LISP, which is devoted to the manipulation of list structures whose *blocks* are all a single type and size. In this case, the total available dynamic storage can be subdivided into a series of blocks, each of the correct size. These blocks can be linked by LINK fields n the first word of each block to form a one-way linear list. A request for a storage block is then handled by a routine similar to Function GET_BLOCK.

**Function** GET_BLOCK(HEAD). Given HEAD, the pointer to the first block on the linked list of available storage blocks, GET_BLOCK returns the address P of an available block.

1. [Overflow?]
      If HEAD = NULL
      then   Return(NULL)
2. [Allocate block]
      P ← HEAD
      HEAD ← LINK(P)
3. [Finished]
      Return(P)                                                          □

In step 1, if we are out of storage (HEAD = NULL), then we can only terminate the job or attempt to recover some storage by techniques we will discuss later in this section. This lack of available storage is denoted by returning a NULL address.

The return of a block to the availability list is equally trivial. Simply attach it as the new first block in the list. We will temporarily defer the question of when blocks are to be returned, however, and simply note that to return a block in this present scheme, all that is needed is P, the block address, and HEAD, the pointer to the first block on the free list.

### 5-6.2 First-fit Storage Allocation

This subsection introduces the problem of fragmentation in storage allocation. Algorithms for first-fit storage allocation are introduced, and various enhancements to the basic technique are discussed.

The situation discussed in the last subsection becomes more complicated if the storage requests can be for blocks of varying sizes, as is common when strings are being handled or when programmer-defined data aggregates of varying sizes are being used. Now we can no longer treat the available storage as a linked list of blocks of the correct size, for there is no correct size. Instead, our linked list can contain blocks of various sizes, each being a potential candidate for allocation or for subdivision into two blocks of smaller size—one for immediate allocation and one for retention on the available list.

With variable-sized blocks, however, we encounter the problem of fragmentation, a problem which did not appear in the case of fixed-size requests. There are two types of memory fragmentation which can arise, namely, internal fragmentation and external fragmentation, both of which are explained as follows.

If a large number of storage blocks are requested and later returned, the linked list of available blocks can be reasonably lengthy (especially if returned contiguous blocks are not fused into one). This means that the average block size becomes small and that there are probably very few blocks which are large. If a request for a large block is received, it may have to be refused because there is no single block on the free list that is big enough, even though the total amount of free storage may be much greater than the requested amount. This phenomenon of decomposing the total available storage into a large number of relatively small blocks is called *external fragmentation*.

We can attempt to inhibit external fragmentation somewhat by occasionally allocating a block that is larger than the requested size (i.e., by refusing to split a block into pieces, one of which might be quite small). If we do this, it could happen that a request for storage must be refused because of the lack of blocks of the required size. This can take place even though the amount of storage that is "wasted" (i.e., allocated but unused) is more than sufficient to satisfy the request. This phenomenon of partitioning the total unused storage into available blocks and allocating these blocks with some portion of the blocks remaining unused, but not available, is called *internal fragmentation*.

Any algorithm for storage management in a context where variable-sized blocks will be used must seek, in some way or another, to minimize the inefficiencies due to fragmentation. Fragmentation is the major factor in making storage management algorithms more complicated than those for fixed-size blocks. In addition, because we cannot know in advance the sizes of blocks, each block generally contains a SIZE field to record its current size, as well as a LINK field to maintain the list structure. For convenience we assume that these fields are in the first word of each block or can be accessed directly once the address of the first word of the block is provided.

If we assume the free list has a list head of the form given in Fig. 5-6.1, with AVAIL being the address of the list head, LINK(AVAIL) being a pointer to the first block on the free list, and SIZE(AVAIL) being set to 0, then a general algorithm for servicing a request for a block of size N can be formulated as follows:

1.  Repeat step 2 while the end of the free list has not been encountered
2.  If the size of the current block is greater than or equal to the requested size
    then split the block
        if the fragment is less than the minimum size allowed
        then release the entire block of storage
        else release a block the requested size
        return the address of the block
    else move on to the next block in the free list
3.  Return no suitable block found

AVAIL ⟶ | SIZE | LINK |

**FIGURE 5-6.1**

A function for performing first-fit storage allocation is now given.

**Function** ALLOCATE_FIRST(AVAIL, N MIN). Given AVAIL, the address of the list head, and N, the size of block requested, this function returns P, the address of a block of length $\geq$ N, with SIZE(P) set to the actual length of the block. The variable MIN records the amount of storage we are willing to waste in order to reduce external fragmentation. That is, no block of size MIN or smaller will be formed by splitting a particular block. K is a local variable which contains the difference between the size of a block and the requested block size. Q is also a local variable and points to the block previous to P in the linked list of available blocks.

1. [Initialize]
       Q ← AVAIL
       P ← LINK(Q)
2. [Find block large enough for request]
       Repeat while P $\neq$ NULL
         If SIZE(P) $\geq$ N
         then   K ← SIZE(P) – N
                If K $\leq$ MIN
                then   LINK(Q) ← LINK(P)
                else   SIZE(P) ← K
                       P ← P + K
                       SIZE(P) ← N
                Return(P)
         else   Q ← P
                P ← LINK(Q)
3. [No suitable block]
       Return(NULL)                                                     □

This algorithm assumes that arithmetic can be performed on addresses. If it is desired to eliminate internal fragmentation completely, simply set MIN to 0, though the utility of a block of size 1 is not very clear, especially since this single location (and perhaps more) is taken up by the SIZE and LINK fields.

The algorithm just given is commonly called a "first-fit" algorithm because the block that is allocated is the first block (or a part) that is found to be larger than the requested amount. One might suspect that a "best-fit" method might be preferable, but, in fact, this is not necessarily the case. The best-fit method does not use the first suitable block found, but instead continues searching the list until the smallest suitable block has been found. This tends to save the larger blocks for times when they are needed to service large requests. However, the best-fit method does have the unfortunate tendency to produce a larger number of very small free blocks, and these are often unusable by almost all requests. Furthermore, the best-fit method requires a search of the entire free list containing, say, M blocks, while the average length of search for first-fit would be M/2 or less, depending on the requested size, though tending to M/2 as the storage usage pattern becomes stable over time. (This latter result follows from a series of simulations carried out by Knuth[1973].)

The choice of methods, in any case, must be made in the context of some knowledge about the type of requests that will be encountered. Given a particular set of circumstances, best-fit might give better performance than first-fit, offsetting the potentially longer search time. It is interesting to note, however, that during the same series of simulations of storage-usage patterns performed in order to compare various management strategies, Knuth discovered that first-fit outperformed best-fit in all cases examined.

To this point, nothing has been said about any ordering imposed on the list of free blocks. This can have a significant effect on performance. If blocks on the free list are ordered by size, then the search time of the best-fit method could be reduced. An ascending-order sort has the effect of converting first-fit to best-fit. Descending order reduces the first-fit's search time to 1 because the first block found would be the largest. However, this can potentially convert first-fit into a method known as "worst-fit," in which the largest block is always used regardless of the size of the request. It may also cause unnecessary generation of many small blocks.

There is another ordering that might be imposed, however. This is to have the blocks on the free list ordered by address (increasing, let us assume). This type of ordering does not necessarily improve search times for blocks of particular sizes, because there is no relation between block address and block size. However, it does make it possible to reduce external fragmentation, and it would tend to reduce all search times because the free list can be shorter. Blocks sorted by address can be checked upon release, and if two consecutive blocks on the list are found to be contiguous, they are fused to form one larger block. This technique tends to keep block sizes larger, and hence to keep the number of blocks smaller. We shall see more of this fusing of blocks when we formulate algorithms for the release of allocated blocks. There is a lot of evidence, though, to suggest that, in the absence of special offsetting conditions, first-fit applied to a free list ordered by address, and hence a list that is essentially an unordered list when considering block size, is quite a good method to adopt.

Another addition that can be made to the first-fit algorithm that can reduce its search time quite noticeably is once again described by Knuth. The modification lies in starting a search for a suitable block at the point the previous search terminated, rather than always with the first block. This tends to distribute smaller blocks more evenly over the entire list, rather than having them concentrated near the front of the list. Function ALLOCATE_FIRST_ROVER is the first-fit algorithm modified to make use of this varying search start point.

**Function** ALLOCATE_FIRST_ROVER(AVAIL, N , MIN, ROVER). Given AVAIL, N, and MIN as before, and ROVER, a pointer to the last examined free node on the previous invocation of this routine, the function returns P, the address of a suitable block, and defines a new value of ROVER. Prior to the first call to this routine, ROVER is assumed to have been initialized to AVAIL. TIME is a flag associated with the traversal of the list. This flag is set to 1 when the end of the list is encountered. K is a local variable which contains the difference between the size of a block and the requested block size. Q is also a local variable and points to the block previous to P in the linked list of available blocks.

1. [Initialize]
   Q ← ROVER
   P ← LINK(Q)
   TIME ← 0
2. [Find large enough block]
   Repeat while TIME = 0 or Q ≠ ROVER
   If P = NULL

```
then    Q ← AVAIL
        P ← LINK(Q)
        TIME ← 1
else    If SIZE(P) ≥ N
        then    K ← SIZE(P) – N
                If K ≤ MIN
                then    LINK(Q) ← LINK(P)
                        ROVER ← Q
                else    SIZE(P) ← K
                        ROVER ← P
                        P ← P + K
                        SIZE(P) ← N
                Return(P)
        else    Q ← P
                P ← LINK(Q)
```

3.  [No suitable block]
        Return(NULL)                                                    □

In his simulation experiments on items, Knuth found, in one case at least, an improvement in the first-fit average length of search from 125 tests (which was M/2, as expected) to 2.8 tests—a significant enhancement. This modified first-fit algorithm operating on a free list ordered by address can serve as a storage-allocation mechanism for many applications.


### 5-6.3  Storage Release

In this subsection we consider the release of an allocated block of storage and its return to the free list. We still ignore the question of when and how the decision is made to free a block of storage and simply assume that a block of storage, starting at address RB, is now considered to be unused and a candidate for reallocation. The case of fixed-size blocks has already been covered, and so we confine the discussion to variable-sized blocks. In this case we assume that a field size. SIZE(RB), in the first word of the block contains the actual size of the block being freed.

The simplest solution is to insert every such freed block as a new first block on an unordered free list. This does, indeed, require a minimum of processing, but it has a serious drawback. After the storage allocation and freeing mechanisms have been operating for a while, the free list is very likely to contain a large number of small blocks. The search time for an allocation routine will become longer and longer, and there will be an ever increasing risk of being unable to meet certain requests because all the blocks are simply too small. The problem is, of course, that in this simple freeing method there is no mechanism running in opposition to the splitting mechanism in the allocation routine. In other words, we never reform big blocks.

The obvious solution is to form one block out of two contiguous free blocks. If every newly released block is checked for contiguity with its predecessor and successor blocks on the free list, and merged with them whenever contiguity occurs, then the free list will always contain the smallest number of blocks. Each block is as large as possible, given the current segments that are allocated. In order for this to work, however, the free list must be kept in order by block address, and this then requires a search of the free list in order to determine the position for insertion of a newly freed block.

The following algorithm can be used to insert a block on the free list, merging it as necessary with contiguous neighbors. Since we have available a second pointer into the free list—the variable search-start point—we can make use of it as a starting point rather than AVAIL on some occasions. It can be shown that this reduces the average length of search from M/2 to M/3. The general algorithm incorporates this modification.

1. If the address of the returned block is greater than the variable starting point
   then start the search at the variable starting point
   else start the search at the list head
2. Find the predecessor and successor of the returned block in the free storage list.
   If an allocated block exists between the freed block and its successor or at the end of the free storage list
   then insert the block in the free list
   else collapse the block with its successor in the free list
3. If an allocated block exists between the freed block and its predecessor or at the front of the free storage list
   then insert the block in the free list
   else collapse the block with its predecessor in the free list

A procedure to insert a block into the free storage list is as follows.

**Procedure**  FREE_BLOCK(AVAIL, RB, ROVER).  Given AVAIL, the address of the list head, ROVER, the variable starting point for searching in the allocation routine, and RB, the address of the block to be inserted, this algorithm inserts block RB into the free list and merges contiguous blocks whenever possible.  This is guaranteed if the list head (with SIZE(AVAIL) set to 0) is the first word of the entire section of memory available for allocation.  We also assume that when the value NULL is compared with a valid address using any of the relational operators, only $\neq$ yields a 'true' result.  Q is a pointer which denotes the predecessor of the node being freed.

1. [Initialize optimally]
```
      If RB > ROVER
      then    Q ← ROVER
      else    Q ← AVAIL
      P ← LINK(Q)
```
2. [Find predecessor and successor in sorted list]
```
      Repeat while P ≠ NULL and RB > P
          Q ← P
          P ← LINK(Q)
```
3. [Collapse with successor, P?]
```
      If P = NULL or RB + SIZE(RB) ≠ P
      then    LINK(RB) ← P
      else    LINK(RB) ← LINK(P)
              SIZE(RB) ← SIZE(RB) + SIZE(P)
              If ROVER = P
              then    ROVER ← RB
```
4. [Collapse with predecessor, Q?]
```
      If Q = AVAIL or Q + SIZE(Q) ≠ RB
      then    LINK(Q) ← RB
      else    LINK(Q) ← LINK(RB)
              SIZE(Q) ← SIZE(Q) + SIZE(RB)
```

5.   [Finished]
     Return                                                                    □

Note that it is the assumption that SIZE(AVAIL) is 0 that prevents the merging of
block RB with the list head when Q is AVAIL, since with AVAIL < RB, we always
have AVAIL − 0 ≠ RB.

To summarize, we now have a storage-allocation method with an average
search time that can be very short, and we have a storage-freeing method with an
average search time of about M/3. Our release technique tends to reduce external
fragmentation because it maintains block sizes as large as possible. The degree of
internal fragmentation is under our control through the variable MIN, though there
is a trade-off between internal fragmentation and both external fragmentation and
search times. Yet looking at these two storage-management mechanisms in terms of
search times, we can see the possibility of the deallocation routine being a bottleneck
because of the M/3 average length of search as compared with the enhanced search
time due to the moving search pointer in the allocation routine. It is therefore
appropriate to consider a deallocation routine that does not require this length of
searching time. The "boundary-tag" method of Knuth is the example chosen.

In the storage-release algorithm just given, it is the search through the blocks
in the sorted list that allows the determination of the predecessor and successor
blocks. Having these, it is simple to determine if they and the released block are
contiguous. Without the search, all that one can do is examine the two words that
are the immediate predecessor and successor of the released block. But unless they
are specially marked with flags, there is no way of telling directly whether the blocks
of which they are a part are on the free list. Consequently, in the boundary-tag
method the first and last words of blocks are made to contain a flag field which
indicates whether the block is allocated. It is also useful to have the last word of a
block contain a size field. From the last word of a block, the address of the first
word can be determined directly. And finally, since searching is being avoided, the
free list is maintained as a doubly linked list. The price paid for eliminating searching is, therefore, more storage being taken up for control fields. This may not be
worthwhile if, because of some conditions of the application, the free list tends to be
fairly short or the average block size is small. In other cases, it may be a very useful
way of speeding up the deallocation of storage. The details can be found in Knuth's
book.

The storage representation of the blocks are of the form given in Fig. 5-6.2a
and b where the blocks are on the free list and allocated, respectively. If the block
starting at address P is free, then the FLAG and FL fields are set to 0; otherwise,
these fields are set to a positive value for a block that is allocated. The fields SIZE
and SZ contain the length of block P SUC(P) and PRED(P) are pointers to the successor and predecessor of block P on the free block list, respectively. We also
assume a list head of the form given in Fig. 5-6.2c, with AVAIL being its address.
The list head is considered to be the successor and the predecessor of the last and
first blocks on the free list. For convenience, we assume that the list head is outside
the segment of storage that is to be managed and that the first and last words of this
segment have the correct flags set to show that these two words have been allocated.
We now proceed to formulate a deallocation algorithm based on this representation.


**Procedure** FREE_BOUNDARY_TAG(AVAIL, RB, ROVER). Given the block structure just described, this algorithm inserts a block with address RB onto the free list

whose head node address is AVAIL, merging it with contiguous blocks as necessary. It also redefines ROVER, the variable-search start point, if required. It is assumed that having the address of the first word of the block is sufficient to access immediately the FLAG, SIZE, SUC, and PRED fields, and that the address of the last word of the block gives direct access to the SZ and FL fields. The procedure itself basically performs an insertion into a two-way linked list. Q is a local variable that points to various blocks during the process of merging.

1.    [Remove predecessor Q and merge?]
      If FL(RB – 1) = 0
      then   Q ← RB – SZ(RB – 1)
               PRED(SUC(Q)) ← PRED(Q)
               SUC(PRED(Q)) ← SUC(Q)
               SIZE(Q) ← SIZE(Q) + SIZE(RB)
               RB ← Q
2.    [Remove successor Q and merge?]
      If FLAG(RB + SIZE(RB)) = 0
      then   Q ← RB + SIZE(RB)
               PRED(SUC(Q)) ← PRED(Q)
               SUC(PRED(Q)) ← SUC(Q)
               SIZE(RB) ← SIZE(RB) + SIZE(Q)
               If ROVER = Q
               then   ROVER ← RB
3.    [Add locations between RB and Q inclusive as new first block]
      Q ← RB + SIZE(RB) – 1
      FLAG(RB) ← FL(Q) ← 0
      SZ(Q) ← SIZE(RB)
      SUC(RB) ← SUC(AVAIL)
      SUC(AVAIL) ← RB
      PRED(RB) ← AVAIL
      PRED(SUC(RB)) ← RB
4.    [Finished]
      Return                           □

In performing the deallocation, we find that four possible cases arise in Procedure FREE_BOUNDARY_TAG and that these are exhibited in Fig. 5-6.3. In the first case, as shown in Fig. 5-6.3a, the freed block pointed to by RB is of size B and has no immediate neighbors that are already marked as free. That is, both the block with a size field of A and the block with size field of C are already allocated and hence their flag fields are marked with a 1. In this case, neither steps 1 or 2 of the procedure are applied and with the application of step 3 the freed block is simply placed at the front of the availability list as depicted in the right-hand side of Fig. 5-6.3a.

The second case is shown in Fig. 5-6.3b. The neighbor block of size A is shown to be on the free list. In this case, step 1 of the procedure collapses the block pointed to by RB and its neighbor of size A to a new block of size A + B. Note that in collapsing the blocks, the block of size A is removed from the free list. Step 2 is not applied in this case and step 3 simply inserts the new collapsed block at the front of the free list.

The third case shows the situation in which the freed block is collapsed with a neighbor that succeeds it in storage. The condition in step 1 is not met, however,

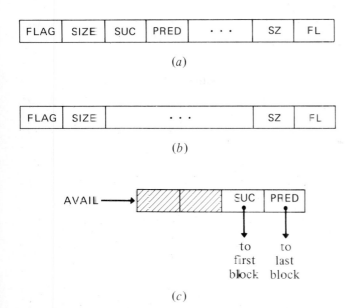

**FIGURE 5-6.2**    Boundary-tag block structure. (a) Free block; (b) allocated block; and (c) list head block.

the condition in step 2 is true. The freed block is collapsed with the block of length C, and the block of length C is removed from the free list. The final step places the collapsed block at the head of the free list.

The fourth case combines the effects of cases two and three discussed previously. Both neighbor blocks are collapsed in steps 1 and 2 and the large collapsed block is again inserted as the first block in the free list.

### 5-6.4 Buddy System

Up to this point the sizes of blocks have been either fixed or completely arbitrary (though larger than some minimum value). Another technique used in some storage management methods is to restrict the sizes of blocks to some fixed set of sizes. All the blocks of each size can be linked together with the intent of speeding up the search for a block of suitable size. For a request for a block of size n, the number m, the smallest of the fixed sizes equal to or larger than n, is determined, and a block of size m is allocated. If no block of size m is available, then a larger block is split into two subblocks (known as buddies ), each also of fixed size, and this process is repeated until a block of size m is produced.

Besides the improvement in search time, there is another advantage in using this technique. The collapsing of two smaller blocks into one larger block is relatively easy, since only the two buddies formed by splitting a larger block may be combined to form this larger block once again. Because the sizes are fixed relative to one another, the address of the buddy of a block is relatively easily determined.

There are, however, some potential disadvantages associated with this technique. Internal fragmentation will be increased generally because of the allocation of blocks which may be somewhat larger than the requested size. As well, there can be an increased amount of external fragmentation due to the fact that two blocks

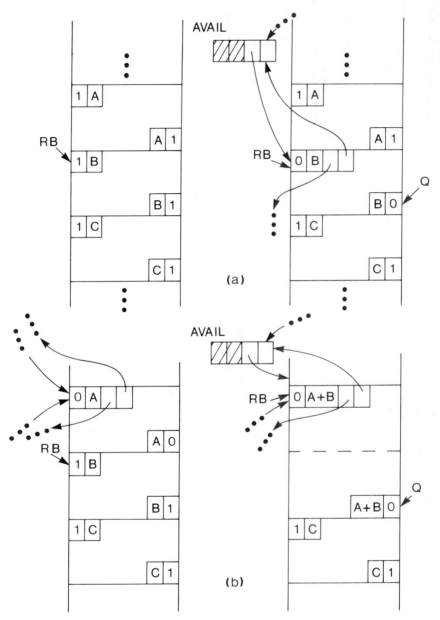

**FIGURE 5-6.3**    An illustration of the four cases of block deallocation in the boundary-tag method.

may be contiguous and yet not merged, because they are not buddies. Generally, though, this technique of storage management has proven to be quite efficient with performance comparable to the previous methods discussed.

The usual approach in implementing this method of storage management is to

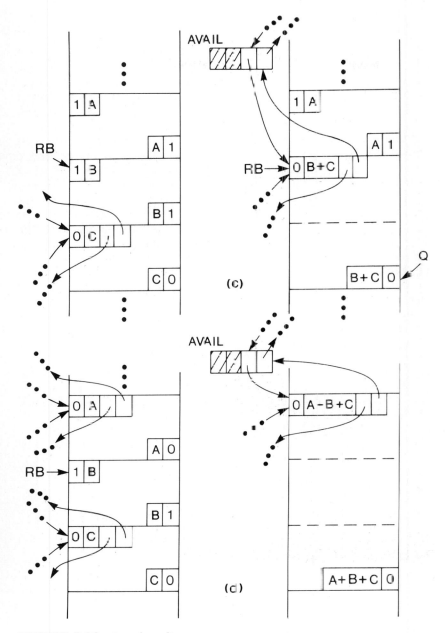

**FIGURE 5-6.3**   (continued)

specify the fixed sizes, $F_0, F_1, ..., F_{MAX}$, for blocks according to some pattern such as the recurrence relation

$$\begin{cases} F_n = F_{n-1} + F_{n-k} & k \leq n \leq MAX \\ F_0 = a, F_1 = b, ..., F_{k-1} = c \end{cases}$$

where a, b, ..., c are minimum block sizes that are used, and k = 1 or 2 or 3 or ....
For example, if k is 1 and $F_0$ is 1, then the block sizes, which are 1, 2, 4, 8, 16, ...,
are the successive powers of 2 and the method is called the buddy system. If k = 2
with $F_0 = F_1 = 1$, then the sizes are just the successive members of the Fibonacci
sequence 1, 1, 2, 3, 5, 8, 13, .... In all likelihood, though, the $F_0$, $F_1$, etc., terms are
not defined to be such small values. Blocks of size 1 are not much use, especially if
they must carry control information so that the allocation and release mechanisms will
work.

The feature that makes this system work is that the merges must correspond
exactly to the splits. By this we mean that the only two blocks that can be merged
are the precise two that were formed by splitting. Furthermore, before each block
can be reformed, each of its subblocks must be reformed from their subblocks.
Consequently, the storage-block pattern formed by the sequence of splits has the
form of a binary tree. The problem with which we are faced is the recording of the
position of a particular block within this tree structure. A rather elegant solution
has been provided by Hinds in a storage-management application.

His solution consists of a coding for each block by which we can reconstruct
the splitting sequence that produced that block. Looking at the recurrence relation
$F_n = F_{n-1} + F_{n-k}$,  if we specify that the $F_{n-1}$ term corresponds to the block that
forms the left branch of a split  (assumed to be at the lower address) and the $F_{n-k}$
term is the right branch, then all we must record for each block is the size of the
block, the number of splits it took to form the block, and whether it is a left block
or a right block. Since one left block and one right block are formed in each split,
we need only record the count of left blocks. In fact, this allows us to code the left
or right factor together with the split count in one coded field. The left block has
the relative split count (a number greater than 0), while the right block has a code of
0. The code for the parent block is thus determined in relation to the left block.
The formulas to use are the following:

*Initially:*   $CODE_{MAX}$  = 0   where $F_{MAX}$ is the entire segment considered to be
                                    a right block

*Splitting:*   $CODE_{LEFT}$  = $CODE_{PARENT}$ + 1

              $CODE_{RIGHT}$  = 0

*Merging:*   $CODE_{PARENT}$ = $CODE_{LEFT}$ − 1

As an example, consider a storage block of 144 cells and the recurrence relation

$$F_n = F_{n-1} + F_{n-2}   2 \leqslant n \leqslant 6$$

$$F_0 = 8, F_1 = 13$$

The entire tree of possible splits is given in Fig. 5-6.4, where the vertex value is the
block size and the superscript is the code value as computed by the above formulas.
Consider the tree cross section that is the set of potential blocks of size 13. A block of
size 13 with code of 0 is the right block formed by splitting a block of size 34. The left
or right nature of this size 34 block is determined by the left buddy for the block of
size 13. If its left buddy (of size 21) has a code of 1, then the size 34 block is a right
block for some larger block of size 89, while if the left buddy has a code greater than

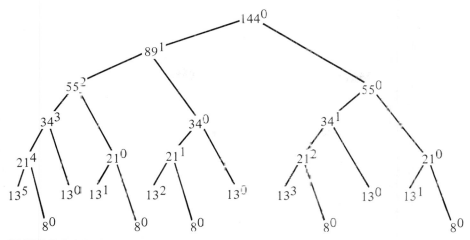

**FIGURE 5-6.4**   Storage-management tree.

1, then the block of size 34 is a left block of some still larger block.  A block of size 13 with a code value greater than 0 is the left block of a split block of size 21.  The numeric value of the code for a left block of size 13 is the number of splits of some higher right block that had to be made to get this left block of size 13.  Or, in other words, the value of the code for a left block is the number of merges that this left block must undergo to become the first 13 locations of some larger block which is finally a right block.

For the algorithms we will present, we assume blocks of the structure given in Figs. 5-6.5$a$ and $b$, which correspond to free and allocated blocks, respectively. FREE(P) is 0 or greater than 0, depending on whether block P is free, SIZE(P) contains the value i for block P of size $F_i$, and SUC(P) and PRED(P) for a free block P are the forward and backward pointers to other free blocks of size $F_i$ in a doubly linked list of all the free blocks of size $F_i$.  The list head with address AVAIL[i] for this list is given in Fig 5-6.5$c$.  CODE(P) for block P is the code giving the left- or right-handedness of block P and the relative split count, if P is a left block.  In addition to the array of list heads AVAIL[0:MAX], we also have the array F[0:MAX], which records the block sizes $F_i$, $0 \le i \le$ MAX, as determined by the recurrence relation.  It is assumed that $F_0$ has a value large enough to allow the storage of the control fields.

The following are two subalgorithms that take care of the insertion and deletion of blocks into and from the above linked lists.

**Procedure**   INSERT(P, I).  Given the arrays and block structures as previously described, parameters I and P, (address of a block of size $F_I$), this procedure inserts P into the list headed by AVAIL[I].

1.   [Insert at front of the list]
        FREE(P) ← 0
        SIZE(P) ← I
        SUC(P) ← SUC(AVAIL[I])
        SUC(AVAIL[I]) ← P

PRED(P) ← AVAIL(I)
PRED(SUC(P)) ← P
2.  [Finished]
    Return                                                            □

**Procedure** DELETE(P). Given the arrays and block structures as previously described and parameter P (the address of a block), this algorithm deletes block P from the list in which it appears.

1.  [Delete block P by unlinking it]
        SUC(PRED(P)) ← SUC(P)
        PRED(SUC(P)) ← PRED(P)
2.  [Finished]
    Return                                                            □

A general algorithm for allocating storage using the buddy system is as follows.

1.  Check that the requested amount of storage is not larger than amount available
2.  Determine the smallest size block larger than or equal to the requested amount of storage
3.  Search list head blocks for smallest free block greater than or equal to the requested size
4.  If such a block does not exist then return
5.  Remove the free block from its linked list
6.  Repeat step 7 until the correct size is reached
7.  Split the block into buddies and place inappropriate buddy on its linked list
8.  Return address of block

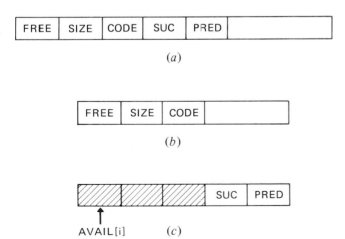

FIGURE 5-6.5   Block structure for storage management.   (a) Free block; (b) allocated block; and (c) list head block.

The following algorithm services the request for storage blocks. The algorithm presumes that the value of K has been fixed so as to determine which recurrence relation is being used.

**Function** ALLOCATE_BUDDY(N). Given the arrays and block structures as previously described, this algorithm receives a request for a block of size N and returns the pointer P set to the address of block of size $F_i$ , which is the smallest size larger than or equal to N. It is assumed that the value of K has been fixed so as to determine which recurrence relation is being used. Local variables include I and J (integers) and Q (pointer).

1.  [Determine size code]
    If N > F[MAX]
    then    Return(NULL)
    else    I ← 0
                Repeat while N > F[I]
                    I ← I + 1
2.  [Find first available block]
    J ← I
    Repeat while SUC(AVAIL[J]) = AVAIL[J]
        J ← J + 1
        If J > MAX
        then    Return(NULL)
    P ← SUC(AVAIL[J])
    Call DELETE(P)
3.  [Split as required until correct size is reached]
    Repeat while J > I and J ≥ K
        Q ← P + F[J – 1]
        CODE(P) ← CODE(P) + 1
        CODE(Q) ← 0
        If I > J – K
        then    Call INSERT(Q, J – K)
                J ← SIZE(P) ← J – 1
        else    Call INSERT(P, J – 1)
                J ← SIZE(Q) ← J – K
                P ← Q
4.  [Allocate block P of size $F_i$]
    FREE(P) ← 1
    Return(P)                                                         □

In the first step of the function, a check is made to ensure the requested amount of storage is not larger than the amount available. If such a condition occurs, a NULL value is returned and appropriate action is assumed to be taken in the calling program. Otherwise, the first step of the algorithm determines the smallest size of block that is larger than or equal to the requested amount of storage. The second step searches the list head blocks for the smallest free block equal to or larger than the required size. If such a block is found, it is removed from its doubly linked list. The third step controls the splitting operation on this block. The if statement in step 3 causes the left buddy of each split block to be placed on the appropriate linked list until one of the buddies satisfies the request size. The inappropriate buddy (either left or right) is placed on the correct linked list, while the other buddy is marked allocated and its address returned.

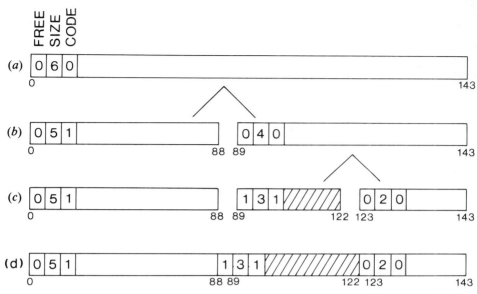

**FIGURE 5-6.6**   Allocate buddy.

Consider the following situation.  A request for a block of storage of size 30 (N = 30) has been received.  The storage allocation system in use is the Fibonacci buddy system described previously (K = 2 and MAX = 6).  Initially, the entire block of size 144 is free, as shown in Fig. 5-6.6a.  The SUC and PRED fields have been dropped to simplify the diagram.  Since the block of size 144 is the smallest block larger then size 30, it is selected.  Figure 5-6.6b shows the first split of this block. The smaller right buddy is still larger than the requested size, so the larger left buddy is marked free, and its CODE is incremented and inserted on the appropriate linked list.  The smaller right buddy is again split as shown in Fig. 5-6.6c.  The new right buddy in Fig. 5-6.6c is less than the request, so it is marked as free, and the CODE is set to zero indicating a right buddy and placed on the appropriate linked list.  The left buddy in Fig. 5-6.6c is the most efficient size for the request.  This block is marked occupied and its address is returned to the calling program.  Figure 5-6.6d shows the segment of memory after the splitting is complete.  The occupied block is indicated by shading.

The following general algorithm controls the return of storage, merging with appropriate buddies whenever possible.  The algorithm assumes K has been set to indicate the recurrence relation being used.

1.   Repeat step 2 until all possible merges have been made
2.   If the code of the freed block is greater than zero
  then determine the address of its right buddy
      if the right buddy is occupied or the wrong size
      then insert the free block on the appropriate list and return
      else remove the right buddy from its linked list and combine buddies
  else determine the address of its left buddy
      if the left buddy is occupied or the wrong size

then insert the free block on the appropriate list and return
else remove the left buddy from its linked list and combine buddies
3.   Insert maximal block on appropriate linked list

A detailed algorithm for this function is now presented.

**Procedure** FREE_BUDDY(P).  Given a block beginning at address P, this algorithm inserts it (or the mergers of it with appropriate buddies) onto the proper free list. It is assumed that the value of K has been fixed so as to determine which recurrence relation is being used.  Q is a local variable.

1.   [Perform all possible merges]
        Repeat step 2 while SIZE(P) < MAX
2.   [Merge blocks]
        If CODE(P) > 0
        then   Q ← P + F[SIZE(P)]
               (P is a left block, Q is address of right block)
               If FREE(Q) > 0 or SIZE(Q) ≠ SIZE(P) – K + 1
               then   (right block is occupied or wrong size)
                      Call INSERT(P, SIZE(P))
                      Return
               else   (combine buddies)
                      CODE(P) ← CODE(P) – 1
                      SIZE(P) ← SIZE(P) + 1
                      Call DELETE(Q)
        else   (P is a right block, Q is address of left block
               Q ← P – F[SIZE(P) + K – 1]
               If FREE(Q) > 0 or SIZE(Q) ≠ SIZE(P) + K – 1
               then   (left block is occupied or wrong size)
                      Call INSERT(P, SIZE(P))
                      Return
               else   (combine buddies)
                      CODE(Q) ← CODE(Q) – 1
                      SIZE(Q) ← SIZE(Q) + 1
                      Call DELETE(Q)
                      P ← Q
3.   [We get here if only if P is the maximal block]
        Call INSERT(P, MAX)
        Return                                                    ☐

The first step of the algorithm controls the merging process.  The second step performs the actual merging of blocks.  If the CODE of the freed block is greater than 0, P is a left block; otherwise it is a right block.  In both these cases, if the neighboring block to the returned block is free and a buddy, the two blocks are combined and the loop continues.  If the neighboring block is not a buddy or is in use, the function places the final block on the appropriate linked list and terminates.

Suppose that the previously allocated block of storage in Fig. 5-6.6 is now released.  The initial situation is given in Fig. 5-6.7c.  The PRED and SUC fields have once more been left out to simplify the diagram.  Since the CODE of the released block is greater than 0, it is recognized as a left block.  Its right buddy is

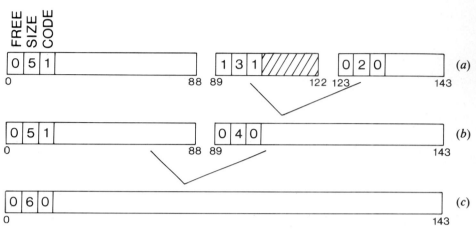

**FIGURE 5-6.7** Free buddy.

examined and found to be free, allowing the two blocks to be merged. The CODE field of the new block is decremented and its SIZE field incremented. The situation after this process is shown in Fig. 5-6.7*b*. The CODE field of this new block is 0, indicating a right block. The left buddy of this block is free, and the two blocks are combined following the same procedure as described above. Since P is now the maximal block, it is inserted on the appropriate linked list and the function terminates. The final result is shown in Fig. 5-6.7*c*.

It should be noted that when K = 1 (when the strategy is in effect the buddy system ), then the addresses of buddies differ from each other by amounts that are integral powers of two. Since all addresses are in binary representation in a computer, the address calculation given earlier could be replaced by a method that makes use of this fact, possibly speeding up these algorithms.

With regard to the performance of the algorithms, Knuth's simulations showed that the buddy system performed quite well, comparable to his boundary-tag method, and in fact, the buddy system has proven itself in practice. Statistical analysis has been performed on the Fibonacci system, and the results appear to show it to be superior to the buddy system (quite possibly because of the wider range of block sizes available for a given segment of storage). The advantage of the Fibonacci system which makes it appear even more useful is that the average amount of wasted storage is less than for the buddy system. This is because there are at least as many Fibonacci numbers less than a given number as there are integral powers of two. In fact, for $n > 4$, there are always more Fibonacci numbers less than or equal to n than there are powers of two, while for $n \leq 4$, there are at least as many Fibonacci numbers. Hence, the Fibonacci system has more sizes available and is more likely to achieve a better fit of allocated amount to requested amount. In summary, then, both of these methods appear to be suitable for use as part of a storage management system.

### 5-6.5 Garbage Collection

Now that we have looked at several methods of allocating and freeing storage, we must still consider the question of how and when the decision to free storage is made. Several algorithms for freeing allocated storage that is no longer being used are introduced.

Deciding when to allocate storage is simple. It is done when the programmer requests it by declaring a structure at program-block entry or by invoking a routine which creates a specific structure at run time. It is also done by the system when, at program-block entry, it processes the temporaries that were discovered at compile time, or when, during program execution, certain data-dependent temporaries are formed.

But to free storage is not as easy a matter. Obviously, at block exit, the storage allocated at entry for local variables can all be freed. The difficult storage to handle is that storage which is dynamically allocated, such as list structure nodes of programmer-created blocks or strings in languages like SNOBOL.

One method is to make the responsibility for freeing storage the programmer's. But this, if applied universally, places too much of a burden on the programmer—it is too easy to forget about some temporaries, structures, etc. Some languages (for example, Pascal) do provide a **dispose** statement to allow programmers some responsibility (if they choose to accept it) for freeing at least some instances of their defined data structures. Most languages (and associated implementation systems), however, reserve for themselves the task of storage release, even if they do provide a **dispose** command by which the programmer can release certain blocks of storage.

Therefore, the problem now becomes one of determining by what means the system decides to free storage. There are several methods. One is to free no storage at all until there is almost none left. Then, all the allocated blocks are checked, and those that are no longer being used are freed. This method is called *garbage collection*. During the program execution, blocks of storage that once were needed but which at some later time became unnecessary and unused are called "garbage." A garbage collection simply goes through and recovers these garbage blocks. Another method is to free each block as soon as it becomes unused. This prevents the accumulation of garbage blocks but requires more run-time checking during processing. This method is generally implemented by means of reference counters—counters which record how many pointers to this block are still in existence in the program.

Two problems arise in the context of storage release. One is the accumulation of garbage as mentioned before; this has the effect of decreasing the amount of free storage available and consequently increasing the chances of having to refuse a request for storage. The other problem is that of "dangling references." A dangling reference is a pointer existing in a program which still accesses a block that has been freed. If ever the block is reallocated and then this dangling pointer is used, the program once again has access to that block which is now being used for completely different purposes. Results can be catastrophic.

It is generally conceded that the dangling reference is potentially the more dangerous of the two problems, and so more effort is taken to minimize its likelihood of occurring. This, by the way, is another reason why not many systems allow the programmer much freedom to deallocate his own storage. It is too easy to do things like the following in Pascal

```
new(p);
    .
    .
    .
q := p;
dispose(p);
```

in which case $q$ has been created as a dangling reference. The system may well set $p$ to **nil**, when it does release the block, in order to break the association between the identifier $p$ and the block, but it can do nothing about $q$, which now records the address of a free block. There is no substitute for disciplined programming, but because many programmers like using "tricks," language implementors tend to try to protect them from their folly by means such as restricting the manner in which they release storage.

In the reference-counter method, as mentioned earlier, a counter is kept that records how many different program elements have direct access (e.g., a pointer) to each block. When the block is first allocated, its reference counter is set to 1. Each time another link is made pointing to this block, the reference counter is incremented; each time a link to it is broken, the reference counter is decremented. When the count reaches 0, then the block is inaccessible, and hence, unsuitable. At this point it is returned to the free list. Notice that this technique completely eliminates the dangling reference problem. The block is returned after there are no references to it in the program.

There are certain drawbacks in using this method, however. First, if the blocks that are allocated form a circular structure, then their reference counts will always remain set to at least 1 and none of the blocks will ever be freed, even if all pointers from outside the circular structure to blocks in the circular list are destroyed. We then have a circle of blocks, each of which is inaccessible from the program, and yet all the blocks will remain allocated—as permanent garbage. There are solutions for this, of course. One is simply to prohibit circular or recursive structures. In a number of applications, however, a circular structure is the most natural and reasonable one to use. Another solution is to flag circular structures as such, thereby signifying that they are to receive special treatment from the point of view of storage release. A third solution is to require that circular structures always use a special list head whose reference counter counts only references from outside the circle, and that all access to blocks in the circular structure are made through this list head. This is then a prohibition against direct accessing of any block in the circle. When the list head counter goes to 0, then the header block and all blocks in the circle can be freed.

Another drawback to the reference-counter method is the overhead involved in maintaining the reference counts. This is a more serious objection because it can increase the execution time of the program significantly. Every processing operation will have to be checked for the effects on the reference counts, and these updated as necessary. For example, the simple statement P = SUC(PRED(Q)) can generate code to do the following, assuming that P and Q are known (perhaps by declarations) to be pointer variables:

*1*   Access block P and decrement its reference count. Let this new reference count be t.
*2*   Test t for zero. If so, free block P.
*3*   Evaluate SUC(PRED(Q)). Let the result be address r.
*4*   Access block r and increment its reference count.
*5*   Assign the value r to the variable P.

Examination of even the simpler algorithms that may be used in a context where dynamic storage allocation and release are reasonable should indicate that the cost of this counter maintenance can easily become excessive.

The other method of determining when to free storage (aside from programmer-commanded release) is garbage collection. This method makes use of a special routine which is invoked whenever the available storage is almost exhausted, or whenever a particular request cannot be met, or perhaps, whenever the amount of available storage has decreased beyond a certain predefined point. Normal program execution is interrupted while this routine frees garbage blocks and is resumed when the garbage collector has finished its work. The garbage-collection algorithm generally has two phases. The first phase consists of a tracing of all the access paths from all the program and system variables through the allocated blocks. Each block accessed in this way is marked. Phase two consists of moving through the entire segment of memory, resetting the marks of the marked blocks, and returning to the free list every allocated block that has not been marked.

Again, this method prevents the generation of dangling references because if there is any path of references leading to a block, this block is marked and is not freed in phase two. Because the garbage collector must trace paths of pointers from block to block, however, it is essential that every time the garbage collector is invoked, all list and block structures are in their normal form with pointers pointing where they should. Otherwise, the garbage collector will not be able to make the proper tracing of all the reference paths, and either some garbage will remain uncollected or, more seriously, blocks still in use will be freed. Since the garbage collector can be invoked by the system at almost any point in program execution, it is required that the use of pointers be disciplined. There are certain algorithms, however, which during their operation, temporarily distort structures—e.g., having pointers pointing up a tree instead of downwards to branches. If the garbage collector is invoked while the program is executing one of these algorithms, it is quite possible that the garbage collector will meet such a distorted tree. The marking phase can then no longer mark the current blocks, and the situation when normal execution resumes can be horrendous.

A solution to this is, of course, to use pointers responsibly, avoiding the kind of algorithm that momentarily distorts structures. Certain applications, however, could well need that type of algorithm; it may be the only way to do the required task. In this case, the algorithm should begin by disabling the garbage collector so that it cannot be invoked while the algorithm is executing. If the algorithm should ever request storage and have the request refused, however, then a stalemate has developed. There is not necessarily any ready solution to this problem other than to terminate the job and rerun with more storage initially allocated to the job.

One of the drawbacks to the garbage collection techniques is that its costs increase as the amount of free storage decreases, and yet, it is at this point that one would hope for efficient and cheap release of storage. When you have little free storage left, you expect the garbage collector to be called more often and you want its use to cost as little as possible. The reason for the inverse relationship is, of course, that when there is little free storage, there is a lot of allocated storage, and hence, the marking process has to trace through many blocks. Because of this factor, and also perhaps to avoid the stalemate situation mentioned earlier, garbage-collection methods are sometimes implemented such that the collector is invoked well before memory gets close to full. For example, whenever the amount of free storage drops below half the total amount, the collector can be invoked intermittently. Also, to eliminate the intolerably repetitive calls to the collector that can result when memory is almost full, some systems consider the memory to be full whenever the garbage collector fails to restore the amount of free storage to a certain level. Such a condition causes the system to terminate when the next unsatisfiable request is encountered.

We now look at some of the algorithms that have been developed for garbage collection. We concentrate on the marking phase because the actual freeing phase, the sequential stepping through memory freeing unmarked blocks, is relatively simple. For fixed-size blocks of size n, with P being the address of the block with the lowest address in the total memory segment, the addresses of all the r blocks that were formed out of the total memory segment are given by $P + i * n, 0 \leqslant i < r$. For variable-sized blocks, with P and Q being the addresses of the first and last words of the total memory segment, the addresses of all the blocks are given by the sequence of P values formed by

$$P_1(=P), P_2(=P_1 + SIZE(P_1)),..., P_m(=P_{m-1} + SIZE(P_{m-1})),$$

where $P_m + SIZE(P_m) = Q + 1$.

In the marking phase, the garbage collector must mark all blocks that are accessible by any path of references that begins with a program or system variable. Consequently, the collection algorithm must have access to a list of all the variables that currently contain references into the dynamic storage area. A scan through the symbol table or current identifier-association table will generally suffice. Once a variable has been found that points to a block of allocated storage, that block must be marked along with all the other blocks that are accessed by pointers within the first block and all blocks accessed from these blocks, etc. Once all blocks accessible from this variable have been marked, the next variable is processed in the same way. When all the variables have been processed, the total memory segment is stepped through and unmarked blocks are freed.

For the convenience of the marking algorithm, we assume that blocks which contain pointers to other blocks, thus forming a list-type structure, have these pointers located so that they are readily accessible given the block address. They can be located in the first words of the block following the block control fields. Therefore, we assume that block P, when allocated, has a structure of the form given in Fig. 5-6.8.

FREE(P) contains a value equal to $1 +$ the number of LINK fields, SIZE(P) is the size of block P (or the coding for the size of block P as in the buddy or Fibonacci allocation system), SAVE(P) is a field to be used in the marking process by which a temporary distortion of the list structure needed for traversal can be eventually undone, MARK(P) is a field, initially set to *false*, which is set to *true* to denote that block P has been marked, and the LINK(P) fields are pointers to other blocks. Note that there need not be any such LINK fields. Note also that the SAVE field is not necessary for the first of the marking algorithms we shall give. In that case, simply assume that it is not there. Observe that the LINK fields can be accessed by the addresses Q, for $P < Q < P + FREE(P)$. (Note that the allocation technique or release method may well require additional control fields. In such cases, simply assume that the correct fields are present.)

The first algorithm we give is very simple. It uses a stack S[1: MAX] to record unprocessed LINK fields encountered in the processing of a particular block. Upon the detection of an empty stack, all blocks on this chain have been marked.

A general algorithm to mark all occupied blocks is as follows.

1. If the first block has no link fields
   then mark the block as occupied and exit
   else stack the address of the block
2. Repeat thru step 4 while the stack is not empty
3. Pop the next block address off the stack

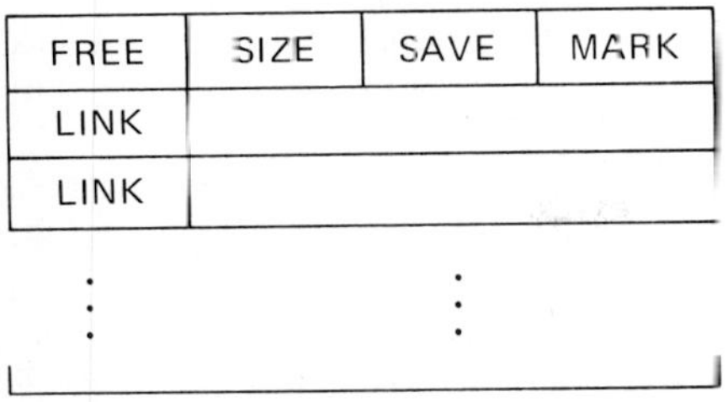

| FREE | SIZE | SAVE | MARK |
|------|------|------|------|
| LINK | | | |
| LINK | | | |

$\vdots$  $\vdots$

**FIGURE 5-6.8**  Block structure for garbage collection.

4.  Repeat for all link fields in the block
    if the block accessed by the link field has not been marked
    then if this block has no link fields
        then mark the block
        else stack the address of the block

5.  Exit

A detailed algorithm for this function is now presented.

**Procedure** STACK_MARK(P).  Given P, the address of a block that is directly accessible via a program or system variable, the stack S, and blocks of the structure just described (without the SAVE field), this routine marks block P and all blocks accessible from block P.

1.  [List structure?]
        If FREE(P) = 1
        then   MARK(P) ← *true*
               Return
        else   TOP ← 1
               S[TOP] ← P
2.  [Process next block]
        Repeat while TOP > 0
            P ← S[TOP]
            TOP ← TOP − 1
            MARK(P) ← *true*
            Q ← P + 1
            Repeat while Q < P + FREE(P)     (stack LINK fields)
                If MARK(LINK(Q)) = *false*
                then   If FREE(LINK(Q)) = 1
                       then   MARK(LINK(Q)) ← *true*
                       else   If TOP + 1 > MAX
                              then   Exit to error routine
                              else   TOP ← TOP + 1
                                     S[TOP] ← LINK(Q)
                Q ← Q + 1
3.  [Finished]
        Return                                              □

It should be noted that, in order to save some unnecessary operations on the stack, only those unmarked blocks which actually have LINK fields ever get pushed onto the stack.

This algorithm will run in time that is proportional to the number of blocks marked, and this is quite good. But the drawback to this method is the use of the auxiliary stack. Presumably, garbage collection is invoked when available storage is getting to be in short supply. There may not be room for the stack, especially if the blocks form a fairly complicated list structure with much cross linking involved. Because of this problem, other algorithms have been proposed, including ones which do not require an auxiliary stack. The following is an algorithm modeled upon one devised by Schorr and Waite.

The algorithm that Schorr and Waite propose works in the following manner. One path of accesses is followed until it ends. In our case, this is the referencing of a block which has no more LINK fields to process or which is already marked because it is also on some other path. As this forward path is followed, the LINK fields which we traverse are set to point to the block from which we came. This temporary distortion of the structure is, however, the factor that enables the one-way path to be retraced. The SAVE field is used to record which of the several LINK fields in a block is currently reversed. When this path is retraced, as we enter a block on the return journey, we reset the altered LINK field to its correct value and then process all other LINK fields of that block as if they initiated subpaths. That is, we follow one to its end, reversing LINK fields, and then trace it backwards, resetting LINK fields and following still further subpaths. It therefore follows that the logical structure of this algorithm involves a considerable degree of "nesting" of path fragments within path fragments. If it were not for the storage shortage, this would make an ideal candidate for a recursive treatment. The actual algorithm follows.


**Procedure**  LINK_MARK(P). Given P, the address of a block which is directly accessible, and blocks with the structure described earlier, this algorithm marks block P and all blocks accessible from P. The pointers P and Q refer to the current block under process and the previous block, respectively. Local variables include T (contains the LINK field that is currently reversed) and TEMP (pointer).


1.  [Initialize]
        Q ← NULL
2.  [Repeat until done]
        Repeat thru step 4 while true    (infinite loop)
3.  [Mark a starting block]
        If MARK(P) = *false*
        then    MARK(P) ← *true*
                SAVE(P) ← 0
        else    (reset a LINK and go backwards one step)
                If Q = NULL
                then    Exitloop
                else    T ← SAVE(Q)
                        TEMP ← LINK(Q + T)
                        LINK(Q + T) ← P
                        P ← Q
                        Q ← TEMP

4.   [Initiate a forward traversal]
        T ← SAVE(P) + 1
        If T < FREE(P)   (reverse a LINK)
        then   SAVE(P) ← T
               TEMP ← LINK(P + T)
               LINK(P + T) ← Q
               Q ← P
               P ← TEMP
5.   [Finished]
        Return                                                              □

It should be noted that this algorithm will run slower than the stack algorithm because each path must must be traced twice. Such a price must be paid for being able to mark in very little space.

The better solution is, of course, to make use of a stack if one is available. If there is some amount of available space. then the stack algorithm should be used initially. If at some point, however, the stack becomes full and there is a block address which must be stacked, then the second algorithm can be used to mark the current block and all blocks accessible from it. When it returns from marking, the stack algorithm can continue because it no longer has to process that block. This blending of the two algorithms couples the speed of the stack algorithm with an additional capability of marking without a stack whenever the stack is full. To blend these two algorithms, all one has to do is alter the phrase "exit to error routine" in Procedure STACK_MARK to "call LINK_MARK(LINK(Q))".

Figure 5-6.9 illustrates a trace of Procedure LINK_MARK for nodes $N_1$, $N_2$, $N_3$, and $N_4$. A snapshot of the state of each node is given when step 2 of the algorithm is executed. Notice that initially the MARK field of all nodes is *false* (i.e., "f") and at the completion of the trace all accessible nodes are marked *true* (i.e., "t").

### 5-6.6  Compaction

As a final topic, we shall briefly discuss compaction as a technique for reclaiming storage and introduce an algorithm to accomplish this task.

Compaction works by actually moving blocks of data, etc., from one location in memory to another so as to collect all the free blocks into one large block. The allocation problem then becomes completely simplified. Allocation now consists of merely moving a pointer which points to the top of this successively shortening block of storage. Once this single block gets too small again, the compaction mechanism is again invoked to reclaim what unused storage may now exist among allocated blocks. There is generally no storage release mechanism. Instead, a marking algorithm is used to mark blocks that are still in use. Then, instead of freeing each unmarked block by calling a release mechanism to put it on the free list, the compacter simply collects all unmarked blocks into one large block at one end of the memory segment. The only real problem in this method is the redefining of pointers. This is solved by making extra passes through memory. After blocks are marked, the entire memory is stepped through and the new address for each marked block is determined. This new address is stored in the block itself. Then another pass over memory is made. On this pass, pointers that point to marked blocks are reset to point to where the marked blocks will be after compaction. This is why the new address is stored right in the block—it is easily obtainable. After all pointers have been reset, then the marked blocks are moved to their new locations. A general algorithm for the compaction routine is as follows.

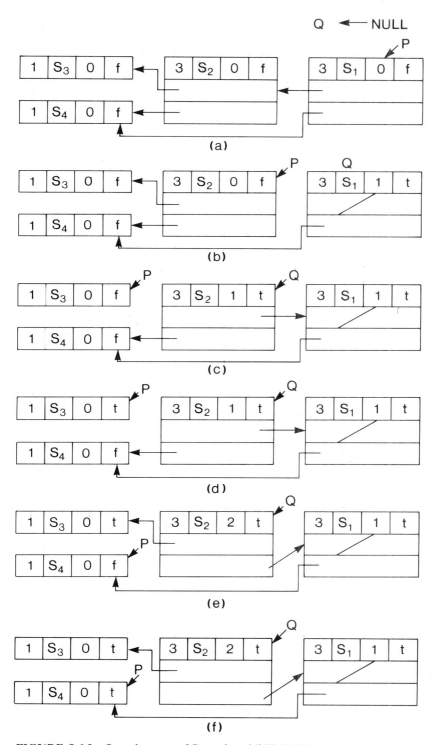

**FIGURE 5-6.9**    Sample trace of Procedure LINK_MARK.

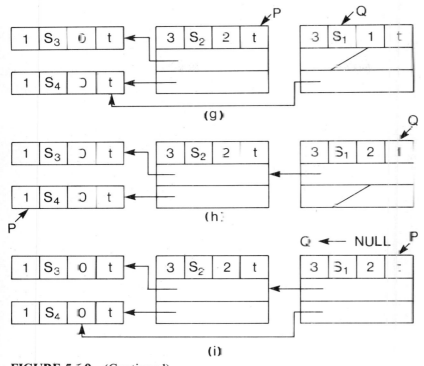

FIGURE 5-5.9   (Continued)

1.   Invoke garbage collection marking routine
2.   Repeat step 3 until the end of memory is reached
3.   If the current block of storage being examined has been marked
     then set the address of the block to the starting address of unused
         memory
         update the starting address of unused memory
4.   Redefine variable references for program and system pointer variables
5.   Define new values for pointers in marked blocks
6.   Repeat step 7 until the end of memory is reached
7.   Move marked blocks into new locations and reset markers

An example of a detailed compaction algorithm is the following one.

**Algorithm** COMPACT.   Given blocks of the structure as described for garbage collection, this algorithm performs a compaction of unused storage into one large block whose starting address is TOP and which extends from TOP to STOP. the highest address in the memory segment. It is assumed that START is the address of the first word of the memory segment. The SAVE field in the marked blocks is used by the compaction routine to record the address of each block. LOC is a pointer to various memory locations. K and T are local variables that are used during the moving of marked blocks to their new locations.

1.   [Mark blocks]
         Invoke garbage collection marking routine to mark blocks.
2.   [Compute new addresses for marked blocks]
         LOC ← TOP ← START
         Repeat while LOC ≤ STOP
             If MARK(LOC) = *true*
             then    SAVE(LOC) ← TOP
                         TOP ← TOP + SIZE(LOC)
             LOC ← LOC + SIZE(LOC)
3.   [Redefine variable references for program and system pointer variables]
         Repeat for each variable
             P ← location of variable
             variable ← SAVE(P)
4.   [Define new values for pointers in marked blocks]
         LOC ← START
         Repeat while LOC ≤ STOP
             If MARK(LOC) = *true*
             then    P ← LOC + 1
                         Repeat while P < LOC + FREE(LOC)
                             LINK(P) ← SAVE(LINK(P))
                             P ← P + 1
             LOC ← LOC + SIZE(LOC)
5.   [Move the marked blocks]
         LOC ← TOP ← START
         Repeat while LOC ≤ STOP
             If MARK(LOC) = *true*
             then    T ← SIZE(LOC)
                         K ← 0
                         Repeat while K < T
                             Copy contents of LOC + K into location TOP + K
                             K ← K + 1
                         MARK(TOP) ← *false*
                         TOP ← TOP + T
                         LOC ← LOC + T
             else    LOC ← LOC + SIZE(LOC)
6.   [Finished]
         Exit                                                                        □

Suppose a request for 125 words of storage is received when memory is allocated as shown in Fig. 5-6.10a. Since no block larger than 100 words is unoccupied, a call to COMPACT is invoked with TOP = 0 and STOP = 399. Figure 5-6.10b shows memory after all pointers have been modified, but no movement of blocks has occurred. After the algorithm has completed movement of storage, memory is as shown in Fig. 5-6.10c. The request for storage can now be met.

It should be noted that this compaction routine is a relatively costly process in terms of execution time because it requires three passes through memory. However, the increased speed of allocation might well make it a reasonable option in certain circumstances. Many implementations of SNOBOL use this compaction algorithm (or a variant), so presumably, it cannot be too very inefficient.

We have now finished our survey of storage management and some of the problems involved in performing it. We have presented a number of different algo-

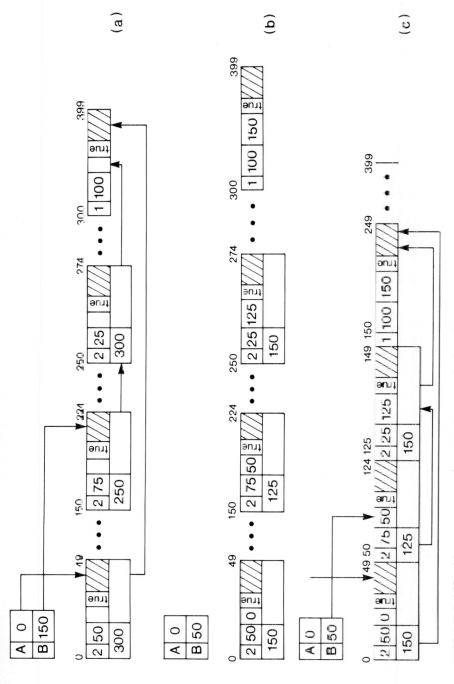

**FIGURE 5-6.10** Memory compaction (a) after step 1; (b) after step 4; and (c) after completion of algoritim.

rithms, ones which are reasonably typical of those that may be found in use. In practice, several of these techniques may be combined. This certainly is feasible; the methods are not necessarily incompatible with each other. In any case, the actual operating environment determines which methods should be used. The practical efficiency of these methods very often depends strongly on many parameters, among which are request frequency, size-of-request distribution, usage (e.g., batch vs. on-line), and the service philosophy of the computer center management.

**Exercises for Sec. 5-6**

1. The equations for the general buddy system were given in the text as

$$F_n = F_{n-1} + F_{n-k} \qquad k \leq n \leq MAX$$

$$F_0 = a, \quad F_1 = b, \quad ..., \quad F_{k-1} = c$$

For the special case of $k = 1$ and $F_0 = 1$, the block sizes obtained by the recurrence equations become 1, 2, 4, 8, 16, ..., and this restricted system is called the "binary" buddy system. The addresses of the buddies for this system differ from each other by amounts that are integral power of two. Assuming a binary representation of numbers in a computer:

   (a) Give the formula for computing the address of the buddies.
   (b) Reformulate a more efficient pair of algorithms (which correspond to Functions **ALLOCATE_BUDDY** and **FREE_BUDDY**) for this restricted binary buddy system. These algorithms should be as efficient as possible. Assume that the size of the memory available for memory requests is $2^m$.

2. For the Fibonacci buddy system described in the text, assume that $k = 4$, MAX $= 8$, $F_0 = 5$, $F_1 = 8$, $F_2 = 13$, and $F_3 = 21$. Generate the values for $F_4$, $F_5$, $F_6$, $F_7$, and $F_8$. Construct a storage management tree which illustrates the breakdown of a block of size $F_8$ into its constituent buddies down to the level of $F_0$, $F_1$, $F_2$, and $F_3$. Show the code for each node.

3. Suppose we are given a string space of size $N = 100$ which is used to store variable-length character strings using the descriptor method of storage representation. A descriptor is a storage cell composed of two fields: the length of string and the starting byte (character position) of the string in string space. For example, S = 'STRING' would be represented as shown in Fig 5-6.11. Assume that descriptors are stored apart from string space and there is no problem with storage overflow of the descriptor area. Also assume that a first-fit storage management scheme is used. In the scheme, descriptors for free blocks are ordered by address and a rotating starting search point is employed with MIN =

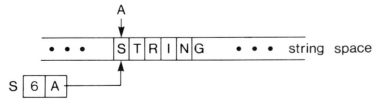

descriptor

**FIGURE 5-6.11**

3. Illustrate the contents of string space and the list of free block and allocated block descriptors after the following string operations.

1. S ← 'COMPUTER□'.
2. S1 ← S ○ 'DATA'
3. S2 ← SUBSTR(S, 1, 3)
4. S ← S ○ S1 ○ '□PROCESSING'
5. C ← 'CMPT-228B'
6. S1 ← SUBSTR(C, 3, 4)
7. S ← S1
8. S3 ← SUBSTR(S2, 3, 2) ○ S
9. S4 ← 'THE□END'

Assume the entire string space of 100 bytes is free initially. The following rules for determining how strings are freed and allocated must be used:

1 *Variable-to-variable assignments* (e.g., statement 7). Copy the descriptor value of the right-hand-side argument into the descriptor for the left side.

2 *Substring assignments* (e.g., statements 3 and 6). The descriptor for the left side is altered so as to point into the string space for the right-hand-side argument.

3 *Concatenate assignments* (e.g., statements 2, 4, and 8). Always request new string space, which is allocated to the variable

4 *Constant assignment* (e.g. statements 1, 5, and 9). Request new string space and allocate this to the variable on the left side.

In all the above cases, the space previously associated with the left-hand-side variable should be freed unless other strings are pointing into that space.

4. In the previous question dealing with the storage management of strings, it was illustrated how string space can become very fragmented after the application of a number of assignment operations. An example string space is given in Fig. 5-6.12, and the list of allocated-string descriptors and the list of free-string descriptors (both of which are ordered by address) are shown. Note that there is some garbage created in string space (for example, due to substring assignments). These garbage spaces are not encompassed by either an allocated-string descriptor or a free-string descriptor.

(a) Derive a garbage collection algorithm which compacts the allocated strings into one contiguous section at the low-order end of string space (i.e., at addresses 1, 2, ..., n. for some n).

(b) Indicate how your compaction algorithm would change the string space in the previous question.

5. Create a garbage collection algorithm that would be invoked in a list-manipulating subsystem when the number of storage cells on the availability list has shrunk to size MIN. The organization of the storage cells in such a subsystem is given in Fig. 5-6.13. Note

i) that more than one variable may point to some cells (e.g., the cells the lists B1 and C have in common in Fig. 5-6.13), and

ii) that due to sublist assignments some cells (see encircled cell in Fig. 5-6.13) may not be accessible through any variable and are not on the availability list.

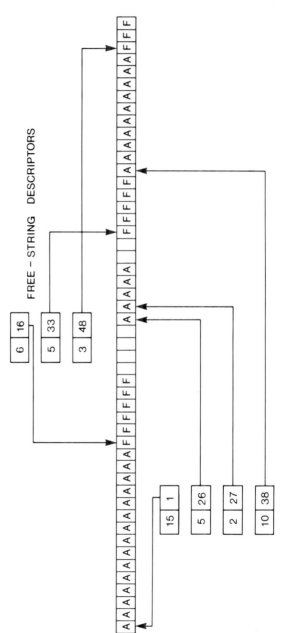

**FIGURE 5-6.12**

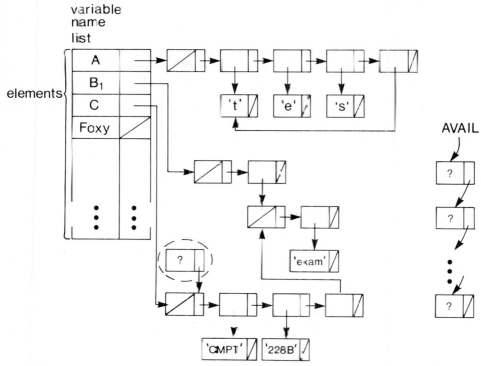

variable
name
list

elements

AVAIL

**FIGURE 5-6.13**

You are to assume that all list nodes are stored in one contiguous area of memory and that each node structure takes precisely m bits of storage which includes any space necessary for flag fields required by the storage management and garbage collection routines. After completing a garbage collection, your algorithm should leave all nodes available for use on the availability list.

6. Let us assume that we have available a heap storage area of 652 words and that size and link fields each require one word of storage for their representation. Suppose that in an application program requests for three types of data blocks (A, B, and C) are made. The blocks are of size 15, 24, and 40 for A, B, and C respectively. The following sequence of commands is a scenario of the storage requests made during the execution of the application program:

```
REQUEST B
REQUEST C
REQUEST B
REQUEST A
REQUEST B(1)
REQUEST A
RELEASE C(1)
REQUEST A
REQUEST B
RELEASE A(2)
```

The parenthesized numbers after a release command determine which copy of a block is released. Therefore, RELEASE B(1) means release the first copy of B that was requested.

You are to provide a trace of how storage would be managed using a first-fit storage management policy (i.e., Function ALLOCATE_FIRST_ROVER and Procedure FREE_BLOCK). Your trace should provide a snapshot of how storage is allocated just prior to and just after each release command.

## BIBLIOGRAPHY

ABRAMS, M. D.: "Data Structures for Computer Graphics," *Proceedings of a Symposium on Data Structures in Programming Languages*, SIGPLAN Notices, Vol. 6, No. 2, February, 1971, pp. 268-286.

AHO, A. V. and J. D. ULLMAN: "The Theory of Parsing, Translation, and Compiling, Vol. 1: Parsing," Prentice-Hall, Inc., Englewood Cliffs, N.J., 1972.

AHO, A. V., J. E. HOPCROFT, and J. D. ULLMAN: "Data Structures and Algorithms," Addison-Wesley Publishing Co., Inc., Reading, Mass., 1983.

AHO, A. V., J. E. HOPCROFT, and J. D. ULLMAN: "The Design and Analysis of Computer Algorithms," Addison-Wesley Publishing Co., Inc., Reading, Mass., 1974.

BERZTISS, A. T.: "Data Structures: Theory and Practice," Academic Press, Inc., New York, 1971.

DAVIDSON, C. H. and E. C. KOENIG: "Computers: Introduction to Computers and Applied Computing Concepts," John Wiley and Sons, Inc., New York, 1967.

DAVIS, S.: "Computer Data Displays," Prentice-Hall, Inc., Englewood Cliffs, N.J., 1969.

ELSON, M.: "Data Structures," Science Research Associates, Inc., Palo Alto, Calif., 1975.

GEAR, C. W.: "Introduction to Computer Science," Science Research Associates, Inc., Palo Alto, Calif., 1973.

GRAY, J. C.: "Compound Data Structures for Computer Aided Design; a Survey," *ACM Professional Development Seminar*.

GRIES, D. E.: "Compiler Construction for Digital Computers," John Wiley and Sons, Inc., New York, 1971.

HARRISON, M. C.: "Data Structures and Programming," Scott, Foresman and Company, Glenview, Ill., 1973.

HINDS, J. A.: "An Algorithm for Locating Adjacent Storage Blocks in the Buddy System," *Communications of the ACM*, Vol. 18, No. 4, 1975, pp. 221-222.

HIRSCHBERG, D. S.: "A Class of Dynamic Memory Allocation Algorithms," *Communications of the ACM*, Vol. 16, No. 10, 1973, pp. 615-618.

KAHN, A. B.: "Topological Sorting of Large Networks," *Communications of the ACM*, Vol. 5, No. 11, 1962, pp. 558-562.

KNUTH, D. E.: "The Art of Computer Programming, Vol. 1, Fundamental Algorithms," Second edition, Addison-Wesley Publishing Co., Inc., Reading, Mass., 1973.

LEVIN, RICHARD I. and CHARLES A. KIRKPATRICK: "Planning and Control with PERT/CPM," McGraw-Hill Book Company, New York, 1966.

LINDSTROM, G.: "Copying List Structures Using Bounded Workspace," *Communications of the ACM*, Vol. 17, No. 4, 1974, pp. 198-202.

MCCARTHY, J., et al.: "LISP 1.5 Programmer's Manual," 2nd edition, M.I.T. Press, Cambridge, Mass., 1969.

NEWMAN, W. M. and R. F. SPROULL: "Principles of Interactive Computer Graphics," McGraw-Hill Book Company, New York, 1973.

PRATT, T. W.: "Programming Languages: Design and Implementation," Prentice-Hall, Inc., Englewood Cliffs, N.J., 1975.

SCHORR, H. and W. M. WAITE: "An Efficient Machine-Independent Procedure for Garbage Collection in Various List Structures," *Communications of the ACM*, Vol. 10, No. 8, 1967, pp. 501-506.

SHEN, K. K. and J. L. PETERSON: "A Weighted Buddy Method for Dynamic Storage Allocation," *Communications of the ACM*, Vol. 17, No. 10, 1974, pp. 558-562.

SUTHERLAND, I. F.: "SKETCHPAD: A Man-Machine Graphical Communication System," Proceedings of the AFIPS 1963 SJCC, Vol. 23, Spartan Books, New York.

TREMBLAY, J. P. and R. M. MANOHAR: "Discrete Mathematical Structures and their Applications to Computer Science," McGraw-Hill Book Company, New York, 1975.

TREMBLAY, J. P. and P. G. SORENSON: "The Theory and Practice of Compiler Writing," McGraw-Hill Book Company, New York, 1985.

VAN DAM, A.: "Data and Storage Structures for Interactive Graphics," Proceedings of a Symposium on Data Structures in Programming Languages, SIG-PLAN Notices, Vol. 6, No. 2, February, 1971, pp 237-267.

WILLIAMS, R.: "A Survey of Data Structures for Computer Graphics Systems," ACM Computing Surveys, Vol. 3 No. 1, March, 1971, pp. 1-21.

# 6

# SORTING AND SEARCHING

In the previous chapters, we have discussed many data structures and their storage representations. Algorithms for a number of operations such as insertion and deletion, which are commonly performed on these structures, were described in detail. This chapter is concerned with two additional operations that are frequently performed on data structures—namely, sorting and searching. We shall see that efficient algorithms for these operations can be realized when data are properly structured.

The algorithms to be discussed progress from the simple to the complex. A quantitative measure of each algorithm is given. The most comprehensive reference to this chapter is Knuth's book on sorting and searching. The methods that are described in this chapter assume that all data are stored in the main memory of the computer, and these methods are therefore, called internal sorting and searching techniques.

## 6-1  SORTING

The operation of sorting is most often performed in business data-processing applications. This operation, however, has also become increasingly important in many scientific applications. The sorting methods which are discussed in this section give a representative sample of the most popular techniques used.

The methods that are described proceed from trivial (and inefficient) algorithms, such as the selection and bubble sorts, to the more complex (and efficient) algorithms, such as quick sort, heap sort, and radix sort. Various data structures such as trees and queues are used to structure the data so as to achieve computational efficiency.

### 6-1.1  Notation and Concepts

Data can occur in many forms. In this section it is assumed that we are given a collection of elements. Each element is represented by a record which contains a number of information fields. The records are combined into a table which represents the information upon which the operation of sorting is to be performed. Each field in a record contains, in general, alphanumeric information. The organization of a record is application dependent and has no bearing on the basic algorithms which will be discussed.

A *table* is assumed to be an ordered sequence of n records $R_1, R_2, ..., R_n$. Each record in a table contains one or more keys. It is with respect to these keys that processing is carried out. For example, the key associated with a record could be an employee number or an employee name. Each record for our purpose will contain a single key field $K_i$ and other additional information which is irrelevant to the present discussion.

Sorting is the operation of arranging the records of a table into some sequential order according to an ordering criterion. The sort is performed according to the key value of each record. Depending on the makeup of the key, records can be sorted either numerically or, more generally, alphanumerically. In numerical sorting, the records are arranged in ascending or descending order according to the numerical value of the key. An example of this type is the sorting of a symbol table according to the internal numeric value of the alphanumeric representation for each variable name. In general, a key can be any sequence of characters, and the ordering imposed by sorting depends on the collating sequence associated with the particular character set which is being used (see Secs. 1-4.6 and 2-3.1). For convenience, it is assumed throughout this section that the key upon which the sorting is performed is numeric. This is not a restrictive assumption since all algorithms to be formulated also apply to any string of characters, given a particular collating sequence.

Most of the algorithms to be discussed involve the movement of records from one place to another in the table. Since records in certain applications can be quite long and consequently expensive to move, the records can be organized in such a manner as to minimize this moving cost while performing a sort.

One method of substantially reducing the cost of moving the records is to arrange the table as a simple linked list. Clearly, the movement of records is efficient when such a representation is used. The additional memory required for a pointer field becomes less significant as the record length increases.

Another method of reducing record movement is to use a pointer vector, each element of which contains the address of one record. As an illustration, Fig. 6-1.1 gives the representation of a small student-record table according to grades before

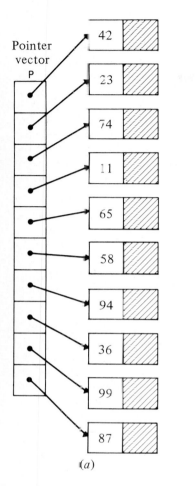
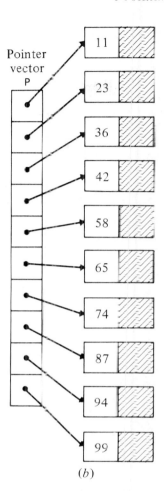

**FIGURE 6-1.1** Representation of a table using a pointer vector. (*a*) Before sorting; (*b*) after sorting.

and after sorting. The hatched area in each record represents information such as name and course number, which can be ignored for our purpose.

All sorting methods to be discussed assume that the entire table can be sorted in the computer's main memory. A number of these methods, such as the merge sort and address-calculation sort, can easily be adapted to tables stored on auxiliary storage devices like disks and drums. Such adaptations are discussed in Chap. 7.

Each sorting method to be described will include an approximate quantitative description of the method as to the number of comparisons and the number of record movements required. Since, as previously mentioned, the expense of record movements can be reduced significantly, the more important factor is the number of comparisons which is required by a particular method.

The sorting methods that are described in the following pages proceed from the trivial to the complex. The suitable structuring of the table, such as in the heap sort, radix sort, and address-calculation sort, can lead to efficient sorting algorithms.

### 6-1.2 Selection Sort

One of the easiest ways to sort a table is by *selection*. Beginning with the first record in the table, a search is performed to locate the element which has the smallest key. When this element is found, it is interchanged with the first record in the table. This interchange places the record with the smallest key in the first position of the table. A search for the second smallest key is then carried out. This is accomplished by examining the keys of the records from the second element onward. The element which has the second smallest key is interchanged with the element located in the second position of the table. The process of searching for the record with the next smallest key and placing it in its proper position (within the desired ordering) continues until all records have been sorted in ascending order. A general algorithm for the selection sort is now presented.

1.  Repeat thru step 5 a total of n – 1 times
2.  Record the portion of the vector already sorted
3.  Repeat step 4 for the elements in the unsorted portion of the vector
4.  Record location of smallest element in unsorted vector
5.  Exchange first element in unsorted vector with smallest element

The following detailed algorithm formalizes this process.

**Procedure** SELECTION_SORT(K, N). Given a vector K of N elements, this procedure rearranges the vector in ascending order; that is, its elements will be in the order $K[1] \leq K[2] \leq ... \leq K[N]$. The sorting process is based on the techniques just described. The variable PASS denotes the pass index and the position of the first element in the vector which is to be examined during a particular pass. The variable MIN_INDEX denotes the position of the smallest element encountered thus far in a particular pass. The variable I is used to index elements K[PASS] to K[N] in a given pass. All variables are of type integer.

1.  [Loop on pass index]
    Repeat thru step 4 for PASS = 1, 2, ..., N – 1
2.  [Initialize minimum index]
    MIN_INDEX ← PASS
3.  [Make a pass and obtain element with smallest value]
    Repeat for I = PASS + 1, PASS + 2, ..., N
        If K[I] < K[MIN_INDEX]
        then    MIN_INDEX ← I
4.  [Exchange elements]
    If MIN_INDEX ≠ PASS
    then    K[PASS] ⟷ K[MIN_INDEX]
5.  [Finished]
    Return                                                                 □

In the algorithm, the search for the record with the next smallest key is called a *pass*. There are n – 1 such passes required in order to perform the sort. This is because each pass places one record into its proper location.

An example of the selection sort is given in Fig. 6-1.2. Each encircled entry denotes the record with the smallest key selected in a particular pass. The elements above the bar for a given pass are those elements that have been placed in order.

| | Unsorted | | | | Pass Number (i) | | | | | Sorted |
|---|---|---|---|---|---|---|---|---|---|---|
| j | $K_j$ | 1 | 2 | 3 | 4 | 5 | 6 | 7 | 8 | 9 |
| 1 | 42 | 11 | 11 | 11 | 11 | 11 | 11 | 11 | 11 | 11 |
| 2 | 23 | 23 | 23 | 23 | 23 | 23 | 23 | 23 | 23 | 23 |
| 3 | 74 | 74 | 74 | 36 | 36 | 36 | 36 | 36 | 36 | 36 |
| 4 | 11 | 42 | 42 | 42 | 42 | 42 | 42 | 42 | 42 | 42 |
| 5 | 65 | 65 | 65 | 65 | 65 | 58 | 58 | 58 | 58 | 58 |
| 6 | 58 | 58 | 58 | 58 | 58 | 65 | 65 | 65 | 65 | 65 |
| 7 | 94 | 94 | 94 | 94 | 94 | 94 | 94 | 74 | 74 | 74 |
| 8 | 36 | 36 | 36 | 74 | 74 | 74 | 74 | 94 | 87 | 87 |
| 9 | 99 | 99 | 99 | 99 | 99 | 99 | 99 | 99 | 99 | 94 |
| 10 | 87 | 87 | 87 | 87 | 87 | 87 | 87 | 87 | 94 | 99 |

**FIGURE 6-1.2** Trace of a selection sort.

We now turn to the performance of this algorithm. During the first pass, in which the record with the smallest key is found, n − 1 records are compared. In general, for the ith pass of the sort, n − i comparisons are required. The total number of comparisons is, therefore, the sum

$$\sum_{i=1}^{n-1}(n-i) = \frac{1}{2}n(n-1)$$

Therefore, the number of comparisons is proportional to $n^2$, i.e., $O(n^2)$. The number of record interchanges depends upon how unsorted the table is. Since, during each pass, no more than one interchange is required, the maximum number of interchanges for the sort is n − 1.

### 6-1.3 Bubble Sort

Another well-known sorting method is the *bubble sort*. It differs from the selection sort in that, instead of finding the smallest record and then performing an interchange, two records are interchanged immediately upon discovering that they are out of order.

When this approach is used, there are at most n − 1 passes required. During the first pass, $K_1$ and $K_2$ are compared, and if they are out of order, then records $R_1$ and $R_2$ are interchanged; this process is repeated for records $R_2$ and $R_3$, $R_3$ and $R_4$, and so on. This method will cause records with small keys to move or "bubble up." After the first pass, the record with the largest key will be in the nth position. On each successive pass, the records with the next largest key will be placed in position n − 1, n − 2, . . ., 2, respectively thereby resulting in a sorted table.

After each pass through the table, a check can be made to determine whether any interchanges were made during that pass. If no interchanges occurred, then the table must be sorted and no further passes are required.

A general algorithm for the bubble sort is as follows.

1. Repeat thru step 4 a total of n − 1 times
2. Repeat step 3 for elements in unsorted portion of the vector
3. If the current element in the vector > next element in the vector
   then exchange elements
4. If no exchanges were made
   then return
   else reduce the size of the unsorted vector by one

We now proceed to the detailed algorithm for this sorting process.

**Procedure** BUBBLE_SORT (K, N).   Given a vector K of N elements, this procedure sorts the elements into ascending (increasing) order using the method just described. The variables PASS and LAST denote the pass counter and position of the last unsorted element, respectively. The variable I is used to index the vector elements. The variable EXCHS is used to count the number of exchanges made on any pass. All variables are integer.

1. [Initialize]
   LAST ← N   (entire list assumed unsorted at this point)
2. [Loop on pass index]
   Repeat thru step 5 for PASS = 1, 2, ..., N − 1
3. [Initialize exchanges counter for this pass]
   EXCHS ← 0
4. [Perform pairwise comparisons on unsorted elements]
   Repeat for I = 1, 2, ..., LAST − 1
       If K[I] > K[I + 1]
       then   K[I] ⟷ K[I + 1]
               EXCHS ← EXCHS + 1
5. [Were any exchanges made on this pass ?]
   If EXCHS = 0
   then   Return   (mission accomplished; return early)
   else   LAST ← LAST − 1   (reduce size of unsorted list)
6. [Finished]
   Return   (maximum number of passes required)                                  □

The algorithm is straightforward. Before each pass, the interchange marker EXCHS is initialized to zero. This marker is incremented each time an interchange is made. If, at the end of a pass, EXCHS has a value of zero, the sort is complete.

Let us consider the analysis of the bubble sort. The best case involves performing one pass which requires n − 1 comparisons. Consequently, the best case is $O(n)$. The worst case performance of the bubble sort is $n(n − 1)/2$ comparisons and $n(n − 1)/2$ exchanges. The average case is more difficult to analyze than the other cases. It can be shown that the average case analysis is $O(n^2)$. The average number of passes is approximately $n − 1.25\sqrt{n}$ (see Stone). For n = 10 the average number of passes is 6, the number of passes required in Fig. 6-1.3. The average number of comparisons and exchanges are both $O(n^2)$.

A number of improvements can be made to the bubble sort. Some of these are considered in the exercises. These refinements, however, do not significantly improve the performance of the method. In summary, the bubble sort may be an

| | Unsorted | | | Pass Number (i) | | | Sorted |
| j | $K_j$ | 1 | 2 | 3 | 4 | 5 | 6 |
|---|---|---|---|---|---|---|---|
| 1 | 42 | 23 | 23 | 11 | 11 | 11 | 11 |
| 2 | 23 | 42 | 11 | 23 | 23 | 23 | 23 |
| 3 | 74 | 11 | 42 | 42 | 42 | 36 | 36 |
| 4 | 11 | 65 | 58 | 58 | 35 | 42 | 42 |
| 5 | 65 | 58 | 65 | 36 | 58 | 58 | 58 |
| 6 | 58 | 74 | 36 | 65 | 65 | 65 | 65 |
| 7 | 94 | 36 | 74 | 74 | 74 | 74 | 74 |
| 8 | 36 | 94 | 87 | 87 | 87 | 87 | 87 |
| 9 | 99 | 87 | 94 | 94 | 94 | 94 | 94 |
| 10 | 87 | 99 | 99 | 99 | 99 | 99 | 99 |

**FIGURE 6-1.3** Trace of a bubble sort.

acceptable method for sorting a table which contains a small number of records (fewer than 15), but it should not be used for larger-sized tables.

### 6-1.4 Merge Sorting

The operation of sorting is closely related to the process of *merging*. In the early days of data processing, merging was performed on cards with the aid of a machine called a *collator*. The collator had as input two separate decks of cards, each of which was sorted, and it proceeded to merge these two decks and to output a single sorted deck of cards. In this section we will formulate a sorting algorithm based on successive merges.

The approach used in this subsection is to give two formulations of a merge sort. The first approach, which is recursive, is simpler to write and analyze. The second approach is iterative and more complex. By comparing both approaches it is obvious that the recursive formulation is superior to its iterative counterpart—even when the data are not organized as a tree or list structure.

First, let us examine the merging of two ordered tables which can be combined to produce a single sorted table. This process can be accomplished easily by successively selecting the record with the smallest key occurring in either of the tables and placing this record in a new table, thereby creating an ordered list. For example, from the tables

```
Table 1     11   23   42
Table 2      9   25
```

we obtain the following trace:

|            |    |    |    |    |    |
|------------|----|----|----|----|----|
| Table 1    | 11 | 23 | 42 |    |    |
| Table 2    | 25 |    |    |    |    |
| New Table  | 9  |    |    |    |    |
| Table 1    | 23 | 42 |    |    |    |
| Table 2    | 25 |    |    |    |    |
| New Table  | 9  | 11 |    |    |    |
| Table 1    | 42 |    |    |    |    |
| Table 2    | 25 |    |    |    |    |
| New Table  | 9  | 11 | 23 |    |    |
| Table 1    | 42 |    |    |    |    |
| Table 2    |    |    |    |    |    |
| New Table  | 9  | 11 | 23 | 25 |    |
| Table 1    |    |    |    |    |    |
| Table 2    |    |    |    |    |    |
| New Table  | 9  | 11 | 23 | 25 | 42 |

Note that the two ordered tables can be assumed to be stored in a common vector. The two tables in the current example could be stored in a vector K as follows:

where the FIRST through the SECOND − 1 elements and the SECOND through the THIRD elements represent the first and second tables respectively. Also note that a temporary vector of the same size is required to hold the results of performing a simple merge.

The following general algorithm performs a simple merge.

1.    Merge two ordered subtables into a temporary vector
2.    Copy the temporary vector into K

The result of performing the first step of this algorithm on the example subtables gives the following representation.

   TEMP:   9   11   23   25   42

where TEMP denotes a temporary vector of the same size as K.

This process is formalized in the following procedure.

**Procedure** SIMPLE_MERGE(K, FIRST, SECOND, THIRD). Given two ordered subtables stored in a vector K with FIRST, SECOND, and THIRD as just described, this procedure performs a simple merge. TEMP is a temporary vector used in the merging process. The variables I and J denote the cursor associated with the first and second subtables, respectively. L is an index variable associated with the vector TEMP.

1.    [Initialize]
         I ← FIRST
         J ← SECOND
         L ← 0
2.    [Compare corresponding elements and output the smallest]
         Repeat while I < SECOND and J ≤ THIRD
            If K[I] ≤ K[J]

```
        then   L ← L + 1
               TEMP[L] ← K[I]
               I ← I + 1
        else   L ← L + 1
               TEMP[L] ← K[J]
               J ← J + 1
```

3.  [Copy the remaining unprocessed elements in output area]
```
        If I ≥ SECOND
        then   Repeat while J ≤ THIRD
                   L ← L + 1
                   TEMP[L] ← K[J]
                   J ← J + 1
        else   Repeat while I < SECOND
                   L ← L + 1
                   TEMP[L] ← K[I]
                   I ← I + 1
```

4.  [Copy elements in temporary vector into original area]
```
        Repeat for I = 1, 2, . . ., L
            K[FIRST - 1 + I] ← TEMP[I]
```

5.  [Finished]
```
        Return                                                    □
```

Note that the timing performance of this procedure is $O(n)$ where n denotes the sum of the sizes of the two subtables to be merged.

The previous algorithm can be generalized to merge k sorted tables into a single sorted table. Such a merging operation is called *multiple merging* or *k-way merging*.

Multiple merging can also be accomplished by performing a simple merge repeatedly. For example, if we have 16 tables to merge, we can first merge them in pairs using Procedure SIMPLE_MERGE. The result of this first step yields eight tables which are again merged in pairs to give four tables. This process is repeated until a single table is obtained. In this example, four separate passes are required to yield a single table. In general, k separate passes are required to merge $2^k$ separate tables into a single table. This strategy can easily be applied to sorting. Given a table containing n records, one merely considers this table to be a set of n tables, each of which contains a single record. Obviously, a table which contains a single record is sorted. The following procedure performs a merge sort.

**Procedure** TWO_WAY_MERGE_SORT_R(K, START, FINISH). Given a vector K it is required to sort recursively its elements between positions START and FINISH (inclusive). SIZE denotes the number of elements in the current subtable to be sorted. MIDDLE denotes the position of the middle element of that subtable.

1.  [Compute the size of the current subtable]
```
        SIZE ← FINISH - START + 1
```
2.  [Test base condition for subtable of size one]
```
        If SIZE ≤ 1
        then   Return
```
3.  [Calculate midpoint position of current subtable]
```
        MIDDLE ← START + ⌈SIZE/2⌉ - 1
```

4. [Recursively sort first subtable]
   Call TWO_WAY_MERGE_SORT_R(K, START, MIDDLE)
5. [Recursively sort second subtable]
   Call TWO_WAY_MERGE_SORT_R(K, MIDDLE + 1, FINISH)
6. [Merge two ordered subtables]
   Call SIMPLE_MERGE(K, START, MIDDLE + 1, FINISH)
7. [Finished]
   Return                                                                  □

The procedure is initially invoked as

   Call TWO_WAY_MERGE_SORT_R(K, 1, N)

where N denotes the size of the initial table to be sorted. The first step determines the size of the current subtable to be sorted. Step 2 performs a return if the size of the subtable is less than or equal to one. The third step finds the position of the middle element in the subtable. Steps 4 and 5 recursively sort the first and second subtables, respectively. The last step performs a simple merge on these two subtables.

Let us consider the timing analysis of this procedure which performs a merge sort. Let $T_{MS}(SIZE)$ denote the order of magnitude for the amount of time required to sort n elements by the previous procedure. From the procedure the timing of steps 1 through 3 is $O(1)$. Similarly, the timing of step 4, step 5, and step 6 is $O(\lfloor SIZE/2 \rfloor)$, $O(\lceil SIZE/2 \rceil)$, and $O(SIZE)$, respectively. The timing analysis then becomes

$$T_{MS}(SIZE) = \begin{cases} O(1), \text{ if SIZE } = 1 \\ O(1) + T_{MS}(\lfloor SIZE/2 \rfloor) + T_{MS}(\lceil SIZE/2 \rceil) + O(SIZE), \text{ otherwise} \end{cases}$$

Note as long as we are only concerned with an order of magnitude estimate the order notation can be dropped. Assuming that the size of a table is an integral power of 2, i.e., $SIZE = 2^k$, then

$$T_{MS}(SIZE) = \begin{cases} 1, \quad \text{ if SIZE } = 1 \\ SIZE + 2 \cdot T(SIZE/2), \text{ otherwise} \end{cases}$$

Such a relation is called a recurrence relation. Recall that a recurrence relation is expressed in terms of itself and a basis condition. This relation can be solved by substitution. Using such an approach on the previous recurrence relation yields the following:

$$T_{MS}(SIZE) = 2 \cdot T(SIZE/2) + SIZE$$

or, when $SIZE = 2^k$,

$$\begin{aligned} T_{MS}(2^k) &= 2 \cdot T(2^{k-1}) + 2^k \\ &= 2 \cdot [2 \cdot T(2^{k-2}) + 2^{k-1}] + 2^k \\ &= 2^2 \cdot T(2^{k-2}) + 2^k + 2^k \\ &= 2^2 \cdot [2 \cdot T(2^{k-3}) + 2^{k-2}] + 2 \cdot 2^k \\ &= 2^3 \cdot T(2^{k-3}) + 3 \cdot 2^k \\ &\quad\quad\quad \cdot \\ &\quad\quad\quad \cdot \\ &\quad\quad\quad \cdot \\ &= 1 \cdot 2^k + k \cdot 2^k \end{aligned}$$

Since $SIZE = 2^k$, we have $k = \log_2(SIZE)$. Therefore,

$$T_{MS}(SIZE) = O(SIZE + SIZElog_2(SIZE))$$

Consequently, the amount of time for the execution of the merge sort is proportional to $SIZE*log_2(SIZE)$. This is a significant improvement over the previous sorting methods discussed such as the selection sort.

The timing analysis can also be performed when SIZE is not an integral power of 2. In this more general case

$$2^k < SIZE \leq 2^{k+1}$$

and the given table can be padded (with some large value) to make it of size $2^{k+1}$. The timing analysis can now be performed on the expanded table. This analysis is left as an exercise.

As mentioned earlier in the subsection, an iterative algorithm can be formulated for the merge sort.

**Procedure** MERGE_PASS(R, N, C, L). Given a table R of N records which is considered to be partitioned into ordered subtables, each of which contains L records (or fewer), this algorithm merges these subtables by pairs. The records of R are denoted by R[1], R[2], ..., R[N]. An auxiliary table C is required in the merging process. The variables P and Q keep track of which pair of subtables are currently being merged. Since N is not necessarily an integral power of 2 the sizes of the subtables being merged are not always the same (that is, L). The sizes of the tables are given by variables N1 and N2. The variables I and J are indices to the corresponding records of the subtables that are to be merged. The index variable S references a record in the output area, and T is a temporary index variable.

1. [Initialize first pass]
   P ← 1
   N1 ← N2 ← L
   Q ← P + L
2. [Perform one pass]
   Repeat thru step 7 while Q ≤ N
3. [Initialize simple merge]
   I ← P
   J ← Q
   S ← P
4. [Compare corresponding records and output smallest]
   Repeat while I − P < N1 and J − Q < N2
       f K[I] ≤ K[J]
       then   C[S] ← R[I]
              I ← I + 1
              S ← S + 1
       else   C[S] ← R[J]
              J ← J + 1
              S ← S + 1
5. [Copy the remaining unprocessed records from a subtable into output area]
   If I − P ≥ N1
   then   Repeat for T = J, J + 1, ..., Q + N2 − 1
              C[S] ← R[T]
              S ← S + 1
   else   Repeat for T = I, I + 1, ..., P + N1 − 1

$$C[S] \leftarrow R[T]$$
$$S \leftarrow S + 1$$

6. [Update and test direct subtable index]

    $P \leftarrow Q + N2$

    If $P > N$

    then   Return

7. [Update Q and check bound of second subtable]

    $Q \leftarrow P + L$

    If $Q + L > N + 1$

    then   $N2 \leftarrow N - Q + 1$

8. [Copy unmatched subtable]

    Repeat for $T = P, P + 1, ..., N$

    $C[T] \leftarrow R[T]$

9. [Finished]

    Return   □

Steps 4 to 6 of the procedure is a rewriting of Procedure SIMPLE_MERGE, where the two ordered subfiles being merged are contained in table R. The resulting ordered table is written out in table C. Since n can be any positive integer, there may arise a case where a particular ordered subtable does not have another subtable with which it can be merged. In such a case, the unmatched subtable is merely copied out into the output area, as shown in step 8. A sample trace is given in Fig. 6-1.4 for Procedure MERGE_PASS.

Procedure MERGE_PASS can now be invoked repeatedly to sort a given table. If $n = 2^k$ for some k, then k passes are required. For any n, however, $\lceil \log_2 n \rceil$ passes are required. A detailed algorithm for this sort is now presented.

**Algorithm** TWO_WAY_MERGE_SORT. Given a vector R containing N records, this algorithm sorts the vector into ascending order by successively invoking Procedure MERGE_PASS. An auxiliary vector C which has the same size as R is needed. L is a variable which specifies the number of elements in each subtable to be merged during a particular pass.

1. [Perform sort]

    Repeat for $L = 1, 2, 4, ..., 2^{\lceil \log_2 N \rceil - 1}$

    If $\log_2 L$ is even

    then   Call MERGE_PASS(R, N, C, L)

    else   Call MERGE_PASS(C, N, R, L)

2. [Recopy if required]

    If $\lceil \log_2 N \rceil$ is odd

    then   Repeat for $I = 1, 2, ..., N$

    $R[I] \leftarrow C[I]$

3. [Finished]

    Exit   □

In step 1, the logarithm of L is tested to determine which area, R or C, is the output area in a particular pass. The same technique is used to determine whether a final recopy operation is required after the table has been sorted. A trace of this algorithm for the sample table is given in Fig. 6-1.5.

As mentioned earlier this sorting method is quite efficient. Since $\lceil \log_2 n \rceil$ passes are required in the sort, the total number of comparisons needed is

Assume L is 2, n is 7

| After Step | p | q | $n_1$ | $n_2$ | $R_1$ | $R_2$ | $R_3$ | $R_4$ | $R_5$ | $R_6$ | $R_7$ | $C_1$ | $C_2$ | $C_3$ | $C_4$ | $C_5$ | $C_6$ | $C_7$ | I | J | L |
|---|---|---|---|---|---|---|---|---|---|---|---|---|---|---|---|---|---|---|---|---|---|
| 1 | 1 | 3 | 2 | 2 | 11 | 13 | 2 | 15 | 14 | 17 | 6 | – | – | – | – | – | – | – | – | – | – |
| 2.1 | | | | | | | | | | | | | | | | | | | | | |
| 3 | | | | | | | | | | | | | | | | | | | 1 | 3 | 1 |
| 4.1 | | | | | | | | | | | | 2 | | | | | | | | 4 | 2 |
| 4.2 | | | | | | | | | | | | | 11 | | | | | | 2 | | 3 |
| 4.3 | | | | | | | | | | | | | | 13 | | | | | 3 | | 4 |
| 5 | | | | | | | | | | | | | | | 15 | | | | | | 5 |
| 6 | 5 | | | | | | | | | | | | | | | | | | | | |
| 7 | | 7 | 1 | | | | | | | | | | | | | | | | | | |
| 2.2 | | | | | | | | | | | | | | | | | | | | | |
| 3 | | | | | | | | | | | | | | | | | | | 5 | 7 | 5 |
| 4.1 | | | | | | | | | | | | | | | | 6 | | | | 8 | 6 |
| 5 | | | | | | | | | | | | | | | | | 14 | 17 | | | 8 |
| 6 | 8 | | | | | | | | | | | | | | | | | | | | |

Exit without ever returning to step 2; repeat loop.

(step 4.i means "the ith iteration within step 4")

**FIGURE 6-1.4** Trace of one pass of Procedure MERGE_PASS.

$O(n \log_2 n)$    Note that this quantity represents the worst case, as well as the average case. One obvious drawback in this method is the large auxiliary area required.

Another approach in performing a two-way merge sort is to take into consideration the degree of order which already exists in the initial table. A sort based on such an approach is given in Fig. 6-1.5. The formulation of the algorithm is left as an exercise.

### 6-1.5 Tree Sorts

In this section we examine two sorting techniques which are based on a tree representation of a given table. The first technique, which is straightforward, is a binary tree sort. The second method, however, although still involving binary trees is much more complex.

Since we have previously introduced all the concepts required to understand the binary tree sort, we merely outline the method here. The algorithm consists of two phases namely, a construction phase and a traversal phase. The construction phase consists of successively inserting a new record in a tree structure in a manner similar to that taken in Sec. 5-2.2, which dealt with the construction of a symbol table. The tree obtained from this first phase can then be traversed in inorder (see Sec. 5-1.2), thus resulting in a sorted table. The average number of comparisons for

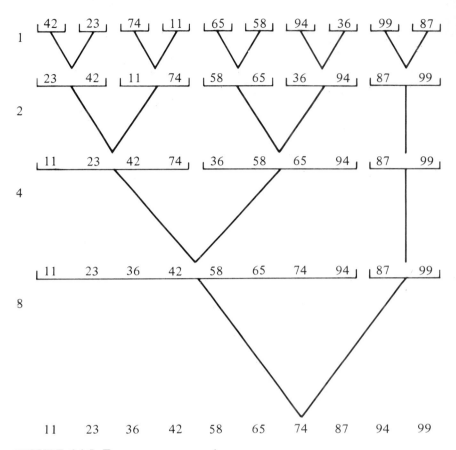

**FIGURE 6-1.5** Two-way merge sorting.

this method is $O(n\log_2 n)$. In the worst case, however, the number of comparisons required is $O(n^2)$, a case which arises when the sort tree is severely "unbalanced." More will be said about unbalanced trees in Sec. 6-2.3.

The second sorting method can be explained in terms of a match-play golf tournament. Assume that this tournament consists of eight players and is to be played according to the schedule given in Fig. 6-1.7. The results of the tournament are also given in the diagram with Paul beating John, Bob beating Rick, etc., and finally Clarence beating Paul. Clarence is consequently declared the winner of the tournament. We now want to find the second best player. This player can be Paul or Bill or Harvey. The second best player can be determined by having Bill play Harvey, and the winner of the match play Paul. The important point to note is that the complete tournament need not be replayed with Clarence absent.

The algorithm which we now formulate is a combination of algorithms by Floyd and Williams. Figure 6-1.8 represents an example table by a particular kind of binary tree called a *heap*. In general, a heap which represents a table of n records satisfies the property

$$K_j \leq K_i \text{ for } 2 \leq j \leq n \text{ and } i = \lfloor j/2 \rfloor.$$

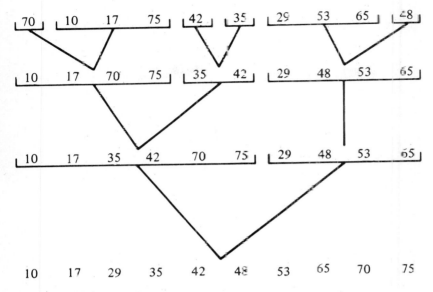

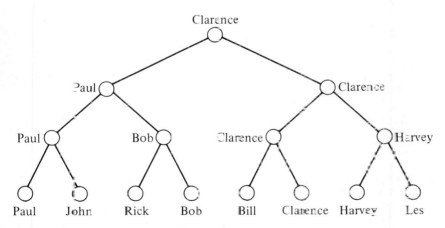

**FIGURE 6-1.6**  An alternate approach to a two-way merge sort.


The binary tree is allocated sequentially such that the indices of the left and right sons (if they exist) of record i are 2 and 2i + 1, respectively. Conversely, the index of the parent of record j (if it exists) is $\lfloor j/2 \rfloor$. It is clear from Fig. 6-1.8 that the tree structure satisfies the definition of a heap.

Once we have a heap representation of a table, the record with the largest key is at the root of the tree (also called the top of the heap). We now formulate an algorithm which will have as input an unsorted sequentially allocated table and produce as output a heap. The starting point is to have a heap initially (e.g., a one-

**FIGURE 6-1.7**  A match-play golf tournament.

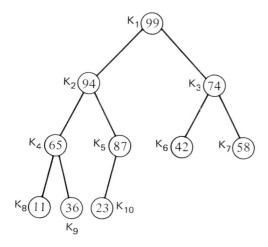

**FIGURE 6-1.8** A heap representation of a sample key set.

record tree is a heap), and then insert a new record into the existing heap such that a new heap is formed after performing the insertion. Insertions are performed repeatedly until all records in the original table form a heap. A general algorithm for creating a heap can now be formulated.

1.  Repeat thru step 7 while there still is another record to be placed in the heap
2.  Obtain child to be placed at leaf level
3.  Obtain position of parent for this child
4.  Repeat thru step 6 while the child has a parent and the key of the child is greater than that of its parent
5.  Move parent down to position of child
6.  Obtain position of new parent for the child
7.  Copy child record into its proper place

A detailed algorithm based on this general strategy follows.

**Procedure** CREATE_HEAP(K, N). Given a vector K (type integer) containing the keys of the N records of a table, this algorithm creates a heap as previously described. The index variable Q controls the number of insertions which is to be performed. The integer variable J denotes the index of the parent of key K[I]. KEY (type integer) contains the key of the record being inserted into an existing heap.

1.  [Build heap]
    Repeat thru step 7 for Q = 2, 3, ..., N
2.  [Initialize construction phase]
    I ← Q
    KEY ← K[Q]
3.  [Obtain parent of new record]
    J ← TRUNC(I / 2)
4.  [Place new record in existing heap]
    Repeat thru step 6 while I > 1 and KEY > K[J]

5.  [Interchange record]
    $K[I] \leftarrow K[J]$
6.  [Obtain next parent]
    $I \leftarrow J$
    $J \leftarrow \text{TRUNC}(I / 2)$
    If $J < 1$
    then  $J \leftarrow 1$
7.  [Copy new record into its proper place]
    $K[I] \leftarrow \text{KEY}$
8.  [Finished]
    Return                                     □

The first step of the algorithm is an iteration statement which controls the building of the desired heap by performing successive insertions. Step 2 selects the record to be inserted in an existing heap and copies this record into KEY. Steps 5 and 6 append the new record (as a leaf) to the existing heap (i.e., a binary tree) and move this record up the tree along the path between the new leaf and the top of the heap. This process continues until the new record reaches a position in the tree that satisfies the definition of a heap. The copying of the new record into its proper place in the tree is accomplished in step 7. A trace of the construction of the heap of Fig. 6-1.8 for the initial key set

    42, 23, 74, 11, 65, 58, 94, 36, 99, 37

is given in Fig. 6-1.9. Each tree in the diagram represents its state after the insertion and reconstruction process is complete. Now that we have represented the initial table by a heap, we can use the notions of the match-play golf tournament to perform the sort. The record with the largest key is presently in $R_1$ and it can be written out directly. This is accomplished by interchanging $R_1$ and $R_n$, and then it reconstructs a new heap consisting of only $n - 1$ records. This is realized in a manner similar to that used in Procedure CREATE_HEAP. The result of this reconstruction process is to place the record with the second largest key in $R_1$. This record can now be exchanged with record $R_{n-1}$. A new heap is then constructed for $n - 2$ records. By repeating this exchange and reconstruction process, the initial table can be sorted. The general algorithm for the sort follows.

1.  Create the initial heap
2.  Repeat thru step 8 a total of $n - 1$ times
3.  Exchange first record with last unsorted record
4.  Obtain the index of the largest son of the new record
5.  Repeat thru step 8 for the unsorted elements in the heap
    and while the current element is greater than the first element
6.  Interchange records and obtain the next left son
7.  Obtain the index of the next biggest son
8.  Copy the record into its proper place

A detailed algorithm for the heap sort is now presented.

**Procedure** HEAP_SORT(K, N). Given a vector K (type integer) containing the keys of the N records of a table and the Procedure CREATE_HEAP which has been previously described, this procedure sorts the table into ascending order. The variable Q represents the pass index. Index variables I and J are used, where the latter is the index of the left son of the former. KEY is an integer variable which contains the key of the record being swapped at each pass.

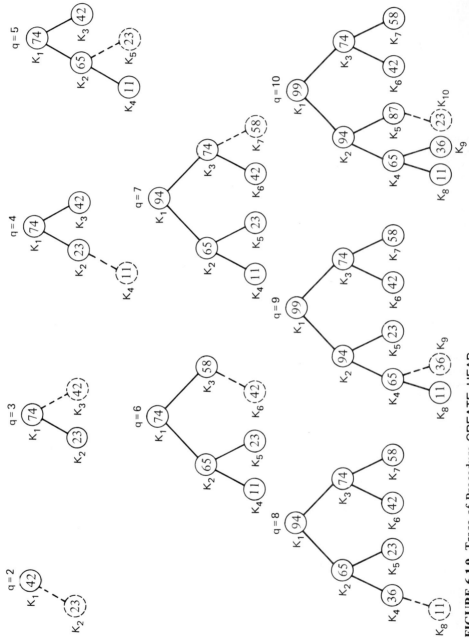

**FIGURE 6-1.9**  Trace of Procedure CREATE_HEAP.

1. [Create the initial heap]
   Call CREATE_HEAP(K, N)
2. [Perform sort]
   Repeat thru step 10 for Q = N, N − 1, .... 2
3. [Exchange record]
   K[1] ⟵⟶ K[Q]
4. [Initialize pass]
   I ← 1
   KEY ← K[1]
   J ← 2
5. [Obtain index of largest son of new record]
   If J + 1 < Q
   then  If K[J + 1] > K[J]
         then  J ← J + 1
6. [Reconstruct the new heap]
   Repeat thru step 10 while J ⩽ Q − 1 and K[J] > KEY
7. [Interchange record]
   K[I] ← K[J]
8. [Obtain next left son]
   I ← J
   J ← 2 * I
9. [Obtain index of next largest son]
   If J + 1 < Q
   then  If K[J + 1] > K[J]
         then  J ← J + 1
   else  If J > N
         then  J ← N
10. [Copy record into its proper place]
    K[I] ← KEY
11. [Finished]
    Return                                                    ☐

The algorithm begins by constructing a heap for the entire table. Step 2 controls the $n − 1$ passes required to sort the table. The remaining steps of the algorithm are very similar to those used in Procedure CREATE_HEAP to construct a new heap after the insertion of a new record. A trace of the sort for Fig. 6-1.8 is given in Fig. 6-1.10, where each tree represents the state of the sort at the end of each pass.

Consider the timing analysis of the heap sort. Since we are using a complete binary tree, the worst case analysis is easier than the average case. Note that the depth of a complete binary tree of $n$ nodes is $\lceil \log_2 n \rceil$. Recall that to sort a given key set we must first create a heap and then sort that heap. The worst case at each step involves performing a number of comparisons which is given by the depth of the tree. This observation implies that the number of comparisons is $O(n \log_2 n)$. As mentioned earlier, the average case is more complex to analyze, but it can be shown that it is also $O(n \log_2 n)$. Also, no extra working storage area, except for one record position, is required.

### 6-1.6 Partition-Exchange Sort

We now consider a sorting method which performs very well on larger tables. At each step in the method, the goal is to place a particular record in its final position

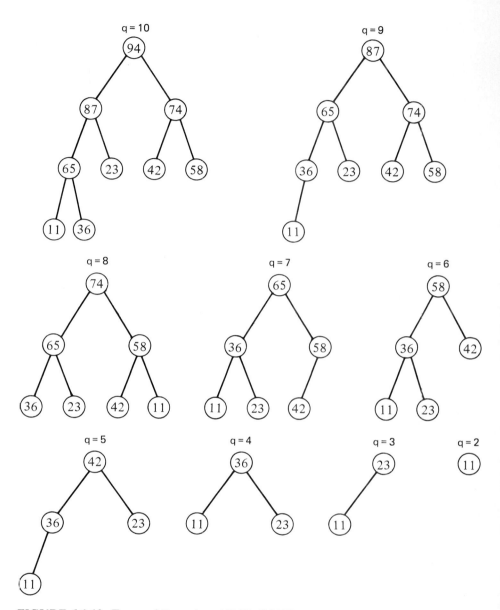

**FIGURE 6-1.10**  Trace of Procedure HEAP_SORT.

within the table. In so doing, all records which precede this record have smaller keys, while all records that follow it have larger keys. This technique essentially partitions the table into two subtables. The same process can then be applied to each of these subtables and repeated until all records are placed in their final positions.

As an example, consider the following key set:

42   23   74   11   65   58   94   36   99   87

We use two index variables, i and j with initial values of 2 and 10, respectively. The two keys 42 and $K_i$ are compared, and if an exchange is required (that is, $K_i < 42$) *then* i is incremented by 1 and the process is repeated. When $K_i \geq 42$, we proceed to compare $K_j$ and 42. If an exchange is required, then j is decremented by 1, and the process is repeated until $K_j \leq 42$. At this point, the keys $K_i$ and $K_j$ (that is, 74 and 36) are interchanged. The entire process is then repeated with j fixed and i being incremented once again. When $i \geq j$, the desired key is placed in its final position by interchanging keys 42 and $K_j$ (that is, keys 42 and 11).

The sequence of exchanges for placing 42 in its final position is given as follows, where the encircled entries on each line denote the keys being compared:

| | | | | | | | | | | |
|---|---|---|---|---|---|---|---|---|---|---|
| (42) | (23) | 74 | 11 | 65 | 58 | 94 | 36 | 99 | 87 | |
| (42) | 23 | (74) | 11 | 65 | 58 | 94 | 36 | 99 | 87 | |
| (42) | 23 | 74 | 11 | 65 | 58 | 94 | 36 | 99 | (87) | |
| (42) | 23 | 74 | 11 | 65 | 58 | 94 | 36 | (99) | 87 | |
| (42) | 23 | 74 | 11 | 65 | 58 | 94 | (36) | 99 | 87 | interchange 74 and 36 |
| (42) | 23 | 36 | (11) | 65 | 58 | 94 | 74 | 99 | 87 | |
| (42) | 23 | 36 | 11 | (65) | 58 | 94 | 74 | 99 | 87 | |
| (42) | 23 | 36 | 11 | 65 | 58 | (94) | 74 | 99 | 87 | |
| (42) | 23 | 36 | 11 | 65 | (58) | 94 | 74 | 99 | 87 | |
| (42) | 23 | 36 | 11 | (65) | 58 | 94 | 74 | 99 | 87 | |
| (42) | 23 | 36 | (11) | 65 | 58 | 94 | 74 | 99 | 87 | interchange 42 and 11 |
| 11 | 23 | 36 | 42 | 65 | 58 | 94 | 74 | 99 | 87 | $i \geq j$ |

The original key set has been partitioned into the subtables, namely, the sets {11, 23, 36} and {65, 58, 94, 74, 99, 87}. The same process can be applied to each of these sets until the table is completely sorted. This partition-exchange method of sorting is also called *quick sort*.

Each time a table is partitioned into two smaller subtables, these can be processed in turn using either an iterative or recursive approach. A general algorithm based on a recursive approach follows:

1. Partition the current table into two subtables
2. Invoke quicksort to sort the left subtable
3. Invoke quicksort to sort the right subtable

A detailed algorithm based on this recursive formulation can now be given.

**Procedure** QUICK_SORT(K, LB, UB). Given a table K of N records this recursive procedure sorts the table, as previously described, in ascending order. A dummy record with key K[N + 1] is assumed where $K[I] \leq K[N + 1]$ for all $1 \leq I \leq N$. The integer parameters **LB** and **UB** denote the lower and upper bounds of the current subtable being processed. The indices I and J are used to select certain keys during the processing of each subtable. KEY contains the key value which is being placed in its final position within the sorted subtable. FLAG is a logical variable which indicates the end of the process that places a record in its final position. When FLAG becomes false, the input subtable has been partitioned into two disjointed parts.

1. [Initialize]
      FLAG ← *true*
2. [Perform sort]
      If LB < UB
      then   I ← LB
             J ← UB + 1
             KEY ← K[LB]
             Repeat while FLAG
                 I ← I + 1
                 Repeat while K[I] < KEY   (scan the keys from left to right)
                     I ← I + 1
                 J ← J − 1
                 Repeat while K[J] > KEY   (scan the keys from right to left)
                     J ← J − 1
                 If I < J
                 then   K[I] ⟷ K[J]   (interchange records)
                 else   FLAG ← *false*
             K[LB] ⟷ K[J]   (interchange records)
             Call QUICK_SORT(K, LB, J − 1)   (sort first subtable)
             Call QUICK_SORT(K, J + 1, UB)   (sort second subtable)
3. [Finished]
      Return                                                                    □

The procedure is invoked initially by the statement

Call QUICK_SORT(K, 1, N)

The behavior of this procedure on the sample key set used earlier is given in Table 6-1.1.

Let us consider the timing analysis of this algorithm. The analysis of Procedure QUICK_SORT is given by

$$T_{QS}(N) = P(N) + T_{QS}(J-LB) + T_{QS}(UB-J)$$

where $P(N)$, $T_{QS}(J-LB)$, and $T_{QS}(UB-J)$ denote the times to partition the given table, sort the left subtable, and sort the right subtable, respectively. Note that the time to partition a table is $O(N)$.

The worst case occurs when, at each invocation of the procedure, the current table is partitioned into two subtables with one of them being empty (that is, J = LB or J = UB ). Such a situation, for example, occurs when the given key set is already sorted. The sorting of the example key set {11, 23, 36, 42} would yield the following sequence of partitions:

```
11   {23    36    42}
11    23   {36    42}
```

$$
\begin{array}{cccc}
11 & 23 & 36 & \{42\} \\
11 & 23 & 36 & 42
\end{array}
$$

Note that in such a situation the present method of sorting is no better than the selection sort  The worst case time analysis, assuming J = LB, then becomes

$$T^W_{QS}(N) = P(N) + T^W_{QS}(0) + T^W_{QS}(N-1)$$

$$= c^*N + T^W_{QS}(N-1)$$

$$= c^*N + c^*(N-1) + T^W_{QS}(N-2)$$

$$= c^*N + c^*(N-1) + c^*(N-2) + T^W_{QS}(N-3)$$

$$\vdots$$

$$= \sum_{k=1}^{N} c^*k + T^W_{QS}(0)$$

$$= c^* \frac{(N+1)(N)}{2} = O(N^2)$$

The worst case can sometimes be avoided by choosing more carefully the record for final placement at each stage.   Instead of always choosing $K_{LB}$ as was done in the previous approach, we could choose a random position in  the interval [ LB, UB ]. Another approach is to take the middle position in the interval.    that is $\lfloor (LB+UB)/2 \rfloor$.   Finally, the position could be chosen to be the median of the keys in the interval, although this option is costly.

The best case analysis occurs when the table is always partitioned in half, that is, $J = \lfloor (LB+UB)/2 \rfloor$.   The analysis becomes

$$T^B_{QS}(N) = P(N) + 2T^B_{QS}(N/2) = c^*N - 2T^B_{QS}(N/2)$$
$$= c^*N + 2c(N/2) + 4T^B_{QS}(N/4)$$

**Table 6-1.1**  Behavior of Procedure QUICK_SORT.

| $K_1$ | $K_2$ | $K_3$ | $K_4$ | $K_5$ | $K_6$ | $K_7$ | $K_8$ | $K_9$ | $K_{10}$ |
|---|---|---|---|---|---|---|---|---|---|
| {42 | 23 | 74 | 11 | 65 | 58 | 94 | 36 | 99 | 87} |
| {11 | 23 | 36} | 42 | {65 | 58 | 94 | 74 | 99 | 87} |
| 11 | {23 | 36} | 42 | {65 | 58 | 94 | 74 | 99 | 87} |
| 11 | 23 | ¯36} | 42 | {65 | 58 | 94 | 74 | 99 | 87} |
| 11 | 23 | 36 | 42 | {58} | 65 | {94 | 74 | 99 | 87} |
| 11 | 23 | 36 | 42 | 58 | 65 | {94 | 74 | 99 | 87} |
| 11 | 23 | 36 | 42 | 58 | 65 | {87 | 74} | 94 | {99} |
| 11 | 23 | 36 | 42 | 58 | 65 | {74} | 87 | 94 | {99} |
| 11 | 23 | 36 | 42 | 58 | 65 | 74 | 87 | 94 | {99} |
| 11 | 23 | 36 | 42 | 58 | 65 | 74 | 87 | 94 | 99 |

$$= c*N + 2c(N/2) + 4c(N/4) + 8T_{QS}^B(N/8)$$

$$= 3*c*N + 8T_{QS}^B(N/8)$$

$$.$$
$$.$$
$$.$$

$$= (\log_2 N)*c*N + 2^{\log_2 N}*T_{QS}^B(1)$$

$$= O(N\log_2 N)$$

The average case analysis of Procedure QUICK_SORT is difficult to perform, but the result of such an analysis is also $O(N\log_2 N)$.

Finally, consider the space analysis of procedure QUICK_SORT. When a table is partitioned into two subtables, the left subtable is chosen to be the current subtable. Consequently, the upper and lower indexes of the remaining subtable must be saved. In the worst case the partitioning process may cause the saving of the indexes for successive subtables of size 1 for later processing. In such a case a maximum of N pairs of indexes may have to be stored. This problem can be alleviated by saving the indexes associated with the largest subtable and processing the smaller subtable. This approach reduces the maximum storage required to $\log_2 N$ pairs of indexes, since the smaller subtable will be no more than half the size of the subtable from which it was derived.

### 6-1.7 Radix Sort

The radix sort is a method of sorting which predates any digital computer. This was performed and is still performed on a mechanical card sorter. Such a sorter usually processes a standard card of 80 columns, each of which may contain a character of some alphabet. When sorting cards on this type of sorter, only one column at a time is examined. A metal pointer on the sorter is used to select any one of the 80 columns. For numerical data, the sorter places all cards containing a given digit in an appropriate pocket. There are ten pockets corresponding to the ten decimal digits. The operator of the sorter combines in order the decks of cards from the ten pockets. The resulting deck has the cards of pocket 0 at the bottom, and those of pocket 9 on top. In general, numbers consisting of more than one digit are sorted. In such a case, an ascending-order sort can be accomplished by performing several individual digit sorts in order. That is, each column is sorted in turn starting with the lowest-order (right-most) column first and proceeding through the other columns from right to left. As an example, consider the following sequence of numbers (one number on each card):

42, 23, 74, 11, 65, 57, 94, 36, 99, 87, 70, 81, 61

After the first pass on the unit digit position of each number we have:

|  | 61 |  |  |  |  |  |  |  |  |
|  | 81 |  |  | 94 |  |  | 87 |  |  |
| 70 | 11 | 42 | 23 | 74 | 65 | 36 | 57 |  | 99 |
| --- | --- | --- | --- | --- | --- | --- | --- | --- | --- |
| Pocket:   0 | 1 | 2 | 3 | 4 | 5 | 6 | 7 | 8 | 9 |

Now by combining the contents of the pockets so that the contents of the "0" pocket are on the bottom and the contents of the "9" pocket are on the top, we obtain:

70, 11, 81, 61, 42, 23, 74, 94, 65, 36, 57, 87, 99

On the second pass, we sort on the higher-order digit, thus yielding

|        |    |    |    |    | 65 | 74 | 87 | 99 |
|        | 11 | 23 | 36 | 42 | 57 | 61 | 70 | 81 | 94 |
| Pocket: | 0 | 1 | 2 | 3 | 4 | 5 | 6 | 7 | 8 | 9 |

By combining the ten pockets in the same order as in the first pass, we complete the sort. This type of sort is called a *radix sort*.

This mechanical method of sorting can be implemented on a computer. Sequential allocation techniques are not practical in representing the pockets, since we do not know how many records will occupy a particular pocket during a certain pass. Our inability to predict the number of records per pocket is solved by using linked allocation. Each pocket can be represented as a linked FIFO queue. At the end of each pass, these queues can be easily combined in the proper order. If the maximum number of digits in a key is m, then m successive passes, from the unit digit to the most significant digit, are required in order to sort the numbers. In the algorithm which follows, we assume that a key K contains m digits of the form $b_m b_{m-1} \ldots b_1$. It is also assumed that a selection mechanism is available for selecting each digit. The initial table is assumed to be arranged as a simple linked list.

A general algorithm to perform a radix sort is now presented.

1. Repeat thru step 6 for each digit in the key
2. Initialize the pockets
3. Repeat thru step 5 until the end of the linked list
4. Obtain the next digit of the key
5. Insert the record in the appropriate pocket
6. Combine the pockets to form a new linked list

The detailed algorithm for the sort is as follows.

**Procedure** RADIX_SORT(FIRST, N). Given a table of N records arranged as a linked list, where each node in the list consists of a key field (K) and a pointer field (LINK), this procedure performs a radix sort as previously described. The address of the first record in the linked table is given by the pointer variable FIRST. The vectors T and B are used to store the addresses of the rear and front records in each queue (pocket). In particular, the records T[I] and B[I] point to the top and bottom records in the Ith pocket, respectively. The variable J is the pass index. The variable I is used as a pocket index, while P is a temporary index variable. The pointer variable R denotes the address of the current record being examined in the table and being directed to the appropriate pocket. NEXT is a pointer variable which denotes the address of the next record to be examined. PREV is a pointer variable which is used during the combining of the pockets at the end of each pass. The integer variable D denotes the current digit in a key being examined.

1. [Perform sort]
    Repeat thru step 4 for J = 1, 2, ..., M
2. [Initialize the pass]
    Repeat for I = 0, 1, ..., 9
       T[I] ← B[I] ← NULL
    R ← FIRST
3. [Distribute each record in the appropriate pocket]
    Repeat while R ≠ NULL
       D ← $b_J$   (obtain Jth digit of the key K(R))

```
          NEXT ← LINK(R)
          If T[D] = NULL
          then    T[D] ← B[D] ← R
          else    LINK(T[D]) ← R
                  T[D] ← R
          LINK(R) ← NULL
          R ← NEXT
4.   [Combine pockets]
          P ← 0
          Repeat while B[P] = NULL
              P ← P + 1
          FIRST ← B[P]
          Repeat for I = P + 1, P + 2, ..., 9
              PREV ← T[I – 1]
              If T[I] ≠ NULL
              then    LINK(PREV) ← B[I]
              else    T[I] ← PREV
5.   [Finished]
          Return                                                         □
```

The algorithm is straightforward. The first step controls the number of passes required to perform the sort. Step 2 initializes the arrays associated with the pockets so that all pockets are empty at the beginning of each pass. Also, the variable R is set to point to the first record in the table in this step. The third step of the algorithm processes each record in the table and directs each such record to the appropriate pocket. Step 4 combines the pockets into a new linked table which is used as input to the next pass. FIRST is set to point to the bottom-most record in the first nonempty pocket (proceeding from pocket 0 through pocket 9). A trace of the algorithm for the previous table is given in Fig. 6-1.11.

This sorting method performs well, providing that the keys are relatively short. For a key of m digits, it requires m * n key accesses.

### 6-1.8 Address-Calculation Sort

As a final sorting method, we now look at the application of hashing functions to sorting. Recall from Sec. 4-3.2 the construction of a symbol table where each name was hashed into a number. Each set of names which was hashed into the same number was called an *equivalence class*. Each equivalence class was represented by a linked list. The same idea can be used to sort a table.

In applying a hashing function to the sorting process, a particular kind of hashing function is required. Let us assume that we have a hashing function H with the property

$$x_1 < x_2 \text{ implies that } H(x_1) \leqslant H(x_2)$$

A function which exhibits this property is called a *nondecreasing*, or *order-preserving, hashing function*. When such a function is used to hash a particular key into a particular number to which some previous keys have already been hashed (that is, a collision occurs), then the new key is placed in the set of colliding records so as to preserve the order of the keys. The result of hashing and inserting the sample key set

42, 23, 74, 11, 65, 57, 94, 36, 99, 87, 70, 81, 61

using a nondecreasing hashing function in which all keys in the ranges 1-20, 21-40, 41-60, 61-80, and 81-100 are each hashed into a different set as sorting proceeds, is shown in Fig. 6-1.12. The five ordered sets obtained during the hash and insert phase can now be trivially merged to yield the desired sorted table.

The separate chaining method of collision resolution with a separate hash table can be used to represent this sorting process. Such a representation of the final sort is given in Fig. 6-1.13.

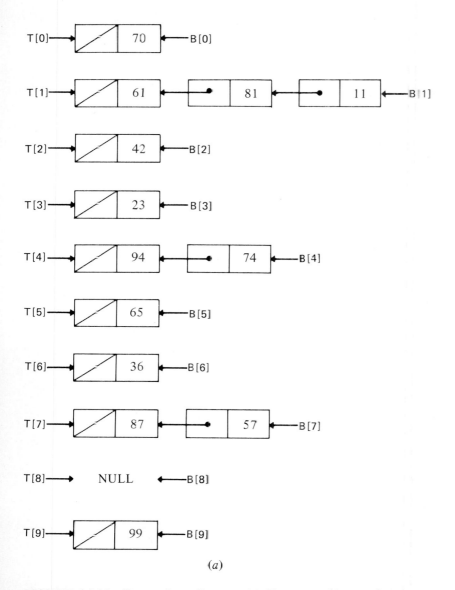

*(a)*

**FIGURE 6-L11**   Trace of a radix sort. *(a)* First pass: *(b)* second pass.

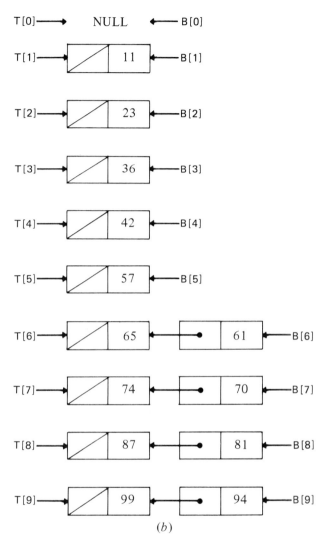

$(b)$

**FIGURE 6-1.11** (Continued)

A general algorithm for this sorting process follows.

1. Initialize hash table entries to null
2. Repeat through step 4 while there are still input records
3. Input and hash a record
4. Insert record into appropriate linked list
5. Concatenate the nonempty linked lists into one

Let us examine some of the details of the general algorithm. We assume the following record structure in the overflow area:

RECORD

| K | DATA | LINK |
|---|------|------|

| Set | 3 records Entered | 6 records Entered | 9 records Entered | 12 records Entered | 13 records Entered |
|---|---|---|---|---|---|
| 1 (1-20) | | 11 | 11 | 11 | 11 |
| 2 (21-40) | 23 | 23 | 23, 36 | 23, 36 | 23, 36 |
| 3 (41-60) | 42 | 42, 57 | 42, 57 | 42, 57 | 42, 57 |
| 4 (61-80) | 74 | 65, 74 | 65, 74 | 65, 70, 74 | 61, 65, 70, 74 |
| 5 (81-100) | | | 94, 99 | 81, 87, 94, 99 | 81, 87, 94, 99 |

**FIGURE 6-1.12**   Behavior of an address-calculation sort.

The important variables for this problem are:

| | |
|---|---|
| M (integer) | Size of hash table |
| HEAD (pointer) | Address of the first record in the sorted table |
| HASH_TABLE (pointer) | Vector of pointers representing the hash table |
| HASH (integer) | Hashing function |
| RECORD (record) | Overflow area record |
| K (integer) | Key of a record |
| DATA (string) | Other relevant information in a record |
| LINK (pointer) | Location of the next record in the list |
| KEY (integer) | Key of the input record |
| INFO (string) | Other relevant information of the input record |
| RANDOM (integer) | Hash address of input record (between 1 and M) |
| NEW (pointer) | Address of newly created overflow record |

The details of the first three steps of the general algorithm are obvious. The fourth step of the algorithm can be detailed by making minor modifications to the algorithm INSORD (see Sec. 4-2.1). The general algorithm's final step is not difficult. The first task involves locating the first nonempty linked list. The following algorithm segment accomplishes this task.

Range                    Equivalence class

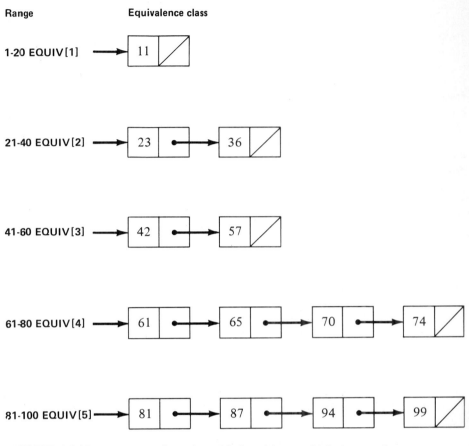

FIGURE 6-1.13 Representation of a table in address-calculation sorting.

```
I ← 1
Repeat while HASH_TABLE[I] = NULL and I < M
     I ← I + 1
HEAD ← HASH_TABLE[I]
J ← I + 1
```

The next task in obtaining a sorted table is to concatenate all nonempty linked lists. This task involves scanning each nonempty linked list for its last node. When this node is found, it is linked to the front node of the next list. The details of this task follow:

```
Repeat while J ≤ M
    If HASH_TABLE[J] ≠ NULL
    then (find tail of linked list)
         P ← HASH_TABLE[I]
         Repeat while LINK(P) ≠ NULL
             P ← LINK(P)
         (link tail of this linked list to the head of the next)
```

```
            LINK(P) ← HASH_TABLE[J]
            I ← J
            J ← I + 1
       else J ← J + 1
```

These details can be incorporated in a detailed algorithm.

**Procedure** ADDR_CAL_SORT. Given input records of the form previously described, this algorithm sorts the records based on address calculation using a hash table with a separate overflow area. An order-preserving hashing function, HASH, is assumed. The sorted table generated is in the form of a linked list, where HEAD denotes the address of its first record. I and J are integer variables. P and S are pointer variables.

1. [Initialize hash table, that is, list heads]
       Repeat for I = 1, 2, ..., M
            HASH_TABLE[I] ← NULL
2. [Input and insert records into appropriate linked lists]
       Repeat thru step 4 while there are still input records
3. [Input and hash a record]
       Read(KEY, INFO)
       NEW ⇐ RECORD
       K(NEW) ← KEY
       DATA(NEW) ← INFO
       LINK(NEW) ← NULL
       RANDOM ← HASH(KEY)
4. [Insert record into appropriate linked list]
       If HASH_TABLE[RANDOM] = NULL
       then   (insert record into empty linked list)
              LINK(NEW) ← HASH_TABLE[RANDOM]
              HASH_TABLE[RANDOM] ← NEW
       else   (insert record in middle or at end of linked list)
              P ← HASH_TABLE[RANDOM]
              S ← LINK(P)
              Repeat while S ≠ NULL and K(S) < KEY
                   P ← S
                   S ← LINK(S)
              LINK(P) ← NEW
              LINK(NEW) ← S
5. [Find first nonempty linked list]
       I ← 1
       Repeat while HASH_TABLE[I] = NULL and I < M
            I ← I + 1
       HEAD ← HASH_TABLE[I]
       J ← I + 1
6. [Concatenate the nonempty linked lists]
       Repeat while J ≤ M
            If HASH_TABLE[J] ≠ NULL
            then   (find tail of linked list)
                   P ← HASH_TABLE[I]
                   Repeat while LINK(P) ≠ NULL
                        P ← LINK(P)
```
```

(link tail of this linked list to the head of the next)
LINK(P) ← HASH_TABLE[J]
I ← J
J ← I + 1

7. [Finished] else J ← J+1
Return □

Assuming that the nondecreasing hashing function uniformly distributes the records of the table among the linked lists, this sort performs in a linear manner; that is, the number of comparisons is $O(n)$. The worst case occurs when all keys are mapped into the same number. In this case the performance of the sorting method degenerates to $O(n^2)$.

### 6-1.9 Summary of Sorting Methods

The sorting methods discussed thus far are summarized in Table 6-1.2. Note that the entries in the table are approximate. The parameter m denotes the number of digits in a key. It is used in the radix sort.

It is difficult to assert that a particular sorting technique is *always* superior to other methods for every key set. Certain properties of a given key set play an important role in the determination of which sorting technique should be used. Properties such as the number, size, distribution, and orderness of keys often dictate which method should be used. The amount of memory available in performing the sort may also be an important factor.

In summary, the selection or bubble sorts can be used if the number of records in the table is small. If n is large and the keys are short, the radix sort can perform well. With a large n and long keys, quick sort, heap sort, or a merge sort can be used. If the table is, initially, almost sorted, then quick sort should be avoided. When the keys, after hashing, are uniformly distributed over the interval $[1,m]$, then an address-calculation sort is a very good method to use.

### Exercises for Sec. 6-1

1. Alter Procedure BUBBLE_SORT to take advantage of the fact that all records below and including the last one to be exchanged must be in the correct order; consequently, these records do not have to be examined again.
2. Modify Procedure BUBBLE_SORT such that alternate passes go in opposite directions. That is, during the first pass, the record with the largest key will be at the end of the table and during the second pass the record with the smallest key will be the first record in the table, etc.
3. Devise an algorithm for performing a selection sort when the table is represented as a linked list.
4. Trace Procedure QUICK_SORT for the sample table given in that subsection.
5. Formulate an algorithm for a binary-tree sort.
6. Trace through Procedure HEAP_SORT for the sample table given.
7. Devise an algorithm for a two-way merge so as to take into consideration the degree of order which already exists in the initial table as suggested at the end of Sec. 6-1.4.
8. Obtain an algorithm for a two-way merge sort using linked-allocation techniques.
9. Change Procedure RADIX_SORT so that the queues are circular.

**Table 6-1.2**  Comparison of Sorting Methods (entries are approximate)

| Algorithm | Average | Worst Case | Space Usage |
|---|---|---|---|
| SELECTION | $n^2/4$ | $n^2/4$ | In place |
| BUBBLE_SORT | $n^2/4$ | $n^2/2$ | In place |
| MERGE_SORT | $O(n\log_2 n)$ | $O(n\log_2 n)$ | Extra n entries |
| QUICK_SORT | $O(n\log_2 n)$ | $n^2/2$ | Extra $\log_2 n$ entries |
| HEAP_SORT | $O(n\log_2 n)$ | $O(n\log_2 n)$ | In place |
| RADIX_SORT | $O(m*n)$ | $O(m*n)$ | Extra space for links |
| ADDRESS_CAL_SORT | $O(n)$ | $O(n^2)$ | Extra space for links |

## 6-2  SEARCHING

In this section we formulate a number of progressively more complex searching algorithms. The linear-search and binary-search methods are relatively straightforward, but they have serious shortcomings for certain operations. Balanced-tree searches are efficient for many operations. A number of search techniques involving the use of hashing functions are also discussed.

### 6-2.1  Sequential Searching

The simplest technique for searching an unordered table for a particular record is to scan each entry in the table in a sequential manner until the desired record is found. An algorithm for such a search procedure is as follows.

**Function** LINEAR_SEARCH(K, N, X). Given an unordered vector K consisting of N + 1 (N ≥ 1) elements, this algorithm searches the vector for a particular element having the value X. Vector element K[N + 1] serves as a sentinel element and receives the value of X prior to the search. The function returns the index of the vector element if the search is successful, and returns 0 otherwise.

1. [Initialize search]
    I ← 1
    K[N + 1] ← X
2. [Search the vector]
        Repeat while K[I] ≠ X
            I ← I + 1
3. [Successful search?]
        If I = N + 1
        then   Write('UNSUCCESSFUL SEARCH')
               Return(0)
        else   Write('SUCCESSFUL SEARCH')
               Return(I)                                                    □

The first step of the algorithm initializes the key value of the sentinel record to x. In the second step, a sequential search is then performed on the n + 1 records. If the index of the record found denotes record $R_{n+1}$ then the search has failed; otherwise, the search is successful and i contains the index of the desired record.

Recall from Sec. 0-3 that the performance of a search method can be measured by counting the number of key comparisons taken to find a particular record. There are two cases which are important, namely, the average case and the worst case. The worst case for the previous algorithm consists of n + 1 key comparisons, while the average case takes (n + 1)/2 key comparisons. The average and worst search times for this method are both proportional to n, that is, of O(n). These estimates are based on the assumption that the probability of a request for a particular record is the same as for any other record.

Let $P_i$ be the probability for the request of record $R_i$ for $1 \leqslant i \leqslant n$. The average length of search (ALOS) for n records is given by

$$E[ALOS] = 1 * P_1 + 2 * P_2 + \cdots + n * P_n$$

where $P_1 + P_2 + \cdots + P_n = 1$.

Now suppose that the probabilities for request for particular records are not equally likely, that is, $P_i \neq 1/n$ for $1 \leqslant i \leqslant n$. The question which naturally arises is: Can we rearrange the table so as to reduce the ALOS? The answer is yes, and the desired arrangement can be obtained by looking at the previous equation for the expected ALOS. This quantity will be minimized if the records are ordered such that

$$P_1 \geqslant P_2 \geqslant \cdots \geqslant P_n \tag{1}$$

For example, letting n = 5 and $P_i = 1/5$ for $1 \leqslant i \leqslant 5$ yields

$$E[ALOS] = 1 * 1/5 + 2 * 1/5 + 3 * 1/5 + 4 * 1/5 + 5 * 1/5 = 3$$

Now, assuming that $P_1 = 0.4$, $P_2 = 0.3$, $P_3 = 0.2$, $P_4 = 0.07$, and $P_5 = 0.03$, the average length of search in this case is

$$E[ALOS] = 1 * 0.4 + 2 * 0.3 + 3 * 0.2 + 4 * 0.07 + 5 * 0.03 = 2.03$$

This number is substantially less than 3. The rearrangement of the initial table according to Eq. (1) is called *preloading*.

If the table is subjected to many deletions, then it should be represented as a linked list. The traversal of a linked table is almost as fast as the traversal of its sequential counterpart. Note that insertions can be performed very efficiently when the table is sequentially represented, assuming the table is not ordered.

If search time is to be improved further, then we must order the elements of the table. This approach is discussed in the next section.

### 6-2.2  Binary Searching

Another relatively simple method of accessing a table is the binary search method. The entries in the table are stored in alphabetically or numerically increasing order. An appropriate method discussed in the previous section can be used to achieve this ordering. A search for a particular item with a certain key value resembles the search for a name in a telephone directory. The approximate middle entry of the table is located, and its key value is examined. If its value is too high, then the key value of the middle entry of the first half of the table is examined and the procedure

**Table 6-2.1** Binary-search trace.

| Search for 275 | | | | Search for 727 | | | |
|---|---|---|---|---|---|---|---|
| Iteration | L | H | M | Iteration | L | H | M |
| 1 | 1 | 10 | 5 | 1 | 1 | 10 | 5 |
| 2 | 1 | 4 | 2 | 2 | 6 | 10 | 8 |
| 3 | 3 | 4 | 3 | 3 | 9 | 10 | 9 |
| 4 | 4 | 4 | 4 | 4 | 10 | 10 | 10 |

|    (*a*)    |    (*b*)    |

is repeated on the first half until the required item is found. If the value is too low, then the key of the middle entry of the second half of the table is tried and the procedure is repeated on the second half. This process continues until the desired key is found or the search interval becomes empty. The following algorithm performs a binary search.

**Function** BINARY_SEARCH(K, N, X). Given a vector K, consisting of N elements in ascending order, this algorithm searches the structure for a given element whose value is given by X. The variables LOW, MIDDLE, and HIGH denote the lower, middle, and upper limits of the search interval, respectively. The function returns the index of the vector element if the search is successful, and returns 0 otherwise.

1. [Initialize]
       LOW ← 1
       HIGH ← N
2. [Perform search]
       Repeat thru step 4 while LOW ≤ HIGH
3. [Obtain index of midpoint of interval]
       MIDDLE ← ⌊(LOW + HIGH) / 2⌋
4. [Compare]
       If X < K[MIDDLE]
       then   HIGH ← MIDDLE − 1
       else   If X > K[MIDDLE]
              then   LOW ← MIDDLE + 1
              else   Write('SUCCESSFUL SEARCH')
                     Return(MIDDLE)
5. [Unsuccessful search]
       Write('UNSUCCESSFUL SEARCH')
       Return(0)                                                  □

A trace of this algorithm for the sample table

75, 151, 203, 275, 318, 489, 524, 591, 647, and 727

is given for x = 275 and 727 in Table 6-2.1*a* and *b*, respectively.

A binary search can also be performed recursively. Such an algorithm can be analyzed with respect to time and space. A recursive algorithm to perform this task is as follows:

**Function** BINARY_SEARCH_R(P, Q, K, X). Given the bounds of a subtable P and Q and a vector K, this algorithm recursively searches for the given element whose value is stored in X. MIDDLE and LOC are integer variables.

1.  [Search vector **K** between **P** and **Q** for value X]
    If P > Q
    then   LOC ← 0
    else   MIDDLE ← ⌊(P + Q)/2⌋
           If X < K[MIDDLE]
           then   LOC ← BINARY_SEARCH(P, MIDDLE−1, K, X)
           else   If X > K[MIDDLE]
                  then   LOC ← BINARY_SEARCH(MIDDLE+1, Q, K, X)
                  else   LOC ← MIDDLE
2.  [Finished]
    Return(LOC)                                                    ☐

with initial call

   POSITION ← BINARY_SEARCH_R(1, N, K, X)

In order to analyze the time of the algorithm, we will make the comparison of X with K[MIDDLE] our active operation. We will assume that one comparison operation with a three-way branch, for <, >, and =, can be used for the branching within a call. Unfortunately, the number of comparisons depends on the location of X. In the best case, X will be in location ⌊(n + 1)/2⌋ so that only one comparison is used and $T_{BS}^B(n) = O(1)$ . The worst case is somewhat more complex. Let W(Q − P + 1) be the function for the worst case number of comparisons in a call of BINARY_SEARCH_R(P, Q, K, X). In the worst case X will not be equal to K[MIDDLE] so that a recursive call is needed. The size of the interval in the recursive call depends on whether Q − P + 1 is even or odd. For Q − P + 1 odd, the interval sizes are

$$Q - \frac{(P + Q)}{2} = \frac{(Q - P)}{2} \quad \text{and} \quad \frac{(P + Q)}{2} - P = \frac{Q - P}{2}$$

For Q − P + 1 even, the interval sizes are

$$Q - \frac{(P + Q - 1)}{2} = \frac{(Q - P + 1)}{2} \quad \text{and} \quad \frac{(P + Q - 1)}{2} - P = \frac{(Q - P - 1)}{2}$$

Thus in the worst case we have the recurrence relation

   W(n) = 1 + W(⌊n/2⌋)  for n = Q − P + 1

The basis condition for the relation is W(1) = 1. To solve the recurrence relation, we expand the relation for a few terms which usually gives us enough information to guess the solution.

   W(n) = 1 + W(⌊n/2⌋)
        = 1 + 1 + W( ⌊n/2²⌋ )
        = 1 + 1 + 1 + W( ⌊n/2³⌋ )

Thus the solution seems to be the power to which 2 must be raised to obtain a value greater than n, that is, $\lfloor \log_2 n \rfloor + 1$. An inductive proof can be used to verify that this is in fact true. Thus we have

$$W(n) = \lfloor \log_2 n \rfloor + 1 \quad \text{and} \quad T_{BS}^W(n) = O(\log_2 n)$$

For the average number of comparisons used by the Procedure BINARY_SEARCH_R(P, Q, V, X), A(Q−P+1), we again need to know the probability distribution for X. This time suppose we assume that each position of V is equally likely and the search is always successful. Thus we have $Q - P + 1$ situations each with probability $1/(Q - P + 1)$. To make the analysis somewhat simpler, assume $n = Q - P + 1$ is one less than a power of 2, that is, $n = 2^k - 1$, where $k = \log_2 (n + 1)$. For other values of n, the answer will be very similar. Let $S_c$ be the number of situations for which the algorithm does c comparisons. Some thought yields that

$$S_1 = 1 = 2^0, \ S_2 = 2 = 2^1, \ S_3 = 4 = 2^2, \ ..., \ S_c = 2^{c-1}, \ c \leqslant k$$

Thus we obtain

$$A(n) = \sum_{c=1}^{k} \frac{S_c}{n} * c = \frac{1}{n} \sum_{c=1}^{k} c * 2^{c-1} = \frac{1}{n} \sum_{c=1}^{k} c(2^c - 2^{c-1})$$

$$= \frac{1}{n} \left\{ \sum_{c=1}^{k} c * 2^c - \sum_{c=0}^{k-1} (c + 1) * 2^c \right\}$$

$$= \frac{1}{n} \left\{ \sum_{c=1}^{k} c * 2^c - \sum_{c=1}^{k-1} c * 2^c - \sum_{c=0}^{k-1} 2^c \right\}$$

$$= \frac{1}{n} \left\{ k * 2^k - (2^k - 1) \right\}$$

$$= \frac{1}{n} \left\{ (k - 1) * (2^k - 1) + k \right\} = (k - 1) + \frac{k}{n}$$

$$= \log_2 (n + 1) (1 + 1/n) - 1 \sim \log_2 n$$

Thus we have $T_{BS}^A(n) = O(\log_2 n)$ so that the order is the same for both average and worst case. Of course both of these are much better than $O(n)$ for the linear search.

We now examine the space requirements of the algorithm. For the binary search algorithm, the analysis is more interesting if we assume the vector is passed by value. This means that each call of BINARY_SEARCH_R has its own local storage for the vector. Thus the local storage of the routine is $O(n)$. Therefore in the best case when only one call is needed, the storage is $O(n)$. In the worst case and average case, $O(\log_2 n)$ calls are needed so that the storage is $O(n \log_2 n)$. On the other hand, if the vector is passed by reference (the standard approach), there is only one copy of the vector. Thus local storage is $O(1)$, so that the worst case requirement for the stack is $O(\log_2 n)$. But now $O(n)$ storage is required globally for the vector so that the total storage is

$$O(n) + O(\log_2 n) = O(n)$$

This saving of storage is one reason why arrays are normally passed by reference rather than by value. The main reason is the time required to copy the values on procedure entry (and perhaps exit). In fact, this copy becomes the active operation, with time $O(n \log n)$, so that the binary search is no longer useful.

The binary-search technique has certain undesirable properties. An insertion of a new record requires that many records in the existing table be physically moved in order to preserve the sequential ordering. A similar situation prevails for deletions. The ratio of insertion time or deletion time to search time is quite high for this method. Binary search is suitable if few insertions and/or deletions are to be made to the table.

One way to improve this search method is to use linked binary trees to represent the table in order to improve the insertion and deletion problems. Such an avenue is discussed in the next subsection.

### 6-2.3 Search Trees

The binary-search method given in the previous subsection can be explained easily in terms of binary trees. Figure 6-2.1 gives a binary tree representation which corresponds to a binary search (according to Procedure BINARY_SEARCH) with n = 10. In Sec. 5-2.2, linked binary trees were used in constructing a symbol table. The same structure can represent a table of records. The search algorithm for such a representation is very similar to Algorithm **TABLE** of Sec. 5-2.2 and is, therefore, omitted here.

The average length of search for this representation is also of $O(\log_2 n)$. The worst case that can be encountered, however, has a search time of $O(n)$, a time which is no better than the worst case for a sequential search. Figure 6-2.2 shows some of the cases which can give this bad search performance. The first two cases involve trees which contain only nonnull left or right links. The remaining two cases represent zigzag structures. Clearly, the search time for these structures takes n comparisons. However, using balanced binary trees, the worst-case search time can be reduced to $O(\log_2 n)$. In this section, we examine the various types of balanced trees.

The first type of balanced trees we look at are height-balanced trees. In such a tree, we attempt to keep each leaf node the same distance from the root. We then examine 2-3 trees, in which each vertex node of the tree must have either 2 or 3 offspring. Next, we look at weight-balanced trees, in which the leaves are organized with the most often searched-for nodes near the top. Finally, we examine the trie structure, which is actually an *m*-ary tree structure.

### 6-2.3.1 Height-Balanced Trees

In order to prevent a tree unbalance, such as the cases given in Fig. 6-2.2, with height-balanced trees we associate a *balance indicator* with each node in the tree. This indicator will contain one of the three values which we denote as left (L), right (R), or balance (B), according to the following definitions:

> *Left:* A node will be called *left heavy* if the longest path in its left subtree is one longer than the longest path of its right subtree.
>
> *Balance:* A node will be called *balanced* if the longest paths in both of its subtrees are equal.
>
> *Right:* A node will be called *right heavy* if the longest path in its right subtree is one longer than the longest path in its left subtree.

In a *balanced tree* each node must be in one of these three states. If there exists a node in a tree where this is not true, then such a tree is said to be *unbal-*

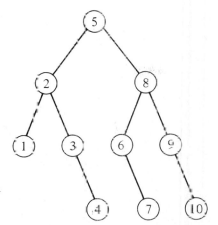

**FIGURE 6-2.1** A binary tree which corresponds to a binary search for $n=10$ .

*anced.* Figure 6-2.3 gives examples of trees which are balanced. while Fig. 6-2.4 represents examples of unbalanced trees.

Let us now look at the operation of inserting a node into a balanced tree. In the following discussion, it is assumed that a new node is inserted at the leaf or terminal node level (as either a left or right subtree). The only nodes which can have their balance indicator changed by such an insertion are those which lie on a path between the root of the tree and the newly inserted leaf. The possible changes which can occur to a node on this path are as follows:

*1*   The node was either left or right heavy and has now become balanced.
*2*   The node was balanced and has now become left or right heavy.
*3*   The node was heavy and the new node has been inserted in the heavy subtree, thus creating an unbalanced subtree. Such a node is said to be a *critical node.*

If condition *1* applies to a current node, then the balance indicators of all ancestor nodes of this node remain unchanged, since the longest path in the subtree

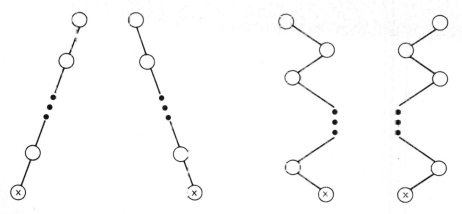

**FIGURE 6-2.2** Worst search time cases for binary trees.

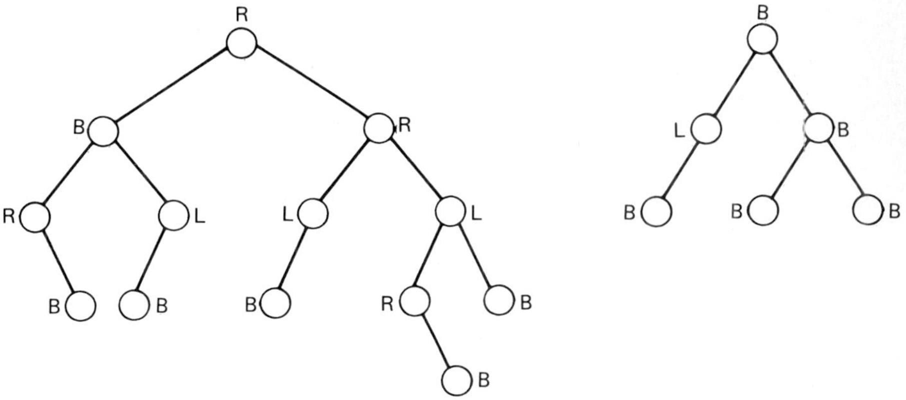

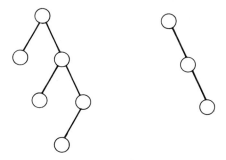

**FIGURE 6-2.3** Balanced trees.

(in which the current node is its root) remains unchanged. When condition 2 applies to a current node, then the balance indicators of the ancestors will change. If condition 3 applies to a current node, then the tree has become unbalanced and this node has become critical. Figure 6-2.5 contains examples of the three cases which can arise. The dotted branch and node denote the new element which is being inserted.

We next turn to the rebalancing of a tree when a critical node has been encountered. There are two broad cases which can arise, each of which can be further subdivided into two essentially similar subcases. A general representation of case 1 is given in Fig. 6-2.6, where the rectangles labeled $T_1$, $T_2$, and $T_3$ represent trees and the node labeled NEW denotes the node being inserted. The expression at the bottom of each rectangle denotes the maximum path length in that tree after insertions. For example, in Fig. 6-2.6a, since node X is critical, then node Y must have been balanced prior to insertion. This case covers the situation when Y has become heavy in the same direction that X was heavy. A concrete example of the second possibility for case 1 is exemplified in Fig. 6-2.7. The PATH and DIREC-TION vectors are defined in the next algorithm. Note that the basic steps involve the changing of three pointers.

**FIGURE 6-2.4** Unbalanced trees.

The second case, which is given in Fig. 6-2.8, is much like the first, except that node Y becomes heavy in an opposite direction to that in which X was heavy. It is clear that node Z must have been balanced prior to insertion. Note that cases $a(i)$ and $b(i)$ are very similar. A specific example of case $2b$ is given in Fig. 6-2.9. Again PATH and DIRECTION refer to vectors that are associated with the next algorithm.

We now proceed to the formulation of an algorithm for the insertion of an element into a balanced tree. The node structure for the tree will consist of a left pointer (LPTR), a right pointer (RPTR) a key field (K), a balance indicator (BI), and an information field (DATA). The name of the node structure is NODE. A list head for the tree is assumed with its left pointer containing the address of the root of the actual tree.

A general algorithm for inserting a node into a height balanced tree is as follows.

1.  If this is the first insertion
    then allocate a node, set its fields and exit

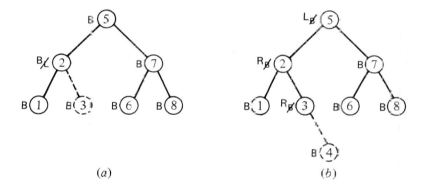

(a)   (b)

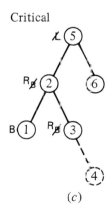

Critical

(c)

**FIGURE 6-2.5** Examples of insertions into a balanced tree.
(a) Condition 1; (b) condition 2; (c) condition 3.

2. If the name is not already in the tree
   then attach the new node to the existing tree
   else write item already present and exit
3. Search for an unbalanced node
4. Adjust the balance indicators, if there is no critical node, exit
5. If the node was balanced and then becomes heavy or
      the node was heavy and then becomes balanced
   then adjust the balance indicators and exit
6. Rebalance the tree and exit

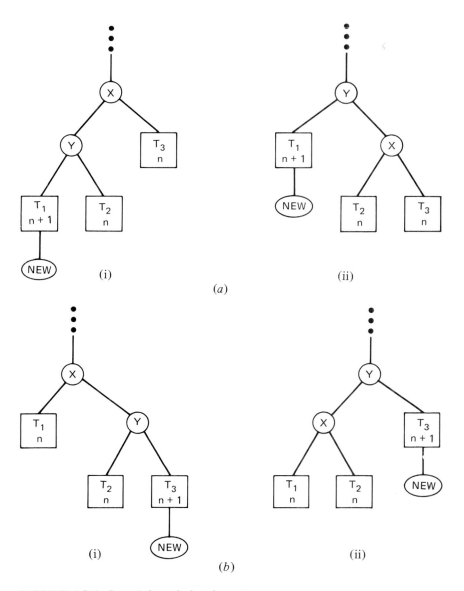

**FIGURE 6-2.6** Case 1 for rebalancing a tree.

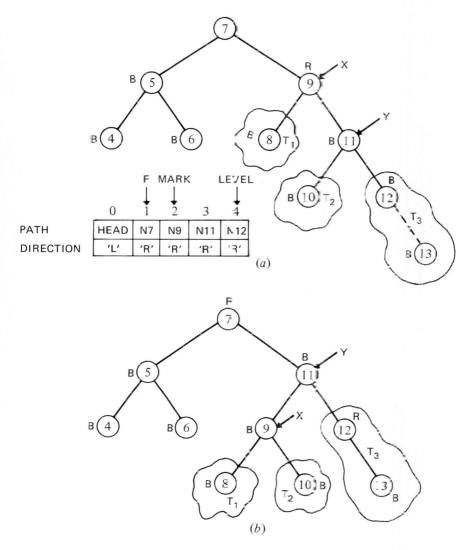

**FIGURE 6-2.7** Example of case 1. (a) Before balancing; (b) after balancing.

The detailed algorithm uses the following procedure which creates a new leaf node.

**Procedure** CREATE_LEAF(NAME, INFO, NEW). Given the key of a new node, NAME, and its associated information, INFO, this procedure creates a new leaf node and initializes its contents. NEW denotes the address of this new leaf.

1. [Create a new leaf node and initialize]
   NEW ⟸ NODE
   LFTR(NEW) ← RPTR(NEW) ← NULL

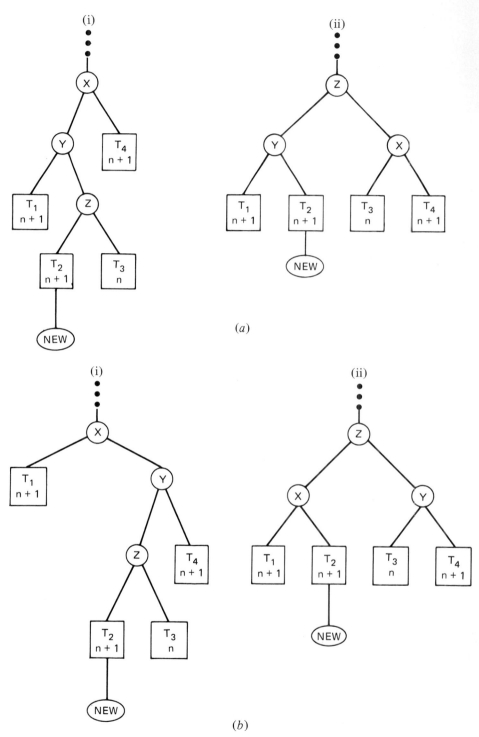

FIGURE 6-2.8 Case 2 for rebalancing a tree.

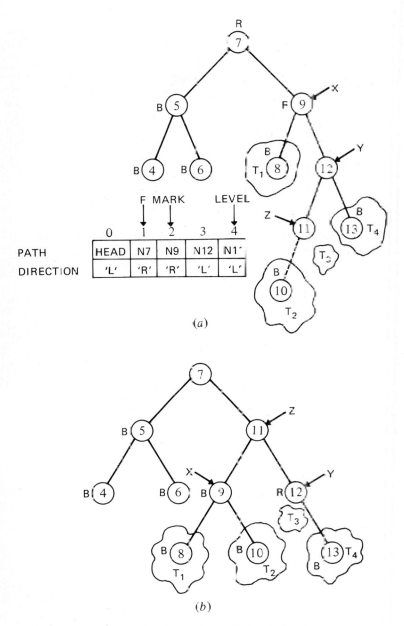

The following data appear within figure (a):

|        | 0 | 1 | 2 | 3 | 4 |
|--------|------|------|------|------|------|
| PATH   | HEAD | N7 | N9 | N12 | N1′ |
| DIRECTION | 'L' | 'R' | 'R' | 'L' | 'L' |

(a)

(b)

**FIGURE 6-2.9** Example of case 2. (a) Before balancing; (b) after balancing.

```
        EI(NEW) ← 'B'
        K(NEW) ← NAME
        DATA(NEW) ← INFO
2.  [Finished]
        Return
```

A formulation of the algorithm follows.

**Function** BALANCED_INSERT(HEAD, NAME, INFO). Given a linked representation of a balanced binary tree with a list head HEAD whose structure has just been described, and the variables NAME and INFO that contain the key value and information contents of the new element being inserted, this algorithm inserts the new element into the tree in such a manner as to maintain the balance property. The function returns **NEW**, the address of the new node created. The vector PATH is used to store the address of the nodes between the list head and the point in the tree where the insertion is made. The corresponding vector DIRECTION is used to store the direction of each branch in this path. The values of 'L' and 'R' are used to denote a left and right branch, respectively. The variable MARK denotes the index of a vector element in PATH that contains the address of the critical node (X). F points to the parent of the critical node before rebalancing takes place. The variables X, Y, and Z are pointer variables whose functions have been previously described. LEVEL is an index variable. T is a temporary pointer used in traversing the tree from the root to the node being inserted.

1. [Is this a first insertion?]
    If LPTR(HEAD) = HEAD
    then   Call CREATE_LEAF(NAME, INFO, NEW)
           LPTR(HEAD) ← NEW
           Return(NEW)
2. [Initialize]
       LEVEL ← 0
       DIRECTION[LEVEL] ← 'L'
       PATH[LEVEL] ← HEAD
       T ← LPTR(HEAD)
3. [Continue until found or inserted]
       **Repeat step 4 forever**   (infinite loop)
4. [Compare and insert, if required]
       If NAME < K(T)
       then   If LPTR(T) ≠ NULL
              then   LEVEL ← LEVEL + 1
                     PATH[LEVEL] ← T
                     DIRECTION[LEVEL] ← 'L'
                     T ← LPTR(T)
              else   Call CREATE_LEAF(NAME, INFO, NEW)
                     LPTR(T) ← NEW
                     LEVEL ← LEVEL + 1
                     PATH[LEVEL] ← T
                     DIRECTION[LEVEL] ← 'L'
                     Exitloop
       else   If NAME > K(T)
              then   If RPTR(T) ≠ NULL
                     then   LEVEL ← LEVEL + 1
                            PATH[LEVEL] ← T
                            DIRECTION[LEVEL] ← 'R'
                            T ← RPTR(T)
                     else   Call CREATE_LEAF(NAME, INFO, NEW)
                            RPTR(T) ← NEW
                            LEVEL ← LEVEL + 1

                    PATH[LEVEL] ← T
                    DIRECTION[LEVEL] ← 'R'
                    Exitloop
          else   (A match; NAME = K(T))
                    Write('ITEM ALREADY THERE')
                    Return(NULL)
5.  [Search for an unbalanced node]
        MARK ← 0
        Repeat for I = LEVEL, LEVEL – 1, ..., 1
            P ← PATH[I]
            If BI(P) ≠ 'B'
            then   MARK ← I
                    Exitloop
6.  [Adjust balance indicators]
        Repeat for I = MARK + 1, MARK + 2, ... LEVEL
            If NAME < K(PATH[I])
            then   BI(PATH[I]) ← 'L'
            else   BI(PATH[I]) ← 'R'
7.  [Is there a critical node?]
        If MARK = 0
        then   Return(NEW)
        D ← DIRECTION[MARK]
        X ← PATH[MARK]
        Y ← PATH[MARK + 1]
        If BI(X) ≠ D
        then   (The node was heavy and now becomes balanced)
                BI(X) ← 'B'
                Return(NEW)
8.  [Rebalancing: case 1]
        If BI(Y) = D
        then   (The node was heavy and now becomes critical)
                If D = 'L'
                then   LPTR(X) ← RPTR(Y)
                        RPTR(Y) ← X
                else   RPTR(X) ← LPTR(Y)
                        LPTR(Y) ← X
                BI(X) ← BI(Y) ← 'B'
                F ← PATH[MARK – 1]
                If X = LPTR(F)
                then   LPTR(F) ← Y
                else   RPTR(F) ← Y
                Return(NEW)
9.  [Rebalancing tree: case 2]
        (a) (Change structure links)
        If D = 'L'
        then   Z ← RPTR(Y)
                RPTR(Y) ← LPTR(Z)
                LPTR(Z) ← Y
                LPTR(X) ← RPTR(Z)
                RPTR(Z) ← X
        else   Z ← LPTR(Y)

```
            LPTR(Y) ← RPTR(Z)
            RPTR(Z) ← Y
            RPTR(X) ← LPTR(Z)
            LPTR(Z) ← X
      F ← PATH[MARK - 1]
      If X = LPTR(F)
      then    LPTR(F) ← Z
      else    RPTR(F) ← Z
      (b) (Change balance indicators)
      If BI(Z) = D
      then    BI(Y) ← BI(Z) ← 'B'
              If D = 'L'
              then    BI(X) ← 'R'
              else    BI(X) ← 'L'
      else    If BI(Z) = 'B'
              then    BI(X) ← BI(Y) ← BI(Z) ← 'B'
              else    BI(X) ← BI(Z) ← 'B'
                      BI(Y) ← D
      Return(NEW)                                          □
```

The algorithm, although lengthy, is straightforward. Steps 1 through 4 are closely patterned after Algorithm TABLE of Sec. 5-2.2. Step 3 attaches the new node to the existing tree, if it is not there already, and stores into vectors PATH and DIRECTION the address of the nodes on the path between the list head and the leaf being inserted, and it stores the direction of the path at each node, respectively. Step 5 of the algorithm searches for an unbalanced node which is closest to the new node just inserted. In step 6 the balance indicators of the nodes between the unbalanced node found in the previous step and the new node are adjusted. Step 7 determines whether there is a critical node. If there is, control proceeds either to step 8 (case 1) or to step 9 (case 2). When no critical node is found, the balance indicator of the unbalanced node found in step 5 is adjusted. The last two steps of the algorithm correspond to case 1 and case 2 in the previous discussion, and rebalancing of the tree is performed in each case. The reader should trace through the algorithm for the examples given in Figs. 6-2.7 and 6-2.9.

Let us now look at the performance of this balanced-tree algorithm. It can be shown that the maximum path length m in a height balanced tree of n nodes is $1.5 \log_2(n + 1)$ (see Stone). The worst ALOS for performing an insertion with any necessary rebalancing is of $O(\log_2 n)$.

Nodes may also be deleted from a balanced tree. The idea of deleting a node from a lexically-ordered binary tree was discussed in Sec. 5-1.3. This same idea can be used to perform a deletion here. A general algorithm for such a deletion follows.

1. Search for the node marked for deletion
2. If the indicated node has two children
   then find the inorder successor of this node
        delete the inorder successor
        replace the node marked for deletion by its inorder successor
   else delete the marked node and replace it by its child (if any)
3. Rebalance the tree along the ancestor path

The first two steps are similar to that used in the deletion algorithm in Chap. 5. The third step is similar to, but more complex than, the insertion rebalance strategy given earlier. The performance of this algorithm can be shown to be $O(\log_2 n)$.

**Exercises for Sec. 6-2.3.1**

1. Show the binary tree built from a sequence of insertions for the following sequence of keys:

   8, 17, 10, 15, 5, 2, 16, 19, 13, 1, 4, 11.

2. Using Function BALANCE_INSERT, show at each step the tree built from a sequence of insertions corresponding to the following keys:

   6, 7, 8, 12, 15, 17, 9, 10.

3. Formulate an algorithm which will delete a node from a balanced tree and leave the resulting tree balanced. (*Hint:* If the node is not a leaf, find its inorder predecessor to see if it can be deleted.)

### 6-2.3.2 2-3 Trees

Another type of height-balanced tree is the 2-3 tree. A 2-3 tree is defined as a tree in which all nonterminal nodes have either 2 or 3 offspring, and all leaf nodes have the same path length from the root node. Note that a tree consisting of a single leaf node is also considered to be a 2-3 tree. Figure 6-2 10 gives an example of a 2-3 tree containing five values.

   In 2-3 trees, only leaves contain values, whereas nonleaf nodes indicate the path taken to the values. When descending the tree during a search, the given key is compared to the two values (indicators) at each nonleaf node. If the key is smaller than or equal to the first value, the left branch is taken; if the key is larger than the first value but less than or equal to the second value, the middle branch is taken; if the key is larger than the second value and a right branch exists, the right branch is taken.

   The first value of a nonleaf node is given by the largest value in the left subtree. Similarly, the second value of a nonleaf node is given by the largest value in the middle subtree. Note also that when a nonleaf node has only two branches, the right branch is the missing one.

   We use two different nodes to represent a 2-3 tree. The leaf nodes are defined as

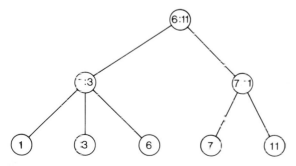

**FIGURE 6-2.10**

LEAF

| TAG | DATA |
|-----|------|

and the nonleaf nodes are defined as:

NONLEAF

| TAG | LDATA | LPTR | MDATA | MPTR | RPTR |
|-----|-------|------|-------|------|------|

A leaf node is indicated by a tag field, where TAG is Boolean, with value *false*, and DATA containing the value of that node. A nonleaf node is indicated by a tag field of *true*. In such a node, LDATA and MDATA indicate the key indicators used to determine the search path, LPTR, MPTR, and RPTR are pointers to other nodes of the tree.

A general algorithm to perform a search on a 2-3 tree is now presented.

1. Repeat step 2 while not a leaf node
2. If key ≤ the first search value in the node
   then move down the left branch
   else if key ≤ the second search value in the node
      then move down the middle branch
      else if a right branch exists
         then move down the right branch
         else unsuccessful search and return
3. If the key has been found
   then successful search and return
   else unsuccessful search and return

A detailed algorithm for this search is now given.

**Function** SEARCH_2_3_TREE(T, KEY). Given a 2-3 tree pointed to by the pointer variable T, this algorithm searches the structure for a given key KEY. The pointer CUR is a temporary variable used to descend the tree.

1. [Initialize]
      CUR ← T
2. [Descend tree]
      Repeat while TAG(CUR)
         If KEY ≤ LDATA(CUR)
         then   CUR ← LPTR(CUR)
         else   If KEY ≤ MDATA(CUR)
                then   CUR ← MPTR(CUR)
                else   If RPTR(CUR) ≠ NULL
                       then   CUR ← RPTR(CUR)
                       else   (Right subtree doesn't exist - key not found)
                              Return(NULL)

3.   [Successful search?]
       If DATA(CUR) = KEY
       then    Return(CUR)
       else    Return(NULL)                              ☐

We now look at the insert operation into a 2-3 tree. There are essentially four cases that can arise.

*Case 1*   The tree before insertion is empty. In this case, we create the node to be inserted, and make this the root of the tree.

*Case 2*   The tree contains just one node. This is the case after an insertion in *case 1*. In this case, a nonleaf node is created, with the previous root node and the node being inserted as the new node's children. This situation is shown in Fig. 6-2.11.

The other two cases occur when there is more than one node in the tree. The procedure is as follows: First, it is determined where the new node would be placed in the tree, then its parent and the search path are found.

*Case 3*   If the parent has two children, insert the new node into its proper position below the parent. If its key value is less than that of the left child, the new node becomes the left child; if its key value is greater than that of the middle child, the new node becomes the right (or third) child; otherwise, it becomes the middle (or second) child. This insertion case is illustrated in Fig. 6-2.12.

*Case 4*   The parent of the new node has three children. In this case the new node becomes a fourth child, in its proper position, of the parent. Next, a new nonleaf node is created and it becomes a brother to the immediate right of the parent node. The two right-most children of the parent node now become the offspring of the new nonleaf node. This case is shown in Fig. 6-2.13. If the addition of the new nonleaf node causes its parent to have four children, the process is repeated on this node. An occurrence of this case is shown in Fig. 6-2.14.

We now formulate a procedure to perform an insertion. Although the procedure is straightforward, it tends to be quite lengthy, so to aid clarity, we use a modular approach.

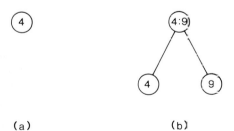

(a)                     (b)

**FIGURE 6-2.11**

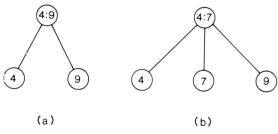

(a)                              (b)

**FIGURE 6-2.12**

A general algorithm for performing an insertion follows.

1. Create a new leaf node
2. If the tree is empty
   then perform an insertion into an empty tree
      return
3. If the tree contains only a leaf
   then create a nonleaf (root) node
         connect the two leaves so as to be ordered
         set the key indicators of the root node
         return
4. a) Obtain the search path from the root node to insertion point
   b) If the parent of the new leaf has two children
      then append new leaf to parent so as to be ordered
            update the key indicators (LDATA and MDATA)
            return
      else determine insert position of new leaf
            call procedure to perform the insertion and rebalance the tree

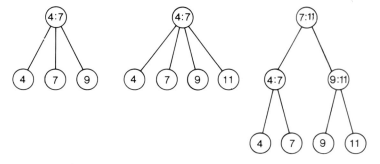

**FIGURE 6-2.13**

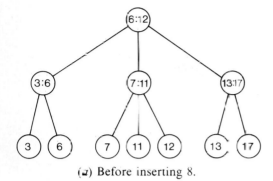

(a) Before inserting 8.

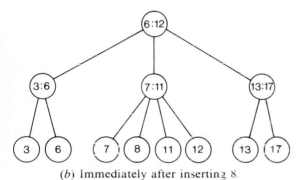

(b) Immediately after inserting 8.

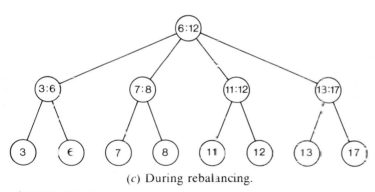

(c) During rebalancing.

**FIGURE 6-2.14**

The algorithm incorporates the various cases in the previous discussion. The first part of this step determines the path from the root node of the tree to the new node's parent. This path can be represented by a stack with its bottom and top nodes representing the root and the parent addresses, respectively. This task can be accomplished by formulating an algorithm similar to the search algorithm discussed earlier.

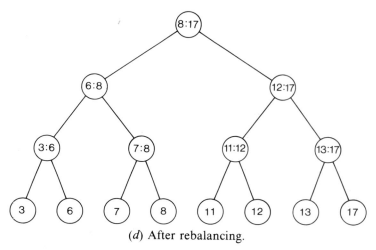

(d) After rebalancing.

**FIGURE 6-2.14**   (Continued)

**Procedure** FIND_PATH(T, KEY). Given a 2-3 tree with the node structure outlined earlier, the root node address T, and the new key to be inserted KEY, this procedure determines the ancestor path for the insertion. A global stack STACK is used to save the node addresses on the path. CUR is a local pointer variable which refers to the current node being processed. PUSH is a procedure which pushes the address of the current node onto the stack.

1. [Initialize]
       CUR ← T
2. [Descend tree]
       Repeat while TAG(CUR)
           Call PUSH(STACK, CUR)
           If KEY ≤ LDATA(CUR)
           then   CUR ← LPTR(CUR)
           else   If KEY ≤ MDATA(CUR)
                  then   CUR ← MPTR(CUR)
                  else   If RPTR(CUR) ≠ NULL
                         then   CUR ← RPTR(CUR)
                         else   CUR ← MPTR(CUR)
3. [Finished]
       Return                                                                  □

This algorithm is simple and requires no further comment.

Next, a general strategy for the rebalancing and insertion of the general algorithm (step 4(b)) can be formulated. We are given the address of the new node, and the position where the new node is to be inserted (i.e., position 1, 2, 3, or 4).

1. Create a new nonleaf brother for the parent node
2. Split the four children between the parent node and its new brother
   Update the key indicators (i.e., LDATA and MDATA)

3.   If the current parent has no ancestor
     then create a new root node
              connect current parent as its left subtree
              connect current parent's brother as its right subtree
              update key indicators of new root node
              return
     else obtain grandparent of current parent
              determine insertion position of current parent's brother (i.e. position
              2, 3, or 4)
              If grandparent has only two children
              then insert current parent's brother
                  update key indicators
                  return
              else recursively invoke rebalancing procedure with the grandparent
                  node which has four children. [Note that the current parent's
                  brother and its position (2, 3, or 4) is made available to the
                  procedure].

The details of this algorithm are the following.


**Procedure** REBALANCE_INSERT(P, NEW, LOC). Given the previous node structures, the parent, P, of the new node, NEW, and the position of the insertion point
LOC, this procedure performs the insertion and rebalancing of the tree. P' is the
address of the brother of P. NROOT denotes the address of the new root node. G
is the parent of P. POP is a stack function for popping the top element from the
stack which represents the search path.

1.   [Create a new nonleaf brother for P]
         $P' \Leftarrow$ NONLEAF
         TAG(P') $\leftarrow$ *true*
         RPTR(P') $\leftarrow$ NULL
2.   [Split the four children between P and P']
         If LOC = 1
         then  LPTR(P') $\leftarrow$ MPTR(P)
               MPTR(P') $\leftarrow$ RPTR(P)
               MPTR(P) $\leftarrow$ LPTR(P)
               LPTR(P) $\leftarrow$ NEW
               LDATA(P') $\leftarrow$ MDATA(P)
               MDATA(P') $\leftarrow$ DATA(RPTR(P))
               MDATA(P) $\leftarrow$ LDATA(P)
               LDATA(P) $\leftarrow$ INFO
         else  If LOC = 2
               then  LPTR(P') $\leftarrow$ MPTR(P)
                     MPTR(P') $\leftarrow$ RPTR(P)
                     MPTR(P) $\leftarrow$ NEW
                     LDATA(P') $\leftarrow$ MDATA(P)
                     MDATA(P') $\leftarrow$ DATA(RPTR(P))
                     MDATA(P) $\leftarrow$ INFO
               else  If LOC = 3
                     then  LPTR(P') $\leftarrow$ NEW
                           RPTR(P') $\leftarrow$ RPTR(P)

LDATA(P') ← INFO
MDATA(P') ← DATA(RPTR(P))

else   LPTR(P') ← RPTR(P)

MPTR(P') ← NEW
LDATA(P') ← DATA(RPTR(P))
MDATA(P') ← INFO

RPTR(P) ← NULL

3. [Create new root node?]

    If STACK is empty

    then   (create a new root and append P and P')

            NROOT ⟸ NONLEAF

            TAG(NROOT) ← *true*

            RPTR(NROOT) ← NULL

            LPTR(NROOT) ← P

            MPTR(NROOT) ← P'

            LDATA(NROOT) ← MDATA(P)

            MDATA(NROOT) ← MDATA(P')

            Return

    else   G ← POP(STACK)

        (determine insert position of P')

        If LPTR(G) = P

        then   LOC ← 2

        else   If MPTR(G) = P

              then   LOC ← 3

              else   If RPTR(G) = P

                   then   LOC ← 4

        If RPTR(G) = NULL

        then   (grandparent has three children after update)

            If LOC = 2

            then   RPTR(G) ← MPTR(G)

                   MPTR(G) ← P'

                   MDATA(G) ← MDATA(P')

            else   If LOC = 3

                 then   RPTR(G) ← P'

        Return

        else   (grandparent has four children after update)

            Call REBALANCE_INSERT(G, P', LOC)      ☐

Note that this procedure is recursive and it permits the expansion of the tree.

    The two previous procedures are used in the following main subalgorithm.

**Function** INSERT_2_3(T, INFO).   Given the root node of a 2-3 tree, T, and the key value, INFO, of a new leaf, this function performs an insertion. The node structures described earlier are assumed. NEW denotes the address of the new leaf node. PARENT contains the address of the parent of the new node. The procedures FIND_PATH and REBALANCE_INSERT are invoked. NROOT denotes the address of a new root node. A stack STACK is also assumed and its associated function POP.

1. [Create a new leaf node]

    NEW ⟸ LEAF

```
      TAG(NEW) ← false
      DATA(NEW) ← INFO
2.  [Perform an insertion into an empty tree?]
      If T = NULL
      then  Return(NEW)
3.  [Perform insertion into a single leaf tree?]
      If not TAG(T)
      then    NROOT ⇐ NONLEAF
              TAG(NROOT) ← true
              RPTR(NROOT) ← NULL
              If INFO < DATA(T)
              then  LPTR(NROOT) ← NEW
                    MPTR(NROOT) ← T
                    LDATA(NROOT) ← INFO
                    MDATA(NROOT) ← DATA(T)
              else  LPTR(NROOT) ← ⁻
                    MPTR(NROOT) ← NEW
                    LDATA(NROOT) ← DATA(T)
                    MDATA(NROOT) ← INFO
              Return(NROOT)
4.  [Perform a general insertion]
        (a) Call FIND_PATH(T, INFO)
            PARENT ← POP(STACK)
        (b) If RPTR(PARENT) = NULL
        then    (parent has two children)
                If INFO < LDATA(PARENT)
                then  (leftmost insertion)
                      RPTR(PARENT) ← MPTR(PARENT)
                      MPTR(PARENT) ← LPTR(PARENT)
                      LPTR(PARENT) ← NEW
                      MDATA(PARENT) ← LDATA(PARENT)
                      LDATA(PARENT) ← INFO
                else  If INFO < MDATA(PARENT)
                      then  (middle insertion)
                            RPTR(PARENT) ← MPTR(PARENT)
                            MPTR(PARENT) ← NEW
                            MDATA(PARENT) ← INFO
                      else  (right insertion)
                            RPTR(PARENT) ← NEW
                Return(T)
        else    (parent has three children, so expand and rebalance tree)
                If INFO < LDATA(PARENT)
                then  POS ← 1
                else  If INFO < MDATA(PARENT)
                      then  POS ← 2
                      else  If INFO < DATA(RPTR(PARENT))
                            then  POS ← 3
                            else  POS ← 4
                Call REBALANCE_INSERT(PARENT, NEW, POS)
5.  [Finished]
      Return(T)                                              □
```

Let us examine the timing analysis of this algorithm. It can be shown that a 2-3 tree of height h  contains between $2^h$  and $3^h$  leaves. This means that the height of a 2-3 tree with n  nodes is at most $\log_2 n$ . Procedure  FIND_PATH is $O(\log_2 n)$ . Also, Procedure REBALANCE_INSERT requires  at most $\log_2 n$  recursive calls. Therefore,  the insertion algorithm is $O(\log_2 n)$ .

A deletion algorithm can be formulated.  The approach is to do the reverse of the insertion algorithm.  If the tree contains only one leaf, it can be removed.  A child can also be removed from a node with three children.  The remaining case involves the deletion of one node from a parent with only two children.  The deletion algorithm is left as an exercise.

The insertion and deletion operations can be programmed easily in Pascal. The node structure can be implemented with variant records in Pascal, as follows.

```
type nodeptr = ↑node;
     nodetype = (leaf, nonleaf);
     node = record
              case tag : nodetype of
                 leaf : (data  : integer );
                 nonleaf : ( ldata : integer;
                             lptr  : nodeptr;
                             mdata : integer;
                             mptr  : nodeptr;
                             rptr  : nodeptr )
            end;
```

The programming of the operations is left as an exercise.


## Exercises for Sec. 6-2.3.2

1.  Formulate an algorithm which performs a deletion in a 2-3 tree.
2.  Implement a Pascal program which uses variant structures for the algorithm obtained in Prob. 1.
3.  Implement a Pascal program for the insert operation.
4.  Prove that a 2-3 tree of height h contains  between $2^h$  and $3^h$  leaves.


### 6-2.3.3  Weight-Balanced Trees

Recall from Sec. 6-2.1, the idea of preloading the keys of a key set into a vector according to their decreasing order of probability of occurrence.  If these probabilities of occurrence are not known, however, something can still be done to improve search performance.  For example, a linear search can be performed on a linked list of keys.  When a particular key is found it can be moved to the front of the list. The reason for this move is the belief that a key which has been just accessed is likely to be accessed again in the near future.  This strategy has worked well in practice.

If the probability of access of a particular key is unknown, the access of such a key can be maintained dynamically.  This subsection describes such a strategy which uses another type of balanced tree called a weight-balanced tree.  Each node of such a tree has an information field which contains the name of the node and the number of times the node has been visited.  Take, for example, the lexically ordered tree $T_1$ given in Fig. 6-2.15.

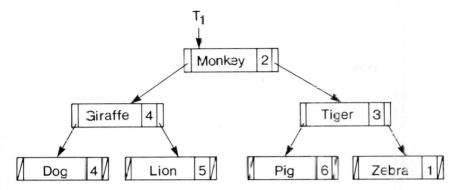

**FIGURE 6-2.15**

$T_1$ is a balanced tree. If we assume that each node is equally likely to be searched for, then a balanced-tree representation provides a minimum average length of search (ALOS). However, the representation for $T_1$ does not take into consideration the probability of accessing a given node. If the number of times a node has been accessed in the past is representative of how often it will be accessed in the future (i.e., the probabilities of access), then we can calculate a weighted ALOS as follows:

$$\text{ALOS}(T_1) = \sum_{i=1}^{n} p_i d_i$$

where $p_i$ is the probability that node i will be accessed based on the proportion of accesses thus far, and $d_i$ is the depth of node i plus one in the binary tree. Therefore,

$$
\begin{aligned}
\text{ALOS}(T_1) &= 2/25 \times 1 + 4/25 \times 2 + 4/25 \times 3 + 5/25 \times 3 \\
&\quad + 3/25 \times 2 + 6/25 \times 3 + 1/25 \times 3 \\
&= .08 + .32 + .48 + .60 + .24 + .72 + .12 \\
&= 2.56
\end{aligned}
$$

An alternative organization of the tree is formed by considering the number of accesses when structuring the tree. The tree $T_2$ of Fig 6-2.16 illustrates this idea. The ALOS of the restructured tree is now

$$
\begin{aligned}
\text{ALOS}(T_2) &= 6/25 \times 1 + 5/25 \times 2 + 4/25 \times 3 - 4/25 \times 4 \\
&\quad + 2/25 \times 3 + 3/25 \times 2 + 1/25 \times 3 \\
&= .24 + .40 + .48 + .64 - .24 + .24 + .12 \\
&= 2.36
\end{aligned}
$$

While this saving does not appear to be significant, it can be very important when considering large tables or files in which accesses must be made to external memory. The rules for placement of an item in a weighted-tree structure can be expressed recursively as follows:

*1*   The first node of a tree (or subtree) is the node with the largest activity count from the set of nodes constituting the tree (or subtree).

*2*   The left subtree of the tree (or subtree) is composed of nodes with values lexically less than the first node.

*3* The right subtree of the tree (or subtree) is composed of nodes with values lexically greater than the first node.

We now formulate algorithms for the insertion and deletion of nodes from a weight-balanced binary tree. For each insertion or request operation concerning a particular node, the access weight of that node is incremented by one. If an access operation is attempted for a node which is not in the tree, then the node is added at its appropriate leaf position in the tree. In this case its weight is initialized to one.

A general algorithm for the access of a given node is the following.

1. Search for the given node and determine the search path followed.
2. If the given node is found
   then update access count of node by one
       rebalance the tree (if required)
   else insert new node
       set its access count to one

In the following algorithms, we assume each node to be represented by a data structure consisting of four fields, LPTR and RPTR, pointers to the nodes descendants, KEY, a string indicating the name of the node, and WEIGHT, an integer indicating the number of times the node has been accessed. The head node of the tree, pointed to by the pointer HEAD, contains a KEY field of 'ZZZZZZZZ' and WEIGHT field of 999999.

We also assume the existence of a stack S which is used to store the path from the head node to the accessed node. Revised PUSH, POP, and PEEP algorithms (see Chap. 3) are used. Procedure PUSH(S, TOP, PTR) pushes the pointer PTR onto the stack S. Function POP(S, TOP) pops the top elements of the stack S, and Procedure PEEP(S, TOP, PTR) places the top element of the stack S into PTR without affecting the stack.

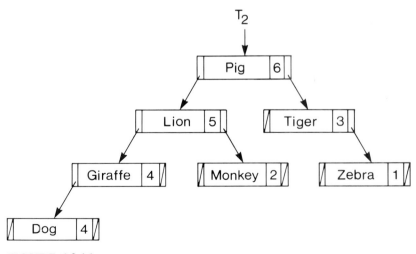

**FIGURE 6-2.16**

**Procedure** ACCESS(NAME). This procedure searches a weight-balanced binary tree for the node with name NAME. If the node is found, its weight is increased by one and the tree is rebalanced if necessary. If the node is not found, a new node is created and inserted at the appropriate position in the tree. The variable CURRENT is a pointer to either the node if found or its parent if not found. The Boolean variable FOUND indicates whether the node has been found. TOP denotes the top element in the stack S. Procedure INSERT handles the insertion of a node into the tree, and Procedure REBALANCE performs the rebalancing of the tree.

1. [Initiate search for given node at head node]
   > CURRENT ← HEAD
   > FOUND ← *false*
   > TOP ← 0
2. [Search until the given key is found or we reach a leaf node]
   > Repeat thru step 4 while not FOUND and CURRENT ≠ NULL
3. [Save address of current node on stack]
   > Call PUSH(S, TOP, CURRENT)
4. [Is there a match?]
   > If NAME = KEY(CURRENT)
   > then   FOUND ← *true*
   > else   (name not found, continue search)
   >        If NAME < KEY(CURRENT)
   >        then   CURRENT ← LPTR(CURRENT)
   >        else   CURRENT ← RPTR(CURRENT)
5. [Perform the access on the node]
   > If FOUND
   > then   WEIGHT(CURRENT) ← WEIGHT(CURRENT) + 1
   >        Call REBALANCE
   > else   (Insert new node)
   >        Call INSERT(NAME, S[TOP])
6. [Completed access]
   > Return                                                          □

Procedure ACCESS calls two procedures, INSERT and REBALANCE. These are now given.

**Procedure** INSERT(NAME, PARENT). This procedure creates a new node with name NAME and inserts it in the appropriate position in the tree. Its parent node is the node whose address is given by PARENT. CHILD is a pointer to the newly created node.

1. [Create the new node]
   > CHILD ⇐ NODE
   > KEY(CHILD) ← NAME
   > WEIGHT(CHILD) ← 1
   > LPTR(CHILD) ← NULL
   > RPTR(CHILD) ← NULL
2. [Insert the new node into the tree]
   > If NAME < KEY(PARENT)
   > then   LPTR(PARENT) ← CHILD
   > else   RPTR(PARENT) ← CHILD

3.  [Finished]
    Return                                                                  □

   There are four cases for rebalancing. However, these are just different instances of the same case. Take the general case illustrated in the tree given in Fig. 6-2.17(a). The node we are accessing is the node labeled CHILD. If this access causes the weight of CHILD to become greater than the weight of PARENT, we must rebalance the tree. The rebalanced tree will have the form given in Fig. 6-2.17(b).

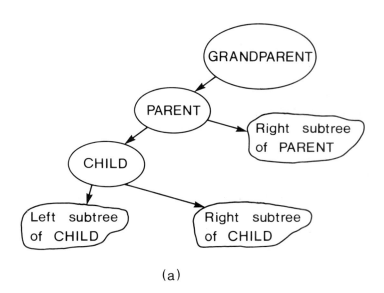

(a)

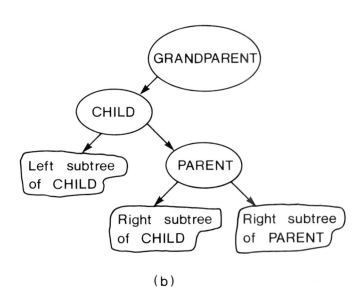

(b)

**FIGURE 6-2.17**

If the weight of CHILD is also greater than the weight of GRANDPARENT, we must again rebalance, with GRANDPARENT now becoming PARENT and its parent becoming GRANDPARENT. This process continues until the weight of CHILD is no longer greater than the weight of PARENT. At this point the tree will be balanced. There are two ways of handling this "bubbling up" the tree. The recursive approach has been used in Procedure REBALANCE, while the iterative approach has been left as an exercise.

**Procedure** REBALANCE. This procedure handles the rebalancing of the tree after an insertion has been performed. It first determines whether the tree does need rebalancing. If it does not, it returns immediately. However, if it does need rebalancing, it makes the appropriate changes to both the tree structure and the search path stack. CHILD is a pointer to the node that has just been accessed; it is the node on the top of the stack. PARENT and GRANDPARENT are the node's parent and grandparent, respectively.

1. [Get the node and its parent from the stack]
   CHILD ← POP(S, TOP)
   PARENT ← POP(S, TOP)
2. [Do we need to rebalance?]
   If WEIGHT(PARENT) ≥ WEIGHT(CHILD)
   then    Return
3. [Get grandparent from stack]
   GRANDPARENT ← POP(S, TOP)
4. [Exchange parent and child]
   If LPTR(PARENT) = CHILD
   then    LPTR(PARENT) ← RPTR(CHILD)
           RPTR(CHILD) ← PARENT
   else    RPTR(PARENT) ← LPTR(CHILD)
           LPTR(CHILD) ← PARENT
   If LPTR(GRANDPARENT) = PARENT
   then    LPTR(GRANDPARENT) ← CHILD
   else    RPTR(GRANDPARENT) ← CHILD
5. [Put grandparent and child on stack]
   Call PUSH(S, TOP, GRANDPARENT)
   Call PUSH(S, TOP, CHILD)
6. [Recursively bubble up tree]
   Call REBALANCE
7. [Finished rebalancing]
   Return                                                                □

We next formulate a general algorithm for the deletion of a node from the weight-balanced tree. There are four cases to consider.

   *1*   The node to be deleted is a leaf node. In this case, we simply remove the pointer from its parent to the node.
   *2*   The node is a branch node, with the right subtree empty, and the node is the left offspring of its parent. In this case, we set the left pointer of the parent node equal to the left pointer of the node marked for deletion. This also holds for the mirror image.
   *3*   The node is a branch node, with the left subtree empty, and the node

marked for deletion is the left offspring of its parent. For this case, we set the left pointer of the parent node equal to the right pointer of the node marked for deletion.

4    The node is a branch node, with both subtrees nonempty.

Case 4 requires further discussion. In this case, directly deleting the node, as is done for unbalanced binary trees, results in unbalancing the tree, and the processing required to rebalance the tree is nontrivial. A much better method is to exchange the node marked for deletion with one of its offspring. To maintain balance, we choose the offspring with the larger weight. After this exchange, we will again be in one of the four mentioned cases. If one of cases 1,2 or 3 occurs, we may delete the node at this point. However, if we are again in case 4, we repeat the procedure until we can delete the node.

A recursive general algorithm for the deletion process is now given.

1. If the node is a leaf node, or has an empty subtree
   then delete the node
2. Replace the node to be deleted with its offspring having the largest weight.
3. Recursively merge the subtree just attached to the parent, and the unattached subtree retaining as the root of this merged subtree the root of the attached subtree.

   This merging is done according to weights and lexical ordering.

The details of the algorithm are left as an exercise.

### Exercises for Sec. 6-2.3.3

1. Formulate a specific algorithm to delete and rebalance a weight-balanced binary tree.
2. Suppose that we have accessed GIRAFFE in tree $T_2$ given in Fig. 6-2.16. The subtree of Fig. 6-2.18(a) would be formed. However, note that if the subtree were rearranged as that given in Fig. 6-2.18(b), then the ALOS would be reduced. Formulate a revised algorithm for handling this rebalancing problem for equal access nodes such as the one given.
3. Formulate an algorithm to change a particular node in a weight-balanced binary tree. The algorithm invocation is to be of the form

   CHANGE(KEY, NEW_WEIGHT)

   where KEY is the key of the node being changed and NEW_WEIGHT is the new weight of that node. Note that NEW_WEIGHT can have a value which can cause the node to move up or down the tree.

### 6-2.3.4 Trie Structures

A previous section discussed the applicability of binary trees to searching. In that discussion the branching at any level in the tree was determined by the entire key value. In this subsection we examine briefly the feasibility of using $m$-ary trees ($m \geq 2$) for searching. The branching criterion at a particular level in such a tree will be based on a portion of the key value rather than its entire key value. A *trie* structure is a complete $m$-ary tree in which each node consists of $m$ components. Typically, these components correspond to letters and digits. Trie structures occur frequently in the area of information organization and retrieval. The method of searching in tries is analogous to the notion of digital sorting. In particular, the

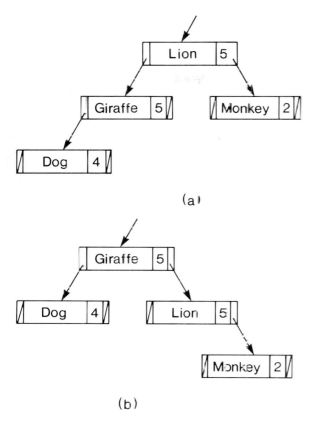

(a)

(b)

**FIGURE 6-2.18**

branching at each node of level $k$ depends on the $k$th character of a key. Table 6-2.2 gives an example of a trie structure for searching a set of 29 English words. This table consists of 12 nodes, each of which is a vector of 27 elements. Each element contains either a dash, or the desired word, or a node number. A blank symbol ($\Box$) is used to denote the end of a word during the scan of the key. Node 1 is the root of the trie.

To insert a value into a trie structure as shown in Table 6-2.2 involves several cases. The simplest case occurs when the calculated position for the key contains a dash. In this case the key may be immediately inserted. If a node number is encountered in the calculated key position, then this value becomes the new node. If another key is encountered in the calculated key position, a new node must be created, and its node value placed where the colliding key was encountered. This process of creating new nodes is continued while the two keys have letters in corresponding positions. A general algorithm to perform a trie insertion is as follows.

1. Repeat thru step 5 for each character in the name
2. Obtain the index from the current character
3. If the calculated position is empty
   then insert the name and return

**Table 6-2.2** A trie structure for a list of words.

|   | Node Number | | | | | | | | | | | |
|---|---|---|---|---|---|---|---|---|---|---|---|---|
|   | 1 | 2 | 3 | 4 | 5 | 6 | 7 | 8 | 9 | 10 | 11 | 12 |
| b | - | - | - | - | - | - | - | - | - | - | - | GO |
| A | ALLOCATE | - | CALL | - | - | - | - | - | - | - | - | - |
| B | 2 | - | - | - | - | - | - | - | - | - | - | - |
| C | 3 | - | - | DCL | - | - | - | - | - | - | - | - |
| D | 4 | - | - | - | - | - | - | - | - | - | END | - |
| E | 5 | BEGIN | - | - | - | - | GET | - | - | - | - | - |
| F | 6 | - | - | - | - | - | - | - | - | - | - | - |
| G | 7 | - | - | - | - | - | - | - | - | - | - | - |
| H | - | - | CHECK | - | - | - | - | - | THEN | WHILE | - | - |
| I | IF | - | - | - | - | - | - | - | - | - | - | - |
| J | - | - | - | - | - | - | - | - | - | - | - | - |
| K | - | - | - | - | - | - | - | - | - | - | - | - |
| L | - | - | CLOSE | - | ELSE | FLOW | - | - | - | - | - | - |
| M | - | - | - | - | - | - | - | - | - | - | - | - |
| N | NO | - | - | - | 11 | - | - | - | - | - | - | - |
| O | OPEN | - | - | DO | - | FORMAT | 12 | - | TO | - | - | - |
| P | 8 | - | - | - | - | - | - | - | - | - | - | - |
| Q | - | - | - | - | - | - | - | - | - | - | - | - |
| R | RETURN | - | - | - | - | FREE | - | PROC | - | WRITE | - | - |
| S | STOP | - | - | - | - | - | - | - | - | - | - | - |
| T | 9 | - | - | - | - | - | - | - | - | - | ENTRY | GOTO |
| U | - | - | - | - | - | - | - | PUT | - | - | - | - |
| V | - | - | - | - | - | - | - | - | - | - | - | - |
| W | 10 | - | - | - | - | - | - | - | - | - | - | - |
| X | - | - | - | - | EXIT | - | - | - | - | - | - | - |
| Y | - | BY | - | - | - | - | - | - | - | - | - | - |
| Z | - | - | - | - | - | - | - | - | - | - | - | - |

4. If a duplicate key is encountered
   then write duplicate key and return
5. If the calculated position contains an index value
   then move to this new location
   else create a new vector and insert colliding name
6. Return

A detailed algorithm to insert a key into a trie structure follows.

**Procedure** TRIE_INSERT(NAME, ROW, TRIE, COL). Given NAME, the name to be searched for, TRIE, an array of 27 by N elements representing a trie structure, where N represents the number of nodes currently required to represent the structure, this procedure inserts a key into a trie structure. The array before the first insertion is a vector (N = 1). The parameters ROW and COL hold the row and column indices of NAME within TRIE, respectively. K is an index which designates the position of the character currently being scanned. If the key is already present, ROW and COL are assigned a value of zero. We assume that NAME contains only alphabetic characters.

1. [Initialize]
   COL ← 1
2. [Perform the insertion]
   Repeat thru step 5 for K = 1, 2, ..., LENGTH(NAME)
   ROW ← INDEX('□ABC...XYZ', SUB(NAME, K, 1))
3. [Enter key in empty position]
   If TRIE[ROW, COL] = '-'
   then  TRIE[ROW, COL] ← NAME
   Return
4. [Check for duplicate key]
   If TRIE[ROW, COL] = NAME
   then  Write('DUPLICATE KEY')
   COL ← ROW ← 0
   Return
5. [Current position occupied]
   If INDEX('0123456789', SUB(TRIE[ROW, COL], 1, 1)) ≠ 0
   then  COL ← TRIE[ROW, COL]
   else  (create new vector N + 1)
   N ← N + 1
   SAVE ← TRIE[ROW, COL]
   TRIE[ROW, COL] ← N
   COL ← N
   ROW ← INDEX('□ABC..XYZ', SUB(SAVE, K + 1, 1))
   TRIE[ROW, COL] ← SAVE
6. [Finished]
   Return                                                                    □

The procedure repeatedly scans the next character from NAME to determine the
position of the key. Step 5 determines if the current calculated key position contains
a node number or another key. If a node number is encountered, COL is updated
and a new row position is calculated from the next letter in NAME. If another key
is encountered, a new vector must be added to the array. This new node number is
placed in the old key's position and a new position for the colliding key is determined. The algorithm continues calculating new row positions for the key until an
empty position or a duplicate key is encountered.

As an example of a search for a word in a trie structure as shown in Table 6-
2.2, we trace through the search for the word END. The letter E tells us that we
should go from node 1 to node 5. The second letter (N) is then used to select the
appropriate element in node 5. The entry corresponding to label N transfers us to
node 11. At this node, the letter D is finally used to find the desired word.

A general algorithm to perform a trie search is now presented.

1. Repeat thru step 5 for each character in the name
2. Obtain the index from the current character
3. Repeat thru step 5 until an empty location is encountered
4. If the calculated position contains the name
   then return its position
5. If the calculated position contains a different name
   then write unexpected name found and return
   else move to this new location
6. Write name not found and return

A detailed algorithm for this search technique follows.

**Procedure**  TRIE_SEARCH(NAME, ROW, TRIE, COL).  Given the parameters as described in Procedure TRIE_INSERT, this procedure performs a search of a trie structure.  If the search fails, ROW and COL are assigned a value of zero.  We again assume that **NAME** contains only alphabetic characters.

1.  [Initialize]
      COL ← 1
2.  [Perform the search]
      Repeat for K = 1, 2, ..., LENGTH(NAME)
         ROW ← INDEX('□ABC...XYZ', SUB(NAME, K, 1))
         Repeat while TRIE[ROW, COL] ≠ '-'
            If TRIE[ROW, COL] = NAME
            then    **Return**
            If INDEX('0123456789', SUB(TRIE[ROW, COL], 1, 1)) = 0
            then    Write('UNEXPECTED', NAME, 'FOUND')
                  ROW ← COL ← 0
                  Return
            else    COL ← TRIE[ROW, COL]
3.  [Missing name]
      Write('NAME NOT FOUND')
      ROW ← COL ← 0
      Return                                                                    ☐

The procedure repeatedly scans the next character from NAME and branches accordingly.  This scanning process stops either when the given name is found or when the search fails.

The example trie given is very wasteful of memory space.  Memory can be saved at the expense of running time if each class of names is represented by a linked tree.  Figure 6-2.19 represents the trie of Table 6-2.2.  Note that this representation is a forest of trees.

The best compromise situation in terms of space and running time occurs when only a few levels of a trie are used for the first few characters of the key and then some other structure, such as a linked list or binary tree, is used in the remainder of the search.

Consider the trie structure given in Fig. 6-2.20.  The top two levels of the trie are made up of 26-ary nodes in an effort to make the structure more space efficient, while the remaining levels contain binary nodes (which make up a binary tree).  Note that the first two levels of the trie structure consist of vectors of 26 elements, each of which corresponds to a letter of the alphabet.  Unlike the trie structure discussed previously, the keys are maintained in a string space, a vector of characters.  More information on string spaces is given in Sec. 2-4.  Instead of an element in a node containing the key itself, as in the previous trie structure, a string descriptor which contains the address of the key in string space and the length of the key must be maintained.  Consequently, each element in an *m*-ary node can be either a pointer to another trie node, a pointer to a binary tree node, or a string descriptor giving the address and length of the key being stored in the string space.  Similarly, the nodes in the binary tree portion of the trie can have two possible makeups.  A nonleaf node contains a left pointer, a right pointer, and a string descriptor.  A leaf node contains only a string descriptor.

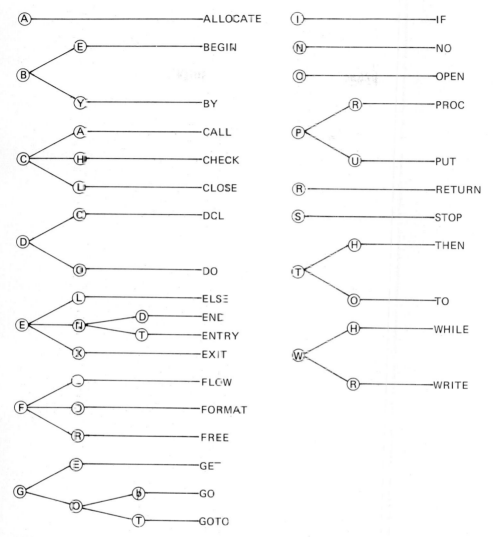

**FIGURE 6-2.19**  A forest representation of the trie given in Table 6-2.2.

**Exercises for Sec. 6-2.3.4**

1. Create an Algorithm TRIE_DELETE which deletes a key from a trie structure as shown in Table 6-2.2.
2. Another representation for a trie is using linked lists to replace the the columns of the trie. Create an insertion algorithm to enter a key in this new structure.
3. Create a search algorithm which searches the structure mentioned in Prob. 2.
4. Create a deletion algorithm to delete a key from the structure mentioned in Prob. 2.
5. Based on the discussion of a trie illustrated in Fig. 6-2.19 give Pascal declarations for this trie structure.

6.  Write a Pascal procedure to perform an insertion based on the declarations obtained in Prob. 5.
7.  Repeat Prob. 6 for a deletion from the trie structure.

### 6-2.4  Hash-Table Methods

The best search method introduced so far (binary search) has a search time which is proportional to $\log_2 n$  for a table of $n$ entries.  In this section we investigate a class of search techniques whose search times can be independent of the number of entries in a table.  To achieve this goal, we must use an entirely new approach to searching.  With this approach, the position of a particular entry in the table is determined by the value of the key for that entry.  This association is realized through the use of a hashing function.  The basic notions of this approach were briefly introduced in Sec. 4-3.2, and subsequently used in Sec. 5-5.4 where topological sorting is presented.  Also recall that in Sec. 6-1.8, a hashing function was used for address-calculation sorting.

The notions and concepts of this new approach are first discussed.  General simple hashing functions are then introduced.  Unfortunately, more than one key can be mapped into the same table position.  In such a case, collisions are said to occur.  These collisions must be resolved using a collision-resolution technique.  Two broad classes of such techniques are examined.

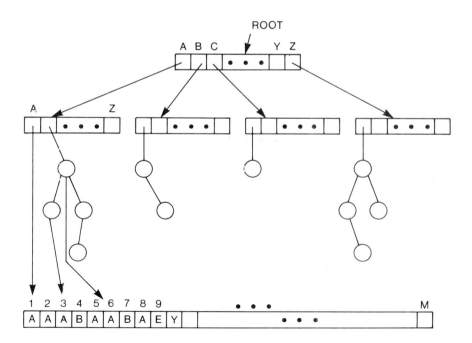

**FIGURE 6-2.20**

### 6-2.4.1 Introduction

The best search method introduced so far is the binary-search technique, which has a search time of $O(\log_2 n)$. The search techniques discussed so far are based exclusively on comparing keys. Another approach, however, is to compute the location of the desired record. The nature of this computation depends on the key set (or space) and the memory-space requirements of the particular table. For example, if we have a table of $n$ employee records, each of which is identified by an employee number key whose value lies between 1 and $n$, the key value of a particular employee, used as a subscript, directly locates the employee in question. Such a convenient key-location relationship rarely exists in real-world applications. This is so because key values are chosen for many reasons, most of which are unrelated to efficient computer processing goals.

For example, in a symbol-table application involving FORTRAN, the key space involves all the valid variable names in that language. This name space has a size of

$$26 + 26 \times 36 + 26 \times 36^2 + \cdots + 26 \times 36^5 \approx 1.6 \times 10^9$$

that is, 26 names of one letter, $26 \times 36$ names of two characters, and so on. For a typical program, this name space is associated with a table space of perhaps 100 or 200 record locations. Consequently, the problem of directly associating a key with the storage location of its associated record in a search is more difficult.

Formally, this *key-to-address transformation* problem is defined as a mapping or a *hashing function* H, which maps the key space (K) into an address space (A). That is, given a key value, a hashing function H produces a table address or location of the corresponding record. The function generates this address by performing some simple arithmetical or logical operations on the key or some part of the key.

Since, as previously indicated, the key space is usually much larger than the address space, many keys will be matched to the same address. Such a many-to-one mapping results in *collisions* between records. A collision-resolution technique is required to resolve these collisions.

Hashing functions fall into two classes, namely, distribution-independent and distribution-dependent functions. A distribution-independent hashing function does not use the distribution of the keys of a table in computing the position of a record. A distribution-dependent hashing function, on the other hand, is obtained by examining the subset of keys corresponding to known records.

In the next subsection we examine some of the most popular distribution-independent hashing functions. Distribution-dependent hashing functions will be discussed in Chap. 7. The collision-resolution problem is examined in a subsequent subsection. The most important operations which are performed on hash tables are those of access and retrieval.

### 6-2.4.2 Hashing Functions

In this subsection we examine several simple hashing functions. Some of the desirable properties of a hashing function include speed and the generation of addresses uniformly. Before describing these functions, however, we introduce the notion of preconditioning as it relates to the key space K. Each element of K often contains alphanumeric characters. Some of these characters may be arithmetically or logically difficult to manipulate. It is sometimes convenient to convert such keys into a form which can be more easily manipulated by a hashing function. This conversion process is often called *preconditioning*. As an example, let us consider the preconditioning of the key RATE1. One possibility is to encode the letters as the numbers 11, 12, ..., 36 and the set of special symbols (for example, +, -, *, /, ...) as 37, 38, 39, .... Using this approach, RATE1 is encoded as 2811301501 (that is, the symbols R, A, T, E, and 1 are replaced by the integers 28, 11, 30, 15, 01, respectively).

Preconditioning is most efficiently performed by using the numerically coded internal representation (for example, EBCDIC or ASCII) of each character in the key. For example, in ASCII, the key A1 is binary-encoded as 1000001 0110001. Interpreted as a 14-digit binary number, this has a decimal equivalent of 8,369. Similarly, the EBCDIC representation of A1 is binary-encoded as 11000001 11110001 or 49,649. In general, the preconditioned result of a key may not fit into a word of memory. In such instances we can ignore certain digits of the preconditioned result. Another approach is to use a hashing function which performs a size-reduction transformation. Frequently, one hashing function generates the preconditioned result, and then a second function maps this result into a table location.

We now proceed to describe seven simple hashing functions. Other more complex functions exist, but they are not generally used with tables that are stored entirely in the main memory of the computer.

## THE DIVISION METHOD

One of the first hashing functions, and perhaps the most widely accepted, is the *division method*, which is defined as

$$H(x) = x \bmod m + 1$$

for some integer divisor m. The operator mod denotes the modulo arithmetic system. In this system the term x mod m has a value which is equal to the remainder of dividing x by m. For example, if x = 35 and m = 11, then

$$H(35) = 35 \bmod 11 + 1 = 2 + 1 = 3$$

The division method yields a "hash value" which belongs to the set $\{1, 2, ..., m\}$.

In mapping keys to addresses, the division method preserves, to a certain extent, the uniformity that exists in a key set. Keys which are close to each other or clustered are mapped to unique addresses. For example, for a divisor m = 31, the keys 1000, 10001, ..., 1010 are mapped to the addresses 9, 10, ..., and 19. This preservation of uniformity, however, is a disadvantage if two or more clusters are mapped to the same addresses. For example, if another cluster of keys is 2300, 2301, ..., and 2313, then these keys are mapped to addresses 7, 8, ..., and 20, and there are many collisions with keys from the cluster starting at 1000. The reason for this phenomenon is that keys in the two clusters yield the same remainder when divided by m = 31.

In general, it is uncommon for a number of keys to yield the same remainder when m is a large prime number. In practice it has been found that odd divisors without factors less than 20 are also satisfactory. In particular, divisors which are even numbers are to be avoided since even and odd keys would be mapped to odd and even addresses, respectively (assuming an address space of $\{1, 2, ..., m\}$).

## THE MIDSQUARE METHOD

Another hashing function which has been widely used in many applications is the *midsquare method*. In this method a key is multiplied by itself and the address is obtained by selecting an appropriate number of bits or digits from the middle of the square. Usually, the number of bits or digits chosen depends on the table size and, consequently, can fit into one computer word of memory. The same positions in the square must be used for all products. As an example, consider a six-digit key, 123456. Squaring this key results in the value 15241383936. If a three-digit address is required, positions 5 to 7 could be chosen, giving address 138. The midsquare method has been criticized by some, but it has given good results when applied to certain key sets.

## THE FOLDING METHOD

In the *folding* method a key is partioned into a number of parts, each of which has the same length as the required address with the possible exception of the last part. The parts are then added together, ignoring the final carry, to form an address. If the keys are in binary form, the "exclusive-or" operation may be substituted for addition. As an example, assume that the key 356942781 is to be transformed into a three-digit address. In the *fold-shifting method*, 356, 942, and 781 are added to yield 079. A variation of the basic method involves the reversal of the digits in the outermost partitions. This variation is called the *fold-boundary method*. In the previous example, 653, 942, and 187 are added together, yielding 782. Folding is a hashing function which is also useful in converting multiword keys into a single word so that other hashing functions can be used.

## DIGIT ANALYSIS

A hashing function referred to as *digit analysis* forms addresses by selecting and shifting digits or bits of the original key. This hashing function is in a sense distribution-dependent. For example, a key 7546123 is transformed to the address 2164 by selecting digits in positions 3 to 6 and reversing their order. For a given key set, the same positions in the key and the same rearrangement pattern must be used consistently. Initially, an analysis on a sample of the key set is performed to determine which key positions should be used in forming an address. Digit positions having the most uniform distributions (that is, the smallest peaks and valleys) are selected. As an example, consider the digit analysis of the sample key set shown in Table 6-2.2. A total of 5,000 ten-digit keys are analyzed to determine which key positions should be used in forming addresses in the address space {0, 1, .., 9999}. Positions 2, 4, 5, and 9 have the most uniform distribution of digits, so they are selected. For example, a key 1234567890 is transformed to the address 9542 by selecting digits in positions 2, 4, 5, and 9, and by reversing their order. This hashing transformation technique has been used in conjunction with static key sets (that is, key sets that do not change over time).

## THE LENGTH-DEPENDENT METHOD

Another hashing technique which has been commonly used in table-handling applications is called the *length-dependent method*. In this method the length of the key is used along with some portion of the key to produce either a table address directly or, more commonly, an intermediate key which is used for example, with the division method to produce a final table address. One function which has produced good results sums the internal binary representation of the first and last characters and the length of the key shifted left four binary places (or, equivalently, the length multiplied by 16). As an example, the key PARTNO becomes 215 + 214 + (6 × 16) = 525 assuming EBCDIC representation. If we treat 525 as an intermediate key and apply the division method with a divisor of **49**, then the resulting address is 36.

## ALGEBRAIC CODING

A hashing method called *algebraic coding* is a cluster-separating hashing function based on algebraic coding theory.   An r-bit key $(k_1 k_2 \cdots k_r)_2$ is considered as a polynomial

$$K(x) = \sum_{i=1}^{r} k_i x^{i-1}$$

If an address in the range 0 to $m = 2^t - 1$ is required, then a polynomial

$$P(x) = x^t + \sum_{i=1}^{t} p_i x^{i-1}$$

is used to divide $K(x)$.  The remainder

$$K(x) \bmod (P(x)) = \sum_{i=1}^{t} h_i x^{i-1}$$

obtained using polynomial arithmetic modulo 2 gives the address $(h_1 h_2 \cdots h_t)_2$.
    Knuth (1973) states that for $r = 15$ and $t = 10$, the divisor polynomial

$$P(x) = x^{10} + x^8 + x^5 + x^4 + x^2 + x + 1$$

will result in a hashing function H such that   $H(y_1)$   and $H(y_2)$   are unequal if   $y_1$ and $y_2$   are distinct binary represented keys different in at most six bit positions. Algebraic coding was originally proposed for implementation in hardware rather than in software.

**TABLE 6-2.3**  Digit Analysis of a Sample Set of 10-Digit Part Numbers

| | Key Position | | | | | | | | | |
|---|---|---|---|---|---|---|---|---|---|---|
| Digit | 1 | 2 | 3 | 4 | 5 | 6 | 7 | 8 | 9 | 10 |
| 0 | 5000 | 531 | 594 | 499 | 590 | 721 | 1565 | 1133 | 562 | 2540 |
| 1 | 0 | 582 | 568 | 536 | 467 | 905 | 874 | 759 | 612 | 1581 |
| 2 | 0 | 571 | 620 | 531 | 563 | 553 | 657 | 606 | 542 | 557 |
| 3 | 0 | 546 | 565 | 511 | 512 | 277 | 555 | 482 | 522 | 332 |
| 4 | 0 | 518 | 529 | 495 | 461 | 0 | 284 | 521 | 546 | 0 |
| 5 | 0 | 503 | 503 | 500 | 463 | 673 | 276 | 469 | 472 | 0 |
| 6 | 0 | 488 | 456 | 469 | 510 | 629 | 263 | 296 | 426 | 0 |
| 7 | 0 | 449 | 411 | 500 | 459 | 0 | 212 | 365 | 425 | 0 |
| 8 | 0 | 422 | 431 | 470 | 457 | 501 | 159 | 310 | 455 | 0 |
| 9 | 0 | 390 | 323 | 489 | 518 | 741 | 155 | 59 | 438 | 0 |

## MULTIPLICATIVE HASHING

Knott (1975) and Knuth claim that another method, the multiplicative hashing function, is quite useful. For a nonnegative integral key x and constant c such that $0 < c < 1$, the function is

$$H(x) = \lfloor m(cx \bmod 1) \rfloor + 1$$

Here cx mod 1 is the fractional part of cx and $\lfloor \ \rfloor$ denotes the greatest integer less than or equal to its contents. This multiplicative hashing function should give good results if the constant c is properly chosen—a choice which is difficult to make.

Knott (1975), Lum et al. (1971), Lordon (1973), Knuth (1973), and Buchholz (1963) present studies of these hashing functions which have been briefly described. Although some of these methods often give a uniform distribution of keys over addresses, it is still necessary to experiment with hashing functions as applied to specific key sets. A performance measure is needed to compare different hashing functions, and the measure most widely adopted is the average length of search (ALOS). For a set of records in a direct file, it is the average number of accesses to the storage device required to retrieve a record. Usually, the best hashing function for use with a particular set of keys minimizes the ALOS. Note that there are other factors beside hashing functions to be considered in minimizing ALOS, as discussed in the following subsections.

Thus far we have described how to perform key-to-address transformations using hashing functions. We have, however, ignored a very important aspect relevant to this process— the problem of colliding records. In general, a hashing function is a many-to-one mapping; that is, many keys can be transformed into the same address. In practice, such a phenomenon happens because there are many more keys than there are addresses. Clearly, two records cannot occupy the same position in a table. Consequently, such collisions among keys must be resolved. We now turn our attention to this problem.

### 6-2.4.3 Collision-Resolution Techniques

As mentioned earlier, a hashing function can, in general, map several keys into the same address. When this situation arises, the colliding records must be sorted and accessed as determined by a *collision-resolution technique*. There are two broad classes of such techniques: open addressing and chaining. In this subsection we formulate algorithms from both classes. Also, we examine certain variations of these basic techniques.

The general objective of a collision-resolution technique is to attempt to place colliding records elsewhere in the table. This requires the investigation of a series of table positions until an empty one is found to accommodate a colliding record. We require a mechanism to generate the series of table positions to be examined. The main criteria for this mechanism are speed (that it determine the positions quickly), coverage (that it will try *every* table position eventually), and reproducibility (that the series produced can be produced again, namely, when it comes time to find the placed record).

With *open addressing*, if a record with key x is mapped to an address location d and this location is already occupied, then other locations in the table are examined until a free location is found for the new record. If a record with key $K_i$ is deleted, then $K_i$ is set to a special value called DELETE, which is not equal to the value of any key. The sequence in which the locations of a table are examined can be formulated in many ways. One of the simplest techniques for resolving collisions is to use the following sequence of locations for a table of m entries:

   d, d + 1, ..., m − 1, m, 1, 2, ..., d − 1

An unoccupied record location is always found if at least one is available; otherwise, the search halts unsuccessfully after scanning m locations. When retrieving a particular record, the same sequence of locations is examined until that record is found or until an unoccupied (or empty) record position is encountered. In this latter case the desired record is not in the table, so the search fails. This collision-resolution technique is called *linear probing*.

   We now formulate an algorithm which performs the table-lookup and insertion operations for a hashed table using the linear probing technique just described. The record to be inserted or located is identified by the key argument X, any other information to be inserted is denoted by **INFO**, and the type of information (lookup or insertion) to be performed is specified by the logical parameter **INSERT**. Values of *true* and *false* indicate the insert and lookup operations, respectively. Furthermore, it is assumed that if a record location never contained a record, then the corresponding key field has a special value called **EMPTY**. A general algorithm for table insertion and lookup using linear probing is as follows.

1.   Calculate the initial position using a hash function
2.   Repeat thru step 4 to examine all locations in the table
3.   If the current location contains the key
       then if not inserting into the table
           then return position of record
           else return error in insertion
4.   If the current location is empty or has a deleted value
       then if inserting into the table
           then insert the record and return its position
           else if the location is empty
               then return error in lookup
5.   Write overflow or lookup error and return

The detailed algorithm we now give is in the form of a function.


**Function**   OPENLP(X, INFO, INSERT). Given the parameters X, INFO, and INSERT introduced earlier, this function performs the table lookup or insertion operations. The function returns the position of the record in question, if successful. Otherwise, an error condition is signaled by a negated position. The hashing function HASH is used to calculate an initial position.

1.   [Calculate initial position]
       d ← HASH(X)
2.   [Perform indicated operation if location is found]
       Repeat for i = d, d + 1, ..., m − 1, m, 1, 2, ..., d − 1
           If X = $K_i$
           then    If not INSERT
                       then    Return(i)    (position of retrieved record)
                       else    Return(−i)    (error in insertion)
           If  $K_i$ = EMPTY or $K_i$ = DELETE
           then    If INSERT
                       then    (perform indicated insertion)

$$K_i \leftarrow X$$
$$DATA_i \leftarrow INFO$$
Return(i)

else     If $K_i$ = EMPTY

then   Return(−i)   (error in lookup)

3.   [Table Overflow]

Write('OVERFLOW OR LOOK-UP ERROR')

Return(0)                                                □

In step 1 an initial position in the table is calculated. Any of the hashing functions which were discussed in the previous subsection can be used in this step. The second step scans the table starting at an initial position d. If the key field and the search argument (X) match, then the table position is returned in the case of a lookup operation. For an insertion, the negated index is returned, indicating that an attempt has been made to insert a duplicate key. If position i of the table is either empty or contains a deleted record, then the new record is entered in this position during an insert operation. On the other hand, an empty location encountered during a lookup operation indicates that the given search key is not in the table. In this case a negated position index is returned. Step 3 indicates that either no record locations are available or that the lookup operation fails. Such a failure is indicated by returning a value of 0.

As an example, let us assume the following:

The name NODE is mapped into 1
The name STORAGE is mapped into 2
The names AN and ADD are mapped into 3
The names FUNCTION, B, BRAND, and PARAMETER are mapped into 9

Assume that the insertions are performed in the following order:

NODE, STORAGE, AN, ADD, FUNCTION, B, BRAND, and PARAMETER

|  |  |  | Number of Probes |
|---|---|---|---|
| $R_1$ | NODE | ///// | 1 |
| $R_2$ | STORAGE | ///// | 1 |
| $R_3$ | AN | ///// | 1 |
| $R_4$ | ADD | ///// | 2 |
| $R_5$ | PARAMETER | ///// | 8 |
| $R_6$ | Empty | | |
| $R_7$ | Empty | | |
| $R_8$ | Empty | | |
| $R_9$ | FUNCTION | ///// | 1 |
| $R_{10}$ | B | ///// | 2 |
| $R_{11}$ | BRAND | ///// | 3 |

**FIGURE 6-2.21**   Collision resolution by using open addressing.

Figure 6-2.21 represents the resulting structure with m = 11. The first three keys are each placed in a single probe, but then ADD must go into position 4 instead of 3, which is already occupied. FUNCTION is placed in position 9 in one probe, but B and BRAND take two and three probes, respectively. Finally, PARAMETER ends up in position 5 after eight probes, since positions 9, 10, 11, 1, 2, 3, and 4 are occupied. A search is completed successfully when the key x is found, or unsuccessfully if an empty record location is encountered. Steps 1 and 3 remain unchanged, so the same comments apply.

Each time that step 2 of Function OPENLP is executed for either insertion or retrieval, one comparison is required. For a table of n records, if all records are stored or retrieved, then the number of times that step 2 is executed divided by n is the ALOS. Knuth gives a probabilistic model for analyzing collision-resolution techniques and develops formulas for the expected average length of a successful search (E[ALOS]) in the case of open addressing. The model assumes that each key has probability $1/m$ of being mapped to each of the m addresses in the table. Therefore, there are $m^n$ ways of mapping keys to the address space.

The ratio $\alpha = n / m$ is known as the *load factor*. E[ALOS] is dependent on the load factor. With n and m as defined previously, Knuth derives the following formulas:

$$E[ALOS] \approx \begin{cases} \dfrac{1}{2}(1 + \dfrac{1}{1 - \alpha}) & \text{for a successful search} \\[2ex] \dfrac{1}{2}(1 + \dfrac{1}{(1 - \alpha)^2}) & \text{for an unsuccessful search} \end{cases}$$

Table 6-2.4 gives representative values for these formulas with a number of different load factors. For a uniformly distributed set of keys, the linear probing technique performs reasonably well when compared to the linear- and binary-search techniques, provided that the table is not too full. That is, the ratio of the number of records being entered (n) to the table size (m) must be less than approximately 0.8. For higher load factors, the linear probe degenerates rapidly. This phenomenon is due to the increased number of collisions as more records are being stored in the table.

The linear probe method of collision resolution has a number of drawbacks. In particular, deletions from the table are difficult to perform. The strategy used here was to have a special table entry with a value of DELETE to denote the deletion of that entry. Such an approach enables the table to be searched in a proper way. As an example, let us assume that the record with key FUNCTION is marked for deletion by assigning a value of DELETE to $K_9$. Now, if we desire to retrieve the record with a key value BRAND, the previously stated algorithm still behaves properly. The question which arises is: Why use a special value such as DELETE to denote deleted entries? If this approach were not used, duplicate entries could occur in the table. For example, in the previous case, our algorithm would find an empty location in position 9 and would assume that BRAND was not in the table. It would then proceed to insert a duplicate copy for BRAND. It is possible to formulate a deletion algorithm which performs deletions immediately by moving records, if necessary. Such an algorithm eliminates the necessity for having records with a value of DELETE. In other words, a record position can be either occupied or

**Table 6-2.4**  $E[ALOS]$ for linear probing.

| Load factor | Number of Probes | |
|---|---|---|
| $\alpha$ | Successful | Unsuccessful |
| .10 | 1.056 | 1.118 |
| .20 | 1.125 | 1.281 |
| .30 | 1.214 | 1.520 |
| .40 | 1.333 | 1.889 |
| .50 | 1.500 | 2.500 |
| .60 | 1.750 | 3.625 |
| .70 | 2.167 | 6.060 |
| .80 | 3.000 | 13.000 |
| .90 | 5.500 | 50.500 |
| .95 | 10.500 | 200.500 |

empty. This approach is not taken, however, because better collision-resolution techniques (based on linked-allocation) are available.

Another drawback of the linear probe method is caused by *clustering* effects, whose severity increases as the table becomes full. This phenomenon is observed by considering a trace of Fig. 6-2.21, which shows the state of the table after performing each insertion. This trace is given in Fig. 6-2.22. When the first insertion is made, the probability of a new element being inserted in a particular position is clearly 1/11. For the second insertion, however, the probability that position 2 will become occupied is twice as likely as any remaining available position namely, the entry will be placed in position 2 if the key is mapped into either 1 or 2. Continuing in this manner, on the fifth insertion the probability that the new entry will be placed in position 5 is five times as likely as its being placed in any remaining unoccupied position. Thus, the trend is for long sequences of occupied positions to become longer. Such a phenomenon is called *primary clustering*.

The detrimental effect of primary clustering can be reduced by selecting a different probing technique. Such a technique exists and is called *random probing*. This method generates a random sequence of positions rather than an ordered sequence as was the case in the linear probing method. The random sequence generated in this fashion must contain every position between 1 and $m$ exactly once. A table is full when the first duplicate position is generated. An example of a random-number generator that produces such a random sequence of position numbers is the statement

$$y \leftarrow (y + c) \bmod m$$

where y is the initial position number of the random sequence and c and m are integers that are relatively prime to each other (that is, their greatest common divisor is 1). For example, assuming that m = 11 and c = 5, the previous statement, starting with an initial value of 2, generates the sequence 7, 1, 6, 0, 5, 10, 4, 9, 3, 8,

After inserting record    Contents of table after insertion

| After inserting record | Contents of table after insertion | | | | | | | | |
|---|---|---|---|---|---|---|---|---|---|
| NODE | NODE | | | | | | | | |
| STORAGE | NODE | STORAGE | | | | | | | |
| AN | NODE | STORAGE | AN | | | | | | |
| ADD | NODE | STORAGE | AN | ADD | | | | | |
| FUNCTION | NODE | STORAGE | AN | ADD | | FUNCTION | | | |
| B | NODE | STORAGE | AN | ADD | | FUNCTION | B | | |
| BRAND | NODE | STORAGE | AN | ADD | | FUNCTION | B | | BRAND |
| PARAMETER | NODE | STORAGE | AN | ADD | PARAMETER | FUNCTION | B | | BRAND |

**FIGURE 6-2.22**

and 2. Adding 1 to each number of this sequence transforms all numbers so that they belong to the interval [1, 11]. We can now formulate a general algorithm which incorporates random probing to insert a value into a table.

1. Calculate the initial position using a hashing function
2. If the initial calculated position is empty or the value has been deleted then insert the key and return
3. Repeat thru step 5 until the first open location is found
4. Calculate the next position using random probing
5. If all positions in the table have been examined then write overflow and return
6. Insert the key and return

A detailed algorithm for this function is now presented


**Function**  OPENRP(X, INFO). Given a record identified by a key X, this function inserts the corresponding INFO into a table represented by the structure R. The hashing function HASH is used to calculate an initial address. C and M are integers relatively prime to each other used for random probing. DELETE and EMPTY serve the same purpose as they did in Algorithm OPENLP.

1. [Calculate the initial position]
   $D \leftarrow HASH(X)$
2. [Perform first probe]
   If $K[D] = EMPTY$ or $K[D] = DELETE$
   then   $K[D] \leftarrow X$
          $DATA[D] \leftarrow INFO$
          Return(D)
3. [Initiate further search]
   $Y \leftarrow D - 1$
   $Y \leftarrow (Y + C) \bmod M$
   $J \leftarrow Y + 1$
   If $J = D$
   then   Write('OVERFLOW')
          Return(0)
4. [Find first open place]
   Repeat step 5 while $K[J] \neq EMPTY$ and $K[J] \neq DELETE$
5. [Scan next entry]
   $Y \leftarrow (Y + C) \bmod M$
   $J \leftarrow Y + 1$
   If $J = D$
   then   Write('OVERFLOW')
          Return(0)
6. [Finished]
   $K[J] \leftarrow X$
   $DATA[J] \leftarrow INFO$
   Return(J)                                                        ☐

The deletion problem becomes more severe with random probing than is the case with linear probing. Therefore, if a table is subjected to many deletions, random probing should not be used.

Although random probing has alleviated the problem of primary clustering, we have not eliminated all types of clustering. In particular, clustering occurs when two keys are hashed into the same value. In such an instance, the same sequence of positions is generated for both keys by the random probe method. The clustering phenomenon is called *secondary clustering*.

One approach to alleviating this secondary clustering problem is to have a second hashing function, independent of the first, select the parameter c in the random probing method. For example, let us assume that $H_1$ is the first hashing function, with $H_1(x_1) = H_1(x_2) = i$ for $x_1 \neq x_2$ where i is the hash value. Now, if we have a second hashing function, $H_2$, such that $H_2(x_1) \neq H_2(x_2)$ when $x_1 \neq x_2$ and $H_1(x_1) = H_1(x_2)$, we can use $H_2(x_1)$ or $H_2(x_2)$ as the value of parameter c in the random probe method. The two random sequences generated by this scheme are different when $H_2$ and $H_1$ are independent. The effects of secondary clustering can, therefore, be curtailed. This variation of open addressing is called *double hashing* (of *rehashing*).

As an example of this method, let

$$H_1(x) = x \bmod m \text{ and } H_2(x) = (x \bmod (m - 2)) + 1$$

for a key x and table size m. For a table size m = 11 and a key value x = 75, $H_1(75) = 9$ and $H_2(75) = 4$. Now, the repeated application of the statement

$$y \leftarrow (y + c) \bmod 11$$

with y = 9 and c = 4 produces the sequence

9, 2, 6, 10, 3, 7, 0, 4, 8, 1, 5

Next, if we choose a key having a value of 42, then

$$H_1(42) = 9 \quad \text{[the same value as } H_1(75) \text{, but } H_2(42) = 7 \text{]}$$

The repeated application of the statement

$$y \leftarrow (y + c) \bmod 11$$

with y = 9 and c = 7, yields the sequence

9, 5, 1, 8, 4, 0, 7, 3, 10, 6, 2

Note that even though $H_1(75) = H_1(42) = 9$, the two random sequences generated are different.

The average length of search for a double hashing technique where $H_1$ and $H_2$ are independent is given by the following pairs of formulas:

$$E[ALOS] \approx \begin{cases} -\dfrac{1}{\alpha} \ln(1 - \alpha) \text{ for a successful search} \\ \\ \dfrac{1}{1 - \alpha} \text{ for an unsuccessful search} \end{cases}$$

Table 6-2.5 gives a summary of representative values for a double hashing method. This technique outperforms the linear probing method, especially as the table becomes full. For example, when a table is 95 per cent full, the average number of probes for the linear probe method is 10.5, while for the double hashing method it is 3.2—a significant improvement!

**Table 6-2.5**  E[ALOS] for random probing with double hashing.

| Load factor | Number of Probes | |
|:---:|:---:|:---:|
| $\alpha$ | Successful | Unsuccessful |
| .10 | 1.054 | 1.111 |
| .20 | 1.116 | 1.250 |
| .30 | 1.189 | 1.429 |
| .40 | 1.277 | 1.667 |
| .50 | 1.386 | 2.000 |
| .60 | 1.527 | 2.500 |
| .70 | 1.720 | 3.333 |
| .80 | 2.012 | 5.000 |
| .90 | 2.558 | 10.000 |
| .95 | 3.153 | 20.000 |

In summary, there are three main difficulties with the open addressing method of collision resolution. First, lists of colliding records for different hash values become intermixed. This phenomenon requires, on the average, more probes. Second, we are unable to handle a table overflow situation in a satisfactory manner. On detecting an overflow, the entire table must be reorganized. The overflow problem cannot be ignored in many table applications where table space requirements can vary drastically. Finally, the physical deletion of records is difficult. We now turn to linked-allocation techniques to resolve these problems.

One of the most popular methods of handling overflow records is called *separate chaining*. In this method the colliding records are chained into a special *overflow area* which is distinct from the *prime area*. This area contains that part of the table into which records are initially hashed. A separate linked list is maintained for each set of colliding records. Therefore, a pointer field is required for each record in the primary and overflow areas. Figure 6-2.23 shows a separate chaining representation of the sample keys used earlier in this subsection. with m = 11 and n = 9. The keys are assumed to be inserted in the order

NODE, STORAGE, AN, ADD, FUNCTION, B, BRAND, and PARAMETER

Note that the colliding records in each linked list are not kept in alphabetical order. When a new colliding record is entered in the overflow area, it is placed at the front of those records in the appropriate linked list of the overflow area.

A useful and more efficient representation of the separate chaining technique involves the use of an intermediate table or hash table. Figure 6-2.24 illustrates how a hash table is used, assuming the same keys, hashing function. and collision-resolution technique as in Fig. 6-2.23. Note that in this representation all the records reside in the overflow area while the prime area contains only pointers. For a table having large records, this approach results in a densely packed overflow area. Furthermore. the hash table whose entries are pointers can be made large without wasting very much storage.

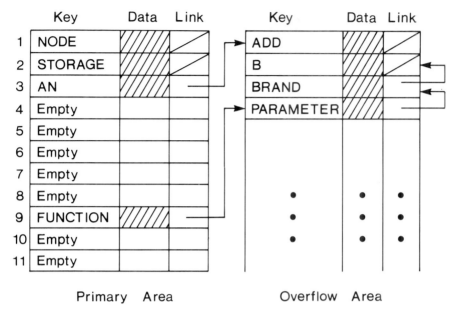

**FIGURE 6-2.23**

An algorithm for entering a key into an existing structure such as that of Fig. 6-2.24 is easily realized. Given a key X, which is to be entered if it is not already in the table, we first proceed to obtain its hash value. The hash table value for this hash value can then be examined. A value of NULL in this position indicates that the corresponding linked list is empty. Therefore, we can insert the given key into an empty list. If, however, the particular linked list in question is not empty, we can search this linked list for the presence of the given key. If the search fails, X becomes the front entry of the updated linked list. An algorithm to perform this function was given in Sec. 4-3.2.

The average length of search for separate chaining is given as follows:

$$E[ALOS] \approx \begin{cases} 1 + \dfrac{\alpha}{2} & \text{for a successful search} \\ \alpha + e^{-\alpha} & \text{for an unsuccessful search} \end{cases}$$

Representative values for this method are given in Table 6-2.6. Note that it is desirable to make the load factor as small as possible. This can be achieved by making m large. This will, however, make many of the lists empty, and space will be wasted for their list heads. Although additional storage is required to store the links using this resolution technique, its performance and versatility make it far superior to open addressing when volatile tables are involved. Furthermore, the performance formulas given hold for $\alpha > 1$!

In terminating this subsection we want to stress the importance of having a suitable hashing function. Ideally, each linked list of colliding records should have the same number of entries. The worst possible case occurs when all keys are mapped to the same hash number (that is, the same linked list), thereby causing the

**Table 6-2.6  E[ALOS] with separate chaining.**

| Load factor | Number of Probes | |
|---|---|---|
| $\alpha$ | Successful | Unsuccessful |
| .10 | 1.050 | 1 005 |
| .20 | 1.100 | 1 019 |
| .30 | 1.150 | 1 041 |
| .40 | 1.200 | 1 070 |
| .50 | 1.250 | 1 107 |
| .60 | 1.300 | 1 149 |
| .70 | 1.350 | 1 197 |
| .80 | 1.400 | 1 249 |
| .90 | 1.450 | 1.307 |
| .95 | 1.475 | 1.337 |

insertion and search operations to be no more efficient than those in a linear search method. In practice it is a nontrivial matter to obtain a good hashing function, since the size of the linked lists of colliding records which it induces depends on the keys being used.

Another important factor pertaining to the efficiency of the separate chaining method of collision resolution is the desirability of keeping the number of records in each linked list relatively small. For example, a hash table of 100 entries would nicely handle 125 records in the overflow area. The average number of comparisons (assuming a uniformly distributed hashing function) for accessing a particular entry in such a situation is slightly greater than 1. From this observation it is clear that the search time in such a table organization is independent of the number of entries in the table.

Finally, since our discussion has been concerned with internal tables (that is, tables that are stored in memory at one time), the hashing function which is used should be simple. The response time to insert or fetch a particular entry is the sum of the times taken to evaluate the hashing function and to perform the indicated operation. It may be more efficient to allow a greater number of comparisons for performing a table operation if a significant reduction in the complexity of the hashing function results.

The ideas introduced so far relate to searching, but the same ideas apply to sorting as well. This possibility was discussed in Sec. 6-1.8, which dealt with address calculation sorting.

## Exercises for Sec. 6-2.4

1. Using the division method of hashing with $m = 101$, obtain the hash values for the following set of keys:

   PAY
   AGE

RATE
NUMBER

Assume an EBCDIC representation of the keys.

2.  Repeat Prob. 1 for the ASCII representation of the keys.

3.  Assuming an open addressing method of collision resolution with linear prob-
    ing, obtain the hash table (as in Fig. 6-2.22) for the following set of keys:

    The names **PAY** and **RATE** are mapped into 1

    The name **TAX** is mapped into 2

    The name **PENSION** is mapped into 4

    The names **DEDUCT, STATUS, DEPENDENTS, SEX,** and **SALARIED** are
    mapped into 8

    Use the division method of hashing with **m** = 11. Also, assume that the inser-
    tions are performed in the following order:

    PAY, RATE, TAX, PENSION, DEDUCT, STATUS, DEPENDENTS, SEX,
    and SALARIED.

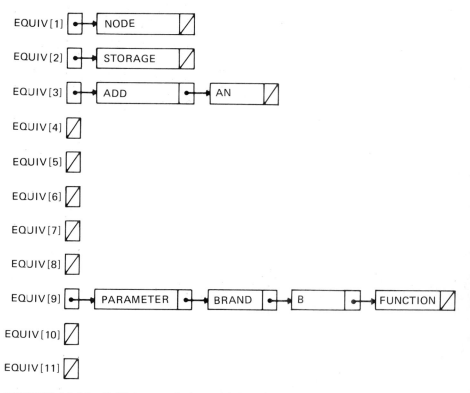

**FIGURE 6-2.24**   Collision resolution with independent chaining.

4. Formulate an algorithm, based on the linear probe method, for deleting a record from a hash table. This algorithm is not to use a special value of **DELETE**. That is, each record position is to be either occupied or empty.

One approach that can be used is first to mark the deleted record as empty. An ordered search is then made for the next empty position. If a record, say y, is found whose hash value is not between the position of the record just marked for deletion and that of the present empty position, then record y can be moved to replace the deleted record. Then the position for record y is marked as empty and the entire process is repeated, starting at the position occupied by y.

5. What happens in Function OPENLP if step 3 is replaced by ← (i + c) mod m + 1? Will this change improve the clustering problem?

6. Trace Function OPENRP for the same sequence of names used in the text.

7. Obtain a searching algorithm based on double hashing.

8. Discuss the problems encountered in the formulation of a deletor algorithm when double hashing is used.

9. Formulate an algorithm for separate chaining where each equivalence class is to be represented as a tree structure, rather than as a one-way chain.

## BIBLIOGRAPHY

ADEL'SON-VEL'SKII, G. M., and E. M. LANDIS: An Algorithm for the Organization of Information, *Dokl. Akad. Nauk SSSR, Mathemat.,* vol. 146, no. 2, pp. 263-266, 1962.

AHO, A. V., J. E. HOPCROFT, and J. D. ULLMAN: "Data Structures and Algorithms," Addison-Wesley Publishing Co., Inc., Reading, Mass., 1983.

AHO, A. V., J. E. HOPCROFT, and J. D. ULLMAN: "The Design and Analysis of Computer Algorithms," Addison-Wesley Publishing Co., Inc., Reading, Mass., 1974.

BERZTISS, A. T.: "Data Structures: Theory and Practice " 2d ed., Academic Press, Inc., New York, 1975.

BROOKS, F. P., and K. E. IVERSON: "Automatic Data Processing System/360 Edition." John Wiley and Sons, Inc., New York, 1969.

BUCHHOLZ, WERNER: File Organization and Addressing, *IBM Systems Journal,* vol. 2, pp. 86-110, June, 1963.

ELSON, MARK: "Data Structures," Science Research Associates, Inc., Palo Alto, California, 1975.

FLORES, IVAN: "Computer Sorting," Prentice-Hall, Inc., Englewood Cliffs, N.J., 1969.

FLOYD, R. W.: Algorithm 245, Treesort 3, *Communications of the ACM.* vol. 7, no. 12, p. 701, December, 1964.

HARRISON, M. C.: "Data Structures and Programming," Scott, Foresman and Company, Glenview, Illinois, 1973.

HOARE, C. A. R.: Algorithms 63 and 64, *Communications of the ACM.* vol. 4, no. 7, p. 321, July, 1961.

ISAAC, E. J., and R. C. SINGLETON: Sorting by Address Calculation, *Journal of the ACM,* vol. 3, pp. 169-174, July, 1956.

KNOTT, GARY D.: Expandable Open-Addressing Hash-Table Storage and Retrieval, *Proceedings of the SIGFIDET Workshop on Data Description, Access, and Control,* ACM, 1971, pp. 187-206.

KNOTT, GARY D.: Hashing Functions, to be published in *The Computer Journal*, 1975.

KNUTH, D. E.: "Sorting and Searching, The Art of Computer Programming," vol. 3, pp. 506-549, Addison-Wesley Publishing Company, Inc., Reading, Mass., 1973.

KRONMAL, R. A. and M. E. TARTER: Cumulative Polygon Address Calculation Sorting, *Proceedings of the 20th National Conference of the ACM*, 1965, pp. 376-385.

LONDON, K. R.: "Techniques for Direct Access," Auerbach Publishers, Inc., Philadelphia, 1973.

LUM, V. Y.: General Performance Analysis of Key-to-Address Transformation Methods Using an Abstract File Concept, *Communications of the ACM*, vol. 16, no. 10, pp. 603-612, 1973.

MAURER, W. D.: "Programming," Holden-Day, San Fransisco, California, 1968.

MAURER, W. D., and T. G. LEWIS: Hash Table Methods, *ACM Computer Surveys*, vol. 7, no. 1, pp. 5-19, March, 1975.

MORRIS, ROBERT: Scatter Storage Techniques, *Communications of the ACM*, vol. 11, no. 1, pp. 38-44, 1968.

PETERSON, WILLIAM W.: Addressing for Random-Access Storage, *IBM Journal of Research and Development*, vol. 1, pp. 130-146, 1957.

PRICE, C. E.: Table Lookup Techniques, *ACM Computing Surveys*, vol. 3, no. 2, pp. 49-65, 1971.

STONE, H. S.: "Introduction to Computer Organization and Data Structures," McGraw-Hill Book Company, New York, 1972.

WILLIAMS, J. W. J.: Algorithm 232, Heapsort, *Communications of the ACM*, vol. 7, no. 6, pp. 347-348, June, 1964.

# FILE STRUCTURES

To this point in the text, a major portion of the discussion has dealt with the representations of and operations on data structures. The storage representations and data manipulations described applied only to data entities which were assumed to reside in main memory. There are at least two reasons why not all information that is processed by a computer should reside in an immediately accessible form of memory. First, there are some programs and data for programs which are so large as not to fit conveniently into main memory, which is typically a scarce resource in a computer system. Second, it is often desirable or necessary to store information from one execution of a program to the next (e.g., in a payroll system). Therefore, large volumes of data and archival data are commonly stored in external memory as special data-holding entities called files.

In this chapter we concentrate on file structures (i.e., the storage representations of files) and operations on files. We begin with a description of external storage devices, the media on which files normally reside. Next, some important concepts and terminology are introduced and later used in the discussion of a number of file organizations—the sequential, indexed sequential, and direct organizations. Notions related to external sorting and searching are discussed in conjunction with these file structures. Virtual memory is presented as an alternative method of handling large volumes of data. VSAM, a file organization used in conjunction with a virtual memory system, is described. Multikeyed access methods for files are examined, and finally the concepts and functions relevant to three types of data-base management systems are outlined.

## 7-1 EXTERNAL STORAGE DEVICES

The storage of information in the main or internal memory of a computer was discussed in Sec. 1-3. Any location in main memory can be accessed very quickly; a typical access time is less than 1 $\mu$sec (= $10^{-6}$ sec). Main memory provides for the immediate storage requirements of the central processor for the execution of programs, including users' programs, assemblers, compilers, and supervisory routines of the operating system.

The storage capacity of main memory is limited by two major factors—the cost of main memory and the technical problems in developing a large-capacity main memory. The storage requirements for programs and the data on which they operate exceed the capacity of main memory in virtually all computer systems. Therefore, it is necessary to extend the storage capabilities of a computer by using devices external to main memory.

An *external storage device* may be loosely defined as a device other than main memory on which information or data can be stored and from which the information can be retrieved for processing at some subsequent point in time. The storage and retrieval operations are referred to as *writing* and *reading*, respectively. External storage devices have a larger capacity and are less expensive per bit of information stored than main memory. The time required to access information, however, is much greater with these devices.

The primary uses for external storage devices include:

*1*   Backup or overlay of programs during execution
*2*   Storage of programs and subprograms for future use
*3*   Storage of information in "files"

In this chapter we are concerned with the third use, although some of the techniques may also be applied to the first and second uses.

A card reader/punch can be considered as a primitive external storage device. However, in this section we are concerned with devices that allow a more rapid transfer of data and a more convenient storage medium than punched cards. We discuss the most common external storage devices in the order of their initial development and use—magnetic-tape, drum, and disk devices. A brief description of physical characteristics as well as certain logical aspects of these devices is given. Some of the new technology relating to mass storage and intermediate storage devices is also described.

### 7-1.1 Magnetic Tapes

The first compact external storage medium to be widely used was magnetic tape. A tape is made of a plastic material coated with a ferrite substance which is easily magnetized. The physical appearance of the tape is similar to the tape used for sound recording, although computer magnetic tape is wider. Several thousand feet of tape are wound on one reel, and information is encoded on the tape character by character. A number of channels or tracks run the length of the tape, one channel being required for each bit position in the binary-coded representation of a character.

An additional channel is usually used for parity check bits. It is possible to encode several hundred characters on one inch of magnetic tape; common encoding densities are 800 and 1,600 bytes per inch. On a 3,600-foot reel of tape which stores 1,600 bytes per inch, a maximum of 1,600 bytes/inch $\times$ 12 inches/foot $\times$ 3,600

feet = 69,120,000 bytes can be stored. (Assuming one byte is used to store a character, a tape can potentially store the text of 25 books the size of this one!) We will
see, however, that this maximum is virtually impossible to achieve.

Information is read from or written on magnetic tape through the use of a
magnetic tape drive. The tape is fed past read/write heads at a typical speed of 125
inches per second. The data transfer rate for such a tape drive when information is
encoded at a density of 1,600 bytes per inch is, therefore, 200,000 bytes per second.

When a tape drive is not reading or writing information, it is in a stopped
position. When a command to read or write is issued by the processor, the tape must
be accelerated to a constant high speed. Following the completion of a read or write
command, the tape is decelerated to a stop position. During either an acceleration or
deceleration phase, a certain length of tape is passed over. This section of tape is
neither read nor written upon. It appears between successive records (groups of
data) and is called an *interrecord gap* (see Fig. 7-1.1a). An interrecord gap varies
from ½ to ¾ inch, depending on the nature of the tape unit. The greater the
number of interrecord gaps, the smaller the storage capacity of the tape. For example, suppose records consisting of 800 bytes each are written one at a time on a tape
having a density of 1,600 bytes per inch. If ½-inch interrecord gaps result, then
only ½ of that tape is used for storing data.

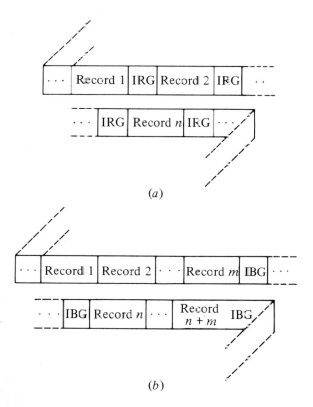

(a)

(b)

**FIGURE 7-1.1**   (a) and (b) Record layout for a magnetic tape.

To circumvent this problem, records are often grouped in *blocks*. If records are blocked, one write command can transfer a number of consecutive records to the tape without requiring interrecord gaps between them, as shown in Fig. 7-1.1*b*. Gaps appropriately called *interblock gaps* are placed between successive blocks. The utilization of a tape's storage capacity increases as the number of records in a block (often called the *blocking factor*) is made larger. If the blocking factor in the previous example is 10, then $800 \times 10 = 8,000$ bytes can be stored between gaps. Thus, the utilization increases to $10/11$ from $\frac{1}{2}$.

The average time taken to read or write a record is inversely proportional to the blocking factor, since fewer gaps must be spanned and more records can be read or written per command. To utilize tape storage efficiently and to minimize read and write time, it appears that the blocking factor should be arbitrarily large. When a block of records is read or written, however, it is transferred to or from an area in main memory called a *buffer*. (More will be said about buffers in Sec. 7-4.1.) Since main memory is very often at a premium, the buffer size cannot be allowed to be arbitrarily large. Obviously, a trade-off exists between tape storage capacity and read/write time on the one hand and the amount of main memory available for buffering on the other.

A limitation of magnetic-tape devices is that records must be processed in the order in which they reside on the tape. Therefore, accessing a record requires the scanning of all records that precede it. This form of access, called *sequential access*, will be discussed in detail in Sec. 7-4. Operations such as rewinding a tape or back-spacing a certain number of records or blocks increase the performance and flexibility of a magnetic-tape device.

Magnetic tape is probably the cheapest form of external bulk storage; currently, the price of a reel of tape is around \$15. In addition, a reel of tape can be easily placed on and removed from a tape drive, and hence it can be used for the off-line storage of data.

Audio cassette tapes have become a very popular and inexpensive form of sequentially accessing external storage for low-cost microcomputer systems. Although more expensive, video tape recording systems are also being used. These systems provide greater capacity and faster read and write times than their audio cassette counterparts.

### 7-1.2  Magnetic Drums

A magnetic drum is a metal cylinder, from 10 to 36 inches in diameter, which has an outside surface coated with a magnetic recording material. The cylindrical surface of the drum is divided into a number of parallel bands called *tracks*, as illustrated in Fig. 7-1.2. The tracks are further subdivided into either *sectors* or *blocks*, depending on the nature of the drum. The sector or block is the smallest addressable unit of a drum. A particular sector or block is directly addressable in the sense that to access a sector or block $n$ of a drum, it is not necessary to access sectors or blocks 1 to $n$ $-1$, as would be the case when using a sequential type of device such as a magnetic tape. For this reason, a drum is referred to as a *direct-access storage device*.

Sectors are fixed-length arcs of a track, and an integral number of sectors make up a track. The size of a sector is the same for all tracks on a drum and is fixed either in the hardware of the drum unit or formatted when the computer system is generated.

Block-addressable drums differ from sector-addressable drums in the sense that a block contains a programmer-defined number of records. (Note that this notion of

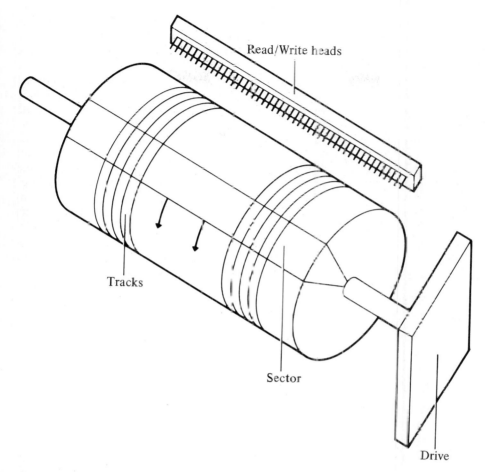

**FIGURE 7-1.2** A magnetic drum with fixed read/write heads.

block is the same as the notion presented in the previous discussion of tapes.) Therefore, the number of blocks which are stored on a track can differ from track to track, and even the size of the blocks stored on a given track can vary. In both sector-addressable and block-addressable drums, however, a complete sector or block, respectively, is read into or written from a buffer at one time.

Because all sectors are the same in size and there are an integral number of sectors per track, a specific sector can generally be located more quickly than a specific block. For a given application, however, the size of a record may not divide exactly into the size of a sector, and space in a sector may thus be wasted. In addition, a record may be larger than a sector, in which case more than one I/O command may be required to read or write the record.

In the discussion throughout this chapter, we will assume block-addressable devices unless stated otherwise. A sector-addressable device can be thought of as a special case of a block-addressable device in which there are an integral number of blocks per track and all blocks are the same size.

Data are transferred to or from the drum as it rotates at a high speed past a number of read/write heads. Two schemes for arranging the read/write heads are used with magnetic drums. The most common scheme is to have *fixed* read/write heads, one for each track, as shown in Fig. 7-1.2. A second architecture is to have a *movable* head in which a group of read/write heads are mounted on a rail and the heads are allowed to traverse the length of the drum. For example, a drum may have 100 tracks with a group of five read/write heads. Such a system permits the group of heads to be moved to any of twenty positions. Five adjacent tracks can be accessed from one position.

For a fixed-head drum, the main component in the time to access a certain location is the *rotational delay* or *latency* L, which is the time in waiting for the drum to rotate to the position where the requested data transfer can commence. Figure 7-1.3 illustrates the conditions of maximum, average, and minimum rotational delay. In movable-head drums, additional time is required to move a read/write head to the desired track. This additional component of the access time is often called the *seek time* S. Therefore the *access time* A(i) associated with a particular I/O operation i can be expressed as the sum of the latency time and the seek time for i. That is,

$$A(i) = L(i) + S(i)$$

An additional component, called the *transmission time* T, is required to calculate the total time to complete a read or write operation. The transmission time, also called the *flow time*, is the time to read or write the record or series of records (as dictated by the I/O operation), given that the heads are positioned over the drum location of the first record to be read or written. The transmission time depends directly on how fast the drum rotates, as does the rotational delay. If we denote the total time to complete an operation i as $\tau(i)$, then

$$\tau(i) = L(i) + S(i) + T(i)$$

For a fixed-head drum, S(i) is considered to be zero.

Note that $\tau(i)$ varies depending on where the heads are positioned, in the case of a movable-head drum, and at what location the first desired record is on the drum circumference associated with a track. Therefore, $\tau(i)$ will continually vary during the computer system's operation. Consequently, a more useful statistic involves the average access time, which is the sum of the average seek time and the average latency. That is,

$$\overline{A}(i) = \overline{L}(i) + \overline{S}(i)$$

Therefore, the average time to complete an I/O operation is

$$\overline{\tau}(i) = \overline{S}(i) + \overline{L}(i) + T(i) = \overline{A}(i) + T(i) \tag{7-1.1}$$

Drums with fixed heads provide a very fast access time and data-transfer rate. They are expensive, however, and are most suitable as backup storage to main memory for programs which are being executed. A movable-head drum usually has a larger storage capacity and is more suitable for storing large volumes of data.

Examples of magnetic-drum devices are given in Table 7-1.1. The available

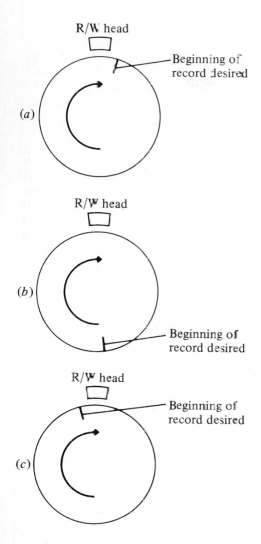

**FIGURE 7-1.3**   Conditions of (*a*) maximum, (*b*) average, and (*c*) minimum rotational delay.

storage capacity, sector capacity, access time, and data-transmission rate are given for each device. Note that IBM drums allow a variable format in storing data.

As mentioned previously, the addressable units (sectors or blocks) on drums are rapidly accessed for data transfers, and no scanning of extraneous data is required as with a magnetic tape. Also, unlike magnetic tape, a drum cannot be removed from its shaft or drive. Hence, the maximum storage capacity for a drum device is limited to the capacity of a single drum.

Of late, magnetic drums have been declining in popularity primarily due to the success of magnetic disk devices with Winchester-based technology.

**Table 7-1.1**  Magnetic drums.

| System | IBM 360 | UNIVAC 1108 | UNIVAC FASTRAND | ICL 1900 |
| --- | --- | --- | --- | --- |
| *Model* | 2301 | FH 432 | II | 1964 |
| Tracks/drum | 200 | 128 | 6,144 | 512 |
| Sector size (chars) | variable | 6 | 168 | 4 |
| Sectors/track | variable | 2,048 | 64 | 1,024 |
| Chars/track | 20,483 | 12,288 | 10,752 | 4,048 |
| Chars/drum | 4,096,600 | 1,572,864 | 132,120,756 | 2,072,574 |
| Avge. latency (ms) | 8.6 | 4.25 | 35 | 20.5 |
| Avge. seek time (ms) | 0 | 0 | 58 | 0 |
| Transmission rate (char/ms) | 1,200 | 1,440 | 153.8 | 100 |

### 7-1.3  Magnetic Disks

The magnetic disk is a direct-access storage device which has become more widely used than the magnetic drum, mainly because of its lower cost. Disk devices provide relatively low access times and high-speed data transfer.

There are two types of disk devices, namely, fixed disks and exchangeable disks. For both types, the disk unit or pack consists of a number of metal platters which are stacked on top of each other on a spindle, as illustrated in Fig. 7-1.4. The upper and lower surfaces of each platter are coated with ferromagnetic particles that provide an information storage media. Often, the outermost surfaces of the top and bottom platters are not used for storing data, as they can be easily scratched or damaged.

The surfaces of each platter are divided into concentric bands called *tracks* (see Fig. 7-1.5). Just as in the case of the magnetic drum, each track is further subdivided into sectors (or blocks) which are the addressable storage units. Note that although the tracks vary in size, all tracks are capable of storing the same amount of information. Therefore, the recording density of the inner tracks is higher than the recording density of the outer tracks.

Information is transferred to or from a disk through read/write heads. Each read/write head floats just above or below the surface of a disk while the disk is rotating constantly at a high speed.

The storage area on the disk to or from which data can be transferred without movement of the read/write heads is termed a *cylinder* or *seek area* (see Fig. 7-1.4). Hence, a cylinder is a set of vertically aligned tracks which reside on the platters of a disk.

With a fixed-disk device, the disk unit is permanently mounted on the drive. Generally, each track of each disk recording surface has its own read/write head. This allows for fast access to data, since the seek time is essentially zero and a rotational delay is the only major component of access time.

An exchangeable-disk device has movable read/write heads. The heads are attached to a movable arm to form a comb-like access assembly, as shown in Fig. 7-1.4. When data on a particular track must be accessed, the whole assembly moves

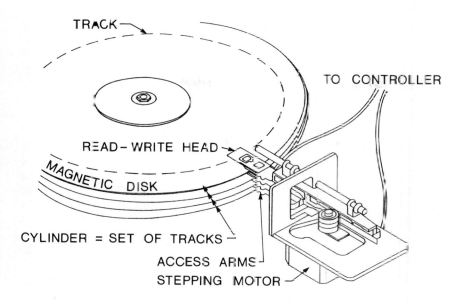

**FIGURE 7-1.4**   Magnetic disk-access mechanisms

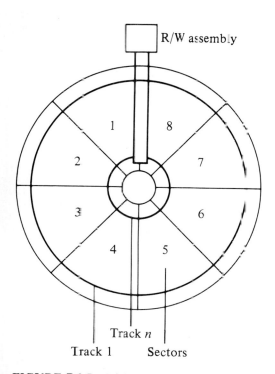

**FIGURE 7-1.5**   Disk surface of a sector-addressable disk

to position the read/write heads over the desired track. While many heads may be in position for a read/write transaction at a given point in time, data transmission can only take place through one head at one time.

In early disk technology, the complete head assembly moved free of the disk pack, thus allowing the pack to be removed and a new pack to be put in its place. In 1973, however, IBM revolutionized the magnetic disk industry with the introduction of what is now called Winchester technology in its Model 3340 disk memory. With this technology the entire set of disks and head assemblies are sealed in a "clean chamber" in which air is continuously recirculated and filtered to exclude large dust particles. Therefore, to remove a disk pack, you simply remove the entire chamber.

Disk storage can be viewed as consisting of consecutively numbered cylinders. A *seek* is a movement of the read/write head to locate the cylinder in which a particular track resides. The time for a seek is the most significant delay when accessing data on a disk, just as it is when accessing data on a movable-head drum. Therefore, it is always desirable to minimize the total seek time. There is also rotational delay or latency in waiting for the disk surface to rotate to a sector or block where a data transfer can commence. Hence, the formula for the average time to complete an I/O operation given previously for magnetic drums applies to disks as well.

Characteristics of magnetic-disk units are summarized in Table 7-1.2. The IBM devices are block-oriented and hence allow variable formats for data rather than the more rigid sector approach. It should also be noted that most of the disk devices have a number of drives and hence a number of units or packs per device. The statistics given are for one unit or pack.

To provide a comparison of transaction times between magnetic drums and magnetic disks, consider the problem of reading 4,096 bytes of information from a track of an IBM 2301 magnetic drum and a track of an IBM 3330 magnetic disk. Using formula 7-1.1, we have

**Table 7-1.2** Magnetic-disk packs.

| System | IBM | | DEC | Commodore |
|---|---|---|---|---|
| Model | 3330 | 3380 | RM80 | D9090 |
| Usable surfaces/unit | 19 | 15 | 7 | 6 |
| Tracks/surface | 404 | 885 | 1,122 | 153 |
| Sector size (chars) | variable | variable | 512 | 256 |
| Chars/track | 13,030 | 47,476 | 15,360 | 8,192 |
| Chars/unit (megabyte) | 100 | 630 | 124 | 9.5 |
| Avge. latency (ms) | 8.3 | 8.3 | 8.3 | 8.3 |
| Avge. seek time (ms) | 30 | 16 | 25 | 153 |
| Transmission rate (char/ms) | 806 | 3,000 | 1,212 | 500 |

$$\overline{\tau}_{\text{IBM 2301}}(\text{read 4,096 bytes}) = 8.6 \text{ ms} - \frac{4,096 \text{ char}}{1,200 \text{ char}/\text{ms}}$$

$$= 8.6 \text{ ms} + 3.4 \text{ ms} = 12.0 \text{ ms}$$

$$\overline{\tau}_{\text{IBM 3330}}(\text{read 4,096 bytes}) = 30 \text{ ms} + 8.3 \text{ ms} + \frac{4,096 \text{ char}}{806 \text{ char}/\text{ms}}$$

$$= 38.3 \text{ ms} + 5.0 \text{ ms} = 43.3 \text{ ms}$$

Observe that the total transaction time using the drum disk is almost one-third of the average seek time for the disk. This clearly illustrates the importance of minimizing seek time for disks with a movable arm.

Unquestionably another form of disk technology that has had a tremendous impact on microcomputer systems is the floppy disk. It is a low-cost disk made of Mylar plastic that is usually 5¼ or 8 inches in diameter and is coated on one or both sides with a magnetic material. There are typically between 8 and 26 sectors per track with each sector holding from 128 to 512 bytes of data. Currently, most floppy disks have a storage capacity of between 125 kilobytes to 1 megabytes, and transmission rates are generally in the range of five to ten characters per millisecond.

In the near future it is expected that floppy disks will be used primarily as an off-line form of data storage, and new and relatively inexpensive hard disks based on Winchester technology will become the standard for on-line auxiliary memory storage for most microcomputer systems.

In summary, disk storage devices are the most versatile storage devices available. They can provide large capacity and fast access time and hence satisfy the needs of most computer systems.

### 7-1.4  Mass Storage Devices

In the early 1960s, several computer manufacturers (NCR, IBM, ICL, and RCA) began marketing direct-access devices, called *card/strip devices*, that have storage capacities on the order of one-half billion characters. A card/strip device consists of groups (decks, magazines, cells, or arrays) of magnetic cards or strips on which data are encoded. The basic principle of operation for these devices involves the selection of a card from a group and the transportation of this card to a revolving cylinder, or *capstan*. The card is wrapped around the capstan and data are then transferred to or from the card via the read/write heads.

Because they are very mechanical in operation, these devices typically have an access time that is greater than one-half second. Their greatest advantage is their large storage capacity; however, magnetic-disk storage devices have been steadily increasing in capacity and decreasing in cost per bit, thus making magnetic card or strip devices obsolete.

While the card/strip devices have fallen into disuse, the principle by which they operate has been applied to the IBM 3851 Mass Storage Facility (MSF). This mass storage device provides a third-level (tertiary) storage facility which contains the archival (permanent) information for the computer system. On-line, multibillion character database systems are now in existence, and with such systems, it becomes too expensive and impractical to store such large amounts of information on disk storage devices. Instead, it is more realistic to store copies of the "often-accessed" programs and data on disk, and to store all programs and data of the system on a cheaper, yet slower, mass storage unit. When a program and its data are required for on-line use, a copy is made on one of the direct-access secondary-memory devices, and it is this copy that is used for as long as is necessary to complete the transactions associated with that particular program and its data. When these transactions are completed, the disk copy is returned to the mass storage device, replacing the old copy.

The IBM system which uses the 3851 Mass Storage Facility is called the 3850 Mass Storage System. IBM 3300 series disk devices (as described in Table 7-1.2) are used as secondary storage. The 3851 MSF uses tape cartridges as its storage media. A tape cartridge is a spool of magnetic tape, 4 inches long and 2 inches in diameter, and has the capacity of one-half of an IBM 3330 disk pack. Access to a particular cartridge is gained after the cartridge is located from a library of cartridges and wrapped around a capstan so that it is properly positioned under a set of read/write heads. Data can be transferred cylinder by cylinder from the IBM 3330 to a tape cartridge and vice versa. The 3851 MSF can contain a maximum of 4,720 tape cartridges, creating a total capacity of 236 billion characters. It had been hoped that mass storage devices such as the IBM 3851 would substantially reduce, if not eliminate, the need for storing large volumes of data off-line on reels of tape or removable disk packs. As yet, this hope has not been met.

### 7-1.5 Intermediate Storage Devices

A new development in the area of external storage devices is the electronic disk. The electronic disk is named "electronic" because it provides fast access times without mechanical movement. It is an intermediate form of storage because it is being developed to fill the gap between main memory and direct-access storage. This is achieved by having a lower cost than main memory and a lower access time than is currently available with external storage devices.

The devices that currently show the greatest potential for being an acceptable electronic disk are *charge-coupled devices.* They are based on semiconductor technology, but their cost per bit should be one-third that of main memory. The average access time they provide is 60 microseconds.

Other candidates for electronic disks include the domain tip propagation, electron beam, and magnetic bubbles technologies.

**Exercises for Sec. 7-1**

1. Calculate the number of 80-column input records that can be stored on a magnetic tape that is 3,600 feet in length assuming:

    (a) One record per block, 1,600 bytes-per-inch density, and ¾-inch interrecord gaps
    (b) Five records per block, 1,600 bytes-per-inch density, and ¾-inch interblock gaps
    (c) Twenty-five records per block, 3,200 bytes-per-inch density, and ½-inch inter-block gaps
    (d) One record per block, 800 bytes-per-inch density, and ½-inch interrecord gaps

2. A number of standard tape densities, such as those given in Exercise 1, are used in the computer industry. Obviously, these are not effective tape density

figures, since they are independent of the block size and the interblock gap size. Derive a formula for the effective tape density (expressed in effective bytes per inch) which is dependent upon three factors: standard density, block size, and gap size.

3. Calculate the effective density for *(a)*, *(b)*, *(c)*, and *(d)* of Exercise 1

4. Suppose average tape speeds of 125 inches per second and 30 inches per second are attained when reading recorded information and passing over gaps, respectively. Calculate the time required to read the tape configurations given in Exercise 1.

5. Direct-access devices are sometimes called *random-access devices*. What is the basis for this synonym-type of relationship?

6. How many tracks of a UNIVAC FASTRAND II drum are required to store a file of 10,000 records each 80 bytes in length, assuming records are not allowed to span sector boundaries? How long does it take to read the file if an initial average access time is included in the timing estimate?

7. Solve Exercise 6 assuming an IBM 2301 drum is available instead. Assume that 14 bytes of system information are stored per block and that a blocking factor of twenty is used. Records are not allowed to span track boundaries.

8. Compute the expected time to locate and read a particular 64-character record residing on the following disks: *(a)* IBM 3380, *(b)* DEC RM80 and *(c)* Commodore D9090. Suppose we are updating the record instead of reading it. In most systems, a read operation takes place immediately after a write operation. This additional read operation, which takes a time of one period of revolution, is needed to verify that the information placed in the direct-access device is correct.

9. Assume an average access time is required to commence reading two files of 64-byte records—one resides on a DEC RM80 and the other resides on an IBM 2301 drum. How many records must be in each of the files in order that the total read time be equal (or approximately equal)? Make the same assumptions about the storage of records as was made in Exercise 7.

## 7-2 DEFINITIONS AND CONCEPTS

Many of the definitions and terminology used in the remainder of this chapter are introduced in this subsection. Because some of the concepts directly relate to external device characteristics, we have chosen to place this subsection after the discussion of external devices. Some of the terms that will be presented have been introduced previously. We reintroduce them here to provide a comprehensive and consistent overview of the hierarchy of information structures associated with file processing.

A *record* (sometimes called a *group* or *segment*) is a collection of information items about a particular entity. For example a record may consist of information about a passenger on an airplane flight, or an article sold at a retail distribution store. An *item* (sometimes called a *field*) of a record is a unit of meaningful information about an entity. The different items of a passenger record may be the passenger's name, address, seat number, and menu restrictions. Generally, an item of a record is an integer, real, or character-string data element. However, items may themselves be composed of aggregates of items, such as an array of items or a sub-collection of nonhomogeneous items. In PL/I, the notion of a record in its most general interpretation can be loosely equated to a structure. For example, a possible structure for a passenger record is declared as follows:

```
DECLARE 1 PASSENGER,
          2 NAME,
              3 INITIALS CHAR(2),
              3 SURNAME CHAR(20),
          2 ADDRESS CHAR(30),
          2 SEAT_NO CHAR(2),
          2 MENU CHAR(35);
```

A collection of records involving a set of entities with certain aspects in common and organized for some particular purpose is called a *file* . For example, the collection of all passenger records for the passengers on a particular flight constitutes a file.

A record item that uniquely identifies a record in a file is called a *key*. In the passenger file, individual passenger records can be uniquely identified by the passenger's name, assuming duplicate names do not occur for a particular flight. The seat-number item can also be used as a key, if desired, since seat numbers are uniquely assigned for a given flight.

It is a common practice to order the records in a file according to a key. Therefore, if the passenger name is selected as the key item, the record for Adams appears before the record for Brown, which appears before the record for Camp in a lexical ordering by surname. Some files are ordered on a particular item, termed the *sequence item*, which may not be unique for each record. For example, in a file of monthly sales for a particular company, several records containing sales information may appear for one customer. The file can be ordered by customer account number with more than one occurrence of a customer sales record type for a given account number.

Thus far we have observed a hierarchy of information structures in which items are composed to form records and records are composed to form files. Files can be composed to form a set of files. If the set of files is used by the application programs for some particular enterprise or application area, and if these files exhibit certain associations or relationships between the records of the files, then such a collection of files is often referred to as a *data base*. Figure 7-2.1 shows the information-structure hierarchy as it applies to file-processing applications.

Items, records, files, and data bases are logical terms in the sense that they have been introduced without any indication as to how they can be realized physically on an external device. A number of file structure concepts are associated with these logical terms. In the last subsection, we described how records are physically stored on several external storage devices. In particular, we pointed out that a logical record, as viewed by the programmer, can be grouped together with several other records to form a single physical entity called a *block* or *physical record*. The blocking of records does not affect the logical processing of those records. However, it does allow the processing to take place more efficiently because the number of read or write commands per logical record, as issued by the operating system, can be reduced significantly.

The term *file* has assumed both a logical and physical interpretation in the data-processing community. Physically, a file is considered to be a collection of physical records which must reside, often contiguously, in external memory. To provide proper access to the physical records in the file, a number of tables are kept by the storage management routines in the operating system. These tables, along with other control information, which is stored in the physical record (such as the length of the record), are transparent to the user who is working with the file at a logical level.

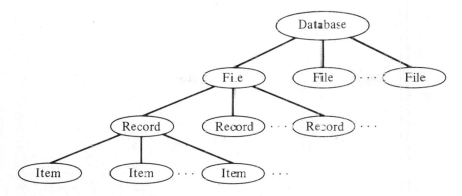

**FIGURE 7-2.1**  Information structure hierarchy for file processing.

In IBM systems, the physical file is often referred to as a *data set*. The physical makeup of the data set is described with a DD (Data Definition) statement in the JCL (Job Control Language) provided. A number of such statements will be described in the file-organization sections of this chapter.

A physical record is composed of fields made up of bytes and words of binary-encoded information. The term *physical field* can be associated with a binary-encoded information element that corresponds to an item or field of a logical record. For simplicity and consistency, we will use the term "field" when describing the field of a physical record and "item" when referring to the field of a logical record. We will discover that there are some fields in a physical record, in particular, fields containing system maintained pointers, which have no counterpart items in the logical description of a record.

Having introduced most of the terminology needed for our discussion of files, let us examine some of the factors that affect the organization of a file The prime factor which determines the organization of a file is the nature of the operations that are to be performed on the file, as dictated by the application. The operations normally performed are the same as those discussed previously in the text, namely, retrieval, addition, deletion, and update. A particular operation involving a record or set of records is called a *transaction*. For example. "Delete Peter Hardie from the passenger list for Flight 279" is a transaction. Transactions are often processed against a file or set of files in the form of *transaction records*. These transaction records contain the keys of the records to be processed, along with the desired operation and any additional information required to complete the operation. In the sections to follow, we will see that the selection of a file organization depends not only on the operations or types of transactions but also on the volume of transactions, the frequency with which transactions are submitted, and the response time required in the completion of a transaction or set of transactions.

The organization of a file is also dependent on the external storage media on which it is to reside. For example, we will discover that the file organization on a sequential device, such as a magnetic tape, differs appreciably from the file organizations that can be accommodated on a direct-access storage device such as a magnetic disk.

Other important concepts which we discuss and illustrate later in this chapter involve file generation and file reorganization.

## 7-3 RECORD ORGANIZATION

In the previous section, we described a record as an entity composed of items or fields. In this section, we concentrate on an important aspect of record organization, namely, the structure of record items.

Before discussing this aspect, the concept of the *domain* of an item must be presented. The domain of an item is simply those values which an item can assume. For example, if we are designing an application dealing with space allocation in a university, then one obvious item is the building location for a room in a record describing the attributes of a particular room. The domain of values for such an item might typically represent the Administration, Agriculture, Arts, Chemistry, Commerce, Education, Engineering, General Purpose, Law, Medical, and Physics buildings. When all the domain values for an item are known, such as in the last example, the item is said to have a *precoordinated domain*. Some record items which contain textual information are not precoordinated. For example, in a record for a bibliography system, an item may be devoted to an abstract of a book. Obviously, not all book abstracts are known prior to the establishment of a file of bibliographic information.

We now present a spectrum of methods for representing both types of items and begin with techniques for precoordinated items.

### Logically-encoded items

For each possible value of a precoordinated item, a single logical value is reserved in a vector or string of logical values which constitute the item. In the item containing a building location of a room, we can allocate a bit value for each building on campus. We let the first value represent the Administration Building, the second value represent the Agriculture Building, and so on, finally letting the eleventh and final value represent the Physics Building. A record item with a value of '01000000000'B in PL/I bit-string notation represents the Agriculture Building if the logical values of 1 and 0 are used to denote the presence and absence of item values, respectively.

A logical-valued format has the tremendous advantage of being capable of representing a multifaceted item (i.e., an item which can take on more than one domain value). For example, '10001000011'B indicates the Administration, Commerce, Medical, and Physics buildings. Of course, such a multifaceted item does not make sense in a record describing the properties of a room. However, if the item appears in the records of a file indicating the availability of certain facilities such as air conditioning, cafeteria services, libraries, etc., then a multifaceted item is needed. Note that a logically encoded item is a fixed-length item which can represent a variable number of values from the domain of an item. This is an important attribute, since variable-length records cannot be processed as efficiently as fixed-length records. Further discussion on this subject takes place at the end of this section.

### Binary-encoded items

A method involving binary encoding utilizes storage more efficiently than the logical-encoding method just discussed. If we assume an item has a domain set of size $n$, then we can encode these item values using a binary scheme in which each element of the scheme is of length $\lceil \log_2 n \rceil$. An example of this type of encoding was given in Table 1-1.1 and discussed in Sec.1-1. Basically, a binary-encoding scheme is established by assigning a unique binary number to each value of the item's domain set. Table 7-3.1 illustrates a binary encoding represented in PL/I bit-string notation for the example set of campus buildings.

First it should be observed that, when using a binary-encoded scheme, an item value can be represented in 4 bits, whereas 11 bits are required for a logically encoded item. However, multifaceted items cannot be represented unless they are incorporated in the encoding scheme (for example, '1111'B could represent the presence of both the Administration and Arts buildings).

### Huffman-encoded items

A Huffman encoding scheme makes use of an assumed set of item-value probabilities for item values in the domain set. Given these probabilities, a minimum average-length binary code can be constructed for each item value in the precoordinated domain. A Huffman encoding of the building location item is given in Table 7-3.2, assuming a priori knowledge of the listed probabilities. This a priori knowledge is essential in the derivation of Huffman-coded items.

In a Huffman coding scheme, a short code is associated with an item value which has a high probability of occurrence, and a long code is assigned to an item value with a low probability of occurrence. The expected or average length of a building-location item is found using the formula

$$\text{Average length} = \sum_{i=1}^{n} l_i \times p_i$$

where $l_i$ and $p_i$ are the length and probability associated with code $i$, respectively. Therefore, the average length of a building location item is

$$2 \times 1/4 + 2 \times 3/16 + 3 \times 1/8 + 3 \times 1/8 - 4 \times 1/16 + 5 \times 1/16$$

$$+ 5 \times 1/16 + 4 \times 1/16 + 5 \times 1/32 + 6 \times 1/64 + 6 \times 1/64$$

$$= 3\ 3/32 \text{ bits} \approx 3.09 \text{ bits}$$

Recall Eq. (1-1.1) from Sec. 1-1, that can be used to compute the average amount of information transmitted from a source. That is,

$$H = -\sum_{i=1}^{n} p_i \log_2 (p_i)$$

**Table 7-3.1**

| Building | Encoded Value | Building | Encoded Value |
|---|---|---|---|
| Administration | '0000'B | Engineering | '0110'B |
| Agriculture | '0001'B | General Purpose | '0111'B |
| Arts | '0010'B | Law | '1000'B |
| Chemistry | '0011'B | Medical | '1001'B |
| Commerce | '0100'B | Physics | '1010'B |
| Education | '0101'B | | |

**Table 7-3.2**

| Location | Probability | Code |
|----------|-------------|------|
| Arts | 1/4 | 10 |
| Engineering | 3/16 | 00 |
| Education | 1/8 | 110 |
| Medical | 1/8 | 011 |
| Commerce | 1/16 | 1110 |
| General Purpose | 1/16 | 11111 |
| Chemistry | 1/16 | 11110 |
| Law | 1/16 | 0101 |
| Agriculture | 1/32 | 01001 |
| Administration | 1/64 | 010001 |
| Physics | 1/64 | 010000 |

Applying this formula to the probabilities of the item values as given in Table 7-3.2, we have

$$H = -1/4 \times \log_2(1/4) - 3/16 \times \log_2(3/16) - \cdots$$
$$- 1/64 \times \log_2(1/64) \approx 3.04 \text{ bits}$$

Therefore the expected length of the building-location item is almost equal to the average amount of information transmitted for a given building-location item. Since $H$ represents the minimum average amount of information needed to transmit a coded-item value, it is apparent that the Huffman coding scheme given in Table 7-3.2 is very efficient from a storage point of view. This efficiency is further supported by the realization that the same item, logically encoded and fixed-length binary encoded, requires 11 and 4 bits, respectively.

Let us briefly explain with the aid of Fig. 7-3.1 how a Huffman code is generated. It is assumed initially that each item value has as its code word an empty string. To produce a Huffman code, we order the item values according to their probabilities—from the item value with the largest probability to the item value with the smallest probability. Next, the item value with the smallest probability has a 0 concatenated at the front of its code word, and the item value with the second smallest probability has a 1 concatenated at the front of its code word. (Note that the second smallest can be equal to the smallest.) These item values are then grouped together to form a new item value with a probability equal to the sum of the two probabilities of the combined values. The table is then reordered, if necessary, and again the last two item values have each of their code words appended with a 0 or 1. These item values are then combined and the process is repeated. The entire procedure is terminated when the table is reduced to a size of two, and the final sets of item values have the appropriate binary values concatenated to the end of their code words. In Fig. 7-3.1, a trace of the derivation of the code word 010000, representing the Physics Building, is illustrated by encircling the entries that participate in its derivation. The development of iterative and recursive algorithms for the derivation of a Huffman code are left as exercises at the end of this section.

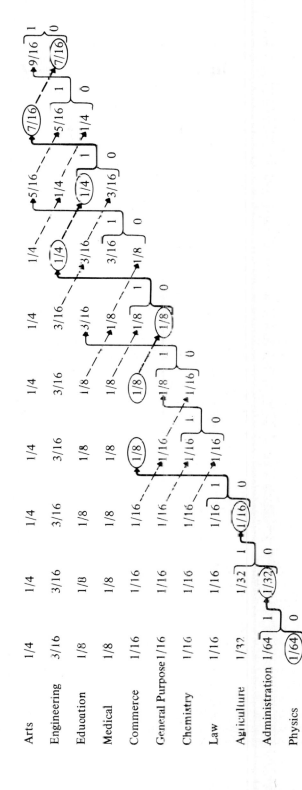

**FIGURE 7-3.1**  Construction of a Huffman code.

Huffman codes have two important properties. First, it can be proven (see Abramson[1963]) that a Huffman code is a minimum average-length binary code. Hence, Huffman-coded record items are minimum average-length items. It should also be noted that Huffman codes have the *prefix property*. That is, no other assigned code in a generated set of codes C is the prefix of another code. Or, for a given y ε C, there does not exist an x ε C such that x ◯ z = y for some nonempty binary string z. Therefore, in a simple linear scan of a Huffman-encoded bit string, we can isolate the next coded-item value because of its unique prefix. For example, suppose we are scanning a record with the binary information '110100011...' to isolate the next value for the building-location item. The Education Building as represented by '110'B is the item value and '100011...' is the remainder of the record. It can be seen that the prefix property is extremely important when decoding a variable-length record item.

Of course the main disadvantage with Huffman codes is that they are variable-length codes. Processing time is required to isolate an item value when it can assume any one of many different lengths.

### Fixed Items

When a record item has a fixed-length value and its domain is too large for an efficient bit encoding, a primitive data-structure (i.e., integer, real, string, etc.) format should be selected for the representation of the item. For example, it is unreasonable to bit-encode an item representing the net sales for the month. Instead, we can declare a record containing such an item in the programming language being used. In PL/I this declaration can be expressed as follows:

```
DECLARE 1 MONTHLY_REPORT,
          2 MONTH CHAR(9),
          2 NET_SALES FIXED(8,2),
          .
          .
          .
```

The net sales item can range in value from -999999.99 to 999999.99. It is unrealistic for the programmer to bit encode such a wide range of item values when the compiler provides an efficient encoding of an item value in binary with a fixed-decimal format. Note that the record item represented by MONTH can be significantly reduced in size if we use a fixed-length binary code of '0000'B for January, '0001'B for February,...., '1011'B for December, and declare the item to be of type BIT(4). Other examples of record items which have domains that are too large to be bit-encoded are surnames and catalogue numbers.

Because both of these items may be considered as fixed-length items, they can technically be called precoordinated. That is, a fixed-length item can only have a finite set of values which can be a priori enumerated. However, we reserve the term precoordinated for those domain sets which are completely established beforehand; in most systems dealing with surnames and catalogue numbers, such a priori knowledge is not available.

Thus far, we have examined record structures in which the items are fixed length, with the exception of Huffman-coded items. Let us now look at some record organizations involving items that often lead to variable-length records.

**Repeating items**

Many applications arise in which the value associated with a record item may be a list of entities. For example, "the degree held" and "the programming languages used at a computer installation" are items which can assume multiple entities. In these instances, the item values may be ' B.Sc., M.Sc., Ph.D." or "COBOL, FOR-TRAN, PL/I, Pascal, BASIC" respectively

The most popular method of handling repeating fields is to create an item which can accommodate up to some maximum number of replications. If we restrict this maximum number to *three*, then the example items can accommodate such information as the three most recent degrees obtained and the three most often used programming languages.

Some computer systems allow the handling of a repeated item as a variable-length item, provided the item appears last in the record definition. This type of variable-length record is permitted in PL/I.

**Tagged items**

A tagged item is an item that contains not only information pertinent to a particular application but also information concerning the structure of the item itself. For example, in a personnel system in which records are kept concerning the history of the employees of a company, several data items may be recorded such as previous addresses, education, previous work experience, yearly achievement reports, etc. Instead of creating repeated items for each of these information fields, it can be more advantageous to store tags with each item. In general, a tag is used in one of two ways. One method assumes a fixed predetermined ordering of items in the record, and tag information is used to delimit items, as shown in Fig. 7-3.2. Item delimiting can be achieved by either a boundary-marker method or length descriptor method as described in Sec. 2-4.

The second approach to record organization using tagged items is to include, in the tag, a description or name of the item, as shown in Fig. 7-3.3. Using this technique, it is not required that item values for a record occur in any predetermined order. Of course, the added flexibility of a tag which dynamically describes the record syntax results in an increase in record length.

```
#117 Birchmount Park, Vancouver, B.C.
Apt. 201, 1492 Columbus Cres, Halifax, N.S.
P.O. 302, Moose Jaw, Sask.
```
```
tag
```
```
M.Sc. Computer Science, Univ. of B.C., 1973
B.Sc. Mathematics, Saint Mary's, 1969
```
```
tag
```
```
No previous work experience
```
```
tag
```

**FIGURE 7-3.2**   Illustration of a preformatted personnel record with tagged items.

| No previous work experience | |
| --- | --- |
| 3 previous addresses | |
| #117 Birchmount Park, Vancouver, B.C.<br>Apt. 201, 1492 Columbus Cres, Halifax, N.S.<br>P.O. 302, Moose Jaw, Sask. | |
| 2 degrees | |
| M.Sc. Computer Science, Univ. of B.C., 1973<br>B.Sc. Mathematics, Saint Mary's, 1969 | |

**FIGURE 7-3.3**    Illustration of self-descriptive tagged items in a personnel record.

**Textual items**

There is a final type of record item which differs from the other item forms discussed thus far. Its difference is primarily due to the size of an item. By a textual item, we mean an item containing a large amount of textual information such as text for a manuscript, for the abstract of a book, for a company report, or for a newspaper's want ad. Typically, records for such items are single-item records. Because of the length of the textual-type record, it is not uncommon to decompose such a record and store it in several physical records or blocks. Data-compression techniques are often necessary to reduce the amount of storage required for textual items. One technique is to use a word-level *concordance* on positions at which that word appears in the text. In a concordance each unique word in the text is stored along with the various positions at which that word appears in the text. For example, a concordance of the previous sentence is given in Table 7-3.3. Usually, the word list for the concordance is arranged in alphabetical order. To restore the text to its "natural" form, it is necessary to concatenate the words together in an order dictated by the numbers in the position field of the concordance. The big saving in terms of compression is in multiple occurrence of words such as "the" and "in," which are stored only once in the concordance.

The Huffman coding scheme discussed earlier might also be used in an attempt to reduce the length of the textual item.

There can be a significant disadvantage to storing text in a compressed format. For example, performing text-editing is virtually impossible unless text is restored to an uncompressed form and therefore if editing operations must be performed often, compression should be avoided. In any application in which text must be manipulated frequently, compression should not be applied.

**Pointer items**

In the remaining sections of this chapter, we will discover that a very important type of record item is an item which contains information that references another record in the file and, in some instances, a record in another file. The pointer information may be in the form of a key of another record, a relative record position in a file, or an absolute physical address based on a cylinder, track, or segment (or block) address. In our discussion of direct files in Sec. 7-9, we will examine pointer items in detail and illustrate their use with some examples.

**Table 7-3.3**

| Word | Position(s) | Word | Position(s) |
|------|-------------|------|-------------|
| a | 2 | stored | 11 |
| along | 12 | text | 9, 24 |
| appears | 21 | that | 19 |
| at | 17 | the | 8, 14, 23 |
| concordance | 3 | unique | 5 |
| each | 4 | various | 15 |
| in | 1, 7, 22 | which | 18 |
| is | 10 | with | 13 |
| positions | 16 | word | 6, 20 |

Before concluding this section, a final comment must be made concerning variable-length records. Variable-length records are used primarily in situations in which the record structure varies considerably from one record item to another in a file. They are used to save storage. Variable-length items such as Huffman-encoded items, repeated items, and tagged items are designed specifically to conserve storage. However, some additional processing time is required to encode and decode a record's format when such items are used. Usually, the development of programs to perform this encoding and decoding are left to the application programmer, since in many situations the format is application-dependent. Therefore, before adopting variable-length record formats, we should be aware of the problems which can arise. In the next section, a detailed description of a file structure used for variable-length records is given. After examining the format of a variable-length record, we can better appreciate the complexity involved in processing such a record.

In summary, we can say that items with a small precoordinated domain can be efficiently represented using one of the binary-encoding schemes. Items with large domains can best be represented in the data description facilities of the programming language in use. Multifaceted and replicated items generate variable-length records, unless they can be logically encoded, and textual information which is subject to very little text processing should be compressed. With a discussion of record organization completed, we can now consider how various types of items discussed in this section can be utilized to form the records that determine the organization of a file.

**Exercises for Sec. 7-3**

1.  Give a practical example of a multifaceted record item for which a logical encoding would be appropriate.
2.  A large multinational company manufactures its products in a number of cities. The value for an item in a record which describes a manufactured product contains one of the following city names: New York, Tokyo, Chicago, London, San Francisco, Paris, Montreal, Detroit, Dusseldorf, Mexico City, and

St. Louis. Design a fixed-length binary code for the values of the item corresponding to a manufacturing location. How many more cities can be added to the list before the code length must be increased?

3. Develop an iterative algorithm for the derivation of a Huffman code given a set of probabilities $p_1, ..., p_n$ for $n$ item values.

4. Design a recursive algorithm for the derivation of a Huffman code given a set of probabilities $p_1, ..., p_n$ for $n$ item values.

5. The item values given in Exercise 2 are known to have the following approximate probabilities of occurrence, respectively, in a record describing a manufactured product: 1/4, 1/6, 1/8, 1/8, 1/12, 1/12, 1/16, 1/24, 1/48, 1/48, 1/48. Generate a Huffman code for these items. What is the expected length of an item using this code?

6. Compute the average amount of information transmitted (i.e., the information entropy) for the record item in Exercise 2 with the probabilities given in Exercise 5. What are the efficiences of the codes derived in Exercise 2 and Exercise 5?

7. Describe how you would organize a record for a personnel file, which involves the following items: *(a)* name, *(b)* address, *(c)* number of years with company, *(d)* work classification (assume a fixed number of classifications are used), *(e)* degrees held, and *(f)* previous jobs held. Create a PL/I structure which is representative of the record.

8. Derive a word-level concordance for the first three sentences in this chapter, excluding the title.

9. What type of storage structures would you choose to represent the following record items?

   *(a)* The number of miles traveled by a salesman per month
   *(b)* The days of the week
   *(c)* Aunt Matilda's favorite recipes
   *(d)* The weather conditions for the day as best described by one of the following categories: clear, cloudy, overcast, raining, snowing, hurricane, or tornado
   *(e)* The same as *(d)*, but assume more than one category name can be used in the daily description
   *(f)* Former places of residence

## 7-4  SEQUENTIAL FILES

In Sec. 7-2, we noted that most operating systems provide a set of basic file organizations that are popular with the users of the system. The three most common types of organizations are sequential, indexed sequential, and direct, which are discussed in this section, Sec. 7-7, and Sec. 7-9, respectively. The presentation of each of these organizations begins with a description of its file structure. Next, the type of processing that can be accomplished with the file organization is examined and then exemplified by algorithms. Finally, each section contains a discussion of how files with that particular type of organization can be processed in PL/I. Applications illustrating each type of organization will be given in separate sections.

### 7-4.1  The Structure of Sequential Files

In a sequential file, records are stored one after the other on a storage device. Of course, a sequential type of storage representation is not new to us. Previously, we discussed the sequential representation of characters in a string, of arrays, and of certain linear and nonlinear lists. Because sequential allocation is conceptually simple, yet flexible enough to cope with many of the problems associated with handling large volumes of data, a sequential file has been the most popular basic file structure used in the data-processing industry.

All types of external storage devices support a sequential-file organization. Some devices, by their physical nature, can only support sequential files. For example, as described in Sec. 7-1, information is stored on a magnetic tape as a continuous series of records along the length of the tape. Accessing a particular record requires the accessing of all previous records in the file. Other devices which are strictly sequential in nature are paper tape readers, card readers, tape cassettes, and line printers.

Magnetic disks and drums provide both direct and sequential access to records and hence support sequential files along with other types of file structures to be described later. A sequential file is physically placed on a drum or disk by storing the sequence of records in adjacent locations on a track. Of course, if the file is larger than the amount of space available on a track, then the records are stored on adjacent tracks. This notion of physical adjacency can be extended to cylinders and even to complete storage devices where more than one device is attached to a common control unit.

The operations that can be performed on a sequential file may differ slightly, depending on the storage device used. For example, a file on magnetic tape can be either an input file or output file, but not both at one time. A sequential file on disk can be used strictly for input, strictly for output, or for update. Update means that, as records are read, the record most recently read can be rewritten on the *same* file, if so desired. Some operating systems provide file-accessing facilities which allow a file to be extended by writing records after the current last record. Also, it is sometimes possible to move backwards and forwards a certain number of records in the file without reading or writing. This extension is beyond the scope of basic sequential-file processing and will not be elaborated upon.

Before discussing the type of processing that is normally applied to sequential files, it is important to examine how information on a file is transmitted to a user program and vice versa. In the previous sections in this chapter, we have defined a logical record and discussed the organization of such a record. In Sec. 7-1.1, it was suggested that it is often advantageous to group a number of logical records into a single physical record or block. Complete blocks and not individual records are transferred between main memory and the external storage.

Note, however, that the execution of a read or write instruction in a high-level programming language such as PL/I corresponds to the handling of only one logical record, as specified in the parameter list of an instruction. For example, consider the PL/I instruction

READ FILE (MASTER) INTO (EMPLOYEE);

where EMPLOYEE is declared to be a PL/I structure as follows:

```
DECLARE 1 EMPLOYEE,
          2 NAME,
            3 SURNAME CHAR(20),
            3 INITIALS CHAR(6),
          2 SOC_INS# FIXED(9),
          2 WAGE_PER_HR FIXED(5,2),
          2 CLASSFCTN CHAR(3);
```

Each time the READ instruction is executed, the next record from the MASTER sequential file is moved into the program area and assigned to the structure EMPLOYEE. However, each time a read or write operation is executed for a particular storage device, a block of logical records is transferred. The apparent difference in a program's read and write statements and the read and write commands issued for a particular device is resolved by using a *buffer* between external storage and the data area of a program. A buffer is a section of main memory which is equal in size to the maximum size of a block of logical records used by a program. The data-management routines of the operating system use buffers for the "blocking" and "deblocking" of records.

To illustrate how the blocking and deblocking of records is accomplished using a buffer, consider the use of the MASTER sequential file as an input file. When the first READ statement is executed, a block of records is moved from external storage to a buffer. The first record in the block is then transferred to the program's data area, as illustrated in Fig. 7-4.1. For each subsequent execution of a READ statement, the next successive record in the buffer is transferred to the data area. Only after every record in the buffer has been moved to the data area, in response to READ statements, does the next READ statement cause another block to be transferred to the buffer from external storage. The new records in the buffer are moved to the data area, as described previously, and this entire process is repeated for each block that is read.

In a similar fashion, WRITE statements cause the transfer of program data to the buffer. When the buffer becomes full (corresponding to a block of logical records), then the block is written on the external storage device immediately after the preceding block of records.

The buffering technique just described is commonly called *single buffering*. *Multiple buffering* makes use of a queue of buffers which are normally controlled by

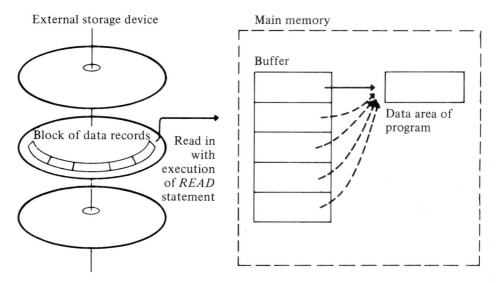

**FIGURE 7-4.1**   Illustration of the reading in of a block of records.

the operating system. The need for more than one buffer arises because of the delay (which is in the order of milliseconds) necessary to read in or write out the next block of records. This delay in the execution of a program only occurs after every n executions of the READ or WRITE statement, when a blocking factor of n and a single buffer is used. However, if the program is executing in an environment where the desired response time is small and where processor and input/output activity need to be overlapped, then it is wise to eliminate this delay by using multiple buffers.

A circular queue of three buffers is shown in Fig. 7-4.2. When the first READ statement is executed, the three buffers A, B, and C are filled with three consecutive blocks, one block per buffer. After all the records in buffer A have been processed, the execution of a subsequent READ instruction results in the transfer of the first record from buffer B to the program's data area. Concurrently, a read command is issued by the operating system and a block transfer from the sequential file on the external storage device to buffer A is initiated. Subsequent executions of READ instructions on the MASTER file cause records to be transferred in sequence from buffer B and then buffer C. By the time the records of buffer C are being processed, buffer A contains a new buffer full of records and buffer B is being refilled. If the process of filling one buffer with new records is generally balanced with the process of reading records from the remaining buffers, then the program should normally experience only one read or write delay, namely, when the buffers are initially being filled.

In some systems, such as an IBM mainframe system, blocks of logical records which constitute a sequential file can be either fixed length (the case we have considered so far) or variable length. A variable-length block contains variable-length records. Therefore, it is not known how many records fit in a block, and hence a maximum length is defined for the block. This maximum length is used to estimate the size of a buffer needed to hold the block, and as many records as possible are grouped into the block by the data-management facilities. Figure 7-4.3 shows the record format for variable-length blocked and unblocked records. Note that a BL (block length) and an RL (record length) must be stored with each block and record, respectively. These lengths are needed when unblocking the records during a READ instruction.

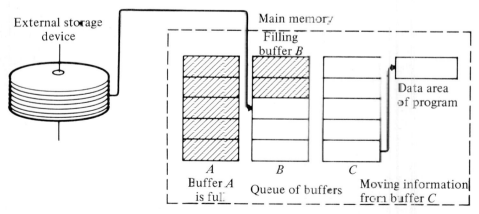

**FIGURE 7-4.2**   Three-buffer system.

| IBG | BL | RL | Record 1 data | IBG | BL | RL | Record 2 data | IBG | BL | RL | Record 3 data | IBG |
|-----|----|----|----|-----|----|----|----|-----|----|----|----|-----|

(a)

| IBG | BL | RL | Record 1 data | RL | Record 2 data | RL | Record 3 data | IBG |
|-----|----|----|----|----|----|----|----|-----|

(b)

**FIGURE 7-4.3**   Record format for variable-length (a) unblocked,
and (b) blocked records.

The maximum length of a block depends on the storage device used for the
file. With magnetic tape, the length depends on the maximum space available for
the buffer in main memory. With disk storage, blocks are generally limited in size to
the capacity of a track. Using a sector-addressable device, a block corresponds to
some maximum number of sectors.

### 7-4.2 Processing Sequential Files

Having discussed the physical layout of a sequential file and how records are
transferred to/from the program area from/to the file, let us examine the types of
processing for which sequential files are most suitable. *Serial processing* is the accessing of records, one after the other, according to the physical order in which they
appear in the file. Obviously, it is an easy matter to process a sequential file serially.
*Sequential processing* is the accessing of records, one after the other, in ascending
order by a key or index item of the record. If, for example, a MASTER file of
employees' records is ordered by employee surname (e.g., the record for ADAMS is
first, BAKER second, ..., ZURCHER last), then sequentially processing the file by
surname is equivalent to serially processing the file. Most sequential files are ordered
by a key or index item such as employee name, student identification number, or
store catalogue number, when the file is created. The key or index item should be
the item which is most often searched for when processing the file. To show the
importance of key selection, assume the MASTER file of employees is ordered by
social insurance number. Suppose we want to find the records of a number of
employees given only their names. Finding the first employee's record, say ADAMS,
is simply a matter of serially processing the file until a record with a name item of
ADAMS appears (ignoring the possibility of name duplications). Consider the processing of a second record, say for BAKER. Since the position of BAKER's record
bears no relationship with the position of ADAM's record, we have no alternative
but to start once again serially processing at the beginning of the MASTER file.
On rare occasions, serial processing is all that is required on a file, irrespective
of the key or item index upon which the file is ordered. For example, if we are to

add a pay increase of $2/hour to the wage item of all employees. it is irrelevant whether the file is sequenced by name or by social insurance number.

In sequential processing, transaction records are usually grouped together (i.e., batched) and are sorted according to the same index item as records in the file. Each successive record of the file is read, compared with an incoming transaction record, and then processed in a manner that is usually dependent upon whether the value of the record's index item is less than, equal to, or greater than the value of the index item of the transaction record.

Sequential and serial processing are most effective when a high percentage of the records in a file must be processed. Since every record in the file must be scanned, a relatively large number of transactions should be batched together for processing. If records are to be added to a file, it is necessary to create a new file unless the records are to be added to the end of the file. In many systems no facilities are provided which allow the direct extension of a sequential file. Records can be deleted from a sequential file by tagging them as "deleted" during a file update. However, this procedure leads to files with embedded "dummy" records, and storage is not efficiently used and processing time is increased. Usually, records to be deleted are physically removed by creating a new file. While creating a new file is sometimes necessary, it should be done as infrequently as possible.

To facilitate a description of file processing, it is necessary to extend our algorithmic notation so that the file-manipulation capabilities present in most programming languages can be expressed. A file is given an identifier name that is not subscripted or qualified by a pointer. We denote this identifier by the syntactic element <file name>. The first requirement before processing a file is to allocate storage for a buffer. It is also popular to identify the operations that can be performed on the file. Can the file be used for input, output, or both (update)? This serves as protection, particularly if we do not wish to write by accident on a file used for input. These functions can be expressed in our algorithmic notation as follows:

*1*   Open <file name> file for input
*2*   Open <file name> file for output
*3*   Open <file name> file for update

Input specifies that records may be read only; output specifies that records may be written only; and update specifies that records may be read and rewritten, or possibly written at the end of the file. Note that it is not possible to rewrite records in a sequential file stored on tape.

When the processing of a file is complete, the buffer space can be deallocated by writing

Close <file name> file

The Open and Close statements also prevent more than one user from accessing the file simultaneously in time-sharing and multiprogramming environments. A program cannot open a file that is currently open for writing by another program until that program closes the file. Some file systems allow several users to read from a file concurrently.

There are two basic operations that can be specified for a sequential file: read and write. The object of a read statement or the source of a write statement should be the identifier of a variable or structure that corresponds to the records in the file. We will denote this identifier by <record name>. A read statement has the form

Read from <file name> file into <record name>

and a write statement has the form

> Write <record name> on <file name> file

A third operation that applies to sequential files stored on direct-access devices is

> Rewrite <record name> on <file name> file

This operation can be used only when the file has been opened for update. It writes a record in the location of the record that it most recently read.

An algorithm is now presented in order to illustrate the basic operations that are performed when processing a file sequentially. Assume that we have a sequential file named MASTER to be processed. The records can be read into a structure MRECORD consisting of MKEY and MDATA. The records are sorted in an ascending sequence according to the value of MKEY. It is assumed that there are no duplicate keys.

The transaction records are stored in a sequential file named TRANSACTION. These records can be read into a structure TRECORD consisting of TKEY, TDATA, and CODE. The transaction records are sorted in ascending sequence by TKEY value, and again, no duplicates exist. CODE has one of three possible values, 1, 2, or 3, that have the following interpretation:

> *1*    Update the record in the file MASTER with key TKEY using TDATA.
> *2*    Add a record to the file MASTER with key TKEY and data TDATA.
> *3*    Delete a record from the file MASTER that has key TKEY.

**Algorithm**  SEQUENTIAL_PROCESSING.  Given the files MASTER and TRANSACTION, it is required to form a new file, NEW_MASTER, by performing the operations specified by the transaction records. NRECORD has a format identical to MRECORD and consists of NKEY and NDATA.

1.  [Open files]
        Open MASTER file for input
        Open TRANSACTION file for input
        Open NEW_MASTER file for output
        Read from TRANSACTION file into TRECORD
        Exit
2.  [**Read** first MASTER file record]
        Read from MASTER file into MRECORD
3.  [Read first transaction]
        Read from TRANSACTION file into TRECORD.
4.  [Loop to read record and do updating]
        Repeat while not end of TRANSACTION file
          If end of MASTER file
          then    Repeat while not end of TRANSACTION file
                If CODE = 2  (add a record)
                then    NDATA ← TDATA
                        NKEY ← TKEY
                        Write NRECORD on NEW_MASTER file
                else    Write('IMPROPER TRANSACTION ', TRECORD)
                Read from TRANSACTION file into TRECORD
          (Terminate algorithm)
          Close MASTER, TRANSACTION, and NEW_MASTER files
          Exit

```
else    If MKEY < TKEY
        then   Write MRECORD on NEW_MASTER file
               Read from MASTER file into MRECORD
        else   If MKEY = TKEY
               then   If CODE = 1   (update a record)
                      then   MDATA ← TDATA
                             Write MRECORD on NEW_MASTER file
                      else   If CODE ≠ 3   (not a deletion)
                             then   Write MRECORD on NEW_MASTER
                                    Write ('ILLEGAL TRANSACTION ',
                                         TRECORD, 'OR DUPLICATE KEY')
                             Read from TRANSACTION file into TRECORD
               else   If CODE = 2   (add a record)
                      then   NDATA ← TDATA
                             NKEY ← TKEY
                             Write NRECORD on NEW_MASTER file.
                      else   Write ('ILLEGAL TRANSACTION ', TRECORD)
                      Read from TRANSACTION file into TRECORD
```

5.  [Transfer remaining records from MASTER file]
      Repeat while not end of MASTER file
         Write MRECORD on NEW_MASTER file
         Read from MASTER file into MRECORD
6.  [Close files]
      Close MASTER, TRANSACTION and NEW_MASTER files
7.  [Finished]
      Exit                                                              □


Algorithm SEQUENTIAL_PROCESSING demonstrates the complications that can arise in checking the TRANSACTION file against the MASTER file. Since either file may end first, the repeat loops in steps 4 and 5 are needed to complete the scanning of TRANSACTION file and MASTER file, respectively. Two kinds of errors can be detected. In step 4, if TKEY and MKEY are equal but neither an update or a deletion is specified, then either an illegal code or the addition of a record with a duplicate key is specified. If TKEY is ever less than MKEY but CODE is not 2, then transactions to update or delete a nonexistent record are ignored.

The requirement that the records in a sequential file be ordered by their keys is not essential if the file is being scanned to perform the same operation on every record.

The important points concerning the sequential processing of sequential files can be summarized as follows:

*1*  Sequential processing is most advantageous if a large number of transactions can be batched to form a single "run" on the file.

*2*  A new file should be created if there are any additions and a significant number of deletions requested.

*3*  Quick response time should not be expected for a transaction or a batch of transactions.

*4*  The requirement that the records in a sequential file be ordered by a particular key is not essential if the file is being scanned to perform the same operation on every record (i.e., serial processing).

In the following sections we will see that certain other file organizations are more suitable if requirements such as quick response time and individual transaction handling exist. If the sequential file resides on a direct-access device (such as disk or drum), it is possible to improve the response time significantly. This can be achieved by performing an external binary search involving track locations within the file and hence accessing records in a nonsequential manner. In some systems, however, the user is not always capable of acquiring specific knowledge concerning track addresses.

### 7-4.3  Sequential Files in PL/I

In the remainder of this section, we describe how sequential files can be created and accessed in PL/I. We do so with the explicit purpose of illustrating how sequential files are handled in a specific programming language. In addition. we heavily rely on this material in the discussion of file applications in Secs. 7-5. 7-8. and 7-10. By tradition, COBOL is the programming language which is used most often in file processing. We will use PL/I because of its similarity with Pascal. the language that has been primarily used throughout this book. Unfortunately, extensive file-handling facilities have not been defined for Pascal. Almost all of the PL/I file-handling facilities discussed in this chapter have counterparts in COBOL.

There are two types of sequential files in PL/I, namely, STREAM files and CONSECUTIVE RECORD files. In this text, we assume some knowledge of the data-, list-, and edit-directed STREAM input/output facilities offered by PL/I, using the standard system files SYSIN and SYSPRINT. We plan to discuss some of the unfamiliar, yet important, properties of STREAM input/output. A comparison of STREAM input/output and CONSECUTIVE RECORD input/output is made. Since RECORD input/output is not assumed to be known by the reader, it will be covered in more detail.

A STREAM-oriented file, as the name suggests, can be considered as a continuous stream of information that flows into the program area via the execution of GET statements and out of the program area via the execution of PUT statements. This stream of information is stored externally on a file in *character form* (e.g., EBCDIC form).  For convenience and efficiency, the information in the file is grouped into physical records or blocks; however, the contents of the blocks bear no relationship to the argument lists of the GET and PUT statements. This aspect will be illustrated presently.

A file is a data-holding entity just as any array or structure is in PL/I. Consequently, all files should be declared with the exception of the standard STREAM files, SYSIN, and SYSPRINT. Consider the following declaration

    DECLARE TRIANGL FILE STREAM INPUT ENVIRONMENT (F(20));

The file TRIANGL is declared to be a STREAM-oriented file which can be used for input (i.e., only GET statements can be applied to this file). The ENVIRONMENT attribute, which can be abbreviated as ENV, contains a list of parameters which are needed by the data-management routines in the operating system.  F(20) is interpreted as specifying a file with a blocksize of twenty characters or bytes which is fixed in length. In the remaining sections of this chapter, we will encounter other types of parameters for the ENV attribute.

In PL/I, files must be opened and closed in order to receive and release buffers from the operating system. This is accomplished with OPEN and CLOSE statements, for example,

```
OPEN FILE (TRIANGL);
CLOSE FILE (TRIANGL);
```

As an example of a simple program involving the nonstandard file TRIANGL, consider Fig.7-4.4. The program reads in three values for A, B, and C, and tests if they form a set of dimensions for a triangle.

Information in the file TRIANGL is stored as illustrated in Fig.7-4.5a. With the initial execution of the GET statement, the first two physical records are read into the two buffers that were allocated with the execution of the OPEN statement. Two buffers are automatically supplied for STREAM-oriented input/output—the reason for this becomes obvious in the following discussion. The character information in the first buffer (see Fig.7-4.5b) is interpreted by the PL/I subsystem for handling STREAM I/O. The information entities which correspond to items A, B, and C are isolated (i.e., intermediate blanks are treated as delimiters) and these entities (5.0, 3.0, and 4.0) are converted from their character formats to floating-point representations. The floating-point representations are assigned to the memory locations for A, B, and C that have been allocated in the program area. Hence, for STREAM input/output, a buffer assumes an additional purpose to that of smoothing out input/output transmission, namely, that of providing an intermediate area from which character conversion can take place.

After the initial execution of the GET statement, a system pointer references the point "a" in the buffer. During the interpretation of the information in the buffer, this pointer is moved along to record the position of the character which is to be scanned next. A second execution of the GET statement results in the interpretation of the next set of three entities in the information stream. The three entities fall across the block boundary, i.e., they reside in both buffers. However, with a two-buffer system this does not present a problem in either the interpretation or the conversion of data. The system pointer is simply moved from the end of one buffer to the front of the other. However, it does graphically illustrate that the amount of data stored in a block is not necessarily related to the argument list in the GET statement, and that a two-buffer system is needed for STREAM input/output. We will see that this is not the case in RECORD input/output.

```
STREAM_EG: PROCEDURE OPTIONS (MAIN);

   DECLARE TRIANGL FILE STREAM INPUT ENV(F(20)),
        (A, B, C) FLOAT BINARY;

   ON ENDFILE (TRIANGL) STOP;
   OPEN FILE (TRIANGL);

   DO WHILE ('1'B);     /* DO UNTIL END OF FILE */

      GET FILE (TRIANGL) LIST (A, B, C);
      IF (A + B) < C | (A + C) < B | (B + C) < A

      THEN PUT SKIP FILE (SYSPRINT) LIST (A, B, C,
            'DOES NOT FORM A TRIANGLE');

      ELSE PUT SKIP FILE (SYSPRINT) LIST (A, B, C,
            'FORMS A TRIANGLE');

   END;

END STREAM_EG
```

**FIGURE 7-4.4**   Example of STREAM-oriented file processing.

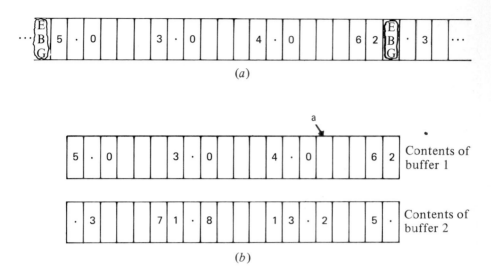

(a)

(b)

**FIGURE 7-4.5**   Representation of (a) a block in the file TRIANGL, and (b) the contents of two buffers after two blocks from the file have been read in. All information is stored in character format.

The effects of the execution of a PUT statement are the opposite to those of a GET statement. With the execution of a PUT statement, the values of the list of arguments are converted to their character representation when moved from the program's data area to the buffers. After a buffer is full, its contents are written out to the specified file which resides on an external storage device. End-of-block characters (interblock gaps in the case of a tape) separate the different blocks. When the file is closed, an end of file (EOF) marker is placed at the end of the final block, along with some other information (often called *trailer information*). STREAM-oriented files should be exclusively used as files associated with off-line sequential devices such as card readers, line printers, and magnetic tapes, since such devices are character-oriented. This does not imply that STREAM-oriented files should not reside on direct-access devices such as disks or drums; often they do. However, direct-access files are typically created as intermediate card files or line printer files by the operating system. Such files avoid the problem of slow program execution, which would arise if each program had to wait for individual cards to be read or lines to be printed. STREAM-oriented files are so commonly used as line printer files that a special type of STREAM file, called a PRINT file, is available in PL/1. A PRINT file allows the user to store in the first character of each block a special ANSI character, which indicates line- and page-skipping control to the printer.

In PL/1 there are many types of RECORD-oriented files (CONSECUTIVE, INDEXED, REGIONAL (1), REGIONAL (2), REGIONAL (3), and TRANSIENT). Only the CONSECUTIVE file is discussed in detail in this subsection. Before doing so, let us identify some properties of RECORD-oriented data transmission which are common to all RECORD files and which clearly distinguish RECORD files from STREAM files.

In record-oriented transmission, data in a file are considered to be a collection of records stored in any internal form (e.g., FLOAT or FIXED numbers, bit strings, character strings, etc.) acceptable by a PL/I program. Hence *no data conversion* need be performed during record-oriented input/output. On input, a READ statement such as

READ FILE(MASTER) INTO (EMPLOYEE);

causes a single record to be transmitted to the program variable (EMPLOYEE) exactly as it is recorded in the file. On output, a WRITE statement such as

WRITE FILE (MASTER) FROM (EMPLOYEE);

or a REWRITE statement (which is described later) causes a single record to be transmitted from the program variable (EMPLOYEE) to the file (MASTER) exactly as it is stored internally.

From the previous statements, it becomes obvious that a record is read into and written from a single program variable. A program variable may be a simple variable, an array variable, or most commonly, a structure variable. Although the PL/I statements used in record-oriented input/output are concerned with records (as dictated by the contents of the program variable), data are actually transmitted to and from a file in blocks of records. Blocks can contain fixed-length or variable-length records in a form described in Sec. 7-1 (in particular, see Fig 7-1.1). Consequently, for RECORD input/output, there is a definite relationship between a logical record, as derived from the contents of the program variable, and a block or physical record. There must be an integral number of logical records in a block—records are not allowed to cross block boundaries. IBM mainframe systems do allow an exception to this rule in the case where a record is unusually large. If the record is so large as to be impossible or inconvenient to store in a single block, it is permissible to have the record span over several blocks. In practice, instances in which this might happen rarely occur.

To understand how sequential processing is performed in PL/I, let us examine the program in Fig. 7-4.6. The program basically follows the logic presented in Algorithm SEQUENTIAL_PROCESSING, in which a master file is updated according to a number of transaction records. The major reason why the program has a different structure is because of the manner in which end of file conditions are handled in PL/I. The program is oriented toward a payroll application in which records from the MASTER file and transaction file (SYSIN) are assumed to be ordered by the social insurance number.

In the program, both MASTER and NEWMTR (meaning "new master") are declared as RECORD-oriented files having the CONSECUTIVE property. The CONSECUTIVE property implies that the records in the file are stored in contiguous locations in external memory. RECORD CONSECUTIVE files are sequential files, since access to a particular record can be gained only by reading all previous records.

Some of the important programming aspects concerning the PL/I program are as follows. First, the standard input file SYSIN containing the transaction record is opened and closed automatically by the operating system—no explicit OPEN or CLOSE statements are needed. Second, the ENV parameter F(370,37) specifies that the MASTER and NEWMTR files are blocked with 10 records, each 37 bytes in length. Hence, the block size and buffer size are 370 bytes. Assuming a basic understanding of Algorithm SEQUENTIAL_PROCESSING, the remainder of the program should be straightforward.

One point that must be noted is that we have not provided enough information in the file declaration statement to identify fully the MASTER and NEWMTR files to

```
SEQPROC: PROCEDURE OPTIONS (MAIN);

/* A PROCEDURE WHICH READS IN TRANSACTION RECORDS AND APPLIES THEM
   TO A MASTER EMPLOYEE FILE. THE TRANSACTION RECORDS ARE OF THE FORM
   <TYPE> <SURNAME> <INITIALS> <SOCIAL INS #> <WAGE/HR> <CLASSIFICATN>
   WHERE    COL 1     <TYPE>: 1=DELETE, 2=ADD, 3=UPDATE
            COL 2-22  <SURNAME>
            COL 22-27 <INITIALS>
            COL 28-36 <SOCIAL INSURANCE NUMBER>
            COL 37-41 <WAGE PER HOUR>
            COL 42-44 <WORK CLASSIFICATION CODE>                    */

DECLARE 1 EMPLOYEE,
          2 NAME,
            3 SURNAME CHAR(20),
            3 INITIALS CHAR(6),
          2 SOC_INS# FIXED(9),
          2 WAGE_PER_HOUR FIXED(5,2),
          2 CLASSIFICATION CHAR(3);

DECLARE 1 TRAN_REC,
          2 NAME,
            3 SURNAME CHAR(20),
            3 INITIALS CHAR(6),
          2 SOC_INS# FIXED(9),
          2 WAGE_PER_HOUR FIXED(5,2),
          2 CLASSIFICATION CHAR(3);

DECLARE MASTER FILE RECORD ENV (CONSECUTIVE F(370,37)),
          NEWMTR FILE RECORD ENV (CONSECUTIVE F(370,37)),
          CODE FIXED(1),
          L(3) LABEL,
          (MASTERDONE, SYSINDONE) BIT(1) INITIAL('0'B);

ON ENDFILE(SYSIN) CALL COMPLETE;
ON ENDFILE(MASTER) CALL EXTEND;
OPEN FILE (MASTER) INPUT;
OPEN FILE (NEWMTR) OUTPUT;

/* INITIAL READING OF MASTER AND TRANSACTION RECORDS */
READ FILE(MASTER) INTO (EMPLOYEE);
GET FILE(SYSIN) EDIT(CODE,TRAN_REC)(COL(1),F(1),A(20),A(6),F(9),
     F(5),A(3));

REPEAT:
    DO WHILE('1'B);    /* REPEAT UNTIL AN END OF FILE CONDITION */
        DO WHILE (EMPLOYEE.SOC_INS# < TRAN_REC.SOC_INS#);
            WRITE FILE (NEWMTR) FROM (EMPLOYEE);
            READ FILE(MASTER) INTO (EMPLOYEE);
        END;
        GO TO L(CODE);

    L(1):   /* DELETE */
        IF EMPLOYEE.SOC_INS# ¬= TRAN_REC.SOC_INS#
        THEN DO;
            PUT SKIP LIST('ERROR* RECORD TO BE DELETED DOES NOT EXIST');
            WRITE FILE (NEWMTR) FROM (EMPLOYEE);
        END;
        READ FILE(MASTER) INTO (EMPLOYEE);
        GO TO NEWTRANS;

    L(2):   /* ADD */
        WRITE FILE (NEWMTR) FROM (TRAN_REC);
        GO TO NEWTRANS;
```

**FIGURE 7-4.6** Processing a sequential file.

```
L(3):    /* UPDATE */
    IF EMPLOYEE.SOC_INS# ¬= TRAN_REC.SOC_INS#
    THEN DO;
        PUT SKIP LIST('ERROR* RECORD TO BE UPDATED DOES NOT EXIST')
        WRITE FILE (NEWMTR) FROM (EMPLOYEE);
    END;
    ELSE WRITE FILE (NEWMTR) FROM (TRAN_REC);
    READ FILE(MASTER) INTO (EMPLOYEE);

NEWTRANS:
    GET FILE(SYSIN) EDIT(CODE,TRAN_REC)(CCL(1),F(1),A(20),A(6),F(9),
        F(5),A(3));

END REPEAT;


COMPLETE: PROCEDURE;
    IF MASTERDONE
    THEN DO;
        CLOSE FILE(MASTER);
        CLOSE FILE(NEWMTR);
        STOP;
    END;
    SYSINDONE = '1'B;
    DO WHILE('1 B);      /* UNTIL END OF MASTER FILE */
        WRITE FILE (NEWMTR) FROM (EMPLOYEE);
        READ FILE(MASTER) INTO (EMPLOYEE);
    END;
END COMPLETE;


EXTEND: PROCEDURE;
    IF SYSINDONE
    THEN DO;
        CLOSE FILE(MASTER);
        CLOSE FILE(NEWMTR);
        STOP;
    END;
    MASTERDONE = '1'B;
    DO WHILE('1'B);     /* UNTIL END OF SYSIN FILE */
        IF CODE = 2 & EMPLOYEE.SOC_INS# < TRAN_REC.SOC_INS#
        THEN DO;
            WRITE FILE (NEWMTR) FROM (TRAN_REC);
            EMPLOYEE.SOC_INS# = TRAN_REC.SOC_INS# ;
        END;
        ELSE PUT SKIP LIST('ERROR – ILLEGAL ADDITION ATTEMPTED');
        GET FILE(SYSIN) EDIT(CODE,TRAN_REC)(COL(1),F(1),A(20),A(6),F(9),
            F(5),A(3));
    END;
END EXTEND;

END SEQPROC;
```

**FIGURE 7-4.6**   (Continued)


the system. Besides the block size and logical record length, a complete description
should include information such as the amount of space required by the file, the
disposition of the file (e.g., whether it exists already or is just being created), and the
type and volume of the device on which the file is to remain on the system. Such
information is commonly described externally through statements in a system command language for the particular installation on which the program is executed. For
example, in IBM systems, the system command language called JCL (Job Control
Language) can be employed to define externally files by the use of a DD (data defin-

ition) statement. The following DD statements coupled with the information in the ENV clauses describe the MASTER and NEWMTR files to the system:

```
//GO.MASTER DD DISP=(OLD,KEEP),UNIT=SYSDA,VOL=SER=USER01,
//    SPACE =(TRK,5)
//GO.NEWMTR DD DISP=(NEW,KEEP),UNIT=SYSDA,VOL=SER=USER01,
//    SPACE =(TRK,5)
```

We are not going to provide the system command information (e.g., the DD statements) for all the programs in this chapter. Since such information can vary from computer installation to installation, it is suggested that a PL/I programmer's guide for a particular installation be consulted when writing programs involving file descriptions.

A final PL/I statement we must discuss before completing this subsection is the REWRITE command. If we want simply to update a file without creating or deleting records, we can do so by using the REWRITE statement if the file resides on a direct-access storage device. Figure 7-4.7 is a segment of a PL/I program which illustrates how the MASTER file can be updated without creating a new file, assuming only update transactions are handled. The declarations for MASTER, EMPLOYEE, and TRAN_REC are assumed to be given and are the same as described in Fig. 7-4.6. The REWRITE command is designed to overwrite the record that was last read. With this capability, it is easy to see how the program can update the MASTER file without creating a new file.

To reinforce our discussion on sequential files, we consider a small billing-system application which makes use of many of the concepts discussed in this section.

```
/* EXAMPLE TO SHOW THE UPDATE OF A FILE WITHOUT CREATING A NEW FILE */

/* 'UPDATES' IS A TRANSACTION FILE OF NEW EMPLOYEE RECORDS TO REPLACE
   CORRESPONDING RECORDS IN THE FILE 'MASTER'. IN BOTH FILES, RECORDS
   MUST BE ORDERED BY SOCIAL-INSURANCE-NUMBER.              */

UPDATE: PROCEDURE OPTIONS (MAIN);

DECLARE MASTER FILE SEQUENTIAL RECORD ENV (CONSECUTIVE F(370,37));
DECLARE UPDATES FILE STREAM;

DECLARE 1 EMPLOYEE,
          2 NAME,
            3 SURNAME  CHAR(20),
            3 INITIALS CHAR(6),
          2 SOC_INS# FIXED(9),
          2 WAGE_PER_HOUR FIXED(5,2),
          2 CLASSIFICATION CHAR(3);

DECLARE 1 TRAN_REC,
          2 NAME,
            3 SURNAME  CHAR(20),
            3 INITIALS CHAR(6),
          2 SOC_INS# FIXED(9),
          2 WAGE_PER_HOUR FIXED(5,2),
          2 CLASSIFICATION CHAR(3);

DECLARE OLD_SOC_INS# FIXED(9) INIT(000000000);
```

**FIGURE 7-4.7**  Updating a sequential file.

```
ON ENDFILE (UPDATES) BEGIN;
    CLOSE FILE (MASTER);
    CLOSE FILE (UPDATES);
    STOP;
    END;

ON ENDFILE (MASTER) BEGIN;
    PUT SKIP LIST ('END OF MASTER FILE');
    CLOSE FILE (MASTER);
    CLOSE FILE (UPDATES);
    STOP;
    END;

OPEN FILE (UPDATES) INPUT;
OPEN FILE (MASTER) SEQUENTIAL UPDATE;

/* READ TO START UP */

READ FILE (MASTER) INTO (EMPLOYEE);


DO WHILE ('1'B)      /* UNTIL END OF UPDATES FILE */

    GET FILE (UPDATES) EDIT (TRAN_REC)
            (CCL(1),A(20),A(6),F(9),F(5,2),A(3))

    IF TRAN_REC.SOC_INS# < OLD_SOC_INS#
    THEN PUT SKIP EDIT ('ERROR* OUT OF ORDER CARD. NUMBER: ',
            TRAN_REC.SOC_INS#,'. NAME: ',TRAN_REC.SURNAME)
            (A,F(9),A,A);

    ELSE DO;

        OLD_SOC_INS# = TRAN_REC.SOC_INS#;

        DO WHILE (EMPLOYEE.SOC_INS# < TRAN_REC.SOC_INS#);
            READ FILE (MASTER) INTO (EMPLOYEE);
        END;

        IF EMPLOYEE.SOC_INS# = TRAN_REC.SOC_INS#
        THEN REWRITE FILE (MASTER) FROM (TRAN_REC);
        ELSE PUT SKIP EDIT ('ERROR* NON-EXISTENT RECORD, NAME:',
                TRAN_REC.SURNAME,'. NUMBER: ', TRAN_REC.SOC_INS#)
                (3 A,F(9));

    END;
END;

END UPDATE;
```

**FIGURE 7-4.7**    (Continued)

### Exercises for Sec. 7-4

1.  Suppose that you are to create a sequential file which contains records describing potential new acquisitions for a library. A key which can be used to access information concerning a new book is the first author's surname Are there any advantages to ordering the file by the first author's surname assuming *(a)* search requests are not batched and *(b)* search requests are batched?

2.  Suppose we are to create a sequential file which contains records describing in detail the descriptions of various course offerings at an educational institution. The class numbers can be used as a key for the file. Examples of class

numbers are CMPT 250, MATH 222, and PHYS 111. Are there any advantages to ordering the files by the class number, assuming *(a)* search requests are not batched and *(b)* search requests are batched? You are to assume that almost all requests concerning classes contain legitimate keys (i.e., a key for which a record exists). Can you propose a better type of ordering than by class number for the situation in which search requests are not batched?

3. Outline the major differences between STREAM input/output and CONSECU-TIVE RECORD input/output in PL/I. For what types of applications should each be used?

4. You are placed in charge of the design and implementation of a small payroll system. The system contains the following employee information:

  *(a)* Employee number (5 digits)
  *(b)* Employee's salary (5 digits)
  *(c)* Social insurance number (9 digits)
  *(d)* Tax exemption (5 digits)
  *(e)* Group insurance premium (3 digits)
  *(f)* Parking (2 digits)
  *(g)* Association dues (3 digits)
  *(h)* Name (up to 37 characters)

Changes to employee information are made via transactions which are applied to the system at the time pay checks are printed (i.e., once a month). Three types of transactions are required, and these are:

  *(a)* *Addition* transaction which must contain the information items for an employee, for example,

  ADD 67823 14400 708312694 01925 320 35 000 LISTOE, A.D.

  *(b)* *Deletion* transaction which contains only an employee number, for example,

  DEL 67823

  *(c)* *Update* transaction which contains the employee number plus an explicit indication of the items to be changed, for example,

  UPD 67823 PARKING = 48 TAX_EMP = 02400

On a month-end run, the system should print pay checks for each member on staff, including an initial pay check for an employee who is added and a final check for an employee who is deleted. Payments consist of a two-part form, as illustrated in Fig. 7-4.8, the check itself and the statement of net earnings.

Income tax is calculated based on a graduated scale which may be approximated using the following formula (N is the taxable income, that is, N = regular pay – exemptions)

Income tax = $(N/2500 + 16)\% \times N$

Therefore, the income tax paid by A. Listoe is

$((1200 - 200)/250 + 16)\% \times (\$1200 - \$200) = \$200$

Pension plan contributions are 8 percent of the income after taxes.

Design in detail and then implement the payroll system just outlined. The design phase should include a detailed discussion of transaction record,

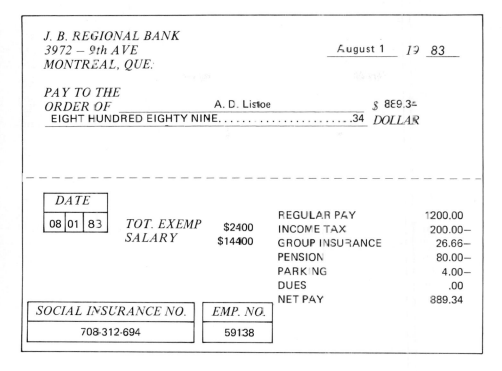

*J. B. REGIONAL BANK*
*3972 – 9th AVE*                                    August 1   19  83
*MONTREAL, QUE.*

*PAY TO THE*
*ORDER OF*            A. D. Listoe                        $ 889.34
 EIGHT HUNDRED EIGHTY NINE. . . . . . . . . . . . . . . . . . . . . .34 *DOLLAR*

---

| *DATE* | | | | |
|---|---|---|---|---|
| 08 | 01 | 83 | *TOT. EXEMP*  $2400 | REGULAR PAY    1200.00 |

*TOT. EXEMP*   $2400
*SALARY*       $14400

REGULAR PAY        1200.00
INCOME TAX          200.00—
GROUP INSURANCE      26.66—
PENSION              80.00—
PARKING               4.00—
DUES                   .00
NET PAY             889.34

| *SOCIAL INSURANCE NO.* | *EMP. NO.* |
|---|---|
| 708-312-694 | 59138 |

**FIGURE 7-4.8**   Sample output for payroll system.

employee payroll record, and output record formats. The stylized printing on the payment forms should be printed as well, even though it would be pre-printed on special forms in a production system.

## 7-5 A SMALL BILLING SYSTEM

The format of this section, as well as the other application sections in this chapter, will consist of analyzing the problem, designing the system (in particular, deciding on the file structure needed in the system), and describing a possible implementation for the system. Each of these three phases of system development will be described in a separate subsection. It would be ideal if systems could be developed using a strict top-down approach that would initially involve a complete system analysis, then the design, and finally the implementation. In the discussion of the applications in this chapter, this ideal will appear at times to be easily achieved. In practice, however, it is almost never realized. As the system develops, we iterate between the analysis and the design phases, and between the design and implementation phases, until the system is complete. (During the development of some systems, there is even iteration between the analysis and implementation phases. This is disastrous and should be avoided at all cost!)

This particular section is concerned with the analysis, design, and implementation of a small billing system. While this example is included primarily as an application using sequential files, it is an interesting application in its own right since everyone, at some time, has interacted with such a system.

### 7-5.1 System Analysis

The Company of Canada, Ltd. operates a chain of small department stores. Recently, the company decided to offer a charge-account service to its customers by means of credit cards. A purchase form indicating the credit-card number, the items purchased, and their cost is filled out by the cashiers at the time of purchase. The form is also designed to show a customer credit in the case of returned articles. The credit card carries a six-digit customer-account number, and an imprinter at the point of sale indicates the date of the transaction.

The forms are sent on an almost daily basis to the head office for processing. The head office sends out monthly statements to all credit-card-carrying customers. All payments on charge accounts are also received at the head office. The company charges interest on these accounts at the rate of 1.5 percent of that part of last month's debit balance for which payments were not received this month.

The company has found it desirable to automate its billing system. The company is small. After some preliminary analysis, it is decided that the company could not afford the ongoing costs of its own computer, and arrangements have been made with another business to rent some magnetic-disk storage and purchase some CPU time once per month.

The company would like as output from each monthly run the following information:

1. A listing of all credit-card-carrying customers. The listing should include for each given account number the name, address, and current balance of account, and it should be ordered by account number.
2. A monthly balance report which should include the total outstanding balance owed to the company, the total of purchases made for the month, the total of payment received, the interest charged, and the new total balance owed to the company.
3. A daily sales report which indicates, for each day, the total of the purchase receipts received at the head office.
4. Monthly statements for all customers which should include an initial balance forward figure, the date, name, and amount of any purchase, the date and amount of any payment on the account, the interest charged (if any), and a final current amount-owing figure. Also included is the customer's address, which is positioned on the statement so as to appear through a see-through window in the statement's envelope. The address must be no more than four lines and a line must be fewer than 30 characters in width.

### The inputs to the billing system include:

1. Credit-card receipts, each of which includes the customer identification number, date of purchase, and description and amount of items purchased.
2. New customer credit-card applications, each of which includes the customer's name, address, and assigned identification number.
3. Payment receipts, each of which includes the customer identification number, the date of payment, and the amount paid.
4. Customer termination information, where each termination must provide the customer identification number and the date of termination.

There are some additional factors which can potentially affect the design of the system. First, all new credit cards must be issued by the head office. Second, as a service to the public, customers are allowed to indicate the termination of their account by writing directly to the head office or by contacting the local business and having them send in a notice of termination.

### 7-5.2 System Design

We proceed with the system design first by deciding on the format for the inputs and outputs, and then by considering the problems of how best to generate the desired outputs. Inputs come from two sources: the point of sale (purchase and termination slips) and the customer (applications for credit cards, payments, and termination notices).

As purchases come in from point-of-sale locations, they are keyed in preparation for data entry to the system. The following format is chosen:

PURCHASE record:

| Position | 1-6: | Customer's identification number |
|---|---|---|
| | 7-12: | Date (two columns of each for month, day, and year) |
| | 13-20: | Amount of purchase |
| | 21-40: | Item description |

The input file that is formed by the encoding of these purchases will be called PURCHASE. Because terminations as well as purchases arrive from the points of sale, it is decided to indicate an account termination by placing the message 'DELETE THIS CUSTOMER' in the description field of the PURCHASE record. Therefore, PURCHASE records must also be created for termination notices that are sent directly to the head office by the customer.

Two separate input files, PAYMENT and NEWACCT, are also created for customer payments and credit-card applications, respectively.

PAYMENT record:

| Position | 1-6: | Customer's identification number |
|---|---|---|
| | 7-12: | Date (two columns each for month, day, and year) |
| | 13-20: | Amount of payment |

NEWACCT record:

| Position | 1-6: | Customer's identification number |
|---|---|---|
| | 7-26: | Customer's name |
| | 27-46: | Customer's street or P.O. box, etc. |
| | 47-65: | Customer's city, province, or state |
| | 66-72: | Customer's postal code |
| | 73-80: | Customer's initial balance (always set to zero) |

An important part of any business system design is the design of output forms and reports. In this application, the greatest effort must be expended on the design of the customer's statement. A format which does satisfy the company's needs is given in Fig. 7-5.1. Note that the boldface print identifies that part of the statement which is common to all statements. This common text should be preprinted on the statement by a printing shop before computer processing. This makes it necessary to print only the dates, purchases, balances, etc., for a specific customer. Such a procedure saves a tremendous amount of time and permits the generation of multicolored statements.

The customer listing as required by the company should be ordered by identification number, and all pertinent customer information should appear in a compact

**THE COMPANY OF CANADA, LTD.**
**4141 THE STREET**
**THE CITY, PROVINCE**
**A0A 1B1**

CUSTOMER'S.NAME. . . .NUMBER
STREET.OR.BOX.NUMBER
CITY, PROVINCE.OR.STATE
POS COD

| Date | TRANSACTION | DEBIT | CREDIT | BALANCE |
|---|---|---|---|---|
| | **BALANCE FORWARD** | $DD.DD | | $BB.BB |
| MM/DD/YY | PURCHASE(ITEM) | $DD.DD | | $BB.BB |
| MM/DD/YY | PAYMENT ON ACCOUNT | | $CC.CC | $BB.BB |
| MM/DD/YY | INTEREST ON: $II.II | $DD.DD | | $BB.BB |
| MM/DD/YY | CURRENT AMOUNT OWING | | | $BB.BB |

**FIGURE 7-5.1**   General format of a customer's statement.

yet readable format. To achieve this, the information pertaining to a single customer is printed on one line with the following format:

ID.NUM NAME...STREET.OR.P.O.BOX...CITY...,STATE...POST.CODE BALANCE

The monthly totals and daily payments received are printed on the same report in an easily readable format. Specific examples for all three of the reports will be illustrated in the next subsection.

We now turn to the design of the program which takes the specified input and creates the desired output properly formatted. Figure 7-5.2 shows a possible design for the system. It is not necessarily the best design, and some improvements will be considered later in this subsection.

An obvious yet important aspect of the system design is that each customer's current balance, along with his or her name, account number, and address, must be kept on a system file from one month's run to the next. We will call this file the CUSTOMER file and create it as a sequential file ordered by account number.

A conceptually simple way of handling new customers is to merge the set of new accounts with the CUSTOMER file and, by necessity, create a new sequential file which we call CUST1. On CUST1, a new account will have a "current-balance" field set to zero. Note that in the system we have designed, the assignment of a new account number is handled manually. While this may result in some extra book-keeping, a sequential card file ordered by account number can be created quite easily during the month and used in assigning new account numbers. This ordered sequential file, called NEWACCT, is the file that is merged with the CUSTOMER file to form CUST1.

To generate a customer's statement, it is necessary to combine the monthly purchases and payments for a customer with his or her previous month's balance.

Grouping all receipts and payments with the previous month's balance would be an inefficient costly process if it were done using a separate run for each customer. However, by sorting the PURCHASE and PAYMENT files by account number and then merging the information in these two files with the information in the CUST1 file, we can produce all the customer statements in one run (i.e., in one pass over each of the three files). The PURCHASE and PAYMENT files each can be sorted by

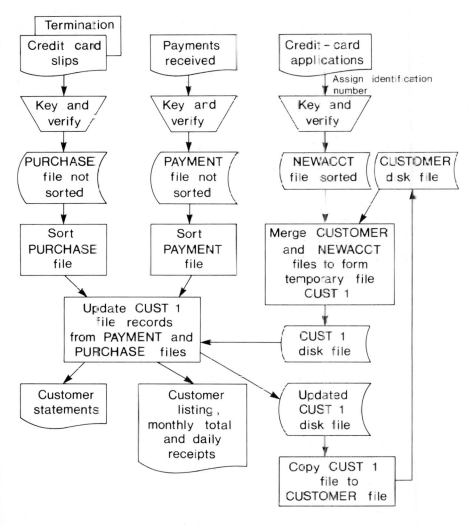

**FIGURE 7-5.2**    A flowchart showing a design of the billing system.

using a system-sort routine, or by writing your own sort procedure, as is indicated in Fig. 7-5.2. The merging of the three files is quite simple and is outlined in the following six steps:

1   Read in a CUST1 record.
2   Read in and process all PURCHASE and PAYMENT records with the same account number as the CUST1 record. (Because the files are ordered by account number, any purchases or payments for the customer designated in the CUST1 record should appear as the "next" records during the sequential processing of the PURCHASE and PAYMENT files.)
3   Compute a new balance.
4   Calculate interest if necessary.
5   Print customer's statement and update CUST1 record.
6   Return to process the next CUST1 record.

The company reports can also be generated during the customer-file updating. A customer's account number, name, address, and balance can be printed immediately after calculating a new balance during the processing of the three files. However, customer statements are printed at the same time, so care must be taken to place the company's customer list and the customer statements on separate files for printing. In the discussion of the system implementation which follows, we will see how this can be accomplished.

The company report containing the monthly totals can be created by accumulating the totals as individual customer records are processed. The final report is output immediately after the updating of all customer records.

The daily sales report is generated by updating a vector of 31 elements, in which each element holds the accumulation of all purchases on a given day. Element $n$ would hold the total of the purchase-slip amounts for the $n$th day of the month.

The final file processing to be completed in a monthly run is that of creating a new CUSTOMER file from the temporary CUST1 file. This involves nothing more than a simple record-by-record (i.e., serial) copying of the records in the CUST1 file into the CUSTOMER file.

In the previous discussion, we purposely neglected the problem of handling accounts which are terminated. One possibility is physically to delete terminating accounts after the processing of these accounts has taken place. The account number is set to 000000 during the merge-update on CUST1, and then all 000000 records are deleted when the new CUSTOMER file is created. The disadvantage with this scheme is that tardy sales slips on terminated accounts may be received the next month, and the account number will have already been removed from the system. An alternative design is considered at the end of the next subsection.

### 7-5.3 Implementation

The PL/I program BILLS given in Fig. 7-5.3 follows the design decisions arrived at in the previous section. BILLS consists of a mainline which is composed of file, record, and temporary-variable declarations, along with a series of five calls to the main modules of the system:

SORT_PURCHASES, SORT_PAYMENTS, MERGE_ACCTS, MERGE_UPDATE, and COPY

```
// EXEC  PL1L=CLG,PARM='ATR,XREF'
//PL1L.SYSIN DD *
```

BILLS: PROCEDURE OPTIONS (MAIN);

```
/*    THIS PROGRAM IS DESIGNED TO HANDLE THE BILLING REQUIREMENTS OF
 THE COMPANY OF THE CANADA, LTD. AS FOLLOWS:

    THE PROGRAM IS COMPOSED OF FIVE LOGICALLY DISTINCT SEGMENTS.
 THE FIRST TWO SORT THE TRANSACTION FILES, PURCHASE AND PAYMENT. THE
 THIRD OF THESE IS USED TO INSERT NEW CUSTOMERS INTO THE FILE OF THE
 CURRENT CUSTOMERS OF THE COMPANY. AND TO DELETE THOSE OLD CUSTOMERS
 WHICH ARE FLAGGED FOR DELETION. THE FOURTH PART OF THE PROGRAM IS
 USED TO UPDATE THE CURRENT BALANCES OF EACH CUSTOMER AND TO PRINT
 HIS MONTHLY STATEMENT. THE PROGRAM ALSO PRINTS A LIST OF TOTALS
 WHICH SERVES AS A MONTHLY SUMMARY REPORT OF THE COMPANY'S CASH FLOW.
 THE FINAL PART CREATES A NEW CUSTOMER FILE AFTER A MONTHLY RUN.      */

/* SOME OF THE IMPORTANT VARIABLES AND FILE NAMES USED IN THIS PROGRAM ARE:

     CUSTOMER — A MASTER FILE OF SEQUENTIAL ORGANIZATION WHICH HOLDS
               THE OLD LIST OF CUSTOMERS AND THEIR OLD BALANCES.
     NEWACCT — A TRANSACTION FILE WHICH CONTAINS A LIST OF NEW
               CUSTOMERS TO BE INSERTED NTO THE CUSTOMER FILE.
     PURCHASE — A TRANSACTION FILE USED TO CONTAIN A RECORD OF ALL
               PURCHASES MADE ON CREDIT IN THE LAST MONTH.
     PAYMENT — A TRANSACTION FILE USED TO CONTAIN A RECORD OF ALL
               PAYMENTS RECEIVED IN THE LAST MONTH.
     CUST1 —   A MASTER FILE, ALSO OF SEQUENTIAL ORGANIZATION, ON
               WHICH IS PLACED THE NEW LIST OF CUSTOMERS.
     STATMENT — A PRINT FILE ON WHICH ALL THE MONTHLY STATEMENTS
               ARE PRINTED.
     CUST —    A STRUCTURE OF THE SAME FORMAT AS THE RECORDS ON
               THE CUSTOMER FILES.
     PURCH —   A STRUCTURE USED TO STORE INTERNALLY THE RECORDS
               FROM THE PURCHASE CARD FILE.
     PAY —     A STRUCTURE USED TO STORE INTERNALLY THE RECORDS
               FROM THE PAYMENT FILE.

     OLD_BALANCE, PURCHASES, PAYMENTS INTEREST, NEW_BALANCE, PAY_DAY:
     AND PAY_DAY ARE VARIABLES USED IN THE CALCULATION OF TOTALS.      */


  DECLARE (CUSTOMER, CUST1) FILE RECORD SEQUENTIAL ENV
          (CONSECUTIVE F(750,75)),
          (NEWACCT,PURCHASE,PAYMENT) FILE STREAM ENV(CONSECUTIVE),
          STATMENT FILE STREAM PRINT,

 1 CUST,
        2 ID FIXED DECIMAL (6,0),
        2 NAME CHARACTER (20),
        2 ADDRESS,
              3 LINE1 CHARACTER (20),
              3 LINE2 CHARACTER (19),
              3 POSTAL_CODE CHARACTER (7),
        2 BALANCE FIXED DECIMAL (8,2),

 1 PURCH,
        2 ID FIXED DECIMAL (6,0),
        2 PDATE,
              3 MONTH CHARACTER (2),
              3 DAY   CHARACTER (2),
              3 YEAR  CHARACTER (2),
        2 AMOUNT FIXED DECIMAL (8,2),
        2 DESCRIPTION CHARACTER (20),
```

**FIGURE 7-5.3**   Small billing system.

```
1 PAY,
     2 ID FIXED DECIMAL (6,0),
     2 PDATE,
          3 MONTH CHARACTER (2),
          3 DAY   CHARACTER (2),
          3 YEAR  CHARACTER (2),
     2 AMOUNT FIXED DECIMAL (8,2),

OLD_BALANCE FIXED DECIMAL (10,2) INITIAL (0),
PURCHASES   FIXED DECIMAL (10,2) INITIAL (0),
PAYMENTS    FIXED DECIMAL (10,2) INITIAL (0),
INTEREST    FIXED DECIMAL (10,2) INITIAL (0),
INT_RATE    FLOAT BINARY INITIAL (.015),
NEW_BALANCE FIXED DECIMAL (10,2) INITIAL (0),
PAY_DAY(31) FIXED DECIMAL (10,2) INITIAL ( (31) 0),
(CUR_BALANCE, INTEREST_AMT) FIXED DECIMAL (8,2),
DELETE BIT(1) INITIAL ('0'B),
(BDATE,TODAY) CHARACTER (8);

/* THIS STATEMENT DETERMINES THE DATE OF THIS RUN TO USE AS THE
   CURRENT DATE ON THE STATEMENTS THAT ARE PRINTED.          */

   TODAY = SUBSTR(DATE,3,2) || '/' || SUBSTR(DATE,5,2) || '/' ||
        SUBSTR(DATE,1,2);

/*              M A I N   L I N E                */

   CALL SORT_PURCHASES;
   CALL SORT_PAYMENTS;
   CALL MERGE_ACCTS;
   CALL MERGE_UPDATE;
   CALL COPY;

/* A PROGRAM SEGMENT WHICH CONTAINS THE THREE INTERNAL PROCEDURES
   SORT_PURCHASES, SORT_PAYMENTS, AND MERGE_ACCTS WOULD NORMALLY FALL
   IN THIS SECTION.                            */


/*****************************************************************/
/*                    M E R G E _ U P D A T E                */

MERGE_UPDATE: PROCEDURE;

/* THIS PROCEDURE READS A RECORD FROM THE CUST1 TEMPORARY FILE
   AND THEN PROCESSES RECORDS FROM THE PURCHASE AND PAYMENTS FILES
   WHICH HAVE THE SAME ID NUMBER. NOTE IT IS REQUIRED THAT THE
   PURCHASE AND PAYMENT FILES ARE ALSO SORTED IN ORDER OF ASCENDING
   ID NUMBERS. (THIS IS ALSO A REQUIREMENT FOR THE NEWACCT FILE IN
   THE MERGE_ACCTS PROCEDURE).                       */

   OPEN FILE (PURCHASE) INPUT,
      FILE (PAYMENT) INPUT,
      FILE (CUST1) UPDATE,
      FILE (STATMENT) OUTPUT;

   ON ENDFILE (CUST1) CALL SUMMARY_REPORT;
   ON ENDFILE (PURCHASE) PURCH.ID = 0;
   ON ENDFILE (PAYMENT) PAY.ID = 0;

   GET FILE (PURCHASE) EDIT (PURCH) (COLUMN(1),F(6),3 A(2),F(8,2),
                    A(20));
   GET FILE (PAYMENT) EDIT (PAY) (COLUMN(1),F(6),3 A(2),F(8,2));
   DO WHILE ('1'B);
      READ FILE (CUST1) INTO (CUST);

/* PRINT STATEMENT HEADINGS AND PREVIOUS BALANCE            */
```

**FIGURE 7-5.3**   (Continued)

```
PUT FILE (STATMENT) EDIT ('THE COMPANY OF CANADA, LTD.',
                '4141 THE STREET',
                'THE CITY, PROVINCE','ADA 1B1')
    (X(22),A,SKIP,X(28),A,SKIP,X(26),A,SKIP,X(32),A)
    (NAME,CUST.ID,ADDRESS)
    (SKIP(3),A(21),F(6),3 (SKIP, A))
    ('DATE','TRANSACTION','DEBIT','CREDIT','BALANCE')
    (SKIP(3),X(2),A(8),A(31),A(11),A(11),A(7))
    ('BALANCE FORWARD',BALANCE)
    (SKIP(2),X(10),A(49),P'$$$$,$$9V.99CR')

IF BALANCE < 0
THEN PUT FILE (STATMENT) EDIT (BALANCE)
            (SKIP(0),X(47),P'$$$$,$$9V.99');

ELSE IF BALANCE > 0
    THEN PUT FILE (STATMENT) EDIT (BALANCE)
            (SKIP(0),X(35),P'$$$$,$$9V.99');

OLD_BALANCE = OLD_BALANCE + BALANCE;
CUR_BALANCE = BALANCE;

/***************************************************************/
/*                    P U R C H A S E S                        */

/* THIS SEGMENT IS SET UP TO HANDLE ALL PURCHASE RECORDS.      */

    DO WHILE (CUST.ID = PURCH.ID);

/* THIS IS WHERE AND HOW THE DELETE FLAG IS SET.               */

        IF DESCRPTION = 'DELETE THIS CUSTOMER'
        THEN DELETE = '1'B;
        ELSE DO;
            PURCHASES = PURCHASES + PURCH.AMOUNT;
            BDATE = PURCH.MONTH || '/' || PURCH.DAY || '/' ||
                    PURCH.YEAR;
            BALANCE = BALANCE + PURCH.AMOUNT;
            IF PURCH.AMOUNT >= 0
            THEN = 5;
            ELSE I = 17;

/* PRINT THE LINE INDICATING A PURCHASE.                       */

            PUT FILE (STATMENT) EDIT (BDATE,DESCRIPTION,
                ABS(PURCH.AMOUNT),BALANCE;
                (SKIP,A(10),A(20),X(I),P'$$$$,$$9V.PP',
                COLUMN(60),P'$$$$,$$9V.99CR');
        END;

        GET FILE (PURCHASE) EDIT (PURCH) (COLUMN(1),F(6),3 A(2)
                F(8,2),A(20));
    END;    /* OF PURCHASE SEGMENT */
```

**FIGURE 7-5.3**   (Continued)

Each module corresponds to a rectangular processing block in Fig. 7-5.2. Because the files CUSTOMER and CUST1 are not input record or print oriented, they are declared as RECORD with the CONSECUTIVE property. CUSTOMER is retained from one run to the next; CUST1 is a temporary file. NEWACCT, PAYMENT, and PURCHASE are all INPUT STREAM files because of their input record orientation. STATMENT is an OUTPUT STREAM file (in particular, a PRINT file) which contains the customer's statements. The record structure CUST is used in the processing

```
/***********************************************************************/
/*                    P A Y M E N T S                          */
/* THIS SEGMENT IS SET UP TO HANDLE ALL PAYMENT RECORDS.        */
    DO WHILE (CUST.ID = PAY.ID);
        BALANCE = BALANCE - PAY.AMOUNT;
        CUR_BALANCE = CUR_BALANCE - PAY.AMOUNT;
        PAYMENTS = PAYMENTS + PAY.AMOUNT;
        PAY_DAY(PAY.DAY) = PAY_DAY(PAY.DAY) + PAY.AMOUNT;
        BDATE = PAY.MONTH || '/' || PAY.DAY || '/' || PAY.YEAR;
        IF PAY.AMOUNT > 0
        THEN I = 17;
        ELSE I = 5;

/* PRINT THE LINE INDICATING A PAYMENT.                        */

        PUT FILE (STATMENT) EDIT (BDATE,'PAYMENT ON ACCOUNT',
                ABS(PAY.AMOUNT),BALANCE)
                (SKIP,A(10),A(20),X(I),P'$$$$,$$9V.99'
                 COLUMN(60),P'$$$$,$$9V.99CR');
        GET FILE (PAYMENT) EDIT (PAY) (COLUMN(1),F(6),3 A(2),
                F(8,2));

    END;    /* END OF PAYMENTS SEGMENT */

/***********************************************************************/
/*        I N T E R E S T   A N D   B A L A N C E   O W I N G      */
/* THIS SEGMENT CALCULATES THE AMOUNT OF INTEREST TO BE CHARGED.
   INTEREST IS CHARGED TO THAT PORTION OF LAST MONTH'S DEFICIT
   BALANCE FOR WHICH PAYMENTS WERE NOT RECEIVED THIS MONTH.     */

    IF CUR_BALANCE > 0
    THEN DO;
        INTEREST_AMT = INT_RATE * CUR_BALANCE;
        BALANCE = BALANCE + INTEREST_AMT;
        INTEREST = INTEREST + INTEREST_AMT;
        PUT FILE (STATMENT) EDIT (TODAY,'INTEREST ON ',
            CUR_BALANCE,':',INTEREST_AMT,BALANCE)
          (SKIP,A(10),A,P'$$$$,$$9V.99',A(3),P'$$$$,$$9V.99',
           COLUMN(60),P'$$$$,$$9V.99CR');
    END;

/* PRINT THE NEW BALANCE OWING (WHICH MAY BE A CREDIT BALANCE)   */

    PUT FILE (STATMENT) EDIT (TODAY,'CURRENT AMOUNT OWING',
            BALANCE)
            (SKIP(2),A(10),A(49),P'$$$$,$$9V.99CR');

    IF DELETE
    THEN DO;
        DELETE = '0'B;
        CUST.ID = 0;
```

**FIGURE 7-5.3**    (Continued)

of the CUSTOMER and CUST1 files, PURCH is used in the processing of the PUR-CHASE file, and PAY is used in the processing of the PAYMENT file. PAY_DAY is the vector used for accumulating the daily receipts. The remaining variables are understandable through their context in the program and the program comments.

The procedures SORT_PURCHASES and SORT_PAYMENTS are not given. A sorting method, such as the merge sort given in Chap. 6, can be used to order the PURCHASE and PAYMENT files. In addition, there exist several special-purpose external sorting methods such as the polyphase and oscillating sorts. These are briefly described in Sec. 7-6.

```
/* IF A CUSTOMER IS DELETED A MESSAGE IS PRINTED TO INDICATE THAT
   THIS IS FINAL STATEMENT.                               */

        PUT FILE (STATMENT) EDIT ('THIS IS YOUR FINAL STATEMENT.',
                          ' THANK YOU FOR YOUR BUSINESS.')
                          (SKIP(3),A,A);
        END;

    NEW_BALANCE = NEW_BALANCE + BALANCE;
    PUT FILE (STATMENT) PAGE;
    REWRITE FILE (CUST1) FROM (CUST);
    PUT FILE (SYSPRINT) EDIT (CUST) (SKIP(1),F(6),X(1),3 A(20),A(7),
                          F(9,2));

    END;    /* END OF MAIN LOOP */

/**********************************************************************/
/*                 S U M M A R Y _ R E P O R T                      */

/* THIS SEGMENT IS USED TO PRINT OUT THE MONTHLY TOTALS             */

SUMMARY_REPORT: PROCEDURE;

    PUT FILE (SYSPRINT) PAGE EDIT ('MONTHLY TOTALS') (A)
                ('OLD BALANCE OWING', OLD_BALANCE,
                 'PURCHASES MADE', PURCHASES,
                 'PAYMENTS RECEIVED', PAYMENTS,
                 'INTEREST CHARGED', INTEREST,
                 'CURRENT BALANCE OWING', NEW_BALANCE)
            (SKIP(1), 5 (SKIP(1),A(23),P'$$$$,$$$,$$9V.99DB'));
    PUT FILE (SYSPRINT) EDIT ('DAILY PAYMENTS RECEIVED THIS MONTH')
                (SKIP(5),A);

    DO I = 1 TO 31;
       IF (PAY_DAY(I) ¬= 0)
       THEN PUT FILE (SYSPRINT) EDIT (I,PAY_DAY(I))
                (SKIP(2),F(2),X(2),P'$$$$,$$$,$$9V.99DB');
    END;
    CLOSE FILE (CUST1), FILE (STATMENT), FILE (PAYMENT),
       FILE (PURCHASE);

END SUMMARY_REPORT;

END MERGE_UPDATE;
```

**FIGURE 7-5.3**   (Continued)


The procedure MERGE_ACCTS is also omitted because of the similarity between the type of processing required in the procedure and that given in the PL/I program in Fig. 7-4.6.

The procedure MERGE_UPDATE involves the sequential processing of the PURCHASE, PAYMENT, and CUST1 files, as was outlined in a six-step general algorithm given in the design subsection. The REWRITE statement is used in the updating of the CUST1 file. Of course, if CUST1 was a tape file instead of a disk file, rewriting would not be allowed and a new file would have to be created. Note also that we have used, to a significant extent, COBOL-like picture formats (i.e., format codes of the form P'$$9V.99') in the printing of the required reports. Such formats allow the placement of '$' adjacent to the left-most nonzero digit in a dollar figure. Also, they provide the ability to automatically place a 'CR' (for credit) or a 'DB' (for debit) following a number, depending on the sign of the number. The reader who is not familiar with COBOL picture formats should consult a COBOL or PL/I reference manual to gain an understanding of this type of formatting.

```
COPY: PROCEDURE;

/* THIS PROCEDURE COPIES THE FINAL CUST1 RECORDS BACK INTO CUSTOMER
   TO SET UP FOR THE NEXT MONTH'S RUN. NOTE THAT THOSE CUSTOMERS WITH
   AN ID OF 000000 ARE THOSE WHICH HAVE BEEN FLAGGED FOR DELETION.    */

   OPEN FILE (CUSTOMER) OUTPUT,
        FILE (CUST1) INPUT;
   ON ENDFILE (CUST1) STOP;
   DO WHILE ('1'B);
      READ FILE (CUST1) INTO (CUST);
      IF (CUST.ID¬= 000000)
      THEN WRITE FILE (CUSTOMER FROM (CUST);
   END;
END COPY;

END BILLS;
//GO.SYSPRINT DD SYSOUT=(J,,7316)
//GO.STATMENT DD SYSOUT=A
//GO.CUST1 DD DSN=&&CUSTOMER,DISP=(NEW,DELETE),UNIT=SYSDA,
//      VOL=SER=USER02,SPACE=(75,(25,5))
//GO.CUSTOMER DD DSN=&&CUSTOM,DISP=(OLD,KEEP),UNIT=SYSDA,
//      VOL=SER=USER02,SPACE=(75,(25,5))
//GO.NEWACCT DD *      (NEWACCT INPUT FILE SHOULD FOLLOW IMMEDIATELY)
//GO.PURCHASE DD *     (PURCHASE INPUT FILE SHOULD FOLLOW IMMEDIATELY)
//GO.PAYMENT DD *      (PAYMENT INPUT FILE SHOULD FOLLOW HERE)
```

**FIGURE 7-5.3**    (Continued)

The final procedure, COPY, involves a simple loop which moves the records in CUST1 to the file CUSTOMER, overwriting the old CUSTOMER records in the process. Records marked with an account number of 000000 are excluded from the new CUSTOMER file.

The JCL for NEWACCTS, PURCHASE, and PAYMENT is given at the end of the program. A set of sample reports for this data is shown in Fig. 7-5.4. Some information is assumed to reside in the CUSTOMER file initially.

To conclude this section, let us consider some changes in design of the system just implemented; remember, system development is an iterative process. Two major changes can be accommodated quite easily. Instead of making a separate pass over the CUSTOMER file to merge it with the NEWACCT file, we can simply include this merge in with the merge/update process, which involves the PURCHASE and PAYMENT files. Note that the temporary file CUST1 is still used. We could place the merged information from the four files immediately back into the file CUSTOMER, but this is risky. If the computer system fails in the middle of the merge/update procedure, the CUSTOMER file will contain both updated and old records. Such a situation would make a billing system restart impossible.

A second change accommodates the problem of tardy accounts — a problem which realistically cannot be ignored. Instead of replacing a terminating account number by 000000, we can copy the information for the account into a file called TERMINAL which is retained from month to month. The terminating account record is removed from the CUSTOMER file. When purchases and payments are applied to an account which is not found in the CUSTOMER file, a search is made of the TERMINAL file. If applicable, the transactions are posted against this file and statements can be generated. Account closures can be completed based on the transactions applied to the TERMINAL file.

```
145203  JOHN C. DRYDEN        BOX 400              JASPER,  AB        TCE 1E0      8.00
504858  PAMELA B. SCHULTZ     1356 OSLER ST.       SASKATOON,  SK     S7N OV2     12.19
     0  PETER L. CLARKE       2337 WEST 10TH AVE.  VANCOUVER,  BC     V2K 1H8     -1.43
529270  DAVID N. PARKER       4534 HIGHLAND ST.    EDMONTON,  AB      T2E 1K6   1353.03
532147  PATRICK L. WATSON     #123-1968 COMOX ST.  VANCOUVER,  BC     V4R 3Z8     37.00
     0  RAYMOND M. JAMES      753 11TH ST. S.      CALGARY,  AB       T3B 2A0      0.00
538494  ALICE H. COCHRANE     2348 MAIN ST.        WINNIPEG, MAN      R5K 7P1      0.00
542137  CINDY L. PARENT       4112 HIGH AVE.       CALGARY,  AB       T7C 5Y6    230.50
556090  DIANNE P. HOLMES      23 ASHTON CRES.      THUNDERBAY, ONT.   M9J 1T4    411.43
563619  PAUL E. JACKSON       1356 AVENUE ROAD     TORONTO, ONT.      M2D 0S9     -3.36
570144  RICHARD D WILLIAMSON  851 CACHE DRIVE      KAMLOOPS,  BC      U5X 3W9    443.30
587542  ROBERT C. SMYTHE      418 AVENUE S         SASKATOON,  SK     S7H 0K1    300.00
591146  LINDA T. GARDNER      2337 49TH ST. E.     CALGARY,  AB       T0M 2A0     25.37
609483  GEORGE H. ELSEY       #4-14015 77TH AVE.   EDMONTON,  AB      T3K 0I0   3457.69
615966  JUDY R. JONES         315 SCARTH ST.       REGINA,  SK        S4N 3D3    -11.70
637263  SUSAN C. FROST        12 1ST ST. N.        KAMLOOPS,  BC      U30 1G5    653.21
643120  JOHN A. THOMPSON      8423 81ST ST.        EDMONTON,  AB      T3F 1S5     29.14
661301  ROY B. ANDERSON       2415 COLONY ST.      SASKATOON,  SK     S7N 0S7      0.10
678007  JAMES P. MACDONALD    4125 ARBUTUS ST.     VANCOUVER,  BC     V4G LS2     39.22
686725  LARRY R. BROWN        4532 HIGHLAND BLVD.  NORTH VANCOUVER, BC V8D 2X3   145.46
693121  PATRICIA L. FOX       4105 36TH ST.        RED DEER,  AB      T5M LU9    183.19
752145  DAVE BROADFOOT        7469 HILL CT.        KAMLOOPS,  BC      U8S 5E5    250.00
```

(a)

```
MONTHLY TOTALS                          DAILY PAYMENTS RECEIVED THIS MONTH

OLD BALANCE OWING       $5,590.58        1          $5.00DB
PURCHASES MADE          $3,331.61
PAYMENTS RECEIVED       $1,428.32        2          $9.00
INTEREST CHARGED           $68.47
CURRENT BALANCE OWING   $7,562.34        3         $25.00

            (b)                          4        $100.00

                                         8         $50.00

                                         9         $25.00

                                        10         $30.00

                                        11        $100.00

                                        12          $5.00

                                        13         $54.32

                                        15        $115.00

                                        18        $200.00

                                        22        $100.00

                                        25        $100.00

                                        29         $50.00

                                        30        $400.00

                                        31         $70.00

                                              (c)
```

**FIGURE 7-5.4**  Sample reports of (a) customer report, (b) monthly balance report,
(c) daily sales report, and (d) a monthly statement.

We have presented in this section a simplified view of a small customer-billing
system. Nevertheless, the system illustrates the use and importance of sequential files
and provides a glimpse of the type of processing necessary in a large billing system.
We now turn our attention to a discussion of external sorting.

```
                 THE COMPANY OF CANADA, LTD.
                      4141 THE STREET
                   THE CITY,  PROVINCE
                        A0A 1B1


DIANNE P. HOLMES        556090
23 ASHTON CRES.
THUNDER BAY, ONT.
M9J 1T4


   DATE      TRANSACTION                DEBIT       CREDIT      BALANCE

             BALANCE FORWARD           $300.24                  $300.24
05/08/74   RECORD                        $5.00                  $305.24
05/08/74   RECORD PLAYER               $253.94                  $559.18
05/08/74   PAYMENT ON ACCOUNT                       $50.00      $509.18
05/22/74   PAYMENT ON ACCOUNT                      $100.00      $409.18
05/20/75   INTEREST ON    $150.24:       $2.25                  $411.43

05/20/75   CURRENT AMOUNT OWING                                 $411.43
```

(d)

**FIGURE 7-5.4**  (Continued)


## 7-6  EXTERNAL SORTING

In the sorting methods described in Chap. 6 we assumed that the list of items being sorted was stored in high-speed main memory. Of course, there are often situations in which we must handle or store in lexicographic order a very large number of items—so large as to not fit in main memory. In particular, it is often necessary to sort a large sequential transaction file by master file key prior to performing a master file merge update as was exhibited in Secs. 7-4 and 7-5. Indeed, even today when on-line direct access applications are so popular one of the most commonly used system utility programs is still the sort facility.

Our purpose in this section is not to present an extensive discussion and analysis of external sorting techniques because sorting packages can normally be invoked with little or no knowledge about how they work. Nevertheless, we believe it is important to have some appreciation of the complexity involved to gain some insight into why it takes as long as it does to sort a large file. For a very definitive discussion of external sorting, the reader is referred to Knuth [1973].

We will review two popular techniques that have typically been used to sort files on magnetic tapes, namely the polyphase and oscillating sorts. Enhancements to these methods and their applicability to sorting on magnetic disks will also be examined. Finally some comments on recent developments that have been affected by technology changes are described. To begin our discussion, however, it is important to introduce the notion of a run list.


### 7-6.1  Run Lists

The general strategy in external sorting is to begin by sorting small batches of records from a file in internal memory. These small batches are commonly called *run lists* (also called *initial runs* or *initial strings*). The size of these run lists depends directly on how much internal memory is set aside to perform the internal sorting. As we will see, the run lists are produced in a piecemeal fashion. They are stored in a target file from which they are later retrieved and merged together again to form fewer but larger run lists. This process of merging run lists to form fewer and larger run lists continues and eventually terminates with the production of a single run list that is the desired sorted file.

Let us assume we have a buffer large enough to hold m records from an unordered file containing n records, where m is usually much smaller than n. A straightforward method of generating run lists is to read m records into the internal buffer, sort them in place using an internal sort, and then write them onto a new target file as a run list of size m. It is recommended that a selection sort be used for m less than approximately 15 and an "in-place" heap sort be adopted for larger values of m. (Both of these sorting techniques were described in Chap. 6.) This run generation process continues until all n records are handled. This obvious way of producing initial run lists is often used and will be assumed throughout our discussion in this chapter whenever initial run lists of a fixed or predetermined length are required.

In fact there is a method to produce longer initial run lists given that the internal sort buffer is limited to size m and this method is commonly called the *replacement selection method*. The details of this method will be described after presenting the various sorting techniques. At that time, its intricacies will be easier to comprehend.

## 7-6.2 Tape Sorting

Traditionally, external sorting has been accomplished using magnetic tapes simply because they have been the most prevalent and cheapest form of external storage. The sequential nature of a tape unit is not a major handicap in performing large external sorts primarily because the process of sorting inherently involves a significant amount of record at a time retrieval and comparision. The major overhead in tape sorting is the amount of tape rewinding that must be done as will be illustrated in the description of the polyphase sort given in the the next subsection. This problem can be overcome to some extent if the tape unit can read both forward and backward. The oscillating sort, discussed in Sec. 7-6.2.2, is designed to take advantage of this feature.

### 7-6.2.1 Polyphase Sorting

One of the best known methods for external sorting on tapes is the *polyphase sort*. The basic strategy of this sort is to distribute ordered initial runs of predetermined size on the available tapes and then to repeatedly merge these runs in multiple phases in which each phase has a predetermined number of merges before a new target tape is selected.

Unquestionably, the initial distribution of the runs on the working tapes is the major consideration affecting the performance of the sort. One simple-minded approach called "balanced merging" can be adopted. This method requires the runs to be distributed evenly on T − 1 of the tapes where T tapes are assumed to be available in total. Each merged run is written on the tape T and redistribution and merging are repeated from the T − 1 working tapes until only one run is formed on tape T. The copying involved in redistributing the runs back on the working tapes adds a significant number of passes to the sort and thus consumes considerable time. It has been found that a perfect Fibonacci distribution of initial runs provides far better performance. The general patterns for this type of distribution was developed by R.L. Gilstad [1960] who also named the sorting technique the *polyphase merge*.

In the polyphase merge with a Fibonacci distribution, the merging procedure is continued until the tape with the least number of run lists is empty. When this occurs the remaining working tapes are "logically rotated" such that the newly emptied tape becomes the new target tape and the old target tape then becomes one of the working tapes to be merged. This strategy never requires any needless copying for the purpose of redistribution and the sort ends when all runs are merged into one.

To exemplify the polyphase sort and exhibit a Fibonacci distribution of initial runs, a small example will be presented. A trace of a sort is illustrated in Fig. 7-6.1 in which a series of 17 records are sorted using four tapes. Originally all the records are on tape 4 as shown in step 1 of Fig. 7-6.1. It should be pointed out that throughout our discussion and in the examples of this section we will represent a record by the sort key for the record only. Of course in general, when an external sort is applied the entire record is moved and not just the key field.

The Fibonacci distribution is perfect for 17 records on 4 tapes. The pth order Fibonacci series is used to determine the number of runs on each tape where $p = T - 1$. This series is defined as follows:

$$F^p_s = F^p_{s-1} + F^p_{s-2} + \cdots + F^p_{s-p},$$
$$F^p_s = 0 \text{ for } 0 \leqslant s \leqslant p - 2,$$
$$F^p_{p-1} = 1$$

for the s-level perfect distribution. In general, the kth tape should be allotted

$$F^p_{s-1} + F^p_{s-2} + \cdots + F^p_{s-k}$$

initial runs in the s-level perfect distribution. Therefore, in the example where $p = 3$, tape 1 receives $F^3_4 = 4$ runs, tape 2 receives $F^3_4 + F^3_3 = 4 + 2 = 6$ runs, and tape 3 receives $F^3_4 + F^3_3 + F^3_2 = 4 + 2 + 1 = 7$ runs for $s = 5$. Based on these recurrence formulae, the initial runs are distributed as shown in step 2 of Fig. 7-6.1.

Table 7-6.1 provides a sample of the s-level perfect numbers for $p = 3$ and several different values for s.

To keep the example in Fig. 7-6.1 simple all initial runs are assumed to be of length 1. In practice these runs should be made as large as possible.

On the first merge pass the initial runs on each of the source tapes 1, 2, and 3 are merged (i.e., the records 14, 6, 12) and the run <6  12  14> is placed on the

**Table 7-6.1**    Perfect tape distributions for $p = 3$.

| Level | Tape | | | Total number |
| s | 1 | 2 | 3 | of runs |
|---|---|---|---|---|
| 1 | 0 | 0 | 1 | 1 |
| 2 | 1 | 1 | 1 | 3 |
| 3 | 1 | 2 | 2 | 5 |
| 4 | 2 | 3 | 4 | 9 |
| 5 | 4 | 6 | 7 | 17 |
| 6 | 7 | 11 | 13 | 31 |
| 7 | 13 | 20 | 24 | 57 |
| 8 | 24 | 37 | 44 | 105 |
| 9 | 44 | 68 | 81 | 193 |

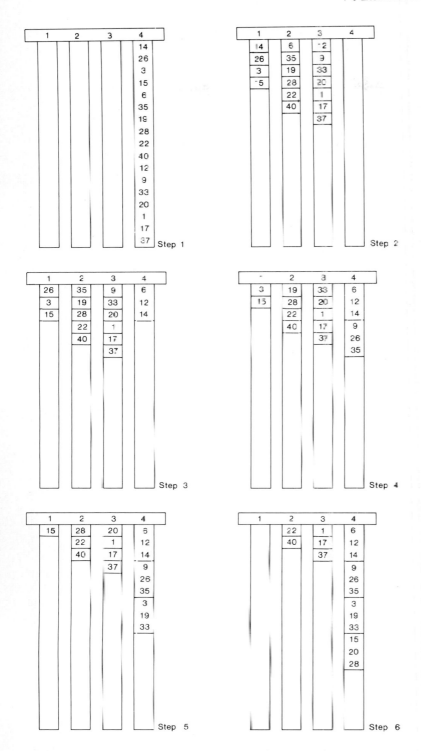

**FIGURE 7-6.1**   A trace of the polyphase sort.

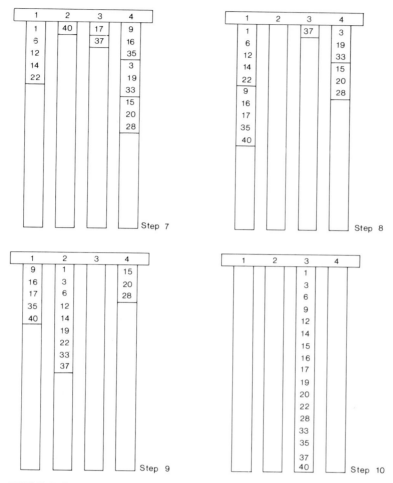

**FIGURE 7-6.1**   (Continued)

initially empty object tape 4. The second, third and fourth merges place the runs <9 26 35>, <3 19 33>, and <15 20 28> on tape 4 as well. This now leaves tape 1 with no more runs left to be read. It is therefore rewound in preparation for its new role as the object tape in the next phase of merges. Tape 4 is also rewound in anticipation of its new role as a source tape. This gives us the situation depicted in step 6.

The next phase begins by merging runs from tapes 2, 3, and 4 which results in the placement of the new run <1 6 12 14 22> on tape 1. On the next merge, the run <9 16 17 35 40> is placed on tape 1 leaving tape 2 exhausted of records. Tapes 1 and 2 are rewound and a third pass is made that places run <1 3 6 12 14 19 22 33 37> on tape 2 (step 9). Tape 3 is now empty of records to be read. It and tape 2 are rewound and the final merge pass places the run, <1 3 6 9 12 14 15 16 17 19 20 22 28 33 35 37 40>, on tape 3 (step 10).

Of course we do not always have a number of records to sort which agrees exactly with a perfect Fibonacci distribution. Nevertheless, it is still possible to sort using the polyphase method by assuming the presence of null or dummy records on the tapes. Enough dummy records should be included to bring the total number of runs up to the next perfect Fibonacci distribution.

There is a problem with the strategy of just filling the final source tape with dummy initial runs in order to arrive at the next perfect number. If we use this approach of filling one tape at a time as was adopted in step 2 of the example in Fig. 7-6.1, then all the dummy runs are placed on the last source tape that is filled (Tape 3 in the example). It can be shown that we are far better off to distribute the dummy runs horizontally across all of the source tapes. This strategy enables us to "merge" dummy runs together very early in the sorting process.

In reality, the dummy runs do not have to be created. Instead, through clever bookkeeping it is possible to keep track of how many there are and where they are located. This can be done by using a series of counters $d_1, d_2, ..., d_T$, where $d_i$ is the number of dummy runs currently residing on tape $i$.

Some horizontal distribution strategies for initial runs are better than others because certain runs are handled more often than others in the merging process. For our example of 17 initial runs and 4 tapes, the number of times each of the initial runs is handled is as follows:

Run number:    1  2  3  4  5  6  7  8  9 10 11 12 13 14 15 16 17

Times
Participating:    4  3  3  2  3  2  2  4  3  3  2  3  2  4  3  3  2

Therefore, runs 1, 8, and 14 are handled the most often and if possible these are where the three first dummy runs should be located.

It is very difficult to determine the optimal placement of dummy runs for the various sizes of perfect distributions. Instead a heuristic procedure is adopted that attempts to distribute the dummy runs as evenly as possible on the various tapes. This procedure, which is adopted in the Algorithm POLYHD to follow, initially distributes the records given in Fig. 7-6.1 in the following manner.

*Tape 1:*    14 15 35 19 40  9  1

*Tape 2:*    26  6 28 12 33 17

*Tape 3:*    3 22 20 37

Observe that if the last three records (i.e., 1, 17, and 37) were missing from the input file, a dummy run should be placed in the last run location of each of the three tapes.

Algorithm POLYHD is for a polyphase sort with horizontal distribution. This is not an optimal polyphase sort but performs at only 2% to 3% below the optimum. It has the added feature of being quite simple when compared to an optimal polyphase which is relatively complex. This algorithm is based on one in Knuth's book on sorting and searching.

**Algorithm** POLYHD(T). Given T the number of tapes used in a polyphase external sort (T ≥ 4), this algorithm performs P-way merging (P = T − 1) making use of a polyphase sort using horizontal distribution. A is a vector of the Fibonacci series in use. D is a vector of the number of dummy runs required. TAPE is a vector of the tapes used to associate the "physical" and "logical" notions of the tapes. The variables j and k are used as standard indices. TYPE is a variable used to denote when dummy runs need to be merged.

1.  [Initialize]
        P = T – 1
        Repeat for j = 1, 2, ..., P
            A[j] ← D[j] ← 1
            TAPE[j] ← j
        A[T] ← D[T] ← 0
        TAPE[T] ← T
        k ← 1
        j ← 1
2.  [Input data runs]
        Repeat while input
            Write one run on tape number j
            D[j] ← D[j] – 1
            If D[j] < D[j + 1]
            then    j ← j + 1
            else    If D[j] ≠ 0
                    then    j ← 1
                    else    k ← k + 1
                            a ← A[1]
                            Repeat for j = 1, 2, ...,P
                                D[j] ← a + A[j + 1] – A[j]
                                A[j] ← a + A[j + 1]
                            j ← 1
3.  [Rewind tapes]
        Rewind all tapes
4.  [Merging of runs to sort]
        Repeat while k ≠ 0
            Repeat until TAPE[P] is empty and D[P] = 0
                TYPE ← 1
                Repeat for j = 1, 2, ..., P
                    If D[j] = 0
                    then    TYPE ← 2
                If TYPE = 1
                then    (merge the dummy runs into one)
                        D[T] ← D[T] + 1
                        Repeat for j = 1, 2, ..., P
                            D[j] ← D[j] – 1
                else    (merge all non-null runs)
                        Merge runs from all TAPE[j] where D[j] = 0
                                onto TAPE[T]
                        Repeat for j = 1, 2, ..., P
                            If D[j] ≠ 0
                            then    D[j] ← D[j] – 1
            k ← k – 1
            Rewind TAPE[P] and TAPE[T]
            (Reassign logical and physical relationship between tapes.)
            {TAPE[1], TAPE[2],..., TAPE[T]
                    ← TAPE[T], TAPE[1],..., TAPE[T – 1]} respectively
            {D[1], D[2],..., D[T] ← D[T], D[1],..., D[T – 1]} respectively

□

In step 1 the general initialization is performed. Step 2 is a loop designed to distribute the runs horizontally on the tapes. A major component of this step is the updating of the vectors A and D. This sets up the number of dummy runs assumed to be present on each tape. It is expected that the input data are either from another part of the system or possibly initially on tape T. After the distribution is completed the tapes are rewound in step 3 to allow them to be read.

Step 4 contains the actual merge and sort. The variable k which was incremented during step 2 serves as a count for the number of times an empty tape will need to be used to hold the next sets of merged runs. In effect, it is used to determine the level number of the next largest perfect Fibonacci distribution. The inner loop controls the merging and rotation of "logical" tapes. The variable TYPE is used to indicate whether or not there are any non-null runs to merge on the given pass. If TYPE = 1 there are only dummy runs and TYPE = 2 indicates that actual merging is necessary. When only dummy runs are being merged the method is simply to readjust the number of dummy runs on each tape. Where non-null runs are present it becomes necessary to merge the non-null runs and place the result on TAPE[T] while readjusting the number of dummy runs on the other tapes. When TAPE[P] is empty of all null and non-null runs the outer loop is reentered. The decrementing of the value of k, the rewinding of tapes, and the rotating of tapes is made in preparation for the next merge pass. Step 4 is repeated until k = 0.

It is worth noting that a major portion of time in the sort is used in the rewinding of the tapes so that they can be read. In fact, at the completion of every pass two of the tapes must be rewound. This time can be reduced if tapes which are readable backwards are used. If a run is written on a tape in ascending order and read backwards from the tape it will be read in descending order. Thus it is necessary to alternate ascending and descending runs on the tapes when using this modified method.

The polyphase method is good for 6 or fewer tapes. Its performance is not as good for a greater number of tapes as other methods such as the oscillating sort.

### 7-6.2.2 Oscillating Sort

While the polyphase sort maximizes the order of the merge to reduce the depth of the merge tree, the *oscillating sort* is able to accomplish this while merging runs of equal length. It is necessary for the tapes to be readable in both directions and able to be quickly reversed. The oscillating sort is superior to the polyphase for more than 6 tape units.

The oscillating sort derives its name from the fact that the sort is performed by oscillating between distribution and merging. Rather than distribute all the inputs to the tapes and then commence merging, some of the inputs are distributed, then merged, and then more are distributed. The process continues in this manner until its conclusion. This method was introduced by Sheldon Sobel [1962]. The sort works exactly if the number of initial runs is a power of T − 1 where T is the number of working tapes used in the sort. When the number of initial runs is not a power of T − 1 it is assumed that dummy runs are present to make up the difference.

The oscillating sort will be illustrated for the first 9 of the sample of numbers used to describe the polyphase sort. In the example trace shown in Fig. 7-6.2, five tapes are used with four of them considered as the working tapes (the first one simply holds the input).

Step 2 shows the first distribution phase in which records with key values of 14, 26, and 3 are distributed on tapes 3, 4, and 5 respectively. In step 3 these are

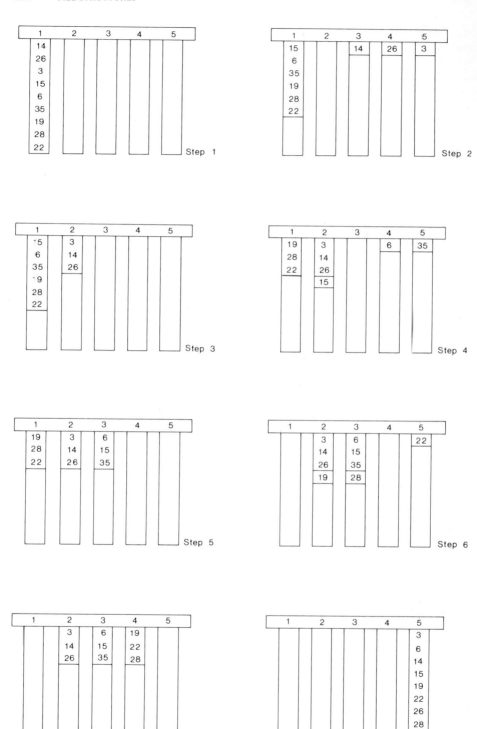

**FIGURE 7-6.2** The trace of an oscillating sort.

merged reading backward and the run <3 14 26> is placed on tape 2. Once more distribution is done in step 4 leaving 15 on tape 2, 6 on tape 4, and 35 on tape 5. These are merged (step 5), again via backward reads, and placed on tape 3. Step 6 is the final distribution phase placing 9, 28, and 22 on tapes 2, 3, and 5, respectively. In step 7 these are merged, via backward reads, and placed on tape 4. At this point we have exhausted the inputs and have three runs of equal length. These three runs are merged using backward reads and placed on tape 5 in step 8.

It is important to remember the alternating nature of the order in which the runs are read from the tapes. For the example just cited the runs would be read and placed on the tapes as shown in Table 7-6.2. In the table, all initial runs are indicated as $A$, all runs produced from a single merge are represented as $B$, and the final run is represented as $C$. A subscript indicates the size of the run and "*" depicts backward reads on the associated tape.

Algorithm OSCIL which follows invokes the recursive procedure OSC in order to perform the oscillating sort. If we realize that the final merge tree that forms the sorted file is, itself, composed of merge trees that are in turn composed of other merge trees, it is easy to see why a recursive implementation of this sorting technique is a natural one. For example, from Fig. 7-6.2 it can be seen that the final run is composed of three separate merge trees that are formed in steps 3, 5, and 7 of the trace.

**Algorithm**  OSCIL(T).  Given T the number of working tapes to be used in an oscillating sort this algorithm is designed to call and use the recursive procedure OSC in order to sort a list of numbers.

1. [Initialize]
    P ← T - 1
    Repeat for J = 1 to T
       D[J] ← 0
    J ← 1
    L ← 0
    TP ← 0
    DIR ← 0
    RTN ← -1
2. [Enter procedure OSC]
    Call OSC (J, L, RTN, TP, DIR)

**Table 7-6.2**  Read patterns for the oscillating sort.

| Step | Tape | | | | |
|---|---|---|---|---|---|
| | T1 | T2 | T3 | T4 | T5 |
| 1 | 9 init. | - | - | - | - |
| 2 | 6 init. | - | $A_1$ | $A_1$ | $A_1$ |
| 3 | 6 init. | $B_3$ | * | * | * |
| 4 | 3 init. | $B_3A_1$ | - | $A_1$ | $A_1$ |
| 5 | 3 init. | $B_3$* | $B_3$ | * | * |
| 6 | - | $B_3A_1$ | $B_3A_1$ | - | $A_1$ |
| 7 | - | $B_3$ | $B_3$ | $B_3$ | - |
| 8 | - | * | * | * | $C_9$ |

3.    [Location and direction of final sorted list]
      If TP = 0 and DIR = 0
      then    write ('There was no input.')
      else    write ('The final list is on tape ', J)
      If DIR = −1
      then    write ('It is in descending order.')
      else    write ('It is in ascending order.')
4.    [Finished.]
      Exit.    □

**Procedure** OSC(NEXT, LEV, RTN, TP, DIR). Given the parameters NEXT—the next tape for merging, LEV—the current level in the sort, RTN—the level which called this one, TP—the tape number where the current final run is located, and DIR—an indicator of whether the run is in ascending or descending order, this recursive procedure serves to distribute initial runs to the tapes and merge them as much as possible. It has a check for end of input which serves as the base condition. The variable TYPE is used to denote whether a merge pass includes only dummy runs or not. The global vector D is used to keep track of the dummy runs on each tape.

1.    [Base—no more input]
      If no input
      then    If RTN < LEV
            then    return.
2.    [Initial level]
      If LEV = 0
      then    Repeat for K = 1, 2, ..., T
            If K ≠ NEXT
            then    If input
                  then    write initial run on tape K
                  else    write dummy run on tape K
                      D[K] ← D[K] + 1
            TYPE ← 1
            Repeat for K = 1, 2, ..., T
              If K ≠ NEXT
              then    If D[K] = 0
                  then    TYPE ← 2
            If TYPE = 1
            then    (merge dummies)
                D[NEXT] ← D[NEXT] + 1
                Repeat for K = 1, 2, ..., T
                  If K ≠ NEXT
                  then    D[K] ← D[K] − 1
            else    merge runs from tapes K = 1, 2, ..., T where K≠ NEXT
                and D[K] = 0 onto tape NEXT.
                Repeat for K = 1, 2, ..., T
                  If K ≠ NEXT
                  then    If D[K] ≠ 0
                      then    D[K] ← D[K] − 1
            TNUM ← NEXT
            FORM ← −1

        If RTN < I
        then    LEV ← LEV + 1
                If NEXT = T
                then    NEXT ← 1
                else    NEXT ← NEXT + 1
                Call OSC(NEXT, LEV, 0, TP, DIR)
        If TP = 0
        then    TP ← TNUM
        If DIR = 0
        then    DIR ← FORM
        Return.

3.  [Rotate if beyond level 1]
        If LEV ≠ 1
        then    If NEXT = T
                then    NEXT ← 1
                else    NEXT ← NEXT + 1

4.  [Number of runs still required in this level]
        If RTN < I
        then    X ← P − 1
        else    X ← P

5.  [Build up level and merge]
        Repeat X times
            CALL OSC(NEXT, LEV − 1, LEV, TP, DIR)
            If NEXT = T
            then    NEXT ← 1
            else    NEXT ← NEXT + 1
        TYPE ← 1
        Repeat for K = 1, 2, ..., T
            If K ≠ NEXT
            then    If D[K] = 0
                    then    TYPE ← 2
        If TYPE = 1
        then    (merge dummies)
                D[NEXT] ← D[NEXT] + 1
                Repeat for K = 1, 2, ..., T
                    If K ≠ NEXT
                    then    D[K] ← D[K] − 1
        else    If LEV is even
                then    merge runs from tapes K = 1, 2, .., T where K ≠ NEXT
                            and D[K] = 0 or to tape NEXT in descending order
                else    merge runs from tapes K = 1, 2, .., T where K ≠ NEXT
                            and D[K] = 0 onto tape NEXT in ascending order
                Repeat for K = 1, 2, ..., T
                    If K ≠ NEXT
                    then    If D[K] ≠ 0
                            then    D[K] ← D[K] − 1
        TNUM ← NEXT
        If LEV is even
        then    FORM ← −1
        else    FORM ← 1

6.  [Prepare for next call]
    If RTN < LEV
    then   LEV ← LEV + 1
           If NEXT = T
           then   NEXT ← 1
           else   NEXT ← NEXT + 1
           OSC(NEXT, LEV, LEV – 1, TP, DIR)
7.  [Finished]
    If TP = 0
    then   TP ← TNUM
    If DIR = 0
    then   DIR ← FORM
    Return                                                           ☐

Procedure OSC can be broken into two major phases. The first (step 1) is responsible for taking the initial runs and dispersing them on the working tapes, occasionally disturbing the distribution process to merge some of the tape contents. The second phase (steps 2 through 7 of the procedure) is responsible for properly merging the runs that have been built up during the first phase. This is accomplished, in part, through additional recursive invocations of OSC and the "unrecurring" processing of all previous invocations. The algorithm uses k-way merging for k = T – 2 where T ≥ 3 tape units.

A final tape sorting technique, the *cascade merge sort*, will not be discussed here but details concerning its operation and performance appear in Knuth [1973]. Like the polyphase sort it starts with a "perfect distribution" of runs. It has been shown to be asymptotically better than the polyphase sort for six or more tapes.

### 7-6.3  SORTING ON DISKS

The capability to access directly a particular record on a magnetic disk is very important when considering the sorting of records in external memory. With direct record access we can ignore the problems of setting up initial runs according to certain merge patterns and having to rewind working tapes. Specifically, we can simply use a *k-way merge strategy* that will allow us to ignore these two problems and thereby reduce significantly the sort time.

Assuming we have r initial runs, it can be shown that the number of passes required to sort a file using a k-way merge is $O(\lceil \log_k r \rceil)$. To appreciate this let us begin by examining a trace of a simple two-way merge as exhibited in Fig. 7-6.3.

In the example, a buffer size of b = 3 is chosen. The first pass is required to create the initial runs of length 3. From this point the merging process is used to create progressively longer runs until the entire file is ordered. It is easy to see that the two-way merge tree is at least depth $\lceil \log_2 r \rceil$ (in the given example, $\lceil \log_2 6 \rceil = 3$ ). Note that because the merge tree is not truly balanced not all records are read in each pass. In particular, in pass 3 only four of the six blocks are involved in the merge*. Therefore, an upper bound on the number of block reads is $r * \lceil \log_2 r \rceil$ .

The storage requirements to perform the merging are two input buffers and one output buffer. More generally, for a k-way merge k + 1 buffers are required. To illustrate why these are sufficient, consider a snapshot of the merging of the first two runs in pass 3 as given in Figure 7-6.4. The snapshot shows that as the records from one input buffer are exhausted they are replaced by another block of records from the same run. The two circled items are the ones being compared at the given

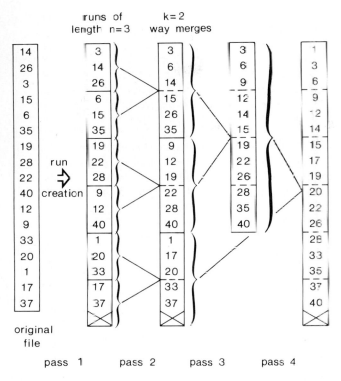

**FIGURE 7-6.3**    Trace of a k-way merge for < = 2

instant in the snapshot and the previous contents of the three active buffers are bounded by broken lines.

The general strategy for the merging process involves the following two steps:

*1*    Form as many initial runs as possible—let the number of runs be r.

*2*    Merge the r runs, k at a time, using a merging algorithm that is a generalization of the simple two-way merging technique discussed in Sec. 6.1.

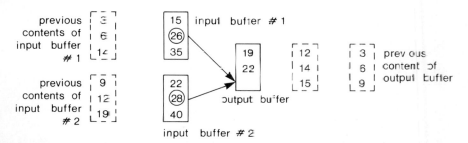

**FIGURE 7-6.4**    Snapshot of a merge illustrating buffer requirements.

In our example we have considered a k-way merge for k = 2. What about merging for larger values of k? Can it improve the performance of a disk sorting strategy? One of the main problems in a general k-way merge is to establish an efficient comparison strategy that involves more than two values. Fortunately, some of the work we described earlier in our discussion of internal sorting in Chap. 6 is very helpful. Specifically, the tree sorting technique used in the heap sort can be applied.

Let us view the records in the k runs that are participating in the merge as players in a tournament. A competition tree can then be formed in which the winner of a particular competition is the record with the smallest sort key. Figure 7-6.5 illustrates an 8-way merge applied to an extended version of our example data. It should be noted that typically such a merge would take place as only one of many in the process of sorting a large file. Broken lines depict the alterations in the competition tree that are necessary to select the second "winner" (3) and place it in an output buffer. The process of altering the tree requires at most $\lceil \log_2 k \rceil$ (i.e., $\lceil \log_2 8 \rceil = 3$ in the example) operations. Therefore, a total of $(k \cdot m) \cdot \lceil \log_2 k \rceil$ comparison operations are necessary to merge k runs each of size m (i.e., $8 \cdot 3 \cdot \lceil \log_2 8 \rceil = 72$ comparison operations in the example). The result of a k-way

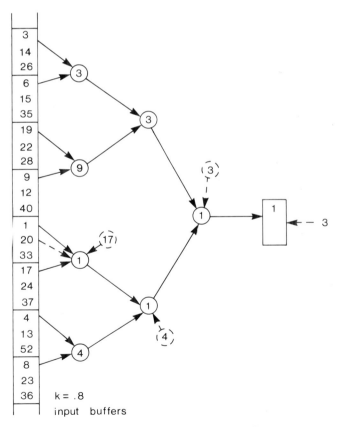

**FIGURE 7-6.5**   Illustrating a k-way merge for k = 8.

merge of k runs, each of size m, is a single run of size k * m. Of course this single run may be divided into several blocks of size b.

The improvement in the sorting time can be quite dramatic when using a k-way merge k > 2 as opposed to a two-way merge. With k-way merging $O(\lceil\log_k r\rceil)$ as opposed to $O(\lceil\log_2 r\rceil)$ passes will be required to merge r initial runs. If each initial run is stored in a single block, as is normally the case, then $O(r*\lceil\log_k r\rceil)$ read operations and hence $O(r*\lceil\log_k r\rceil)$ write operations will be required, since a block is written for each block that is read in the sort-merge process.

This performance improvement does not come without the cost of additional cpu time in performing the merge process and, more importantly, additional memory space for buffers. As observed earlier, k + 1 buffers as opposed to 3 buffers are necessary for a k-way merge.

An algorithm for a general k-way merge will not be given as it is similar to the tree sorting algorithm in Chap. 6. It is left as an exercise at the end of this section.

The crucial question of how long will the entire sorting process take given that we initially have a file of n records stored in blocks of size b can now be addressed. Let $\overline{\tau}$ as defined in Sec. 7-1 represent the expected time to perform a disk I/O operation on a block of size b. The expected time to sort a file of n records can be broken down into two steps:

Step 1:  Perform initial pass to create runs of size b.
         ($2*r$ I/O operations + $r*\lceil\log_2 b\rceil$ comparisons are required)
Step 2:  Perform k-way merges until the sorted file is achieved.
         ($2*(r*\lceil\log_k r\rceil)$ I/O operations + $\lceil\log_k r\rceil*n*\lceil\log_2 k\rceil$ comparisons are required)

where $r = \lceil n/b\rceil$ is the number of initial runs that are created in blocks of size b, and $\lceil\log_k r\rceil$ is a bound on the number of passes that will be required in the k-way merge. Note that the factor of 2 is included in I/O operations to account for both the reading and writing of records. Therefore, the total expected time would be $2r(\lceil\log_k r\rceil+1)$ I/O operations and $r\lceil\log_2 b\rceil+n\lceil\log_k r\rceil\lceil\log_2 k\rceil$ comparisons.

To gain an appreciation of a bound on the expected sort time, left us assume we wish to sort 51,200 records each 300 bytes in length blocked at 100 records per block on an IBM 3380 disk device using an 8-way merge. Let us also assume that a conservative estimate of the time to perform a "within memory" comparison plus associated housekeeping activities is 10 msecs. Therefore, from the statistics for an IBM 3380 given earlier in Table 7-1.2, we have

$$\overline{\tau} = 8.3 \text{ msec} + 16 \text{ msec}$$
$$+ (300 \text{ char/rec} * 100 \text{ rec})/(3000 \text{ char/msec})$$
$$= 34.3 \text{ msec}$$

Hence, the total expected sort time (given that $r = 51,200/100 = 512$) is

$$2 * 512 * (\lceil\log_8 512\rceil + 1) * 34.3 \text{ msec}$$
$$+ 512 * \lceil\log_2 100\rceil * .01 \text{ msec}$$
$$+ 51200 * \lceil\log_8 512\rceil * \lceil\log_2 8\rceil * .01 \text{ msec}$$
$$\approx (351,232 + 33 + 13,824) \text{ msec} = 365,089 \text{ msec}$$
$$\approx 6.08 \text{ minutes}$$

Observe that the primary contribution to the total expected time is the time to perform the I/O operations. Of course, the previous estimate is based on the assumption that the sorting routine is the only program executing in the system. This is not a realistic assumption in a shared multiprogramming environment.

As a final comment, it should be noted that if double buffering is used in the k-way sort an improvement by a factor of 2 is possible. Let us assume that 2k as opposed to k input buffers and 2 as opposed to 1 output buffers are available. Then if the input and output files for each pass are stored on disk devices that are on separate channels, it is possible to overlap the input and output I/O activity. Of course, double buffering is required to ensure that an I/O operation can take place at the same time as the merging process is being carried out. Without double buffering, the merging process must come to a halt whenever an input buffer becomes empty or an output buffer becomes full.

### 7-6.4 Generating Extended Initial Runs

Throughout this section we have been assuming that all initial runs are of a fixed length, say m. They are created by reading records from an unordered file, sorting these records using an internal sort, and placing the initial run in one of the source files in preparation for the merging phase. It is, however, possible to produce longer runs (which we will call *extended runs*) by applying a *replacement selection technique* to the records as they are read into memory.

To illustrate this technique, let us consider the generation of extended runs for our example unordered file. Run generation, as depicted in Fig. 7-6.6, commences with the placement of the first three records into an empty buffer that we will call the *merge buffer*. In our example, the merge buffer is of size m = 3. A selection procedure is then invoked which simply isolates the record with the least key and copies this record into an output buffer. The next record in the input file is then moved into the merge buffer to replace the previously selected record (i.e., the record with the key of 15 replaces the record with the key of 3 in the first replacement in Fig. 7-6.6). The selection procedure is then reapplied and *the record with the least key that is greater than the key of the record that was last selected* is copied into the output buffer. Notice that if the least key is selected and it is less than the key of the last selected record, it should not be placed in the output buffer because to do so would terminate the current run. In an effort to extend a run as long as possible, the best strategy is to always select the least key possible that does not terminate the current run. Of course, eventually the merge buffer becomes filled with records of keys that are less than the previously selected key and the current run is terminated and a new run must be initiated.

The trace in Fig. 7-6.6 shows that a first run of length five can be generated before there are not any keys available that are greater than the last selected key. This occurs when (6, 19, 28) are in the merge buffer and 35 was the key of the last record moved to the output file. At this point, a second run is started and the same selection and replacement process is applied. Eventually two new runs of length five and a final run of length two are formed.

The development of a formal algorithm for the generation of extended runs using the selection and replacement strategy is quite straightforward and is left as an exercise at the end of the section.

It is possible to adapt both the polyphase and the oscillating sorts to take advantage of extended runs, although for the polyphase sort the gains are minimal due to the precise merge patterns that must be created. It is also the case that the k-way disk merge can be improved and the adaption of this technique using extended runs is left as an exercise at the end of this section.

It can be shown empirically that the average length of an extended run is 2m assuming that the unordered records are in random order and a merge buffer of size

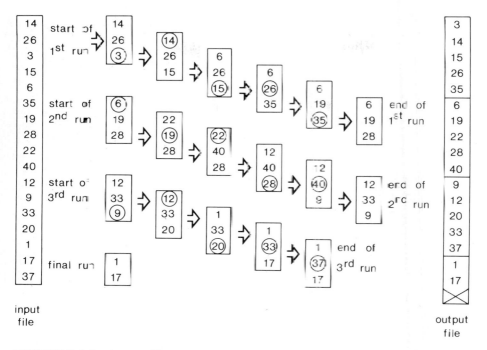

**FIGURE 7-6.6** A trace illustrating the generation of extended runs.

m is used. It should be pointed out, however, that the extended merge strategy does not provide a substantial improvement unless the merge buffer is significantly larger than the input buffer (the buffer into which records are initially read). In the previous example, we did not explicitly state the block size of the input file. Let us assume that it is blocked at size m implying that an input buffer of size m is required. If the merge buffer is also of size m, then a total space requirement of size 2m must be allotted to guarantee extended runs with expected length of size 2m. However, using our standard strategy involving an internal sort on a buffer of size 2m we can also generate runs of length 2m—in fact, fixed-length runs of size 2m. Note that if we have buffer space of size 3m available, it is possible to produce extended runs with an average length of 4m by allocating an input buffer of size m and a merge buffer of size 2m. In general, if we devote km space to buffers, extended runs of average size $(k - 1) * 2m$ are possible; whereas, initial runs of length km are only possible using the standard approach.

### 7-6.5 Recent Developments

It can be seen from our discussion that the methods used on disks are often adaptations of those used for tapes. These do not make optimal use of the assets of a disk which are not present on tapes. Bayer and Haerder [1978] performed work with preplanning the allocation of merge blocks on disks. The aim of this preplanning is to minimize access time where moveable head disks are involved. The overlapping of input and output in the sort/merge is also considered to cut down on the time involved. Their cost model shows substantial time savings of up to a factor of three are to be expected.

It is also important to note that sorting is possible on other external memory devices. Some work has also been done involving sorting on the more recent charge-coupled devices or magnetic bubble memories. Chung, Luccio, and Wong [1980] discuss the parameters to be considered along with some usable models. The basic ability of switches to route bubble streams is enhanced to allow routing according to contents by use of *compare and steer* switches. The important parameters monitored in their models are the number of compare and steer switches, the number of control states, and the number of steps to sort data. Work done by Chen et al [1977] on uniform ladders, another device based on magnetic bubbles, was expanded by Chin and Fok [1980] to derive two algorithms for sorting on this device. The algorithms are based on those of Chen and on the odd-even transposition sort. They are designed to allow maximum overlap. For a one ladder sort the sorting process is completely embedded in the input/output time of 2n periods for n records on the ladder. Where the number of input records requires the use of more than one ladder, only a negligible non-overlapped sorting time is found.

**Exercises for Sec. 7-6**

1. Provide a detailed trace of Algorithm POLYHD when applied to the unordered input file given in Fig. 7-6.1. Assume initial runs of size 1 and four tapes are available.
2. Provide a detailed trace of Algorithm POLYHD when applied to an input file that contains the following records.

   6 29 1 10 23 48 17 13 16 12 10 2 3 7

   Assume initial runs of size 2 and two tapes are available.
3. Write a Pascal or PL/I program that simulates the polyphase sort outlined in Algorithm POLYHD. Use vectors to represent the contents of the real tapes.
4. Give a table, similar to Table 7-6.1, of perfect Fibonacci tape distributions for $p = 4$, and $s = 1$ through 9.
5. Provide a detailed trace of Algorithm OSCIL when applied to the unordered input file given in Fig. 7-6.2.
6. Illustrate the contents of $k = 4$ tapes for an oscillating sort operating on the input file given in Fig. 7-6.1. Assume initial runs of size 1.
7. Write a Pascal or PL/I program that simulates the oscillating sort outlined in Algorithm OSCIL. Use vectors to represent the contents of the real tapes.
8. Write a Pascal or PL/I program that performs a k-way disk merge. Use vectors to represent the k different input buffers and the single output buffer.
9. Illustrate the contents of the input buffers for a four-way disk merge operating on an input file with the following contents:

   { 12, 6, 22, 93, 14, 78, 16, 22, 47, 16, 44, 32, 53,
     63, 8, 92, 58, 29, 31 }

   Assume the size of an input buffer is $b = 2$.
10. Illustrate how the replacement selection technique would operate on the input file given in Prob. 9 to create extended runs. Assume a merge buffer of size $m = 4$.
11. Provide an algorithm that specifies in detailed steps how the replacement selection technique works.
12. Suggest how you might adapt the oscillating and k-way merge sorts to take advantage of extended runs.

## 7-7 INDEXED SEQUENTIAL FILES

In the design of the billing system in Sec. 7-5, we did not allow inquiries about the status of an account, except on a monthly basis. As the company expands its operation, it may become desirable or necessary to provide store clerks at the point of sale, the facility to validate a customer account. Customers who exceed their credit limit and stolen or lost credit cards are two facets of business the company must deal with. Validation at a store's counter must be instantaneous, for customers become irate if they are unnecessarily delayed.

A query on a customer's status can be handled, with slight modifications, using the system already implemented; however, the system's performance would undoubtably be less than satisfactory. Since CUSTOMER (the main permanent file of the system) is a sequential file, it may be necessary to search almost the entire file before a desired record is located. The delay associated with such an activity can be prohibitively high. For example, suppose we have 5,000 records stored on the CUSTOMER file and we access the file sequentially at an average delay (including seek time, latency, and transmission time) of 30 milliseconds per record. The expected time taken to access the final record on the file is approximately 150,000 milliseconds, or 2.5 minutes!

If customers are to obtain a reasonable response time for an on-line query from a salesperson, the ability to go directly to the required record must be available. In this section, we will examine how a record can be directly accessed. In addition to a direct-access capability, it is also advantageous to retain in a small billing system the sequential ordering of the file. This should be done to allow for the sequential processing of the CUSTOMER file when generating monthly reports and statements. We can process monthly reports by accessing customer records in a direct yet nonsequential fashion. However, a tremendous amount of seek-time overhead is incurred due to the quasi-random movement of the disk heads as generated by the nonsequential processing of the records of the file. Therefore, the file structure that is required for such a billing system with on-line inquiry must support both a direct and sequential form of access. In this section, we examine a file organization which allows both types of access capabilities.

### 7-7.1 The Structure of Indexed Sequential Files

An important aspect affecting the file structure is the type of physical medium on which the file resides. The capability of directly accessing a record based on a key (or unique index) can only be achieved if the external storage device used supports this type of access. In particular, devices such as card readers and tape units allow the access of a particular record only after reading all the other records that physically appear before a desired record in the file. Hence, direct record access is impossible for these types of devices. The types of external storage devices that support both direct and sequential access are magnetic drums and disk units.

The file-structure concepts relating to indexed sequential files are best exemplified when considering a magnetic disk as the storage medium. In fact, because of their low price/performance ratio and large total storage capacity, disks are generally chosen when using indexed sequential files. Hence, the discussion to follow assumes that the file structures are mapped onto such a device.

We will present two types of indexed sequential-file organizations—the first one is due to IBM, and the second is used by CDC. An IBM indexed sequential file consists of three separate areas: the prime area, the index area, and the overflow area. The *prime area* is an area into which data records are written when the file is first created. The file is created sequentially, that is, by writing records in the prime area in a sequence dictated by the lexical ordering of the keys of the records. The writing process starts at the second track of a particular cylinder, say the $n$th cylinder, of a disk. When this cylinder is filled, writing continues on the second track of the next $(n + 1)$th cylinder and continues in this fashion until the file's creation is completed. If the newly created file is accessed sequentially according to the key item, the records are processed in the order they were written.

The second important area of an indexed sequential file, the *index area*, is created automatically by the data-management routines in the operating system. A number of index levels may be involved in an indexed sequential file. The lowest level of index is the *track index*, which is always written on the first track (named track 0) of the cylinders for the indexed sequential file. The track index contains two entries for each prime track of the cylinder—a *normal entry* and an *overflow entry*. The normal entry is composed of the address of the prime track to which the entry is associated and of the highest value of the keys for the records stored on that track. If there are no overflow records, the overflow entry is set equal to the normal entry. The significance of the overflow entry is described later in this subsection during a discussion of overflow records. Figure 7-7.1 illustrates the file structure for an indexed sequential file of customer records in which the key item is a six-digit account number. Only one cylinder is shown with a prime area of m tracks.

In the same manner as a track index describes the storage of records on the tracks of a cylinder, the *cylinder index* indicates how records are distributed over a number of cylinders. A cylinder index references a track index—one cylinder index entry per track index.

A final level of indexing exists in this hierarchical indexing structure. A *master index* is used for an extremely large file where a search of the cylinder index is too time consuming. This index forms the root node of the tree of indices used in an indexed sequential file. Figure 7-7.2 illustrates the relationships between the different levels of indices discussed.

Locating the record corresponding to the customer with account number 089631 involves a search of the master index to find the proper cylinder index with which the record is associated (e.g., cylinder index 1). Next, a search is made of the

Normal entry    Overflow entry

| Track 0 | 020028 | Trk 1 | 020028 | Trk 1 | 028761 | Trk 2 | 028761 | Trk 2 | · · | 094415 | Trk m | 094415 | Trk m |
|---|---|---|---|---|---|---|---|---|---|---|---|---|---|

| Track 1 | 010213 | Customer data | 011120 | Customer data | · · · | 020028 | Customer data |
|---|---|---|---|---|---|---|---|

| Track 2 | 023612 | Customer data | 024121 | Customer data | · · · | 028761 | Customer data |
|---|---|---|---|---|---|---|---|

| Track m | 089213 | Customer data | 089725 | Customer data | · · · | 094415 | Customer data |
|---|---|---|---|---|---|---|---|

**FIGURE 7-7.1**   Track index and prime area of an indexed sequential file.

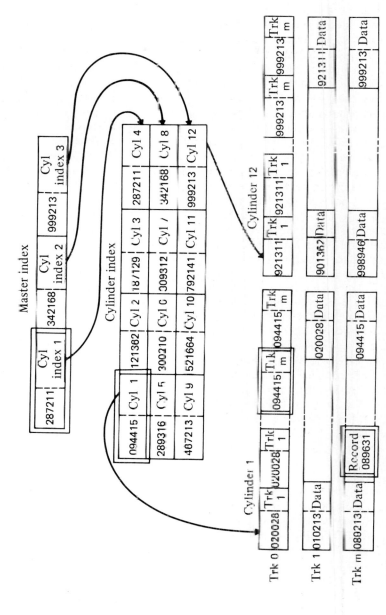

**FIGURE 7-7.2**  Relationships between the different levels of indices.

cylinder index to find the cylinder on which the record is located (e.g., cylinder 1). A search of the track index produces the track number on which the record resides (e.g., track m). Finally, a search of the track is required to locate the desired record. This searching process is described in Algorithm INDEXED_SEQ_ACCESS, which is given later in this section after we have discussed overflow records. It should be noted that a master index is not always necessary, and it should only be requested for large files. When it is used, it should reside in main memory during all of the processing of an indexed sequential file.

If records are added to a sequential file, a new sequential file must be created. We can use the same approach when handling additions for an indexed sequential file. However, because it is possible to access records directly in an indexed sequential file, this type of file is generally used in a more volatile and quick-response demanding environment, i.e., an environment in which many additions and deletions arise from on-line transactions or small batches of transactions. Such deletions and additions must be immediately reflected in the file; one cannot wait until the month's end.

The problems of adding records are handled by creating an overflow area or areas, usually on the same device on which the file resides. Two types of overflow areas are possible—a cylinder overflow area or an independent overflow area. A *cylinder overflow area* is a number of dedicated tracks on a cylinder that contains a number of prime-area tracks. If, through the addition of a record, an overflow is created in the prime-area tracks of the cylinder, then the overflow records are stored in the cylinder overflow area.

The effect that an overflow record has on the structure of the file is illustrated in Fig. 7-7.3. Note that we make the unrealistic yet simplifying assumption that one track contains only three records. Initially, a customer record with an account number of 026924 is added to the file, as depicted in Fig. 7-7.3a. The record with account number 028761 must be moved to the cylinder overflow area at track m + 1 to preserve the sequential ordering of records in track 2 of the prime area. This change necessitates two other alterations to the file. First, the normal entry in the track index for track 2 must be changed from 028761 to 026924, since the latter number is now the highest key value for the track. Secondly, the overflow entry is adjusted so that its first subentry contains the largest key value of any record for track 2 (i.e., the value 028761) and the second entry is set to the track/record address of the overflow record with the *smallest* key value for track 2.

An overflow record is identical to a prime record, except that a track/record address field is added to the end of the record. This track/record address field contains a pointer to the overflow record with the next largest key value in the list of overflow records for a particular track. Therefore, when the record with the key value 026924 becomes an overflow record with the addition of the record with a key value of 021008, the track/address field is set to point to the record with key value 028761. Figure 7-7.3, by necessity, presents a simplified view. In general, there may be a number of cylinder overflow tracks, and the overflow records for each track are grouped together in a linked list. The head of the link list is given by the track/record address in the track index. The final record in the linked list is specified by placing the number of the associated prime track in the track/record address field of the overflow record (e.g., track 2 is placed in the link field of overflow record 028761).

As more and more records are added to the indexed sequential file, the cylinder overflow area becomes full. When this happens, further overflow records are transferred to an *independent overflow area,* providing such an area is specified

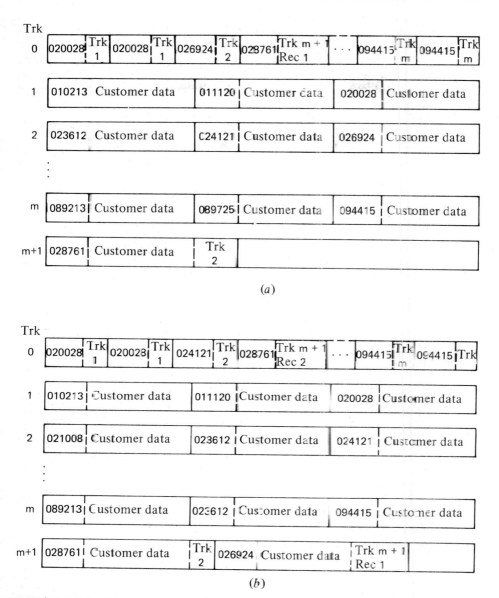

**FIGURE 7-7.3** The effects of an overflow in an indexed sequential file. (a) The addition of a record with a key of 026924. (b) the addition of a record with a key of 021008.

when the file is created. The independent overflow area resides on a cylinder or cylinders apart from any prime-area cylinder. Overflow records are linked together in the same manner as they are in the cylinder overflow area. Note, however, that for disks with movable heads, the use of independent overflow areas should be discouraged as a significant number of seeks are generated when the access arm is moved between the prime and independent overflow areas.

Thus far we have discussed the addition of records; let us now turn to the deletion of records. In IBM's indexed sequential organization, deleted records are not physically removed from a file, but are merely marked as deleted by placing '11111111' B (all ones) in the first byte of the record. If a new record is added later which has the same key as a record previously deleted, then the space occupied by a deleted record is recovered.

Records which are placed in an overflow area are never moved back into the prime area because of a deletion. Only by reorganizing the file can an overflow record be placed in the prime area. Reorganization is achieved by sequentially copying the records of the file into a temporary file and then recreating the file by sequentially copying the records back into the original file. Because the retrieval of overflow records can carry a large overhead, the amount of disorganization in an indexed sequential file should be monitored closely. A good rule of thumb when using movable head disks is to reorganize when records must be placed in the independent overflow area.

We now leave the discussion of IBM's indexed sequential-file organization to consider briefly another file structure for an indexed sequential file. We return to the IBM organization when considering the processing of indexed sequential files in the next subsection.

The SCOPE monitor for the Control Data 6600 and CYBER series of machines provides an indexed sequential file that is structured very differently from the IBM system. A SCOPE Indexed Sequential (SIS) file is organized into *data blocks* and *index blocks*. Both blocks are handled as logical records which are allocated and transferred to and from main storage under the guidance of the SCOPE monitor. The user has no control over the physical placement of the blocks on the external storage device. This strict system control is a necessary requirement because SCOPE allows the simultaneous sharing of disk files in a multiuser environment. The user does have control of the size of the data and index blocks.

A data block is composed of data records, keys with pointers to the data records within the data block, and padding space into which overflow records are placed. A set of data blocks is shown in Fig. 7-7.4. Note that the user may specify the size of the padding area as a factor of the size of the complete block (i.e., .5 means that half of the data block is assigned as padding).

The index blocks form a tree-structured hierarchy of keys and pointers much as the index areas do in the IBM system. An index block contains pairs of keys and addresses, and padding space for the addition of such pairs. A key/address pair is composed of the lowest key of a particular data block or a "lower level" index block and the address of the data or index block in which this key resides. Figure 7-7.4 shows the relationship between index blocks and data blocks in a two-level index block file. Note that the user may select a padding factor for the index blocks and may specify the number of index levels for the file when it is created. In Fig. 7-7.4, the master index block (MB) references three subordinate index blocks (SIB1, SIB2, and SIB3). These index blocks point to data blocks (DB1, DB2, ..., DBm).

Again we are presenting a somewhat unrealistic situation by allowing only three records in a data block. However, with the addition of two records with keys of 010943 and 010000, we can illustrate how overflow records are handled in the SCOPE system. Figure 7-7.5a shows the local effect the addition of record 010943 has on DB1. Figure 7-7.5b depicts the more global effects the addition of record 010000 has on DB1, SIB1, and MB. A by-product of this addition is the creation of a new data block, DBm + 1, which contains half the records that would have resided in DB1 if there had been enough space.

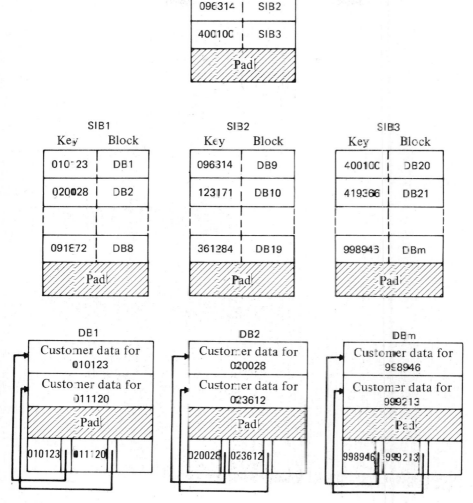

**FIGURE 7-7.** Index and data blocks in a SCOPE indexed sequential file.

As more data blocks are created, the index block becomes full. Overflows in an index block are handled in the same manner as for data blocks. A new block is created and half the index records in the full index block are moved to the new index block. The reason for splitting an overflow block is to eliminate the problem of continually having to move overflow records from a full block into a separate overflow area, as is done with prime-area overflows in the IBM system. Of course, the "splitting" process requires more memory than a "record-at-a-time" overflow process, because of the padding space that must be reserved.

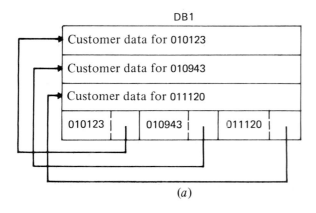

(a)

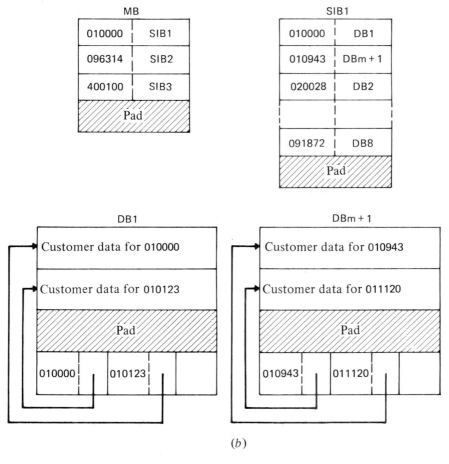

(b)

**FIGURE 7-7.5** The effects of the addition of (a) record with key 010943 and (b) record with key 010000.

In the CDC SCOPE system, deleted records are "garbage collected." That is, the holes left by deleted records are replaced by the active records with higher key values in the block. Hence, both the active record area and the padding areas are always contiguous areas in a block.

Let us now examine the type of processing that is performed when using an indexed sequential file.

### 7-7.2 Processing Indexed Sequential Files

By now it should be clear that the organization of an indexed sequential file is much more complex than that of a sequential file. Because of this complexity, most operating systems provide access facilities or methods which handle the file structure changes that can result from the insertion and deletion of records. In the discussion to follow, we point out those aspects of indexed sequential-file processing which are normally performed by system access methods and those that are left to the user.

The main advantage of an indexed sequential file is that records can be processed either sequentially or directly. In this subsection, we describe both types of processing as they relate to IBM's indexed sequential file. The formulation of algorithms for sequential and direct processing of CDC's SCOPE indexed sequential file is left as an exercise at the end of this section.

The sequential processing of an indexed sequential file is logically identical to the sequential processing of a sequential file, i.e., records are processed in a sequence determined by the index item. The types of transactions that are performed are the reading, alteration, addition, and deletion of records. These are accomplished at a user level with READ, WRITE, and REWRITE statements, as described in Sec. 7-4. While the types of transactions and the operations used to effect these transaction types are usually the same for the sequential processing of sequential and indexed sequential files, the manner in which the records are accessed is substantially different, due to the differences in the file structures.

Algorithm IS_SEQUENTIAL outlines how records are processed sequentially in an indexed sequential file. In the algorithm, we purposely do not specify the type of transactions which are processed. Typically, a variety of transaction types would be handled, such as the addition, deletion, and alteration of records. The processing of these transaction types was described in Algorithm SEQUENTIAL_PROCESS in Sec. 7-4 and, therefore, is not presented again here. Instead, in the algorithm the statement "process transaction" indicates that section in which transaction processing would take place. Algorithm IS_SEQUENTIAL simply shows how the sequential accessing of a particular record in a sequential file differs from the sequential accessing of a record in an indexed sequential file.

**Algorithm** IS_SEQUENTIAL. Given an indexed sequential file called MASTER which contains records that are each made up of a key and a set of information items, an algorithm is provided for accessing the records sequentially. During processing, the MASTER file records are read into a variable MTR_REC which contains KEY and INFO items. A prime-area record is denoted by the variable PRIME_REC, with subitems of KEY and INFO. The track index, TRK_INDEX, is considered to be a vector M in length in which each element contains four items: NORMAL_KEY, NORMAL_ADDR, OVFLOW_KEY, and OVFLOW_ADDR. An overflow record is referred to using the variable OVFLOW_REC, which consists of the three items: KEY, INFO, and LINK. For a given overflow record, LINK contains the track/record address of the overflow record with the next largest key value. The variables CYL and TRK denotes the cylinder and track which is being accessed. ADDR is a special pointer variable which contains the track/record address of the next record to be processed. ADDR is implicitly initialized to point at the first record in the file when the file is opened.

1.  [Initialize]
    Open MASTER for input.
2.  [Process records from the first cylinder (represented by K) to the last cylinder (represented by N) as derived from the cylinder index]
    Repeat thru step 5 for CYL = K, K + 1, ..., N
3.  [Process prime-track records and their associated overflow records for a given cylinder]
    Repeat thru step 5 for TRK = 1, 2, ..., M
4.  [Read records on a prime track and process]
    ADDR ← first pointer location in track TRK
    Repeat while KEY of PRIME_REC(ADDR) ≠
                    NORMAL_KEY of TRK_INDEX[TRK]
        Read PRIME_REC at ADDR from MASTER file into MTR_REC
        ADDR ← beginning of next track record
        Process transactions posted against MTR_REC
    Read PRIME_REC at ADDR from MASTER file into MTR_REC
5.  [Read from linked list of overflow records and process]
    If NORMAL_KEY of TRK_INDEX[TRK] ≠
                    OVFLOW_KEY of TRK_INDEX[TRK]
    then   (Initialize ADDR)
           ADDR ← OVFLOW_ADDR of TRK_INDEX[TRK]
           Repeat while ADDR ≠ TRK
               Read OVFLOW_REC at ADDR
                        from MASTER file into MTR_REC
               ADDR ← LINK of OVFLOW_REC
               Process transactions posted against MTR_REC
6.  [Finished]
    Exit                                                          □

Algorithm IS_SEQUENTIAL begins by opening the MASTER file, which involves the allocation of buffer space for processing of the MASTER file. The records for a particular prime track are processed in step 4. Note the use of the pointer variable ADDR when referencing a particular prime record [i.e., PRIME_REC (ADDR)]. In step 5, overflow records are read by following the overflow links for records in the cylinder overflow area and in the independent overflow area, if applicable. This processing continues for all tracks of all cylinders containing the indexed sequential file. The algorithm presupposes that the space allotted for an indexed sequential file is an integral number of cylinders. This supposition is true for IBM systems.

Algorithm IS_SEQUENTIAL illustrates the complex processing involved simply to read the next record in sequence. However, for the user, the sequential processing of an indexed sequential file is no different than the sequential processing of a sequential file which is ordered by a desired key. It involves two steps:

*1* Open MASTER file for input.
*2* Repeat while not end of MASTER file:
>    read the next record;
>    process transactions posted against MTR_REC.

Therefore, the system access facilities automatically handle the incrementing of counters CY_ and TRK and the updating of the variable ADDR in Algorithm IS_SEQUENTIAL.

The direct processing of an indexed sequential file differs substantially from the sequential processing just outlined. Algorithm IS_DIRECT shows how direct processing is accomplished given a transaction record which specifies the reading, alteration, or deletion of an existing record, or the addition of a new record. The algorithm assumes an input of just one transaction. This is realistic since, in practice, direct processing is used when a quick response time is needed for a number of individual requests, and yet there is not sufficient time to batch the requests and achieve a higher system throughput of requests. A transaction record is of the form

<transaction record>::= <transaction type> <key> <info>

where the <transaction type> and the corresponding <info> field are given in Table 7-7.1.

**Algorithm** IS_DIRECT. Given an indexed sequential file called MASTER which contains records each made up of a key and a set of information items, this algorithm accesses a record directly and performs the desired transaction on this record. The cylinder index, CYL_INDEX, is considered to be a vector P in length in which each element contains the two items CYLNO (meaning cylinder number) and KEY. The transaction record is referenced using the variable TRAN_REC which is composed of the items TRANS, KEY, and INFO. The remaining variables take on the roles described in Algorithm IS_SEQUENTIAL.

1. [Initialize]
>    Open MASTER file for update
>    Read TRAN_REC
2. [Examine cylinder index]
>    CYL ← CYLNO of CYL_INDEX[P]
>    Repeat for I = 1, 2, ..., P − 1
>        If KEY of TRAN_REC ≤ KEY of CYL_INDEX[I]

**Table 7-7.1**

| <transaction type> | <key><info> |
| --- | --- |
| READ | key of record only (no <info>) |
| ALTER | key and new information items |
| DELETE | key of record only (no <info>) |
| ADD | key and information items of new record |

    then CYL ← CYLNO of CYL_INDEX[I]
       Exitloop

3. [Examine track index for CYL]
    Repeat for J = 1, 2, ..., M
      If KEY of TRAN_REC ≤ OVFLOW_KEY of TRK_INDEX[J]
      then If KEY of TRAN_REC ≤ NORMAL_KEY of TRK_INDEX[J]
         then ADDR ← NORMAL_ADDR of TRK_INDEX[J]
            (ADDR is initially pointing at the first record
            on the prime track)
            If TRANS = 'ADD'
            then Call IS_PRIME_INSERT(ADDR)
              Exit
            Repeat while KEY of PRIME_REC(ADDR) <
                   KEY of TRAN_REC
              ADDR ← beginning of next prime track record
         else If KEY of PRIME_REC(ADDR) ≠ KEY of TRAN_REC
            then Write('TRANSACTION KEY DOES NOT MATCH',
                ' A FILE KEY')
              Exit
            ADDR ← OVFLOW_ADDR of TRK_INDEX[J]
            (ADDR is initially pointing to first record
            in list of overflow records)
            If TRANS = 'ADD'
            then Call IS_OF_INSERT(ADDR)
              Exit
            Repeat while KEY of OVFLOW_REC(ADDR) <
                   KEY of TRAN_REC
              ADDR ← LINK of OVFLOW_REC(ADDR)
            If KEY of OVFLOW_REC(ADDR) ≠ KEY of TRAN_REC
            then Write('TRANSACTION KEY DOES NOT MATCH',
                ' A FILE KEY')
              Exit
         Read track record at ADDR from MASTER file into MTR_REC
         If TRANS of TRAN_REC = 'DELETE'
         then Delete track record at ADDR from MASTER file.
            Exit
         If TRANS of TRAN_REC = 'ALTER'
         then Rewrite track record at ADDR in MASTER file
            with KEY and INFO of TRAN_REC
            Exit
         Write('ILLEGAL TRANSACTION SPECIFIED')
         Exit

4. [Compare keys and change CYL_INDEX if necessary]
    If TRANS = 'ADD'
    then KEY of CYL_INDEX[P] ← KEY of TRAN_REC
       Call IS_OF_INSERT(ADDR)
       Exit
    else write('ILLEGAL TRANSACTION')
       Exit            □

Before describing Algorithm IS_DIRECT, it must be pointed out that a master index is not used in the algorithm. If it were considered, an extra step would be necessary to locate the proper cylinder index before executing step 2.

The algorithm begins by opening the MASTER file and reading in a transaction record. The track location of the MASTER file record corresponding to the key in the transaction record is found by searching the cylinder-index table in step 2. The track index table is examined in step 3 to determine if the prime or overflow area should be searched. Once located, the desired record is updated based on the transaction type that is input. Step 4 handles the unusual yet possible situation of the addition of a record with a key that is greater than the keys of all other records in the file. When this occurs, the cylinder index must be updated and the record is added to the overflow area for the last cylinder.

Two procedures are invoked from Algorithm IS_DIRECT, namely, Procedure IS_PRIME_INSERT and Procedure IS_OF_INSERT. Procedure IS_PRIME_INSERT is responsible for establishing the record location for a given prime track at which the record from the transaction should be inserted. If a dummy or deleted record has the same key as the transaction key, then the new record is inserted at the dummy or deleted record location. A dummy record is simply a record that is written into a file, usually when the file is created. The record contains no meaningful information other than its key. This record is created in anticipation that it will store meaningful information later in the "life" of the file.

If no dummy or deleted record corresponds to the transaction key, then records with keys greater than the transaction key must be moved further along the prime track to leave room for the insertion of the record. Such a movement of records results in the transfer of the last record on the track to the overflow area. This new overflow record contains the lowest key of the overflow records for the prime track under consideration. Hence, the overflow track/record address field for the corresponding element of the track index table must be altered to point to the new overflow record. A step-by-step description of Procedure IS_PRIME_INSERT is left as an exercise. The second procedure for record insertion, Procedure IS_OF_INSERT, however, is described as follows.

**Procedure** IS_OF_INSERT(ADDR). Given the track/record address ADDR of the first overflow record of a particular track J, a new record which is contained in the transaction record is inserted at its proper location in the ordered list of overflow records for the given track. NEWLOC is a variable that is assigned the track/record location at which the new record is written. PREVADDR is a temporary address needed to insert the new record into the linked list of overflow records. OVFLOW_AVAIL is a pointer to the next available record location from a list of unused overflow record locations.

1. [Write the new record into next available overflow location]
        NEWLOC ← OVFLOW_AVAIL
        Update OVFLOW_AVAIL pointer
        Write KEY and INFO of TRAN_REC on MASTER file at location NEWLOC
2. [Initialize search for positioning of new record in overflow list]
        If KEY of OVFLOW_REC(ADDR) > KEY of TRAN_REC
        then  (add to head of list)
                OVFLOW_ADDR of TRK_INDEX[J] ← NEWLOC
                LINK of OVFLOW_REC(NEWLOC) ← ADDR
                Return

3.  [Insert in middle of overflow list]
        PREVADDR ← ADDR
        ADDR ← LINK of OVFLOW_REC(ADDR)
        Repeat while KEY of OVFLOW_REC(PREVADDR) ≠
                    OVFLOW_KEY of TRK_INDEX[J]
            (continue until end of list)
            If KEY of OVFLOW_REC(ADDR) ≥ KEY of TRAN_REC
            then   LINK of OVFLOW_REC(PREVADDR) ← NEWLOC
                    LINK of OVFLOW_REC(NEWLOC) ← ADDR
                    Return
            PREVADDR ← ADDR
            ADDR ← LINK of OVFLOW_REC(ADDR)
4.  [Insert at end of overflow list]
            LINK of OVFLOW_REC(ADDR) ← NEWLOC
            (Set link field to track ADDR)
            LINK of OVFLOW_REC(NEWLOC) ← J
            OVFLOW_KEY of TRK_INDEX[J] ← KEY of TRAN_REC      □

In the algorithm, it is assumed that a special pointer, OVFLOW_AVAIL, is used in managing available record space in the overflow area. The logic of Procedure IS_OF_INSERT varies little from the logic of many of the algorithms presented in Sec. 4-2.1 and, therefore, should be comprehensible without a detailed explanation.

It should be evident from the discussion thus far that if the system access facilities for indexed sequential files are not provided, the file-management routines which the user would have to write would be very complex. However, if record searching and handling is accomplished by system facilities (as generally happens), we can express the user-level commands required for the direct processing of an indexed sequential file in the following six steps:

1.  Open MASTER file for update, and read TRAN_REC
2.  If TRANS = 'ADD'
        then Write INFO of TRAN_REC
              with key of TRAN_REC on MASTER file
              Exit
3.  Read from MASTER file into MTR_REC with key of TRAN_REC
4.  If TRANS = 'ALTER'
        then Rewrite INFO of TRAN_REC
              with key of TRAN_REC on MASTER file
              Exit
5.  If TRANS ='DELETE'
        then Delete from MASTER file the record with key KEY of TRAN_REC
              Exit
6.  If TRANS ≠ 'READ'
        then Print 'ILLEGAL TRANSACTION'
              Exit

Note that before a record is deleted or rewritten, it is read. This is done purposely to remain consistent with the access method used in IBM systems. The read statement is used to locate a record. If a desired record does not exist, a condition code is set by the system. The user can intercept this code and thus avoid executing a rewrite or delete command which can cause a system error. In our discussion of PL/I indexed sequential file processing in the next subsection, we demonstrate how the condition code can be used.

To conclude this subsection, let us summarize the important properties relating to indexed sequential files:

1 Indexed sequential files provide reasonably fast access to records using either sequential or direct processing.

2 For relatively static files, the independent overflow area can be eliminated and the cylinder overflow area can be minimized, thus giving a high percentage of disk utilization.

3 For highly volatile files, the access time for a record becomes excessive as overflow areas become filled.

4 Indexed sequential access facilities are generally provided in most systems, thus relieving the programmer of a large amount of housekeeping detail in maintaining indexes and linked overflow areas. At the programmer level, the sequential processing of an indexed sequential file appears identical to the sequential processing of a sequential file.

### 7-7.3 Indexed Sequential Files in PL/I

An indexed sequential file is identified in a PL/I program through a declaration statement of the form

DECLARE MASTER FILE RECORD KEYED ENV(INDEXED);

Two other sets of attributes are commonly associated with a declaration statement or are supplied in the OPEN statement for the file. These are the accessing-type attributes, namely, DIRECT or SEQUENTIAL, and the processing-mode attributes: INPUT, OUTPUT, or UPDATE. For example, to create an indexed sequential file, say MASTER, we use either

OPEN FILE(MASTER) SEQUENTIAL OUTPUT;

or we add the attributes SEQUENTIAL and OUTPUT to the file declaration. Remember all indexed sequential files must be created sequentially and thereafter can be accessed directly or sequentially.

A number of different PL/I input/output statements are provided to perform operations on an indexed sequential file. Table 7-7.2 gives a list of these statements for the file CUSTOMER with the key of ACCT_NO. CUST is the record containing the specific information identified by the key ACCT_NO.

Many of these I/O statements are illustrated in the PL/I program given in Fig. 7-7.6. The program is composed of three major segments. The first segment creates the file CUSTOMER sequentially. The second segment updates the CUSTOMER file directly in a similar manner to that described in Algorithm IS_DIRECT given in the last subsection. The single-letter transaction codes are: 'A' meaning 'ADD,' 'C' meaning 'CHANGE,' 'D' meaning 'DELETE' and 'R' meaning 'READ'. Note again that we must read a record before it can be rewritten or deleted during a file update.

The third segment reads the file sequentially, printing the contents of each record while doing so. It should be observed that the KEYTO form of a SEQUEN-TIAL READ statement has been used. This form of READ statement is necessary if the key for a record is not embedded in the record. The clause KEYTO(ACCT_NO) causes the value of the nonembedded key to be assigned to ACCT_NO and thus allows the printing of the account number along with the other pertinent customer information. If we omitted the KEYTO clause, we could not recover the account number, since it does not reside in the customer record.

**Table 7-7.2**

| Processing Mode | Access Type | Purpose | Sample I/O Statements |
|---|---|---|---|
| OUTPUT | SEQUENTIAL | To create a new indexed sequential file | WRITE(CUSTOMER) FROM (CUST); /* OR */ WRITE FILE(CUSTOMER) FROM (CUST) KEYFROM(ACCT_NO); |
| INPUT | SEQUENTIAL | To process all the records in sequence | READ FILE(CUSTOMER) INTO (CUST); /* OR */ READ FILE(CUSTOMER) INTO (CUST) KEYTO(ACCT_NO); |
| INPUT | DIRECT | To process selected records | READ FILE(CUSTOMER) INTO (CUST) KEY(ACCT_NO); |
| UPDATE | SEQUENTIAL | To modify all records | REWRITE FILE(CUSTOMER); /* OR */ REWRITE FILE(CUSTOMER) FROM (CUST); |
| UPDATE | DIRECT | To modify selected records | REWRITE FILE(CUSTOMER) FROM (CUST) KEY(ACCT_NO); |
| UPDATE | DIRECT | To add new records to the file | WRITE FILE(CUSTOMER) FROM (CUST) KEYFROM(ACCT_NO); |
| UPDATE | DIRECT | To delete a specific record from the file | DELETE FILE(CUSTOMER) KEY (ACCT_NO); |

The differences in record structure for records with embedded and nonembedded keys are illustrated in Figs. 7-7.7 and 7-7.8. To tell the file-management facilities of the location and length of a recorded key, we use the DCB parameters RKP (relative key position) and KEYLEN (key length). For example, suppose that we wish to embed the key ACCT_NO in the CUST structure. Then CUST would be declared as indicated in the following statements:

```
DECLARE 1 CUST,
          2 DELETE_FLAG BIT(8),
          2 ACCT_NO CHARACTER (6),
          2 INFO,
              3 NAME CHARACTER(20),

                    .
                    .
                    .
              3 BALANCE FIXED DECIMAL(7,2);
```

In this case, RKP = 1 and KEYLEN = 6 would be used as DCB parameters. The RKP specifies the number of bytes from the first byte of a record at which the embedded key is found. An RKP of zero is the default value and indicates that a nonembedded key is used.

```
//  EXEC  PL1FCLG
//PL1L.SYSIN DD *

INDX_EG: PROCEDURE OPTIONS (MAIN);

/*                INITALIZATION                        */

    DECLARE CUSTOMER FILE RECORD KEYED ENV(INDEXED F(770 77)),
            TRANFILE FILE STREAM INPUT,
                1 CUST,
                    2 DELETE_FLAG BIT(8),
                    2 INFO,
                        3 NAME CHARACTER(20),
                        3 ADDRESS,
                            4 LINE1 CHARACTER(20),
                            4 LINE2 CHARACTER(19),
                            4 POSTAL_CODE CHARACTER(7),
                        3 BALANCE FIXED DECIMAL(7,2),
            ACCT_NO CHARACTER(6),  /* USED AS A KEY ITEM FOR RECORDS */
            CODE CHARACTER(1),
            LAB(0:4) LABEL;
    DELETE_FLAG = (8) '0'B;

/*                CREATING FILE                        */

    ON ENDFILE(SYSIN) GO TO UPDTE;
    OPEN FILE (CUSTOMER) SEQUENTIAL OUTPUT;
    DO WHILE ('1'B);    /* UNTIL END OF FILE SYSIN */
        GET EDIT (ACCT_NO,CUST.INFO)
            (COL(1),A(6),2 A(20),A(19),A(7),F(7,2));
        WRITE FILE (CUSTOMER) FROM (CUST) KEYFROM (ACCT_NO);
    END;
UPDTE:
    CLOSE FILE (CUSTOMER);

/*                UPDATING FILE                        */

    OPEN FILE (CUSTOMER) DIRECT UPDATE;
    OPEN FILE (TRANFILE);
    ON ENDFILE (TRANFILE) GO TO OTPT
    ON KEY (CUSTOMER) BEGIN;
        IF ONCODE = 51
        THEN PUT SKIP LIST (ACCT_NO,' NOT FOUND');
        IF ONCODE = 52
        THEN PUT SKIP LIST ('DUPLICATE ACCOUNT' ACCT_NO);
    END;
```

**FIGURE 7-7.6**   Example of a PL/I program using an indexed sequential file.

For variable-length records, the minimum RKP is 4 and implies a nonembedded key. The offset of four bytes is accounted for by the block- and record-length indicators that must accompany variable-length records. Therefore, the position of an embedded key is 4 plus the relative offset of the key from the beginning of the record.

The DD statements for the file CUSTOMER in Fig. 7-7.5 tell the system how to structure the indexed sequential file. The DSNAME parameters INDEX, PRIME, and OVFLOW specify the three different areas of the file. The DD statement with the INDEX parameter describes the file space needed for the cylinder index, the DD statement with the PRIME parameter describes the file space needed for the prime area, and the DD statement with the OVFLOW parameter describes the file space needed for the independent overflow area. No space has been allocated for a cylinder overflow area. If we wish to create a file with no cylinder index, no

```
    DO WHILE ('1'B);
        GET FILE (TRANFILE) EDIT (CODE)(COL(1),A(1));
        I = INDEX('ACDR',CODE);
        GO TO LAB(I);

LAB(0): /* ILLEGAL TRANSACTION CODE */
    PUT SKIP LIST ('ILLEGAL TRANSACTION CODE ',CODE);
    GO TO NEXT_TRAN;

LAB(1): /* A - ADDITION TRANSACTION */
    GET FILE (TRANFILE) EDIT (ACCT_NO,CUST.INFO)
            (A(6),A(20),A(20),A(19),A(7),F(7,2));
    WRITE FILE (CUSTOMER) FROM (CUST) KEYFROM (ACCT_NO);
    GO TO NEXT_TRAN;

LAB(2): /* C - CHANGE OR ALTER TRANSACTION */
    GET FILE (TRANFILE) EDIT (ACCT_NO)(A(6));
    READ FILE (CUSTOMER) INTO (CUST) KEY (ACCT_NO);
    GET FILE (TRANFILE) EDIT (NAME,ADDRESS) (2 A(20),A(19),A(7));
    REWRITE FILE (CUSTOMER) FROM (CUST) KEY (ACCT_NO);
    GO TO NEXT_TRAN;

LAB(3): /* D - DELETE TRANSACTION */
    GET FILE (TRANFILE) EDIT (ACCT_NO)(A(6));
    READ FILE (CUSTOMER) INTO (CUST) KEY (ACCT_NO);
    DELETE FILE (CUSTOMER) KEY (ACCT_NO);
    GO TO NEXT_TRAN;

LAB(4): /* R - READ TRANSACTION */
    GET FILE (TRANFILE) EDIT (ACCT_NO)(A(6));
    READ FILE (CUSTOMER) INTO (CUST) KEY (ACCT_NO);

NEXT_TRAN:
    END;    /* DO WHILE PROCESSING TRANFILE */

OTPT: CLOSE FILE (CUSTOMER);




/*              O U T P U T   F I L E                        */

OPEN FILE (CUSTOMER) INPUT SEQUENTIAL;
ON ENDFILE (CUSTOMER) STOP;
DO WHILE ('1'B);    /* UNTIL END OF CUSTOMER FILE */
    READ FILE (CUSTOMER) INTO (CUST) KEYTO (ACCT_NO);
    PUT SKIP EDIT (ACCT_NO,CUST.INFO)(5 (A,X(1)), F(7,2));
END;

END INDX_EG;
//GO.CUSTOMER DD DSNAME=BILLING(INDEX),DISP=(NEW,KEEP),UNIT=SYSDA,
//   VOL=SER=USER02,DCB=(DSORG=IS,RKP=0,KEYLEN=6,OPTCD=L),SPACE=(CYL,1)
//       DD DSNAME=BILLING(PRIME),DISP=(NEW,KEEP),UNIT=SYSDA,
//   VOL=SER=USER02,DCB=(DSORG=IS,RKP=0,KEYLEN=6,OPTCD=L),SPACE=(CYL,3)
//       DD DSNAME=BILLING(OVFLOW),DISP=(NEW,KEEP),UNIT=SYSDA,
//   VOL=SER=USER02,DCB=(DSORG=IS,RKP=0,KEYLEN=6,OPTCD=L),SPACE=(CYL,1)
//GO.SYSIN DD *
134679MR. JOHN Q. BROWN    445 5TH AVE. N.    SASKATOON, SASK.    S7K 2H6 123.45
654821MRS. ALICE W. SMITH 285 VANCOUVER AVE.  WINNIPEG, MAN.      R4T 5S5 512.34
753981MORE O THESAME       2 LITTLE DATUM RD.  ANYTOWN, ANYWHERE  A1A 1A1
987654MR GIGO DATA         12345 DATA AVE      DATA, DATA         D5A 4T1 123.56
//GO.TRANFILE DD *
A321548MR. JOHN W. SMITH   321 MONTREAL AVE.   CALGARY, ALTA.     R4T 2D9321.54
R134679
D987654
C654821MRS. ALICE W. SMITH 286 VANCOUVER AVE.   WINNIPEG, MAN.    R4T 5S5
```

**FIGURE 7-7.6** (Continued)

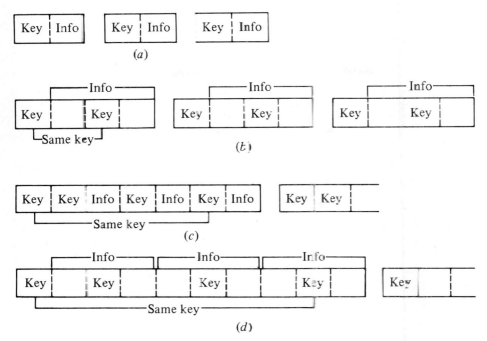

**FIGURE 7-7.7** Structure of fixed-length records in an indexed sequential file. (*a*) Unblocked records—nonembedded keys; (*b*) unblocked records—embedded keys; (*c*) blocked records—nonembedded keys; (*d*) blocked records—embedded keys.

independent overflow area, and a cylinder overflow area of three tracks per cylinder, we would use the following DD statement:

```
//GO.CUSTOMER DD DSNAME=BILLING(PRIME),DISP=(NEW,KEEP),
//      UNIT=SYSDA,VOL=SER=USER02,DCB=(DSORG=IS,
//      RKP=0,KEYLEN=6,CYLOFL=3),SPACE=(CYL,3)
```

The ON KEY type of ON condition is very important when processing files in PL/I. Its use is illustrated in Fig. 7-7.6. If an unusual condition occurs during an I/O statement, this condition is detected by the operating system and a condition code is assigned. A PL/I program can intercept this unusual condition using the ON KEY ON unit. The condition code is assigned to a special PL/I pseudo variable, ONCODE, which can be used to warn the programmer of the I/O error and to allow alternate action to be taken. A list of ONCODE values that can be checked for are as follows:

ONCODE
- 50  KEY signal, used to test ON KEY conditions by setting the pseudo variable KEY to a legitimate ONCODE value
- 51  keyed record not found
- 52  attempt to duplicate key
- 53  key sequence error, used when creating IS file
- 54  key conversion error, character string not used for key
- 55  key specification error

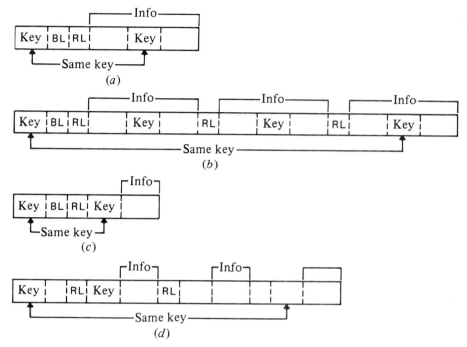

**FIGURE 7-7.8** Structure of variable-length records in an indexed sequential file. (a) Unblocked variable-length records, RKP > 4; (b) blocked variable-length records, RKP > 4; (c) unblocked variable-length records, RKP = 4; (d) blocked variable-length records, RKP = 4.

    56    keyed region outside data set limit, used in REGIONAL files
    57    no space available to add keyed record (or LMTCT reached)

As a final comment relating to the program in Fig. 7-7.6, it should be pointed out that the programmer is responsible for leaving a one-byte field for a delete flag indicator, if records are to be deleted from the file during UPDATE DIRECT processing. A **DELETE** statement marks a record as a dummy by putting (8)'1'B in the first byte of the record.

There are many other interesting file-processing features associated with indexed sequential files. For example, the GENKEY (generic key) ENVIRONMENT option allows the access of records according to their key class, as determined by a generic key. For example, the recorded keys '692138', '693112', '694761', and '698882' are all members of the class of keys identified by the generic key '69'.

To illustrate how the GENKEY option can be used, consider the following PL/I statements:

```
DECLARE CUSTOMER FILE RECORD SEQUENTIAL KEYED UPDATE
    ENV(INDEXED GENKEY);
        .
        .
        .
```

```
READ FILE(CUSTOMER) INTO(CUST) KEY('69');
    .
    .
    .

LOOP:  READ FILE(CUSTOMER) INTO(CUST);
    .
    .
    .

GO TO LOOP;
```

The first READ locates and reads the first record with key beginning '69'. The second READ reads the remaining records with keys which belong to the generic key class '69'.

To obtain a more comprehensive understanding of how to create and use indexed sequential files in PL/I, read the appropriate sections of the IBM PL/I Programmer's Guide.

Let us now turn to an example application which helps illustrate many of the concepts presented in this section.

**Exercises for Sec. 7-7**

1.  Formulate Algorithm IS_SEQ_SCOPE which depicts how records are processed sequentially in an indexed sequential file on the CDC Scope System.
2.  Formulate Algorithm IS_DIR_SCOPE which depicts how records are processed directly in an indexed sequential file on the CDC Scope System.
3.  Construct Procedure IS_PRIME_INSERT which places a record which is to be added to an indexed sequential file (IBM variety) in its proper prime area location. Note that the placement of the new record may generate an overflow involving the last record on the prime track.
4.  Assume that we always access a certain file sequentially. Under what conditions, if any, is it advantageous to have the file organized as an indexed sequential rather than a sequential file?
5.  An important application area within many business systems is sales analysis. Sales analysis produces information giving management a review of sales data on customers, items, and salespeople. There are two basic methods of handling sales data—the *detail method* and the *summary method*. Using the detail approach, detailed sales-transaction information is accumulated until the end of an established period (say, a month), at which time it is sorted and then analyzed to produce customer, item, and salesperson information. Obviously, a sequential file can be used to store this accumulated information.

    The summary method is based on sales values accumulated daily from sales information associated with order entry and invoicing, and inventory accounting. Individual inquiries return up-to-date information on customer, salesperson, and item sales. An indexed sequential organization should be considered to ensure immediate responses to such queries.

    Write a PL/I program which takes as input the following information as gathered from customer invoices: salesperson's number, customer's account number, amounts sold (or returned) for each of article types A, B, C, and D and the total amount sold (or returned). Two files, a customer file and a salesperson file, should be created and maintained for summary reports. The customer file is keyed on the customer's account number and contains an accumulated total of the purchases made to date by the customer. The salesperson file is keyed on the salesperson's number and retains the total number of sales for each of the article types *A, B, C,* and *D,* and the total sales to date for the salesperson. To thoroughly test your programs, intermix inquiries concerning the status of certain customer accounts or the performance of certain salespeople with the invoice information which is read in. Customer inquiries are keyed on account numbers and return the total purchases to date. Salesperson inquiries are keyed on a salesperson's name—a table relating salesperson's name and number is required—and the sales-to-date figures are returned for each article type *A, B, C,* and *D,* plus the total sales-to-date figure.

## 7-8 CLASS-RECORDS RETRIEVAL SYSTEM

In this section, we describe a system for retrieving, maintaining, and processing students' marks on a class-by-class basis. When compared to most data-processing systems, the Class-Records Retrieval (CRR) System is small in size. Nevertheless, it is illustrative, comprehensible, and involves an application area familiar to everyone. Again, the development of the system will be presented in three phases—the system analysis, system design, and the implementation phases.

### 7-8.1 System Analysis

A group of professors within the Department of Computer Science has decided to reduce the bookkeeping chores related to the recording of students' grades. A small computerized retrieval system is proposed as the tool to aid in the efficient and accurate handling of the class records. The desired system facilities the professors feel are necessary are the following:

*1* The ability to produce a complete listing of the students' names, numbers, and marks for all students in a particular class.
*2* The ability to compute weighted averages for each student and a class average on any given assignment and final grades.
*3* The ability to insert records for new students or to delete the records of students who cancel out.
*4* The ability to insert or update marks.

It is desirable that the system be on-line to provide immediate access.

The form of input to the system should be in easy-to-learn English-like statements which allow the user to express requests such as

LIST OF STUDENTS WITH MARKS ON ASSIGNMENT 3 > 80
or  LIST OF STUDENTS, IDS, MARKS, GRADES

The term "grade" means the weighted final mark or weighted final mark to date if all term marks have not been recorded as yet.

The output should be in an easy-to-read format and printed in an order determined by the alphabetical ordering of the students' names. This ordering is the most convenient for transcribing marks to the official statements of standings for the university, which lists the students in alphabetical order.

## 7-8.2  System Design

We proceed with a top-down approach to the design of the system, beginning with the formulation of a query language and ending with the design of the file structures and file processing routines.

The design of the query language is one of the most important steps in the development of a system, especially a system that can be used in an on-line environment. The users must be able to express their requests in a manner which fits the nature of the application. The CRR System is not the type of system which is used daily by a professor. Therefore, the language should not have a highly structured format with abbreviations for commands and command operands. In a system such as an airline reservation system, rigorous and abbreviated languages are acceptable, and even desirable, since the terminal operators are using their consoles hourly in a role which demands quick customer service.

The following BNF-like description defines a query language which is natural-language-oriented yet does not introduce the complexity of a full English query language. Grammatical expressions of the form {A} mean that the syntactic unit represented by A can appear 0, or 1, or 2, ..., of $n$ times for $n$ equal to any non-negative integer. Expressions of the form [A] mean that the syntactic unit represented by A appears once, or not at all.

```
<query> ::= <proposition>
              | <maintenance function>
              | <marks weighting function>
<proposition> ::= <subject1> <object1>
              | <subject2> <object2>
<subject1> ::= LIST OF | NUMBER OF
<subject2> ::= AVERAGE | MIN[IMUM] | MAX[IMUM]
<object1> ::= <object head1> { <objective1> }
              | { <objective2> } <object2>
<object2> ::= <object head2> [ <relational statement> ]
                { <objective1> } { <objective2> }
<object head1> ::= STUDENT[S] [ <name list> ]
              | ID[S]
              | <object head2>
<object head2> ::= GRADE[S]
              | MARK[S] [ON ASSIGNMENT <number> ]
<objective1> ::= <buzz word> <object head1>
<objective2> ::= <buzz word> <object head2>
                [ <relational statements> ]
<buzz word> ::= WITH | FOR | ,
<relational statement> ::= <relation> <number> | <connector>
                <relation> <number> ]
<relation> ::= < | = | > | # | >= | <=
<connector> ::= AND | OR
<number list> ::= <number> | <number> , <number list>
<number> ::= <digit> | <digit> <number>
<digit> ::= 0 | 1 | 2 | 3 | 4 | 5 | 6 | 7 | 8 | 9
<name list> ::= <name> | <name> , <name list>
<name> ::= <letter> | <letter> <name>
<letter> ::= A | B | C | ... | X | Y | Z | & | . | -
```

&lt;maintenance function&gt; ::= DELETE &lt;name list&gt;
            | INSERT [MANY]
            | &lt;update head&gt;
&lt;update head&gt; ::= UPDATE ASSIGNMENT &lt;number&gt; [ALL]
&lt;marks weighting function&gt; ::= WEIGHTING &lt;number list&gt;

Example queries from this language are as follows:

LIST OF STUDENTS WITH MARKS ON ASSIGNMENT 3 > 80
LIST OF IDS, GRADES
LIST OF STUDENTS, IDS, MARKS, GRADES
AVERAGE MARKS, GRADES
MINIMUM GRADE
MAXIMUM MARK ON ASSIGNMENT 1
DELETE HARPER.B
INSERT MANY
UPDATE ASSIGNMENT 2
WEIGHTING 33, 34, 33

The first seven queries should be self-explanatory. The two system maintenance functions, INSERT and UPDATE, must be elaborated upon. When either of
these requests is made, the system should be designed to prompt the user with the
required input. For example, when a student is inserted into the system, initial information such as student name, student identification number, college, and year must
be provided. A reliable way of ensuring that the necessary information is given is to
lead the user with prompting *-commands such as

*ENTER THE STUDENT'S NAME...
 HARPER.B
*ENTER THE STUDENT'S IDENTIFICATION NUMBER...
 724115
*ENTER THE STUDENT'S COLLEGE...
 COMMERCE
*ENTER THE STUDENT'S YEAR...
 3
*HARPER.B HAS BEEN SUCCESSFULLY INSERTED.

The UPDATE command performs in a prompting mode also. The WEIGHTING command sets the relative weighting of the term assignments and exams. The list of
numbers following the WEIGHTING keyword must total 100. Hence, a weighting of
34 in the second element of the list indicates that $34/100$ of the final grade is
based on the mark on assignment 2.

After adopting this query language, the next step in the design is to formulate
the scanning and parsing (i.e., the syntactic analysis) strategies for the recognition of
statements from the query language. The scanner, which is responsible for detecting
the basic word-like units of the language, isolates the keywords such as LIST,
NUMBER, OF, MIN, MINIMUM, GRADE, GRADES, AND, OR, DELETE, INSERT,
etc., as well as the &lt;name&gt; and &lt;number&gt; syntactic units. (Refer to Sec. 2-5.2 for
a more complete description of the function of a scanner.)

There are many different parsing techniques which can be employed in the
recognition of query statements. We have described two general strategies, top-down
and bottom-up parsing, in Chaps. 2 and 5 of the text. A description of most of the
very powerful techniques is beyond the scope of this text (see Gries [1971]). How-

ever, one of the simplest parsing strategies to implement is recursive descent, which was discussed in Sec. 5-2.3. Since the query language is described with a relatively small grammar, the inefficiencies of this method can be tolerated, and we have adopted this as the parsing strategy. Figure 7-8.1 illustrates the relationship of the query analysis phase with the complete system design. Notice that scanning errors (e.g., the input of a character like '?' which does not belong to the alphabet of the language) and parsing errors (e.g., an incorrect input like 'NUMB STUDENTS' instead of 'NUMBER OF STUDENTS') are identified and an error message is sent to the user.

If a query belongs to our previously defined query language, it must be acted upon. For the CRR System this action is either a correct response, as determined by

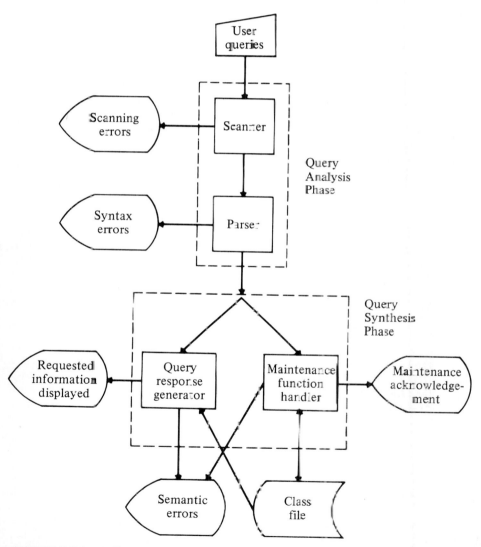

**FIGURE 7-8.1**   A flow diagram illustrating the design of the CRR system.

the retrieval of an appropriate set of information, or the system data base (i.e., the set of student records) is manipulated correctly. Figure 7-8.1 depicts this logical breakdown of the query synthesis phase. The query-response generating section handles data-retrieval requests as expressed in the LIST OF, NUMBER OF, AVERAGE, MIN, and MAX commands. Most of these retrieval requests demand the sequential processing of a file of student records. For example, the query

NUMBER OF STUDENTS WITH GRADE > 80

suggests the examination of each student record to determine if that student scored higher than 80. For each such score, a counter is incremented and the value of this counter is printed after all records have been examined. A similar form of processing is required to handle most of the other retrieval requests, except for those commands referring to specific students by name. For example,

LIST OF STUDENTS COOPER.R, RIDGWAY.W, NYLANDER.L<br>WITH MARKS ON ASSIGNMENT 1 > 90

requires the examination of only three specific student records. Hence, the ability to access directly student records by student name is a definite asset. Note that we could have designed the query language so as to insist that student identification numbers, rather than student names, be used to identify a student record in the system. However, such a design decision is not appealing from the user's point of view. Both professors and students communicate on a name, rather than number, basis. If we are designing a university-wide registration system, then student identification by number has many definite advantages, including record anonymity and a unique identification scheme for each student, which is not necessarily the case when names are used for identification. Of course, student numbers were derived initially for registration systems.

The direct referencing of records is also needed when performing the system-maintenance function. We delete and update records by student name. When adding a new record, the student name along with other student information is requested. Hence, the file processing required in this application involves the examination of records in a sequential fashion, the printing of record information in alphabetical order of student name, and the direct processing of selected records based on a student name index. Clearly, the indexed sequential-file organization satisfies these processing needs, and an indexed sequential class-record file keyed on the student name item should be used. This file is referred to as the "class file" in Fig. 7-8.1.

To retain all the information required by the users of the system, a record in the class file must contain the student's name, I.D., college, year, marks up to a reasonable number of assignments (say 12), and the student's final grade. Ideally, we should create a different file for each class. However, the minimum amount of space that can be allocated to an indexed sequential file for the IBM system is one cylinder. Assuming we are to implement the CRR System on an IBM system using an IBM 3330 disk pack, this minimum space is much too large for a file of records for only one class.

There are 13,030 bytes/track $\times$ 18 tracks/cylinder = 234,540 bytes/cylinder of prime and cylinder overflow area on a cylinder of an IBM 3330. Even assuming as much as ½ of the bytes are devoted to overhead space, i.e., space for overflow chains, record-length descriptors, and other record-storage information, 117,270 bytes remain for storing record information. Approximately 40 bytes are needed to store the information for a student. (This figure will be confirmed in the next subsection when we discuss the implementation.) Therefore, one cylinder can hold 2,931 records (using an extremely conservative estimating procedure). It would be extremely wasteful of disk storage to devote a cylinder to each class.

A better approach is to place the records from all classes on a common cylinder and to make use of the GENKEY option when retrieving records for a particular class. The adoption of this strategy means that the key for the indexed sequential class file must be prefixed with a class number. For example, the key for D. Smith's record in class CMPT 316 is '316SMITH.D', and the key of D. Jones' record in class CMPT 441 is '441JONES.D'. All records in the class CMPT 316 can be accessed in PL/I by first using the generic key '316', as described at the end of Sec. 7-7.3.

An initial class list is usually compiled when course lectures begin. The indexed sequential class file is created sequentially by writing the student records on file as ordered by the class number/student name key. From this initial file, updates, deletions, and alterations can be made without requiring a large overflow area.

There are three forms of output generated from the query synthesis phase. First, there is the information which is retrieved from the query-response commands such as LIST and MAXIMUM. The output form should be clearly readable. Some example output is presented in the next subsection. Second, semantic errors can arise during the processing of requests. Attempts to delete a student who is not in the file or to add a student who is already in the file are examples of a semantic error. Third, an output response to the user by the system acknowledging the completion of a maintenance command, such as a deletion, is extremely helpful.

We have completed a description of the design phase and now turn to a discussion of the implementation.

### 7-8.3  Implementation

The implementation of the CRR System involves the writing of programs for the four main modules in Fig. 7-8.1, namely, the scanner, the parser, the query-response generator, and the maintenance-function handler. The scanner is realized through a procedure called SCAN. The parser is composed of 19 procedures, many of which are recursive in nature because of the recursive-descent parsing strategy we have adopted. The parser is initially invoked by a call to the procedure QUERY, which invokes either directly or indirectly the other 18 parser procedures. Both the query-response generator and maintenance-function handler facilities reside in a procedure named RESPONSE.

These three procedures, SCAN, QUERY, and RESPONSE, are initially called in the CRR System mainline, as shown in Fig. 7-8.2. Also included in this figure is the declaration and initialization of many of the program variables. Specifically, we should note the entry statements for the different procedures and the A_STUDENT structure declaration which is a description of the records that are stored in the indexed sequential file named CLASS. The procedure MSG is responsible for printing most of the user messages. The procedure SCAN is not given, except for a dummy heading. A discussion of the important aspects of the scanner, as they relate to data structures, was given in Sec. 2-5.2.

The mainline program begins by prompting the user with a 'HELLO' message and requesting a class number entry. After some initialization of system variables, the procedures SCAN, QUERY, and RESPONSE are invoked in order and repetitively until the user terminates the session.

```
CRR: PROCEDURE OPTIONS (MAIN);
```

```
/* THIS PROGRAM IS DESIGNED TO PERFORM A RETRIEVAL FUNCTION ON A DATA
   SET THAT CONTAINS RECORDS WITH INFORMATION PERTAINING TO A CLASS.
   FOR THIS REASON IT IS KNOWN AS THE CLASS RECORDS RETRIEVAL SYSTEM
   (CRR). A QUERY LANGUAGE IS USED TO EXTRACT THE DESIRED INFORMATION
   FROM THE FILE. THE PROGRAM IS COMPOSED OF TWO LOGICALLY DISTINCT
   PHASES. THE FIRST SCANS THE INPUT QUERY AND THEN TESTS IT FOR
   SEMANTIC VALIDITY. THE SECOND PORTION OF THE PROGRAM PERFORMS THE
   ACTUAL RETRIEVAL OF INFORMATION.                              */
```

```
DECLARE SCAN       ENTRY RETURNS (CHARACTER (30) VARYING),
        MSG        ENTRY (CHARACTER (*)),
        QUERY      ENTRY,
        RESPONSE   ENTRY;
```

```
/* THE FOLLOWING LIST OF PROCEDURES ARE USED IN THE PARSING OF THE
   INPUT QUERY. A RECURSIVE DESCENT PARSE HAS BEEN IMPLEMENTED.    */
```

```
DECLARE PROPOSITION          ENTRY RETURNS (BIT(1)),
        MAINTENANCE          ENTRY RETURNS (BIT(1)),
        WEIGHTING            ENTRY RETURNS (BIT(1)),
        SUBJECT1             ENTRY RETURNS (BIT(1)),
        SUBJECT2             ENTRY RETURNS (BIT(1)),
        OBJECT1              ENTRY RETURNS (BIT(1)),
        OBJECT2              ENTRY RETURNS (BIT(1)),
        OBJECT_HEAD1          ENTRY RETURNS (BIT(1)),
        OBJECT_HEAD2          ENTRY RETURNS (BIT(1)),
        OBJECTIVE1           ENTRY RETURNS (BIT(1)),
        OBJECTIVE2           ENTRY RETURNS (BIT(1)),
        REL_STAT             ENTRY RETURNS (BIT(1)),
        NAME               ENTRY RETURNS (BIT(1)),
        NAME_LIST            ENTRY RETURNS (BIT(1)),
        RELATION             ENTRY RETURNS (BIT(1)),
        NUMBER               ENTRY RETURNS (BIT(1)),
        NUMBER_LIST           ENTRY RETURNS (BIT(1)),
        UPDATE_HEAD           ENTRY RETURNS (BIT(1)),
```

```
/* THE FOLLOWING IS A LIST OF BIT STRING FLAGS WHICH ARE SET DURING THE
   PARSING PROCEDURE AND THEN REFERENCED DURING THE RETRIEVAL OF
   INFORMATION. DECLARATIONS OF TEMPORARY VARIABLES ARE INCLUDED AS
   WELL.                                                     */
```

```
        (NUM,LIST,MIN,MAX,AVERAGE,DUMMY,STUDENT,GRADE,ID,
         MARK,DELETE,INSERT,UPDTE,WEIGHT,ASNMT) BIT (1),
        ERROR BIT (1) INITIAL ('0'B),
        NEXTSYM CHARACTER (30) VARYING,
        RELATE (5) CHARACTER (2) VARYING,
        ST_NAMES (15) CHARACTER (20) VARYING,
        ASSIGN(16) CHARACTER (7) VARYING INITIAL ( (16) '-1'),
        LOOP BIT (1),
        COLUMN_SCAN FIXED,
        WORK CHARACTER (3),
        W(12) FIXED BINARY INITIAL ( (12) -1 ),
        NO_ST FIXED BINARY INITIAL (0),
        (STN,ASN) FIXED;
```

**FIGURE 7-8.2**   Main-line program for the CRR system.

The QUERY procedure and the recursive procedure for identifying the syntactic unit <OBJECT HEAD1> are shown in Fig.7-8.3. Both procedures illustrate the direct relationship that exists between a given syntactic description and the set of procedure calls used to check the validity for that description. In the procedure OBJECT_HEAD1, the global-bit-string flags STUDENT and ID may be set, depending on the form of the query. These bit-string variables, as well as a number of

```
/* THIS CLASS FILE IS THE FILE ASSOCIATED WITH THE DATA SET WHICH
CONTAINS THE CLASS RECORDS. THE STRUCTURE: 'A_STUDENT' IS USED TO
MANIPULATE THE RECORDS INTERNALLY. THE STRUCTURE SERVES TO INDICATE
THE FORMAT AND CONTENTS OF EACH RECORD                        */

     DECLARE CLASS FILE RECORD KEYED ENVIRONMENT (INDEXED GENKEY),
           1 A_STUDENT,
                 2 FILLER CHARACTER (1),
                 2 S_ID CHARACTER (6),
                 2 S_CLASS CHARACTER (4),
                 2 S_NAME CHARACTER (20),
                 2 S_COLLEGE CHARACTER (14),
                 2 S_YEAR CHARACTER (1),
                 2 S_MARKS (12) FIXED DECIMAL (3),
                 2 S_AVERAGE FIXED DECIMAL (5,2);

MSG: PROCEDURE (MESSAGE);
/* THE MSG PROCEDURE IS USED BY ALL PORTIONS OF THE PROGRAM TO PRINT
ALL MESSAGES TO THE USER. . . .                        */
     DECLARE MESSAGE CHARACTER (*)
     PUT EDIT (MESSAGE) (SKIP (2), A);
     END MSG;

/***************         S C A N          *******************/
SCAN: PROCEDURE RETURNS (CHARACTER (30) VARYING);

/* THE 'SCAN' PROCEDURE SCANS THE INPUT MESSAGE RETURNING THE NEXT
LEXICAL UNIT TO BE USED BY THE PARSER. . . .                */
END SCAN;

/******* Q U E R Y   P A R S I N G    P R O C E D U R E S **********/
/******                         &
/***** Q U E R Y   S Y N T H E S I S   P R O C E D U R E S *********/
/****                         F A L L   H E R E


/**************** M A I N   L I N E ***************************/
/* THIS SECTION OF THE PROGRAM INTRODUCES THE USER TO THE SYSTEM AND
THEN INITIALIZES A NUMBER OF SYSTEM VARIABLES AND CALLS THE QUERY
PROCESSING ROUTINES.                        */

     ON ENDFILE(SYSIN) GO TO DONE;

     LOOP = '1'B;
```

**FIGURE 7-8.2**   (Continued)

other bit-string flags, are declared in Fig. 7-8.2 and are used in the response-generating section of the program. It is these variables which determine what system functions should be performed and what information should be retrieved.

Because our main emphasis in this section is on the application of indexed sequential files, we will present a more detailed discussion of the operations performed on the class file. These operations arise in the query synthesis phase, which is implemented as the procedure RESPONSE. A skeleton version of the RESPONSE procedure is given in Fig. 7-8 4.

A module for handling queries requesting the minimum or maximum mark for a specified list of students is given as an example from the response-generator section of the RESPONSE procedure. This program segment illustrates how the indexed sequential file CLASS is accessed directly via the class number/student name key. Note that we have used the ON KEY condition to detect inquiries involving students not in the file for a given class

```
DO WHILE(LOOP);
    PUT EDIT('HELLO ','PLEASE ENTER YOUR CLASS NUMBER (E.G. ',
        '313B,441A,102,ETC)','')
        ( (2) (COLUMN(1),A),A,COLUMN(1),A(0));
    GET EDIT (STRING) (COLUMN(1),A(72));
    I = 1;
    NEXTSYM = SCAN;
    IF (LENGTH(NEXTSYM) = 3) | LENGTH(NEXTSYM) = 4)
    THEN DO;
        YOUR_CLASS = NEXTSYM;
        CALL MSG ('THANKYOU');
        LOOP = '0'B;
    END;
    ELSE CALL MSG ('CLASS NUMBER IS TOO LONG OR TOO SHORT');
END;   /* OF DO WHILE (LOOP); */

LOOP = '1'B;
ON ENDFILE (SYSIN) LOOP = '0'B;

DO WHILE (LOOP);
    FILLER = LOW (1);
    NUM,LIST,MIN,MAX,AVERAGE,STUDENT,ID,GRADE,MARK,DELETE,
    INSERT,UPDTE,WEIGHT,ASNMT = '0'B;
    DO J = 1 TO 16;
        IF J <= 5
        THEN RELATE (J) = '';
    END;
    COLUMN_SCAN = 81;
    NEXTSYM = SCAN;
    IF¬ERROR
    THEN CALL QUERY;
    IF¬ERROR
    THEN DO;
        CALL RESPONSE;
        CLOSE FILE(CLASS);
    END;
    ERROR = '0'B;
    PUT EDIT (' ') (COLUMN(1),A(0));
END;
DONE:
    PUT SKIP LIST ('THIS RUN OF CRR IS NOW ENDED.');
END CRR;
```

**FIGURE 7-8.2**    (Continued)

The module for finding the minimum or maximum mark for a particular assignment is not given. It should be clear, however, that such a module involves the sequential access of all student records for a class. The other modules which are devoted to retrieval-oriented commands such as LIST, NUMBER, and AVERAGE also require the reading of student records directly and sequentially. The records are accessed directly when a query relates to a particular list of students and sequentially when all student records are involved.

To exhibit the file operations other than the read operation, we must examine the maintenance functions of the system. The program modules for the DELETE, UPDATE, and INSERT functions are also exhibited in Fig. 7-8.4. Again the ON KEY feature is used to detect erroneous student-record specifications. The DELETE function is implemented with the aid of the PL/I DELETE instruction. This instruction marks the first byte of each of the specified student records with '11111111'B, thereby indicating that these records cannot be read.

The program section for the INSERT function is designed to prompt the user and thereby helps to ensure that all the information items for a student record are

```
QUERY: PROCEDURE;

/* 'QUERY' IS THE PROCEDURE CALLED INITIALLY IN THE RECURSIVE DESCENT
PARSER. ALL OTHER PROCEDURES ARE CALLED EITHER DIRECTLY OR INDIRECTLY
FROM THIS PROCEDURE.                                          */

/* BNF NOTATION WILL BE USED WITH THE FOLLOWING ADDITIONS AND CHANGES:

    "WILL BE USED IN PLACE OF BRACES
    ( WILL BE USED IN PLACE OF THE LEFT SQUARE BRACKET
    ) WILL BE USED IN PLACE OF THE RIGHT SQUARE BRACKET         */


/* <QUERY> ::= <PROPOSITION>
      | <MAINTENANCE FUNCTION>
      | <MARKS WEIGHTING FUNCTION>                      */

    IF ¬PROPOSITION &¬ERROR
    THEN IF¬MAINTENANCE &¬ERROR
        THEN IF¬WEIGHTING &¬ERROR
            THEN CALL MSG ('FIRST WORD OF COMMAND',
                                ' IS INVALID');
        COLUMN_SCAN = 81;
END QUERY;

/* A TYPICAL PROCEDURE IN THE RECURSIVE DESCENT PARSER IS SHOWN FOR THE
PRODUCTIONS INVOLVING THE NON-TERMINAL OBJECT_HEAD1.            */

OBJECT_HEAD1: PROCEDURE RECURSIVE RETURNS (BIT(1));

/* <OBJECT HEAD1> ::= STUDENT(S)
              | STUDENT(S) <NAME LIST>
              | ID(S)
              | <OBJECT HEAD2>                  */

    IF NEXTSYM = 'STUDENT' | NEXTSYM = 'STUDENTS'
    THEN DO;
        NEXTSYM = SCAN;
        STUDENT = '1'B;
        IF (NEXTSYM¬='WITH' & NEXTSYM¬='FOR' & NEXTSYM¬=','
                    & NEXTSYM¬='*')
        THEN DO;
            IF¬NAME_LIST
            THEN RETURN('0'B);
        END;
        RETURN ('1'B);
    END;

    IF NEXTSYM = 'ID' | NEXTSYM = 'IDS
    THEN DO;
        NEXTSYM = SCAN;
        ID = '1'B;
        RETURN ('1'B);
    END;

    IF OBJECT_HEAD2
    THEN RETURN ('1'B);
    RETURN ('0'B)
END OBJECT_HEAD1;
```

**FIGURE 7-8.3** Examples of procedures for syntactically analyzing queries.


provided. The WRITE instruction is used to place the new record in the file based on the class number/student name key.

The UPDATE function can be used to update the marks on a specific assignment for the entire class or the mark for a specified student on a specific assignment.

```
RESPONSE: PROCEDURE;

/* THE 'RESPONSE' PROCEDURE IS USED TO EVALUATE A QUERY AND TO
PERFORM THE NECESSARY RETRIEVAL OF INFORMATION. IT ALSO PERFORMS ALL
UPDATE FUNCTIONS WHICH ARE REQUIRED BY THE QUERY'S.          */

/************* M A I N T E N A N C E   F U N C T I O N S *************/
   IF STN > O        /* INDEX INTO ARRAY ST_NAMES */
   THEN DO;
      OPEN FILE(CLASS) DIRECT UPDATE;

/* THE DELETION OF A RECORD. NOTE THAT THERE IS A CHECK TO SEE IF THE
RECORD TO BE DELETED ACTUALLY EXISTS ON FILE.               */

   IF DELETE
   THEN DO;
      ON KEY (CLASS)
      BEGIN;
         CALL MSG ('THE STUDENT YOU ARE TRYING TO DELETE — '
            || ST_NAMES(J) || '— IS NOT IN THE FILE');
         GO TO RET;
      END;

      DO J = 1 TO STN;
         IF ST_NAMES(J)¬= '&&WEIGHTS&&'
         THEN DO;
            DELETE FILE (CLASS) KEY (YOUR CLASS || ST_NAMES(J));
            NO_ST = NO_ST – 1;
            CALL MSG (ST_NAMES(J) || ' HAS BEEN SUCCESSFULLY ' ||
                  'DELETED ');
         END;
         ELSE CALL MSG ('&&WEIGHTS&& IS A PROTECTED NAME AND '
               || 'MAY NOT BE DELETED FROM THE FILE.');

         ERROR = '0'B;
      END;
      RETURN;
   END;

/* INSERT A RECORD. NOTE THAT THERE IS A CHECK TO MAKE SURE THAT THE
RECORD TO BE INSERTED IS NOT ALREADY ON FILE.               */

   IF INSERT
   THEN DO;
      ON KEY (CLASS)
      BEGIN;
         CALL MSG ('THE STUDENT YOU ARE TRYING TO INSERT — '
               || S_NAME   || ' — IS ALREADY IN THE FILE');
         GO TO RET;
      END;

      ST_NAMES(15) = NEXTSYM;

P2:   PUT EDIT('ENTER THE STUDENT''S NAME',' ')
         (COLUMN(1),A,COLUMN(1),A(0));
      STRING = S_NAME;
      GET EDIT(S_NAME  ) (SKIP(1),A(20));
      COLUMN_SCAN = 1;
```

**FIGURE 7-8.4**  A procedure for handling query responses.

The program segment for the former update capability is given in Fig. 7-8.4. Of course, to update the indexed sequential class file, the REWRITE instruction is used. The value of ASSIGN(I) indicates which assignment is to be updated. The W array contains the relative weights of the assignments.

```
      NEXTSYM,S_NAME = SCAN;
      IF S_NAME = 'END'
      THEN RETURN;
      IF 1NAME
      THEN DO;
          ERROR = '0'B;
          GO TO P2;
      END;
```

/* PROMPTING CYCLES TO ENSURE ENTRY OF STUDENT IDENTIFICATION NUMBER,
YEAR, AND COLLEGE SHOULD APPEAR AT TH S POINT IN THE PROGRAM. . . .  */

```
      S_AVERAGE = 0;
      S_CLASS = YOUR_CLASS;

      WRITE FILE (CLASS) FROM (A_STUDENT)
               KEYFROM(S_CLASS || S_NAME);
      NO_ST = NO_ST + 1;
      PUT EDIT (S_NAME || ' HAS BEEN SUCCESSFULLY INSERTED ')
          (COLUMN(1),A);
      IF ST_NAMES(15) = 'MANY'
      THEN GO TO P2;
      RETURN;
  END;
```

/* THIS SEGMENT HANDLES THE UPDATING OF MARKS ON A SPECIFIED
ASSIGNMENT FOR ALL STUDENTS IN THE CLASS.                   */

```
  IF UPDTE
  THEN DO;
```

  /* WORK IS USED AS A TEMPORARY CHARACTER STRING VARIABLE        */

```
      IF NEXTSYM = 'ALL'
      THEN DO
         CLOSE FILE (CLASS);
         OPEN FILE (CLASS) SEQUENTIAL UPDATE;
         ON ENDFILE (CLASS)
         BEGIN;
            STM = 0;      /* STUDENT INDEX SET TO ZERO    */
            S_NAME = 'I';  /* STUDENT NAME SET TO 'I'     */
         END;
         READ FILE (CLASS) INTO (A_STUDENT) KEY (YOUR_CLASS);
         IF S_NAME = '&&WEIGHTS&&'
         THEN READ FILE (CLASS) INTO (A_STUDENT);
```

**FIGURE 7-8.4**    (Continued)


When performing an update, the user is again prompted by the system—this time a message containing the name of the next student to be updated is presented. In the case of an update for a specific student on a specific assignment, the user is prompted as follows:

```
  UPDATE ASSIGNMENT 4
  *ENTER THE STUDENT'S NAME
  THOMSON.C
  *ENTER THE STUDENT'S MARK
  91
  *MARK FOR THOMSON.C WAS UPDATED SUCCESSFULLY.
```

We have prefixed the system-generated commands with a * for clarity. In an interactive system, this would not be necessary, but it is desirable for aiding in a review of the output from a terminal session.

```
    DO WHILE (STN = 1);
    P6: PUT EDIT('ENTER THE MARK FOR ',S_NAME,' ')
            (COLUMN(1),A,A,COLUMN(1),A(0));
        GET EDIT(WORK) (SKIP(1),A(3));
        STRING = WORK;
        SUBSTR(STRING,76,5) = ' * * ';
        COLUMN_SCAN = 1;
        NEXTSYM = SCAN;
        ERROR = '1'B;
        IF⌐NUMBER
        THEN DO;
            ERROR = '0'B;
            CALL MSG ('THE VALUE ENTERED AS A MARK IS ' ||
                    'NON-NUMERIC');
            GO TO P6;
        END;
        ERROR = '0'B;
        DO WHILE (SUBSTR(WORK,3,1) = ' ');
            WORK = ' ' || SUBSTR(WORK,1,2);
        END;
        S_AVERAGE = 0;
        S_MARKS(ASSIGN(1)) = WORK;
        DO K = 1 TO 12;
            S_AVERAGE = S_AVERAGE + ROUND(W(K) * 0.010000
                        * S_MARKS(K), 2);
        END;
        REWRITE FILE (CLASS) FROM (A_STUDENT);
        PUT EDIT ('THE MARK FOR ',S_NAME,' HAS BEEN ',
                'UPDATED ') (COLUMN(1),4 (A));
    R6: READ FILE (CLASS) INTO (A_STUDENT);
        IF S_NAME = '&&WEIGHTS&&'
        THEN GO TO R6;
        IF S_CLASS⌐= YOUR_CLASS
        THEN STN = O;
    END;

    RETURN;
END;

/* THE NEXT SECTION SHOULD HANDLE THE UPDATE OF THE MARKS FOR
A SPECIFIC STUDENT AND A SPECIFIC ASSIGNMENT. . . .            */


/* FOR ALL INFORMATION RETRIEVAL FUNCTIONS TO BE PERFORMED ON A
SPECIFIED LIST OF STUDENTS, A CHECK IS MADE TO ENSURE THAT EACH
STUDENT IN THE LIST IS ON THE FILE.                          */

    ON KEY (CLASS)
    BEGIN;
        CALL MSG('THIS STUDENT —' || ST_NAMES(J) || ' — IS '
        || 'NOT IN THE FILE');
        GO TO RET;
    END;
```

**FIGURE 7-8.4**   (Continued)

The "skeleton" system presented is not provided with the capability of self-monitoring the file activity. This is an important aspect in any system—especially systems using indexed sequential files. When the prime area of an indexed sequential file is full or nearly full, an overflow record can be generated with each insert. On the other hand, if a large number of deletion-type transactions are applied to the file, much of the file will contain "dummy" deleted records. Again, performance will be degraded. The number of insertions and deletions should be recorded, and after a certain level of insertion and deletion activity has been attained, the file should be

```
/********* Q U E R Y   R E S P O N S E   F U N C T I O N S *********/
/* FINDING THE MINIMUM OR MAXIMUM MARK FOR SPECIFIED STUDENTS.     */

    IF MIN | MAX
    THEN IF MARK | ASNMT
      THEN DO;
        CALL MSG('WHEN REFERRING TO SPECIFIC STUDENTS, THE '
          || 'MIN(IMUM) OF MAX(IMUM) FUNCTIONS MUST ' ||
          'REFER TO ALL MARKS OF THOSE STUDENTS');
        RETURN;
      END;

      ELSE DO;
        DO J = 1 TO STN;
          READ FILE(CLASS) INTO (A_STUDENT)
                    KEY (YOUR_CLASS || ST_NAMES(J))
          IF MIN
          THEN WORK = 101;
          ELSE WORK = -1;
          DO K = 1 TO 12;
            IF MIN
            THEN IF ((S_MARKS(K) < WORK) &
                  (S_MARKS(K) ¬= -1))
                THEN WORK = S_MARKS(K);
                ELSE;
            ELSE IF ((S_MARKS(K) > WORK) &
                  (S_MARKS(K) ¬= -1))
                THEN WORK = S_MARKS(K);

          END;
          IF WORK = 101 | WORK = -1
          THEN WORK = 0;
          PUT EDIT (S_NAME,WORK) (COLUMN(1),A(21),A);
        END;
        RETURN;
      END;

/* THE REMAINING INFORMATION PROCESSING FUNCTIONS SUCH AS AVERAGE
CALCULATIONS, LISTING STUDENTS AND GRADES. ETC. APPEAR IN THIS
SECTION OF THE PROGRAM. . . .                          */

    RET: RETURN;
END RESPONSE;
```

**FIGURE 7-8.4**   (Continued)

reorganized by recreating it sequentially. There are many other system enhancements that can be made to the CRR System; nevertheless, the simple system presented adequately illustrates the important concepts related to indexed sequential files.

In the last two sections, we have investigated a file organization which allows the direct and sequential access of records. In order to permit both access capabilities, a significant amount of overhead is incurred, particularly with respect to the movement of records in the prime area and the creation and update of pointers in the index and overflow areas. In the next section, we examine a file organization which does not necessarily provide the capability of sequentially accessing records, but does enable quicker direct access and does not require as much file-management overhead.

## 7-9  DIRECT FILES

To illustrate the type of file processing associated with a direct file, let us return momentarily to our small billing system example. We introduced the example as an application of sequential files in Sec. 7-5 and reviewed it in the introduction to indexed sequential files in Sec. 7-7. In Sec. 7-7, it was pointed out that in order to accommodate any form of on-line processing which concerns the status of an account, individual customer records must be accessed directly. It was also desirable to have the records ordered sequentially by account number. This is necessary to generate monthly customer bills based on receipts which are received in batches from points of sale.

It is relatively easy to hypothesize that in the near future our small company will want a billing system which does away with the process of filling out purchase slips at the point of sale and then sending these to the main office for computer processing. A simpler but more expensive approach is to have a purchase or return posted against a customer account immediately via on-line terminals operated by point-of-sale clerks. On-line terminals would be remote from a computer yet tied directly to it via telephone lines. If purchases and returns can be handled at the point of sale, it would be unnecessary to batch all of the customer receipts and sequentially process them against the account via the merge procedure described in Sec. 7-5. With the need for sequential processing eliminated, we can design a system that requires only the capability of direct access. In this section, we consider a number of file structures which provide efficient direct access. This efficiency of access is gained because we remove the criterion that the file must be organized so that it can be accessed both sequentially and directly.

The section is again divided into three parts—file structures, direct file processing, and direct files in PL/I. In Sec. 7-10, we examine an application which involves the processing of direct files in an on-line banking system.

### 7-9.1  The Structure of Direct Files

In a *direct* (also called *random*) file, a transformation or mapping is made from the key of a record to the address of the storage location at which that record is to reside in the file. One mechanism used for generating this transformation is called a *hashing algorithm*. In Sec. 6-2.4, we examined hashing algorithms as they applied to the placement of records in a hash table. It was pointed out that a hashing algorithm consists of two components—a *hashing function*, which defines a mapping from the key space to the address space, and a *collision-resolution technique*, which resolves conflicts that arise when more than one record key is mapped to the same table location.

The hashing algorithms used for direct files are very similar to those used for tables, and therefore it is necessary to have a complete understanding of Sec. 6-2.4 before reading this section. The main conceptual differences are due to the physical characteristics of external storage, which differ from the directly addressable storage characteristics assumed for tables in Chap. 6. In particular, the time to access a record in a table in main memory is in the order of microseconds, while the time to access a record in external memory is in the order of milliseconds. In addition, records in a file are stored in *buckets* in which each bucket contains b record locations, as opposed to just one location. The number of records in a bucket is called the *bucket capacity*. Basically, we can think of a bucket as a sector in a sector-addressable device, or as a block in a block-addressable device. For a particular record to be isolated, the bucket in which the record resides must be located, the contents of the bucket brought into a buffer in memory, and then the desired record extracted from the buffer.

Let us define an *address space* A of size m such that $A = \{C + 1, C + 2,....,C + m\}$, where C is an integer constant. Then mb records can be accommodated by A, and the load factor for the direct file is $n/(mb)$, assuming a key set of size n is mapped into the address space.

A key set of $S = \{X_1, X_2, \cdots, X_n\}$ is a subset of a set K of possible keys which is called the *key space*. If the size of K is equal to the number of record locations in A, and the key is consecutive, then a transformation can be defined which assigns to each bucket of A exactly b keys from K. This type of one-to-one transformation is termed *direct addressing* and is an array-reference form of addressing.

In most situations, however, S is a small subset of K, and direct addressing results in a ridiculously low utilization of direct-access storage. Instead, *indirect addressing* is implemented. That is, S is mapped into A with the distinct possibility that enough records will be assigned to the same bucket so that a bucket *overflow* takes place. When this happens, a bucket-overflow handling technique must be used to store any overflow records. We will discover later in this subsection that the techniques for handling bucket overflow are very similar to those for collision resolution in a table.

Having reviewed some of the concepts related to hashing algorithms, let us examine in more detail the possible organizations for a direct file. We begin by reexamining the hashing functions which can be used for address translation. A more in-depth investigation of the overflow handling techniques is then considered.

In Sec. 6-2.4, hashing functions were divided into two general classes—distribution-independent and distribution-dependent hashing functions. The three most significant analyses of distribution-independent hashing functions were performed by Buchholz [1963], Lum et al. [1971], and Lum [1973]. The results from the three investigations indicated that the division method, using a prime divisor or a divisor that is relatively prime with the size of address space, yielded the best performance on the average. This is not to say that, for certain key sets with certain load factors and bucket capacities, one of the other methods discussed in Sec. 6-2.4 cannot outperform the division method.

Recently there has been tremendous interest in hashing techniques that enable a file to grow dynamically without requiring a significant amount of rehashing. These techniques are particularly applicable to direct file organization. Although they involve more complicated address transformations, they do result in a significantly reduced number of collisions. We will discuss these techniques in detail in Sec. 7-11. For this section and the next section, we will, however, adopt the division method as the standard hashing function because it is simple to use and yields reasonable performance.

The second aspect of a hashing algorithm is the collision-resolution technique. In a direct file, the smallest addressable unit is the bucket, which may contain many records that have been mapped to the same address. Hence, in a direct file with a given bucket capacity, a certain number of collisions are expected. When there are more colliding records for a given bucket than the bucket capacity, however, then some method must be found for handling these overflow records. The term *overflow handling technique* is used in place of collision-resolution technique, which is commonly adopted for hash-table methods.

In Sec. 6-2.4, two classes of collision-resolution techniques were given—open addressing and chaining. The same general classification can be applied to overflow handling techniques. When we use a bucket with a capacity greater than 1, we are in fact imposing a restricted linear-probe form of open addressing. When a record is added to a bucket which is not full, the new record is added at the next open location. Of course, the next open record location is in the bucket and is already reserved for records which are mapped to that bucket address.

In the discussion to follow, we refer to the bucket referenced by the address calculation of a record as the *primary bucket* for that record. If a record is not present in the primary bucket, it is located in an *overflow bucket,* or it is not in the file.

Since the complete contents of a bucket are brought into main memory with one request, it is extremely beneficial if the desired record is located somewhere in the primary bucket. If the record is not in the primary bucket, a request must be made to bring in an overflow bucket, as determined by the overflow handling method.

If a linear-probe open-address overflow handling method is used, then a successive search is made of the records in the remaining buckets in the file. The search is terminated successfully when the record is located. It is terminated unsuccessfully, however, if an empty (dummy) record is encountered, or if the search returns to the original bucket tested.

A random-probe form of open addressing or double hashing are not necessarily good overflow methods to use for direct files. In both methods the sequences of overflow buckets which are examined do not exhibit the property of physical adjacency. That is, two buckets which are adjacent in the overflow sequence are not necessarily physically adjacent. Physical adjacency can be important, since records which are not physically adjacent have a higher probability of requiring a seek in a movable-head storage device. The extra seek time may be prohibitive.

Overflow records can be chained from the primary to a separate overflow area. An overflow record should reside in an overflow bucket which is in the same seek area (e.g., the same cylinder) as the primary area for the overflow record. A particularly good strategy is to reserve the last few buckets of a seek area strictly for overflow records from the primary buckets in that area. That is the strategy adopted in using the cylinder overflow area in the indexed sequential organization. However, it may be difficult to adopt such a configuration strategy, since the overflow buckets would break up the linear-addressing scheme required for direct addressing (i.e., groups of prime area buckets and overflow buckets will be interspersed throughout the file space). Therefore, an independent overflow area which is totally separate from the prime area may be required.

A final overflow strategy also involves chaining. Knuth [1973] refers to the method as *chaining with coalescing lists.* With this method, overflow records are placed in available buckets in the prime area of the direct file, and overflows are located using pointers from one bucket to another. Therefore, when a key is hashed to a bucket, a search commences through a chain of buckets until the required record or an empty storage location is found. Keys may be mapped to buckets which are not the first in a chain, so it is necessary that lists be coalesced. In a chain of buckets, keys which are originally hashed to different addresses may be found.

A comparative analysis of the overflow handling methods is described in Knuth [1973]. It is shown that chaining with separate lists requires the smallest average length of search of the three overflow handling techniques discussed. However, this apparent advantage is gained because of two factors. First, the separate overflow area is not counted as part of the total file space. Hence, if n records are added to the file, all n records are placed in the primary area, using open addressing or chaining with coalescing lists.    If there are m overflows, however, then only n – m records are placed in the primary area when using chaining with separate lists. Therefore, the effective load factor is less for chaining with separate lists.

The second factor contributes to the better performance of any chaining method over an open address method. For a chaining method, information concerning the location of the next overflow record is stored in the record itself. Hence, to access a particular overflow record, there is no need to examine a number of intermediate records which may not be overflow records. It must be noted, however, that the storage of overflow links enlarges the record size. This may be an important file-design consideration, especially if the file consists of many small records.

A final point that should be kept in mind is that access to an independent overflow area will most likely result in a seek request. Therefore, if moving-head external devices are being used, chaining to an independent overflow area may not be an efficient method. A possible compromise is to adopt chaining with coalescing lists. However, this method has not, as yet, been thoroughly investigated and is rarely used in practice.

So far we have centered the discussion of file structures for direct files on hashing (or address-translation) techniques. There are other ways of organizing a direct file which are less popular but nevertheless may be applicable in some situations.

If the number of records in the file is relatively small and the record size is relatively large (i.e., only a few records per bucket is achievable), then it may be worthwhile to consider a direct-addressing scheme. Several methods for achieving direct-address translation involve the use of cross referencing or indexing. A *cross-reference table* is simply a table of keys and addresses in which a unique external storage address is assigned to each key. Figure 7-9.1 illustrates a cross-reference table of surnames and external storage addresses for a sector-addressable device. A cross-reference table is merely an associative list as discussed in Sec. 4-4.  Locating a

| Surname | External Address (Cyl., Trk., Sector) |
|---------|---------------------------------------|
| Ashcroft | 1,07,04 |
| Barnsley | 1,07,05 |
| Bernard | 1,08,15 |
| Duke | 1,06,09 |
| Edder | 1,07,00 |
| Groff | 1,06,10 |
| Katz | 1,06,12 |
| Murray | 1,08,13 |
| Paulsen | 1,06,00 |
| Smith | 1,06,03 |
| Thomas | 1,06,04 |
| Tollard | 1,06,11 |
| Yu | 1,07,01 |

**FIGURE 7-9.1**   Cross-reference table.

record given its key is simply a matter of retrieving the external address associated with the key and then issuing an I/O command which directly retrieves the desired record. In most programming languages, however, associative lists are not provided and the programmer must maintain the cross-reference table. The table can be kept as an unordered list and, therefore, can accommodate additions with ease. A linear search is then required to find an address. Alternatively, the table can be implemented as a list ordered by the key set and a binary search can be employed to locate an address more rapidly. Record additions and deletions, however, present problems because the table must be maintained in order.

Indexing methods involving binary trees, m-ary trees, and trie structures can also be chosen to achieve direct addressing in direct files. With tree-structured methods (which were discussed in Sec. 6-2.3), record additions and deletions can be handled more effectively. A binary-tree indexing scheme for the cross-reference table given in Fig. 7-9.1 is shown, in part, in Fig. 7-9.2.

In the discussion throughout this subsection, we have assumed that if a desired record is not located in its primary bucket, then a series of I/O commands is issued. Each command brings in an overflow bucket which is scanned in search of the required record. The search strategy just outlined is true for external memory units which are sector-addressable. Some record-addressable devices such as the IBM 3380, however, are capable of locating, via hardware, a particular record on a given track based on the key of the record. In the discussion of PL/I direct files in Sec. 7-9.3, we will discover that this hardware capability can help to eliminate much of the scanning of overflow buckets in main memory that must be done using sector-addressable devices.

Let us now turn out attention to the type of processing that is associated with direct files.

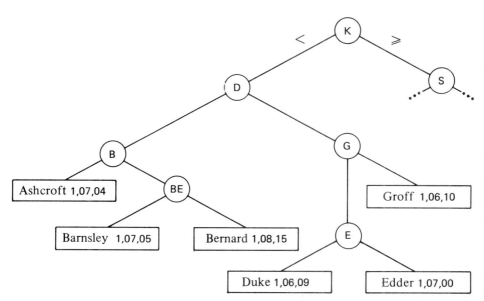

**FIGURE 7-9.2**   Binary-tree cross-reference indexing scheme.

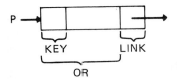

**FIGURE 7-9.3**   Representation
of an overflow node.

### 7-9.2 Processing Direct Files

The processing of a direct file is dependent on how the key set for the records is transformed into external device addresses. In the previous subsection, we reviewed a number of transformation methods. It is impractical to discuss direct-file processing for each method; therefore, we have chosen to present, as a representative example, the direct processing of a file which is accessed via a hashing algorithm using chaining with separate lists for overflow handling. Algorithms involving the processing of this form of organization are presented in this subsection.

Direct files are primarily processed directly. That is, a key is mapped to an address, and depending on the nature of the file transaction, a record is created, deleted, updated, or accessed at that address or possibly at some subsequent address if a collision takes place. Of course, the subsequent address is determined by the overflow handling technique which is adopted.

When overflow handling is accommodated using chaining with separate lists, a pointer to a linked list of overflow records is included in each bucket. A representation of an overflow record in the separate list area is shown in Fig. 7-9 3. Each overflow location in the overflow area consists of two major parts—OR, containing an overflow record, and LINK, a pointer containing the address of the next location in a chain. KEY is the key of the record contained in OR.

A pointer to a chain of overflow records is included in each bucket, and for the ith bucket, this pointer is designated by $PTR_i$ . If there are no overflow records for a bucket, then $PTR_i$  has the value NULL; otherwise, it has the value of the address of the first record in the overflow chain for that bucket. The following algorithm inserts a record into a direct file which is organized according to the specifications given earlier.

**Algorithm** DIRECT_INSERT.   Given a record R with key x, it is required to insert R into a direct file with n primary buckets $B_1, \ldots B_n$, in which a particular bucket $B_i$ contains m record locations $b_{i1}, b_{i2}, \ldots, b_{in}$.   If a record is resident at location $b_{ij}$, then its key is denoted by $k_{ij}$.   If no record is present, then the key field is represented with a negative number. [There are many other conventions that can be adopted to represent an empty record location. We will see in the next subsection that the placement of $(8)'1'B$ in the first record has been adopted by IBM.] If an overflow condition results, then R is stored in a location on a list of overflow locations for the primary bucket. The hashing function H is used to calculate an address.

1.   [Apply hashing function]
     $i \leftarrow H(x)$

2. [Scan the bucket indicated]
    If $PTR_i$ = NULL
    then   Repeat for j = 1,2,...,m
            If $k_{ij} < 0$
            then  $b_{ij} \leftarrow R$
            Exit
3. [Put R in overflow storage at the head of overflow list]
    Obtain an overflow location and assign its address to P
    $OR(P) \leftarrow R$
    $LINK(P) \leftarrow PTR_i$
    $PTR_i \leftarrow P$
    Exit        □

In step 2, the record is placed in the bucket it is hashed to if a record location is available. Otherwise, an overflow node is obtained, its address is assigned to P, record R is placed at location P, and the pointers LINK(P) and $PTR_i$ are altered so that the new node is the first in the overflow chain for bucket i.

It should be noted that a check is not made to see if the key of the record being added matches the key of a record presently in the file. This checking should be done to prevent duplicate or inconsistent data. The necessary extensions to Algorithm DIRECT_INSERT to effect this checking are left as an exercise.

The algorithm for retrieving a record from a direct file using chaining with separate lists follows.

**Algorithm** DIRECT_RETRIEVE. Given a key x, it is required to retrieve the record identified by that key from the direct file with primary buckets $B_1, \ldots, B_n$ and the separate overflow storage.

1. [Apply hashing function]
    $i \leftarrow H(x)$
2. [Search the bucket indicated]
    Repeat for j = 1,2,...,m
        If $x = k_{ij}$
        then  $R \leftarrow b_{ij}$
            Exit
        else  If $k_{ij}<0$
            then  Exit unsuccessfully
    $P \leftarrow PTR_i$
3. [Search the overflow chain]
    Repeat while true
        If P = NULL
        then  Exit unsuccessfully
        If KEY(P) = x
        then  $R \leftarrow OR(P)$
            Exit
        else  $P \leftarrow LINK(P)$    □

In step 2, the required record is assigned to R if it is found in bucket $B_i$. If the bucket is not full and the record is not located, then the search ends unsuccessfully. Otherwise, in step 3 each successive node of the overflow chain is examined until the record is found or the end of the linked list is encountered.

If these algorithms are implemented using disk storage, overflow nodes should be located in a common seek area, and ideally, in the same area as their associated primary buckets. This is done so that extra seeks are not required to scan a linked list of overflow records.

Knuth [1973] has analytically derived formulae for the expected average length of search using a model which assumes chained overflow with bucket capacities of 1 or greater. Before using chained overflow, the reader is encouraged to review these algorithms. The extensions of these algorithms to make them applicable to direct files are left as an exercise.

Thus far, the only type of processing we have considered for direct files is direct processing. In some instances, it may be necessary to perform an identical transaction on all or nearly all records in the file. For example, in the small billing system, which we have often used to illustrate the material on file organization, it may be desirable to print monthly bills even though individual customer accounts can be accessed directly in an on-line mode. The generation of monthly bills can be accomplished by accessing the records in a physically sequential or serial manner.

Serial access of a direct file is not necessarily sequential access. That is, $x_1 \leq x_2$ for keys $x_1$ and $x_2$ does not imply $H(x_1) \leq H(x_2)$ for some hashing functions H. The fact is that we relinquished this ability of sequential access in favor of a quicker direct access when we proceeded from indexed sequential to direct files.

For most direct organizations, serial access presents no problems. Access commences at the physical beginning and terminates at the physical end of the file. If the file uses a separate overflow area, however, it may be difficult to access this area in a serial fashion independent of the prime area. Difficulties arise because the overflow area may be unblocked or blocked in a different manner than the prime area. A logically consistent, yet potentially time-consuming method, of serial access of a separate overflow area is to read all the records in the first prime area bucket, followed by all the overflow records for this bucket, and then return to read the next prime area bucket, followed by its overflow records, etc., until all records in the file have been accessed.

A final aspect of direct-file processing which we should consider is file maintenance. Many systems which support direct files simply mark deleted records and only recover the space occupied by these records when a new record can be added to the file at the marked location. The space occupied by a deleted record may require needless examination in search of a record in the prime bucket. In addition, deleted records affect performance when probing or chaining through a file in search of an overflow record. It is sometimes possible to remove deleted records logically, especially where chaining is involved; however, this is rarely done. Instead it is the programmer's responsibility to monitor the activity of the file and to reorganize it whenever performance degrades significantly. Reorganization can be accomplished by reading the file serially and creating a new direct file that involves only the active records of the old file.

We complete this subsection by summarizing the important properties related to direct files:

1    Direct access to records in a direct file is rapid, especially for files with low load factors and few overflow records.

2    Because a certain portion of the file remains unused in order to prevent an excessive number of overflow records, the space utilization for a direct file is poor when compared to the other file organizations we have discussed.

3    The performance attained using a direct file is very dependent upon the key-to-address transformation algorithm adopted. The transformation that is used is application-dependent and is generally implemented and maintained through users' programs.

4    Records can be accessed serially but not sequentially unless a separate ordered list of keys is maintained.

### 7-9.3  Direct Files in PL/I

In PL/I, a direct file is called a *regional* file. There are three types of regional files available; namely, REGIONAL(1), REGIONAL(2), and REGIONAL(3). Each of these is examined in this subsection.

To appreciate fully the differences between these three direct file organizations, we must discuss in some detail the track formats for record-addressable storage devices as exemplified by IBM's 3330 and 3380 disks. While much of the discussion in this section is device-dependent, such emphasis is warranted because the PL/I instructions for regional files are heavily oriented toward, but not necessarily dependent upon, record-addressable direct-access devices.

There are two track formats on IBM direct-access storage devices. They are called *count-data* and *count-key-data formats,* and these are illustrated in Fig. 7-9.4.

For both formats, the count area is ten bytes in length and contains the record's location in terms of the cylinder, head, and record number, the record's key length (which is 0 if no key is used), and the record's data field length. If a key is used, the key area holds a key that is between 1 and 255 bytes (characters) in length. The data area contains the user-provided data for the record. The maximum length of this field is determined by the device's track capacity. The data area can be thought of as a block (bucket or region) which may consist of several logical records. However, if more than one logical record is stored in a data area, blocking and unblocking is the responsibility of the user. This aspect is not discussed in this

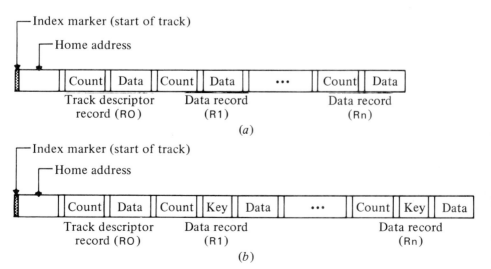

**FIGURE 7-9.4**  Track formats. (*a*) Count-data; (*b*) count-key-data.

subsection. Note that record R0 is a special record maintained by the system. It contains information related to the status of a track, such as whether the track is defective and, if defective, the address of an alternate track.

All REGIONAL files are divided into *relative regions*, each of which is identified by a *region number*. The regions are numbered successively from 0 to 16777215 ($2^{24}-1$).    A record is accessed by specifying its region number in a record-oriented I/O statement in one of two ways, namely, relative record or relative track.

A *relative record* is referenced by a number relative to the first record in the file. Figure 7-9.5a depicts the sectioning of a disk surface into relative records. In a relative record scheme, which is used in REGIONAL(1) and REGIONAL(2) files, only one record is allowed per region.

A *relative-track* specification refers to a particular track relative to the first track of the file. Figure 7-9.5b illustrates this type of organization. Each region is a track, and more than one record can be stored in a region. REGIONAL(3) files provide this type of organization.

Before considering each of the three types of REGIONAL files, we must introduce and clearly distinguish between the notions of a source key and a recorded key. A *source key* is a character string specified in the record-oriented I/O statements following the KEY or KEYFROM options. For example, in

READ FILE(INVEN) INTO (STORE_ITEM) KEY(CATLG#)

CATLG#, which typically may have a value such as 'A2E01101241', is the source key.

In a REGIONAL(1) file, the source key consists of a region number only, and it is this number which uniquely identifies a particular record. Hence, the source

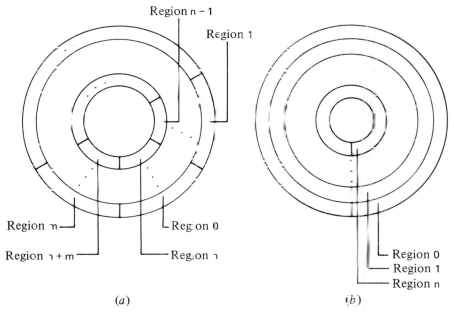

(a)     (b)

**FIGURE 7-9.5**  Regional specifications.  (a) Relative record; (b) relative track.

key for a REGIONAL(1) organization consists of an eight-position character string which is capable of representing the region numbers in the range of 0 to 16777215. Because there is no stored key in a REGIONAL(1) organization, a count-data track format is used.

The source key for REGIONAL(2) or REGIONAL(3) files has two logical parts—the *comparison key* and the *region number*. The region number is found in the rightmost eight characters of the source key, and the comparison key is generally formed from the remainder of the source key. Therefore, the source key with a value of 'A2E01101241' designates the region number '01101241' and comparison key of 'A2E'.

The portion of the source key that is stored in the key area of a record is called the *recorded key*. The recorded key may be from 1 to 255 characters in length. The length is specified through the KEYLENGTH option of the ENVIRONMENT clause or as a DCB parameter of the form KEYLEN = n in a DD job control statement.

The recorded key takes on the value of the comparison key. Therefore, to declare the file INVEN to be a REGIONAL(2) file with a recorded key equal to the comparison key based on the CATLG# source key, we write

    DECLARE INVEN FILE RECORD KEYED
              ENV (REGIONAL(2) KEYLENGTH = 3);

Hence, the first three characters of the catalogue number form the recorded key. If we specify a KEYLENGTH of 1 or 4, then the comparison key and the recorded key for 'A2E01101241' become 'A' or 'A2E0', respectively. Therefore, part of the source key may be unused, and the comparison key and the recorded key can include part or all of the region number.

The distinction between the comparison key and recorded key is a strictly functional one. On output, the comparison key is written as the recorded key, and on input, the comparison key is compared with the recorded key. The format of the I/O statements for PL/I direct files is identical to the format for the I/O statement for indexed sequential files. An example READ statement for the file INVEN was given earlier in this section. A WRITE statement for directly writing into the INVEN file is as follows:

    WRITE FILE(INVEN) FROM (STORE_ITEM) KEYFROM(CATLG#);

DELETE and REWRITE statements are available as well. All these instructions will be illustrated in an example given later in this subsection.

Other similarities exist between direct and indexed sequential files in PL/I. Direct files can also be opened for INPUT, OUTPUT, or UPDATE. The DIRECT and SEQUENTIAL attributes can be used to specify the manner in which the records in the file are accessed. The DIRECT attribute designates that records are accessed by use of a key. SEQUENTIAL specifies that the records are accessed according to their physical sequence in the file. In other words, SEQUENTIAL implies serial access.

Let us now describe the three different REGIONAL organizations.

### REGIONAL(1) files

REGIONAL(1) files are designed for applications involving direct-address translation (i.e., every key in the file corresponds to a unique external storage address). The source key for a REGIONAL(1) file is a region number, and it is this relative record address that is translated into a unique external storage address It is a common occurrence in direct-address translation that not all record locations are filled. Those locations that are not filled with user information are identified as dummy records by placing the constant (8)'1'B in the first byte of the record (just as we did for indexed sequential files). Dummy records can be replaced by any valid data.

REGIONAL(1) files, and indeed any REGIONAL file, can be created sequentially or directly. However, when the SEQUENTIAL OUTPUT attribute is used to create a REGIONAL file, the records must be handled in ascending order by region number. An error in the sequence, or a duplicate key, will cause the KEY condition to be raised. Any region that is omitted during creation is filled with a dummy record. If the file is created directly, all of the space allocated to the file is filled with dummy records when the file is opened.

REGIONAL(1) files can be accessed serially (which is also sequentially by region number) and directly. The standard file operations of retrieval, addition, deletion, and alteration can be achieved using READ, WRITE, DELETE, and REWRITE statements. These operations are illustrated in the example program given in Fig. 7-9.6.

The program accepts transaction records of the form

<transaction type> <car license number> [detailed car information]

The <transaction type> can be 'REQUEST', 'ADD', 'UPDATE', and 'DELETE'. A <car license number> can be a license-plate number of six or fewer digits which conveniently is used as a region number. The detailed car information is not required and does not appear in the transaction records requesting or deleting information about a vehicle.

### REGIONAL(2) files

Each record in a REGIONAL(2) data set is uniquely identified by a recorded key. However, the position of a record in the file relative to other records is determined by the region number as derived from the source key of the WRITE statement which created the record. When a record is added to the file, it is written with its recorded key in the first available space after the beginning of the track that contains the region specified. To read, rewrite, or delete a particular record, a search begins at the start of the track containing the specified region and continues until a record is found with the appropriate recorded key. This search continues across track boundaries and can progress to the end of the file. The search can be limited to a certain number of tracks by the LIMCT DCB parameter (i.e., LIMCT = n for some nonnegative integer n) of a job control language DD statement.

Let us look at an example of how records are placed in a REGIONAL(2) file. Assume we are using as a source key the CATLG# described earlier in this section. If we use the first three characters of the 11-character catalogue number as the recorded key, then 'A1E00000000' specifies a record with a region number of zero and a recorded key of 'A1E'. Let us assume that there are four regions (i.e., records) per track as illustrated in Fig. 7-9.7. The records with source keys of 'A1E00000000' and 'B2L00000002' are already created. If the instruction

WRITE FILE(INVEN) FROM (SALES_ITEM) KEYFROM('Z6K00000003');

is executed, then this record is added to the file in region 1. It is placed at this location because region 1 is the first available space after the beginning of the track that contains the region specified.

```
// EXEC PL1LFCLG,PARM=' ATR,XREF'
//PL1L.SYSIN DD *
 REG1_EG: PROCEDURE OPTIONS(MAIN);

    DECLARE CARS RECORD KEYED ENV(F(115) REGIONAL(1)),
           1 INFO,
                2 DEL_CODE BIT(8),
                2 NAME CHAR(30),
                2 ADDR CHAR(80),
                2 AGE FIXED(2),
                2 OFF# FIXED(2),
           TRANSACTION CHAR(7),
           LICENSE# CHAR(6),
           I FIXED,
           TRAN(0:4) LABEL,
           TYPE_STR CHAR(28) INITIAL('REQUESTADD   UPDATE  DELETE ');

    ON KEY(CARS) BEGIN;
       PUT SKIP LIST('RECORD REQUESTED IS NOT PRESENT OR ATTEMPTING'||
           ' TO ADD A DUPLICATE RECORD — ONKEY IS: ', ONKEY);
       STOP;
    END;

    OPEN FILE(CARS) DIRECT UPDATE;
    ON ENDFILE(SYSIN) STOP;    /* SYSIN CONTAINS TRANSACTION RECORDS */

    DO WHILE('1'B);
       GET EDIT(TRANSACTION,LICENSE#) (COL(1),A(7),A(6));
       I = (INDEX(TYPE_STR,TRANSACTION) + 6) / 7;
       IF I¬= 2 & I¬= 0 /* NOT AN 'ADD' TRANSACTION */
       THEN READ FILE(CARS) INTO(INFO) KEY(LICENSE#);
       GO TO TRAN(I);  /* I DETERMINES TRANSACTION TYPE */

    TRAN(0):   /* ILLEGAL TRANSACTION */
       PUT SKIP LIST('ILLEGAL TRANSACTION');
       GO TO CONTINUE;

    TRAN(1):   /* 'REQUEST' TRANSACTION */
       PUT SKIP EDIT('THE INFORMATION CONCERNING LICENSE NUMBER ',
          LICENSE#, 'IS AS FOLLOWS:','NAME: ',NAME,'ADDRESS: ',ADDR,
          'AGE: ',AGE,'NUMBER OF PREVIOUS OFFENSES: ',OFF#)
          (3 A,SKIP,2 A,SKIP,2 A,SKIP,A,F(2),SKIP,A,F(2));
       GO TO CONTINUE;

    TRAN(2):   /* 'ADD' TRANSACTION */
       GET EDIT(NAME,ADDR,AGE,OFF#) (COL(1),A(20),COL(1),A(80),2 F(2));
       WRITE FILE(CARS) FROM(INFO) KEYFROM(LICENSE#);
       GO TO CONTINUE;

    TRAN(3):   /* 'UPDATE' TRANSACTION */
       GET EDIT(NAME,ADDR,AGE,OFF#) (COL(1),A(20),COL(1),A(80),2 F(2));
       REWRITE FILE(CARS) FROM(INFO) KEY(LICENSE#);
       GO TO CONTINUE;

    TRAN(4):   /* 'DELETE' TRANSACTION */
       DELETE FILE(CARS) KEY(LICENSE#);

    CONTINUE:
       END;   /* OF DO WHILE */
END REG1_EG;
//GO.CARS DD DSN=LICENSE,DISP=(OLD,KEEP),UNIT=SYSDA
//GO.SYSIN DD *
(DATA GO HERE)
 /*
```

**FIGURE 7-9.6**  Example of a REGIONAL(1) file.

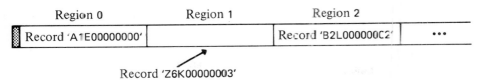

**FIGURE 7-9.7**   The insertion of a record in a REGIONAL(2) file.

When REGIONAL(2) files are created sequentially, the records must be presented in ascending order by region number. Any region that is omitted is assigned a dummy record, and if there is an error in the sequence or an attempt to place more than one record in the same region, the KEY condition is raised.

If a REGIONAL(2) file is created directly, the entire file space is filled with dummy records. Records can be presented in any order, and a KEY condition is *not* raised if there is a duplicate recorded key, duplicate region, or duplicate key or region. Hence, duplicate records are stored. To protect against such duplication, one is wise to execute a READ statement, using the source key of the record to be added, prior to the execution of the WRITE statement. If the READ statement fails and a KEY condition is invoked, then the record can be safely written.

When a REGIONAL(2) file is accessed sequentially, the KEYTO option can be used to extract the recorded key. For example, the execution of the statement

READ FILE(INVEN) INTO (SALES_ITEM) KEYTO(CATLG#);

causes the next record, in order of ascending region number, to be read.   The recorded key is concatenated with the region number and then is assigned to the variable CATLG#.

When records with duplicate recorded keys are accessed for retrieval, deletion, or update the record closest to the beginning of the file is the record affected.

Figure 7-9.8 is an example program involving the generation and update of invoices in an order entry and invoicing system. A region number is equated to an invoice number, and the recorded key is the invoice number prefixed by one of four letters: 'C' meaning "on order"; 'S' meaning "shipped"; 'R' meaning "received and paid"; and 'D' meaning "some defective items returned." In most instances, there is a single invoice per region number (i.e., direct addressing is used). In some situations, however, the goods corresponding to a particular invoice may be received, and then later some of them returned as defective. In this case, two records with the same region number are created for the invoice.   To accommodate the spatial demands generated by allowing records with duplicate region numbers, invoice numbers ending with a zero are not used.

The program in Fig. 7-9.8 illustrates how REGIONAL(2) files can be used in a direct-addressing mode. Indirect addressing can be applied to REGIONAL(2) files as well. For example, in a parts-department application, many of the parts come from different manufacturers, each of whom has a different parts numbering scheme. Example part numbers are TC103, 176-232, and 6225AX. Assuming a direct file is a desirable type of file for the parts application, then a hashing function can be applied to a part number to generate a region number. If the actual part number is adopted as the recorded key, then records with duplicate region numbers are uniquely identified by the recorded key. Therefore, the region is used as a primary area and indicates the relative position of the record, and the recorded key is used to locate the desired record within this relative area.

```
// EXEC PL1LFCLG,PARM=' SM=(2,80,1)'
//PL1L.SYSIN DD *
 REG2_EG: PROCEDURE OPTIONS (MAIN);

    DECLARE INVOICE RECORD KEYED ENV (REGIONAL(2) F(92)),
         1 RECORD,
              2 DELETE_CODE BIT(8),
              2 DATE FIXED (6),
              2 ITEM_COUNT FIXED (1),
              2 TOTAL_PRICE FIXED (10,2),
              2 ITEM (5),
                   3 PART# CHAR(6),
                   3 MANUF# CHAR(3),
                   3 QUANTITY FIXED (2),
                   3 UNIT_PRICE FIXED (8, 2),
         (TYPE_CODE, NEW_TYPE_CODE) CHAR (1),
         INVOICE# CHAR (8),
         TRANSACTION CHAR (7),
         TYPE_STR CHAR (28) INITIAL ('REQUESTADD   UPDATE  DELETE'),
         I FIXED,
         LABEL (0:4) LABEL;

    ON KEY (INVOICE) BEGIN;
         PUT SKIP LIST ('ERROR — KEY CONDITION RAISED','ONKEY=',ONKEY);
    END;

    OPEN FILE (INVOICE) DIRECT UPDATE;

    ON ENDFILE (SYSIN) STOP;

LOOP:    DO WHILE ('1'B);

         GET FILE (SYSIN) EDIT (TRANSACTION, TYPE_CODE, INVOICE#)
                   (COL(1), A(7), A(1), A(8));
         I = (INDEX(TYPE_STR, TRANSACTION) + 6) / 7;
         IF I¬= 2 & I¬= 0  /* NOT AN 'ADD' */
         THEN READ FILE(INVOICE) INTO(RECORD) KEY(TYPE_CODE || INVOICE#);
         GO TO LABEL(I);

    LABEL(0):  /* ILLEGAL TRANSACTION */
         PUT SKIP LIST ('ILLEGAL TRANSACTION :', TRANSACTION);
         GO TO CONTIN;

    LABEL(1):  /* 'REQUEST' TRANSACTION */
         PUT SKIP EDIT ('INVOICE #',INVOICE#, 'DATE ',DATE,
            'PART','MANUFACTURER','QUANTITY','UNIT PRICE')
            (2 A,X(10),2 A,COL(1),A,COL(10),A,COL(30),A,COL(50),A);
         PUT SKIP EDIT ( (ITEM(I)  DO I = 1 TO ITEM_COUNT) )
            ((ITEM_COUNT)(COL(1),A,COL(15),A,COL(33),F(2),COL(50),F(11,2)));
         PUT SKIP EDIT ('TOTAL PRICE', TOTAL_PRICE)
                 (COL(30),A,COL(48),F(13,2));
         GO TO CONTIN;

    LABEL(2):  /* 'ADD' TRANSACTION */
         GET EDIT (DATE, ITEM_COUNT, TOTAL_PRICE)
              (COL(1), F(6), F(1), F(10,2));
         GET EDIT ( (ITEM (I)  DO I = 1 TO ITEM_COUNT) )
              ( (ITEM_COUNT)(COL(1),A(6),A(3),F(2),F(8,2)) );
         WRITE FILE (INVOICE) FROM(RECORD) KEYFROM(TYPE_CODE ||INVOICE#);
         GO TO CONTIN;

    LABEL(3):  /* 'UPDATE' TRANSACTION */
         GET EDIT (NEW_TYPE_CODE) (COL(1), A(1));
         GET EDIT (DATE, ITEM_COUNT, TOTAL_PRICE)
              (COL(1), F(6), F(1), F(10,2));
```

**FIGURE 7-9.8**    Example of a REGIONAL(2) file.

```
      GET EDIT ( (ITEM (I)  DO I = 1 TO ITEM_COUNT) )
             ( (ITEM_COUNT)(COL(1),A(6),A(3),F(2),F(8,2)) );
      IF TYPE_CODE = NEW_TYPE_CODE
      THEN REWRITE FILE(INVOICE) FROM(RECORD) KEY(TYPE_CODE ||INVOICE#);
      ELSE DO;
         WRITE FILE (INVOICE) FROM (RECORD)
             KEYFROM (NEW_TYPE_CODE || INVOICE#);
         GO TO LABEL(4); /* TO DELETE OLD RECORD */
      END;
      GO TO CONTIN;

   LABEL(4):   /* 'DELETE' TRANSACTION */
      DELETE FILE (INVOICE) KEY (TYPE_CODE || INVOICE#);

   CONTIN:
      END LOOP;

END REG2_E3;
//GO.INVOICE DD DSN=INVEN,DISP=(OLD,KEEP),UNIT=SYSDA
//   DCB=(DSORG=DA,KEYLEN=9)
//GO.SYSIN DD *
(DATA GO HERE)
/*
```

**FIGURE 7-9.8**   (Continued)

#### REGIONAL(3) files

A REGIONAL(3) file differs from a REGIONAL(1) or REGIONAL(2) file in the following respects. Each region in a REGIONAL(3) file is a track on a direct-access device (see Fig. 7-9.5b) and the region number can be at most 32767. Probably the most significant differences are that a region can contain one or more records and records can be fixed or variable in length.

If the file is created sequentially, the records must be presented in ascending order of region numbers. Identical region numbers, however, can be specified for successive records. When a track is filled with records, the corresponding region number is automatically incremented. A further attempt to add a record with the previous region number will raise the KEY condition, as will any sequence error.

If the file is created directly with fixed-length records, the whole file space is initialized with dummy records when the file is opened. For variable-length records, only one dummy record is created per region, and this can occupy the entire track. As in the case of REGIONAL(2) records, no condition is raised by duplicate keys in the same region. When a record is added to a region, it is assigned to the first dummy record location encountered. For variable-length records, the record is located in the first available space on the track.

A record is accessed directly by scanning a particular track (as designated by the region number given in the source key) until a match is found between the comparison key and the recorded key. It should be noted that the space occupied by deleted variable-length records is not available. In addition, one cannot replace a variable-length record with a record that is larger. An attempt to do so can be detected using the ON RECORD condition.

An example program illustrating the processing of a REGIONAL(3) file is shown in Fig. 7-9.9. The file contains a number of abstracts of civil court case proceedings. The first ten characters of a record are a case-proceedings number which is used to obtain a detailed copy of the proceedings as compiled by the courtroom recorder. The remaining portion of a record contains a variable number of eighty-character lines of text which forms the abstract of the case proceedings.

```
// EXEC PL1LFCLG,PARM='SIZE=999999,SM=(2,80,1)'
//PL1L.SYSIN DD *
 REG3_EG: PROCEDURE OPTIONS (MAIN);
    DECLARE ABSTRACTS FILE RECORD KEYED ENV (REGIONAL(3) V(1618)),

/* THE RECORD IS COMPOSED OF A TEN CHARACTER CASE NUMBER FOLLOWED BY A
VARIABLE LENGTH CASE ABSTRACT.                              */
    RECORD CHAR (1610) VARYING,
    RECDS CHAR (80),
    EOF BIT (1) INIT ('0'B),
    REQUEST CHAR (8),
    REQUEST_STR CHAR (32) INIT ('RETRIEVEADD    DELETE  REPLACE '),
    (I, TYPE) FIXED,
    NAMES CHAR (17),
    HASH ENTRY (CHAR(*)) RETURNS (CHAR(8)),
    GETRECDS ENTRY,
    PROC (0:4) LABEL;

 ON ENDFILE (SYSIN) EOF = '1'B;
 ON KEY (ABSTRACTS) BEGIN;
    PUT SKIP EDIT ('ERROR IN REQUEST: ',REQUEST, 'NAMES: ',NAMES)
            (2 A,X(10),2 A);
    IF ONCODE = 51
    THEN DO;
       PUT SKIP LIST ('RECORD NOT FOUND');
       CALL GETRECDS;
    END;
    GO TO CONTINUE;
 END;

 OPEN FILE (ABSTRACTS) DIRECT UPDATE;

 GET FILE (SYSIN) EDIT (RECDS) (A(80));

DO_LOOP: DO WHILE (¬EOF);

       REQUEST = SUBSTR(RECDS,2,8);
       NAMES = SUBSTR(RECDS,10,17);
       TYPE = (INDEX(REQUEST_STR, REQUEST) + 7) / 8;
       GO TO PROC(TYPE);

 PROC(0):   /* BAD REQUEST */
    PUT SKIP LIST ('UNKNOWN REQUEST :', REQUEST);
    CALL GETRECDS;
    GO TO CONTINUE;

 PROC(1):   /* 'RETRIEVE' REQUEST */
    READ FILE (ABSTRACTS) INTO (RECORD) KEY (NAMES || HASH (NAMES));
    PUT SKIP(2) EDIT('CASE',NAMES,'PROCEEDINGS #',SUBSTR(RECORD,1,10))
            (A, X(4), A, COL(35),2 A);
    PUT SKIP(2) LIST ('ABSTRACT :');
    DO I = 11 BY 80 WHILE (I < LENGTH (RECORD));
       PUT SKIP LIST (SUBSTR(RECORD,I,80));
    END;
    PUT SKIP;
    CALL GETRECDS;
    GO TO CONTINUE;

 PROC(2):   /* 'ADD' REQUEST */
    CALL GETRECDS;
    WRITE FILE (ABSTRACTS) FROM (RECORD)
          KEYFROM(NAMES || HASH(NAMES));
    GO TO CONTINUE;
```

**FIGURE 7-9.9**   Example of a REGIONAL(3) file.

```
PROC(3):    /* 'DELETE' REQUEST */
    DELETE FILE (ABSTRACTS) KEY (NAMES | HASH(NAMES));
    CALL GETRECDS;
    GO TO CONTINUE;

PROC(4):    /* 'UPDATE' REQUEST */
    CALL GETRECDS;
    REWRITE FILE (ABSTRACTS) FROM (FECORD)
            KEY (NAMES || HASH (NAMES));

CONTINUE:
    END DO_LOOP;


    GETRECDS: PROCEDURE;
/* READ PROCEEDINGS NO. AND ABSTRACT (IF NEEDED) AND GET NEXT REQUEST */

    GET FILE (SYSIN) EDIT(RECDS) (A (80));
    IF SUBSTR (RECDS,1,1) = '*'
    THEN RETURN;
    RECORD = SUBSTR (RECDS,1,10);
    GET FILE (SYSIN) EDIT (RECDS) (A (30))

    DO WHILE (¬EOF & SUBSTR(RECDS,1,1)¬= '*');
        RECORD = RECORD || RECDS;
        GET FILE (SYSIN) EDIT (RECDS) (A (80));
    END
    END GETRECDS;

HASH: PROCEDURE (KEY) RETURNS (CHAR (8');

    DECLARE KEY CHAR (*),
        (I, HASHED) FIXED;

    I = INDEX (KEY, '-') +1;

    HASHED = MOD (UNSPEC (SUBSTR(KEY,1,3)) +
            UNSPEC (SUBSTR(KEY,I,3)), 997);
    RETURN (HASHED);

END HASH;

 END REG3_EG;
//GO.ABSTRACT DD DSNAME=CASES,DISP=(OLD,KEEP),UNIT=SYSDA.
//    DCB=(DSORG=DA,KEYLEN=17)
//GO.SYSIN DD *
(DATA GOES HERE)
 /*
```

**FIGURE 7-9.9** (Continued)


The source key is made up of a twenty-five character comparison key which contains the names of the principal parties involved (e.g., HARTENGER-WILSON) and an eight-digit region number of which the first five characters are zeros and the last three characters are determined by a hashing function. The hashing function is based on the division method and uses the EBCDIC representation of the first three characters of the two names of the parties [e.g., for HAR and WIL we have $(C8C1D9)_{16}$ and $(E6C9D3)_{16}$ or 13,156,625 and 15,124,947, respectively]. These numbers are added together and the result modulus 997 (the greatest prime less than 1000) is taken to be the region number (for the example, the region is 670).

Transaction records are composed, in part, of a command—either *RETRIEVE, *ADD, *DELETE, or *REPLACE—which together with the names of the principal parties involved form the first line of a transaction. For the *ADD and *REPLACE commands, the additional information items (i.e., the case-proceedings number and the case abstract) are required.

By now it should be evident that the REGIONAL file organizations differ from the organizations discussed earlier in the chapter with respect to the handling of collisions. With REGIONAL files there are no apparent collisions. There is an implicit assumption that the external device is capable of locating a particular record based on its key. An IBM 3380 (record-addressable) device has this capability, and it is not necessary to bring records into main memory for examination. In REGIONAL(2) and REGIONAL(3) files, records are added directly to the file without checking to see if there is another record with the same region number, i.e., there is no check for collisions. Instead, a record is placed at the first open location of the track associated with the record's region number. Of course, if this track is full, a search is made for an open record location on the succeeding tracks. Therefore, one can conceptually think of a track as being a bucket in which a REGIONAL(2) or REGIONAL(3) record resides. If a desired record is not located on the primary track (as dictated by the region number), then a progressive overflow-handling technique is followed.

In contrast, devices which are sector-addressable require more processing to locate an overflow record. First, the primary bucket (i.e., sector) is brought into memory and a scan of its contents is made to determine if the bucket holds the desired record. If it does not, then an overflow bucket is brought into memory and examined. A progression of such overflow records may be considered before the correct record is located. Of course, the necessity to bring the contents of a bucket into memory and then to scan these contents for a particular record makes direct access on a sector-addressable device slower than on a record-addressable device.

In the section to follow we discuss an on-line banking system as an application of direct files. Since a PL/I implementation is considered, much of the material presented in this subsection will be pertinent.

### Exercises for Sec. 7-9

1. In what ways does the bucket capacity affect the performance of an information system in which direct files are used?

2. List the advantages and disadvantages of chained overflow with separate lists when compared to an open-addressing technique.

3. Formulate algorithms for inserting, deleting, and retrieving records from a direct file assuming chaining with coalescing lists is used as the overflow technique.

4. Formulate Algorithm DIRECT_SEQ for reading the records of a direct file in which chaining with separate lists is used as the overflow technique.

5. List the advantages and disadvantages of having a direct file on a record-addressable device (such as the IBM 3330) over having the file reside on a sector-addressable device.

6. Can you suggest why variable-length records are disallowed in REGIONAL(1) and REGIONAL(2) files?

7. A type of on-line information system which is familiar to all is an airline reservation system. One function the system must handle instantaneously is the reservation (and confirmation) of a passenger on a particular flight. In this question, you are to design and implement this part of the total system. Assume that two sets of information items are received when handling a flight reservation. The first item is in the form of a request made for a certain type

of ticket (economy or first class) for a particular flight (for example. TW937) on a particular day. The system must immediately determine if such a request can be fulfilled. If it can, then a second set of information—the passenger's name and phone number—is received and used to complete the reservation.

Write a PL/I program in which a direct file [REGIONAL(3) file] is used in the reservation of a passenger. A flight name of the form <abbreviated airline name> <three digit number> is used as part of the key for the direct file. Example flight names are AM666, AC125, CP098, EA930, LU002, NW794, and TW365. The region number of a PL/I source key should be associated with each airline. Flight numbers and the date of the flight are used to distinguish flights within a given region of the file. Therefore, AM666 on January 5, 1983, is translated into the PL/I source key 66600519830000C001 if the region number 00000001 is associated with American Airlines. The field 666 is the flight number, 005 is the fifth day of the year, and 1983 is the year.

The REGIONAL(3) file should contain an initial three records which hold the number of seats for each class which have not been reserved and the total number of seats available for the flight. The remaining records are source key values for a REGIONAL(1) file which contains records each holding a passenger's name and phone number. For example, when an economy-class passenger is added to a flight, he or she is assigned a number which serves as a source key in the REGIONAL(1) file. This number is placed in the REGIONAL(3) file, and the second record in the file is decremented by 1. The name and phone number of the passenger are stored at the appropriate record locations in the REGIONAL(1) file, completing the reservation. Cancellations of reservations are handled in a obvious manner. Be sure to place error-checking procedures into the system and test the system thoroughly.

8.  What are the advantages and disadvantages of using two files instead of one file [i.e., only the REGIONAL(3) file] in Exercise 7?

## 7-10 AN ON-LINE BANKING SYSTEM

To demonstrate the use of direct files. we have chosen an application involving an on-line banking system which handles savings accounts. The PL/I implementation of the system illustrates the use of two types of direct files: REGIONAL(1) and REGIONAL(2). The system described is pedagogical and does not have many of the refinements that are now appearing in most modern banking systems. Nevertheless, an examination of its development is informative and interesting.

### 7-10.1 System Analysis

The system should permit bank customers to perform monetary transactions  by interacting with a teller, who keys in the transactions, and to have these transactions registered instantaneously in the customer's account. The current status of the account is available to the customer in a permanent form through the use of a pass-book in a special recording slot in a terminal, and the current transaction plus all previously unrecorded transactions are printed in the passbook. There are a number of special banking terminals on the market, and a typical transaction keyboard is shown in Fig. 7-10.1.

It is important that the system be designed to handle monetary transactions without a customer's passbook; customers are notoriously forgetful or lazy. Interest is calculated monthly on the lowest balance of the past month. This calculation is

Message
prompting window

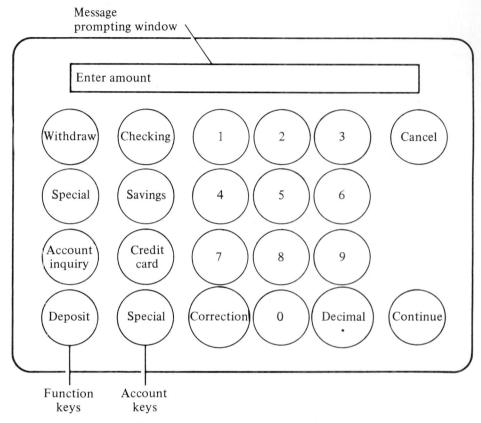

**FIGURE 7-10.1**   Transaction-oriented keyboard for a banking system.

performed automatically and is entered into the passbook the first time the book is presented in the month. Should the passbook not be presented during some month, the interest is accumulated until the passbook is brought in, at which time all necessary entries are made.

The system will accommodate only one type of customer account—a savings account—for which the following transactions are permitted:

*1*   A new account may be opened.
*2*   Money may be deposited into an existing account.
*3*   Money may be withdrawn from an existing account (checking privileges are not allowed).
*4*   Passbooks may be updated.
*5*   An existing account may be closed.

The system should be designed to handle accounts from a number of different branches located in the same geographic area. Therefore, a customer need not be forced to go to the same branch for all transactions.

As a final requirement, the system should be reliable. If the computer responsible for updating customer accounts fails, then a backup mode of operation must be present. Ideally, a second computer should be simultaneously in operation and performing the same transactions as the first computer. If the first fails, the second can continue handling accounts without interruption of banking services. A less expensive form of backup is to employ a microcomputer to store on tape all monetary transactions which take place while the main system is down. When the system recovers, the transactions are sent in batch mode to the main computer. A final alternative is to revert to a manual method of recording in the event of a main-system failure. When the main system becomes operable again, delayed transactions are entered when time is available for the teller to do so. In the next subsection, however, we will only consider the design of the main system and will ignore the problem of system backup.

## 7-10.2 System Design

We begin by examining those aspects of the system's design that most directly affect the user—the transaction entry facility. In a fully automated banking system, tellers ideally key in customer transactions through a keyboard similar to that shown in Fig. 7-10.1. In our system, however, we will assume a standard input device (such as a CRT) is available. We make this assumption primarily to demonstrate clearly the interaction between a keyed request and the resulting file transaction in the PL/I implementation phase. In addition, specialized banking terminals are luxuries not all banks can afford.

It should be obvious that if a query language is used in an on-line banking system, it should be a terse language. Since tellers are constantly interacting with the system, an abbreviated command structure aids in efficiency and reduces keyboard errors, which are more likely to occur if long textual commands are required. Also, it is useful, wherever possible, to prompt the teller if prompting is requested. The inexperienced teller can be aided by such a facility. The experienced teller can turn this feature off.

The five customer transactions that normally occur in banking are *account opening, withdrawal, deposit, inquiry,* and *account closing.* Since the opening and closing of an account are relatively rare, yet very important events, special status is often given to these transactions. In some banking systems, only managers are allowed to complete these transactions and do so by keying in special function codes of which they alone have access. Other banking systems do not handle deposits on-line for reasons of security.

The type of processing that is necessary in an on-line banking system is quite rudimentary. An input that is representative of a customer transaction is first examined. Once the nature of the transaction is determined, a system routine is available for each customer transaction type. Figure 7-10.2 shows the general flow of system execution. A special module for scanning and identifying the basic lexical units of an input message is invoked several times per input by the input-evaluation routine. Such a module is not required in a function keyboard system such as that in Fig. 7-10.1.

Let us now turn to an examination of the file structures and file-level transactions required by the system.

In almost all modern-day banking systems, access to information concerning a bank account is gained through an account number. This is true of computerized or manual systems. An account number is the vehicle for providing a unique and somewhat anonymous method for account identification.

The uniqueness property makes account numbers ideal primary keys for accessing account information in a computerized system. If we assume an on-line

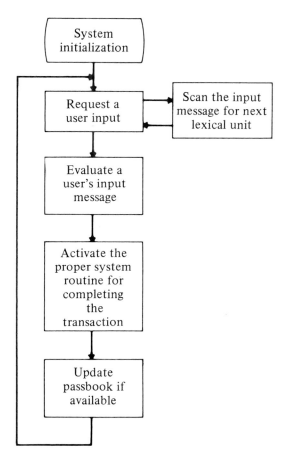

**FIGURE 7-10.2**   A flow diagram illustrating
the handling of customer transactions in a
banking system.

system for a relatively small bank, then the following account-numbering scheme
may be adopted. A five-digit account number is used, with the first two digits referring to a specific branch. If a branch is particularly large, several two-digit combinations can be assigned to the same branch. The final three digits are customer-
identifying digits.

Such an account-numbering scheme lends itself extremely well to a direct file
in which the first two digits are used to locate the relative region in which a customer record resides, and the last three digits are used to isolate the desired record. In
PL/I, a REGIONAL(2) organization models this form of access and is therefore
adopted. Henceforth, we refer to this file as the account file.

To permit the deposit of money into and/or the withdrawal of money from an
account without presenting a passbook, the on-line system needs a file which records
those transactions not as yet printed in passbooks. For a given account, we must be

able to determine if unrecorded entries exist. If they do, it is desirable that access to these records be achieved directly.

While there are various ways of handling the problem of unrecorded entries, we will examine one method which uses a direct file with direct addressing. For example, we can create a file containing 100 records numbered 0 through 99. The records are organized initially as a linear linked list with record $n$ pointing to record $n + 1$ for $1 \leq n \leq 98$ and record 99 containing a link field value of $-1$ (indicating the end of the list). Record 0 is a special record in that it contains two pointers: one pointing to the current head of the list (initially set to 1) and the other pointing to the current tail of the list (initially set to 99). Record 0 is, in effect, a special list head.

A relationship exists between the account file and the unrecorded transaction file. Each record in the account file contains a pointer item which either references a linked list of records in the unrecorded-transaction file or contains a $-1$ (which is the initial value), indicating there are no unrecorded transactions for that account. Figure 7-10.3 depicts a relationship which can exist for an account file with just three accounts. In the figure, broken arrows represent the links of the list of available record locations and solid arrows represent the links containing unrecorded transactions.

A series of independent lists are formed in the unrecorded-transaction file, with one list for each account which has unrecorded transactions. When a passbook for one of these accounts is presented, it is updated by generating an entry for each node in the unrecorded-transaction list for that account. All nodes in the processed list are then available for other unrecorded transactions which later occur. Hence, an availability list with a list head of record 0 is used to manage free unrecorded-transaction file records. It should be clear that a REGIONAL(1) organization, with its direct-addressing capability, can be adopted for the unrecorded-transaction file.

There are many other design considerations that should be included in the design of a banking system. For example, it is desirable to be able to place an account on hold pending the settlement of a deceased customer's estate. System security features must be provided in a computerized system. Archival files are needed to record all transactions from the previous six months (or thereabouts) for auditing procedures and to provide a customer with an updated statement of his or her account if the passbook is lost or stolen. Provisions must be available to change erroneous transactions that have already been applied against an account. This aspect is very important in the design of a user-oriented system. If errors cannot be easily and promptly corrected, users soon get frustrated and take their business elsewhere. Finally, the system we are examining only handles savings accounts. Checking, checking-savings, and loan accounts, along with credit-card accounting, are other facilities a banking system should accommodate.

### 7-10.3 Implementation

The implementation of the on-line banking system involves the programming of a number of submodules which are called from a mainline module, as was the case with the implementations of the other system described in this chapter. The submodules, which are named EVALUATE, SCAN, ACTIVATE, and PASSWRITE, correspond to the processing boxes shown in Fig. 7-10.2.

The initialization section, the procedure SCAN, skeletons of the procedures EVALUATE and ACTIVATE, the procedure PASSWRITE, and the mainline section

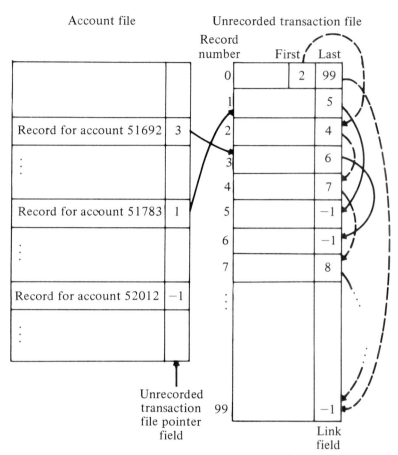

**FIGURE 7-10.3** The relationship between the account file and the unrecorded transaction file.

of the program are given in Fig. 7-10.4. The ACCT and TRANS files correspond to the account and unrecorded-transaction files as discussed in the previous subsections. ACCOUNT and TRANSACTION are the record descriptions which are associated with the ACCT and TRANS files, respectively. The procedure SCAN is called from the EVALUATE procedure whenever a new lexical unit from a user input must be isolated. The EVALUATE procedure will not be given, mainly because of its length and because it is not directly relevant to our discussion of file structures. However, it should be capable of interacting with a user in a manner exemplified by the following session:

```
*ENTER TRANSACTION
W 7812B 2150
*INVALID ACCOUNT NUMBER—REENTER TRANSACTION
W 78127 21.500
*INVALID AMOUNT—REENTER TRANSACTION
V 78127 21.50
```

```
// EXEC PL1LFCG
//PL1L.SYSIN DD *
```

```
/*          ON-LINE BANKING SYSTEM                    */
BANKS: PROCEDURE OPTIONS (MAIN);
```

```
/* THIS PROGRAM IS DESIGNED TO SIMULATE AN ON-LINE BANKING SYSTEM.   */
```

```
/* THIS IS A RATHER SIMPLIFIED SYSTEM AS ONLY SAVINGS ACCOUNTS ARE
   DEALT WITH. THE FOLLOWING TRANSACTIONS MAY BE PERFORMED ON THESE
   ACCOUNTS: MONEY MAY BE WITHDRAWN OR DEPOSITED, NEW ACCOUNTS MAY
   BE OPENED AND OLD ONES MAY BE CLOSED. ALSO, A SIMPLE PASSBOOK-
   UPDATE FUNCTION MAY BE PERFORMED. INTEREST IS CALCULATED AT THE
   GENEROUS RATE OF 1% PER MONTH, AND IS AUTOMATICALLY GIVEN TO THE
   CUSTOMER WHEN THE PASSBOOK IS PRESENTED.
```

```
   SOME OF THE KEY VARIABLES USED IN THIS PROGRAM ARE:
       INSTRUCTION: A CHARACTER VARIABLE USED TO HOLD THE INCOMING
               INSTRUCTION (OR PORTION THEREOF).
       PART: A CHARACTER VARIABLE USED TO HOLD THE PORTIONS OF THE
               INSTRUCTION AS THEY ARE RETURNED BY THE SCANNER.
       SCAN: A PROCEDURE USED TO SCAN THE INPUT INSTRUCTIONS AND
               SEPARATE ITS INDIVIDUAL COMPONENTS.
       SOURCE_KEY: A SOURCE KEY COMPOSED OF THE ACCOUNT NUMBER AND
               THE FIRST TWO DIGITS OF IT — IT IS USED TO
               REFERENCE THE RECORDS STORED ON THE ACCOUNT FILE
               WHICH HAVE RECORDED KEYS.
       ACCT_NO: A VARIABLE USED TO TEMPORARILY HOLD THE ACCOUNT
               NUMBER AS IT IS IDENTIFIED BY THE SCANNER.
       T_TYPE: A VARIABLE USED TO TEMPORARILY STORE THE TRANSACTION
               TYPE AS IT IS IDENTIFIED BY THE SCANNER.
       SAVE: A VARIABLE USED TO HOLD THE AMOUNT OF THE TRANSACTION
               AS IDENTIFIED BY THE SCANNER.
       PASSBK: A PRINT FILE USED TO PRINT OUT RECORDS OF TRANS-
               ACTIONS ONTO PASSBOOKS.
       TRANS: A DISK FILE HAVING DIRECT ACCESS CAPABILITIES, USED
               TO HOLD RECORDS OF ALL TRANSACTIONS MADE WHEN NO PASS
               BOOK WAS PRESENTED.
       ACCT: A FILE HAVING DIRECT ACCESS CAPABILITIES WHICH HOLDS
               ALL THE CUSTOMER ACCOUNTS INCLUDING THE CURRENT BALANCE
               FOR EACH CUSTOMER'S ACCOUNT.
       ACCOUNT: A STRUCTURE USED TO INTERNALLY HOLD RECORDS FROM THE
               ACCT FILE. IT GIVES THE READER A LOOK AT THE
               INFORMATION STORED ON THAT FILE.
       TRANS_POINT: A FIELD OF ACCOUNT WHICH POINTS INTO THE TRANS
               FILE, TRANS_POINT POINTS TO A LIST OF UNRECORDED
               TRANSACTIONS INVOLVING THAT ACCOUNT.
       TRANSACTION: A STRUCTURE USED TO INTERNALLY HOLD RECORDS
               FROM THE TRANS FILE. IT ALSO IS A DESCRIPTION
               OF CONTENTS OF EACH RECORD ON THE FILE
       LINK: A FIELD OF TRANSACTION. LINK IS USED TO FORM A SINGLY-
               LINKED LIST OF THE UNRECORDED TRANSACTIONS FOR EACH
               CUSTOMER. THE FIRST RECORD OF THIS FILE CONTAINS A
               POINTER TO THE NEXT AVAILABLE NODE OF THIS LIST (THAT
               IS, THE NEXT FREE RECORD IN THE FILE) AND A POINTER TO
               THE LAST NODE IN THE LIST. THESE POINTERS ARE UPDATED
               WHEN RECORDS ARE ADDED TO THE FILE OR WHEN LISTS ARE
               DELETED FROM THE FILE. THE DELETED SUBLISTS ARE
               TACKED ON TO THE END OF THE LIST OF AVAILABLE NODES.
               THUS, WE HAVE AN EXTERNAL LINEAR LINKED LIST.         */
```

```
    DECLARE
        INSTRUCTION CHARACTER(74) VARYING.
        PART CHARACTER(10) VARYING,
        SCAN ENTRY RETURNS (CHARACTER(10) VARYING),
```

**FIGURE 7-10.4**  Mainline and submodules for the on-line banking system.

```
          (I,J,L) FIXED BINARY,
          SOURCE_KEY CHARACTER(13),
          ACCT_NO CHARACTER(5),
          (FIRST,LAST,TEMP) FIXED DEC(2,0),
          T_TYPE CHAR(1),
          SAVE FIXED DEC (9,2),
          PASSBK FILE STREAM PRINT,
          TRANS FILE RECORD KEYED ENVIRONMENT(F(20) REGIONAL(1)),
          ACCT FILE RECORD KEYED ENVIRONMENT(F(90) REGIONAL(2)),
          1 ACCOUNT,
               2 FILLER CHAR(1),
               2 TYPE CHAR(1),
               2 NUMBER CHAR(5),
               2 NAME CHAR(20),
               2 ADDRESS(3) CHAR(15),
               2 BALANCE FIXED DECIMAL(9,2),
               2 LAST_DATE CHAR(6),
               2 INT_BAL FIXED DECIMAL(9,2),
               2 TRANS_POINT FIXED DECIMAL(2,0),
          1 TRANSACTION,
               2 FILLER CHARACTER(1),
               2 TYPE CHARACTER(1),
               2 NUMBER FIXED DECIMAL(9,2),
               2 DAY CHARACTER(6),
               2 AMOUNT FIXED DECIMAL(9,2),
               2 LINK FIXED DECIMAL(2,0),
          PASSBOOK BIT(1);


     SCAN: PROCEDURE RETURNS(CHARACTER(10) VARYING);

/* THE SCAN PROCEDURE IS USED TO ISOLATE THE INDIVIDUAL COMPONENTS
   OF THE INPUT INSTRUCTION. NOTE THAT IT IS ASSUMED THAT THE
   COMPONENTS ARE DELIMITED FROM ONE ANOTHER BY AT LEAST ONE BLANK.   */

          DECLARE ELEMENT CHARACTER(10) VARYING;
          INSTRUCTION = SUBSTR(INSTRUCTION,VERIFY(INSTRUCTION,' '));
          /* TRIMS LEADING BLANKS */
          ELEMENT = '';
          IF SUBSTR(INSTRUCTION,1,1) = '*'
          THEN RETURN(ELEMENT);
          ELEMENT = SUBSTR(INSTRUCTION,1,(INDEX(INSTRUCTION,' ')-1));
          /* ELEMENT IS ASSIGNED THE VALUE OF THE FIRST WORD OF */
          /* THE INSTRUCTION.                    */
          INSTRUCTION = SUBSTR(INSTRUCTION,INDEX(INSTRUCTION,' '));
          /* FIRST WORD IS DELETED FROM INSTRUCTION. */
          RETURN (ELEMENT);
     END SCAN;



     EVALUATE: PROCEDURE;

/* EVALUATE IS A PROCEDURE USED TO EVALUATE THE INPUT TRANSACTION.
   THIS PROCEDURE CALLS 'SCAN' TO ACCESS THE INDIVIDUAL PARTS OF THE
   INSTRUCTION AND THEN CHECKS THESE COMPONENTS FOR VALIDITY. IT WILL
   REQUEST CORRECT INFORMATION IF ANY OF THAT WHICH IS SUPPLIED IS
   FOUND TO BE INVALID.                            */

                    .
                    .
                    .
     END EVALUATE;


     PASSWRITE: PROCEDURE;

/* THIS SHORT PROCEDURE IS USED TO OUTPUT THE LINES ONTO THE PASSBOOK
   FILE.                                  */
```

**FIGURE 7-10.4**   (Continued)

```
          PUT FILE(PASSBK) EDIT(SUBSTR(DAY,5,2),SUBSTR(DAY,3,2),
                         SUBSTR(DAY,1,2))
                         (COLUMN(1),3 (X(1),A(2)));
          IF TRANSACTION.TYPE = 'W'   /* WITHDRAWAL */
          THEN PUT FILE(PASSBK) EDIT(AMOUNT,'') (F(11,2),X(20),A);
          ELSE DO;
              PUT FILE(PASSBK) EDIT(AMOUNT) (X(12),F(10,2));
              IF TRANSACTION.TYPE = 'I'   /* INTEREST */
              THEN PUT FILE(PASSBK) EDIT('INTEREST') (X(1),A);
              ELSE PUT FILE(PASSBK) EDIT('') (X(9),A(0));
          END;
          PUT FILE(PASSBK) EDIT(TRANSACTION.NUMBER) (F(11,2));
          RETURN
       END PASSWRITE;


       ACTIVATE: PROCEDURE;

  /* THE ACTIVATE PROCEDURE PROCESSES THE INSTRUCTIONS AND PRINTS
     THE TRANSACTION ONTO EITHER THE PASSBOOK FILE, OR
     THE TRANS FILE.                              */




       END ACTIVATE;


  /* * * * * * * * * * * * *  M A I N L I N E  * * * * * * * * * * * * * */

  /* THE MAINLINE SECTION OF THE PROGRAM.                   */

       OPEN FILE(TRANS) DIRECT UPDATE,
          FILE(ACCT) DIRECT UPDATE,
          FILE(PASSBK) OUTPUT;

  /* THE FIRST RECORD OF THE TRANSACTION FILE IS READ IN TO DETERMINE
     THE AVAILABLE NODES OF THE TRANSACTION FILE.            */
       READ FILE(TRANS) INTO(TRANSACTION) KEY('0');
       LAST = LINK;
       FIRST = TRANSACTION.NUMBER;
       ON ENDFILE(SYSIN) GO TO DONE;
       PUT FILE(PASSBK) EDIT('DATE','WITHDRAWAL','DEPOSIT','COMMENTS',
                   'BALANCE') (COLUMN(1),X(3),A(7),A(11),X(2),
                        A(9),A(9),X(3),A(7));
       DO WHILE('1'B);
          PUT FILE(PASSBK) EDIT(' ') (COLUMN(1),A(0));
          PASSBOOK = '1'B;
          CALL EVALUATE;
          CALL ACTIVATE;
       END;

  DONE:    TRANSACTION.NUMBER = FIRST;

          LINK = LAST;
          WRITE FILE(TRANS) FROM(TRANSACTION) KEYFROM('0');
          CLOSE FILE(TRANS),
             FILE(ACCT),
             FILE(PASSBK);

  END BANK3;
  //GO.TRANS DD UNIT=SYSDA,VOL=SER=USER02,SPACE=(20,100),
  //      DSN=TRNDATA,DISP=(OLD,KEEP)
  //GO.ACCT DD UNIT=SYSDA,VOL=SER=USER03,SPACE=(95,411),
  //      DSN=ACTDATA,DCB=(KEYLEN=5,LMTCT=10),DISP=(OLD,KEEP)
  //GO.SYSIN DD *
          (INCOMING TRANSACTIONS)
   /*
```

**FIGURE 7-10.4**   (Continued)

*INVALID TRANSACTION TYPE—REENTER TRANSACTION
W 78127 21.50

This session illustrates the type of syntactic errors that should be detected by the EVALUATE function. An '*' is placed before each system message to delineate it from user input. Each message is of a prompting nature.

The processing of a customer transaction is performed by the ACTIVATE procedure, as shown in Fig. 7-10.5. The five types of transactions are handled by five different segments within the procedure. Account openings are processed first. They are unique from the other transactions in that no check is made for a valid existing account number, no writing is performed in a passbook, and a considerable amount of personal information about the customer is required. For each open transaction, a check is made to ensure that the assigned number is unique. The following is a sample session involving the opening of an account:

```
*ENTER TRANSACTION
O 71444 .00
*ENTER CUSTOMER'S NAME
GAIL W. WALKER
*ENTER THE FIRST LINE OF THE ADDRESS
1002 LANDSDOWNE CRESCENT
*ENTER THE SECOND LINE OF THE ADDRESS
WINNIPEG, MANITOBA
*ENTER THE THIRD LINE OF THE ADDRESS (IF THERE IS ONE),
 OR A NULL LINE
S7K3J5 CANADA
```

```
ACTIVATE: PROCEDURE;

    DECLARE TRANS#(0:4) LABEL;

/* * * * * * * * * * * * * * OPEN * * * * * * * * * * * * * * * */
/* WHEN AN ACCOUNT IS TO BE OPENED, A TEST IS MADE TO SEE IF AN
   ACCOUNT BY THAT NUMBER EXISTS. IF SO, THE OPEN FUNCTION IS NOT
   PERFORMED.                                     */
    IF T_TYPE = 'O'
    THEN DO;
        ON KEY(ACCT) GO TO INITIALIZE;
        READ FILE(ACCT) INTO (ACCOUNT) KEY(SOURCE_KEY);
        PUT EDIT('THE ACCOUNT NUMBERED ',ACCT_NO,' HAS ALREADY ',
            'BEEN OPENED.') (COLUMN(1),4 A);
        RETURN;

INITIALIZE:
    ACCOUNT.FILLER = LOW(1);
    ACCOUNT.TYPE = 'S';
    ACCOUNT.NUMBER = ACCT_NO;
    BALANCE = AMOUNT;
    LAST_DATE = DATE;
    IF SUBSTR(DATE,5,2) = '01'
    THEN INT_BAL = AMOUNT;
    ELSE INT_BAL = 0;
    TRANS_POINT = -1;
```

**FIGURE 7-10.5**   The procedure ACTIVATE for processing customer transactions.

```
/* WHEN OPENING AN ACCOUNT ADDITIONAL INFORMATION ABOUT THE CUSTOMER
   IS NEEDED. THE PROGRAM REQUESTS THIS INFORMATION ONE LINE AT A TIME. */

   P2:  PUT EDIT('ENTER THE CUSTOMER''S NAME',') (COLUMN(1),A);
        GET EDIT(NAME) (COLUMN(1),A(20));
        IF NAME = ''
        THEN GO TO P2;
   P3:  PUT EDIT('ENTER THE FIRST LINE OF THE ADDRESS',')
             (COLUMN(1),A);
        GET EDIT(ADDRESS(1)) (COLUMN(1),A(15));
        IF ADDRESS(1) = ''
        THEN GO TO P3;
   P4:  PUT EDIT('ENTER THE SECOND LINE OF THE ADDRESS',')
             (COLUMN(1),A);
        GET EDIT(ADDRESS(2)) (COLUMN(1),A(15));
        IF ADDRESS(2) = ''
        THEN GO TO P4;
        PUT EDIT('ENTER THE THIRD LINE OF THE ADDRESS (IF THERE '
          || 'IS ONE), OR A NULL LINE',') (COLUMN(1),A);
        GET EDIT(ADDRESS(3)) (COLUMN(1),A(15));
        WRITE FILE(ACCT) FROM(ACCOUNT) KEYFROM(SOURCE_KEY);
        PUT FILE(PASSBK) EDIT(SUBSTR(DATE,5,2),SUBSTR(DATE,3,2),
                    SUBSTR(DATE,1,2),AMOUNT,'NEW',
                    AMOUNT) (COLUMN(1),3 (X(1),A(2)),
                    X(12),F(10,2),X(4),A(6),F(10,2));
        RETURN;
      END;

   SAVE = AMOUNT;
/* FOR ALL OTHER CASES A CHECK IS MADE ON THE VALIDITY OF THE ACCOUNT
   NUMBER BEING PROCESSED. THAT IS, A CHECK IS MADE TO SEE WHETHER OR
   NOT AN ACCOUNT BY THAT NUMBER EXISTS.                        */
      ON KEY(ACCT)
      BEGIN;
         PUT EDIT('THE FOLLOWING ACCOUNT NUMBER IS INVALID:',
              SUBSTR(SOURCE_KEY,1,5),'') (COLUMN(1),A);
         GO TO RET1;
      END;

      READ FILE(ACCT) INTO(ACCOUNT) KEY(SOURCE_KEY)

/* THIS SECTION UPDATES THE PASSBOOK IF THERE ARE TRANSACTIONS FOR
   WHICH THE CUSTOMER DID NOT HAVE HIS PASS BOOK PRESENT.          */
      IF PASSBOOK & TRANS_POINT ¬= -1
      THEN DO;
         IF FIRST = -1
         THEN FIRST = TRANS_POINT;
         ELSE DO;
            READ FILE(TRANS) INTO(TRANSACTION) KEY(LAST)
            LINK = TRANS_POINT;
            WRITE FILE(TRANS) FROM(TRANSACTION) KEYFROM(LAST);
         END;
         LAST = TRANS_POINT;
         READ FILE(TRANS) INTO(TRANSACTION) KEY(TRANS_POINT);
         CALL PASSWRITE;
         DO WHILE(LINK ¬= -1);
            LAST = LINK;
            READ FILE(TRANS) INTO(TRANSACTION) KEY(LINK)
            CALL PASSWRITE;
         END;
         TRANS_POINT = -1;
      END;

/* THIS SEGMENT CALCULATES THE INTEREST OWING THE CUSTOMER, IF THE
   DATE OF HIS LAST VISIT TO THE BANK WAS NOT IN THE SAME MONTH AS
   THE CURRENT VISIT. INTEREST ENTRIES ARE CREATED FOR EACH MONTH.  */
```

**FIGURE 7-10.5**   (Continued)

```
          .
          .
          .
    LAST_DATE = DATE;
    GO TO TRANS#(INDEX('PWDC',T_TYPE));

/* * * * * * * * * * P A S S B O O K  * * * * * * * * * * * * * * * */
/* IF THE ONLY PURPOSE OF THIS VISIT TO THE BANK WAS TO UPDATE A
PASSBOOK, THEN THE PROCESSING IS HALTED.                          */
    TRANS#(1):
       REWRITE FILE(ACCT) FROM(ACCOUNT) KEY(SOURCE_KEY);
       RETURN;

/* * * * * * * * * * * W I T H D R A W A L S  * * * * * * * * * * * * */
/* THIS SEGMENT HANDLES 'WITHDRAWAL' TYPE TRANSACTIONS.             */
    TRANS#(2):
       BALANCE = BALANCE - SAVE;
       IF INT_BAL > BALANCE
       THEN INT_BAL = BALANCE;
       IF PASSBOOK
       THEN PUT FILE(PASSBK) EDIT((SUBSTR(LAST_DATE,J,2) DO J
                  = 5 BY -2 TO 1),SAVE,BALANCE)
                  (COLUMN(1),3 (X(1),A(2)),F(11,2),
                  X(20),F(11,2));
       ELSE DO;
          IF FIRST = -1
          THEN DO;
             PUT EDIT('*** WARNING *** THE TRANSACTION FILE IS'
                  || ' FULL', 'THE FOLLOWING TRANSACTION '
                  || 'CANNOT BE STORED:')
                  (COLUMN(1),A,COLUMN(1),X(17),A)
                  ('WITHDRAW: ',SAVE,'; NEW BALANCE: ',
                  BALANCE) (COLUMN(1),A,F(10,2),A,F(10,2));
             RETURN;
          END;
          IF TRANS_POINT ¬= -1
          THEN DO;
             TEMP = TRANS_POINT;
             READ FILE(TRANS) INTO(TRANSACTION) KEY(TEMP);
             DO WHILE (LINK ¬= -1);
                TEMP = LINK;
                READ FILE(TRANS) INTO(TRANSACTION) KEY(LINK);
             END;
             LINK = FIRST;
             WRITE FILE(TRANS) INTO(TRANSACTION) KEYFROM(TEMP);
          END;
          ELSE TRANS_POINT = FIRST;

          READ FILE(TRANS) INTO(TRANSACTION) KEY(FIRST);
          TRANSACTION.FILLER = LOW(1);
          TRANSACTION.TYPE = 'W';
          TRANSACTION.NUMBER = BALANCE;
          AMOUNT = SAVE;
          DAY = DATE;
          TEMP = FIRST;
          FIRST = LINK;
          LINK = -1;
          WRITE FILE(TRANS) FROM(TRANSACTION) KEYFROM(TEMP);
       END;
       REWRITE FILE(ACCT) FROM(ACCOUNT) KEY(SOURCE_KEY);
       RETURN;
```

**FIGURE 7-10.5**    (Continued)

```
/* * * * * * * * * * * * *   D E P O S I T S   * * * * * * * * * * * * * */
/* THIS SEGMENT HANDLES 'DEPOSIT' TYPE TRANSACTIONS.               */
      TRANS#(3):
          BALANCE = BALANCE + SAVE;
          IF INT_BAL > BALANCE
          THEN INT_BAL = BALANCE;
          IF PASSBOOK
          THEN PUT FILE(PASSBK) EDIT((SUBSTR(LAST_DATE,J,2) DO J
                      = 5 BY -2 TO 1),SAVE , BALANCE)
                      (COLUMN(1),3 (X(1),A(2)),X(11),F(11,2),
                      X(9),F(11,2));
          ELSE DO;
             IF FIRST = -1
             THEN DO;
                 PUT EDIT('*** WARNING *** THE TRANSACTION FILE IS'
                       || ' FULL','THE FOLLOWING TRANSACTION '
                       || 'CANNOT BE STORED:')
                       (COLUMN(1),A,COLUMN(1),X(17),A)
                       ('DEPOSIT: ',SAVE,'; NEW BALANCE: ',
                       BALANCE) (COLUMN(1),A,F(10,2),A,F(10,2));
                 RETURN;
             END;
             IF TRANS_POINT = -1
             THEN TRANS_POINT = FIRST;
             ELSE DO;
                 TEMP = TRANS_POINT;
                 READ FILE(TRANS) INTO(TRANSACTION) KEY(TEMP);
                 DO WHILE (LINK = -1);
                     TEMP = LINK;
                     READ FILE(TRANS) INTO(TRANSACTION) KEY(LINK);
                 END;
                 LINK = FIRST;
                 WRITE FILE(TRANS) FROM(TRANSACTION) KEYFROM(TEMP)
             END;

             READ FILE(TRANS) INTO(TRANSACTION) KEY(FIRST);
             TRANSACTION.FILLER = LOW(1);
             TRANSACTION.TYPE = 'D';
             TRANSACTION.NUMBER = BALANCE;
             AMOUNT = SAVE;
             DAY = DATE;
             TEMP = FIRST;
             FIRST = LINK;
             LINK = -1;
             WRITE FILE(TRANS) FROM(TRANSACTION) KEYFROM(TEMP);
          END;

          REWRITE FILE(ACCT) FROM(ACCOUNT) KEY(SOURCE_KEY);
          RETURN;

/* * * * * * * * * * * * *   C L O S E   * * * * * * * * * * * * * * * */
/* THIS SEGMENT IS USED TO CLOSE OFF ANY ACCOUNT WHEN SUCH AN ACTION
   HAS BEEN REQUESTED BY THE TELLER                        */
      TRANS#(4):
          IF ¬PASSBOOK
          THEN DO;
             PUT EDIT('PASSBOOK MUST BE PRESENTED WHEN CLOSING AN'
                    || ' ACCOUNT','') (COLUMN(1),A);
             RETURN;
          END;

          AMOUNT = BALANCE;
          BALANCE = 0;
```

**FIGURE 7-10.5**   (Continued)

```
        IF AMOUNT > 0
        THEN PUT EDIT('THE FOLLOWING AMOUNT IS TO BE RETURNED TO'
                || ' THE CUSTOMER: ') (COLUMN(1),A);
        ELSE IF AMOUNT < 0
            THEN PUT EDIT('THE CUSTOMER OWES THE BANK:  ')
                    (COLUMN(1),A);
            ELSE PUT EDIT('THE CUSTOMER''S ACCOUNT IS  EMPTY .',
                    '') (COLUMN(1),A);
        IF AMOUNT ⌐= 0
        THEN PUT EDIT(AMOUNT,'') (F(11,2),COLUMN(1),A(0));
        PUT FILE(PASSBK) EDIT((SUBSTR(DATE,J,2) DO J = 5 BY -2
                    TO 1),AMOUNT,'CLOSED',BALANCE)
                    (COLUMN(1),3 (X(1),A(2)),F(11,2),
                    X(13),A(8),F(10,2));
        DELETE FILE(ACCT) KEY(SOURCE_KEY);
RET1:    RETURN;


    END ACTIVATE;
```

**FIGURE 7-10.5**    (Continued)


Transaction types other than an account opening are handled after passbooks are updated and the interest is calculated for the previous months. The calculation of interest payments is left out—once again for brevity. The four modules corresponding to the customer transactions—PASSBOOK, WITHDRAWAL, DEPO-SIT, and CLOSE—illustrate the use of each of the I/O commands which are available in PL/I for direct files. A number of semantic errors and special conditions can occur with a transaction, such as an attempt to take more money from an account than is currently in the account, a transaction-file full warning, and the closure of an account without a passbook. These conditions are detected in the ACTIVATE procedure. The procedure PASSWRITE is invoked form ACTIVATE and is responsible for printing customer's transactions in the passbook.

This section concludes our discussion of direct files. The banking-system example helps to exhibit the most important property of a direct file—the ability to access a specific record quickly without the necessity of sequentially searching through a large number of records in the file.


## 7-11  EXTERNAL SEARCHING

The discussion on external searching in this section is restricted primarily to those techniques which are based on hashing. Recall from Sec. 6-2.4 that hashing techniques can be applied successfully to internal tables. Here we wish to apply these techniques to external files. Other techniques that are based on tree structures such as balanced trees and tries could also be used as a basis of searching external files. Throughout the discussion we use the terms table and file interchangeably. The first subsection deals with distribution-dependent hashing functions. The remaining subsection introduces the notion of dynamic hashing.


### 7-11.1  Distribution-Dependent Hashing Functions

Four distribution-dependent functions are discussed in this section. All functions except the first are discussed in detail. Knott has published discussions of such distribution-dependent functions and characterizes them as follows.

For $S \subset K$ it is required to find a hashing function $H$ which maps the elements of $S$ to the address space $\{1, 2, ..., m\}$ uniformly. The required function can be obtained from the discrete cumulative distribution function $F_Z(x) = P(Z \leq x)$, where $Z$ denotes a random variable that assumes values of keys in $S$. If $S$ contains n distinct keys, then the random variable $F_Z(Z)$ is such that $P(F_Z(Z) \leq k/n) = k/n$ for $0 \leq k \leq n$. It follows that $F_Z(Z)$ and $mF_Z(Z)$ have a discrete uniform distribution on $\{(1/n), ..., [(n - 1)/n]1\}$, and $\{(m/n), (2m/n), ..., m\}$, respectively. Therefore $\lceil MF_Z(Z) \rceil$, where $\lceil \ \rceil$ denotes the least integer greater than or equal to its contents (i.e., the ceiling function), is approximately uniform on $\{1, 2, ..., m\}$. This is particularly the case when $m \leq n$. Consequently, the distribution-dependent hashing function $H$ for a given key $x$ is defined by $H(x) = \lceil mF_Z(x) \rceil$

Since in many cases $F_Z$ is not known, it must be approximated. The distribution-dependent hashing functions discussed here (except the digit analysis method) vary only in the approach used to estimate $F_Z$. One or more scannings of the subset of keys corresponding to the known records must be performed before these functions can be defined. Since frequent insertions into and deletions from the file may change this subset drastically, periodic redefinition of the hashing function and reorganization of the direct file may be required.

Four such estimations of $F_Z$ are now described, using algorithms and mathematical notation. It should be emphasized, however, that the first method to be discussed does not involve the computation of an estimate of $F_Z$.

*Digit analysis* is a hashing transformation which is, in a sense, distribution dependent. Recall from Sec. 6-2.4 that digits or bits of the original key are selected and then shifted in order to form addresses. As an example, a key 123456789 would be transformed to an address 7654 if digits in positions 4 through 7 were selected and their order reversed. For a given key set, the same positions of the key and the same rearrangement pattern must be used consistently. The key positions to be used in forming an address are selected on the basis of an analysis which is performed on a sample of the key set.

A *piece-wise linear function* is a second distribution-dependent hashing function that can be used to approximate $F_Z$. Isaac and Singleton [1956] first suggested this method. A formulation of the necessary function was presented by Kronmal and Tarter [1965]. The key space consists of integers in the interval (a, d). This interval is divided into j equal subintervals of length $L$, i.e., $L = (d - a)/j$. The interval location of a given key $x$ is found by the formula

$$i = 1 + \lfloor (x - a)/L \rfloor.$$

The j intervals can be described as:

$$l_i = \begin{cases} (a, a + L), i = 1 \\ (a + (i - 1)L, A + L), 2 \leq i \leq j \end{cases}$$

Let $N_i$ be defined as the number of keys from $S$ contained in the interval $l_i$, and $G_i$ be the corresponding number of keys less than $A + iL$. Therefore, $N$ and $G_i$ are the frequency and cumulative frequency respectively of the interval $l_i$. Using $N_i$ and $G_i$, the equation

$$P_i(x) = (G_i + ((x - a)/L - i)N_i)/n$$

gives a linear appproximation of the cumulative frequency distribution function $F_Z$ for $x$ in the interval $l_i$. The required hashing function for a key $x$ on interval $l_i$ is, therefore, $H_i(x) = \lceil mP_i(x) \rceil$, $1 \leq i \leq j$ for an address space of size m.

The following algorithm illustrates how the piece-wise linear function for indirect addressing is calculated.

**Algorithm** PIECE_WISE. (Piece-wise linear parameter calculation). Given $j$, $a$, $d$, $m$, and $n$ as previously defined and a key set $\{x_1, x_2, ..., x_n\}$, it is required to calculate interval length L and the frequencies and cumulative frequencies $N_i$ and $G_i$, $1 \le i \le j$, for the piece-wise linear function.

1. [Initialize array N to zero]
      Repeat for $i = 1, 2, ..., j$
        $N_i \leftarrow 0$
2. [Determine interval length and interval frequencies]
      $L \leftarrow (d - a)/j$
      Repeat for $k = 1, 2, ..., n$
        $i \leftarrow 1 + \lfloor (x_k - a)/L \rfloor$
        $N_i \leftarrow N_i + 1$
3. [Calculate interval cumulative frequencies]
      $G_1 \leftarrow N_1$
      Repeat for $i = 2, 3, ..., j$
        $G_i \leftarrow G_{i-1} + N_i$
4. [Finished]
      Exit                                        ⬜

This simple algorithm requires only one scan of the key set in order to determine the N and G vectors. From the given parameters, the following assignment statements can be used to calculate an address H from a key $x$ in the interval $(a, d)$.

    $i \leftarrow 1 + \lfloor (x - a)/L \rfloor$
    If $G_i \ne 0$
    then $H(x) \leftarrow \lceil m(G_i + ((x - a)/L - i)N_i)/n \rceil$
    else $H(x) \leftarrow 1$

Note that if $G_i$ is zero, then the hash value returned for a key in a dynamic key set (i.e., a key set involving the addition of a record with a key that was not in the original key set) must be 1 to avoid returning a value outside the address space. This should rarely happpen but, unfortunately, must be checked for explicitly.

As an example of this method, consider the case where $a = 0$, $d = 1000$, $j = 10$, $n = 220$, and the vectors N and G are as given in Table 7-11.1. Then $L = (1000 - 0)/10 = 100$. For a key value $x = 410$, with $m = 250$,

    $i = 1 + \lfloor (410 - 0)/100 \rfloor = 5$

and

    $H(x) = \lceil 250(80 + ((410 - 0)/100 - 5)18))/220 \rceil = 73$.

Another estimate of $F_Z$ has been devised by Deutscher et al. It involves the use of multiple frequency distributions. In this method an initial piece-wise linear estimate of the frequency distribution of the subset S of the key space is used to map that subset into an equivalent key space instead of the address space. This tends to spread out clusters of keys and condense sparsely populated intervals. The total effect is that the distribution of keys in the key space becomes more uniform.

**Table 7-11.1**

| i | N | G |
|---|---|---|
| 1 | 10 | 10 |
| 2 | 16 | 26 |
| 3 | 30 | 56 |
| 4 | 6 | 62 |
| 5 | 18 | 80 |
| 6 | 26 | 106 |
| 7 | 40 | 146 |
| 8 | 32 | 178 |
| 9 | 24 | 202 |
| 10 | 18 | 220 |

The piece-wise linear estimate of the distribution of the transformed keys is found and may be used in conjunction with the first piece-wise linear function to form a hashing function. Alternatively, a number of iterations may be performed until the hashing function obtained is judged to be good. The criterion used for determining the number of iterations is to stop iterating when the average length of search does not decrease by more that an insignificant amount (say .02) from one iteration to the next. A key from the original key set S is used to generate an address by being transformed through a number of key sets. A different piece-wise linear estimate is used for each transformation.

This hashing method is designated as the *multiple frequency distribution function* and can be described by using variables similar to those given in the description of the piece-wise linear function.

**Algorithm** MULTIPLE_FREQUENCY    (Multiple frequency address calculation). Assume that n keys in the subset S have been transformed into a second key set, then to a third key set, and so on up to a $(q + 1)$st key set. This requires q transformations using piece-wise linear functions for each transformation. All key sets are in the interval (a, d), and the length of all subintervals is L. Let $N_{ik}$ be the number of keys in interval $l_i$ of the kth key set, and let $G_{ik}$ be the number of keys less than a + iL in the same key set k. It is required to calculate H, the value of the function H(x) for a key x from the initial key set, using q frequency distribution mappings.

1. [Initialize auxiliary variable]
       $y \leftarrow x$
2. [Transform through key sets]
       Repeat for k = 1, 2, ..., q
           $i \leftarrow 1 + \lfloor (y - a)/L \rfloor$
           $F \leftarrow (G_{ik} + ((y - a)/ \_ - i) N_{ik} )/n$
           If $k < q$
           then   $y \leftarrow \lfloor (d - a)F + a \rfloor$

3. [Calculate an address]
    If $F \neq 0$
    then  $H \leftarrow \lceil mF \rceil$
    else  $H \leftarrow 1$
4. [Finished]
    Exit                                              □

Observe that in the algorithm an explicit test is again made for the situation in which a new record is being inserted at the beginning of the file (i.e., when $F = 0$).

The determination of the number of transfomations, q, requires an algorithm for calculating the ALOS. Two such algorithms use open addressing and chaining as collision resolution techniques. $N_{ik}$ and $G_{ik}$ for $1 \leq i \leq j$ and $k = 1$ are calculated using Algorithm PIECE_WISE. The ALOS is determined for the set of keys under consideration. Following this, the piece-wise linear function is used to map the keys to a second key set and $N_{ik}$ and $G_{ik}$ for $k = 2$ are calculated. The ALOS using the two piece-wise linear functions is determined, and if it does not decrease by more than .02 from the first ALOS, then the multiple frequency function is complete and q is 2. If the ALOS increases in comparison to the first ALOS, then only the first piece-wise linear estimate should be used in forming the function, so q is 1.

In tests performed by Deutscher the process of using previous piece-wise linear functions to determine another set of $N_{ik}$ and $G_{ik}$ elements is continued until ALOS does not decrease by more than .02 or until $q = 5$. If i distributions are formed in the construction of this function, then $i + 1$ scans of the keys in a key set are required. If each successive distribution decreases the ALOS, then q is equal to i. If the final distribution increases ALOS, however, then q is equal to $i - 1$. Thus, either $q + 1$ or $q + 2$ scans of the key set are necessary.

Deutscher et al. devised another function for estimating the frequency distribution of a key set. This function is also based on a piece-wise linear estimate. The key space is initially divided into an arbitrary number of equally-sized intervals. The storage of a subset S of keys is then simulated. If the ALOS of an interval is greater than a predetermined ALOS, then this interval is further subdivided, so that a better estimate of the frequency distribution can be obtained for that interval. This interval-splitting process is performed in an iterative manner so that subintervals may also be split. The hashing function thus obtained is denoted as the *piece-wise linear function with interval splitting*. The process requires the use of a data structure that can be represented by an array. An example of the interval-splitting process and its representation is given in Fig. 7-11.1.

The range of the key space (a, d) in Fig. 7-11.1 is initially divided into 10 intervals of length $(d - a)/10$. $N_i$ denotes the frequency of the ith interval. If this interval has not been split, then $G_i$ has a value which represents the cumulative frequency for that interval. If $G_i$ contains a negative value, however, then the absolute value of $G_i$ gives the location of the first of two consecutive pairs of array elements $N_{|G_i|}$ and $G_{|G_i|}$, and $N_{|G_i|+1}$ and $G_{|G_i|+1}$. These elements correspond to the half-intervals of interval i. Each half-interval has a length of $(d - a)/20$. The values $N_{|G_i|}$ and $N_{|G_i|+1}$ denote the frequencies of the first and second half-intervals of interval i respectively. Let k be either $|G_i|$ or $|G_i| + 1$. A nonnegative value of $G_k$ indicates that it represents the cumulative frequency of the corresponding half-interval. For negative $G_k$, $|G_k|$ indicates the location of the first of two consecutive pairs of array elements which give information for the two quarter-intervals of the corresponding half-interval. This process is continued to obtain eighth-intervals and so on.

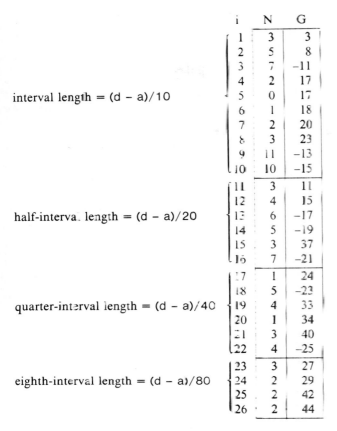

| i | N | G |
|---|---|---|
| 1 | 3 | 3 |
| 2 | 5 | 8 |
| 3 | 7 | -11 |
| 4 | 2 | 17 |
| 5 | 0 | 17 |
| 6 | 1 | 18 |
| 7 | 2 | 20 |
| 8 | 3 | 23 |
| 9 | 11 | -13 |
| 10 | 10 | -15 |
| 11 | 3 | 11 |
| 12 | 4 | 15 |
| 13 | 6 | -17 |
| 14 | 5 | -19 |
| 15 | 3 | 37 |
| 16 | 7 | -21 |
| 17 | 1 | 24 |
| 18 | 5 | -23 |
| 19 | 4 | 33 |
| 20 | 1 | 34 |
| 21 | 3 | 40 |
| 22 | 4 | -25 |
| 23 | 3 | 27 |
| 24 | 2 | 29 |
| 25 | 2 | 42 |
| 26 | 2 | 44 |

interval length = $(d - a)/10$

half-interval length = $(d - a)/20$

quarter-interval length = $(d - a)/40$

eighth-interval length = $(d - a)/80$

**FIGURE 7-11.1**  Representation of a data structure for the piece-wise linear function with interval splitting.

Consider interval 9 with $N_9 = 11$ and $G_9 = -13$. A negative value for $G_9$ indicates that this interval is split, so $|G_9| = 13$ references $N_{13}$, $G_{13}$, $N_{14}$, and $G_{14}$. These entries contain information on the half-intervals of interval 9. $N_{13}$ is 6 and since $G_{13} = -17$ the first half-interval is also split. $N_{17}$, $G_{17}$, $N_{18}$, and $G_{18}$ correspond to its quarter-intervals. The first quarter-interval, having one key in it, is not split. The second quarter-interval however, is split, as indicated by $G_{18} = -23$. $N_{23}$, $G_{23}$, $N_{24}$, and $G_{24}$ give the frequencies and cumulative frequencies for the eighth-intervals of the second quarter-interval. The eight-intervals are not split, as indicated by $G_{23} = 27$ and $G_{24} = 29$. Consequently, the splitting process for the first half-interval of interval 9 terminates at this point. By repeating this splitting process for other intervals, the splitting of the original key set can be observed.

The algorithm which follows calculates a hashing function based on the piece-wise linear function with interval splitting. It is assumed that intervals may be split to no less than $(1/2)^{p-1}$ of their initial size. Consequently, if $p = 1$, then the algorithm computes the piece-wise linear function.

**Algorithm** INTERVAL_SPLITTING. Given L, a, m, n, and p as previously defined and arrays N and G whose content is exemplified by Fig. 7-11.1, it is required to calculate an address H in {1, 2, ..., m} from the key x.

1. [Calculate initial interval number]
   $$r \leftarrow i \leftarrow 1 + \lfloor (x - a)/L \rfloor$$
2. [Calculate interval number and array index if interval or subinterval is split]
   Repeat for k = 1, 2, ..., p − 1 while $G_i < 0$
   $$r \leftarrow 1 + \lfloor (x - a)/(L/2^k) \rfloor$$
   $$i \leftarrow -G_i - (r \bmod 2) + 1$$
3. [Calculate address]
   If $G_i \neq 0$
   then    $H \leftarrow \lceil m(G_i + ((x - a)/(L/2^{k-1}) - r)N_i)/n \rfloor$
   else    $H \leftarrow 1$
4. [Finished]
   Exit                                                                   □

In step 2, note that the computed value for r is such that $1 \leq r \leq 2^k j$. This value of r is used in the address calculation of step 3, and is also used to adjust $-G_i$ in step 2. If r is odd, then $-G_i$ is unchanged, but if it is even, then $-G_i$ is incremented by 1. This calculation determines i, the index to the array elements corresponding to the required half-interval. In step 2, note that k is incremented before it is compared with p − 1 and $G_i$ is tested.

An algorithm for constructing the N and G arrays has slow execution time. It requires that the key set be scanned 2p − 1 times.

The major conclusion derivable from two experiments by Deutscher et al is that distribution-dependent functions (in particular, the multiple frequency distribution function) can give very good results when used in conjunction with open addressing. Insertion and deletion activity is possible with the multiple frequency distribution function, but one must be aware of the distribution of keys to which this function is applied.

### 7-11.2 Dynamic Hashing Techniques

One of the principal drawbacks of conventional hashing as a means of organizing external files for fast access is that the size of the hash table must be estimated in advance. Two problems can arise: if the hash table is too small, access speed becomes unacceptably slow as the table fills or overflows, and if the table is too large, unacceptably low storage utilization results (Knott [1971]). Hopgood [1968] suggested that all keys should be rehashed to a new hash table of appropriate size, and provided an algorithm for deciding when this rehashing should take place. In this algorithm the number of times each key will be accessed is first estimated. By considering the average length of search for keys before and after a projected rehashing, the expected decrease in search time which will result from rehashing is determined. The table is completely rehashed if this decrease in search time is greater than the cost of rehashing. Bays [1973] reaffirmed Hopgood's conclusion that rehashing the complete table is the best way of improving the performance of a hash table.

Ways of varying the size of the hash table are considered in this subsection. Of particular interest are a number of *dynamic hashing techniques* which avoid the costly rehashing of the whole file by changing the hashing function rather than moving a large number of records. In the first subsection, the terminology is introduced and some measures that can be applied to a hash table are described. The second subsection describes linear hashing. Virtual hashing is explained in the third subsection. The performance of the methods is considered in the fourth subsection. Four other methods, extendible hashing, dynamic hashing, modified dynamic hashing and spiral hashing, are described in the last subsection.

### 7-11.2.1 Organizing Direct Files with Hashing

This subsection describes the organization of a hash table corresponding to a direct file and the terminology used to describe such a table. In addition, several measurements which can be applied to a hash table are discussed.

To simplify the discussion, assume that the direct file is divided into a *primary area* consisting of a set of equal-sized *primary buckets* and an *overflow area* consisting of a set of equal-sized *overflow buckets*. Note that the primary buckets are not necessarily the same size as the overflow buckets. The primary buckets are numbered 0, 1, 2, ..., and access to a particular bucket can be gained simply by specifying its number. Overflow buckets are accessed by pointers. Originally all overflow buckets are unused. When an overflow bucket is required, an unused one is allocated in the same manner as a linked list element is allocated.

Consider a direct file containing M buckets, including $M_P$ primary buckets (numbered 0,1,2,..., $M_P-1$) and $M_V$ overflow buckets as shown in Fig. 7-11.2. Note that $M = M_P + M_V$. Each primary bucket can hold up to $B_P$ records, and each overflow bucket can hold up to $B_V$ records. At most $M_P B_P$ records can be held in the primary area of the direct file. Records are identified by a key k. The remainder of this discussion will ignore the non-key fields of the records, and refer to the problem of storing and accessing keys rather than records.

Suppose that a hashing technique is used to organize this direct file. A hashing technique requires a hashing function and a collision-resolution technique. The area of the direct file can be thought of as a hash table containing $M_P$ elements (i.e., the buckets). To determine the location of a key in the file, a hashing function yielding a value in the range 0,1,2,..., $M_P-1$ is required. The result of applying such a hashing function to a key is the number of the primary bucket for that key. This primary bucket can then be sequentially scanned until the key is found. As long as no more than $B_P$ keys are hashed to any location, all keys stored in the table can be retrieved by accessing one bucket. A brief example is presented before turning to a discussion of cases where overflow buckets are necessary.

Consider the following simple hashing function.

**Function** HASH(KEY, TABSIZE). This function uses the division method to obtain a position for key KEY in a hash table of size TABSIZE. The *mod* operator results in the remainder after division of the first argument by the second argument.

1.   [Determine and return position]
        Return (KEY mod TABSIZE)                       □

To determine the position of key 513 in the hash table shown in Fig. 7-11.2, Function HASH is called with KEY = 513 and TABSIZE = $M_P$ = 8. The value 513 mod 8 = 1 is returned, indicating that key 513 should be stored at location 1, either

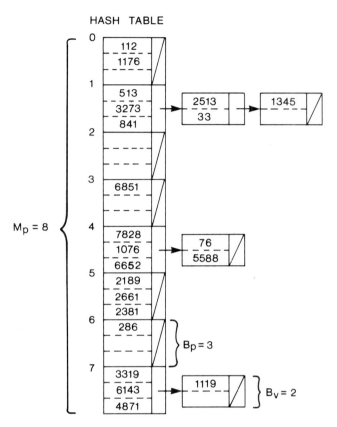

**FIGURE 7-11.2**   Organization of a hash table.

in the primary bucket or an overflow bucket. The locations of the other keys shown in Fig. 7-11.2 can be determined in a similar manner.

*A collision* results when an attempt is made to insert a record at a location with a full primary bucket. A collision resolution method is used to suggest an alternate location for a record which can not be placed in its primary bucket. In Fig. 7-11.2 the bucket chaining collision-resolution method is used. With this method, each primary bucket contains a pointer to a linked list (or chain) of overflow buckets. When more than $B_P$ keys are hashed into a location L, an overflow bucket is allocated and associated with the primary bucket at location L. When more than $B_P + B_V$ keys are hashed to location L, a second overflow bucket is added to the first. Further overflow buckets are added to the end of the linked list as necessary. In the diagram shown in Fig. 7-11.2, the hash table contains 8 primary buckets (i.e., $M_P = 8$); of these, buckets 1, 4, 5, and 7 are full. Additional insertions at locations 1, 4, and 7 have resulted in the creation of overflow buckets at these locations.

In Table 7-11.2, the construction of the hash table shown in Fig. 7-11.2 is traced. The first column gives the keys in order of insertion, the second column gives the location of the primary bucket for each of these keys, and the last column notes the details of the insertion. From Table 7-11.2, one can see that keys 513,

**Table 7-11.2**   Trace of hash table construction.

| Key | Location | Comment |
|-----|----------|---------|
| 7828 | 4 | |
| 513 | 1 | |
| 112 | 0 | |
| 3319 | 7 | |
| 3273 | 1 | |
| 2189 | 5 | |
| 2661 | 5 | |
| 841 | 1 | |
| 2513 | 1 | allocated  first  overflow  bucket , added  there |
| 33 | 1 | added  to  first  overflow  bucket |
| 286 | 6 | |
| 1076 | 4 | |
| 2381 | 5 | |
| 6652 | 4 | |
| 6143 | 7 | |
| 76 | 4 | allocated  first  overflow  bucket , added  there |
| 4871 | 7 | |
| 1119 | 7 | allocated  first  overflow  bucket , added  here |
| 1176 | 0 | |
| 1345 | 1 | allocated  second  overflow  bucket , added  there |
| 5588 | 4 | added  to  first  overflow  bucket |
| 6851 | 3 | |

3273, and 841 are added to primary bucket 1 without complications. When an attempt is made to insert key 2513, primary bucket 1 is full. An overflow bucket is allocated and the pointer at location 1 is set to point to this overflow bucket. Key 2513 is inserted in this overflow bucket. Later, key 33 is also inserted in this overflow bucket. When key 1345 is added, a second overflow bucket is added to the first at location 1. If further keys were added to location 1, more overflow buckets would be added to the end of the linked list of overflow buckets. Note that primary buckets 0, 2, 3, 5, and 6, which have no overflow buckets associated with them, have null pointers.

The number of keys in the primary buckets is denoted by $N_c$, the number in first overflow buckets is denoted by $N_1$, the number in second overflow buckets is denoted by $N_2$, and so on. N denotes the total number of keys inserted; N can be calculated using the following formula:

$$N = \sum_{i=0}^{\infty} N_i$$

In the example, $N_0 = 16$, $N_1 = 5$, $N_2 = 1$, and $N_i = 0$ for all $i \geq 3$. Thus,

$$N = \sum_{i=0}^{\infty} N_i = 16 + 5 + 1 + 0 = 22$$

Three measurements used to assess the effectiveness of hashing strategies are the load factor ($\alpha$), the storage utilization ($\beta$), and the average length of search

(ALOS). The *load factor* ($\alpha$) gives the ratio between the number of keys in the hash table and the space available in the primary buckets. It is calculated as follows:

$$\alpha = \frac{N}{M_P B_P}$$

For the hash table shown in Fig. 7-11.2, $\alpha$ is

$$\alpha = \frac{22}{8(3)} = .9167$$

The *storage utilization* ($\beta$) tells what fraction of the space available for storing keys is currently occupied. It is calculated as follows:

$$\beta = \frac{N}{M_P B_P + M_V B_V}$$

For the hash table shown in Fig. 7-11.2, $\beta$ is

$$\beta = \frac{22}{8(3) + 4(2)} = .6875$$

To assess the performance of hashing strategies, Knuth [1973] relied on $\alpha$, but later researchers, such as Larson [1980], have recognized that $\beta$ provides a better indication of the storage efficiency of a hashing strategy. A value of .6875 for $\beta$ indicates that 68.75% of the memory space allocated for storing records in the direct file actually contains records. Note that this calculation ignores the memory space used for the pointers to the overflow buckets.

The *length of search* (LOS) refers to the number of buckets which must be accessed to retrieve a key. For example, in the hash table shown in Fig. 7-11.2, LOS (2661) = 1 since key 2661 can be found in one access to primary bucket 5. On the other hand, LOS (1345) = 3 because primary bucket 1 and its two overflow buckets must be accessed before the key is found. The LOS provides a good indication of the access time for a key since each bucket access will typically require a separate access to secondary storage. Thus, extra time will be required to access a key stored in an overflow bucket at the end of the linked list.

Assuming that all stored keys are equally likely to be accessed, the *average length of search* (ALOS) is calculated as follows:

$$\text{ALOS} = \sum_{i=0}^{i} \frac{(i+1)^* N_i}{N}$$

For the example table, $N_i = 0$ for $i \geq 3$, and thus the ALOS is calculated as follows:

$$\text{ALOS} = \sum_{i=0}^{2} \frac{(i+1)^* N_i}{N} = \frac{1(16) + 2(5) + 3(1)}{22} = 1.318$$

On the average, 1.318 buckets must be examined to find a record stored in the hashed file shown in Fig. 7-11.2.

This method of computing the ALOS only applies to attempts to retrieve keys that are present in the file. The ALOS for unsuccessful searches (i.e., attempted retrievals of keys not in the file) can also be estimated. For example, only one bucket must be accessed to determine that a key is not in location 1, but 3 buckets must be accessed to determine that one is not stored in location 2. The ALOS for unsuccessful searches depends on the relative frequency of searching the locations.

The reader is referred to Sec. 6-2.4 for a more complete discussion of means of calculating the ALOS.

The ALOS serves as an indicator of the access performance, i e., the amount of time necessary to access a key. As overflow buckets continue to be added, the ALOS will rise and the access performance will deteriorate. The following subsections describe dynamic hashing techniques, which dynamically modify hashing functions to address a hash table that changes in size. Such techniques can be used to overcome the problem of deteriorating access performance.

### 7-11.2.2  Linear Hashing

Linear hashing is described in Litwin [1980]. In linear hashing, the table is gradually expanded by splitting the buckets in order until the table has doubled its size. *Splitting* refers to the rehashing of a bucket b and its overflows in order to distribute the keys in them among b and one other primary location. Overflow buckets may still be required. but if the hashing function selected for the rehashing is well chosen, the ALOS can be significantly reduced. Once the table has been doubled in size, the same method of gradual expansion is applied to the enlarged table, and so on. The original table size is denoted by $M_0$. After d doublings, the size of the table is $2^d M_0$;  therefore $M_p = 2^d M_0$.

Linear hashing requires the use of a series of hashing functions, $H_0$, $H_1$, $H_2$, ... Originally, hashing function $H_0$ is used to produce a number between 0 and $M_0-1$. When the size of the table is doubled, $H_1$ is used to give a number between 0 and $2M_0-1$. In general, $H_d$ is used to give a number between 0 and $2^d M_0 - 1$.  Note that the subscript d associated with H tells how many times the table has been doubled in size, and can be calculated as follows:

$$d = \lceil \log_2 \frac{M_P}{M_0} \rceil$$

These hashing functions can be used to split buckets; i.e., during the first doubling of the table hashing function $H_1$ is used to split the buckets, during the second doubling $H_2$ is used, and so on.

In this book, the Function HASH, given in the preceding subsection, is used instead of a series of hashing functions. HASH(KEY, $M_0$) replaces $H_0$(KEY), HASH(KEY, $2M_0$) replaces $H_1$(KEY). HASH(KEY, $4M_0$) replaces $H_2$(KEY), and so on. In general, $H_d$(KEY) is replaced by HASH(KEY, $2^d M_0$). Function HASH could be replaced by any other function satisfying what will be called the the Litwin condition. A hashing function HASH meets the *Litwin condition* if for any key KEY and any integer d ≥ 0, either

HASH(KEY, $2^{d+1}M_0$) = HASH(KEY, $2^d M_0$)

or

HASH(KEY, $2^{d+1}M_0$) = HASH(KEY, $2^d M_0$) + $2^d M_0$

In other words, the Litwin condition ensures that when the table is doubled in size, the hashing function maps a key to the same location as before or to the corresponding location in the new half of the table, i.e., the location $2^d M_0$ (the number of positions in the undoubled table) positions beyond it in the table. For example, keys mapped to position 157 in a 256-bucket table are mapped to either position 157 or position 157 + 256 = 413 in a 512-bucket table.

Consider the example hash table presented in Fig. 7-11.2. Suppose that the table is doubled in size whenever an insertion at a position with a full primary bucket is to be made and the ALOS for the table is already greater than 1.3. Now consider the insertion of key 3820 into the table. Hashing function $H_0$ suggests placing key 3820 at position 4, which has a full primary bucket.    Since the ALOS = 1.318, which is greater than 1.3, the table is expanded in size before the key is added.    To expand slightly the hash table shown in Fig. 7-11.2, the first bucket is rehashed using function $H_1$, a hashing function which distributes the contents of bucket 0 between buckets 0 and 8. Although bucket 4 has the most items, it is not split first. Buckets are split in sequence, not according to fullness. Figure 7-11.3 illustrates the expansion of the linear hash table. In Fig. 7-11.3a, a hash table after the splitting of bucket 0 is presented. In the diagram, the table's fully doubled size is indicated with ticked lines. The ALOS is unchanged by this slight expansion, so expansion continues until the ALOS is reduced below $ALOS_{MAX}$.    Bucket 1 is split, reducing the ALOS to 1.182, which is below $ALOS_{MAX}$ = 1.3. Then key 3820 is inserted. The hash table which results after this insertion is shown in Fig. 7-11.3b.

Table 7-11.3 gives a trace for the construction of the linear hash table shown in Fig. 7-11.3b. Information about the number of the current doubling (d), the number of the bucket which will be split next (s), the ALOS, the load factor and the storage utilization is indicated after each insertion of a key. Note that before key 3820 is inserted, the doubling of the table has not yet begun, and consequently d = 0. During this time, s remains pointing to bucket 0. When doubling begins, d is set to 1 and s advances to point to the bucket which will be split next.

Linear hashing requires only three pieces of information: $M_0$ (the original size of the hash table), d (the number of the current doubling of the table), and s (the bucket in the table which will be split next).    Consider a hash table of $2^d M_0$ buckets. The table has three parts. Buckets 0, 1, ..., s – 1 are the *split* buckets, buckets s, s + 1, ..., $2^{d-1}M_0$ – 1 are the *unsplit* buckets, and buckets $2^{d-1}M_0$, $2^{d-1}M_0$ + 1, ..., $2^{d-1}M_0$ + s – 1 are the *new* buckets. $H_d$ is used with split and new buckets, and $H_{d-1}$ is used with unsplit buckets. In the example hash table shown in Fig. 7-11.3a, $M_0$ = 8, d = 1 (since the table is being doubled for the first time), and s = 1 (since primary bucket 1 will be split next).    In this hash table, bucket 0 is a split bucket, buckets 1 through 7 are unsplit buckets, and bucket 8 is a new bucket.

We now present Function LFIND, a functional algorithm which finds the location of the primary bucket for a given key in a linear hash table. This algorithm is based on one given in Litwin [1980].


**Function**    LFIND(KEY, s, d, $M_0$).    This subalgorithm determines the location of the primary bucket of key KEY in a linear hash table. The hash table, which originally contained $M_0$ buckets, is currently being doubled for the $d^{th}$ time. The next bucket to be split is bucket s. Function HASH, which was presented earlier, uses the division method to obtain a position in a hash table. Assuming that the key is in an unsplit bucket, BUCKET_LOC gives the location of the key's bucket.


1.  [Unexpanded table]
      If d = 0
      then    Return (HASH (KEY, $2^d M_0$))

2.  [Assume key is in an unsplit bucket]
      BUCKET_LOC ← HASH (KEY, $2^{d-1}M_0$)

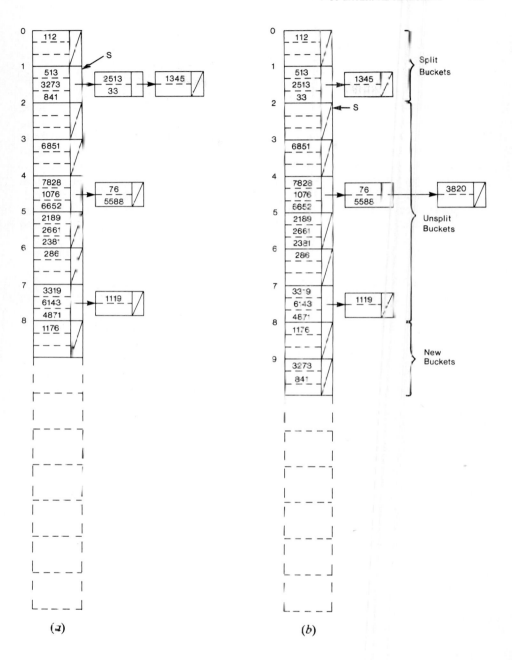

**FIGURE 7-11.3**    Linear hash table (*a*) After splitting bucket 0; (*b*) after inserting key 3320.

3.   [If bucket has been split, determine resulting location]

    If BUCKET_LOC < s

    then   Return (HASH (KEY, $2^dM_0$))

    else   Return (BUCKET_LOC)          ☐

Step 1 determines where KEY would be placed using $H_{d-1}$. If the suggested bucket is a split bucket, $H_d$ must be used to determine the location of the key. Otherwise, the suggested bucket is the bucket being sought. Although a simple hashing function based on the division method is used in this algorithm, any hashing function satisfying the Litwin condition could be used instead.

    As an example, consider using Function LFIND to find key 1076 in the hash table shown in Fig. 7-11.3$b$. KEY = 1076, s = 2, d = 1, and $M_0$ = 8. In step 1, nothing is done because d is not equal to 0. In the next step, BUCKET_LOC is set to HASH(1076, 8) = 4. In step 3, BUCKET_LOC = 4 is not less than s = 1, and consequently 4 is returned. An examination of Fig. 7-11.3$b$ shows that key 1076 is indeed at location 4. As another example, consider finding key 3273 in the same hash table. Again, nothing is done in step 1 because d is not equal to 0. In step 2, BUCKET_LOC is calculated to be HASH(3273, 8) = 1. Since BUCKET_LOC = 1 is less than s = 2, bucket 1 has been split during the current doubling of the hash

**Table 7-11.3**   Trace of the construction of a linear hash table.

| Key | d | NEXT_SPLIT | ALOS | Load Factor | Storage Utilization |
|-----|---|-----------|------|-------------|---------------------|
| 7828 | 0 | 0 | 1.0000 | 0.0417 | 0.0417 |
| 513 | 0 | 0 | 1.0000 | 0.0833 | 0.0833 |
| 112 | 0 | 0 | 1.0000 | 0.1250 | 0.1250 |
| 3319 | 0 | 0 | 1.0000 | 0.1667 | 0.1667 |
| 3273 | 0 | 0 | 1.0000 | 0.2083 | 0.2083 |
| 2189 | 0 | 0 | 1.0000 | 0.2500 | 0.2500 |
| 2661 | 0 | 0 | 1.0000 | 0.2917 | 0.2917 |
| 841 | 0 | 0 | 1.0000 | 0.3333 | 0.3333 |
| 2513 | 0 | 0 | 1.1111 | 0.3750 | 0.3462 |
| 33 | 0 | 0 | 1.2000 | 0.4167 | 0.3846 |
| 286 | 0 | 0 | 1.1818 | 0.4583 | 0.4231 |
| 1076 | 0 | 0 | 1.1667 | 0.5000 | 0.4615 |
| 2381 | 0 | 0 | 1.1538 | 0.5417 | 0.5000 |
| 6652 | 0 | 0 | 1.1429 | 0.5833 | 0.5385 |
| 6143 | 0 | 0 | 1.1333 | 0.6250 | 0.5769 |
| 76 | 0 | 0 | 1.1875 | 0.6667 | 0.5714 |
| 4871 | 0 | 0 | 1.1765 | 0.7083 | 0.6071 |
| 1119 | 0 | 0 | 1.2222 | 0.7500 | 0.6000 |
| 1176 | 0 | 0 | 1.2105 | 0.7917 | 0.6333 |
| 1345 | 0 | 0 | 1.3000 | 0.8333 | 0.6250 |
| 5588 | 0 | 0 | 1.3333 | 0.8750 | 0.6563 |
| 685 | 0 | 0 | 1.3182 | 0.9167 | 0.6875 |
| 3820 | 1 | 2 | 1.2609 | 0.7667 | 0.6053 |

table's size. The value returned is therefore HASH(3273, 16) = 9. Checking Fig. 7-11.3b shows that key 3272 is at location 9.

The next subalgorithm inserts a given key in a linear hash table.

**Function**   LINSERT(KEY, s, d, $M_0$).   This subalgorithm inserts key KEY in a linear hash table. The hash table, which originally contained $M_0$ buckets, is currently being doubled for the $d^{th}$ time. The next bucket to be split is bucket s; note that s is passed by reference. The function returns *true* if the key is successfully inserted and *false* if it is not. BUCKET_LOC is the location of the key's primary bucket. ALOS gives the current average length of search and $ALOS_{MAX}$ is the maximum value ALOS is allowed to attain. FULL_BUCKET is a function which determines whether a bucket is full. The ADD_KEY procedure adds one key to a partially empty primary bucket. The ADD_OVERFLOW function adds one key to the overflow chain associated with a full bucket; if it fails to obtain the necessary space, it returns *false*. The DOUBLE_TABLE function allocates $2^d M_0$ new buckets; it returns *false* if insufficient space is available. The REHASH_BUCKET procedure splits a given bucket by rehashing it with function $H_d$ (where d is the second argument of the procedure). Four of the subprograms, ADD_KEY, ADD_OVERFLOW, DOUBLE_TABLE, and REHASH_BUCKET, update ALOS as necessary.

1.   [Determine location for key in current table]
      BUCKET_LOC ← LFIND (KEY, s, d, $M_0$).
2.   [Simple insertion]
      If not FULL_BUCKET (BUCKET_LOC)
      then   Call ADD_KEY (KEY, BUCKET_LOC)
            Return (*true*)
3.   [Expand table in a linear manner]
      Repeat thru step 5 while ALOS > $ALOS_{MAX}$
4.   [If necessary, double table]
      If d = 0 or s = $2^{d-1} M_0$
      then   d ← d + 1
            If not DOUBLE_TABLE ( )
            then   Return (*false*)
            s ← 0
5.   [Rehash next bucket]
      Call REHASH_BUCKET (s, d)
      s ← s + 1
6.   [Redetermine key's location in expanded table]
      BUCKET_LOC ← LFIND (KEY, s, d, $M_0$).
7.   [Add key to primary or overflow bucket]
      If not FULL_BUCKET (BUCKET_LOC)
      then   Call ADD_KEY (KEY, BUCKET_LOC)
      else   Return (ADD_OVERFLOW (KEY, BUCKET_LOC))
8.   [Finished]
      Return (*true*)   □

In step 1, Function LFIND is used to find the location at which the key would be inserted in the current table. In the second step, Function FULL_BUCKET decides whether or not an insertion at this location results in a collision. If no collision occurs, a simple insertion is made. Otherwise, buckets are split as necessary in the loop controlled by step 3. If all buckets are now being accessed using $H_d$ (i.e, $s = 2^{d-1}$, the first bucket produced by splitting bucket 0 using $H_{d-1}$), splitting of buckets begins again at bucket 0. To start the next doubling, d is incremented, the table is physically doubled in size, and the s pointer is reset to primary bucket 0. Buckets are split until a sufficiently low ALOS is achieved. In step 6, the location at which the key is to be inserted is recomputed using Function LFIND. Finally, in step 7, the key is inserted in either its primary bucket or an overflow bucket, depending on the fullness of the primary bucket.

Consider the insertion of key 3820 into the hash table presented in Fig. 7-11.2. Since the doubling of the table has not yet begun, $d = 0$. Suppose that $ALOS_{MAX} = 1.3$.   When Function LFIND is called in step 1, it computes BUCKET_LOC as 4 (i.e., HASH(3820, 0) = 4) and returns this result. In step 2 of LINSERT, a collision is detected. The while loop is entered in step 3, because ALOS = 1.318 is greater than $ALOS_{MAX} = 1.3$.   Since d is 0, d is incremented to 1, and the table is physically doubled in size. Bucket 0 is split (which moves key 1176 to bucket 8), and s is incremented to 1. The resulting hash table has already been displayed in Fig. 7-11.3a. Since the ALOS is unchanged, the loop is repeated. This time, d is not equal to 0 and $s = 1$ is not equal to $2^{d-1}M_0 = 2^0 * 8 = 8$. The rest of step 4 is ignored. In step 5, Procedure REHASH_BUCKET is called to split bucket 1. Keys 3273 and 841 are moved to primary bucket 9, s is incremented to 2, and control returns to step 3. On this occasion, the ALOS is 1.182, and the loop is exited. In step 6, the desired location of key 3820 is recomputed, and again is bucket 4. Since bucket 4 is full (in spite of the splitting), key 3820 is inserted in an overflow bucket.

As another example, suppose that the insertion of 3820 did not occur until the table was being doubled for the third time, as shown in Fig. 7-11.4. Suppose that s = 14. In step 1 of Function LINSERT, Function LFIND is called with KEY = 3820 and d = 3. In step 1 of Function LFIND, BUCKET_LOC is set to HASH(3820, 2) = 12. Since BUCKET_LOC = 12 is less than s = 14, bucket 12 has already been split using $H_3$.   When the location of the key is recomputed using $H_3$,   the value HASH(3820, 3) = 44 is returned to Function LINSERT. Suppose that when the FULL_BUCKET function is called in step 2 of Function LINSERT, bucket 44 is found to be not full. Then procedure ADD_KEY is called to add key 3820 to bucket 44, and the algorithm is exited.

Larson [1980a], [1980b], and [1980c] proposed a variation of linear hashing called *linear hashing with partial expansions*. Hashing strategies work best when keys are distributed as evenly as possible among the primary buckets. Larson observed that linear hashing departs from this distribution since the number of keys in a

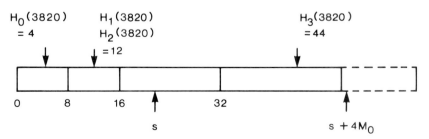

**FIGURE 7-11.4**   Expanded linear hash table.

bucket which has been split is approximately half that in a bucket which has not been split. On the basis of this observation, Larson suggested a method of improving performance by creating a more uniform density in the hash table. In linear hashing with partial expansions, the hash table is doubled by means of a series of partial expansions. For example, if a table is expanded by two partial expansions, it is first increased to 3/2 times its original size, and then to twice its size. Likewise, if three partial expansions are used, the table is expanded first to 4/3 its original size, then to 5/3 its original size, and finally to twice its original size. In general, to expand a table using p partial expansions (where $p \in I$ and $p > 1$), the ratio of the table's size to its original size successively becomes $\dfrac{p+1}{p}$, $\dfrac{p+2}{p}$, $\dfrac{p+p}{p} = 2$.

Consider in more detail the doubling of a hash table by means of 2 partial expansions, as shown in Fig. 7-11.5. Assume that the hash table originally contains an even number of buckets. The number of buckets in the original hash table is $M_0$ or $2M_H$, where $M_H$ gives the number of buckets in half the table. The first partial expansion begins with the creation of bucket $2M_H$ and the movement of some keys from buckets 0 and $M_H$ to it (see Fig. 7-11.5a) Then bucket $2M_H+1$ is created and some keys from buckets 1 and $M_H + 1$ are moved to it (see Fig. 7-11.5b). This process continues until bucket $3M_H-1$ is created and partly filled with keys from buckets $M_H-1$ and $2M_H-1$ (see Fig. 7-11.5c). At this point, the table is 1.5 times its ori-

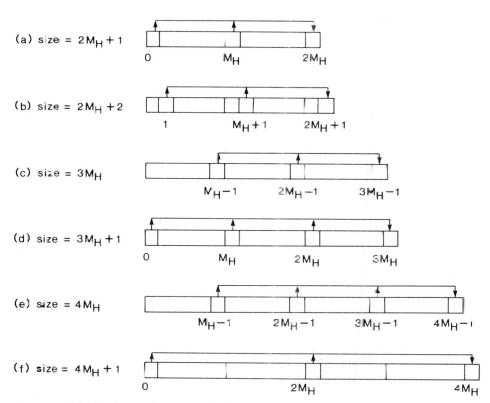

**FIGURE 7-11.5**   Linear hashing with partial expansions.

ginal size. The second partial expansion starts with the creation of bucket $3M_H$ and the movement of keys from buckets 0, $M_H$, and $2M_H$ to it (see Fig. 7-11.5d). Expansions using keys from three buckets continue until keys from buckets $M_H-1$, $2M_H-1$, and $3M_H-1$ are placed in newly created bucket $4M_H-1$ (see Fig. 7-11.5e). At this time, the table contains $4M_H$ buckets and has been doubled in size. To expand the table further, a new set of partial expansions is performed. First a partial expansion from size $4M_H$ buckets to size $6M_H$ buckets is made; this expansion begins by placing keys from buckets 0 and $2M_H$ in newly created bucket $4M_H$ (see Fig. 7-11.5f). Then another partial expansion from size $6M_H$ to size $8M_H$ buckets is performed, completing the doubling of the table. In general, the $d^{th}$ doubling of the table is performed from size $2^dM_H$ buckets, first to size $1.5 * 2^dM_H$ buckets, and then to size $2^{d+1}M_H$ buckets.

A method of choosing which keys to move is necessary to linear hashing with partial expansions. When two partial expansions are used, a method of choosing keys from two buckets is required during the first partial expansion, and a method of choosing keys from three buckets is required during the second expansion. The function used to select from three buckets should do so without requiring that any keys be moved around among these three buckets. Larson [1980a] proposed a method called the rejections technique for choosing which keys to move. This method requires a series of functions that hash keys uniformly and independently. In particular, Larson suggested that a series of pseudo-random functions would be suitable. The interested reader is referred to Larson's article for a more complete discussion of the rejections technique and its application to linear hashing.

Partial expansions are a useful addition to linear hashing. Although the use of partial expansions complicates the algorithms, the average value for ALOS during table doublings can be reduced through their use. Partial expansions require additional calculations, but such calculations are probably worthwhile for accessing hash tables stored in secondary storage. Partial expansions also increase the complexity of making insertions. Since partial expansions never cause a higher value for ALOS during searches than does ordinary linear hashing, their use is particularly recommended for tables on which many more searches than insertions are made.

### 7-11.2.3  Virtual Hashing

Litwin [1978a] proposed a new type of hashing called virtual hashing, and Litwin [1978b] presented performance measurements for the method. Litwin suggested that the term *virtual hashing* refer to any hashing function which dynamically adapts to changes in the table being accessed. In this book, the term is restricted to the VH1 Algorithm described by Litwin [1978a] and [1978b]. This subsection provides a high-level description, an example, and a formal description of virtual hashing. Then the effectiveness of the strategy is evaluated.

When virtual hashing is used, the size of the table is doubled whenever the table becomes too full. A new hashing function is used with those buckets in the original table that overflow. This new hashing function maps some of the records of an overflowing bucket to the corresponding bucket in the new half of the table. A bit table is used to indicate with which positions the new hashing function is employed.

Virtual hashing requires the use of a series of hashing functions, $H_0$, $H_1$, $H_2$, ... These hashing functions must meet the Litwin condition. Originally, hashing function $H_0$ is used to produce a number between 0 and $M_0 - 1$ where $M_0$ is the starting table size. When the size of the table is doubled, $H_1$ is used to give a number between 0 and $2M_0 - 1$. In general, $H_d$ is used to give a number between 0 and $2^d * M_0 - 1$. Note that the subscript associated with H tells how many times the table has been doubled in size, and can be calculated as follows:

$$d = \lceil \log_2 \frac{M_P}{M_0} \rceil$$

A separate vector of $2M_0$ bit flags, called the IN_USE table, tells which positions in the second half of the table are in use. As the hash table is increased in size, the IN_USE table grows proportionally. Litwin [1978a] assumes that no table will ever shrink smaller than its starting size. If this assumption is made, the IN_USE table can be $M_0$ bits smaller since the first $M_0$ bits will always remain set to *true*. To avoid complicating the algorithms, this assumption is not made in this book. For example, consider a table of starting size 8 which has been doubled 5 times and now has a size of 256. Since the first 8 positions are always in use, only 248 bits are required in the IN_USE vector. If no bits are associated with the first 8 locations, special checks must be inserted in all routines accessing the IN_USE vector to differentiate between the positions corresponding to the original table and those corresponding to all other positions. It is unlikely that the saving of a few bits offsets the cost of making these checks.

Consider the example hash table presented in Fig. 7-11.6. Suppose that the table is doubled in size whenever an insertion at a position with a full primary bucket is to be made and the ALOS for the table is already greater than 1.3. Now consider the insertion of key 3820 into the table. The resulting hash table is shown in Fig. 7-11.7. Hashing function $H_0$ suggests placing key 3820 at position 4, which has a full primary bucket. Since the ALOS = 1.318, which is greater than 1.3, the table is doubled in size, i.e., $M_P$ is changed from 8 to 16. At the same time, the IN_USE table is doubled in size and bits 8 through 15 of this table are set to 0. Function $H_1$ yields results from 0 to 15 (since $2 * M_0 - 1 = 2(8) - 1 = 15$), and thus can be used to select positions anywhere within the expanded table.

As mentioned, $H_0$ hashes key 3820 to position 4. Rather than adding key 3820 as an overflow, all entries at position 4 are rehashed using $H_1$. When Function $H_1$ is used to split bucket 4, keys 6652 and 76 are moved to bucket 12. Since position 12 is now in use, IN_USE[12] is set to 1. Using $H_1$, the suggested location for 3820 is position 12. Finally, key 3820 is inserted in position 12, producing the table which was presented in Fig. 7-11.7.

The reader should note that the keys in position 1 are not rehashed using $H_1$. When $H_0$ suggests position 1 for another insertion, a collision will be detected, and all keys at position 1 will be immediately rehashed using $H_1$.

To find a key, its position according to the hashing function associated with the current table size (in this case, $H_1$) is used. If the bit on this position is *false*, then the hashing function with a subscript one smaller than the current one's (in this case, $H_0$) is tried. This continues until some hashing function results in a position for which the bit in the IN_USE table is *true*. (If $H_0$ is reached, the search must stop because the first $M_0$ bits remain set to *true*.) The position where the bit is set is the location of the desired key or, if a collision has occurred, the location at which to begin to search for the desired key.

A subalgorithm for finding the primary bucket for a given key in a virtual hash table follows. (The function is loosely based on Algorithm VH1 given in Litwin [1978a].)

IN_USE          HASH TABLE

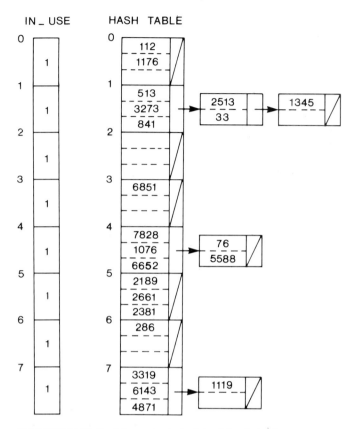

**FIGURE 7-11.6**   Unexpanded virtual hash table.

**Function**   VFIND(KEY, d, $M_0$).   This function determines the location of the primary bucket for key KEY in a virtual hash table.  d indicates how many times the table has been doubled in size, and $M_0$ gives the number of buckets in the original table.  BUCKET_LOC is the bucket location currently being considered as the primary bucket for KEY.

1.   [Assume function $H_d$ was used]
        $n \leftarrow d$
2.   [Determine location using this function]
        BUCKET_LOC $\leftarrow$ HASH(KEY, $2^n * M_0$)
3.   [Try functions $H_d, H_{d-1}, ...$, until correct function is found]
        Repeat while not IN_USE[BUCKET_LOC]
            $n \leftarrow n - 1$
            BUCKET_LOC $\leftarrow$ HASH(KEY, $2^n * M_0$)
4.   [Return location of KEY]
        Return(BUCKET_LOC)                                              □

The parameter d tells how many times the original table has been doubled in size. In the algorithm, $H_n(KEY)$  is computed using HASH(KEY, $2^n * M_0$).   A simple HASH function (introduced earlier) based on the division method is assumed.

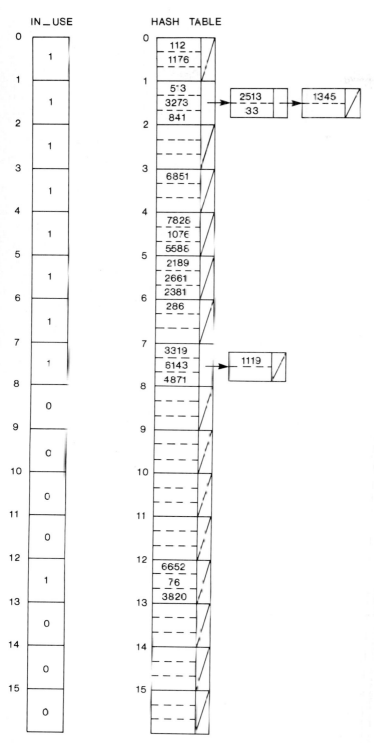

**FIGURE 7-11.7**   Expanded virtual hash table.

To locate the primary bucket for key 2189 in the hash table shown in Fig. 7-11.7, Function VFIND is called with KEY = 2189, d = 1, and $M_0$ = 8. In step 1, n is set to 1 and BUCKET_LOC is set HASH(2189, $2^1 * 8$) = 2189 mod 16 = 13. Since IN_USE[13] is *false*, the loop in step 3 is entered. Then d is set to 0, and BUCKET_LOC is recomputed as HASH(2189, $2^0 * 8$) = 2189 mod 8 = 5. Since IN_USE[5] is *true*, the algorithm proceeds to step 4 where position 5 is returned. An examination of Fig. 7-11.7 shows that key 2189 does indeed have bucket 5 as its primary bucket.

Before an insertion algorithm for virtual hashing can be formulated, the criterion for doubling the size of the table must be chosen. The table is doubled in size whenever splitting a bucket requires a larger table than that currently in use. Thus, if a bucket being accessed by $H_d$ requires splitting, the table is doubled in size and d is increased by 1. Two criteria which can be used for deciding when a bucket should be split are the average length of search (ALOS) and the load factor $\alpha$.

When a collision occurs, the possibility of splitting the bucket is considered. Suppose that the decision whether to split the bucket or to add the key to the current bucket's overflow chain depends on the current ALOS. If the current ALOS is less than or equal to some maximum allowable ALOS, denoted by $ALOS_{MAX}$, the collision is resolved using bucket chaining. Bucket chaining is used even if the addition of one more key to an overflow bucket increases the ALOS past $ALOS_{MAX}$. On the other hand, if the current ALOS is greater than $ALOS_{MAX}$, the table is doubled in size and the bucket is split. This split is performed regardless of whether or not space remains in an existing overflow bucket of this primary bucket.

The following algorithm formalizes the preceding discussion of insertion using the ALOS splitting criterion.

**Function** VINSERT(KEY, d, $M_0$). This function attempts to insert key KEY in a hash table and then returns *true* or *false* depending on the successfulness of this attempt. The hash table is organized according to a virtual hashing strategy and collisions are resolved using a bucket chaining method. IN_USE, $M_0$, d, n, and HASH are as previously described. BUCKET_LOC is the bucket location currently being considered for the key's location. ALOS gives the current average length of search and $ALOS_{MAX}$ is the maximum value ALOS is allowed to attain. FULL_BUCKET is a function which determines whether a bucket is full. The ADD_KEY procedure adds one key to a partially empty primary bucket. The ADD_OVERFLOW function adds one key to the overflow chain associated with a full bucket; if it fails to obtain the necessary space, it returns *false*. The DOUBLE_TABLE function allocates $2^d * M_0$ new buckets; it returns *false* if insufficient space is available. The REHASH_BUCKET procedure splits a given bucket by rehashing it with function $H_d$ (where d is the second argument of the procedure). Four of the subprograms, ADD_KEY, ADD_OVERFLOW, DOUBLE_TABLE, and REHASH_BUCKET, update the ALOS as necessary.

1. [Find the primary bucket for the key]
   n ← d
   BUCKET_LOC ← HASH(KEY, $2^n * M_0$)
   Repeat while not IN_USE[BUCKET_LOC]
       n ← n − 1
       BUCKET_LOC ← HASH(KEY, $2^n * M_0$)

2.  [Attempt to locate a partially empty bucket]
    Repeat while FULL_BUCKET(BUCKET_LOC)
        If n = d   (presently using a hashing function which covers table)
        then   If ALOS ≤ $\text{ALOS}_{MAX}$
            then   (access speed is not sufficiently slow
                   to justify doubling table's size)
                   Return(ADD_OVERFLOW(KEY, BUCKET_LOC))
            else   (double table size)
                   If not DOUBLE_TABLE()
                   then   Return(*fail*)
                   else   d ← d + 1
        IN_USE[BUCKET_LOC + $2^n * M_0$] ← *true*
        n ← n + 1
        Call REHASH_BUCKET(BUCKET_LOC, n)
        BUCKET_LOC ← HASH(KEY, $2^n * M_0$)
3.  [Add key to partially empty bucket]
    Call ADD_KEY(KEY, BUCKET_LOC)
4.  [Finished]
    Return(*true*)                                                        ☐

Step 1 finds the primary bucket associated with the key in the same manner as Function VFIND does. If this primary bucket is not full, the algorithm proceeds to step 3 where the key is added to this bucket. If, on the other hand, a collision occurs (i.e., the bucket is full), another bucket is sought. If the hashing function associated with this bucket maps to the complete table, then depending on the ALOS, the key is either added to the bucket's overflow chain (and the function is exited) or the table is doubled in size. The remainder of step 2 splits the current bucket, and then the step is repeated. Eventually, either splitting a bucket results in a partially empty bucket or the key is added to an overflow chain.

Previously, the insertion of key 3820 into the hash table shown in Fig. 7-11.5, was described in general terms. Now consider how Function VINSERT would operate with KEY = 3820, d = 0, and $M_0$ = 8. Suppose that $\text{ALOS}_{MAX}$ = 1.3. In step 1, n is set to 0, and BUCKET_LOC is computed as HASH(3820, $2^0 * 8$) = 3820 mod 8 = 4. Since IN_USE[4] is *true*, the loop in step 1 is not entered. Primary bucket 4 is full, and therefore the loop in step 2 is entered. Since n = d = 0 and ALOS = 1.318 is greater than $\text{ALOS}_{MAX}$ = 1.3, Function DOUBLE_TABLE is called to double the table's size and c is incremented to 1. Next, IN_USE[4 + $2^0 * 8$] = IN_USE[12] is set to *true* and n is incremented to 1. Procedure REHASH_BUCKET is called to split bucket 4. This procedure moves keys 6652 and 76 to bucket 12. Key 5588 is moved from the overflow bucket to primary bucket 4 and the overflow bucket is deleted from the hash table. The location of key 3820 is recalculated in the newly expanded table as HASH(3820, $2^1 * 8$) = 3820 mod 16 = 12. Control returns to the top of the loop in step 2. Since bucket 12 is not full, the algorithm continues on to step 3. In step 3, key 3820 is added to partially empty bucket 12. Finally, in step 4, the function returns the value *true*.

So far, only the ALOS has been considered as a splitting criterion. Litwin [1978a] suggested this splitting criterion. This criterion prevents a degradation in access performance below $\text{ALOS}_{MAX}$. However, to calculate the ALOS it is necessary to maintain independent totals for the number of keys in primary buckets, in first overflow buckets, in second overflow buckets, and so on. These totals must be adjusted during insertions and rehashings. Also, if more than a bucketful of keys are all repeatedly rehashed to the same bucket, the table may be doubled several times, resulting in an extremely low storage utilization.

Litwin [1978b] suggested that the load factor, $\alpha$, be used instead of the ALOS. Although $\alpha$ does not provide direct control over the number of accesses required, it does prevent the ALOS from rising to too high a value in all but a few, pathological cases. $\alpha$ is much more easily calculated than the ALOS since only N, $M_P$, and $B_P$ need be available (and only N changes in value). Function VINSERT could be modified to incorporate $\alpha$ split control by changing the condition If ALOS $\leq$ $ALOS_{MAX}$ to If $\alpha \leq \alpha_{MAX}$ where $\alpha_{MAX}$ is the maximum acceptable load factor.

The storage utilization, $\beta$, does not provide a good splitting criterion. $\beta$ is less sensitive to poor access performance than $\alpha$: as overflow chains lengthen, $\beta$ does not increase as quickly as $\alpha$.

Both the ALOS and $\alpha$ are good splitting criteria. If minimizing the number of buckets accessed is of paramount importance, the ALOS should be used, but if space efficiency is a factor, $\alpha$ may be a better choice. A combination of the two criteria provides a compromise solution: the table is doubled only if the ALOS is greater than $ALOS_{MAX}$ and $\alpha$ is greater than $\alpha_{MAX}$.

Another criterion results from considering the possibility of doubling the table size for insertions other than those resulting in collisions. For example, if the $\alpha$ split criterion is used, an insertion which does not result in a collision may cause $\alpha$ to exceed $\alpha_{MAX}$. Function VINSERT could be modified to compare $\alpha$ and $\alpha_{MAX}$ on all insertions rather than only on those which result in collisions. This modification would probably result in poorer access performance. Keys which can be inserted without a collision have a LOS of 1. Thus, access performance could not be improved by the modification. Such insertions increase $\alpha$, but a high value for $\alpha$ is avoided only as an indirect means of controlling access performance; an increasing $\alpha$ during insertions with no collisions signifies more efficient use of storage, rather than declining access performance. The modification would cause buckets to be split when they contained fewer keys than ordinary, but the philosophy of virtual hashing is to split buckets only as necessary to maintain good access performance. Therefore, only during collisions should the table be doubled in size or buckets split.

The performance of virtual hashing has not been reported extensively in the literature. Litwin [1978a] estimated the effectiveness of his algorithm but provided no experimental results. He stated that with $M_S = 7$, $B_P = 20$, and $ALOS_{MAX} = 1.15$, a 7200-byte buffer for the IN_USE table would allow 1,032,132 keys to be added to the hash table. While the hash table is being expanded to $2^{13} = 8192$ times its original size, the load factor remains in the range $.45 \leq \alpha \leq .90$.

Litwin did not describe in detail the manner in which the size of the hash table is reduced when virtual hashing is used. Both the ALOS and the load factor were suggested as criteria for table expansion, but of these two, only the load factor provides a suitable indicator for table contraction. The ALOS is not a good criterion for halving the table because no value for the ALOS is so low as to be unsatisfactory. Instead, the load factor is chosen as the halving criterion. If $\alpha$ falls below some minimum, such as $\alpha_{MIN}$, all keys in buckets in the upper half of the table are added to the corresponding buckets in the lower half of the table. At the same time, all bits in the top half of the IN_USE table are set to *false*. To prevent repeated doubling and halving of the hash table, $\alpha_{MIN}$ should be less than or equal to $0.5\alpha_{MAX}$ since doubling the size of the table halves the load factor. Also, $\alpha_{MIN}$ should be sufficiently less than $0.5\alpha_{MAX}$ to prevent one or two deletions from causing the halving of a newly doubled table.

There are a number of limitations to virtual hashing. If the splitting criteria are poorly chosen, the table may be unnecessarily expanded to a large size. For example, if all collisions are resolved by table doubling, the insertion of a single key can cause the table to expand to 8 or 16 (or more) times its previous size. The IN_USE bit table expands at the same rate as the hash table, but must be kept in core no matter how large it becomes to prevent a deterioration of access performance. In previous studies of hashing, researchers have found that the best choices for the number of buckets in a hash table are prime numbers (Buchholz [1963]), with integers with no factors smaller than 20 as second choices (Lum et al. [1971]). Since large virtual hash tables are obtained by repeatedly doubling the size of much smaller tables, the number of buckets in them is almost certainly a multiple of 2, 4, and 8. The division method and several other hashing methods perform poorly on tables whose size is a multiple of these numbers.

Virtual hashing allows the size of the hash table to change without requiring the rehashing of the complete table. Virtual hashing preserves a low ALOS by choosing only buckets which are overflowing for splitting. The next subsection gives performance of dynamic hashing techniques.

### 7-11.2.4 Experimental Results with Dynamic Hashing Techniques

This subsection gives a brief description of the performance of two dynamic hashing techniques, linear and virtual hashing. Litwin was the first to describe the performance of the two methods (Litwin [1978b] and Litwin [1980]). Both methods are capable of achieving very good access performance with uniformly distributed key sets, especially when large bucket sizes are used. Virtual hashing with $M_0 = 7$, $B_P = 5$, and $ALOS_{MAX} = 1.15$ results in a load factor in the range 0.45 to 0.90 (Litwin [1978a]). Using the $\alpha$ splitting criterion with $M_0 = 7$, $B_P = 5$, and $\alpha_{MAX} = 0.90$, virtual hashing causes the ALOS to range from 1.00 to 1.30 (Litwin [1978b]). Access performance is improved by using a larger bucket size; when $B_P$ is changed from 5 to 50 in the simulation just described, ALOSs in the range 1.00 to 1.19 result. For these settings, linear hashing causes the ALOS to range from 1.00 to 1.60. However, if $\alpha_{MAX}$ is reduced to 0.75, linear hashing gives ALOS in the range 1.00 to 1.13 (Litwin [1980]). In Litwin's experiments with virtual and linear hashing, the hash table is expanded to over 8000 times its original size without access performance deterioration.

To better compare the performance of the two methods, a series of simulations were conducted at the University of Saskatchewan (Hamilton [1983]). These experiments employed both uniformly and non-uniformly distributed key sets. From the results of these experiments, the following conclusions are drawn. For a given setting of $ALOS_{MAX}$, virtual hashing gives better access performance than linear hashing, but is much less storage efficient. In cases where similar access performance is observed, virtual hashing is less storage efficient than linear hashing. Storage utilization is lower when key sets do not have linear distributions. Overall, linear hashing gives much more predictable and constant behavior than virtual hashing. For example, when the ALOS splitting criterion is used with linear hashing, the ALOS remains close to the value of $ALOS_{MAX}$ but when it is used with virtual hashing, the ALOS varies in the range 1 to $ALOS_{MAX}$. A virtual hash table containing a given number of keys is as large or larger than a linear hash table containing the same number of keys. By considering the nature of linear and virtual hashing, one can see that in expanding hash tables to the same size, virtual hashing splits fewer primary buckets than linear hashing. Virtual hashing only splits overflowing buckets. Linear hashing, on the other hand, splits all primary buckets in order regardless of their fullness. The number of primary buckets split during the insertion of a given number of keys is affected by the size of the hash table required and the number of primary buckets that must be split to produce a hash table of that size. As a consequence, either virtual or linear hashing may split more primary buckets during the insertion of a given number of keys. In fact, linear hashing requires fewer splits when the key set has a uniform distribution, but virtual hashing requires fewer splits when it has a non-uniform distribution. When the number of both primary and overflow buckets is considered, virtual hashing splits fewer total buckets. Although each of the methods has strong points, linear hashing's amenability to control gives it a significant advantage over virtual hashing. As well, linear hashing does not require the IN_USE bit table that virtual hashing needs.

### 7-11.2.5  Other Dynamic Hashing Techniques

This subsection gives a brief description of four other dynamic hashing techniques.

### EXTENDIBLE HASHING

Fagin *et al.* [1979] proposed *extendible hashing,* which combines radix search trees or tries (Fredkin [1960]) and hashing. The method is similar to dynamic hashing but employs an alternate organization for the index table. To represent the index, an extendible trie structure is used instead of a binary tree (see Figs. 7-11.8, 7-11.9, and 7-11.10). The index table contains $2^d$ positions, where d is the number of leftmost bits currently being used to address the index table. The leftmost d bits of a key, when interpreted as a number, give the position in the index table of the pointer to the bucket containing the key.

Originally, the table contains only one position, which holds a pointer to the single bucket in use. When this bucket fills, the table is doubled in size, a new bucket is created, and keys are appropriately rearranged. This expansion is illustrated in Fig. 7-11.8; dotted lines indicate the new portion of the index table and the new data bucket. When one of these buckets (say bucket 0) fills, the index table is again doubled in size (see Fig. 7-11.9). The keys from the overflowing bucket are redistributed among it and a new bucket (in this case, bucket 2). One of the new pointers in the index table is set to point to the new bucket, and the other to the bucket which did not overflow, i.e., bucket 1 in Fig. 7-11.9. Note that there are now two pointers to the bucket which did not overflow. As additional keys are added, the index table is doubled in size whenever a distinction based on more bits of the keys is required to avert a bucket overflow. Suppose bucket 1 is the next bucket to be split. In this case, no expansion of the table is required. Now suppose bucket 0 again requires splitting: another doubling of the size of the index table is necessary. Splitting in succession buckets 1 and 0 of the hash table of Fig. 7-11.9 yields the hash table depicted in Fig. 7-11.10.

Since key sets often do not have a uniform distribution, Fagin *et al.* suggest that a hashing function be applied to the keys, and the resulting pseudo-keys be used to determine a position in the index table and subsequent placement in a bucket. A serious drawback to this scheme is that the index table soon grows to be too large to fit in main memory. When part or all of the index table is stored on secondary storage, extra accesses are required to consult this table.

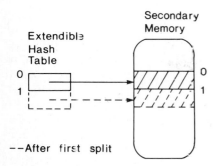

**FIGURE 7-11.8**   Extendible hash table.

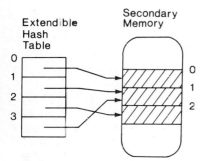

**FIGURE 7-11.9**   Extended version of hash table.

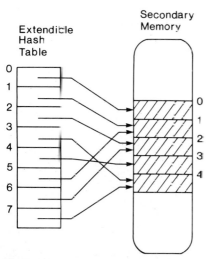

**FIGURE 7-11.10**   Further extended hash table.

## DYNAMIC HASHING

Larson [1978a] described *dynamic hashing,* which uses prefix binary trees (i.e., prefix trees with b = 2) to resolve collisions (see Fig. 7-11.11). A hash table is used as an index to data buckets kept in secondary storage. Originally, all positions of this table contain pointers to data buckets. In Fig. 7-11.11, positions 0, 2, and 3 have remained in this original state. When a data bucket overflows, it is split into two data buckets. At the same time, the index table is updated. The original pointer to the data bucket is replaced by a pointer to a prefix binary tree, originally containing two nodes. For example, position 1 of the hash table in Fig. 7-11.11 originally pointed to data bucket 1. When data bucket 1 overflowed, part of its contents were moved to data bucket 6. A prefix binary tree was created at position 1 of the hash table. The leaves of this tree contain pointers to data buckets 1 and 6. Pointers to the two data buckets are stored in these two nodes of the prefix binary tree. When one of these data buckets overflows, it is split into two buckets, and the prefix binary tree is expanded to point to both of these buckets. The tree at position 4 of the hash table in Fig. 7-11.11 shows the result of such a split.

With dynamic hashing, data buckets are split on the basis of the binary representations of the keys stored in them. For the first split, the first bit of the binary representation is examined: if it is a 0, the key is left where it is, and if it is a 1, the key is moved to the new bucket. When either of the two buckets is split, the second bits of the keys are examined, and so on for subsequent splits. For example, note that the binary representation of all keys in data bucket 5 of Fig. 7-11.11 must begin with '10', whereas all those in bucket 7 must begin with '11'. Note that those in bucket 4 may begin with either '00' or '01'. A hashing function could be applied to key sets with non-uniform distributions and the resulting values used instead of the binary representations of the keys during splitting. In particular, Larson mentions that a pseudo-random function yielding 0 or 1 with equal probability could be initialized (i.e, *seeded)* with a key value and used to produce a bit series. Whether or not the key was moved at the $i^{th}$ split would be determined by the $i^{th}$ value of this bit series.

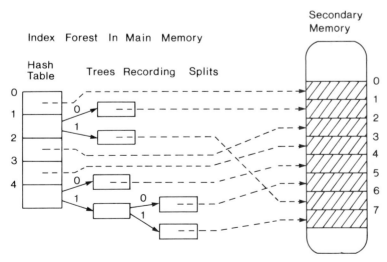

**FIGURE 7-11.11**    Dynamic hash table.

As long as the index table is kept in main memory, all keys can be found in one access to secondary memory. Unfortunately, for large hash tables or smaller ones which have been greatly expanded, the index table is indeed too large to be kept in main memory and extra accesses to secondary storage are required.

## MODIFIED DYNAMIC HASHING

Scholl [1981] presented two schemes based on Larson's dynamic hashing: dynamic hashing with deferred splitting and dynamic hashing with linear splitting. Only the first scheme will be discussed here. Dynamic hashing with deferred splitting is a simple variation of dynamic hashing designed to increase storage utilization and decrease directory size. In ordinary dynamic hashing, each leaf node points to one bucket, but in dynamic hashing with deferred splitting, each leaf node points to a chain of buckets (see Fig. 7-11.12). Instead of splitting a bucket as soon as it becomes full, overflows are permitted until $\gamma b$ keys (where $\gamma > 1$ and $b$ is the bucket size) have been stored in the chain of buckets. In Fig. 7-11.12 $\gamma$ is set to 2. This approach decreases the index size by a factor of approximately $\gamma$. The storage utilization using this approach is increased, although Scholl does not estimate the size of this increase either experimentally or analytically. The advantages of reduced index size and increased storage utilization are offset by an increase in the ALOS from 1 to $\gamma$. But by decreasing the index size, dynamic hashing with deferred splitting permits a larger hash table to be addressed while still storing its index in main memory.

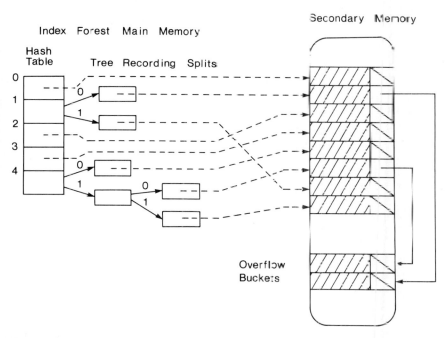

**FIGURE 7-11.12**   Dynamic hashing with deferred splitting.

## SPIRAL HASHING

Martin [1979] proposed spiral hashing, another hashing technique suitable for hash tables which vary in size. The name *spiral hashing* is derived from considering memory space to be organized in a spiral rather than in a line. In Fig. 7-11.13a, the conceptual view of memory as an exponential spiral is shown. Fig. 7-11.13b relates this conceptual view to the ordinary view of memory as a linear space.

The hash table is considered to lie along one revolution of the spiral; in Fig. 7-11.13, the hash table occupies locations $c_3$ through $c_4$. To expand the table, keys from the inner portion of the table are rehashed to positions outside the current table. For example, the hash table shown in Fig. 7-11.13 could be expanded slightly by rehashing all keys stored between positions $c_3$ and $d_3$ to positions between $c_4$ and $d_4$. After this rehashing, the table would occupy positions $d_3$ through $d_4$. Expanding the table by rehashing the inner end of the spiral works particularly well if the innermost locations have the most dense concentration of keys. The table can be contracted in an analogous manner by rehashing keys at the outer end to inner positions.

In an exponential spiral, each successive revolution is proportionally as large when compared to the previous revolution, as that revolution was when compared to the revolution previous to it. This proportion is called the *growth factor, g.* A spiral hash table occupies one revolution outward from its starting point. To obtain a starting point, an arbitrary number of revolutions, s, is chosen and the starting location is specified as $\lfloor g^s \rfloor$. All keys are assumed to be real numbers in the range [0, 1). The primary location for each key k is specified by the following formula:

$$\lfloor g^{\lceil s-k \rceil + k} \rfloor$$

where g, s, k $\in$ R, g > 1, and k $\in$ [0, 1). To expand the hash table, s is increased in value, and to contract it, s is decreased.

Ordinarily, a spiral hash table consists of two parts, each in key order. The inner part is located at the end of one revolution of the spiral, and the outer part at the beginning of the next revolution. The inner part contains keys which have not been rehashed during the current expansion, and the outer part contains keys which have been rehashed. Note that immediately after a revolution has been completely rehashed, all keys are located in a single spiral. No directory is required with spiral hashing: only the value of s is altered as the hash table changes size. To perform an insertion of a key k, the key's primary bucket location $\lfloor g^{\lceil s-k \rceil + k} \rfloor$ is first determined. If this bucket is not full, the key is inserted in it. If, on the other hand, the bucket is full, either an overflow bucket is added or the table is expanded, depending on the expansion criterion being used. To expand the table, s' is chosen such that s' > s. Then all keys k in the range (s − $\lfloor s \rfloor$, s' − $\lfloor s' \rfloor$] are rehashed using $\lfloor g^{\lceil s'-k \rceil + k} \rfloor$. During an expansion, s can be increased either by a constant amount or by the amount necessary to rehash a single bucket or an integral number of buckets.

Spiral hashing causes the hash table to move through memory. This movement is inconvenient because storage must be continually allocated at one end of the table and freed at the other end. Martin [1979] suggested that the locations generated by spiral hashing be treated as locations within a large virtual space. Locations in the virtual space can then be mapped to a smaller *constant-origin* address space. The lower boundary of a constant-origin address space is fixed and the other boundary varies with the current size of the hash table.

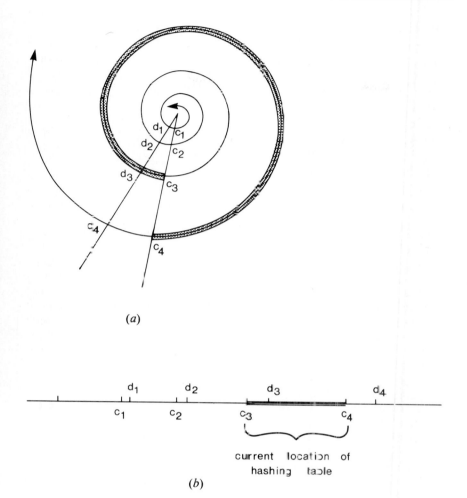

(a)

(b)

**FIGURE 7-11.13**   A spiral view of a hashing table. (a) Spiral view; (b) linear view.

When spiral hashing locations are mapped to a constant-origin address space, storage is reused whenever possible. When the location at the inner end of the spiral is no longer needed for the hash table, it is reused instead of being freed. Only when a new location is required, and no location can be freed, is new storage allocated. During rehashing, the same constant-origin bucket is used for the virtual bucket being rehashed and the new virtual bucket being created to hold a portion of its contents. Thus, constant-origin mapping also reduces the number of keys that must be moved from a bucket during rehashing.

Although ordinary spiral hashing keeps keys in order (in each of the two parts of the tables), constant-origin mapping destroys this ordering. In spite of this, the buckets can be accessed in order by determining the order in which the virtual buckets should be accessed and then accessing the corresponding constant-origin buckets in the same order. This method accesses each bucket only once.

## Exercises for Sec. 7-11

1. Construct a table with 6 columns (key, location, d, s, ALOS, and comment) tracing the insertion of the keys listed below into a linear hash table originally containing 5 primary buckets. Use a primary bucket size of 2 and an overflow bucket size of 1. Use the ALOS bucket-splitting criterion with $ALOS_{MAX}$ set to 1.35. Draw two diagrams resembling that shown in Fig. 7-11.3b displaying the hash table immediately after the insertion of key 2661 and of key 33. Calculate the load factor, storage utilization, and ALOS for the final hash table. Show your calculations.

    112  1176  513  3273  841  6851  7828  1076  6652  2189

    2661  2381  286  3319  6143  4871  2513  33

2. In Function LINSERT buckets are split as long as the ALOS is greater than specified maximum $ALOS_{MAX}$. Modify Function LINSERT to use a bucket splitting criterion based on the load factor $\alpha$ instead of on the ALOS. Now modify it to use a criterion based on the storage utilization.

3. As mentioned in Sec. 7-11.2, the hash table's physical size is sometimes completely doubled as soon as the doubling process begins. The number of requests to the operating system is greatly reduced by requesting memory space only once for each doubling rather than each time a new primary bucket is required. Specify formulas for computing $M_0$ with each of the two approaches. You may use the variable s in your formulas. Notice that $M_0$ is required in the formula for computing the load factor ($\alpha$) given in Sec. 7-11.2.1. Compute $\alpha$ for the hash table shown in Fig. 7-11.3 using each of the methods of calculating $M_P$. Which approach would be most appropriate for very large tables? Small tables? Explain why.

4. Bucket chaining, a collision resolution technique based on separate chaining, was used in Sec. 7-11.2.2. Describe the problems which would result if open addressing were used instead of bucket chaining.

5. Repeat Prob. 1 for virtual hashing, replacing the column for s with one for size of hash table.

6. Repeat Prob. 2 for virtual hashing.

7. Implement functions LFIND and LINSERT in a programming language of your choice. To simplify your program, leave out all parts of the records but the keys. Create two sets of keys, one with a uniform distribution and the other with a non-uniform distribution. Compare the performance of linear hashing on these two key sets, making particular reference to the ALOS, the load factor, the storage utilization, the number of primary buckets rehashed, and the total number of buckets rehashed.

8. Repeat Prob. 7 for virtual hashing. Compare your results with those you obtained in Prob. 7. Are your conclusions in agreement with those presented in Sec. 7-11.2.4?

9. Formulate Functions EXFIND and EXINSERT for performing extendible hashing. Use Functions LFIND and LINSERT as your models.

10. Formulate Functions DFIND and DINSERT for performing dynamic hashing. Indicate how Scholl's modification could be incorporated into your functions.

11. Formulate Functions SFIND and SINSERT for performing spiral hashing.

12. Methods for allowing hash tables to grow have been studied extensively in this subsection. Sometimes many deletions may result in the hash table being too

large. Describe how the size of a hash table could be decreased when each of the following techniques are used:

(a) linear hashing
(b) virtual hashing
(c) extendible hashing
(d) dynamic hashing
(e) spiral hashing.

## 7-12 OTHER METHODS OF FILE ORGANIZATION

An important concept that is affecting the way data (and programs) are organized in many computer systems is virtual memory. We begin this section by describing what virtual memory is, by examining a number of schemes for implementing a virtual memory system, and by discussing the effects such systems have and will have on the development of file systems. Our investigation of virtual memory is by no means detailed, and the interested reader who is knowledgeable in operating systems is invited to delve into some of the references that are provided.

The second part of this subsection introduces a type of file organization, VSAM, that is designed to co-exist with a virtual memory system. It encompasses all three of the organizations described thus far in the chapter.

### 7-12.1 Virtual Memory

In the introduction to this chapter two reasons were given for storing information in files on an external medium. The first reason was to provide for the inexpensive storage of large amounts of data—amounts so large that the data could not fit into main memory at one time. The second reason related to the archival property of some data. For certain applications, it is desirable or necessary to store information from one execution of a program to the next (e.g., a payroll application). The information should be stored on a readily accessible medium (e.g., tape or disk) but not in main memory, which is a critical system resource shared by other programs on a continuous basis.

If main memory becomes extremely inexpensive, say .00001 cents per byte, and if billions and even trillions of bytes were directly addressable, then files, as they have been discussed thus far, would not be required. The data structures presented in Chaps. 1 through 5 would be sufficient to handle most programming problems.

While as yet main memory technology is not advanced to the degree just described, efforts have been made to extend main memory in a logical sense. One type of system which provides this logical extension is called a *virtual memory system*. A virtual memory system performs a dynamic mapping from a virtual address space. In a virtual memory system, all currently active programs and data are allocated space (i.e., assigned virtual addresses) in virtual memory. The programs and data may not (in fact, usually do not) reside in main memory, but instead are located on fast auxiliary storage devices such as drums or fixed-head disks. When a program is executing and referencing data, all virtual addresses are translated automatically by the operating system into real main-memory addresses. If a program is called upon for execution and currently is not residing in main memory, then this fact will be detected during the virtual-to-real memory address translation. Automatically (i.e., without user initiation or knowledge), the program or a section of it which is scheduled for execution is brought into main memory so that execution on that program can continue. With this form of automatic address translation, we are able to enlarge our main memory to an effective size which is equivalent to that of a gigabyte virtual address space.

Before discussing how virtual memory systems help to solve some of the problems related to file processing, let us examine briefly three types of virtual memory systems—paging systems, segmentation systems, and segmented paging systems.

### Paging systems

*Paging* is a memory-management technique in which the virtual address space is split into fixed-length blocks called *pages.* Main memory space is divided into physical sections of equal-size subsections called *page frames.* A page frame and a page are the same size. The transformation from a virtual address to a main (or real) address involves the mapping of a page to a page frame.

A virtual address in a paging system is made up of two components $p$ and $d$, where $p$ designates a page and $d$ denotes the displacement within page $p$. The translation of this two-component address to a main memory address generally requires a page table and a paging algorithm.

A *page table* is associated with each user job (i.e., set of user programs and data). Each entry in the page table contains:

*1* A presence bit (a flag indicating whether the page is in the main memory)
*2* The location of the page (in main or in auxiliary storage)
*3* Protection bits that are used to check the type of access that is allowed for the page

To examine a particular example illustrating how paging is performed, let us refer to Fig. 7-12.1a. In this example, we assume a page size of 1,000 bytes (in most paging machines, page sizes are between 1,000 and 4,000 bytes in length), a rather small virtual memory address space of 2,000,000 bytes, and a main memory of 50,000 bytes. An address such as 0630 can be expressed as a two-level address 0, 630, where the first number is the page number and the second number is a displacement from the beginning of the page. For convenience, we have placed the programs and data for a sample job in the first six pages of virtual memory.

When an address such as 4444 (or 4,444) is encountered during execution, the page table for that job is entered. The entry corresponding to page number $p$ in the page table contains a pointer to the desired page which may or may not reside in main memory. Page 4 is located in main memory and may be found in page frame 3. By moving $d$ locations down the page, the desired memory location can be reached. Therefore, the instruction LOAD 2110 is found 444 locations from the beginning of page 4 (i.e., page frame 3).

The execution of the machine-level instruction "LOAD 2110" requires that the data stored at the virtual address 2110 be loaded into a central processing unit register. When a virtual-to-real memory address translation is initiated, it is discovered in the page table that page 2 does not reside in main memory currently. In order to continue executing the job, it is necessary that page 2 be brought in from external storage and placed in a page frame of main memory.

A *paging algorithm* (or page replacement strategy) is required to decide which of the pages that currently reside in main memory must be replaced by page 2. A variety of page replacement strategies have been analyzed and used in paging systems, and these are described in a number of advanced-level operating systems texts such as Madnick and Donovan [1974], Shaw [1974], and Tsichritzis and Bernstein [1974]. A detailed discussion of this topic is outside the scope of this text.

During the time period in which the selected page is removed and placed in auxiliary memory and then the required page is fetched from auxiliary memory, execution can begin on another user's job. At some later point in time, after the required page is brought into main memory, the job can commence execution with the instruction "LOAD 2110".

Some important advantages from a data-management point of view are gained by using a paging system. First, data is brought into main memory without any explicit user program specifications such as read instructions. The notions of a file and a system directory containing file names can be discarded. Secondly, since a complete page of information is brought into memory at one time, subsequent access of data on the same page may be achieved without having to read in or write out individual records. This is only possible if the page is not pulled from memory before such accesses take place. This property is particularly beneficial when data accesses are highly localized, as is the case for sequential processing. These first two advantages apply to all virtual memory systems discussed in this section.

In a paging system, all pages are of equal size, and therefore, a memory management problem does not exist. Any given page can be replaced by any other page. It should also be noted that in most paging systems, virtual-to-real address translation is performed by a special hardware unit. Therefore, the accessing of a data item which is in a page that is not in main memory can still be handled fairly efficiently.

A major disadvantage with paging is the internal fragmentation that develops because the programs and data are placed in fixed-sized blocks (i.e., pages). The concepts of fragmentation are discussed in Sec. 5-6. Since the program and data for two different jobs are not allowed to reside in a common page, a large proportion of some pages may not be used.

Let us examine an alternative memory-management scheme which eliminates the problem of internal fragmentation.

### Segmentation systems

Programs and their associated data are generally composed of a number of logical units such as procedures, program blocks, and data areas. *Segmentation* is a scheme in which the addressing structure of a program is based upon logical program divisions. In segmentation, each program's virtual memory address space is divided into variable-sized blocks, called *segments,* each of which contains one of these logical program divisions. To access a word within a user's address space, we again use a two-part address as we did with paging. An address $s$, $d$, specifies the location of a segment $s$ and the displacement $d$ within the segment.

The translation of a virtual memory address to a real address is a logically identical process for paging and segmentation. A segment table, as opposed to a page table, contains the actual address (i.e., the main memory or auxiliary memory address) for the beginning of a particular user segment. Each user job has its own segment table like the one illustrated in Fig. 7-12.2. To access a particular location such as "<DATA1>, 52" of the instruction "LOAD <DATA1>, 52", it is necessary first to locate the element in the segmentation table associated with "<DATA1>". (A discussion of how this is accomplished automatically is outside the scope of the text.) If the segment "<DATA1>" resides in main memory, which can be determined by the presence bit, then access can be achieved directly. If the segment is

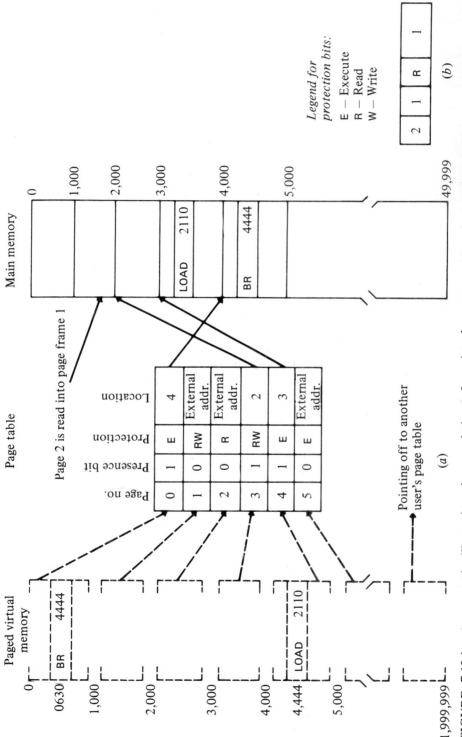

**FIGURE 7-12.1**    An example illustrating the translation of a virtual memory address in a paging system.

not in main memory, however, the external address is used to fetch the segment. The placement of the segment in main memory presents a problem, as did the placement of a page in a paging system. If there does not exist a contiguous unused area in main memory which can contain the segment, then a *segmentation replacement policy* must be called upon to remove a segment and place the required segment in the vacated area.

There are a number of possible segmentation replacement strategies that can be adopted, just as there are a wide variety of paging replacement schemes. It should be observed, however, that a segment replacement strategy is confronted with a memory-management problem which does not exist in paging systems. Because segments are variable-length blocks, *external fragmentation* arises. That is, a segment $A$ may replace another segment, say $B$, in which the space occupied by $B$ is slightly larger than the space required by $A$. A small unused section of main memory is created. After this type of replacement has happened thousands of times, memory becomes so fragmented with small sections as to become unusable. Therefore, a segmentation replacement strategy must be chosen so as to reduce this type of fragmentation. Some of the memory management strategies such as first-fit, best-fit, and the buddy system (these were described in Sec. 5-6) have been tried as segmentation replacement policies.

Regardless of which replacement rule is adopted, external fragmentation grows as more jobs are executed. The free space fragments which are generated must, on occasion, be collected and compacted into one contiguous area. Some of the garbage-collection techniques discussed in Sec. 5-6 can be used for the compaction process.

Many of the advantages of segmentation are advantages of any virtual memory system—in particular, the first two advantages listed for paging systems. Because segmentation divides virtual memory into logical units, the notion of a file can still assume some meaning. It is possible to associate a name with a particular data area just as it is possible to associate a name with a file in some systems. The programmer can find this aspect, which is not available on paging systems, particularly appealing. In addition, there are other advantages to segmentation, such as ease of linking procedures and ease of sharing and protecting programs and data, which we will not discuss.

While the problem of internal fragmentation is overcome by using segmentation, the new and potentially more disturbing problem of external fragmentation arises. In an effort to minimize the effects of external fragmentation and yet adopt some of the virtues of segmentation, many virtual memory systems have been developed which are hybrids of the two approaches.

### Segmented paging systems

In unifying the two approaches, a virtual memory address has three components $s$, $p$, and $d$, where $s$ is a segment name (or address into a segment table), $p$ is an index into the page table for segment $s$, and $d$ is the displacement within a page designated by the index $p$. Virtual memory space is now divided into a number of variable-length segments which are composed of smaller fixed-length pages.

Figure 7-12.3 illustrates the tables necessary to perform a virtual-to-real memory address translation for a segmented paging system. An address such as "<DATA1>, 3, 98" is translated into a real address by first finding the segment-table element corresponding to <DATA1>. The page table for this segment is then located. The element in the page table designates a page frame if the page resides in

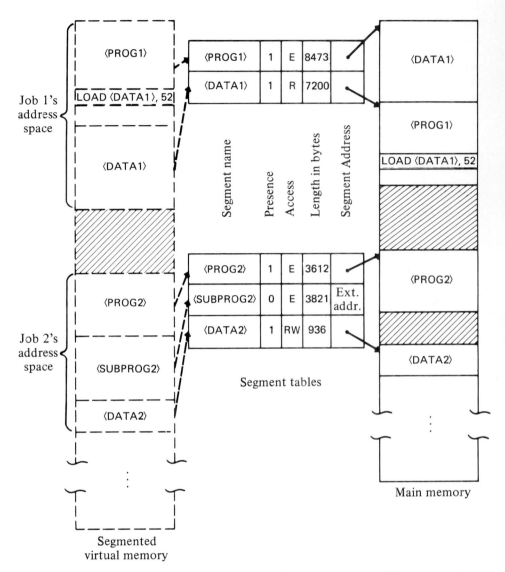

**FIGURE 7-12.2** Address translation in a virtual memory system with segmentation.

main memory. For our example address, a displacement of 98 is used to locate the desired word.

If, during the translation, the segment <DATA1> is not marked as present in main memory, then all pages for this segment are fetched. Once a segment is brought in, its pages may be replaced on a demand basis. That is, if certain pages of the segment are seldom or never referenced, they may be pulled out of memory and replaced by more active pages from another segment. Therefore, during the translation process, it is possible that a page from a currently active segment may have to be retrieved because it was replaced due to its previous inactivity.

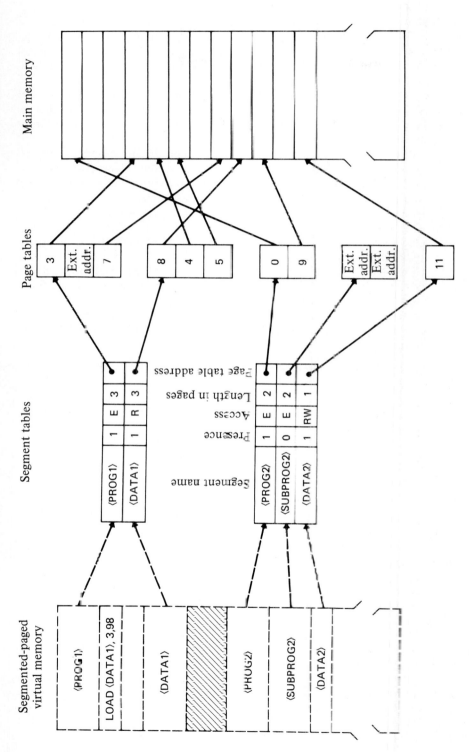

**FIGURE 7-12.3**    Address translation in a virtual memory system with segmented paging.

Segmented paging systems attempt to provide most of the advantages of paging and segmentation systems. External fragmentation is not present, since the basic unit of information handled by the system is the page. Data sharing, program linking, and protection are enhanced because the concept of a segment persists. Internal fragmentation is still present, and this can only be reduced by reducing the size of a page.

There are two disadvantages, namely, increased hardware costs and processor overhead which are incurred because of the three-level address translation that is necessary. In addition, more main memory is required to store the additional address translation tables (i.e., both segment and page tables).

Before describing the ramifications of virtual memory on file structures and file systems, it is important to point out that a number of commercially available systems provide virtual memory capability. Paging was first used on the Atlas computer (Fotheringham [1961]) and later was adopted in the XDS 940 system. Segmentation was implemented in the Burrough's B5000 series of computer (MacKenzie [1965]). The IBM/370 and the Honeywell 6180 (Bensoussan [1969]) systems used a segmented paging form of virtual memory management. Most current-day multiuser systems employ some form of virtual memory system.

It is clear that virtual memory systems will be present for some time in the future. Their effect on the management of data cannot be ignored. Currently, there are two schools of thought concerning the relationship between file-management systems and virtual memory systems. One is to integrate the file system and the segmentation and paging facilities, as exemplified in MULTICS (Madnick [1974]). This can easily be accomplished if the following similarities are recognized:

1    The notions of a file and a segment are similar notions both involving the logical organization of information.

2    Both files and segments require a two-dimensional form of addressing—a file name and a record address, and a segment name and word address, respectively.

3    Both files and segments may be variable in size—they grow and shrink dynamically.

4    Memory buffers can be considered to be functionally similar to page frames.

A main disadvantage of this approach is that a request for one record from a data segment (i.e., file) results in the fetching of a whole segment. This can lead to a tremendous amount of overhead when processing only a few records from each file for a large number of files. In addition, even if the entire segment is fetched, there is no guarantee that certain pages in the segment may not have to be re-retrieved later because of a certain pattern of record references.

The second school of thought suggests that the similarities between files and segments should be ignored and that separate mechanisms should be established for each. The OS/VS operating system follows this philosophy, and a discussion of the file mechanism provided by the system will be described in the next subsection. One of the advantages of this approach is that a file is an entity somewhat removed from the direct memory management of the system and, therefore, can be easily copied on a transportable device (i.e., a removable disk or tape) and used on another system. Of course, the disadvantage with this approach is that the user must be familiar with a special data-holding entity, a file, which must be explicitly referenced and treated in a manner different than the other data-holding entities in a program.

If the file system is incorporated within the virtual memory system, the two reasons for the existence of a file, as cited at the beginning of this subsection, disappear. If the two entities are separated, a file system is required only for archival and transportability purposes.

### 7-12.2 VSAM Files

In 1972, IBM announced a new access method called VSAM (Virtual Storage Access Method) for its series of 370 virtual storage machines. A discussion of a file organization for VSAM is important because of the capabilities of this access method provides. VSAM was designed to replace all the access methods (sequential, indexed sequential, and direct access methods) that IBM previously supported. In particular, we will see that the keyed access facility provided by VSAM is a significant departure from IBM's ISAM and resembles quite closely the indexed sequential facilities available in CDC's SCOPE monitor discussed in Sec. 7-7.1. The reader is invited to reexamine the section of the text dealing with CDC's indexed sequential organization before continuing to read this subsection.

In this subsection, we begin by describing the possible file structures of a VSAM file. The types of processing that are associated with VSAM are then considered.

Two types of file structures exist for a VSAM file—namely, a *key-sequenced structure* and *entry-sequenced structure*. In a key-sequenced file, records are loaded in an ordered sequence defined by the collating sequence of the content of the key field in each record. Direct access to a record can be gained via the unique value in the key field. In an entry-sequenced file, records are loaded according to the order in which they are entered into the file. A record's position is independent of its contents. Direct access to a record is gained via a relative byte address (RBA) from the beginning of the file. Let us first discuss the concepts relevant to a key-sequenced VSAM file, and later determine how these notions relate to an entry-sequenced VSAM file.

A key-sequenced VSAM file is composed of continuous fixed-length areas of direct-access external storage called *control intervals*. A control interval is the unit of information that is transferred between virtual and auxiliary storage by the VSAM access facilities. The size of a control interval may vary from one file to another; however, for a given file the size of each control interval is fixed. The size may be chosen by the user or by VSAM, which attempts to select an optimal size for the type of direct-access storage device used.

Records in a control interval may be either fixed or variable in length—VSAM treats them identically. Control information describing the data records is placed at the end of the control interval. A *stored record* is the combination of a data record and its control information, even though they are not physically adjacent. Stored records may not span across control-interval boundaries, and when a file is defined, enough buffer space must be allocated to accommodate the largest stored record.

Parts of a control interval may be unused as is illustrated in Fig. 7-12.4. Later in this subsection, we describe how records can be added or deleted so as to keep this area contiguous. In general, free space can be initially distributed throughout a key-sequenced file in two ways—by leaving space at the end of all the used control intervals and by leaving some control intervals empty.

A data record is addressed by its displacement (in bytes) from the beginning of the file (i.e., its relative byte address). VSAM considers the control intervals to be

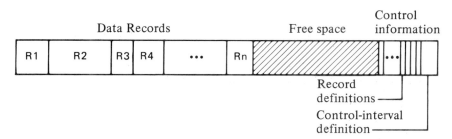

**FIGURE 7-12.4**   The relative placement of data, free space, and control information in a control interval.

contiguous and treats a file as though it is stored in virtual storage beginning at address 0.

A set of control intervals can be logically grouped together to form a *control area*. This relationship is shown in Fig. 7-12.5. Relating these concepts to ISAM, it is best to think of a control interval as a logical track, and a control area as a logical cylinder. A set of indices is created for each control area and a particular set contains relative byte address pointers to the control intervals forming the control area. The indices for a control area form a *sequence-set element* and the sets of indices for all control areas in the file is called the *sequence set*.

Indices at higher levels can be constructed also. Each index is contained in a record, and the set of all such index records is called the *index set*. At the highest level of indices, only one index is allowed. An entry in an index-set record consists of the highest key that an index record in the next lower level contains, together with a pointer to the lower-level index record. For a sequence-set record, an entry consists of the highest key in a control interval and a pointer to that control interval.

In order to increase the number of entries in an index record, VSAM uses a technique called *key compression* in which it eliminates from the front and back of a key those characters that are not necessary to distinguish it from adjacent keys. Because the size of keys in index entries is reduced by compression, either a smaller index or an index with more entries is achievable.

Key-sequenced VSAM files can be processed in three ways—namely, *sequential, skip sequential,* and *direct.* In the sequential processing of a key-sequenced file, records are accessed in an order determined by the sequence of keys in the file. When the file is opened for sequential processing, the access facilities secure the RBA of the first record in the file and sequential processing continues from this address. Alternatively, a specific key or a generic key may be supplied with the first I/O statement which is executed. Sequential processing can then begin at the record with the given key or the first of the records having the generic key.

Skip-sequential processing involves the accessing in order of a subset of the records in a file. Assume we are given an ordered set of keys which forms a subset of the keys for the records in the file. When processing a next record based on the ordered set of keys, the horizontal links in the sequence set are used to locate the appropriate element from the sequence set records. The addressing information in this element is used to isolate the control interval for the desired data record. This control interval is brought into virtual memory, and the requested record is processed.

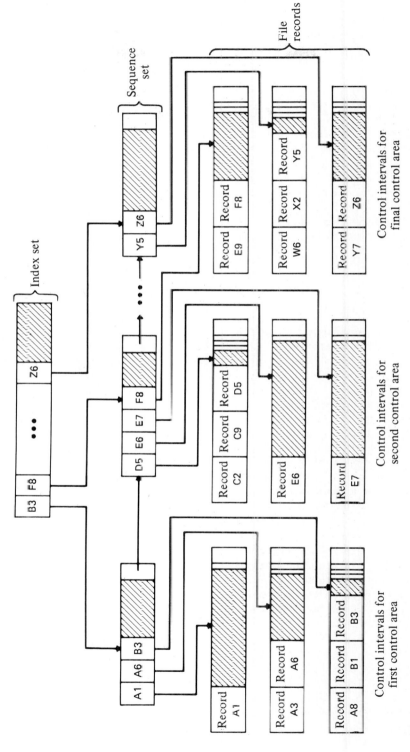

**FIGURE 7-12.5**   The structure of a VSAM file.

As an example illustrating skip-sequential processing, let us examine the file as depicted in Fig. 7-12.5. Suppose the records we are interested in accessing are identified by the ordered set of keys {A3, E7, N6, Q3, Y5}. Processing begins by directly accessing the record identified by the key A3 (i.e., by searching through the index set and the sequence set to isolate the second control interval in the first control area). The next record to be accessed has the key E7. Instead of directly accessing the record by following the vertical pointers from the highest level of index down to the sequence set, we can proceed along the horizontal pointers at the sequence-set level. Therefore, in the example, we can move to the second sequence-set element, and thereby eventually find the record with key E7 without tracing through the higher index levels. Of course, the requirement that the set of search keys be ordered is crucial to the success of this method of access.

Direct access to a record in a key-sequenced VSAM file is gained by traversing the tree of index records down to the sequence set. The appropriate control interval is then retrieved and the desired record is accessed in virtual memory. VSAM supports a very general and powerful form of record retrieval. A key can be used to specify the retrieval of

1    A particular record (i.e., the key is an exact key)

2    A record with the next largest key (i.e., the key is an approximate key)

3    A record which is the first record to satisfy a generic key (i.e., the key is a generic key)

The most interesting features of VSAM are related to the management of data records when deletion, addition, and update operations are performed. When records are deleted from a key-sequenced file, the amount of space occupied by the record is recovered and added to the free-space section of a control interval. This recovery of available space is accomplished by moving data records in the control interval to ensure that the data-record sections and free-space section each remain contiguous areas. Figure 7-12.6 illustrates the effect of removing the record with a key of A8 from the third control interval of the file shown in Fig. 7-12.5. Note that if record B3 is removed from this interval, the third entry in the first sequence-set record and the first entry in the index-set record must be altered to indicate that B1 is now the largest index in that particular control interval and control area, respectively.

When a record is added to a key-sequenced file, VSAM may move some of the existing records over to keep the records within a control interval physically in key sequence. For example, suppose a record with key A9 is added to the third control interval in Fig. 7-12.5. The result of this insertion is shown in Fig. 7-12.7. The records B1 and B3 are moved, displacing some of the free-space area.

An obvious question arises: What if there is not enough room in a control interval to accommodate the insertion of a new record? VSAM handles this situation by performing a *control-interval split* which is almost identical to a data-block split in a CDC Scope indexed sequential file. In a control-interval split, stored records in

| Record B1 | Record B3 | |
|---|---|---|

**FIGURE 7-12.6**   The third control interval after removing record A8.

| Record A8 | Record A9 | Record B1 | Record B3 | |
|---|---|---|---|---|

**FIGURE 7-12.7**   The third control interval after the addition of record A9.

the control interval are moved to an empty control interval in the same control area, and the new record is inserted in its proper key sequence. Just how the interval is split depends on the type of processing that is taking place. For a sequential insertion, the new record is placed in the original control interval, if possible, and all subsequent records are placed in the new control interval. Such a control-interval split is illustrated in Fig. 7-12.8a for the insertion of a small record with key B2 in the control interval shown in Fig. 7-12.7. If the new record is too large to be placed in the original control interval, it and all remaining records in the original control interval are placed in the new control interval. Figure 7-12.8b depicts such an insertion involving a large record with key B2. When VSAM detects that two or more records are to be inserted in sequence a technique called *mass sequential insertion* is used to save I/O operations by buffering the records being inserted.

For direct insertion, approximately one-half of the records in a control interval are moved when a control-interval split occurs.

If there is not a free control interval in a control area when performing a control-interval split, a *control-area split* results. In such an operation, a new control area is established by making use of the space already allocated, or by extending the file if the initially allocated file space is full. Approximately half of the control intervals are moved from the full control area to an equal-sized new control area. The new record is placed in one of the control areas as dictated by the key value. Control-area splitting should be performed very infrequently, as it results in a major and expensive file reorganization

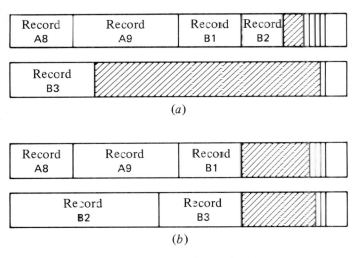

(a)

(b)

**FIGURE 7-12.8** A control-interval split involving the insertion of (a) a small record B2 and (b) a large record B2.

The process of updating a record with a new record that is different in length precipitates the same type of file reorganization as a deletion or insertion. If the new record is shorter than the old record, then the extra space is returned to the free-space area in a similar manner as that used in returning space from a deleted record. If the new record is larger than the old record, then the extra space required is accommodated in the same manner as that adopted when acquiring space for the insertion of a record. Hence, control-interval splits and control-area splits can result from the expansion of an updated record. By now it should be evident that the file-processing facilities required to support key-sequenced VSAM files must be extremely sophisticated.

Now let us examine entry-sequenced VSAM files. The most noticeable difference between a key-sequenced and an entry-sequenced file is that no index is associated with the latter type of VSAM file. When a record is added sequentially to an entry-sequenced file, VSAM returns its RBA (Relative Byte Address). Using these RBAs, it is possible for us to create our own index or index set to aid in fast direct access.

If we wish to create and access the file directly, then we should preformat the file with blank records. For a data record to be stored, it is necessary to transform the key item of the record to an RBA and retrieve the preformatted record at that RBA. If the record location as determined by the RBA is empty, the new record is stored at that location. If the record location already contains a data record, then a user-written collision-resolution procedure must be invoked which determines an alternate RBA for the record.

It can be concluded that entry-sequenced VSAM files provide very few file-processing facilities for the user. The development of file structures to enhance file access capabilities is entirely left to the user. A summary of the important differences between key-sequenced and entry-sequenced files is given in Table 7-12.1.

VSAM and other B-tree types of file structures have gained widespread acceptance in recent years. This acceptance is due primarily to the capability of these file organizations to react to the dynamic insertion and deletion requirements of many of the modern, online applications.

**Exercises for Sec. 7-12**

1. Formulate an algorithm containing the steps necessary to locate a particular word in virtual memory, as described by the three-level address $s$, $p$, $d$, where $s$ is a segment name, $p$ is an index into the page table for segment $s$, and $d$ is the displacement within page $p$. Assume segment tables and page tables are of the form illustrated in Fig. 7-12.3.

2. Suppose you are converting a file-based information system from a machine with data-management facilities which support sequential, indexed sequential, and direct files to a virtual memory system with segmented paging. The file system is similar to that available in MULTICS in that the file system is integrated with the segmented paging system. Outline what you feel are potential advantages and disadvantages of such a conversion assuming sequential, indexed sequential, and direct files were used in the original information system.

3. In the virtual memory systems discussed in this section, it was pointed out that when a page or segment must be brought into main memory, a page or segment currently in main memory must be replaced. What is wrong with selecting the page or segment to be replaced on a strictly random basis? Can you suggest a better replacement strategy?

**Table 7-12.1** A comparison of key-sequenced and entry-sequenced VSAM files.

| Key-Sequenced File | Entry-Sequenced File |
|---|---|
| Records are ordered by key | Records are ordered by their sequence of entry |
| Access is by key, although RBA access is possible | Access is by RBA |
| A record's RBA can change with additions and deletions | A record's RBA cannot change |
| By distributing free space, it is possible to insert records and change the length of records relatively easily | Only space at the end of the file can be used to create new record locations |
| Within a control interval, the space available due to a deleted or shortened record is automatically reclaimed | Records cannot be physically deleted; however, the space can be reused for a record of the same length |

4. Derive algorithms for accessing a VSAM file in a skip sequential manner and in a direct manner. Use notation consistent with that given in this section.
5. List the advantages of key-sequenced VSAM file over an indexed sequential file (IBM variety). Are there any disadvantages?

## 7-13 MULTIPLE-KEY ACCESS

The file structures discussed thus far provide us with the ability to access a record based on a single key, often called the *primary key*. In many applications, however, it may be desirable or even necessary to access a record using any one of a number of keys. One such application, from which several examples will be drawn in this section, involves a hospital administration system designed to aid in the distribution of drugs to hospital patients. The users of such a system ask questions such as:

Which patients are in recovery rooms?
Which patients of Dr. Novak require the drug XEN-02?
How many patients are currently in the pediatric ward?
Is John Brown a patient at the hospital?

Figure 7-13.1 depicts the records of a patient's file which is ordered by a state-wide hospitalization number. This number uniquely identifies each record of the file, and hence can be used as the primary key. The other given items of a patient's record are called *secondary index items* (also commonly called *secondary keys*, although this may be somewhat of a misnomer since they do not necessarily uniquely identify a record). A secondary index item is important in handling inquiries based on the value of the item, and it is used in a manner similar to or in conjunction with the primary key to access a record directly. For example, "Which patients are in recovery rooms" can be answered by printing the names, plus any other information deemed to be important, of the patients with bed numbers beginning with *R*.

The nonindexed items in Fig. 7-13.1 may contain information such as the patient's address and a list of the different facilities and services used by the patient during his or her period of confinement (e.g., cobalt-treatment facilities and labor and delivery services). Some of the nonindexed items can also be considered as secondary index items if inquiries relevant to these items are in demand. For example, "Which patients require physiotherapy" is one such inquiry which may be handled most efficiently by adopting one of the secondary access methods to be described in this section for the facilities' item of a patient record.

In this section, we examine a number of file structures which aid in the retrieval of information for inquiries based on secondary index items. In particular, the *multilist* (multiple threaded list) and the *inverted-list* organizations are introduced. A structural continuum of these two methods is created simply by placing restrictions on the length of a multilist structure. Two file structures from this continuum—multilist with controlled list length and multilist with cellular partitions—are presented.

We will purposely emphasize secondary access methods, since these are the techniques which are used to effect multikey access given today's technology. Undoubtably in the future, sophisticated hardware systems will be developed which will allow a record to be accessed directly by any one of a number of keys.

| Primary Key | Secondary Indexed Items | | | | |
|---|---|---|---|---|---|
| Hospitalization Number | Patient's Name | Bed Number | Patient's Doctor | Drug Prescribed | Nonindexed Information |
| 0913628 | Brown, J.H. | R67 | Novak | XEN-02 | |
| 0931762 | Copeck, J.A. | A02 | Turtle | HYPOCH | |
| 1013761 | Rollie, R.K. | A04 | Black | SULPH-3 | |
| 1029372 | Cristie, L.H. | B21 | Novak | CRYOL | |
| 3056718 | Jones, W.I. | R69 | James | RESIN-A | |
| 3084255 | Watson, W.P. | B23 | Turtle | CRYOL | |
| 3931768 | Andrews, A.K. | A09 | Novak | NEOBEN | |
| 4111234 | McCord, G.A. | B24 | James | HYPOCH | |
| 4450902 | Tash, R.R. | I33 | King | SULPH-3 | |
| 6331313 | Whyte, E.A. | A08 | Black | LAX | |
| 7614009 | Dree, T.P. | R68 | James | NEOBEN | |
| 7729310 | Bent, K.E. | A03 | Novak | SULPH-3 | |

(*Bed number legend*: A = General Ward, B = Pediatric Ward, I = Intensive Care, M = Maternity Ward, R = Recovery Room.)

**FIGURE 7-13.1**   Records for a hospital administration system.

It should be noted that multikey access generally is not used in batch processing. The main reason for this is that in batch-processing systems all inquiries can be batched together, and all requests and updates can be handled on a record-by-record basis during a sequential scan of the entire file.

### 7-13.1 Multilist Organization

In a multilist organization, records which have equivalent values for a given secondary index item are linked together to form a list. Since a particular item usually assumes a number of values, say $n$, then $n$ lists are created, one for each item value (hence the term multilist).

Figure 7-13.2 illustrates two multilists—one for the patient's doctor and one for the drug prescribed. Note that for brevity the name items, bed-number items, and the nonindexed items are omitted from the records. To provide a clear picture, lists for only three item values are shown, and a unique method is used for representing the links for each item in the diagram. An index is needed for each multilist, and each entry in the index contains three fields—the name of an item value, a link to the first record in a list of records containing that item value, and the length of the list. In effect, each index entry in the multilist structure is a list head with the addition of a length field.

The length field is extremely important when handling conjunctive queries such as "Which patients of Dr. Novak require the drug CYROL?" To service such a request, we must locate the patient records with a doctor item of Novak and a drug item of CYROL. The length field is used to detect which is the shorter list—the list of patients each of whom has a doctor named Novak, or the list of patients taking the drug CYROL. Obviously, for this example, it is more efficient to retrieve the two records corresponding to patients taking CYROL and examine the patient's doctor item for the value Novak than to retrieve the four patient records corresponding to Novak and examine the drug item for the value CYROL. Note that for some elements of the index, there may not exist any records with that item value. In such instances, conjunctive queries can be handled without accessing records from the main file, since no record contains information satisfying the query.

For some applications, a secondary index such as the doctor index or the drug index may be so large that it becomes necessary to store the index in a separate file. Access to a particular element in the file may be gained sequentially (using a sequential file), directly (using a direct file with the item value assuming the role of the key), or either sequentially or directly (using an indexed sequential file). It is often the case, however, that an index is small enough to reside as a table in main memory, and one of the search strategies discussed in Sec. 6-2 can be used to locate a particular element. To speed up the searching process, it is advantageous to have the index elements ordered as in the case for the drug index in Fig. 7-13.2.

The address field of an index element and the link field of the indexed item are depicted with arrows emanating from them in Fig. 7-13.2. In practice, these address fields contain either an absolute auxiliary memory address or a primary key value. An auxiliary memory address provides for quicker access; however, it is affected by the physical movement of records. For example, if the record corresponding to patient 3931768 is moved in a reorganization of the patient file, then all links pointing to this record must be updated. Such an update is nontrivial for a singly linked list. Primary key values, on the other hand, remain unaffected by the physical movement of records. Access to a record is slower, however, because a primary key must be transformed into an auxiliary address before the record can be

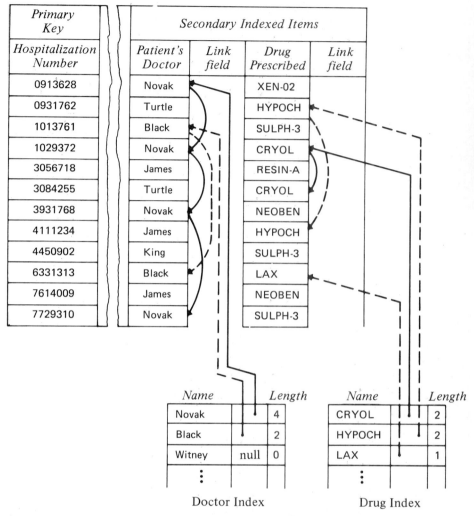

**FIGURE 7-13.2**   Multilist organization for doctor and drug items.

located. Figure 7-13.3 depicts a primary-key type of linkage for the doctor index using only the first five records. Note also that if we are programming an information system using a high-level language such as PL/I or COBOL, we are responsible for creating tables for secondary indices. Since auxiliary memory addresses generally are not available at this level of programming, we are forced to use primary keys for record linkages.

The greatest disadvantage of the multilist organization is that in order to respond to a query with a conjunctive term, all records corresponding to the term having the shortest list must be individually brought into main memory for examination. The principal advantages are the simplicity of programming and the flexibility in performing updates, which are described later in this section.

| Primary Key | | Secondary Index Item | |
|---|---|---|---|
| Hospitalization Number | | Patient's Doctor | Link Field |
| 0913628 | | Novak | 1029372 |
| 0931762 | | Turtle | 3084255 |
| 1013761 | | Black | 6331313 |
| 1029372 | | Novak | 3931768 |
| 3056718 | | James | 4111234 |

| Name | Key | Length |
|---|---|---|
| Novak | 0913628 | 4 |
| Black | 1013761 | 2 |
| Witney | null | 0 |

**FIGURE 7-13.3**  Multilist using primary-key link fields.

### 7-13.2  Inverted-List Organization

One way of overcoming the major disadvantage of the multilist approach (i.e., the necessity to access all records on the shortest list of the terms for a conjunctive query) is to remove all linkages from the file area and to place the list in the secondary index, that is, to create an *inverted list*. Figure 7-13.4 shows the inverted lists created for the patient's name and bed-number record tems of the patient file. Figure 7-13.4a illustrates the inversion process associated with the formation of an inverted list. Normally, access to a particular patient name in the patient file is gained via the primary key, which is the hospitalization number. The inverted list (or table) in Fig. 7-13.4a provides an inverse relationship; that is, given a particular

| Patient's Name | Primary Key |
|---|---|
| Andrews, A.K | 3931768 |
| Bent, K.E. | 7729310 |
| Brown, J.H. | 0913628 |
| Copeck, J.A. | 0931762 |
| Cristie, L.H. | 1029372 |
| Dree, T.P. | 7614009 |
| Jones, W.I. | 3056718 |
| McCord, G.A. | 4111234 |
| Rollie, R.K. | 1013761 |
| Tash, R.R. | 4450902 |
| Watson, W.P. | 3084255 |
| Whyte, F.A. | 6331313 |

| Ward | Primary Key |
|---|---|
| General(A) | 0931762 |
| | 1013761 |
| | 3931768 |
| | 6331313 |
| | 7729310 |
| Pediatric(B) | 1029372 |
| | 3084255 |
| | 4111234 |
| Intensive(I) | 4450902 |
| Maternity(M) | null |
| Recovery(R) | 0913628 |
| | 3056718 |
| | 7614009 |

(a)                               (b)

**FIGURE 7-13.4**  Inverted lists for (a) patients' names, and for (b) patients' wards.

name, the corresponding hospitalization number can be located. The inverted list of patients' names allows for quick access in response to inquiries involving specific patients, such as "Who is W.I. Jones' doctor?"

Figure 7-13.4*b* shows only a partial inversion of the bed-number record item. The list represents an inversion to the ward-level only, and hence is helpful in the handling of inquiries about a particular ward such as "How many patients are in recovery?" If queries are required concerning individual beds (for example, "What drug is the patient in bed A04 receiving?"), then a complete inversion may be warranted.

An inverted list can appear as a sequential, indexed sequential, or direct file, depending on how quickly we desire a response to a query. If a list is not extremely long, then it may be possible to retain it in main memory while processing user requests. Internal searching methods then can be applied. For many large applications, however, this may not be possible, especially with lists which have an entry for every record in the main file such as the patient's name list in Fig. 7-13.4*a*. Note that the patient's ward list in Fig. 7-13.4*b* is really composed of five sublists. It is possible to leave selected sublists in main memory for such an inverted structure.

For highly volatile files, it may be worthwhile to invert a secondary index item using a tree-type structure. Figure 7-9.2 illustrates such a structure for a primary index of a direct file. Additions and deletions can be handled very easily with this type of structure.

In Fig. 7-13.4, we have used the primary key as a pointer to the patient record(s) associated with a given inverted list element. We could also have used an external memory address. The advantages and disadvantages of the two types of linkage were discussed for the multilist structure. The arguments cited then apply when considering linkages in an inverted list or any of the other secondary processing methods discussed in this section.

One of the major advantages credited to the inverted list structure is its ability to handle queries with conjunctive terms. For example, the query "Is R.K. Rollie in pediatrics?" can be answered by first locating Rollie's hospitalization number in the patient's name list (Fig. 7-13.4*a*). The hospitalization number of all patients in pediatrics can be found in the patient's ward list (Fig. 7-13.4*b*), and it is easy to determine if Rollie is in pediatrics by comparing Rollie's hospitalization number with those of patients on the pediatrics ward. In fact, we can answer this question without accessing a record in the patient file! This is not true if a multilist structure is used for the name and bed-number items. In general, a query involving the conjunction of two terms which have associated inverted lists can be handled with the examination of only those records containing information satisfying the query statement. For example, the query "Which patients of Dr. Novak require the drug CYROL?" as discussed in the last subsection requires only one patient-record retrieval, if the doctor and drug index items are inverted. Recall that two record retrievals were required using multilist structures.

Another advantage of using an inverted list is that statistics concerning the number of times a secondary index item has been used can be easily kept. An extra numeric field in the inverted list can be incremented each time a particular secondary index item is required. Such an entry can also be included in a multilist structure; however, the master file record must be rewritten each time the field is incremented.

One of the major disadvantages of the inverted list is that the item values being inverted generally have to be included in both the inverted list and the master file. For example, the patients' names are present in the inverted list (Fig. 7-13.4*a*) and the patient file (Fig. 7-13.1). If the only time a patient's name is used is in an inquiry function (for example "Who is J.H. Brown's doctor?"), and it never appears as information in response to a query, then it is possible to remove the patient's name item from the patient record. Note that this same item can be removed if we use a multilist structure. However, in practice, this probably would not be the case. In a multilist structure, secondary index items are not duplicated, and therefore, it is storage-wise more efficient than an inverted list.

Later in this section we will discover that the maintenance of an inverted list is nontrivial.

### 7-13.3 The Controlled List Length Multilist Organization

In an effort to minimize the disadvantages of the multilist and inverted list structures, we now consider a compromise which involves controlling the length of a multilist. Figure 7-13.5 typifies this type of structure. The multilists for the bed-number item are restricted to a maximum length of three. As a consequence of this restriction, the patient records with general-ward bed numbers are placed on two lists. Of course, the example we are using is very limited in size; however, it is easy to visualize that for larger files, a given item value may have several lists associated with it.

| Primary Key | | Secondary Indexed Item | |
|---|---|---|---|
| Hospitalization Number | | Bed Number | Link field (primary key) |
| 0913628 | | R67 | 7614009 |
| 0931762 | | A02 | 7729310 |
| 1013761 | | A04 | null |
| 1029372 | | B21 | 3084255 |
| 3056718 | | R69 | null |
| 3084255 | | B23 | 4111234 |
| 3931768 | | A09 | null |
| 4111234 | | B24 | null |
| 4450902 | | I33 | null |
| 6331313 | | A08 | 3931768 |
| 7614009 | | R68 | 3056718 |
| 7729310 | | A03 | 1013761 |

| Ward | Bed | Link | Length |
|---|---|---|---|
| General | A02 | 0931762 | 3 |
| General | A08 | 6331313 | 2 |
| Pediatric | B21 | 1029372 | 3 |
| Intensive | I33 | 4450902 | 1 |
| Maternity | nil | null | 0 |
| Recovery | R67 | 0913628 | 3 |

**FIGURE 7-13.5**   Multilist with controlled list length.

The restriction on the length of a list provides two enhancements to the multilist. First, the breakdown of lists into sublists, each having their own list head entries in the secondary index, contributes to a faster average access time. For example, in Fig. 7-13.5, the accessing of information concerning bed A09 can be accomplished by first scanning and making comparisons with the "general-ward" entries in the index (that is, A02 and A08), and then proceeding down the "A08 list" until the record of the patient residing in bed A09 is located. Therefore, only two records need to be retrieved, as opposed to as many as five records in the multilist case. It must be observed, however, that all records corresponding to the term of a conjunctive query with the shortest list must still be scanned for a controlled list length organization. For example, if we assume Dr. Novak had six patients and the patient's doctor item is considered as a secondary index item, then the inquiry "List all patients of Dr. Novak who are in the general ward" must involve the searching of the records on both the general-ward lists, as given in Fig. 7-13.5. Nevertheless, there can be an advantage to having a long list split into several smaller sublists. If the individual lists reside on separate external-device modules (i.e., separate cylinders or units), it is sometimes possible to overlap the list accesses so that the processing of one list and the reading of another can take place in parallel.

By now, it should be evident that the multilist with a controlled list length of one is simply an inverted list structure, and that the multilist with a controlled list length of infinity is the multilist structure discussed earlier. As a hybrid structure, the multilist with a controlled list length carries some of the disadvantages of both "parent" structures. We have already discussed how the problems associated with conjunctive-term queries are not significantly reduced by controlling the list length of a multilist structure. The disadvantage of having to include indexed items redundantly in an inverted list and the records of the master file creeps into a controlled list length multilist structure. As more sublists are created, more entries appear in the secondary index. Each entry in the index contains a name field which is duplicated in the master file record.

We will look at some of the problems associated with maintaining a controlled list length multilist structure later in this section.

### 7-13.4 Cellular Partitioned Structures

To this point, we have almost completely ignored the physical placement of records in the secondary access methods which have been considered. An alternative is to take advantage of the cellular boundaries (i.e., the block or sector boundaries) of the direct-access storage medium being used. If possible, an attempt should be made to load records with a common attribute (e.g., records for patients with a common doctor) in the same cellular pattern. With this form of partitioning, all or many of the records with a common attribute can be accessed with only one read operation.

Most files, however, are organized based on their primary key, and the positioning of records with respect to a secondary key (or index item) often appears to be arbitrary. Even in this situation, it can be advantageous to organize secondary indices or inverted list structures based on the cellular partitioning of the file.

To illustrate what is meant by cellular partitioning, let us begin by considering a multilist structure such as the one in Fig. 7-13.6. An entry in the secondary index is created on each occasion an item value appears one or more times in a cellular partition. Therefore, the value "Novak" has three entries, since Novak appears in all three partitions, whereas "King" has but one entry, since it only appears in cell 3.

| Primary Key | Secondary Index Item | |
|---|---|---|
| Hospitalization Number | Patient's Doctor | Link Field |
| 0913628 | Novak | • |
| 0931761 | Turtle | null |
| 1013761 | Black | null |
| 1029372 | Novak | null |

| | | |
|---|---|---|
| 3056718 | James | • |
| 3084255 | Turtle | null |
| 3931768 | Novak | null |
| 4111234 | James | null |

| | | |
|---|---|---|
| 4450902 | King | null |
| 6331313 | Black | null |
| 7614009 | James | null |
| 7729310 | Novak | null |

Secondary Index
Relative
Record

| Name | Position | Cell # | Length |
|---|---|---|---|
| Novak | 1 | 1 | 2 |
| | 3 | 2 | 1 |
| | 4 | 3 | 1 |
| Turtle | 2 | 1 | 1 |
| | 2 | 2 | 1 |
| Black | 3 | 1 | 1 |
| | 2 | 3 | 1 |
| James | 1 | 2 | 2 |
| | 3 | 3 | 1 |
| King | 1 | 3 | 1 |

**FIGURE 7-13.6**   Multilist structure with cellular partitioning.

The relative position in the cell of the first record in a chain is included in the index to aid in the direct accessing of a record after it has been read into main memory. The length field is included as an informational aid when performing conjunctive query operations.

It should be noted that when handling queries which contain a conjunction of terms, some preprocessing can be carried out at the cellular level. For example, consider the query "How many of Dr. James' patients receive HYPOCH?" Suppose the drug item is treated as a secondary index item accessible via a multilist list structure with cellular partitioning. Then "HYPOCH" appears in records in cells 1 and 2. Since "James" appears in records in cells 2 and 3, an intersection operation at the cell level indicates that all of James' patients (if any) taking HYPOCH can be found in cell 2.

A multilist structure with cellular partitioning is primarily useful when there is a large number of records residing in a cell. The additional space required by the link field is warranted if it significantly reduces the time to access a list of records in a cell. If there are relatively few records per cell, as in the case in Fig. 7-13.6, it is better to omit the link field and examine the record of a cell in a serial fashion. An index for this type of structure, as it relates to partitions of the patient file in Fig. 7-13.6, is illustrated in Fig. 7-13.7a. Note that neither the relative record position or the length fields are included. Lefkovitz [1969] refers to this type of structure as a *cellular serial* structure. Martin [1975] presents a similar type of structure, which he terms a *cellular inverted list*. The index for such a structure is a binary matrix in which each element of the matrix indicates that a secondary index value is present

| Name | Cell # |
|------|--------|
| Novak | 1 |
| | 2 |
| | 3 |
| Turtle | 1 |
| | 2 |
| Black | 1 |
| | 3 |
| James | 2 |
| | 3 |
| King | 3 |

(a)

| | Secondary Index Item | Cellular Partitions | | |
|---|------|---|---|---|
| | | 1 | 2 | 3 |
| Doctor | Novak | 1 | 1 | 1 |
| | Turtle | 1 | 1 | 0 |
| | Black | 1 | 0 | 1 |
| | James | 0 | 1 | 1 |
| | King | 0 | 0 | 1 |
| Drug | XEN-02 | 1 | 0 | 0 |
| | HYPOCH | 1 | 1 | 0 |
| | SULPH-3 | 1 | 0 | 1 |
| | CRYOL | 1 | 1 | 0 |
| | NEOBEN | 0 | 1 | 1 |
| | LAX | 0 | 0 | 1 |
| | RESIN-A | 0 | 1 | 0 |

(b)

**FIGURE 7-13.7** Secondary index tables for the (a) cellular serial and (b) cellular inverted-list structures.

(1 value) or absent (0 value) in a particular cellular partition. Figure 7-13.7b illustrates such a structure for both the doctor and drug items. The latter type of organization can be used very efficiently in the processing of queries involving the logical "oring" (disjunction) and "anding" (conjunction) of query terms. For example, to determine the cells which contain information satisfying the query "List all those who are patients of Dr. Black or are receiving LAX" involves the logical operation 101 V 001 = 101. Therefore, we need only serially search cells 1 and 3 to find all the information pertinent to the query.

A major advantage of cellular partitioning is the capability of being able to initiate simultaneously several read operations and to overlap these operations with the processing of a query and the generation of a response. Some search time can be reduced by first performing logical operations at the cellular partition level. If records with common item values are not clustered in a few cells (i.e., if item values are spread over a number of cells with only one or two records per cell containing common item values), then it is more advantageous to use an inverted list structure. The more spread out common item values are over the partitions of the file, the more entries are needed in the secondary index and the longer it takes to access a set of records having a common item value.

Thus far we have introduced a number of file structures which are used for secondary access, provided examples of each structure, and discussed the advantages and disadvantages of each in terms of the retrieval process (i.e., how easily each facilitates the handling of inquiries). Let us now examine how easy or difficult it is to maintain each of these structures. The types of maintenance operations we will be considering are the addition, deletion, and the updating of records in a file.

### 7-13.5 Maintenance of a Multilist

The addition of a record to a file can cause a substantial reorganization of the file due to the creation of overflow records and the changes in primary-key indexes that are necessitated. These effects were discussed in earlier sections of this chapter. If multikey access is provided, then the addition of a record can also alter the secondary index tables that are associated with each secondary key of the file. Additions can be handled relatively easily in a multilist structure. If the lists are not ordered, then an addition can be accommodated most easily by placing the new record at the logical head of the list. This simply involves a change in the address of the index entry for each secondary index-item value present in the new record. Figure 7-13.8 shows the effect of such a change on the doctor item. If the list must be ordered according to some criterion such as the primary key, then the new record may be inserted logically somewhere in the middle of a list. Finally, if the list is ordered by an activity count (i.e., a count of the number of times a particular record in the list is accessed), then the record should be inserted at the logical end of the list. In this case, it is helpful for faster insertion to keep the location of the last record of the list as an index entry. Note that the length field of the index entry must be incremented by 1 for each addition.

The deletion of a record involving a multilist structure can be treated as an inverse process of record insertion. The index entry corresponding to each secondary index-item value in the deleted record is located. Using the list head information provided by the index entry, we can chain through the list structure for the item value, locate the desired record, and delete it from the list by altering the link field. A process similar to Algorithm DELETE in Sec. 4-2.1 can be used to achieve the deletion. This process can be long and involved if there are a number of items in the deleted record which are in multilist structures.

We can reduce the time required to perform a deletion by simply marking the record as being deleted instead of logically removing the record from the multilist. The disadvantage with this approach is that we must consider deleted records as well as active records when accessing a particular list in a multilist structure. For volatile files, the overhead incurred by leaving deleted records in the multilist chains can be very costly. Performance can be improved by deleting the inactive records periodically using low-priority background processing.

If the system requires both on-line maintenance and retrieval, bidirectional links should be considered in the multilist structures. The deletion of an item from a doubly linked list was described in Algorithm DOUBLDEL in Sec. 4-2.3. With this algorithm, a record can be deleted without having to chain through a linked structure starting from the list head. Hence, deletions can be performed more quickly with the additional storage overhead of a link field for every secondary item in the record.

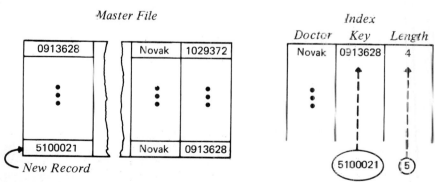

**FIGURE 7-13.8**    Addition of a new record to a multilist structure.

For some applications, it is necessary to delete a secondary index item from a record and yet not delete the whole record. One of the following alternatives can be adopted to achieve item deletion. First, a special value can be used to indicate that no meaningful item value is present (i.e., a "nil" value is used). Second, a bit accompanying the item can be used to denote if the item is deleted from the list or not. Leftovitz [1969] suggests this method. Thirdly, the item can be logically deleted from a linked list using the techniques just discussed for record deletion, and then the record can be rewritten with the item removed. Let us now turn our attention to the problems related to record updates in a multilist structure.

Whenever records are rewritten, some item is altered. If an item belonging to a multilist changes in value, then the record must be removed from one list and added to another list of the structure. The update involves the invocation of the deletion and addition algorithms for linked structures, which have already been discussed several times. Updates involving the addition of an item or the deletion of an item from a record are similarly straightforward to achieve. Depending on how the records are organized in the file, the addition of an item may involve the relocation of the record.

A final important consideration relevant to the maintenance of a multilist structure concerns system recovery in the event of a hardware failure (e.g., an external-device unit failure during a write operation) or a software failure (e.g., a programming error which erases a record). If the failure occurs while a pointer is being updated, then the result may be an erroneously written pointer. Recovery can be achieved relatively easily if the multilist structure is doubly linked (e.g., a backward link can be used to restore an erroneously written forward link). Recovery is difficult, if not impossible, using a singly linked structure.

### 7-13.6 Maintenance of an Inverted List

The addition of a record which contains one or more items that have been inverted can cause some substantial reorganizational problems. If the inverted list is maintained as a sequentially allocated table or sequential file, then the addition of a new record with an inverted item results in the movement of table entries or sequential file records to leave room for the new entry. As an example, consider what effects the addition of a patient record with a hospitalization number of 6293109, a name field of A.A. Atwood, and bed number of A07 would have on the inverted lists shown in Fig. 7-13.4. If the inverted list is maintained in a direct or indexed sequential file, then the new inverted item can create an overflow record. If the inverted structure is maintained as a tree or a linked list, an addition causes very few problems—simply the creation of a node in the list structure and the alteration of a few link fields. The addition of a new item value, such as the creation of a psychiatric (P) ward, to the ward list in Fig. 7-13.4 results in the formation of a completely new sublist within the current inverted list structure. In most applications, however, additions can be completed more quickly on an inverted list structure than a multilist structure, simply because the reading of master file records is avoided.

Deletion of records containing inverted items requires that the pointers to each such item be removed from the inverted list. For example, the removal of the patient record 3931768 results in the deletion of the element corresponding to Andrews in the patient's name list, and of an element from the general ward sublist in the patient's ward list for the inverted lists depicted in Fig. 7-13.4. Again, the difficulty of removing a pointer is dependent upon the storage (or file) structure associated with the list. Rather than physically removing the pointer, it may be more efficient to associate a deletion flag with each inverted list element if a sequential storage structure is adopted. Periodically, such inverted lists can be reorganized and the deleted items can be removed physically. The removal of individual inverted items presents no additional problems from those already discussed concerning the removal of entire records. Similarly, the updating of records constitutes no new conceptual difficulties, and it can best be viewed as a process of removing an element from one inverted list and inserting a new element in another.

### 7-13.7 Maintenance of Constrained Multilist and Cellular Structures

The addition, deletion, or update of records with items which are designated as secondary keys increases or decreases the number of records on a particular list within a multilist structure. Therefore, maintaining a structure such as the controlled list-length multilist can involve some additional processing not required by the multilist with an indefinite list length. For example, the addition of a patient record with hospitalization number 6912488 and bed number A01 causes a major reorganization of the controlled list-length multilist structure exhibited in Fig. 7-13.5. The record with bed number A04 must be moved to the head of second sublist for the general ward and the new record with bed number A01 is placed at the head of the first sublist. Note that the addition of yet another patient to the general ward necessitates the creation of a new sublist and a new element in the secondary index.

The deletion of an element requires less processing since a new list cannot be generated. Nevertheless, index elements may have to be altered or removed completely if a list length drops to zero. A deletion bit can be used to speed up on-line deletions. Major reorganizations, which take into consideration maximum allowable list lengths, can be completed off-line. Updates to secondary keys constitute a deletion-insertion activity.

A cellular partitioned structure is more easily maintained than a controlled list-length multilist structure. Whenever possible, records should be placed so as to promote the clustering of common secondary index items in cellular partitions. This may be difficult or impossible to achieve because of the sequencing of records dictated by the primary key. For cellular multilist structures, index entries may have to be altered with the addition and deletion of records or individual secondary index items. Note that such changes are minimal when using a cellular serial or cellular inverted list structure.

### 7-13.8 Summary of Secondary Access Methods

Table 7-13.1 provides a summary of the advantages and disadvantages of the secondary access methods discussed in this section.

Unless we can take advantage of a certain degree of parallelism in read/write operations, the multilist and inverted list are the secondary access methods generally adopted. Multilist structures are ideal for systems which are constrained in terms of main memory and/or are oriented toward single-term queries and/or do not require fast response times. The simplicity of programming a system using multilist structures is an added benefit. For most large information systems, however, the inverted list structure is the best structure to use if fast response time is a system requirement.

In this section we have equated multikey access with secondary access. To a large degree, this association reflects the state of the art. Multikey access facilities are now becoming part of the data-management routines provided by the operating

**TABLE 7-13.1** A summary of the results for secondary access methods.

| Method | Advantages | Disadvantages |
|---|---|---|
| Multilist | Easily programmed. Easily updated especially if bidirectional links are used. Efficient use of storage, especially if secondary index item is not stored in master file record. Ordering lists by accession rate can improve speed of access. Good for queries involving a single secondary key, since all records in the list must be examined. | Slow access, since many master file records may have to be examined. Queries with conjunctive terms are not easily handled as they require a transfer to memory of all records from the shortest list. |
| Inverted list | Fastest access of all the methods and especially good for queries with conjunctive terms. Updating is relatively fast, especially if lists reside in main memory. Good for keeping track of file statistics for secondary access. | Deletions and additions can create problems if list is sequentially allocated. Inefficient storage use if secondary index item values appear in inverted list and master file records. No great advantage over multilist for single-term queries, unless records can be accessed in parallel. |
| Controlled list-length multilist | Parallel access may be possible. Lists are divided into sublists, and if it can be determined in which sublist a conjunctive term resides, then query handling is faster than for multilist. Can be altered relatively easily to take on the appearance of a multilist or an inverted list, depending on system demands. | All sublists of a list may have to be searched serially for certain conjunctive queries. Updating more difficult than for multilist. Many of disadvantages of the multilist or the inverted list as the sublist lengths are allowed to grow longer or are kept shorter, respectively. |
| Cellular multilist | Designed to take advantage of parallel access. Query handling can be enhanced by performing conjunctive operations at the cell level. Relatively easy to update when compared to controlled list-length multilist. | Scattering of secondary index terms yields poor performance. Many of the disadvantages of the multilist. |

**Table 7-13.1**   A summary of the results for secondary access methods (continued).

| Method | Advantages | Disadvantages |
|---|---|---|
| Cellular-serial and cellular-inverted list | Very little index maintenance; better than cellular multilist if there are only a few records per cell. Bit-encoded index scheme provides fast logical operations on secondary index items at the cell level. | Scattering degrades performance. If there are many records per cell, then access time may be large. |

system. For example, IBM's VSAM now supports secondary indexes quite capably. In addition, the development of associative memories is certain to play a major role in future multikey access systems.

**Exercises for Sec 7-13**

1.  Design an algorithm for answering a query of the form "List all items with properties $x$ and $y$," where $x$ and $y$ are item values for two distinct items in a master file record. If a particular record in the file has these properties, then the value of a third item, say $z$, is returned. An example query is, "List the names of all patients in the general ward who are taking CYROL." In this case, "the general ward" and "CYROL" correspond to $x$ and $y$, and "the names of all the patients" corresponds to an output $z$. The algorithm should be designed assuming that the items for $x$ and $y$ each provide secondary access through multilist structures. All assumptions concerning the forms of tables containing the secondary indices should be stated.

2.  Answer Prob. 1 assuming inverted lists are used as secondary access methods for the $x$ and $y$ values.

3.  Answer Prob. 1 assuming controlled list-length multilists are used as secondary access methods for the $x$ and $y$ values.

4.  Answer Prob. 1 assuming cellular-serial access is used for the $x$ and $y$ values.

5.  If two multilist structures are involved in a conjunctive query, then we should examine records from the shorter list. Suppose one term of the conjunctive query provides secondary access through an inverted list and a second term provides secondary access through a multilist. What criteria for record selection should we use in this situation?

6.  An *involute structure* is a multilist structure in which all item values for secondary index items are removed from the master file and only link fields appear in their place. Figure 7-13.9 illustrates such a structure for the hospital-administration-system example. Discuss the advantages and disadvantages of such a structure.

7.  Design a general algorithm for handling a conjunctive query involving $r$ terms (e.g., "How many items have properties $x_1$ and $x_2$ and $x_3$ and . . . and $x_r$"), assuming all items provide secondary access through an inverted list structure.

| Primary Key | Secondary Index Item Link Fields | |
|---|---|---|
| Hospitalization Number | Doctor Link | Drug Link |
| 0931762 | 2066766 | 1010123 |
| 0955128 | 1967892 | null |
| 1010123 | 7936129 | 1967892 |
| 1967892 | 3077990 | null |
| 2066766 | null | 8813762 |
| . | . | . |
| . | . | . |

| Doctor Index | | |
|---|---|---|
| Doctor | Link | Length |
| Brown | 0955128 | 3 |
| Douglas | 1010123 | 2 |
| Hastings | 0931762 | 2 |
| . | . | . |
| . | . | . |
| . | . | . |

| Drug Index | | |
|---|---|---|
| Drug | Link | Length |
| COBALT | 2066766 | 2 |
| CRYOL | 0955128 | 1 |
| DETRI | 0931762 | 3 |
| . | . | . |
| . | . | . |
| . | . | . |

**FIGURE 7-13.9**    An involute structure.

8.  Throughout this section we considered each patient record to have a drug item
    in which only one drug per patient was accommodated. This is unrealistic,
    since many patients often receive more than one drug. Discuss the problems
    associated with treating a repeated field item as a secondary index item. In
    particular, point out the advantages and disadvantages of using (*a*) a multilist
    and (*b*) an inverted list for such an item.

## 7-14  AN INTRODUCTION TO DATA-BASE SYSTEMS

In Sec. 7-2, the notion of a data base was introduced. A data base was defined as a
collection of files used by the application programs for some particular enterprise
such that these files exhibit certain associations or relationships at the record level.
In this section, we begin by elaborating on some general concepts relating to data-
base systems and then discuss three approaches which have been adopted in managing systems with large data bases. These are the hierarchical, network, and relational
approaches.

### 7-14.1  General Concepts in Data-Base Systems

The definition just given for a data base is sufficient from a structural point of view,
but it omits an important property which ideally characterizes systems designed
using the "data-base approach." This important property is termed *data independence,* and it can be described as a condition in which the data and the application
programs are independent in the sense that either may be changed without changing
the other. Hence, for example, application programs can be left unaffected by
changes made to the data and the way they are organized.

To provide a clearer understanding of data independence, we can describe how such a term might relate to a manual filing system. Suppose we ask the secretary to retrieve information in the "Albert file." Any changes to the location of the file (i.e., changing the file from drawer $A$ to drawer $B$), to the internal numbering of the file, or to the number of subfiles created from the main Albert file should not seriously affect the ability to retrieve the desired information. Therefore, the request for information is to a certain degree independent of how that information is stored or organized. However, if data independence is carried to an extreme (e.g., we remove Albert as an index in our filing system and subsume the file's information in a number of other files), then retrieval becomes difficult and time-consuming. We shall see that the degree of data independence which is achievable in a data-base system depends in part on the data-base management approach adopted.

Besides providing some degree of data independence, integrated data-base systems should offer a centralized control operation. This form of operation aids in:

1   Reducing the amount of redundancy in the stored data

2   Promoting data integrity and avoiding problems of data inconsistency, i.e., inconsistencies due to changing one instance of a fact but leaving other instances of the same fact unchanged

3   Enhancing the sharing of data between users

4   Providing more uniform and effective controls for the security and privacy of user data

Martin [1975] describes in some detail how these goals can be achieved.

Figure 7-14.1 shows the general organization of a data-base system. This figure, as well as much of the terminology adopted in this section, follows that used by Date [1981]. The figure depicts the various levels at which we can view a data-base system. The top level is the user level. A user interacts with the system in a workspace using an application-dependent language. Several classes of users employing several different languages may coexist on one system while using the same data base. Statements in a user language are translated to *data sublanguage expressions*. Sublanguage expressions are then analyzed and retrievals are made from the data base, or modifications may be made on the data base. Examples of data sublanguages will be given later in this section.

To facilitate data independence, a *data model* or *schema* is created and is administered by a person (or group of persons) called *data-base administrator(s)*. The data model provides a logical view of the stored information. This logical view should be significantly independent of the physical representation of the data. For example, access to a particular record may appear as an associative type of retrieval at the logical level, while the information is stored in a direct file which is really accessible using an address-transformation algorithm. Of course, changing this physical representation to one involving an indexed sequential file does not change the logical view.

Within the data-base system there may be data submodels (i.e., submodels of the data model) which are presented to special sectors of the data-base system community. These submodels provide restrictive views of the total data model, and such views may be necessary for security reasons.

We have already mentioned the very important mapping from the data model to the storage structure of the data base. Usually, this mapping involves the file-access methods provided by the data-management facilities of the operating system. The software necessary for this mapping, in addition to the software for performing

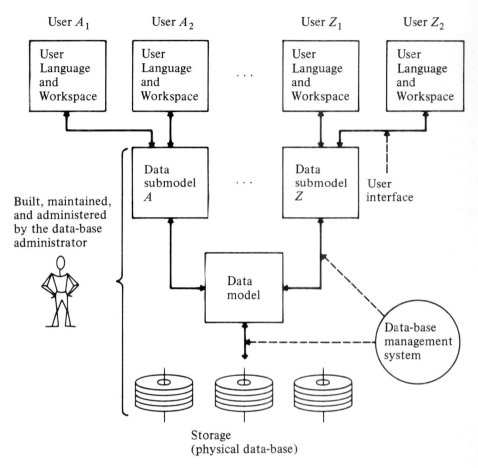

**FIGURE 7-14.1**   An architecture for a data-base system. Solid arrows refer to mappings which are realized in software.

the other mappings viewed in Fig. 7-14.1, constitutes the *data-base management system,* or DBMS.

It should be obvious that the role of data-base administrator is an important one, and an elaboration of his or her duties is given in Date [1981]. They include deciding upon the information content of the data base, deciding upon the storage structure, providing liaison with users, defining authorization checks, defining backup and recovery strategies, and monitoring system performance and user behavior.

In the description of each of the three data-base management approaches which follows, we present a data model, describe how information can be accessed using a data sublanguage compatible with the data model, and discuss some of the advantages and disadvantages of the approach. Throughout the discussion, we will use an example based on an application involving the inventory control of parts. This example was popularized by Codd [1970]. The information items relevant to the example application are:

| | | | | | |
|---|---|---|---|---|---|
| *1* | Supplier name | | *5* | Part name | |
| *2* | Supplier number | | *6* | Part number | |
| *3* | Supplier location | | *7* | Part size | |
| *4* | Supplier delivery time | | *8* | Supplier's quantity of part | |

An instance of a data base which we will work with is shown in Fig. 7-14.2.

### 7-14.2  Hierarchical Approach

A hierarchical data-base system is a system in which the user views the data base as consisting of trees of segments. These segments may contain several sublevels of segments which culminate at the item level in the information hierarchy. A *segment* is a term due to IBM and refers to a basic quantum of data which can be manipulated by the data-base management software. Roughly speaking, a segment can be a record or an aggregate of items.

The data-processing industry has, by tradition, adopted the hierarchical structuring of data, as demonstrated by the acceptance of the COBOL record and the PL/I structure. Consequently, a number of modern data-management systems are hierarchical in nature. IBM's Information Management System (IMS) exemplifies this type of approach.

For the suppliers-parts application, it is possible to structure the information using a hierarchical data model as exhibited in Figs. 7-14.3 and 7-14.4. Figure 7-14.3a shows an example data model in which a supplier segment is composed of a number of entities, including a parts segment, and Fig. 7-14.3b is an instance of the data model. Figure 7-14.4 depicts another model for the same data base. In this case, PART is the parent segment and SUPPLIER is a subservient segment.

We now discuss a data sublanguage for accessing information in a hierarchical data base. The language is functionally similar to DL/I, the data sublanguage used in IMS. Table 7-14.1 summarizes the important operations of this sublanguage.

| SUPPLIER# | SNAME | DELVRY_TIME | CITY | PART# | PNAME | PSIZE | QTY |
|---|---|---|---|---|---|---|---|
| S1 | Black | 2 | New York | P1 | Nut | 3/4 | 3 |
| S1 | Black | 2 | New York | P2 | Bolt | 3/4-2 | 1 |
| S2 | Lee | 1 | Toronto | P5 | Spring | 2 | 4 |
| S2 | Lee | 1 | Toronto | P6 | Sprocket | 4 | 2 |
| S3 | Waters | 1 | Chicago | P1 | Nut | 3/4 | 3 |
| S3 | Waters | 1 | Chicago | P2 | Bolt | 3/4-2 | 4 |
| S3 | Waters | 2 | Chicago | P3 | Bolt | 3/4-1 | 2 |
| S3 | Waters | 1 | Chicago | P6 | Sprocket | 4 | 2 |
| S4 | Dyck | 3 | St. Louis | P4 | Screw | 1/4-1 | 6 |
| S5 | Jones | 1 | Montreal | P4 | Screw | 1/4-1 | 2 |
| S5 | Jones | 1 | Montreal | P5 | Spring | 2 | 5 |
| S5 | Jones | 1 | Montreal | P6 | Sprocket | 4 | 4 |
| S6 | Whyte | 2 | Los Angeles | P1 | Nut | 3/4 | 3 |
| S6 | Whyte | 2 | Los Angeles | P2 | Bolt | 3/4-2 | 1 |
| S6 | Whyte | 2 | Los Angeles | P3 | Bolt | 3/4-1 | 2 |

**FIGURE 7-14.2**   Data for supplier-part application.

```
1 SUPPLIER,
    2 SUPPLIER#,
    2 SNAME,
    2 DELVRY,
    2 CITY,
    2 PART[N],
        3 PART#,
        3 PNAME,
        3 SIZE,
        3 QTY.
```

| S1 | Black | 2 | New York |
|----|-------|---|----------|
| | P1 | Nut | 3/4 | 3 |
| | P2 | Bolt | 3/4-2 | 1 |

*(a)*                         *(b)*

**FIGURE 7-14.3**   *(a)* and *(b)* Data model with SUPPLIER as parent segment.

```
1 PART,
    2 PART#,
    2 PNAME,
    2 SIZE,
    2 SUPPLIER[N],
        3 SUPPLIER#,
        3 SNAME,
        3 DELVRY,
        3 CITY,
        3 QTY.
```

| P2 | Bolt | 3/4-2 | | |
|----|------|-------|--|--|
| | S1 | Black | 2 | New York | 1 |
| | S3 | Waters | 1 | Chicago | 4 |
| | S6 | Whyte | 2 | Los Angeles | 1 |

*(a)*                         *(b)*

**FIGURE 7-14.4**   (a) and (b) Data model with PART as parent segment.

**Table 7-14.1** DL/I operations.

| Operation | Semantics |
|-----------|-----------|
| GET UNIQUE | Direct retrieval |
| GET NEXT | Sequential retrieval |
| GET NEXT WITHIN PARENT | Sequential retrieval under current parent |
| GET HOLD UNIQUE, GET HOLD NEXT, GET HOLD NEXT WITHIN PARENT | Operations as above, but subsequent DELETE and REPLACE operations can be performed |
| INSERT | Add new segment |
| DELETE | Delete existing segment |
| REPLACE | Replace existing segment |

Let us now examine how we may answer two queries assuming the data model depicted in Fig. 7-14.4.

Question 1: Find the supplier numbers for the suppliers who supply part P3:

```
PART_NOT_FOUND = '1'B; /*TRUE*/
GET UNIQUE PART (PART# ='P3')
        SUPPLIER;
DO WHILE (PART_NOT_FOUND);
    print SUPPLIER#;
    GET NEXT WITHIN PARENT SUPPLIER;
    IF end of parent segment
    THEN PART_NOT_FCUND = '0'B; /*FALSE*/
END;
```

Question 2: Find the part numbers for parts supplied by supplier S2:

```
ALL_PARTS_NOT_FOUND = '1'B; /*TRUE*/
DO WHILE (ALL_PARTS_NOT_FOUND);
    GET NEXT PART;
    IF end of file
    THEN ALL_PARTS_NOT_FOUND = '0'B; /*FALSE*/
    ELSE DO;
        GET NEXT SUPPLIER (SUPPLIER# ='S2');
        IF supplier S2 is present
        THEN print PART#;
    END;
END;
```

Both of the queries are formulated in a high-level language (a "bastardized" PL/I) within which the data sublanguage operations are embedded. The practice of embedding a data sublanguage in a "host" language is not uncommon; for example, both PL/I and COBOL are host languages for DL/I.

It is obvious that the data model as given in Fig. 7-14.4 is much more conducive to the retrieval of the information necessary to answer Question 1 than Question 2. In answering Question 1, it is necessary only to locate the parent segment with a part number of P3 and then search sequentially the subordinate SUPPLIER segment and print out the SUPPLIER#'s. To answer Question 2, however, it is necessary to access all PART segments, searching each for a supplier segment with a supplier number of S2, which is an extremely time-consuming task.

On the other hand, the data model given in Fig. 7-14.3 facilitates the answering of Question 2 but not Question 1. This illustrates a major problem with the hierarchical approach. Even though the two queries are symmetric, the data sublanguage procedures necessary to answer each question are not symmetric for a given data model. One of the procedures is unnecessarily complex. The user can reduce this complexity by requesting the data administrator to expand one of the data models to include both data models. Such a data model expansion, however, may require the duplicate storage of many data items.

There are additional disadvantages to the hierarchical approach which relate to maintaining the data base. For example, with the data model given in Fig. 7-14.3, we must introduce a dummy part before a new supplier can be introduced. This may not always be desirable. Similarly, in some hierarchical systems, deleting all occurrences of parts for a particular supplier may cause the supplier to be deleted as well. If we change the part size for a particular part, say P2, in the data model given in Fig. 7-14.3, then we must change the size item of every occurrence for that part.

In concluding our introduction to hierarchical data-base systems, we can say that the major advantage of the approach is that it reflects the hierarchical structuring of data that does exist in some "real world" applications. However, because of the strict hierarchical structure that is imposed with this approach, the user must spend time overcoming difficulties which are introduced by the model and are not intrinsic to the questions being posed.

### 7-14.3 Network Approach

A network data-base system is a system in which the user views the data base as a number of individual record occurrences in which a given node (i.e., item or item aggregate) may have any number of immediate superior or subordinate nodes. By superior node we mean a node which incorporates some given node. A network structure is equated to a graph structure, as discussed in Chap. 5, and differs from a hierarchical structure in that a node is not limited to a maximum of one superior.

With a network structure, it is possible to represent many-to-many relationships (e.g., many suppliers can supply many parts) instead of simply one-to-many relationships (e.g., one supplier supplying many parts, as shown in Fig. 7-14.3, or one part being supplied by many suppliers, as indicated in Fig. 7-14.4). This more general type of relationship is made possible by using link items within records. Figure 7-14.5a shows the general relationship that can exist in a network data model for the part-supplier application, and Fig. 7-14.5b depicts some instances of the data model as taken from the data in Fig. 7-14.2. The upper-level links on the supplier-part records link the parts and the associated quantity-on-hand for a given supplier. The lower-level links on the supplier-part records indicate the list of suppliers and their associated quantity-on-hand for a given part. The dotted-line segments illustrate that other supplier-part records reside in the chain, if the entire data base as given in Fig. 7-14.2 were to be shown.

Before considering the advantages and disadvantages of this approach, let us examine a data sublanguage which is feasible for retrieving and maintaining a network data base. The data sublanguage we introduce is based on the operations available in the COBOL DML (Data Manipulation Language) as described in CODASYL's DBLTG (Data Base Language Task Group) proposal [1971]. A summary of the important operations is given in Table 7-14.2.

Two important terms appearing in Table 7-14.2 must be elaborated upon. First, the *current occurrence of run-unit* refers to the most recently accessed record in the execution of a program involving the data sublanguage. A *set* is defined in the data model to have a certain record type as its owner and records of another record type (or types) as its members. For example, we can define S-SP to be a set in which the record type SUPPLIER is its owner and the record type SP (supplier part) is its member. A set is an information-carrying entity which defines the links between two record types. The data model as given in Fig. 7-14.5a is not complete, as it lacks any set definitions which describe the linkages between the record types as are shown in Fig. 7-14.5b. Therefore, to complete the data model we should include set definitions similar to those given in Fig. 7-14.6. The complete data model formed by combining Figs. 7-14.5a and 7-14.6 is sometimes called a *schema* (a term used by the DBLTG). Generically, a schema can be defined as any chart of all the data-item types and record types stored in a data base (Martin [1975]). It should be

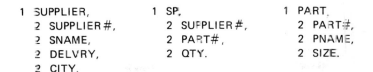

```
1  SUPPLIER,          1  SP,              1  PART,
   2  SUPPLIER#,         2  SUPPLIER#,        2  PART#,
   2  SNAME,             2  PART#,            2  PNAME,
   2  DELVRY,            2  QTY.              2  SIZE.
   2  CITY.
```

(*a*)

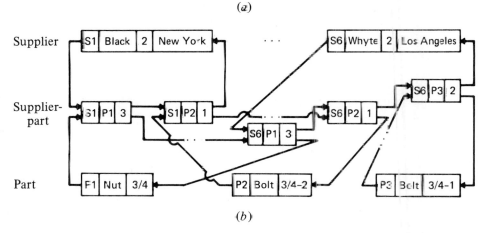

(*b*)

**FIGURE 7-14.5**    Network approach. (*c*) The general data model; (*b*) instances of the model.

reiterated that the schema definition given only captures the flavor of what is a formally defined notion by the DBLTG, and for an accurate description the reader should check the references cited in the Bibliography.

**Table 7-14.2** Data sublanguage commands for a network data-base system.

| Operation | Semantics |
|---|---|
| FIND | Locates and establishes an existing record occurrence as the current active run-unit |
| GET | Retrieves the current occurrence of run-unit |
| STORE | Creates a new record occurrence and establishes it as the current occurrence of run-unit |
| MODIFY | Updates the current occurrence of run-unit |
| INSERT | Inserts the current occurrence of run-unit into one or more set occurrences |
| DELETE | Deletes the current occurrence of run-unit |
| REMOVE | Removes the current occurrence of run-unit from one or more set occurrences |

SET S-SP;
    MODE IS CHAINED;
    ORDER IS SORTED;
    OWNER IS SUPPLIER;
    MEMBER IS SP;
        ASCENDING KEY IS PART# IN SP
            WITH DUPLICATES NOT ALLOWED;


SET P-SP;
    MODE IS CHAINED;
    ORDER IS SORTED;
    OWNER IS PART;
    MEMBER IS SP;
        ASCENDING KEY IS SUPPLIER# IN SP
            WITH DUPLICATES NOT ALLOWED;

**FIGURE 7-14.6**   Set definitions for S-SP and P-SP.


Let us now return to answer the two questions which were addressed in the previous subsection given the data model (or schema) and the data sublanguage just described.

Question 1: Find the supplier numbers for the suppliers who supply part P3.

```
                MOVE 'P3' TO PART# IN PART.
                FIND PART RECORD.
                FIND FIRST SP RECORD OF P-SP SET.
                IF ERROR-STATUS = 0307 (end of set occurrence)
                    GO TO ENDING.
AGAIN.          GET SP.
                (add SUPPLIER# in SP to list of supplier numbers)
                FIND NEXT SP RECORD OF P-SP SET.
                IF ERROR-STATUS = 0307 (end of set occurrence)
                    GO TO ENDING.
                GO TO AGAIN.
ENDING.     ...
```

Question 2: Find the part numbers for parts supplied by supplier S2.

```
                MOVE 'S2' TO SUPPLIER# IN SUPPLIER.
                FIND SUPPLIER RECORD.
                FIND FIRST SP RECORD OF S-SP SET.
                IF ERROR-STATUS = 0307 (end of set occurrence)
                    GO TO ENDING.
AGAIN.          GET SP.
                (add PART# in SP to list of part numbers)
                FIND NEXT SP RECORD OF S-SP SET.
                IF ERROR-STATUS = 0307 (end of set occurrence)
                    GO TO ENDING.
                GO TO AGAIN.
ENDING.     ...
```

The answers to the questions are formulated in the data sublanguage which is embedded in a COBOL-like host language. For example, the MOVE instruction constitutes an assignment in COBOL.

It should be obvious that these programs are completely symmetric and therefore reflect the symmetry of the two questions. Hence, the major disadvantage with the hierarchical approach is avoided. This symmetry can be realized without duplicating large quantities of data (only SUPPLIER# and PART# are duplicated). It is actually possible to define the SP record without including the SUPPLIER# and PART# items; however, there are certain disadvantages to this which we will not consider in our discussion here. Notice also that we can add a new supplier, say S7, without having to generate dummy part information. Initially, there are no links for the new supplier; its chain consists of a single pointer from the SUPPLIER record to itself. We can delete all parts for a supplier without deleting the supplier, and an update to the size of a particular part involves only one change—namely, to the SIZE item in the PART record.

Probably the major disadvantage with the network approach is the necessity to describe the relationships which exist between records using chains. As we have seen earlier in the text, a link is very much a storage-structure concept, and therefore it can be argued that the network model is partly a storage-structure model. There is thus a danger that the user will become locked into a particular storage structure (Date [1981]). This is contrary to the goal of data independence.

### 7-14.4 Relational Approach

A relational data-base system can best be described as a system in which the user views the data base as a number of interrelated "flat" files or tables. Figure 7-14.2, for example, depicts the data base as one large table in which the combined items of SUPPLIER# and PART# uniquely identify a row within the table.

The relational approach has its basis in a mathematical theory of relations. The term *relation* can be defined as follows. Given the sets $D_1, D_2, ..., D_n$ (not necessarily mutually distinct), $R$ is a relation on these sets if it is a set of ordered $n$-tuples $<d_1, d_2, ..., d_n>$ such that $d_1$ belongs to $D_1$, $d_2$ belongs to $D_2$, $d_n$ belongs to $D_n$, where the sets $D_1, D_2, ..., D_n$ are called the *domains* of $R$. $R$ is said to be a relation of degree $n$.

Some important properties are associated with a table that represents a relation in the data base:

*1*    No two rows (that is, $n$-tuples) can be identical.
*2*    The ordering of these rows is insignificant.
*3*    The ordering of the columns is insignificant.

Usually, the primary key of a relation is denoted by underlining it and placing it in the first column of the table. In some instances, however (such as in Fig. 7-14.2), the primary key may involve more than one domain and hence cannot appear in the first column.

A final important property of a relation is that each data item in its domains should be atomic (i.e., nondecomposable, such as an integer or character string). When this property along with the previous three holds, the relation is called *normalized*. A normalized relation is also said to be in the *first normal form* (1NF), which is a notation due to Codd [1972].

Two problems exist when using a first-normal-form relation. One is the apparent redundancy of data (e.g., how many times does 'S3' appear?). Of course, updating a particular nonkey item such as CITY constitutes a major search effort on a large data base in order to guarantee that all occurrences of CITY for a particular supplier are altered. The second and potentially more serious problem relates to certain nonfully functional dependencies which are allowed to exist in a 1NF relation.

We say that domain $Y$ is *functionally dependent* on domain $X$, where $X$ and $Y$ are domains of a relation $R$, if and only if each $X$ value has associated with it only one $Y$ value at any one time. For example, SNAME is functionally dependent on SUPPLIER#. A domain $Y$ is *fully functionally dependent* on domain $X$ if it is functionally dependent on $X$ and not functionally dependent on any subset of $X$ (where $X$ can be a composite domain). For example, QTY is fully functionally dependent on the combined domains PART#-SUPPLIER#; however, CITY is not fully functionally dependent on PART#-SUPPLIER# because it is functionally dependent on SUPPLIER#, but not PART#. Figure 7-14.7 illustrates these functional dependencies.

Because not all domains in the relation shown in Fig. 7-14.2 are fully functionally dependent upon the combined key domains of PART#-SUPPLIER#, some restrictions arise when maintaining our data base. First, we cannot add the fact that a particular supplier is located in a particular city with a particular delivery time, until that supplier is able to supply at least one part. The addition cannot be made because no appropriate primary key exists. Similarly, if we delete all occurrences of parts for a supplier, we must delete the supplier information, since no primary key with that supplier number will remain.

To alleviate these anomalies, Codd [1972] suggests the formulation of relations in *second normal form* (2NF). A normalized relation $R$ is in 2NF if and only if the nonkey domains of $R$ are fully functionally dependent on the primary key of $R$. A breakdown of our original data base, as given in Fig. 7-14.1, into three 2NF relations is shown in Fig. 7-14.8a, and the functional dependencies which exist for these new relations are depicted in Fig. 7-14.8b.

An obvious question involving the definition of 2NF concerns the restriction that full functional dependency should exist between nonkey and primary key domains only. What about functional dependencies which exist between nonkey domains? Can problems arise if such functional dependencies exist? From Fig. 7-14.8a it can be seen that the nonkey item DELVRY_TIME is not only functionally dependent on CITY but also transitively functionally dependent on SUPPLIER#. It may be desirable to express this functional dependency between the two nonkey items DELVRY_TIME and CITY apart from a SUPPLIER#. That is, if it is known that a new supplier is going to supply parts from VANCOUVER and the

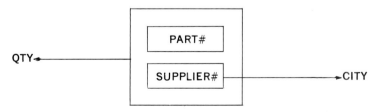

**FIGURE 7-14.7**    Functional dependencies in supplier-part application.

SP relation

| SUPPLIER# | PART# | QTY |
|-----------|-------|-----|
| S1 | P1 | 3 |
| S1 | P2 | 1 |
| S2 | P5 | 4 |
| S2 | P6 | 2 |
| S3 | P1 | 3 |
| S3 | P2 | 4 |
| S3 | P3 | 2 |
| S3 | P6 | 2 |
| S4 | P4 | 6 |
| S5 | P4 | 2 |
| S5 | P5 | 5 |
| S5 | P6 | 4 |
| S6 | P1 | 3 |
| S6 | P2 | 1 |
| S6 | P3 | 2 |

Part Relation

| PART# | PNAME | PSIZE |
|-------|-------|-------|
| P1 | Nut | 3/4 |
| P2 | Bolt | 3/4-2 |
| P3 | Bolt | 3/4-1 |
| P4 | Screw | 1/4-1 |
| P5 | Spring | 2 |
| P6 | Sprocket | 4 |

Supplier relation

| SUPPLIER# | SNAME | CITY | DELVRY_TIME |
|-----------|-------|------|-------------|
| S1 | Black | New York | 2 |
| S2 | Lee | Toronto | 1 |
| S3 | Waters | Chicago | 1 |
| S4 | Dyck | St. Lou s | 3 |
| S5 | Jones | Montreal | 1 |
| S6 | Whyte | Los Angeles | 2 |

(a)

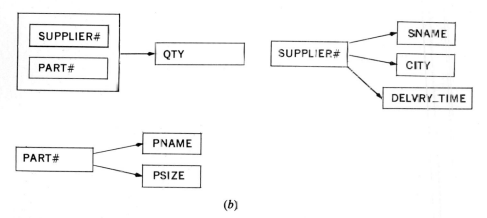

(b)

**FIGURE 7-14.8**   Formulation of supplier-part data base in 2NF. (a) The data base; (b) functional dependencies within the data base.

DELVRY_TIME for this city is 3, then we should be able to express this relationship in the system prior to knowing the new supplier's name or number. Figure 7-14.9 exhibits such a breakdown of the supplier relation shown in 7-14.8.

Codd [1972] recognized the problems associated with the presence of nonkey dependencies and suggested a third normal form for a relation to eliminate these problems. A normalized relation $R$ is said to be in *third normal form* (3NF) if and only if the nonkey domains of $R$ are (1) mutually independent and (2) fully functionally dependent in the primary key of $R$. Nonkey items are *mutually independent* if no functional dependencies exist between them. Therefore, the SUPPLIER relation in Fig. 7-14.9 is in 3NF, while the SUPPLIER relation in Fig. 7-14.8a is in 2NF but not in 3NF. Because of the manner in which we have defined the normal forms, it can be concluded that any relation that is in 3NF is in 2NF and 1NF, and any relation in 2NF is also in 1NF, and a hierarchy of normal forms is created.

Let us now look at a data sublanguage for the relational approach. Two types of languages have been formulated: the *relational algebra* (Codd [1972]) and the *relational calculus* (Codd [1972]). We examine only the relational calculus here. The relational calculus is a nonprocedural notation based on predicate calculus statements. (See Tremblay and Manohar [1975] for a discussion of the predicate calculus.) These statements involve the quantifiers "there exists" and "for all." Let us introduce the language by giving a number of examples assuming the 3NF relations in Fig. 7-14.8a. First, we answer the two questions posed earlier in the section.

Question 1: Find the supplier numbers for the suppliers who supply part P3.

{SP.SUPPLIER#: SP.PART# ='P3'}

Therefore, it is stated that we want to retrieve the SUPPLIER# values from the SP relation which are such that the associated PART# value is P3. The expression on the left of the colon indicates what is to be retrieved, the colon reads "such that," and the expression on the right is the predicate, which if satisfied returns the corresponding information as dictated by the left side.

Question 2: Find the part numbers for parts supplied by supplier S2.

{SP.PART#: SP.SUPPLIER# ='S2'}

This statement is symmetric with that given in answer to Question 1. Some other more complicated queries can be easily formulated in the relational calculus.

| Supplier relation | SUPPLIER# | SNAME | CITY |
|---|---|---|---|
| | S1 | Black | New York |
| | S2 | Lee | Toronto |
| | S3 | Waters | Chicago |
| | S4 | Dyck | St. Louis |
| | S5 | Jones | Montreal |
| | S6 | Whyte | Los Angeles |

| Delivery relation | CITY | DELVRY_TIME |
|---|---|---|
| | New York | 2 |
| | Toronto | 1 |
| | Chicago | 2 |
| | St. Louis | 3 |
| | Montreal | 1 |
| | Los Angeles | 2 |
| | Vancouver | 3 |

**FIGURE 7-14.9**   The decomposition of the SUPPLIER relation into 3NF.

For example,

> Quest on 3: For each supplier, find part numbers and supplier's cities from which the parts may be obtained.

$$\{(SP.PART\#, SUPPLIER.CITY): \; SP.SUPPLIER\# = SUPPLIER.SUPPLIER\#\}$$

> Question 4: Find the supplier numbers for suppliers who are from Toronto or Montreal and who supply a part of size 3/4.

$$\{SP.SUPPLIER\#: \exists PART \exists \; SUPPLIER(PART.SIZE = '3/4' \land$$

$$PART.PART\# = SP.PART\# \land SP.SUPPLIER\# = SUPPLIER.SUPPLIER\# \land =$$

$$(SUPPLIER.CITY = 'TORONTO' \lor SUPPLIER.CITY + 'MONTEAL'))\}$$

Question 4 demonstrates that the queries can become quite complicated. Try formulating the same query in the hierarchical or network-system data sublanguages!

Because the relational calculus is nonprocedural (i.e., no step-by-step specification is given), we have not shown the underlying operations necessary for the manipulation and retrieval of information from the relations. Set algebraic operations such as joins, projections, and divisions are required, and these are part of the relational algebraic approach. A detailed discussion of these operations is outside the scope of this text but may be found in Date [1981].

### 7-14.5 Summary

One of the major points that can be made in this section is that a data-base system consists of data entities and a description of the relationships between these entities. In the hierarchical approach, these relationships are implicitly bound by the relative positions of the data entities or segments in the record definition. For example, a part may be a subordinate or superior entity to a supplier, depending on how the data model is defined.

In the network approach, relationships are exhibited explicitly by means of links. A data entity is subordinate, superior, or nonrelated to another entity, depending on the presence or absence of a pointer.

In the relational approach, relationships are also exhibited explicitly; however, the relationships and the data entities themselves both appear in relations (i.e., both are considered to be the same type of object). Hence, it is possible to provide a uniform look for the data base (i.e., both the entities and relationships) without considering storage and access details such as parent nodes or pointers.

Which approach is superior is not of significant importance in this text at this time—all approaches have been and will be used. What is important is that the wide variety of data structures and their associated storage representations that we have discussed in the text are very pertinent to the area of data-base systems. Even from this brief introduction to data-base systems, it is obvious how relevant the data structures such as trees, graphs, and associative structures (along with the many file structures) are to an understanding of data-base systems. Indeed, the text provides a sound basis for further study in this relatively new and expanding area.

## BIBLIOGRAPHY

ABRAMSON, N.: "Information Theory and Coding," McGraw-Hill Book Company, New York, 1963.

BAYER, R. and T. HAERDER: "Preplanning of Disk Merges," *Computing 21*, no. 1, 1978, Springer-Verlag, pp. 1-16.

BAYER, R. and T. HAERDER: "A Performance Model for Preplanned Disk Sorting," *Computing 21*, no. 1, 1978, Springer-Verlag, pp. 17-35.

BAYS, C.: "The Reallocation of Hash-Coded Tables," *CACM*, vol. 16, no. 1, 1973, pp. 11-14.

BENSOUSSAN, A.: Overview of the Locking Strategy in the File System, "Multics Systems Programmers Manual," Section B.G. 19.00, November 1969, pp. 1-10.

BUCHHOLZ, WERNER: File Organization and Addressing, *IBM Systems Journal*, vol. 2, June 1963, pp. 86-110.

CHEN, T. C., K. P. ESWARAN, V. Y. LUM, and C. TUNG: "Simplified Odd-Even Sort using Multiple Shift-Register Loops," IBM Tech. Report RJ 1919 (27428), Jan. 1977.

CHIN, F. Y. and K. S. FOK: "Fast Sorting Algorithms on Uniform Ladders (Multiple Shift-Register Loops)," *IEEE Tranactions on Computers C-29*, no. 7, 1980, pp. 618-631.

CHUNG, K., F. LUCCIO, and C. K. WONG: "On the Complexity of Sorting in Magnetic Bubble Memory Systems," *IEEE Transactions on Computers C-29*, no. 7, 1980, pp. 553-562.

"CODASYL Data Description Language Committee," *Journal of Development*, June 1973.

CODD, E. F.: A Relational Model of Data for Large Data Banks, *Communications of the ACM*, vol. 13, no. 6, 1970, pp. 377-387.

CODD, E. F.: Further Normalization of the Data Base Relational Model, *Data Base Systems*, Courant Computer Science Symposia Series, vol. 6, Prentice-Hall, Englewood Cliffs, N.J., 1972.

"Data Base Task Group of CODASYL Programming Language Committee Report," April 1971. (Available from ACM.)

DATE, C.J.: "An Introduction to Database Systems," third edition, Addison Wesley Publishing Company, Reading, Mass., 1981.

DEUTSCHER, R.F., P.G. SORENSON, and J.P. TREMBLAY: Distribution Dependent Hashing Functions and Their Characteristics, *Proceedings of the International Conference of the Management of Data, ACM/SIGMOD*, May 14-15, 1975, San Jose, pp. 224-236.

DEUTSCHER, R. F., J. P. TREMBLAY, and P. G. SORENSON: A Comparative Study of Distribution-Dependent and Distribution-Independent Hashing Functions, *Proceedings of the ACM Pacific 75*, April 17 and 18, 1975, San Fransisco, pp. 172-178.

ESSELID, T.J.: "On Replacement Selection and Dinsmore's Improvement," *BIT*, no. 18, 1976, pp. 133-142.

FAGIN, R., J. NIEVERGELT, N. PIPPENGER, and H.R. STRONG: "Extendible Hashing—A Fast Access Method for Dynamic Files," *TODS*, vol. 4, no. 3, 1979, pp. 315-344.

FOTHERINGHAM, J.: Dynamic Storage Allocation in the Atlas Computer, Including an Automatic Use of Backing Store, *Communications of the ACM*, vol. 4, October 1961, pp. 435-436.

FREDKIN, E.: "Trie Memory," *CACM*, vol. 3, no. 9, 1960, pp. 490-499.

GILSTAD, R. L.: "Polyphase Merge Sorting-an Advanced Technique," *Proc. AFIPS Eastern Jt. Computer Conf.,* vol. 18, Dec. 1980, Spartan Books, New York, pp. 143-148.

GRIES, D.E.: "Compiler Construction for Digital Computers," John Wiley and Sons, Inc., New York, 1971.

HAMILTON, H. J.: *"Dynamic Hashing Techniques,"* M. Sc. Thesis, Dept. of Comp. Sc., University of Saskatchewan, Saskatoon, Canada, 1983.

HOPGOOD F. R. A.: "A Solution to the Table Overflow Problem for Hash Tables," *Comp. Bulletin,* no. 11, 1968, pp. 297-300.

HUGHES, J K.: "PL/I Programming," John Wiley and Sons, New York, 1973.

"IBM System/360 Operating System PL/I(F) Language Reference Manual," IBM Form No. GC28-8201.

"IBM System/360 Operating System PL/I(F) Programmer's Guide." IBM Form No. GC28-6594.

"Information Management System/360 Version 2 General Information Manual," IBM Form No. GH20-0765.

"Information Management System/360 Version 2 Utilities Reference Manual," IBM Form No. SH20-0915.

"Introducing the IBM 3600 Finance Communication System," IBM Form No. GA27-2764.

ISAAC, E. J., and R. C. SINGLETON: "Sorting by Address Calculation," *Journal of the ACM,* vol. 3, July, 1956, pp. 169-174.

KINDRED, A.R.: "Data Systems and Management," Prentice-Hall, Englewood Cliffs, N.J., 1973.

KNOTT, GARY D.: "Expandable Open-Addressing Hash-Table Storage and Retrieval,' *Proceedings of the SIGFIDET Workshop on Data Description, Access, and Control,* ACM, 1971, pp. 187-206.

KNUTH, D.E.: "The Art of Computer Programming, vol. 3, Searching and Sorting," Addison-Wesley Publishing Company, Reading, Mass., 1973.

KRONMAL, R. A., and M. E. TARTER: "Cumulative Polygon Address Calculation Sorting," *Proceedings of the 20th National Conference of the ACM,* 1965, pp. 376-385.

LARSON, P. A. "Dynamic Hashing," *BIT,* no. 18, 1978, pp. 184-201.

LARSON, P. A. "Linear Hashing With Partial Expansions." *Proc. 6th Int. Conf. on Very Large Data Bases,* Montreal, 1980a.

LARSON, P. A. "Linear Hashing with Partial Expansions," Swedish University of Abo, Abo, Finland, 1980b.

LARSON, P. A.: "Performance Analysis of Linear Hashing with Partial Expansions," Swedish University of Abo, Abo, Finland, 1980c.

LEFKOVITZ, D.E.: "File Structure for On-line Systems," Spartan Books, New York, 1969.

LITWIN, W.: "Virtual Hashing: A Hashing Which May Be Dynamically Changed," *CIPS Session '78 Proceedings,* Toronto, 1978a, pp. 401-405.

LITWIN, W.: "Virtual Hashing: A Dynamically Changing Hashing," *Proc. 4th Int. Conf. on Very Large Data Bases,* Berlin, 1978b, pp. 517-523.

LITWIN, W.: "Linear Hashing: A New Tool for File and Table Addressing." *Proc. 6th Int. Conf. on Very Large Data Bases,* Montreal, 1980, pp. 212-223.

LONDON, K.R.: "Techniques for Direct Access," Auerbach Publishers, Philadelphia, 1973.

LUCCIO, F.: "Weighted Increment Linear Search for Scatter Tables," *CACM,* vol. 15, no. 12, 1972, pp. 1045-1047.

LUM, V.Y.: General Performance Analysis of Key-to-Address Transformation Methods Using an Abstract File Concept, *Communications of the ACM*, vol. 16, no. 10, 1973, pp. 603-612.

LUM, V.Y., P.S.T. YUEN, and M. DODD: Key-to-Address Transformation Techniques: A Fundamental Performance Study on Large Existing Formatted Files, *Communications of the ACM*, vol. 14, no. 4, 1971, pp. 228-239.

MACKENZIE, F.B.: Automated Secondary Storage Management, *Datamation 11*, 1965, pp. 24-28.

MADNICK, S.E. and J.J. DONOVAN: "Operating Systems," McGraw-Hill Book Company, New York, 1974.

MARTIN, G. N. N.: "Spiral Storage: Incrementally Augmentable Hash Addressed Storage," Theory of Computation Report No. 27, University of Warwick, Coventry, England, 1979.

MARTIN, J.: "Computer Data-Base Organization," Prentice-Hall, Englewood Cliffs, N.J., 1975.

MEADOWS, C.T.: "The Analysis of Information Systems," 2d ed., Melville Publishing, Los Angeles, 1973.

MULLINS, J.K.: An Improved Indexed Sequential Access Method Using Hashed Overflow, *Communications of the ACM*, vol. 15, no. 5, May 1972, pp. 301-307.

"OS/VS Virtual Storage Access Method (VSAM) Planning Guide," IBM Form No. GC26-3799.

"PDP-11 Peripherals Handbook," Digital Equipment Corporation, 1975.

PHILIPPAKIS, A.S. and L.J. KAZMIER: "Information Systems Through COBOL," McGraw-Hill Book Company, New York, 1974.

"Reference Manual for IBM 3330 Series Disk Storage," IBM Form No. GA26-1615.

SCHOLL, M.: "New File Organizations Based on Dynamic Hashing," *ACM Transactions on Database Systems*, vol. 6, no. 1, March, 1981, pp. 194-211.

"SCOPE Indexed Sequential System," Control Data Corporation, CDC-60305400A.

SHAW, A.C.: "The Logical Design of Operating Systems," Prentice-Hall, Englewood Cliffs, N.J., 1974.

TOONG, H.D. and A. GUPTA: "Personal Computers," *Scientific American*, December 1982, pp. 87-106.

TREMBLAY, J.P. and R.P. MANOHAR: "Discrete Mathematical Structures with Applications to Computer Science," McGraw-Hill Book Company, New York, 1975.

TSICHRITZIS, D.C. and P.A. BERNSTEIN: "Operating Systems," Academic Press, New York, 1974.

WEINBERG, G.M.: "PL/I Programming: A Manual of Style," McGraw-Hill Book Company, New York, 1970.

WHITE, R.M.: "Disk-Storage Technology," *Scientific American*, August 1980, pp. 138-148.

# INDEX